# The Complete Illustrated Book of DEVELOPMENT DEFINITIONS

# The *Complete* Illustrated Book of DEVELOPMENT DEFINITIONS

FOURTH EDITION

HARVEY S. MOSKOWITZ
CARL G. LINDBLOOM
DAVID LISTOKIN
RICHARD PREISS &
DWIGHT H. MERRIAM

Routledge
Taylor & Francis Group
LONDON AND NEW YORK

First published 2015 by Transaction Publishers

Published 2017 by Routledge
2 Park Square, Milton Park, Abingdon, Oxon OX14 4RN
711 Third Avenue, New York, NY 10017, USA

First issued in paperback 2017

*Routledge is an imprint of the Taylor & Francis Group, an informa business*



Library of Congress Catalog Number: 2014035417

Library of Congress Cataloging-in-Publication Data

Moskowitz, Harvey S.
The complete illustrated book of development definitions / Harvey S. Moskowitz, Carl G. Lindbloom, David Listokin, Richard Preiss, and Dwight H. Merriam. -- Fourth edition.
pages cm
Revised edition of Harvey S. Moskowitz's and Carl G. Lindbloom's The latest illustrated book of development definitions, published in 2004.
ISBN 978-1-4128-5504-4
1. City planning--United States--Dictionaries. 2. Zoning--United States--Dictionaries. 3. City planning and redevelopment law--United States--Dictionaries. 4. Rural development--United States--Dictionaries. I. Moskowitz, Harvey S. Latest illustrated book of development definitions. II. Title.
HT167.M683 2015
307.1'2160973--dc23

2014035417

ISBN 13: 978-1-138-51559-8 (pbk)
ISBN 13: 978-1-4128-5504-4 (hbk)

# About the Authors

**HARVEY MOSKOWITZ**, PP, FAICP, is a planning consultant and a former member and past president of the New Jersey Board of Professional Planners. He has a PhD in urban planning and policy development from Rutgers University and an MPA from New York University. Moskowitz was formerly on the board of directors of the American Planning Association and the New Jersey Site Improvement Advisory Board. Dr. Moskowitz holds New Jersey professional planners license #12 and is a charter member of the American Institute of Certified Planners. He was the first New Jersey planner elected to the College of Fellows of the American Planning Association in 1983, and he received an outstanding alumnus award from the Edward J. Bloustein School of Planning and Public Policy in 1995. He has worked in over 250 municipalities and other governmental entities in the United States throughout his career.

**CARL LINDBLOOM**, AICP, is a planning and urban design consultant with over fifty years' experience in both the private and public sector. He was a member of the Princeton New Jersey Planning Board and provided consulting services for numerous municipalities throughout the state. Early in his career, he worked in England as an architect/planner for the London County Council and the Greater London Council. He has an undergraduate degree in architecture (1954) and a graduate degree in city design (1956) from Miami University, Oxford, Ohio. He is the author of *Environmental Design Review*, a guide for the development of municipal site plan review ordinances, and the coauthor of *A Guide for Residential Design Review*. He illustrated this volume and all three earlier editions.

**DAVID LISTOKIN** is a professor at the Edward J. Bloustein School of Planning and Public Policy at Rutgers, The State University of New Jersey. For over forty years, he has conducted studies for international and national clients on the subjects of development impact assessment, historic preservation, public finance, land use, and housing. He is the author of numerous monographs and articles on these subjects. His research on subdivision regulations was adopted in the New Jersey Residential Site Plan Improvement Standards, and he contributed to New Jersey's "smart building" code to encourage building rehabilitation and historic preservation. At Bloustein, he codirects the Center for Urban Policy Research. He holds master's degrees in urban planning and public administration and a doctorate in urban planning. Dr. Listokin has served as a visiting professor at Harvard and Cornell Universities.

**RICHARD PREISS**, P.P., has served as a principal of Phillips Preiss Grygiel LLC, a planning and real estate consulting firm in New York City and now in Hoboken, New Jersey, for over thirty years. Richard has a bachelor's degree in town and regional planning from the University of Witwatersrand (South Africa) and a master's degree in planning from the University of Oregon. He has drafted zoning ordinances for entire cities (Yonkers, Newark) and small towns (Larchmont, Roslyn Harbor), as well as amendments for over a hundred communities. He was also instrumental in drafting a Model Zoning Ordinance for cities and counties in the State of Oregon. Richard has served as a planning expert in numerous trials on a range of planning issues—religious uses, sexually oriented businesses, affordable housing, large-lot zoning, condemnation, housing and health care facilities, and classic constitutional issues (whether the zoning is arbitrary, discriminatory, or confiscatory). In 2012, Mr. Preiss received the Achievement in Planning Award from the New Jersey Planning Officials.

**DWIGHT MERRIAM**, a fellow and past president of the American Planning Association's American Institute of Certified Planners, founded Robinson & Cole's Land Use Group in 1978. He represents landowners, developers, governments, and individuals in land use matters. Dwight is the former chairman of the American Bar Association's Section of State and Local Government Law, a former director of the American Planning Association, a former chair of APA's Planning and Law Division, the Connecticut member of Owners' Counsel of America, a fellow of the Royal Institution of Chartered Surveyors, a fellow of the American Bar Foundation, a member of the Rocky Mountain Land Use Institute National Advisor Board, a fellow of the Connecticut Bar Foundation, a counselor of real estate (CRE), a member of the Anglo-American Real Property Institute, and a fellow of the American College of Real Estate Lawyers. He received his BA (cum laude) from the University of Massachusetts, his master's of regional planning from the University of North Carolina, where he was invited back as the graduation speaker in 2011, and his JD from Yale. He teaches land use law at the University of Connecticut School of Law and the Quinnipiac University School of Law and previously taught for eighteen years at the Vermont Law School. He has published over two hundred articles and nine books, including *Inclusionary Zoning Moves Downtown*, *The Takings Issue*, *The Complete Guide to Zoning*, and *Eminent Domain Use and Abuse: Kelo in Context*.

# Contents

# Illustrations

# Preface

*The Complete Illustrated Book of Development Definitions* is the fourth edition of the series that began in 1981 with *The Illustrated Book of Development Definitions*. A second edition, *The New Illustrated Book of Development Definitions*, was published in 1991; and most recently, a third edition, *The Latest Illustrated Book of Development Definitions*, was published in 2004.

The fourth edition differs significantly from the previous editions in a number of respects. The most important is the addition of legal annotations to virtually all of the definitions. The legal annotations add citations from court decisions and other sources from around the country that are pertinent to the definition and that bridge the gap between theory and real-world applications. The legal annotations were provided by Dwight Merriam, Esq., FAICP, past president of the American Institute of Certified Planners and a partner in the law firm of Robinson & Cole, LLP of Hartford, Connecticut.

A second major change from the previous editions is the addition of two prominent planners, one of whom is an academic, to the staff as researchers/writers/editors. David Listokin, PhD, is professor of planning at Rutgers University and codirector of the Rutgers University Center for Urban Policy Research. The second addition is Richard Preiss, PP, principal of Phillips Preiss Grygiel LLC, a planning and real estate consulting firm with offices in Hoboken, New Jersey.

The fourth edition also includes a significant number of new definitions relating to more current planning issues. For example, a number of new terms and phrases relating to natural and industrial disasters, such as Hurricanes Katrina and Sandy and the oil spill in the Gulf of Mexico, have been added. In the same vein, also prominent in this edition are definitions and illustrations relating to sustainability, new urbanism, and green communities, as well as pedestrian- and bicycle-related terms, reflecting a new focus on these older and perhaps long-neglected forms of transportation. Various housing types and living accommodations are reexamined and redefined where necessary, in light of changing development and demographics patterns. In all, the fourth edition contains 2,198 definitions, or 243 more than the third edition. The fourth edition contains 109 illustrations and legal annotations for almost all of the definitions. There were no legal annotations in the previous editions.

The original intent of the authors was to prepare a book of definitions that could be used directly, or with only slight modifications, in any zoning, subdivision, or land development ordinance. This presented certain obvious problems, such as attempting to write a single definition that would be appropriate for a wide variety of municipalities located in different states, each with its own enabling statutes and idiosyncratic practices. In execution, however, this objective was not as difficult to achieve as it first appeared. One of the principles that the authors used and believe should be followed in writing any definition is not to include the standard that is being defined in the definition itself. Indeed, the standard itself may vary within the municipality by zoning district. For example, the definition for height can be constructed in such a manner that it can be applied universally while recognizing that the maximum or minimum standard will vary from municipality to municipality, and even within municipalities. At the same time, how the height should be measured—from what point at the base of the structure to what point at the top—is equally applicable in New York City as it is in East Alton, Illinois.

The attempt at universality and direct application is obviously made more difficult when one learns that two or even more equally adequate definitions can cover the same word or term. For example, the definitions of *retail services*, *personal services*, *business services*, and *social services* overlap to a great extent. However, in these circumstances the reader may find one more appropriate than another for a particular municipality.

Commentaries and annotations suggest how the definition is designed to be used in development regulations; they also offer some discussion pertinent to the definition. Although the commentaries are used primarily as a guide to the reader, the authors suggest that commentaries can be useful in local ordinances as well. Very often the background and legislative intent can be included in a preamble or a purpose section of an ordinance, a device often used in state legislation but less so in local codes.

Throughout the book, the terms *zoning ordinance* and *land development ordinance* are used synonymously. Actually, a land development ordinance is much broader in scope and application, covering all aspects of development including, in addition to zoning, subdivision and site-plan regulations, stormwater management, environmental impact, and similar controls. The trend today is to unify all such development regulations into a unified code, referred to as a "land development ordinance" or "development regulations ordinance." More recently, such regulations are being translated into Form-Based Codes or hybrid codes combining aspects of both, an outgrowth of the new urbanist movement and a new and compelling way of expressing land development controls. Whatever the title or format, all codes need definitions. We hope that this fourth edition will assist all those responsible for drafting, interpreting or implementing such codes.

# Acknowledgments

Most zoning or land-development ordinance definitions are "borrowed," "inherited," or "stolen" from other ordinances. Indeed, most ordinances are written in this way. If a planner is particularly astute, early on he or she will start collecting definitions, then add, discard, or modify as the planner comes across new definitions or finds old ones not working. Many of the definitions in this book came about in this manner, but we would like to acknowledge the following contributions to this fourth edition.

A major source of many of the new definitions and assistance in developing more cohesive, insightful, and useful commentaries was the American Planning Association and its excellent publications. These include the well-researched and comprehensive material produced for the Planning Advisory Service (PAS), cases, articles, and commentaries in *Planning* Magazine.

The North American Industry Classification System (NAICS) supersedes the US Standard Industrial Classification (SIC) system. Both the NAICS and SIC manuals contain the best source of definitions of all types of economic activity. More planners should use NAICS to allow definitions of various types of use activities to become standardized.

The New Jersey Site Improvement Advisory Board was established in 1993 to prepare uniform residential site improvement standards. The resulting Residential Site Improvement Standards (RSIS), NJAC 5:21, provides an excellent source for many of the technical definitions relating to site improvements, including streets, sanitary sewers, stormwater management, and potable water supplies. In fact, one of the authors of the RSIS, David Listokin, PhD, is a coauthor of this fourth edition, and another coauthor, Richard Preiss, conducted studies of subdivision and site plans in order to generate standardized regulations for all residential developments in the RSIS.

For specific issues and topics, such as FORM-BASED CODES and OFFICE HEADQUARTERS, prominent persons in the field were contacted, and their names are listed as part of the commentary related to the topic. Special thanks to Susan Blickstein, PhD, PP, AICP, for her expertise on transportation issues; to Janice Talley, PP, AICP, for municipal planning recommendations; and to Howard Wolf, for his input on FEMA regulations and definitions. We also acknowledge with gratitude Elizabeth C. McKenzie, PP, AICP, our go-to planner when we needed another perspective on a definition or comment. Very smart, very articulate, and very direct.

We discovered that adding the legal annotations was a much bigger job than we thought initially. Most of the heavy lifting over a year and a half's time was done by Emily C. Deans, a student at the University of Connecticut School of Law and already a rising star. She received the CALI Award for the highest grade in her land use law course. Remember her name: you will most certainly see it in the future. Emily researched and did drafts for the letters B–P and W–Z. Linnea C. McCaffrey, AICP, a land use analyst at Robinson & Cole LLP, helped pull together the text from different formats, did part of the letter S, and with Sorell Negro, a lawyer at Robinson & Cole LLP, did the letter A. Michele Maresca, a lawyer at Robinson & Cole LLP, did part of the letter V.

Special thanks and our deep appreciation go to Arlene Pashman, former senior editor of the Center for Urban Policy Research (CUPR) Press. Her impressive editing skills, uncommon common sense, and eye for detail materially improved the 2004 edition of our definitions (published by CUPR Press), and the 2004 version provided a critical foundation for the current fourth edition. We are most grateful to this very special person.

The authors wish to particularly thank John Richkus of Phillips Preiss Grygiel LLC, who typed many drafts of this fourth edition in a very competent and expeditious manner. Besides the authors, no person worked harder or more diligently on the fourth edition.

We also acknowledge the contributions of many people, including planners, lawyers, builders, developers, educators, and public officials, who made important and timely recommendations and suggestions for this fourth edition. They include Eileen Banyra, Robert W. Burchell, Leslie Burer (Princeton), Philip Caton, Richard Chaiken, Ross Chapin, Pamela S. Chasek, Richard Coppola, Robert Cotter, Frank DeMaio, John DePinto, Andrew Feranda, Alan Finkel, Robin Finn, Paul Grygiel, Mary Hammon, Thomas B. Harvey, Mitchel Hirsh, David Hoder, Keenan Hughes, George Jacobs, Liz Jordan, Michael Jovishoff, David Karlback, Al Kaplan, Allan Kehrt, Kate Keller, Robert Kirkpatrick, Josette Kratz, Elizabeth Leheny, Jacob Lehrfeld, Niev Lindbloom, Christopher Looney, Allan Maitlin, Diana Marsh, Maser Consulting PA, Deborah Moskowitz, Diane Moskowitz, Leonard J. Moskowitz, Ross Moskowitz, Steven Moskowitz, Moy Pang, Paul Phillips, Sherry Preiss, Bob Regan, Maurice Ruberman, Megan Seel, Robert L. Shapiro, Mark Silance, Kiersten Skog, Gary Stephenson, Michael Sullivan, Katie Thielman-Puniello, Deborah Van Renterghem, Jerry Walters, and Joe Weber.

Finally, the authors thank President Mary Curtis and the talented and energetic staff of Transaction Publishers for their yeoman, professional assistance and for enabling the continued legacy of development definitions.

To all who assisted, whether directly or indirectly, we give our thanks. Naturally, the authors alone accept the responsibility for any mistakes that may appear in the book.

# Introduction

How much lighter is light industry than heavy industry? Is there a difference between an advertising sign and a business sign? Are the terms *floodplain*, *flood hazard area*, and *flood fringe area* interchangeable? The answers to these questions obviously depend on how we define our terms. Like it or not, all professional fields develop a language of their own. These "words of art" have meanings not anticipated by Webster. The purpose of *The Complete Illustrated Book of Development Definitions*, therefore, is to define some of the more common planning, development, and environmental terms.

## THE PURPOSE OF DEFINITIONS

Webster (1976) defines *definition* as "a word or phrase expressing the essential nature of a person or thing or class of persons or of things, a statement of the meaning of a word or word group." However, definitions do more than that. When used in complex legal documents such as zoning ordinances or other development regulations, they have a threefold purpose:

1. *They simplify the text*. By defining our terms, it is possible to combine into a single word long phrases, lists of words, or similar terms that, from a zoning or control point of view, may be treated alike. For example, rather than repeat *application for site plan approval*, *permission to build in a floodplain*, *soil removal application*, or *application for subdivision* in an ordinance regulating development, the phrase *application for development* can be defined to mean all of the preceding terms. Similarly, the term *manufacturing* is defined to mean:

   > *Establishments engaged in the mechanical or chemical transformation of materials or substances into new products, including the assembling of component parts, the creation of products, and the blending of materials such as lubricating oils, plastics, resins, or liquors.*

   Think how long an ordinance would be if the definiens (the words used to describe the term to be defined) had to be repeated throughout the ordinance.

2. *Definitions precisely establish the meaning of a word or term that may be subject to differing interpretations*. The precise definition eliminates ambiguity and vagueness. It focuses on the essential elements of a word or phrase and clearly marks off and limits its application or interpretation. For example, a zone may permit light industrial uses. Everyone knows what light industry is—right? Industry is—well, work. Or is it manufacturing, and is warehousing included? Webster has five definitions of industry, and the North American Industry Classification System, or NAICS, includes retailing, finance, and real estate under the broad definition of industry. So it is not quite that apparent, and even experts can impart different meanings to the word.

If we consider defining *industry* difficult, we must acknowledge the equally difficult problem of defining *light* in conjunction with it. Does *light* refer to the end product, the raw material, or the machines used in the process? Or does it refer to something else entirely?

By precisely defining *light industry* in an ordinance, we eliminate the vagueness and ambiguity that, at best, result in confusion, and, at worst, end up in costly lawsuits and delays.

3. *Definitions translate technical terms into usable and understandable terminology.* Definitions enable us to convert sometimes-abstract technical terms into meaningful standards to control and guide development. For instance, returning to our favorite example, the word *light* as used in *light industry* may be defined in terms of a number of variables, such as trip generation, bulk controls, and nuisance characteristics. Each of these terms requires further definition to make the original *light industry* term meaningful and enforceable.

   Thus, one nuisance characteristic may be smoke emission, and the defined characteristic of *light industry* in terms of smoke emission is that the smoke density cannot exceed a certain level on the Ringlemann Chart, or some other authoritative standard, for measuring smoke density. Another nuisance characteristic is noise, and *light industry* can be further defined in terms of the maximum noise level as measured at the lot line.

## WHAT DEFINITIONS ARE NOT

Given that definitions simplify, clarify, and translate, it might be wise to point out what definitions should not be. The most important limitation is that the definition should not contain the control elements or standards that regulate the defined word or phrase.

For example, most ordinances attempt to define home occupations in terms of the standards or controls under which the home occupation can be established. These controls usually include the percentage of floor area that can be occupied, limitations on nonresident employees, parking requirements, lot sizes, and sign controls. These controls belong in the body of the ordinance and may vary depending upon the zone in which the home occupation is permitted. To locate the standards in the definition precludes this flexibility. Another example of misplaced standards is illustrated in our previously cited example, *light industry*. Two definitions are considered in this book: one that precisely lists all those activities or uses that would fall under the term *light industry*—a "use-specific definition"—and a second, "performance-based standard," in which the definition of *light industry* might read as follows:

**INDUSTRY, LIGHT Industrial uses that meet the specific performance standards, bulk controls, and other requirements contained in this ordinance.**

Utilizing this second "performance-based" approach would require one to spell out the performance standards and bulk controls to which *light industry* must conform. In fact, as illustrated below, the controls on *medium industry* and *heavy industry* also could be included, and the definitions of *medium industry* and *heavy industry* need not be substantially different from *light industry* on every control element.

A typical control chart, which would be part of the zoning chapter, might read as follows:

| ***Control Elements, Industry*** | ***Light Industry*** | ***Medium Industry*** | ***Heavy Industry*** |
|---|---|---|---|
| Minimum Lot Size | No minimum | 5 Acres | 10 Acres |
| Maximum Lot Size | 5 Acres | 10 Acres | No limit |
| Maximum FAR | 0.5 | 1.0 | 2.0 |
| Maximum Building Height<br>maximum Number of Vehicle Trips Per Peak Hour | 2 Stories/30'<br>100 | 4 Stories/40'<br>300 | 6 Stories/60'<br>No limit |
| Maximum Noise Level | 70 dBA | 75 dBA | 82 dBA |
| Maximum Smoke Density On Ringle-mann Chart | #1 | #1 | #2 |
| Vibration | None permitted beyond building wall | None permitted beyond zone line | None permitted beyond zone line |
| Air Quality | 50% of maximum allowed by state law | 75% of maximum allowed by state law | As permitted by state law |
| Buffers | 25' around property line | 40' around property line | 50' around property line |

*Note:* The list of control elements noted above is not complete, and standards suggested are for illustration purposes only. The chart does illustrate the point: The definition is only a few lines and simple; the standard in the ordinance may be long and detailed. We would also point out that some states do not permit a local ordinance to impose more stringent standards than permitted in the state law. This may be true of noise or air-quality standards.

Definitions should not run counter to the generally accepted meaning of words and phrases. As pointed out, "If it quacks like a duck, walks like a duck, looks like a duck . . . it must be a duck." Very often this problem manifests itself in a negative manner. A zoning ordinance may establish a retail commercial zone and then exclude an obvious retail use because of local pressures, fear of competition, or perceived impacts. The point is that the generally accepted meaning of words and phrases should not be radically altered in an ordinance.

Cox (2003, 114) quotes a New Jersey case—*Essex County Retail, etc., v. Newark, etc. Beverage Control*, 77 N.J. Super. 70, 77 (App. Div. 1962):

> *Ordinances are to receive a reasonable construction and application, to serve the apparent legislative purpose. We will not depart from the plain meaning of language which is free of ambiguity, for an ordinance must be construed according to the ordinary meaning of its words and phrases. These are to be taken in the ordinary or popular sense, unless it plainly appears that they are used in a different sense.*

Similarly, common words and phrases often take on a specific meaning in a technical field, and these may differ substantially from the generally accepted definition. Some examples are *affordable housing*, *cellar*, *basement*, or *home occupation*. The courts also may restrict or expand commonly accepted definitions. The best illustration is the word *family*, which recent state court decisions have expanded to include an unlimited number of nonrelated individuals living as a single housekeeping unit.

# SOME GENERAL OBSERVATIONS ABOUT DEFINITIONS IN DEVELOPMENT ORDINANCES

1. *Don't define it if it is not used in the ordinance.* There are two schools of thought on whether to include a word or phrase that is not subsequently included in the ordinance. For example, in a rural farming municipality, should the term *high-rise apartment* be defined? Conversely, in a built-up urban area, should the term *farm* be defined?

   Many drafters believe that if there is a possibility that the phrase will be used in the future, it should be included. The authors have a different opinion. If it is not used, either as a permitted use or one specifically excluded, it should not be defined. The reason is that it may confuse the intent of the framers. If high-rise apartments are not permitted, then there is no reason to include that term anywhere in the ordinance. In addition, where there may be a question as to the intent of whether or not a particular use is allowed in a zone, the fact that it is defined gives credence to the position that the intent was to allow the use. If the author of a zoning ordinance is fearful that undefined, unlisted uses will be perceived as being permitted, the way to ameliorate that possibility is to include a general provision which indicates that "all uses not specifically listed as being permitted or conditionally permitted are hereby prohibited."

2. *Use federal, state, or county definitions if available.* More and more categories of land use are no longer under local control, or they may require federal, state, or county licenses or approvals even when the municipality exercises location control. To avoid conflicts, the local definition should be consistent with the "higher" definition, to the extent possible. It also more clearly defines the intent of the framers in allowing a specific type of use or activity in a zone. For example, all states license schools. If the local intent is to permit elementary schools in residential neighborhoods, then the definition can be "any school licensed by the State and which meets the State requirements for elementary education." This eliminates private business schools or vocational schools. County requirements and definitions relating to roads and streets are particularly appropriate for inclusion in local development codes. One word of caution, however. What may be appropriate on a federal or state level, and defined as such, may be inappropriate on a local level. This is particularly true of public utilities and essential services.

3. *Use nationally accepted definitions if available.* We noted in the introduction to a previous edition of this book that, at that time, the best single source of use definitions was the *Standard Industrial Classification Manual*. The SIC grouped all land-use activities in a series of categories from very broad activity classes (residential, manufacturing, trade, services, and so on) to very specific and detailed land-use categories. The SIC has been replaced by the North American Industry Classification System (NAICS). It classifies business establishments into twenty two-digit broad categories as compared with the ten divisions in the old SIC. The twenty broad categories are then further subdivided into three-, four-, five-, and six-digit categories. A total of 1,170 different industries and business activities are identified. It is important to keep in mind that the NAICS defines uses; zoning controls are needed to regulate scale, intensity, and impacts.

4. *Words should be defined within the context of the legislative intent of the zone district and by the other examples of uses permitted in the district.* While these limitations may seem obvious, applicants may attempt to use uncommon or rare permutations of words in order to establish the legality of other uses. For example, a residential zone permitting single-family detached houses, home occupations, and studios as principal permitted uses does not contemplate professional office buildings or motion picture studios if one considers the legislative intent of the zone

(residential) or the context of home occupations and studios in terms of scale and uses normally permitted in a single-family residential district.

5. *Legal and technical input are necessary in preparing definitions for development ordinances.* Legal review is needed to ensure that the definition does not run afoul of state or federal laws or counter to court decisions. Engineering, architectural, and environmental review is needed for definitions encompassing those fields.

## SUMMARY

Using in part the Planning Advisory Service (PAS) Report No. 72 *Zoning Ordinance Definitions* (1955), the general "rules" relating to definitions are as follows:

- The term being defined
  a. Must be exactly equivalent to the definition.
  b. Should not appear in the definition.
  c. Cannot be defined by a synonym.
  d. Should not be defined by other indefinite or ambiguous terms.

- Definitions phrased in positive terms are preferable to definitions phrased in negative terms.
- Definitions should not include standards, measurements, or other control regulations.
- Anything not specifically included in a definition is automatically excluded.
- A defined term can have none other but the defined meaning throughout the entire ordinance.
- If a group of objects is being divided into two or more groups by definitions, be sure that all members of the group are included in one or the other of the groups.
- Use particular care in the grammatical construction of definitions.
- Do not define terms that are not used in the ordinance.
- Check definitions in related local ordinances, and make sure they do not conflict.
- Use county, state, or federal definitions where appropriate.
- Use standard definitions from national organizations or agencies when they are available.
- Words can be further defined in context with other examples or in terms of the legislative intent of the zone where located.
- Legal and technical review is needed to ensure the legality of terms and their technical correctness.

## A WORD ABOUT LEGAL ANNOTATIONS, BY DWIGHT MERRIAM

The coauthors of this new edition decided that one way to enhance an understanding of how the definitions work in practice would be to research the law and annotate the definitions with legal references. In most instances, relevant case law was easy to find and has been included. Sometimes, a definition is so new or rare that there is no case law, and those definitions are annotated with statutes or regulations. Finally, with just a handful of the definitions, no useful case law, statutes, or regulations could be found.

The annotations are illustrative only. They are not necessarily legal precedent. Interestingly, in researching the annotations, several instances were found where courts have cited a prior edition of this book as authority for a definition. It is appropriate to cite to definitions in this book as authority for the meaning of the term and to make note of the annotation, though it would be prudent to check the annotation to make sure that it has not been overruled or distinguished in some way and is precedent in the jurisdiction. This is best done with one of the legal search engines such as Westlaw or Lexis.

If the reader is interested in reviewing the full case, statute, or regulation, it is easy to do with the information provided in the annotation. All of the cases are available on Google Scholar, and the full decisions can be found by searching the case name or a phrase from the annotation (in quotes) in Google Scholar: http://scholar.google.com. Make sure to click on "Case Law" and not "Articles" on the home page. Statutes and regulations are available, assuming the Web links are not broken (a problem now called "link rot"), at the Web addresses provided. If a link is broken, you will likely be able to find the full text by searching a phrase (do it in quotes) from the annotation on your Web browser.

If you have a better annotation for any of the definitions, please send it to us for inclusion in the next edition.

# Abbreviations and Acronyms

Abbreviations and acronyms used in the definitions and comments:

| | |
|---|---|
| AADT | average annual daily traffic |
| AASHTO | American Association of State Highway and Transportation Officials |
| ADT | average daily traffic |
| AGD | Attention-getting device |
| AICP | American Institute of Certified Planners |
| ANSI | American National Standards Institute |
| APA | American Planning Association |
| App | Appellate |
| ARC | Application Review Committee |
| ASTM | ASTM International (formerly ASTM [American Society for Testing and Materials]) |
| ATM | automated teller machine |
| ATV | all-terrain vehicle |
| AVR | average vehicle ridership |
| B&B | bed-and-breakfast |
| BID | business improvement district |
| BMP | best management practice |
| BOCA | Buildings Officials and Code Administrators (national building code) (*Editor's note:* In 1994, the International Code Council [ICC] was established, combining three organizations: BOCA, ICBO [International Conference of Building Officials], and SBCCI [Southern Building Code Congress International].) |
| BOD | biological oxygen demand |
| BTU | British Thermal Units |
| CAFO | concentrated animal feeding operation |
| CBD | central business district |
| CCO | continued certificate of occupancy |
| CCRC | continuing care retirement community |
| CFS | cubic feet per second |
| CIP | capital improvement program |

| | |
|---|---|
| CO | certificate of occupancy |
| CPC | current planning capacity |
| CRDD | community residences for the developmentally disabled |
| Ct | Court |
| dBA | A-weighted sound level decibel |
| DRC | Development Review Committee |
| DRI | developments of regional impact |
| DO | dissolved oxygen |
| DU | dwelling unit |
| EIS | environmental impact statement |
| EMF | electromagnetic field |
| EPA | Environmental Protection Agency |
| FAR | floor area ratio |
| FBC | form-based code |
| FCC | Federal Communications Commission |
| FEMA | Federal Emergency Management Agency |
| FIA | fiscal impact analysis |
| FIRM | flood insurance rate map |
| FIRE | finance, insurance, and real estate |
| GDP | general development plan |
| GFA | gross floor area |
| GHz | gigahertz |
| GIS | geographic information system |
| GLA | gross leasable area |
| HAZ | hazardous material |
| Hz | hertz |
| HOV | high-occupancy vehicle |
| HUD | US Department of Housing and Urban Development |
| ICF | intermediate care facility |
| IESNA | Illuminating Engineering Society of North America |
| ITE | Institute of Transportation Engineers |
| ITS | Intelligent Transportation Systems |
| KHz | kilohertz |

| | |
|---|---|
| kV/m | kilovolts per meter |
| LDO | land development ordinance |
| LDR | land development regulations |
| LEED | leadership in energy and environmental design |
| LRT | light rail transit |
| LUI | land-use intensity |
| MG | milligauss |
| MGD | millions of gallons per day |
| MHz | megahertz |
| MP | master plan |
| MSA | metropolitan statistical area |
| MXD | mixed-use development |
| NAAQS | National Ambient Air Quality Standards |
| NAICS | North American Industry Classification System |
| NEPA | National Environmental Policy Act |
| NGO | nongovernmental organization |
| NIMBY | not in my backyard |
| NRI | Natural Resources Inventory |
| NRPA | National Recreation and Park Association |
| ORV | off-road vehicle |
| PAS | Planning Advisory Service |
| PCD | planned commercial development |
| PD | planned development |
| PID | planned industrial development |
| PILOT | payment in lieu of taxes |
| POD | portable on-demand storage |
| PPP | public private partnership |
| PRT | personal rapid transit technology |
| PUD | planned unit development |
| PURD | planned-unit residential development |
| RHCF | residential health-care facility |
| RIUIPA | Religious Land Use and Institutionalized Persons Act |
| ROW | right-of-way |

| | |
|---|---|
| RSIS | (NJ) Residential Site Improvement Standards |
| SID | special improvement district |
| SLM | shared lane marking |
| SOB | sexually oriented business |
| $SO_2$ | sulfur dioxide |
| SRO | single-room occupancy |
| TCC | technical coordinating committee |
| TDM | transportation demand management |
| TDR | transfer of development rights |
| TIF | tax increment financing |
| TLR | transit, light rail |
| TMA | transportation management association |
| TND | traditional neighborhood development |
| TOD | transit-oriented development |
| TSM | transportation systems management |
| WiFi | wireless Internet access |
| WQMP | water quality management plan |
| ZO | zoning ordinance |

# A

## ABANDONED VEHICLE

See *Motor Vehicle, Abandoned.*

## ABANDONMENT

**The relinquishment of property, or a cessation of the use of the property, by the owner or lessee without any intention of transferring rights to the property to another owner or of resuming the use of the property.**

***Comment***: In zoning, abandonment of a nonconforming use requires (1) a discontinuance of the use and (2) an intent to abandon. Since intent is often difficult to prove, many zoning ordinances sidestep the issue by stating that a nonconforming use not exercised for a continuous period of time (one year, for example) cannot be resumed. Nonuse may not be enough, however, and absent any significant changes to suggest an intent to abandon the nonconforming use, the nonconforming rights remain (Cox 2003). Conversion of a nonconforming use to a conforming one, though, is always indicative of an intent to abandon the use.

***Legal Annotation***: "**Abandonment** is proved only when both essential elements are established: (1) intent to abandon and (2) implementation of the intent, i.e., actual abandonment." *In Re: The Appeal of SIIKA, LLC v. Jackson Township* (Pa. Cmwlth. 2011) (citing *Heichel v. Springfield Township Zoning Hearing Bd.* [Pa. Cmwlth., 2003]).

## ABATEMENT

**The method of reducing the degree and intensity of pollution.**

***Legal Annotation***: Section 313 of the Clean Water Act "provides that if an agency of the federal government is engaged in discharge of pollutants, or if it owns a property, it must comply with all local and state laws and regulations involving **abatement** of water pollution." *Oneida Tribe of Indians of Wisconsin v. Village of Hobart* (E.D. Wis., 2011).

## ABATTOIR

**A place where livestock are killed and prepared for distribution to butcher shops and food markets.**

***Comment***: An abattoir is a very intensive use, often requiring a rail siding. It is usually a twenty-four-hour operation, noisy, and often odorous, with special solid and septic waste considerations. Some abattoirs have small retail operations selling directly to consumers.

***Legal Annotation***: Section 21.1.70 of the Crosby Township Zoning Resolution prohibits specific uses such as **abattoirs**, slaughterhouses, vinegar manufacture, and yeast plants. *Engel v. Crosby Township Bd. of Zoning Appeals* (Ohio App., 2009).

"The first section forbids the landing or slaughtering of animals whose flesh is intended for food within the city of New Orleans and other parishes and boundaries named and defined, or the keeping or establishing any slaughterhouses or **abattoirs** within those limits except by the corporation thereby created." *The Slaughter House Cases* (U.S., 1873).

## ABSORPTION

**(1) The penetration of one substance into or through another; (2) the length of time it takes for a product or real estate to be sold or rented.**

***Comment***: Absorption in development terms is critical in determining whether a project is economically viable. Developers often speak of absorption rates of so many dwelling units (by type) per year or the square footage of floor area rented or leased over a fixed period of time.

*Legal Annotation*: "Because Fenton Centre is presently only 50% occupied . . . whether or not there is equity above the Bank's debt will largely turn on the **absorption** rate at which the court concludes the vacant space will lease up." *In Re: FRE Real Estate, Inc.* (Bankr. N.D. Texas, 2011).

## ABSORPTION BED OR FIELD

**A large pit or system of trenches containing coarse aggregate and distribution pipe through which the septic tank effluent may seep into the surrounding soil (Toenjes 1989).**

*Legal Annotation*: "[I]mproper grading and insufficient swales and berms (all to divert surface water from flowing over the absorption field), and . . . a lack of appropriate sodding or ground cover the **absorption field** . . . allowed raw sewage to run on the ground and drain downhill toward the neighbor's yard." *Smith v. Taylor Built Construction Co.* (Ala. Civ. App., 2000).

## ABUT

**To physically touch or border on; or to share a common property line but not overlap.**

*Legal Annotation*: "Defendant's 'property does not **abut** the portion of the sidewalk where plaintiff fell[,]' and he therefore 'did not have a duty to maintain th[at] portion of the sidewalk . . . in a reasonably safe condition.'" *Montalbano v. 136 W. 80 St. CP* (N.Y. App. Div., 2011).

## ABUTMENT

**(1) A structure that supports the end of a bridge or arch; (2) the side of an earth bank that supports a dam (Toenjes 1989).**

*Legal Annotation*: "Affirming trial court's findings that '[t]he present bridge **abutments** and surrounding fill serve to significantly restrict the width of Strickland Brook and the adjacent wetlands.'" *Eisenberg v. Tuchman* (Conn. App. 2006).

## ACCELERATION LANE

**An added roadway lane that permits integration and merging of slower-moving vehicles into the main vehicular stream.** ***See Figure 1.***

*Comment*: Frequently used in connection with the entrance to a major traffic generator.

*Legal Annotation*: "[T]he Texas Department of Transportation devised [a] proposed plan . . .

**Figure 1**

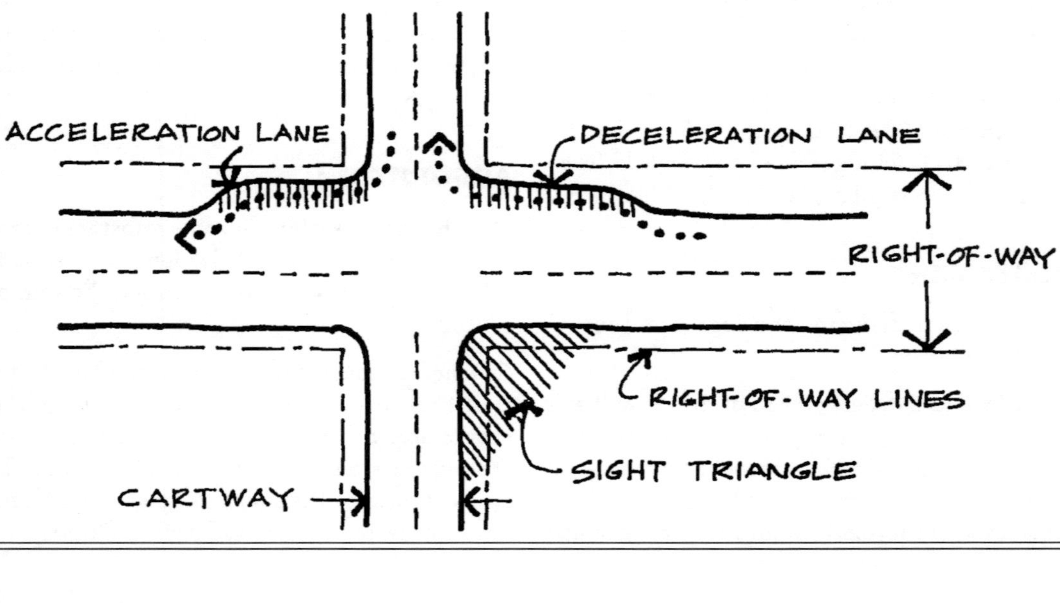

which provided a . . . corresponding **acceleration lane** for vehicles exiting the property and returning to the highway." *Texas v. PR Investments & Specialty Retailers, Inc.* (Texas App., 2005).

## ACCEPTABLE RISK

**That level of risk (likelihood of occurrence and consequence of impact) for any activity or situation that is sufficiently low that society (or an organization within society that is managing the risk) is comfortable with it. Society (and an individual organization) does not generally consider expenditure in further reducing such risks justifiable. (Adapted from Australian National 1994). http://www.gwu.edu/~icdrm/publications/PDF/GLOSSARY%2002-19-2007.pdf**

***Legal Annotation***: "Of course, if the Administrator cannot find that there is an acceptable risk at any level, then the Administrator must set the level at zero." *Natural Resources Defense Council v. USEPA* (D.C. CT. App., 1987).

## ACCESS

**A way or means of approach to provide vehicular or pedestrian physical entrance to a property.**

***Legal Annotation***: Conn. Gen. Stat. "Section 13a-55 grants the plaintiff a private right of **access** over Old Huckleberry Hill Road [to its property] and does not purport to reinstate a right of public **access**." *KJC Real Estate Development, LLC v. Zoning Bd. of Appeals* (Conn. App., 2011).

## ACCESS CLASSIFICATION

**A hierarchical rating system for streets and highways based on function, environment, and traffic characteristics, used to determine applicable access standards. See *Access Code*.**

***Comment***: Part of a growing number of regulations governing access to state highways and, where applicable, to local and county roads. Access standards may include a minimum spacing of distance between driveways.

***Legal Annotation***: In 1969, pursuant to Section 17 of the Federal Aid Highway Act of 1968, the NHDPW&H inventoried the State's highway system and **functionally classified** all state **highways**. *No East-West Highway Committee, Inc. v. Whitaker* (D. N.H., 1975).

## ACCESS CODE

**The highway access management code adopted pursuant to appropriate legislation. See *Access Classification; Access Level; Access Management Plan; Access Permit; Alternate Work Arrangement Programs; Employee Transportation Coordinator; Major Traffic Generator; Peak-Hour Traffic; Rational Nexus; Significant Increase In Traffic; Traffic Growth Rate; Traffic Impact Study; Transportation Demand Management Plan; Transportation Management Association.***

***Comment***: Where permitted by states, municipalities and counties can adopt access codes providing for access management plans and standards of access to local and county roads.

***Legal Annotation***: The NJ Department of Transportation "regulates the number, placement, and configuration of driveways along State highways pursuant to the Access Act and the State Highway **Access** Management **Code** (Access Code)." *In the Matter of the Issuance of Access Conforming Lot* (N.J. Super., 2010).

## ACCESS LEVEL

**The allowable turning movements to and from access points on a highway segment based on the highway access classification.**

***Legal Annotation***: "(i) The Department may allow modifications to an existing private point of access abutting a Category 2 or 3 highway including relocation of the point of access within the limits of the property, if such modification or change will benefit the operation and safety of the highway, bring the **access level** of the highway into greater conformance with the access category, or be in the interest of public health, safety, and welfare." Utah Administrtaive Code R930-6-7

Design Requirements http://www.rules.utah.gov/publicat/code/r930/r930-006.htm

## ACCESS MANAGEMENT PLAN

**A plan showing the design of access for every lot on a highway segment developed jointly by the state, the municipality in which the highway is located, and the county, if a county road intersects the segment.**

***Comment***: In states with highway access regulations, counties and municipalities are permitted to enact access management plans for various categories of roads under their jurisdiction. These plans may include the minimum distance between road access points and the roadway design.

***Legal Annotation***: The town's environmental impact statement called for an **access management plan**, which "involves planning for the entry and exit of traffic on major roads in such a way as to keep interference with traffic flow to a minimum." *Eadie v. Town Bd.* (N.Y. App., 2006).

## ACCESS PERMIT

**A permit issued by the appropriate governmental agency for the construction, maintenance, and use of a driveway or public street connecting to a highway.**

***Legal Annotation***: The Secretary of the Interior's "regulations provide . . . that an **access permit** must be obtained before operating heavy, off-road vehicles in the [Yukon-Charley Rivers National] Preserve." *United States v. Vogler* (9th Cir., 1988).

## ACCESS POINT

**The location of the intersection of a highway or street or driveway with the highway.**

***Legal Annotation***: "We have held that access to a business was not materially and substantially impaired when one **access point** was closed, but another access point on a public street remained unaffected." *City of San Antonio v. TPLP Office Park* (Texas, 2007).

## ACCESS POINT OFFSET

**The distance between the centerlines of access points on opposite sides of undivided highways and the distance between the centerlines of an access point and a median opening on a divided highway.** ***See Figure 2.***

***Legal Annotation***: "That this particular provision of the ordinance which requires a 300-foot distance between '**access points**' of a site located upon an admittedly major traffic thoroughfare bears a direct and reasonable relationship to the safety and general welfare of the public travelling upon this particular vehicular artery is beyond question." *Sun Oil Co. v. Zoning Board of Adjustment* (Pa. 1961).

**Figure 2**

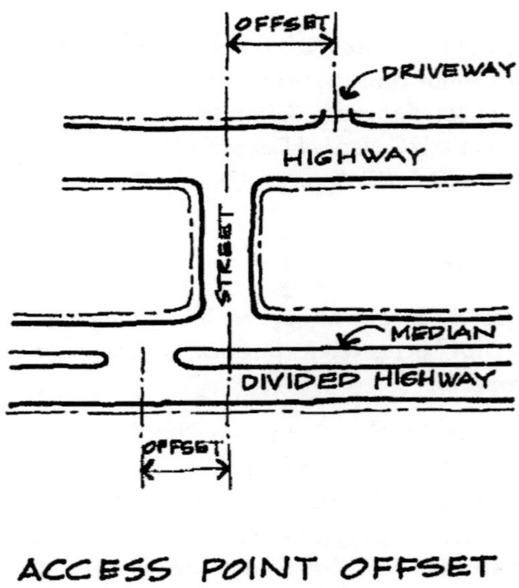


## ACCESS ROAD

See *Street, Local.*

## ACCESSIBLE DESIGN

**Accessible generally means that environments, objects, and systems meet prescribed requirements for accessibility for people with disabilities. See *People with Disabilities*.**

***Comment***: "Mandatory requirements for accessible housing vary widely and are found in state, local, and model building codes, in agency regulations such as in the Department of Housing and Urban Development's program 202 and 811, section 504, the Fair Housing Amendments Act requirements, and the Americans with Disabilities Act. They are also found in standards such as the American National Standards Institute's A117.1 (ANSI A117.1-1986, 1998) and the Uniform Federal Accessibility Standards (UFAS).

"Accessible features in dwellings include items such as wide doors, sufficient clear floor space for wheelchairs, lower countertop segments, lever and loop type handles on hardware, seats at bathing fixtures, grab bars in bathrooms, knee spaces under sinks and counters, audible and visual signals, switches and controls in easily reached locations, entrances free of steps and stairs and an accessible route through the house. Most 'accessible' features are permanently fixed in place and very apparent." See *Adaptable Design*. http://www.ncsu.edu/ncsu/design/cud/pubs_p/docs/Fact%20Sheet%206.pdf *See also* Skinner 2009, 11.

***Legal Annotation***: "H.R. Rep. No. 101-485(III) at 60, reprinted at 1990 U.S.C.C.A.N. 445, 483 ('Because it costs far less to incorporate **accessible design** into the planning and construction of new buildings and of alterations [as compared to retrofitting existing structures], a higher standard of "readily accessible to and usable by" persons with disabilities has been adopted in the ADA for new construction and alterations')." *Independent Living Resources v. Oregon Arena Corp.* (D. Ore., 1997).

## ACCESSIBLE PLAYGROUND

See *Playground, Accessible*.

## ACCESSIBLE PRINCIPAL ARTERIAL

**A roadway that is part of an interconnected network of continuous routes serving transportation corridors with high traffic volumes and long trips, the primary function of which is to provide safe and efficient service for major traffic movements in which access is subordinate.**

***Legal Annotation***: "The classification of a road determines whether the state, county, or city is financially responsible for its upkeep and maintenance. . . . DOT determines the classification and jurisdictional assignment of roads in urban areas. . . . Points are assigned to each road according to its function and characteristics. Roads with the highest points are classified as urban **principal arterial roads**; the number of miles in the principal and minor arterial road classifications is limited by Rule 14-12.016(1)(b)4." *City of Palm Bay v. State DOT* (Fla. Dist. Ct. App., 1991).

## ACCESSIBLE ROUTE

**A continuous, unobstructed path connecting all accessible elements and spaces of a building or facility.**

***Comment***: Accessible routes are required as part of the Americans with Disabilities Act of 1990. See *Americans with Disabilities Act (ADA)*.

***Legal Annotation***: "The remaining question is whether an obstacle, like the Del Taco concrete trash container, blocking an **accessible route** of travel to an entrance, presents a breach of this duty under the ADA." *Madden v. Del Taco, Inc.* (Calif. App. Ct., 2007).

## ACCESSORY APARTMENT

**A dwelling unit with a separate means of ingress and egress containing separate kitchen, bathroom, and sleeping facilities, that is (1) physically attached to or contained within an existing single-family house or (2) occupies the second story of an existing garage or accessory building on the same lot as the principal dwelling.**

***Comment***: Accessory apartments, often referred to as "accessory dwelling units," "granny flats," "mother-in-law" housing, or "garage apartments," can be an important resource in providing housing for elderly, one- or two-person households, and lower-income families. Accessory apartments can be listed as permitted units in appropriate areas or conditional uses where site plan approval is warranted. Regulations vary by municipality but are usually concerned with health and safety issues, as well as maintaining the basic character of the neighborhood. These objectives can be achieved by using designated minimum and maximum floor areas for the accessory apartments, setback and height limits, requiring off-street parking, and prohibiting any change in the basic single-family appearance of the structure (Andrews 2005, 8; Selige 2012). Also, City of Santa Cruz, California, Accessory Dwelling Unit Development Program and Chapter 2416, part 2 of the Zoning Ordinance of the City of Santa Cruz, California, Accessory Dwelling Unit Development Program. See *Dwelling, Garage Apartments; Dwelling, End Gap; Dwelling, Micro-Unit.*

***Legal Annotation***: "On September 27, 2005, Nikolas's application for an **accessory apartment** came before the City Council for a hearing and vote." *Nikolas v. City of Omaha* (D. Neb., 2009).

## ACCESSORY DWELLING

**A dwelling unit either attached to a single-family principal dwelling or located on the same lot and having an independent means of access. See *Accessory Apartment; Accessory Structure; Party Wall; Party Driveway*.**

***Comment***: An accessory dwelling differs from an accessory apartment in that, if permitted by local ordinance, it has a separate means of access and can be a separate structure on the lot.

***Legal Annotation***: "The County stated that it would encourage **accessory dwelling** units in single-family zones." *Kitsap County v. C. Puget Sound Growth Management Hearings Bd.* (Wash. Ct. App., 2007).

## ACCESSORY STRUCTURE

**A structure detached from a principal building located on the same lot and customarily incidental and subordinate to the principal building or use. *See Figure 3*.**

***Comment***: The accessory structure must be on the same lot as the principal structure unless the ordinance specifically permits it to be located on another lot. An example of this is a parking structure for a commercial establishment required to be located within a certain radius but not necessarily on the same lot as the establishment. It is desirable to place limits on the number and size of accessory structures, particularly in residential areas.

***Legal Annotation***: "In response to the Nunleys' petition for a variance to construct a garage, the board of zoning appeals 'eventually granted the Nunleys a modified variance, permitting an **accessory structure** no closer than five feet from the northern projected boundary and no closer than 15 feet from the eastern projected

**Figure 3**

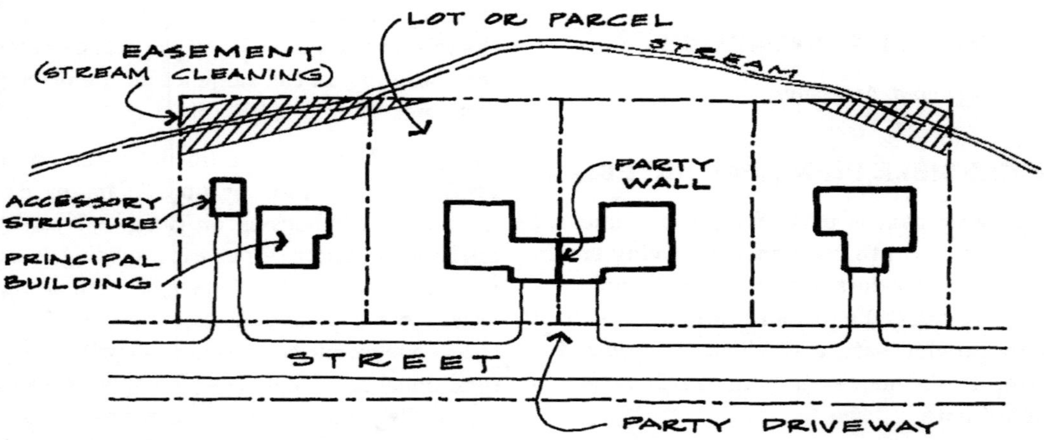

boundary of the property.'" *Cochran v. Fairfax County Bd. of Zoning* (Va., 2004).

## ACCESSORY USE

**A use of land or of a building or portion thereof customarily incidental and subordinate to the principal use of the land or building and located on the same lot with the principal use.**

***Comment***: A New Jersey case noted the following characteristics of an accessory use: commonly, habitually, and by long practice as being established or reasonably associated with the primary use (*Charley Brown of Chatham v. Board of Adjustment*, 202 N.J. Super. 312, App. Div. [1985]). What constitutes an accessory use changes over time. For example, many ordinances now define a child-care facility as an accessory use to large-scale office or industrial buildings. Other facilities such as bank branches, gyms, restaurants, and gift shops, which primarily serve the employees in major office developments (and have the added benefit of reducing lunchtime vehicular trips), may also be defined as accessory uses.

It may be advisable to physically limit the accessory use to prevent it from becoming the principal use. For example, a retail outlet in a warehouse, selling those products stored in the warehouse, could be considered an accessory use. The local ordinance should limit the floor area of the retail use. A reasonable standard might be a maximum of 5 percent of the warehouse floor area, or five thousand square feet, whichever is less. Other limits might include the number of employees. Where the accessory use is not confined to a specific physical area or the number of employees is difficult to establish, the approving agency might have to determine that the planning impacts of the proposed accessory use are, in fact, significantly less than the principal use. In other words, if the principal use generates one hundred vehicle trips during the peak hour, and the proposed accessory use generates 125 trips, the accessory use can no longer be considered an accessory use

***Legal Annotation***: The Zoning Commission concluded that "the weekly, sizable prayer meetings were not a customary **accessory use** in a single-family residential area." *Murphy v. New Milford Zoning Comm'n* (2d Cir., 2005).

## ACCIDENTAL SPACES

**"Specific, definable public or quasi-public locations within communities used for productive purposes other than or in addition to their intended purpose" (Zelinka and Johnston 2005, 42).**

***Comment***: "Accidental spaces may be divided into three types: people-centered, activity-linked, and event-based. In all three cases, the spaces are used for purposes other than those originally intended. People-centered accidental spaces are spontaneously claimed by people for individual or collective non-organized activities, such as socializing, exercising theatrical performances and eating. Activity-linked accidental spaces are regularly claimed by a business or organization for an ongoing use directly linked to its primary activity, such as a city-sponsored rock climbing wall on a bridge footing or outdoor dining as an accessory use to a restaurant. Event-based accidental spaces are used by an organization for regular activity that is directly tied to its organizational mission or purpose, such as farmers' markets. All three types of accidental spaces share the following traits: a unique character and sense of place; comfort and the perception of safety; proximity to activity generators such as paths, roads, and businesses, and visibility" (Zelinka and Johnston 2005, 42).

***Legal Annotation***: "Public Art, '**accidental spaces**' and well designed street furniture could inform the character of the squares and spaces.".East Village (Calgary, Canada) Master Plan Executive Summary 29.

http://www.calgaryherald.com/pdf/East_Village_Master_Plan_ExSummary.pdf

## ACCLIMATIZATION

**The physiological and behavioral adjustments of an organism over time to changes in its environment.**

*Legal Annotation*: The court considers, in determining habitual residence of a child, "whether there was 'an actual change in geography' coupled with the 'passage of an appreciable period of time, one sufficient for **acclimatization** by the children to the new environment.'" *Boehm v. Boehm* (Md. Dist. Ct., 2011).

## ACCRETION

**The creation of land by the recession of a lake or stream or by the gradual deposit of solid material by water.**

*Legal Annotation*: "[U]nder the doctrines of erosion, reliction, and **accretion**, the boundary between public and private land is altered to reflect gradual and imperceptible losses or additions to the shoreline." *Walton County v. Stop the Beach Renourishment, Inc.* (Fla. 2008).

## ACID RAIN

**Rain containing dissolved acidic compounds, resulting from chemical pollution of the atmosphere by sulfur and nitrogen compounds.**

*Comment*: When deposited, these increase the acidity of the soil and water, causing agricultural and ecological damage (Blanchard 2007, 37).

*Legal Annotation*: "Acid deposition—often referred to as '**acid rain**'—is believed to occur when certain pollutants are transported through the atmosphere and chemically altered by atmospheric processes before being deposited in either dry or wet form." *Thomas v. State of New York,* (D.C. Ct. App., 1986).

## ACRE

**A measure of land containing 43,560 square feet.**

*Comment*: Many ordinances use a "builder's acre" of forty thousand square feet. Other ordinances define a "net acre," which excludes existing rights-of-way, public use area dedications, easements, and similar limitations to development. See *Net Area of Lot.*

*Legal Annotation*: "Density restrictions permit the appellants to build between one and five single-family residences on their 5-**acre** tract." *Agins v. City of Tiburon* (U.S., 1980).

## ACRE-FOOT

**The volume of water, one foot deep, covering an acre of land.**

*Comment*: This term is often used in defining storm or potable water storage capacity.

*Legal Annotation*: "The stormwater treatment element of the project includes collection of stormwater in an eight-**acre-foot** detention pond which occupies three to four acres of the Legacy Park site." *Santa Monica Baykeeper v. City of Malibu* (Calif. Ct. App., 2011).

## ACTIVATED SLUDGE PROCESS

**The process of using biologically active sewage sludge to hasten the breakdown of organic matter in raw sewage during secondary waste treatment.**

*Legal Annotation*: "Meanwhile, the **activated sludge** that had settled in the final clarifiers was pumped from the bottom of the clarifiers. A certain portion was returned to the aeration basins, while the remainder, known as waste **activated sludge** ('WAS'), was pumped to WAS holding tanks. From the holding tanks, the WAS could either be returned to other phases of the treatment process or hauled away to a different sewage treatment facility." *United States v. Weitsenhoff* (9th Cir., 1993).

## ACTIVE RECREATION

**See** ***Recreation, Active.***

## ACTIVITY CENTER

**A community focal point providing for the combination, rather than scatteration, of general retail, service commercial, professional office, higher density housing, and appropriate public/quasi-public uses. http://www.pgplanning.org/Resources/Tools_On-line/Glossary.htm**

*Legal Annotation*: "The proposed center would also have a youth **activity center**, gymnasium, and study rooms for after school youth programs." *Cottonwood Christian Center v. Cypress Redev. Ag.* (Calif. D.C. C.D., 2002).

## ACT OF GOD

**An unintentional hazard event (usually a natural hazard) whereby society feels that no individual or organization is responsible for the hazard occurrence or its impact; i.e., an "accident."**

*Comment*: This is an increasingly narrow category of hazards in the USA, as society has begun to view almost all hazards or their impact as predictable, and that mitigation actions could be undertaken. In particular, risk management has presented the view that technological hazards are expected outcomes of planned risk behavior, and even that technological failure from a natural hazard is usually predictable and could have been avoided. For example, almost all motor vehicle crashes are now viewed as expected outcomes of speed, substance use, distracted drivers or other behavior, failure of mechanical equipment, or road design, and are now referred to as "crashes" rather than motor vehicle accidents. http://www.gwu.edu/~icdrm/publications/PDF/GLOSSARY%2002-19-2007.pdf

*Legal Annotation*: "Nevertheless, plaintiffs suggest we should construe '**act of God**' in this section to mean 'any catastrophe beyond the control of the owner.'" *Korean Am. Legal Advocacy Foundation v. City of Los Angeles* (Calif. Ct. App 2nd, 1994).

## ADAPTABLE DESIGN

**"An adaptable dwelling unit has all the accessible features that a fixed accessible design unit has but allows some items to be omitted or concealed until needed so the dwelling units can look the same as others and be better matched to individual needs when occupied." (Center for Universal Design 2006). See *Accessible Design*.**

*Comment*: For example, "in an adaptable dwelling, wide doors, no steps, knee spaces, control and switch locations, grab bar reinforcing and other access features must be built in. Grab bars, however, can be omitted and installed when needed. Because the necessary blocking is already provided, the bars can simply be screwed in place without opening the existing walls to install reinforcing. Knee spaces can be concealed by installing a removable base cabinet that can simply be unscrewed from adjacent cabinets and slipped out when needed or by installing self-storing cabinet doors that fold and slide back. Counter tops and closet rods can be placed on adjustable supports rather than fixed at lower heights as required for some wheelchair users. Standards for adaptable design have been incorporated into both ANSI and UFAS. These standards specify adaptability criteria, which will provide a level of full accessibility when adjustments are made."(Center for Universal Design 2006).

*Legal Annotation*: "Plaintiff sues under the Americans with Disabilities Act (hereinafter 'ADA'), 42 U.S.C. §§ 12181, *et seq.*, contending that the properties at issue do not contain, in areas comprising 'public accommodations,' e.g., leasing offices, parking lots, sidewalks, and restrooms, certain features of minimum accessibility and **adaptable design** as required by law." *Equal Rights Center v. Equity Residential (*D. Md., 2007).

## ADAPTATION

**A change in the structure or habit of an organism resulting from an adjustment to its environment.**

*Legal Annotation*: "In the area of **adaptation**, Dr. Lynn opined that Plaintiff is moderately limited in her ability to respond appropriately to changes in the work setting, and to set realistic goals or make plans independently of others." *Edmonds v. Astrue* (S.D. Ala., 2010).

## ADAPTIVE REUSE

**The development of a new use for an older building or for a building originally designed for a special or specific purpose.**

*Comment*: Adaptive reuse is a particularly useful technique for preserving older buildings of historic or architectural significance. It also applies to the conversion of other special-use structures, such as gas stations, train stations, or school buildings, that are no longer needed for their original use.

***Legal Annotation***: "Hartland applied to the Burlington Development Review Board (DRB) for a zoning permit for the **adaptive reuse** or residential conversion of an existing 16.500 square-foot industrial warehouse located on 0.65 acres at 237 North Avenue." *In Re: Hartland Group N. Avenue Permit* (Vt., 2008).

## ADDITION

**(1) A structure added to the original structure at some time after the completion of the original; (2) an extension or increase in floor area or height of a building or structure.**

***Comment***: "At some time after" is usually defined as after the certificate of occupancy has been issued for the original structure.

***Legal Annotation***: "The Association indicated that it would approve an **addition** larger than 1,500 square feet in exchange for [defendants] replacing the aluminum siding on the Kerrigan House with wooden siding." *Bjork v. Draper* (Ill. App. Ct., 2008).

## ADJACENT LAND

**See *Adjoining Lot or Land.***

***Legal Annotation***: "This appeal requires us to address issues regarding the statute of limitations that is applicable to claims for damage to real property occasioned by rainwater draining from **adjacent land**." *Sexton v. City of Mason* (Ohio, 2008).

## ADJOINING LOT OR LAND

**A lot or parcel of land that shares all or part of a common lot line with another lot or parcel of land. See *Abut; Contiguous*.**

***Legal Annotation***: "[T]he Association has not established the nature of its claimed property right. It is not clear whether its right-of-way was established by easement over the land of **adjoining lot** owners or by fee simple title." *Big Bass Lake Cmty. Ass'n v. Warren* (Pa. Commw. Ct., 2008).

## ADMINISTRATIVE OFFICE

**An establishment primarily engaged in overall management and general supervisory functions, such as executive, personnel, finance, legal, and sales activities, performed in a single location or building for other branches or divisions of the same company.**

***Comment***: The term "administrative office" is obsolete, given changes in the way business is conducted. Moreover, in terms of impact, there is very little difference between an administrative office and other types of business offices, with the possible exception of a corporate headquarters office. Corporate headquarters offices usually have fewer employees per square foot and more conference rooms than other types of offices, but here again, bottom-line considerations are eliminating these differences as well.

***Legal Annotation***: Appellant "thereafter created a two-phase plan for the development of a student center on Site 653 (the Project), the first phase of which involved [appellant]'s continued operation of an **administrative office** at the 8976 Cliffridge Avenue residence and its provision of limited religious services there." *Taxpayers for Responsible Land Use v. City of San Diego and Hillel of San Diego* (Calif. Ct. App., 2009).

## ADMINISTRATIVE OFFICER

**The designated governmental official charged with administering land development regulations.**

***Comment***: The administrative officer is often identified as a specific official, such as the municipal clerk, planning commission secretary, or zoning officer. Many land development ordinances will often add in the definition section, "For purposes of this ordinance, the administrative officer shall be the . . ."

***Legal Annotation***: "The **Administrative Officer** . . . performs all administrative and managerial work, including circulating materials to the Board members, preparing all official correspondence and compiling all records required to be kept, and providing notice of meetings under the Open Public Meetings Act or the Municipal Land Use Law; and maintaining custody of all records." *Hopewell Valley Citizens' Group, Inc. v. Berwind Property Group Dev. Co.* (N.J., 2011).

## ADULT BOOKSTORE

See *Adult Use.*

***Legal Annotation***: "[W]hen an establishment such as an **adult bookstore** is the subject of the [nuisance] abatement action, something more is added to the balance: not only does the landowner have a First Amendment interest in selling protected material, but the public has a First Amendment interest in having such material available for purchase." *County of Santa Clara v. Superior Ct. of Santa Clara County* (Calif., 2010).

## ADULT DAY CARE

**A nonresidential facility typically operating several hours per day, providing meals and social and recreational activities under general supervision for elderly persons and/or persons with disabilities.**

***Comment***: Adult day care centers may focus on providing care for persons with Alzheimer's and related dementias, and/or for adults with disabilities. Additional services may include transportation, personal care, and counseling. Some may provide the services of a medical assistant or nurse.

***Legal Annotation***: "In Delaware, **Adult Day Care** is defined as a program for functionally-impaired persons that provides a variety of supervised therapeutic, social and recreational activities for participants who cannot live independently (due to a physical or mental impairment), but do not require 24-hour institutional care." www.AdultDayCare.Org

## ADULT DAY CARE CENTER

**A facility typically operating for several hours per day, providing meals and social and recreational activities for elderly persons and/or persons with disabilities.**

***Comment***: Adult day care centers are nonresidential facilities focused mostly on providing care for elderly persons, some with Alzheimer's and related dementias, or disabled and/or functionally disabled adults. Additional services may include transportation, personal care, and counseling. Some centers may provide rehabilitation services or those of a medical assistant or nurse. Planning issues include parking for staff and visitors. By definition, day care does not include overnight facilities.

***Legal Annotation***: "The interpretation which forms the crux of this appeal compared the kitchen with a boarding house, the **adult daycare center** with a rooming house, and construed the offices as an accessory use." *Allen v. City of Burlington Bd. of Adjustment* (N.C. Ct. App., 1990).

"In 1978, Donald Goncher, the administrator of Acre View, sought the opinion of the village officials as to whether a day-care center for older adults was a permitted use within the terms of the special use permit. The village manager responded by letter that the 'conversion of Acre View from a nursing home operation to an **Adult Day Care Center** appears to be within the scope of your special use permit.'" *Palella v. Leyden Family Service & Mental Health Center* (Ill., 1980).

## ADULT RETIREMENT COMMUNITY

**A planned development designed for active older people that emphasizes social and recreational activities but may also provide personal services, limited health facilities, and transportation. See *Retirement Community*.**

***Comment***: Dwellings in adult retirement communities are generally for sale, but occasionally rental units are available. Dwellings may be in the form of detached and attached houses, duplexes, or apartments. Activities may include a clubhouse, tennis, golf, swimming, and other recreation resources appropriate for older residents. Services, such as transportation and limited medical care, may also be provided. A manager is usually responsible for the general maintenance and upkeep of the community, and a monthly fee is generally charged for these services. Regulations usually require a certain minimum entrance age. The 1988 amendment to the Federal Fair Housing Act provides some guidance on age restrictions.

***Legal Annotation***: "The dispute in this case centers on various disagreements pertaining to the control and management of common areas and a golf course in an active **adult retirement community**." *Pierce v. CRB Partners, LLC* (Texas Ct. App., 2010).

## ADULT USE

**(*Note*: Much of the material used in defining adult use and the recommendations on regulations are adapted from Eric Damian Kelly, "Local Regulation of Lawful Sex Businesses," *Land Use Law & Zoning Digest* 51, September 1999, 9; and Eric Damian Kelly and Connie Cooper, *Everything You Always Wanted to Know About Regulating Sex Businesses*, Planning Advisory Service Report No. 495/496, December 2000. The authors are indebted to Professor Kelly and Ms. Cooper, as well as to the American Planning Association, for permission to use the material.)**

An establishment consisting of, including, or having the characteristics of any or all of the following:

*ADULT BOOKSTORE, NEWSSTAND, VIDEO STORE, OR COMBINATION:* An establishment having more than 40 percent of its stock-in-trade, floor area, or display area used for the sale or rental of books, magazines, publications, tapes, or films that are distinguished or characterized by the emphasis on sexually oriented material depicting, describing, or relating to sexual activities or anatomical genital areas.

*SEX SHOP:* Any establishment offering, for sale or rent, items from any two of the following categories: sexually oriented books, magazines, and videos; leather goods marketed or presented in a context to suggest their use for sexual activities; sexually oriented toys and novelties; or video viewing booths; or an establishment that advertises or holds itself out in any forum as a sexually oriented business.

*VIDEO VIEWING BOOTHS:* Often referred to as peep shows and characterized by small private booths rented to individuals to view sexually explicit films or tapes.

*ADULT MOTION PICTURE THEATER:* A building used for presenting films distinguished or characterized by an emphasis on matter depicting, describing, or relating to sexual activities or anatomical genital areas.

*ADULT CABARET:* An establishment, either with or without a liquor license, offering sexually oriented live entertainment, which may include topless and go-go dancers, strippers, or male or female impersonators.

***Comment***: Adult uses are now more commonly referred to as "sexually oriented businesses," or SOBs. As noted earlier, many of the definitions and recommendations on regulations are from Kelly and Cooper's research work (American Planning Association, Planning Advisory Service Report No. 495/496, 2000). Of particular relevance is the discussion in the report about various court decisions and how they influence the regulation of adult uses.

Kelly and Cooper establish the parameters of regulation of adult uses clearly and unequivocally by stating that "local government clearly can regulate the location of sexually oriented businesses through zoning and, in many states, some or all local governments can also regulate the conduct of the business directly through licensing" (Kelly 1999: 3). But they also point out that "some of the products handled by sexually oriented businesses—certain sexually oriented books, magazines, videos, and movies—enjoy First Amendment protection" (Kelly 1999: 3).

Some of the regulatory guidelines they suggest are as follows:

1. Dispersal ordinances or similar provisions in local zoning ordinances have been generally found to be legal. These ordinances establish minimum distances between adult uses and between adult uses and other uses such as child-oriented uses, houses of worship, and schools. The minimum distance figures vary from five hundred to fifteen hundred feet.

But Kelly points out that if the result is to eliminate all possible sites, the restriction can be considered unreasonable.

2. Licensing is probably the best way to control adult uses with on-premises entertainment. As Kelly (1999, 9) notes, "zoning deals well with locational and basic design issues . . . [and] concerns about how customers will act when enjoying entertainment . . . [and] falls squarely within the scope of licensing laws."
3. General and content-neutral regulations have a better chance of being upheld, as opposed to content-based or content-oriented regulations. For example, not all business districts permit movies or cabarets. But trying to bar only sexually oriented movies or adult cabarets from districts that allow other types of movies or cabarets can be risky. Another example is the regulation of hours of operation. Such restrictions may be unreasonable if they apply only to adult uses and not to other uses in the zone.
4. Reasonable operating restrictions covering lighting, monitoring of booths, the age of customers, and displays are usually acceptable. But here again, licensing may be better than zoning to impose these controls.
5. Establishments that allow one-on-one interaction between patrons and employees, such as encounter booths, massage parlors (other than for licensed therapists), and escort services, may not enjoy First Amendment protection (PAS Report 495/496 cited above). Note that none of the definitions of adult uses list one-on-one interaction activities. If a municipality wants to exclude such activities, it probably should list them as prohibited activities.
6. A clear delineation should be made between adult uses that feature predominantly on-site entertainment (such as movies and cabarets) and relatively benign uses (such as adult bookstores or shops). In other words, there are good reasons to prohibit all types of on-premises entertainment in neighborhood business zones because of their potential adverse impact on the neighborhood. But it would be difficult to make the same case for a bookstore selling or renting adult books or tapes.

Finally, Kelly (1999: 9) makes a strong case that "findings in support of the action are important" and should be undertaken at the time the ordinance is enacted and not when the lawsuit is filed. The findings should clearly demonstrate that the proposed action is the minimum necessary to achieve the purposes. While local studies are best, material detailing the experience of other communities on the issue can also be used.

"In *City of Renton v Playtime Theaters*, 475 US 41, 89 L Ed 2d 29, 106 S Ct 925 (1986), the United States Supreme Court presented a four (4) part test for determining when it is permissible to use zoning to single out **adult uses** without violating the First Amendment of the US Constitution. In determining the constitutional validity of a zoning regulation, courts must consider whether:

1. The predominant purpose of zoning is to suppress the sexually explicit speech itself, or rather, to eliminate the "secondary effects" of adult uses;
2. The zoning regulation furthers a substantial governmental interest;
3. The zoning regulation is "narrowly tailored" to affect only those uses which produced the unwanted secondary effects; and
4. The zoning regulation leaves open reasonable alternative locations for adult uses."

The Massachusetts Appeals Court ruled in June 2006 that a zoning ordinance drafted so as to leave no land available for adult businesses was unconstitutional (*T&D Video, Inc. v. City of Revere)* (Lawlor, 2006, 53).

http://www.dos.ny.gov/cnsl/1u03.htm

***Legal Annotation***: "[I]n 1994, the Town enacted an **adult use** ordinance limiting adult use to three zoning districts: shopping center business (SCB), light industry (LI) and heavy industrial (HI)." *People of New York Town of Smithtown v. 490 West Jericho Realty Corp.* (Suffolk, N.Y. Dist. Ct., 2008).

## ADVANCED WASTE TREATMENT

**Wastewater treatment beyond the secondary or biological state that includes removal of nutrients, such as phosphates and nitrates, and a high percentage of suspended solids.**

*Comment*: Advanced waste treatment, known as tertiary treatment, is the "polishing state" of wastewater treatment and produces a high-quality effluent.

*Legal Annotation*: "The purpose of Memorandum 79-7's rigorous review of **advanced waste treatment** projects is to insure that Clean Water Act funds are used in the manner which will achieve the most progress in water quality at the least cost." *California v. U.S. EPA* (D.C. Cir., 1982).

## ADVERSE DRAINAGE CONDITION

**The absence of stormwater maintenance facilities that would provide adequately for stormwater runoff, or that would prevent flooding, erosion, silting, or other damaging effects to a street, road, drainage structure, or property, or that would remove the threat of such damage. See *Stormwater Maintenance Facilities*.**

*Legal Annotation*: "Final approval by the city was denied at that time due to concerns that the plat would result in **adverse drainage problems**, which were the responsibility of the county to remedy before the plat could be approved." *McCary v. City of Fairhope* (Ala. Ct. Civ. App., 1992).

## ADVERSE IMPACT

**A condition that creates, imposes, aggravates, or leads to inadequate, impractical, unsafe, or unhealthy conditions on a site proposed for development or on off-tract property or facilities.**

*Comment*: Adverse impacts usually relate to circulation, drainage, erosion, potable water, and sewage collection and treatment. They may also relate to lighting and glare, aesthetics, quality of life, and impact on the environment.

*Legal Annotation*: Appellants "argued that the [access] condition could not be imposed absent evidence that their proposed development would have a direct **adverse impact** on public access to the beach." *Nollan v. Cal. Coastal Comm'n* (U.S., 1987).

## ADVERSE POSSESSION

**The right of an occupant to acquire title to a property after having continuously and openly used and maintained a property over a statutory period of time without protest from the owner of record.**

*Legal Annotation*: "**Adverse possession**, although not a favored method of procuring title, is a recognized one. It is a necessary means of clearing disputed titles and the courts adopt it and enforce it, because, when **adverse possession** is carefully and fully proven, it is a means of settling disputed titles and this is desirable." *Walling v. Przybylo* (N.Y., 2006).

## ADVERTISING DISPLAY

**See *Sign*.**

*Legal Annotation*: San Diego enacted an ordinance prohibiting **advertising display** signs, and the "California Supreme Court subsequently defined the term '**advertising display** sign' as 'a rigidly assembled sign, display, or device permanently affixed to the ground or permanently attached to a building or other inherently permanent structure constituting, or used for the display of, a commercial or other advertisement to the public.'" *Metromedia, Inc. v. City of San Diego* (U.S., 1981).

## ADVISORY COMMITTEE

**See *Focus Group*.**

*Legal Annotation*: "[W]e hold that the zoning ordinance . . . was rendered invalid because of the non-public activities of the citizens planning **committee**, which **committee** was established by the Town Council, active on behalf of the Council in an advisory capacity, and participated in the formulation of the zoning plan." *Town of Palm Beach v. Gradison* (Fla., 1974).

## ADVOCACY PLANNING

**Planning for groups often underrepresented in the planning profession (e.g., minorities and the poor), notably when resisting destructive**

**schemes by planning authorities, government agencies, or similar bodies.**

*Comment*: Paul Davidoff is known as the "father of advocacy planning" (Knack 2005, 18).

*Legal Annotation*: "It received a grant from OEO under section 232 of the Economic Opportunity Act, 42 USC § 2825, to conduct a research and pilot program in '**advocacy planning.**' The goal of the program was to organize community groups in the East Oakland and Fruitvale areas." *East Oakland-Fruitvale Planning Council v. Rumsfeld* (9th Cir., 1972).

## AERATION

**The process of being supplied or impregnated with air.**

*Comment*: Aeration is used in wastewater treatment to foster biological and chemical purification.

*Legal Annotation*: "The cities of Gilroy and Morgan Hill jointly operate a municipal sewage wastewater treatment plant in south Santa Clara County. Wastewater is treated in **aeration** ponds in the facility and then discharged into 230 acres of evaporation-percolation ponds." *Comm. for a Progressive Gilroy v. State Water Resources Control Bd.* (Calif. Ct. App., 1987).

## AERIAL MAP

**A map created from a process involving the taking of photographs from the air with predetermined reference points marked on the ground.**

*Legal Annotation*: A member of the County Planning and Zoning Department "displayed an **aerial map** indicating the surrounding homes, and stated that a 153-foot tower at the proposed site would 'visually dominate an otherwise residential area.'" *Sprint Spectrum, L.P. v. Platte County* (8th Cir., 2009).

## AEROBIC

**Life or processes that can occur only in the presence of oxygen.**

*Legal Annotation*: "The [waste] water then flows to the **aerobic** lagoon, where most of the remaining organic matter is consumed by **aerobic** bacteria (bacteria that do need oxygen)." *American Meat Institute v. Environmental Protection Agency* (7th Cir., 1975).

## AEROSOL

**A suspension of liquid or solid particles in the air.**

*Legal Annotation*: "We must also consider the fact graffiti can be created with a wide variety of implements . . . an **aerosol** paint container, a felt tip marker, or any other marking substance." *In re Daniel R., a Person Coming Under the Juvenile Court Law. The People v. Daniel R.* (Calif., 2008).

## AESTHETIC

**The perception of artistic elements or elements in the natural or created environment that are pleasing to the eye.**

*Legal Annotation*: "Declarants use these areas along with their families, children, and pets, for a variety of recreational and **aesthetic** pursuits." *Resurrection Bay Conservation Alliance, et al. v. City Of Seward, Alaska* (D. Alaska, 2008).

## AESTHETIC ZONING

**Regulations designed to preserve or improve building and/or site development design so as to reflect community design goals and objectives.**

*Comment*: Planning has always had an aesthetic orientation. The origins of city planning were in the City Beautiful movement beginning with the 1893 World's Columbian Exposition held in Chicago. While early court decisions failed to sustain aesthetics as the sole basis for the exercise of the police power, later cases suggest a more pragmatic approach. In *City of Lake Wales v. Lamar Advertising Association of Lakeland*, 414 So.2d 1030 (Fla. 1982), the court noted: "Zoning solely for aesthetic purposes is an ideal whose time has come; it is not outside the police power." A New Jersey case (*State v. Miller*, 83 N.J. 402, A.2d 821, 1980) upheld aesthetics as a legitimate goal of zoning and "no longer a matter of luxury or indulgence." In fact, the New Jersey *Municipal*

*Land Use Law* (N.J.S.A. 40:55D1 et seq.) lists as one of the purposes of the act: "To promote a desirable visual environment through creative development techniques and good civic design and arrangements." Finally, the U.S. Supreme Court in *Berman v. Parker* (348 U.S. 26, 1954) recognized the right of the legislature to determine that beauty is a valid objective of police power authority. Ordinances that purport to regulate aesthetics, however, often have problems with standards upon which to judge the "aesthetics" of an application, particularly with respect to building design. Unless an area is an official historic district, architectural design control remains difficult to achieve unless "the architectural standard . . . can be objectively administered and judiciously reviewed for arbitrariness, and yet not so confining as to unlawfully inhibit expression through architectural design" (Frizell & Pozycki 1989: 117). Even in historic districts, specific standards are required to allow applicants to know in advance the standard of review.

A well-prepared community design plan that provides supporting data and policy guidelines for design-related regulations offers the best chance for such ordinances to be upheld by the courts. As noted in Planning Advisory Service Report 489/490, "No trend is more clearly defined in planning law than that of courts upholding regulations whose primary basis is aesthetics. Only a few die-hard states do not permit local governments to adopt aesthetic-based police power regulations. While local governments must still proceed carefully in enacting and implementing aesthetic-based laws . . . they generally have great leeway in acting to protect community aesthetics" (American Planning Association, *Aesthetics, Community Character, and the Law,* Planning Advisory Service Report 489/490, 1999). See *Architectural Control; Building Mass; Building Scale; Community Design Plan; Compatible Design; Design Continuity; Design Fit; Design Review; Design Standards; Development Context; Harmonious Relationship; Human Scale; Urban Context; View Protection Regulation.*

***Legal Annotation***: "The concept of the public welfare is broad and inclusive. . . . The values it represents are spiritual as well as physical, **aesthetic** as well as monetary." *Berman et al., Executors v. Parker et al.* (U.S., 1954).

## AFFORDABLE (HOUSING)

**Housing with a sales price or rent within the means of a low-, middle-, or moderate-income household as defined by state or federal legislation.**

***Comment***: The definition or parameters of "affordable" may vary by state. In New Jersey, for example, affordable housing for moderate-income households is 80 percent of the median family income for a particular area, adjusted for household size and with not more than 30 percent of the income used for rent (including utilities) or 28 percent for purchase (including principal and interest, taxes, condo fees, and insurance). The applicable figure for low-income households is 50 percent of median family income. In Florida, on the other hand, affordable housing is defined as housing capable of being acquired with 30 percent of gross income.

While affordable housing is most often thought of as subsidized housing, this is not necessarily so. Market housing, meeting low- and moderate-income targets, with affordability controls in place, may also qualify. There are numerous local and regional efforts in the United States to provide affordable housing (Meck et al. 2003).

***Legal Annotation***: "We clarified and reaffirmed the constitutional mandate set forth in Mt. Laurel I, imposing an affirmative obligation on every municipality to provide its fair share of **affordable** housing." *Holmdel Builders Association v. Township of Holmdel* (N.J., 1990).

## AFFORESTATION

**The establishment of a tree cover on an area from which it has always or very long been absent, or the planting of open areas that are not presently in forest cover. http://www.pgplanning.org/Resources/Tools_On-line/Glossary.htm**

***Comment***: Afforestation differs from reforestation in that the latter describes the replanting of land that presently is, or recently was, planted with trees. See *Reforestation.*

***Legal Annotation***: Citing President Franklin Roosevelt: "[T]he potential public *usefulness* of the entire Tennessee River . . . transcends mere power development: it enters the wide fields of flood control, soil erosion, **afforestation**, elimination from agricultural use of marginal lands, and distribution and diversification of industry." *State Of Alabama v. Tennessee Valley Authority et al.* (5th Cir., 1981).

## AFTERBURNER

**An air pollution abatement device that removes undesirable organic gases through incineration.**

***Legal Annotation***: The EPA's regulations "exempt changes such as the addition of an **afterburner** to a control system to reduce odors even though particulate emissions may increase due to the afterburner." *National-Southwire Aluminum Co. v. United States Environmental Protection Agency* (6th Cir., 1988).

## AGGRESSIVE SOILS

**Soils that may be corrosive to metallic pipe or tubing (NJAC 5:21-1.4).**

***Comment***: These soils include dump areas, swamps, marshes, alkaline soils, cinder beds, polluted river bottoms, etc., that are considered to be potentially corrosive.

***Legal Annotation***: **"**The trial court found that the water main in question was installed in 1924 and . . . that the presence of corrosion was a substantial cause of the break in the water main; that the water main's break occurred at two separate points where external loss of materials occurred due to **corrosive soil conditions**; [and] that the corrosion of the water main was so extensive that a rupture was imminent without the need for any large surge of pressure to cause it to break." *McMahan's of Santa Monica v. City of Santa Monica* (Calif., Ct. of App., 1983).

## AGING IN PLACE

**"The ability to live in one's own home and community safely, independently and comfortably, regardless of age, income or ability level" (Center for Disease Control, Healthy Places Terminology). http://www.cde.gov/healthyplaces/terminology.htm**

***Comment***: The provision of assistance with the daily chores and health-care needs of an aging population that allows seniors to remain in their homes, independently or semi-independently, is thought to enhance their health, well-being, happiness, and longevity. Land use policies or regulations that allow housing to be adapted to accommodate the changing needs of seniors as they age and become more dependent on outside services, or that provide several types of housing—independent units, congregate care, assisted living, and nursing homes in a single health-care or life-care campus—foster aging in place. "In December 2011, the AARP Policy Institute and National Conference of State Legislatures issued a report entitled 'Aging in Place: A State Survey of Liability Policies and Practices,' to foster aging in place (for seniors) by giving state legislators examples of how laws, policies and programs can support this goal. In addition to such governmental initiatives, livability can be optimized through the incorporation of universal design principles, telecare, and other assistive technologies. Assistive technologies include communications, health and wellness monitoring, home safety and security. Purposeful aging in place has grown in popularity and is celebrated by the National Aging in Place Week and the National Aging in Place Council that promotes the positive outcomes of older adults having a choice in their care and living arrangements." See *Housing, Multigenerational.* http://en.wikipedia.org/wiki/Aging_in_place

***Legal Annotation***: "Mr. Heisler, testifying on behalf of appellant, stated that it was the State's policy to promote affordable and accessible housing for the elderly and to encourage '**aging in place**,' described as being able to stay in the home they have chosen as their health deteriorates." *Colandrea v. Wilde Lake* (Md. Ct. App., 2000).

## AGRARIAN

**Relating to land, particularly agriculture.**

***Legal Annotation***: "[T]he common **agrarian** conception of property limited owners to 'natural' uses of their land prior to and during much of the 18th century." *Lucas v. South Carolina Coastal Council* (U.S., 1992, Justice Blackmun dissent)

## AGRICULTURAL ASSESSMENT

**A government program in which land used for agricultural purposes is assessed based on its value as agricultural land as opposed to a higher valuation, such as for development purposes.**

***Comment***: Owners of land in agricultural assessment programs need to prove the land is actually being used for agricultural purposes by showing a minimum annual monetary return (usually set by the state) for the sale of agricultural products. In addition, if the land is eventually sold for other than agricultural purposes, a three- to five-year "giveback" is usually assessed on the land. The giveback is the taxes based on the non-agricultural value of the land for the giveback period. http://www.pgplanning.org/Resources/Tools_On-line/Glossary.htm

***Legal Annotation***: "The PTAB held that Elder's use of the parcel brought it within the definition of 'farm' for property **tax** purposes." *McLean County Bd. of Teview v. PTAB* (Ill. App. 1997).

## AGRICULTURAL BUILDING

**A structure on agricultural land designed, constructed, and used to house farm implements, livestock, or agricultural produce or products grown or raised on the premises.**

***Legal Annotation***: "Being on agricultural property did not transform the residence into an **agricultural building**." *The County of De Kalb v. Vidmar et al.* (Ill., 1993).

## AGRICULTURAL LAND, PRIME

**Land that qualifies for a rating as Class I in the US Department of Agriculture (USDA) Soil Conservation Service land-use capability classification.**

***Comment***: Capability classification is the grouping of soils that shows, in a general way, their suitability for various kinds of farming. It is a practical classification based on limitations of the soils, the risk of damage when they are used, and the way they respond to treatment. Capability classes are designated by Roman numerals I–VIII. As the numerals increase, they indicate progressively greater limitations and narrower choices for practical use.

The best soils for agricultural use, Classes I and II, are described by the USDA as

> Class I: Soils that have few limitations that restrict their use
>
> Class II: Soils that have some limitations that reduce the choice of plants or require moderate conservation practices

The particular soil types for each class are detailed in the County Soil Survey for each state.

***Legal Annotation***: "[W]hether land is **prime agricultural land** is a question of fact because neither the legislature, nor any other state agency, has mapped out and designated certain areas of the state as 'agricultural land.'" *Red Hill Coalition, Inc. v. Town Plan and Zoning Commission of the Town of Glastonbury* (Conn., 1989).

## AGRICULTURAL MARKET

**See *Farm Stand*.**

## AGRICULTURAL POLLUTION

**The liquid, gaseous, and solid wastes from all types of farming, including runoff from pesticides, fertilizers, and feedlots, erosion and dust from plowing, animal manure and carcasses, and crop residue and debris.**

***Legal Annotation***: "The regulations sought to exempt from 33 U.S.C. § 1311 unconcentrated **agricultural pollution** such as rain water runoff containing fertilizer." *United States of America v. Frezzo Brothers, Inc.* (E.D. Pa., 1982).

## AGRICULTURAL SERVICES

**Establishments primarily engaged in supplying soil preparation services, crop services,**

**landscaping, horticultural services, veterinary and other animal services, and farm labor and management services.**

*Legal Annotation*: "'Seasonal **agricultural services' are** defined by IRCA as 'the performance of field work related to planting, cultural practices, cultivation, growing and harvesting of fruits and vegetables of every kind and other perishable commodities, as defined in regulations by the Secretary of Agriculture.'" *Morales v. Yeutter* (N.D. Ill., 1990)

## AGRICULTURAL SOLID WASTE

**Solid waste that is generated by the rearing of animals and the producing and harvesting of crops or trees.**

*Legal Annotation*: "**Agricultural solid waste** is defined as waste produced in either the rearing of animals; the production of crops or trees. Materials excluded from the RCRA solid waste definition include domestic sewage; waste from irrigation return flows; point source discharges into navigable waters which are permitted for release under the National Pollutant Discharge Elimination System (NPDES) of the Clean Water Act (FE770).

The Florida Handbook of Solid and Hazardous Waste Regulation: Resource Conservation and Recovery Act (RCRA)1

http://edis.ifas.ufl.edu/document_fe762

## AGRICULTURAL ZONING

**Regulations that protect the agricultural land base by limiting nonagricultural uses, prohibiting high-density development, requiring houses to be clustered on small lots, and restricting subdivision of land into parcels that are too small to farm.**

***Comment***: An example of agricultural zoning is in the Pinelands, an environmentally significant area in southern New Jersey. The area is preserved and regulated by the New Jersey Pinelands Commission. Farmers in designated agricultural areas may build only one house unrelated to farming on a one-acre lot within each forty-acre agricultural section. In 1991, the New Jersey Supreme Court ruled that these regulations did not amount to an unconstitutional confiscation of property, because the land could still be used for farming and had not, therefore, been rendered valueless. The court added that "there exists no constitutional right to the most profitable use of property" and also stated that the unique and ecologically fragile nature of the Pinelands justified the area's special treatment.

Conflicts between farmers and residents of new subdivisions are serious problems and can be expected to increase as new development expands into agricultural areas. Most new residents are attracted to these areas because of the bucolic impression created by farms. However, after moving into their new homes, many find that farming is an intensive industry, conducted mostly outdoors. These new residents find themselves subjected to noise from farm machinery, smells from livestock and animals, dust created by plowing, and chemicals from pesticides and fertilizers. Traffic bottlenecks created by slow-moving farm equipment are not uncommon.

On the other hand, farmers have legitimate complaints resulting from the encroachment of urban development, including having to respond to complaints from neighbors, vandalism of farm equipment, trespassing, and restrictions placed on farming operations.

Many of these problems can be addressed through smart planning and education. Some of the tools available to municipalities are noted below and are more fully discussed in "The Conflict at the Edge" (Thompson 1997a).

***BUFFERS***: Much of the conflict between farms and residential developments can be avoided by requiring wide buffers between new development and the farms. Minimum buffers would vary by type of farming. For example, the city of Napa, California, requires a minimum of eighty feet from the property line to any dwelling. The local ordinance also requires that at least fifteen of the eighty feet be planted with trees, shrubs, berms, or fences. In addition, noise-reducing design and building construction includes window and door orientation and the use of double-pane windows. In San Luis Obispo County, California, buffer distances are four hundred to eight hundred feet for vineyards, three hundred to eight hundred feet for irrigated orchards, and one hundred to four hundred feet for field crops.

*NUISANCE DISCLAIMERS*: Disclaimers inform potential purchasers of homes adjacent to or near farms as to what they can expect from normal farming operations. While the disclaimer does not reduce the conflict, it does make it more difficult for the homeowner to claim he or she was not aware of the potential problems. In some cases, the disclaimer is noted on the deed and recorded, so that it becomes part of the official record describing the lot.

*LARGE LOT ZONING*: This technique is simply to zone land proposed to be preserved for farming into large parcels. This could be as "small" as six acres to as large as forty acres. While this technique works, it often runs afoul of the farmer's ultimate goal of eventually selling out when retirement beckons and "the last crop is blacktop." Alternatives are participation in farmland preservation programs, now available in most states, in which the development rights are purchased, often through a cooperative program using state, county, and local funding, or through lot averaging or cluster planning. See *Cluster Subdivision; Lot Averaging*.

*RIGHT-TO-FARM ORDINANCES*: All states have right-to-farm ordinances, which essentially protect farmers from nuisance suits resulting from normal farming operations. These educate the homeowner as to what can be expected in the new environment. Many municipalities require that a copy of the right-to-farm ordinance be made available to prospective purchasers of homes in farm areas.

*COMMUNICATION*: Laura Thompson (1997a) presents examples in which better communication can mitigate complaints and conflicts. Her article cites programs whereby farmers inform the municipality of plans to fertilize or lay down pesticide and this information is disseminated to surrounding residents, or where farmers inform surrounding residents of plowing and planting schedules.

*Legal Annotation*: "The **[agricultural] zoning scheme** of Hopewell Township unquestionably has some relationship to the goal of preserving farmland, merely by reason of the fact that tracts of such land are restricted in the extent to which they can be diverted to non-agricultural uses." *Hopewell Township Board of Supervisors and Hopewell Township Zoning Hearing Board v. Edward B. Golla et al.* (Pa., 1982).

## AGRICULTURE

**The production, storage, keeping, harvesting, grading, packaging, processing, boarding, or maintenance, for sale, lease, or personal use, of plants and animals useful to humans, including but not limited to: forages and sod crops; grains and seed crops; dairy animals and dairy products; poultry and poultry products; livestock, including beef cattle, sheep, swine, horses, ponies, mules, or goats or any mutations or hybrids thereof, including the breeding and grazing of any or all of such animals; bees and apiary products; fur animals; trees and forest products; fruits of all kinds, including grapes, nuts, and berries; vegetables; nursery, floral, ornamental, and greenhouse products; or lands devoted to a soil conservation or forestry management program. See *Agricultural Zoning; Horse Farm; Horticulture*.**

***Comment***: The definition is contained in the *New Jersey Farmland Assessment Act* (Chapter 48, Laws of 1964) and is broadly applied. It includes intensive agricultural activities, such as feedlot operations, chicken farms, and agribusiness activities, some of which may not be appropriate in all areas. See *Concentrated Animal Feeding Operation*.

The definition does not cover activities that are often connected with farms but are peripheral to the principal activities (for example, horse shows, mazes [in cornfields], and "pick your own"). Mazes and pick-your own are not particularly intense operations and attract few participants over a short period of time. They can be easily accommodated with some consideration for parking.

Horse shows may take place two to four times a year and include the sale of horses, races, and similar activities. Horse shows can generate crowds of people, vehicles, and animals. Municipalities should decide whether these activities are accessory to the principal farm use or require special permits. The permits can specify the maximum number of shows per year and requirements for review of parking, circulation, and accommodations for crowds.

***Legal Annotation***: "All **agriculture** conducted for profit is commercial in some degree. . . . The term '**agriculture**' has a broad meaning." *Cumberland Farms Of Connecticut, Inc. vs. Zoning Board of Appeal of North Attleborough* (MA, 1971).

## AGRICULTURE, HOME

**The on-site production, principally for use or consumption of the property owner or tenant, of plants, animals, or their products, including, but not limited to, gardening, fruit production, poultry, and livestock production. This does not include the sale of products produced off-site but does include the sale of products produced on-site to others as long as such sales are incidental to the principal use of the property as a residence.**

***Comment***: This definition requires that the agricultural products be produced on-site and that any sales to non-residents or non-tenants be of a minor or incidental use of the property.

***Legal Annotation***: "There is no evidence in the record that the garden was used for any purpose other than the growing of marijuana, such as the growing of **vegetables for home consumption.**" *People v. Stork* (Ill. App. Ct., 1990).

## AGRICULTURE, URBAN

**"The growing, processing, and distribution of food and other products through intensive plant cultivation and animal husbandry, in and around cities" (Bailkey and Nasr 2000, 6; *see also* Thibert 2012, 351 and Hendrickson and Porth 2012, 60).**

***Comment***: In recent years, urban agriculture has been encouraged (Hodgson, Campbell and Bailkey 2011) for a variety of reasons: health, food security, jobs, open space, economic development, urban environmental considerations, and sustainable development. urpl.wise.edu/ecoplan/content/lit_urbanag.pdf

But permitting urban agriculture is not without problems and should be integrated into a city's comprehensive land use system (Thibert 2012). For example, should urban agriculture be permitted in all zoning districts, and is animal husbandry a permitted use?

*See* Mukherji and Morales (2010) for discussion of zoning for urban agriculture.

***Legal Annotation***: "**Urban agriculture** is the practice of producing food in and around the urban area, including the cultivation of crops and sale of produce." City of Sacramento Urban Agriculture Ordinance

http://portal.cityofsacramento.org/Community-Development/Planning/Long-Range/Urban-Agriculture

## AGRITAINMENT

**Events and activities, such as corn mazes, hayrides, and petting zoos, that allow for recreation, entertainment, and tourism in conjunction with agriculture support and services directly associated with ongoing agricultural activity on-site (American Planning Association 2004, 3). See also *Agritourism***

***Legal Annotation***: "'**Agritainment**' is simply providing an opportunity for entertainment in an agricultural setting. Visitors or customers can provide a wide range of revenue-generating opportunities for farms." *Agritainment* Penn State Extension

http://extension.psu.edu/business/ag-alternatives/farm-management/agritainment

## AGRITOURISM

**Agricultural uses such as farms, ranches, and vineyards that, through promotion and advertising, facilities, and activities seek to attract visitors and guests.**

***Comment***: Agritourism includes dude ranches on active cattle ranches; guest facilities, including eating and sleeping; vineyards; and summer camps, particularly oriented to children, on active farms. See *Agriculture*.

***Legal Annotation***: "At the hearing, Mr. Vecchione argued, however, that he was in the '**agritourism**' business. He stated that at various times he used his land, which I take to be a reference to the Mendon Street property, for recreational activities open to the public for a fee, including ice skating, skate sharpening, sledding, hayrides and archery. He also stated that two years ago he grew pumpkins and watermelons on land other than the Mendon Street property owned by a third party. He also stated he used that land for excavation of gravel and fill. According to Mr. Vecchione, these activities make him a farmer eligible to file a chapter 12 case." *In re Vecchione* (Bankr. Court, D.Mass., 2013).

## AIR PARK

**A planned development that includes an airport, with accessory and support services.**

***Legal Annotation***: "[P]laintiff **Air Park** Estate Zoning Committee [obtained a temporary injunction] restraining defendant's completion of an aircraft hangar. . . . The development contemplated that persons buying lots would build both a hangar and a residence on each lot." *Ivan Harrison v. Air Park Estates Zoning Committee* (Texas, 1976).

## AIR POLLUTION

**Introduction into the atmosphere of contaminants—such as smoke, fumes, or odors—that are of sufficient quantity, concentration, or duration as to have a negative effect on human, animal, or plant life or on human activities.**

***Comment***: Air pollution may be classified by physical form (e.g., mobile source, stationary source, indirect source) or by some other useful characteristic, such as degree of severity.

***Legal Annotation***: "The ordinance [prohibiting issuance of residential building permits] states that it was enacted to further the health, safety, and welfare of the citizens of Livermore and to contribute to the solution of **air pollution**." *Associated Home Builders of The Greater Eastbay, Inc. v. City Of Livermore et al.* (Calif., 1976).

## AIR POLLUTION EPISODE

**The occurrence of abnormally high concentrations of air pollutants, usually resulting from low winds and temperature inversion, that may be accompanied by increases in illness and death. See *Inversion*.**

***Legal Annotation***: "[The slash-and-burn of timberland] was subject to automatic suspension in the event an **air pollution episode** was declared by the Department of Ecology." *Simpson Timber Company v. Olympic Air Pollution Control Authority, The Department Of Natural Resources* (Wash., 1976).

## AIR QUALITY CONTROL REGION

**An area designated by the federal government where two or more communities, either in the same or different states, share a common air pollution problem.**

***Legal Annotation***: Citing Section 110 (a) (2), 42 U. S. C. § 1857c-5 (a) (2)(E): "[the plan shall include] measures necessary to insure that emissions of air pollutants from sources located in any **air quality control region** will not interfere with the attainment or maintenance of such primary or secondary standard in any portion of such region outside of such State or in any other air quality control region." *Train v. Natural Resources Defense Council, Inc.* (U.S., 1975).

## AIR QUALITY CRITERIA

**The levels of pollution and length of exposure at which adverse effects on health and quality of life occur. See *Criteria Pollutant*.**

***Legal Annotation***: "[The Clean Air Act] requires the Administrator of the EPA to promulgate NAAQS for each air pollutant for which '**air quality criteria**' have been issued." *Whitman v.*

*American Trucking Associations, Inc., et al.* (U.S., 2001).

## AIR QUALITY STANDARDS

**The prescribed level of pollutants in the outside air that cannot be exceeded legally during a specified time in a specified geographical area. See *Criteria Pollutant*.**

***Legal Annotation***: "The heart of the [Clean Air Act] Amendments is the requirement that each State formulate, subject to EPA approval, an implementation plan designed to achieve national primary ambient **air quality standards**." *Union Electric Co. v. Environmental Protection Agency et al.* (U.S., 1976).

## AIR RIGHTS

**Unused or excess development rights capable of being transferred from one building lot to another (Finn 2013).**

***Comment***: Air rights are actually a form of transfer of development rights. When permitted by state enabling legislation, and implemented in local zoning or land development ordinances, excess or unused floor area, height, or density can be transferred from a vacant or underdeveloped lot to another, usually vacant or underdeveloped parcel. But the actual implementation can be complicated. For example, many ordinances permit only contiguous lots or lots sharing a common lot line to transfer the rights. Other ordinances specify sending and receiving zones.

Still others establish "banks" where property owners can sell their air/development rights to the bank and developers can purchase the rights from the bank. This process works well in preserving farmland and open space and creating urban centers.

In New York City and other large cities, the sale of air rights over historic buildings has become an important method of historic preservation. The purchase of the air rights allows the construction of taller and/or denser buildings on non-historic properties, with the monies secured from the sale of the air rights being used to preserve the historic building or site.

(Discussions with Robin Finn, *New York Times*; Phillip B. Caton, PP, FAICP; Clarke, Caton, Hintz, Trenton, NJ; Ross Moskowitz, Esq., Stroock, Stroock & Lavan LLP, New York City; and Robert I. Shapiro, City Center Real Estate, New York City). See *Transfer of Development Rights; Density Transfer; Non-Contiguous Parcel Clustering*.

***Legal Annotation***: "[Appellants] urge that the Landmarks Law has deprived them of any gainful use of their '**air rights**' above the [Grand Central] Terminal." *Penn Central Transportation Co. et al. v. New York City et al.)* (U.S., 1978).

## AIR TRANSPORTATION

**Establishments engaged in transportation by air, including airports and flying fields, as well as terminal services.**

***Legal Annotation***: "In 1960 FAA rejected a proposed restriction on jet operations at the Los Angeles airport between 10 p. m. and 7 a. m. because such restrictions could 'create critically serious problems to all **air transportation** patterns.' 25 Fed. Reg. 1764-1765." *City of Burbank et al. v. Lockheed Air Terminal, Inc., et al.* (U.S., 1973).

## AIRPORT

**A place where aircraft can land and take off, usually equipped with hangars, facilities for refueling and repair, and various accommodations for passengers.**

***Comment***: From a zoning and planning perspective, allowing airports in a particular zone district calls for some consideration as to the type of airport, which, in turn, requires different types of accessory services or uses and has widely differing impacts on the municipality. See *Airport Zoning*.

***Legal Annotation***: "Thus Congress has not only appropriated the airspace necessary for planes to fly at high altitudes throughout the country but has also provided the low altitude airspace essential for those same planes to approach and take off from **airports**." *Griggs v. Allegheny County* (U.S., 1962).

## AIRPORT HAZARD

**Any structure, vegetation, or use of land that would exceed federal airport obstruction standards or is otherwise hazardous to the landing or takeoff of aircraft. *See Figure 4*.**

*Legal Annotation*: "'**Airport hazard**,' as defined by RCW 14.08.010(1) by reference to RCW 14.04.020(14), means: '. . . any structure, object of natural growth, or use of land, which obstructs the airspace required for the flight of aircraft in landing or taking off at an airport or is otherwise hazardous to such landing or taking off.'" *Helen Hilyard Mills v. Orcas Power & Light Company* (Wash., 1960).

## AIRPORT ZONING

**A specific set of controls intended to protect the integrity of an airport, its airspace, and its environs (Schalk and Ward 2010).**

***Comment***: While the major control is the height of buildings or structures near airports, with permitted maximums increasing with the distance from runways, airport zoning also limits electronic interference with navigational equipment and some types of uses, primarily places of human assembly, to reduce accident risks. Many communities have, in addition, made special provisions for airport surroundings by zoning them for compatible uses (for example, warehousing, industry, and certain commercial uses) and excluding residential uses and places of assembly (American Planning Association, *The Language of Zoning*, Planning Advisory Service Report No. 322, 1976).

*Legal Annotation*: "'[T]he defendants have no standing in this court to question the reasonableness of the height limits prescribed by the **airport zoning** regulation.'" *Harrell's Candy Kitchen, Inc. v. Sarasota-Manatee Airport* Authority (Fla., 1959).

## AIRPORT-RELATED USE

**A use that supports airport operations, including, but not limited to, aircraft repair and maintenance, flight instruction, and aircraft chartering.**

*Legal Annotation*: "The classic example is recently Kansas City very nearly was able to get McDonnell Douglas into an **airport-related use** adjacent to the airport. We agree that the trial court erred in ruling that such aviation-related uses do not fit within the definition of a public use." *City of Kansas City v. Hon* (Mo: Ct. App., 1998).

## AIRSPACE

**"The area above or below a highway's established grade line, beneath an elevated highway**

**Figure 4**

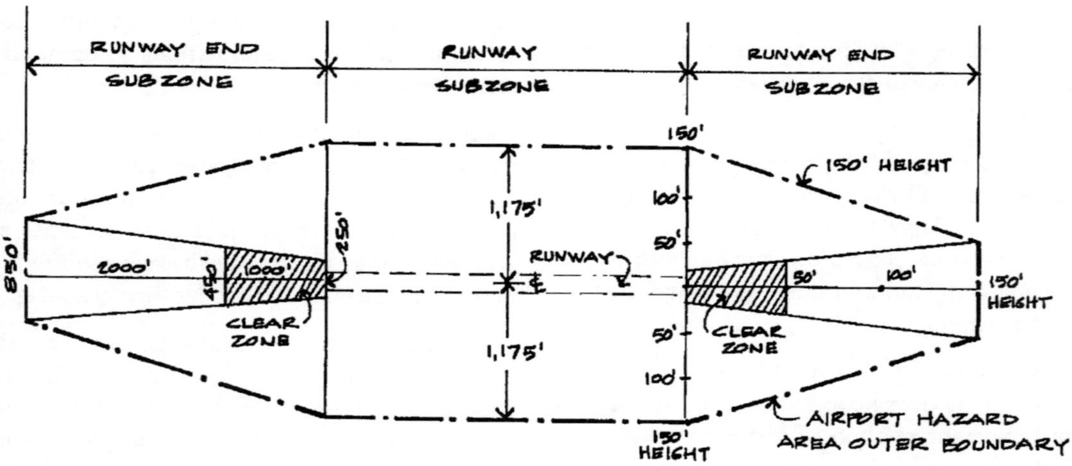


AIRPORT HAZARD AREA HEIGHT RESTRICTIONS

**structure, or adjacent to the roadway and located within the approved right-of-way boundary" (Wells 2003: 17–18).**

***Comment***: "Airspace leasing involves a wide range of uses, including farming, parking lots, commercial and government buildings and telecommunication facilities, such as underground fiber optic lines and wireless transmission towers" (Wells 2003: 18).

***Legal Annotation***: "[T]he County enacted Ordinance 1599, which adopted '**Airspace** Zoning Maps,' including an Aircraft Departure Critical Area Map for McCarran Airport. According to the map, Sisolak's property was located in the departure critical area and was therefore placed under an 80:1 slope restriction (limiting an owner's use of **airspace** one foot above ground level for every 80 feet from the runway), resulting in height restrictions of 3 to 10 feet above ground level. Ordinance 1599 provided for a variance procedure similar to that in Ordinance 1221." *McCarran Int'l Airport v. Sisolak* (Nev., 2006).

## AISLE

**The traveled way by which cars enter and depart parking spaces. *See Figures 73 and 74.***

***Legal Annotation***: "[T]he difficulty of access to the second driveway [was] because parking space 101 blocked passage from one parking **aisle** to the next." *Bettman v. Michaelis et al., Board of Zoning Appeals of the Town of Hempstead* (N.Y. Sup. Ct., 1961).

## ALGAE BLOOM

**A proliferation of living algae and/or other aquatic plants on the surface of lakes or ponds.**

***Legal Annotation***: "A 1996 volume of the *Muckraker* . . . [d]escribed a 'massive **algae bloom**' that had occurred earlier that year, explained that water quality 'changed drastically' after construction of canals in the early part of the century and in the 1950's, and that '[n]ot since the decade of 1950–59 has the river been so heavily polluted.'" *Mildenberger v. US* (Fed. Cir., 2011).

## ALL-TERRAIN VEHICLE (ATV)

**See *Vehicle, Off-Road.***

***Legal Annotation***: "Harris owns a small piece of land in the County which he has used for various business purposes including renting **all-terrain vehicles** (ATVs)." *Harris v. County of Riverside* (9th Cir., 1990).

## ALLEY

**A service roadway providing a secondary means of access to abutting property and not intended for general traffic circulation. *See Figure 97.***

***Comment***: Found in many older, grid-pattern neighborhoods and providing access to garages, alleys have now found favor in traditional neighborhood designs by eliminating front-lot driveways, thereby improving the appearance of small lot layouts. In residential areas they are called "rear lanes" and are paved only in the center part of the right-of-way to a width of ten to twelve feet. Commercial-area alleys tend to be paved over the entire right-of-way.

"Cities across the United States are transforming older alleys, especially those in downtown neighborhood commercial districts, into dynamic, design-orientated places that are safe and interesting for pedestrians and often serve as access points to festive plazas, secondary storefronts, and outdoor dining areas. Examples include the transformation of Seattle's Post Alley and Santa Cruz's Alleywalk" (Zelinka and Beattie 2003: 25).

***Legal Annotation***: "The Board affirmed the denial of a permit, finding that the **alley** was within a residential district [prohibiting] . . . commercial vehicular access. . . . [Alley defined as] A vehicular way providing secondary access to the side or rear of abutting property." *City Of Atlanta Board of Zoning Adjustment V. Midtown North, Ltd. et al.* (Ga., 1987).

## ALLUVION

**That increase of land area on a shore or bank of a stream or sea by the force of the water, as by a current or by waves, that is so gradual**

**that it is impossible to determine how much is added at each moment of time. See *Accretion*.**

***Legal Annotation***: "[T]he doctrine of accretion was applied in respect of a lot of **alluvion** or batture in the Mississippi River fronting the city of New Orleans, in favor of the riparian proprietor." *Jefferis v. East Omaha Land Co.* (U.S., 1890), citing *Saulet v. Shepherd* (U.S., 1867).

## ALTERATION

**Any change or rearrangement in the supporting members of an existing building, such as bearing walls, columns, beams, girders, or interior partitions, as well as any change in doors, windows, or means of ingress or egress; or any enlargement to or diminution of a building or structure, whether horizontally or vertically; or the moving of a building or structure from one location to another. See *Alteration, Incidental*.**

***Comment***: The definition of alteration is important because most ordinances do not permit any expansion of a nonconforming structure or use. All expansions are alterations, but not all alterations are expansions. This definition excludes normal repairs and maintenance, such as painting or roof replacement, but includes more substantial changes. See *Structural Alteration*.

***Legal Annotation***: "It would not be fair, indeed would deprive a person of property without due process, to prosecute or require substantial building **alteration** under a law not in force at the time of initial construction." *154 East Park Avenue Corp. v. City of Long Beach* (N.Y. Sup. Ct., 1973).

## ALTERATION, INCIDENTAL

**Modifications to an existing structure that are of a cosmetic nature, replacement of utilities, or rearrangement of non-load-bearing partitions.**

## ALTERNATIVE ENERGY SOURCES

**Energy sources that do not involve the burning of fossil fuels or the splitting of atoms.**

***Comment***: Alternate energy sources include solar, wind energy, geothermal, tides, and hydroelectric (Wolcott 2004: 4).

***Legal Annotation***: "16 U. S. C. § 824a-3 . . . seeks to encourage the development of cogeneration and small power production facilities. Congress believed that increased use of these sources of energy would reduce the demand for traditional fossil fuels. But it also felt that two problems impeded the development of nontraditional generating facilities: (1) traditional electricity utilities were reluctant to purchase power from, and to sell power to, the nontraditional facilities, and (2) the regulation of these **alternative energy sources** by state and federal utility authorities imposed financial burdens upon the nontraditional facilities and thus discouraged their development." *FERC v. Mississippi* (U.S., 1982).

## ALTERNATIVE LIVING ARRANGEMENT

**An arrangement in which households maintain private rooms yet share kitchen and bathroom facilities, central heat, and common areas. See *Single-Room Occupancy*.**

***Comment***: Alternate living arrangements include boarding homes, residential health-care facilities, group homes for the developmentally disabled and mentally ill, and congregate living arrangements.

***Legal Annotation***: The court noted that "[a]lthough more detailed and far-reaching rights—including the right to habilitation in the least restrictive **alternative living arrangement**—have been located by district courts in the federal constitution and federal law, in this case it is likely that all such . . ." *Lelsz v. Kavanaugh* (5th Cir., 1987).

## ALTERNATE WORK ARRANGEMENT PROGRAMS

**Programs that vary the traditional workday arrival and departure times for employees to avoid peak-hour congestion, or that allow employees to work from home.**

*Comment*: These programs may include flextime, compressed workweek, staggered hours, and job sharing. Newer forms of alternative work arrangement programs allow employees to work from home.

*Legal Annotation*: "Plaintiff requested 'becoming a participant in the "**alternate work arrangement**" program ("AWA") . . . [because she] was tired and . . . sick and . . . needed to be able to work from home if possible on the days when [she] could not make it into the office.'" *Leslie Trout v. Electronic Data Systems Corp.* (6th Cir., 2005).

## ALTERNATIVE ACCESS

**(1) The ability to enter a highway indirectly through another improved roadway instead of from a direct driveway entrance from the principal highway frontage; (2) the availability of another means of access to a roadway or property in addition to the primary access.**

*Legal Annotation*: "[W]hen there is no question that direct access has been taken and no frontage or service road has been provided . . . [t]he availability of **alternative access** and its reasonableness would be appropriate considerations in awarding damages." *Department of Transportation v. Harkey* (N.C., 1983).

## AMATEUR RADIO TOWER

**See *Tower, Amateur Radio*.**

## AMBIANCE

**The character of an area, as determined by building scale and design, amount and type of activity, intensity of use, location and design of open space, and related factors that influence the perceived quality of the environment.**

*Legal Annotation*: The township's three-acre lot zoning "removes it as a target for smaller lot development detrimental to preservation of the rural **ambiance** of the Township." *Sod Farm Associates v. Springfield Tp. Planning Bd.* (N.J., 1995).

## AMBIENT AIR

**Any unconfined portion of the atmosphere; the outside air.**

*Legal Annotation*: "[T]he Environmental Protection Agency should publish proposed regulations describing national quality standards for the '**ambient air**,' which is the statute's term for the outdoor air used by the general public." *Train v. Natural Resources Defense Council, Inc.* (U.S., 1975).

## AMBIENT AIR QUALITY STANDARD

**A maximum permissible air pollution standard. See *Criteria Pollutant*.**

*Legal Annotation*: "Section 109(b)(1) of the [Clean Air Act] instructs the EPA to set '**ambient air quality standards** the attainment and maintenance of [which] . . . are requisite to protect the public health.'" *Whitman v. American Trucking Assns., Inc.* (U.S., 2001).

## AMBIENT NOISE LEVEL

**The normal or existing level of noise from existing conditions or activities at a given location.**

*Legal Annotation*: "The existing **ambient noise level** of 72.1 dBA already exceeds the Department of Health's recommended maximum of 70 dBA." *Los Angeles Unified Sch. Dist. v. City of Los Angeles* (Calif., 1997).

## AMBULATORY CARE FACILITY

**See *Clinic*.**

*Legal Annotation*: "GWU also intended to consolidate in [the building addition] various medical functions . . . [to] serve as a comprehensive outpatient or **ambulatory care facility**." *Draude v. Board of Zoning Adjustment* (D.C., 1990).

## AMENITY

**A natural or created feature that enhances the aesthetic quality or visual appeal or makes more attractive or satisfying a particular property, place, or area.**

*Legal Annotation*: "A river is more than an **amenity**, it is a treasure. It offers a necessity of life that must be rationed among those who have power over it." *New Jersey v. New York* (U.S., 1931).

## AMERICANS WITH DISABILITIES ACT (ADA)

**A 1990 federal law designed to bring Americans with disabilities into the economic mainstream by providing them equal access to jobs, transportation, public facilities, and services ("Zoning and the Americans with Disabilities Act," *Zoning News*, February 1992). See *Accessible Route; Area Of Rescue Assistance; Clear Floor Space; Disability; Major Life Activities*. See *Figure 5*.**

***Comment***: The ADA has had a significant impact on planning and zoning activities, including public services, public accommodations, and commercial facilities. For example, every public meeting must be accessible. As the previously cited *Zoning News* states, a building or facility is accessible if it has no barriers to people with disabilities. This may mean a central location with public transportation, accessible rest rooms, signage, materials, and information a visually impaired person can use, and meetings in which people with hearing and speech impairments can participate and communicate. Posters announcing public hearings can be mounted in senior citizen housing and meal sites, group homes, and other public centers to reach more people with disabilities.

The *Zoning News* article also made an important point about zoning ordinances. Most communities continue to produce zoning ordinances only in written form, with limited availability to the public. Zoning administrators need to think carefully both about how zoning ordinances are published and about which citizens are excluded when the city is creating, modifying, and reviewing the ordinance. Under the ADA, other methods of communication must be adopted. Some cities use computer databases with a publicly accessible terminal to allow persons with disabilities to comment on proposed ordinance modifications. Cities will have to apply creative alternatives so that people with disabilities can read and use important documents, such as the city's zoning ordinance.

*Legal Annotation*: "Both Title II of the **ADA** and section 508 of the Rehabilitation Act prohibit

**Figure 5**

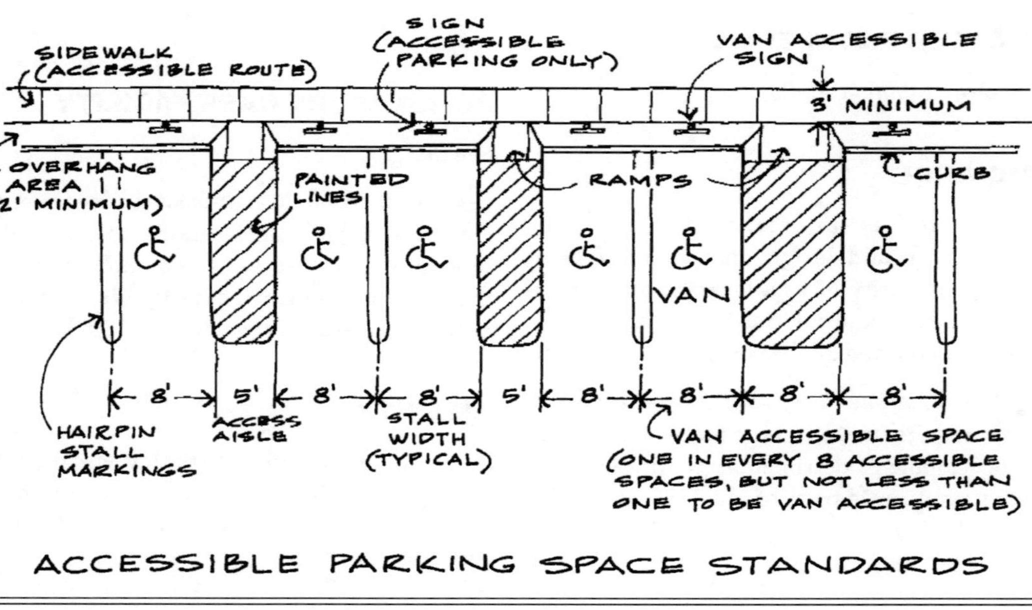

discrimination based on a disability by a public entity. . . . [B]oth clearly encompass zoning decisions by the City because making such decisions is a normal function of a governmental entity." *Innovative Health Systems v. City of White Plains* (2nd Cir., 1997).

## AMORTIZATION OF NONCONFORMING USES

**A method of eliminating nonconforming uses by requiring the termination of the nonconforming use after a specified period of time.**

***Comment***: The legality of requiring the amortization of nonconforming uses remains unclear. The most likely candidates for amortization are junkyards and signs that, in addition to not having a great deal of capital investment, are highly visible nuisances that may have significant adverse impacts on surrounding uses. See *Sign, Nonconforming*.

***Legal Annotation***: "A legislative body may well conclude that the beneficial effect on the community of the eventual elimination of all nonconforming uses by a reasonable **amortization** plan more than offsets individual losses." *City of Los Angeles v. Gage* (Calif., 1954).

## AMUSEMENT AND RECREATION SERVICES

**Establishments engaged in providing entertainment for a fee, including such activities as dance halls, studios, theatrical productions, bands, orchestras, and other musical entertainment; bowling alleys and billiard and pool establishments; commercial facilities, such as arenas, rings, rinks, and racetracks; public golf courses; coin-operated devices, amusement parks, membership sports and health clubs, amusement and bathing beaches, swimming pools, riding academies, carnival operations, expositions, game parlors, and horse rides.**

***Comment***: The above definition is very broad and covers all types of amusement and recreational facilities. Many of the facilities listed are obviously not suited for all zones.

***Legal Annotation***: The plaintiff asked the Zoning Board of Adjustment for "a determination that article III, section 1 (d) 16 entitled '**Amusement and recreation services**' permitted the erection and operation of an outdoor drive-in theater." *Tremblay v. Town of Hudson* (N.H., 1976).

## AMUSEMENT ARCADE

**A primarily outdoor area or open structure, open to the public, that contains coin-operated games, rides, shows, and similar entertainment facilities and devices. See *Recreation Facility*.**

***Legal Annotation***: "The slower turnover of an audience listening to live entertainment justifies the conclusion that such a use does not pose the same problems of noise and congestion as is posed by the operation of an **amusement arcade**." *America's Best Family Showplace Corp. v. The City of New York, Dept. of Buildings* (D. N.Y., 1982).

## AMUSEMENT, COMMERCIAL, INDOOR

**Amusement and recreation services that are wholly enclosed in a building.**

***Legal Annotation***: "Plaintiff Franken Equities, LLC ('Franken') filed a motion for preliminary injunction asking the Court to enjoin the enforcement of an Evanston City ordinance that requires a conditional use permit to operate an '**indoor amusement** and video establishment.'" *Franken Equities, LLC v. City of Evanston* (D. Wyo., 1997).

## AMUSEMENT, COMMERCIAL, OUTDOOR

**Amusement and recreation services where any portion of the activity takes place outside a building.**

***Legal Annotation***: "The County's zoning staff determined the City's request was for an **outdoor commercial amusement** use and that the SE zoning classification of the Ochylski property did not permit construction of the proposed softball complex." *Fox v. Polk County Bd. Of Sup'rs.* (Iowa, 1997).

## AMUSEMENT MACHINE OR DEVICE

**Any coin- or token-operated machine or device, whether mechanical, electrical, or electronic, that is ready for play by the insertion of a coin or token and operated by the public for use as a game, entertainment, or amusement.**

***Comment***: Examples of an amusement machine or device are kiddie rides, games of chance, pool or billiards, pinball machines, shuffleboard, bowling, rotary merchandise, dartboards, target games, basket hoops, and electronic and video games.

***Legal Annotation***: "[P]etitioners, who are the owners of many coin-operated **amusement devices** and juke boxes located in Newport" asked the court to find the city's ordinance null and void "in so far as it imposed a license fee and prohibited use of the machines by minors under the age of eighteen years." *Newport Amusement Company v. Maher* (R.I., 1960).

## AMUSEMENT PARK

**A facility, primarily outdoors, that may include structures and buildings where there are various devices for entertainment, including rides, booths for the conduct of games or sale of items, and buildings for shows, entertainment, restaurants, and souvenir sales.**

***Comment***: Amusement parks, better known as theme parks and family entertainment centers, are multiuse facilities often covering thousands of acres. Disney World is probably the best-known example of a theme park, but smaller ones include a variety of indoor and outdoor activities such as traditional rides (carousels, roller-coasters, Ferris wheels, and other "thrill rides"), shooting galleries, and games of skill and chance. Newer parks include music and craft shops, recreation (miniature golf, bowling, golf driving ranges, batting cages, and water sports), entertainment events, movie theaters, bumper boats, go-kart and roller rinks, arcades, and simulation and video games. Larger parks have hotels, retail stores, and many restaurants, ranging from typical fast-food operations to "silver service" establishments. Finally, theme parks host concerts, conventions, business meetings, and similar events. Modern parks are mostly all-year-round facilities and can be an important boost to the local economy. They are difficult neighbors, however, often generating significant amounts of traffic, lights, noise, and other nuisance characteristics. These impacts need to be addressed in the local zoning ordinance by requiring adequate buffers, limits on the hours of operation, adequate parking facilities, and restrictions on fireworks, outdoor concerts, and similar activities.

In addition, larger parks can create major off-site demands for tourist-related facilities such as lodging, food, and retail uses, as well as impacts on services and utilities. Without proper planning and adequate controls, this can result in a "strip-city" environment.

***Legal Annotation***: "Marine Attractions obtained an occupational license to operate 'kiddie rides,' the fee therefor covering the operator, Marine Attractions, and ten devices. Early in January, the city took action to stop the erection of what seems a large-scale **amusement park**, with a Ferris wheel and other rides." *Marine Attractions v. City of St. Petersburg Beach* (Fla. Dist. Ct. App., 1969).

## ANAEROBIC

**Refers to life or processes that occur in the absence of oxygen.**

***Legal Annotation***: "**[A]naerobic** bacteria, those which live out of contact with air, attack animal bodies soon after their death." *City of Milwaukee v. Activated Sludge* (7th Cir., 1934).

## ANCHOR STORE

**See *Anchor Tenant; Magnet Store.***

***Legal Annotation***: "The modern trend in retail, according to appellee's experts, is to have a large **anchor store** surrounded by smaller stores." *Loreto Dev. Co. v. Village of Chardon* (Ohio, 1996).

## ANCHOR TENANT

**The major store or stores within a shopping center.**

*Comment*: The anchor tenant usually is a major department store, often in excess of one hundred thousand square feet. It is the most important tenant in a shopping center and the one that generates the customer traffic. Superregional centers (750,000 square feet or more) may have three or more anchor stores. See *Retail Store, Large Scale.*

*Legal Annotation*: "Each shopping center will feature a 220,000-square-foot [WalMart] Supercenter as its primary **anchor tenant**." *BCLC v. City of Bakersfield* (Calif. Ct. App., 2004).

## ANCILLARY USE

See *Accessory Use.*

## ANIMAL

**A living organism other than a plant or bacterium, including fish, amphibians, reptiles, birds, and mammals, excluding humans.**

*Legal Annotation*: "**Animal**: Any living vertebrate creature, domestic or wild oher than humans.". Cillicothe, Missouri Zoning Ordiance Sec. 5-1 http://www.chillicothecity.org/chap5_animals.html

## ANIMAL HOSPITAL

See *Veterinary Hospital.*

## ANIMAL KENNEL

**Any structure or premises in which animals are boarded, groomed, bred, or trained for commercial gain. See *Kennel.***

*Legal Annotation*: "[Defendants] say that an **animal kennel** is 'similar in character' to a hatchery and 'no more offensive than a truck line terminal or milk processing plant.'" *Township of Pittsfield v. Malcolm* (Mich., 1965).

## ANIMAL SHELTER

**A facility used to house or contain stray, homeless, abandoned, or unwanted animals and that is owned, operated, or maintained by a public body, established humane society, animal welfare society (such as the Society for the Prevention of Cruelty to Animals), or other nonprofit organization devoted to the welfare, protection, and humane treatment of animals.**

*Legal Annotation*: "[T]he court found that over 1,000 stray animals are located within this single-family residential district; there are no buildings used in connection with the operation of this **animal shelter** (this does not mean that there are no pens or structures)." *Life for God's Stray Animals v. New North & C. Assn.* (Ga., 1984).

## ANIMAL UNIT

**(1) A unit of measurement that compares various animal types based on the amount of waste that they generate (*Land Use and Zoning Digest*, Volume 55, No. 2, footnote 5; S. Mark White, "Regulation of Concentrated Animal Feeding Operations: The Legal Context"); (2) the equivalent of one cow, four hogs, ten sheep, ten goats, one hundred poultry, one horse, one pony, one mule, or one hundred rabbits, or an equivalent combination thereof (Dade County, Wisconsin, ordinance).**

*Comment*:

(1) The first definition is designed to control large feedlot and concentrated feeding operations (COFA). The basic standard used in determining animal units is the beef cow. Conversion factors are then used to compare various animal types, as shown in table A-1.

The maximum number of animal units permitted in a particular zone is used to determine the size of the animal feeding operation as well as the various bulk controls, size of parcel, distance to residences, minimum area required for manure distribution, and so on. See *Concentrated Animal Feeding Operation*.

(2) The second definition is used to limit the number of animals on lots of one acre or more that are primarily residences and not farms in suburban areas. For example, not more than one animal unit per acre would be allowed in these districts. The standard is flexible enough to allow some negotiation between the enforcement officer and the homeowner to arrive at various combinations. In addition, the local ordinance can

**TABLE A-1: Animal Units by Type of Livestock**

| Type of Livestock | U.S. EPA* | Illinois | Nebraska | Notes |
|---|---|---|---|---|
| Slaughter/feed cattle | 1.0 | 1.0 | 1.0 | *The Environmental Protection Agency's regulations do not specifically cite a conversion factor for poultry animals, but the numbers used here are inferred from the overall numbers used in defining COFAS. |
| Mature dairy cattle | 1.4 | 1.4 | 1.4 | |
| Young dairy cattle | – | 0.6 | – | |
| Swine | 0.4[a] | 0.4 | 0.4 | |
| Swine (under 55 lbs.) | – | 0.03 | – | |
| Sheep | 0.1 | 0.1[b] | 0.1 | |
| Horses | 2.0 | 2.0 | 2.0 | |
| Turkeys | 0.018 | 0.02 | 0.02 | |
| Ducks | 0.2 | 0.2 | 0.2 | |
| Laying hens or broilers[c] | 0.01 | 0.01 | – | |
| Laying hens or broilers[d] | 0.03 | 0.03 | – | |
| Chickens | – | – | 0.01 | |

a Factor is for swine over 55 lbs.
b Factor includes goats.
c At facilities with continuous overflow watering.
d At facilities with liquid manure handling systems.

Source: Jim Schwab, *Planning and Zoning for Concentrated Feed Lot Operations*, Planning Advisory Service Report No. 482, December 1998; Jim Schwab, *Planning and Zoning for Concentrated Feed Lot Operations* (Chicago: Planners Book Service, 1999).

establish minimum setbacks from property lines for buildings that house animals, where animals are fed, and where they are permitted to graze, root, or wallow. (See "Living with Animals," *Zoning News*, January 1993, for complete discussion of animals and pets.)

***Legal Annotation***: "The ordinance at issue assigns **animal-unit** equivalencies for certain livestock based upon the odor-producing characteristics of the animal's waste." *Richardson v. Township of Brady* (6th Cir., 2000).

## ANIMAL, DOMESTIC

**Any animal that has been bred and/or raised to live in or about the habitation of humans and is dependent on people for food and shelter.**

***Comment***: The ordinance might list the domestic animals acceptable to the community, or exclude by weight or other characteristics those animals deemed to be unacceptable. See *Household Pet.*

***Legal Annotation***: "Corti testified that she had pointed out to the board that a horse was a **domestic animal**. . . . We conclude that within the context of these regulations . . . a horse is not a 'household pet.'" *Kaeser v. Zoning Board of Appeals* (Conn., 1991).

## ANIMATED SIGN

See *Sign.*

## ANNEXATION

**The incorporation of a land area into an existing community with a resulting change in the boundaries of that community.**

***Comment***: Annexation may include newly incorporated land or land transferred from one municipality to another.

***Legal Annotation***: "The [legislature's] act authorized the consolidation of . . . Pittsburgh and

Allegheny [cities]. . . . [Plaintiff alleges] the taxes of the citizens of Allegheny would be increased by **annexation** to Pittsburgh." *Hunter v. Pittsburgh* (U.S., 1907).

## ANNUAL FLOOD

**The most significant flood event in any given year.**

*Legal Annotation*: "The **annual flood** is usually considered the single greatest event each year. The 10-year flood, for example, is the discharge that will exceed a certain volume which has a 10% probability of occurring each year." Organization of American States, Primer on Natural Hazard Management in Integrated Regional Development Planning, Chapter 8: Floodplain Definition and Flood Hazard Assessment http://www.oas.org/osde/publications/Unit/oea66e/Insert ch08.htm

## ANTENNA

**A device used to transmit and/or receive radio or electromagnetic waves between terrestrially and/or orbitally based structures. See *Satellite Dish Antenna; Wireless Telecommunications Towers And Facilities*.**

*Legal Annotation*: "[R]espondent was using his **antennas** to provide a commercial service, in violation of a City ordinance requiring a 'conditional-use permit' . . . for commercial antenna use." *Rancho Palos Verdes v. Abrams* (U.S., 2005).

## ANTIDEGRADATION CLAUSE

**A provision in air quality and water quality laws that prohibits deterioration of air or water quality in areas where the pollution levels are currently below those allowed.**

*Legal Annotation*: "The exception assumes that some groundwater degradation is permitted by the Order and that constitutes a recognition that the **antidegradation clause** applies to the Order." *Asociacion de Gente Unida por el Agua v. Central Valley Regional Water Quality Control Bd.* (Calif. App., 2012).

## APARTMENT, GARDEN

**See *Dwelling, Garden Apartment*.**

## APARTMENT, HIGH-RISE

**See *Dwelling, High-Rise*.**

## APARTMENT, MID-RISE

**See *Dwelling, Mid-Rise*.**

## APARTMENT, HOTEL

**A facility offering transient lodging accommodation to the general public and where rooms or suites may include kitchen facilities and sitting rooms in addition to the bedroom. See *Hotel*.**

*Comment*: The apartment hotel, also known as hotel suites, differs from the typical hotel in that transients are likely to rent rooms or suites for longer periods than the traditional one or two nights.

*Legal Annotation*: "[T]he high rise apartment house structure, itself similar in design and purpose as the so-called **apartment hotel**, would not have been provided for in the ordinance." *Moyer v. Board of Zoning Appeals* (Me., 1967).

## APARTMENT HOUSE

**A structure containing three or more dwelling units. See *Dwelling, Multifamily*.**

*Legal Annotation*: "With particular reference to **apartment houses**, . . . the development of detached house sections is greatly retarded by the coming of **apartment houses**, which has sometimes resulted in destroying the entire section for private house purposes; that in such sections very often the **apartment house** is a mere parasite, constructed in order to take advantage of the open spaces and attractive surroundings created by the residential character of the district." *Village of Euclid v. Ambler Realty Co.* (U.S., 1926).

## APARTMENT UNIT

**One or more rooms with private bath and kitchen facilities constituting an independent,**

**self-contained dwelling unit in a building containing three or more dwelling units.**

*Legal Annotation*: "The BZA . . . noted that density would be greater if the basement . . . remained a place for from four to five roomers than if conversion of the basement into a third **apartment unit** were allowed." *Wolf v. Dist. Of Columbia Bd. Of Zoning* (D.C. Ct. App., 1979).

## APARTMENT UNIT, EFFICIENCY

See *Dwelling Unit, Efficiency.*

## APPLICANT

**Any person, firm, partnership, corporation, or public agency submitting an application for development.**

*Legal Annotation*: "[A] zoning board of appeals is required . . . to engage in a balancing test, weighing the benefit to the **applicant** against the detriment to the health, safety and welfare of the neighborhood or community." *Matter of Ifrah v. Utschig* (N.Y., 2002).

## APPLICATION FOR DEVELOPMENT

**The application form and all accompanying documents and exhibits required of an applicant by an approving authority for development review and approval purposes.**

*Legal Annotation*: "In assessing the significance of petitioner's failure to submit **applications to develop** the upland area it is important to bear in mind the purpose that the final decision requirement serves." *Palazzolo v. Rhode Island* (U.S., 2001).

## APPLICATION REVIEW COMMITTEE (ARC)

**An advisory committee to a municipal agency or approving authority that provides nonbinding reviews of development applications. See *Technical Coordinating Committee*.**

*Legal Annotation*: "[T]he Architectural **Review Committee** gave concept approval to the site plan . . . as to the number of bedrooms in each unit, the exterior design, the square footage of each building, the size and shape of the roads and parkways, and the number, size, and shape of the parking facilities." *Del Monte Dunes v. City of Monterey* (9th Cir., 1990).

## APPRAISAL

**An estimate or opinion of the value of real or personal property or an interest or estate in that property as determined by a qualified appraiser.**

*Legal Annotation*: "The plaintiff's expert, whose **appraisal** the referee adopted, gave consideration to the comparative sales approach, as well as to the reproduction-cost approach. He concluded, however, that the income approach was the most suitable method to use in arriving at an estimate of the value of the property." *Stanley Works v. New Britain Redevelopment Agency* (Conn., 1967).

## APPROVABLE SITE

**(1) A site that meets all the bulk requirements of the local ordinance and is capable of accommodating permitted development; (2) a site that may be developed for low- and moderate-income housing in a manner consistent with the regulations of all agencies with jurisdiction over the site.**

*Comment*: With respect to low- and moderate-income housing, a site may be approvable although not currently zoned for low- and moderate-income housing.

*Legal Annotation*: "Sites should be 'available, suitable, developable and approvable' . . . '**approvable site**' [i]s a site that may be developed for low and moderate income in a manner 'consistent with the regulations of all agencies with jurisdiction over the site.'" *In re Township of Denville* (N.J., 1991).

## APPROVED PLAN

**A plan that has been granted final approval by the appropriate approving authority.**

*Legal Annotation*: "The procedure for land development . . . requires first of all that there be a general plan for development approved by the Village Board of Trustees. This condition was met; there is an **approved plan** for the plaintiffs' tract." *Coniston Corp. v. Village of Hoffman Estates* (7th Cir., 1988).

## APPROVED STREET

See *Street*.

*Legal Annotation*: "[A] road which is no longer a publicly **approved street** is not a 'public right of way' as that term is used in the Brentwood zoning ordinance." *Metzger v. Brentwood* (N.H., 1975).

## APPROVING AUTHORITY

**The agency, board, group, or other legally designated individual or agency that has been charged with the review and approval of plans and applications.**

*Legal Annotation*: "The plan-**approving authority** . . . must act on all plans submitted within forty-five days from receipt thereof." *United Land Corp. of America v. Clarke* (4th Cir., 1980).

## APPURTENANCES

**The visible, functional, or ornamental objects accessory to, and part of, buildings or structures (American Planning Association, *Appearance Codes for Small Communities,* Planning Advisory Service Report No. 379, 1983).**

*Legal Annotation*: "Necessary **appurtenances** to structures and movables made immovable by attachment, which are defective or have fallen into ruin, also may be included within that term 'building' for purposes of the building-owner's delictual responsibility." *Dunn v. Tedesco* (La., 1958).

## AQUACULTURE

**The propagation, rearing, and harvesting of aquatic organisms in controlled or selected environments, and the subsequent processing, packing, and marketing (*New Jersey State Development and Redevelopment Plan,* 2002).**

*Legal Annotation*: "The plan designated Orion's property as 'aquatic,' a designation that foreclosed dredging and filling the tidelands. . . . The only possible uses of any particular value were nonintensive recreation and **aquaculture**, the latter of which required a conditional use permit." *Orion Corporation v. State* (Wash., 1987).

## AQUARIUM

**A building where collections of fish, live water plants, and marine animals are exhibited (Minton 2003: 14).**

*Legal Annotation*: "[T]his doesn't mean that a corporation operating an **aquarium** attraction can build a separate amusement park and describe it as a use accessory to the nonconforming **aquarium**." *Marine Attractions v. City of St. Petersburg Beach* (Fla., 1969).

## AQUATIC ORGANISMS

**Finfish, mollusks, crustaceans, aquatic plants, and similar creatures and species (*New Jersey State Development and Redevelopment Plan* 2002).**

*Legal Annotation*: "These [cooling water intake] structures pose various threats to the environment, chief among them the squashing against intake screens (elegantly called 'impingement') or suction into the cooling system ('entrainment') of **aquatic organisms** that live in the affected water sources." *Entergy Corp. v. Riverkeeper, Inc.* (U.S., 2009).

## AQUATIC PLANTS

**Plants that grow in water, either floating on the surface, growing up from the bottom of the body of water, or growing under the surface of the water.**

*Legal Annotation*: "The new regulations permitted the following uses as of right: . . . raising of **aquatic plants**, fish and fish food." *Morris County Land, etc. v. Parsippany-Troy Hills Tp.* (N.J., 1963).

## AQUIFER

**A geologic formation, group of formations, or part of a formation capable of storing and**

yielding groundwater to wells or springs. *See Figure 6*.

*Legal Annotation*: The county's resolution stated, "The subject property area overlies one of the most permeable aquifers in the world, the Biscayne **Aquifer**. This **aquifer** serves as the source of virtually all drinking water in Dade County and must be protected from contamination." *Moviematic Ind. v. Bd. Of Cty. Com'rs* (Fla., 1977).

## AQUIFER RECHARGE AREA

**The surface land or water area through which an aquifer is replenished (*New Jersey State Development and Redevelopment Plan*, 2002).**

*Comment*: Growing concern over water supply and quality has led to increasing protection of aquifer recharge areas. For example, San Antonio, Texas has limited impervious cover in such areas (Robbins 2006, 32).

*Legal Annotation*: "If the long-range productivity of the aquifer and **aquifer recharge area** as a natural resource will be substantially reduced by mining, additional acres should be designated as unsuitable for mining." *Village of Pleasant City v. Ohio Dept. of Natl. Resources* (Ohio, 1993).

## ARABLE

**Land capable of being cultivated for sod, grains, and seed crops.**

*Legal Annotation*: "'**Arable land**' **is** land fit for plowing or tillage." 6 C.J.S., p. 142; Black's Law Dictionary, p. 95 (5th ed. 1979). *Knowles v. Moore* (Mo. Ct. App., 1981).

## ARBORIST

**An individual trained in arboriculture, forestry, landscape architecture, horticulture, or related fields and experienced in the conservation and preservation of native and ornamental trees.**

*Legal Annotation*: "[T]he tree ordinance here requires a significant exercise of discretion, primarily by the County **Arborist**, in several instances." *Greater Atlanta H'bldrs v. DeKalb County* (Ga., 2003).

## ARCADE

**A continuous passageway parallel to and open to a street, open space, or building, usually covered by a canopy or permanent roofing, and accessible and open to the public. *See Figure 20*.**

*Legal Annotation*: "The main lobby of the [Carew Tower] complex, the '**Arcade**,' runs between the office and hotel spaces at ground level and spans the distance of a city block between two streets." *Emery Realty, Inc. v. NLRB* (6th Cir., 1988).

## ARCHAEOLOGICAL SITE

**Land or water area that shows evidence of artifacts of human, plant, or animal activity,**

**Figure 6**

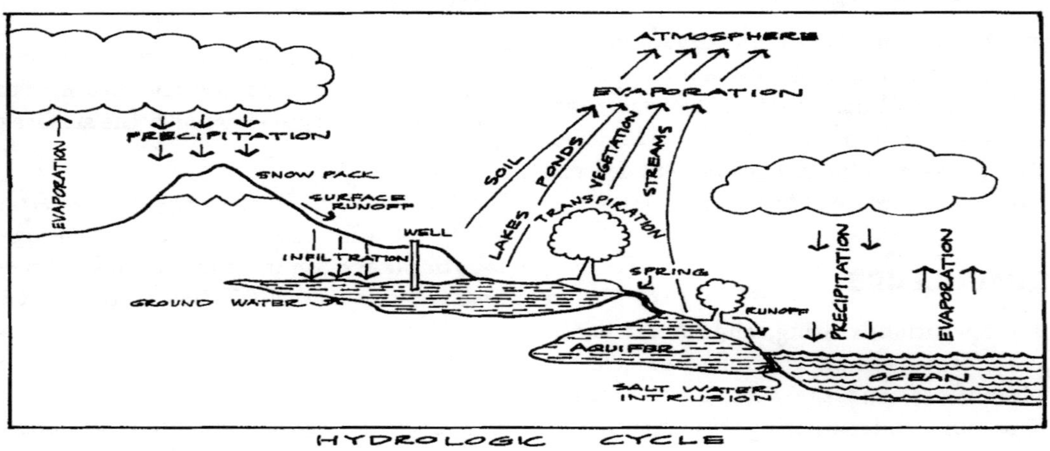

**usually dating from periods of which only vestiges remain.**

***Legal Annotation***: "Compadres, a partnership, owns about 20 acres of land in San Diego County on which, Society claims, is located a significant and rare **archaeological site**, 3,000–7,000 years old." *San Diego Cty. Archaeological Society v. Compadres* (Calif., 1978).

## ARCHERY RANGE

**An outdoor facility, which may include buildings or structures, used for target practice with bows and arrows. See *Amusement, Commercial, Outdoor*.**

***Legal Annotation***: "The regulations define private outdoor recreation as a 'yacht club, golf course, trap, skeet and **archery range** . . . tennis court, recreation stadium and skiing facility." *In re Scheiber* (Vt., 1998).

## ARCHITECTURAL CONCEPT

**The basic aesthetic idea of a building, or group of buildings or structures, including the site and landscape development that produce its distinctive character (American Planning Association, *Appearance Codes for Small Communities,* Planning Advisory Service Report No. 379, 1983).**

***Legal Annotation***: "The Guidelines contain an '**Architectural Concept**' section that explains that Association's architecture is a homogenous Spanish style reminiscent of California early days." *Chapala Management Corp. v. Stanton* (Calif., 2010).

## ARCHITECTURAL CONTROL

**Public regulation of the exterior design of private buildings to preserve, enhance, or develop the character of a particular area.**

***Comment***: Aesthetics is the major reason architectural controls are imposed. In all ordinances calling for architectural controls, the standards upon which to judge a particular building must be precise and carefully drawn to avoid charges of vagueness and improper delegation of authority. See *Aesthetic Zoning; Design Standards.*

***Legal Annotation***: "The courts have repeatedly sustained the validity of **architectural control** ordinances as police power regulation, especially when historic or touristic districts like the Vieux Carré are concerned." *Maher v. City of New Orleans* (5th Cir., 1975).

## ARCHITECTURAL FEATURE

**A prominent or significant part or element of a building, structure, or site (APA, *Appearance Codes for Small Communities,* Planning Advisory Service Report No. 379, 1983).**

***Legal Annotation***: "The openings built into the wall over right field are an **architectural feature** of Three Rivers Stadium which are not an inherent feature of the spectator sport of baseball." *Jones v. Three Rivers Management Corporation and Pittsburgh Athletic Company, Inc.* (Pa., 1978).

## ARCHITECTURAL PROJECTIONS

**Building projections that are permitted to intrude into required front, rear, and side yards.**

***Comment***: The text of the ordinance should indicate the extent to which the projection is permitted. For example, on dwellings, bay windows, chimneys, and roof overhangs might be limited to two feet into the yard. Unroofed steps and landings could extend up to ten feet but could not occupy more than 20 percent of the building width. On nonresidential buildings, these projections may include the covered awning or canopy from the curb to the entrance.

***Legal Annotation***: "The height of fences and/or retaining walls is determined by measuring the exposed face of the fence and/or wall at its tallest point, from finished grade at the base, to the top of the fence and/or wall, including all ornamental and **architectural projections**." *Elan and Reverend Oracle v. Santa Cruz County Planning Department et al.* (N.D. Ca., 2010).

## ARCHITECTURAL STYLE

**The characteristic form and detail of buildings of a particular historic period (APA, *Appearance Codes for Small Communities,* Planning**

Advisory Service Report No. 379, 1983). See *Historic Building Styles*.

*Legal Annotation*: "The predominant **architectural style** found in the area is Victorian, the characteristics of which are readily identifiable." *A-S-P Associates v. City Of Raleigh*) (N.C., 1979).

## AREA OF RESCUE ASSISTANCE

**An area with direct access to an exit where people who are unable to use stairs may remain temporarily in safety to await further instructions or assistance during emergency evacuation.**

*Comment*: Part of the Americans with Disabilities Act, 1990.

*Legal Annotation*: "There is no means of emergency egress or **area of rescue assistance** provided at the facility, violating the requirements of Section 4.3.10 of the ADAAG." *Caldarola v. Rosner Realty LLC* (Fla. Dist. Ct., 2014).

## AREA PLAN

**A plan that provides specific planning and design proposals for a defined geographic area.**

*Comment*: Area, neighborhood, or district plans are urban design plans that are often prepared after the adoption of the local master plan. They provide the specific local planning detail, which may be adopted as amendments to the master plan.

*Legal Annotation*: "Rank Two plans may be either Facility Plans or **Area Plans** that typically cover 15 or more square miles, and specify important development standards." *West Bluff Neighborhood Association v. City of Albuquerque* (N.M. Ct. App., 2002).

## AREA SCALE

**A graphic display of the relationship between map areas and actual areas. See *Scale*. *See Figure 7*.**

*Legal Annotation*: "These maps are made part of this report and are identified as follows: Map No. 1:

**Figure 7**

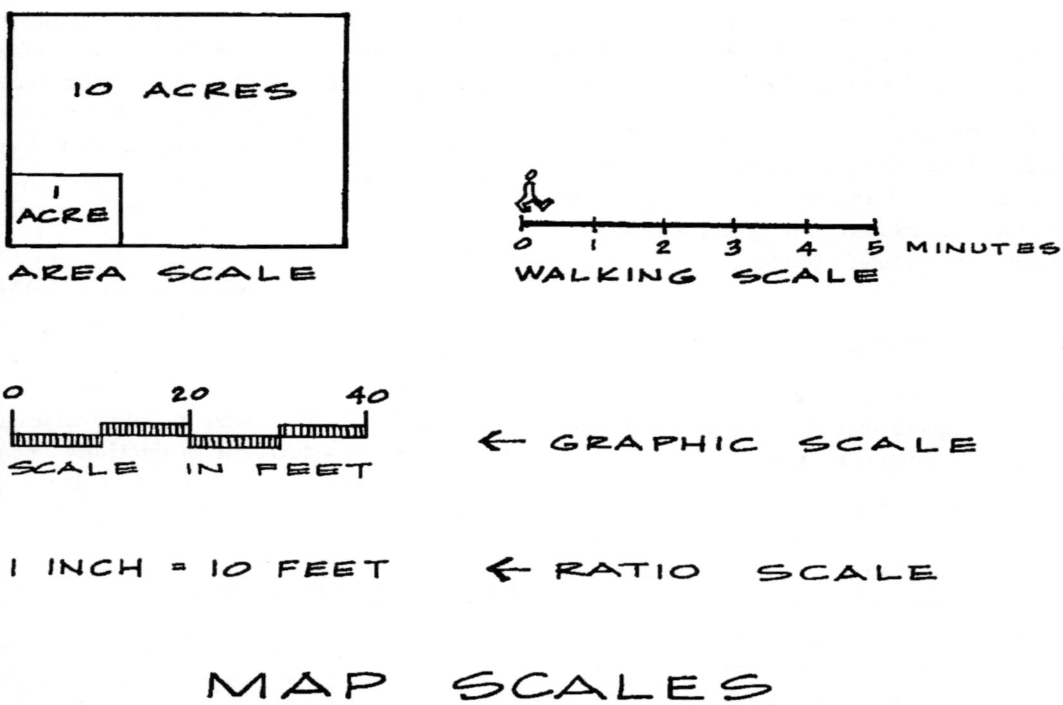

Cadastral Map of the Big Bend **Area**, **scale** 2,000 feet to the inch; Map No. 2: Cadastral Map of the oil field region, in two sheets, Nos. 1 and 2, scale 500 feet to the inch." *Oklahoma v. Texas* (U.S., 1924).

## AREA SOURCE

**In air pollution, any small individual fuel combustion source, including any transportation source. See *Point Source*.**

***Comment***: This is a general definition; area source is usually specifically set forth and precisely defined in appropriate federal statutes.

***Legal Annotation***: "An '**area source**' is 'any stationary source . . . that is not a major source,' and does not include 'motor vehicles or nonroad vehicles subject to regulation under [42 U.S.C. §§ 7521-7590].' 42 U.S.C. § 7412(a)(2)." *National Mining Association v. United States Environmental Protection Agency* (D.C. Cir., 1995).

## ARTERIAL STREET

**See *Street, Major Arterial*.**

## ARTESIAN AQUIFER

**An aquifer in which water is confined under pressure between layers of impermeable (aquiclude) material.**

***Legal Annotation***: "Water in the **artesian aquifer** is under pressure. One artesian aquifer is known as the Floridan aquifer. It underlies most of the state and furnishes most of the well-water supplies of the state." *The Village of Tequesta v. Jupiter Inlet Corporation* (Fla., 1979).

## ARTICULATE

**To divide into distinct and significant parts.**

***Comment***: Design standards for large buildings can require that building walls or facades over a certain length be "articulated," or divided into distinct and significant parts. See *Warehouse*.

***Legal Annotation***: "[T]he design of the proposed south wing would avoid the effect of a massive wall along Connecticut Avenue through the use of vertical shafts, recessed courts, and a highly **articulated** facade." *Cathedral Park Condominium Committee v. District Of Columbia Zoning Commission* (D.C. Ct. App., 2000).

## ARTICULATION

**For structures, a change in the depth of the building plane, roofline, or height. See *Articulate*.**

***Legal Annotation***: "The record demonstrates that the Wal-Mart building will include significant **articulation**, roofline modulation, and façade variation, and it will incorporate numerous exterior treatments, design features, and landscaping." *Friends of North Kelsey v. City of Monroe* (Wash. Ct. App., 2013).

## ARTIFICIAL RECHARGE

**Adding water to an aquifer by artificial means, such as specially designed wells or ditches, or through other constructed methods.**

***Legal Annotation***: "The Water Court determined that: (1) **artificial recharge** activities involving the movement of underground water into, from, or through aquifers underlying the surface lands of the Landowners would not constitute a trespass." *The Board of County Commissioners of the County of Park v. Park County Sportsmen's Ranch, LLP* (Colo., 2002).

## ARTIST'S STUDIO

**A place of work for an artist, artisan, or craftsperson, including persons engaged in the application, teaching, or performance of fine arts such as, but not limited to, drawing, vocal or instrumental music, painting, sculpture, and writing.**

***Comment***: An artist's studio may include the dwelling of the artist.

***Legal Annotation***: "In 2003 the former owner of the subject property applied for permission to convert the third floor to an **artist's studio** and residence, which was a permitted use by special permit." *Sonne v. Board of Trustees of Village of Suffern* (N.Y. Sup. Ct., 2009).

## ARTS CENTER

**A structure or complex of structures for the visual and/or performing arts.**

***Comment***: Arts centers are often owned and/or operated by public or semipublic agencies. In any zone permitting arts centers, accessory needs, such as parking, must be considered and adverse impacts, such as noise, lighting, traffic, and hours of operation, must be carefully evaluated and addressed.

***Legal Annotation***: Section 18-116 of the New York City Code "[a]uthorized the City to construct a parking garage 'under the public park property in Lincoln Square Performing **Arts Center** for the purpose of accommodating persons using the facilities included in the Performing **Arts Center** and the adjacent public parks.'" *Hotel Employees & Restaurant Employees Union v. City of NY Dept. of Parks & Recreation* (2nd Cir., 2002).

## AS-BUILT PLANS

**Accurate and precise drawings of post-construction site features and characteristics, including all buildings, structures, infrastructure, boundaries, and natural features (source: Brian Curran, building surveyor, November 2013).**

***Legal Annotation***: According to Arizona Revised Statutes (A.R.S.) section 32-152(B)(2008),[2] "as built plans" are "plans that document the registered or certified professional's final plans and that include all changes made to the plans in the actual project construction." Smith v. Maricopa County (Ariz., 2013).

## ASSEMBLAGE

**The merger of separate properties into a single tract of land. See *Consolidation*.**

***Legal Annotation***: "These may include such diverse matters as irregularity of the plots, inadequacy of the streets, diversity of land ownership making **assemblage** of property difficult, incompatibility of the existing mixture of residential and industrial property, overcrowding, the incidence of crime, lack of sanitation, the drain an area makes on municipal services, fire hazards, traffic congestion, and pollution." *Yonkers Community Development Agency v. Morris* (N.Y., 1975).

## ASSESSED VALUATION

**The value at which property is appraised for tax purposes. See *Assessment Ratio*.**

***Legal Annotation***: "The amount of revenue which a district can raise in this manner thus depends largely on its tax base—i.e., the **assessed valuation** of real property within its borders. . . . Although private residential and commercial patterns may be partly responsible for the distribution of **assessed valuation** throughout the state, such patterns are shaped and hardened by zoning ordinances and other governmental land use controls which promote economic exclusivity." *Serrano v. Priest* (Calif., 1971).

## ASSESSMENT RATIO

**The relation between the assessed value of a property and its true market value.**

***Comment***: Sometimes referred to as sales assessment ratio or equalization ratio. For a number of reasons, the assessed value of property may not reflect market value. In some states, communities are permitted to assess at a percentage of true market value. In addition, in jurisdictions that do not reassess or revalue frequently, the discrepancy between assessed valuation and true market value often increases over time. To equalize all properties within a given taxing jurisdiction, some regional or state agency will assign an assessment ratio to a community's property. The planner must consider this equalization ratio in undertaking any cost-benefit analysis.

***Legal Annotation***: "[T]he common **assessment ratio** was from the beginning given recognition under the old constitutional and statutory standard of 'true value.' . . . But this is not true of the 'average' **assessment ratio** of true value, an arithmetical mean of varying ratios of true value, necessarily making for unequal proportions of value between the individual property owners and thus for the inequality of treatment and burden obnoxious to basic principle." *Switz v. Township of Middletown* (N.J. 1957).

## ASSIMILATION

**The ability of a body of water to purify itself of organic pollution.**

***Legal Annotation***: "And in discussing how surface coal mining affects water resources and in turn interstate commerce, the House Committee explained: . . . Reduced recreational values, fishkills, reductions in normal waste **assimilation** capacity, impaired water supplies . . . are some of the most obvious economic effects that stem from mining-related pollution and sedimentation." *Hodel v. Virginia Surface Mining & Reclamation Association* (U.S., 1981).

## ASSISTED LIVING FACILITY

**Residences for the frail elderly that provide rooms, meals, personal care, and supervision of self-administered medication. They may provide other services, such as recreational activities, financial services, and transportation. See *Residential Health Care Facilities; Retirement Community*.**

***Comment***: Assisted living facilities (or assisted care facilities) range in size from a few rooms to more than a hundred. A typical development might be 110 to 115 units on three to five acres. The facilities are sometimes combined with other types of housing, such as congregate apartment housing for the elderly and residential health-care facilities.

***Legal Annotation***: "We consider here whether, in the circumstances presented, federal antidiscrimination statutes require a municipality to make accommodations in order to permit construction of an '**assisted living facility**'—a facility designed to provide care, in a residential environment, for individuals with certain disabilities—on land zoned for commercial uses only." *Forest City Daly Housing, Inc. v. Town of North Hempstead* (2nd Cir., 1999).

## AT GRADE

**See *Grade Level*.**

## ATMOSPHERE

**The layer of air surrounding the earth. *See Figure 6*.**

***Legal Annotation***: "A well-documented rise in global temperatures has coincided with a significant increase in the concentration of carbon dioxide in the **atmosphere**. Respected scientists believe the two trends are related. For when carbon dioxide is released into the **atmosphere**, it acts like the ceiling of a greenhouse, trapping solar energy and retarding the escape of reflected heat." *Massachusetts v. EPA* (U.S., 2007).

## ATTACHED DWELLING UNIT

**See *Dwelling, Attached*.**

## ATTENTION-GETTING DEVICE

**A device designed or intended to attract by noise; sudden, intermittent, or rhythmic movement; or physical change or lighting change, such as banners, flags, streamers, balloons, propellers, whirligigs, searchlights, and flashing lights.**

***Legal Annotation***: "In addition, **AGDs** containing certain types of written messages are considered 'signs' and are subject to the Sign Code's provisions. Section 28-37(a) states: [A]ny device otherwise defined as an **attention-getting device** which contains or displays any written message, business name, pictorial representation, logo, corporate symbol, silhouette or other visual representation representing or advertising a particular business, good, service, or merchandise sold or available for sale on the premises where the device is erected, displayed or maintained shall be a 'sign.'" *Houston Balloons & Promotions, LLC v. City of Houston* (S.D. Texas, 2008).

## ATTIC

**That part of a building that is immediately below and wholly or partly within the roof framing. See *Story, Half. See Figure 8*.**

*Legal Annotation*: "The unabridged *Webster's Third New International Dictionary* sets out the following definitions of '**attic**': 1a: a low story or wall above the main order or orders of a facade in the classical styles; b: a room or rooms behind an **attic**; c: the part of a building immediately below the roof and wholly or partly within the roof framing: a garret or storage space under the roof." *Kalorama Citizens Association v. District of Columbia Board of Zoning Adjustment* (D.C. Ct. App., 2007).

## ATTRIBUTES

**Physical, natural, constructed, or demographic characteristics that define and describe a building, site, or entity.**

*Comment*: Examples of attributes include physical characteristics of a building or structure, length and width of a road, and demographic data of a municipality or census tract.

*Legal Annotation*: "The nonconforming **attributes** of the building, however, existed at the time when the front yard setback and building coverage requirements were adopted by the town's planning and zoning commission." *Moon v. Zoning Board of Appeals of Town of Madison* (Conn., 2009).

**Figure 8**

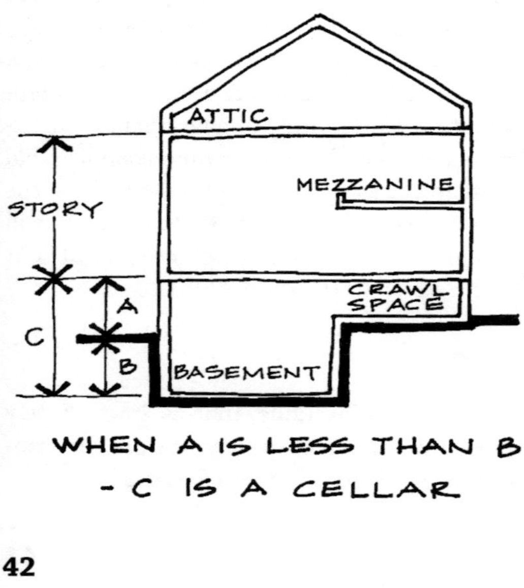


## AUCTION HOUSE

**A place where objects of art, furniture, and other goods are offered for sale to persons who bid on the object in competition with each other.**

*Legal Annotation*: "Unlike a traditional **auction house**, eBay is not actively involved in the listing, bidding, sale and delivery of any item offered for sale on its website." *Hendrickson v. eBay, Inc.* (D.C. Calif., 2001).

## AUDIOMETER

**An instrument for measuring hearing sensitivity.**

*Legal Annotation*: "On the day of the examination, the **audiometer**, the instrument used to test hearing, was not in operation, and that fact was brought to the attention of the examinees, including Whitaker." *United States v. Callaway* (E.D. Pa., 1974).

## AUTHORITATIVE SOURCE

**A person, document, professional organization, or institution whose expertise, based on education, research, study, and experience of a given subject or in a given field, is generally accepted by other experts on the subject or practitioners in the field.**

*Comment*: Many ordinances allow flexibility and discretion in applying certain standards, particularly with respect to engineering and construction requirements. For example, an ordinance might require that all road improvements must meet AASHTO (American Association of State Highway and Transportation Officials) standards or standards from some other "authoritative source." One state enabling act, citing a specific document, allows changes or modifications "in light of any recommended . . . standards promulgated under similarly authoritative auspices of any academic or professional institution or organization" (*New Jersey Municipal Land Use Law*, C. 40:55D-40.4, dealing with site improvement standards).

Many problems arise in attempting to differentiate between an authoritative source and a recognized source. While there is some overlap, a recognized source is one that has general acceptance but is not necessarily an authoritative source. The determination requires a case-by-case analysis. Other conflicts can arise when the authoritative source has a vested interest in the outcome. National organizations promoting education, libraries, or recreation, for example, or the use of certain materials such as plastic, concrete, or asphalt, often conduct research and publish recommended standards. These may be considered authoritative sources if the research used in developing the standards is carefully designed to remove any possible taint of bias. But the source still has to be considered, and the methods used in arriving at the standard should be examined.

*Legal Annotation*: "When valuing such individual units, an **authoritative source** for the appraisal industry recognizes that individual units should not be valued by valuing the entire project and then allocating total value to individual units." *Seaside Investments LLC v. Clatsop County Assessor* (Ore., Tax Ct., 2013).

## AUTOMATED CONVENIENCE STORE

See *Vending Machine.*

## AUTOMATED TELLER MACHINE (ATM)

**An automated device that performs banking financial functions at a location that may be separate from the controlling financial institution.**

*Legal Annotation*: "Under the statute, **ATM** networks may not prohibit a Nevada bank from charging transaction fees to an **automated teller machine (ATM)** cardholder who withdraws funds from the Nevada bank's ATM but whose account is with another bank." *Valley Bank of Nevada v. Plus System, Inc.* (9th Cir., 1990).

## AUTOMATIC CAR WASH

**A structure containing facilities for washing automobiles and automatic or semiautomatic application of cleaner, brushes, rinse water, and heat for drying.**

*Comment*: Many gas stations are incorporating on-site automatic car wash facilities. Zoning considerations include drainage and possible freezing of runoff, water use, drying areas, vehicle stacking capacity, and litter and debris.

*Legal Annotation*: "In March 1984 respondents Gulf Oil Corp. and Fenley & Nichol Co. (Gulf) applied for a permit to erect a prefabricated metal **automatic car wash** on their property, which is used as a gas station—a nonconforming legal use. The **automatic car wash** was to replace a self-service car wash." *In the Matter of Sun-Brite Car Wash v. Board of Zoning and Appeals of Town of North Hempstead* (N.Y., 1987).

## AUTOMOBILE

**A self-propelled, free-moving vehicle with four wheels, usually used to transport not more than six passengers and licensed by the appropriate state agency as a passenger vehicle.**

*Legal Annotation*: "The Code defines '**automobile**' as a 'self-propelled, free-moving vehicle, primarily for conveyance on a street or roadway.'" *Hitchcock v. Zoning Board of Adjustment of City of Pittsburgh* (Pa. Comm. Ct., 1991).

## AUTOMOBILE, COMPACT

See *Compact Car.*

## AUTOMOBILE DEALERSHIP, USED

See *Automobile Sales, Used.*

## AUTOMOBILE MALL

**A single location containing more than one automobile dealership that provides display and sales space primarily for new motor vehicles, as well as centralized services, which may include vehicle servicing and repair, financing, insurance, leasing and rental, and other related services.**

*Comment*: Auto malls are very large establishments, often consisting of several dealerships. They are the result of the increasing cost of retail auto sales and cost efficiencies from combining services facilities. Because of their size, they are usually located on the outside of the central business district and developed commercial areas. They require large tracts of land, often in excess of thirty acres with good access. Planning considerations include controls on lighting and signage and requirements for screening and landscaping. A major problem is that because of their large size and combined repair facilities, auto malls may generate significant environmental problems, including pollution and runoff ("Acres of Automobiles," *Zoning News*, June 1997).

***Legal Annotation***: "Plaintiff, a franchised motor vehicle dealer for . . . intended to use this property to consolidate some of its car dealerships, then at different locations, into an 'autoplex' or **automobile mall** where customers could come and shop for cars from different manufacturers." *Grossinger Motorcorp Inc. v. American National Bank & Trust Co.* (Ill. App. Ct., 1992).

## AUTOMOBILE REPAIR

**See *Automotive Repair Services And Garages; Garage, Repair.***

## AUTOMOBILE REPAIR SERVICES, MAJOR

**General repair, rebuilding, or reconditioning of engines, transmissions, or other major systems of motor vehicles or trailers, including bodywork, welding, and major painting service.**

***Comment***: Also referred to as automotive repair garages, wherein major repairs are undertaken.

***Legal Annotation***: "[A]nd the making of repairs to motor vehicles except **repairs of a major type** which are defined to be spray painting, body, fender, clutch, transmission, differential, axle, spring and frame repairs, major overhauling of engines requiring the removal of engine cylinder head or crankcase pan, repairs to radiators requiring the removal thereof or complete recapping or retreading of tires." *Lesser v. City of Cleveland* (Ohio Ct. App., 1995).

## AUTOMOBILE REPAIR SERVICES, MINOR

**The replacement or repair of any automobile part that does not require removal of the engine head or pan, engine transmission, or differential but may include incidental body and fender work, minor painting, and upholstering service.**

***Comment***: Also referred to as automotive repair garages, wherein minor repairs are undertaken.

***Legal Annotation***: "Moreover, Rink's Auto Repair is limited to conducting **minor automobile repair services** as are permitted at service stations." *Lesser v. City of Cleveland* (Ohio Ct. App., 1995).

## AUTOMOBILE SALES

**The use of any building, land area, or other premise principally for the display, sale, rental, or lease of new or used automobiles (but may include light trucks or vans, trailers, or recreation vehicles), and including any vehicle preparation, warranty, or repair work conducted as an accessory use.**

***Legal Annotation***: "The parcel is occupied at one end by a building used as an **automobile sales** agency, service station and as a gasoline station." *Incorporated Village of Great Neck v. Green* (N.Y. Sup, Ct., 1957).

## AUTOMOBILE SALES, USED

**The use of land and buildings for the display and sale of primarily used motor vehicles, which may include repair and service facilities as well as financing and leasing services.**

***Comment***: While the sale of used motor vehicles is customarily an accessory use to new car dealerships, where used car sales are a principal or primary use, they are often defined as such and may be subject to more stringent regulations. Sometimes used car sales are even excluded from zones that allow new car sales. Used-car superstores are a recent phenomenon, akin to the big box retailers. They usually provide one-stop shopping in the sale of used vehicles and include servicing, financing, and similar services. They occupy large land areas, usually on the outskirts of built-up areas. Good access and visibility are critical. As with auto malls, planning considerations include site design, landscaping, lighting, signage, and pollution ("Acres of Automobiles," *Zoning News*, June 1997).

***Legal Annotation***: "Plaintiff entered into a lease agreement for a parcel of land (the 'Site') on which Plaintiff intends to operate a **used automobile sales** business." *Goldstar Auto Sales, LLC v. Town of Halfmoon* (N.D. NY, 1999).

## AUTOMOBILE SERVICE STATION

**Any building, land area, or other premises, or portion thereof, used for the retail dispensing or sales of vehicular fuels; minor or light servicing and repair of automobiles; and including as an accessory use the sale and installation of lubricants, tires, batteries, and similar vehicle accessories.**

***Comment***: The name "automobile service station" is probably a misnomer as more and more stations convert to fuel sales only and no longer undertake vehicle repairs. In addition, many gas-only stations provide a convenience store on-site selling snack food, tobacco, drinks, newspapers, and similar convenience goods. While convenience stores are often treated as a second principal use, their ubiquity has led most jurisdictions to permit them as an accessory use, or jointly with fuel sales as a singular use. Some additional parking may be needed if a convenience store is provided along with fuel dispensing. Other zoning considerations include circulation, signage, and landscaping. See *Minimart*.

***Legal Annotation***: "Umatilla County Development Code (UCDC) 152.003 defined '**automobile service station**' as '[a]ny building, land area or other premises or portion thereof, used or intended to be used for the retail dispensing or sale of vehicular fuels; and including as an accessory use the sale and installation of lubricants, tires, batteries and similar accessories.' Thus, the restaurant, convenience store, and **automobile service station** uses were permitted on the property without a conditional use permit." *Western Land & Cattle, Inc. v. Umatilla County* (Ore. Ct. App., 2009).

## AUTOMOBILE WRECKING YARD

**An establishment that cuts up, compresses, or otherwise disposes of motor vehicles. See *Junkyard*.**

***Comment***: Wrecking yards may also store and sell salvaged auto parts, but if so, they function as junkyards.

***Legal Annotation***: "Mr. Kockelman, a land use expert and a city and regional planner, testified that an **automobile wrecking yard** is a refinement of a junkyard and that a junkyard involves three operations: (1) The collection and storage of material; (2) dismantling and resale; (3) scrapping and destruction." *Racine County v. Plourde* (Wis., 1968).

## AUTOMOTIVE REPAIR SERVICES AND GARAGES

**Establishments primarily engaged in furnishing automotive repair, rental, leasing, and parking services to the general public.**

***Comment***: This term is outdated, and few such establishments still exist today. However, this term applies to establishments in which all major components of the automotive industry (except the dispensing of gas and oil directly into the vehicles) are provided, including parking lots and structures, all types of repairs, car washes, and rental and leasing activities. See *Automobile Repair Services, Major And Minor*.

***Legal Annotation***: "The BZA found that revocation was warranted because petitioner was operating an **automobile repair** garage, a use outside the scope of petitioner's Certificate of Occupancy . . . and not permitted in its zoning district without a special exception. . . . Their testimony was corroborated by photographs of petitioner's garage, copies of work orders, and petitioner's own business card, advertisements and signage offering a full range of auto repair services (e.g., 'brakes,' 'exhaust,' 'alignment,' 'transmission,' 'electrical,' 'body work,' 'engine overhauls,' 'air conditioning/heating') and asserting that petitioner had 21 service bays, ASE certified technicians, and the capability to 'service and repair all cars domestic & foreign.'" *Kuri v. Bd of Zoning Adj.* (D.C. Ct. App., 2006).

## AUXILIARY LANE

**A part of the roadway striped for use but not for through traffic.**

***Legal Annotation***: "However, in the traffic rules and regulations chapter of the Utah Code, the legislature has defined this type of lane as an '**auxiliary lane**' not as an 'acceleration or deceleration lane.' Utah Code Ann. § 41-6-53.5(1)(b) (Supp. 2004) (stating that a 'general purpose lane' does not include an '**auxiliary lane** that begins as a freeway on-ramp and ends as part of the next freeway off-ramp')." *Young Electric Sign Co., Inc. v. Utah* (Utah Ct. App., 2005).

## AVAILABLE SITE

**A site with clear title, free of encumbrances that preclude development for low- and moderate-income housing (New Jersey Council on Affordable Housing 1993).**

***Legal Annotation***: "'**Available site**' is one with clear title free of encumbrances which preclude development of low and moderate income housing." *In re Petition for Substantive Certification Filed by Township of Denville* (N.J. Super. Ct., 1991).

## AVERAGE ANNUAL DAILY TRAFFIC (AADT)

**The total yearly traffic volume in both directions of travel divided by 365.**

***Comment***: Generally replaced by Average Daily Traffic (ADT) counts. See *Average Daily Traffic (Adt)*.

***Legal Annotation***: "A more specific unit of measure is known as **average annual daily traffic volume ('AADT')**. **AADT** is determined by dividing the total yearly volume by the number of days in the year. **AADT** can also be estimated in terms of hourly traffic volume, which is the primary datum used in evaluating and designing roadways." *Conservation Law Foundation v. Federal Highway Administration* fn. 11 (D.C. N.H., 2007).

## AVERAGE DAILY TRAFFIC (ADT)

**The average number of motor vehicles at a given location over a twenty-four-hour period.**

***Comment***: ADT counts have generally replaced average annual daily traffic counts (AADT) as the norm. Traffic engineers usually will take a sample of three to seven days of traffic to determine representative ADT counts.

***Legal Annotation***: "Mr. Thomas further testified that in front of the site of the subject property, the **average daily traffic** totaled 900 vehicles for a 24-hour count in both directions." *American Oil Co. v. Board of Appeals of Montgomery County* (Md. Ct. App., 1973).

"The general unit of measure used to quantify roadway usage is **average daily traffic ('ADT'),** which is defined as the total traffic volume during a given time period divided by the number of days in that period."*Conservation Law Foundation v. Federal Highway Administration* fn. 11 (D.C. N.H., 2007).

## AVERAGE FINISHED GRADE

**See *Grade, Finished.***

## AVERAGE SETBACK

**The average distance from the street right-of-way of buildings on both sides of a lot.**

***Comment***: In built-up neighborhoods, many ordinances establish the prevailing setback as the standard to which new houses must conform. Thus, if the houses on both sides of a vacant lot are set back twenty and thirty feet, respectively, the average would be twenty-five feet. In some ordinances, all setbacks within a specific distance of the lot (two hundred to three hundred feet) are averaged. Some ordinances will specify both a minimum and maximum setback.

***Legal Annotation***: "This was in accordance with the 60-foot minimum setback requirement of the zoning ordinance, unless a larger minimum setback is compelled by a clause in the ordinance providing that the setback line shall be not less than the **average setback** of all other buildings on the same side of a street." *In the Matter of Sierra Construction Co., Inc. v. Board of Appeals of the Town of Greece* (N.Y., 1962).

## AVERAGE VEHICLE RIDERSHIP (AVR)

**A numerical value calculated by dividing the number of employees scheduled to start work between 6:00 AM and 10:00 AM by the number of vehicles arriving at the worksite between 6:00 AM and 10:00 AM. See *Access Code*.**

*Legal Annotation*: "'**Average vehicle ridership**' means the total number of attendees arriving in vehicles parking in areas controlled by the event center, divided by the total number of those vehicles parking in areas controlled by the event center." *California Health and Safety Code Section 40717.8.*

"**AVERAGE VEHICLE RIDERSHIP (AVR)** is the current number of employees scheduled to report to work during the window for calculating **AVR** divided by the number of vehicles arriving at the worksite during the same window." *South Coast (Calif.) AQMD Rule 2202* (Amended February 6, 2004).

## AVIARY

**A place for the keeping of birds for the purpose of racing, exhibiting, or selling.**

*Legal Annotation*: "The term '**aviary**' is commonly understood to mean a large enclosure where birds fly freely. The definition of '**aviary**' used in the ordinance ('a place for keeping birds confined') is a standard definition which appears to mean that it is the place that confines the bird." *Hodges v. Marion County* (Fla. Dist. Ct. App., 1999).

## AVIATION EASEMENT

**See *Easement, Aviation*.**

## AVULSION

**The sudden or perceptible loss of or addition to land by the action of the water or a sudden change in the bed of a lake or the course of a stream (*Board of Trustees of the Internal Improvement Trust Fund v. Sand Key Associates, Ltd.* [FL: Supreme Court 1987], http://tinyurl.com/nkm3aa8).**

***Comment***: Avulsion often occurs as the result of severe flooding or when a stream shifts course over a period of time. "The U.S. Supreme Court ruled [June 2010] in *Stop the Beach Renourishment, Inc. v. Florida Dept. of Environmental Protection* that Florida's beach renourishment program was not a compensable taking, and it rejected the novel idea of a 'judicial taking'. The Texas Supreme Court saw things differently in November [2010], when it ruled against the state in another beach case [*Severance v. Patterson, November 5 (2010), 54 Tex. Sup. Ct. F. 172 (Tex.)]*. Carol Severance bought three properties on Galveston Island's West Beach in April 2005. As required by law, her purchase contract included a notice that her property line could change if the coastline shifted. Hurricane Rita plowed through in September of that year, moving the vegetation line so that Severance's house fell on the seaward side. State General Land Commissioner Jerry Patterson offered $40,000 to Severance—and other property owners in the same situation—to help her remove her house from the public beach. Severance and her neighbors filed suit against the state, alleging a taking. . . . The Texas Supreme Court ruled in favor of Severance and other property owners, concluding that a public easement that existed seaward of the vegetation line could 'roll' onto private property with the natural and gradual changes of the vegetation line, but not with the sudden changes, also known as avulsion, that occur with hurricanes. The court's decision on Severance's claim could throw the beach restoration program into a tailspin" (Lucero 2011: 9).

*Legal Annotation:* "**Avulsion** is defined as '[a] sudden and perceptible loss or addition to land by the action of water, or a sudden change in the bed or course of a stream .... The removal of a considerable quantity of soil from the land of one man, and its deposit upon or annexation to the land of another, suddenly and by the perceptible action of water.' Black's Law Dictionary (5th Ed.); see 5 Powell, Real

Figure 9

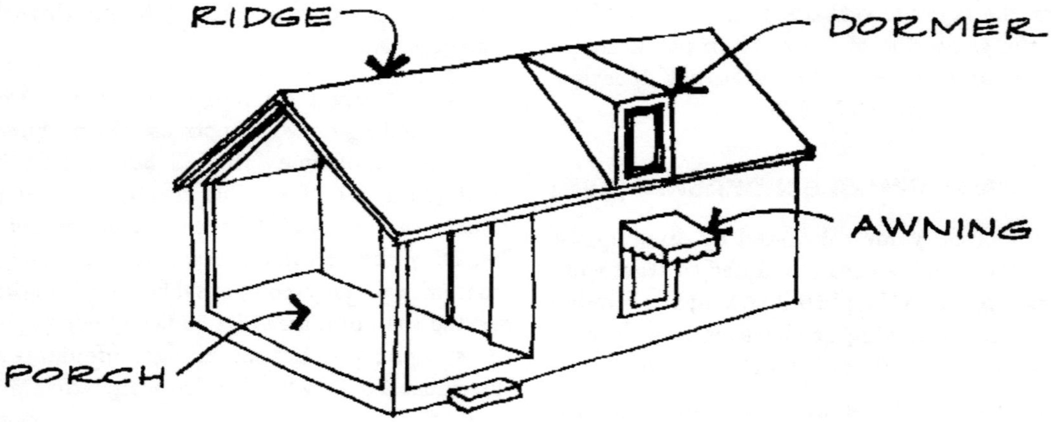


Property (1981) ¶ 719. *Roche v. Fairfield* (Conn., 1982).

## A-WEIGHTED SOUND LEVEL (dBA)

**The sound level in decibels as measured on a sound-level meter using the A-weighting network.**

***Comment***: The A-weighting scale is "a scale for sound measurement that is meant to simulate the subjective response of the human ear" (American Planning Association, *Industrial Performance Standards for a New Century,* Planning Advisory Service Report No. 444, 1993).

***Legal Annotation***: "Leq is the average or equivalent sound level, 'which corresponds to a steady-state **A-weighted sound level** containing the same total energy as a time-varying signal over a given time period (usually one hour). . . . **A-weighted sound levels (expressed as dBA)** have a strong correlation with the community response to noise.'" *Citizens for a Healthy Community v. City of Red Bluff* (Calif. Ct. App., 2011).

## AWNING

**A roof-like cover that projects from the wall of a building for the purpose of shielding a doorway or window from the elements.** ***See Figure 9.***

***Comment***: Awnings may be temporary or portable devices or may be permanent and fixed. Some are "retractable," which allow the awning to be periodically retracted to the face of the building. If an awning is permanent and incapable of being retracted, then all setbacks should be measured from the end of the awning. Otherwise, most ordinances permit them to project into required yards.

***Legal Annotation***: "In a broad fashion, the main issues in three of the cases relate to the legality of a retractable **awning** and windscreen (temporary enclosure) that enclosed an outdoor dining area on a preexisting, nonconforming deck attached to the rear of the restaurant." *Raymond v. Zoning Board of Appeals of the City of Norwalk* (Conn. App. Ct., 2003).

## AWNING, FIXED

**An awning constructed with a rigid frame that cannot be retracted, folded, or collapsed.**

***Legal Annotation***: "No marquee or **fixed awning** shall hereafter be erected or maintained so as to project over any public sidewalk, street or alley except with the official approval of the city council and subject to the condition of section 217(c) of the building code." *Ver Hoiven W. Chevrolet, Inc. v. Dunkirk* (Mich., 1958).

## AWNING, ILLUMINATED

**A fixed awning covered with a translucent membrane that is, in whole or part, illuminated by light passing through the membrane from within the structure.**

***Comment***: Illuminated awnings covering the width of a storefront are seen by some as unattractive and having a visually detrimental impact on a commercial streetscape. In such cases, illuminated awnings are sometimes specifically prohibited accessory structures. Some jurisdictions prohibit signage to be placed on awnings (apart from a street address) or only allow such signage in lieu of a wall or window sign.

***Legal Annotation***: "The Lechters' space was renovated and an **illuminated awning** was affixed to the building by Lechters below respondent's apartment." *169 East 69th Street Corp. v. Leland* (NYC Civ. Ct., 1992).

# B

## BACK-TO-BACK LOTS

**Separate land parcels that have at least half of each rear lot line coterminous.** ***See Figure 10.***

*Legal Annotation*: "It appears that Lot 53 was held in common ownership in 1930 together with Lot 11 (a **'back-to-back' lot** fronting on a parallel street) and Lot 54 (adjoining on the north) and thus, as respondents concede, the O'Donnells do not have a vested right to build in a manner not conforming to rear yard [sic] minimum requirements." *Point Lookout v. Zoning Board* (N.Y. Sup. Ct., 1981).

## BACKFILL

**Material used to refill a ditch or other excavation, or the process of doing so.**

*Legal Annotation*: "The contract permitted CCI to use certain of the excavated materials as **backfill**, but it prohibited CCI from filling the excavated areas with construction debris or 'other objectionable material.' That prohibition was designed to ensure that the **backfill** consisted only of properly compacted materials that would provide adequate support for the channel." *Commercial Contractors, Inc. v. United States* (Fed. CCt. App., 1998).

## BACKGROUND LEVEL

**Amounts of pollutants present in the ambient air.**

*Comment*: Background level is also referred to as the ambient level and is the base from which measurements are calculated or made.

*Legal Annotation*: "In all urban environments, there is a level of asbestos in the ambient air. This level, often called **background level**, varies from location to location and ranges from .000001 to .01 f/cc." *Bartel v. Crane* (N.D. Ohio, 2004).

## BACK LANE

See *Alley*.

**Figure 10**

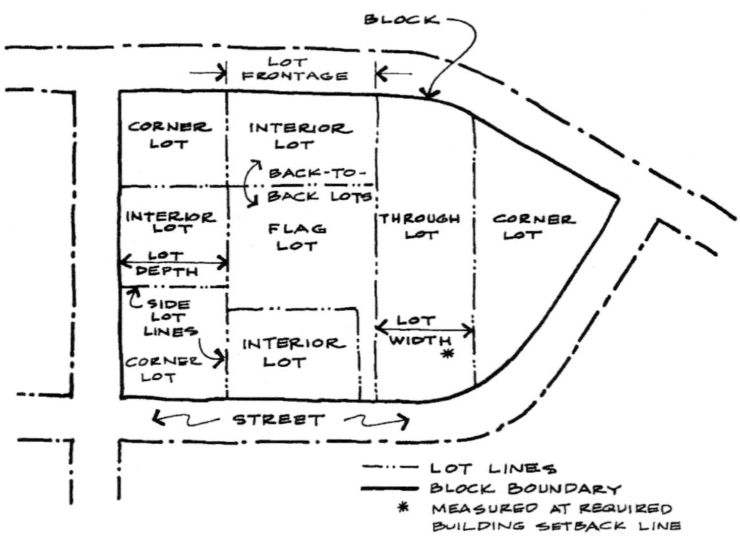

## BAFFLE

**Any deflector device used to change the direction or the flow of water, sewage, products of combustion (such as fly ash or coarse particulate matter), or sound waves.**

*Legal Annotation*: "Adjoining the coagulating room was the **baffle** area, described as a vertical chamber open from the roof to the basement. The purpose of the **baffle** chamber was to '**baffle**' the water back and forth for further mixing." *Tenenbaum v. City of Chicago* (Ill., 1975).

## BALING

**A means of reducing the volume of solid waste by compaction.**

*Legal Annotation*: "Specifically, it is contended that the operation of the ***baling*** machine involved is similar to that of a 'cutting machine having a guillotine action,' a 'corrugating' machine, a 'stamping' machine or an 'embossing' machine, or that his attempt to remove a piece of material from the baler can be classified as 'cleaning machinery in motion or assisting therein.' The machine involved is a power-driven, hydraulic **baler** used for the compressing and compacting of cardboard boxes into bales for convenient storage, handling and shipping." *Dubiel v. Laneco Inc.* (N.J. Super. Ct., 1978).

## BALLISTIC SEPARATOR

**A machine that separates inorganic from organic matter in a composting process.**

## BANDWIDTH

**In traffic analysis, the time in elapsed seconds between the passing of the first and last possible vehicle in a group of vehicles moving at the design speed of a progressive traffic signal system.**

## BANKED PARKING

**See *Parking, Banked*.**

## BANQUET FACILITY

**An establishment that provides food prepared and served in a formal setting for special occasions such as weddings, bar/bat mitzvahs, family reunions, corporate award ceremonies, charitable benefits and other special events. See *Catering Establishment*.**

*Legal Annotation*: "Our review of the record further establishes that during its meeting of October 30, 2003, the BZA interpreted the meaning of the zoning ordinance in determining whether Holmes' proposed facility met the definition of a commercial recreational use and concluded that a **banquet hall-wedding reception facility** qualified as such use." *Green v. Hancock Cty. Bd. of Zoning Appeals* (Ind. Ct. App., 2006).

## BAR

**An establishment in which alcoholic beverages are served for on-site consumption, primarily by the drink. See *Tavern*.**

*Legal Annotation*: "[A] bar is defined as '[a]n establishment used primarily for the sale and dispensing of liquor by the drink to the general public for on-site consumption.'" *529 Waterfront Prop. v. Nugent Group (N.J. Super., 2009).*

## BAR SCREEN

**In wastewater treatment, a device that removes large floating and suspended solids.**

*Legal Annotation*: "The domestic and industrial effluent treated by the wastewater treatment plant enters the system through a **bar screen** with two-inch grids designed to catch large items of debris. It is then raised by large pumps and flows by gravity through the rest of the plant. It next passes through a smaller **bar screen** and grid chamber, which removes additional debris and sand, and from there goes to one of four primary clarifiers where the primary (thicker) sludge is separated and pumped to holding tanks adjacent to the heat treatment facility." *Aiken County v. BSP Division of Envirotech Corp.* ($4^{th}$ Cir., 1989).

## BARRIER

**A device that prevents traffic from crossing into the path of traffic flowing in an opposite direction. See *Median Island*.**

*Legal Annotation*: "With medians 46 feet or wider, regardless of traffic volume, the benefits of preventing cross-median accidents and injuries by **barrier** placement are outweighed by the disadvantages of the accidents and injuries generated by a **barrier**." *Alvarez v. State* (Calif. Ct. App., 1999).

## BARRIER CURB

**A steep-faced curb intended to prevent median crossing. See *Curb*.**

*Comment*: While traffic safety is its primary function, barrier curbs also facilitate stormwater runoff collection from road surfaces.

*Legal Annotation*: "He further testified that a **barrier curb** is a curb that is generally about eight inches high and is used to provide a separation between a roadway and the sidewalk; it forms a gutter to facilitate drainage of water from the crowned surface of a roadway to a catch basin." *Chunhye Kang-Kim v. NY City* (N.Y. Sup. Ct. App. Div., 2006).

## BARRIER ISLAND

**Land area, separated on all sides by water, usually elongated and formed by the action of the sea on land, that protects the mainland from sea action.**

*Legal Annotation*: "By definition, a **barrier island** acts as a shield to protect the mainland from the direct force and effect of the Atlantic Ocean." *Nature Conservancy v. Machipongo Club Inc.* (E.D. Virginia, 1976).

## BARRIER-FREE

**An environment that will permit a person with disabilities to operate independently with comparative ease under normal circumstances and with little or no other assistance. See *Americans With Disabilities Act; Facility For Handicapped People; Handicapped Person; Minimal Accessibility; Nonambulatory Handicap; Nonslip; Physical Handicap; Principal Entrance; Public Assembly Area; Ramp*.**

*Legal Annotation*: "'Accessible' is defined as 'an environment that will permit a handicapped person to operate independently with comparative ease under normal circumstances and with little or no other assistance. This term is synonymous with the term '***barrier-free***.'" *DIAL Inc. v. NJ Dept. of Community Affairs* fn. 3 (N.J. Super. Ct, App. Div., 1992).

## BARRIER-FREE DESIGN

**"The design of a site, building, facility, or portion thereof that can be approached, entered, and used by the physically impaired" (Source: AASHTO Glossary, http:/trt.trb.org/trt.aspPnn=Esuh).**

*Legal Annotation*: "The purpose of this legislation is further echoed in administrative regulations. Pursuant to section 4450, the State Building Code[5] requires: 'In buildings and facilities, floors of a given story shall be a common level throughout, or shall be connected by pedestrian ramps, passenger elevators, or special access lifts.'[6] (Cal. Code Regs., tit. 24, § 2-522, subd. (e).) The purpose of this part is: 'To assure that barrier free design is incorporated in all buildings, facilities . . . to which this Code applies to assure that they are accessible to, and usable by, physically handicapped persons.' (Cal. Code Regs., tit. 24, § 2-101, subd. (b).)

*Donald v. Café Royale, Inc.* (Calif. Ct. App., 1990).

## BASE FLOOD

**The minimum magnitude flood to be used by a community as a basis for its floodplain management regulations; presently required by regulation to be "that flood which has a one-percent chance of being equaled or exceeded in any given year." (Blanchard 2007, 37) See *Base Flood Elevation*.**

*Comment*: The term *base flood* is used in the National Flood Insurance Program. The base flood is also known as a hundred-year flood.

(*Legal Annotation*: "The SFIP defines a '**base flood**' as the 100-year flood, i.e., the flood 'having a one percent chance of being equaled or exceeded in any given year.'" *Carneiro Da Cunha v. Standard Fire Ins./Aetna Flood Ins.*, ($11^{th}$ Cir., 1997).

## BASE FLOOD ELEVATION

**The highest point, expressed in feet above sea level, of the level of floodwaters occurring in the regulatory base flood.**

*Comment*: Flood elevations are calculated by engineering techniques, and observed experiences may be used to verify reliability. The base flood elevation represents the estimated height that waters will reach given a storm of certain magnitude; that is, one-year, two-year, hundred-year, or five-hundred-year. Regulations promulgated by various agencies, such as the US Department of Housing and Urban Development, permit construction in certain flood-prone areas provided that the new construction is elevated or raised a given distance from the base flood elevation (usually one foot above the hundred-year flood elevation) and that other flood damage prevention measures are taken.

*Legal Annotation*: "A '**base flood elevation**' is a measurement of 'the potential water level height during a base flood.'" *Great Rivers Habitat Alliance v. FEMA* ($8^{th}$ Cir., 2010).

## BASE MAP

**A map having sufficient points of reference, such as state, county, or municipal boundary lines, streets, easements, and other selected physical features, to allow the plotting of other data.**

*Legal Annotation*: "After the area to be shown has been determined, the plaintiff's files are examined to ascertain if there is a suitable **base map** for the area. If none is available one is made. . . . The amount and kind of detail added to a **base map** depends largely on the purpose for which the new map is being produced and its scale." *C.S. Hammond & Co. v. International College Globe, Inc.* (S.D. NY, 1962).

## BASEMENT

**A space having one-half or more of its floor-to-ceiling height above the average level of the adjoining ground and with a floor-to-ceiling height of not less than 6.5 feet. See *Cellar*. See *Figure 8*.**

*Comment*: The Building Officials and Code Administrators (BOCA) Basic/National Building Code (1996) defines "basement" as that portion of a building that is partly or completely below grade. Use of this definition eliminates the distinction between basements and cellars. Ordinances should specify when the basement or cellar is counted as a story and when the floor space is used in computing the intensity of development.

Whether the basement is counted as a story depends on how great the vertical distance of the basement ceiling is over the average adjoining grade. Some ordinances call it a story if that distance is greater than five feet.

Generally speaking, if a basement is used only for heating, mechanical, and similar equipment and parking, it is not included in computing the intensity of development as measured by floor area ratio. The only exception is whether parking is also computed as part of the floor area ratio. If the basement is used for storage purposes for the principal use, for dwelling unit purposes, or for office space or a similar function, it is included in whatever standards are used to control the intensity of development.

*Legal Annotation*: "If the **basement** or garden level is 'substantially below grade' then a portion of it, by definition, can be partially above grade, which would necessarily put the floor of the next level up—the first floor—somewhat above grade." *Covered Bridge Inc. v. Town of Vail* (Colo. Ct. App., 2008).

## BASE STATION

**In wireless communications, a fixed, local radio station used to communicate with a portable or mobile radio.**

*Comment*: A base station includes equipment to receive and generate radio frequency signals and an antenna. See *Wireless Telecommunications Towers and Facilities*.

***Legal Annotation***: "When a wireless telephone is turned on, it searches for a **base station** (usually a tower) within range. A **base station** is a fixed transmitter containing antennae and electronic equipment that communicates with the transmitter in a wireless telephone." *Pinney v. Nokia, Inc.* (4th Cir. 2005).

## BASIN

**An area drained by the main stream and tributaries of a large river. See *Detention Basin; Retention Basin.***

***Legal Annotation***: "This 'NPDES Permit' authorizes the permittees to discharge combined storm/sewer drainage from the Bloomfield Village Combined Sewer Overflow Area only if a **basin** is constructed to retain and treat the drainage before it discharges into the Rouge River." *Ahern v. Charter Township of Bloomfield* (6th Cir. 1996). http://tinyurl.com/ow4xven

## BASIS POINT

**One one-hundredth of a percentage point.**

***Comment***: A full percentage point is 100 basis points. For example, if mortgage rates fall from 7.50 percent to 7.47 percent, then they've declined three basis points. http://www.realtor.com/home-finance/mortgages/terms-glossary.aspx?source=web

***Legal Annotation***: "The time value of money approach takes an appropriate risk-free rate and adds a risk premium, measured in **basis points**, sufficient to compensate the holder of a secured claim for the inherent risks imposed upon it by the proposed plan." *In re SM 104 Ltd.* (Bankr. Ct. S.D. Fla., 1993).

## BAYSCAPES

**Areas that conserve water, create a diverse landscape and wildlife habitat, and use integrated (nonchemical) pest management.**

***Comment***: Bayscapes are garden-type environments and are popular in bay areas, riverfront communities, and high-water locations. They provide an alternative to lawns and may include bogs, rock gardens, butterfly gardens, wildflower meadows, perennial gardens, ground cover, and shrubs, all connected with paths (Shirley 1999: 24).

***Legal Annotation***: "Kent County Growth Allocation Policy ('the Policy') provides: '4. Site location and development will use innovative design features to minimize negative impacts on water quality, habitat protection areas, woodlands, and forests. Examples include but are not limited to the use of buffer areas to protect habitat, wildlife corridors, and other important natural areas, the use of conservation landscapes or **bayscapes**, and limitation of impervious surfaces through clustering and shared roadways.'" *Smith v. Kent County* (Md: Ct. App., 2011).

## BEACH

**A nearly level stretch of pebbles and/or sand beside a body of water that may be artificially created or created by the action of the water. See *Intertidal Area. See Figure 11.***

***Legal Annotation:*** "The **beach** is defined as the area between the mean low tide mark and the seaward edge of the first permanent vegetation zone on the dunes or seawall, whichever is closer to the Atlantic Ocean." *Loggerhead Turtle v. County Council of Volusia County* (M.D. Fla., 2000).

## BEACH NOURISHMENT

**The placement of sand extracted from an offshore source to an eroding shoreline to restore its form and to reinforce a beach's protective function.**

***Comment***: A beach fill plan typically includes a berm (that slopes to the sea floor) backed by a dune. Together, the dune and the berm combine to prevent erosion and inundation damages to leeward areas. Beach nourishment requires periodic replacement of sand to offset erosion of the beach fill in order to maintain the design level of protection.

Figure 11

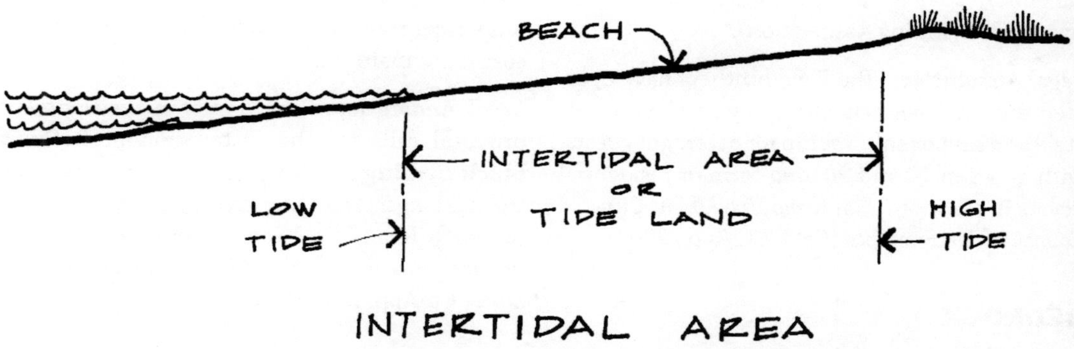


*Legal Annotation*: "The Act establishes procedures for '**beach** restoration and **nourishment** projects,' § 161.088, designed to deposit sand on eroded beaches (restoration) and to maintain the deposited sand (**nourishment**)." *Stop the Beach Ren. v. Fla. Dept. of Env. Prot.* (U.S., 2010).

## BEAUFORT SCALE

**Numerical scale from 0 to 12, indicating wind force.**

0-calm
1-light air
2-light breeze
3-gentle breeze
4-moderate breeze
5-fresh breeze
6-strong breeze
7-strong wind
8-gale
9-strong gale
10-storm
11-violent storm
12-hurricane

http://training.fema.gov/EMIWeb/edu/docs/terms%20and%20definitions/Terms%20and%20Definitions.pdf

*Legal Annotation*: "The wind on the day in question apparently did not exceed 23 mph and under the **Beaufort scale** would be characterized as 'moderate breeze' to 'fresh breeze.'" *Lee v. Milwaukee Gas Light Co.*, (Wisc., 1963).

## BED AND BREAKFAST (B&B)

**Overnight accommodations and a morning meal in a dwelling unit provided to transients for compensation. See *Boardinghouse*.**

*Comment*: Bed and breakfast accommodations, also referred to as B&Bs or tourist homes, differ from rooming and boardinghouses in that they are truly transient accommodations, with guests rarely staying more than a few days. In addition, the owner almost always lives in the facility. The impact of a B&B should not be much greater than that of a private home with frequent houseguests, with the exception of parking demand. Many B&Bs are not accessible by public transit, and consequently guests usually arrive by car. Zoning regulations should address parking requirements, the number of rooms that can be rented out, and signs, and require the owner or renter of the facility to live on the premises. Some ordinances limit meals (breakfasts to guests only) and limit the length of time a guest may stay—often a maximum of one week. Some municipalities permit B&Bs with accommodations for three or fewer guests as a matter of right, and as a conditional use for those renting to more than three guests. This recognizes that larger facilities have a greater impact on the neighborhood, requiring site plan approval and the opportunity for neighbors to comment on the application. Other municipalities require larger B&Bs to be licensed, with annual renewal requirements, to determine compliance with health and fire codes ("Keeping Tabs on Bed and Breakfasts," *Planning*, August

1987; "Bed and Breakfasts: An Accommodating Neighbor," *Zoning News*, December 1989; both American Planning Association).

*Legal Annotation*: "The Field brothers have operated the establishment primarily as a European-style **bed and breakfast** inn for overnight guests, with between 10 and 20 long-term or residential guests in addition." *San Remo Hotel, LP v. City and County of San Francisco* (Calif. Ct. App., 2000).

## BEDROCK

**Any solid body of rock, with or without fractures, that is not underlined by soil or unconsolidated rock material.**

*Legal Annotation*: "Unfortunately, it is impossible to predict whether high levels of toxic dioxin or other hazardous contaminants remain in the karst soil beneath the Denney farm, presenting future possibilities of exposure, if the permeability of the soil and **bedrock** allow the substances to flow toward the Calton Creek." *US v. Northeastern Pharmaceutical and Chemical Co.* (W.D. Mo., 1984).

## BEDROOM

**A private room planned and intended for sleeping, separated from other rooms by a door, and accessible to a bathroom without crossing another bedroom.**

*Comment*: When is a den a bedroom? The distinction may be important when other standards, such as parking, are based on the number of bedrooms.

*Legal Annotation*: "Codified Ordinance § 1357.03(h)(1) [d]efines '**bedroom**' as 'a habitable room designed for sleeping purposes, and which has a minimum habitable floor area of eighty square feet.'" *Fair Housing Advocates Assn. v. City of Richmond Heights* (N.D. Ohio, 1998).

## BELGIAN BLOCK CURB (GRANITE BLOCK)

**A type of paving stone generally cut in a truncated pyramidal shape, laid with the base of the pyramid down. See *Curb* and *Figure 27*.**

*Comment*: While Belgian block curbing is considered more attractive than concrete curbing, it is more expensive, more vulnerable to damage, and costlier to maintain.

*Legal Annotation*: "The Cameron development proposal calls for the installation of **Belgian block curbing** and storm drains and pipes along the full length of its property on the easterly side of North Road." *Cameron & Cameron, Inc. v. The Planning Board of the Township of Warren, NJ* (N.J. Super Ct. App. Div., 1991).

## BELTWAY

**A highway, usually of limited access, around a developed area. *See Figure 97*.**

*Legal Annotation*: "It is true that there is an area on the opposite side of the **Beltway** which has been zoned for apartment use. But this limited access road undoubtedly will create quite a barrier between that property and the property with which we are concerned." *Board of County Commissioners of Prince George's County v. Kines* (Md. Ct. App., 1965).

## BENDWAY WEIR

**A specialized weir that is placed in a bend of a river and consists mostly of large rocks designed to reduce water flow in navigable waterways yet still allow water traffic.**

*Comment*: In small streams and rivers, bendway weirs are strategically placed smaller rocks designed to minimize erosion to natural banks.

*Legal Annotation*: "A **bendway weir** is a similar structure. It is anchored into an eroding bank and diverts the current away from the bank, creating a habitat for fish and narrowing the channel so as to make it flow faster and carry more sediment." *Upper Salt Fork Drainage Dist. v. DiNovo* (Ill. App. Ct., 2008).

## BERM

**A mound of earth or the act of pushing earth into a mound. *See Figures 12 and 68*.**

*Comment*: Berms are usually two to six feet high and are used to shield, screen, and buffer undesirable views and to separate incompatible land uses. They also provide visual interest, decrease noise, control the direction of water flow, and act as dams. Landscaping on berms, particularly on or near the top, often suffers from lack of water and needs an ensured water supply.

*Legal Annotation*: "When the ditch was excavated, the soils were cast to either side of the ditch, creating upland **berms** approximately four feet wide along the banks of the ditch. The **berm** edging the Carabells' property serves to block immediate drainage of surface water out of the parcel into the ditch." *Carabell v. US Army Corps of Engineers* (6th Cir., 2004).

## BEST MANAGEMENT PRACTICE (BMP)

**State-of-the-art technology as applied to a specific problem and including a schedule of activities, prohibited practices, and maintenance procedures.**

*Comment*: BMPs are often required as part of major land development projects. The BMP presents physical, institutional, or strategic approaches to environmental problems, particularly with respect to nonpoint-source pollution control.

*Legal Annotation*: "The **best management practices** are only guidelines for use in forestry activities. . . . The State Forester cannot issue special orders solely for the violation of a best management practice." *Dail v. York County* (Va., 2000).

## BEST PRACTICES

**"Peer-validated techniques, procedures, and solutions that prove successful and are solidly grounded in actual experience in operations, training, and exercises" (FEMA, HSEEP Glossary, 2008). See *Best Management Practices*. http://training.fema.gov/EMIWeb/edu/docs/terms%20and%20definitions/Terms%20and%20Definitions.pdf)**

*Legal Annotation*: "Whether defendants' actions were consistent with FEMA's '**best practices**' and other agency materials is irrelevant to whether plaintiff's claim can proceed." *Hofstetter v. Chase Home Finance, LLC* (N.D. Calif., 2010).

## BICYCLE (BIKE)

**A device propelled solely by human power having two or more wheels in tandem, including children's bicycles, except a toy vehicle intended for use by young children, such as a tricycle. http://safety.fhwa.dot.gov/ped_bike/tools_solve/fhwasa12018/#chap1.6**

*Comment*: There has been a significant increase in all types of bicycle use in recent years. According to the League of American Bicyclists, the national organization promoting bicycling since 1880, there was a 10 percent increase in bicycle commuting (riding a bike to and from work) from 2011 to 2012. Since 2000, there has been a 58 percent increase in bicycle commuting. The increase in recreational bike use has been even more dramatic. As noted by Rick Pruetz, FAICP, new recreational bicycling trails

**Figure 12**

have generated significant economic benefits to towns and cities along the routes. He noted the recent opening of the thirty-three-mile "super bikeway" from Pittsburgh to Washington, DC, officially called the Great Allegheny Passage/ C&O Canal Towpath. Eighteen towns along the Towpath have reported significant benefits to the local economies and quality of life for residents. The towns have worked together to create a "welcoming environment" for trail users (Pruetz 2013).

The increase in bicycle use has been due in part to additional support and funding from the federal government and state programs implementing legislation promoting bicycling. Examples include funding from the 2005 Safe Accountable, Flexible, Efficient Transportation Equity Act: a Legacy for Users (SAFETEA-LU), the 1991 Intermodal Surface Transportation Efficiency Act (ISTEA), and the 1998 Transportation Equity Act for the 21st Century (TEA-21).

The following definitions include all bicycle definitions from the previous editions and new research and new material from the "Glossary of Bicycle Transportation Terms" from the American Association of State Highway Transportation Officials (AASHTO), the US Department of Transportation, International Bicycle Fund, as well as other sources. http://www.ibike.org/engineering/glossary.htm

In the following definitions, the terms "bicycle" and "bike" are used interchangeably.

*Legal Annotation*: "**Bicycle** Defined—39000. '**Bicycle,**' for the purposes of this division, means any device upon which a person may ride, which is propelled by human power through a system of belts, chains, or gears having either two or three wheels (one of which is at least 20 inches in diameter) or having a frame size of at least 14 inches, or having four or more wheels." California Vehicle Code Section 39000-39011 *Amended Ch. 421, Stats. 1978* (Effective January 1, 1979).

## BICYCLE ACCESS

**The ability of bicyclists to have access to roads and trails.** http://www.ibike.org/engineering/glossary.htm

*Legal Annotation*: "Plaintiff is a nonprofit Oregon corporation that is an advocate for increased **bicycle access,** use and safety in the City of Portland." *Bicycle Transp. Alliance v.* Portland (Ore. Ct. App., 1995).

## BICYCLE BOULEVARD

**A street segment (or series of contiguous street segments) that has been modified to accommodate through bicycle traffic but discourage through motor traffic. http://safety.fhwa.dot.gov/ped_bike/tools_solve/fhwasa12018/#chap1.6**

*Legal Annotation*: "ActiveTrans is looking for suggestions as to where in Chicago to place a **Bicycle Boulevard. Bicycle Boulevards** are 'bike-friendly' roadways." *Illinois Bicycle Law.* http://www.illinoisbicyclelaw.com/2010/04/chicago-department-of-transportation-to.html

## BICYCLE-COMPATIBLE ROADWAY

**A road designed to accommodate the shared use of the roadway by motor vehicles and bicycles.** *See Figure 14.*

*Legal Annotation*: "'**Bicycle-Compatible Roadway**' means a road designed to accommodate the shared use of the roadway by bicycles and motor vehicles." *Title 5. Community Affairs—Chapter 21. Residential Site Improvement Standards—N.J.A.C. 5*:21 (2013). http://www.state.nj.us/dca/divisions/codes/codreg/pdf_regs/njac_5_21.pdf

## BICYCLE DOORING

**"Being clipped by a parked car opening its door into the bicycle lane" (Arvidson 2012: 13).**

*Legal Annotation*: "**Dooring**. No person shall open any door of a vehicle unless it is safe to do so and can be done without interfering with moving traffic." *DC Dept. of Transp. Bicycle and Pedestrian Regulations.*

## BICYCLE FACILITY

**A general term denoting improvements and provisions to accommodate or encourage bicycling, including parking facilities (Class I, II, III), maps, and all bikeways (Class I, II, III, IV). See *Bicycle Parking.* http://www.ibike.org/engineering/glossary.htm**

***Legal Annotation***: "The parking related conditions include . . . (4) the **bicycle facility** has been required to exceed standard requirements to encourage alternative modes of transportation." *Sanders v. City of Pleasant Hill* (Calif. Ct. App., 2008).

## BICYCLE FACILITIES, CLASSIFICATION OF

**Bicycle facilities are classified as follows:**

*"SEPARATE FACILITY (a.k.a. Class I)*—A non-motorized facility, paved or unpaved, physically separated from motorized vehicular traffic by an open space or barrier. Also called Bicycle Path (*Figure 15*), Bike Trail, Non-motorized Trail, Multi-purpose Trail or some combination thereof." http://www.ibike.org/engineering/glossary.htm

*"BIKE LANE (a.k.a. Class II)*—A portion of road that is designated by striping, signing, and pavement markings for the preferential or exclusive use of bicyclists. Most often these are done in couplets, each one being one way and adjacent to the outside through travel lane. Also called Bicycle Lanes." (*See Figure 15.*) http://www.ibike.org/engineering/glossary.htm

*"BIKE ROUTE (a.k.a. Class III)*—A segment of road designated by the jurisdiction having authority, with appropriate directional and informational markers, but without striping, signing and pavement markings for the preferential or exclusive use of bicyclists. Also called Bicycle Route" (*See Figure 15.*) http://www.ibike.org/engineering/glossary.htm

*"BIKE FRIENDLY (a.k.a. Class IV)*—A roadway not designated by directional and informational markers, striping, signing nor pavement markings for the preferential or exclusive use of bicyclists, but containing appropriate bicycle-friendly design standards such as wide-curb lanes and bicycle safe drain gates." http://www.ibike.org/engineering/glossary.htm

Bike-friendly urban design factors also include:

- Public facilities such as bicycle racks on streets or by public buildings
- Regulations that allow riders to take bicycles on board buses, trains, etc.
- Accessibility such as the position of bicycle paths relative to roads, quality of the terrain, presence of curb cuts, etc.
- Safety features such as lighting, security measures, and protection from on-road vehicles
- Aesthetics of bicycle paths and their surrounding areas

http://safety.fhwa.dot.gov/ped_bike/tools_solve/fhwasa12018/#chap1.6

***Comment***: "Many communities are providing an expanded array of bicycle facilities in order to foster enhanced bicycling for commuting and recreation. An example is a bicycle-only bridge opened in Minneapolis, MN, as the last phase of the Midtown Greenway, a five-mile, crosstown bike route in a former industrial corridor" (Arvidson 2008: 6). Vancouver, British Columbia has added twelve-foot bicycle lanes in its downtown and has a total of two hundred miles of bike lanes (Newcomb 2011).

## BICYCLE PARKING FACILITIES, CLASSIFICATION OF

***"LONG TERM PARKING (a.k.a. Class I)*—Bicycle parking facility intended for long-term parking and protected against theft of the entire bicycle and its components and accessories." http://www.ibike.org/engineering/glossary.htm**

***"MEDIUM TERM PARKING (a.k.a. Class II)*—Bicycle parking facility intended for medium- or short-term parking and consisting of a stationary object in which the user can lock the frame and both wheels with a user-provided lock. The facility should be designed to protect the lock from physical assault." http://www.ibike.org/engineering/glossary.htm**

*"SHORT TERM PARKING (a.k.a. Class III)*—**Bicycle parking facility intended for short-term parking, consisting of a stationary object to which the user can lock the frame and both wheels with a user-provided 6 foot cable (or chain) and lock." http://www.ibike.org/engineering/glossary.htm**

***Comment***: "Three common ways of providing Class I bicycle parking are:

a. Fully enclosed lockers accessible only by the user;
b. a continuously monitored facility that provides at least Class II bicycle parking facilities;
c. a restricted access facilities in which Class II racks are provided and access is restricted only to the owners of the bicycles stored therein." (http://www.ibike.org/engineering/glossary.htm)

## BICYCLE LANE, CONTRAFLOW

**"A bicycle lane that allows bicyclists to travel the opposite direction of motor vehicle traffic on a one-way street."** http://safety.fhwa.dot.gov/ped_bike/tools_solve/fhwasa12018/#chap1.6

## BICYCLE, LENGTH

**"Relates to space needed for longitudinal clearance, which may be especially critical at intersections where motor vehicles, bicycles, and pedestrians share space." http://safety.fhwa.dot.gov/ped_bike/tools_solve/fhwasa12018/#chap1.6**

***Comment***: "Longitudinal space should consider the varying lengths of bicycles that are expected to use a facility and the impact on safety (*see Figure 13*). For example, at a midblock crossing of a shared use path, the space dedicated to a cyclist in the refuge area may need to adequately accommodate a bicycle and trailer without encroaching on the roadway." http://safety.fhwa.dot.gov/ped_bike/tools_solve/fhwasa12018/#chap1.6

**Figure 13**

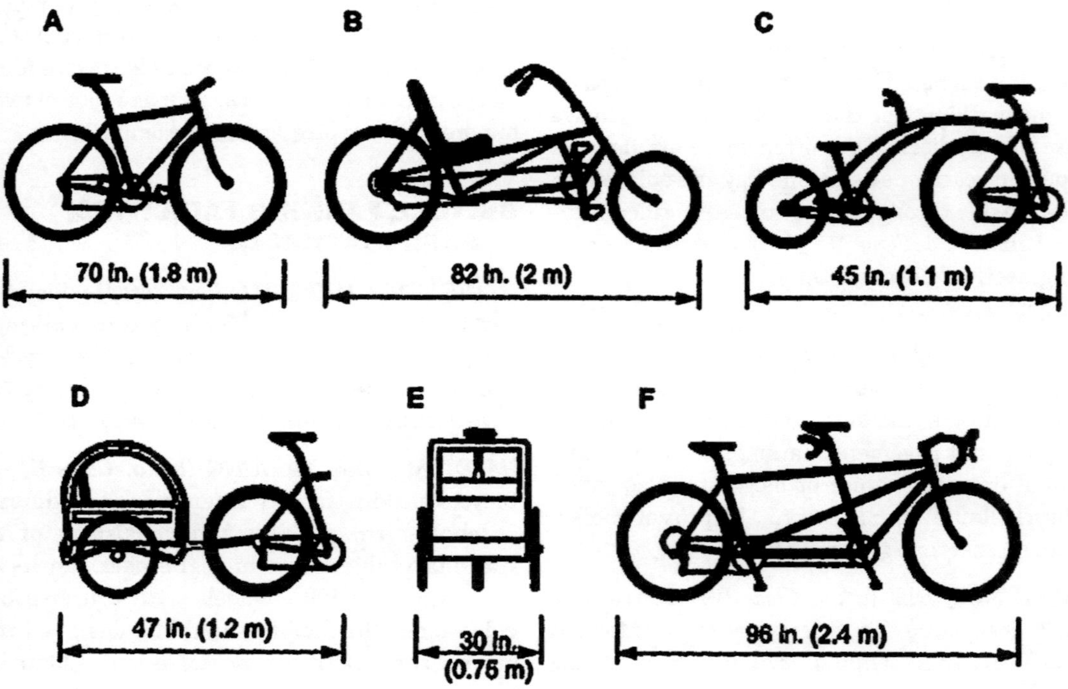

## BICYCLE TRACK

**A bicycle facility, typically unidirectional, that is separated from motor vehicle travel lanes, as well as sidewalks and pedestrians, by a physical barrier such as on-street parking or a curb, or is grade-separated. http://safety.fhwa.dot.gov/ped_bike/tools_solve/fhwasa12018/#chap1.6**

*Comment*: By way of background, "many cities are attempting to minimize dooring [*see* BICYCLE DOORING] and the fear of it by creating more exclusive bike space for bicycles. There are several ways to do this. The bicycle lane can be widened from four or five feet (typical widths) to six. Alternatively, planners can consider the total width from the curb to the outer edge of the bike lane and provide up to 14.5 feet for the parking and bicycle facility. Wider lanes allow a bicyclist room to get around an open door without entering traffic lanes.

"Another way to make space between doors and bicyclists is to create a striped buffer between parking and the bike lane. Buffered bike lanes allow for a driver 'loading zone' that does not conflict with through-riding bicyclists. A bicycle track takes the buffering concept one step further by placing the bicycle facility at the very edge of the road-way, separated from the traveled lanes by a raised curb, a planted median, or parking. Bicycle tracks can be one- or two-way. They essentially create a trail at the side of the roadway, when a cycle track is located between parking and the curb the thinking goes it is safer from dooring because many cars lack passengers" (Arvidson 2012: 14–15).

## BICYCLE TWO-STAGE TURN QUEUE

**Allows cyclists to make a safe left turn from a separate track located on the left side of the street.**

*Comment*: "Bicyclists can have a difficult time turning left from a cycle track or buffered lane located on the right side of the street. They are blocked from moving into traffic and must often resort to pedestrian crosswalks or making a very long left through the middle of the vehicular intersection. A two-stage turn queue creates a special bicycle waiting zone right out in the intersection. First, a bicyclist moves from the bike lane or bicycle track straight ahead on the green light, ending in the waiting zone, which is a colored box located in front of traffic on the cross street. The cyclist stays there until the opposing signal turns green, then proceeds across the intersection, ahead of the cross-street traffic. Though rare in the U.S. (there are examples in Portland and New York), this design is fairly common in northern Europe" (Arvidson 2012: 15–16).

## BICYCLIST (BICYCLIST, RIDER OR BIKE RIDER)

**A person who is riding a bicycle as bicycle is defined here. http://safety.fhwa.dot.gov/ped_bike/tools_solve/fhwasa12018/#chap1.6**

*Legal Annotation*: "316.2065 Bicycle regulations.—

(1) Every person propelling a vehicle by human power has all of the rights and all of the duties applicable to the driver of any other vehicle under this chapter, except as to special regulations in this chapter, and except as to provisions of this chapter which by their nature can have no application." *Fla. Stat.* (2013).

## BIFURCATED DRIVEWAY

**A roadway with two separate road openings, one for ingress to, and one for egress from, a street or highway.**

*Legal Annotation*: "Defendant Piper's hillside home was on the lower side of the elongated turnaround, and the **bifurcated** segment of the original Piper **driveway** between the Piper home and the lower side of the narrow, elongated, unpaved island within the paved turnaround (that segment being identified as the lower level) was lower than the **bifurcated** segment of the original Piper **driveway** on the opposite and upper side of the unpaved island (that segment being identified as the upper level)." *Burger v. Wood* (Sprngfld. Ct. App. Mo., 1969).

## BIG-BOX RETAIL

See *Retail Store, Big-Box*.

## BIG-BOX STORE

**A large, freestanding, single-story retail store, of generally more than fifty thousand square feet, and usually part of a regional or national chain.**

***Comment***: Initially, big-box stores were defined as large, freestanding retail stores in excess of one hundred thousand square feet. In recent years, the average size of big-box stores has fallen, and some are even below the fifty-thousand-square-foot standard in the definition. Thus the definition can and should be modified based upon the intent of the regulations pertaining thereto in the ordinance. Typically big-box retail stores fall into three categories: those that sell general dry goods similar to a department store (e.g., Wal-Mart and Target); those that are limited to a particular specialty, sometimes referred to as "category killers" (Staples, Best Buy, Barnes & Noble); and those that sell mostly groceries (e.g., Wegmans). Architecturally, the stores are rectangular, built on concrete slabs, with concrete-block or masonry siding, and with flat roofs and ceiling trusses made of steel. Planning concerns include the economic impact on smaller established downtown merchants, heavy traffic, generic and lackluster architectural treatment, and the sprawl-inducing aspects of such developments.

Big-box stores usually require sites with maximum access and visibility. Interstate interchanges and major arterials are the preferred locations. However, some of the big-box retailers have also located in downtowns and in industrial and warehousing districts, often adapting size, building, and site design to reflect an area's traditional architecture, scale, and fabric.

If the local master plan and land development ordinance reflect municipal land-use policy to permit big-box development, either as standalone buildings or as part of large-scale shopping centers, the following controls should be addressed: minimum and maximum lot and tract size, floor area ratio and impervious coverage, setbacks and buffers, and parking requirements. In general, minimum lot and tract sizes encourage mall-type or center development, while a maximum lot or building size will discourage centers and encourage stand-alone buildings.

Parking requirements for big-box stores, either as stand-alones or in malls, are not too dissimilar from current retail parking requirements, ranging from four to eight parking spaces per one thousand square feet of gross leasable area. However, some categories of big-box stores, such as warehouse clubs, claim to have half the traffic demand of a conventional shopping center. Big-box retailers do generate significantly more truck traffic than conventional retail establishments. As part of the site plan review process, testimony from qualified traffic engineers can be extremely helpful as to parking demand and truck loading and unloading requirements.

In addition to the conventional controls, design criteria become increasingly more important for big-box buildings. The most frequent complaint is that they look like "big, faceless boxes." One publication describes them as "blank, windowless facades, flat roofs, lack of architectural detail, and minuscule, hard to see entries . . . big box stores are boring at best and future eyesores at worst" (Duerksen 1996). The publication goes on to report how Fort Collins, Colorado, addressed these issues and the controls implemented there to prevent and avoid many of the design deficiencies, as follows:

- Uninterrupted façades in excess of one hundred horizontal feet are prohibited. Façades greater than one hundred feet in length must incorporate recesses and projections along at least 20 percent of the length of the façade. Windows, awnings, and arcades must total at least 60 percent of the façade length abutting a public street.
- Smaller retail stores that are part of a larger principal building are required to have display windows and separate outside entrances.
- Greater architectural interest in the main structure is encouraged by directing the use

of a repeating pattern of change in color, texture, and material modules. The ordinance requires that one of these elements shall repeat horizontally and all elements shall repeat at intervals of no more than thirty feet, either horizontally or vertically.

- Variation in rooflines is required to reduce the massive scale of these structures and add visual interest. Roofs must have at least two of the following features: parapets concealing flat roofs and rooftop equipment, overhanging eaves, sloping roofs, and three or more roof slope planes.

The Fort Collins ordinance, as reported by Duerksen, requires that each principal building have a clearly defined, highly visible customer entrance with features such as canopies or porticos, arcades, arches, wing walls, and integral planters.

Color and materials are also carefully addressed in the Fort Collins ordinance. For example, smooth-faced concrete block, tilt-up concrete panels, or prefabricated steel panels are prohibited as the predominant exterior building materials. Brick, wood, sandstone or other native stone, and tinted or textured concrete masonry units are encouraged.

Facade colors are required to be of low reflectance, subtle, neutral, and earth-tone colors. The use of high-intensity colors, metallic colors, black, or fluorescent colors is prohibited.

The Fort Collins ordinance addresses the relationship of the superstores to the surrounding community and public streets and calls for berms and landscaping to buffer the stores from adjacent residential uses.

Pedestrian circulation features require sidewalks of at least eight feet in width along all lot sides that abut a public street and a continuous internal pedestrian walkway from public sidewalks to the principal customer entrance. The internal walkway requires landscaping, benches, and other such materials and facilities for no less than 50 percent of its length. Internal pedestrian walkways must provide weather-protection features such as an awning within thirty feet of all customer entrances, and the internal pedestrian walkways must be distinguished from driving surfaces through the use of special paving brick or scored concrete to enhance pedestrian safety and the attractiveness of the walkways.

Finally, the Fort Collins ordinance allows only 50 percent of the required off-street parking for the entire property to be located between the front facade of the principal building and the primary abutting street.

An excellent discussion of all aspects of big-box retail development, and from which much of the first part of this commentary was derived, is contained in a memo entitled "Big Box Retail" (New Jersey Office of State Planning 1995). As noted above, the summary of the Fort Collins ordinance pertaining to big-box retailers is contained in Duerksen 1996.

***Legal Annotation***:"We are satisfied that notice of a proposed 'main retail store of 150,000 s.f.' adequately informed laypersons that a major '**big box**' store was proposed for the site and alerted them to the possible concerns, such as traffic, commonly associated with those stores, and, indeed, such concerns were expressed by members of the public at the hearings." *Shakoor Supermark v. Old Bridge* (N.J. App. Ct., 2011).

## BIKE BOX

**A designated area, painted and appropriately marked, at a signalized roadway intersection, where bicycle riders can pull in front of and in full view of waiting traffic, to await the green signal to proceed.**

*Comment*: By allowing cyclists to wait in front of waiting auto traffic, bike boxes reduce the risk of collisions in which a driver makes a right turn without seeing a cyclist in his path. The bike box is located in front of the motor vehicle stop line but behind the pedestrian crosswalk. It usually extends over one travel lane but might include another lane if bicycle traffic is heavy (Arvidson 2012, 15). (*See Figure 14.*)

**Figure 14**

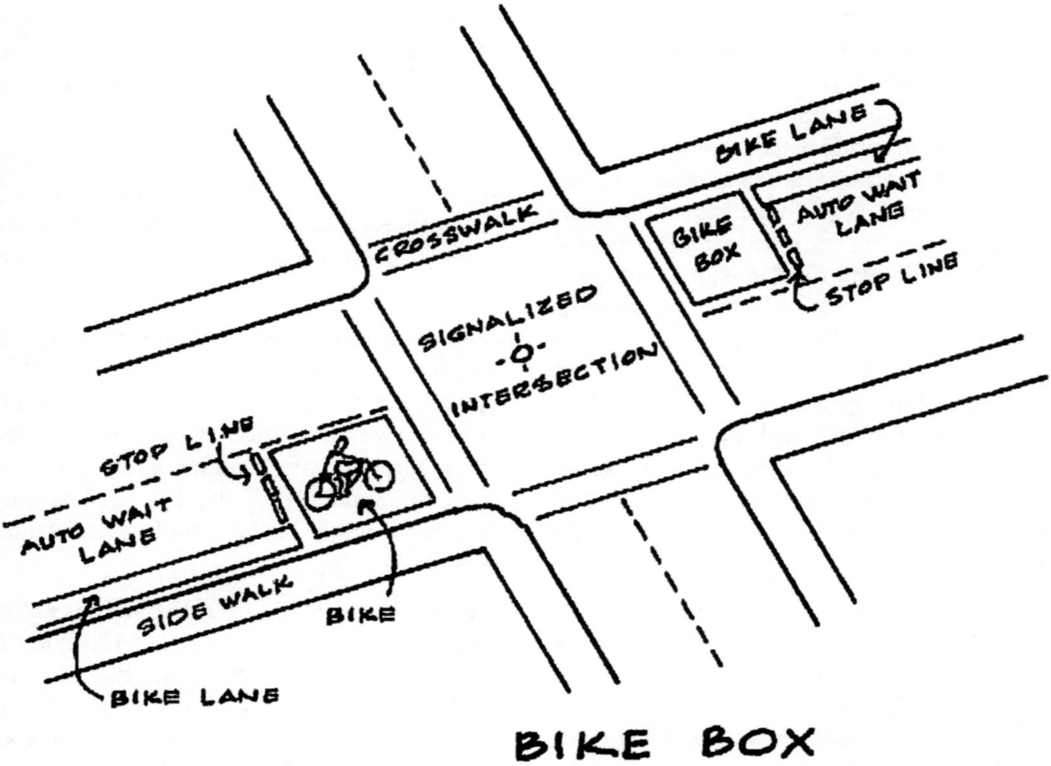


## BIKE/BUSWAY

**A vehicular right-of-way or portion thereof that is reserved exclusively for the use of bikes and buses.**

*Comment*: The exclusive reservation may be limited to peak traffic hours.

## BIKE LANE

**See** ***Bicycle Facilities, Classification (Class Ii)*** **and** *Figures 14 and 15.*

*Legal Annotation*: "At the time, she was proceeding on the east side of Beach Avenue, a one-way residential street, in a southerly direction facing traffic in a designated pedestrian-bicycle lane (**bike lane**)." *Atalese v. Long Beach Township* (N.J. Super. Ct. App. Div., 2003).

"Streets and Highways Code section 890.4 provides: '[B]ikeways shall be categorized as follows: [¶] . . . (b) Class II bikeways, such as a "**bike lane**," which provide a restricted right-of-way designated for the exclusive or semiexclusive use of bicycles with through travel by motor vehicles or pedestrians prohibited, but with vehicle parking and crossflows by pedestrians and motorists permitted.'" *Farnham v. City of Los Angeles* (Calif. Ct. App., 1998).

## BIKE PATH

**A designated right-of-way for bicycles, separated from pedestrians and motor vehicles. See** ***Bicycle Facilities, Classification (Class I)*** **and** ***Figure 15.***

*Comment*: Most bike paths are designed exclusively for bicycles, although in some instances they can be shared with pedestrians. In those cases, it is better to specify them as such or provide a separate regulation or definition of "combined paths," indicating their shared function.

*Legal Annotation*: "Streets and Highways Code section 890.4 provides: '[B]ikeways shall be categorized as follows: (a) Class I bikeways, such as a "**bike path**," which provide a completely separated right-of-way designated for the exclusive use of bicycles and pedestrians with crossflows by motorists minimized.'" *Farnham v. City of Los Angeles* (Calif. Ct. App., 1998).

## BIKE ROUTE

**See Bicycle Facilities, Classification (Class III) and *Figure 15*.**

*Legal Annotation*: "Streets and Highways Code section 890.4 provides: '[B]ikeways shall be categorized as follows: . . . (c) Class III bikeways, such as an onstreet or offstreet "**bike route**," which provide a right-of-way designated by signs or permanent markings and shared with pedestrians or motorists.'" *Farnham v. City of Los Angeles* (Calif. Ct. App., 1998).

## BIKE ROUTES, NATIONAL

**A national network of bike routes that may span multiple states or have national or regional significance.http://safety.fhwa.dot.gov/ped_bike/tools_solve/fhwasa12018/#chap1.6**

## BIKE SHARING

**"A service in which bicycles are made available for shared use to individuals on a . . . short term basis." http:/en.wikipedia.org/wiki/bicycle_sharing_system**

*Comment*: Bike sharing is designed to increase mobility in urban settings by providing bicycles at designated locations or docking stations where, utilizing interface technology, bikes may be obtained or returned.

Bike sharing can provide a low-cost expansion to communities' existing transportation services without creating additional congestion or pollution and is less expensive to purchase and maintain than conventional rail, bus or auto modes. Bike sharing programs are particularly suitable in areas of short-term trip demands such as city centers, college campuses, and tourist settings.

For additional information see Amiton 2011; Kaiser 2010; "Taking Off the Stabilisers" 2013.

*Legal Annotation*: "Transportation improvements would include the realignment of the Muni M-Oceanview light-rail line through the Project Site, redesign and redevelopment of all public streets within the Project Site to meet the City's Better Streets design standards, provision of car-share and **bike-sharing** stations throughout the Project Site, pedestrian safety and traffic improvements to intersections adjacent to the Project Site, construction of new bicycle paths, provision of a free shuttle service to Daly City BART and other items detailed in the Transportation Plan." *San Francisco Tomorrow v. San Francisco* (Calif. Ct. App., 2014).

## BIKEWAY

**"A generic term for any road, street, path, or traveled way that is in some manner specifically or legally designated for bicycle travel, regardless of whether such facilities are designated for the exclusive use of bicycles or are to be shared with other transportation modes." (See Figure 15.) http://safety.fhwa.dot.gov/ped_bike/tools_solve/fhwasa12018/#chap1.6**

*Legal Annotation*: "Streets and Highways Code section 890.4 provides: 'As used in this article, "**bikeway**" means all facilities that provide primarily for bicycle travel.'" *Farnham v. City of Los Angeles* (Calif. Ct. App., 1998).

## BILLBOARD

**See *Sign, Billboard*.**

## BIOLOGICAL OXYGEN DEMAND (BOD)

**A measure of the amount of oxygen consumed in the biological processes that break down organic matter in water.**

**Figure 15**

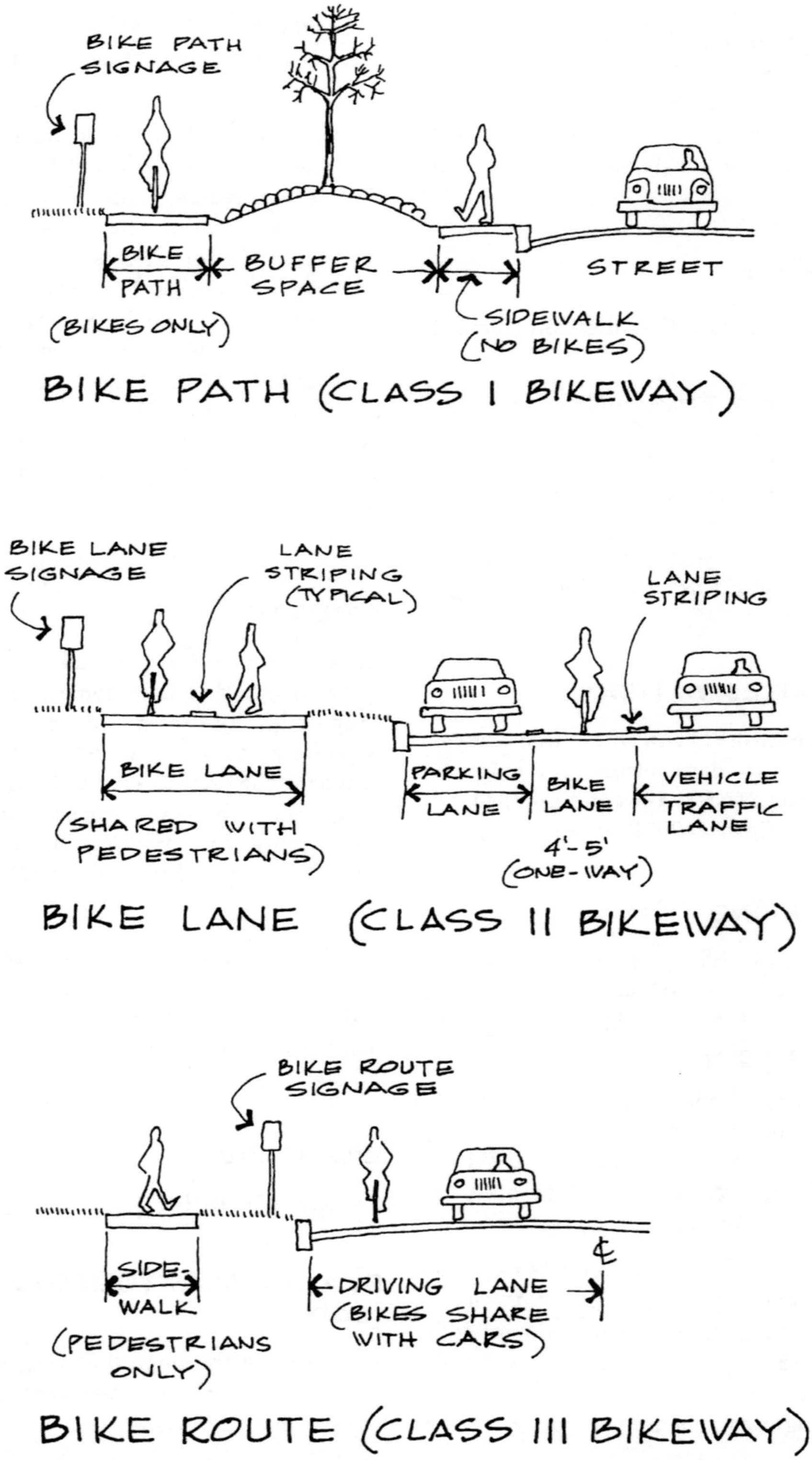
BIKE PATH SIGNAGE
BIKE PATH
(BIKES ONLY)
BUFFER SPACE
SIDEWALK (NO BIKES)
STREET
BIKE PATH (CLASS I BIKEWAY)
BIKE LANE SIGNAGE
LANE STRIPING (TYPICAL)
LANE STRIPING
BIKE LANE
(SHARED WITH PEDESTRIANS)
PARKING LANE
BIKE LANE
VEHICLE TRAFFIC LANE
4'-5' (ONE-WAY)
BIKE LANE (CLASS II BIKEWAY)
BIKE ROUTE SIGNAGE
SIDE-WALK
(PEDESTRIANS ONLY)
DRIVING LANE (BIKES SHARE WITH CARS)
℄
BIKE ROUTE (CLASS III BIKEWAY)

*Comment*: Large amounts of organic waste use up large amounts of dissolved oxygen; thus, the greater the degree of pollution, the higher the BOD.

*Legal Annotation*: "BOD, **biological oxygen demand**, indicates the oxygen consuming capacity of organic matter in the wastewater." *FMC Corp. v. Train* (4th Cir., 1976).

## BIODEGRADABLE

**Capable of being decomposed by the action of microorganisms.**

*Legal Annotation*: "Since the sole noteworthy distinction between the two is that the imported soft alkylate could be used to produce a detergent which was **biodegradable** after use, the question may be more narrowly phrased as whether the attribute of being **biodegradable**, that is to say, capable of being naturally decomposed, detracts from the otherwise demonstrably similar and competitive nature of the two." *John S. Connor, Inc. v. US* (U.S. Cust. Ct., 1 975).

## BIODIVERSITY

**The variety of biological species within ecosystems together with the genetic variation within each species (New Jersey State Development and Redevelopment Plan 2002).**

*Legal Annotation*: "The elimination of all or even some of these endangered species would have a staggering effect on **biodiversity**—defined as the presence of a large number of species of animals and plants—in the United States and, thereby, on the current and future interstate commerce that relies on the availability of a diverse array of species." *National Ass'n of Home Builders v. Babbitt* (D.C. Cir., 1997).

## BIOLOGICAL CONTROL

**A method of controlling pests by means of introduced or naturally occurring predatory organisms, sterilization, or the use of inhibiting hormones, or similar methods, rather than by mechanical or chemical means.**

*Legal Annotation*: "The work of Dr. Robert van den Bosch, a professor of entomology at the University of California at Berkeley, is principally concerned with the control of agricultural pests through **biological control**, which consists of the utilization of biotic natural enemies, that is, parasites and predators that affect these pests." *Uribe v. Howie* (Calif. Ct. App., 1971).

## BIOLOGICAL OXIDATION

**The process by which bacterial and other microorganisms feed on complex organic materials and decompose them. Also known as biochemical oxidation.**

*Comment*: Biological oxidation is the basis for the self-purification of waterways and activated sludge and trickling filter wastewater treatment processes.

*Legal Annotation*: "The second theory, entitled **biological oxidation**, is that microorganisms, indigenous to the soil, consumed petroleum products." *Sharp v. Wyatt, Inc.* (Conn. App. Ct., 1993).

"Biochemical Oxygen Demand is defined as 'the quantity of dissolved oxygen required for **biochemical oxidation** of decomposable matter under aerobic conditions in a period of five days at a temperature of 20 degrees centigrade.'" *Chicago Allis Mfg. Corp. v. The Metropolitan Sanitary District of Greater Chicago* (Ill., 1972).

## BIOMONITORING

**The use of living organisms to test the suitability of effluent for discharge into receiving waters and to test the quality of such waters downstream from a discharge.**

*Comment*: Also referred to as "effluent biomonitoring."

*Legal Annotation*: "The 1992 permit also requires Coats American to develop, upon EPD request, a program for 'whole effluent **biomonitoring**' if EPD believes the Facility discharge includes toxic substances in concentrations or combinations harmful to humans, fish or aquatic life." *Culbertson v. Coats American, Inc.* (D.C. Ga., 1995).

## BIOSPHERE

**That part of the earth and its atmosphere capable of supporting life.**

***Legal Annotation***: The purposes of NEPA are: "[T]o declare a national policy which will encourage productive and enjoyable harmony between man and his environment; to promote efforts which will prevent or eliminate damage to the environment and **biosphere** and stimulate the health and welfare of man; to enrich the understanding of the ecological systems and natural resources important to the Nation." 83 Stat. 852, 42 U. S. C. § 4321. As cited in *Andrus v. Sierra Club* (U.S., 1979).

## BIOSTABILIZER

**A machine used to convert solid waste into compost by grinding and aeration.**

***Legal Annotation***: "These include some of the performance requirements and the prohibition against on-site storage of compost, but not the specified **biostabilizer** process including the 'composting' described above." *Dano Resource Recovery, Inc. v. District of Columbia* (District of Columbia Court of Appeals, 1993). **http://tinyurl.com/nf4fjd7**.

## BIOTA

**All the species of plants and animals occurring within a certain area.**

***Legal Annotation***: "Dr. Wahtola defined diversified aquatic **biota** as the presence of various trophic levels: phytoplankton, zooplankton, benthos and fish. He then testified that although his tests revealed that a diversified aquatic **biota** was present, it could not be satisfactorily maintained because of the unstable environment present in the stream." *Modine Manufacturing Co., v. The Pollution Control Board* (Ill. App. Ct., 1976).

## BLANK WALL

**An exterior building wall with no openings and generally constructed of a single material, of a uniform texture, and on a single plane (Nelessen 1994: 271).**

***Legal Annotation***: "The rear line abuts a **blank wall** of a building used as a residence." *Poster Advertising Company, Inc. v. Zoning Board of Adjustment* (Pa., 1962).

## BLENDING

**The joining of two or more materials that combine chemically to form a new product that differs chemically from either of the original materials.**

***Comment***: The process of blending usually involves gases, liquids, or chemicals, but it may involve solids that are physically combined in a manner in which the individual components lose their original identities. Blending usually is classified as a manufacturing activity but is also typically part of small retail and service establishments, such as bakeries and restaurants.

***Legal Annotation***: "According to Bituminous, ABPC's routine **blending** of chemicals in an open dirt pit constituted intentional behavior of an ongoing nature and thus, any spills or leaks could not have been 'sudden or accidental.'" *Drexel Chemical Company v. Bituminous Insurance Company* (Tenn. Ct. App., 1996).

## BLIGHTED AREA

**An area characterized by deteriorating and/or abandoned buildings; inadequate or missing public or community services; and vacant land with debris, litter, lack of utilities, accumulation of trash and junk and impacted by adverse environmental nuisances, such as odor, noise, and heavy traffic.**

***Comment***: An alternative definition could refer to appropriate state enabling legislation. A blighted area has specific legal meaning in the application of federal and state funding. Under the Housing Act of 1949 as amended, and various state acts, an area that meets a blight definition can be acquired by public agencies by eminent domain and resold to private developers for the purpose of redevelopment and renewal. Blighted areas also may be eligible for certain favorable tax treatment and funding. An alternative, less derogatory term, "area in need of redevelopment," is used in more recent state enabling legislation. Blighted areas were formerly referred to as "slums," a term that is no longer used.

***Legal Annotation***: "In *Berman v. Parker*, the Supreme Court '[u]pheld a redevelopment plan targeting a **blighted area** of Washington, D. C., in which most of the housing for the area's 5,000 inhabitants was beyond repair.'" *Kelo v. City of New London* (U.S., 2005).

## BLOCK

**A unit of land bounded by streets or by a combination of streets and public land, railroad rights-of-way, waterways, or any other barrier to the continuity of development.** ***See Figure 10.***

***Legal Annotation***: "[T]he court defined the word 'block' as follows: 'Ordinarily the word **"block"** . . . refers to a space in a city, usually rectangular, enclosed by streets and used or intended for buildings.'" *State of Kansas v. The City of Kansas City* (Kan., 1957).

## BLOCK STATISTICS

**United States census information tabulated on a block basis.**

***Legal Annotation***: "Plaintiffs urge that the proceedings are fatally defective because the planning board considered information contained in **block statistics** published by the United States Bureau of the Census. . . . The **block statistics** show housing characteristics of the city by blocks." *Stahl v. Paterson Bd. of Finance* (N.J. Super. Ct., 1960).

## BLOW-OFF

**An outlet in a pipe through which water or sediment can be discharged from a lower sewer.**

***Legal Annotation***: "Appellants further contend that when they made the decision to purchase the property, none of the appellees informed them of the easement, which contained pipes below the surface and a **blow-off** valve onto the property where appellants contend they wished to build an addition." *Sevin v. Kelshaw* (Pa. Super. Ct., 1992).

## BOARD OF ADJUSTMENT

**An officially constituted body whose principal duties are to hear appeals and, where appropriate, grant variances from the strict application of the zoning ordinance.**

***Comment***: The name and work of boards of adjustment vary by state. In some states, boards of adjustment are called boards of standards and appeals, zoning hearing boards, or zoning boards of adjustment. In most states, the board of adjustment interprets the zoning ordinance and the zoning map, can grant variances from the bulk and dimensional requirements of the ordinance, and can grant a variance for a use not specifically permitted in the zone.

***Legal Annotation***: "The power to grant use variances has been shifted from the governing body, whose responsibilities include enactment of the zoning ordinance, to the **board of adjustment**. This shift of authority undoubtedly reflects the legislature's determination **that boards of adjustment** possess special competence to decide use-variance applications, and that absent an appeal no participation by the governing body is necessary." *Medici v. BPR Co.* (N.J., 1987).

## BOARDER

**An individual other than a member of the family occupying a dwelling unit who, for a consideration, is furnished sleeping accommodations and meals and may be provided personal care, financial services, counseling, or other such services.**

***Comment***: Many older ordinances made a distinction between temporary and permanent boarders, which is not a particularly meaningful distinction, and also excluded the provision of meals or other services, restricting their function to solely providing sleeping accommodations. These distinctions are not important from a zoning perspective.

*Legal Annotation*: "[A] person who is enjoying accommodations at an inn or hotel under such conditions of permanency as to make the place his home or residence for the time being is not a guest but a **boarder**, or a lodger if he simply has rooms without meals." *Jackson v. Engert* (St. Louis Ct. App., 1970).

## BOARDING HOME FOR SHELTERED CARE

**A nonprofit or for-profit group home for the sheltered care of persons with special needs, which, in addition to providing food and shelter, may also provide some combination of personal care, social or counseling services, and transportation. See *Assisted Living Facility; Boardinghouse; Community Residences For The Developmentally Disabled; Community Shelters For Victims Of Domestic Violence; Family; Handicap*.**

*Comment*: The sheltered care facility serves as a substitute for the residents' own homes, furnishing facilities and comforts normally found in a home but providing, in addition, such service, equipment, and safety features as are required for safe and adequate care of the residents. These may include: (1) supervision and assistance in dressing, bathing, and in the maintenance of good personal hygiene; (2) care in emergencies or during temporary illness; (3) supervision in the taking of medications; and (4) other services conducive to the residents' welfare. Group homes for sheltered care should be treated as boardinghouses in zoning terms unless they qualify under state licensing requirements as houses for battered spouses and children or community residences for the developmentally disabled.

Group homes for the developmentally disabled are subject to the provisions of the federal Fair Housing Act (42 U.S.C.A. §3601). The Fair Housing Act, as amended, prohibits municipalities from "applying different rules to the handicapped than are applied to others" (49 ZD 131, *Land Use Law*, April 1997: 17). Spacing requirements (minimum distance between homes) and limits on the number of residents would not be permitted.

*Legal Annotation*: "Dr. Desai explained that a **sheltered care home** is intended to house people who are not capable of independent living and who need some type of nursing care. A nursing home is distinguished from a sheltered care home in that residents of a nursing home need more skilled nursing." *City of Evanston v. Ridgeview House, Inc.* (Ill., 1976).

"Ill. Rev. Stat. 1973, ch. 111 1/2, par. 35.16 . . . [d]efines a sheltered care home as follows: 'Sheltered care home' means a county sheltered care home or a sheltered care home operated as part of a county nursing home . . . or a private **boarding home**, institution, building, residence, or other place whether operated for profit or not which, through its ownership or management, provides sheltered care to 3 or more persons who are not related to the applicant or owner by blood or marriage.'" *City of Evanston v. Ridgeview House, Inc.* (Ill., 1976).

## BOARDING STABLE

**A structure designed for the feeding, housing, and exercising of horses not owned by the owner of the premises and for which the owner of the premises may receive compensation. See *Horse Farm*.**

*Legal Annotation*: "Although there was abundant evidence that the parcel itself was unsuitable for farm use, respondents Moore argued to the county that they were 'willing' to use petitioners' property as an adjunct of their neighboring **boarding stable**, where they board and pasture horses and provide for recreational riding." *Moore v. Coos County* (Ore. Ct. App., 1996).

## BOARDINGHOUSE

**A dwelling unit or part thereof in which, for compensation, lodging and meals are provided and personal and financial services may be offered. See *Boarding Home For Sheltered Care; Personal Services*.**

*Comment*: Over the years, the distinction between boardinghouses and rooming houses has narrowed. Traditionally, rooming houses provided only rooms and boardinghouses rooms and meals, but this distinction is no longer meaningful. The principal concern from a zoning point of view is how many rooms should be permitted to be rented as a matter of right, beyond which the rooming house or boardinghouse would be restricted to certain zones with controls, permitted only as a conditional use, or licensed. Another concern is how to ensure that the rooming houses and boardinghouses remain safe and sanitary.

Communities have addressed these problems by licensing boardinghouses and rooming houses, requiring periodic inspections, limiting the number of guests, prohibiting cooking facilities in guest rooms, requiring adequate parking (in terms of both number and location of spaces), and establishing a minimum floor area for guest rooms. For boardinghouses in residential zones, communities require the owners or operators to maintain their residence on-site and personally collect rents, to ensure that the structure remains principally a private dwelling unit.

Concerns over abuses of residents, especially the poor, aged, or special groups, have prompted some states to require state licenses for boardinghouses. In New Jersey, accommodations for two or more unrelated boarders require a state license, and a distinction is made between rooming houses, which provide only rooms or rooms and meals, and boardinghouses, which provide personal or financial services as well. However, the location and conditions of approval still remain local prerogatives.

Some boarding homes serve special populations, and these homes may be referred to as assisted living facilities, boarding homes for sheltered care, community residences for the developmentally disabled, and community shelters for the victims of domestic violence.

***Legal Annotation***: "Berwick, Me., Land Use Ordinance § 2.2 defines a '**boardinghouse**' as: '[a]ny residential structure including congregate housing where lodging and/or meals are provided for compensation for a period of at least one week, and where a family residing in the building acts as proprietor or owner. There shall be no provisions for cooking in any individual guest room.'" *Malonson v. Town of Berwick* (Maine, 2004).

## BOARDWALK

**An elevated public pedestrian walkway constructed over a public street or along an oceanfront or beach.**

***Legal Annotation***: "For many years, there existed a wooden **boardwalk** or walkway (wooden walkway) over a portion of EAP's property that the plaintiffs and the Dodds maintained and used to access White Beach." *Murphy v. EAPWJP, LLC* (Conn. App. Ct., 2010).

## BOAT RAMP

**A facility designed to launch and retrieve recreational watercraft from a trailer.**

***Legal Annotation***: "In 1965 the State constructed a **boat ramp** facility to permit members of the public to launch boats from the ramp onto the lake." *Reitsma v. Pascoag Reservoir & Dam, LLC* (R.I., 2001).

## BOAT SLIP

**A space designed for the mooring of a single watercraft.**

***Legal Annotation***: "Further, the court defined a '**boat slip**' as 'one parking space for one single boat, vessel, yacht or watercraft (boat) at, and tied to, the piers and/or fingers attached to said piers' and limited the defendant to a maximum number of seventy-five boat slips." *Reichenbach v. Kraska Enterprises* (Conn. App. Ct., 2008).

## BOATEL

**A combination of a motel and marina that is accessible to boats as well as automobiles and may include boat sales and servicing facilities, overnight accommodation for transients, and eating and drinking facilities.**

***Legal Annotation***: "A **boatel** can best be described as a shore facility having docking accommodations. Whenever a boat is secured to such a dock, its occupants can go ashore to the **boatel** where they can enjoy such amenities as hot and cold water, a full-size bed and clean bed linens." *Northeastern Corp. v. Zoning Bd. of Review of the Town of New Shoreham* (R.I., 1987).

## BOATHOUSE

**An enclosed or partially enclosed structure designed for the use and storage of private watercraft.**

*Legal Annotation*: "The creek is located on the eastern end of Lake Ontario near the mouth of the St. Lawrence River and is lined with commercial and private **boathouses**. Speach's property, undeveloped but for an existing single slip **boathouse**, is located within a 'lakefront district' as designated by local ordinances adopted in 1991 and is a 'special permit' use." *Matter of Sasso v. Osgood* (N.Y., 1995).

## BOATYARD

See *Marina*.

## BOG

**Wet, spongy land, usually poorly drained, highly acid, and rich in plant residue.**

*Legal Annotation*: "According to common definitions from the *Random House Webster's College Dictionary* (2001 ed), a '**bog**' is 'wet, spongy ground with soil composed mainly of decayed vegetable matter.'" *People v. Kozak* (Mich. Ct. App., 2008).

## BOLLARD

**A short post used to divert or block vehicular traffic.**

*Comment*: Originally designed to secure ships, bollards are a useful and decorative street furniture element. They often incorporate low-level lighting and, with appropriate spacing, they can restrict vehicular travel while permitting unimpeded pedestrian movement.

*Legal Annotation*: "Further, the evidence demonstrated that appellee had marked the concrete pedestrian sidewalk adjacent to the asphalt parking lot in front of the store with three red **bollards** in front of the store entrance . . . a yellow **bollard** in front of the crosswalk by the store entrance with a stop sign attached to it and a pedestrian crossing sign attached above the stop sign." *Christian v. Wal-Mart Stores East, LP* (Ohio Ct. App., 2011).

## BONUS ZONING

See *Incentive Zoning*.

## BOROUGH

**An incorporated, self-governing municipality.**

*Legal Annotation*: "The general and specific powers of a **borough** are enumerated in the **Borough** Code at 53 P.S. §§ 46201 and 46202. Nowhere in those or any other sections is the power to build and operate a cable television system expressly granted to boroughs, with the sole exception of municipal cable systems already in operation on July 1, 1979, which are grandfathered in." *Warner Cable Com. v. Borough of Schuylkill Haven* (E.D. Pa., 1992).

## BOULEVARD

**A collector street that includes landscaped medians.**

*Comment*: The most attractive boulevards are those with landscaping in the medians and a double row of trees, framing the sidewalks, along the outside of each roadway. For additional information on boulevards, *see* Jacobs, MacDonald, and Rofe (2002).

*Legal Annotation*: "Inverrary **Boulevard** is a 4-lane divided roadway, with a landscaped median, that meanders generally north and south through a golf course called Inverrary Country Club." *McFall v. Inverrary Country Club, Inc.* (Fla. Dist. Ct. App. 1993).

## BRACKISH WATER

**A mixture of fresh and salt water.**

*Legal Annotation*: "The present case involves the purchase of waterfront property located on **brackish water** near the confluence of the Sakonnet River and the Atlantic Ocean, and only about two miles from the ocean itself." *Stebbins v. Wells* (R.I., 2001).

## BRANDING

**The application of directed publicity and marketing techniques to enhance the image of and favorable perception of a state, county, or municipality.**

*Comment*: Municipalities, states, and other jurisdictions are using branding techniques to sell themselves to the public in order to create a positive image of the jurisdiction which in turn will attract tourists, visitors, commerce, and industry, and attract and encourage new development, home buyers, and residents. The branding includes extensive programs highlighting art, entertainment, location, history, natural resources, recreational facilities, educational and cultural resources, good government, and a favorable living environment. Along with such programs are eye-catching slogans and mottos; for example, "The Big Apple" (New York City), "The Cradle of Liberty" (Boston), "The Entertainment Capital of the World" (Las Vegas), "The City of Presidents" (Quincy, Massachusetts), "America's Sailing Capital" (Annapolis, Maryland.), "The Scenic City" (Chattanooga, Tennessee), and "The City That Was So Nice They Named It Twice" (Walla Walla, Washington).

How various municipalities have effectively used branding techniques is featured in Green (2007). Franchises also emphasize branding (Fleming 2002).

## BREAKAWAY WALL

**A wall that is not part of the structural support of a building and is intended, through its design and construction, to collapse under specific lateral loading forces without causing damage to the elevated portion of the building or supporting foundation system.**

*Legal Annotation*: "A **breakaway wall** is a non-bearing wall that is designed to fail under low stress conditions without endangering or bringing about the collapse of the structure." *Easton's Point v. Coastal Resources Management* (R.I., 1989).

## BREAKWATER

**A protective structure, usually built offshore for the purpose of protecting the shoreline or harbor areas from wave action.**

*Legal Annotation*: "The fact that the land . . . had been filled in by the railroad company in the construction of the tracks for its railroad and for the **breakwater** on the shore west of it, did not deprive the city of its riparian rights. The exercise of those rights was only subject to the condition of the agreement with the city, under which the tracks and **breakwater** were constructed by the railroad company, and that was for . . . the continuance of the **breakwater** as a protection of its works and the shore from the violence of the lake." *Illinois Central Railroad Co. v. Illinois* (U.S., 1892).

## BREEDING FARM

**An agricultural establishment where animals are impregnated either naturally or by artificial insemination and whose principal purpose is to propagate the species.**

*Legal Annotation*: "In 1907 the decedent purchased a farm of 75 acres in the suburbs of Cleveland and equipped it as a **breeding farm** or nursery for trotting and pacing horses, with stables, a dwelling house for a superintendent, bungalow for a caretaker, a blacksmith shop, and other out buildings." *Clark v. Commissioner of Internal Revenue* (Bd. Tax App., 1931).

## BREW PUB

**A restaurant that prepares handcrafted natural beer intended for consumption on the premises as an accessory use.**

*Comment*: Also known as a microbrewery. Some ordinances place limitations on the yearly production of beer, and/or on the percent of gross floor area of the primary restaurant occupied by the brewery operation.

*Legal Annotation*: "As a **brew pub,** appellee is a licensed restaurant that brews beer on-site for consumption by its patrons." *Boston Beer Co. v. Slesar Bros. Brewing Co.* (1st Cir., 1993).

## BRIDGE

**A structure having a clear span of more than twenty feet designed to convey vehicles and/or pedestrians over a watercourse, railroad, public or private right-of-way, or any depression.**

*Comment*: Structures having a clear span of less than twenty feet are usually designated as culverts.

*Legal Annotation*: "It charged that the defendants . . . were engaged in the construction of a **bridge** across the Ohio River, at Wheeling, which would obstruct its navigation, to and from the ports of Pennsylvania, by steamboats and other craft which navigate the same." *State of Pennsylvania v. The Wheeling & Belmont Bridge Co.* (U.S., 1852).

## BRITISH THERMAL UNIT (BTU)

**The amount of heat required to raise the temperature of one pound of water, at one atmosphere, one degree Fahrenheit.**

*Legal Annotation*: "The dispute arose over the method of computing the number of **British Thermal Units** contained in the gas delivered. A **British Thermal Unit**, generally known as a 'BTU', is defined as the amount of heat required to raise the temperature of one pound of water one degree Fahrenheit." *The Kansas Power & Light Co. v. Hugoton Production Co.* (10th Cir., 1958).

## BROADCAST APPLICATION

**The application of a chemical or seeds over an entire field, lawn, or other area.**

*Legal Annotation*: "All **broadcast application**, aerial or otherwise, must be prohibited in coastal counties or parishes and on or near rivers, streams, lakes, ponds, and other aquatic areas. I also believe it necessary to restrict aerial or other **broadcast application** in non-coastal, nonaquatic areas to Federal, State, county, or local authorities." *Save America's Vital Environment, Inc. v. Butz* (N.D. Ga., 1972).

## BROOK

**A small stream or creek.**

*Legal Annotation*: "No excavation shall be permitted within seventy-five (75) feet of any great pond, navigable river, or other standing body of water ten (10) acres or more in area, or within twenty-five (25) feet of any other stream, river or **brook** which normally flows throughout the year, or any naturally occurring standing body of water smaller than ten (10) acres, prime wetland as designated in accordance with RSA 482-A:15, I or any other wetland larger than five (5) acres as defined by the Wetlands Board." Sharon, N.H., Earth Excavations Regulations § I (2010). *SAN-Ken Homes, Inc. v. Town Of Sharon* (N.H., 2013).

## BROWNFIELDS

**Abandoned, idled, or underutilized industrial and commercial facilities where expansion or redevelopment is complicated by real or perceived environmental contamination (US EPA, cited in *PAS Report 491/492*).**

*Comment*: The term "brownfields" is often applied to sites with confirmed levels of contamination as well as to sites that are believed to be contaminated although actual contamination is unverified. Brownfields, often located in older urban areas but also evident in rural areas, offer potential opportunities for redevelopment in areas with a scarcity of vacant land. Recent changes in federal regulations allow for a variety of cleanup methods and standards, depending on the reuse of the property. For example, brownfield sites to be used only for parking can be rendered usable by paving the site.

*Legal Annotation*: "Many initiatives have been instituted by California and the federal government to 'expedite the cleanup of these '**Brownfields**', and reduce the cost and burden of returning such properties to beneficial use." *Fireman's Fund Insurance Co. v. City of Lodi* (9th Cir., 2002).

## BUFFER AREA

**An area of land within a property or site, generally adjacent to and parallel with a property line, to allow adequate screening of view, noise, or activity taking place within the property or site from adversely affecting an adjoining property, site, or the public right-of-way. See *Buffer Strip*.**

*Legal Annotation*:"The term 'upland area' is used to describe the nonregulated area outside of the wetlands, watercourses and upland review **(buffer) area** of the proposed development." *River Bend Associates v. Conservation and Inland Wetlands Cmmmission* (Conn., 2004).

## BUFFER STRIP

**Open spaces, landscaped areas, fences, walls, berms, or any combination thereof used to physically separate or screen one use or property from another so as to visually shield or block noise, lights, or other nuisances. See *Berm*. See *Figures 12 and 68*.**

*Comment*: Basic criteria for buffers are the width of the buffer and the type of material to be planted or installed. In design of buffers, the ordinance should allow flexibility and permit fences and berms to be used in conjunction with the landscaping (American Planning Association, *Zoning News*, February 1990). *See* Berm.

*Legal Annotation*: "To require by zoning regulation a **buffer strip** between one zone of a particular classification and another zone of a different class in one specific instance and not in other instances when zones of these two zone classifications abut clearly violates the statutory uniformity requirement and is exactly the arbitrary and discriminatory use of the police power which the statute was designed to prevent." *Vesekis v. Bristol Zoning Commission* (Conn., 1975).

## BUFFER ZONE

**See *Transition Zone*.**

## BUILDABLE AREA

**The area of a lot remaining after the minimum yard and open space requirements of the zoning ordinance have been met. See *Figure 16*.**

*Comment*: The buildable area should be actually buildable. If a lot is largely wetlands, very steep slopes, or easements, it may be difficult to locate a building or improvements on the land. In some ordinances, such areas of environmental constraints are deducted from "buildable area" calculations. The zoning regulations should specify that a minimum building area must be available to accommodate a building, driveway, and where required, a well and septic system.

*Legal Annotation*: "To determine whether a lot is large enough to be developed, the ordinance requires a percentage reduction of the property's gross area depending upon the degree of the property's slope, which yields the **buildable area**." *Matter of Anello v. Zoning Board of Appeals of the Village of Dobbs Ferry* (N.Y., 1997).

## BUILDING

**Any structure having a roof supported by columns or walls and intended for the shelter, housing, or enclosure of any individual, animal, process, equipment, goods, or materials of any kind and intended for use in one place.**

*Legal Annotation*: "In using the term '**building** or structure,' the Court encapsulated the common understanding of the word '**building**'—a structure designed for occupancy that is intended for use in one place." *US v. Grisel* (9th Cir., 2007).

## BUILDING, ACCESSORY

**A subordinate structure on the same lot as the principal or main building or use. See *Accessory Structure*. See *Figure 3*.**

*Legal Annotation*: "An **accessory Building** is a subordinate building, separated from or attached to the main building, the use of which is incidental to that of the main building or the use of the premises." *Lowry v. City of Mankato* (Minn., 1950).

**Figure 16**

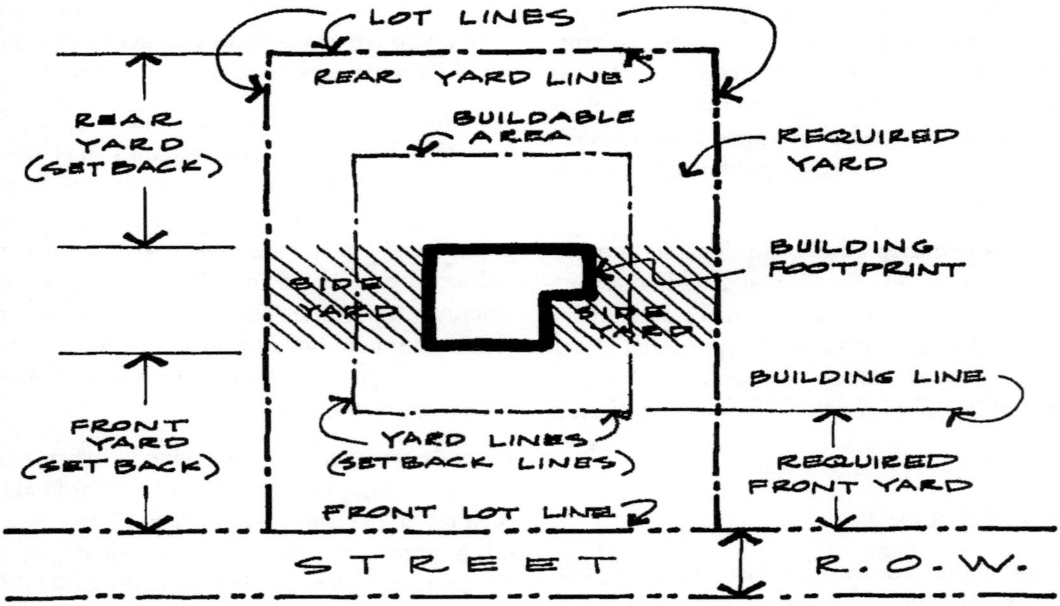


## BUILDING, PRINCIPAL

**A building in which is conducted the principal use of the lot on which it is located.** *See Figure 3.*

*Legal Annotation*: "A '**Principal building**' is defined as '[a] building in which is conducted the main or principal use of the lot on which the building is located.'" *Marshall Township Board of Supervisors v. Marshall Township Zoning Hearing Board* (Pa. Comm. Ct., 1998).

## BUILDING COVERAGE

**The ratio of the horizontal area, measured from the exterior surface of the exterior walls of the ground floor, of all principal and accessory buildings on a lot to the total lot area.**

*Comment*: In single-family residences, porches and decks usually are excluded. For multifamily and nonresidential structures, more meaningful controls over the intensity and environmental impact of development are limits on impervious surfaces and floor area ratio, coupled with open-space requirements.

*Legal Annotation*: "By its plain language, this provision refers to **building coverage** within the entire setback area rather than the **building coverage** of one particular building, and therefore, the thirty percent increase should be measured in comparison to all the buildings in the setback area rather than one particular building within that area." *Rockland Plaza Realty Corp. v. City of Rockland* (Maine, 2001).

## BUILDING ENVELOPE

See *Zoning Envelope*.

*Legal Annotation*: "The trial justice contrasted the definitions of '**building envelope**' and 'lot building coverage' as set forth in the zoning ordinance. He noted that § 17.08.010 of the zoning ordinance defines the term '**[b]uilding envelope**' as 'the three-dimensional space within which a structure is permitted to be built on a lot and which is defined by regulations governing building setbacks, maximum height, and bulk' and that the term 'lot building coverage' was defined as 'that portion of the lot that is or may be covered by buildings and accessory buildings.'" *Lloyd v. Zoning Board of Review for City of Newport, RI* (R.I., 2013).

## BUILDING FOOTPRINT

**The area encompassed by a building's outer wall at ground level. *See Figure 16*.**

***Legal Annotation***: "Schunkewitz and Meckler had prepared 'conceptual sketch architectural drawings' of the **building 'footprint'**—the shape or outline of the building on the land surface—and surrounding parking areas." *Sparaco v. Lawler, Matusky, Skelly, Engineers, LLP* (2nd Cir., 2002).

## BUILDING HEIGHT

**The vertical distance from finished grade to the top of the highest roof beams on a flat or shed roof, to the deck level on a mansard roof, and the average distance between the eaves and the ridge level for gable, hip, and gambrel roofs (BOCA National Building Code, slightly modified). *See Figure 17*. See *Grade, Finished*.**

***Comment***: Mechanical equipment, chimneys, air conditioners, elevator penthouses, church spires and steeples, water towers, and similar appurtenances are usually exempted from height restrictions. However, the exclusion should apply only to those elements that are usually appurtenant to a building. For example, antennas are often excluded from height restrictions. This might result in radio broadcasting antennas, often two hundred feet or higher, to be placed on the roof of a building in a zone with a maximum height of

**Figure 17**

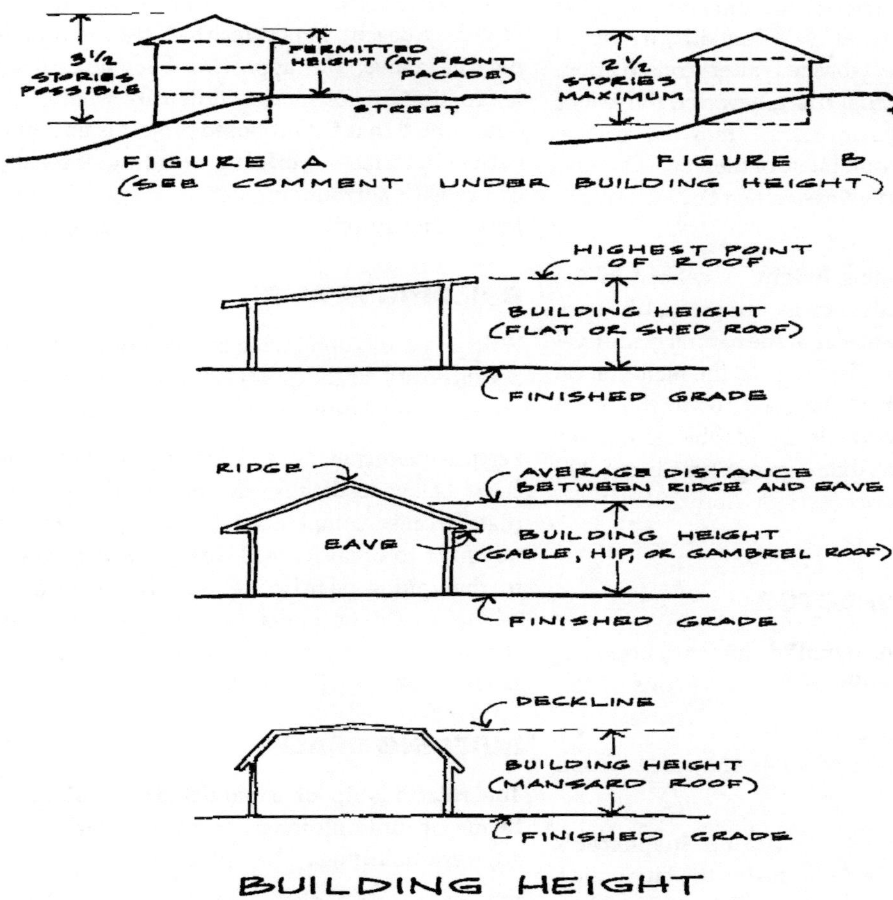

thirty-five feet. One way to preclude this is to specify that the excluded elements cannot exceed the maximum height by more than twenty-five feet.

Note, however, that the FCC regulations affecting amateur radio and satellite antennas may override local controls. *See* Satellite Dish Antenna; Tower, Amateur Radio.

Measuring height on sloping ground can be a problem; consequently, some limit on the number of stories is needed, at least in residential zones. Although height measurements are usually taken from the average finished grade, without a story limitation a building on sloping land could result in the situation shown in *Figure 17A*. With a typical limit of thirty-five feet or two and one-half stories, whichever is less, the result would be as shown in *Figure 17B*. *See* Grade, Finished.

***Legal Annotation***: "They contend the 35-foot **building height** restriction contained in RCW 90.58.030(3)(e)(vi) and .320 should be measured from the grade established after construction. We agree with the trial court, however, the height restriction must be measured from the average grade level in the natural state of the land." *The Dept. of Ecology v. Pacesetter Construction Co., Inc.* (Wash., 1977).

"Additionally, 'building **height**' is defined in the Phoenix Zoning Ordinance as, 'the vertical distance measured from the higher of the natural grade level or the finished grade level . . . to the highest level of the roof surface of flat roofs; or to the mean height between eaves and ridge of gable, gambrel or hip roofs.' Phoenix, Ariz., Zoning Ordinance § 202 (2011)." *Price v. Kravitz* (Ariz. Ct. App., 2012).

## BUILDING INSPECTOR

**The individual designated by the appointing authority to enforce the provisions of the building code.**

***Comment***: Also referred to as the construction official.

***Legal Annotation***: "The **building inspector's** job was to execute or administer the city policy, established by the city council in its building code." *Bennett v. City of Slidell* (5th Cir., 1984).

## BUILDING LINE

**A line parallel to the street right-of-way line touching that part of a building closest to the street. See *Setback Line*. See *Figure 16*.**

***Comment***: The building line is important because many ordinances prohibit parking or other uses between the street and the building line.

***Legal Annotation***: "Another ordinance, as amended July 11, 1924, creates a set-back or **building line**, with relation to the street, to which all buildings subsequently erected must conform." *Gorieb v. Fox* (U.S., 1927).

## BUILDING MASS

**The three-dimensional bulk of a structure: height, width, and depth.**

***Legal Annotation***: "The 'escape clause' in Section 4.4.13(I)(1) of the Code of Ordinances of the City of Delray Beach . . . [s]tates that 'Notwithstanding the above, the approving body may deny an application for increased density where it is determined that the proposed project is not compatible in terms of **building mass** and intensity of use with surrounding development.'" *Rectory Park, LC v. City of Delray Beach* (S.D. Fla. 2002).

## BUILDING PERMIT

**Written permission issued by the proper municipal authority for the construction, repair, or alteration of a structure, or addition to a structure.**

***Legal Annotation***: "A motion was made in the court below to dismiss the bill on the ground that, because complainant [appellee] had made no effort to obtain a **building permit** or apply to the zoning board of appeals for relief as it might have done under the terms of the ordinance, the suit was premature." *Village of Euclid v. Amber Realty Co.* (U.S., 1926).

## BUILDING SCALE

**The relationship of a particular building, in terms of building mass, to other nearby and adjacent buildings.**

***Legal Annotation***: "That subsection provides that development adjacent to a historic landmark should be compatible in **building scale** and other design aspects and have no adverse impact on the landmark." *Cathedral Park Condo v. DC Zoning Com'n* (D.C. Ct. App., 2000).

## BUILDOUT ANALYSIS

**An estimate of the projected population, employment, traffic, utilities, and types/sizes of land uses in a project area or other designated area in accordance with the current zoning ordinance and other applicable regulations.**

*Comment*: A buildout analysis can also include the consideration of other impacts. For example, the local regulations might require, for large projects, an analysis of visual impacts, specific utility demands, school impacts, and recreation needs.

*Legal Annotation*: "[T]he County AFEIS contains a 'population growth study and **buildout analysis**' using three alternative models for projected development within the geographical area served by OCSD over the next thirty years." *Matter of Town of Woodbury v. County of Orange* (NY: Supreme Court, Orange, 2012).

## BUILT ENVIRONMENT

**Artificially created fixed elements, such as buildings, structures, utilities, roads, and surfaces, that together create the physical character of an area. See *Urban Area*.**

*Legal Annotation*: "Under these rules, the 1990 Plan Update EIS should identify and discuss any elements of the natural and **built environment**, including historic and cultural preservation, in which there is a probable significant, adverse impact under the nonproject solid waste management plan." *Citizens v. Klickitat County* (Wash., 1993).

## BUILT-UP AREA

**An area where less than 25 percent of the land is vacant.**

*Comment*: While the figure of 25 percent is somewhat arbitrary, it is at this figure (75 percent developed) that an area gives the observer the impression of being totally developed.

*Legal Annotation*: "In the Rochester case the board gave as one of its reasons for denial of the application that to allow these proposed uses in this **built-up area** inhabited by people who have chosen to live there because it was strictly residential, would change the character of the residential use and enjoyment of the area." *Matter of Jewish Ctr v. Village of Garden City* (N.Y., Sup.Ct., 1956).

## BULK ENVELOPE

**See *Zoning Envelope*.**

*Legal Annotation*: "[T]he increase in FAR is a function of the previously approved Phase I building and is within the existing **bulk envelope** in light of the Phase II development. In other words, consistent with Phase I, the more intensive use of the space permitted the IMF's special needs to be met in accord with the exceptional working environment in Phase II." *Foggy Bottom v. DC Zoning Commission* (DC: Ct. App., 1994).

## BULK PLANE

**See *Sky Exposure Plane*.**

*Legal Annotation*: "Neighborhood Inspection Services (NIS) . . . determined that the roofline projected four feet through the north side **bulk plane**, in violation of the Denver Revised Municipal Code (D.R.M.C.)." *Egle v. City and County of Denver* (Colo. Ct. App., 2004).

## BULK REGULATIONS

**Standards applying to individual lots that control the placement, intensity, and character of development and include the amount of open space on the lot, the height of structures, setbacks from property lines and public rights-of-way, impervious coverage, floor area ratio, and density (*Designing New Jersey*. Trenton, NJ: Office of State Planning, Department of Community Affairs, 2000).**

*Legal Annotation*: "In R-1 districts, **bulk regulations**, which govern the size and setback of buildings and structures on a lot . . . require side yards to be a minimum of five feet in width." *People ex* *rel. Wordell v. City of Chicago* (Ill: Appellate Court, 1st Dist., 1978). http://tinyurl.com/o36eg8p

## BULK STORAGE

**The storage of chemicals, petroleum products, grains, and other materials in structures for subsequent resale to distributors or retail dealers or outlets.**

***Comment***: Bulk storage is essentially a warehousing and wholesaling operation. The products are primarily sold for eventual resale and not directly to the consuming public.

***Legal Annotation***: "In 1984, DEC promulgated a petroleum **bulk storage** code (the Code) that required petroleum storage facilities to meet certain State-wide minimum standards and addressed leak detection, corrective action, registration and access to records and facilities." *Con Edison Co. v. Department of Environmental Conservation* (N.Y., 1988).

## BULKY WASTE

**Large items of solid waste such as household appliances, furniture, large auto parts, trees, branches, stumps, and other oversize waste whose large size precludes or complicates their handling by normal solid waste collection, processing, or disposal methods. See *Waste*.**

***Legal Annotation***:"That section defines '**bulky waste**' as 'landclearing debris and waste resulting directly from demolition activities other than clean fill' and then includes '**bulky waste**' within the definition of 'special wastes' or 'non-hazardous solid wastes which require special handling. . .' *Connecticut Building Wrecking Co. v. Carothers* (Conn., 1991).

## BULKHEAD

**A retaining wall created along a body of water behind which fill is placed.** *See Figure 19.*

***Legal Annotation***: "Plaintiffs constructed a **bulkhead** or retaining wall in front of their lot on the lake side and later defendants constructed a retaining wall in front of their lot which abutted plaintiffs' retaining wall." *Carpentier v. Ellis* (Texas Ct. App., 1972).

## BULKHEAD DOOR

**Doors that open outward from a lower-level enclosed space to the outdoors.** *See Figure 18.*

***Legal Annotation***:"The violations included installation of a fence without a permit, a keyed padlock which impeded egress from the laundry area in the basement to the back yard, and debris rendering a **bulkhead** inoperable." *Hancock v. Chambers* (Mass. App. Ct., 2014).

## BULKHEAD LINE

**A line along a navigable waterway offshore of which no fill or structure is permitted. *See Figure 19*.**

***Comment***: The bulkhead line defines the permanent shoreline of navigable waterways or lakes. The top is usually stated in feet above sea level. **See *Pierhead Line*.**

***Legal Annotation***: "F.S. Sec. 253.122, F.S.A., was construed to authorize the establishment of a **bulkhead line** only at a point where, in fact, 'a further extension of land or islands outward would be an interference with the servitude in favor of commerce and navigation.'" *Gies v. Fischer* (Fla., 1962).

## BULLETIN BOARD SIGN

**See *Sign, Bulletin Board*.**

## BUMPER BLOCKS

**Permanent devices in parking stalls that block the front wheels of a vehicle.**

***Comment***: Also called wheel stops. Typical precast concrete wheel stops can be a problem in that they crack easily, make it difficult to clear parking areas of snow, trap debris, and are a hazard to pedestrians. A better arrangement is to widen the adjacent walkways or parking lot islands, install curbing, and permit the cars to overhang the curb.

**Figure 18**

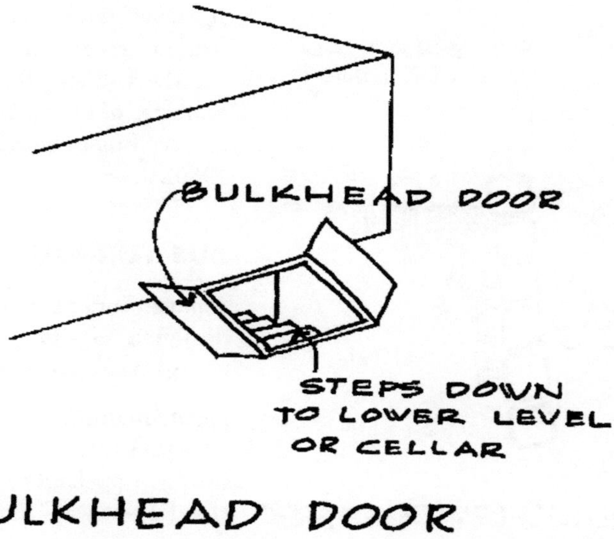


*Legal Annotation*: "The wheels of the truck were close to a cement '**bumper block**' lying at the head of the parking space, and the edge of the **bumper block** protruded slightly beyond the left front wheel." *Gable v. Shoney's Inc.* (Ala., 1995).

## BUS/BIKEWAY

See *Bikeway, Busway*.

## BUS LANE

**A designated part of a roadway intended primarily for bus use during specified periods. See *Busway*.**

*Legal Annotation*: "The express **bus lane** regulations consist of an order that the state construct such lanes along specified corridors according to EPA blueprint and a requirement for the submission of a compliance schedule." *District of Columbia v. Train* (D.C. Cir., 1975).

## BUS POOL

**A bus service, usually administered by an employer, with limited pickup and destination stops, guaranteed seats, and advance ticket purchase.**

## BUS RAPID TRANSIT (BRT)

**"A flexible rubber-tired bus rapid transit mode that combines stations, vehicles, service, running ways, and intelligent transportation system elements into an integrated system" (Swope 2006, 54).**

*Comment*: "BRT has greater operating flexibility and potentially lower capital and operating costs than light rail and can be especially desirable in large cities with high potential ridership and enough bus traffic to justify dedicated running ways" (Swope 2006, 54).

*Legal Annotation*: "FEIS concludes that **bus rapid transit** would not meet purpose and need of the Project because buses would still operate in mixed traffic, congestion would not be alleviated, and it would not have encouraged growth in the project corridor Honolulu Traffic." *Comm. v. Federal Transit Administration* (D.C. Hawaii, 2012).

## BUS SHELTER

**A small, roofed structure, usually having three walls, located near a street and designed primarily for the protection and convenience of bus passengers. *See Figure 20*.**

**Figure 19**

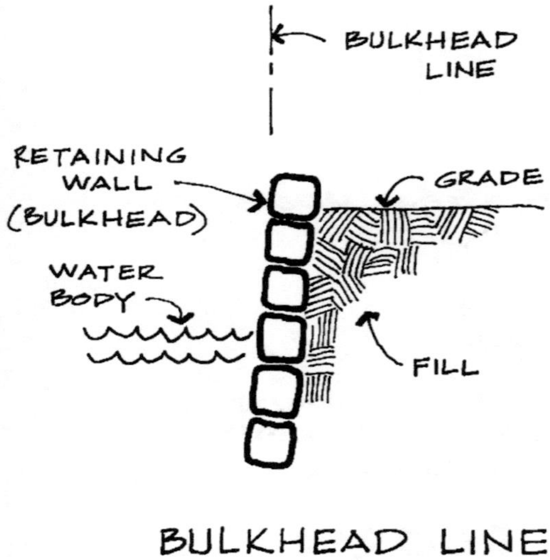


*Comment*: Shelters are often constructed of see-through materials for safety reasons.

*Legal Annotation*: "He was alone in a three-sided Plexiglas **bus shelter** open to the street in downtown Milwaukee." *State v. Stewart* (Wis., 1988).

## BUS TERMINAL OR BUS STATION

**Any premises for the storage or parking of motor-driven buses and the loading and unloading of passengers.**

*Comment*: Bus terminals may include ticket purchase facilities, toilets, restaurants, and stores.

*Legal Annotation*: "The first part of the document showed that Trailways Terminal was then constructing a '**bus station**' with built-in facilities 'for the operation of a restaurant, soda fountain, and news stand.' . . . In short, as Terminal and Restaurant agreed, 'the operation of the restaurant and the said stands shall be in keeping with the character of service maintained in an up-to-date, modern **bus terminal**.'" *Boynton v. Virginia* (U.S., 1960).

## BUS TURNOUT

**A paved indentation at the side of a roadway designed to allow buses to pick up and discharge passengers.** ***See Figure 20.***

*Legal Annotation*: "This case concerns the permissible uses of an easement for a public road right-of-way. Appellants installed a **bus turnout** on the right-of-way." *State v. Homar* (Wyo., 1990).

## BUSINESS CLUSTER ANALYSIS

**An economic development technique that analyzes the economic base of a region as part of the economic element of the local master plan.**

*Comment*: Business cluster analysis is designed to provide insight into a region's economic activities as a basis for attracting new firms and activities. It does so by defining the existing business clusters that share infrastructure, suppliers, business services, support facilities, and distribution facilities. It provides a focus for future efforts in attracting and keeping industries and employment in an area. A community can then develop land-use policies and capital programs to strengthen the base that initially attracted these business clusters.

**Figure 20**

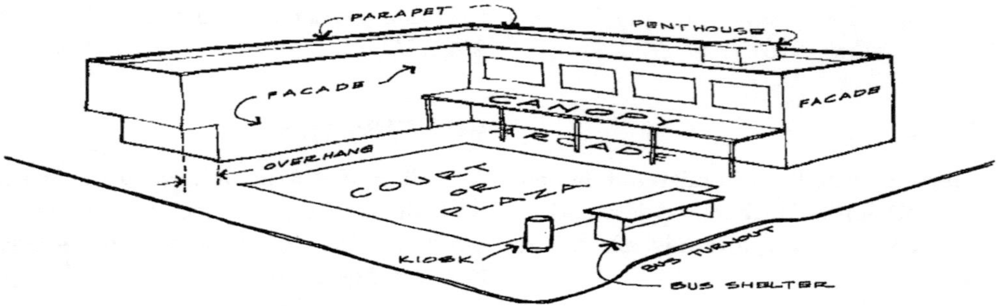

## BUSINESS IMPROVEMENT DISTRICT (BID)

**The BID is a designated area designed to improve an area, often the downtown, by providing enhanced security, cleanup, promotion, and other services, with the costs of these services paid for by the beneficiaries of these enhanced activities—businesses and others in the improvement district (Houston 2004). See *Special Improvement District*.**

*Comment*: BIDs have been very effective in assisting in the revitalization of and maintaining the competiveness of local business areas. Their work primarily focuses on cleanliness, maintenance, and safety but also includes recommendations on building facades and signage, coordinating special events and programs, facilitating streetscape improvements, developing off-street parking, providing liaison to the public and private sector, and providing district maintenance. Some BIDs deploy "community service representatives"—uniformed individuals who "serve as the eyes and ears for other code enforcement agencies." An important reason for the effectiveness of BIDs is their ability to tax themselves in addition to regular taxes and channel the additional revenues into programs directly benefiting the BID (Levy, 2001).

*Legal Annotation*: "Quapaw Central **Business Improvement District** was created by the Little Rock City Board of Directors for the purpose of providing funds to construct improvements to streets, sidewalks, utilities, curbs and gutters, street lighting, landscaping, and other improvements within the district." *Quapaw Cent. Business Improvement Dist. v. Bond-Kinman, Inc.* (Ark., 1994).

## BUSINESS INCUBATOR

**"An organization [or physical space] designed to accelerate the growth and success of entrepreneurial companies through an array of business support resources and services that could include small business-appropriate physical space, capital, coaching, common services, and networking connections." See *Business Services; Flex Space*. http://www.entrepreneur.com/encyclopedia/business-incubator.carney (See also 2009.)**

*Comment*: For discussion of different definitions of a business incubator and the evolution of this term, see http://worldbusinessincubation.wordpress.com/2012/12/10/business-i.

*Legal Annotation*: "He contemplated renovating two existing buildings into a '**business incubator**' office complex where fledgling companies could lease office space and have access to on-site support services." *Hunkins v. City of Minneapolis* (Minn. Ct. App., 1993).

## BUSINESS SERVICES

**Establishments primarily engaged in rendering services to business establishments on a fee or contract basis, such as advertising and mailing; building maintenance; employment services; management and consulting services; protective services; equipment rental and leasing; commercial research, development, and testing; photo finishing; and personal supply services.**

## BUSINESS SIGN

**See *Sign, Business*.**

## BUSWAY

**A road, or lane within a road or highway, specifically designed and reserved solely for the use of buses. See also *Bike/Busway*.**

*Legal Annotation*: "The accident occurred when Mrs. Galvin attempted to cross the busway, a section of roadway used by buses pulling into the station, located between a drop-off island in the parking lot and the platform where passengers board and disembark from buses." *Neagle v. Massachusetts Bay Transportation Authority* (Mass. Ct. App., 1998). http://tinyurl.cm/nror5rr

## BUY-DOWNS

**The purchase of previously owned market-rate dwelling units and offering of them in sound**

**condition at affordable prices to low- and moderate-income households.**

***Comment***: A buy-down program, if permitted by state and local enabling legislation, is a fast and efficient way municipalities can provide low- and moderate-income housing. Since the buy-down program buys existing units, it addresses community concerns with growth, increased densities, or the lack of available land for new housing. In addition, it is particularly cost-effective when the housing market is soft and mortgage rates are low. When purchases are in existing developments with homeowners' associations, exterior maintenance is provided. A buy-down program provides for instant scattered-site housing without concerns about too many low- and moderate-income units in a single location (McGowan and Richter-Reba 1998).

***Legal Annotation***: "Therefore, money to finance approved affordable housing techniques, such as Regional Contribution Agreements . . . rehabilitation programs . . . accessory apartments . . . or write down/**buy down** units . . . must come through development fees." *Bi-County Development of Clinton, Inc. v. Borough of High Bridge* (N.J., 2002).

# C

## CABARET

**A restaurant or bar that has a stage upon which some form of live entertainment such as music, song, dance, recitation, or drama is performed. See *Nightclub*.**

*Comment*: Cabarets are different from nightclubs in that the audience sits at tables at which they are served food and drink, before and sometimes during the performance.

*Legal Annotation*: "A '**cabaret**' is defined as 'an adult club, restaurant, theater, hall or similar place which features topless dancers, go-go dancers, exotic dancers, strippers, male or female impersonators or similar entertainers exhibiting specified anatomical areas[2] 849*849 or performing specified sexual activities.[3]'" Philadelphia Zoning Code § 14-102(24). *Maj v. Zoning Bd. of Adj.* (Pa. Common. Ct., 2008)

## CAFÉ

**A small restaurant primarily serving coffee drinks and light meals, sandwiches and/or desserts and which often includes an outdoor seating area and provides table service indoors and out.**

*Comment*: A café is similar to a coffee shop or espresso bar, but it provides table service and a broader range of food choices. Its menu tends to be oriented to lunchtime food and desserts and is more limited than a full-service restaurant.

*Legal Annotation*: "As we have pointed out, the use of the building in question as a **cafe** would be a permitted use under the general provisions of the zoning regulations, and if the building were to be used for a **cafe** the only nonconformity would be in the failure to provide the off-street parking spaces required by the off-street parking regulations." *Bora v. Zoning Board of Appeals* (Conn., 1971).

## CAFETERIA

**A restaurant in which patrons wait on themselves, carrying their food from counters, where it is displayed and served, to their tables.**

*Legal Annotation*: "DOE-promulgated definitions define a **cafeteria** in terms of the method of food service and available seating facilities. . . . This definition is consistent with the dictionary definition that defines a **cafeteria** as 'a restaurant in which the customers serve themselves or are served at a counter and take the food to tables to eat.' *Webster's Ninth New Collegiate Dictionary* 195." (1991). *Nish v. Rumsfeld* (10th Cir., 2003).

## CALIPER

**The diameter of a tree trunk. *See Figure 21*.**

*Comment*: The measurement distance from ground level should be specified. The usual distance is six inches for trees up to four inches in diameter and twelve inches for larger-diameter trees (American Association of Nurserymen standard). The diameter standard, which may be used to require certain mature trees to remain on a site or require planting of minimum-age trees, will vary with the species. Certain trees, such as birches or dogwoods, are normally thinner; consequently, the standard for such trees would be different from that for other species.

*Legal Annotation*: "According to testimony at trial, **caliper** measures the tree diameter at six inches above the root crown." *New Jersey Shore Builders Ass'n v. Township of Jackson* (N.J., 2009).

## CAMP

**See *Campground; Camping Unit*.**

**Figure 21**

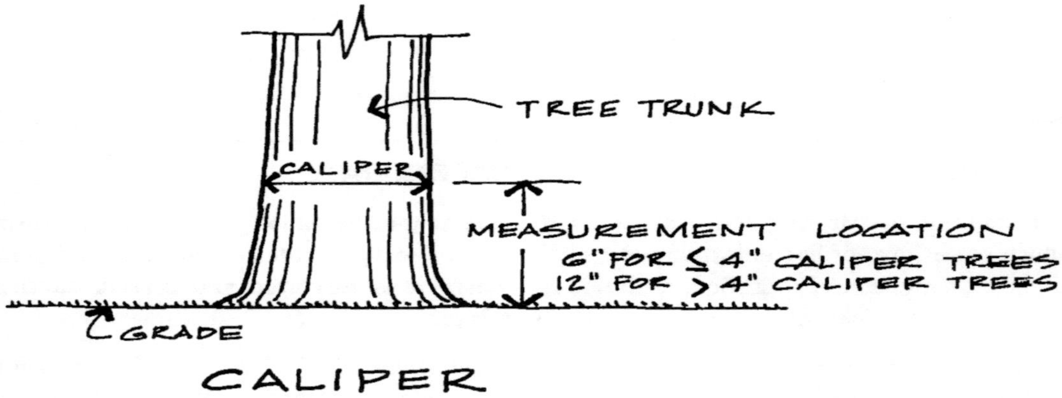


## CAMPER

**Any individual who occupies a campsite or otherwise assumes charge of, or is placed in charge of, a campsite. See *Camping Vehicle, Recreational Vehicle*.**

***Legal Annotation***: "The complaining **camper** also told a park ranger that the campers at the adjacent site received a call warning them that a ranger was coming to investigate the site and that the voice on the call sounded like plaintiff. Following the camper's complaint, plaintiff was reprimanded and suspended with pay for improperly reserving the campsite and her comment to the camper." *Kerns v. State* (Mich. Ct. App., 2010).

## CAMPGROUND

**A plot of ground on which two or more campsites are located, established, or maintained for occupancy by camping units as temporary living quarters for recreation, education, or vacation purposes. See *Camping Unit*.**

***Comment***: Most states regulate campgrounds under a state campground code or sanitary code. Any state definition should be used in the local ordinance. The state code also may prescribe minimum standards, including the amount of space required for each campsite, provision of sanitary facilities, and similar requirements. Local ordinances usually are required to be as strict as the state's, but in some states, they may be stricter. Many state or local ordinances also prohibit occupancy for longer than a specified period of time, often ninety continuous days, in order to prevent these temporary accommodations from becoming permanent.

***Legal Annotation***: "The plaintiff purchased his 85.77-acre **campground** in 1979 for $125,000. The prior owner had built twenty-nine campsites on the property after receiving the required State approval. Without seeking State or local authorization, the plaintiff further developed the land. Nine years later, the campground had approximately 130 campsites, each with water, sewer, and electrical hookups, and several tent sites with limited utility hookups." *Quirk v. Town of New Boston* (N.H., 1995).

## CAMPING UNIT

**Any tent, trailer, cabin, lean-to, recreational vehicle, or similar structure established or maintained and operated in a campground as temporary living quarters for recreation, education, or vacation purposes.**

***Legal Annotation***: "Because plaintiff intends to construct 203 sites in an area of approximately 30 acres, the Board contends that the lot space for each **camping unit**, either tent or camping vehicle, is less than the three-acre minimum for a 'dwelling' under the above provision." *Robinson v. Board of Appeals, Town of Kennebunk* (Maine, 1976).

## CAMPING VEHICLE

**See *Recreational Vehicle*.**

***Legal Annotation***: "These **campers** are mobile and are either towed or driven upon the land. They are titled by the Division of Motor Vehicles. Generally, when in place, the campers are supported by jacks or bricks which are placed under them on the ground. However, such supports, although desirable, are not necessary. The campers are suitable for use as temporary dwellings, and, occasionally, some defendants sleep in them overnight. Electric and natural gas utilities are connected to the campers." *Marks v. Wingfield* (Va., 1985).

## CAMPSITE

**Any plot of ground within a campground intended for exclusive occupancy by a camping unit or units under the control of a camper.**

***Legal Annotation***: "With the annexation of the additional parcels, the campsite consisted of approximately 100 acres. Having satisfied the American Camping Association's requirement that there be one acre of land per camper, the Boys' Club was then accredited by the Association." *Boys' Club of Clifton, Inc. v. Township of Jefferson* (N.J., 1977).

## CAMPUS

**The grounds and buildings of a public or private college, university, school, or institution.**

***Legal Annotation***: "Webster's Dictionary defines '**campus**' as 'the grounds and buildings of a university, college, or school.' *Webster's Ninth New Collegiate Dictionary* 200 (1983)." *Hartman v. Bethany College* (N.D. Va., 1991).

## CANAL

**An artificial waterway for transportation or irrigation.**

***Legal Annotation***: "The Court below held that the mere capability of navigability in commercial use and/or the fact that the canal was subject to the ebb and flow of the tide was sufficient to establish Corps' jurisdiction even over a private and artificial canal." *United States v. DeFelice* ($5^{th}$ Cir., 1981).

## CANDLEPOWER

**Luminous intensity expressed in candelas.**

***Comment***: Candlepower is a measure of illuminating power that has generally been replaced by the foot-candle. For those technically inclined, the luminous intensity is defined as the luminous flux per unit solid angle in a given direction. See *Foot-Candle; Lumen*.

***Legal Annotation***: "Although not clearly stated, we infer from this comment that the report was referring to '**candlepower**,' a measure of luminous intensity. *Webster's II New College Dictionary* 161 (2001)." *Zack v. State* (N.J. App. Div., 2012).

## CANOPY

**See *Awning. See Figure 20.***

## CANTILIVER

**A part of a beam or structure projecting beyond its support. *See Figure 22***

Comment: The local zoning ordinance should specify whether cantilevered elements, such as a porch, balcony, or some other overhang, can project beyond the minimum setback line. Often, if the projection is only minimal, two to four feet for example, and less than six to eight feet wide, projection beyond the required setback line may be permitted.

**Figure 22**

## CAPABILITIES-BASED PLANNING

**Capabilities-based planning is defined in the National Preparedness Goal as "planning, under uncertainty, to provide capabilities suitable for a wide range of threats and hazards while working within an economic framework that necessitates prioritization and choice."**

***Comment***: Capabilities-based planning addresses uncertainty by analyzing a wide range of scenarios to identify required capabilities. This approach seeks to provide a means for the nation to answer three fundamental questions: "How prepared do we need to be?", "How prepared are we?", and "How do we prioritize efforts to close the gap?" At the heart of this capability-based planning process is the Target Capabilities List (TCL) (version 2.0). The TCL identifies thirty-six national preparedness capabilities, provides a description of each capability, and presents guidance on the levels of capability that federal, state, local, and tribal entities will be expected to develop and maintain. http://www.gwu.edu/~icdrm/publications/PDF/GLOSSARY%2002-19-2007.pdf

***Legal Annotation***: "As such, while this directive is intended to galvanize action by the Federal Government, it is also aimed at facilitating an integrated, all-of-Nation, **capabilities-based** approach to preparedness." *Presidential Policy Directive / PPD-8*: *National Preparedness* (March 30, 2011).

## CAPACITY, ROADWAY

**The maximum hourly rate at which vehicles can reasonably be expected to traverse a point or uniform section of a lane or roadway during a given time period under the prevailing roadway, traffic, and control conditions (Transportation Research Board 2000). See *Level of Service*.**

***Comment***: Roadway capacity is defined in terms of levels of service. Six levels of service are described, designated from A through F, with A representing the best operating conditions and level F the worst. Level C is usually designated as the level minimally uncongested.

Briefly, the level of service A represents free flow, B stable flow, and C also stable but starting to be affected by other drivers. Level of service D starts to experience some congestion, with speed and freedom to maneuver restricted. Level of service E is a level in which the road is operating at or near capacity, speed is slow, and comfort and convenience are poor. Level F is forced or breakdown flow, with severe congestion.

***Legal Annotation***: "The township contends that its roadway system lacks the capacity to serve the existing population and future development. To address this problem it has adopted a capital improvement program to increase **roadway capacity**." *Toll Bros. v. West Windsor Tp.* (N.J. App. Div., 1998).

## CAPACITY ANALYSIS

**Determining and evaluating the capacity of natural systems, infrastructure, and social and fiscal systems to define the carrying capacity for existing development and future growth of a municipality or region (*New Jersey State Development and Redevelopment Plan* 2000).**

***Comment***: Capacity analysis is a useful planning tool for evaluating the impacts of alternative growth scenarios.

***Legal Annotation***: "It does make clear, however, that the recreation plan itself cannot be read as imposing a duty on FERC to block development solely in light of any particular level of carrying capacity, or to assess proposals in light of a carrying **capacity analysis**." *Brady v. Federal Energy Regulatory Commission* (D.C. Ct. App., 2005).

## CAPITAL FACILITIES

**The land, buildings, and other physical facilities under public ownership, or operated or maintained for public benefit, that are necessary to support development and redevelopment and to protect the public health, safety, and welfare.**

***Legal Annotation***: "The quality of a district's **capital facilities** is directly proportional to the value of real property within the district." *Roosevelt Elem. School Dist. V. Bishop* (Ariz., 1994).

## CAPITAL IMPROVEMENT

**An acquisition of real property, major construction projects, or acquisition of expensive equipment expected to last a long time. See *Improvement*.**

***Comment***: Capital improvements are usually large, nonrecurring items. They are often financed by the sale of bonds. Many ordinances specify a minimum expenditure or cost to qualify as a capital improvement.

***Legal Annotation***: "It questioned whether certain items were properly included in the **capital improvement** budget, contending that they were routine maintenance items that should be funded exclusively by the City Board." *Liddell v. State of Missouri* (8th Cir., 1984).

## CAPITAL IMPROVEMENTS PROGRAM (CIP)

**A timetable or schedule of all future capital improvements to be carried out during a specific period, listed in order of priority, together with cost estimates and the anticipated means and sources of financing each project.**

***Comment***: The capital improvements program is usually a six-year program, with the first year being the capital improvements budget.

***Legal Annotation***: "Second, the Town maintains that the trial court's reliance on the Town's lack of a **capital improvements program** (CIP), which is a growth management tool, was error, because the subdivision denial was based on the violation of subdivision regulations, which are different from growth control regulations." *Zukis v. Town of Fitzwilliam* (N.H., 1992).

## CAPITAL OUTLAY

**Direct expenditure for contract or force account construction of buildings, grounds, and other improvements, and purchase of equipment, land, and existing structures.**

***Comment***: Capital outlay includes amounts for additions, replacements, and major alterations to fixed works and structures. However, expenditure for repairs to such works and structures is classified as current operation expenditure. http://census.gov/govs/local/definitions.htm

*Legal Annotation*: "The term 'current expenses' is defined in Black's Law Dictionary as follows: 'Ordinary, regular, and continuing expenditures for the maintenance of property, the carrying on of an office, municipal government, etc.' In the same work, **capital outlay** is defined as: 'Money expended in acquiring, equipping, and promoting an enterprise.'" Osage County Excise Bd. v. Missouri-Kansas-Texas Railroad Co. (Ok. 1959).

## CAPPED SYSTEM

**A completed water supply and/or sewerage system, put in place for future use, rather than to meet immediate development needs.**

*Comment*: The capped system may be needed to accommodate a proposed expansion of the development or the installation or the expansion of treatment or supply facilities.

## CARBON DIOXIDE ($CO_2$)

**A colorless, odorless, nonpoisonous gas that is a normal part of the ambient air and is a product of fossil fuel combustion.**

*Legal Annotation*: "We hold that the Clean Air Act and the EPA actions it authorizes displace any federal common law right to seek abatement of **carbon-dioxide** emissions from fossil-fuel fired power plants. Massachusetts made plain that emissions of carbon dioxide qualify as air pollution subject to regulation under the Act." *American Elec. Power Co. v. Connecticut* (U.S., 2011).

## CARBON MONOXIDE (CO)

**A colorless, odorless, highly toxic gas that is a normal by-product of incomplete fossil fuel combustion.**

*Legal Annotation*: **"[C]arbon monoxide** is not only defined in common dictionaries as a 'colorless odorless very toxic gas' . . . but it is also regulated by the federal government as a 'pollutant.'" *American States Ins. Co. v. Koloms* (Ill., 1997).

## CARPOOL, CARPOOLING

**Two or more people sharing car journeys by means of a privately owned vehicle, either using one car and sharing expenses or alternating vehicles so that no money changes hands.**

*Comment*: Carpooling is similar to vanpooling but differs in that in carpooling, the driver is usually the car owner. In vanpooling, the vehicle is usually owned by the employer, and the driver rides free in return for maintaining the van and serving as driver. From a zoning perspective, carpooling reduces the number of parking spaces needed for any use that employs the system. Zoning regulations might permit an applicant with a viable carpooling program to request relief from installing all of the required off-street parking. The site plan would show the required parking for which relief is requested, but it would not have to be installed unless a new occupant without a carpooling plan moved into the premises.

*Legal Annotation*: "Five members of the crew . . . traveled to and from the drilling site in a **carpool**; that is, each member of the crew owned an automobile and each fifth working day used his automobile to transport himself and the others, at his own expense, from Yorktown to the drillsite in going to work and from the drillsite to Yorktown in returning home." *Janak v. Texas Employers' Insurance Association* (Texas, 1964).

## CARPORT

**A roofed structure providing space for the parking of motor vehicles and enclosed on not more than three sides.**

*Legal Annotation*: "The **carport** . . . was contiguous to the dwelling. It consisted of a cement slab, a roof that was flush with the roof of the dwelling, and four aluminum poles supporting the roof. The **carport** shared a wall with the dwelling, and the kitchen door opened onto the **carport**. The

**carport** was no longer used for parking vehicles and contained miscellaneous items." *State v. Burston* (Fla. Ct. App., 1997).

## CARRYING CAPACITY

**The maximum sustainable capacity that a system can accommodate indefinitely.**

*Comment*: Carrying capacity originated as an ecological term, defined as the maximum population that a biological species could attain in a specific environment. The term has been coopted and adapted in traffic engineering, environmental impact assessment, and land use planning, where the maximum sustainable capacity of the natural or built environment is in question. The definition herein is therefore deliberately broad and general and needs to be further refined in terms of the specific system and what capacity is measured and how. For example, the carrying capacity of a roadway system can be defined in terms of the maximum number of vehicles the roadway system can accommodate during peak traffic hours. Utility systems (potable water, storm water drainage, sewerage, electricity, etc.) can be similarly quantified. Carrying capacity can be applied to the impact of development (existing and/or proposed) on the natural environment (air quality, open space, plant and animal habitat, for example) and the built environment (schools, recreational opportunities, medical and health facilities, housing by type and density, and jobs, goods and services).

In the final analysis, carrying capacity determines the extent and intensity of development and is reflected in the various controls and laws that regulate development. See *Buildout Analysis; Holding Capacity.*

*Legal Annotation*: "The 'average annual **carrying capacity**' is defined as 'the average number of animal units which can be supported by a section of grazing land with due consideration for sustained production of the forage consistent with conservative range management.' A.R.S. § 37-101(3)." *Ariz. State Land Dept. v. R. H. Fulton* (Ariz. Ct. App., 1978).

## CARRYOUT COLLECTION

**Collection of solid waste from a storage area proximate to a business or other establishment.**

## CARRYOUT RESTAURANT

**An establishment that by design of the physical facilities, service, or packaging, sells prepared ready-to-eat foods intended primarily to be consumed off the premises. See *Restaurant, Take-Out*.**

*Comment*: Many primarily carryout restaurants also have tables, further blurring the distinction between conventional restaurants and carryout places. If space for parking is limited, the number of tables should be restricted.

*Legal Annotation*: "After this brief conversation, Byrd decided to go instead to a nearby **carryout restaurant** and buy something that was already prepared so that he would not have to cook it when he got home." *Hairston v. United States* (D.C. Ct. App., 2006).

## CAR SHARING

**A computerized private membership auto rental system that provides, at designated locations, vehicles that are reserved, accessed, used, and then returned to designated locations by system members.**

*Comment*: Car sharing is a relatively new activity found in large urban areas and at college campuses. It offers easy access to motor vehicles for persons and businesses that require short-term use of a car on an intermittent basis. The cost of gas, insurance, maintenance, and reserved parking is usually included in the membership rental fee. Municipal permission for the use of street locations for car-sharing vehicles is not unlike taxi stands and designated locations for official vehicles and cars with special license plates. Car-sharing members find car locations through digital technology and have membership cards to gain access to the vehicles.

Hertz on Demand, Enterprise WeCar, and U Car Share are examples of current car-sharing operations. According to the Transportation

Sustainability Research Center at the University of California, Berkeley, membership in car-sharing organizations were expected to exceed six hundred thousand by the end of 2013 with over ten thousand available cars (Biesczat and Schwieterman 2012: 38).

*Legal Annotation*: "FlightCar is a startup **car sharing** company which allows vehicle owners to park their cars for free at a FlightCar lot, usually located close to an airport, provided that FlightCar can, in turn, rent out the vehicle while the owner is away." *Flightcar v. City of Millbrae* (N.D. Calif., 2014).

## CAR WASH

**Any building or premises used for washing motor vehicles.**

***Comment***: Car wash establishments usually perform polishing, and many provide detailing and minor body-repair services. Some car washes have vacuum machines to allow owners to clean the interiors of their vehicles. See *Automatic Car Wash*.

*Legal Annotation*: "[M]rs. Tryon worked regularly at the 'Rapid **Car Wash**', a business owned by Mr. Tryon devoted to washing, cleaning and polishing automobiles for automobile dealers and the public." *Tryon v. Casey* (Mo. Ct. App., 1967).

## CARTWAY

**The paved area of a street or road between the curbs, including travel and parking lanes and acceleration and deceleration lanes, but not including shoulders, curbs, sidewalks, or swales. *See Figure 1.***

***Comment***: Where there are no curbs, the cartway is that part between the edges of the paved, or hard-surface, width.

*Legal Annotation*: "The regulations define '**cartway**' as 'the actual road surface area from curbline to curbline' and 'curb' as 'a stone, concrete, or other improved boundary marking the edge of the roadway or paved area.'" N.J.A.C. 5:21-1.4. *Norris v. Borough of Leonia* (N.J., 1999).

## CASINO

**A room or rooms or building in which legal gaming is conducted.**

*Legal Annotation*: "The Taj Mahal will be the largest **casino**/hotel complex in Atlantic City, with approximately twice the room capacity and **casino** space of many of the existing **casino**/hotels in Atlantic City." *In re Donald J. Trump Casino Securities Litigation* (D.C. N.J., 1992).

"The Sands consists of a **casino** and simulcasting facility, which contains approximately 2,000 slot machines and 125 table games; a hotel with 532 rooms, six restaurants, two cocktail lounges and two private lounges." *In re Greate Bay Hotel & Casino, Inc.* (Bankr. Court, D. N.J., 2000).

## CASINO HOTEL

**See *Hotel, Casino*.**

## CATALYTIC CONVERTER

**An air pollution abatement device that removes organic contaminants by oxidizing them into carbon dioxide and water through chemical reaction and that is used to reduce nitrogen oxide emissions from motor vehicles.**

*Legal Annotation*: "A **catalytic converter** can reduce carbon monoxide emissions by 60–80 percent by promoting a chemical reaction among the carbon monoxide, hydrocarbons, and oxygen." *Chrysler Corp. v. US Environmental Protection* (D.C. Ct. App., 1980).

## CATCH BASIN

**An inlet designed to intercept and redirect surface waters.**

*Legal Annotation*: "'C/B' is an abbreviation for '**catch basin**,' which is essentially an open box set into the street and covered by a metal grate. Its purpose is to collect water." *Bruni v. City of New York* (N.Y., 2004).

## CATEGORY KILLER

**See *Retail Store, Category Killer*.**

## CATERING ESTABLISHMENT

**An establishment in which food is prepared and typically served or delivered to an off-site location. See *Banquet Facility*.**

*Comment*: Catering establishments can be provided in standalone buildings and deliver their prepared food to a home, a social hall, or another off-site venue. A catering establishment that also serves the food on-site in a formal setting is a banquet facility. Sometimes catering can be conducted within a restaurant or other eating or drinking establishment as an accessory use. Note that the term does not include mobile catering, in which the food service is delivered directly to customers from a vehicle (cart or truck).

*Legal Annotation*: "In 2007, after receiving complaints from some of the Church's neighbors (to which the Church responded), the DOB issued a Notice of Intent to Revoke the previously given permit. That Notice stated that 'the **catering establishment** is not an accessory use because . . . it appears to be a principal commercial establishment at the premises.'" *Third Church of Christ v. City of New York*, (2nd Cir., 2010).

## CELLAR

**A space with less than one half of its floor-to-ceiling height above the average finished grade of the adjoining ground. A space with more than one half of its floor-to-ceiling height above the average grade of the adjoining ground that has a floor-to-ceiling height of less than six and a half feet is also a cellar. See *Basement; Story. See Figure 8.***

*Comment*: Cellars are typically used only for storage or for HVAC or utility equipment accessory to the principal structure, or for uninhabitable space. In such circumstances, they are not counted as a story or in the computation of the intensity of land use, such as floor area ratio. In some jurisdictions, cellars that have floor-to-ceiling heights over six and a half feet are considered to be "basements," and the habitable space is counted toward the FAR. However, they are still not considered to be a "story."

*Legal Annotation*: "The Zoning Resolution defines '**cellar**' in R3 zoning districts as: 'a space wholly or partly below the base plane with more than one-half its height (measured from floor to ceiling) below the base plane.'" *MTR Raritan Dev. Corp. v. Silva* (N.Y., 1997).

## CELLS

**With respect to solid waste disposal, earthen compartments in which solid wastes are dumped, compacted, and covered over daily with layers of earth.**

*Legal Annotation*: "[B]rackenrich agreed to furnish various services, which included the design of increased disposal **cell** capacity for solid waste disposal and the addition of a constructed wetland system to treat leachate from the landfill waste disposal cells before its discharge into the environment." *Webster County v. Brackenrich & Assoc.* (W. Va., 2005).

## CELLULAR TOWER SITE

**See *Wireless Telecommunications Towers and Facilities*.**

## CEMETERY

**Property used for the interment of the dead.**

*Comment*: Most development ordinances do not include provisions for cemeteries. They are so unusual a use that they are generally handled by variance. When cemeteries are regulated in the development ordinance, height and setback standards should be established for crematories and mausoleums, where the bodies are interred above ground in stacked vaults. In areas with high water tables, this is a fairly common type of burial.

*Legal Annotation*: "The plaintiff was organized in 1938 as The Mason **Cemetery** Association, Inc., for the purpose of 'maintaining and operating a cemetery for the burial of deceased members of the Masonic order in good standing and their families and relatives, and for the burial of such other human remains as may subsequently be provided for by the Board of Directors.'" *Fairlawns Cemetery Assn., Inc. v. Zoning Commission* (Conn., 1952).

## CENSUS

**An official periodic enumeration of a designated geographic area's population, housing, and related characteristics.**

***Legal Annotation***: "The Census Bureau (Bureau) has announced a plan to use two forms of statistical sampling in the 2000 Decennial **Census** to address a chronic and apparently growing problem of 'under counting' certain identifiable groups of individuals." *Dept. of Commerce v. United States House of Representatives* (U.S., 1999).

## CENSUS TRACT

**Small areas into which large cities and adjacent areas have been divided for statistical purposes.**

***Legal Annotation***: "The rate of nonresponse follow-up in a tract would vary with the mail response rate to ensure that the Bureau obtains census data from at least 90 percent of the housing units in each **census tract**." *Dept. of Commerce v. US House of Representatives* (U.S., 1999).

## CENTER ISLAND NARROWING

**See *Traffic Calming*.**

## CENTERLINE OFFSET

**The distance between the centerline of roads intersecting a common road, as measured along the centerline of the common road. See *Access Point Offset*.**

***Legal Annotation***: "Thus, even assuming the intersection here has a **centerline offset** of less than 125 feet, the plain language of the ordinance indicates this is a recommendation and not a requirement." *Neighbors v. Valley County* (Idaho., 2007).

## CENTRAL BUSINESS DISTRICT (CBD)

**The largest, most intensively developed mixed-use area within a city, usually containing, in addition to major retail uses, governmental offices; service uses; professional, cultural, recreational, and entertainment establishments and uses; residences; hotels; appropriate industrial activities; and transportation facilities.**

***Comment***: There is no hard-and-fast rule as to what the CBD may include. In fact, all uses are appropriate, providing they do not adversely infringe on other uses or diminish the traditional retail, office, cultural, and entertainment functions. Controls on industry in the CBD, for example, might restrict them from prime, first-floor locations, which should be used for retail activities. Even open space and passive recreational facilities have a place in the CBD.

***Legal Annotation***: "The City zoned its **central business district** commercial (C-3) with the intent of establishing 'a community-regional commerce district . . . in recognition of the existing downtown commercial development and of the need for its future expansions, rehabilitation and redevelopment.'" *Cornerstone Bible Church v. City of Hastings* (8th Cir., 1991).

## CERTIFICATE OF APPROPRIATENESS

**A certificate issued by the approving authority on approval of the exterior architectural features of any new building construction or alterations to an existing building located within a historic zone.**

***Comment***: Certificates of appropriateness are often required in historic or other special design districts before the issuance of a building or zoning permit and are typically limited to the exterior architectural features of a building. In some historic district ordinance procedures, the application review is carried out by a special design review committee of local experts, and their nonbinding recommendations are forwarded to the approving authority for consideration and action.

In a historic district, the review is usually limited to architectural features that are visible from a public street. For a special design district (a central business district, for example), the basis for review is typically the conformance of the development proposal to the adopted area design plan. See *Certificate of Compliance.*

***Legal Annotation***: "Second, the owner may apply to the Commission for a **certificate of 'appropriateness.'** . . . Such certificates will be granted if the Commission concludes—focusing upon aesthetic, historical, and architectural values—that the proposed construction on the landmark site would not unduly hinder the protection, enhancement, perpetuation, and use of the landmark." *Penn Central Transp. Co. v. New York City* (U.S., 1978).

## CERTIFICATE OF COMPLIANCE

**A document issued by the proper authority certifying that the plans for a proposed use meet all applicable codes and regulations.**

*Legal Annotation*: "On 6 June 1991, the Durham City-County Inspections Department issued a **Certificate of Compliance** for the house. The certificate stated that the house was in substantial compliance with applicable building and zoning ordinances." *Nolan v. Paramount Homes* (NC, 1999).

## CERTIFICATE OF NEED

**A document required to be obtained before certain facilities can be constructed or expanded.**

***Comment***: Certificates of need are usually required before a health facility can be constructed and/or an existing one expanded. Certificates of need may also be required for subsidized housing facilities and may be a condition for certain other public uses. In many states, when a certificate of need is required, it provides the critical proof for the grant of a variance or approval of a conditional use.

***Legal Annotation***: "Included in these guidelines is the requirement that each State establish a '**certificate of need**' program under which all new institutional health facilities must seek state approval prior to construction." *National Gerimedical Hospital and Gerontology Center v. Blue Cross of Kansas City* (U.S., 1981).

## CERTIFICATE OF OCCUPANCY (CO)

**A document issued by a governmental authority allowing the occupancy or use of a building and certifying that the structure or use has been constructed and will be used in compliance with all the applicable municipal codes and ordinances.**

***Comment***: One of the questions with respect to COs is whether a temporary CO is a viable regulatory device. In theory, if an applicant does not meet certain conditions of approval by certain dates, the CO is lifted. In practice, once issued, COs are difficult to revoke. A better arrangement is to require the posting of bonds or a letter of credit to guarantee the completion of all required improvements. Some local jurisdictions require a Continuing Certificate of Occupancy when a building's tenant or ownership changes—referred to as a "CCO." See *Temporary Permit.*

***Legal Annotation***: "The occupancy of the building at 14 Norwich Avenue has been changed from residential use to business use. The building is to remain vacant and no occupancy is permitted until the **Certificate of Occupancy** has been issued by this office." *Brady v. Town of Colchester* (2nd Cir., 1988).

## CERTIFICATION

**A written statement by the appropriate officer that required constructions, inspections, tests, or notices have been performed and comply with applicable requirements.**

***Legal Annotation***: "The Act requires that a utility seeking to build in California any electric power generating plant, including a nuclear powerplant, must apply for **certification** to the State Energy Resources Conservation and Development Commission (Energy Commission)." *Pacific Gas & Electric Co. v. State Energy Resources Conservation and Development Commission* (U.S., 1983).

## CESSPOOL

**A covered pit with open, jointed lining where untreated sewage is discharged, the liquid portion of which is disposed of by seepage or**

**leaching into the surrounding porous soil; the solids, or sludge, being retained in the pit.**

*Legal Annotation*: "The rest of the Nassau and Suffolk County residents depend upon **cesspools**, septic tanks and other individual disposal systems for their sewage. The seepage of untreated wastewater from these **cesspools** and septic tanks has, by contamination, threatened the quality of underground water which serves as the sole drinking water supply." *Environmental Defense Fund v. Costle* (E.D. N.Y., 1977).

## CFS

**Cubic feet per second.**

*Comment*: The measure of the amount of liquid or gas passing a given point.

*Legal Annotation*: "The annual flow of the Connecticut [river] at the Massachusetts-Connecticut boundary is about 17,000 **cubic feet per second**, approximately 11,000 million gallons a day." *Connecticut v. Massachusetts* (U.S., 1931).

## CHAIN

**A lineal measure equal to sixty-six feet.**

*Comment*: This surveyor's measure is no longer in use. Many street right-of-way widths were laid out as thirty-three feet, or half a chain.

*Legal Annotation*: "In older deeds, distances were measured in **chains** with links of a known length, such as a Gunter's Chain. The Gunter's **Chain** was designed and introduced in the early 1600's by English clergyman and mathematician Edmund Gunter to enable plots of land to be accurately surveyed and plotted. One **chain** equals 66 feet." *Muldrow v. Jones*, (Fla. Ct. App., 2010).

## CHAIN STORE

**Retail outlets with the same name, selling similar types of merchandise, operating under a common merchandising policy, and usually owned or franchised by a single corporate entity.**

*Legal Annotation*: "The prime function of petitioner's **chain store** system is to sell groceries at retail. Like most large chains, however, petitioner has found it economically feasible to perform and integrate both the retail and wholesale functions of the grocery business." *AH Phillips, Inc. v. Walling* (U.S., 1945).

## CHANGE OF USE

**(1) A change from one use classification in the zoning ordinance to another use classification; (2) any use that differs substantially from the previous use of a building or land.**

*Comment*: Change of use is important in that where such change is substantial, site plan approval may be required. Most courts have indicated that a change of occupancy or a change of ownership in and by itself should not be construed as a change of use. However, many ordinances require site plan approval where a change of use is proposed. This level of review should, however, be reserved only in those circumstances where the new use is substantially different from the previous use. Thus, a retail clothing store selling men's clothes would not be substantially different from a retail store selling women's shoes, and site plan approval would not be required. Whether a retail clothing store would be considered substantially different from a drugstore, and whether site plan approval would be required under such circumstances, is debatable.

From a zoning perspective, change of use is important only if it affects any of the usual elements involved in site plan review: parking, drainage, traffic, circulation, landscaping, signage, building arrangements, and nuisance factors, such as lighting and noise. If they remain the same, it is questionable as to why a new site plan is needed, and a waiver of that requirement may be appropriate.

A New Jersey Supreme Court case (*Belleville v. Parrillo's, Inc.*, 83 N.J. 309 [1980]) provides further insight as to when a change of use takes place. Cox (2003) writes:

> In that case a restaurant was changed to a "disco" and a proceeding was brought in the Municipal Court charging violation of the zoning

ordinance. The defendant's conviction was reversed by the Appellate Division, which held that there was not a change of use, but the Supreme Court disagreed. The Appellate Division had found that each aspect of the "new" business had been conducted previously, e.g., food had been served previously and continued to be; there had been music in the restaurant and continued to be; there was serving of alcoholic beverages previously and continued to be. The Supreme Court held that this quantitative analysis was improper and that the focus in cases of this type must be on the quality, character and intensity of the use viewed in their totality and with regard to the overall effect on the neighborhood and zoning plan (83 N.J. 309 at 314). As a restaurant it had been open every day but now was open only one day and three evenings; the primary use of the dance hall had been incidental to dining but was now a primary use; the music was formerly provided by live bands and was now recorded; admission charges were now made whereas there had been none; the bulk of the prior business was food catering, which now was discontinued. The Court concluded that there had indeed been a change of use and that the defendant was properly convicted. . . . The Supreme Court [also] noted that "an increase in the time period during which a conforming use is operated may justifiably be the basis for finding an unlawful extension thereof, just as changes in the functional uses of the land or increases in the area of use have been." *(Belleville v. Parrillo's, Inc.* at 317–18.)

***Legal Annotation***: "Since we cannot properly exercise our function of judicial review without a record of adequate findings by the board or the Planning Commission on which it based its decision to allow a **change of use** within a zone, it is within our province to require such findings as an essential part of the Board's procedure." *Roseta v. County of Washington* (Ore., 1969).

## CHANNEL

**A watercourse with a definite bed and banks that confine and conduct the normal continuous or intermittent flow of water.**

***Legal Annotation***: "A natural watercourse is defined as a course or **channel** consisting of well-defined banks and a bottom through which water flows in a definite direction for a substantial period each year." *Gasway v. Lalen* (Ind. Ct. App., 1988).

## CHANNELIZATION

**(1) The straightening and deepening of channels and/or the surfacing thereof to permit water to move rapidly and/or directly; (2) a traffic control device that forces vehicles into certain traffic flows or turning movements.**

***Legal Annotation***: "The Master Plan consists of the **channelization** of Murrieta Creek and its major tributaries and includes several concrete lined open channels and a small network of underground storm drains." *Endangered Habitats League, Inc. v. St. Water Red. Ctrl. Bd.* (Calif. Ct. App., 1997).

## CHARACTER

**Special physical characteristics of a structure or area that set it apart from its surroundings and contribute to its interest and/or individuality.**

***Comment***: Examples of an area's character might include: a residential gridiron pattern; tree-lined streets with alleys for garage access and trash removal; a business district with uniformity in building scale, materials, setbacks, street furniture, and sign design; or a waterfront promenade with fountains, public art, and design-coordinated street furniture of benches, light standards, and trash receptacles. (Source: *New Jersey Planner*, Winter 2005–2006: 10. Court case discussing inappropriate character for the neighborhood.)

***Legal Annotation***: "We hold, therefore that a provision in a restrictive covenant as to the **character** of the structure which may be located upon a lot does not by itself constitute a restriction of the premises to a particular use." *JT Hobby & Son, Inc. v. Family Homes, Etc.* (N.C., 1981).

## CHARGING STATION

**The physical device that provides a connection from a power source to an electric vehicle.**

*Comment*: Also referred to as an electric vehicle charging station, or EVCS.

*Legal Annotation*: **"Electric vehicle charging station** means a public or private parking space that is served by battery charging station equipment that has as its primary purpose the transfer of electric energy (by conductive or inductive means) to a battery or other energy storage device in an electric vehicle. An electric vehicle charging station equipped with Level 1 or Level 2 charging equipment is permitted outright as an accessory use to any principal use." *Section V-T Electric Vehicle Charging Stations and Electric Vehicle Battery Exchange Stations, Metheun, MA* (approved 10/27/2010).

## CHARITABLE USE

**A use that provides essential goods or services, such as food, housing, clothing, counseling, aid, or assistance, to those in need, for no fee or compensation or at a fee recognized as being significantly less than the cost of the goods or services.**

*Legal Annotation*: "A **charitable use**, where neither law nor public policy forbids, may be applied to almost anything that tends to promote the well-doing and well-being of social man." *Ould v. Washington Hospital for Foundlings* (U.S., 1877).

## CHARRETTE

**A highly focused, broad-based public work effort to develop consensus on a variety of design issues.**

*Comment*: A charrette is named after the horse-drawn cart that, during the Beaux Arts period, collected the elaborate drawings and models prepared by French architecture students for their design projects. Even though their projects were imminently due, the students would often ride in the cart with their drawings, adding finishing touches as they and their work were conveyed across town to be judged by the faculty (Lardner/Klein Landscape Architects 1998).

The National Charrette Institute distinguishes charrettes from other workshops by their intense, collaborative nature, their holistic approach, and their focus on a feasible solution (Lennertz 2006; Lennertz 2011).

*Legal Annotation*: "Deller invited Clark and his colleagues at DDG to do a '**charrette**'—design and architectural parlance for 'a workshop with one's client or his team.' As Deller described it, the plan was 'to design the whole project, in essence,' to develop a design concept and a 'master plan,' and to begin creating models." *Development Design Group, Inc. v. Deller* (D.C. Md., 2012).

## CHATTEL

**Personal property as contrasted with real estate.**

*Legal Annotation*: "*Black's Law Dictionary*, Seventh Edition, defines **chattel** as movable or transferable property, especially personal property." *Evans v. Woodard* (Ark. Ct. App., 2007).

## CHECK CASHING

**See *Financial Service Center*.**

## CHECKERBOARDING

**Undersized adjoining lots being owned alternately by two individuals.**

*Comment*: Cox tells of the case of a husband and wife who owned a number of adjoining lots as tenants by the entirety. Prior to a new zoning amendment that upgraded minimum lot sizes, they conveyed the lots alternately to each other in an attempt to circumvent the upgrading requirements. The local board of adjustment rejected an application for a variance since adjacent land was available at a reasonable price to bring the lots up to the minimum required by the ordinance. In addition, any hardship would be considered self-created (Cox 2003).

*Legal Annotation*: "'**Checkerboarding**' refers to a practice by which a large landowner divides his property into single lots held by 'straws.' Ownership of the property is then divided so as to avoid having two adjacent lots held by one person. Employing the graphics of the checkerboard, Mr. X holds all the black squares, while Mr. Y holds all the red ones and neither 'owner' holds two contiguous squares. Thus using two 'straws,' a large parcel of land could be divided between two parties. The two 'straws' were protected from any subsequent increases in minimum frontage or area requirements as owners of single noncontiguous lots under the old zoning enabling act, G.L.c. 40A, § 5A." *Baldiga v. Board of Appeals of Uxbridge* (Mass., 1985).

## CHEMICAL OXYGEN DEMAND (COD)

**A measure of the amount of oxygen required to oxidize organic and oxidizable inorganic compounds in water.**

***Comment***: The COD test, like the BOD (biological oxygen demand) test, is used to determine the degree of pollution in an effluent.

***Legal Annotation***: "**COD** measures the amount of oxygen removed by the chemical oxidation of biodegradable and non-biodegradable materials, while BOD measures only the amount of oxygen removed by the biological degradation of organic matter." *FMC Corp. v. Train* (4th Circ., 1976).

## CHICANES

**See *Traffic Calming*.**

## CHILD-CARE CENTER

**An establishment providing for the care, supervision, and protection of children.**

***Comment***: Child care emerged as one of the critical planning issues of the 1980s and will continue to be critical because of the number of women in the workforce with children under the age of six years. Regulations vary by state or municipality, including restrictions relating to the number of children permitted. The general definition is all-inclusive and requires further refinement for zoning use. Some of these refinements are suggested below.

EXEMPT CHILD-CARE CENTER: Many states permit child care in private residences as permitted uses for a specified number of children—five or fewer, for example. This type of child care is the most widely used and, according to some experts, the preferred method. It is referred to as "family day care" because it is provided in a private residence occupied by the provider of the day care.

FAMILY DAY-CARE CENTER/HOME OCCUPATION: New Jersey and some other states use a different approach and require municipalities to treat family day-care centers as any home occupation is treated. If home occupations are allowed in residential zones, family day-care centers must also be permitted. No additional or more restrictive controls are permitted (N.J.S.A. 40:55D-66.4). The problem in using general home occupation criteria for family day-care centers is that they often limit the amount of square footage that the home occupation can occupy. The home occupation requirements must be carefully reviewed to ensure that they are not onerous.

Typically, a family day-care center is defined as a private residence, approved by a public or nonprofit agency, in which child-care services are regularly provided to no less than three and no more than five children for no less than fifteen hours per week. Children legally related to the provider are not included in the care limits, nor are children who are part of a cooperative agreement between parents for the care of their children by one or more of the parents and where no payment for the care is being provided.

LICENSED CHILD-CARE CENTER: A third category of child-care centers is the licensed center that is regulated by a governmental agency (usually the state) and that by definition meets stringent licensing requirements. The requirement for state licensing is often triggered by the number of children in the center.

The planner has to decide in which zones licensed centers are appropriate. They could be permitted in residential zones, for instance, as conditional uses. In nonresidential districts, many states have followed the lead of New Jersey, which makes child-care centers permitted uses in all nonresidential districts, eliminates all off-street parking requirements, and exempts the floor area from any density or floor area ratio limits (N.J.S.A. 40:55D-66.6).

Recent unpublished court cases have also recognized child-care centers in nonresidential zones as customary accessory uses.

*Legal Annotation*: "[Iowa Code § 237A.1 defines] a '**child care center**' as 'a facility providing child care or preschool services for seven or more children, except when the facility is registered as a child development home.'" *Doe v. Miller* (S.D. Iowa, 2004).

## CHIMNEY

**A structure containing one or more flues for drawing off emissions from stationary sources of combustion. See *Stack*.**

*Legal Annotation*: "The changes included adding a porch, constructing a concrete driveway and sidewalk, and encasing the **chimney** in such materials as would resemble a traditional **chimney**." *Knight v. Town of Knightdale* (N.C. Ct. App., 2004).

## CHLORINATED HYDROCARBONS

**A class of usually long-lasting, broad-spectrum insecticides.**

*Comment*: The best known of the chlorinated hydrocarbons is DDT, first used for insect control during World War II. The characteristics of persistence and effectiveness against a wide variety of insect pests were long regarded as highly desirable in agriculture, public health, and home uses. Later research has revealed that these same qualities may represent a potential hazard through accumulation in the food chain and persistence in the environment.

*Legal Annotation*: "Although there is a conflict in the testimony as to the duration of the leakage and the extent thereof, it is clear that the soil of much of the 550 acres of swamp is permeated to some degree with **chlorinated hydrocarbons**, which are toxic and which are, for all practical purposes, non-biodegradable." *Ewell v. Petro Processors of Louisiana, Inc.* (La. Ct. App., 1978).

## CHLORINATION

**The application of chlorine to drinking water, sewage, or industrial waste for disinfection or oxidation of undesirable compounds.**

*Legal Annotation*: "These are byproducts of **chlorination**, the most widely used technique for ensuring the safety of drinking water. **Chlorination** plays a significant role in the control of microbial pathogens and in turn in the protection of public health." *Chlorine Chemistry Council v. EPA* (D.C. Ct. App., 2000).

## CHLORINATOR

**A device for adding a chlorine-containing gas or liquid to drinking water or wastewater.**

*Legal Annotation*: "The evidence of record shows that two chlorine tanks were attached to a V-100 **chlorinator** system on the premises of Lakeshore Marine, Inc. The **chlorinator** system was used to chlorinate the water in the restaurant located on the premises." *Lakeshore Marine v. Hartford Acc. & Co.* (Ga. Ct. App., 1982).

## CHOKERS

**See *Traffic Calming*.**

## CHRISTMAS TREE FARM

**A land area cultivated for the growing, harvesting, and marketing of evergreen trees.**

*Legal Annotation*: "The planting of evergreen trees for either a saw cut operation or a 'cut your own' **Christmas tree farm** is within the commonly understood meaning of agriculture or horticulture." *Henry v. Board of Appeals of Dunstable* (Mass., 1994).

## CHURCH

**A place of worship. See *Megachurch; Place of Worship; Religious Use*.**

*Legal Annotation*: "The new ordinance became effective after the oral argument in this Court. Under that ordinance, '**churches** and similar places of worship' are now a conditional use in an

R-15 zone, and a **church** is defined as a 'building or structure where persons regularly assemble for worship, which by design and construction are primarily intended for the conducting of organized religious services and accessory uses associated therewith.' *State v. Cameron* (N.J., 1985).

## CINEPLEX

See *Megaplex; Motion Picture Theater*.

## CIRCULATION

**Systems, structures, and physical improvements for the movement of people, goods, water, air, sewage, or power by such means as streets, highways, railways, waterways, towers, airways, pipes, and conduits and the handling of people and goods by such means as terminals, stations, warehouses, and other storage buildings or trans-shipment points.**

*Legal Annotation*: "The plan or plans of the municipality shall be prepared in order to promote, in accordance with present and future needs, the safety, morals, order, convenience, prosperity and general welfare of the citizens; and may provide, among other things, for efficiency and economy in the process of development, for the appropriate and best use of land, for convenience of traffic and **circulation** of people and goods, for safety from fire and other dangers, for adequate light and air in the use and occupancy of buildings, for healthful and convenient distribution of population, for good civic design and arrangement, for adequate public utilities and facilities, and for wise and efficient expenditure of funds." Ark.Stat.Ann. § 19-2825(a) (Repl.1980) as cited in *Mings v. City of Fort Smith* (Ark., 1986).

## CISTERN

**A tank or reservoir used for storing rainwater.**

*Legal Annotation*: The governing body of the city has the power "[t]o provide, or cause to be provided, the city with water; to make, regulate and establish public wells, pumps and **cisterns**, hydrants and reservoirs in the streets or elsewhere within said city or beyond the limits thereof, for the extinguishment of fires and the convenience of the inhabitants, and to prevent the unnecessary waste of water." Tex.Rev.Civ. Stat.Ann. Art. 1015, § 30 (Vernon 1963) cited in *City of Lucas v. North Texas Mun. Water Dist.* (Texas Ct. App., 1986).

## CITIZEN PARTICIPATION

**Public involvement in governmental policy formation and implementation.**

*Comment*: The Internet and other new technology can foster citizen participation (Groc 2005, 30).

*Legal Annotation*: "And the Congress apparently was sufficiently pleased with the operation of the citizen suit section of the Clean Air Act to essentially duplicate the provision in the subsequently enacted Water Pollution Control Act of 1972. . . . Thus the Act seeks to encourage **citizen participation** rather than to treat it as curiosity or a theoretical remedy." *Friends of the Earth v. Carey* (2nd Cir., 1976).

## CITY PLANNING

**The decision-making process in which goals and objectives are established, existing resources and conditions analyzed, strategies developed, and legislation and policies enacted and adopted to achieve the goals and objectives as they relate to cities and communities.**

*Legal Annotation*: "The City presented affidavits from two city planners containing little more than conclusory statements that excluding churches from the C-3 zone is consistent with the **City's planning** process and historical land-use." *Cornerstone Bible Church v. City of Hastings* (Cir., 1991).

## CIVIC CENTER

**A building or complex of buildings that houses government offices and services and that may include cultural, recreational, athletic, convention, and entertainment facilities.**

*Comment*: Broadly speaking, ownership and operation by a governmental agency is no longer a critical element in the definition of a civic center. Governmental participation and/or sanction of a private endeavor would still meet the definition.

*Legal Annotation*: "Appellants are members of groups residing or having their businesses in an area of lower Manhattan called 'The Manhattan **Civic Center**' which comprises not only various courthouses, government buildings and businesses, but also residential housing, including cooperative apartments in two buildings close to the MCC and various similar apartments and tenements in nearby Chinatown." *Hanly v. Kleindienst* ($2^{nd}$ Cir., 1972).

## CLARIFICATION SYSTEM

**In wastewater treatment, a system used for the removal of turbidity and suspended solids by settling, often aided by centrifugal action and chemically induced coagulation.**

*Legal Annotation*: "[F]&H, a general contractor hired by a water agency to upgrade a water treatment plant, purchased a water **clarification system** from Kruger." *F&H Construction, Inc. v. I. Kruger, Inc.* (Calif. Ct App., 2010).

## CLARIFIER

**In wastewater treatment, a settling tank that mechanically removes settled solids from water.**

*Legal Annotation*: "A waste water treatment plant comprising an aeration chamber and a clarification chamber within said aeration chamber, said **clarifier** chamber being formed by a partition in the form of an inverted, truncate cone-like member . . . a passageway between the aeration chamber and the lower end of the clarification chamber to cause the waste water to flow upwardly in the clarification chamber without turbulence to allow large solid particles to fall downwardly through the upwardly moving waste water and reenter the aeration chamber." *Clearstream Wastewater Systems v. Hydro-Action* (Fed. Cir., 2000).

## CLEAN AIR ACT

**A federal act establishing national air quality standards.**

*Legal Annotation*: "The **Clean Air Act** of 1963 . . . authorized federal authorities to expand their research efforts, to make grants to state air pollution control agencies, and also to intervene directly to abate interstate pollution in limited circumstances. Amendments in 1965 . . . broadened federal authority to control motor vehicle emissions and to make grants to state pollution control agencies." *Train v. Natural Resources Defense Council* (U.S., 1975).

## CLEAR-CUTTING

**The large-scale, indiscriminate removal of trees, shrubs, and undergrowth with the intention of preparing real property for non-agricultural development purposes (American Planning Association,** *A Survey of Planning Definitions,* **Planning Advisory Service Report No. 421, 1989).**

*Comment*: In a tree preservation ordinance, the removal of dead trees and selective cutting in accordance with a forest management plan (often required to be prepared by a certified forester) is usually permitted. The approving agency, in considering any development plan for a heavily wooded tract, should require submission of a tree retention plan. In addition to the removal of trees and vegetation, changes in grades and other significant cutting and filling can have deleterious impacts on the remaining trees. Many agencies require that trees to be retained be marked and protected by placing fencing around them at the drip line. This protects them, at least in theory, from construction activities. *See Figure 98.*

*Legal Annotation*: "Fairview is in Management Prescription 3.2, and the plan authorizes logging there by the method known as 'even-aged management,' and specifically by **clear-cutting**. (If all the trees in a tract are cut down at once, the new trees that grow in their place will be of roughly the same age.)" *Cronin v. US Dept. of Agriculture* ($7^{th}$ Cir., 1990).

## CLEAR FLOOR SPACE

**The minimum unobstructed floor or ground space required to accommodate a single, stationary wheelchair and occupant. See *Americans With Disabilities Act*.**

*Legal Annotation*: "56 Fed. Reg. 9511 '[g]uidelines provide that usable kitchens require "a **clear floor space** at least 30 inches by 48 inches that allows a parallel approach by a person in a wheelchair . . . at the range or cooktop and sink."' *United States v. Quality Built Const., Inc.* (D.C.N.C., 2003).

## CLEAR VISION TRIANGLE

**See *Sight Triangle*.**

## CLERGY

**Men and women who conduct religious services and undertake the duties prescribed by religious orders or denominations.**

*Legal Annotation*: "As a general rule, if the employee's primary duties consist of teaching, spreading the faith, church governance, supervision of a religious order, or supervision or participation in religious ritual and worship, he or she should be considered '**clergy**.'" *Rayburn v. General Conf. of Seventh-Day Adventists* (4th Cir., 1985).

## CLERGY RESIDENCE

**The home of a member of the clergy, usually located on the same parcel as the house of worship.**

*Comment*: Also referred to as a parsonage, vicarage, manse, or rectory. When located on the same lot as the house of worship, the clergy residence is a customary accessory use. When located on a separate lot, it is a single-family home. When the house is a clergy residence, bible studies, prayer meetings, counseling, committee meetings, and similar activities in the clergy residence are customary accessory uses.

*Legal Annotation*: "We are led to this conclusion when we consider that in many places the **clergy's residence** was on the premises used also for religious worship, but some of them were elsewhere." *City of Houston v. South Park Baptist Church* (Texas Ct. App., 1965).

## CLINIC

**An establishment where patients are admitted for examination and treatment on an outpatient basis by physicians, dentists, other medical personnel, psychologists, or social workers and where such examination and treatment generally require a stay of less than twenty-four hours.**

*Comment*: The clinic is now more accurately described as an ambulatory health-care facility in which outpatient treatment is provided.

*Legal Annotation*: "Because patients or their doctors can choose to have problems treated either in a hospital or in an outpatient **clinic** or doctor's office in a significant number of cases, the court finds that certain **clinics** and other providers of outpatient services compete with the defendants' hospitals to treat various medical needs." *US v. Carilion Health Service* (D.C. Va., 1989).

## CLOVERLEAF

**A grade-separated, multiple-highway interchange that, by means of curving ramps from one level to another, permits traffic to move or turn in any of four directions without interference. *See Figure 97*.**

*Comment*: Often referred to as "cloverleaf interchanges." Partial cloverleafs permit traffic movements in fewer than four directions.

*Legal Annotation*: "In each of these cases, the expropriation was made for the construction of a **cloverleaf** design interchange (sometimes called a 'modified cloverleaf design') at the intersection of Interstate Highway 12 and U.S. Highway 190 in St. Tammany Parish." *State Dept. of Highways v. Wax* (La. Ct. App., 1974).

## CLUB

**A group of people organized for a common purpose to pursue common goals, interests, or**

**activities and usually characterized by certain membership qualifications, payment of fees and dues, regular meetings, and a constitution and bylaws.**

*Comment*: Older zoning ordinances usually permitted clubs in residential neighborhoods under the phrase "clubs, lodges, and social buildings." Such clubs were assumed to draw their membership from the neighborhood. Today, clubs have become much more regionally oriented; consequently, there is little reason to permit them in low-density residential areas. The definition above is restricted to nonprofit clubs. "Clubs," however, can also include "recreational clubs," which have the same organizational framework but are formed for the purposes of particular sports or recreational pursuits and may be commercial in nature. A distinction should therefore be made between nonprofit clubs organized for religious, social, cultural, or educational purposes and those that usually are commercial in nature and primarily recreational, such as tennis and racquetball clubs. See *Fraternal Organization.*

*Legal Annotation*: "The Bohemian **Club** is a distinguished private nonprofit association whose membership is limited to men professing devotion to the arts." *Bohemian Club v. Fair Employment & Housing Com.* (Calif. Ct. App., 1986).

"After a membership drive to raise funds, the Association obtained zoning as a 'community pool' and constructed its facility near Silver Spring, Maryland. The Association is essentially a single-function recreational **club**, furnishing only swimming and related amenities." *Tillman v. Wheaton-Haven Recreation Assn., Inc.* (U.S., 1973).

## CLUBHOUSE

**A building, or portion thereof, used by a club.**

*Legal Annotation*: "The Presidio Golf Club appeals the district court's summary judgment . . . in the Club's action challenging the environmental and historic review process undertaken by the government and its concessioner, Arnold Palmer Golf Management Company, in connection with efforts to build a new public **clubhouse** at the Presidio Golf Course of San Francisco, near a century-old private **Clubhouse** which the Club seeks to preserve." *Presidio Golf Club v. National Park Service* (Court of Appeals, 9th Circuit, 1998).

## CLUSTER

**A development design technique that concentrates buildings on a part of the site to allow the remaining land to be used for recreation, common open space, and preservation of environmentally sensitive features. See *Cluster Subdivision*.**

*Legal Annotation*: "**Cluster** development is an optional planning technique permitting Planning Boards to exercise greater flexibility in subdivision approval for the purpose of achieving more efficient use of land containing unusual features (e.g., the wetlands and steep slopes in petitioner's land), for facilitating economical provision for streets and utilities, as well as for preserving the natural and scenic qualities of open lands." *Bayswater v. Planning Bd. of the Town of Lewisboro* (N.Y., 1990).

## CLUSTER SUBDIVISION

**A form of development that permits a reduction in lot area and bulk requirements, provided there is no increase in the number of lots permitted under a conventional subdivision or increase in the overall density of development, and the remaining land area is devoted to open space, active recreation, preservation of environmentally sensitive areas, or agriculture. *See Figure 23.***

*Comment*: The cluster subdivision is an excellent planning concept that has been used successfully in many communities. Some communities require the developer to submit a conventional subdivision plan to establish the number of developable lots possible and a cluster subdivision plan to determine the appropriateness of cluster design for the site. Cluster should not be used to subsidize a developer who buys a piece of land with development constraints, such as steep

**Figure 23**

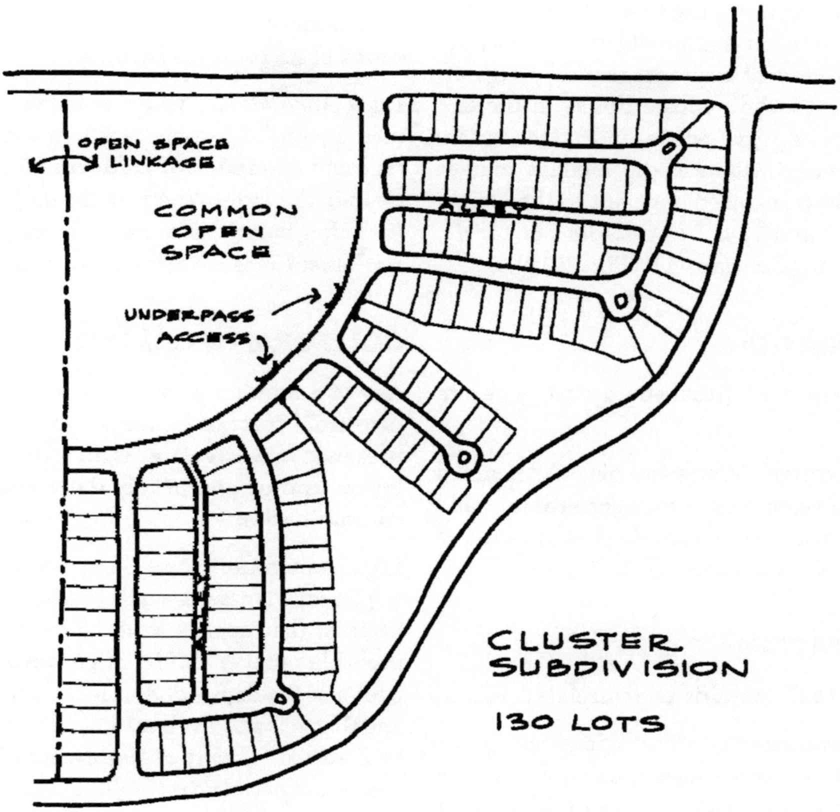


slopes, wetlands, and floodplains, and expects the yield to be the same as if the land were completely developable. See *Critical Area*.

The cluster subdivision technique can be used in conjunction with an area-wide plan for a system of pathways and bikeways or the conservation of wildlife corridors or riverside areas. This approach means that implementation of a circulation system, recreation program, or the conservation of environmentally sensitive areas can be achieved through the development process. Cluster subdivisions can also be used to preserve lands in agricultural uses, thus serving as an alternative to the purchase of development rights. See *Conservation Area*.

***Legal Annotation***: "Section 15-200 of the Ordinance . . . [d]efines **'cluster' subdivision** as '[a]n alternative means of subdividing a lot premised on the concept of reducing lot size requirements for the provision of open space in conjunction with the development.'" *Board of Sup'rs v. Machnick* (Va., 1991).

## C.O.

**Certificate of occupancy. See *Certificate of Occupancy*.**

## COFFEE HOUSE

**An establishment that serves primarily prepared coffee and other hot drinks as well as light snacks.**

***Comment***: A coffee house has indoor and often outdoor seating, and orders are placed and picked up directly from the preparer. There is no waiter or waitress service.

*Legal Annotation*: "The Society of Lloyd's, London, is not an insurance company, but rather a British organization that provides infrastructure for the international insurance market. Originating in Edward Lloyd's **coffee house** in the late seventeenth century, where individuals gathered to discuss insurance, the modern market structure was formalized pursuant to the Lloyd's Acts of 1871 and 1982." *Underwriters at Lloyd's, London v. Osting-Schwinn,* (11th Cir., 2010).

## COGENERATION

**The conversion of heat energy to generate electricity.**

*Legal Annotation*: "Congress also determined that the development of **cogeneration** and small power production facilities would conserve energy." *FERC v. Mississippi* (U.S., 1982).

## COHABITATION

**Household that contains two unrelated adults.**

*Legal Annotation*: "The statute does not define '**cohabitation**,' but we have construed the term in this statute as follows: 'The essential elements of "cohabitation" are (1) sharing of familial or financial responsibilities and (2) consortium.'" *State v. Carswell* (Ohio, 2007).

## COHOUSING

**"Privately-owned housing units and commonly-owned areas, with a participatory governance structure" (Henderson 2005, 61).**

*Comment*: According to *The Cohousing Handbook* (Scotthanson and Scotthanson 2005), cohousing helps foster community interaction.

*Legal Annotation*: "**Co-housing** projects like the one cohousing contemplated here place an emphasis on open space and communal living. Because Cohousing requires the groups on whose behalf it undertakes development to commit to a certain threshold level of funding before Cohousing becomes involved, Cohousing's projects have a relatively high probability of coming to fruition." *Kunelius v. Town of Stow*, (1st Cir., 2009).

## COLIFORM INDEX

**An index of the purity of water based on a count of its coliform bacteria.**

*Legal Annotation*: "Water pollution is generally measured in important degree in terms of bacteria count and **index of coliform** microorganisms (*B. coli*), the latter reflecting the degree of animal (including human) excrement." *Borough of Westville v. Whitney Home Builders* (N.J. App. Div., 1956).

## COLIFORM ORGANISM

**Any of a number of organisms common to the intestinal tract of humans and animals whose presence in wastewater is an indication of pollution and of potentially dangerous bacterial contamination.**

*Legal Annotation*: "The State Board found that the Basin Plan set a water quality objective for bacteria that applies to groundwater at a most probable number (MPN) of **coliform organism** over a seven-day period of less than 2.2/100 ml, and that was also the level at which coliform could be detected." *County of Sacramento v. State Water Resources Control Board* (Calif. Ct. App., 2007).

## COLLECTION

**The act of removing solid waste (or materials that have been separated for the purpose of recycling) from a central storage point.**

**Legal Annotation**: "Congress has explicitly found that the field of solid waste collection is properly subject to state regulation. See 42 U.S.C. § 6901(A)(4) (stating that 'the collection and disposal of solid waste should continue to be primarily the function of State, Regional and local agencies'). The Supreme Court has consistently held that a state's power to regulate commerce is at its zenith in areas traditionally of local concern." *Kleenwell Biohazard Waste V. Nelson* (9th Cir, 1995).

## COLLECTION FREQUENCY

**The number of times collection is provided in a given period of time.**

## COLLECTOR STREET

**A street that collects traffic from local streets and connects with minor and major arterials but also provides access to abutting properties.**

*Legal Annotation*: "A Class V collector street is defined as '[a] roadway which assembles traffic from local streets and distributes it to the nearest arterial street, providing direct primary access to low/medium density land uses and designed to carry low to moderate traffic volumes at low to moderate speeds.' *Myers Park Homeowners Association v. City of Charlotte* (N.C. Ct. App., 2013).

## COLLEGE

**An institution of higher education and research that provides undergraduate degrees.**

*Comment*: Although the term "college" is used interchangeably with "university," generally most colleges do not offer a postgraduate education.

*Legal Annotation*: "The ordinance designated 'private **colleges**' as a special use that might be permitted in limited districts. Zoning Ordinance No. 99, however, established no limited business districts. The comprehensive plan map showed Nazareth Hall, Bethel **College**, and a proposed bible **college** to be 'semi-public uses,' and listed '**colleges**' as a subcategory of 'schools.'" *Northwestern College v. City of Arden Hills* (Minn., 1979).

## COLLIERY

**A coal mine, including buildings and equipment.**

*Legal Annotation*: "[T]he legislature ha[s] power under the Constitution to establish reasonable police regulations for the operating of mines and **collieries**, and that an act providing for the health and safety of persons employed in coal mines, which required the owner or agent of every coal mine or **colliery** employing ten men or more, to make or cause to be made an accurate map or plan of the workings of such coal mine or **colliery**, was not unconstitutional." *Holden v. Hardy* (U.S., 1898).

## COLOSSEUM

**A large auditorium or stadium used for spectator sports, concerts and the like.**

*Legal Annotation*: "The **COLOSSEUM** convention center in no way resembled the ancient Roman Coliseum. It did not have elevated seating and was rectangular in shape." *Caesars World, Inc. v. Milanian* (D.C. Nev., 2003).

## COMBINED SEWERS

**A sewerage system that carries both sanitary sewage and stormwater runoff.**

*Legal Annotation*: **"Combined sewers**, which are mostly older sewer systems, are designed to carry both storm water and sanitary waste in the same pipes." *Friends of Milwaukee's Rivers v. Milwaukee Metropolitan Sewerage Dist.* (7th Cir., 2004).

## COMBUSTION

**Burning.**

*Comment*: Technically, combustion is a rapid oxidation accompanied by the release of energy in the form of heat and light.

*Legal Annotation*: "The CISWI Definitions Rule defines a 'commercial or industrial solid waste incineration unit,' in relevant part, as 'any **combustion** unit that combusts commercial or industrial waste (as defined in this subpart)' and then defines 'commercial or industrial waste' to include only waste that is combusted at a facility that cannot or does not use a process that recovers thermal energy from the combustion for a useful purpose." *Natural Resources Defense Council v. EPA* (D.C. Cir., 2007).

## COMMERCIAL CONDOMINIUM

**See *Condominium*.**

## COMMERCIAL GARAGE

**See *Garage, Public*.**

## COMMERCIAL GREENHOUSE

**A structure in which plants, vegetables, flowers, and similar materials are grown for sale.**

*Legal Annotation*: "The plant material sold by the taxpayer is produced in a **commercial greenhouse** which extends over an area of approximately nine acres of land. The greenhouse consists of an enclosure constructed out of metal tubing and polyethylene film with shading, irrigation and ventilation systems which operate together to provide the optimum environment for plant production." *Revenue Dept. v. Greiling* (Wis., 1983).

## COMMERCIAL SOLID WASTE

**All types of solid wastes generated by stores, offices, restaurants, warehouses, and other nonmanufacturing activities; excludes multifamily residential, residential, and industrial wastes.**

*Legal Annotation*: *"Municipal solid waste landfill (MSWLF)* units means a discrete area of land or an excavation that receives household waste. . . . A MSWLF unit also may receive other types of RCRA Subtitle D wastes, such as **commercial solid waste**, nonhazardous sludge, conditionally exempt small quantity generator waste and industrial solid waste." *Marcas v. Bd. of County Com'rs of St. Mar's Cty*. (D.C. Md., 2011).

## COMMERCIAL USE

**Activity involving the sale of goods or services carried out for profit.**

*Legal Annotation*: "The notable and famous have the 'exclusive right during life to control and profit from the **commercial use** of their name and personality.'" *Memphis Development Foundation v. Factors Etc., Inc.* ($6^{th}$ Cir., 1980).

## COMMERCIAL VEHICLE

**Any motor vehicle licensed by the state as a commercial vehicle.**

*Comment*: Current practice is to permit only certain types of commercial vehicles in residential zones, such as passenger vehicles licensed as commercial vehicles, or vans or small trucks of up to a certain carrying capacity or gross vehicle weight limitation.

*Legal Annotation*: "The trooper believed Herrera's truck to be a **commercial vehicle** under Kansas law because it had '[d]ual wheels on the back and a utility bed with a heavy lift hydraulic lifter on the back, and also there was a sign on the back, a paint sign for a paint company.' Herrera's truck, however, did not have a Department of Transportation ('DOT') number displayed, as a commercial vehicle would have." *US v. Herrera* ($10^{th}$ Cir., 2006).

## COMMINUTION

**Mechanical shredding or pulverizing of waste, converting it into a homogeneous and more manageable material.**

*Comment*: Used in solid waste management and in the primary stage of wastewater treatment.

*Legal Annotation*: "The common meaning of '**comminution**' is the reduction of particle size through force." *Rolite v. Wheelabrator Technologies, Inc.* (Dist Court, ED Pennsylvania, 1995).

## COMMINUTOR

**A device that grinds solids to make them easier to treat.**

*Legal Annotation*: "A **comminutor**, which was utilized to break down the raw sewage, had not been operable for several months, and the screen used to filter the sewage through the treatment process had a large hole in it." *Brown v. Scioto City Board of Commissioners* (Ohio Ct. App., Appeals, 1993).

## COMMON ELEMENTS

**Land amenities; certain areas of buildings, such as lobbies, corridors, and hallways; central services and utilities; and any other elements and facilities owned and used by all condominium unit owners and designated in the master deed as common elements.**

*Legal Annotation*: "Section 711.06(1) (a) provides that the term **common elements** includes '[t]he land on which the improvements are located and any other land included in the condominium property whether or not contiguous.' Each unit owner possesses, as an appurtenance to his unit, an undivided share in the **common elements**." *Ackerman v. Spring Lake of Broward, Inc.* (Fla. Ct. App., 1972).

## COMMON LATERAL SEWER

**A sewer pipe serving more than one (1) unit or user.**

***Legal Annotation***: "A collector sewer is defined as 'the **common lateral sewers**, within a publicly owned treatment system, which are primarily installed to receive wastewaters directly from facilities which convey wastewater from individual systems, or from private property.' A **lateral sewer** is defined as 'pipes that run under city streets and receive the sewage from homes and businesses.'" C.C. Lee, *Environmental Engineering Dictionary* 344–45 (2d ed. 1992). As cited in *Town of Front Royal v. Front Royal & Warren City Industrial Park Corp.* (Va.,1994).

## COMMON OPEN SPACE

**See *Open Space, Common*.**

## COMMON OWNERSHIP

**Ownership by two or more individuals in any form of ownership.**

***Legal Annotation***: "The Uniform Condominium Act approved by the National Conference of Commissioners on Uniform State Laws in 1977 defines 'condominium' as meaning 'real estate, portions of which are designated for separate ownership and the remainder of which is designated for **common ownership** solely by the owners of those portions.' This Act has been adopted in ten states, but Massachusetts is not among them." *Noble v. Murphy* (Mass. App., 1993).

## COMMON PASSAGEWAY

**A commonly shared or used pedestrian or vehicular way that connects or serves two or more properties. See *Party Driveway*.**

***Legal Annotation***: "If a landlord may be liable for a tenant's injury caused by a defect on a common premises such as a rusted handrail or a rotted step, why should he be released from liability where the injury is caused by a natural accumulation of snow and ice which is negligently permitted to remain upon the surface of the **common passageway**." *Fuller v. Housing Authority of Prov.* (R.I., 1971).

## COMMUNAL AUTOMOBILE

**See *Car Sharing*.**

## COMMUNICATION USE

**Establishments furnishing point-to-point communication services, whether by wire or wireless means, either aurally, visually, or by radio frequency, including radio and television broadcasting stations and the exchange or recording of messages. See *Wireless Telecommunications Towers and Facilities*.**

***Comment***: Some care must be exercised in permitting all communication uses, since the term covers a wide range of uses and impacts. For example, radio broadcast stations often include high, multitower antennas covering large areas. Point-to-point communication services using cable, on the other hand, may be indistinguishable from a typical office use.

***Legal Annotation***: "The Zoning Hearing Board is a political subdivision of Bucks County, Pennsylvania that has the authority to either approve or deny applications for use variances to construct wireless **communication** facilities." *Liberty Towers v. Zoning Hearing Bd.* (E.D. Pa., 2010).

## COMMUNITY ASSOCIATION

**A homeowners' association organized to own, maintain, and operate common facilities and to enhance and protect their common interests.**

***Legal Annotation***: "Homeowners in the Garden Lakes subdivision in Avondale, Arizona are members of the homeowners association known as the Garden Lakes **Community Association**,

Inc. ('Association')." *Garden Lakes Community Association, Inc. v. Madigan* (Ariz. Ct. App., 2003).

## COMMUNITY BUS

**A smaller bus, accommodating between twelve and twenty passengers, which may run on fixed routes or on-demand calls for service, acting as a feeder to other traditional, larger main or fixed-route transit buses, bus rapid transit, or rail service.**

***Comment***: Typically used as a mode of travel for the elderly and infirm, or as a jitney service for commuters who live beyond walking distance to transit stops or rail service. Properly marketed, community buses have proved effective in encouraging commuters to forego the use of a car to get to and from transit hubs.

***Legal Annotation***: "Courts have commonly confirmed DHCR determinations that required ancillary services include garage facilities and parking spaces, laundry room facilities, courtyard and backyard use, a swimming pool, a community room, and **mini-bus** service." *Broome JV LLC v. Goldstein* (N.Y. Sup. Ct., 2014).

## COMMUNITY CENTER

**Concentration of activities, services, and land uses that serve, and are focal points for, the immediate neighborhoods and used for recreational, social, educational, and cultural activities. http://www.pgplanning.org/Resources/Tools_On-line/Glossary.htm**

***Legal Annotation***: "The **Community Center** is situate[d] in a public park and includes, in addition to the Community Theater, a junior museum, swimming pools, a soft-ball park, junior playground, tennis courts, scout headquarters, administration offices of the city recreation department, a power generating plant, a firehouse, a grammar school, and a parking lot, all owned by appellant." *Rhodes v. City of Palo Alto* (Calif. Ct. App., 1950).

## COMMUNITY CHARACTER

**The image of a community or area as defined by such factors as its built environment, natural features and open space elements, type of housing, architectural style, infrastructure, and the type and quality of public facilities and services. See *Character*.**

***Legal Annotation***: "Thus, the impact that a project may have on population patterns or existing **community character**, with or without a separate impact on the physical environment, is a relevant concern in an environmental analysis since the statute includes these concerns as elements of the environment." *Chinese Staff v. City of NY* (N.Y., 1986).

## COMMUNITY DESIGN PLAN

**An element or subplan element of a local master plan that provides supporting data and policy guidelines for the enactment of design-related land development regulations and for the review of community development proposals.**

***Comment***: The end product of the urban planning process is the built environment. If that end product is to be a visual as well as social, economic, and functional success, there must be three-dimensional design input into that process. Depending on community size and needs, community design plan proposals may range from a set of general policy statements or guidelines to detailed urban design plans and standards for every neighborhood. In addition, the community design plan may also provide design guidelines for development application review by the municipal planner and planning board; provide design guidelines for all municipal departments, agencies, and commissions in decisions affecting community design in their own operations; inform architects, builders, and developers of design guidelines for development that are considered important to the community; and provide general education in community design to increase public awareness of the issues, focus the efforts of improvement groups, and influence the many small design decisions that collectively affect the character of the community. See *Compatible Design*.

***Legal Annotation***: "[H]e has only been deprived of his right to 'cut it up' into individual units for conveyance to separate individuals, to what reasonably appears would be to the public detriment and at variance with the dictates of the city's overall **plan of community design**.'" *Clemons v. City of Los Angeles* (Calif., 1950).

## COMMUNITY DEVELOPMENT BOUNDARY

**See *Urban Growth Boundary; Urban Service Boundary*.**

***Legal Annotation***: "The DEP . . . '[e]xpects that municipalities will examine the coastal center delineations in relation to their own planning efforts and development and redevelopment issues, and in many cases, seek a different **community development boundary** and formal center designation or plan endorsement by the State Planning Commission.'" *In re Protest of Coastal Permit* (N.J. App. Div., 2002).

## COMMUNITY FACILITY

**A building or structure owned and operated by a governmental agency to provide a governmental service to the public.**

***Legal Annotation***: "The Second Circuit and the Ninth Circuit . . . '[h]ave made it clear that even in those comparatively rare instances where there is a market value for the **community facility** taken (for example a possible sale of a public building for private use) the government's duty to indemnify is to provide the cost of a more expensive public substitute facility.'" *US v. 564.54 Acres of Land, Etc.* (3rd Cir., 1974).

## COMMUNITY GARDEN

**"Any piece of land gardened by a group of people" (American Community Gardening Association, http://www.community garden.org/learn). See *Agriculture, Urban*.**

***Comment***: The ACGA emphasizes the broad breadth of what a community garden entails. It can be urban, suburban, or rural. It can grow flowers, vegetables, or other community food. Community gardeners generally are not permitted to sell the products of their labor for profit; most community gardens are for personal use only. Community gardens can have a variety of owners: institutions, community groups, land trusts, or private citizens.

***Legal Annotation***: "Although Friends acknowledges that its formation was motivated by the City's efforts to sell Congress Square Park, its initiative does not solely involve the Park: the amendments would add many other properties to the land bank, including some of the City's most heavily used open spaces. Indeed, there is no meaningful difference between the designation of parcels as land bank properties and the legislative adoption of a zoning scheme that creates open space districts and lists specific parks by name for inclusion within those districts. See, e.g., Boston, Mass., Zoning Code, vol. I, art. 33, §§ 33-5, 33-17 (2014) (establishing open space districts, including '**Community Garden**,' 'Parkland,' 'Recreation,' and 'Urban Plaza' subdistricts, and including a list of so-designated existing city parks)." *Friends of Congress Square Park v. City of Portland*, (Maine, 2014).

## COMMUNITY IMPACT STUDY

**See *Impact Analysis*.**

## COMMUNITY LAND TRUST (CLT)

**"Nonprofit corporation that develops and stewards affordable housing, community gardens, civic buildings, commercial spaces and other community assets on behalf of a community" (http://en.wikipedia.org/wiki/Community_land_trust).**

***Comment***: For example, with respect to housing, CLTs (often sponsored by a community development corporation), "provide affordable housing in perpetuity through land leasing and homeownership. While the trust owns the land, they then lease the land to homeowners, who own the structure on the land. The separation in ownership of land and house, allows future buyers to purchase the house only. The trust continues to own the land and lease the land to the next homeowner. In this way, the community is continually able to maintain a stock of affordable housing" (http://www.lincolninst.edu/subcenters/community-land-trusts/. *See* Finkel 2005, 24).

*Legal Annotation*: "In the second case, *Rockingham Area* Community Land Trust *v. Town of Rockingham*, taxpayer Kathleen Margaret (Margaret) owns a house subject to a housing-subsidy covenant granting the **land trust** a ninety-day purchase option and ostensibly capping the amount she will receive upon the sale of her home to her original contribution, plus twenty-five percent of its appreciation and capital improvements." *Franks v. Town of Essex* (Vt., 2013).

## COMMUNITY OF PLACE

**A dynamic, diverse, compact, and efficient center that has evolved and been maintained at a human scale, with an easily accessible central core of commercial and community services, residential units, and recognizable natural and built landmarks and boundaries that provide a sense of place and orientation (*New Jersey State Development and Redevelopment Plan* 2000). See *Human Scale; Sense of Place*.**

*Legal Annotation*: "The plan's goal is to create a '**community of place**' within Mount Laurel. . . . [T]he township is trying to address the need to provide a **community of place**, or a defined identity that characterizes the township. *Mount Laurel Township v. Mipro Homes* (NJ.J. App. Div., 2005).

## COMMUNITY RESIDENCES FOR THE DEVELOPMENTALLY DISABLED (CRDD)

**Residential facilities, licensed by the state, providing food, shelter, and personal guidance, with supervision, to developmentally disabled or mentally ill persons who require assistance, temporarily or permanently, in order to live in the community. (Adapted from the New Jersey *Municipal Land Use Law* [N.J.S.A. 40:55D-66.2].) See *Boarding Home for Sheltered Care*.**

*Comment*: CRDDs normally include group homes, halfway houses, intermediate-care facilities, and supervised apartment living arrangements.

*Legal Annotation*: New Jersey law provides that "**Community residences for the developmentally disabled** . . . shall be a permitted use in all residential districts of a municipality, and the requirements therefor shall be the same as for single family dwelling units located within such districts." *Easter Seal Soc. v. Township of North Bergen* (D.N.J., 1992).

## COMMUNITY RESIDENTIAL HOME

**A dwelling unit licensed to provide a living environment for unrelated residents who operate as the functional equivalent of a family, including such supervision and care by supportive staff as may be necessary to meet the physical, emotional, and social needs of an aged person, a person with disabilities, a developmentally disabled person, a non-dangerous mentally ill person, and a child as defined in the appropriate statute. See *Congregate Residences*.**

*Comment*: A community residential home is similar to congregate residences. In both cases, the residents served may be defined under a specific state statute. It would be important to cite the statute to provide a more specific definition of whom the home is designed to serve.

*Legal Annotation*: "The Orange County Code defines '**community residential home**' as 'a dwelling unit licensed to serve clients of the state department of health and rehabilitative services, which provides a living environment to unrelated "residents" who operate as the functional equivalent of a family, including such supervision and care by support staff as may be necessary to meet the physical, emotional, and social needs of the "residents."'" *Open Homes Fellowship, Inc. v. Orange County, Fla.* (M.D. Fla., 2004).

## COMMUNITY SHELTERS FOR VICTIMS OF DOMESTIC VIOLENCE

**A residence providing food, shelter, medical care, legal assistance, personal guidance, and other services to persons who have been victims of domestic violence, including any children of such victims, and who temporarily require shelter and assistance in order to**

**protect their physical or psychological welfare. (Adapted from the New Jersey *Municipal Land Use Law* [N.J.S.A. 40:55D-66.1].) See *Community Residences for the Developmentally Disabled*.**

*Legal Annotation*: New Jersey law provides that **[C]ommunity shelters for victims of domestic violence** shall be a permitted use in all residential districts of a municipality, and the requirements therefor shall be the same as for single family dwelling units located within such districts." *Easter Seal Soc. v. Township of North Bergen* (D.N.J., 1992).

## COMMUNITY SHOPPING CENTER

**A facility containing a junior department store with approximately 150,000 to 250,000 square feet of gross leasable area, and having a site area of ten to twenty-five acres. Its clientele draw is typically a radius of a ten-minute drive of the center.**

*Legal Annotation*: "The focus on pedestrian-oriented facilities and the stated intention to limit strip-type commercial development directly contrasts with the purpose of the C-3 District, which includes, 'to provide for a carefully designed **community shopping center** meeting the commercial needs of the residents of Northampton Township.'" *Appeal of Richboro CD Partners, L.P.* (Pa. Comm. Ct., 2014).

## COMMUNITY SUPPORTED AGRICULTURE (CSA)

**Describes a variety of direct farm marketing practices with certain common characteristics, including**:

- emphasis on community and/or local produce;
- shares/subscriptions that are sold prior to the season's beginning; and
- weekly deliveries to members/subscribers.

*Comment*: "CSA is relatively new to the United States, beginning in Massachusetts in 1986 and growing to 60 CSA farms in the U.S. in 1990. The CSA structure grew significantly in popularity among both producers and consumers during the 2000s. In 2005, a CSA database reported over 1,150 CSA farms. . . . It is estimated that there are currently more than 4,000 CSAs in the U.S.; some estimates even place the number of CSAs as high as 6,000 nationally. This marketing channel continues to increase in popularity, especially among consumers around urban centers" (Ernst and Woods 2013: 1).

*Legal Annotation*: "Now that the conventional view of Iowa agriculture as the production of corn, soybeans, cattle, and hogs is being challenged by the emergence of **Community Supported Agriculture** involving smaller farms growing fruits, vegetables, and livestock, it is critical that county boards of adjustment do not employ a litmus test for the number of acres necessary to qualify for an agricultural exemption." *Lang v. Linn County Board of Adjustment* (Iowa Ct. App., 2012).

## COMMUTER SHED

**The area from which people will commute from their homes to a specific workplace area, based on an analysis involving assumptions of travel time, mode, costs, and distance.**

*Legal Annotation*: "I am certain that the commuter standing at a roadside in Scotch Plains would not fail to see that a Trailways bus that roars through the community on its route between Miami and Boston is not engaged in the same business as a bus company that provides public transportation from that point to another point within the **commuter shed**. There really should be no question in the minds of the majority that intercity bus service is an entirely distinct commodity from commuter bus service." *Continental Trailways v. Director, Div. of Motor* (N.J., 1986).

## COMPACT CAR

**Any motor vehicle that does not exceed fifteen feet in length, bumper to bumper, and five feet, nine inches in width.**

*Legal Annotation*: "A **compact sedan** is defined in passenger & cargo volume (cu. ft.) as 100 to 109 by the US Dept. of Energy." http://tinyurl.com/pky5l9h

"With respect to parking, the BZA concluded that Gateway would provide one normal-sized space and one **compact-car** space." *Gladden v. Dist. of Columbia Zoning Adj.* (D.C. Ct. App., 1995).

## COMPACT CAR PARKING

**Parking spaces, in parking lots and parking structures, intended for compact cars only, of smaller dimensions than those provided for standard-sized or larger-sized cars.**

***Legal Annotation***: "Notably, there are different measurements for compact cars depending on the agency. Some define compact cars based on passenger and cargo volume while municipalities and parking authorities look to standard length and width for **compact car parking** spaces (examples of parking dimensions range from 7.5 ft wide to 9 ft wide and 14 to 16.5 ft; long)." *Carrboro, NC, Board of Aldermen Agenda Item Abstract* (March 24, 2012).

## COMPACTION

**Reducing the bulk of solid waste by rolling, tamping, and compression.**

***Legal Annotation***: "A packer blade sweeps through this trash hopper area during the **compaction** cycle, and pushes the trash into the storage area of the truck." *Uloth v. City Tank Corp.* (Mass., 1978).

## COMPATIBILITY

**The concept that new development or rehabilitation of existing properties in an area must "fit in" with the current surroundings and match certain criteria and characteristics common of that area. See *Compatibility Design, Compatible Land Use; Community Character*.**

***Comment***: In 2008, "the Arkansas Supreme Court declared that a county planning ordinance that requires new development to be 'compatible' with existing development withstands constitutional scrutiny" (*Benton County Stone, Inc. v. Benton County Planning Board, October 30, 2008 WL 4754805,* in "Compatibility Defined" 2009: 10).

***Legal Annotation***: "(c) In applying the principle of **compatibility**, the commission shall consider the following factors, as applicable:

(1) The general design, character and appropriateness to the designated landmark or designated historic district of the proposed alteration or new construction;

[. . .]

(3) Texture, materials, and color and their relation to similar features of other properties in the neighborhood of the designated historic district;

(4) Visual **compatibility** with surrounding properties or the designated historic district . . .

(5) The importance of historic, architectural or other features to the significance of the property or the designated historic district.

(d) The commission shall prepare and adopt guidelines that contain suggested standards of **compatibility** elaborating upon the principles set forth above regarding the future development of and the preservation of properties, buildings and structures within the district." *Matter of Lachaud v. Zoning Bd. of Appeals of the Inc. Vil. of Bellport* (N.Y. Sup. Ct., 2013).

## COMPATIBLE DESIGN

**The visual relationship between adjacent and nearby buildings and the immediate streetscape, in terms of a consistency of materials, colors, building elements, building mass, and other constructed elements of the urban environment, such that abrupt or severe differences are avoided.**

***Comment***: Two of the major problems facing planners today with respect to compatible design are "teardowns" and "poptops" (American Planning Association, *Planning*, October 1999). Teardowns are buildings (usually dwellings) purchased for the specific purpose of replacement, almost always on a larger scale than the original. Poptops are second-story additions, usually considerably higher than the surrounding structures.

Many planners would agree that residential teardowns are part of the natural evolutionary process that takes place within neighborhoods. As noted by Charles Crook, planning director of Lake Forest (Illinois), in the previously cited planning article, "Some houses deserve to be torn down . . . [but] you need to control what you put up in their place" (ibid., p. 7).

A number of different techniques have been suggested to ensure that replacement homes or major expansions still remain compatible with the surrounding homes and reflect the neighborhood fabric. These techniques include FAR (floor area ratio) limits, building scale calculations, encroachment planes, and similar methods. With the exception of FAR limits, these techniques appear to be complicated and labor-intensive.

Generally speaking, the techniques that seem to work include making house size a function of lot size; that is, smaller houses on smaller lots. Thus, a five-thousand-square-foot lot with a maximum FAR of .30 would permit a fifteen-hundred-square-foot house. Larger lots would allow larger houses, but the FAR would probably have to be reduced in order to keep the houses compatible with the neighborhood. A fifteen-thousand-square-foot lot with the same FAR as the one permitted for the five-thousand-square-foot lot (.30) would result in a house with forty-five hundred square feet. This probably would be inconsistent with the overall neighborhood design. A FAR of between .20 and .25 would probably be appropriate. The exact FAR would have to be determined after more detailed studies of the prevailing FAR in the neighborhood, possibly as part of the design element of the master plan.

More important, however, new houses or expansions of existing houses should take place on the lot only in such a manner that the character of the existing streetscape is not seriously affected. This requires that the existing front yard and side yard setbacks remain the same, or in the case of the side yards, any encroachment takes place toward the rear of the lot. Building heights can be increased, but that part of the roof that is raised should be set back farther from the front building line.

One additional point worth noting is that most houses are not built to existing setback requirements, except on very small lots. In other words, on moderately sized and larger lots, with the exception of the front building line, many houses can be expanded to the rear and sides and still conform to existing codes. But this type of expansion or new house will be significantly different from the existing neighborhood character. A detailed survey of the existing development characteristics is needed to establish a realistic and effective set of controls. This type of survey can best be done by the use of aerial photography. See *Community Design Plan; Design Fit*.

***Legal Annotation***: Tampa City Code Section 27-216(m) states, "**Compatible design** shall mean architectural design and construction that will fit harmoniously into the district or the landmark site. New construction shall be compatible in scale, materials and quality of construction with adjacent buildings and structures that have been designated." As cited in *City of Tampa v. City Nat. Bank of Florida* (Fla. Ct. App., 2007).

## COMPATIBLE LAND USE

**A use of land and/or building(s) that, in terms of development intensity, building coverage, design, bulk and occupancy, traffic generation, parking requirements, access and circulation, site improvements, and public facilities and service demands, is consistent with and similar to neighboring uses and does not adversely affect the quality of life of persons in surrounding or nearby buildings. See *Quality of Life; Compatible Design*.**

*Comment*: The definition spells out the specific criteria that should be examined but also includes a determination as to whether the use adversely affects the quality of life of the neighborhood residents. Compatible land uses may include different land uses that are mutually supportive and necessary, providing goods and services, economic opportunities, and a healthy and safe environment.

***Legal Annotation***: "As indicated earlier in this report, certain actions by State and local public agencies, such as zoning to assure **compatible land use**, are a necessary part of the total attack on aircraft noise." *Burbank v. Lockheed Air Terminal, Inc.* (U.S., 1973).

## COMPLETE APPLICATION

**An application for development completed as specified by ordinance and the rules and regulations of the approving authority and the provisions of all required documents.**

*Comment*: Most states require that a determination of completeness be made within a specific period of time and on the meeting of all requirements specified in the ordinance and in the rules and regulations of the approving authority. On the day it is so certified by the administrative officer, the time period for action by the approving authority begins. Problems occasionally occur when a required document, on initial review, does not appear to substantially meet the ordinance requirements. For example, a landscaping plan showing only foundation plants surrounding a building on a ten-acre site may be rejected outright as incomplete. However, a better way to handle questionable submissions is to certify them as complete but, after detailed review, to reject the questionable or unacceptable element as not in conformance with the technical or design standards set forth in the ordinance

*Legal Annotation*: "As stated previously, however, it appears that College is simply adverse to complying with the PUD ordinance's requirements. The City's ordinance imposes no restriction whatsoever on College's religious exercise; it merely requires College to submit a **complete application**, as is required of all applicants." *San Jose Christian College v. Morgan Hill* (9th Cir., 2004).

## COMPLETE STREETS

See *Street, Complete*.

## COMPONENT FACTORS

**The various parts of a road, including right-of-way, grading, surface and subsurface drainage provisions, curbs, gutters, catch basins, foundations, shoulders and slopes, wearing surfaces, bridges, culverts, retaining walls, intersections, private entrances, guide rails, trees, illumination, guideposts and signs, ornamentation, and monuments.**

## COMPOST

**Relatively stable decomposed organic matter.**

*Legal Annotation*: "The **compost** is comprised mainly of hay and horse manure mixed with water and allowed to ferment outside on wharves." *United States v. Frezzo Bros, Inc.* (3rd Cir., 1979).

## COMPOSTING

**A controlled process of degrading organic matter by microorganisms.**

*Comment*: Composting may be achieved by several methods: (1) mechanical—a method in which the compost is continuously and mechanically mixed and aerated; (2) ventilated cell—compost is mixed and aerated by being dropped through a vertical series of ventilated cells; and (3) windrow—an open-air method in which compostable material is placed in windrows, piles, or ventilated bins or pits and occasionally turned or mixed. The process may be anaerobic or aerobic.

*Legal Annotation*: "Dano was to receive daily amounts of waste from the District and place it in large tubular biostabilizers, which initiated the **composting** process by way of tumbling and aeration. The waste was to 'stabilize' at a temperature of 140 degrees for twenty-four hours to help eliminate pathogens, then be discharged from the biostabilizers and sifted through grates." *Dano Resource v. District of Columbia* (D.C. Ct. App., 1993).

## COMPREHENSIVE PLAN

See *Master Plan*.

## COMPRESSED WORKWEEK PROGRAM

**A program that allocates the working hours into fewer than five days per week or fewer than ten days per two-week period, such as a four-day workweek or a nine-day, eighty-hour schedule.**

*Legal Annotation*: "According to the Society of Human Resource Management, 51% of companies have flexible work schedule options such as a change of start or stop times or **compressed work weeks** (four ten-hour days; '9-80s'—80 hours worked over nine days, etc.)." "Mitigate or Litigate: Flexible Working and Legal Exposure," Littler Mendelson (Feb. 2011). http://tinyurl.com/kwrz9j3

## CONCENTRATED ANIMAL FEEDING OPERATION (CAFO)

**A parcel of land, with or without buildings, used or intended to be used for the confined feeding, breeding, raising, or holding of animals in excess of two hundred animal units and specifically designed to store and accumulate animal manure and other waste products in holding areas and lagoons.**

***Comment***: Concentrated (the term "confined" is also used) animal feeding operations (also known as feedlots) are industrial operations with enormous potential for air, water, and soil pollution. While experts agree that the most serious problems come from hog operations, all CAFOs can have major adverse impacts over large areas in proximity to the operation unless careful management procedures and processes are undertaken and implemented. These might include large setbacks to residential areas, injection of manure rather than spraying, and the use of covered lagoons. The topic is complex and calls for the assistance of qualified agricultural engineers to address these potential problems. In addition, many states have included CAFOs under their "right to farm" legislation, making it difficult to apply zoning as a means of controlling these uses. In these states, as well as in states where zoning is used, some controls have been included as part of local health and environmental legislation.

While the definition specifically calls for a maximum of two hundred animal units, the local ordinance may establish higher or lower limits. The definition of *animal unit* notes that each swine over fifty-five pounds constitutes 0.4 animal units. A typical family farm might have five hundred swine (Barrette 1996) or two hundred animal units. An ordinance allowing up to a maximum of two hundred animal units on a farm would then clearly preclude CAFOs.

One approach recommended by James Duncan and Associates (1996) for Minnesota communities divides agricultural uses into limited agricultural and general agricultural zones. The limited agricultural category does not permit any livestock production, while the general agricultural permits large-scale uses and feedlots. Obviously, the requirements for each are significantly different, and the general agricultural zones can be located in areas where their impact on existing or potential new development is minimized.

In addition to controlling the operation of these uses, some provision should be included for returning the soil to a viable, non-feedlot agriculture use when the CAFO is discontinued or abandoned. This may call for escrow or bonds to avoid the creation of "rural brownfields" (Schwab 1998).

A comprehensive discussion of CAFO is found in the American Planning Association's Planning Advisory Service Report No. 482, *Planning and Zoning for Concentrated Animal Feeding Operations,* by Jim Schwab, December 1998. The October 1996 issue of APA's *Zoning News* also discusses feedlots in the Barrette article. See *Feedlot*.

***Legal Annotation***: "With more than 5000 cattle, the dairies operate a '**concentrated animal feeding operation**' ('CAFO'). **CAFOs** are animal feeding operations where animals are stabled or confined for a total of 45 days or more in any 12 month period in an area where neither crops, vegetation nor crop residue is sustained." *Community Ass'n for Restoration v. Bosma Dairy* (9th Cir., 2002).

## CONCEPT PLAN

**A schematic or conceptual design for land development, prepared for informal review purposes, that carries no vesting rights or obligations on any party. See *Plan, Sketch*.**

***Comment***: Many approving authorities use the informal concept plan review process to alert applicants to problems and requirements before the submission of a formal development application. Use of the concept plan review can save time and money for all parties.

*Legal Annotation*: "At the conclusion of the hearing, the Board of Commissioners approved the **concept plan** of the PUD conditionally upon resolution of issues regarding natural stream flows, the development's impact on the city of Victor, traffic flow, impact on county services, sewer system capacity, and density." *Evans v. Teton County* (Idaho, 2003).

## CONCURRENCY

**A finding or requirement by the approving authority that basic services and facilities are adequate to serve a proposed development.**

*Comment*: Concurrency requirements may be very stringent, such as in Florida, which requires that public facilities must be in place before a development can be built; or less stringent, such as in Colorado, which requires only a finding as to the adequacy of sewer, water, and access before approval.

Basic services may include water, sewers, roads, schools, parks, and recreation facilities. The definition of "adequate" requires that, to the extent possible, objective standards be established to measure any deficiencies so that the applicant can be required to provide his or her fair share of bringing these services up to the standard.

*Legal Annotation*: "The Growth Management Act . . . vests counties with the primary authority to plan future development, including **concurrency** planning with providers of public services." *Whatcom County Fire Dist. v. Whatcom County* (Wash. Ct. App., 2009).

## CONDEMNATION

**The exercise by a governmental agency of the right of eminent domain. See *Eminent Domain*.**

*Legal Annotation*: "The city council also authorized the NLDC to purchase property or to acquire property by exercising eminent domain in the City's name. . . . As a consequence, in November 2000, the NLDC initiated the **condemnation** proceedings that gave rise to this case." *Kelo v. New London* (U.S., 2005).

## CONDITIONAL USE

**A use permitted in a particular zoning district when it is shown that such use in a specified location will comply with all the conditions and standards for the location or operation of the use as specified in the zoning ordinance and authorized by the approving authority. See *Permitted Use*.**

*Comment*: Conditional uses are permitted uses and are appropriate in the zoning district only when all conditions are met. For example, houses of worship may be desirable in a residential area, but controls over parking, circulation, setbacks, and landscaping may be needed to prevent them from adversely affecting surrounding residences. By classifying them as conditional uses, separate regulations can be imposed to mitigate the adverse impacts. In some states, conditional uses are classified as special-exception uses. In all cases, the conditions must be specific.

*Legal Annotation*: "A special exception or **conditional use** refers to a permissive land use category authorized by a zoning or administrative body pursuant to the existing provisions of the zoning law and subject to guides, standard and conditions for such special use which is permitted under provisions of the existing zoning law." *Mayor and Council of Rockville v. Rylyns Enterprises, Inc.* (Md. Ct. App., 2002).

## CONDITIONAL USE PERMIT

**A permit issued by the approving authority stating that the conditional use meets all conditions set forth in local ordinances.**

*Legal Annotation*: "It suggests that in rare situations the government may grant another type of permit, such as a **conditional use permit**, which affords substantially the same specificity and definition to a project as a building permit, and that in such instances a builder might acquire a vested right even though the document was not designated a 'building permit.'" *Avco Community Developers v. South Coast Regional Com.* (Calif., 1976).

## CONDITIONS OF APPROVAL

**Requirements established by the approving authority before preliminary or final approval of an application for development becomes effective.**

*Comment*: Applications for development are often approved by the responsible authority subject to certain changes, corrections, or compliance with other agency reviews or approval. These changes and corrections, usually minor in nature, and compliance with other agency reviews or approvals, usually statutory, must be achieved before the application is deemed approved. Required signatures, for example, are withheld until the municipal engineer or planner certifies that all conditions are met. Any time limits for appeals, building permits, and so on run from the time all conditions of approval have been met.

*Legal Annotation*: "The appellants seek reversal of a district court order that upheld two requirements imposed on the developer by appellee Larimer County Board of County Commissioners (Board) as **conditions of approval** of the master plan for the Beaver Meadows PUD." *Beaver Meadows v. Board of County Commissioners* (Colo., 1985).

## CONDOMINIUM

**A building, or group of buildings, in which dwelling units, offices, or floor area are owned individually and the structure, common areas, and facilities are owned by all the owners on a proportional, undivided basis.**

*Comment*: By definition, a condominium has common areas and facilities, and there is an association of owners organized for the purpose of maintaining, administering, and operating the common areas and facilities. It is a legal form of ownership of real estate and not a specific building style. The purchaser has title to his or her interior space in the building and an undivided interest in parts of the interior, the exterior, and other common elements. The property is identified in a master deed and recorded on a plat with the local jurisdiction. The common elements usually include the land underneath and surrounding the building, certain improvements on the land, and such items as plumbing, wiring, and major utility systems, the interior areas between walls, public interior spaces, exterior walls, parking areas, private roads, and recreational facilities.

Most states do not permit zoning ordinances to differentiate among various forms of ownership. Thus, an ordinance could not limit the principal use as a condominium or cooperative as opposed to rental housing or leased space.

*Legal Annotation*: "Lakeside Village is a large **condominium** development in Culver City, Los Angeles County. It consists of 530 units spread throughout 12 separate 3-story buildings. The residents share common lobbies and hallways, in addition to laundry and trash facilities." *Nahrstedt v. Lakeside Village Condominium Assn* (Cali., 1994).

## CONDOMINIUM ASSOCIATION

**The community association that administers and maintains the common property and common elements of a condominium.**

*Comment*: Condominium associations differ from other forms of community associations in that the condominium association does not have title to the common property and facilities. These are owned by the condominium owner on a proportional, undivided basis.

*Legal Annotation*: "Ownership of a unit includes membership in the project's homeowners association, the Lakeside Village **Condominium Association** (hereafter Association), the body that enforces the project's CC&R's, including the pet restriction." *Nahrstedt v. Lakeside Village Condominium Assn* (Calif., 1994).

## CONDOMINIUM HOTEL

**A building constructed, maintained, and operated and managed as a hotel in which each room is individually owned and in which some or all of the rooms are available to transients for rent, and where the structure, common**

**areas, and facilities are owned by all the owners on a proportional, individual basis.**

*Legal Annotation*: "In 1965, a hotel was built at the base of the ski area, which, in 1985, was swept up in a joint venture (of which Recreational Industries is the remaining venturer) to establish a **condominium/hotel** project." *Council of Unit Owners v. Recreational Industries* (D. Md., 1992).

## CONFERENCE CENTER

**A facility used for conferences and seminars, with accommodations for sleeping, food preparation and eating, recreation, entertainment, resource facilities, meeting rooms, fitness and health center, and retail stores and services primarily for conference center guests.**

*Comment*: The definition could also include a minimum and maximum number of rooms and a minimum floor area for seminar and conference facilities related to the number of rooms. An informal study of conference centers found approximately ninety square feet of meeting and seminar room space per sleeping room. A hundred-room conference inn would have about nine thousand square feet of meeting rooms.

Communities also must decide whether or not to allow conference centers to rent rooms and facilities to transients other than those attending conferences. Very often a specific percentage of rooms must be reserved for conference participants, with the remainder available for transients.

*Legal Annotation*: "The prospectus represented that these lodge units would form an integral part of an 'inter-related resort village' called Stratton Mountain Village, to contain, in addition to the condominium units, a 16–18,000 square foot **conference center**." *Finkel v. Stratton Corp.* (2nd Cir., 1992).

## CONFERENCE HOTEL

**A hotel with a primary focus on conference center activities. See *Conference Center; Hotel*.**

*Legal Annotation*: "Parcel 1 is designated for a waterfront **conference hotel** at the center of a 'small urban village' that will include restaurants and shopping. This parcel will also have marinas for both recreational and commercial uses." *Kelo v. New London* (U.S., 2005).

"The Township of Readington, NJ, Code defines **Conference Inn** in Land Development Code Section 148-9 as a "building or group of buildings containing sleeping rooms, eating and cooking facilities, meeting rooms, fitness facility/health center and customary and usual accessory uses. The fitness facility/health center shall consist of a pool, exercise room and lockers and shall be restricted to conference inn guests and available to the general public on a membership basis only." http://ecode360.com/8741408

## CONGESTION PRICING

**A fee or surcharge imposed on automobiles entering a designated area during peak traffic hours.**

*Comment*: The objective of congestion pricing, as applied to traffic, is to reduce traffic congestion, encourage drivers to drive during off-peak hours, and to encourage the use of mass transit. Introduced in central London in 2003, it has been credited with reducing traffic flow, improving circulation, reducing commuter time, and improving air quality. Congestion pricing can also be applied to electricity, water and sewer service, and other public goods and services to ease peak-hour demands (Litman 2006; O'Connor 2004; Replogle 2008).

While the prime objective of congestion pricing is to speed traffic flow by reducing the number of vehicles entering designated areas, it also has improved air quality. In addition to London, Singapore introduced a congestion charge in 1975. "Oslo, Bergen and five other Norwegian cities adopted their own charges between 1986 and 2004, both to manage traffic and to finance transportation projects. Stockholm, Milan, Rome, and other cities have similar initiatives" (Replogle 2008: 5).

## CONGREGATE RESIDENCES

**Apartments and dwellings with communal dining facilities and services, such as**

**housekeeping, organized social and recreational activities, transportation services, laundry, and other support services appropriate for the residents and designed to provide a relatively independent lifestyle. See *Community Residential Home*.**

***Comment***: Also known as "congregate care" of "congregate housing." Congregate apartment residences are often developed in conjunction with assisted living facilities. Long-term care is sometimes added as well, so that a range of accommodations and a continuum of care can be provided.

Congregate residences may also function as boarding homes for sheltered care, community residences for the developmentally disabled, and community shelters for the victims of domestic violence. For these groups, specialized on-site support services may also be provided. See *Assisted Living Facility; Boarding Home for Sheltered Care; Community Residences for the Developmentally Disabled; Community Shelters for Victims of Domestic Violence; Continuing Care Retirement Community.*

***Legal Annotation***: "The Uniform Housing Code states: 'Floor Area. Dwelling units and **congregate residences** shall have at least one room which shall have not less than 120 square feet . . . of floor area. Other habitable rooms, except kitchens, shall have an area of not less than 70 square feet. . . . Where more than two persons occupy a room used for sleeping purposes, the required floor area shall be increased at the rate of 50 square feet . . . for each occupant in excess of two.'" *College Area Renters & Landlord Association v. City of San Diego* (Calif. Ct. App., 1996).

"The facility was described . . . as something between traditional senior citizen housing consisting of fully self-contained apartments and a nursing home. This description applies not only to the modicum of support services implicit in the **congregate housing** plan but to its physical attributes as well." *Jayber, Inc. v. Municipal Council* (N.J. App. Div., 1990).

## CONNECTIVITY

**"Describes the extent to which" spatial forms or development patterns "permit (or restrict) movement of people or vehicles" http://en.wikipedia.org/wiki/Permeability_(spatial_and_transport_planning).**

***Comment***: Connectivity "is generally considered a positive attribute of" a neighborhood "design, as it permits ease of movement and avoids isolating neighborhoods." Urban or suburban forms that lack connectivity, such as having long cul-de-sacs, "are considered to discourage movement on foot and encourage longer journeys by car" http://en.wikipedia.org/wiki/Permeability_(spatial_and_transport_planning). See *Handy, Paterson, and Butler* (2003) on planning for street connectivity.

***Legal Annotation***: "The Commission specifically found that '[the proposal] complies with the Oldham County Subdivision Regulations including the **connectivity** to improve EMS Fire Protection.'" *Croftboro Homeowners Association, Inc. V. Oldham County Planning* (Ky. Ct. App., 2011).

## CONSENSUS DESIGN

**Making a decision based on the input of many individuals.**

## CONSERVATION AREA

**Environmentally sensitive area with characteristics such as steep slopes, wetlands, floodplains, high water tables, forest areas, endangered species habitat, or dunes, or areas of significant biological productivity or uniqueness that have been designated for protection from any activity that would significantly alter their ecological integrity, balance, or character (American Planning Association, *A Survey of Zoning Definitions*, Planning Advisory Service Report No. 421, 1989). See *Cluster Subdivision; Critical Area*.**

***Comment***: Local ordinances could specify more specific standards, such as the percentage of slope considered steep (often 20 percent) or how high a water table (less than three feet). Environmentally sensitive areas may also have been mapped as part of the open space and conservation element of a comprehensive plan.

*Legal Annotation*: "Sarasota County has zoned approximately 2,971 acres on the site as a **conservation area**, which includes the most valuable areas of upland wetland habitat on the Walton Tract and adjoins other preserve areas off-site. These preserved lands combine with adjacent properties to form a continuous unit of potentially suitable Florida Panther habitat and serve as a barrier between the Myakka River ecosystem and further development from the west." *Fund for Animals, Inc. v. Rice* (11th Cir., 1996).

## CONSERVATION DISTRICT

See *Soil Conservation District.*

## CONSERVATION DISTRICT, HISTORIC

See *Historic Area.*

## CONSERVATION EASEMENT

See *Easement, Conservation.*

## CONSIDERATION

**An inducement to a contract.**

*Legal Annotation*: "Essential elements of a contract include an offer, acceptance, contractual capacity, **consideration** (the bargained for legal benefit and/or detriment), a manifestation of mutual assent and legality of object and of **consideration**." *Kostelnik v. Helper* (Ohio, 2002).

## CONSISTENCY

**A requirement that all land development regulations be consistent with the comprehensive or master plan of the municipality, county, or state.**

*Comment*: New Jersey, as do many other states, requires that all zoning "either be substantially consistent with the land use plan element and the housing plan element of the master plan, or designed to effectuate such plan element" (N.J.S.A. 40:55D-62a, NJ *Municipal Land Use Law*). In states with consistency requirements, ordinance amendments that are inconsistent can be successfully attacked in court. In some states, where inconsistent amendments are permitted, they may require a supermajority (a majority of the fully authorized membership of the governing body, as opposed to a majority of the members present) and a statement citing the reasons for the inconsistency.

In states where a separate written comprehensive plan is not required and a municipality has chosen not to adopt one, consistency may have to be evaluated in terms of municipal goals and objectives, adequate findings, and consideration of neighboring land uses (Dennison 1996).

*Legal Annotation*: "Section 163.3194(3), Florida Statutes (1991), explains **consistency** as follows: '(a) A development order or land development regulation shall be consistent with the comprehensive plan if the land uses, densities or intensities, and other aspects of development permitted by such order or regulation are compatible with and further the objectives, policies, land uses, and densities or intensities in the comprehensive plan and if it meets all other criteria enumerated by the local government.'" *Board of City Commissioners of Brevard v. Snyder* (Fla., 1993).

## CONSOLIDATION

**The removal of lot lines between contiguous parcels.**

*Comment*: Consolidation of several lots into a single lot or tract is usually considered an exempt subdivision. See *Assemblage; Subdivision.*

*Legal Annotation*: "Property lines can be eliminated in a variety of ways, including through local regulations concerning vacation or **consolidation** of lots or parcels." *Weyerhaeuser Real Estate Development Company v. Polk County* (Ore. Ct. App., 2011).

## CONSTRUCTION AND DEMOLITION WASTE

**The waste building materials, packaging, and rubble resulting from construction,**

**remodeling, repair, and demolition operations on pavements, houses, commercial buildings, and other structures.**

*Legal Annotation*: "Phoenix C & D Recycling, Inc. is in the business of acquiring **construction and demolition waste** materials (C&D) and recycling such materials for other uses. One use of C&D waste is as alternative daily cover (ADC) in landfills." *Phoenix C & D Recycling, Inc. v. Des Moines Metropolitan Area Solid Waste Agency* (Iowa Ct. App., 2010).

## CONSTRUCTION LOAN

**A temporary loan that is used to pay for the building of a house. (http://www.realtor.com/home-finance/mortgages/terms-glossary.aspx?source=web)**

*Legal Annotation*: "This case involves competing claims of lien priority between the seller of real property, which took back a security interest on property sold to a developer, and the bank which financed development of the project through a **construction loan**. . . . The CLA provides that loan funds shall be used only for constructing and equipping the project." *Citizens Business Bank v. Gevorgian* (Calif. Ct. App., 2013).

## CONSTRUCTION OFFICIAL

See *Building Inspector*.

## CONSTRUCTION PERMIT

See *Building Permit*.

*Legal Annotation*: "It presents the question whether the Commission erred in continuing in effect a provisional **construction permit** which authorizes the petitioner Power Reactor Development Company to construct, but not to operate, a fast-neutron breeder reactor for the generation of electric power." *Power Reactor Co. v. Electricians* (U.S., 1961).

## CONTAINER

**Any portable device in which a material is stored, transported, treated, disposed of, or otherwise handled.**

*Legal Annotation*: "In July 2011, the Township's enforcement officer Robert Rehman (Enforcement Officer Rehman) issued an enforcement notice stating that the use of the Property was in violation of Sections 403.1 and 902.1 of the Zoning Ordinance because it was being used as junk yard without a zoning permit . . . [the Joneses] have placed shipping **containers** without chassis on the [Property] and thus have placed structures on the [Property] without permits as the term 'structure' is defined in the Ordinance." *Jones v. Hamilton Township Zoning Hearing Board* (Pa. Comm. Ct., 2013).

## CONTAINER YARD

**A site, usually associated with ports or truck terminals, upon which storage containers are temporarily kept, often stacked, after being unloaded from ships or trailers, or awaiting loading onto ships or trailers, or until sold or rented for reuse.**

*Comment*: Container yards become problems when, for a variety of reasons, such as during a period of economic recession, they become long-term storage yards for empty containers. They are large and often unsightly or in poor condition. Container storage should be carefully designated on industrial sites to minimize their visual impact on surrounding uses. Maximum stacking heights should be considered.

*Legal Annotation*: "The cranes move these containers to a **container yard** at the edge of a marine terminal where containers are stored. One such yard in the Port of New York District where containers are placed in the **Container Yard** at the Global Marine Terminal. Continental 'pick[s] up containerized freight' from the Global Marine Terminal's **Container Yard** and transports it to its facilities." *Continental Terminals, Inc. v. Waterfront Commission of New York Harbor* (S.D.N.Y., 2013).

## CONTEXT

See *Development Context*.

## CONTEXTUAL ZONING

**The requirement that new construction and rehabilitation of existing properties in largely built-up areas reflect the characteristic bulk, and height and style, of existing buildings (Oser 2003: 7). See *Compatibility, Devlopment Context.***

***Legal Annotation***: "Consistent with this goal, the City sought to map '**contextual zoning** districts to regulate the height and bulk of new buildings, their setback from the street line, and their width along the street frontage, to produce buildings that are more consistent with existing neighborhood character.'" *In the Matter of Jakobson Props. v. City of New York* (N.Y. Supreme Ct., 2010).

## CONTIGUOUS

**Next to, abutting, or touching and having a boundary, or portion thereof, that is coterminous. See *Abut; Adjoining Lot or Land.***

***Legal Annotation***: "Under New York City's zoning laws, owners of real property who have not developed their property to the full extent permitted by the applicable zoning laws are allowed to transfer development rights to **contiguous** parcels on the same city block." *Penn Central Transp. Co. v. New York City* (U.S., 1978).

## CONTINUING CARE RETIREMENT COMMUNITY (CCRC)

**An age-restricted development that provides a continuum of accommodations and care, from independent living to long-term bed care, and enters into contracts to provide lifelong care in exchange for the payment of monthly fees and an entrance fee in excess of one year of monthly fees.**

***Comment***: What distinguishes a CCRC from other types of mixed residential development is (1) a contract for lifelong care; (2) monthly maintenance fees; and (3) a substantial entrance fee always greater than one year of monthly fees. Because of the substantial amounts of money required to enter a CCRC and the long-term commitment, many states have established stringent controls over CCRCs, including licensing, certificates of need, and full financial disclosure.

A CCRC typically includes independent living units, congregate residences, assisted care units, and a long-term bed care section. All units are age restricted. The independent living units may be single-family detached or attached housing or apartments.

CCRCs include health-care services and meals, with common dining facilities, physical therapy facilities and activities, meeting rooms, social activities, recreation facilities, on-site services and shops, and other ancillary services customarily accessory to the principal permitted use.

From a zoning perspective, CCRCs should be designated as conditional uses. Public water and sewer are necessary, and the appropriate location is within, or at the edge of, a residential area. Since the traffic generation of a CCRC is significantly lower than non-age-restricted housing, a higher density can be accommodated. Setbacks typical of multifamily uses are also appropriate for CCRCs. See *Assisted Living Facility; Congregate Residences; Retirement Community.*

***Legal Annotation***: "Passavant is a **continuing care retirement community**, providing various levels of nursing services in its skilled nursing facility, separate assisted-living units, and independent-living apartments and cottages." *Passavant Retirement & Health Center v. NLRB* (3rd Cir., 1998).

## CONTINUING EASEMENT

**See *Easement, Continuing.***

## CONTOUR LINE

**A line on a map that connects all points of the same ground elevation. See *Topographic Map. See Figure 24.***

***Comment***: Contour maps are the standard way of representing ground form. The contour lines on topographic maps indicate the slope of the land. The closer the lines are to each other, the steeper the slope. Conversely, the farther apart the contour lines, the flatter the slope. The contour lines

**Figure 24**

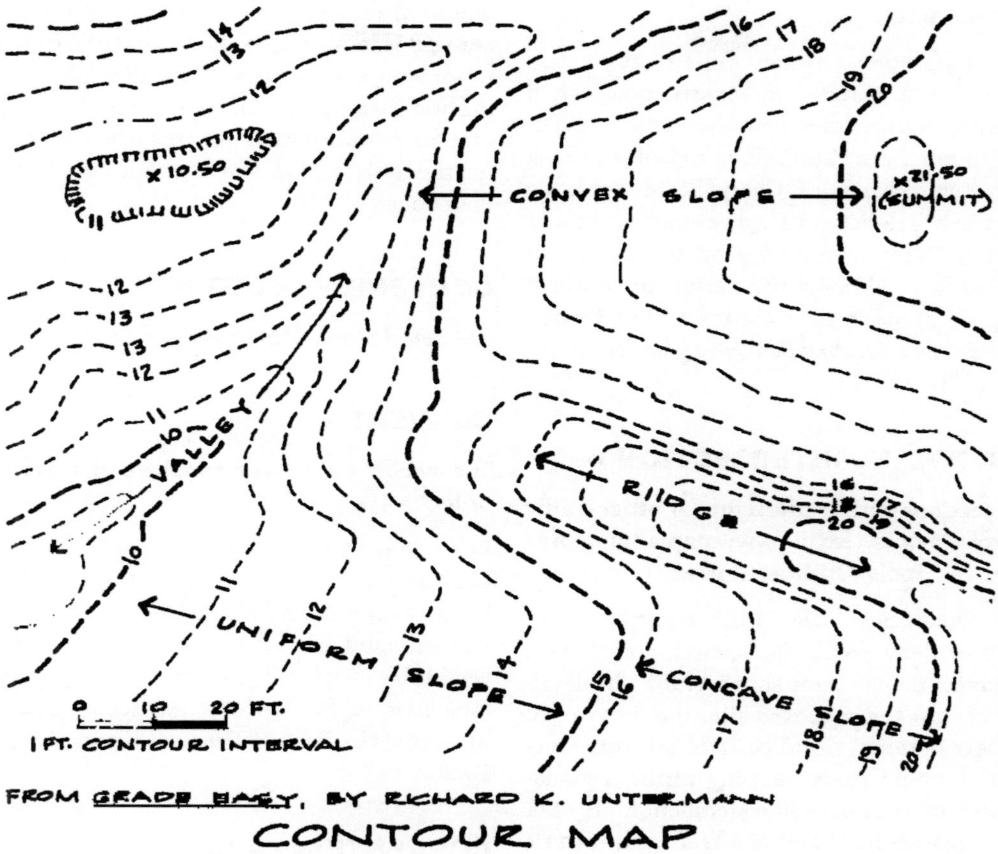


*All points on a contour line have the same elevation. A contour line connects points of the equal elevation. A contour line that closes on itself is either a summit or a depression. Both are indicated by a spot elevation at the highest or the lowest point. A depression is also indicated by placing hachure marks on the low side of the contour line. Contour lines never cross other contours except where there is an overhanging cliff, natural bridge, or similar condition. On a convex slope (gentler slope at the summit), the higher contours are spaced farther apart than the lower ones. On a concave slope (steeper slope at the summit), the lower contour lines are spaced farther apart than the higher ones.*

*Source*: Richard K. Untermann, *Grade Easy* (American Society of Landscape Architects, 1989).

represent a vertical interval. In relatively flat areas, a topographic map using a one- or two-foot contour interval is necessary for planning design and review purposes. For areas with steep slopes, a five- or ten-foot contour interval may be adequate.

***Legal Annotation***: "The land in question is located between the 715-foot **contour line** and Lake Travis. The 715-foot **contour line** is a line 715 feet above mean sea level as established by the United States Geological Survey Bench Marks." *Wall v. Lower Colorado River Authority* (Texas Ct. Civ. App., 1976).

## CONTRACTOR'S STORAGE YARD

**A lot or portion of a lot or parcel used to store and maintain construction equipment and other materials and facilities customarily**

**required in the building trade by a construction contractor.**

*Legal Annotation*: "Duran Construction . . . engages in a variety of construction-related activities, from building new homes and subdivisions to processing and selling topsoil and rock to other contractors. . . . Cheryl Easterwood, the department's director, issued a compliance order requiring Duran to cease topsoil processing and apply for a conditional use permit to continue using the property as a **contractor's storage yard**." *Duran v. City and Borough of Juneau, Alaska* (Alaska, 2005).

## CONTROLLED INTERSECTIONS

**Intersections with traffic lights or other traffic control devices. http://www.pgplanning.org/Resources/Tools_On-line/Glossary.htm**

*Legal Annotation*: "The other commissioners, voting to deny T&C's application, stated their reasons for denial were: 'shoehorning' the development into the proposed site; the distance of the development from **controlled intersections**; a traffic study showing traffic degradation; setting an undesirable precedent for the B-1 zone; negative neighborhood feedback; historic preservation; parking problems; and, meeting the character of the B-1 zone and neighborhood." *Town & Country Foods, Inc. v. City of Bozeman* (Mont., 2009).

## CONVALESCENT CENTER

**A facility that provides short-term, primarily inpatient care, treatment, and/or rehabilitation services for persons recovering from illness or injury who do not require continued hospitalization. See *Intermediate Care Facility*.**

***Comment***: Convalescent centers are now generally referred to as rehabilitation centers. Unlike nursing homes and similar extended and long-term care facilities, convalescent homes are similar to short-term care facilities that assist patients in physical rehabilitation and recovery from illness or injury. They may also include outpatient services.

*Legal Annotation*: "The convalescent and rehabilitation center (hereinafter the **convalescent center**) is located a few hundred yards from the retirement community. It is essentially a nursing home with a full-time nursing staff providing care for 'custodial' type patients who cannot care for themselves." *Estate of Smith v. Commissioner* (Tax Court, 1982).

## CONVENIENCE STORE

See *Retail Store, Convenience*.

## CONVENT

**The dwelling of female members of a religious order.**

*Legal Annotation*: "As proposed, the **convent** would contain a chapel, living and dining areas for the nuns, and a work area where religious and educational literature and tapes would be displayed for sale to the public." *Daughters of St. Paul, Inc. v. Zoning Board of Appeals of the Town of Trumbull* (Conn. App. Ct., 1988).

## CONVENTION FACILITY

**A building or portion thereof designed to accommodate three hundred or more people in assembly. See *Conference Center*.**

***Comment***: The definition is admittedly broad, and the figure three hundred is arbitrary. It is designed to give the municipality as much control over these very intensive uses as possible. Most municipalities restrict them to central business districts. Standards have to be established relating to parking, setbacks, signs, landscaping, and circulation. As many communities have built convention facilities, often with public support, they can be "risky investments" (Minton 2006: 19).

*Legal Annotation*: "A '**convention facility**' is therefore a means used to facilitate the assembly of members of a particular group." *Alexander v. Macon-Bibb County Urban Development Authority* (Ga., 1987).

## CONVENTIONAL ENERGY SYSTEM

**Any energy system, including supply elements, furnaces, burners, tanks, boilers, related controls, and energy-distribution components, that uses any source(s) of energy other than solar energy and windmills.**

*Comment*: The sources of conventional energy systems include the usual fossil fuels, such as gas, oil, and coal, as well as nuclear fuels.

*Legal Annotation*: "Duke **Energy's system** of electrical generating facilities includes nuclear, hydroelectric, gas-fired combustion turbine, and coal-fired generating plants." *US v. Duke Energy Corporation* (M.D.N.C., 2003).

## CONVERSION

**A change in the use of land or a structure.**

## COOLING TOWER

**A device to remove excess heat from water used in industrial operations, notably in electric power generation.**

*Legal Annotation*: "All three states sought to introduce evidence intended to show that operation of the facility without a **cooling tower** system for reducing the temperature of water discharged into the river would harm the natural resources of the river." *State of New Hampshire v. Atomic Energy Commission* (1st Cir., 1969).

## CORNER LOT

**See *Lot, Corner*.**

## CORNICE

**Any horizontal member, structural or nonstructural, projecting outward from the exterior walls at the roofline, including eaves and other roof overhang. *See Figure 25*.**

*Legal Annotation*: "Indeed, the evidence suggests that the board has refused to grant any height variances in the Back Bay neighborhood in the past ten or more years in order to 'maintain the architectural integrity of the neighborhood as manifested in original, unbroken roof and **cornice** lines.'" *Steamboat Realty, LLC v. Zoning Board of Appeal of Boston* (Mass. App. Ct., 2007).

**Figure 25**

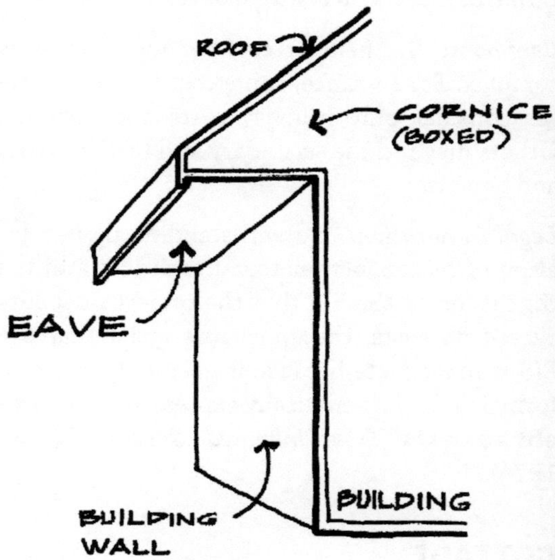


## CORPORATION STOP

**Also known as corporation cock. A valve is placed in a building's water or gas service pipe near its junction with the public water or gas main.**

*Legal Annotation*: "A **corporation stop** is a device that cuts off the water supply from the main water service line." *FNB v. Mountain Cascade, Inc.* (Calif. App. Ct., 2000).

## CORRECTIONAL FACILITY

**A public or privately operated facility housing persons awaiting trial or persons serving a sentence after being found guilty of a criminal offense.**

*Legal Annotation*: "The PLRA provides: 'No action shall be brought with respect to prison conditions under section 1983 of this title, or any other Federal law, by a prisoner confined in any jail, prison, or other **correctional facility** until such administrative remedies as are available are exhausted.'" *Woodford v. Ngo* (U.S., 2006).

## COST-BENEFIT ANALYSIS

**An analytical method whereby the costs of a proposed project are measured against the benefits to be received from the project (Mary Edwards). See *Also Fiscal Impact Analysis*.**

***Comment***: The field of cost-benefit analysis is complex. For instance, some cost-benefit analyses consider only primary costs and benefits. Others may include secondary and tertiary costs and benefits.

***Legal Annotation***: "Notwithstanding this evaluation of reasonably related alternatives and the conclusion of the EIS that the project's benefits exceed its costs, the appellants insist that the EIS is inadequate because it does not contain a formal and mathematically expressed **cost-benefit analysis**." *Trout Unlimited v. Morton* (9th Cir., 1974).

## COTTAGE

**A small, detached dwelling unit.**

***Comment***: A cottage is usually an outbuilding on a larger tract of land. Originally, the cottage may have been a seasonal dwelling without heat but later converted to an all-year-round dwelling. Local ordinances should specify minimum standards for space, heating, and sanitary facilities as a condition of conversion.

***Legal Annotation***: "In 1939 Annette and James Darnell conveyed most of the tract to Harry and Roscoe Baldwin by a warranty deed which reserved 'the small **cottage** and a half acre garden plot' to the Darnells." *Guido v. Baldwin* (Ind. Ct. App., 1977).

## COTTAGE INDUSTRY

**A home occupation.**

***Comment***: "Cottage industry" is an obsolete term previously used to describe manufacturing and assembly carried out in the home, often on a contract basis, with the entire family working. In later years, cottage industry was accessory to the principal residential use and was often carried out in an outbuilding or accessory structure. It is now used to describe start-up businesses or occupations carried out by single practitioners in their homes.

***Legal Annotation***: "The home occupation issue is not as easily resolved. The Superior Court judge tracked the factual findings of the board, which essentially are not in dispute. The plaintiff began applying her own floral designs to premanufactured clothing in 1985. What originated as a one-person craft operation became a successful **cottage industry**." *Burnham v. Town Of Hadley* (Mass. App. Ct., 2003).

## COUNCIL OF GOVERNMENTS

**A regional planning and review authority whose membership includes representation from all communities in the designated region.**

***Legal Annotation***: "Defendant delegated to the Orange County **Council of Governments** (OCCOG), another public agency created under section 6500 that includes the County of Orange and the incorporated cities within its boundaries, 'the responsibility for providing data that would be used by [defendant] when [it] applied the methodology used to determine the allocation of housing units to jurisdictions within Orange County.'" *City of Irvine v. Southern California Association of Governments* (Calif. Ct. App., 2009).

## COUNTRY CLUB

**A recreational facility, usually restricted to members and their guests, that generally includes a clubhouse, dining and eating establishments, and recreational facilities such as golf courses, tennis courts, and swimming pools.**

***Comment***: While most country club facilities are restricted to members and their guests, some clubs make available their facilities to nonmembers for weddings, banquets, golf tournaments, dances, conferences, and so forth. In addition, the restaurants may be open to the general public, and some country clubs offer limited memberships for specific facilities such as golf, swimming, or tennis. The expanded use of the country club to nonmembers often creates a year-round, active, and heavily patronized facility. When these clubs are located in residential areas, the heavy use can create friction between surrounding residents and club patrons.

Another factor to be considered is the fact that the golf course, almost always a feature of a country club, is a significant user of water and is heavily dependent on pesticides and fertilizers. New clubs should be required to indicate water sources and a best-management protocol limiting the use of chemical pesticides and fertilizers.

*Legal Annotation*: "It is mutually understood by the parties that both conveyance and loan before mentioned are in consideration of the construction by the Club of a first-class **country club** on said property, including an eighteen-hole golf course, and adequate club house and recreational facilities." *Country Club Estates, Inc. v. Commissioner of Internal Revenue* (Tax Court, 1954).

## COUNTY MASTER PLAN

**The official master plan for the physical development of a county.**

*Legal Annotation*: "The Planning Commission argues, however, that the provisions of 3.08 of Article 66B . . . permits the Board to reject the subdivision on grounds of non-compliance with the presently existing Cecil **County Master Plan**. The Board feels that the short answer to this contention is the fact that while the **Master Plan** constitutes a useful, effective, and necessary guideline in the planning and zoning area, it does not have statutory effect until implemented by the Zoning Ordinance." *Board of County Commissioners v. Gaster* (Md. Ct. App., 1979).

## COURT

**Any open space, unobstructed from the ground to the sky, that is bounded on two or more sides by the walls of a building that is on the same lot. See *Plaza; Square. See Figure 20 and 26.***

*Comment*: As indicated in Figures 20 and 26, there are two types of courts: inner and outer courts.

*Legal Annotation*: "Chapter 66 of the [Chicago Zoning Ordinance] Municipal Code provides the following criteria: 66-1.1 (a) **Court**. A **court** is an open, unobstructed space on the same lot with the building." *Baron v. Abt* (Ill. App. Ct., 1965).

**Figure 26**

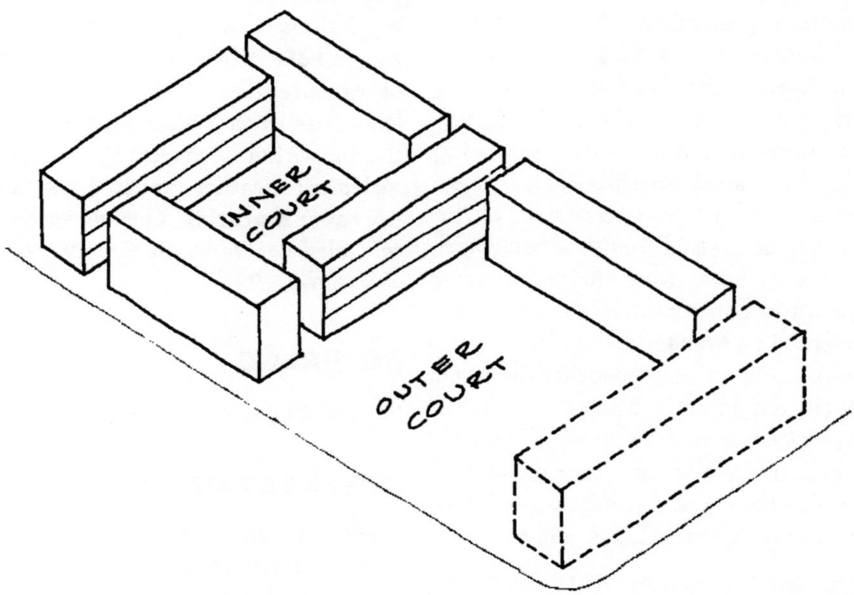

**"Inner Court.** An **inner court** is a court entirely surrounded by building walls or lot lines or any court not defined as a through or outer court." Chapter 66 of the [Chicago Zoning Ordinance] *Municipal Code*; 66-1.1 (e).

**"Outer Court.** An **outer court** is a court open on one end to an open space not less than thirty feet wide. The open space shall be a public way, yard or through court or any combination of two or more such areas." Chapter 66 of the [Chicago Zoning Ordinance] *Municipal Code*; 66-1.1 (d).

## COURTYARD

**"Landscaped outdoor areas that are walled for privacy" (Paguette 2004: 11).**

***Comment***: "'The concept of an outdoor private area has always been popular in warmer climates, but now wherever buildable lots have gotten smaller, the private area has gotten smaller, and courtyards are just starting to be constructed in the Northeast,' said Michael Medick of the Baltimore-based Medick Architects and Town Planners and a member of the National Association of Home Builders' 20-member design committee, which follows design trends. He said a courtyard for a home on a small lot can often raise the price of the house by up to 25 percent. According to another committee member, Michael Kephart who has a community planning and architectural firm in Denver, the creation of courtyards began more than 100 years ago in the Southwest when residents constructed overhanging roofs over outdoor areas for shade and privacy. Today, they are built in about 50 percent of the homes in the region, he said. 'In this modern age,' Mr. Kephart said, 'even with air-conditioning, people enjoy sitting outdoors, and one of the most valued elements in a home is the quality of outdoor space with privacy.' He noted that the trend has already taken hold in the Midwest. 'Probably the New York region is as far as it will go,' he said. Areas far north of the city are not prime targets because the weather is not warm for a good part of the year, he said" (Paguette 2004: 11).

***Legal Annotation***: "In addition, he testified that SWAP planned to create an open **courtyard**; connect the buildings with a roofline; and use a composite material with clapboards and shingles for the buildings' sheathings." *Carello v. Zoning Board of Review of City Of Providence* (R.I. Super. Ct., 2013).

## COVE

**A small bay or inlet or a sheltered recess in a cliff face.**

***Legal Annotation***: "The mouth of the **cove** lies on its west side between two rocky points directly to the north and south. The **cove** lies just east of a sloping rocky foreshore which rises from the ocean up to a rocky sill—also called a 'bench' and a 'dam' in the testimony—which then opens into the **cove**." *McDonald v. Halvorson* (Ore., 1989).

## COVENANT

**See *Restrictive Covenant*.**

## COVER MATERIAL

**Soil that is used to cover compacted solid waste in a sanitary landfill.**

***Legal Annotation***: "A landfill no longer in use must be sealed or closed in accordance with Mississippi Nonhazardous Waste Management Regulation No. PC/S-1. . . . Section D-19 of the regulations reads in part: A final cover of at least two feet of earthen material, compacted in layers of no more than 12 inches, shall be placed over the entire surface of each completed portion of the fill within 30 days after completion unless inclement weather prevents the application of dry **cover material**." *Commission on Environmental Quality v. Chickasaw County board of Supervisors* (Miss., 1993).

## COVERAGE

**See *Building Coverage; Lot Coverage*.**

## COVERED EMPLOYMENT

**Employees covered by the state's unemployment compensation law.**

***Comment***: In some states, covered employment and covered employment trends are used in formulas to determine lower-income housing needs. The amount of change is measured by a linear regression equation over a time span sufficiently long—seven years, for example—to minimize the impact of short-term fluctuations.

***Legal Annotation***: "In our view, the term 'participant' is naturally read to mean either 'employees in, or reasonably expected to be in, currently **covered employment**,' or former employees who 'have . . . a reasonable expectation of returning to **covered employment**' or who have 'a colorable claim' to vested benefits." *Firestone Tire & Rubber Co. v. Bruch* (U.S., 1989).

## CRAFTSPERSON

**An individual having creative skills in manufacturing or arrangement of materials resulting in a finished product or commodity such as wearing apparel, home decorations, jewelry, toys, furniture, leather goods, dried flowers, or similar products.**

***Legal Annotation***: "Arts and Cultural Affairs Law § 12.01 provides that notwithstanding any custom or agreement to the contrary, whenever 'an artist . . . delivers . . . a work of fine art, craft or a print of his own creation to an art merchant for the purpose of exhibition and/or sale on a commission, fee or other basis of compensation, the delivery to and acceptance thereof by the art merchant establishes a consignor/consignee relationship as between such artist or **craftsperson**.'" *Koeniges v. Woodward* (N.Y. Cnty. Civ. Ct., 2000).

## CRAWL SPACE

**A space of no more than four and a half feet high below the first floor or between the ceiling of one story and the floor of the next story, which usually contains pipes, ducts, and wiring and lighting fixtures, and permits access but is too low for an individual to stand. *See Figure 8.***

***Comment***: The crawl space may be a cellar area or, if between a ceiling and a flat or shed roof, a cockloft.

***Legal Annotation***: "[D]avid Berkel, the chief of police of Lenox, entered a **crawl space** under the defendant's first-floor apartment on Housatonic Street with the permission of the owner of the property. The crawl space is used for access to pipes and wiring." *Commonwealth v. Panetti* (Mass: Supreme Judicial Court 1989).

## CREDIT SCORE

**A single numerical score, based on an individual's credit history, that measures that individual's credit worthiness.**

***Comment***: A widely used credit score is called FICO for Fair Issac Co., which developed it (http://www.mtgprofessor.com/glossary.htm).

## CREEK

**A small stream somewhat larger than a brook.**

***Legal Annotation***: "The appellate court quoted *Black's Law Dictionary's* definition of a '**creek**,' stating, 'A **creek** is "[a] small stream less than a river. The term imports a recess, cove, bay or inlet in the shore of a river and not a separate or independent stream."'" *People v. Village of Hawthorn Woods* (Ill. App. Ct., 2012).

## CRITERIA POLLUTANT

**One of the six air pollutants used by the federal Environmental Protection Agency to measure ambient air quality under the Clean Air Act.**

***Comment***: The six air pollutants are nitrogen dioxide, sulfur dioxide, particulate matter, lead, ozone, and carbon monoxide. See *Performance Zoning.*

***Legal Annotation***: Section 110 of the Clean Air Act "ensures that levels of certain **'criteria' pollutants** in the ambient air do not exceed specified healthful levels. For each **criteria pollutant**, EPA promulgates NAAQS [national ambient air quality standards] sufficient to protect the public health with an adequate margin of safety and to protect the public welfare." *Michigan Dept. of Environmental Quality v. Browner* ($6^{th}$ Cir., 2000).

## CRITICAL AREA

**An area with one or more of the following environmental characteristics: (1) steep slopes;**

**(2) floodplain; (3) soils classified as having high water tables; (4) soils classified as highly erodible, subject to erosion, or highly acidic; (5) land incapable of meeting percolation requirements; (6) land formerly used for landfill operations or hazardous industrial use; (7) fault areas; (8) stream corridors; (9) estuaries; (10) mature stands of native vegetation; (11) aquifer recharge and discharge areas; (12) wetlands and wetland transition areas; and (13) habitats of endangered species. See *Conservation Area*.**

*Comment*: The purpose of classifying certain lands as critical areas is to focus attention on these lands and to set standards to regulate development in these areas. Local ordinances should specify standards within these general categories, such as the percentages of slope considered steep (often 20 percent) or water table height. The additional requirements may also include the preparation and submission of an environmental impact statement or requirement that the applicant specifically address what measures will be taken with respect to the critical elements. Local development ordinances can also provide for shifting development from critical areas to noncritical areas of the site. This transfer provision often results in greater cooperation from builders, since the development potential of the site is preserved. See *Cluster Subdivision*.

*Legal Annotation*: "In 1984, the General Assembly enacted the Chesapeake Bay **Critical Area** Protection Program . . . embracing several key policy choices, namely that the Chesapeake Bay and its tributaries 'are natural resources of great significance to the State and the nation' [and] that the shoreline constitutes 'a valuable, fragile, and sensitive part of this estuarine system.'" *Critical Area Commission v. Moreland* (Md. Ct. App., 2011).

## CRITICAL HABITATS

**Biologically diverse areas containing habitats of endangered or threatened plant or animal species; contiguous freshwater wetland systems, defined as the zone of biological diversity primarily supported by wetlands and wetland systems; and prime forested areas, including mature stands of native species. See *Biodiversity*.**

*Legal Annotation*: "The District Court found that closure of the dam and the consequent impoundment of the reservoir would 'result in the adverse modification, if not complete destruction, of the snail darter's **critical habitat**,' making it 'highly probable' that 'the continued existence of the snail darter' would be 'jeopardize[d].'" *TVA v. Hill* (U.S., 1978).

## CROP

**A harvestable product, planted, grown, and cultivated in the soil.**

*Legal Annotation*: "Except in regions of large-scale production, wheat is usually grown in rotation with other **crops**; for a nurse crop for grass seeding; and as a cover crop to prevent soil erosion and leaching." *Wickard v. Filburn* (U.S., 1942).

## CROSSWALK

**Any portion of a roadway distinctly indicated for pedestrian crossing by lines or other surface markings or by a change in surface material. *See Figure 14*.**

*Legal Annotation*: "[R]esidents in the neighborhood of that intersection made it known to County officials that they were having difficulty crossing Pacheco to get to and from the bus stop; in response, the County painted a **crosswalk** at the intersection. Other than bus patrons, few pedestrians used the **crosswalk**." *Bonanno v. Central Contra Costa Transit Authority* (Calif., 2003).

## CUBIC CONTENT SPACE

**The volume of space contained within the walls of a room or building, found by multiplying the height, width, and length.**

*Legal Annotation*: "In Arizona, condominium ownership consists of individual ownership of a horizontal layer of **cubic content space**, subject to the owner's exclusive control, together with a fractional interest held in common with other unit owners in the common elements." *Mountain View Condo Ass'n v. Scott* (Ariz. Ct. App., 1994).

## CUBIC FEET PER SECOND

See *CFS*.

## CUL-DE-SAC

See *Street, Cul-De-Sac; Street, Dead-End.*

## CULTURAL EUTROPHICATION

**Acceleration of the natural aging process of bodies of water.**

*Comment*: Eutrophication often takes place because of runoff from cultivated lawns or the use of septic systems that introduce nutrients into the water, thus hastening the growth of algae and underwater plants.

*Legal Annotation*: "In **cultural eutrophication**, high levels of nutrients are added to a lake, dissolved oxygen levels are lowered, and the lake experiences a rapid growth in rooted plants along the shore and algae in the water." *Stoddard v. Western Carolina Regional Sewer Auth.* (4th Cir., 1986).

## CULTURAL FACILITIES

**Establishments that document the social and religious structures and intellectual and artistic manifestations that characterize a society and include museums, art galleries, and botanical and zoological gardens of a natural, historic, educational, or cultural interest (*New Lexicon Webster Dictionary* 1989).**

*Comment*: While these activities may charge admission fees, the bulk of their expenses is usually borne by public agencies, foundations, or donations. Cultural facilities can foster city revitalization (Knack 2008).

*Legal Annotation*: "The District is 'formed for the express purposes of "Molding fairs, expositions and exhibitions for the purpose of exhibiting all of the industries and industrial enterprises, resources and products of every kind or nature of the state with a view toward improving, exploiting, encouraging, and stimulating them," and "[c] onstructing, maintaining, and operating recreational and **cultural facilities** of general public interest."'" *Bame v. City of Del Mar* (Calif. Ct. App., 2001).

## CULVERT

**A drain, ditch, or conduit, not incorporated in a closed system, that carries drainage water under a driveway, roadway, railroad, pedestrian walk, or public way, or other type of overhead structure.**

*Legal Annotation*: "Consequently, he designed a five-foot **culvert** under the bypass to handle normal rainfall drainage from the area west of the bypass. Downs admitted that this **culvert** was inadequate to drain the creek's other normal overflows." *Heins Implement v. Hwy. Transp. Com'n* (Mo., 1993).

## CUMULATIVE IMPACT

**The total impact that results from an individual action under consideration, when added to the impacts of other past, present, and reasonably foreseeable future actions (*New Jersey State Development and Redevelopment Plan* 2002).**

*Comment*: The cumulative impact analysis is particularly important in assessing traffic and utility capacities. See *Capacity Analysis.*

*Legal Annotation*: "A **cumulative impact** on the environment 'results from the incremental impact of the action when added to other past, present, and reasonably foreseeable future actions.' 40 C.F.R. § 1508.7. **Cumulative impacts** may result from 'individually minor but collectively significant actions taking place over a period of time.'" *Blue Mountains Biodiversity Project v. Blackwood* (9th Cir., 1998).

## CUPOLA

**A small dome-like structure on the roof of a building or structure and designed to provide ventilation and/or decoration.**

*Legal Annotation*: "At this northeast corner of the city hall, there seems to be an old bell tower, which forms a **cupola**. The roof of the **cupola**, which is hip-roof construction, comes down on the north and east side of the building." *Ritgers v. City of Gillespie* (Ill. App. Ct., 1953).

## CURB

**A stone, concrete, or other improved boundary marking the edge of the roadway or paved area. See *Belgian Block Curb*. See *Figures 27 and 28*.**

*Legal Annotation*: "Now, you are hereby instructed that a **curb** is defined as a stone or row of stones or a similar construction of concrete, wood, or other material along the margin of the roadway as a limit to the roadway and a restraint upon and protection to the adjoining sidewalk space." *Hyatt v. Sierra Boat Co.* (Calif. App. Ct., 1978)

*Legal Annotation*: "In particular, the expert found 'no protective **curb** surrounding the concrete sidewalk curb ramp,' that is, '[t]he street asphalt [met] the curb ramp directly.' He thus concluded that either the City or its agents had constructed the curb ramp without a protective **curb** in place and without ensuring that the ramp was flush with the street, or the **curb** had sunk relative to

**Figure 27**

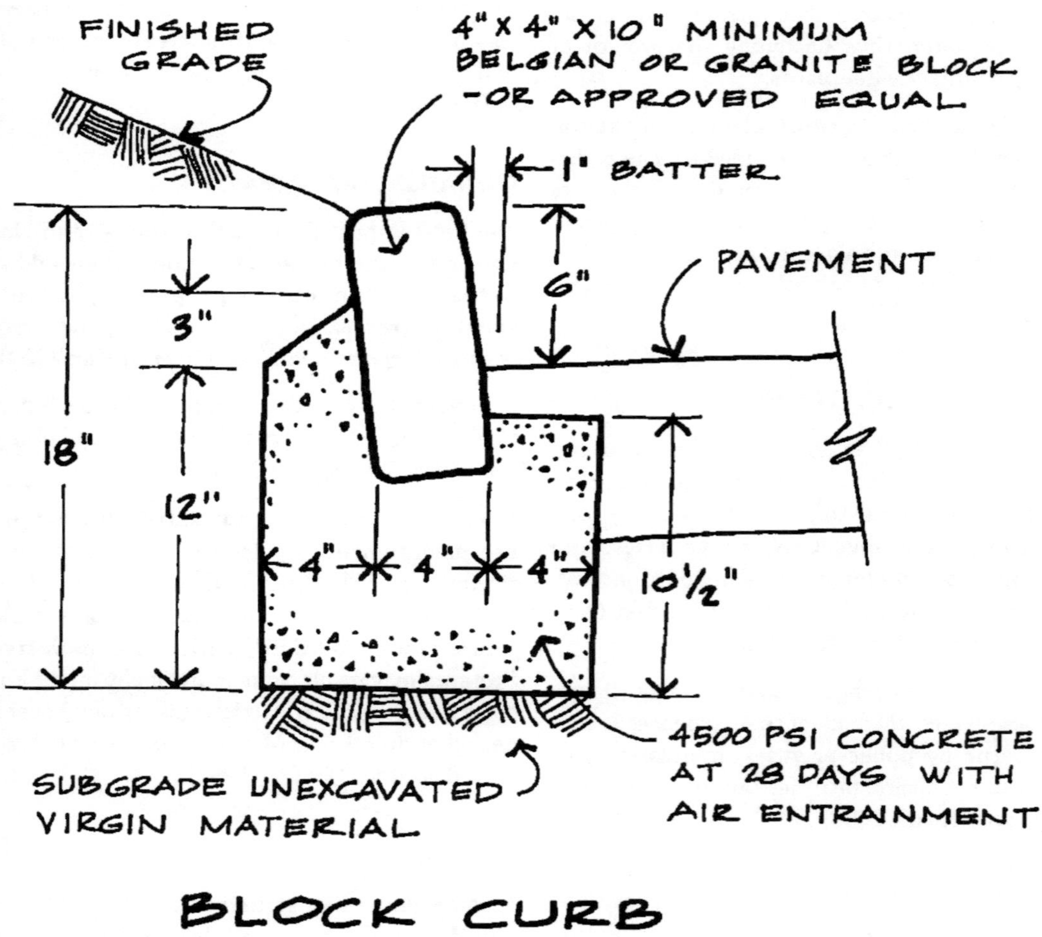

**Figure 28**

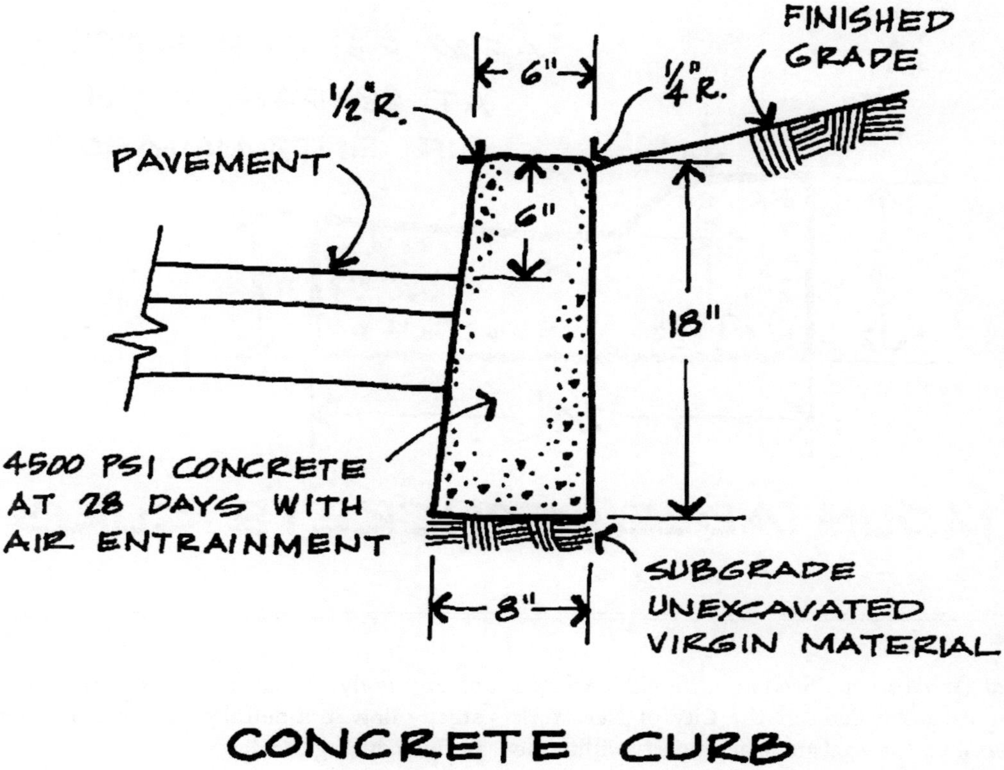


the ramp and had been paved over." *Ortiz v. City of New York* (N.Y. App. Div., 2009).

### CURB, MOUNTABLE

**A low curb with a slope designed to be crossed easily. *See Figure 29.***

*Legal Annotation*: "The curb in question is a **mountable curb**, which by its very design is meant to be used by pedestrians exiting their automobiles." *Bessard v. State DOTD* (La. Ct. App., 1994).

### CURBSIDE COLLECTION

**The collection of solid waste placed adjacent to a street.**

*Legal Annotation*: "ABC provides **curbside collection** and disposal of solid waste and recycling for participating households and small businesses. ABC employees driving company trucks have on occasion caused damage to the trucks and to personal property of third parties." *Camara v. Attorney General* (Mass., 2011).

### CURB CUT

**The opening along the curb line at which point vehicles may enter or leave the roadway. *See* Figure 74.**

*Legal Annotation*: "In conjunction with the proposed redesign of their house, in 1994, the Dadians sought a 6" side variance from the Village, which was approved, and a **curb cut** for a front driveway." *Dadian v. Village of Wilmette* (7th Cir., 2001).

### CURB LEVEL

**The permanently established grade of the curb top in front of a lot.**

Figure 29

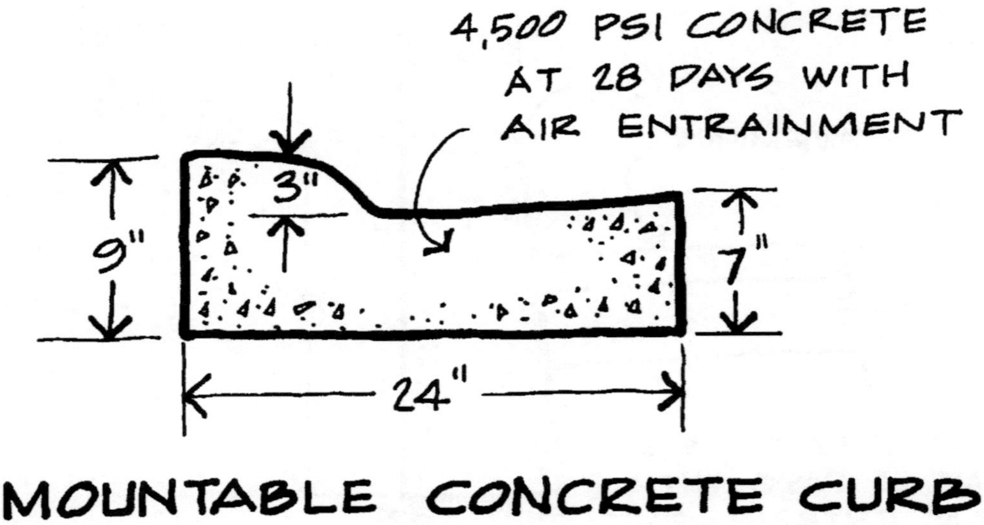


*Legal Annotation*: 'Section C26-562.0 of the Administrative Code of the City of New York determines the legal grade of property within the city. . . . [I]t provides: 'Regulation of lots. —The regulation of lots, in conformity with the street on which they are situated, shall be calculated at **curb level**.' . . . This necessarily means that the grade of a lot must be determined by the grade at **curb level**, but there is nothing in the law which compels an owner to erect his property level with the grade of the curb." *People v. Wittman* (N.Y.Ct. Spec. Sess., 1954).

## CURB RETURN

**The connecting link between the street curb and the ramp or driveway curb. *See Figure 30*.**

*Legal Annotation*: "The section of the curb that is curved between the two tangent points is called the **curb return."** *News Printing Co. v. Borough of Totowa* (N.J. Super. Ct., 1986).

## CURRENT

**(1) The volume of water passing a given point measured in cubic feet per second; (2) the part of any body of water that has more or less steady flow in a definite direction for certain periods during the day.**

*Legal Annotation*: "The trial court . . . dismissed the complaint on the ground that there was no right under the constitution and laws of the State of Idaho to appropriate the **current** of the river so as to render it impossible for others to apply the otherwise unappropriated waters of the river to beneficial uses." *Schodde v. Twin Falls Land & Water Co.* (U.S., 1912).

## CURRENT EXPENDITURES

**All expenditures, with the exception of capital outlay. Includes current operations, assistance and subsidies, interest on debt, and insurance benefits and payments (http://www.census.gov/govs/local/definitions.html).**

*Legal Annotation*: "If the court finds that the local government is 'reasonably certain to fail to make a debt service payment or reasonably certain to not have sufficient revenue to pay **current expenditures**,' it will appoint a fiscal administrator." *State Ex Rel. Caldwell v. Town of Jonesboro* (La. Ct. App., 2012).

**Figure 30**

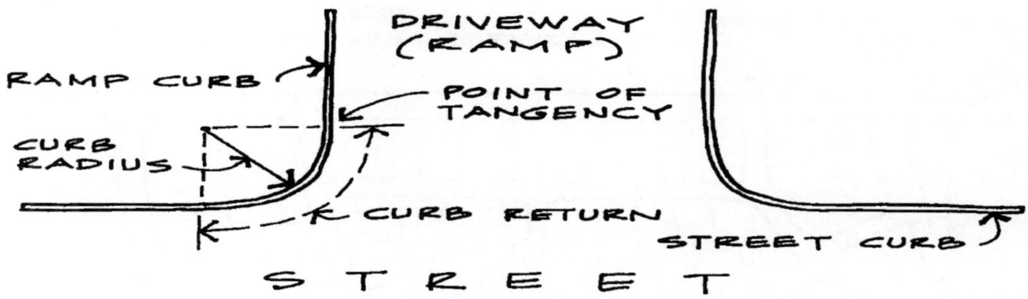


## CURRENT PLANNING CAPACITY (CPC)

**A measure of the ability of a region to accommodate growth and development within the limits set by existing infrastructure and natural resource capabilities. See *Capacity Analysis; Cumulative Impact*.**

***Comment***: Generally, CPC is defined by water supply, water and air quality, sewage capability, highway capacity, and available community facilities. Some development ordinances award points for various infrastructure improvements and subtract them when certain environmental constraints are noted. The higher the number of points, the higher the permitted development density. In Florida, a "CPC-like" point system, included in an Urban Area Residential checklist (part of the County Comprehensive Plan), permits applicants to request higher densities based on the following: proximity to commercial or employment centers; vehicular access to an arterial; access to mass transit; fire protection; water supply and sewers; percentage of affordable housing to be provided; access to schools; and proximity to parks and recreation. It is important to keep in mind that CPC does not necessarily yield appropriate or desired densities or levels of development. It often represents a cap.

***Legal Annotation***: "Appellant argues under Point IV of its brief that the RMP violates N.J.S.A. 13:20-8(a) because it fails to recommend adequate receiving zones for transfer development rights in the Highlands Region and fails to designate the **development capacity** of each receiving zone." *Toll Brothers, Inc. v. Corzine* (N.J. App. Div., 2011).

## CURTAIN WALL

**A nonstructural exterior building wall, usually window- or window panel-dominated.**

***Legal Annotation***: "A **curtain wall** is not a part of the structural skeleton of the building, as would be a weight bearing wall. It simply spans an upper and lower deck (or floor) of the building, enclosing that floor." *Village of Cross Keys v. US Gypsum* (Md. Ct. App., 1989).

## CURVILINEAR STREET SYSTEM

**A pattern of streets that is curved. *See Figure 31*.**

***Legal Annotation***: "**Curvilinear Street System** - A pattern of streets which is curved." *Bolivar, Tenn. Subdivision Regulations* (2013).

## CUT

**A portion of land surface or area from which earth has been removed or will be removed by excavation; the depth below the original ground surface or excavated surface. *See Figure 47*.**

***Legal Annotation***: "At about the same time, the slushing operation was going on in the area to receive the fill or embankment and the appellant was not able to proceed with a large **cut** or excavation to move the earth as there was no place to receive it." *Gasparini Excavating Co. v. Pennsylvania Turnpike Commission* (Pa., 1963).

Figure 31

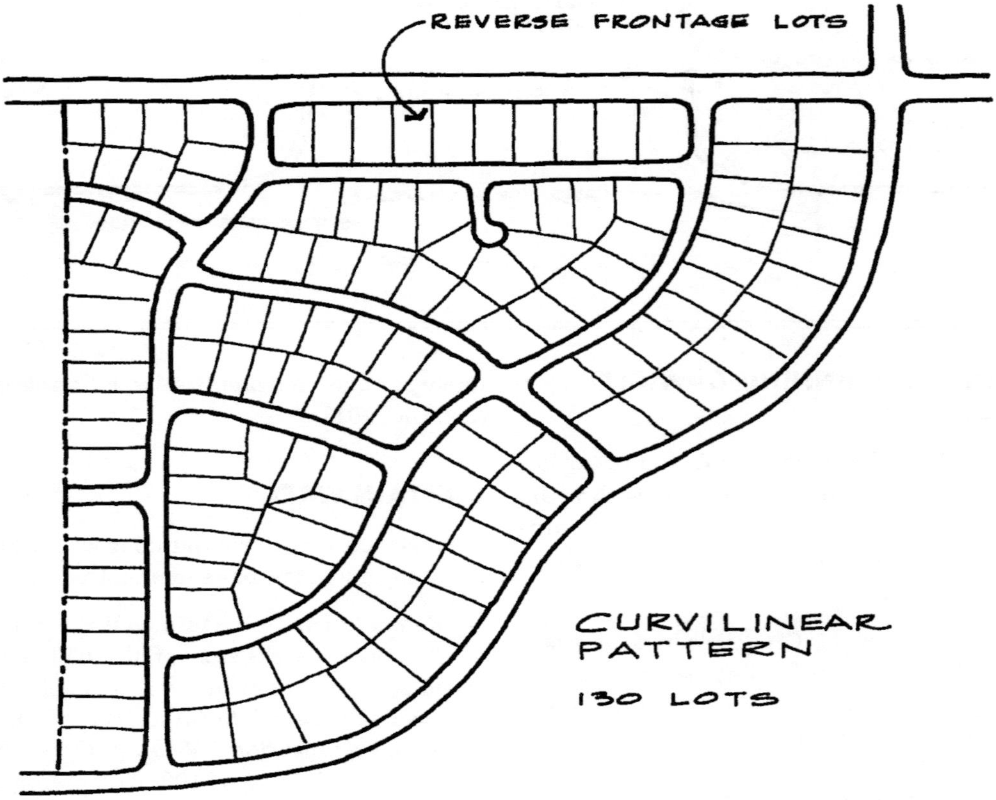


## CUTOFF

**The point at which all light rays emitted by a lamp, light source, or luminaire are completely eliminated at a specific angle above the ground (Kendig et al. 1980).**

*Legal Annotation*: "The OLC requires that display lot lighting fixtures must either be fully shielded, thus permitting no light rays to be emitted at an angle above the horizontal plane of the fixture, or be designed or provided with sharp **cut-off** capability, so as to minimize up-light, spill-light, and glare." Footnote 4, *Ellet Media Co. v. City of Tuscon* (Ariz: Court of Appeals, 2nd Div. 2000).

## CUTOFF ANGLE

**The angle formed by a line drawn from the direction of light rays at the light source and a line perpendicular to the ground from the light source, above which no light is emitted (Kendig et al. 1980).**

*Legal Annotation*: "Limits on **Cutoff Angle**. Cutoff from a lighting source that illuminates an outdoor recreational use may exceed an angle of ninety (90) degrees from the pole, provided that the luminaries are shielded to prevent light and glare to spill over to adjacent residential properties." Chap. 1167, *Lighting Regulations*, Wooster, Ohio.

## CUTOFF LIGHTING

**A lamp or source of illumination with elements such as a shield, reflector, or refractor panels that direct and cut off the light at a cutoff angle less than ninety degrees (Kendig et al. 1980).**

***Legal Annotation***: "The Board approved the Church's application for the conditional use permit subject to the following conditions: . . . 7. All lighting on the site shall be full **cut-off lighting** with the point source of light not visible from adjacent properties." *Arnold v. Woodford County Board of Adjustment Members* (Ky. Ct. App., 2007).

## CYBER

**Usually used in connection with references to automated systems, both in terms of hardware and software (VHA Emergency Management Guidebook 2005). http://www.gwu.edu/~icdrm/publications/PDF/GLOSSARY%2002-19-2007.pdf**

***Legal Annotation***: "Plaintiffs contend that Flava Works' '**cyber**-business' is unnecessarily burdened by this ordinance because its business does not impose any of the nuisances on residential zones that traditional businesses do. The fact that an internet-based business may, in some respects, be different than a 'traditional' business is inapposite." *Flava Works, Inc. v. City of Miami, Fla.* (S.D. Fla., 2011).

## CYCLONIC SEPARATOR

**See *Industrial Separator*.**

# D

## DAM

**Any artificial dike, levee or other barrier, together with appurtenant works, that is constructed for the purpose of impounding water, on a permanent or temporary basis, that raises the water level five feet or more above the usual mean low water height when measured from the downstream toe-of-dam to the emergency spillway crest or, in the absence of an emergency spillway, the top-of-dam. See *Embankment*.**

***Legal Annotation***: "When fully operational, the **dam** would impound water covering some 16,500 acres—much of which represents valuable and productive farmland—thereby converting the river's shallow, fast-flowing waters into a deep reservoir over 30 miles in length." *TVA v. Hill* (U.S., 1978).

## DAMAGE ASSESSMENT

**An appraisal or determination of the effects of the disaster on human, physical, economic, and natural resources (NFPA 1600, 2004). http://www.gwu.edu/~icdrm/publications/PDF/GLOSSARY%2002-19-2007.pdf**

***Legal Annotation***: "Desvousges opined that a natural resource's lost services and uses 'play a critical role in **damage assessment**' and are a commonly accepted component of natural resources economics. He stated that compensable damages cannot be calculated unless the lost services and uses resulting from contamination are identified and quantified." *New Jersey Department of Environmental Protection v. Essex Chemical Corporation* (N.J. Super. Ct., 2012).

## DATUM

**A reference point, line, or plane used as a basis for measurements.**

## DAYCARE

**A building or structure where care, protection, and supervision are provided on a regular schedule for a fee *(Ware v. Zoning Board of Appeals, Village of Fairfax;* Lawlor 2006: 31).**

***Legal Annotation***: "'**Day care**' is defined as non-medical care provided on less than a 24-hour basis." *Brown v. County of San Joaquin* (E.D. Calif., 1985).

## DAY-CARE CENTER/DAY NURSERY

**See *Child-Care Center*.**

## DAY LABORER

**A worker hired and paid by the day, with no promise of work in the future.**

***Comment***: According to the US Department of Labor, approximately one hundred and twenty thousand day laborers congregate daily at over four hundred locations throughout the USA, seeking daily work, usually in construction, or as painters, roofers, farm workers, or other manual laborers. They usually congregate on street corners along major thoroughfares, although some communities have established hiring halls, and churches and other nonprofit organizations have provided similar space for day laborers (Downey 200:, 9).

## dBA

**The unit of measurement for the total sound level of all noise as measured with a sound level meter using the A-weighted network. See *A-Weighted Sound Level*.**

***Comment***: The unit, dBA, is based on a reference sound pressure of .0002 microbars. In the A-weighted network system, decibel values are corrected for low frequency and are thought to better indicate the injurious nature of noise on human hearing. https://www.osha.gov/SLTC/noisehearingconversation

*Legal Annotation*: "The threshold set by the City of Berkeley's noise ordinance for the Institute, an R-3 zoned property, was 65 **dBA**." *Save Strawberry Canyon v. US Dept. Of Energy* (N.D. Calif., 2011).

## DEAD-END STREET

**See *Street, Dead-End*.**

## DECELERATION LANE

**An added roadway lane that permits vehicles to slow down and leave the main vehicle stream. *See Figure 1*.**

*Legal Annotation*: "Savala's design combines two preexisting adjacent approaches into a single upgraded encroachment that will include a new left-turn bay, a right-hand **deceleration lane**, and a merging lane to allow eastbound traffic to drive straight past the approach—all of which are features that will mitigate concerns about drivers on Highway 55 having to slow down or swerve to avoid traffic entering the highway from Savala's approach." *Vickers v. Lowe* (Idaho, 2011).

## DECIBEL

**A unit of measurement for sound pressure or the relative loudness of sound that is abbreviated as dB.**

*Comment*: The decibel (abbreviated dB) is used to express noise level. The reference level is a sound pressure of 20 micronewtons per square meter. Zero decibels, the starting point of the scale of noise level, is about the level of the weakest sound that can be heard by someone with very good hearing in an extremely quiet location. The noise level in an average residence is about fifty decibels; twenty feet from a subway train, the noise level is about ninety decibels; and two hundred feet from a jet, it is 120 decibels. **See *Table D*-1.**

*Legal Annotation*: "This conclusion is supported by the EPA, which has stated that 'adding a 60 **decibel** sound to a 70 **decibel** sound only increases the total sound pressure level less than one-half **decibel**.'" *Mid States Coal for Progress v. Surface Transp. Bd.* (8th Cir. 2003).

## DECIDUOUS

**Plants that drop their foliage annually before becoming dormant.**

*Comment*: In specifying landscaping for buffer areas, there should be a mix of deciduous and evergreen trees, with the predominant emphasis on evergreens, which provide an all-year-round buffer.

*Legal Annotation*: "Omnipoint reassured the Board that the proposed tower would have minimal visual impact on the community because a tower disguised as a tree would blend in, camouflaged by the local 'mature and **deciduous** tree line.'" *Omnipoint Communications v. City of White Plains* (2nd Cir. 2005).

## DECK

**(1) An unroofed platform, either freestanding or attached to a building that is supported by pillars or posts; (2) a pier or landing for a boat.**

*Legal Annotation*: "The denied request was for an area variance to the side setback requirements so that the plaintiffs could build a screened **deck** on the north side of their home. The ZBA denied this request on the ground that there were 'feasible alternatives for achieving the desired benefit without a variance—including an unroofed **deck** . . . or a porch located in the front—without substantial hardship.'" *Colla v. Town of Hanover* (N.H., 2006).

## DECK LINE

**The intersection of two roof surfaces of a mansard roof forming the highest horizontal line of the steeper roof slope.**

*Legal Annotation*: "The vertical distance measured from the level of approved street grade opposite the middle of the front of a building to the highest point of roof surface of a flat roof; to the **deck line** of a mansard floor; and to the mean height level between eaves and ridge of a gable, hip or gambrel roof." *Permanent Fin. Corp. v. Montgomery City* (Md. Ct. App., 1986).

**Table D-1: Sound Levels And Human Response**

| ***Common Sounds*** | ***Noise Level*** | ***Effect*** |
|---|---|---|
| Carrier deck | 140 | Painfully loud |
| Jet operation | | |
| Air raid siren | | |
| Jet takeoff (200 feet) | 130 | |
| Thunderclap | | |
| Discotheque | 120 | Maximum vocal effect |
| Auto horn (3 feet) | | |
| Pile drivers | 110 | |
| Chain saw (2 feet) | | |
| Garbage truck (50 feet) | 100 | |
| Power lawn mower (4 feet) | | |
| Heavy truck (50 feet) | 90 | Very annoying |
| City traffic (8 hours) | | Hearing damage |
| Alarm clock (2 feet) | 80 | Annoying |
| Hair dryer | | |
| Vacuum cleaner (5 feet) | | |
| Noisy restaurant | 70 | Telephone use difficult |
| Freeway traffic | | |
| Man's voice (3 feet) | | |
| Air-conditioning unit (20 feet) | 60 | Intrusive |
| Light auto traffic (100 feet) | 50 | |
| Living room | 40 | Quiet |
| Bedroom | | |
| Quiet office | | |
| Library | 30 | Very quiet |
| Soft whisper (15 feet) | | |
| Broadcasting studio | 20 | |
| | 10 | Just audible |
| | 0 | Hearing begins |

Source: City of Chula Vista, California, *Noise Control Ordinance*, p. 108

## DECOMPOSITION

**Reduction of the net energy level and change in chemical composition of organic matter because of the actions of aerobic or anaerobic microorganisms.**

***Legal Annotation***: "The rate of oxygen depletion depends primarily on the volume of water in the hypolimnion (the more water, the more oxygen is available for **decomposition**), its temperature (**decomposition** occurs more slowly in cold water and colder water also contains more dissolved oxygen), and the quantity of organic matter it contains (the more organic matter, the greater the oxygen demands for **decomposition**)." *National Wildlife Federation v. Gorsuch* (D.C.Cir., 1982).

## DECONSTRUCTION

**"Deconstruction is the systematic disassembly of a structure in order to salvage its components for reuse" (McKeon 2010: 32).**

***Comment***: Deconstruction is an alternative to demolition. "Unlike architectural salvage, which usually targets a few valuable pieces from a building, the aim of deconstruction is to consider reuse or recycling of the entire structure, including ordinary materials such as structural timbers and floorboards" (McKeon 2010: 32).

***Legal Annotation***: "Lamar **deconstructed** the old billboard and built the new billboard before intervening in View's appeal in April 2007. . . . On February 21, 2007, Lamar reused some of the parts from the old billboard and constructed a new billboard on the Trust property." *Lamar Advertising, Inc. v. View Outdoor Advertising, LLC* (Ind. Ct. App., 2010).

## DECONTAMINATION

**The reduction or removal of a chemical, biological, or radiological material from the surface of a structure, area, object, or person (FEMA State and Local Guide 101). http://www.gwu.edu/~icdrm/publications/PDF/GLOSSARY%2002-19-2007.pdf**

***Legal Annotation***: "On November 16, 2010, the City issued its Invitation to Bid wherein it requested bids from qualified contractors able to provide, inter alia, a demolition plan, asbestos abatement and building **decontamination**, demolition, and removal of materials from the demolition site." *Matter of Dan's Hauling & Demo Inc. v. City of Troy* (N.Y. Sup. Ct., 2011).

## DEDICATION

**The transfer of property by the owner to another party.**

***Comment:*** Such transfer is conveyed by written instrument and is completed with an acceptance. The dedication is often for a specific use. Typically, dedication of land for roads, utilities, and open space is a requirement of subdivision or site plan approval. Where dedication is impractical because of costs or other reasons, an easement may suffice. See *Easement*.

***Legal Annotation***: "Petitioner challenges the decision of the Oregon Supreme Court which held that the city of Tigard could condition the approval of her building permit on the **dedication** of a portion of her property for flood control and traffic improvements." *Dolan v. City of Tigard* (U.S., 1994).

## DEDICATION, FEE IN LIEU OF

**Payments in cash as an alternative to dedication of land or construction of improvements.**

***Comment***: In some states, mandatory construction of improvements or dedication of land for open space, recreation, services, or utilities may be a requirement for development approval. Where such construction or dedication is physically impossible or untimely, a fee in lieu of dedication may be substituted, based on a formula established by ordinance.

***Legal Annotation***: "The developer may instead pay a **fee in lieu of dedication** or reservation: Unless land within a proposed subdivision is dedicated or reserved . . . final approval of the subdivision shall be contingent upon payment of a park development fee from the developer to King County." *Trimen Development Co. v. King County* (Wash., 1994).

## DEED

**A legal document conveying ownership of real property.**

***Legal Annotation***: "Under Oregon law '[b]eneficiary means the person named or otherwise designated in a trust **deed** as the person for whose benefit a trust **deed** is given.'" *Beyer v. Bank of America* (D. Ore., 2011).

## DEED RESTRICTION

See *Restrictive Covenant*.

## DEFENSIBLE SPACE

**Design or redesign of the built environment to reduce opportunities for crime.**

*Comment*: Defensible space or "crime prevention through environmental design" is based on three principles: natural surveillance by placing physical features, activities, and people to maximize visibility; natural access control through the judicial placement of entrances, exits, fencing, landscaping, and lighting; and territorial reinforcement using buildings, fences, pavement, signs, and landscaping to express ownership (Brennan et al. 1997; Newman 1996).

## DEFICIENT HOUSING UNIT

**A housing unit that is not decent, safe, or sanitary, as determined through census surrogates or on-site inspection, and that does not comply with local codes or other housing standards. See *Surrogate*.**

*Comment*: Surrogates for deficient housing include age of structure, overcrowding, lack of central heat, shared bathroom facilities, inadequate kitchen facilities, inadequate access, and lack of elevators in mid- and high-rise buildings.

*Legal Annotation*: "A rehabilitated unit is a 'previously **deficient housing unit** [that] has undergone significant renovation to meet municipal or other applicable housing code standards.'" N.J.A.C. 5:93-1.3. *FSHC v. Township of Cherry Hill* (N.J., 2002).

## DELINEATED STREAM

**Those streams that have been studied by the state and assigned flood hazard areas.**

*Legal Annotation*: "The regulations also formulate land use restrictions imposed in flood plains. 'In the floodway of a **delineated stream** . . . virtually all construction of structures and addition of fill is prohibited.'" *Asdal Builders, LLC v. New Jersey Department of Environmental Protection* (N.J. App. Div., 2012).

## DE MINIMIS

**A minimal deviation from the norm or standard.**

*Comment:* A *de minimis* exception is often used to justify the grant of a design waiver or variance. In fact, Black says *de minimis* is "[of] a fact or thing so insignificant that a court may overlook it in deciding an issue or case" (*Black's* 1999). In planning and zoning, *de minimis* means that the approval will not affect the basic standard and may not even be noticed, if granted. No attempt has been made to quantify what minimal means, and it varies with each application.

*Legal Annotation*: "Several of the non-settling defendants argue that EPA's definition of **de minimis**—those responsible for less than one percent of the volume of waste—is arbitrary and unfair." *US v. Cannons Engineering Corp.* (D. Mass. 1989).

## DEMOGRAPHIC MULTIPLIERS

1. Residential multiplier: A statistical measure that indicates the average number of persons and/or schoolchildren generated by a specific residential use, defined by housing type and number of bedrooms.
2. Non-residential multiplier: A statistical measure that indicates the average number of employees generated by a specific nonresidential land use and expressed on the basis of floor area (e.g., four employees per one thousand square feet of gross floor area).

*Comment*: Demographic multipliers form one basis for fiscal impact analysis (FIA), a key planning tool used in determining the future fiscal, service, and capital needs of the municipality. For example, knowing that five hundred single-family detached homes are expected to be built in the municipality over the next several years and that each single-family unit will generate one schoolchild will enable municipal officials to estimate how many schoolchildren can be expected, the amount of parkland that will be needed, and what to expect in terms of municipal services to meet the new population base.

*Legal Annotation*: "Yet based on United States Census data in **Demographic Multipliers** for

Common Configurations of Standard Housing Types for School Age Children, the District also provided substantial evidence that the proposed housing units would generate approximately .78 FTE students per single family lot and .39 FTE per multi-family unit. Applying those standards, the development alone would generate approximately 60 new students." *E. Paul Detray & Land Ho, Inc. v. City of Lacey* (Wash. Ct. App., 2006).

## DEMOGRAPHY

**The study of population and its characteristics.**

***Legal Annotation***: "In so concluding, our guiding lights are the trial court's conclusions that the Jefferson County system has been effectively desegregated and is unitary and that these three one-race schools are the products of geography and **demography** alone." *Stout v. Jefferson County Board of Education* (5th Cir., 1976).

## DEMOLITION PERMIT

**Official authorization to remove part, or all, of a building or structure.**

***Comment:*** Demolition permits are usually authorized by the construction official or building inspector. The grant of a demolition permit may be contingent on fulfilling certain requirements, such as rodent control, insurance in place, and protection against erosion.

***Legal Annotation***: "Where the landlord both owns habitable property and does not wish to rebuild, a **demolition permit** will be granted only upon a finding that (1) the building is not occupied by persons of low or moderate income, (2) cannot be afforded by persons of low or moderate income, (3) removal will not adversely affect the housing supply and (4) the owner cannot make a reasonable return on his investment." *Nash v. City of Santa Monica* (Calif., 1984).

## DENSITY

**The number of families, individuals, dwelling units, households, or housing structures per unit of land.**

***Comment:*** The most common standard is dwelling units per acre. Ordinances regulating density must make it clear as to whether the standard is stated in net or gross density. Gross density includes all the area within the boundaries of the specific area. Net density usually refers to the developable areas only, excluding streets, easements, water areas, lands with environmental constraints, parklands, and undevelopable lands. Table D-2 shows some typical gross densities for various types of housing.

Allowable densities may vary, depending on occupancy characteristics. For example, senior citizen apartments are typically built at higher

**Table D-2: Gross Density Ranges For Housing Types**

| | ***Typical Density Ranges (units per gross acre)*** | | |
|---|---|---|---|
| ***Type of Unit*** | ***Suburban Area*** | ***Town*** | ***Urban Center*** |
| Single-family detached | 1–4 | 4–8 | 8–15 |
| Two-family | 6–8 | 8–12 | 20–40 |
| Townhouses | 6–10 | 10–20 | 20–30 |
| Flats, two- and three-story | 10–18 | 15–30 | 25–40 |
| Mid-rise | 20–40 | 30–50 | 40–60 |
| High-rise | – | 50–60 | 70+ |

densities than non-age-restricted units, since overall impact of such factors as vehicle trip generation, schoolchildren, persons per acre, and so forth is less. Mixed-type structures containing townhouses and flats, for instance, may have densities somewhere between the two types. Single-family detached variations, such as zero lot line homes, are often built at densities of about six to ten dwelling units per net acre.

Stuart Meck, principal investigator for the American Planning Association's *Growing Smart* project, suggests that low density is one to seven dwelling units per acre; medium density is seven to fourteen dwelling units per acre; and high density is fourteen or more dwelling units per acre. He notes that in an article on density by Ruth Eckdish Knack ("Dense, Denser, Denser Still," *Planning*, August 2002), the densities are similar to Lynch and Hack's (1994) categories in *Site Planning*. See *Critical Area; Net Area Of Lot. See Also* Haughey (2008).

***Legal Annotation***: "Moreover, as a general proposition, I see no constitutional infirmity in a town's limiting the **density** of use in residential areas by zoning regulations which do not discriminate on the basis of constitutionally suspect criteria." *Village of Belle Terre v. Boraas* (U.S., 1974).

## DENSITY BONUS

**The granting of additional floor area or dwelling units, beyond the zoned maximum, in exchange for providing a public benefit or preserving an amenity at the same or a separate site.**

***Comment***: For a residential site, the amenity or public benefit might be the preservation and restoration of a historic home or site, or the inclusion of affordable housing; for a commercial development, the amenity might be the inclusion of a generous plaza dedicated to use by the public. The methodology for calculating the amount of the bonus should be specified in the ordinance, perhaps as a maximum allowable percentage increase in gross floor area or dwelling units per acre.

***Legal Annotation***: "[A]ffected municipalities must provide realistic opportunities for their fair share of lower income housing, and require the municipality to provide **density bonuses** for the construction of multi-bedroom units . . . (a **density bonus** allows the developer to build more units per acre if certain kinds of units are included in the project)." *So. Burlington City NAACP v. Mount Laurel Tp* (NJ., 1983).

## DENSITY MODIFICATION FACTOR

**See *Cluster Subdivision*.**

## DENSITY TRANSFER

**The transfer of all or part of the permitted density on a parcel to another parcel.**

***Comment***: "Density transfer" is also known as the transfer of development rights (TDR). TDR must be permitted by a state enabling act and then enacted in the local ordinance. Usually, density transfers are made from designated sending districts to designated receiving districts. Both types of districts must be identified in the zoning ordinance. Density transfer may be used to preserve farmland, open space, historic areas, and critical areas. See *Air Rights; Lot Averaging; Noncontiguous Parcel Clustering; Transfer of Development Rights*. http://tinyurl.com/kzcz6z4

***Legal Annotation***: "When Steven Horn of the State Coastal Conservancy testified that '**density transfer**' programs were a 'difficult and uncertain' approach due to difficulty in finding receiver sites, he was addressing specific density transfers being proposed." *Sierra Club v. California Coastal Commission* (Calif. Ct. App., 1993).

## DENSITY ZONING

**Averaging residential density over an entire parcel without restriction as to lot sizes (American Planning Association, *The Language of Zoning*, Planning Advisory Service Report No. 322, 1976).**

***Comment:*** Density zoning is often confused with cluster development. Technically, it is more akin to lot averaging, in which the size of the lots may vary if the number of dwelling units remains the same. Density zoning may also be used to permit any housing type, provided the number of units does not exceed the maximum density permitted in the ordinance. See *Lot Averaging*.

*Legal Annotation*: "On the subject of cluster or open space zoning, the master plan report suggested an optional system parallel to that enacted in the zoning ordinances under attack here, but applicable only in zones with a minimum lot size of 45,000 square feet and allowing reductions of minimum lot sizes but not minimum frontages. The planning consultants label this recommended scheme 'density zoning,' stressing that no more homes can be built in a subdivision despite smaller size lots, because the land thus saved must be deeded to the municipality." *Chrinko v. South Brunswick Township* (N.J. Super. Ct., 1963).

## DESALINIZATION

**Salt removal from seawater or brackish water.**

***Legal Annotation***: "There is simply no evidence that **desalinization** could provide a substantial and reliable source of water for the County." *James City County, Va. v. USEPA* (4th Cir., 1992).

## DESCRIPTIVE SUMMARY

**A statement accompanying an application to a planning board, board of adjustment, or government agency that covers the main points of the application concisely, but without overwhelming details, in a manner that serves to clearly describe the nature of the application to the board or agency (Lawlor 2004).**

***Comment***: In *Glazbrook v. Spotslyvania County,* decided in October 2004, the Virginia Supreme Court opined on the meaning of a descriptive summary in a proposed ordinance amendment (Lawlor 2004).

***Legal Annotation***: "In sum, this statute provides that public hearing notices must contain three specific elements: (1) a **descriptive summary** of the proposed amendments." *Gas Mart Corporation v. Board of Supervisors of Loudoun County* (Va. Ct. App., 2005).

## DESIGN CONTINUITY

**A unifying or connecting theme or physical feature for a particular setting or place, provided by one or more elements of the natural or created environment.**

***Legal Annotation***: "Earls testified that the Lees also agreed that she could resurface her side of the fence with grape stakes so there would be some **design continuity** with her other fences." *Earls v. Lee* (Calif. Ct. App., 2008).

## DESIGN FIT

**Consistency in scale, quality, or character between new and existing development so as to avoid abrupt and/or severe differences. See *Compatible Design; Compatible Land Use*.**

## DESIGN FLOOD

**The magnitude of a flooding event that a facility is designed to accommodate.**

***Comment***: The design flood is the basis of the delineation of the floodway, the flood hazard area, and the water surface elevations. http://tinyurl.com/mauzat9

***Legal Annotation***: "The flood hazard area is determined by the 'flood hazard area **design flood**,' which is defined as the 100-year storm in nondelineated areas and the 100-year storm plus 25% (the '25% add-on') in delineated areas." *American Cyanamid v. State of NJ Dept. of Enviro. Protection* (N.J. App. Div., 1989).

## DESIGN REVIEW

**Site or building design review by a design review body constituted to comment or make recommendations on the design or to grant approval. See *Site Plan Review*.**

***Comment***: Three American Planning Association Planning Advisory Service (PAS) publications offer a most useful overview on the background, legality, and function of the design review process, with suggestions for the preparation and implementation of design review guidelines. These include: Robert Lee Fleming, *Saving Face*:

*How Corporate Franchise Design Can Respect Community Identity,* PAS Report Number 452 (1994); Mark L. Hinshaw, *Design Review*, PAS Report Number 454 (1995); and Christopher J. Duerksen and R. Matthew Goebel, *Aesthetics, Community Character and the Law*, PAS Report Number 489/490 (1999). *See Also* Hamid Shirvani, *Urban Design Review: A Guide For Planners* (Washington, DC: Planners Press, 1981).

***Legal Annotation***: "City of Davis Design Review Commission Architectural and Landscape Architectural Standards . . . explains that anyone seeking a permit for the construction of a building with three or more living units, duplexes when required by the planning commission, single-family attached units, and commercial and industrial developments and additions, must submit to **design review**." *Friends of Davis v. City of Davis* (Calif. Ct. App., 2000).

## DESIGN STANDARDS

**A set of guidelines defining parameters to be followed in site and/or building design and development. See *Design Review*.**

***Comment***: Design standards can be quite specific and required in a historic or other special design district. They can also be more general guidelines, adopted as part of the local master plan, to provide direction to decision makers, design professionals, and the public regarding site, building, landscaping, and infrastructure design in the preparation and review of development applications.

***Legal Annotation***: "Those regulations were to include **design standards**, which must be 'consistent with the minimum guidelines and requirements issued by the Architectural and Transportation Barriers Compliance Board.'" *Independent Living Resources v. Oregon Arena Corp.* (D. Ore., 1997).

## DETENTION BASIN (POND)

**A facility for the temporary storage of stormwater runoff.**

***Comment***: Detention basins or ponds differ from retention basins in that the water storage is only temporary, with water often released by mechanical means at such time as downstream facilities can handle the flow. Basins are generally designed to regulate the rate of flow to predevelopment conditions. Usually the basins are planted with grass and, if large enough, can be used for open space or recreation in periods of dry weather. Basins also serve to recharge groundwater and are not considered impervious surfaces.

***Legal Annotation***: "It would also build a water runoff **detention basin** to improve storm water flow; deposit sufficient money in an interest-bearing escrow account to maintain that detention basin." *Matter of Village of Tarrytown v. Planning Board of Village of Sleepy Hollow* (N.Y. App. Div., 2002).

## DETERIORATION

**The marked diminishing of the physical condition of structures or buildings. See *Deficient Unit; Surrogate*.**

***Comment***: In a development context, deterioration may also be used to describe worsening levels of pollution.

***Legal Annotation***: "The Administrator, in recent testimony before Congress, indicated that he had declined to require state implementation plans to provide against significant **deterioration** of the existing clean air areas—i. e., areas with levels of pollution lower than the secondary standard—because he believed that he lacked the power to act otherwise." *Sierra Club v. Ruckelshaus* (D.D.C., 1972).

## DEVELOPABLE LAND

**Parcels or sites free of constraints to development such as, but not limited to, wetlands, steep slopes, water bodies, unstable soils, easements, and legal impediments and that have frontage on or access to an improved roadway and can be served by public or private utilities and facilities such as sewer, water, electricity, and gas.**

*Legal Annotation*: "Zoning a great proportion of the **developable land** in a municipality noncumulatively for nonresidential uses may have the effect of forcing the price of land zoned for residential purposes up beyond the reach of persons with low or moderate incomes." *Southern Burlington County NAACP v. Township of Mount Laurel* (N.J., 1975).

## DEVELOPER

**The legal or beneficial owner or owners of a lot or of any land included in a proposed development, including the holder of an option or contract to purchase or other persons having enforceable proprietary interests in such lands. See *Applicant*.**

*Legal Annotation*: "[W]e must decide whether the **developer** of a subdivision may acquire a vested right to construct buildings on its land without a permit from the California Coastal Zone Commission." *Avco Community Developers v. South Coast Regional Commission* (Calif., 1976).

## DEVELOPMENT

**The division of a parcel of land into two or more parcels; the construction, reconstruction, conversion, structural alteration, relocation, or enlargement of any structure; any mining, excavation, landfill, or land disturbance; or any use or extension of the use of land.**

*Legal Annotation*: "After the appellants acquired five acres of unimproved land in the city of Tiburon, Cal., for residential **development**, the city was required by state law to prepare a general plan governing both land use and the development of open-space land." *Agins v. City of Tiburon* (U.S., 1980).

## DEVELOPMENT, CONVENTIONAL

**Development other than planned development or cluster development.**

*Legal Annotation*: "Section 14 of the Memphis and Shelby County zoning ordinance provides relief from zoning requirements designed for more **conventional development** only when a planned development meets the standards of the pre-existing ordinance." *McCallen v. City of Memphis* (Tenn., 1990).

## DEVELOPMENT, MAJOR

**Any development involving more than three lots and/or involving a land area of more than five acres, and/or requiring the extension of any new streets or other municipal or governmental facilities. See *Development, Minor*.**

*Legal Annotation*: "The principal statutory guidance for the Commission's designation power is found in Section 380.05(2), which provides: 'An area of critical state concern may be designated only for: . . . (c) A proposed area of **major development** potential, which may include a proposed site of a new community, designated in a state land development plan.'" *Cross Key Waterways v. Askew* (Fla. Ct. App., 1977).

## DEVELOPMENT, MINOR

**Any development involving three or fewer lots and/or involving a land area of less than five acres and not requiring the extension of any new streets or other municipal or governmental facilities. See *Development; Development, Major*.**

*Comment*: The definition of development is sufficiently broad to cover all types of activity relating to land and building. The designation of an application as a minor development relieves the applicant of the need to meet the more stringent requirements of a major application, including advertising, notification of neighbors, and a public hearing. The number of lots and land area is strictly a local determination. In many built-up communities, where the streets and major infrastructure are already installed, five lots or less may be considered a minor subdivision. In urban areas, the five-acre standard for site plans may be too large, and a smaller maximum may be desirable.

There are two recurring problems with respect to minor developments. The first is the danger that the land will come in at some subsequent time for another minor development application, a phenomenon referred to as "the creeping major."

This problem can be addressed by requiring any application involving land previously approved as a minor development to be submitted as a major application. The second problem is how the developer proposes to use the remaining land. While applicants will often claim that they have no intention of developing the remainder, the prudent board will require at least a concept plan for the remaining land to ensure that the minor development does not pose future problems.

***Legal Annotation***: "Section 11-33 of the Zoning Regulations of the City of New York . . . provides, in part, that a right to construct shall vest if the foundations are completed in the case of a **minor development**." *Matter of Tetmkin v. Karagheuzoff* (N.Y., 1974).

## DEVELOPMENT, PLANNED

**See *Planned Development*.**

## DEVELOPMENT ANALYSIS STUDY

**An analysis of potential uses and markets, whether permitted by zoning or not, for a parcel of real estate to determine the type and intensity of development. See *Feasibility Study*.**

***Comment***: Development analysis differs from impact analysis, which analyzes the impact of a specific development in terms of water and sewer use, traffic, and impact on community facilities, such as schools, recreation, environment, and public services. If the purpose of the analysis is to determine whether the development meets the minimum thresholds of viability, the development analysis study is often called a feasibility study.

***Legal Annotation***: "[T]hree documents . . . memorialize IHDA's investigation of the development and of the character of the surrounding neighborhood [including] an undated '**Development Analysis**,' [in which] the 'Site/Market Characteristics' were described." *Greer v. Illinois Housing Development Authority* (Ill., 1988).

## DEVELOPMENT CONTEXT

**The three-dimensional character of the buildings, structures, streetscape, and immediate surroundings of a given building or site.**

***Comment***: An important consideration in site plan review is how the proposed site development respects the contextual character of its location. Contextual elements include building design (roof shape, mass, fenestration, materials, and color), setbacks, street furniture, street and sidewalk width, fences, street trees, street lighting, open spaces, and the like, as well as how well the proposed development is harmonious with the nature or character of the land uses which surround it. See *Character; Community Character; Compatible Design; Compatible Land Use; Design Fit; Urban Context.*

***Legal Annotation***: "Mayor Ghilardi testified that the purpose of the public hearing in the zoning and **development context** was to provide an opportunity for input on a legislative process that results in a policy decision." *People ex rel. Klaeren v. Village of Lisle* (Ill., 2002).

## DEVELOPMENT REGULATION

**Any zoning, subdivision, site plan, official map, floodplain or wetlands regulation, or other governmental regulation that affects the use and intensity of land development.**

***Comment***: The current trend is to combine all development regulations into a single land development ordinance since procedures, informational requirements, public hearings, and notices are the same or similar for all development applications.

***Legal Annotation***: "In order to constitute an innovative zoning technique consistent with the overall meaning of the Act, a **development regulation** must satisfy the Act's mandate to conserve agricultural lands for the maintenance and enhancement of the agricultural industry." *King County v. Central Puget Sound* (Wash., 2000).

## DEVELOPMENT REVIEW COMMITTEE (DRC)

**See *Technical Coordinating Committee*.**

## DEVELOPMENT RIGHT

**The right to develop property.**

*Comment*: Fee simple ownership of property involves a bundle of rights, including but not limited to mineral rights, air rights, easements, and such. These may be sold, dedicated, or transferred in their entirety or in part. Purchase of development rights has become a method to preserve farmland, open space, or historic structures. Usually a governmental agency purchases the development rights to the property at a fair appraisal price. The owner keeps title to the property and may continue to farm the land and live on the property. Development rights can also be transferred. See *Density Transfer.*

*Legal Annotation*: "The amendments permitted ranchers in the valley to sell to other property owners in the valley the **right to develop** within the regulations of the community. A purchaser could accumulate more than one **development right**." *Barancik v. County of Marin* (9th Cir., 1989).

## DEVELOPMENT TIMING

**Regulating the rate and/or geographic sequence of development over time.**

*Comment*: Large-scale developments are often broken down into a number of phases, with the number of units and geographic area specified on a phase-by-phase basis. The approving authority has to ensure that each phase can stand on its own in terms of the supporting infrastructure (e.g., circulation, utilities, and drainage) in the event subsequent phases are delayed, left incomplete, or abandoned. This can be done by requiring that the infrastructure designed to serve a specific project phase are completed before the first buildings in that phase are granted certificates of occupancy, and also by requiring performance guarantees.

*Legal Annotation*: "A reading of the relevant statutory provisions reveals that there is no specific authorization for the **'sequential' and 'timing' controls** adopted here. . . . It has utilized its comprehensive plan to implement its timing controls and has coupled with these restrictions provisions for low and moderate income housing on a large scale. Considered as a whole, it represents both in its inception and implementation a reasonable attempt to provide for the sequential, orderly development of land in conjunction with the needs of the community, as well as individual parcels of land, while simultaneously obviating the blighted aftermath which the initial failure to provide needed facilities so often brings." *Golden v. Planning Board of the Town of Ramapo* (N.Y., 1972).

## DEVELOPMENTS OF REGIONAL IMPACT (DRI)

**Projects or development activities that have impacts that extend beyond local government borders or that affect more than one community.**

*Comment*: The impacts can be traffic, stormwater flow, aesthetics, noise, glare, and similar development characteristics. Some ordinances classify any development activity within one hundred yards of another municipality as a DRI. States that have specific standards and review procedures for DRIs include Colorado, Florida, Georgia, Maine, Massachusetts, Minnesota, Vermont, and Washington.

*Legal Annotation*: "In 1975, the American Law Institute adopted the Model Land Development Code, which provided for procedural and planning reforms at the local level and increased state participation in land use decision-making for **developments of regional impact** and areas of critical state concern." *Board of County Commissioners of Brevard County v. Snyder* (Fla., 1993).

## DIAGONAL DIVERTERS

**See *Traffic Calming*.**

## DIFFUSED LIGHTING

**Soft lighting created by passing direct lighting through a screen to decrease its intensity or by using an indirect light source. See *Lighting Plan; Foot-Candle*.**

*Comment*: Lighting standards often specify diffused lighting for signs or outdoor displays in order to reduce the impact on surrounding properties and/or streets. Lighting standards should also include a maximum foot-candle limit to be measured at the property line.

*Legal Annotation*: "All illuminated signs shall be either indirectly lighted or of the **diffused lighting** type. No sign shall be lighted by means of flashing or intermittent illumination. All lights used for the illumination of any use or building or the areas surrounding them or for the illumination or display of merchandise or products of business establishments shall be completely shielded from the view of vehicular traffic using the road or roads abutting such business properties." *Quick Chek Food Stores v. Springfield Tp.* (N.J., 1980).

## DIGITAL BILLBOARD

See *Sign, Digital*

## DILAPIDATION

**A deterioration of structures or buildings to the point of being unsafe or unfit for human habitation or use.**

*Legal Annotation*: "Physical conditions that cause blight are defined as follows: '(1) Buildings in which it is unsafe or unhealthy for persons to live or work. These conditions can be caused by serious building code violations, **dilapidation** and deterioration, defective design or physical construction, faulty or inadequate utilities, or other similar factors.'" *Friends of Mammoth v. Agency* (Calif. Ct. App., 2000).

## DILUTION RATIO

**The ratio of the volume of water of a stream to the volume of incoming waste.**

*Comment*: To maintain the quality of water in streams that are subject to discharges of wastewater, maximum dilution ratios are often mandated.

*Legal Annotation*: "In 1978, petitioner's discharge permit was amended to allow it to discharge the effluent into a nearby creek which runs into the river, provided that a 20:1 **dilution ratio** of water to effluent was maintained." *SCA Chemical Waste Services, Inc. v. Board of Appeals of the Town of Porter* (NY: Court of Appeals 1981). http://tinyurl.com/jwlclym.

## DIRECT (AGRICULTURAL) MARKETING

**Includes any marketing method whereby farmers sell their products directly to consumers.**

*Comment*: Examples of direct marketing channels include farmers' markets, on-farm retail markets, roadside farm stands, U-Pick/Pick-Your-Own/Cut-Your-Own operations, and community-supported agriculture (CSA) (Bruch and Ernst 2010: 1). http://utextension.tennessee.edu/publications/Documents/PB1796.pdf

*Legal Annotation*: "The legal issues in this case pertain to the scope of the **farm stand** statute, ORS 215.283(1)(o), as implemented by OAR 660-033-0130(23). More specifically, we must determine the scope of the statute's allowance of 'fee-based activit[ies] to promote the **sale of farm crops** . . . **sold at the farm stand**' and what limitations are placed on the use of structures in connection with a farm stand." *Greenfield v. Multnomah County* (Ore. Ct. App., 2013).

## DISABILITY

**The consequence of an impairment that may be physical, cognitive, mental, sensory, emotional, developmental, or some combination of these that creates difficulty for persons with disabilities in executing a task or action or limits them from involvement in life situations (1988 amendments to the Fair Housing Act, 42 U.S.C. §3602[h]). See *Americans With Disabilities Act*.**

*Comment*: As noted by Mandelker (1994), the ADA "affects land use restrictions on group homes that are contained in statutes and local ordinances. The act includes as discrimination the refusal *to make reasonable accommodations* in rules, policies, and practices where such accommodations are necessary to afford handicapped persons an opportunity to use and enjoy a dwelling" (Mandelker 1994: 3). A number of court cases have interpreted "reasonable accommodation" to mean that municipalities have to amend zoning regulations to accommodate people with disabilities. For example, ramps needed by persons in wheelchairs should be considered exceptions to front-yard setback requirements. Treating group homes differently from other residences, for example, would be discriminatory under the Fair Housing Act (Mandelker 1994; Connor 1998). See *Major Life Activities*.

***Legal Annotation***: "[A] **disability** is defined [in the ADA] as: '(A) a physical or mental impairment that substantially limits one or more of the major life activities of such individual; (B) a record of such an impairment; or (C) being regarded as having such an impairment.'" *Sutton v. United Airlines, Inc.* (U.S., 1999).

## DISASTER

**A major detrimental impact of a hazard upon the population and economy, society, and environment of the affected area.**

***Comment***: Logically, a natural disaster results from the impact of a natural, as opposed to a human-caused or technological, hazard upon the built environment of the affected area. But as used by federal agencies (FEMA, for example), the term is broadly defined to include disasters and emergencies that may be caused by any natural or man-made event (*FEMA Glossary*). Hurricanes Katrina and Sandy, and other such events have evoked post-disaster planning (Beckman, Bartholomew, and Rookwood 2006).

***Legal Annotation***: "The restoration of nonconforming buildings after an Act of God, natural **disaster**, or fire is governed by paragraph 6 of Section 22-8, which states: 'Restoration. A legally nonconforming building destroyed by fire, storms, or other acts of God or a public enemy may be repaired or rebuilt, provided the restoration is accomplished with no increase in cubical content and no increase in floor area over the building existing immediately prior to damage.'" *Williams v. Parish of St. Bernard* (La. Ct. App., 2010).

## DISASTER HOUSING

**Temporary housing supplied by emergency management officials to disaster victims whose homes or dwellings are no longer habitable due to damage sustained in a declared disaster (*FEMA Glossary*).**

***Comment***: From a planning perspective, disaster housing can vary from tents to mobile homes, or even modified nonresidential buildings converted to emergency shelter. The major objective is to quickly provide disaster victims with safe and durable housing.

***Legal Annotation***: "HANO issued an emergency no bid contract to MFR to perform accounting and administration services for the Displaced Housing Program. MFR issued a sub-contract to Inspeq to perform the required inspections as it had no experience in this field, and Inspeq had the only local certified inspectors. Both MFR's emergency contract and Inspeq's sub-contract relative to the **Disaster Housing** Program were set to expire on August 31, 2009." *Zeigler v. Housing Authority of New Orleans* (La. CT. App., 2013).

## DISCHARGE OF HAZARDOUS WASTE

**The accidental or intentional spilling, leaking, pumping, pouring, emitting, emptying, or dumping of hazardous waste into or on any land or water.**

***Legal Annotation***: "Moreover, for a party to be liable under the Spill Act, the **discharge of hazardous waste** at issue 'must be tied to the discharge by that operator [of the property] and not another.'" *Heller Urban Renewal, LLC v. FER Boulevard Realty Corp.* (D.N.J., 2104).

## DISCOTHEQUE

**A public hall for dancing to recorded popular music. See *Nightclub*.**

***Comment***: Discotheque is a term that is no longer used very often. These are more frequently referred to as "nightclubs" or simply as "clubs."

***Legal Annotation***: "By banning topless dancing only in every 'cabaret, bar or lounge, dance hall, **discotheque**, restaurant or coffee shop within the Town of North Hempstead,' the Town's aim was to narrow the broad reach of the ordinance sufficiently to meet constitutional muster." *Salem Inn, Inc. v. Frank* (2nd Cir., 1975).

## DISCOUNT CENTER

**A group of retail stores offering merchandise for sale at lower-than-usual retail prices.**

***Comment***: Discount centers comprising several discount stores are now major forces in retailing. The stores in discount centers are often characterized by very large structures, often converted warehouses, with merchandise offered for sale on steel industrial shelving in original shipping boxes. Such single stores are now more commonly referred to as "big-box stores," and centers that are composed of several big-box stores are referred to as "power centers." See *Big-Box Retail Store; Power Center; Retail Outlet Store; Retail Store, Large-Scale; Retail Warehouse Outlet.*

***Legal Annotation***: "**Discount store** operation is defined as a retail establishment which regularly sells a major portion of its merchandise at off prices or at prices below normal retail, or advertises or holds itself out to the public as a discount house or store as regularly selling off price." *Cook United, Inc. v. Waits* (Ky. Ct. App., 1974).

## DISCOVERY

**(1) The act or process of finding or learning something that was previously unknown; (2) compulsory disclosure, at a party's request, of information that relates to the litigation (*Black's* 1999).**

***Comment***: Black notes that "[t]he primary discovery devices are interrogatories, depositions, and requests for production" (p. 478). Since many planners will testify in a court of law at some time or other during their careers, they will most likely experience the discovery process. Except for privileged communications, usually from or to attorneys, all material in the planner's file used to prepare reports or opinions is subject to discovery. The planner's attorney should be consulted as to what files, letters, and notes must be produced for the discovery process.

***Legal Annotation***: "Thus a leading legal dictionary first defines '**discovery**' to mean, 'In a general sense, the ascertainment of that which was previously unknown; the disclosure or coming to light of what was previously hidden,' and gives as example, 'the granting of a new trial for newly "discovered" evidence.' (*Black's Law Dict.* [6th ed. 1990] p. 466, italics added.) But the same work also defines the word in its specifically legal sense, as 'The pre-trial devices that can be used by one party to obtain facts and information about the case from the other party in order to assist the party's preparation for trial,' and gives as examples such formal procedures as depositions, interrogatories, requests for admission, and motions for production of documents." *Arnett v. Dal Cielo* (Calif., 1996).

## DISPLACEMENT

**The act of removing, moving, or forcing residents, businesses, or occupants out of buildings, neighborhoods, or communities.**

***Comment***: Displacement can occur as a result of intentional acts, indirectly as a result of changes in land use policy, or unintentionally. An example of intentional displacement is condemnation and relocation. Indirect relocation may result from changes in zoning that increase development yields and land values, resulting in gentrification. Unintentional displacement can occur where buildings are destroyed or damaged beyond repair through natural disasters like floods or fire.

***Legal Annotation***: "[This legislation] recognizes that relocation is a serious and growing problem in the United States and that the pace of **displacement** will accelerate in the years immediately ahead." *A&E North, LLC v. Mayor & City Council of Baltimore* (Md. Ct. App., 2013).

## DISPOSAL

**The discharge, deposit, injection, dumping, spilling, leaking, or placing of any solid or hazardous waste into or on any land or water so that such solid waste or hazardous waste or any constituent thereof may enter the environment by emissions into the air or discharge into any water, including groundwater.**

***Legal Annotation***: "The City is a third-class city organized and operating under a home rule charter (Charter). Pursuant to Act 101 and its powers under the Charter, the City adopted an ordinance regulating the collection, transportation, storage and **disposal** of solid waste and recycling and imposing separate fees for these services on persons owning property located within its borders." *City of Reading v. Iezzi* (Pa. Comm. Ct., 2013).

## DISPOSAL AREA

**The entire area used for underground dispersion of the liquid portion of sewage.**

***Comment***: The disposal area usually consists of the seepage pit or a disposal field or a combination of both. "Disposal area" is also sometimes used in connection with sanitary landfills, where solid waste is "disposed."

***Legal Annotation***: "Section 3.0.2 of the Glastonbury building zone regulations permits a special exception for a sanitary landfill **disposal area** when the board determines that the public welfare will be served and the appropriate use of neighboring property will not be substantially or permanently injured." *Rocchi v. Zoning Board of Appeals* (Conn., 1968).

## DISPOSAL BED

**That part of a disposal field used for sanitary sewage.**

***Comment***: The disposal bed is an area from which the entire earth contents have been removed and the excavation partially filled with satisfactory filtering material in which distribution lines have been laid. The entire area is then covered with topsoil and suitable vegetative cover.

***Legal Annotation***: "Section 308(B) of the zoning ordinances provides that: 'No disposal trench, **disposal bed**, cesspool, seepage pit or other facility designed to leach liquid wastes into the soil shall be located within 150 feet of an intertidal salt marsh or within 150 feet of the line of mean high water of any tidal water body.'" *Gara Realty v. Zoning Board of Review* (R.I., 1987).

## DISPOSAL FACILITY

**A facility or part of a facility at which waste is intentionally placed into or on any land or water, and at which waste will remain after closure.**

***Legal Annotation***: "In August 1976, Tri-County Industries, Inc. and Edward and Margaret Vogel first filed an application for solid waste disposal (Phase I application) with the Department of Environmental Resources (DER, later known as DEP, and referred to as DEP throughout this opinion for clarity) seeking a permit for 90 acres on a 212-acre site. In that application, there was a section requesting information regarding zoning, and in the answers to the questions posed in the application, the applicants represented that there was no zoning ordinance and that the site was previously used for a landfill. . . . The pertinent portion of that order stated that Tri-County did not presently have a permit to operate a solid waste **disposal facility** on its property in Mercer County." *Tri-County Landfill, INC. v. Pine Township Zoning Hearing Board* (Pa. Comm. Ct., 2014).

## DISPOSAL FIELD

**An area consisting of a combination of disposal trenches and a disposal bed. *See Figure 32.***

***Comment***: The disposal field is used for dispersion of the liquid portion of sanitary sewage into the ground as close to the surface as possible. See *Septic System*.

***Legal Annotation***: "The County Development Code contains the following regulations for on-site systems: 'Section 402.09: . . . All sewage shall be treated in the septic tank and the septic tank effluent shall be discharged to the **disposal field**.'" *Town of Grant v. Washington County* (Minn., 1982).

## DISPOSAL TRENCH

**A shallow ditch used for solid waste disposal with vertical sides and a flat bottom partially filled with a satisfactory filtering material in which a single distribution line has been laid and covered with topsoil and a suitable vegetative cover.**

***Legal Annotation***: "The Town moved east to the opposite side of the tract, dug a landfill **disposal**

**Figure 32**

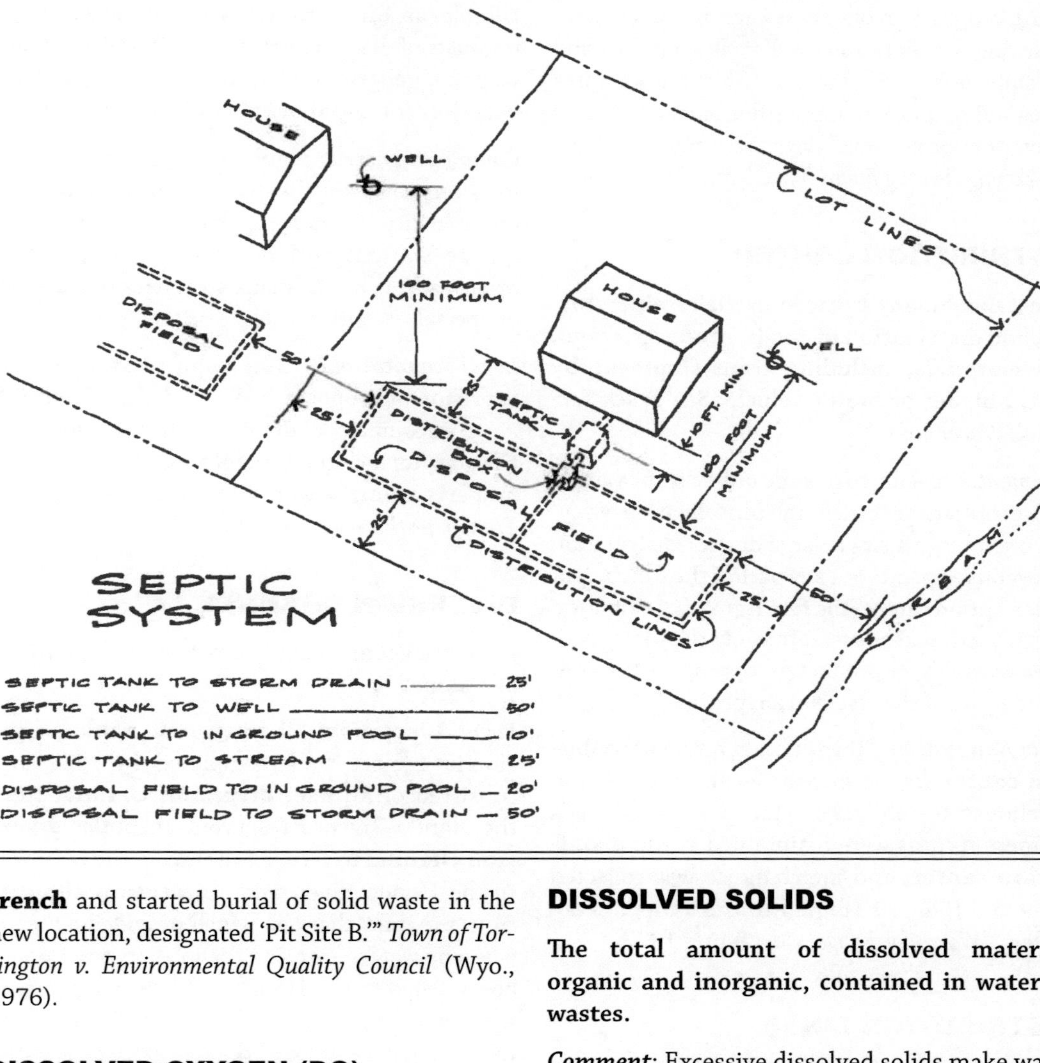


**trench** and started burial of solid waste in the new location, designated 'Pit Site B.'" *Town of Torrington v. Environmental Quality Council* (Wyo., 1976).

## DISSOLVED OXYGEN (DO)

**The oxygen dissolved in water or sewage.**

*Comment*: Adequate DO is necessary for the life of fish and other aquatic organisms. Low DO concentrations generally are due to a discharge of excessive organic solids, the result of inadequate waste treatment.

*Legal Annotation*: "Also, a river low in oxygen has limited ability to break down pollutants and other organic matter. Because **dissolved oxygen** is important both for fish and for breakdown of organic matter, it is an important measure of water quality." *National Wildlife Federation v. Gorsuch* (D.C.Cir., 1982).

## DISSOLVED SOLIDS

**The total amount of dissolved material, organic and inorganic, contained in water or wastes.**

*Comment*: Excessive dissolved solids make water unpalatable for drinking and unsuitable for industrial uses.

*Legal Annotation*: "The mere presence of **dissolved solids** in ground water does not necessarily indicate a water quality problem." *Stokes v. Morgan* (N.M., 1984**)**.

## DISTRIBUTION BOX

**A watertight structure that receives sanitary sewage effluent from a septic tank and distributes such sewage effluent in equal portions to two or more pipelines leading to the disposal field.** ***See Figure 32.***

*Legal Annotation*: "This application, which is in the record, proposes an on-site sewage disposal system consisting of a septic tank, a **distribution box** and a drainfield to accommodate effluent from three stores and an office containing five toilets to be used by five or more persons." *Fretz, Inc. v. Hilltown Township Zoning Hearing Board* (Pa. Comm. Ct., 1975).

## DISTRIBUTION CENTER

**An establishment engaged in the receipt, storage, and distribution of goods, products, cargo, and materials, including trans-shipment by boat, rail, air, or motor vehicle. See *Truck Terminal; Warehouse*.**

*Comment*: Breakdown of large orders from a single source into smaller orders and consolidation of several orders into a single large one for distribution to several recipients is a key part of the function of a distribution center. The functions of distribution centers and warehouses often overlap, but retail sales, assembly, or product processing are not considered part of the distribution process.

*Legal Annotation*: "The function of the **distribution center** was to provide a central office and warehouse for Kroger's retail outlets. Kroger's business records were maintained at the **distribution center**, and merchandise was collected there and then distributed to the various retail outlets." *Worrall v. Kroger Co.* (Tenn., 1977).

## DISTRIBUTION LINES

**A series of open, jointed, or perforated pipes used for the dispersion of sewage into disposal trenches or disposal beds. *See Figure 32*.**

*Legal Annotation*: "These plants consist of buildings, pumps, tanks, **distribution lines** and other equipment for the treatment of water and sewage, and are alleged to be, for the most part, real property under the laws of Florida." *CD Utility Corp. v. Maxwell* (Fla. Ct. App., 1966).

## DISTRICT

**(1) A part, zone, or geographic area within the municipality within which specific zoning or development regulations apply; (2) An area of a community with a unique character identifiable as different from surrounding areas because of its distinctive architecture, street pattern, geographic features, diversity of land uses, and/or social or cultural characteristics.**

*Comment*: District regulations must be uniform for all uses within the district. For example, if a municipality wants to apply a larger lot size to service stations within a district compared to other uses, it has to make such uses conditional or special-exception uses.

*Legal Annotation*: "[T]he plain meaning of the provision of Proposition 62 . . . defines '**district**' . . . to encompass all districts within the terms of the statute, including therefore districts without property taxing power." *Santa Clara County Local Transp. Authority v. Guardino* (Calif., 1995).

## DIVERSION CHANNEL

**A channel constructed across or at the bottom of a slope.**

*Legal Annotation*: "The irrigation works of the Hondo Project were completed in 1907 and consisted of an inlet **diversion channel** from the Hondo River, a reservoir, an outlet **diversion channel** to return water from the reservoir to the Hondo River, and a **diversion channel** from the inlet channel, which provided a means whereby waters entering the inlet channel would be returned to the Hondo River before reaching the reservoir." *Kelley v. Carlsbad Irrigation Dist.* (N.M., 1966).

## DIVERSITY

**Consisting of or composed of a variety of different elements, qualities, or characteristics. See *Diversity Index*.**

*Comment*: Geographic areas (neighborhoods, municipalities, states, regions, etc.) can be described in a variety of ways: land use, population, natural features, cultural activities, and economic factors, to name a few. Urban planners may be principally concerned with population characteristics, including race, age, ethnicity, country of origin, and economic status, with a goal of encouraging neighborhood diversity. Diversity of land use is also a principal objective of many comprehensive plans calling for mixed neighborhoods of various types of residences, stores, and business uses.

*Legal Annotation*: "On June 9, 2008, plaintiffs submitted an application to defendants to develop ten residential condominiums at 26 Oak Crest, Darien, as affordable housing units to 'provide much needed **diversity** of housing options and increased opportunity for a wider range of income levels.'" *Hamer v. Darien Planning and Zoning Commission* (D.Conn., 2013).

## DIVERSITY INDEX

**A quantitative measurement of how different a population is in a given geographic or defined area.**

*Comment*: Diversity can be used to describe the population of an area in terms of age, race, income, gender, and even height or weight, as well other characteristics. Using an urban neighborhood as an example, a typical question that might arise is how diverse is the neighborhood in terms of ethnicity. The six general population groups that are typically considered are non-Hispanic white; black; Hispanic; Asian and Pacific Islanders; and persons of two or more races. The diversity index depends on how many groups are in the population and the number of persons in each group. A completely diverse population would result in two persons selected at random to be from two different groups.

*Legal Annotation*: "After that, the '**Diversity Index**' handles further assignments. 'Under the **Diversity Index** process, the school district calculates a numerical profile of all student applicants. The current **Diversity Index** is composed of six binary factors: socioeconomic status, academic achievement status, mother's educational background, language status, academic performance index, and home language.'" *Parents Involved in Community Schools v. Seattle School District* (9th Cir., 2005).

## DIVIDED HIGHWAY

**(1) A highway having access on only one side of the direction of travel; (2) a highway having a median island or other barrier separating opposing moving lanes. See *Street, Dual*.**

*Legal Annotation*: "A **divided highway** is defined in LSA-R.S. 32:1(15) as follows: '"Divided highway" means any highway divided into roadways by a median, physical barrier, or clearly indicated dividing section so constructed as to impede vehicular traffic.'" *Dagnall v. Louisiana Dept. of Highways* (La. Ct. App., 1983).

## DIVIDED STREET

**A street having a center island or other barrier separating opposing directions of traffic.**

*Legal Annotation*: "Gerhart Street, in the county of Los Angeles, is 100 feet wide, and runs north and south. It is **divided** into two paved roadways, each 35 feet wide, by a 30-foot center strip, which is planted with trees and grass and bounded by curbs." *De Yo v. Umina* (Calif. Ct. App., 1953).

## DOG PARK

**See *Park, Dog*.**

## DOMICILE

**A residence that is a permanent home to an individual.**

*Legal Annotation*: "That standard was described as follows: 'In reviewing a claim of in-state status, the issue becomes essentially one of **domicile**. In general, the **domicile** of an individual is his true, fixed and permanent home and place of habitation. It is the place to which, whenever he is absent, he has the intention of returning.'" *Martinez v. Bynum* (U.S., 1983).

## DONATION

**A voluntary gift for which no valuable consideration is given in exchange.**

*Legal Annotation*: "The *American Heritage Dictionary* defines '**donation**' as 'the act of giving to a fund or cause' and alternatively as 'a gift or grant.' Similarly, *Webster's Dictionary* defines '**donation**' as 'the act of giving or bestowing' and 'that which is given as a present.' Therefore, '**donation**' can be interpreted to mean either the act of giving or the gift itself." *Huber v. Kenna* (Colo., 2009).

## DORMER

**A projection from a sloping roof that contains a window.** *See Figure 9.*

*Legal Annotation*: "There were two **dormer** window areas. The smaller, with its low peak, was fitted out with a long pad and cushions at the window for lounging, reading, and the like. In the larger **dormer** area there was a built-in couch along one side." *Paxman v. Commissioner of Internal Revenue* (Tax Ct., 1968).

## DORMITORY

**A building used as group living quarters for a student body or religious order as an accessory use to a college, university, boarding school, convent, monastery, or similar institutional use.**

***Comment***: Court cases on the definition of family (for instance, *State of N.J. v. Dennis Baker,* A-59, Supreme Court of New Jersey) make the distinction between dormitories and households of unrelated individuals less precise. Regulations based on living space or other performance standards may offer the most positive method of control. The basic difference between dormitories and dwelling units is that (1) a dormitory is an accessory use to an institutional use while a dwelling unit is a principal use; and (2) a dwelling unit is designed to be occupied by one or more persons functioning as a household. Dormitories do not usually include individual kitchen facilities or private bathroom facilities as do dwelling units.

***Legal Annotation***: "Our interpretation of the Ordinance's provisions is consistent with the four definitions of '**dormitory**' in the record that were supplied to the Boards. Each of the four definitions include two alternative definitions: (1) a room, or rooms, or a large room with many beds, for sleeping; and (2) a building housing a number of persons at a school or college." *Peregrine Developers v. Town of Orono* (Maine, 2004).

## DOUBLE-WIDE UNIT

**Two manufactured housing components, attached side by side, to make one complete housing unit.**

*Legal Annotation*: "A **double-wide unit** is simply two single-wide units bolted together with siding material applied to the exterior to cover the seam." *Dempsey v. Apache Shores Property Owners* (Tex: Court of Appeals, 3rd Dist. 1987). http://tinyurl.com/jvqpysu

## DOWNZONE

**To decrease the intensity of use by lowering the permitted density or floor area ratio or otherwise decrease the extent of development previously permitted. See *Upzone*.**

***Comment***: Downzoning means fewer dwelling units or less floor area on the site. It is the opposite of upzoning, but the terms are often confused.

***Legal Annotation***: "The Hailey Planning and Zoning Commission (Zoning Commission) was requested to '**downzone**' the property in question from Business District to General Residential District in 1990 and again in 1992, and the Zoning Commission denied both requests." *Sprenger Grubb & Assoc. v. Hailey* (Idaho, 1995).

## DOWNZONING

**A popular term for an action that changes a property to a lower density, in effect limiting development to less-intense uses than previously permitted. http://www.pgplanning.org/Resources/Tools_On-line/Glossary.htm**

***Legal Annotation***: "This appeal presents our first opportunity to consider the standard to be applied in judicial review of the validity of a zoning ordinance, enacted on motion of the zoning authority, which effects a piecemeal reduction of permissible residential density (**downzoning**). With respect to the validity of a piecemeal **downzoning** ordinance such as that here involved, we are of opinion that when an aggrieved landowner makes a prima facie showing that since enactment of the prior ordinance there has been no change in circumstances substantially affecting the public health, safety, or welfare, the burden of going forward with evidence of such mistake, fraud, or changed circumstances shifts to the governing body. If the governing body produces evidence sufficient to make reasonableness fairly debatable, the ordinance must be sustained. If not, the ordinance is unreasonable and void." *Board of Super. of Fairfax Cty. v. Snell Const. Corp.* (Va., 1974).

## DRAINAGE

**(1) Surface water runoff; (2) the removal of surface water or groundwater from land by drains, grading, or other means, which include runoff controls to minimize erosion and sedimentation during and after construction or development.**

***Legal Annotation***: "The anticipated increased storm water flow from the subject property to an already strained creek and **drainage** basin can only add to the public need to manage the stream channel and floodplain for **drainage** purposes." *Dolan v. City of Tigard* (Ore., 1993).

## DRAINAGE AREA

**That area in which all of the surface runoff resulting from precipitation is concentrated into a particular stream or waterbody.**

***Legal Annotation***: "Appellants' position is that in its natural state the surface water from the **drainage area** of Dry Creek would not have flooded their lands; the over-all development of this **drainage area** by means of buildings, paved streets . . . and the changes made in the natural watercourse within the city all combined to increase the volume of water and the rapidity of its flow into Dry Creek beyond its capacity." *Perry v. City of Wichita* (Kan., 1953).

## DRAINAGE DISTRICT

**A district established by a governmental unit to build and operate facilities for drainage.**

***Legal Annotation***: "The **Drainage District** consists of approximately 1,060 acres and the southern portion of said District which is the area where the assessments are in question is within the City limits of Spencer. Drainage facilities which were installed in said **District** in the area within the city limits of Spencer include a bridge or large culvert." *Drainage District No. 119 v. Incorporated City of Spencer* (Iowa, 1978).

## DRAINAGE FACILITY

**Any man-made component of the drainage system.**

***Legal Annotation***: "That section further provides that the system should be designed to adequately 'handle the run-off from a twenty-five (25) year storm.' Sections 5.d.2, 5.d.3 and 5.d.4 provide that, when it is anticipated that additional runoff from a subdivision will overload an existing downstream **drainage facility** during a 50-year storm, the PZC shall not approve the plan unless the applicant improves the existing system to meet those conditions." *Pappas v. Town of Enfield* (D. Conn., 2014).

## DRAINAGE SYSTEM

**Pipes, swales, natural features, and constructed improvements designed to carry drainage.**

***Comment***: The system may carry the drainage to storage facilities, streams, or retention or detention basins.

***Legal Annotation***: "Thus, the Commission required that petitioner dedicate the portion of her property lying within the 100-year floodplain for improvement of a storm **drainage system** along Fanno Creek and that she dedicate an additional 15-foot strip of land adjacent to the floodplain as a pedestrian/bicycle pathway." *Dolan v. City of Tigard* (U.S., 1994).

## DRAINAGEWAY

**Any natural or artificial watercourse, trench, ditch, swale, or similar depression into which surface water flows.**

***Legal Annotation***: "It is not important to characterizing a manmade **drainageway** as a 'natural **drainageway**' that it has artificial elements. . . . '[T]he mere presence of an artificial element in a **drainageway** does not destroy its characterization as a natural **drainageway**. It is only where an essential part of the **drainageway** is artificial or manmade that such characterization may be precluded.'" *Gruber v. County of Dawson* (Neb., 1989).

## DRAWDOWN

**(1) A lowering of the surface water elevation of a stream as it approaches and flows through a bridge or culvert; (2) the lowering of the water level in a storage facility, such as a reservoir or well; (3) in construction, the receipt of funding in portions over time to finance the construction of a project.**

***Comment***: In the first definition above, drawdown is the measure of difference of the water surface elevation upstream from the bridge or culvert and a short distance downstream from their entrances (*FEMA Glossary*).

***Legal Annotation***: "Winter **Drawdown**—The findings of fact contain numerous pros and cons of maintaining the winter **drawdown** of the lake levels (under the DNR's proposed order) and eliminating the winter **drawdown** under the Petition. The findings generally point to adverse impacts on wetlands, wildlife, water quality, and riprap structures if the winter **drawdown** were eliminated." *Rock-Koshkonong Lake Dist. v. DNR* (Wis., 2013).

## DREDGE AND FILL

**A process that creates land by dredging material from the bottom of a body of water and depositing this material on land, usually adjacent to the water.**

***Legal Annotation***: "The third is for the development of a marina and ecological enhancement of the Ballona flood control channel which will **dredge and fill** 9.8 acres of wetlands in Area A. Of that, 3.7 acres are a man-made drainage ditch and 8.1 acres are scattered, degraded wetlands." *Wetlands Action Network v. US Army Corps of Engineers* (9th Cir., 2000).

## DREDGE SPOIL

**See *Spoil*.**

## DREDGING

**A method of deepening streams, swamps, or coastal waters by removing solids from the bottom.**

***Comment***: Dredging and filling can disturb natural ecological cycles. For example, dredging can destroy shellfish beds and other aquatic life; filling can destroy the feeding and breeding grounds for many fish species. The dredging and filling of navigable waterways and most wetland areas are regulated by the federal government.

***Legal Annotation***: "The appellant's operation involves the removal of earth from the bottom of the bay. In the plain and ordinary sense of the term, this procedure is '**dredging**.'" *English Bay v. Island County* (Wash., 1977).

## DRIP LINE

**The ground line around a tree that defines the limits of the tree canopy. *See Figure 103.***

***Comment***: During construction, excavation within the drip line of a tree or paving within the drip line with impervious materials can lead to substantial damage and/or kill the tree. Some tree protection ordinances restrict such activities within the drip line.

***Legal Annotation***: "He also explained the 'broadest root system can be what we refer to as **drip line** distances out. The **drip line** is from the trunk to the edge of the canopy crown.'" *Moreno v. City of Imperial Beach* (Calif. Ct. App., 2008).

## DRIVE-IN RESTAURANT

**See *Restaurant, Drive-In*.**

## DRIVE-IN THEATER

**See *Theater, Drive-In*.**

## DRIVE-IN USE

**An establishment that by design, physical facilities, service, or packaging procedures encourages or permits customers to receive services, obtain goods, or be entertained**

**while remaining in their motor vehicles on the premises.**

***Legal Annotation***: "It is undisputed plaintiffs did not timely appeal the Architectural Commission's decision disallowing **drive-in use** of their property, but commenced operation of their restaurant in compliance with the conditions the commission imposed. Therefore plaintiffs' vested rights claim, which is dependent upon a valid underlying permit, is barred because plaintiffs never contested the City's withdrawal of the permit." *Freeman v. City of Beverly Hills* (Calif. Ct. App., 1994).

## DRIVEWAY

**A private roadway providing access to a street or highway.**

***Comment***: Driveways may be paved or unpaved and are not considered streets, roads, or highways.

***Legal Annotation***: "'**Driveway**' is defined in *Webster's New World Dictionary* (1951) page 443, as 'a path leading from a garage or house to the street, used especially by automobiles.'" *Dolske v. Gormley* (Calif., 1962).

## DRIVEWAY WIDTH

**The narrowest width of driveway measured perpendicular to the driveway.**

***Legal Annotation***: "City ordinances in effect since 1945 require a minimum residential **driveway width** of ten feet." *Pugh v. Zoning Board of Adjustment of the City of Asbury Park* (N.J. App. Div., 2010).

## DROP MANHOLE

**A manhole provided for inspection and maintenance of sewers where an incoming sewer is considerably higher than the outgoing.**

***Legal Annotation***: "Defendant contracted with Kenny Construction Company in July 1958 to do work on the Calumet Intercepting Sewer. On October 18, 1958, Woodrow Green, the putative father of the minor plaintiffs and an employee of Kenny, was working with an air spade (as a clay-cutter) in the vicinity of Doty Road and 130th Street in Chicago on an excavation for a **drop manhole**. Green was killed as the result of a cave-in in the excavation." *Bradley v. Metropolitan Sanitary Dist.* (Ill. App. Ct., 1965).

## DROP PIPE

**A vertical pipe used to convey water or sewage from a higher to a lower elevation.**

***Legal Annotation***: "The mechanics of a pitless unit may be described as follows: well water is pumped up from the well through a **drop pipe** and into a spool which is contained in the sleeve." *Baker Manufacturing Co. v. Whitewater Manufacturing Co.* (E.D.Wisc., 1969).

## DRUGSTORE

**A store where the primary business is the filling of medical prescriptions and the sale of drugs, medical devices and supplies, and nonprescription medicines but where nonmedical products may be sold as well.**

***Comment***: A drugstore may be distinguished from a pharmacy, which deals primarily with preparing and dispensing drugs and medicines. The non-medicine-related products may be cards, candy, and cosmetics. In recent years, however, the variety of nonmedical products has expanded substantially, particularly with the advent of national drugstore chains. See *Pharmacy*.

***Legal Annotation***: "Courts are not supposed to be ignorant of that which everybody knows; and everybody in this state knows that **drug stores** are not limited in their stock in trade to drugs only; that they carry tobacco, cigars, candies, soaps, toilet articles, and the like, as well as medicines and drugs." *City of Birmingham v. Tomerlin* (Ala. Ct. Crim. App., 1976).

## DRY LINES

**See *Capped System*.**

## DRY WELL

**A covered pit with an open, jointed lining through which water is piped or directed from roofs, basement floors, other impervious**

**Figure 33**

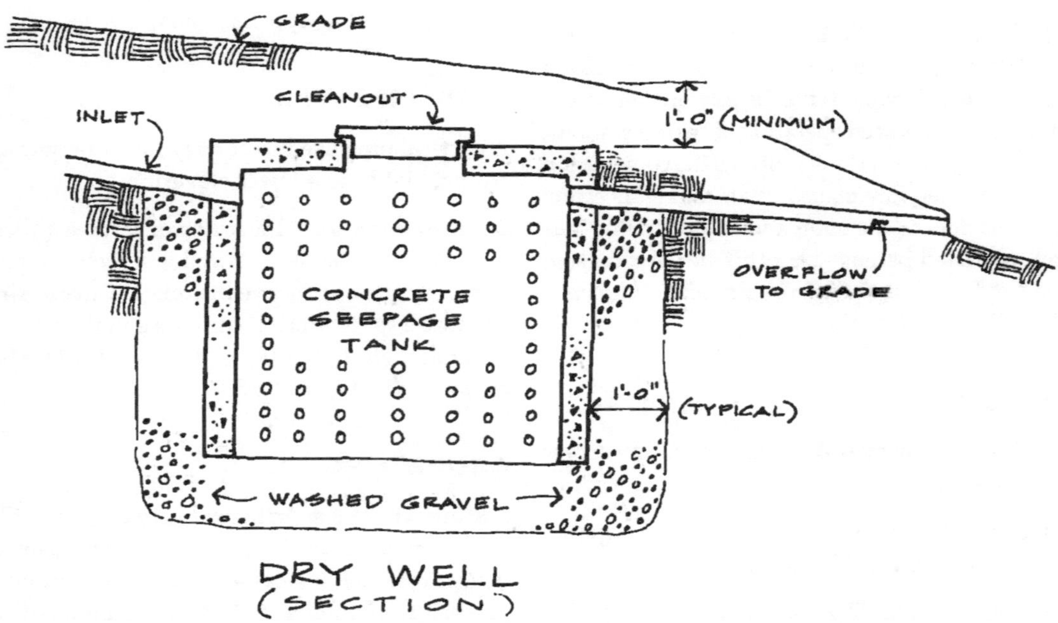


**surfaces, swales, or pipes to seep or percolate into the surrounding soil.** *See Figure 33.*

*Legal Annotation*: "According to the testimony, a **dry well** is a large hole embedded in the ground, with porous sides, where water is collected and dissipated into the surrounding soil." *Nat'l Cash Reg. Co., v. Haak* (Pa. Super. Ct., 1975).

## DUMP

**A land site used primarily for the disposal by dumping, burial, burning, or other means, and for whatever purposes, of garbage, sewage, trash, refuse, junk, discarded machinery, vehicles or parts thereof, and other waste, scrap, or discarded material of any kind.**

*Legal Annotation*: "In 1960, the township contracted with Vaughan Collett to use the site as a **dump** for town residents, for 'waste' but not 'garbage' (a distinction that was never defined)." *US v. Township of Brighton* (6th Cir., 1998).

## DUMPSTER™

**An exterior waste container designed to be mechanically lifted by and emptied into or carted away by a collection vehicle.**

*Comment*: The unregulated placement and control of trash bins or containers, particularly in commercial and multifamily developments, can be visually detrimental to the urban environment. Site plan regulations should include standards for trash bin size, placement, screening, and maintenance. In multifamily developments, bins should be housed in fully enclosed, roofed structures that match the architectural character of the development. *See Figure 34.*

*Legal Annotation*: "The **Dumpster** is alleged to be a large metal waste container designed for easy emptying, with two lids on top which could remain open or closed. It had sleeves about midway up on the outside which received the pickup forks." *Hall v. Witzel* (Fla. Ct. app., 1973).

## DUPLEX

**A building containing two single-family dwelling units totally separated from each other by an unpierced wall extending from basement to roof. See *Dwelling, Two-Family; Dwelling, Semi-Detached. See Figure 41.***

*Comment*: One major advantage of a duplex is that each dwelling unit can be sold in fee simple.

**Figure 34**

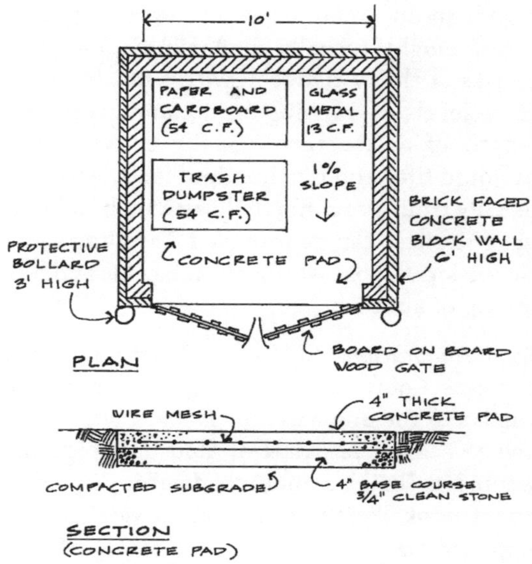


TRASH ENCLOSURE DESIGN

The two-family type with one apartment over another requires condominium ownership. In some areas, the duplex is known as a twin or as a semi-detached dwelling.

*Legal Annotation*: "From this definition, it is apparent that the plain and ordinary meaning of the term '**duplex**' is a home divided for use by two families." *Board of Directors of Bass Lake v. Brewer* (Ind. Ct. App., 2004).

## DWELLING

**A structure or portion thereof that is used exclusively for human habitation.**

*Legal Annotation*: "RCW 9A.04.110(7) . . . defines '**dwelling**' as 'any building . . . or a portion thereof, which is used or ordinarily used by a person for lodging.' The New Mexico statute defines **dwelling** house as 'any structure, any part of which is customarily used as living quarters.'" *State v. Murbach* (Wash. Ct. App., 1993).

## DWELLING, ATTACHED

**A one-family dwelling with ground-floor outside access, attached to two or more one-family dwellings by common vertical walls without openings.**

*Comment*: Also known as a townhouse.

*Legal Annotation*: "Wrightstown Township's Zoning Ordinance, Section 102.3, reveals the following uses under the 'Dwelling' definition: 'Single-Family **Attached Dwelling** (Townhouse): A building designed for and occupied exclusively as a residence for only one family and having a party wall on at least one side (or both sides) in common with an adjacent building.'" *MA Kravitz Co., Inc. Appeal* (Pa. Comm. Ct., 1980).

## DWELLING, DETACHED

**A dwelling that is not attached to any other dwelling by any means.**

*Comment*: The detached dwelling does not have any roof, wall, or floor in common with any other dwelling unit.

*Legal Annotation*: "Wrightstown Township's Zoning Ordinance, Section 102.3, reveals the following uses under the 'Dwelling' definition: 'Single-Family **Detached Dwelling**: A building designed for and occupied exclusively as residence for only one family and having no party wall in common with an adjacent building.'" *MA Kravitz Co., Inc. Appeal* (Pa. Comm. Ct., 1980).

## DWELLING, END GAP

**Small apartment units located at the end of a street between a detached house and a major road.**

*Comment*: End gap housing is part of a mix of housing units (single-family detached, duplex, attached, apartments, etc.) that might be part of a neighborhood. **See *Dwelling, Garage Apartment; Dwelling, Micro-Unit*.**

## DWELLING, GARAGE APARTMENT

**A single-family apartment over an attached or detached garage on a lot containing an existing single-family detached house. See *Accessory Apartment*.**

*Comment*: Garage apartments (sometimes referred to as "granny flats"), are accessory dwelling units that many municipalities are encouraging as alternate housing for lower-income, one- and two-person households. St. Petersburg, Florida, permits garage apartments as part of their Traditional Neighborhood Residential District, with controls on access, minimum size units, and privacy.

***Legal Annotation***: "The court found that the board 'could not reasonably conclude that the Wisemans' garage apartment constituted a nonconforming use or a hardship' and that 'the **garage apartment** does not qualify as a permitted use under the zoning regulations.'" *Greenfield v. Reynolds* (Conn: App. Ct., 2010).

## DWELLING, GARDEN APARTMENT

**One or more two- or three-story, multifamily structures, generally built at a gross density of ten to fifteen dwelling units per acre, with each structure containing eight to twenty dwelling units and including related off-street parking, open space, and recreation facilities. See *Dwelling, Multifamily.* See *Figure 35.***

***Comment***: A garden apartment is actually a multifamily development. Development controls should define the commonly accepted configuration of a garden apartment in terms of density (usually ten to fifteen dwelling units per acre in a suburban community, somewhat higher in an urban area and lower in a rural area), height (usually a maximum of three stories or thirty-five feet, with a maximum of three levels of dwelling units), and maximum length of a structure (usually between one hundred fifty and two hundred feet). Access is usually from a common hall, although individual entrances can be provided. Dwelling units can be located back-to-back, adjacent, and one on top of another.

***Legal Annotation***: "In *Hamer v. Town of Ross,* the Supreme Court considered a spot zoning case similar to the one here. In *Hamer*, the plaintiff owned a 2.2-acre parcel of land on which she wanted to build a multiple-**dwelling garden apartment**." *Ross v. City of Yorba Linda* (Calif. Ct. App., 1991).

## DWELLING, HIGH-RISE

**An apartment building of eight or more stories. *See Figure 36.***

***Comment***: High-rise apartment buildings often have health club facilities and other services for the residents.

***Legal Annotation***: "The Edenboro property is located in an apartment district where the right to build multiple-**dwelling, high-rise** structures has existed at all times." *Sautto v. Edenboro Apartments, Inc.* (N.J. App. Div., 1964).

**Figure 35**

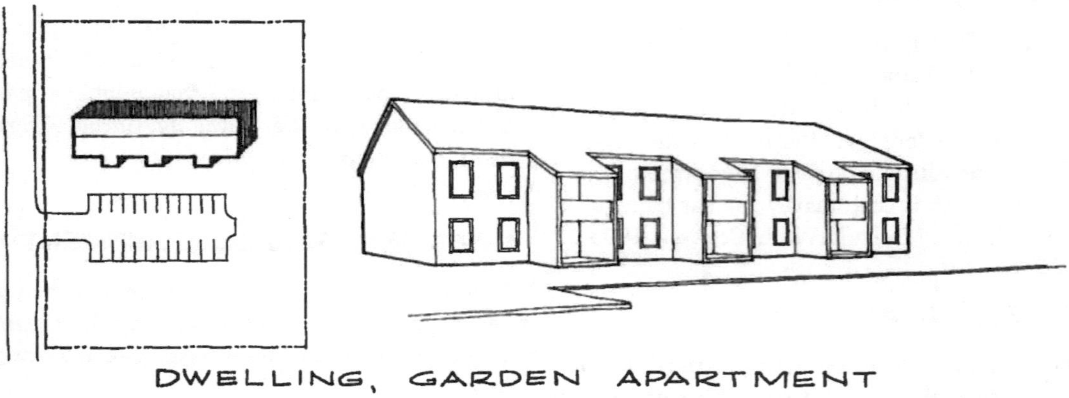

**Figure 36**

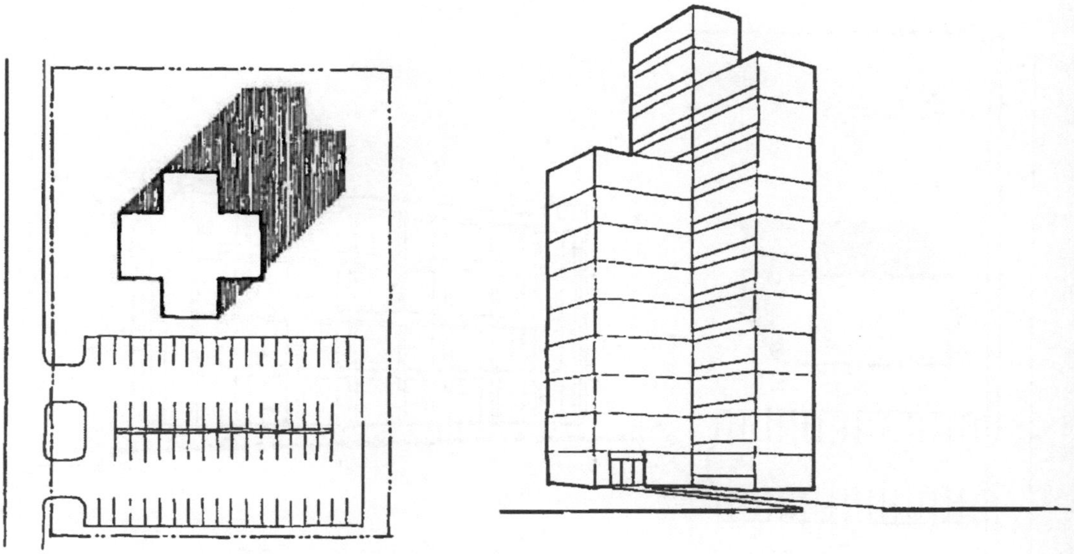

DWELLING, HIGH-RISE

## DWELLING, MICRO-UNIT

**A type of dwelling unit between two hundred fifty to four hundred square feet containing a kitchen, bathroom, and sleeping accommodations.**

*Comment*: The micro-unit is designed to provide affordable housing to single persons and couples. The size of micro-units differs by jurisdiction and purpose. Most cities usually have minimum area requirements for apartment housing (four hundred fifty square feet, for example) that would have to be changed if micro-units are to be permitted. Newer forms of "rooming houses" composed solely of micro-units are now being built to cater to young singles who want to live away from home in smaller, affordable units. The micro-units in such modern rooming houses may be as small as one hundred to two hundred square feet, including a small kitchen and compact bath. See *Micro Hotel.*

*Legal Annotation*: "**Micro-units** are by definition smaller in floor area than what the current New York City Zoning Resolution allows. ZR Section 28-21 requires a minimum dwelling unit size of 400 sf for residential developments pursuant to the Quality Housing Program. An override of ZR Section 28-21 would allow the construction of dwelling units with floor area less than the current 400 square foot minimum. The size of the proposed micro-units would range from 250 to 350 gsf." NYC EQR 13HPD058M "Micro-Units Development EAS," http://cbsix.org/wp-content/uploads/2013/06/13HPD058M_EAS-3.4.131.pdf

## DWELLING, MID-RISE

**An apartment building containing from three to seven stories. *See Figure 37*.**

*Legal Annotation*: "Brody, in turn, testified that the highest and best use of defendant's property was a **mid-rise building** containing 92 residential units." *County of Monmouth v. Hilton* (N.J. App. Div., 2000).

## DWELLING, MULTIFAMILY

**A building containing three or more dwelling units, including units that are located one over another.**

*Comment*: Multifamily buildings typically include all housing types that contain three or more attached units, such as garden apartments,

**Figure 37**

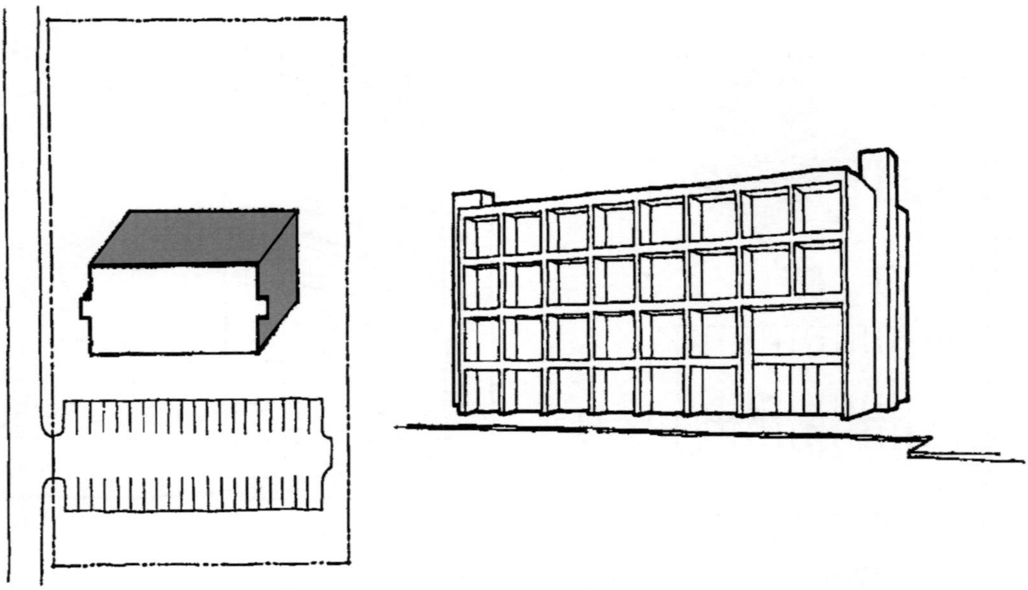


mid- and high-rise apartment buildings, townhouses, row houses, triplexes, and quadruplexes.

*Legal Annotation*: "The applicants applied pursuant to § 906.3(C) of the City of Warwick Zoning Code of Ordinances (ordinance) to demolish the existing residential structure and replace it with a two-and-a-half story brick **multifamily dwelling** that would contain six one-bedroom units." *Newton v. Zoning Board of Review of Warwick* (R.I., 1998).

## DWELLING, PATIO HOME

**A dwelling on a separate lot with open space setbacks on three sides. See *Dwelling, Zero Lot Line*. See *Figure 38*.**

*Comment*: There is no significant difference between a patio home and a zero lot line house, in that at least one side of the dwelling rests on a lot line. Both uses would require an access easement on the adjoining lot permitting dwelling

**Figure 38**

owners to maintain that side of the dwelling that rests on the lot line.

*Legal Annotation*: "'**Patio home**' is defined as '[a] single-family home . . . often with one outside wall of the structure sitting on the property line. **Patio homes** have no common structural walls with adjoining properties.'" *Southland Development Corp. v. Battle* (Ga. Ct. App., 2005).

## DWELLING, QUADRUPLEX

**Four attached dwellings in one building in which each unit has two open-space exposures and shares one or two walls with adjoining unit or units. *See Figure 39.***

*Legal Annotation*: "[T]he following land uses may be allowed provided the permitted use is compatible . . . and standards for development are met . . . [:] Multifamily residences (in existing platted areas only or in lieu of clustering single family units at a density of one unit per lot of record and requiring the recombination of said lots. For example, a duplex requires two lots to be recombined into a single parcel, a **quadruplex** four lots, etc.)." *Katherine's Bay LLC v. Fagan* (Fla. Ct. App., 2010).

## DWELLING, SEASONAL

**A dwelling unit that is not used as a principal residence and may be occupied weekends and for brief periods during the year.**

*Comment*: " Brief period" is difficult to define. Seasonal dwellings in oceanfront or lake areas may be occupied for three to four months. In ski areas, six months may be the norm. At one time, seasonal units often lacked heat and insulation. Today, most municipalities do not make any distinction between seasonal and all-year-round units; both must meet the same standards.

*Legal Annotation*: "The zoning regulations of the town of Old Lyme define '**seasonal dwelling**' as '[a] dwelling unit, designed, used, or intended to be used for seasonal use.' The regulations define 'seasonal use' as '[t]he use of a structure for dwelling purposes between April 1 and November 15, only.'" *Francini v. Zoning Board of Appeals* (Conn., 1994).

## DWELLING, SINGLE-FAMILY DETACHED

**A building containing one dwelling unit and that is not attached to any other dwelling by any means and is surrounded by open space or yards. See *Dwelling, Detached. See Figure 40.***

*Legal Annotation*: "We have reference to young and elderly couples, single persons and large, growing families not in the poverty class, but who still cannot afford the only kinds of housing realistically permitted in most places—relatively high-priced, **single-family detached dwellings** on sizeable lots and, in some municipalities, expensive apartments." *Southern Burlington County NAACP v. Township of Mount Laurel* (N.J., 1975).

**Figure 39**

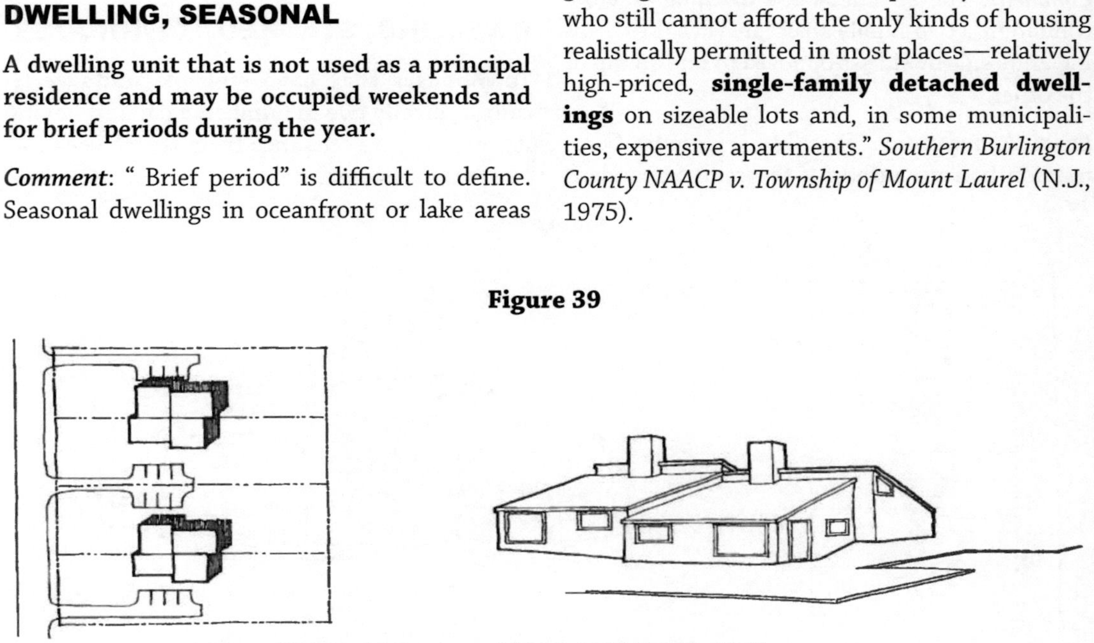

DWELLING, QUADRUPLEX

**Figure 40**

## DWELLING, SINGLE-FAMILY SEMIDETACHED

**A one-family dwelling attached to one other one-family dwelling by a common vertical wall, with each dwelling located on a separate lot. See *Duplex*. See *Figure 41*.**

***Comment***: The semidetached dwelling is most commonly a two-family structure with the dwelling units side by side as opposed to one on top of the other.

***Legal Annotation***: "The City Planning Commission had no authority to grant respondent a special exception permit to convert his one-family dwelling, situated in an R-1 single-family residential district, into two **single-family semidetached dwelling** units." *Williams v. City Planning Commission of the City of Rochester* (N.Y. App. Div. 1988) (Boomer, J. Dissenting).

## DWELLING, STACKED TOWNHOUSE

**Townhouses that have multiple units vertically, typically two in number, each unit having its own private entrance from the street or at least from the outside.**

**Figure 41**

*Comment*: An increasingly popular hybrid of condominium apartments and conventional townhouses, which have characteristics of both. Stacked townhouses afford many of the advantages of conventional townhouses, such as multiple vertical floors, but with a separate entrance either from the street or from an enclosed garage located at ground level. Typically the first level contains the two separate enclosed garage spaces (one for each of the two stacked townhouses), with living space on the remainder of the ground level for Unit A. The bedrooms for Unit A are provided on half of the second level. Unit B's enclosed garage space contains a staircase that leads up to the second level, where a half of that level provides for Unit B's living space. The third level above that is devoted entirely to the bedrooms for Unit B. Essentially, each of the stacked townhouse units has one and a half levels of living space and bedrooms, and also an enclosed garage. The obvious advantage of building stacked townhouse units is the ability to substantially increase the density of development that can be accommodated in comparison to conventional townhouse units.

## DWELLING, TOWNHOUSE

**A one-family dwelling in a row of at least three such units in which each unit has its own front and rear access to the outside, no unit is located over another unit, and each unit is separated from any other unit by one or more vertical common fire-resistant walls.** ***See Figure 42.***

*Comment*: Townhouses usually have separate utilities, such as individual hot water and heating systems and separate electric meters. However, in some condominium developments, the homeowners' association may arrange for the bulk purchase of certain utilities and distribute them to individual dwelling units. Consequently, the definition above could include a requirement for separate utility systems. In some states—Florida, for example—one-story townhouses are called "villas." See *Dwelling, Attached.*

***Legal Annotation***: "We first note that the Board found that, although no separate **townhouse** district was established by the Zoning Ordinance, 'the intention of the drafters was to permit **townhouse** development as well as other multifamily dwellings to be located in the R-4 District.'" *Appeal of MA Kravitz Co., Inc.* (Pa., 1983).

## DWELLING, TRIPLEX

**A building containing three dwelling units, each of which has direct access to the outside or to a common hall.**

**Figure 42**

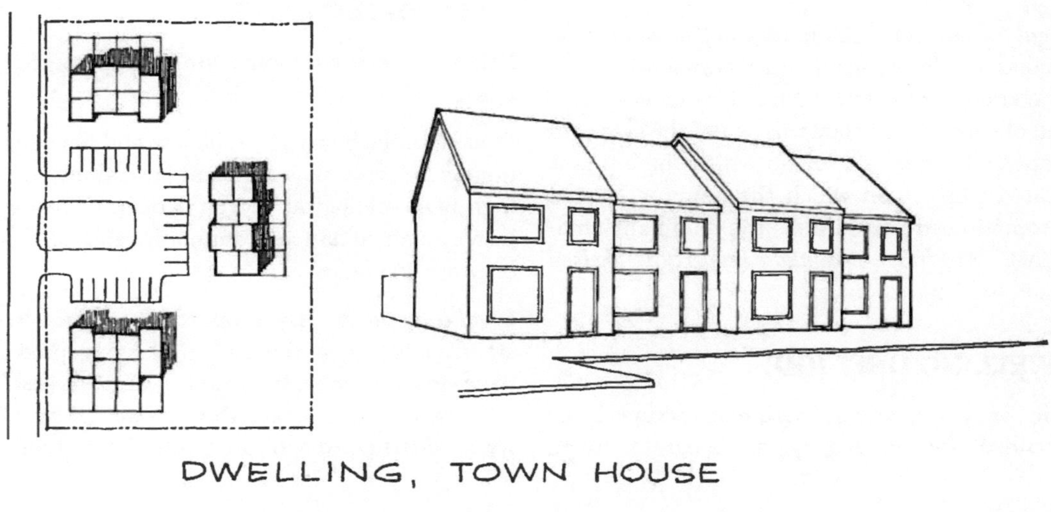

*Legal Annotation*: "The pertinent use regulations for such a district are set forth in Section 3 thereof and a triplex or three family dwelling is not included as a permissible use unless a three family dwelling or **triplex** qualified, on June 6, 1929, as a legal non-conforming use in accordance with Section 10 (b) thereof." *Audubon Area Zoning Association v. Krushevski* (La. Ct. App., 1955).

## DWELLING, TWO-FAMILY

**A single building containing two dwelling units. See *Duplex; Semi-Detached Dwelling*.**

*Legal Annotation*: "A **two-family dwelling** consists of a basement and not less than four living rooms and a bathroom for each family; and is further described as a detached dwelling for the occupation of two families, one having its principal living rooms on the first floor and the other on the second floor." *Village of Euclid v. Ambler Realty Co.* (U.S. 1926).

## DWELLING, ZERO LOT LINE

**A dwelling located on a lot in such a manner that at least one of the dwelling's sides rests on a lot line. See *Dwelling, Patio Home*. See *Figure 38*.**

***Comment***: A three- to four-foot-wide access easement on the adjoining lot is necessary for the zero lot line (and patio home) dwelling occupants to maintain the side of the dwelling that rests on the lot line.

*Legal Annotation*: "The homes in the Woodridge Escondido development (development) are a type known as '**zero lot line**.' One exterior side wall of each home is built on one of the side yard property lines of the lot on which the home is located (the lot on which the home is located is sometimes referred to as the dominant tenement)." *Woodridge Escondido Property v. Nielsen* (Calif. Ct. App., 2005).

## DWELLING UNIT (DU)

**One or more rooms, designed, occupied, or intended for occupancy as separate living quarters, with cooking, sleeping, and sanitary facilities provided within the dwelling unit for the exclusive use of a single family maintaining a household. See *Echo Housing; Housing Unit*.**

*Legal Annotation*: "The City's Community Development Code states 'Floor Area. Every **dwelling unit** shall have at least one room which shall have not less than 120 square feet of floor area. Other habitable rooms, except kitchens, shall have an area of not less than 70 square feet.'" *City of Edmonds v. Oxford House Inc.* (U.S., 1995).

## DWELLING UNIT, EFFICIENCY

**A dwelling unit consisting of not more than one habitable room, together with kitchen or kitchenette and sanitary facilities.**

***Comment***: Efficiency units, also known as studio apartments, typically contain between four hundred and five hundred square feet. See *Dwelling, Micro-Unit*.

*Legal Annotation*: "In the zoning ordinance an **efficiency unit** is defined as 'a dwelling unit consisting of one room exclusive of bathroom, kitchen, hallway, closets, or dining alcove directly off the principal room, providing such dining alcove does not exceed 125 square feet in area.'" *City of Chicago v. Exchange Nat. Bk.* (Ill., 1972).

## DYSTROPHIC LAKES

**Lakes between eutrophic and swamp stages of aging.**

***Comment***: Such lakes are shallow and have high humus content, low nutrient availability, and high BOD (biological oxygen demand). They are heavily stained and are commonly referred to as brown-water lakes.

*Legal Annotation*: "**Dystrophic lake**: A lake that stands midway in the biological aging process between a eutrophic lake and a swamp." *Leelanau (County, Michigan) General Plan, Appendix D.* http://www.leelanau.cc/downloads/appendix_d_1.pdf

# E

## EASEMENT

**A grant of one or more of the property rights by the property owner to and/or for use by the public, a corporation, or another person or entity. *See Figure 3.***

***Comment***: An easement may be a more acceptable and less expensive way to achieve certain public goals, since not all of the property rights are being purchased. For instance, where property owners are reluctant to donate land for road-widening purposes, an easement may be an acceptable alternative. The property owner keeps the title, but the road can be widened. This is particularly important in rural areas where land is sold by the acre. Another example is slope rights to permit roadway grading.

***Legal Annotation***: "The Glen Arbor Zoning Ordinance '[d]efines "**easement**" as "a right or privilege that a person or persons may use another's land."'" *Keen v. Oak Shores, LLC* (Mich. Ct. App., 2008).

## EASEMENT, AFFIRMATIVE

**An easement that gives the holder a right to make some limited use of land owned by another. See *Easement In Gross*.**

***Legal Annotation***: "An **affirmative easement** is one which grants the owner of the dominant estate the right to make active use of the servient estate or to do some act thereon or in respect thereto which, were it not for the easement, he would not be privileged to do or which would otherwise be unlawful." *Rahabi v. Morrison* (N.Y. App. Div., 1981).

## EASEMENT, APPURTENANT

**An easement benefiting, attaching to, and running with a designated parcel of land.**

***Legal Annotation***: "An appendant or **appurtenant easement** must inhere in the land, concern the premises, have one terminus on the land of the party claiming it, and be essentially necessary to the enjoyment thereof. It attaches to, and passes with, the dominant tenement as an appurtenance thereof." *Sandy Island Corp. v. Ragsdale* (S.C., 1965).

## EASEMENT, AVIATION

**An air rights easement that protects air lanes around airports.**

***Legal Annotation***: "These cases simply hold that where the government has taken an **aviation easement** by use of certain kinds of airplanes, the statute of limitations does not bar a claim based on the use of different aircraft which created a greater noise." *De Anza Properties X, Ltd. v. County of Santa Cruz* (9th Cir., 1990).

"This real estate, which consisted of approximately 10.9 acres, was located adjacent to City's municipal airport; 2.35 acres of which was included in an **aviation easement** that restricted its use as a safety zone for the airport." *City of Brookings v. Mills* (S.D., 1987).

## EASEMENT, CONSERVATION

**The grant of a property right requiring that the described land will remain in its existing natural state in perpetuity.**

***Comment***: Conservation easements are useful tools in preserving open space, environmentally sensitive areas, scenic views, or wetlands and wetlands buffers. However, while approving agencies usually identify those areas suitable for easement protection, follow-up is often lax. In a survey of 322 easements on thirty-three properties in Hopewell Township, New Jersey, easement violations were found on 80 percent of the sites by the Stony Brook-Millstone Watershed Association (*Watershed Watch*, June 2001). The association recommended a number of steps that municipalities could take to monitor conservation easements effectively:

- Ensure that all easements are referenced by lot and block number and the details of restrictions are shown in the master plan. If a municipality has an official map, the easements should be shown on the map.
- Ensure that easements are shown on the documents filed with the official filing agency. For example, in New Jersey, easements are filed with the county and not the municipality.
- Establish a routine by which all easements are inspected on a regular basis and, if practical, photographed to guard against any violations.
- Provide a regular funding source to provide for effective and routine monitoring.

In addition to the monitoring of easements, another major problem is providing for the maintenance and/or replacement of vegetation. A typical example is where a stream cuts across a parcel proposed to be subdivided. Good platting practice would have the rear lot lines follow the stream course, and the stream, wetlands, and vegetation on both sides of the stream course should be included as part of a conservation easement. However, trees and vegetation die, plants sometimes crowd out others, noxious plants grow, and storms and insect infestation can significantly alter the original character of the area proposed to be conserved.

Property owners should be permitted to undertake minor maintenance and replacement of vegetation in conservation easements. The minor maintenance includes removal of dead or diseased plants, thinning of undergrowth that does not reduce shielding or buffering, and the removal of noxious or poisonous plants. Minor maintenance should be limited to hand tools, excluding electric, motor, or engine-powered tools. Removal of dead trees should be considered major maintenance.

Where major maintenance or changes are proposed, the municipality should be informed and a municipal official, often the municipal engineer or planner, should be given the opportunity to review and comment on the changes. In addition, the changes should be indicated on a written document so that the official approval of the site plan or subdivision can be properly amended.

It is also important that neighbors be given notice of any proposed major changes to a conservation easement area. The existence of the easement may have been a factor in the purchase of their property, and changes to the easement could affect their views, drainage, or privacy.

If a conservation easement is under the ownership and control of a homeowners' association, they should also have the right to review and approve any major changes to the easement.

Finally, in some cases, conservation easements along streams can be linked together to form publicly accessible greenways. In order to do this, however, the original conservation easement should specify that the municipality (or other governmental agency) has the right to construct a pathway through the conservation easement.

While conservation easements have been in place for many years, their utilization has increased in recent years. The number of acres with such easements has increased nationally from 1.4 million in 1993 to 5.0 million in 2003 (Magers 2006: 22).

***Legal Annotation***: "The [perpetual **conservation**] **easement**, which did not extend to other neighboring lands also owned by defendant, was granted for the benefit of the general public and precludes defendant from removing vegetation, excavating soil, erecting structures, dumping trash, and engaging in any activity that might be detrimental to drainage, flood control, potable water, erosion control, or soil conservation. Except as specifically permitted, it prohibits any act or use detrimental to the preservation of the Property in its natural state." *Village of Ridgewood v. Bolger Foundation* (N.J., 1986).

## EASEMENT, CONTINUING

**An easement that is self-perpetuating and runs with the land.**

***Legal Annotation***: "A **continuing easement** is '[o]ne that is self-perpetuating, independent of human intervention, as, the flow of a stream.'" *Brown v. Tomilson* (Ga., 1980).

## EASEMENT, CROSS ACCESS

See *Easement, Private Access*

## EASEMENT, DISCHARGE

**The grant of a property right to allow runoff in excess of the previous quantity and/or rate of flow, or for the purpose of facilitating discharge off the property.**

***Legal Annotation***: "The E[nhanced] U[se] L[easing] leases property . . . 'TOGETHER WITH the right to access to an area outside of the Project for [purposes] of constructing and maintaining a discharge line from the [wastewater treatment] Facility to the discharge channel pursuant to the terms of the **discharge easement** as more specifically described in Exhibit A-1.'" *Clark County v. City of North Las Vegas* (D. Nev., 2011).

## EASEMENT, DRAINAGE

**Land required for the installation of stormwater sewers or drainage ditches and/or required for the preservation or maintenance of a natural stream or watercourse or other drainage facility.**

***Legal Annotation***: "Although the subdivision map shows the location of the five-foot-wide reserved storm **drainage easement** on either side of the property line between plaintiffs' and their neighbor, the pipe was not located there. The City's Storm Drainage Inventory Maps erroneously show a non-existent storm drainage, corrugated metal culvert within the reserved storm **drainage easement**." *DiMartino v. City of Orinda* (Calif. Ct. App., 2000).

## EASEMENT, EXPRESS

**An easement that is expressly created by a deed or other instrument.**

***Legal Annotation***: "The character of an **express easement** is determined by the nature of the right and the intention of the parties creating it." *Tupper v. Dorchester County* (S.C., 1997).

## EASEMENT, FACADE

**An easement that prohibits or restricts any changes to the facade of a building that would alter or damage its historic integrity or architectural character.**

***Legal Annotation***: "The subject is deductions on the couple's joint returns of the asserted value of Lorna Kaufman's donation to the National Architectural Trust of a **façade easement** restricting alterations on her Boston house." *Kaufman v. Shulman* (1st Cir., 2012).

## EASEMENT, MAINTENANCE

**A part of a lot free of structures reserved to an adjacent lot to allow access to repair or maintain a structure located on the adjacent lot.**

***Legal Annotation***: "The document as a whole does not reflect a permanent easement, but rather a **maintenance easement** that was restricted to the sole purpose of dredging the ditch during the road construction." *Koenigs v. Mitchell County Bd. Of Sup'rs* (Iowa: Supreme Court 2003). http://tinyurl.com/nlz7jlj

## EASEMENT, NEGATIVE

**An easement that precludes the owner of the land from doing that which the owner would be entitled to do if the easement did not exist.**

***Comment***: Negative easements historically have been limited to easements for light, air, views, and conservation.

***Legal Annotation***: "A **negative easement** has been defined as one the effect of which is to preclude the owner of the land subject to the easement from doing that which, if no easement existed, he would be entitled to do, or one which curtails the owner of the servient tenement in the exercise of some of his rights in respect of his estate in favor of the owner of the dominant tenement or tenements." *City of Olympia v. Palzer* (Wash., 1986).

## EASEMENT, PRIVATE ACCESS

**An easement created for the purpose of providing vehicular or pedestrian access across one property to another.**

*Comment*: Private access easements are often used to provide access to property that does not front on a public road. If the easement provides access to a residence or building lot, the ordinance or legal document providing for the easement should specify that the private access easement should be improved to permit passage by emergency vehicles (ambulance, police car, or fire truck). The easement agreement should also specify who is responsible for maintaining the easement.

*Legal Annotation*: "Owners of property abutting a once public road continue to have a **private access easement** over that road to their property even after the road loses its character as a public road." *Hall v. Pippin* (Tenn. Ct. App., 1998).

## EASEMENT, SCENIC

**An easement designed to limit development in order to preserve a viewshed or scenic area. See *Easement, Conservation; Viewshed. See Figure 106.***

*Legal Annotation*: "The concept of the **scenic easement** springs from the idea that there is enjoyment and recreation for the traveling public in viewing a relatively unspoiled natural landscape, and involves the judgment that in preserving existing scenic beauty as inexpensively as possible a line can reasonably be drawn between existing, or agricultural (and in these cases very limited residential) uses, and uses which have not yet commenced but involve more jarring human interference with a state of nature." *Kamrowski v. State* (Wis., 1966).

## EASEMENT, UTILITY

**The right-of-way acquired by a utility or governmental agency to locate utilities, including water, sewer, stormwater and gas mains, and telephone and electric poles, cables, pylons, and towers.**

*Comment*: Most utility easements have restrictions on their use; however, in some instances utility providers allow such easements to be utilized as walkways and bike paths, buffer or transition areas, community gardens and parking.

*Legal Annotation*: "Thus, consistent with the nature of the other specified properties, and harmonizing the statute's subsections, '**utility easement**' can reasonably be read to cover only public easements, that is, those easements dedicated to the public's use." *Marcus Cable Associates, LP v. Krohn* (Texas, 2002).

## EASEMENT, VIEWSHED

**An easement that places restrictions on the development of private land in order to preserve a viewshed. See *Viewshed. See Figure 106.***

*Comment*: An example is limiting the heights of new buildings within or adjacent to the sightline between two places so as to preserve the ability to view a landmark or scenic vista. In Portland, Oregon, for example, the height of certain downtown blocks is limited to preserve views of Mount Hood from the West Hills.

*Legal Annotation*: "There is no easement guaranteeing an unobstructed view of the golf course in the deeds of either Murphy or Rossi, and no such **viewshed easement** is guaranteed or provided for in the HOA's Declaration of Covenants." *Murphy v. Rossi* (Pa. Comm. Ct., 2010).

## EASEMENT IN GROSS

**An easement created for the personal benefit of the holder and not benefiting, attaching to, and running with a designated parcel of land.**

*Legal Annotation*: "An **easement**, or right-of-way, **in gross** is a mere personal privilege to the owner of the land and incapable of transfer by him, and is not, therefore assignable or inheritable." *Sandy Island Corp. v. Ragsdale* (S.C., 1965).

## EATING AND DRINKING PLACES

**Retail establishments serving food or drink for immediate consumption on the premises,**

**including restaurants, lunch counters, refreshment stands, ice cream parlors, and luncheonettes, but excluding drive-in or drive-through restaurants and bars or taverns.**

*Comment*: The above definition is typically provided to permit restaurants and other dining-related establishments whose primary purpose is the serving and consumption of prepared food on the premises. For this reason, drive-through or drive-in establishments are not included, and establishments where predominantly liquor is served are excluded. Eating and drinking places are also typically permitted as accessory uses within hotels, motels, sports arenas, and other amusement places. Note that the above definition can be tailored to meet the specific conditions and desires of each community—such as deleting some of the exclusions, or indeed, adding to the list of exclusions.

*Legal Annotation*: "In the present instance, however, further consideration of the problem is required because of the enactment by the legislature of the Act of May 23, 1945, P.L. 926, entitled: 'For the protection of the public health by regulating the conduct and operation of public **eating and drinking places** within this Commonwealth; requiring their licensing; imposing certain duties on the Department of Health of this Commonwealth and on the local health authorities; and providing penalties.'" *West. Pa. Restaurant Assn. v. Pittsburgh* (Pa., 1951).

## EAVE

**The projecting lower edges of a roof overhanging the wall of a building.** ***See Figures 17 and 25.***

*Comment*: In zoning ordinances, minimum setback requirements to buildings typically exempt eaves provided they do not significantly extend beyond the wall of a building (e.g., one and a half or two feet).

*Legal Annotation*: "This extension of the roof and roof covering beyond the south wall of what we now refer to as the gable end will be hereinafter determined to be an **eave** as applied to the facts and record in this case, so we will refer to it as an **eave**." *Hanna v. Nowell* (Mo. Ct. App., 1959).

## ECHO HOUSING

See *Housing, Echo*.

## ECOLOGICAL IMPACT

**The total effect of an environmental change, either natural or man-made, on the ecology of an area. See** ***Environmental Impact Statement.***

*Legal Annotation*: "Thus an area such as the River Common is to be avoided altogether for highway purposes if possible, but, if there is no feasible alternative, may be utilized in such a way as to minimize the environmental or **ecological impact** of the use." *Payne v. Kassab* (Pa., 1976).

## ECOLOGY

**The interrelationship of living things to one another and to their environment, or the study of such relationships.**

*Legal Annotation*: "Permitted uses in the shorelines of the state shall be designed and conducted in a manner to minimize, insofar as practical, any resultant damage to the **ecology** and environment of the shoreline area and any interference with the public's use of the water." *Dept. of Ecology v. Ballard Elks* (Wash., 1974).

## ECONOMETRICS

**Statistical analysis and techniques applied to economic information and used for modeling and projection.**

*Legal Annotation*: "**Econometrics** is 'the application of statistical and mathematical techniques in solving problems as well as in testing and demonstrating theories.'" *State of Ohio Ex Rel. Montgomery v. Trauth Dairy* (S.D. Ohio, 1996).

## ECONOMIC BASE

**The system of production, distribution, and consumption of goods and services within a planning area.**

*Comment*: "Economic base," as the term is used in planning, is the sum of all activities that result in income for the area's inhabitants. The definition, however, is significantly broad to include all geographic and functional elements that may have an impact on the planning area even if not physically part of the area. Economic base analysis identifies and measures the components of an area's economic base and highlights strengths and weaknesses of the local economy. "Economic base" is different from "base economy," which is a term used by economists to identify that part of a region's economy that is sold outside the region.

*Legal Annotation*: "Congress emphasized the need to fashion new remedies . . . to achieve its objectives: '[W]hat is needed here . . . are new approaches that will deal not only with individuals, but also with the **economic base** through which those individuals constitute such a serious threat to the economic well-being of the Nation.'" *Russello v. United States* (U.S., 1983).

## ECONOMIC DEVELOPMENT

**Policies, strategies, and programs adopted and implemented by various levels of government to attract new jobs, expand the existing job base, increase tax ratables and generally improve the economic well-being of an area. See *Economic Base*.**

*Comment*: Economic development programs include tax abatement for new or expanding industries, sale or lease of government-owned land to new plants and facilities, and extension or expansion of needed infrastructure such as water, sewer, or transportation. Many municipalities have found that long-term programs to improve livability by expanding the local education system and encouraging new housing are effective in encouraging economic development. Also, local "business improvement committees" or "industrial commissions" can identify problems in the local business or industrial environment that discourage new development. The adoption of redevelopment plans to replace blighted or significantly underutilized land, or downtown revitalization plans, is also a form of economic development facilitated by land use planning (Moore et al. 2006).

*Legal Annotation*: "In the aftermath of World War II, the Legislature authorized the formation of community redevelopment agencies in order to remediate urban decay. . . . The Community Redevelopment Law 'was intended to help local governments revitalize blighted communities.'... It has since become a principal instrument of **economic development**, mostly for cities, with nearly 400 redevelopment agencies now active in California." *California Redevelopment Assn. v. Matosantos* (Calif., 2011).

## ECOSYSTEM

**The interacting system of all living organisms and the physical environment in a specific geographic area.**

*Comment*: An ecosystem can be the entire biosphere, an ocean, a parcel of land, or an aquarium, depending on the context of use.

*Legal Annotation*: "The birds inhabit the sage-steppe **ecosystem** found in ten western states, including Idaho. They are sagebrush obligates, and rely on sagebrush all year to provide roosting, cover and food. The sagebrush-steppe (or sage-steppe) **ecosystem** is found across the 'Great Basin' region, defined by the BLM to include much of southern Idaho and northern Nevada, plus portions of Oregon, California and Utah. . . . The sage-steppe **ecosystem** features sagebrush in the overstory; native grasses, forbs, and litter in the understory; and biological soil crusts filling interspaces between vegetation." *Western Watersheds Project v. Salazar* (D. Idaho, 2012).

## ECOTOURISM

**Tourism designed to contribute to or raise awareness of unspoiled natural resources, and carried out in a manner that is intended to have the least possible impact on the environment.**

*Legal Annotation*: "Second, the Seminole Tribe argues that the Ordinance approved uses incompatible with the adjacent Big Cypress Reservation, in violation of LDC section 1-53-5.4. Specifically, the Seminole Tribe was concerned with the impact that the approved uses would have on water, **ecotourism**, and wildlife on the

Reservation." *Seminole Tribe of Florida v. Hendry* (Fla. Ct. App., 2013).

## EDGE CITY

**"A suburb that has developed its own political, economic and commercial base independent of the central city." www.meriam-webster.com/dictionary/edge%city**

*Comment*: According to Joel Garreau (1991), who coined the term, an edge city has such characteristics as having at least five million square feet of office space and six hundred thousand square feet of retail space, and "is perceived by the population as one place" (Garreau 1991: 7). According to Robert Lang (2003), edge cities are being superseded by "edgeless cities" (Kohut 2004: 26).

*Legal Annotation*: "This is a large site. It's on one hundred and thirty-five acres in a township that has been characterized as an **edge city**, almost an urban place. One hundred thirty-five acres of vacant land is significant. This is not a small, incidental piece of ground and it's certainly not comparable at least in the size of the context to anything surrounding it." *In Re Realen Valley Forge Greenes* (Pa., 2003).

## EDGE CLEARANCE

**The distance measured along the curb line from the extended property lot line to the driveway. *See Figure 43.***

*Legal Annotation*: "By an August 7, 1997 letter, the DOT advised the property owner that it would be constructing improvements to Route 206 and, as part of the improvements, closing the southerly driveway on Route 206, one of two existing egresses fronting Route 206. The reason given for the closing was that the southerly egress was in violation of an **edge clearance** regulation . . . and a corner clearance at signalized intersection regulation." *In Re I/M/O Route 206 New Amwell Rd.* (N.J. App. Div., 1999).

## EDGE DEFINITION

**A way of demarcating the traveled way, as distinguished from the nontraveled way.**

**Figure 43**

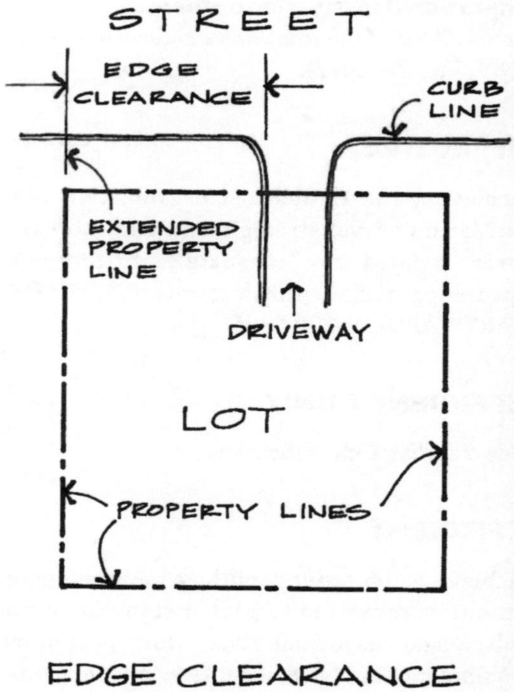


*Comment*: The edge may be demarcated by the use of railings, bollards, wheel stops, curb, or edge plantings.

*Legal Annotation*: "Curb requirements may be waived only in extremely narrow circumstances, and if waived, a comparable means of '**edge definition** and stabilization' is required. In contrast, the dictates for sidewalk construction lack uniformity and vary according to the net density and location of the development." *Norris v. Borough of Leonia* (N.J., 1999).

## EDUCATIONAL INSTITUTION

**A place where people of all ages gain an education, including preschools; child care; elementary, middle, and high schools; community colleges; colleges; and universities.**

*Legal Annotation*: "Thereafter, in accordance with the new Comprehensive Plan, the Town considered a specific zoning amendment . . . to 'permit adult student housing as a conditional use [by special permit] in all residential zones,' as an accessory to an approved postsecondary **educational institution** on the same site." *Matter of Village of Chestnut Ridge v. Town of Ramapo* (N.Y. Sup. Ct., 2012).

## EFFECTIVE

**Achieving the established organization-wide and/or unit-level strategic and tactical objectives (related to "adequate"). http://www.gwu.edu/~icdrm/publications/PDF/GLOSSARY%2002-19-2007.pdf**

## EFFICIENCY UNIT

See *Dwelling Unit, Efficiency*.

## EFFICIENT

**Achieving objectives with a minimum of resources compared to past or standard methods. Resources include time, effort, personnel, equipment, supplies, facilities, and expense. http://www.gwu.edu/~icdrm/publications/PDF/GLOSSARY%2002-19-2007.pdf**

*Legal Annotation*: "Our review begins with WIS. STAT. § 281.31, the 'Navigable waters protection law.' Subsection (1) provides: 'To aid in the fulfillment of the state's role as trustee of its navigable waters and to promote public health, safety, convenience and general welfare, it is declared to be in the public interest to make studies, establish policies, make plans and *authorize municipal shoreland zoning regulations* for the **efficient** use, conservation, development and protection of this state's water resources.'" *Hegwood v. Town of Eagle Zoning Board of Appeals* (Wis. Ct. App., 2013).

## EFFLUENT

**A discharge of liquid waste, with or without treatment, into the environment.**

*Comment*: The term is generally used to describe discharges from a treatment plant, a sewer, or an industrial outfall into a river or the sea.

*Legal Annotation*: "In addition, the analysis of an **effluent's** composition, examination of other sources' discharges into the water, and the study of chemical reactions of various compounds present in water at various points along miles of a river to determine the causes of odor, foam or color at another specific place on the river are not simple examinations which a lay person could conduct. These determinations would have to be made in order to prove that the defendant's actions of discharging its **effluent** in North Carolina caused the interference complained of at the plaintiff's property in Tennessee." *Freeman v. Blue Ridge Paper Products, Inc.* (E.D. Tenn., 2012).

## EFFLUENT, BIOMONITORING

See *Biomonitoring*.

## EGRESS

**A place or means of exiting a property.**

*Legal Annotation*: "In affirming the trial court's judgment, the Appellate Court concluded that the plain language and context of the regulations demonstrate that they apply to both existing and newly proposed dead-end streets . . . and that a loop road, such as Eastwood Drive, fits within the definition of a dead-end street because it has only one means of ingress or **egress**." *Kraiza V. Planning and Zoning Commission of Town of Hartland* (Conn., 2012).

## ELDER COTTAGE HOUSING

See *Echo Housing*.

## ELDER HOUSING

See *Housing for the Elderly*.

## ELECTRIC VEHICLE CHARGING STATION (EVCS)

See *Charging Station*.

## ELEEMOSYNARY OR PHILANTHROPIC INSTITUTION

**A private or public organization that is organized and operated for the purpose of providing a service or carrying on a trade or business without profit and for charitable purposes.**

*Comment*: Eleemosynary or philanthropic organizations generally provide services or goods to disadvantaged persons. Their nonprofit aspects are recognized by the Internal Revenue Service. However, these uses should be located in areas according to the activities that are conducted on their premises rather than according to their nonprofit status. For example, a nonprofit fund or foundation that distributes grants functions as an office use; however, a nonprofit organization that trains disabled individuals to restore and repair furniture should be located in an industrial area. The primary factors in locating these uses should be the type of use or service it provides, and the actual impacts on the surrounding area.

*Legal Annotation*: "Thus we see that the doctrine in Virginia was established that a charitable or **eleemosynary institution** is liable to beneficiaries of the charity for negligence of its employees if it fails to exercise ordinary care in the selection and retention of its employees." *Memorial Hospital v. Oakes* (Va., 1959).

## ELEVATION

**(1) A vertical distance above or below a fixed reference level; (2) a fully dimensioned drawing of the front, rear, or side of a building, showing features such as windows, doors, and relationship of grade to floor level.**

*Legal Annotation*: "The only definition in the same dictionary for '**elevation**' which specifically refers to a building, and has reference to construction plans, is 'a geometrical projection (as of a building) on a plane perpendicular to the horizon: orthographic [characterized by perpendicular lines or right angles] projection on a vertical plane.' Thus, an **'elevation'** on construction plans is the side view showing the structure, or a portion thereof, projected against the horizon." *Villas of Lake Jackson, Ltd. v. Leon County* (N.D. Fla., 1995).

## EMBANKMENT

**An elevated deposit of soil, rock, or other materials, either constructed or natural. See *Dam*.**

*Legal Annotation*: "There was no element of common knowledge that the result would follow the action, such as is present where an **embankment** is built so close to plaintiff's land, and so steep and high, that the forces of gravity or of rainfall are quite certain to cause the earth to slide or be washed over plaintiff's land." *Wisconsin Power & Light Co. v. Columbia County* (Wis., 1958).

## EMERGENCY

**Any incident, natural or man-made, that requires responsive action to protect life or property.**

*Comment*: Emergencies are events that have the potential to cause immediate adverse physical, social, psychological, economic, or political effects and that challenge the ability of governmental and private aid organizations to rapidly and effectively respond. They require a stepped-up capacity and capability (call-back procedures, mutual aid, etc.) to meet the expected outcome, and they commonly require change from routine management methods to an incident command/management process in order to achieve the expected outcome. (**See *Disaster*** for important contrast between the two terms).

Federal and state laws carefully prescribe which officials may declare an emergency, areas so designated, and the type of assistance that may be provided. Under the Robert T. Stafford Disaster Relief and Emergency Assistance Act, an emergency means any occasion or instance for which, in the determination of the president, federal assistance is needed to supplement state and local efforts and capabilities to save lives and to protect property and public health and safety, or to lessen or avert the threat of a catastrophe in any part of the United States. http://www.gwu.edu/~icdrm/publications/PDF/GLOSSARY%2002-19-2007.pdf

*Legal Annotation*: "To this analysis, the Court would add the numerous points made above in this Decision and Order, including the following: . . . the fact that any New York State statute authorizing the establishment of local response plans and/or teams to assists persons with household pets following a *natural disaster* or the declaration of a *local state of* ***emergency*** does not somehow give rise to a failure-to-train claim by Plaintiff against the County Defendants under the circumstances." *Bruno v. City of Schenectady* (N.D.N.Y., 2014).

## EMERGENCY MANAGEMENT

**The science of managing complex systems and multidisciplinary personnel to address emergencies and disasters, across all hazards, and through the phases of mitigation, preparedness, response, and recovery.**

***Comment***: Emergency management involves organized analysis, planning, decision-making, and assignment of available resources to mitigate, prepare for, respond to, and recover from the effects of all hazards. The goal of emergency management is to save lives, prevent injuries, and protect property and the environment if an emergency occurs (FEMA 1995: I-6). http://www.gwu.edu/~icdrm/publications/PDF/GLOSSARY%2002-19-2007.pdf

***Legal Annotation***: "Local governments and emergency management organizations, such as fire departments and sheriff's offices, may formally enter into various types of agreements, such as mutual aid agreements and **emergency management** plans, to respond to each other's emergencies." *Hauber v. Yakima* County (Wash., 2002).

## EMERGENCY PREPAREDNESS

**Activities and measures designed or undertaken to prepare for or minimize the effects of a hazard upon the civilian population, to deal with the immediate emergency conditions that would be created by the hazard, and to effectuate emergency repairs to, or the emergency restoration of, vital utilities and facilities destroyed or damaged by the hazard (Stafford Act). http://www.gwu.edu/~icdrm/publications/PDF/GLOSSARY%2002-19-2007.pdf**

## EMERGENCY SHELTER

**A facility providing temporary housing for one or more individuals who are otherwise temporarily homeless.**

***Comment***: Emergency shelters are usually provided by governmental agencies and religious, eleemosynary, or philanthropic institutions. In addition to housing, some shelters provide food, clothing, and other ancillary services. Emergency shelters generally serve the poor, primarily indigent, or needy; however, persons displaced by emergencies (such as fire and natural disasters) may also be temporarily housed in emergency shelters.

***Legal Annotation***: "In 1987, the Council of the District of Columbia, responding to similar concerns, enacted D.C.Law 7-86, the **Emergency Shelter** Services for Families Reform Amendment Act of 1987 (the Family Shelter Act), which established a homeless shelter program for eligible homeless families." *Atchison v. District of Columbia* (D.C. Ct. App., 1991).

## EMERGENCY SPILLWAY

**See *Spillway, Emergency*.**

## EMINENT DOMAIN

**The authority to acquire or take or to authorize the taking of private property for public use or public purpose (Shingley 2007; Weinstein 2006). See *Taking; Just Compensation*.**

***Comment***: While eminent domain is largely the prerogative of government, utilities and independent agencies may also have the right of eminent domain if permitted under state law. The US Constitution requires just compensation for any taking, and the taking must be for a public purpose.

***Legal Annotation***: "Government, through its **eminent domain** authority, may condemn certain property and assign it to public use, subject to reasonable compensation to the owner of the land." *Stelpflug v. Town Board, Town of Waukesha* (Wis., 2000).

## EMISSION

**A discharge of pollutants into the air.**

***Legal Annotation***: "EPA based its order upon an interpretation of the Clean Air Act which requires that national air quality standards be met by continuous **emission** limitations to the maximum extent possible, and that intermittent controls and dispersion systems by used only when continuous **emission** controls are not economically feasible." *Kennecott Copper Corp. v. Train* ($9^{th}$ Cir. 1975).

## EMISSION FACTOR

**The average amount of a pollutant emitted from each type of polluting source in relation to a specified amount of material processed.**

***Comment***: The emission factor is used in establishing a performance standard. Most of the factors and standards themselves are now specified and regulated by state or federal agencies.

***Legal Annotation***: "In computing the '**emission factor**' upon which his results were based, Bray took the amount of total emissions generated during the test and divided by the total weight of finished product to come up with a figure of emissions per ton of finished production." *US v. Louisiana-Pacific Corp.* (D. Colo. 1988).

## EMISSION STANDARD

**The maximum amount of a pollutant legally permitted to be discharged from a single source, either mobile or stationary.**

***Legal Annotation***: "Once issued, a permit may be revoked or modified for failure to comply with the terms and conditions of the permit, with **emission standards** applicable to the air contaminant source, or with the ambient air standards for the area in which the air contaminant source is located." *Hancock v. Train* (U.S., 1976).

## EMPLOYEE TRANSPORTATION COORDINATOR

**The person who develops, implements, and administers an employee transportation program.**

***Comment***: Also referred to as a rideshare coordinator. Duties may include registering employees for a ride-match program; coordinating the formation of car, van, and bus pools; promoting the use of public transit; and monitoring employee participation in the program.

***Legal Annotation***: "(3) A commute trip reduction program of a major employer shall consist of, at a minimum (a) designation of a **transportation coordinator** and the display of the name, location, and telephone number of the coordinator in a prominent manner at each affected worksite; (b) regular distribution of information to employees regarding alternatives to single-occupant vehicle commuting; (c) a regular review of employee commuting and reporting of progress toward meeting the single-occupant vehicle reduction goals to the county, city, or town consistent with the method established in the commute trip reduction plan and the rules established by the department of transportation . . . and (d) implementation of a set of measures designed to achieve the applicable commute trip reduction goals adopted by the jurisdiction." *RCW 70.94.531 Transportation demand management—Requirements for employers.*

## ENABLING ACT

**A legislative act authorizing a county, municipal, or other governmental agency to undertake actions or activities.**

***Legal Annotation***: "The fundamental objective of (the) constitutional amendment and the implementing Municipal Zoning **Enabling Act** was local control of zoning and planning for the purpose of effecting the public good." *South Burlington County NAACP v. Township of Mount Laurel* (N.J., 1975).

## ENCLOSURE

**An area, enclosed or semi-enclosed by a wall or fence, at ground or slightly below ground level, and adjacent to a building.**

***Comment***: Enclosures are used for limited storage, parking, deliveries and similar ancillary uses, as well as secondary building access. The enclosure area is not usually included as part of net floor area calculations.

***Legal Annotation***: "The Court states that curtilage questions are often resolved through evaluation of four factors: 'the proximity of the area claimed to be curtilage to the home, whether the area is included within an **enclosure** surrounding the home, the nature of the uses to which the area is put, and the steps taken by the resident to protect the area from observation by people passing by.'" *United States v. Dunn* (U.S., 1987).

## ENCROACHMENT

**Any obstruction or illegal or unauthorized intrusion in a delineated floodway or right-of-way, or on adjacent land. *See Figure 48.***

***Legal Annotation***: "The movement of development closer to the ocean creates the prospect of **encroachment** on public tidelands, because of fluctuation in the mean high-tide line." *Nollan v. California Coastal Commission* (U.S., 1987).

## ENDANGERED SPECIES

**Species whose prospects for survival are in immediate danger because of a loss of or change in habitat, overexploitation, predation, competition, disease, disturbance, or contamination and designated as such by a governmental agency.**

***Legal Annotation***: "The plaintiffs' principal argument is that the NMFS violated the **Endangered Species** Act ('ESA') because it based the fishing restrictions on declines in sub-regions rather than in the entire population of the **endangered species**." *Alaska v. Lubchenco* (9th Cir., 2013).

## ENLARGEMENT

**An increase in the size of an existing structure or use, including the physical size of the property, building, parking, and other improvements.**

***Comment***: What constitutes an enlargement is especially critical when it comes to nonconforming uses. While a physical expansion always constitutes an enlargement, other changes, such as alterations, may or may not be considered an enlargement. This was noted in a New Jersey Supreme Court (the state's highest court) decision (*Burbridge v. Mine Hill Twp.,* 117 N.J. 376 [1990]), in which the court said, "Applications to expand nonconforming uses offer boards opportunities to impose conditions, frequently aesthetic, which will help integrate the use with its surroundings"(Cox 2003).

***Legal Annotation***: "In contrast to 'intensification' are the concepts of 'expansion and **enlargement**' of the nonconforming use. Expansion and **enlargement** of a nonconforming use contrary to a properly enacted zoning ordinance is unlawful." *Baxter v. City of Preston* (Idaho, 1989).

## ENRICHMENT, NUTRIENT

**The addition of nitrogen, phosphorus, and carbon compounds or other nutrients to a lake or other waterway.**

***Comment***: Nutrient enrichment greatly increases the growth potential for algae and aquatic plants. Most frequently, nutrient enrichment results from the inflow of sewage effluent or from fertilizer runoff.

***Legal Annotation***: "The STAC report issued January, 1986 . . . concluded that recent studies demonstrated nitrogen, as well as phosphorus, play vital roles in **nutrient enrichment** in the Chesapeake Bay Region, and that deteriorating water quality was directly correlated with increased **nutrient enrichment**." *Howard County v. Davidsonville Civic & Potomac River Assn., Inc.* (Md. Ct. Spec. App., 1987).

## ENVIRONMENT

**All external conditions and influences affecting the life, development, and ultimately the survival of an organism.**

***Comment***: In a development context, *environment* is used in a more location-specific context and typically refers to all of the physical conditions and influences affecting a particular area, both natural and man-made.

***Legal Annotation***: "The Guidelines . . . define '**environment**' as 'the physical conditions which exist within the area which will be affected by a proposed project including land, air, water, minerals, flora, fauna, ambient noise, objects of historic or aesthetic significance.'" *Topanga Beach*

*Renters Assn. v. Dept. of General Services* (Calif. Ct. App., 1976).

## ENVIRONMENTAL CONSTRAINTS

**Features, natural resources, or land characteristics that are ecologically sensitive to improvements and may require conservation measures or the application of creative development techniques to prevent their degradation, or may require limited development, or in certain instances may preclude development.**

***Legal Annotation***: "The chancellor emphasized that **environmental constraints** on Biloxi's land post-Katrina, especially the fact that of much of the Biloxi peninsula was reclassified as a flood zone, demonstrated a need for Biloxi to expand. The chancellor noted that D'Iberville had many of the same environmental issues as Biloxi. The chancellor concluded that both cities are subject to heightened **environmental constraints** and influences, such as flood plains, wetlands, and severe slopes, due to their proximity to the Gulf of Mexico." *In Re Enlarging, Extending and Defining* (Miss., 2013).

## ENVIRONMENTAL IMPACT

**See *Ecological Impact*.**

## ENVIRONMENTAL IMPACT STATEMENT (EIS)

**A report that discusses the effect of proposed development and/or other major private or governmental actions on the environment.**

***Comment***: The purpose of an EIS is to provide the community with information needed to evaluate the effects of a proposed project upon the environment. The statement usually consists of an inventory of existing environmental conditions at the project site and in the surrounding area. The inventory includes air and water quality, hydrology, geology, soil type, topography, vegetation, wildlife, aquatic organisms, demography, land use, community character, aesthetics, history, and archaeology. An EIS also includes a project description and may include a list of all licenses, permits, or other approvals required by law. The EIS assesses the probable impact of the project on all the inventory items and includes a listing of adverse environmental impacts that cannot be avoided. The statement also includes what steps the applicant proposes to take to ameliorate or minimize adverse environmental impacts during construction and operation and whether there are alternatives to the project that could lessen its adverse environmental impacts. Both federal and state laws may require an EIS (Amur 2007).

***Legal Annotation***: "Section 102 (2) (C) of the National Environmental Policy Act of 1969[1] (NEPA) requires that all federal agencies include a detailed statement of environmental consequences—known as an **environmental impact statement**— 'in every recommendation or report on proposals for legislation and other major Federal actions significantly affecting the quality of the human environment.'" *Kleppe v. Sierra Club* (U.S., 1976).

## ENVIRONMENTAL RESOURCE INVENTORY

**See *Natural Resources Inventory*.**

## ENVIRONMENTALLY SENSITIVE AREA

**A geographic area that contains one or more significant natural or ecological resources that are both particularly susceptible to damage or degradation resulting from disturbance or construction, and that are important to its ecology, including surface waters, sources of water supply, bay islands and corridors, beaches, dunes, wetlands and wetland transition areas, critical wildlife habitats, prime fishing areas, finfish migratory pathways, submerged vegetation habitats, shellfish harvesting areas, forest areas, habitats for threatened or endangered species, vegetated wilderness areas, and wild and scenic corridors. See *Critical Area*.**

***Comment***: It should be noted that certain natural features such as shallow bedrock or groundwater may be environmental constraints but are not in and of themselves environmentally sensitive areas. The key to determining whether an environmental features is sensitive is the degree to which disturbance increases the probability of its degradation or demise.

*Legal Annotation*: "Section 30107.5 provides this two-part test for ESHA status (numbering ours): '**Environmentally sensitive area**' means any area [1] in which plant or animal life or their habitats are either rare or especially valuable because of their special nature or role in an ecosystem and [2] which could be easily disturbed or degraded by human activities and developments." *Sierra Club v. California Coastal Commission* (Calif. Ct. App., 1993).

## EQUALIZATION RATIO OR RATE

**A ratio or rate of total assessed value for properties in a community to those properties' true market values. Also referred to as "assessment-to-sales ratio."**

*Comment*: "The equalization ratio or rate represents the state or locality's judgment of how closely assessed values match the market value. For example, an equalization ratio or rate of 90% would mean that, on average, the property in a community is being assessed at 90% of its market value" (http://taxes.about-com/od/statetaxes/a/equalization-rate.htm). In formula terms:

$$\frac{\text{Total assessed value}}{\text{Total market value}} = \text{Equalization Rate (Ratio)} \times \text{Total market value}$$

$$\text{Total assessment value} = \text{Total Market Value} \times \text{Equalization rate}$$

*Legal Annotation*: "Thus, the state appraiser found the best estimate of fair market value to be $174,300. Applying an **equalization ratio** of 99.79%, the state appraiser found the listed value of the property to be $173,900." *Franks v. Town of* Essex (Vt., 2013).

## EQUALIZED OR EFFECTIVE PROPERTY TAX RATE

**The amount of the property tax divided by the market value of the property.**

*Comment*: The equalized or effective property tax rate provides the true rate or measure of this tax. Comparing the equalized or effective property tax rate in multiple taxing jurisdictions gives an "apples to apples" comparison of the true tax burden of properties in different locations. This is not the case in comparing the statutory (or nomimal or posted) property tax rates, which can be misleading, given differences in the equalization ratio or rate or "assessment-to-sales" ratio in different taxing jurisdictions. http://eyeonhousing.wordpress.com/2011/08/09/new-nahb-report-on-effective-property-tax-rates/

*Legal Annotation*: "Sohm noted that 'no adjustment . . . for the **effective property tax rate** is required' because 'rent is projected on a triple net basis.'" *Truserv Corp v. Lane County Assessor* (Ore. Tax Ct., 2011).

## EROSION

**The detachment and removal of soil or rock fragments or the wearing away of the land surface by water, wind, ice, and gravity.**

*Legal Annotation*: "In general, three methods are used to manage the problem of shoreline **erosion**: armoring the beach with 'hard' erosion control devices; renourishing the beach with sand; and retreating from the beach altogether." *SC Coastal Conservation v. SC Department of Health and Environmental Control* (S.C. Ct. App., 2001).

## EROSION CONTROL PLAN

**A plan designed to minimize erosion, ensure proper waste disposal, and protect trees on a building site.**

*Comment*: The objectives of the erosion control plan can be achieved by implementing a number of important measures. These include requiring that grading and excavation be confined to the smallest area of the site as possible; protecting exposed areas with vegetation, sod, or tarps; or seeding and mulching where soils are exposed, soon after the ground has been disturbed. Other measures include the requirement that fill be kept clean of topsoil, organic matter, and rocks, and that it be stored away from any protected vegetation and stabilized by mulching, vegetation, or tarps. An erosion control plan should also provide for sedimentation basins for disturbed areas of more than ten acres, and silt fences or straw bales should be employed to keep the soil from moving off the site. The plan should provide for "no-disturbance setbacks" from streams or ponds, with appropriate vegetation in place to filter stormwater before it enters water bodies. Another important means of minimizing erosion is to insist upon utilizing a grading plan that minimizes the importation of fill or the removal of excess material from the site.

Other measures call for using gravel or paved driveways to prevent mud from being tracked onto public roads, with pads that remove mud from construction vehicles before leaving the site. Any mud left on public roads should be the responsibility of the contractor and should be swept up, rather than washed away.

The erosion control plan should also address waste disposal and specifically prohibit construction debris and other waste being buried on the site. Finally, an important element of the plan should be the saving of as many trees on the site as possible and protecting trees during the construction period. Fencing around saved trees avoids harmful compaction, grading, and excavation around the root system. It may also be necessary to prune the tree crown to reduce the demand on the roots for nutrients and water.

The erosion control plan should include: a construction schedule; a maintenance plan for keeping erosion control equipment in good repair; maps showing proposed locations for temporary and permanent channels, fencing, vegetation, and fill areas; drawings of erosion control devices whose locations should be specified; and cut-and-fill calculations.

***Legal Annotation***: "This permit is part of an overall **erosion control plan** required of defendant in connection with construction of its plant. Part of the **erosion control plan** is a storm water detention pond from which water is periodically released." *Sierra Club v. Hyundai America, Inc.* (D. Ore., 1997).

## ERUV

**A symbolic technical boundary demarcating an area in which Orthodox (traditional-oriented) Jews may conduct certain activities normally forbidden by traditional Jewish law on the sabbath (Saturday). (Derived, with modifications, from www.thefreedictionary.com/eruv.)**

***Comment***: According to traditional Orthodox Jewish rules, "it is forbidden to carry or push any item—regardless of its weight, size, or purpose [e.g., house key, baby stroller, or wheelchair]—on the Shabbat . . . from a 'private' domain into a 'public' one, or vice versa." For the purpose of this law, "'private' and 'public' do not refer to ownership, but rather to the nature of the area. An enclosed area is considered a private domain, whereas an open area is considered public." (www.chabad.org/library/article_cdo/aid/700456/jewish/What Is). An eruv symbolically demarcates an area as a "private" domain. An eruv can consist of numerous objects, such as a physical wall, a waterway or other boundary, existing telephone or utility poles and lines, poles and lines added specifically for eruv purposes, or a combination of the above.

There are at least two hundred eruvim in communities large and small in the United States and abroad (e.g., portions of Boston; New York City; Las Vegas; Washington, DC; London; and Melbourne [Eruv.org]). The first eruv in the United States was constructed in St. Louis in 1894. An eruv may involve construction (e.g., building permit for the added poles and lines) and planning considerations. For example, the San Diego Planning Commission (SDPC) considered approval of a "Site Development Permit to allow the establishment and installation of an eruv line of demarcation using eight new utility poles within the public right-of-way" (SDPC 2013: 1). The SDPC even considered the environmental aspects of this matter under the California Environmental Quality Act. In this case the SDPC approved the eruv line demarcation.

***Legal Annotation***: "An **eruv** is an unbroken demarcation or delineation of an area. An eruv may be established in a number of ways, including the attachment of wooden or plastic strips, called 'lechis,' to telephone or utility poles. Plaintiffs propose to establish an **eruv** within the three defendant municipalities. The perimeter, outline, or delineation of the proposed **eruv** would be the existing overhead utility wires, existing structures and natural boundaries." *East End Eruv v. Village of Westhampton Beach* (E.D.N.Y., 2013).

## ESCARPMENT

**A cliff or steep slope generally separating two levels of gently sloping areas.** *See Figure 44.*

***Comment***: Also known as a scarp (*FEMA Glossary*).

***Legal Annotation***: "After a storm in 2006, the condominium's access to the beach, a wooden staircase, was partially buried by the municipality in attempt to restore the shoreline. In 2009, erosion resulted in a steep **escarpment** from the bottom of the staircase to the beach. As a result, the DEP permitted the Association to install temporary aluminum stairs to bridge the **escarpment**." *Weiss v. 2100 Condominium Ass'n, Inc.* (S.D. Fla., 2013).

## ESCROW

**A deed, bond, cash, or other security delivered to a third person or agency and delivered by the third person to the grantee only upon fulfillment of a condition.**

***Comment***: Applicants for development are often required to post escrows to ensure payment of review and inspection fees.

***Legal Annotation***: "The term '**escrow**' is defined in ORS 696.505(2), which provides, in part: '"Escrow" means any transaction wherein any written instrument, money, evidence of title to real or personal property or other thing of value is delivered to a person."' *Cost Security v. Real Estate Agency* (Ore., 2000).

**Figure 44**

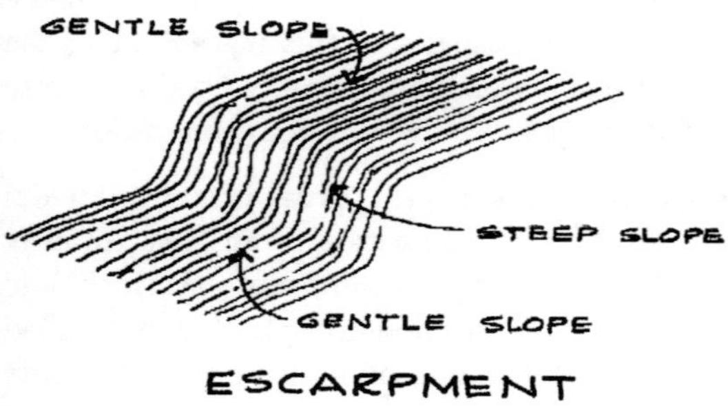


## ESSENTIAL SERVICES

**Services and utilities needed for the health, safety, and general welfare of the community, such as underground, surface, or overhead electrical, gas, telephone, steam, water, sewerage, and other utilities and the equipment and appurtenances necessary for such systems to furnish an adequate level of service for the area in which they are located.**

***Comment***: The definition of *essential services* is limited to utility-type services as opposed to other services, such as police, fire and ambulance services, which are termed "emergency services" and which are obviously equally important. Improvements necessary to deliver essential services are typically either permitted or conditional uses in all zones, but larger facilities that generate or handle them are typically confined to nonresidential zones; some distinction is necessary for the equipment, facilities, and appurtenances associated with the service. For example, sewer lines and lift stations may be located in residential areas, but a sewage treatment facility is not appropriate in a residential zone. **See *Public Utility***.

***Legal Annotation***: "Under the balancing approach outlined in Mathews, some administrative procedure for entertaining customer complaints prior to termination is required to afford reasonable assurance against erroneous or arbitrary withholding of **essential services**." *Memphis Light, Gas & Water Div. v. Craft* (U.S., 1978).

## ESTABLISHMENT

**An economic unit where business is conducted or services or industrial operations are performed.**

***Comment***: An establishment is generally at a single physical location, but not necessarily so. An establishment may include, for example, one or more manufacturing plants and several retail sales outlets.

*Legal Annotation*: "But if, as we believe, Congress used the word '**establishment**' as it is normally used in business and in government—as meaning a distinct physical place of business—petitioner's enterprise is composed of 49 retail establishments and a single wholesale establishment." *AH Phillips, Inc. v. Walling* (U.S., 1949).

## ESTUARIES

**Areas where fresh water meets salt water, such as bays, mouths of rivers, salt marshes, and lagoons.**

*Comment*: Estuaries are notable for two major attributes: as important breeding grounds for all types of aquatic and bird life; and for being especially vulnerable and intolerant of pollution and/or disturbance.

*Legal Annotation*: "The term '**estuaries**' as used in this provision means 'waters, including coastal lagoons, located at the mouths of streams which serve as mixing zones for fresh and ocean waters.'" *Central Delta Water Agency v. State Water Resources Control Board* (Calif. Ct. App., 1993).

## EUTROPHIC LAKES

**Shallow water bodies, often weed-choked and very rich in nutrients.**

*Comment*: Eutrophic lakes are characterized by large amounts of algae, poor water transparency, low dissolved oxygen, and high BOD (biological oxygen demand).

*Legal Annotation*: "A **eutrophic lake** is one which is rich in nutrients favoring plant life over animal life." *City of Maple Lake v. American States* (Minn. Ct. App., 1993).

## EUTROPHICATION

**The normally slow aging process by which a lake evolves into a bog or marsh and ultimately assumes a completely terrestrial state and disappears.**

*Legal Annotation*: "**Eutrophication** is the 'normally slow aging process by which a lake evolves into a bog or marsh. . . . During eutrophication the lake becomes so rich in nutritive compounds (especially nitrogen and phosphorus) that algae and other microscopic plant life become superabundant, thereby "choking" the lake.'" *Arkansas v. Oklahoma* (U.S., 1992).

## EVALUATION

**A process to measure the success of an activity and how closely the results meet the anticipated outcome.**

*Legal Annotation*: "As the [Supplemental Information Report] demonstrates, the Corps conducted a reasoned **evaluation** of the relevant information and reached a decision that, although perhaps disputable, was not 'arbitrary or capricious.'" *Marsh v. Oregon Natural Resources Council* (U.S., 1989).

## EVAPORATION PONDS

**Shallow, artificial ponds where sewage sludge is pumped, permitted to dry, and either removed or buried by more sludge.**

*Comment*: Evaporation ponds are also used to store and treat liquid hazardous wastes.

*Legal Annotation*: "The hazardous waste management activities conducted by CWM at Denver-Arapahoe include the operation of three surface impoundments, or **evaporation ponds**, known as Ponds 1, 2, and 3. The ponds were built to store and treat liquid hazardous wastes by the process of evaporation." *Chemical Waste Management, Inc. v. USEPA* (D.D.C., 1986).

## EVERGREEN

**A plant that retains its foliage and that remains green year-round.**

*Legal Annotation*: "As a minimum, a wall, fence or compact **evergreen** hedge or other type of **evergreen** foliage or a combination of fence and shrubbery at least six (6) feet in height shall be provided along the side and rear lot lines of the commercial or industrial property." *Richland County v. Kaiser* (S.C. Ct. App., 2002).

## EXACTION

**Contributions or payments required as an authorized precondition for receiving a development permit (American Planning Association, *The Language of Zoning,* Planning Advisory Service Report No. 322, 1976).**

***Comment***: Exactions may refer to mandatory dedications, such as for road widenings or low-income housing. In all cases, there must be a nexus between the amount of the exaction and the purpose for which it is used. Thus, an exaction fee from an office use, based on the number of square feet, could be used for improvements to roadways that are directly proportional to the impacts created by the added traffic generated by the additional office area.

***Legal Annotation***: "Instead, the court read Nollan to mean that an '**exaction** is reasonably related to an impact if the **exaction** serves the same purpose that a denial of the permit would serve.'" *Dolan v. City of Tigard* (U.S., 1994).

## EXCAVATION

**Removal, displacement, or recovery by any means whatsoever of soil, rock, minerals, mineral substances, or organic substances from water or land, on or beneath the surface thereof, or beneath the land surface, whether exposed or submerged.**

***Legal Annotation***: "Section 2.3 of the Underground Utility Facilities Damage Prevention Act defines '**excavation**' as: 'any operation in which earth, rock, or other material in or on the ground is moved, removed, or otherwise displaced by means of any tools, power equipment or explosives, and includes, without limitation, grading, trenching, digging, ditching, drilling, augering, boring, tunneling, scraping, cable or pipe plowing, and driving.'" *Quality Saw and Seal v. Illinois Commerce Commission* (Ill. App. Ct., 2007).

## EXCEPTION

**Permission to depart from the design standards in the ordinance. See *Waiver*.**

***Comment***: Exceptions often refer to design standards such as length of cul-de-sacs, location and type of improvements, and landscaping requirements. The granting of exceptions is dictated by the circumstances related to the specific application that makes the design requirement for which the exception is requested unnecessary or unreasonable. As in the case of waivers, the approving agency must make findings and conclusions before granting the exception.

## EXCLUSIONARY ZONING

**Development regulations that result in the exclusion of low- and moderate-income and minority families from a community.**

***Comment***: Exclusionary zoning may also serve to keep out, or limit, additional development. Exclusionary zoning provisions include allowing only large-lot, single-family detached dwellings; bulk regulations in excess of those needed for health and safety; limiting or barring of multifamily development; and excessive improvement requirements that generate unnecessary costs (Knapp et al. 2007).

***Legal Annotation***: "The misuse of the municipal zoning power at issue in this case, generically described as '**exclusionary zoning**,' . . . involves two distinct but interrelated practices: (1) the use of the zoning power by municipalities to take advantage of the benefits of regional development without having to bear the burdens . . . and (2) the use of the zoning power by municipalities to maintain themselves as enclaves of affluence or of social homogeneity." *South Burlington County NAACP v. Township of Mount Laurel* (N.J., 1975).

## EXCLUSIVE-USE DISTRICT

**A zoning district that allows only one use or a limited range of uses.**

***Legal Annotation***: "So let us consider those criteria, noting by way of background that originally zoning was 'cumulative'—that is, 'higher uses,' such as residential land uses, were permitted in districts in which 'lower uses,' such as manufacturing, were permitted, though the 'lower uses' were excluded from districts zoned for the higher ones. Cumulative zoning soon gave way to noncumulative **(or 'exclusive') zoning**, in which specified land uses were confined to specified districts and thus could be and often were separated." *River of Life Kingdom Minist. v. Hazel Crest, Ill.* (7th Cir., 2010).

## EXECUTIVE HEADQUARTERS

**An office building occupied almost entirely by the principal office of a business or corporation. See *Office Headquarters*.**

***Comment***: Usually, the executive headquarters (or corporate headquarters) bears the name of the corporation and is designed to project a favorable corporate image. The buildings are often of a higher quality and cost more to construct than multi-tenanted or speculative office buildings. Headquarters buildings have fewer employees per square foot, since the executives typically have large offices and the buildings have a significant number of meeting rooms. From a planning and zoning perspective, there is no guarantee that a headquarters building will always remain so. Corporations are sold, functions change, and cost-cutting requires cutbacks. The fewer parking spaces allowed for a headquarters building may not be sufficient when the building no longer functions as originally approved.

***Legal Annotation***: "A company's principal place of business is where its 'nerve center' is located, or, more concretely, where its **executive headquarters** are located." *Illinois Bell Telephone Co. v. Global Naps* (7th Cir., 2008).

## EXISTING GRADE OR ELEVATION

**The existing vertical location of the ground surface before excavating or filling.**

***Comment***: Existing grade or existing elevation is sometimes an important reference point with respect to measuring the height of buildings or structures after construction is completed. Communities are often concerned that the ultimate height or elevation of such structures may be substantially greater if the finished grade or elevation is used as a reference point for measuring such height, instead of existing grade or elevation.

***Legal Annotation***: "In paragraph 5 the parties also agreed that, 'All walls and foundations shall be removed one (1) foot below the elevation of the **existing grade** of the sidewalk adjacent to it.'" *Fourth Ocean v. Interstate* (N.Y., 1985).

"Thus, a special exception, with particular conditions, was required for any permitted use which involved a change in any drainage ditch, for the removal of earth products, such as gravel, sand, fill-dirt and peat, and for the diking, damming or filling of any land within the zone with an **existing elevation** of less than 175 feet above sea level (apparently this limitation would encompass practically all the land in the zone)." *Morris County Land, Etc. v. Parsippany-Troy Hills Township* (N.J., 1963).

## EXISTING USE

**The use of a property at the time that an application for development or redevelopment is made.**

***Legal Annotation***: "EPA has explained that under its antidegradation regulation, 'no activity is allowable . . . which could partially or completely eliminate any **existing use**.' Thus, States must implement their antidegradation policy in a manner 'consistent' with **existing uses** of the stream." *PUD No. 1 of Jefferson City v. Washington Dept. of Ecology* (U.S. 1994).

## EXIT

**The location where egress from a lot or structure is afforded.**

***Legal Annotation***: "That code provision applies to 'interior stairs,' which are defined as 'stair[s] within a building, that serve as a required **exit.**' . . . By all accounts, the stairs from where plaintiff fell did not serve as an '**exit**' as defined by the Administrative Code . . . but rather as a means of walking from the first floor to the basement." *Cusumano v. City of New York* (N.Y., 2010).

## EXIT RAMP, ENTRANCE RAMP

**Access lanes leading to and from a limited-access highway.**

*Legal Annotation*: "Near the top of the hill there is an overpass with an **exit ramp** allowing southbound traffic to exit the interstate and an **entrance ramp** allowing northbound traffic to enter the interstate." *Walden v. State* (Mont., 1991).

## EXPERT

**A person who, through education and/or experience, has developed skill or knowledge in a particular subject so that he or she may form an opinion that will assist the fact-finder (*Black's* 1999).**

*Comment*: Other tests as to the qualifications of an individual are whether the expert has been accepted by his or her peers as such, or whether the individual has been qualified as an expert before other courts or agencies.

*Legal Annotation*: "Rule 702, governing expert testimony, provides: 'If scientific, technical, or other specialized knowledge will assist the trier of fact to understand the evidence or to determine a fact in issue, a witness qualified as an **expert** by knowledge, skill, experience, training, or education, may testify thereto in the form of an opinion or otherwise.'" *Daubert v. Merrell Dow Pharmaceuticals, Inc.* (U.S., 1993).

## EXPRESS RETAIL STORE

**See *Retail Store, Express*.**

## EXPRESSWAY

**A divided arterial highway for through traffic and with full or partial control of access and, generally, with grade-separated intersections. *See Figure 97*.**

## EXTENDED CARE FACILITY

**A long-term facility or a distinct part of a facility licensed or approved as a nursing home, infirmary unit of a home for the elderly, or a governmental medical institution. See *Long-Term Care Facility*.**

*Legal Annotation*: "An '**extended care facility**' is 'A facility primarily engaged in providing to in-patients the nursing care and related services for patients who require twenty-four (24) hour medical, nursing, or rehabilitation services." *City of Torrance v. Transitional Living Centers* (Calif., 1982).

## EXTENDED PROPERTY LOT LINE

**A line, radial or perpendicular to the street centerline, at each end of the frontage, extending from the right-of-way line to the curb line. *See Figure 43*.**

*Legal Annotation*: "**Extended Property Lot Line—**A line, radial or perpendicular to the street centerline, at each end of the frontage, extending from the right-of-way line to the curb line." *Clearfield County, Pennsylvania Zoning Ordinance, Article II, Section 202 "Meaning of Words."*

## EXTENSION

**(1) An increase in the amount of existing floor area beyond the exterior wall, or an increase in the dimension of a structure; (2) extending the length of time an approving authority can act on an application for development, or the period of time for which a permit remains valid.**

*Legal Annotation*: "The testimony and exhibits clearly establish that an exterior wall of the garage is an **extension** of an exterior wall of the warehouse. The exterior wall is, in fact, one wall. From this evidence, the garage is, at the very least, an enclosed **extension** of the warehouse." *Orland Fire PD v. Intrastate Piping and Controls, Inc.* (Ill. App. Ct., 1994).

## EXTERIOR WALL

**Any wall that defines the exterior boundaries of a building or structure.**

*Legal Annotation*: "The testimony and exhibits clearly establish that an exterior wall of the garage is an extension of an **exterior wall** of the warehouse. The **exterior wall** is, in fact, one wall. From this evidence, the garage is, at the very least, an enclosed extension of the warehouse. *Orland Fire PD v. Intrastate Piping and Controls, Inc.* (Ill. App. Ct., 1994).

## EXTRACTIVE INDUSTRIES

**Enterprises that excavate and remove rock, stone, ore, soil, gravel, sand, minerals, and similar materials from the surface and/or subsurface.**

***Comment***: Extractive industries are quarries, sand and gravel pits, mines, and soil removal operations. They are intensive operations, generating large amounts of truck traffic, noise (including blasting), and dust. Much of the activity takes place outdoors, and the result can be a continuing, unaesthetic scar on the landscape, with ore, gravel, sand, and rock piled high on the property. In addition, customary accessory uses provide their own special nuisance impacts, such as odors from asphalt plants; noise and dust from sifters, crushers, and loading and unloading trucks; as well as runoff from washing material and cleaning operations and water sprayed to keep the dust down. Blasting, an integral part of quarry operations, can be particularly bothersome to adjacent properties and at times, due to miscalculation, dangerous as rock is exploded and thrown beyond the boundaries of the site.

Because of the potential adverse impacts of such activities, extractive industries are governed by special rules. As Cox (2003) notes, "Since by the very nature of the use they must continually expand over a larger area, the 'diminishing asset theory' provides that such an industry may expand to the boundaries of its property." However, Cox also quotes a court decision (*Mt. Bethel Humus v. State*, 273 N.J. Super, 421 Appellate Div. 1994) in which the court noted that nonconforming uses of this type are still subject to the regulations adopted by the municipality, such as soil removal regulations, and applicable state laws, such as, for example, wetlands protection regulations.

While development regulations may prohibit such uses in all zones or restrict them to only appropriate industrial districts, annual or biennial licensing requirements by the municipality appear to be the most effective way of regulating and controlling these uses. The licensing can require that a reuse plan be presented to the approving authority and that all activities be directed to the ultimate implementation of the plan. The licensing requirement can require adherence to a program of material extraction, showing locations where the material is to be extracted and time schedules. At the time of license renewal, the applicant would have to demonstrate, through aerial maps and surveys, that the locations and schedules have been followed. In addition, adequate buffered setbacks from surrounding areas should be established, and special routing for trucks can be required. Hours of operation and limits on blasting, with adequate insurance in place in case of a mishap, can also be part of the licensing requirement. The licensing requirement can also specify that piles of materials, asphalt plants, rock crushers, conveyers, and truck loading and unloading areas be located on the site in such a way as to minimize their impact on surrounding properties. Finally, some municipalities levy an escrow fee at the time of license renewal to cover inspection costs and necessary repairs to roads resulting from the heavy truck use on local roads. Others levy a per-cubic-yard extraction fee to cover the same costs.

***Legal Annotation***: "The amendments here at issue . . . prohibit businesses engaged in **extractive industries** from 'expand[ing] horizontally in surface area by more than 25% of [their] existing excavated area' unless they first obtain a special use permit." *South County Sand & Gravel Co. v. Town of South Kingstown* (1st Cir., 1998).

"Expansion of a prior nonconforming use to a larger area of the lot ordinarily is not permitted without satisfying the positive and negative criteria for a 'd' variance. . . . Expansion of such a use is not favored . . . and '[e]xcept in the case of the extractive industries' such as quarrying or **soil removal**, our courts have rejected attempts to expand prior nonconforming uses 'to the boundaries of the property.' William M. Cox, New Jersey Zoning and Land Use Administration Ch. 11-6.1 at 254-55 (2000)." *McDowell, Inc. v. Bd. of Adjustment* (N.J. App. Div, 2000).

## EXTRATERRITORIAL ZONING

See *Zoning, Extraterritorial*.

## EXURBAN AREA

The fringe area between a suburbanized area and rural area, subject to development pressures.

*Legal Annotation*: "[T]he only objective evidence of the industry's investment backed expectations is a quote from a 1972 guide which indicated that a project located 'in a growing suburban or **exurban area**, it may increase in value over the years, thus creating substantial residual profits to the investors upon sale or other disposition.'" *CCA Associates v. US* (Fed. Cir., 2011).

# F

## FABRICATION AND ASSEMBLY

**The manufacturing from standardized parts of a distinct object, differing from the individual components.**

*Comment*: The term "fabrication and assembly" is often used to describe a general class of permitted uses. It usually involves materials with form and substance (as opposed to liquid or gas), with a physical (as opposed to chemical) mating or joining of the individual parts.

*Legal Annotation*: "Y-12 is primarily engaged in the **fabrication and assembly** of nuclear weapons components." *Legal Environmental Assistance Foundation v. Hodel* (E.D. Tenn., 1984).

## FACADE

**The exterior portion of a building exposed to public view. *See Figure 20.***

**Comment:** While "facade" refers to any wall or face of a building that can be seen by the public, the term is used primarily in reference to special architectural treatments that are meant to enhance the building's aesthetics. Design or architectural standards or guidelines may have particular requirements for facades as opposed to other exterior surfaces of a building (e.g., color, materials, style, or articulation.).

*Legal Annotation*: "The requirements in these sections that **facades** have windows, doorways, and decorative architecture cannot be reconciled with the Board's interpretation in this case that the **facade** includes the decorative architecture, but not the dealership's glass front and entranceway." *MMR Holdings, LLC v. City of Charlotte* (N.C. Ct. App., 2005).

## FACADE, PRINCIPAL

**That face of a building which is most exposed to public view, such as a street, park, or plaza.**

*Legal Annotation:* "At the second floor line of the two **principal facades** there are full length iron balconies supported by ornate limestone brackets." *Losch v. Commissioner* (Tax Ct., 1988).

## FACILITY

**A place where an activity occurs.**

*Comment*: The word "facility" (or "facilities") is a general term describing one or more buildings, structures, or locations in, on, or at which something, other than a random occurrence, is happening. Land development ordinances provide controls of where in the municipality a particular facility is permitted as well as its physical characteristics, such as size, height, setbacks, etc. The land development ordinance may also establish controls on the activity itself, such as how many parking spaces are required, the location of lighting, how many signs are allowed, and similar characteristics.

*Legal Annotation*: "'**Facility**' is defined in CERCLA as follows: '"**Facility**" means (A) any building, structure, installation, equipment, pipe or pipeline (including any pipe into a sewer or publicly owned treatment works), well, pit, pond, lagoon, impoundment, ditch, landfill, storage container, motor vehicle, rolling stock, or aircraft, or (B) any site or area where a hazardous substance has been deposited, stored, disposed of, or placed, or otherwise come to be located.'" *US v. Conservation Chemical Co.* (W.D. Mo., 1985).

## FACILITY FOR PEOPLE WITH DISABILITIES

**Any ramp, handrail, elevator, door, specially treated surface, or similar design, convenience, or device that facilitates the health, safety, or comfort of people with disabilities.**

*Comment*: The Americans with Disabilities Act (ADA) requires all public facilities and certain other buildings to incorporate features that facilitate access and navigation by people with disabilities. They are mandatory requirements in building codes and are now more frequently being incorporated into zoning and site plan ordinances.

## FACTORY

**A building in which raw material and semifinished or finished materials are converted to a different form or state, or where goods are manufactured, assembled, treated, or processed.**

***Legal Annotation***: "[K]itco operates a **factory** in Bluffton, Indiana, where workers turn hot molten rubber into various automobile parts." *Kitco, Inc. v. Corp. for General Trade* (Ind. Ct. App., 1999).

## FACTORY-BUILT HOUSING

**Structures designed for long-term residential use, including modular homes, mobile homes, and manufactured homes (American Planning Association, *Manufactured Housing: Regulation, Design Innovations, and Development Options,* Planning Advisory Service Report No. 478, 1998). See *Manufactured Home; Mobile Home; Modular Home.***

***Comment***: Once considered inferior to conventionally "stick-built" housing and subject to discriminatory zoning practices, advances in the quality and durability of factory-built housing have led to wider acceptance in most jurisdictions. The primary advantage of factory-built housing is the reduction in time and construction cost compared to conventionally built housing.

***Legal Annotation***: "The Town of Helena zoning ordinance defined Factory-built housing in § 24-4-2(2), Code 1975: '(2) **FACTORY-BUILT HOUSING**. Any structure, or component thereof, designed primarily for residential occupancy which is wholly, or in substantial part, made, fabricated, formed or assembled in manufacturing facilities for installation, or assembly and installation, on the building site. Mobile Homes . . . are specifically excluded from the provisions of this chapter.'" *Town of Helena v. County Mobile Homes, Inc.* (Ala., 1980).

## FAIR MARKET VALUE

**A price at which a buyer and seller, with reasonable knowledge of the pertinent facts and not acting under any compulsion, are willing to do business.**

***Comment***: Used most commonly in appraisals or real estate transactions, the term is used in connection with real property—the land and any buildings or structures attached thereto. The definition describes an ideal, abstract situation. In real-life situations, brokers use a variety of methods to establish the fair market value, including comparable sales, income capitalization, and replacement value.

***Legal Annotation***: "The **fair market value** is the price at which the property would change hands between a willing buyer and a willing seller, neither being under any compulsion to buy or to sell and both having reasonable knowledge of relevant facts. Treas. Reg. § 20.2031-1 (b)." *United States v. Cartwright* (U.S., 1973).

## FAIR SHARE PLAN

**A plan or proposal by which a municipality would satisfy its obligation to create a realistic opportunity to meet its fair share of the low- and moderate-income housing needs of its region and that details the affirmative measures the municipality proposes to undertake to achieve its fair share of low- and moderate-income housing.**

*Comment*: The above definition was derived from New Jersey's Supreme Court *Mt. Laurel II* case, *Southern Burlington County NAACP v. Mt. Laurel Township*, 92 N.J. 158 (1983).

***Legal Annotation***: "Satisfaction of the Mount Laurel obligation shall be determined solely on an objective basis: if the municipality has in fact provided a realistic opportunity for the construction of its **fair share** of low and moderate income housing, it has met the Mount Laurel obligation to satisfy the constitutional requirement; if it has not, then it has failed to satisfy it." *So. Burlington Cty. NAACP v. Mount Laurel Township* (N.J., 1983).

"West Windsor claims that the trial court's consideration of market demand led to the erroneous conclusion that the Township's **fair share plan** failed to reflect adequately the actual and anticipated demand for various types of affordable housing." *Toll Bros, Inc. v. Tp. of West Windsor* (N.J., 2002).

## FALLOW LAND

**Farmland left uncultivated.**

***Legal Annotation***: "[T]he usual, customary and practical way of dry farming the lands in question is to crop one-half the land each year and to let the other one-half of the land lie idle and fallow; and that such **fallow land** is usually plowed and planted in August or September of one year and the ensuing crop harvested the next year." *Rudeen v. Howell* (Idaho, 1955).

## FAMILY

**A group of individuals, not necessarily related by blood, marriage, adoption, or guardianship, living together in a dwelling unit as a single housekeeping unit; but not including any society, club, fraternity, sorority, association, lodge, federation, or like organization, or any group of individuals who are in a group living arrangement as a result of criminal offenses (Merriam and Sitkowski 1999). See *Household*.**

***Comment***: The key words in the definition are "single housekeeping unit," which is defined as "common use and access to all living and eating areas, bathrooms, and food preparation and serving areas." In addition to the single housekeeping unit, a family also represents an intentionally structured relationship and implies a permanent and long-term voluntary relationship as opposed to one that is short-term, transient, and mandated by law.

The above definition places no limit on the number of unrelated individuals that may occupy the dwelling unit, save the specific exceptions noted. However, a limitation on unrelated individuals living together is constitutional under the US Constitution following the US Supreme Court decision in the *Village of Belle Terre v. Boraas* case (U.S., 1974). In that case, a maximum of two unrelated individuals was deemed to constitute a family. However, as Merriam and Sitkowski note, "a law can be legal under the U.S. Constitution but not under that of a state constitution." Indeed, state courts in several states, interpreting their individual and unique state constitutions, have held that the restrictive *Belle Terre*-type of definition, typical of most zoning regulations across the country, is unconstitutional in their states as a matter of state law. That means the definition is not enforceable in that state, regardless of what the US Supreme Court decided in *Belle Terre*. For example, in *State v. Baker* (N.J., 1979) the New Jersey Supreme Court invalidated a local ordinance that established a limit on the number of unrelated individuals. It suggested that by limiting the number of unrelated individuals, it prohibited much reasonable occupancy, such as unrelated widows, bachelors, or "even judges." The decision said that the municipality could regulate density by relating the number of occupants to the number of bedrooms or bathrooms, or a minimum number of square feet per occupant. It also said that traffic could be restricted by limiting the number of vehicles.

The City of Santa Barbara, California, had this definition of family: "1. An individual or two (2) or more persons related by blood, marriage or legal adoption living together as a single housekeeping unit in a dwelling unit. . . . 2. A group of not to exceed five (5) persons, excluding servants, living together as a single housekeeping unit in a dwelling unit." The California Supreme Court held that this definition was unconstitutional as a matter of state law because it violated the state constitution, which provides, in relevant part, "All people . . . have inalienable rights. . . . Among these [inalienable rights] are enjoying . . . life and liberty . . . possessing . . . property, and pursuing and obtaining . . . happiness, and privacy" (*City of Santa Barbara v. Adamson* [Calif., 1980]).

***Legal Annotation***: "The provision, governing areas zoned for single-family dwelling units, defines '**family**' as 'persons [without regard to number] related by genetics, adoption, or marriage, or a group of five or fewer [unrelated] persons.'" *City of Edmonds v. Oxford House, Inc.* (U.S., 1995).

"The word '**family**' as used in the ordinance means, '[o]ne or more persons related by blood, adoption, or marriage, living and cooking together as a single housekeeping unit, exclusive of household servants. A number of persons but not exceeding two (2) living and cooking together as a single housekeeping unit though not related by blood, adoption, or marriage shall be deemed to constitute a **family**.'" *Village of Belle Terre v. Boraas* (U.S., 1974).

## FAMILY ENTERTAINMENT CENTER

**See *Amusement Park; Theme Park.***

***Legal Annotation***: "The debtor is the lessee of a real estate lease dealing with improvements in the form of a **family entertainment center** including bowling lanes, restaurant facility, go-cart track and other entertainment venues." *In the Matter of Husker Bowl, LLC* (Bankr. Ct. D. Neb., 2010).

## FANNIE MAE

**A company chartered by Congress to provide liquidity, stability, and affordability to the United States housing and mortgage markets. See *Freddie Mac.***

***Comment***: Fannie Mae purchases mortgages from lenders and finances its purchases by packaging mortgages into pools and then issuing securities against the pools. (Another Congressionally chartered entity, Freddie Mac, does the same.) From 2009 through 2014, Fannie Mae provided $4.1 trillion in liquidity to the mortgage market.

***Legal Annotation***: [A]ppellants contend that **FNMA** should not be treated as a federal instrumentality. The reasons advanced for this contention are: (1) that FNMA is a privately owned corporation and (2) that **FNMA** engages in certain non-governmental functions. Responding to the argument that **FNMA** should be treated like a private lending institution, we are persuaded that such a contention is contrary to the intent expressed when the Act creating the present corporate structure of FNMA was enacted by Congress." *Rust v. Johnson* (9th Cir., 1979).

## FARM OR FARMLAND

**A parcel of land or waterbody used for agricultural production. See *Agriculture; Agricultural Zoning; Horse Farm.***

***Comment***: While most definitions of *farm* are restricted to farmland, a pond or other waterbody used for aquaculture for the commercial production of fish or shellfish may also be classified as a "farm" or "farming."

***Legal Annotation***: "The RTFA defines '**farmland**' as 'land or freshwater ponds devoted primarily to the production, for commercial purposes, of livestock, freshwater aquacultural, or other agricultural commodities. . . . Similarly, a '**farm**' is 'the land, buildings, freshwater ponds, freshwater culturing and growing facilities, and machinery used in the commercial production of farm products.'" *Vicwood Meridian Partnership v. Skagit Sand & Gravel* (Wash. Ct. App., 2004).

## FARM STAND

**A structure for the display and sale of farm products primarily grown on the property upon which the stand is located.**

***Comment***: In farming communities or municipalities where farms exist, farm stands are customary accessory uses and very much part of the farming operation. Reasonable restrictions are appropriate, however, to ensure that the stands are operated in a safe manner and do not constitute a nuisance to surrounding nonfarm properties. Controls include maximum size of the stand, setbacks from the road and side property lines, signage, parking, and litter control.

Farm stands should be a maximum of two hundred fifty square feet in order to reflect their temporary and accessory nature. Setbacks of twenty-five feet from the side property lines and road provide some nuisance protection for adjacent properties and allow cars to safely pull off the road. The local zoning officer or planner should review a sketch plan to determine that adequate parking is provided and that provisions are made to control litter.

Some municipalities impose the additional restriction that the farm products sold at the stand must be raised on the farm or the land on which the stand is located. In actual practice, this has proven to be impractical and difficult to enforce. On the other hand, most towns would not like to see a "garden center" on each farm. The definition requires the products to be "primarily grown on the property, etc." This allows some flexibility and also provides an indication of the intent of the ordinance.

*Legal Annotation*: "Both cases involve a proposal to construct and operate a **farm stand** for the sale of farm products on certain farm land in Norwell (locus)." *Prime v. Zoning Board of Appeals of Norwell* (Mass. App. Ct., 1997).

## FARM STRUCTURE

**Any building or structure used for agricultural purposes.**

*Legal Annotation*: "A '**farm structure**' is defined as 'a building, enclosure, or fence for housing livestock, raising horticultural or agronomic plants, or carrying out other practices associated with accepted agricultural or farming practices, including a silo, as "farming" is defined in § 6001(22), but excludes a dwelling for human habitation.'" *In re Moore Accessory Structure Permit and Use* (Vt., 2013).

## FARMERS' MARKET

**The seasonal selling or offering for sale at retail of vegetables or produce, flowers, orchard products, and similar nonanimal agricultural products, occurring in a predesignated area, where the vendors are individuals who have raised the vegetables or produce or have taken the same on consignment for retail sale.**

*Comment*: Municipalities or local business associations usually sponsor farmers' markets. They consist of booths, tables, or stands, indoors or outdoors. They are probably best regulated by licensing and a separate farmers' market ordinance, which would include general regulations establishing who can sell and what may be sold, hours and days of operation, responsibilities for cleanup, fees for the rental of spaces and stalls, liability requirements, and so on. The land development ordinance should establish the zones where farmers' markets could be located and provide for site plan review to ensure adequate circulation, safe access, and controls over signage and lighting. If permitted by the local ordinance, farmers' markets may also include home-produced crafts and restaurants.

Farmers' markets are usually held in business areas, often on existing parking lots and/or closed-off streets. They can be important elements of an overall plan to revitalize urban areas. They serve to attract more people into these areas and increase the market for existing merchants. Observers of farmers' markets have noted that "they encourage community interaction, establish community cohesion, and evoke a community spirit" (Linowes 1985). An illustrative book dealing with organizing, maintaining, and selling in a farmers' market is Corum et al. 2001. (Also Stephenson 2008 and Groe 2008). As farmers' markets have become more popular, there have been growing issues concerning their exact definition and function. http://farmersmarketcoalition.org/definition-task-force-announcement

*Legal Annotation*: "The Columbus **Farmers Market** is owned . . . by the State of Georgia, and operated by the State Department of Agriculture. Individuals who wish to sell their produce at such market must acquire a license . . . and rent space therein. The market consists of three separate selling areas from which individual growers sell their produce to the general public." *Smith v. Department of Agriculture of State of GA* (5th Cir., 1980).

## FAST FOOD

**Food that can be prepared with preheated or precooked ingredients and served very quickly to a customer in packaged form, both for consumption on the premises or takeout.**

*Legal Annotation*: "Although the lease does not define 'so-called **fast food**,' the Parties do not dispute that IHOP is not a **fast food** restaurant under any definition of '**fast food**' or 'quick service'— the industry descriptor for fast food establishments. McDonald's and Defendants both state that IHOP is a full service, family style restaurant." *McDonald's Corp. v. Rappaport* (D. Mass., 2008).

## FAST-FOOD RESTAURANT

**See *Restaurant, Fast Food.***

## FAULT

**A fracture in the earth's surface resulting from the horizontal and/or vertical displacement at the juncture of two tectonic plates (*FEMA Glossary*).**

*Legal Annotation*: "Real Parties proposed a project to develop approximately 64 acres along the Oakland Estuary and the Embarcadero, converting a maritime and industrial area into residential, retail/commercial, open space, and marina uses (the project or the Oak to Ninth Project). Building heights would range from six to 24 stories. In its discussion of seismicity, the EIR noted that the project site was approximately three and one-half miles from the Hayward **fault** zone and 15 and one-half miles from the San Andreas fault zone, both active fault zones capable of generating major earthquakes, and that other **faults** were also capable of producing significant ground shaking at the project site. The EIR identified various seismic hazards; of particular relevance here were the potential for strong ground shaking and liquefaction." *Oakland Heritage Alliance v. City of Oakland* (Calif. Ct. App., 2011).

## FEASIBILITY STUDY

**An analysis of a specific project or program to determine if it can be successful.**

*Comment*: Feasibility studies can cover a wide range of subjects. The most common is the financial feasibility study to determine whether the project will turn a profit. Other feasibility studies may cover law and various elements of planning, such as traffic, environment, building size, and so forth. The feasibility study relates capacity to demand but may also cover political and social benefits and costs. Banks may require feasibility studies to determine the estimated rate of return on investment. See *Cost-Benefit Analysis; Marketability Study*.

*Legal Annotation*: "The EPA also contracted with Ecology & Environment, Inc., for the preparation of a **feasibility study** for the cleanup of the Denney farm site." *US v. Northeastern Pharmaceutical* (8th Cir., 1986).

## FEE SIMPLE ABSOLUTE

**The most complete set of private property land rights, including mineral rights below the surface, surface rights, and air rights. See *Easement*.**

*Legal Annotation*: "A fee simple, also referred to as **fee simple absolute**, is an estate over which the owner has unlimited power of disposition in perpetuity without condition or limitation." *Walker v. Foss* (Texas Ct. App., 1996).

## FEEDLOT

**A confined area, or structure, pen, or corral, used to fatten livestock prior to final shipment. See *Concentrated Animal Feeding Operation*.**

*Legal Annotation*: "The testimony indicated that cattle in a commercial **feedlot** will produce 35 to 40 pounds of wet manure per day, per head, or over a million pounds of wet manure per day for 30,000 head of cattle, and that despite the admittedly good **feedlot** management and good housekeeping practices by Spur, the resulting odor and flies produced an annoying if not unhealthy situation as far as the senior citizens of southern Sun City were concerned." *Spur Industries, Inc. v. Del E. Webb Development Co.* (Ariz., 1972).

## FEMA

**The Federal Emergency Management Agency.**

*Legal Annotation*: "Congress established the National Flood Insurance Program (NFIP) in 1968 in order to reduce the burden on the public fisc after flood disasters. . . . The program created a unified national system of flood insurance coverage, which is administered by the Federal Emergency Management Agency (**FEMA**). Id. § 4011. Under this program, FEMA promulgated the Standard Flood Insurance Policy (SFIP). . . . FEMA regulations authorize private insurance companies, referred to as 'Write Your Own' (WYO) insurers, to issue these flood policies." *Dickson v. American Bankers Ins. Co. of Florida* (8th Cir., 2014).

## FENCE

**An artificially constructed barrier of any material or combination of materials erected to enclose, screen, or separate areas. *See Figures 45 and 46.***

*Comment*: Development regulations should include provisions for fences. Generally, they should be divided into categories of open, semi-open, and closed fences, and regulations should establish maximum heights and setbacks for the different categories. For example, an open fence, such as a split-rail fence, might be permitted anywhere on a particular lot. Solid fences, such as board-on-board fences, might be restricted to a maximum height of six feet and be required to meet all setback requirements for principal structures in the zone. Most definitions restrict fences to those which are constructed of building materials and do not include vegetation. (**See *Hedge*.**) A fence may or may not include a gate, but a gate does not include a fence. (**See *Gate*.**)

**Figure 45**

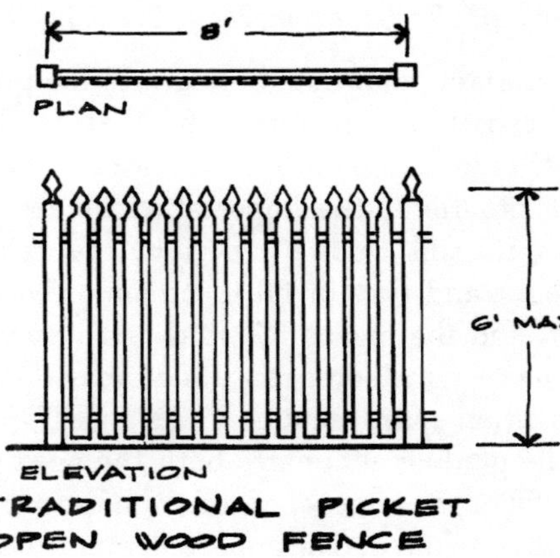


*Legal Annotation*: "*Black's Law Dictionary* '[d] efines "**fence**" as "a hedge, structure, or partition, erected for the purpose of inclosing a piece of land."'" *Piper v. State* (Ark. Ct. App., 2013).

## FENCE, OPEN

**A fence constructed with openings between the materials used in its construction. *See Figure 45.***

*Legal Annotation*: "Section 1101.7(b) of the Ordinance [specifies] . . . that '[a] security fence provided for any purpose including schools, playgrounds and parks, in any District, shall be an **open fence** with the ratio of the open portion to the solid portion of not less than six-to-one (6:1), not more than five (5) feet in height.'" *Northampton T. Appeal* (Pa. Comm. Ct., 1984).

## FENCE, SOLID

**A fence, including any gates, constructed of solid material, wood or masonry, through which no visual images may be seen. *See Figure 46.***

**Figure 46**

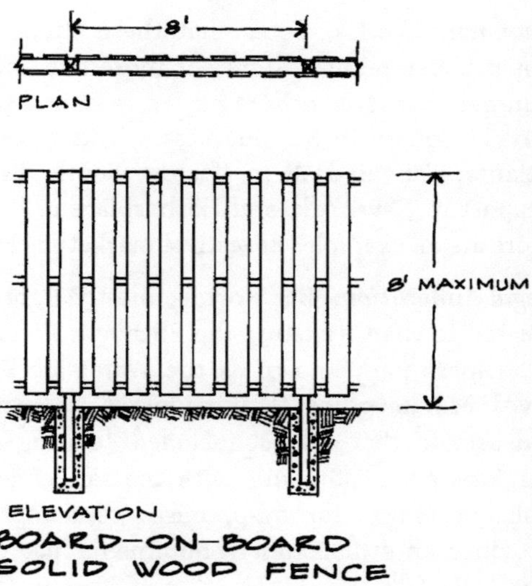


*Legal Annotation*: "The entire operation of the proposed automobile repair garage shall be enclosed with either a **solid fence**, solid wall, or dense living hedge not less than six feet in height shall be provided along north and west lot line." *Ledford v. Board of Zoning Appeals* (Ohio Ct. App., 2007).

## FENESTRATION

**Windows and other openings on a building facade. See *Facade*.**

*Legal Annotation*: "The requirement that, for retail use, **fenestration** occupy 60% of the first floor building space also applies throughout the Redevelopment Area, and is not specific to the Stadium District. . . . . Accordingly, the deviation will avoid the need for placing windows in inappropriate areas such as storage facilities and unused areas." *Lester M. Entin Associates v. Town of Harrison, NJ* (N.J. App. Div., 2009).

## FESTIVAL MARKETPLACE

**An anchorless retail center with a mix of small specialty shops offering one-of-a-kind merchandise, with an emphasis on gifts and crafts supplied locally and food offerings, often located in a unique architectural setting (Sawicki 1989).**

***Comment***: Sawicki notes that these shops are not primary retail centers but more like entertainment centers anchored by restaurants. Ghirardelli Square in San Francisco, Underground Atlanta, Faneuil Hall in Boston, South Street Seaport in New York, and Harborplace in Baltimore are all examples of festival marketplaces.

***Legal Annotation***: "Bar Norfolk and the Café are located in the City along the Elizabeth River in a business park known as the Waterside **Festival Marketplace** (Waterside). . . . Permitted uses in that district included '[e]ating and drinking establishments' with the sale of alcoholic beverages for on-premises consumption provided an establishment obtained a 'use permit.'" *Norfolk 102, LLC v. City of Norfolk* (Va., 2013).

## FIELD CHANGES

**Adjustments to approved plans based on actual conditions found during construction.**

***Comment***: Field changes are usually approved by the municipal engineer, municipal planner, or construction official. They are minor in nature, such as the need to shift a pipe a few feet, change the location of a catch basin, or substitute a plant or tree species. Field changes are typically small in nature and do not involve violation of zoning design standards that would necessitate the grant of variances or design waivers. (Changes of such a nature would require approval by an authorized board or agency.) After approval, a field change memo is usually prepared by the approving official and placed in the project file. The actual change is also reflected in the final "as-built" plans submitted by the applicant.

***Legal Annotation***: "The board found that these changes, in general, consisted of (1) **field changes** to adapt the work to the conditions encountered, and (2) design changes to structures occasioned by discovery that a structure as originally specified would not accomplish its intended purpose or did not meet the requirements of the owner of existing facilities." *Seger v. United States* (Ct. Cl., 1972).

## FILL

**Sand, gravel, earth, or other materials of any composition whatsoever placed or deposited by humans. *See Figure 47*.**

## FILLING

**The process of depositing fill in a low-lying area. See *Land Reclamation; Made Land; Infill*.**

*Comment*: Many municipalities control the process or restrict the amount of fill that can be taken off or brought onto a construction site. In most situations, the importation or exportation of fill will require a permit, specifying the amount and type of fill to be imported or exported and the means by which such movement can occur, including route and times. Some municipalities may require a "balanced" job where the grading eliminates both the need to bring in fill or the removal of soil from the property. If fill is required to be imported, municipalities often require that the fill be from a virgin source and/or tested to ensure that the material is free from contaminants. Filling regulated by such permits does not include placing fill in wetlands, marshy areas, or waterbodies. Filling of these sites is governed by state and/or federal statutes.

***Legal Annotation***: "Section 4:02 of 302 Code Mass. Regs. defines '**Filling**' as 'the placing of any material that raises, either temporarily, or permanently, the existing elevation of any

Figure 47

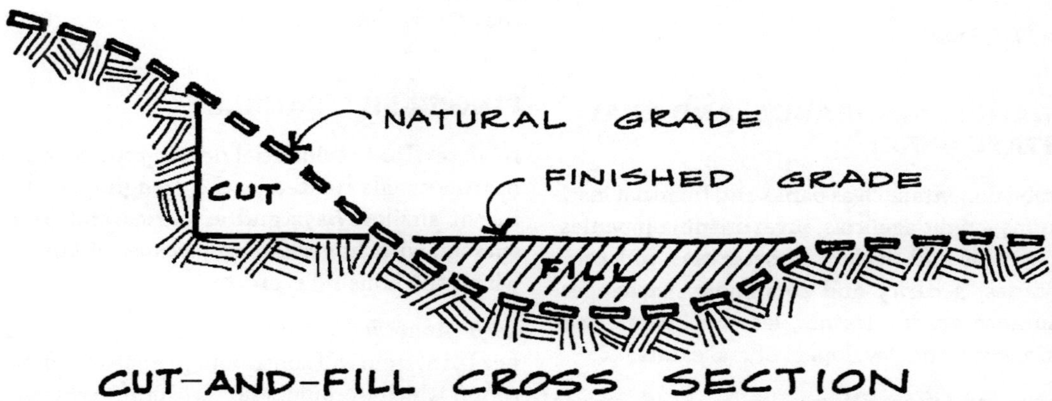


coastal wetland.'" *Roberts v. Dept. of Environmental Quality Engineering* (Mass., 1989).

## FILLING STATION

**See *Automobile Service Station*.**

***Comment***: *Filling station* is synonymous with gasoline or automobile service station but is a term no longer in use in most zoning ordinances.

***Legal Annotations***: "A 'drive-in' **filling station** is defined to be one which automobiles can enter or depart from only by being driven across the sidewalk. In other words, it is inside the property line with the sidewalk between it and the street pavement." *City of San Antonio v. Rubin* (9th Cir., 1930).

## FILTRATION

**In wastewater treatment, the mechanical process that removes particulate matter from water, usually by passing it through coal or sand.**

***Legal Annotation***: "When it set effluent limits for the primary metals industry, EPA used as its model technology a waste treatment process called lime, settle and **filtration** (L, S & F). Briefly, this treatment technique works in the following way: adding lime to wastewater increases the pH. . . . At different pHs, different metals . . . emerge from solution and become suspended as solids in the wastewater. Eventually, most solids settle at the bottom of the tank. The precipitate can then be disposed of separately from the wastewater. The wastewater is often subsequently filtered through coal or sand in order to remove additional suspended solids." *Kennecott v. United States EPA* (4th Cir., 1985).

## FINAL APPROVAL

**The last official action of the approving agency taken on a development plan that has been given preliminary approval, after all conditions and requirements of preliminary approval have been met and either the required improvements have been installed or guarantees properly posted for their installation, or approval has been granted subject to the posting of such guarantees.**

***Comment***: In most jurisdictions, lots may not be sold until final subdivision approval has been granted, and construction may not begin until final approval on all permits, including building permits, has been granted. However, in some cases, construction may begin after preliminary site plan approval is obtained, but certificates of occupancy are withheld until final site plan approval and other permits have been satisfied.

***Legal Annotation***: "Construction may begin only after an additional environmental analysis (although it is not clear that a second EIS need always be prepared) and **final approval** of the developer's master plan." *Robertson v. Methow Valley Citizens Council* (U.S., 1989).

## FINAL PLAT

See *Plat, Final*.

## FINANCE, INSURANCE, AND REAL ESTATE (FIRE)

**Establishments such as banks and financial institutions, credit agencies, investment companies, brokers of and dealers in securities and commodities, security and commodity exchanges, insurance agents, lessors, lessees, buyers, sellers, agents, and developers of real estate.**

***Comment***: Often referred to as FIRE in use groupings.

***Legal Annotation***: "Equally compelling, the general definitional section of the Code explicitly recognizes insurance agents as a separate potential land use and includes them in the category of '**Finance, Insurance, and Real Estate**' ('[e]stablishments operating primarily in the fields of . . . insurance . . . such as . . . insurance agents . . . and similar establishments')." *Geaghan v. City of Bath* (Me., 1989).

## FINANCIAL SERVICE CENTER

**A nonbank entity that does not accept deposits or make loans like traditional banks or financial institutions but that provides monetary services that include the sale or redemption of traveler's checks or money orders, money wire transfers, check cashing, and currency exchange.**

***Comment***: Financial service centers may also provide electronic bill payments, automatic teller machine access, sale of debit and phone cards, deposit acceptance services, public transportation fare and token sales, postage stamp sales, fax and copy services, and electronic tax preparation. They are characterized by mostly on-site customer service. This term is usually synonymous with "check cashing" establishments, but the industry has replaced the term because of negative connotations sometimes associated with the former name.

***Legal Annotation***: "The letter specified the **financial service center's** operating hours and indicated that Plaintiff is the sole employee of the center." *Smith v. Flying J, Inc.* (D.N.M., 2010).

## FINGER-FILL CANALS

**In waterfront residential developments, deep, narrow canals created by the dredging and filling of shallow bays and estuaries and interspersed with fingerlike projections of land on which the housing is erected.**

***Legal Annotation***: "The proposed project's **finger fill** system will contribute to increased urban runoff which in conjunction with the excessively deep **canals** will contribute to eutrophication of adjacent waters." *Gables by the Sea, Inc. v. Lee* (S.D.Fla., 1973).

## FINISHED ELEVATION

**The proposed elevation of the land surface of a site after completion of all site preparation work. See *Grade, Finished; Grade, Existing*. See *Figure 47*.**

***Legal Annotation***: "The document also specifies that topsoil would be stripped and stockpiled, that the **finished elevation** of the pit would have a 6:1 slope so that surface water would stand in the pit, that the pit would be topsoiled and grassed, and that any access road and other disturbed areas would be restored to their original state." *Taylor v. Commissioner* (Tax Ct., 1987).

## FINISHED PRODUCT

**The end result of a manufacturing process that is ready for utilization or consumption by the ultimate consumer (NAICS 1997). See *Semifinished Product*.**

***Legal Annotation***: "A second, related rationale is that '**finished product** manufacturers know exactly what they intend to do with a component or raw material and therefore are in a better position to guarantee that the component or raw material is suitable for their particular applications.'" *Taylor v. Elliott Turbomachinery Co., Inc.* (Calif. Ct. App., 2009).

## FIRE HAZARD ZONE

**An area where, because of slope, fuel, weather, or other fire-related conditions, the potential loss of life and property from a fire necessitates special fire protection measures.**

***Legal Annotation***: "The project is located in a declared high **fire hazard zone** due to the vegetation type, fire history, and rough topography in the area." *Preserve Wild Santee v. City of Santee* (Calif. Ct. App., 2012).

## FIRE LANE

**An unobstructed paved or improved surface area clearly defined by pavement markings and signs, at least twelve feet wide, and designed to provide access for fire-fighting equipment.**

*Comment*: Fire lanes are recommended for shopping centers and larger office buildings to ensure access to the building for fire-fighting equipment. The lanes should not be used for parking but may be part of the overall circulation system.

***Legal Annotation***: "The plan shows a **fire lane** extending to the rear of the building. The centerline radius of this drive is 43.5 feet, which is a minimal radius for access. The difficulty with the **fire lane** as shown is that exiting the **fire lane** will require backing a vehicle around this same tight radius with the edge of the drive within two feet of the building." *Lapid-Laurel v. Zoning Board of Adjustment of Township of Scotch* (3rd Cir., 2002).

## FIRE ZONE

**An area clearly delineated and marked to facilitate access to hydrants and buildings as designated by the chief of the fire district in which the building, structure, or use is situated.**

***Legal Annotation***: [T]rucks presently park and are stored in the **fire zone**, which will become worse if the density of the development is allowed to increase; . . . " *Witherow v. Burlington Township Planning Board* (N.J. App. Div., 2010).

## FISCAL IMPACT ANALYSIS (FIA)

**A study designed to estimate the public costs and revenues associated with a specific development or land use change. See also *Cost-Benefit Analysis*.**

***Comment***: FIAs are also known as cost-revenue analyses. They can be simple or sophisticated, depending in part on whether secondary and tertiary impacts are considered. FIA has a significant influence and is practiced throughout the United States. FIA can be a required report or proffered ("volunteered") by a developer. It can be a stand-alone report or be part of a larger impact analysis (e.g. environmental impact statement or EIS).

***Legal Annotation***: "On completion of the plan or amendment, the planning board shall transmit the plan or amendment to the district council, and also transmit copies of the plan or amendment to the County Executive. Within 60 days, the County Executive shall transmit a **fiscal impact analysis** to the district council with any other comments and recommendations the County Executive deems appropriate." *Montgomery Preservation v. Park & Planning* (Md. Ct. Spec. App., Appeals 2011).

## FISCAL YEAR

**The twelve-month period at the end of which the government or any government agency determines its financial condition and the results of its operations and closes its books. *http://www.census.gov/govs/local/definitions.html***

***Legal Annotation***: **"[F]iscal year"** is defined as 'an accounting period of twelve months ending on the last day of any month other than December.' *Guaranty Trust Co. v. Commissioner of Internal Revenue* (U.S., 1938).

## FISH FARM

**An area devoted to the cultivation of fish and other seafood for commercial sale. See *Aquaculture*.**

*Legal Annotation*: "The land in question was used as a **fish farm** and contained several fish rearing ponds." *United States v. Corbin* (10th Cir., 1970).

## FISHING, HUNTING, TRAPPING

**Establishments primarily engaged in commercial fishing, including shellfish marine products, operating fish hatcheries, and fish and game preserves, and the killing of animals by shooting or capture in mechanical or other types of devices, for commercial gain.**

*Legal Annotation*: "Idaho Code section 36-103(b) provides that: [b]ecause conditions are changing and in changing affect preservation, protection, and perpetuation of Idaho wildlife, the methods and means of administering and carrying out the state's policy must be flexible . . . and fix the needs for regulation and control of **fishing, hunting, trapping**, and other activity relating to wildlife." *State v. Thurman* (Idaho Ct. App., 1999).

## FITNESS CENTER

**See *Health Club*.**

## FLAG LOT

**See *Lot, Flag*.**

## FLASH FLOOD

**A flood that crests in a short period of time and is often characterized by high velocity flow—often the result of heavy rainfall in a localized area (NOAA). http://www.gwu.edu/icdrm/publications/PDF/GLOSSARY%20 02-19-2007.pdf**

*Legal Annotation*: "In common parlance, a 'flash flood' is 'a local flood of great volume and short duration generally resulting from heavy rainfall in the immediate vicinity.' (Merriam-Webster's Collegiate Dict. (10th ed. 2001) p. 442; see Scott v. Continental Ins. Co. (1996) 44 Cal.App.4th 24, 29 ['In seeking to ascertain the ordinary sense of words, courts in insurance cases regularly turn to general dictionaries'].) A flash flood is a type of 'flood,' as demonstrated by the fact that it is defined in terms of a flood." *Horvath v. State Farm General Insurance Company* (Calf. Ct. App., 2014).

## FLEA MARKET

**A temporary or seasonal market that can be held indoors or outdoors, where secondhand or inexpensive goods are sold or bartered. See *Temporary Outdoor Activity*.**

***Comment***: Also referred to as a "swap meet," flea markets are seasonal—for example, held on Saturdays over the summer.

*Legal Annotation*: "That the primary use of the real estate owned by the defendant is the operation of a **flea market** business. That the defendant has allowed vendors or customers to park vehicles on the real estate which fall within the description of travel trailers under the ordinance as an incidental or accessory use of the real estate." *Woods v. Brown County Plan Commission* (Ind., Ct. App., 1983).

## FLEX SPACE

**A building, or parts of a building, suitable for or capable of being changed to accommodate a variety of permitted uses, and designed to be used on a short- or long-term basis. See *Business Incubator*.**

***Comment***: Flex space evolved from light industrial warehouses being converted to office space. In certain real estate markets, flex space refers to large warehouse buildings in which a small percentage of the space (typically ± 5 percent) is used as office space for administering the storage or warehouse operation. In broader land-use parlance, flex space refers to buildings designed to be subdivided into smaller spaces (three hundred square feet or larger), for a variety of uses such as offices, storage, assembly, research, service, information technology, instruction, etc., and for variable periods of time (thirty days or longer, for example). The space can be equipped with necessary support facilities such as conference rooms, desks, cable, etc. Warehouses and big-box retail stores lend themselves for conversion to flex-space buildings.

*Legal Annotation*: "**Flex Space**: A building shall be deemed devoted to '**flex space**' use if 50%or more of its gross leasable area is devoted to office use andthe remaining portion of such building is devoted to light industrial, warehouse, distribution, light assembly or retail use. Such a building must have fenestration, docking location, screening and landscaping which are consistent with the commercial and retail character of the B-3 district. Office space may be decreased to 20% provided that such reduction has been authorized by an approved Special Use Permit." *Village of Romeoville, Illinois Zoning Code* Sec. 159.03 Definitions. http://www.romeoville.org/comdev/PDF/ZONING-CODE.pdf

## FLEXTIME

**The ability of an employee to determine his or her starting and finishing times.**

*Comment*: Flextime is used to spread peak-hour traffic loads and may be required as part of traffic management systems. Employers usually determine a range of starting times, such as 6:30 AM to 9:30 AM, and finishing times, such as between 3:30 PM and 6:30 PM, and core hours when all employees have to be on the premises.

*Legal Annotation*: "MHRI requires its employees to fill out daily time sheets under a '**flex-time**' schedule that allows all employees to start work any time between 7:00 and 9:00 AM and leave for the day after they have worked seven and a half hours." *Ward v. Massachusetts Health Research Institute* (1st Cir. 2000). http://tinyurl.com/jvuadlk

## FLOATING ZONE

**An unmapped zoning district where all the zone requirements are contained in the ordinance and the zone is fixed on the map only when an application for development meeting the zone requirements is approved.**

*Comment*: Floating zones have generally declined in popularity because of charges that they closely resemble spot zoning or contract zoning, both illegal under current case law. The most appropriate application of floating zones appears to be in rural communities, where large tracts of land may be developed in accordance with planned development regulations, providing that the ordinance requirements are met for conversion of the land from the previous rural designation to a development zone. Some of these ordinance regulations might require direct access to major roads, availability of public water and public sewer, and proximity to other municipal facilities and services.

In recent years, floating zones have also been used to provide lower-income housing in built-up municipalities. Such floating zones typically require that when previously unavailable land (such as a farm, surplus municipal land, or redevelopment areas) above a minimum area (for example, two acres) is proposed to be developed for residences, a percentage of the units must be reserved for low- and moderate-income households. An alternative to floating zones is to make the planned development or lower-income housing a conditional use in those zones deemed appropriate.

*Legal Annotation*: "The P-R zone adopted by the 1963 ordinance is of the type known as a '**floating zone**,' so-called because the ordinance creates a zone classification authorized for future use but not placed on the zoning map until its use at a particular location is approved by the governing body." *Fasano v. Board of County Commissioners of Washington City* (Ore., 1973).

## FLOCCULATION

**In wastewater treatment, the process of separating suspended solids by chemical creation of clumps or floes.**

*Legal Annotation*: "'**Flocculation**,' the joining of the smaller particles into bigger ones, was absolutely critical to the success of the wastewater treatment system. Absent proper **flocculation**, contaminants would remain suspended in the water and the water could not be discharged into the sewer." *Cambridge Plating Co., Inc. v. Napco, Inc.* (1st Cir., 1996).

## FLOOD OR FLOODING

**A general and temporary condition of partial or complete inundation of normally dry**

**land areas from: (1) the overflow of inland or tidal waters and/or (2) the unusual and rapid accumulation or runoff of surface waters from any source. See *Base Flood Elevation; Flood-Prone; Flood, Regulatory Base; Flood, Regulatory Base Discharge; Flood Fringe Area; Flood Hazard Area; Flood Hazard Design Elevation; Flood Insurance Rate Map; Flood Of Record; Floodplain; Floodway; Floodway, Regulatory*.**

***Legal Annotation***: "The sixth edition of *Black's Law Dictionary* defines '**flood**' as follows: 'An inundation of water over land not usually covered by it. Water which inundates area of surface of earth where it ordinarily would not be expected to be.' *BLACK'S LAW DICTIONARY* 640 (6th ed.1990)." *In re Katrina Canal Breaches Litigation* (5th Cir., 2007).

## FLOOD, BASE FLOOD ELEVATION

See *Base Flood Elevation*.

***Legal Annotation***: "A '**base flood elevation**' is a measurement of 'the potential water level height during a base flood.'" *Great Rivers Habitat Alliance v. FEMA* (8th Cir., 2010).

## FLOOD DAMAGE POTENTIAL

**The susceptibility of a specific land use at a particular location to damage by flooding and the potential of the specific land use to increase off-site flooding or flood-related damages.**

***Legal Annotation***: "[T]he chief flood plain management division of defendant, David R. Boyer, concluded that 'the proposed construction . . . will actually decrease the flood profile and will also decrease the flood velocities. This would indicate that there will be no increase in the **flood damage potential** of the adjacent flood plain properties.'" *Beverly Bank v. Illinois Dept. of Transportation* (Ill., 1991).

## FLOOD FRINGE AREA

**The area outside of the floodway of delineated streams that is needed to store the hundred-year storm plus 25 percent. See *Flood, Regulatory Base; Flood, Regulatory Base Discharge; Floodway*. See *Figure 48*.**

***Comment***: The flood fringe area serves as a temporary storage area for floodwaters during a flood. Inundated during the flood, waters recede once the flood is over.

***Legal Annotation***: "Outagamie County Shoreland-Floodplain-Wetland Zoning Ordinance provides: 'In all cases, a variance . . . (h) Shall not permit a lower degree of flood protection in the floodway area than the flood protection elevation. . . . In the **flood fringe area** a lower degree of flood protection than the flood protection elevation may be allowed.'" *State v. Outagamie City Board of Adjustment* (Wis., 2001).

**Figure 48**

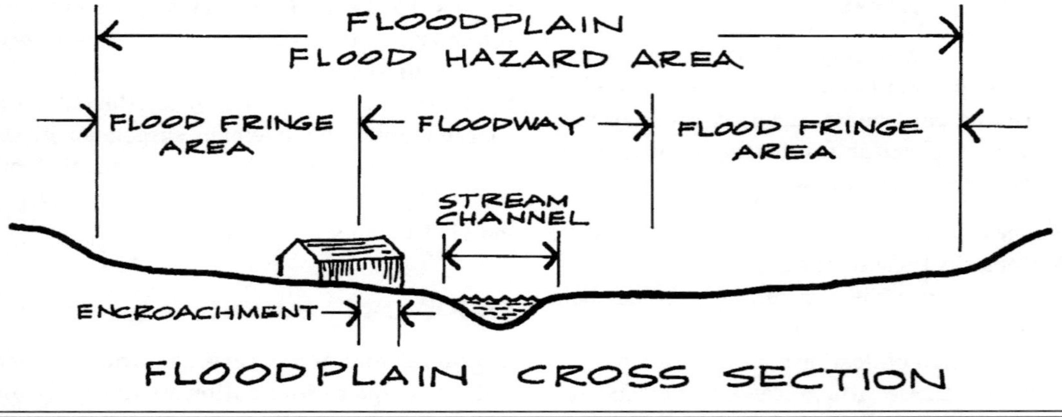

"**Flood Fringe Area**—That portion of the flood hazard area outside of the floodway based on the total area inundated during the regulatory base flood plus twenty-five percent of the regulatory base flood discharge." *Terner v. Spyco* (N.J. App. Div., 1988) (quoting *The Illustrated Book of Development Definitions* 1988).

## FLOOD HAZARD AREA

**The floodway and flood fringe area of a delineated stream or the floodplain of a non-delineated stream. *See Figure 48.***

***Legal Annotation***: "It appears, therefore, that some of the flood damage is caused by properties within the **flood hazard area** 'which are inadequately elevated, floodproofed or otherwise protected from flood damage.'" *Responsible Citizens v. City of Asheville* (N.C., 1983).

## FLOOD HAZARD DESIGN ELEVATION

**The highest elevation, expressed in feet above sea level, of the level of floodwaters that delineates the flood fringe area.**

***Legal Annotation***: "N.J.A.C. 13:4-7(d)(1) provides: 'The volume of net fill and structures to be placed on an applicant's property shall be limited to occupying 20 percent of the total volume of net-fill which: . . . ii. Which is also from between the natural or existing ground surface, whichever is lower, and the level of the **flood hazard design elevation** along delineated streams or the 100-year storm elevation along non-delineated streams.'" *Society for Environmental Economic Development v. New Jersey DEP* (N.J. App. Div., 1985).

## FLOOD INSURANCE RATE MAP (FIRM)

**The official map delineating flood prone areas and used by FEMA to set rates under the National Flood Insurance Program.**

***Comment***: Maps depicting flood-prone areas can become obsolete as the result of changes in land use and/or development, increase in stormwater runoff volume, and inadequate stormwater management or flood mitigation programs.

***Legal Annotation***: "FEMA assesses the flood risk within each flood-prone community by conducting a Flood Insurance Study. . . . FEMA presents the results of a flood study on a map referred to as a **Flood Insurance Rate Map** (a 'flood map') and also in a narrative format." *National Wildlife Federation v. FEMA* (W.D.Wash., 2004).

## FLOOD OF RECORD

**A past flood for which there are accurate local records available and that is used as the reference flood.**

***Legal Annotation***: "[I]n the Court's opinion, the evidence at the February hearing indicates that, statistically, a flood such as that which occurred in 1968 (the maximum **flood of record** on the Cossatot River) can be expected to occur with a frequency of once in between 100 and 200 years." *Environmental Defense Fund v. Corps of Engineers of US Army* (E.D.Ark., 1971).

## FLOODPLAIN

**The channel and the relatively flat area adjoining any natural or man-made stream, pond, lake, river, or any other body of water that is subject to flooding during a storm. *See Figure 48.***

***Legal Annotation***: "The year-round flow of the creek renders the area within the creek's 100-year **floodplain** virtually unusable for commercial development. The city's comprehensive plan includes the Fanno Creek **floodplain** as part of the city's greenway system." *Dolan v. City of Tigard* (U.S., 1994).

## FLOODPLAIN MANAGEMENT

**Floodplain management means the operation of an overall program of corrective and preventive measures for reducing flood damage, including but not limited to emergency preparedness plans, flood control works, and floodplain management regulations (*CFR***

*2004)*. http://www.gwu.edu/icdrm/publications/PDF/GLOSSARY%2002-19-2007.pdf

*Legal Annotation*: "**Floodplain management** is 'the operation of an overall program of corrective and preventive measures for reducing flood damage and preserving and enhancing, where possible, natural resources in the floodplain, including but not limited to emergency preparedness plans, flood control works, floodplain management regulations, and open space plans.'" *Kmart v. The Kroger Co.* (N.D. Miss., 2013).

## FLOOD, BASE FLOOD ELEVATION

**See *Base Food Elevation*.**

## FLOOD, REGULATORY BASE DISCHARGE

**The rate of flow produced by the regulatory base flood measured in cubic feet per second (CFS).**

*Legal Annotation*: "Flood Fringe Area—That portion of the flood hazard area outside of the floodway based on the total area inundated during the regulatory base flood plus twenty-five percent of the **regulatory base flood discharge**." *Terner v. Spyco* (NJ.J. App. Div., 1988) (quoting *The Illustrated Book of Development Definitions* 1988).

## FLOOD-PRONE

**A land area adjoining a river, stream, watercourse, or lake for which a floodway and floodplain has not been determined with respect to any specific flood frequency, but for which the potential for flooding has been identified by soils, geological evidence, or other data.**

*Legal Annotation*: "These ordinances and Ordinance No. 73-14 essentially declared a moratorium on construction on certain lands in the borough within what is referred to as the **flood-prone** or flood-plain area of Fleischer Brook, unless a special exception use permit was obtained from the governing body on recommendation of the board of adjustment." *Cappture Realty Corp. v. Board of Adjustment of Elmwood Park* (N.J. Super. Ct., 1973).

"The Board concluded in the June 28, 1995 findings, that, among other things, the proposed development complied with the goals and objectives of the Valley County Comprehensive Plan . . . and that the proposed filling of part of the project complied with the **Flood-Prone** Areas section of the 1982 Ordinance." *Payette River Property Owners Association v. Board of Commissioners of Valley County* (Idaho, 1999).

## FLOODPROOFING

**A combination of structural provisions and changes or adjustments to properties and structures subject to flooding for the reduction or elimination of flood damage to properties, water and sanitary facilities, and other utilities, structures, and the contents of buildings.**

*Legal Annotation*: "Under the Pierce County Code, any modification of a nonconforming structure in a floodplain, including **floodproofing**, requires a land use permit." *Johnson v. Pierce County Zoning Board of Adjustment* (Wis. Ct. App., 2012).

## FLOOD-WALL

**A flood barrier constructed of materials such as concrete or masonry (*FEMA Glossary*).**

## FLOODWAY

**The channel of a natural stream or river and portions of the floodplain adjoining the channel, which are reasonably required to carry and discharge the floodwater or flood flow of any natural stream or river. See *Floodway, Regulatory*. See *Figure 48*.**

*Legal Annotation*: "Studies by the Army Corps of Engineers show the Cedar River has a long history of flooding. In 1966, the Corps of Engineers established 100-year-cycle **floodway** and floodway-fringe lines along the river." *Maple Leaf v. Dept. of Ecology* (Wash., 1977).

## FLOODWAY, REGULATORY

**The channel of a river or other watercourse and the adjacent land areas that must be reserved in order to discharge the base flood without cumulatively increasing the water surface elevation more than 0.2 foot.**

*Legal Annotation*: "FEMA uses these base flood elevation determinations to prepare flood insurance rate maps. . . . These maps, among other things, delineate the minimum **regulatory floodway** that a community must adopt to comply with NFIP." *Columbia Venture LLC v. SC Wildlife Federation* (4th Cir., 2009).

## FLOOR AREA

**Area of all floors of buildings or structures. See also *Gross Floor Area; Net Floor Area; Net Leasable Floor Area, and Floor Area Ratio*.**

*Legal Annotation*: "The statutory language could not be clearer. As noted above, a cellar is defined within the Zoning Resolution in terms of its physical location in a building. '**Floor area**' includes dwelling spaces when not specifically excluded and "cellar space," without further qualification, is expressly excluded from FAR calculations." *MTR Raritan Dev Corp v. Silva* (N.Y.,1997).

## FLOOR AREA, GROSS (GFA)

**The sum of the gross horizontal areas of all enclosed floors of a building, including cellars, basements, mezzanines, penthouses, corridors, and lobbies, from the exterior face of exterior walls, or from the centerline of a common wall separating two buildings, but excluding any space with a floor-to-ceiling height of less than six feet, six inches (Institute of Real Estate Management 1985). See *Net Floor Area*.**

*Legal Annotation*: "Section 59-A-2.1 [of the Montgomery County Building Code] defines '**gross floor area**' as follows: The sum of the gross horizontal areas of the several floors of all buildings on the lot, measured from the exterior faces of exterior walls and from the center line of walls separating two buildings." *Permanent Fin. Corp. v. Montgomery Cty.* (Md. Ct. App., 1986).

## FLOOR AREA RATIO (FAR)

**The gross floor area of all buildings on a lot divided by the lot area. *See Figure 49*.**

*Comment*: Some care should be exercised in applying this definition. It includes all buildings and structures and the *entire* lot area. The New Jersey cases (*Manalapan Builders v. Tp. Committee*, 290 N.J. Super. 295 [App. Div. 1992] and *Crow--New Jersey 32 Ltd v. Township of Clinton*, 718 F. Supp. 378 [D. N.J. 1980]) set aside FAR definitions that excluded environmentally sensitive land from the ordinance definition of FAR. In the Manalapan case, the judge noted that if the site had extensive environmentally constrained areas, the FAR should be adjusted accordingly.

**Figure 49**

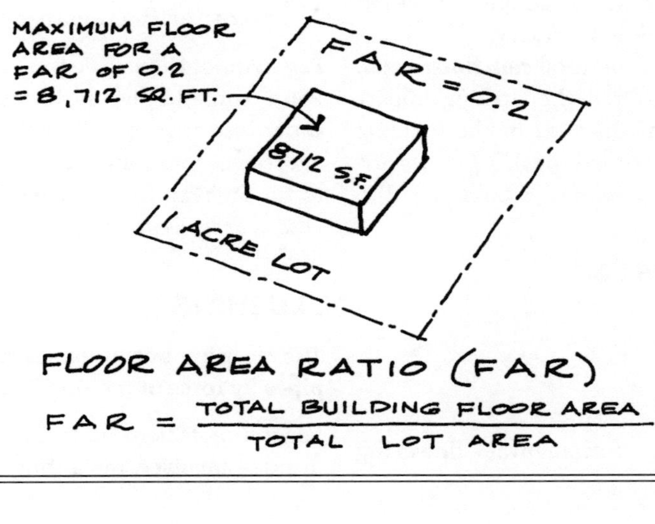

However, in a subsequent case, *Rumson Estates v. Borough of Fair Haven* (795 A2d 290 [2002]), the appellate court let an ordinance stand that created a separate definition and regulation relating to a "maximum habitable floor area," which differed from "floor area ratio," citing the broad scope of the general enabling provisions of the state statute.

*Legal Annotation*: "In calculating the **Floor Area Ratio (FAR)** for zoning purposes, floor area includes the total amount of 'floor space used for dwelling purposes, no matter where located within a building, when not specifically excluded. . . . However, the floor area of a building shall not include . . . cellar space.'" *Matter of Raritan Development Corp. v. Silva* (N.Y., 1997).

## FLOOR AREA, NET

**The total of all floor areas of a building, excluding stairwells and elevator shafts, equipment rooms, interior vehicular parking or loading, and all floors below the first or ground floor, except when these are used or intended to be used for human habitation or service to the public.**

*Comment*: Very often, for ease of administration, net floor area is expressed as gross floor area minus a certain percentage. Stairwells, elevator shafts, equipment rooms, and utility rooms generally average out to about 15 percent of the gross floor area. Thus, net floor area may be defined as gross floor area minus 15 percent.

*Legal Annotation*: "However, because proposed development will have a sanctuary which comprises less than 5% of the total **net floor area**, staff has instead analyzed the parking impact using an aggregate of the uses in the building (sanctuary, offices and classrooms)." *Church of Scientology v. City of Sandy Springs* (N.D.Ga., 2012).

## FLOOR AREA, USAGE

**See *Floor Area, Net*.**

## FLORICULTURE

**The cultivation of ornamental flowering plants.**

*Legal Annotation*: "In fact, the evidence of record indicates that the greenhouses and cold frames were used in conjunction with plaintiffs' horticulture and **floriculture** commercial business that is located on the south parcel." *Papadelis v. City of Troy, Mich.* (Mich. Ct. App., 2009).

## FLOWMETER

**In wastewater treatment, a meter that indicates the rate at which wastewater flows.**

*Legal Annotation*: "After an inspection of the existing sewer lines, the Utility Board directed Sunrise Village to install a flow meter where its sewer lines met the city's sewer system. The **flow meter** measures the volume of materials which flow into the city's system from Sunrise Village." *Underwood v. City of Jasper Municipal Utility* (Ind. Ct. App., 1997).

## FLUE GAS

**A mixture of gases, resulting from combustion, that emerges from a chimney.**

*Legal Annotation*: "'**Flue gas**' is created with temperatures of up to 3000 F when the ground coal is ignited in the boiler's furnace. The **flue gas**, which contains sulfur dioxide, ash particles or particulate matter, and nitrogen oxides, passes around the tubes and tube assemblies." *US v. Duke Energy Corp.* (M.D.N.C., 2003).

## FLUME

**A constructed channel that carries water.**

*Legal Annotation*: "The project included the Mill Pond dam and diversion works, which diverted water into a wooden **flume** and canal system to a forebay, from which the water was transported to the Sullivan Creek powerhouse." *Public Utility Dist. v. State Dept. of Ecology* (Wash., 2002).

## FLUSHING

**The cleaning out of debris and sediment from pipes by force of moving liquid, usually water.**

*Legal Annotation*: "Catania indicated that work in issue involved replanting a yard, **flushing** a pipe, and performing general clean-up construction material and/or debris." *In re Creative Conservation, Inc.* (E.D.Pa., 1991).

## FLY ASH

**All partially incinerated solids that are carried in a gas stream.**

***Legal Annotation***: "NIPSCO operated a generating station that produced electricity by using steam-driven turbines powered by coal-fired boilers. As a result of this process, coal ash is produced. This coal ash, also known as **fly ash**, is used in the production of concrete." *Marks v. Northern Indiana Public Service* (Ind. Ct. App., 2011).

## FLY-IN DEVELOPMENT

**A residential development planned and integrated with airport facilities and directly accessible to recreational flyers.**

***Legal Annotation***: "The project is designed as a **'fly-in' development** with airport, runway and hangar facilities for residents who commute to and from their homes by means of small aircraft." *Chandler Flyers, Inc. v. Stellar Development Corp.* (Ariz. Ct. App., 1979).

## FOCUS GROUP

**A group of people formed to gather qualitative information related to their perceptions, opinions, beliefs, and attitudes toward a product, service, concept, idea, advertisement, or packaging.**

***Comment***: Adapted from social sciences and market research, in land-use planning, focus groups are typically composed of approximately five to fifteen individuals organized to research, investigate, gather information, develop goals and objectives, and make recommendations on land-use issues, plans, or policies. In such instances, focus groups are usually appointed by the local governing body or planning agency. They generally consist of local residents, business people, and officials of service organizations, with specialized knowledge or interest in a specific element of the master plan, such as circulation, open space and recreation, schools, economic development, land-use environment, utilities, public services, etc. Focus groups usually receive assistance from the local planning staff, but the findings, opinions, goals and objectives, and recommendations are citizen-generated to give the planning agency or governing body a fresh perspective on the particular area of interest. See *Visioning*.

***Legal Annotation***: "On December 5, 1988, shortly before a scheduled hearing on various motions pending in connection with the criminal prosecution, counsel for Cinema Blue informed Gilchrist of the particulars of Dr. Scott's '**focus group**' proposal. Gilchrist immediately expressed concern that the proposed **focus group** exhibition would itself constitute a violation of the state obscenity statute." *Cinema Blue of Charlotte, Inc. v. Gilchrist* (4th Cir., 1989).

## FOOD CART, FOOD TRUCK

**See *Retail Food Establishment, Mobile*.**

## FOOD COURT

**An area in which a variety of prepared meals, beverages, and desserts are available from several establishments for purchase and for consumption within a common seating area on the premises.**

***Comment***: These establishments are found in regional shopping malls, major office and retail complexes, resort and entertainment centers, gambling casinos, and the like. Appropriate accessory or adjacent uses often include entertainment, recreation, child-care facilities, and restrooms. When located within a shopping mall or other major complex, food courts will typically provide, in addition to interior access, direct access to the exterior of the facility.

***Legal Annotation***: "As part of the renovation, a '**food court**' area on the bottom level of the mall was constructed, which included ten restaurants and several stores." *Cornucopia, Inc. v. Wagman* (Mo. Ct. App., 1986).

## FOOD STORE

See *Retail Food Establishment; Retail Store, Convenience.*

## FOOD-PROCESSING ESTABLISHMENT

**An establishment in which food is processed or otherwise prepared for eventual human consumption but is not consumed on the premises.**

*Comment*: A food-processing establishment covers a wide range of businesses, all involving food. It may be a caterer or a flour mill. The zoning implications are based on impacts and size of the establishment.

***Legal Annotation***: "Albuquerque, N.M., Code of Ordinances . . . states 'It shall be unlawful for any person to operate a food-service or **food processing establishment** within the city who does not possess a valid permit issued to him by the enforcement authority.'" *Camuglia v. The City of Albuquerque* (10th Cir., 2006).

## FOOT-CANDLE

**(1) The unit of illumination when the foot is the unit of length. *See* Figure 45. (2) A unit of illumination produced on a surface, all points of which are one foot from a uniform point source of one candle (Kendig et al. 1980). *See Figure 50.***

*Comment*: Lighting requirements in local ordinances usually establish a minimum and sometimes a maximum foot-candle level required for different types of outdoor areas, such as walkways, parking lots, and open space. These are shown in subdivision or site plans as isofootcandle diagrams, where all the points on the line represent the same level of illumination. The diagrams are often drawn around light standards to show the level and extent of lighting on the site.

Important issues in evaluating lighting plans are the extent of light spillage from a site onto adjoining sites and roadways as well as the potential for overhead "sky glow" created by intense, unshielded site lighting. (*See* SKY GLOW.) Most municipalities require shielding of light fixtures or special "cutoff" light fixtures to limit the penetration of light into areas where it is not desired. (See *Cutoff*.)

**Figure 50**

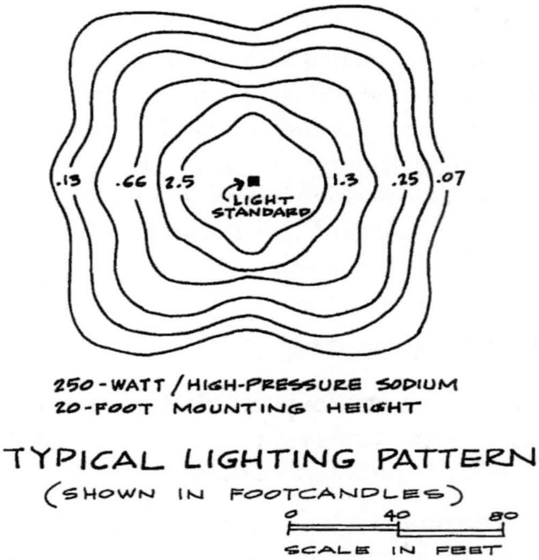


Suggested levels of illumination for various outdoor public areas are presented in Table F-1 and are based upon information contained in the tenth edition of the *Lighting Handbook*, published by the Illumination Engineering Society of North America (2014).

***Legal Annotation***: "PMC section 17.40.080, pertaining to outdoor lighting, provides in pertinent part at subdivision (A) that '[n]o lighting on private property shall produce an illumination level greater than one **footcandle** on any property within a residential zoning district except on the site of the light source.'" *Residents for a Healthy Environment v. City of Pasadena* (Calif. Ct. App., 2009).

## FOOTING

**The enlarged base of a foundation wall or vertical member (such as a pier, post, or column) for a house or other structure, including a floodwall.**

***Comment***: A footing provides support by spreading the load of a structure so that the bearing capacity of the soil is not exceeded (*FEMA Glossary*).

**TABLE F-1: Illumination Guidelines for Street, Parking and Pedestrian Areas**

**A. Street Illumination**

| | AREA CLASSIFICATION | | |
|---|---|---|---|
| **Street Hierarchy** | **Commercial Foot-candles** | **Intermediate Foot-candles** | **Residential Foot-candles** |
| Major | 1.2 | 0.9 | 0.6 |
| Collector | 0.8 | 0.6 | 0.4 |
| Local | 0.6 | 0.5 | 0.3 |

**B. Parking Illumination (Open Parking Facilities)**

| | ILLUMINATION OBJECTIVE | |
|---|---|---|
| **Level of Activity** | **Vehicular Use Only Foot-candles** | **General Parking and Pedestrian Safety Foot-candles** |
| Low activity | 0.5 | 0.2 |
| Medium activity | 1.0 | 0.6 |
| High activity | 2.0 | 0.9 |

**C. Pedestrian Way Illumination**

| **Walkway and Bikeway Classification** | **Minimum Average Horizontal Levels Foot-candles** | **Average Levels for Special Pedestrian Safety Foot-candles** |
|---|---|---|
| Sidewalks (roadside) and Type A Bikeways[a] | | |
| Commercial Areas | 1.0 | 0.2 |
| Intermediate Areas | 0.6 | 0.1 |
| Residential Areas | 0.6 | 0.5 |
| Walkways distant from roadways and type B Bikeways[b] | 0.5 | 0.5 |
| Pedestrian tunnels | 4.3 | 5.4 |

*Notes:*

a Type A bikeways are on-street areas reserved for bikes.

b Type B bikeways are separate designated bikeways.

*Source:* David Listokin and Carole Walker, *The Subdivision and Site Plan Handbook* (New Brunswick, NJ: Center for Urban Policy Research, 1989).

***Legal Annotation***: "It is his opinion that the mode of wall failure was primarily by sliding of the **footing** which occurred when the excavation contractor violated the limits of the influence line for the **footing**. For the two days between the excavation and the collapse, the foundation wall was in a precarious state of equilibrium." *Colombo v. Merchants Ins. Group* (N.Y. Sup. Ct., 2010).

## FORCED-TURN ISLANDS

See *Traffic Calming*.

## FOREST

**Areas or stands of trees, the majority of which have a caliper of greater than twelve inches, covering an area greater than one-quarter acre; or groves of mature trees, without regard to minimum area, consisting of substantial numbers of individual specimens.**

***Comment***: The twelve-inch requirement does not apply to certain species, such as birches and dogwoods, and trees found in pinelands. The minimum caliper should represent a mature tree. "Substantial numbers" is difficult to define. It represents more of a visual impression than a specific number.

***Legal Annotation***: "[R]CW 36.70A.030(8) defines **forest** land as 'land primarily useful for growing trees.'" *City of Redmond v. Central Puget Sound* (Wash., 1998).

## FOREST MANAGEMENT PLAN

**A plan establishing best conservation and management practices for a forested area or forest, including schedules and responsible agencies.**

***Legal Annotation***: The National Forest Management Act of 1976 Section 4(d)(1) states, "It is the policy of the Congress that all forested lands in the National Forest System shall be maintained in appropriate forest cover with species of trees, degree of stocking, rate of growth, and conditions of stand designed to secure the maximum benefits of multiple use sustained yield management in accordance with land **management plans.**"

"The National Forest Service, which manages the System, develops land and resource **management plans** pursuant to NFMA, and uses these **forest plans** to 'guide all natural resource management activities.' . . . In developing the plans, the Service must take both environmental and commercial goals into account." *Ohio Forestry Assn. v. Sierra Club* (U.S., 1998).

## FORESTRY

**The operation of timber tracts, tree farms, or forest nurseries; or the gathering of forest products; or the performing of forest services.**

***Legal Annotation***: "Moreover, the **forestry** rules governing the preparation of THP's require that the cumulative impact of the proposed timber harvesting be considered as a substantive criterion for evaluating the environmental impact of the proposed project." *Friends of Old Trees v. Dept. of Forestry & Fire* (Calif. Ct. App., 1997).

## FORM-BASED CODE

**A development regulation methodology, incorporating graphic and design illustrations including mass, height, and location of buildings and amenities as well as their relation to streets, rights of way, and civic spaces.**

***Comment***: Form-based codes (FBC), in one form or another, have played a role in the development of the urban environment from ancient times (Greek, Roman, and Chinese civilizations) to near-modern times (Paris, Philadelphia, and Washington, DC) and up to the present. In 1977, architect Christopher Alexander published "a compendium of physical rules for designing humane building places" (*A Pattern Language*). In the 1980s, Ian McHarg published "systematic tools" to promote development that was sensitive to environmental conditions. But it was not until 1982 that the first modern form-based code was created. It was for the Florida resort town of Seaside, and the plan was prepared by the husband-and-wife design team of Andres Duany and Elizabeth Plater-Zyberk. As noted in Wikipedia, "Realizing that designing an entire town would be . . . overwhelming . . . they created a design code that established basic physical standards mapped to parcels and then invited developers and their architects to put their own distinctive stamp on their projects—but within those standards". http:en.wikipedia.org/wiki/form-based-code

The result proved very successful and provided a framework for future form-based code endeavors. In 2006, Duany/Plater-Zyberk revised their basic FCB into a SmartCode transect-based code designed to be calibrated to local needs. How form-based codes work and what they include follows:

> Form-based codes address the relationship between building facades and the public realm, the form and mass of buildings in relation to one another, and the scale and types of streets and blocks. The regulations and standards in form-based codes are presented in both words and detailed diagrams and other visuals. They are keyed to a regulating plan that designates the appropriate form and scale (and therefore, character) of development, rather than only distinctions in land-use types. This approach contrasts with conventional zoning's focus on the micromanagement and segregation of land uses, and the control of development intensity through abstract and uncoordinated parameters (e.g., FAR [floor area ratio], dwellings per acre, setbacks, parking ratios, traffic LOS [levels of service]), to the neglect of an integrated built form. Not to be confused with design guidelines or general statements of policy, form-based codes are regulatory, not advisory. They are drafted to implement a community plan and to realize a community vision.
>
> Form-based codes commonly include the following elements:

- Regulating Plan. A plan or map of the regulated area designating the locations where different building form standards apply, based on clear community intentions regarding the physical character of the area being coded.
- Public Space Standards. Specifications for the elements within the public realm (e.g., sidewalks, travel lanes, on-street parking, street trees, street furniture, etc.).
- Building Form Standards. Regulations controlling the configuration, features, and functions of buildings that define and shape the public realm.
- Administration. A clearly defined application and project review process.
- Definitions. A glossary to ensure the precise use of technical terms.

Form-based codes may also include:

- Architectural Standards. Regulations controlling external architectural materials and quality.
- Landscaping Standards. Regulations controlling landscape design and plant materials on private property as they impact public spaces (e.g., regulations about parking lot screening and shading, maintaining sight lines, ensuring unobstructed pedestrian movement, etc.).
- Signage Standards. Regulations controlling allowable signage sizes, materials, illumination, and placement.
- Environmental Resource Standards. Regulations controlling issues such as stormwater drainage and infiltration, development on slopes, tree protection, solar access, etc.
- Annotation. Text and illustrations explaining the intentions of specific code provisions. http://www.formbasedcodes.org/what-are-form-based-codes

Sources: Wikipedia, Form-Based Codes; Parolek et al., 2008; Purdy 2007; Interviews with Andres Duany, principal of Duany Plater-Zyberk & Company; William, M. Spikowski, FAICP, principal of Spikowski Planning Associates; Brian Falk, director of publications, Center for Applied Transect Studies; Alan Mammoser, AICP, program director, Form-Based Code Institute; Peter Katz, consultant.

***Legal Annotation***: "**Form-based** zoning focuses on the physical appearance of streets and buildings to achieve a predictable, aesthetic result. Conventional zoning, by comparison, focuses on the segregation of land uses, which contributes to sprawl." Richard S. Geller, *The Legality of Form-Based Zoning Codes*. http://www.law.fsu.edu/journals/landuse/vol26_1/geller.pdf

"Alternatives to traditional zoning have arisen over the years, such as '**form based zoning**' or 'mixed use zoning.' S. Mark White, Classifying and Defining Uses and Building Forms: Land-Use Coding for Zoning Regulations, American Planning Association Zoning Practice, Sept. 2005, at 2-3; Sonia Hirt, The Devil is in the Definitions, 73 Journal of the American Planning Association, at 436 (Autumn 2007). '"**[F]orm-based zoning"** is the latest trend in the planning profession.'

White, supra, at 3. It is 'based on the theory that design controls can resolve inconsistencies between land uses. Design controls for [**form-based zoning**] ordinances include building envelope standards, building frontage requirements, fenestration (window and entryway), facade coverage, and traditional facade modulation techniques.' Id. at 2. In contrast, 'mixed use zoning' mixes a number of different uses in respective zones rather than limiting mixed uses. Hirt, supra, at 436. Many urbanists believe that mixed use districts are the key to restoring vibrancy to American cities. Id. However, traditional 'use districting remains the mainstay of most zoning ordinances' and 'this is expected to continue for the foreseeable future.' White, supra, at 3." *Town of Rhine v. Bizzell* (Wis., 2008).

## FOSSIL FUELS

**Fuels derived from the remains of ancient plant and animal life, such as coal, oil, and gas.**

***Legal Annotation***: "Gas, fuel oil, coal and other **fossil fuels** are used to provide chemical energy resulting from the chemical reactions occurring through the process of combustion or burning." *AFG Industries, Inc. v. Cardwell* (Tenn., 1992).

## FRACKING

**See *Hydraulic Fracturing*.**

***Legal Annotation***: "On January 13, 2012, R&J applied to Buffalo County for a CUP. R&J sought permission to establish a '[f]rac sand mining operation' on property that was zoned agricultural. . . . 'Frac sand' is a high-purity quartz sand with very durable and very round grains. It is a crush-resistant material produced for use by the petroleum industry. It is used in the hydraulic fracturing process (known as '**fracking**') to produce petroleum fluids, such as oil, natural gas and natural gas liquids from rock units that lack adequate pore space for these fluids to flow to a well." *O'Connor v. Buffalo County Board of Adjustment* (Wis. Ct. App., 2014).

"The industry uses two techniques that enhance recovery of natural gas from these 'unconventional' gas wells: hydraulic fracturing or '**fracking**' (usually slick-water fracking) and horizontal drilling. Both techniques inevitably do violence to the landscape. Slick-water fracking involves pumping at high pressure into the rock formation a mixture of sand and freshwater treated with a gel friction reducer, until the rock cracks, resulting in greater gas mobility. Horizontal drilling requires the drilling of a vertical hole to 5,500 to 6,500 feet—several hundred feet above the target natural gas pocket or reservoir—and then directing the drill bit through an arc until the drilling proceeds sideways or horizontally. One unconventional gas well in the Marcellus Shale uses several million gallons of water. The development of the natural gas industry in the Marcellus Shale Formation prompted enactment of Act 13." *Robinson Township v. Commonwealth* (Pa. Comm. Ct., 2013).

## FRANCHISE

**(1) The right or authority to provide specified goods or services to a defined geographic area. (2) A retail store of a particular regional or national brand, utilizing a common name, logo, and business model, based upon an established successful model or prototype, but owned and operated by a party other than the franchisor.**

***Comment***: The most common use of franchise in planning in the first definition above is with respect to utility franchises. Exclusive franchises are often granted to utility companies to provide service to a geographic area.

***Legal Annotation***: "O.S. Supp.1999 § 802(5) [d]efines '**franchise**' under the Oklahoma Business Opportunity Sales Act as agreement between seller and purchaser whereby franchisee is granted right to engage in business under marketing plan prescribed in substantial part by franchiser." *Gabler v. Holder and Smith, Inc.* (Okla. Ct. Civ. App., 2000).

## FRATERNAL ORGANIZATION

**A group of people formally organized for a common interest, usually cultural, religious, or**

**entertainment, with regular meetings, rituals, and formal written membership requirements.**

*Comment*: Examples of such groups are Masons or the Knights of Columbus. The clubhouses for fraternal organizations were usually located in residential neighborhoods, but newer ordinances properly locate them in business areas or classify them as conditional uses with carefully drawn requirements for parking, buffering, lighting, and solid waste disposal, because they usually draw their membership from a wide geographic area. In addition, the club facilities are often used for weddings, bingo, and weekend catering and can become nuisances to surrounding residences. See *Club; Membership Organization*.

*Legal Annotation*: "ORS 307.134 defines a **fraternal organization** as a corporation: . . . (b) Which is not solely a social club but is established under the lodge system with ritualistic form of work and representative form of government; [and] (c) Which regularly engages in or provides financial support for some form of beneficial or charitable activity with the purpose of doing good to others rather than for the convenience of its members." *Falkenstein v. Department of Revenue, State of Oregon* (D.Ore., 1972).

## FRATERNITY HOUSE

**A building containing sleeping rooms, bathrooms, common rooms, and a central kitchen and dining room maintained exclusively for fraternity members and their guests or visitors and affiliated with an institution of higher learning.**

*Comment*: A fraternity house is a distinct and separate use. It is not a dwelling unit or multifamily structure. The members do not constitute a family in the zoning sense, since they do not function as a single household unit. See *Family*.

*Legal Annotation*: "[D]efendant maintains that the sole purpose of the house is to provide a place for fraternity members to live while attending school. . . . Payment of dues by members who reside at the house is in addition to the fee charged for room and board. The **fraternity house** is a nonprofit organization." *Gilhooly v. Zeta Psi Fraternity* (N.J. Super. Ct., 1990).

## FREDDIE MAC

**A company chartered by Congress to provide liquidity, stability, and affordability to the United States housing and mortgage markets. See *Fannie Mae*.**

*Comment*: Freddie Mac purchases mortgages from lenders and finances its purchases primarily by packaging mortgages into pools and then issuing securities against the pools. (Another congressionally chartered entity, Fannie Mae, does the same.) From 2009 to 2014, Freddie Mac provided $2.3 trillion in liquidity to the mortgage market.

*Legal Annotation*: "The State and County plaintiffs sued the Federal National Mortgage Association (Fannie Mae), the Federal Home Loan Mortgage Corporation (**Freddie Mac**), and the Federal Housing and Finance Agency in an effort to collect state and local real estate transfer taxes that plaintiffs claim are owed for real property transfers made by defendants. . . . Defendant **Freddie Mac** is also a corporation chartered by Congress for substantially the same purposes as Fannie Mae." *County of Oakland v. Fed. Housing Finance Agency* (6th Cir., 2013).

## FREE PARKING PROGRAMS

**A program in which parking spaces in privately held parking garages are leased by a governmental entity and provided free to the public to encourage shopping.**

*Comment*: Such programs are used mostly in downtowns competing with suburban malls. In downtown Fort Worth, proponents of this tax increment-financed program indicate that it has spurred economic growth, new downtown housing, and increased property values. Opponents point to the hidden costs of the program and say the money should be spent on offering better mass transit options to reduce vehicular dependency.

*Legal Annotation*: "In order to finance and administer its economic development and its **free parking programs**, the City enacted ordinances for the levying of certain taxes. An ordinance allowed for an ad valorem real property tax by the City on real property in the District; another ordinance provided for a tax of $2.50 per $1,000 of gross retail sales and receipts from non-professional businesses within the District; and a third imposed a tax of $40 on professional businesses within the District for each quarter of the year per each professional and each employee of a professional." *Jarvill v. City of Eugene* (Ore., 1980).

## FREEWAY

See *Street, Freeway*.

## FREIGHT FORWARDING

**Establishments primarily engaged in the transshipment of goods from shippers to receivers for a charge, covering the entire transportation route and, in turn, making use of the services of other transportation establishments in effecting delivery.**

*Legal Annotation*: "A **freight forwarder** is defined as 'any person which (otherwise than as a carrier . . . [by rail, motor vehicle or water]) holds itself out to the general public as a common carrier to transport or provide transportation of property . . . and which . . . (A) assembles and consolidates . . . shipments . . . and (B) assumes responsibility for the transportation of such property . . . and (C) utilizes, for the whole or any part of the transportation of such shipments, the services of' a rail, motor vehicle or water carrier." *American Trucking Assns., Inc. v. Atchison* (U.S., 1967).

## FREIGHT-HANDLING FACILITIES

**Terminals with the capability of handling a large variety of goods, involving various forms of transportation, and providing multimodal shipping capabilities, such as rail-to-truck and truck-to-air.**

*Comment*: Freight-handling facilities are terminals that have a variety of equipment and storage facilities and space to handle shipboard, truck, rail, and air-freight containers and often liquid and raw agricultural products. They differ from warehouses in that they do not usually store the freight for any period of time, although they may have warehouses associated with them (Schultz and Kasen 1984).

*Legal Annotation*: "Plaintiff has leased to T. & P. Motor Transport Company a space 60 feet by 70 feet in its New Orleans **freight handling facility** in the warehouse on Annunciation Street for its operation under the latter agreement. It now develops that this meant that the breaking out as well as the delivering of LTL ex-pool trailer freight within the New Orleans commercial zone would be done by T. & P." *Texas Pacifc-Missouri Pacific Terminal Railroad of New Orleans v. Brotherhood of Railway & Steamship Clerks* (E.D.La., 1964).

## FRESHWATER WETLAND

See *Wetland, Freshwater*.

## FRINGE AREA

**The area of transition between two different dominant land uses or other recognizable characteristics, including social, economic, or cultural (Schultz and Kasen 1984).**

*Legal Annotation*: "Plainly the legislature considered that chapter 236 did not provide communities with all the tools needed to deal with **fringe area** growth." *Boucher Lincoln-Mercury v. Madison Planning Commission* (Wis. Ct. App., 1993).

## FRONT FOOT

**A measure of land width, being one foot along the front lot line of a property.**

*Comment*: Front-foot measurements are usually used in assessment formulas.

*Legal Annotation*: "While **front foot** or square foot methodologies for apportioning costs of special improvement projects are more traditional, other methods are permissible." *City of Boca Raton v. State* (Fla., 1992).

## FRONT LOT LINE

See *Lot Line, Front*.

*Legal Annotation*: "The **front lot line** is ordinarily understood to be the lot line toward which the residence faces." *Orange Gardens Civic Association v. Harris* (Fla. Ct. App., 1980).

## FRONT YARD

**See *Yard, Front*.**

*Legal Annotation*: "The Thornbury Zoning Ordinance of 1983 defines '**front yard**' as 'a yard extending the full width of the lot along the front line and extending in depth from the lot line to the nearest point of the permitted principal or accessory buildings or buildings on the lot.'" *Caln Nether Co. v. Board of Supervisors of Thornbury Township* (Pa. Comm. Ct., 2004).

## FRONTAGE

**That side of a lot abutting a street; the front lot line. *See Figure 16.***

*Comment*: On unbuilt or unimproved corner or through lots, the frontage may be designated by the owner, but it should be consistent with the orientation of buildings on the other lots and improvements on the same side of the street. On improved corner or through lots, the frontage is usually the side where the main building entrance is located and in the general direction in which the principal building faces.

*Legal Annotation*: "*Black's Law Dictionary* 602 (5th ed. 1979) defines '**frontage**' as denoting a line of a property on a street and the extent of front along the road or street. The definition for 'fronting and abutting' is also given as signifying abutting, adjoining, or bordering on, depending largely on the context." *Federici v. Zoning Hearing Board* (Pa. Comm. Ct., 1990).

## FRONTAGE ROAD

**A service road, usually parallel to a highway, designed to reduce the number of driveways that intersect the highway. Also referred to as a "local service road."**

*Legal Annotation*: "G.S. 1955 Supp. 68-1901 (c) defines '**Frontage road**' as '. . . a highway, road or street which is auxiliary to and located on the side of another highway, road or street for service to abutting property and adjacent areas and for control of access to such other highway, road or street.'" *Franks v. State Highway Commission* (Kan., 1957).

## FUEL DISPENSER

**The vertical structure(s) at gasoline stations that contains the hoses from which fuel is dispensed directly into motor vehicles.**

*Comment*: Formerly referred to as gas pumps, they did, at one time, contain the pump that transferred fuel from underground storage tanks into motor vehicles. Now, all pumps are located in the underground storage tanks themselves. Modern fuel dispensers typically have one hose on each side that can pump regular, plus, or high-octane fuel. Most fuel service stations now offer diesel fuel, necessitating a second pump on one of the fuel dispensers. In all cases, however, only two motor vehicles can be serviced at any time (i.e., one on each side of the fuel dispenser). Older ordinances often specified the number of "gas pumps" on a site, to limit the size of the station.

*Legal Annotation*: "The terms of 17 O.S. Supp.2003 § 620 provide: 'Except as otherwise provided in this section, retail facilities that sell motor fuel shall not be required to post information regarding fuel additives on the motor **fuel dispenser** or anywhere else on the premises of the facilities.'" *Rogers v. Quiktrip Corp.* (Okla., 2010).

## FUEL PUMP

**See *Fuel Dispenser*.**

## FULL CLOSURES

**See *Traffic Calming*.**

## FUNERAL HOME

**A building used for the preparation of the deceased for burial and the display of the deceased and rituals connected therewith before burial or cremation.**

## FUNERAL HOME

***Comment***: Funeral homes are generally very stable uses and are extremely well maintained. The only potential problem is the necessity for adequate off-street parking and stacking room for cars lined up for the funeral procession.

***Legal Annotation***: "The amending ordinance contains a proviso that the premises shall be used only as a **funeral home** and that no embalming shall be done on the premises." *Cassel v. City of Baltimore* (Md. Ct. App., 1950).

# G

## GABION

**A wire mesh basket filled with stone or riprap and principally used in retaining wall construction, erosion control, temporary flood walls, and dams. *See Figure 51*.**

*Comment*: Largely due to their modularity, gabion baskets have several advantages over more rigid structures: basket size can be varied, the baskets can adjust to ground movement, and their strength may increase as silt and vegetation fill basket voids and reinforce the structure. http://www.gabions.net.welcome.html

***Legal Annotation***: "The two **gabion** walls are made of 'basketball' size rocks. One wall is situated at the western boundary of the Property along Southlawn Lane, and the other is situated on the eastern side of a stormwater management pond that is also on the western side of the Property." *Srour v. Montgomery County* (Md. Ct. App., 2008).

## GAMBLING GAME

**Any betting or percentage game played for money, property, or any representative of value with cards, dice, or any device or machine and located exclusively within a facility licensed for such activity.**

***Legal Annotation***: "In Missouri, chance must be a material element in determining the outcome

**Figure 51**

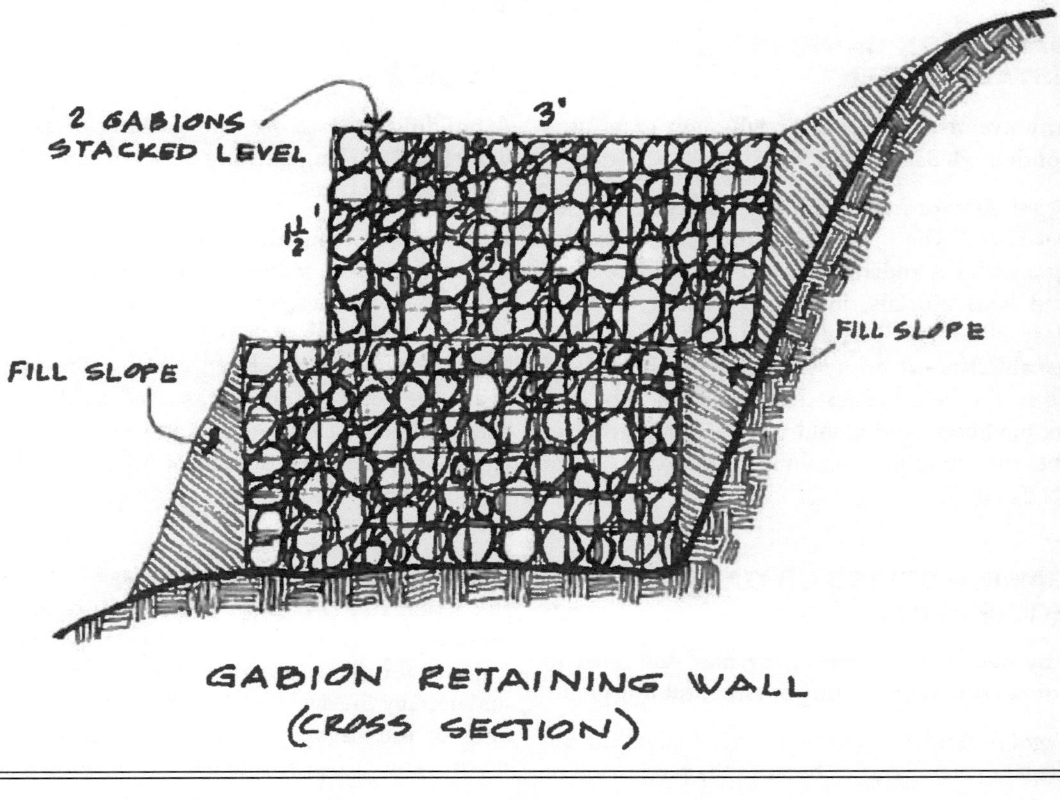

of a **gambling game**." *Thole v. Westfall* (Mo. Ct. App., 1984).

## GAMING OR GAMBLING

**The dealing, operating, carrying on, conducting, maintaining, or exposing for pay of any game.**

***Legal Annotation***: "Section 572.010: '**Gambling**,' a person engages in '**gambling**' when he stakes or risks something of value upon the outcome of a contest of chance or a future contingent event not under his control or influence, upon an agreement or understanding that he will receive something of value in the event of a certain outcome." *Thole v. Westfall* (Mo. Ct. App., 1984).

"In accordance with the generally accepted view that the terms '**gaming**' and '**gambling**' are synonymous, they are used interchangeably. See, e.g., *Black's Law Dictionary* (5th ed), which defines 'gaming' as 'the practice or art of gambling.'" *Automatic Music and Vending Corp. v. Liquor Control Comm.* (Mich., 1986).

## GAMING OR GAMBLING ESTABLISHMENT

**Any premises wherein or whereon gaming is conducted. See *Casino*.**

***Legal Annotation***: "Gaming, however, will be permitted when 'the Secretary, after consultation with the Indian tribe and appropriate State and local officials, including officials of other nearby Indian tribes, determines that a **gaming establishment** on newly acquired lands would be in the best interest of the Indian tribe and its members, and would not be detrimental to the surrounding community.'" *Dalton v. Pataki* (N.Y., 2005).

## GAMING DEVICE OR GAMING EQUIPMENT

**Any device, contrivance, or machine used in connection with gaming or any gambling game.**

***Legal Annotation***: "These forms of gambling are illegal in Nebraska . . . because the possession or operation of a '**gambling device**,' including 'any mechanical gaming device, computer **gaming device**, electronic gaming device, or video gaming device which has the capability of awarding something of value,' is prohibited." *US v. Santee Sioux Tribe of Nebraska* (8th Cir., 1998).

## GAP ANALYSIS

**(1) In traffic engineering, the study of available time between vehicles in a stream of traffic to determine the capability of vehicles to enter or cross that stream of traffic from an intersecting road or driveway; (2) in retail trade, the difference between actual spending on certain categories of goods or services and the potential spending on such goods and services.**

***Legal Annotation***: "However, the Board had requested plaintiff to submit to the expert a '**gap analysis**' study to determine the gaps in traffic on Route 206 to enable the Board to gauge how much delay would be involved in getting in and out of the development." *El Shaer v. Planning Board of Township of Lawrence* (N.J. App. Div., 1991).

## GARAGE

**A building utilized for the parking of motor vehicles, including parking decks or multilevel parking structures.**

***Comment***: In regulating garages as a principal or accessory use, a distinction should be made between short- and long-term parking and the storage of vehicles such as that associated with auto sales and unregistered vehicles. For many years the term "garage" was used to describe establishments that serviced and repaired vehicles. Today this practice, along with the term, is no longer utilized. See *Automotive Repair Services*.

***Legal Annotation***: "[A] private **garage** is defined in Section 200 (14) (a) of the Ordinance as: 'An accessory building or a part of a principal building used for the storage of motor vehicles owned and used by the owner or tenant of the premises, and for the storage of not more than two (2) motor vehicles owned and used by persons other than the owner or tenant of the premises. Not more than two (2) commercial vehicles or trucks may be stored in a private **garage**.'" *Sojtori v. Zoning H. Bd. & Moyere* (Pa. Common. Ct., 1972).

## GARAGE, MUNICIPAL

**A structure owned or operated by a municipality and used primarily for the parking and storage of vehicles owned by the general public.**

***Legal Annotation***: "The ordinance in question is entitled:

'An Ordinance Providing for the Construction of a **Municipal Garage**, accessory improvements and appurtenances, the appropriation of the monies necessary therefor, and the issuance of bond anticipation notes for the financing of said work.' It provides that a new **municipal garage**, accessory improvements and appurtenances be constructed on a portion of the premises known as Lot 1, Block 785, in the Town of Westfield. These premises are part of that area of Westfield known as Tamaques Reservation, a municipal park area, and are presently zoned for the highest one-family residential use—Zone 'A.'" *Scotch Plains Tp. V. Town of Westfield* (N.J. Super. Ct. 1964).

## GARAGE, PRIVATE CUSTOMER AND EMPLOYEE

**A structure that is accessory to a nonretail, commercial, or manufacturing establishment, building, or use and is primarily for the parking and storage of vehicles operated by the customers, visitors, and employees of such building and that is not available to the general public.**

***Legal Annotation***: "Cheryl explained to the officers that the car had been parked in an **employee garage** all day, and that the officers had made a mistake." *Horne v. City of Cincinnati* (Ohio Ct. App., 2004).

## GARAGE, PRIVATE RESIDENTIAL

**A structure that is accessory to a single- or two-family dwelling, is used for the parking and storage of vehicles owned and operated by the residents thereof, and is not a separate commercial enterprise available to the general public.**

***Comment***: The combination of narrow lots and two-car attached garages can result in visually unattractive "snout houses" or "garage door" streetscapes. Solutions include using detached garages set back from the house with street access, or fronting detached garages on alleys behind the homes. In both cases, a covered walkway to the house can be provided. Side-entry garages are another alternative but usually require a wider lot (at least 115 feet wide). Another solution is sharing the driveway access and necessary turning courts with the adjacent lot. In this last example, three-bay side-entry garages can be accommodated with no detriment to the streetscape. See *Snout House*.

***Legal Annotation***: **"Private garage**: 'An attached or detached building or part thereof, used as an accessory to a main building or dwelling, with a capacity for the storage of not more than three motor vehicles and in which no occupation or business for profit is carried on.'" *Roselle v. Wright* (N.J., 1956).

## GARAGE, PUBLIC

**A structure or portion thereof, other than a private customer and employee garage or private residential garage, used primarily for the parking and storage of vehicles and available to the general public.**

***Legal Annotation***: "A "**public garage**" is defined in the 1973 Zoning Order as 'a building or portion thereof, designed or used for the storage, sale, hiring, care or repair of motor vehicles, which is open for commercial purposes.' (Emphasis supplied)." *Schaefer v. Neumann* (Mo. Ct. App., 1977).

## GARAGE, REPAIR

**Any building, premises, and land in which or upon which a business, service, or industry involving the maintenance, servicing, repair, or painting of vehicles is conducted or**

**rendered. See *Automotive Repair Services And Garages*.**

***Comment***: See also the ***Comment*** under GARAGE relating to the fact that the term "garage" is most often used in relation to the parking and storage of vehicles and not their repair. Such establishments are now referred to as automobile repair establishments.

*Legal Annotation*: "Other improvements consist of a large maintenance and **repair garage** and an employee parking lot." *Highway Commission v. Great Lakes Express Co.* (Mich. Ct. App., 1973).

## GARAGE, SHARED RESIDENTIAL

**A garage used exclusively for the parking and storage of vehicles owned or operated by residents of nearby dwelling units and their guests, and which is not available to the general public.**

*Legal Annotation*: "The appellate court agreed with the trial court's conclusion 'that [the owner of the dominant tenement] was entitled to exclusive use of the garage as "a necessary incident" of the easement, reasoning that a **shared garage** would generate disputes about allocation of parking spaces, security, and maintenance costs.'" *Gray v. McCormick* (Calif. Ct. App., 2008).

## GARAGE SALE

**The sale or offering for sale to the general public of items of personal property by the owner or tenant of an improved lot in a residential district, whether within or outside any building.**

***Comment***: This definition limits sales to residential districts, appropriate to the noncommercial nature of this occasional activity. Some local regulations require a permit and fee, with restrictions on hours of operation, a restriction on the days of the week when it may be held (typically weekends only), a limit of two sales per household per year, and requirements for the removal of signs after the sale. Garage sales are also known as patio sales, yard sales, or porch sales.

*Legal Annotation*: "About a month before he moved out of the Canyon Drive house, appellant held a **garage sale** at which paintings, furniture and a red Mercedes were offered for sale." *People v. Feinberg* (Calif. Ct. App., 1997).

## GARBAGE

**Food waste—animal and vegetable waste resulting from the handling, storage, sale, preparation, cooking, and service of foods—or any discarded useless or unwanted materials. See *Food Waste and Solid Waste*.**

*Legal Annotation*: "Oregon defines 'solid wastes' as 'all putrescible and nonputrescible wastes, including but not limited to **garbage**, rubbish, refuse, ashes, waste paper and cardboard." *Oregon Waste Systems v. Department of Environmental Quality* (U.S., 1994).

## GARDEN APARTMENT

**See *Dwelling, Garden Apartment*.**

## GARDEN CENTER

**See *Nursery, Retail*.**

## GAS PUMP

**See *Fuel Dispenser*.**

## GASOLINE STATION AND CONVENIENCE CENTER

**A retail facility combining a gasoline station and a convenience store.**

***Comment***: In such establishments, attempts to distinguish whether one of the uses is principal and the other secondary or accessory are of little value. Convenience stores on the same lot as gasoline stations have become so commonplace that where the size of the parcel of land can accommodate both and land use regulations permit them, they are now almost always provided together.

*Legal Annotation*: "This appeal involves the law of zoning and its application to the proposed construction of a 'corner gas station' and neighborhood convenience center. . . . It is [the plaintiff's] position that a **gas station and convenience center** should be permitted to be built on their property." *Buhrmaster v. County of Du Page* (Ill. App. Ct., 1973).

## GATE

**(1) An opening in a fence; (2) an artificial barrier capable of being opened and closed, permitting or denying access across a driveway or path.**

*Legal Annotation*: "Thus, in the absence of a demonstrated intent to provide otherwise, a landowner burdened by an express easement of ingress and egress may narrow it, cover it over, **gate** it or fence it off, so long as the easement holder's right of passage is not impaired." *Lewis v. Young* (N.Y., 1998).

## GATED COMMUNITIES

**Residential developments that limit access to residents, invited guests, and authorized service and delivery vehicles.**

*Comment*: Gated communities are often high-end residential subdivisions and multifamily enclaves, located largely in the suburbs. The types of gates can range from elaborate guardhouses to simple electronic barriers. Residents may enter by electronic cards, identification stickers, codes, or remote-control devices. Visitors and service and delivery vehicles must stop to be verified for entry ("Gated Communities," *Planning and Zoning News*, March 1999).

Gated communities can be a disruptive force to the functional continuity of a neighborhood. If permitted, they should be located only in areas that are already physically or geographically separated from the larger community. For a full discussion of gated communities, see Blakeley and Snyder (1997).

*Legal Annotation*: "Mr. and Mrs. Landry own a home in Hilton Head Plantation, a **gated community** that is open only to residents and their guests. The Landrys paid a premium on the price of their home because it is located in this **gated community** with common recreational areas." *Landry v. Hilton Head Prop. Owners Association* (S.C. Ct. App., 1994).

"**Gated communities** come in three different types: lifestyle communities, elite communities, and security zone communities. All of these community types differ in their inhabitants, but they all serve the same basic service, to keep unwanted individuals out. **Lifestyle communities** provide security and separation for leisure activities and the amenities offered inside. . . . The second type of a **gated community** is known as an **elite community**. 'These communities are primarily occupied by the rich and famous, the top one fifth of Americans.' These developments focus on exclusion and status. In these communities, the primary focus is on image. The gates represent a barrier of status to all who are outside and looking in. Security is another major concern due to the resident's status within the community. Like lifestyle communities, the developers of the elite communities build walls and gates as a marketing strategy. . . . The final type of **gated community** is the **security zone community**. Unlike the other two communities, security zone communities are gated by the residents themselves and can somewhat represent a 'fortress' mentality. 'The fortress mentality is perhaps clearest here, where groups of people band together to shut out their neighbors.' Many of these new communities are located in inner city and lower income neighborhoods where the residents see crime increasing. The fear of crime and outsiders is the major reason that these people gate themselves in." *State v. Tecza* (Wis. Ct. App., 2008).

## GATEWAY

**A major entrance or point of access into a neighborhood, district, community or region (New Jersey State Development and Redevelopment Plan 2002).**

*Comment*: Gateways are often defined or reinforced by features that emphasize the transition and create a sense of arrival and departure. Gateway features are often vertical elements and can be constructed, such as taller buildings, pylons, or arches; or they may be natural, such as a river gorge or a valley (*New Jersey State Development and Redevelopment Plan* 2002).

*Legal Annotation*: "On February 7, 1950, the City of Louisville conveyed by deed to the Department of Highways and the Commonwealth of Kentucky those portions of Cherokee Park embraced in Eastern Parkway from its **gateway entrance** at Bardstown Road and Eastern Parkway to Willow Avenue." *City of Louisville v. Milton* (Ky. Ct. App., 1952).

## GAZEBO

**An accessory building consisting of a detached, covered, freestanding, open-air structure not exceeding three hundred square feet.**

*Comment*: The limitation on the size of a gazebo is important to maintain its accessory-use status. The public use of a gazebo as, for example, a bandstand, may require a size exemption.

*Legal Annotation*: "A picturesque **gazebo**, suitable for anything from political rallies to orchestral performances, stands on the northwest corner. Indeed, a number of public and private events take place on the courthouse lawn and at the **gazebo**." *Green v. Board of County Commissioners of County of Haskell* (E.D. Okla., 2006).

## GENERAL DEVELOPMENT PLAN (GDP)

**A plan showing general land use, circulation, open space, utilities, stormwater management, environmental factors, community facilities, housing, and phasing for parcels of land in excess of one hundred acres and proposed to be constructed as a planned development.**

*Comment*: The GDP is a concept plan that vests for up to twenty years the right of the applicant to submit various phases for preliminary and final site plan approval. Both the vesting period and minimum acreage are usually set by local ordinances in accordance with state enabling legislation.

The GDP differs from concept plans in that the latter provide no vesting. Most GDP legislation calls for sufficient detail to allow the approving agency to determine that the plan as submitted will work. The long vesting period is needed because of the high up-front investment in improvements. The applicant requires assurances that the zoning will not be amended or rescinded before the project is completed.

*Legal Annotation*: "[The City] maintains that Chapter 23.71 SMC, which regulates land use and development . . . provides that '[a]fter a **General Development Plan** has been approved, the applicant may develop in accordance with the approved plan.'" *Thornton Creek Legal Defense Fund v. City of Seattle* (Wash. Ct. App., 2002).

## GENERAL PUBLIC

**Any and all individuals without prior qualifications.**

*Comment*: When a facility is "open to the general public," there are no restrictions or limitations other than a possible admission fee for the persons attending.

*Legal Annotation*: "Ordinance 75-1994, codified as Article 711 of the Codified Ordinances of the city of Erie, provides in relevant part: 'Public Place' includes all outdoor places owned by or open to the **general public**, and all buildings and enclosed places owned by or open to the **general public**, including such places of entertainment, taverns, restaurants, clubs, theaters, dance halls, banquet halls, party rooms or halls limited to specific members, restricted to adults or to patrons invited to attend, whether or not an admission charge is levied." *Erie v. Pap's AM* (U.S., 2000).

## GENTRIFICATION

**The process of restoration, renewal, and/or rebuilding of deteriorating or deteriorated urban areas as a result of an influx of middle-class or affluent people into a neighborhood, a phenomenon that increases property values but displaces poorer residents and small businesses. See also *Displacement*.**

*Comment*: Gentrification generally carries a negative connotation as a result of the displacement of poorer residents and small business entities. However, gentrification can also revitalize a city, creating a market for new businesses and eventually putting pressure on schools and other government institutions to better respond to the needs of constituents. Gradual gentrification by individuals buying up and improving old buildings and effecting subtle changes in existing neighborhoods tends to have less of a negative connotation than large-scale, government-sponsored urban renewal programs (Dictionary.com; *Merriam-Webster*).

***Legal Annotation***: "The tenor of the complaint is evident from the section headed 'Statement of Facts,' which principally alleges that the Plan unlawfully deprived Watkins of suitable housing and employment options as far back as 12 years ago: Chicago's **gentrification** policy is displacing thousands of Black families from neighborhoods that they have resided in for generations to other Black neighborhoods that are already struggling with their own marginalization.

"As part of this **gentrification**, poor residents who are left on the Near Southside of Chicago are being denied access to living wage jobs and contracts let to develop their social culture.

"As a result, the impact of **gentrification** is indirectly responsible for discriminatory practices that denied plaintiff and other public housing residents access to fair housing, jobs and contracts." *Watkins v. Chicago Housing Authority* ($7^{th}$ Cir., 2013).

## GEOGRAPHIC INFORMATION SYSTEM (GIS)

**A computer-generated mapping system for collecting, storing, analyzing, and integrating information about physical and man-made features on maps.**

***Legal Annotation***: "In the alternative, however, FEMA provided Plaintiff with sixteen '**Geographic Information System (GIS)** maps of the 27 communities that have a flood hazard designated by FEMA where the flooding source is the San Juan, Animas, or Rio Grande Rivers.'" *Forest Guardians v. US Federal Emergency Management Agency* ($10^{th}$ Cir., 2005).

## GLARE

**The effect produced by light from a luminaire with an intensity sufficient to cause annoyance, discomfort, or loss in visual performance and visibility.**

***Comment***: The definition is subjective but can be applied in a given situation by establishing a reference line (usually the lot or zone line) and maximum foot-candle reading. *See* ***Foot-Candle***.

***Legal Annotation***: "Uses specifically permitted under the Chester Township regulations are only allowed 'provided such uses do not emit or create any danger to health and safety in the surrounding area, and do not create any offensive noise, vibration, smoke, dust, heat, **glare**, flame, air pollutants or other objectionable influences.' Chester Township Zoning Resolution Section 5.02.01." *Dinardo v. Chester Twp. Bd. of Zoning Appeals* (Ohio Ct. App., 2010).

## GOLF COURSE

**A tract of land laid out for at least nine holes for playing the game of golf, and that may include a clubhouse, dining and snack bars, pro shop, and practice facilities. See *Country Club*.**

***Comment***: Golf courses are fairly intensive uses. Most require significant quantities of water for irrigation and make extensive use of pesticides and fertilizers, although some golf courses today are attempting to lower their utilization of such resources. Most golf courses have clubhouses that include dining rooms, locker facilities, and pro shops. Many dining rooms are open to the public and, if permitted, may be rented for weddings and other social events. Adequate parking for all functions, some of which overlap, must be considered. Maintenance, storage sheds, and garages are typically part of a golf course.

The Middlesex County, New Jersey, Open Space and Recreation Plan 2003 has standards for county golf courses that are generally applicable to all golf courses, as follows:

*Golf courses can be one of three types*:

1. *Regulation golf courses have a minimum par of 72 and a minimum of 6,000 yards as measured from the middle tees.*

*2. Executive golf courses have a total par ranging from 55 to 68 and an average of 3,000 to 4,500 yards.*
*3. Par 3 golf courses have a par on each hole of 3 and an average of 2,000 to 2,500 yards.*

*Typical ancillary facilities include a practice range, a clubhouse with dining facilities, and a pro shop. Other recreation activities may occur on portions of the property not developed for golf. The minimum acreage for each type of course is:*

| | |
|---|---|
| *Regulation:* | *150 acres* |
| *Executive:* | *40-75 acres* |
| *Par 3:* | *30 acres* |

*A total land area of 250 acres or more is preferred to accommodate 27 holes at each course. Potential for possible future expansion should be considered. The site should have topography, soils, and a configuration that will efficiently support golf course development. The site should be capable of withstanding intensive public use and should include adequate parking facilities to accommodate employees and guests. The course should be capable of being developed and operated in a fashion compatible with any significant environmental features. Land uses within or adjacent to the site should not unduly constrain the site or golf course operation. An adequate water supply for irrigation is required.*

(Adapted from the Open Space and Recreation Plan 2003, Middlesex County, New Jersey.)

***Legal Annotation***: "As Plaintiffs point out, the policy defines '**golf course** grounds' as including 'greens, tees, and fairways; practice putting greens, practice driving areas; fairways, rough, sand traps, bunkers, and other outdoor grounds at the premises described, specifically designed and maintained for the game of golf; and trees, plants, shrubs.'" *Crestview Country Club v. St. Paul Guardian Ins. Co.* (D.Ma.ss, 2004).

"A **golf course** consists of a large tract of land, supporting facilities and improvements devoted to the sport of golf." *Phxaz Ltd. Partnership v. Maricopa County* (Ariz. Ct. App., 1998).

## GOVERNING BODY

**The chief legislative body of the municipality. See *Local Authority; Municipality*.**

***Legal Annotation***: "'**Governing body**' is defined... to mean: the multimember board, commission, committee, council, or other policy or rule-making body of a public agency, or any committee thereof when the committee acts on behalf of the governing body, conducts hearings, or takes testimony or public ***Comment***." *Clark v. City of Lakewood* (9th Cir., 2001).

## GOVERNMENT AGENCY

**Any department, commission, independent agency, or instrumentality of the United States, of a state, county, incorporated or unincorporated municipality, township, authority, district, or other governmental unit.**

***Legal Annotation***: "The GEPA requires a '**government agency**' to prepare an environmental effects report before proceeding with any governmental action that could 'significantly adversely affect the quality of the environment.' . . . The Act defines '**government agency**' as 'any department, board, bureau, commission, authority, or other agency of the state.'" *Thornton v. Clarke County School Dist.* (Ga., 1999).

## GRADE

**(1) When used in conjunction with the terms "existing," "finished," or "natural," *grade* is the same as "elevation"; (2) when used as a measurement, *grade* refers to the percentage of rise or descent of a sloping surface. See *Slope*.**

***Comment***: In the first definition, when grade is referenced as existing finished, or natural, it is meant to describe a fixed reference point and is measured in feet above sea level. In the second definition, when it is used to describe the extent of a sloping surface, there is a distinction between percentage of slope and degree of slope. For example, a forty-five-degree slope is a 100 percent grade. *See Figures 17 and 52.*

***Legal Annotation***: "The quantity of material necessary for each layer of the project was calculated based on the length, width, slope and desired **grade** elevation of the roadbed." *AGE Corp. v. State* (S.D., 2006).

Figure 52

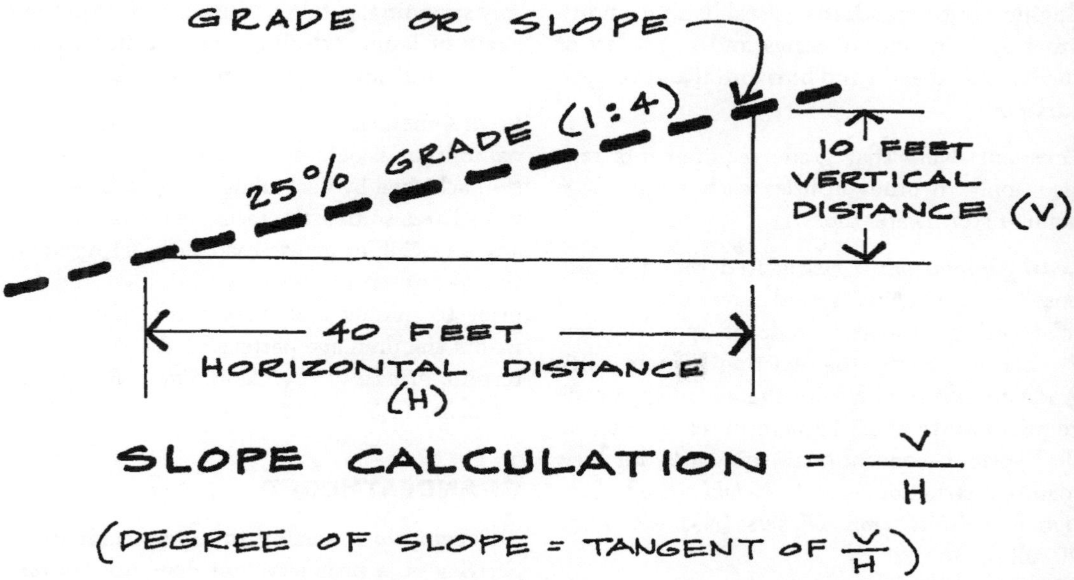


"The term '**grade**' is defined in Portland City Code 33.910.030 to mean: The lowest point of elevation of the finished surface of the ground, paving, or sidewalk within the area between the building and the property line or, when the property line is more than 5 feet from the building, between the building and a line 5 feet from the building." *Tirumali v. City of Portland* (Ore. Ct. App., 2000).

## GRADE, FINISHED

**The final elevation of the average ground level adjoining a building at all exterior walls after development (BOCA 1996: 55). See *Finished Elevation*. See *Figures 17 and 47*.**

***Legal Annotation***: "Petitioners contended, inter alia, that the city erred by allowing respondents to use an artificial, earth-filled '**finished grade**,' rather than the 'original grade' of the sloping property, in fixing the 'base point' for measuring the height of respondents' building." *Tirumali v. City of Portland* (Ore. Ct. App., 2000).

## GRADE, NATURAL

**The elevation of the ground level in its natural state, before construction, filling, or excavation. See *Natural Ground Surface*. See *Figure 47*.**

***Legal Annotation***: "Where seepage occurs as a result of the **natural grade** of property, in the absence of any claim that such grade was created for the express purpose of diverting water onto another's property, there can be no nuisance or trespass liability therefor." *Congregation B'nai Jehuda v. Hiyee Realty Corp.* (N.Y., App. Div., 2006).

## GRADE LEVEL

**That level of a building or structure which is at the same elevation as the ground around it, or very close to the same elevation.**

***Comment***: "Grade level" (or "at grade") differs from "below grade" or "above grade." All use the existing grade, whether finished or natural, as the reference.

***Legal Annotation***: "Building a highway along the contours of every hill and dale would leave every property at **grade level**, but at considerable difficulty, discomfort, delay, and danger to the traveling public." *County of Bexar v. Santikos* (Texas, 2004).

## GRADE REQUIREMENTS

**Engineering standards establishing minimum and maximum slopes and geometry of roads, such as radii and horizontal and vertical curves.**

*Comment*: Note that grade requirements may also apply to other utilities such as sewerage main or stormwater pipes.

*Legal Annotation*: "Clark stated that the proposed new roadway would have a section of road with a proposed grade of approximately 23 percent along the existing ground. This grade did not comply with the maximum **grade requirements** of 13-18 percent as set forth in the 'current conventional standards for new road construction.'" *ATR Neighborhood Association v. GMH Prop. Owners* (N.C. Ct. App., 2010).

## GRADE SEPARATION

**Structures that physically separate various modes of transportation and intersecting flows of traffic from one another in a vertical manner.**

*Legal Annotation*: "The only difference between the 'controlled access arterial highway' and the 'expressway,' as defined in sec. 29 (c) is that 'cross streams of traffic need not be eliminated at every intersection by means of **grade separation** structures.'" *State Roads Comm. v. Jones* (Md. Ct. App., 1966).

## GRADED AREA

**Any area of land that has had its grade altered, to provide either a level or a very slightly sloping surface.**

*Legal Annotation*: "Mr. Jensen described the terrain as follows: 'Someone had attempted to grade, drain off areas to outline the road. There was no roads there. There was a proposed area to be used for road that had a drain culvert or drain, **graded area** to let the water drain off the edge and drain onto the lower areas.'" *City of Sacremento v. Jensen* (Calif. Ct. App., 1956).

## GRADING

**Any stripping, cutting, filling, or stockpiling of earth or land, including the land in its cut or filled condition, to create new grades.**

*Legal Annotation*: "The term 'approximate original contour' is defined as 'that surface configuration achieved by backfilling and **grading** of the mined area so that the reclaimed area, including any terracing or access roads, closely resembles the general surface configuration of the land prior to mining and blends into and complements the drainage pattern of the surrounding terrain.'" *Hodel v. Virginia Mining & Reclamation Ass'n. Inc.* (U.S., 1981).

## GRANDFATHERED

**An exemption relating to a particular use or activity on a property that does not conform to applicable rules or regulations because of its establishment prior to the enactment of such rules or regulations.**

*Legal Annotation*: "We are likely to have cases in the future challenging zoning ordinances that are harder to classify, as variances and special-use permits and **grandfathered** nonconforming uses blur the character of particular zoning districts. But should a municipality create what purports to be a pure commercial district and then allow other uses, a church would have an easy victory if the municipality kept it out." *River Of Life Kingdom Minist. V. Hazel Crest, Ill.* (7th Cir., 2010).

## GRANDFATHERING

**The act of exempting a use or condition on a property that does not conform to current rules or regulations because of its establishment prior to the enactment of such rules or regulations.**

*Legal Annotation*: "Contrary to the plaintiffs' contention, § 240-66C(2) is not a **grandfathering** provision requiring as a precondition that a lot subject to its 'protection' have conformed to dimensional requirements in effect at the time the lot was created. Instead, by its terms, the section sets out alternative dimensional regulations applicable to lots that meet its criteria." *Jenkins v. Zoning Board of Appeals of Falmouth* (Mass. App. Ct., 2013).

## GRANITE BLOCK

See *Belgian Block*.

## GRANNY FLAT

See *Echo Housing; Dwelling, Garage Apartment*.

## GRANT

**(1) An instrument by which property is transferred by deed or writ; or (2) an instrument that conveys some estate or interest in the lands that it embraces; or (3) an outright gift of money for the purpose of study or research.**

*Legal Annotation*: "Although such a requirement, constituting a permanent **grant** of continuous access to the property, would have to be considered a taking if it were not attached to a development permit, the Commission's assumed power to forbid construction of the house in order to protect the public's view of the beach must surely include the power to condition construction upon some concession by the owner, even a concession of property rights, that serves the same end." *Nollan v. California Coastal Commission* (U.S., 1987).

## GRAPHIC SCALE

See *Scale*.

## GRAVEL PIT

See *Extractive Industries*.

## GREASE TRAP

**A device in which the grease present in wastewater is intercepted and congealed by cooling and from which it may be skimmed off liquid wastes for disposal.**

*Legal Annotation*: "When Hayes acquired title to her property in 1969, the easement was being used for sewer pipes and a **grease trap.** Although the **grease trap** has since been removed, the sewer pipes running underground between Matoush's property and the alley are still in use." *Matoush v. Lovingood* (Colo., 2008).

## GREEN AREA

**Land shown on a development plan, master plan, or official map for conservation, preservation, recreation, landscaping, or park. See *Open Space*.**

*Legal Annotation*: "There was evidence that there was almost a total lack of open space or **green area** within the CBD and that the scale and intensity of development in such a small area caused traffic congestion, inadequate parking, aggravating noise, and visual pollution." *Montgomery County v. Woodward & Lothrop, Inc.* (Md. Ct. App., 1977).

## GREENBELT

**An open area that may be cultivated or maintained in a natural state surrounding development, used as a buffer between land uses or to mark the edge of an urban or developed area. See *Open Space, Natural*.**

*Comment*: The famous greenbelt surrounding the metropolitan area of London, England, includes large-scale open recreation areas and low-intensity public and semipublic facilities and uses. In the United States, the planned community of Greenbelt, Maryland, was developed in 1937 during the Depression era as the largest of three "green" towns under the Resettlement Administration to ease a housing shortage and to help stimulate the national economy. The two other green towns are Greendale, Wisconsin, and Greenhills, Ohio. A fourth town, Roosevelt, New Jersey, was not developed to the same large scale as Greenbelt. All three planned communities provide significant green areas of public parks and open space (Stein 1989; "Greenbelts" 2008; "Over 70" 2008).

*Legal Annotation*: "First, they cite the preservation of open space and the creation of a '**greenbelt**' which, as most present day *Commentators* impress upon us, are worthy goals. While in full agreement with these goals, we are convinced that four acre minimum zoning does not achieve the creation of a **greenbelt** in its technical sense." *National Land & Investment Co. v. Easttown Township Board of Adjustment* (Pa., 1965).

## GREEN BUILDING

**Practices that consider the impacts of buildings on the local, regional, and global environment; energy and water efficiency; reduction of operation and maintenance costs; minimization of construction waste; and eliminating the use of harmful building materials. http://www.pgplanning.org/Resources/Tools_On-line/Glossary.htm**

***Legal Annotation***: "According to the United States **Green Building** Council, 'LEED' is defined as follows: [A]n internationally recognized **green building** certification system, providing third-party verification that a building or community was designed and built using strategies aimed at improving performance across all the metrics that matter most: energy savings, water efficiency, CO2 emissions reduction, improved indoor environmental quality, and stewardship of resources and sensitivity to their impacts. Developed by the U.S. **Green Building** Council (USGBC), LEED provides building owners and operators a concise framework for identifying and implementing practical and measurable **green building** design, construction, operations and maintenance solutions." *Burchick Construction Company, Inc. v. Pennsylvania State System of Higher Education* (Pa. Comm. Ct., 2010).

## GREEN INFRASTRUCTURE PLANNING

**Planning that integrates outdoor recreation, open space, cultural resources, and conservation lands into ongoing, environmentally sensitive planning and land-use management decisions.**

***Comment***: Using green infrastructure, land planning guides development to less environmentally sensitive lands, which reduces time needed for permits, lowers costs of development, protects water quality, and creates sustainable communities. Opportunities for strategically linking linear corridors of land together in this planning process maximizes environmental, habitat, and human benefits of development and better meets the needs of growing populations. http://www.dcr.virginia.gov/recreational_planning/giback.shtml

***Legal Annotation***: "Further, the analysis noted that the site was within a '**Green Infrastructure** Hub,' which was identified by the Department of Natural Resources ('DNR') as 'one of the most ecologically sensitive Green Infrastructure areas.' . . . Counsel explained that the **green infrastructure** was meant to protect wildlife species by setting aside a sufficient area to allow the species to flourish. He reiterated that 'this is the worst place in the world to have this' development, and would 'open up one of the last protected areas' in the County." *Pomeranc-Burke v. Wicomico Env.* (Md. Ct. Spec. App., 2011).

## GREEN MARKET

**See *Farmer's Market*.**

## GREEN MASTER PLANNED COMMUNITIES

**Communities that are large in scale, comprehensively designed, and developed to take account of ecology. They often have compact, discrete urban centers with more intensive land uses and are surrounded by a greenbelt.**

***Comment***: Found mostly in European new towns and new urbanist neighborhoods in the United States. Advantages are more efficient use of land and savings on energy used for transportation, heating, cooling, and infrastructure. Sustainable green features include the redevelopment of brownfields, light rail systems, centralized recycling and composting systems, use of green building technologies, and bicycle and pedestrian networks.

***Legal Annotation***: "Good governance considers restrictive covenants, including eco-friendly practices. Guidance on solar panels may be a matter of community preference. Similarly, some communities see clotheslines as aesthetically pleasing as flowering fields, while others do not. Communities will create the rules that fit the vision and mission of that association. That said, more and more state legislatures have passed laws superseding governing documents that prohibit both solar panels and clotheslines." *Best Practices Report #9* ***Green Communities*** *CAI* (2014). http://www.cairf.org/research/bpgreen.pdf

## GREENFIELD

**Farmland and open areas where there has been no previous industrial or commercial activity.**

***Comment***: The term *greenfield* was originally used in construction and development to reference land that has never been used (e.g., green or new), where there was no need to demolish or rebuild any existing structures. Today, the term *greenfield project* is used in many industries, including software development, where it means to start a project without the need to consider any prior work. http://www.webopedia.com/TERM/G/greenfield.html

***Legal Annotation***: "In addition, lenders are often reluctant to extend credit for the purchase and cleanup of brownfield sites, fearing future liability or diminution of the value of the property held as collateral should the site prove to require more extensive and costly cleanup than initially thought. Consequently, financing such a purchase may be more difficult than financing a purchase of a **greenfield** site." *Pointe v. NY S. Dept.* (N.Y., 2010).

## GREENHOUSE

**A building or structure whose roof and sides are made largely of glass or other transparent or translucent material and in which the temperature and humidity can be regulated for the cultivation of fragile or out-of-season plants for subsequent sale or for personal enjoyment. See *Nursery, Retail*.**

***Legal Annotation***: "This warm and humid atmosphere is not conducive to normal human activity and therefore all of the human activity that does occur within the **greenhouse** is directly related to the production of the commercially grown flowering and foliage crops." *Stuppy, Inc. v. United States* (W.D.Mo., 1978).

## GREENHOUSE EFFECT

**A term describing the warming of the earth's atmosphere as the result of accumulated carbon dioxide and other gases in the upper atmosphere.**

***Comment***: These gases absorb energy radiated from the earth's surface, trapping it in the same manner as a greenhouse traps heat.

***Legal Annotation***: "This '**greenhouse effect**' is a natural phenomenon, without which the planet would be significantly colder and life as we know it would not be possible." *Mass. v. EPA* (D.C. Cir., 2005).

"Calling global warming 'the most pressing environmental challenge of our time,' a group of States, local governments, and private organizations, alleged in a petition for certiorari that the Environmental Protection Agency (EPA) has abdicated its responsibility under the Clean Air Act to regulate the emissions of four **greenhouse gases**, including carbon dioxide. Specifically, petitioners asked us to answer two questions concerning the meaning of § 202(a)(1) of the Act: whether EPA has the statutory authority to regulate **greenhouse gas** emissions from new motor vehicles; and if so, whether its stated reasons for refusing to do so are consistent with the statute." *Mass. v. EPA* (U.S., 2007).

## GREEN PLAN

**Comprehensive management plans that have the final goal of achieving environmental and economic sustainability. See *Sustainable Development*.**

***Legal Annotation***: "While the Court agrees that the City need not await an emergency before enacting 'green' initiatives to address future problems, the evidence in the record establishes that the City has taken almost no action to implement its **'green' plan**." *National Solid Wastes Management v. City of Dallas* (N.D., 2012).

## GREEN ROOF

**A roof covered with vegetation, designed for its aesthetic value and to optimize energy conservation.**

*Comment*: Planted with low-growing sedums, native grasses, herbs, and shrubs, green roofs slow the rate that precipitation runs into the stormwater system, reduce energy needed for heating and cooling, and reduce the urban "heat island" effect (Snodgrass et al., no date).

*Legal Annotation*: "10. '**Green roof**' shall mean an addition to a roof of an eligible building that covers at least fifty percent of such building's eligible rooftop space and includes (a) a weatherproof and waterproof roofing membrane layer that complies with local construction and fire codes, (b) a root barrier layer, (c) an insulation layer that complies with the Energy Conservation Construction Code of New York State and local construction and fire codes, (d) a drainage layer that complies with local construction and fire codes and is designed so the drains can be inspected and cleaned, (e) a growth medium, including natural or simulated soil, with a depth of at least two inches, (f) if the depth of the growth medium is less than three inches, an independent water holding layer that is designed to prevent the rapid drying of the growth medium, such as a nonwoven fabric, pad or foam mat or controlled flow roof drain, unless the **green roof** is certified not to need regular irrigation to maintain live plants, and (g) a vegetation layer, at least eighty percent of which must be covered by live plants such as (i) sedum or equally drought resistant and hardy plant species, (ii) native plant species, and/or (iii) agricultural plant species." *New York Real Property Tax—Title 4-B—§ 499-AAA Definitions.*

"**Green roofs** are rooftops planted with vegetation. Intensive green roofs have thick layers of soil (6 to 12 inches or more) that can support a broad variety of plant or even tree species. Extensive roofs are simpler green roofs with a soil layer of 6 inches or less to support turf, grass, or other ground cover. U. S. Environmental Protection Agency Heat Island Effect Glossary, http://www.epa.gov/heatisland/resources/glossary.htm (last visited Feb. 22, 2010)." *Critical Area Commission for the Chesapeake and Atlantic Coastal Bays v. Moreland, LLC* (Md. Spec. Ct. App., 2010).

*Legal Annotation*: "[T]he 'building features a **"green" roof**, efficient energy systems, and re-used materials throughout.' (Id. at 93.) He testified that those features add value through 'efficient ventilation and heating and energy savings.'" *CLP Elements v. Benton County Assessor* (Ore. Tax Ct., 2011).

## GREENWAY

**(1) A linear open space established along either a natural corridor, such as a riverfront, stream valley, or ridgeline, or over land along a railroad right-of-way converted to recreational use, a canal, a scenic road, or another route; (2) any natural or landscaped course for pedestrian or bicycle passage; (3) an open-space connector linking parks, natural reserves, cultural features, or historic sites with each other and with populated areas; (4) locally, certain strip or linear parks designated as a parkway or greenbelt (Little 1990).**

*Legal Annotation*: "If petitioner's proposed development had somehow encroached on existing **greenway** space in the city, it would have been reasonable to require petitioner to provide some alternative **greenway** space for the public either on her property or elsewhere." *Dolan v. City of Tigard* (U.S., 1994).

## GRAY WATER

**Wastewater from domestic sinks and tubs, but excluding that part of the plumbing waste stream that includes human wastes.**

*Legal Annotation*: "Shortly after moving into the house, defendants experienced problems with the septic system, which they subsequently found to consist of a 300-gallon concrete tank for '**grey water**' (i.e., water from the sink, bath and shower), a separate 275-gallon tank for toilet waste, and a leach field." *Meldrim v. Hill* (N.Y. App. Div., 1999).

## GRID SYSTEM

**A map coordinate system that allows identification of a land area by using two coordinate figures. *See Figure 53*.**

*Legal Annotation*: "In setting out this **grid system**, wooden stakes were placed at 100 foot intervals and identified as to location by a letter of the alphabet indicating its position on a north-south coordinate line, and a number indicating its position on a west-east coordinate line. This grid system was later used on all sections by taxpayer." *Santa Fe Pacific Railroad Co. v. United States* (N.D. Ill., 1965).

**Figure 53**

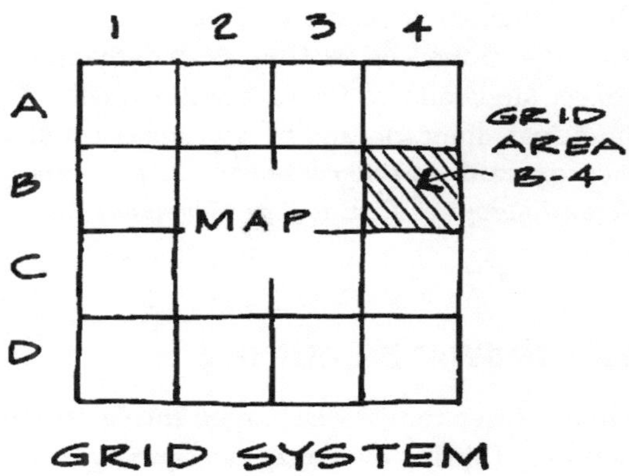


## GRIDIRON PATTERN

**A street and block system of formal, regular rectangular blocks and resulting four-way intersections.**

*Comment*: The gridiron pattern, characteristic of older city neighborhoods, fell into disfavor because of its insensitivity to topography, the excessive areas required for streets, and inflexible platting. It was replaced in the late 1930s by the curvilinear layout. Recently completed traditional neighborhood developments have shown that the gridiron system deserves reexamination because of its pedestrian orientation and scale, ease of access, multipathway opportunities, and mixed-use potential. See *Traditional Neighborhood Development*.

*Legal Annotation*: "Prudential planned to develop the area as a residential suburb of Somerville and subdivided it into a **gridiron pattern** of small lots, blocks and streets." *Levin v. Township Committee of Township of Bridgewater* (N.J., 1971).

## GROSS FLOOR AREA

**See *Floor Area, Gross And Floor Area, Net*.**

## GROSS HABITABLE FLOOR AREA

**See *Floor Area, Net*.**

## GROSS LEASABLE AREA (GLA)

**The total floor area for which the tenant pays rent and that is designed for the tenant's occupancy and exclusive use, including any basements and mezzanines.**

*Comment*: GLA does not include public or common areas, such as utility rooms, stairwells, and malls.

*Legal Annotation*: "The annual rent and certain other expenses are calculated on the basis of '**gross leasable area**', which is defined in the lease as 'measured from the outside face of the front and rear exterior walls and the midpoint of the common walls on either side of the Demised Premises.'" *British American Development Corp. v. Fay's Drug Co.* (N.Y. App. Div., 1991).

## GROUND COVER

**Grasses or other low-growing plants and landscaping.**

*Comment*: Ground cover has many functions and benefits as compared to lawn. It adds variety to the vegetative characteristics of open space. It can help to limit soil erosion by forming a dense mat covering an area, which over time prevents soil from being blown or washed away. It also prevents the growth of unwanted plants. Ground cover also generally requires less watering, mowing, fertilizer, and maintenance than lawns.

*Legal Annotation*: "The ordinance requires minimum barrier curbs and landscaping areas equal to at least ten percent of the paved area within a lot, **ground cover** (shrubs, ivy, pine bark or similar landscape materials) and at least one tree for every eight parking spaces." *Parking Association of Georgia, Inc. v. City of Atlanta* (Ga., 1994).

## GROUND COVERAGE

See *Lot Coverage*.

## GROUND FLOOR

**The first floor of a building other than a cellar or basement.**

*Legal Annotation*: "In computing the **ground floor** area, one must base his calculation upon the horizontal plane at 'ground floor level'. Although '**ground floor** level' is not defined within the ordinance, the plain and ordinary meaning of the term ground floor area manifests a calculation based upon the floor which is level to the ground." *Jones v. Hendricks County Plan Commission* (Ind. Ct. App., 1982).

## GROUNDWATER

**(1) The supply of fresh water under the surface in an aquifer or geologic formation that forms the natural reservoir for potable water; (2) the water contained within the interconnected pores, cracks, or fractures located below the water table of a confined or unconfined aquifer. *See Figure 6*.**

*Legal Annotation*: "Section 46-635, R.R.S.1943, defines '**ground water**' as: '. . . that water which occurs or moves, seeps, filters, or percolates through the ground under the surface of the land.'" *Prather v. Eisenmann* (Nebr., 1978).

## GROUNDWATER CONTAMINATION

**The presence of any substance designated by federal or state authorities as a primary or secondary water-quality parameter in excess of the maximum allowable contaminant level.**

*Legal Annotation*: "Determination of the magnitude of the damage includes recognition that the disposal of toxic waste may cause a variety of harms, including **ground water contamination** via leachate, surface water contamination via runoff or overflow, and poison via the food chain." *NJ Department of Environmental Protection v. Ventron Corp.* (N.J., 1983).

## GROUNDWATER RECHARGE

**The natural process of infiltration and percolation of rainwater from land areas or streams through permeable soils into water-holding strata or soils that provide underground storage.**

*Legal Annotation*: "[T]he district seeks to divert waters from the Platte River and a tributary of Prairie Creek in order that it might store the diverted waters and thus replenish the supplies of irrigation waters now being withdrawn from the ground water sources underlying the project lands and to improve water quality for municipal, domestic, and livestock uses through such **ground water recharge**." *Central Platte Natural Resources Dist. v. City of Fremont* (Nebr., 1996).

## GROUNDWATER RUNOFF

**Groundwater that is discharged into a stream channel as spring or seepage water.**

*Legal Annotation*: "The conditions attached to the approval, set forth more fully in the margin, generally require detailed geotechnical studies and reports verifying that particular building sites can be safely developed and that storm and **groundwater runoff** can be limited to predevelopment levels." *Meyer v. City of Portland* (Ore. Ct. App., 1984).

## GROUP CARE FACILITY

See *Boarding Home For Sheltered Care*.

## GROUP HOME

See *Boarding Home For Sheltered Care*.

## GROUP LIVING QUARTERS

See *Boardinghouse; Dormitory; Fraternity House*.

## GROUP RESIDENCES

See *Boarding Home For Sheltered Care; Boardinghouse; Dormitory; Fraternity House.*

## GROWTH MANAGEMENT

**Techniques used by the government to control the rate, amount, location, timing, and type of development.**

*Legal Annotation*: **"Growth management** hearings boards are charged with adjudicating GMA compliance and, when necessary, with invalidating noncompliant comprehensive plans and development regulations." *City of Burien v. Central Puget Sound Growth Management Hearings Board* (Wash. Ct. App., 2002).

## GUARANTEES

**Cash, letters of credit, bonds, or similar financial instruments deposited with the municipality to ensure that required improvements will be constructed or installed.**

*Comment*: Guarantees are required before a development application receives final approval or before a governmental agency accepts an improvement. They are designed to ensure that all streets, sidewalks, utility lines, street lighting, and similar improvements are completed and in place before certificates of occupancy are issued. Performance guarantees protect the municipality against a developer who may go bankrupt or who is unable to complete the improvements for any reason. In such cases, the guarantee is used by the municipality to complete the improvement. Maintenance guarantees ensure that the improvement will function for a period of time (usually eighteen months to two years); if not, the developer is responsible for correcting the problem. See *Maintenance Guarantee; Performance Guarantee*.

*Legal Annotation*: "Section 3066(c) of The First Class Township Code, 53 P.S. § 58066 (c), provided: '[B]efore approving any subdivision plan for recording, the board of township commissioners shall either require that the necessary grading, paving and other street improvements . . . or that the township be assured by means of a proper completion **guarantee** in the form of a bond or the deposit of funds or securities in escrow sufficient to cover the cost of the required improvements . . . that the said improvements will subsequently be installed by the owner.'" *Safford v. Board of Commissioners* (Pa. Comm. Ct., 1978).

## GUIDE RAIL

**A safety barrier designed to protect motor vehicles from driving off the road or falling into hazardous areas.** *See Figure 54.*

*Legal Annotation*: "The New York State Department of Transportation (hereinafter the DOT) responded by commissioning a study, which

**Figure 54**

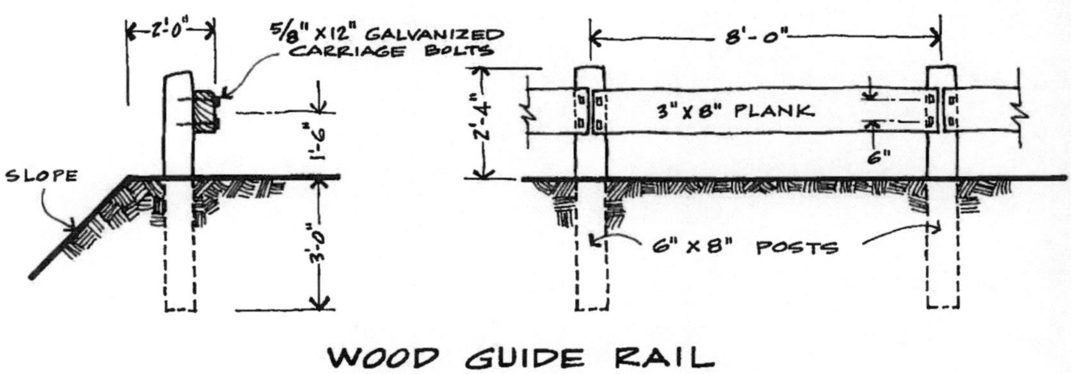

recommended the installation of a **guide rail** at the point where vehicles had previously mounted the concrete barrier." *Giske v. State* (N.Y. App. Div., 1993).

## GUTTER

**A shallow channel, usually set along a curb or the pavement edge of road, for purposes of catching and carrying off runoff water (N.J.A.C. 5:21-1.4).**

*Legal Annotation*: "The city plan commission refused to approve the plat unless one of the proposed streets was extended . . . and unless the width of the bituminous streets was increased to 25 feet, and curb and **gutter** and suitable storm water drainage facilities were provided." *Petterson v. City of Naperville* (Ill., 1956).

## GYM

**The abbreviated term for gymnasium, which is an enclosed facility for exercise and athletics.**

*Comment*: The above definition is most often associated with facilities provided at schools and colleges for the pursuit of exercise and athletics. More recently the term has been used interchangeably with health or fitness clubs. See *Health Club*.

*Legal Annotation*: "A '**gym**nasium' is 'a large room used for various indoor sports . . . and equipped with gymnastic apparatus" as well as "a building . . . containing appropriate space and equipment for various indoor sports activities. . . .' WEBSTER'S THIRD NEW INTERNATIONAL DICTIONARY 1014 (1986)." *Hass v. Turbot Township Zoning Hearing Board* (Pa. Comm. Ct., 2009).

# H

## HABITABLE FLOOR AREA

**The total floor area of all the habitable rooms in a dwelling unit.**

*Legal Annotation*: "Every dwelling unit shall contain at least one hundred and fifty (150) square feet of **habitable floor area** for the first occupant thereof and at least one hundred (100) additional square feet of **habitable floor area** for every additional occupant thereof, but in no case shall any dwelling unit contain less than two hundred and fifty (250) square feet of **habitable floor area**." *Nolden v. East Cleveland City Commission* (Ohio Ct. Comm. Pleas, 1966).

## HABITABLE ROOM

**Any room in a dwelling unit other than a kitchen, bathroom, closet, pantry, hallway, cellar, storage place, garage, or unfinished basement, cellar, or attic.**

*Legal Annotation*: "'A **Habitable Room**' is a room or enclosed floor space used or intended to be used for living, sleeping or eating purposes, excluding bathrooms, toilet rooms, laundries, pantries, dressing rooms, storage spaces, foyers, hallways, utility rooms, heater rooms, boiler rooms, basement recreation rooms, and areas used for kitchen purposes." *Nolden v. East Cleveland City Commission* (Ohio Ct. Comm. Pleas, 1966).

## HABITAT

**The sum total of all the environmental factors of a specific place that is occupied by an organism, a population, or a community.**

*Legal Annotation*: "The FS defines **habitat** capability as '[t]he estimated ability of an area, given existing or predicted habitat conditions, to support a wildlife, fish or plant populations.'" *San Juan Citizens Alliance v. Stiles* (D. Colo., 2010).

## HABITAT PROTECTION AREA

**A designated area wherein disturbance or destruction of the natural environment is prohibited or restricted in order to conserve rare, threatened, or endangered species of fauna and flora.**

*Legal Annotation*: "[M]r. Serey asserted that the project 'would severely impact sensitive portions' of the Critical Area Buffer, a designated **habitat protection area**, by permitting development not necessarily associated with water development facilities; improperly disturb steep slopes; remove all trees in a two-acre area, possibly adversely impacting a forest interior dwelling, bird habitat, etc., all in violation of the State's Critical Area Criteria and Kent County's Local Program." *Wharf at Handy's Point, Inc. v. Department of Natural Resources* (Md. Ct. App., 1992).

## HAIRPIN MARKING

**A double painted line separating parking stalls.** ***See Figure 55.***

*Comment*: Hairpin marking or striping of parking stalls is particularly advantageous where narrower parking stalls are proposed (e.g., eight-and-a-half-foot spaces), because they narrow the space in which a vehicle has to park. This helps to center the vehicle and to make sure it is not parked to one side of the space, thereby infringing on the adjacent parking space.

*Legal Annotation*: "C. The minimum size of standard parking spaces shall be nine feet by 19 feet where spaces are provided with 'looped' or

**Figure 55**

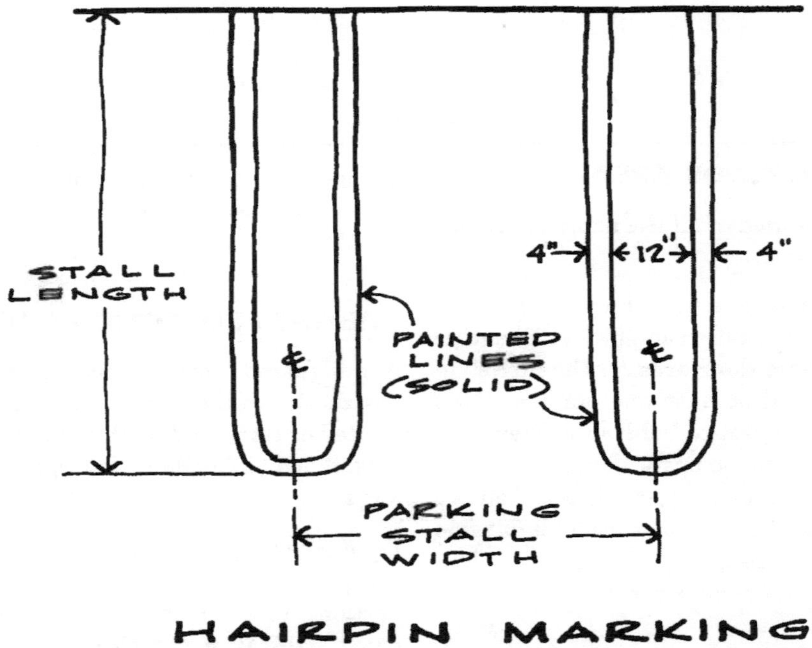


'**hairpin**' stall markings, or 10 feet by 19 feet where spaces are provided with single-line stall markings. The minimum size of large vehicle parking spaces shall be 12 feet by 45 feet where the spaces are provided with 'looped' or '**hairpin**' stall markings, or 13 feet by 45 feet where spaces are provided with single-line stall markings. Looped or **hairpin** markings shall provide that the center line of the loop or **hairpin** shall be a minimum of four inches on-center to either inside edge of the loop or hairpin marking." *Township of Wall, NJ PART I, ADMINSTRATIVE LEGISLATION § 140-218. General requirements.*

## HALF-CLOSURES

See *Traffic Calming*.

## HALF-STORY

See *Story, Half*.

## HALFWAY HOUSE

See *Boarding Home For Sheltered Care*.

## HAMLET

**A small settlement or village.**

***Comment***: *The New Jersey State Development and Redevelopment Plan* (2002) defines *hamlet* as a small-scale, compact residential settlement with one or more community-related functions that accommodates development in a compact form. In New York State, hamlets are unincorporated settlements within towns.

***Legal Annotation***: "These sections are legislative authority only for the creation of a **hamlet** or village into a municipality, and they do not authorize the citizens within a village or **hamlet** to create a municipality embracing such village or **hamlet** and including territory within such municipality which is in no manner connected with the village or **hamlet** sought to be incorporated into a municipality." *US v. Heyward* (5th Cir., 1938).

## HAMMERMILL

**A broad category of high-speed equipment that uses pivoted or fixed hammers or cutters**

**to crush, grind, chip, or shred material into smaller pieces.**

*Comment*: In development, hammermills are most commonly referenced in the context of solid waste management.

*Legal Annotation*: "At some point after arriving at the processing site, the limestone is loaded into a **hammermill** to commence the process of transforming the raw material into Portland cement." *In Re Lafarge Midwest/Martin Tractor Co.* (Kans., 2012).

## HANDICAP

**See *People With Disabilities*.**

*Comment*: The term "handicap" has been replaced in this 4th Edition by the term "disability," and "handicapped persons" with the term "people with disabilities." For persons with disabilities, the term "handicapped" is now considered insulting.

*Legal Annotation*: "General Laws c. 151B, § 1 (17), defines '**handicap**' as '(a) a physical or mental impairment which substantially limits one or more major life activities of a person; (b) a record of having such impairment; or (c) being regarded as having such impairment.' . . . Federal legislation now uses the term 'disability' rather than 'handicap.'" *Dahill v. Police Dept. of Boston* fn. 6-7 (Mass., 2001).

## HANDICAPPED PARKING SPACE

**Parking spaces reserved for people with disabilities, typically marked with the International Symbol of Access. *See Figure 5*.**

*Comment*: Parking in such spaces carries the requirement that a placard of those who have satisfied the requirement to receive it is displayed within the vehicle. The provision of a certain number of such spaces in all public parking lots was mandated by the Americans with Disabilities Act in 1990 along with other provisions to make rights-of-way, buildings, and facilities accessible to people with disabilities. Such spaces are also required to be located closest to the building entrances and have features that facilitate access, such as curb ramps and wider spaces to accommodate side-loading lifts.

*Legal Annotation*: "Section 27-710.1.E—requiring one **handicapped parking space** for every one to twenty-five parking spaces, and one additional **handicapped parking space** for every additional one to twenty-five parking spaces." *Gould v. Zoning Hearing Board of Bristol Borough* (Pa. Comm. Ct., 2011).

## HANDICAPPED PERSON

**See *People With Disabilities; Americans With Disabilities Act*.**

## HARDSCAPE

**Nonliving components of a landscape design, such as walls, sculpture, paved walkways, patios, stone and gravel areas, benches, fountains, and similar hard-surface areas and objects.**

*Legal Annotation*: "While Taylor works primarily in the building of commercial structures, it won a '**hardscape**' contract to do the aesthetic landscaping and concrete work on the grounds of the Central Park office complex in Atlanta, Georgia." *Ed Taylor Construction v. OSHRC* (11th Cir., 1991).

## HARDSHIP VARIANCE

**See *Variance, Hardship*.**

## HARMONIOUS RELATIONSHIP

**The design, arrangement, and location of buildings or other created or natural elements of the urban environment that are sufficiently consistent in scale, character, and siting with other buildings or created or natural elements in the area to avoid abrupt or severe differences. See *Development Context*.**

*Comment*: The objective of a harmonious relationship is an appropriate consideration in evaluating the quality of life to be experienced in an environment. It applies equally to residential and nonresidential areas.

*Legal Annotation*: "The Commission finds that the proposed subdivision with the interior lots does not comply with '[t]he provision for creation of a **harmonious relationship** between proposed and existing buildings in the vicinity; specifically with regard to the visual relationship of said buildings in terms of their terrain, use, scale proportions and, particularly, the historic significance of the existing buildings.'" *Irwin v. Planning & Zoning Commission* (Conn., 1998).

## HAZARD

**(1) A potential or actual force, physical condition, or agent with the ability to cause human injury, illness, and/or death, and significant damage to property, the environment, critical infrastructure, agriculture and business operations, and other types of harm or loss; (2) something that is potentially dangerous or harmful, often the root cause of an unwanted outcome (*NIMS*). http://www.gwu.edu/~icdrm/publications/PDF/GLOSSARY%2002-19-2007.pdf**

***Legal Annotation***: "[T]the ZHB found that Appellants failed to present evidence to demonstrate the following: the proposed use would not create a public safety **hazard**, including fire, toxic or explosive hazards." *Above & Beyond, Inc. v. Zoning Hearing Board of Upper Macungie Township* (Pa. Common. Ct., 2010).

## HAZARDOUS AIR POLLUTANT

**A pollutant for which no ambient air quality standard is applicable and that may cause or contribute to an increase in mortality or serious illness.**

***Comment***: Examples of hazardous air pollutants are asbestos, benzene, and formaldehyde.

***Legal Annotation***: "The statute requires the Administrator to publish a list containing each hazardous pollutant for which he intends to adopt an emission standard, to publish proposed regulations and a notice of public hearing for each such pollutant, and then, within a specified period, either to promulgate an emission standard or to make a finding that the particular agent is not a **hazardous air pollutant**." *Natural Resources Defense Council v. USEPA* (D.C. Cir., 1987).

## HAZARD MITIGATION

**Measures taken in advance of a disaster aimed at decreasing or eliminating its impact on society and environment (UN 1992: 41; Schwab 2010). http://www.gwu.edu/~icdrm/publications/PDF/GLOSSARY%2002-19-2007.pdf**

*Legal Annotation:* "York County **Hazard Mitigation** Plan provides, in relevant part, '[a]ccording to the PA [Department of Conservation and Natural Resources], the susceptibility to landslides in York County is considered generally low, but this does not imply that given the right combination of factors a landslide could not occur.' (R.R. at 1352a.) This general statement is not substantial evidence of record which demonstrates that the SSCO provisions were supported by the York County **Hazard Mitigation** Plan." *Boyer v. Board of Supervisiors Franklin Township* (Pa. Common. Ct., 2013).

## HAZARD RISK

**A quantitative product of the probability of a hazard occurring and the projected consequence of the impact. http://www.gwu.edu/~icdrm/publications/PDF/GLOSSARY%2002-19-2007.pdf**

*Legal Annotation:* "The zoning ordinance itself recognizes the heterogeneous character of the neighborhood because of the permitted uses contained in the ordinance. In fact, the ridiculous nature of the denial of a variance in this case may be demonstrated by placing the alleged reasons for denial side by side with some of the permitted uses in the same ordinance: greater fire **hazard risk** of tavern . . ."

*Cutone v. Anaconda Deer Lodge* (Mont., 1980).

## HAZARDOUS SUBSTANCE

**Any substance or material that, by reason of its toxic, caustic, corrosive, abrasive, flammable, oxidizing, asphyxiating, biohazardous, pathogenic, allergenic, or otherwise injurious properties, may be detrimental or deleterious to the health of any person handling or otherwise coming into contact with such material or substance. Includes hazardous materials. See *Hazmat*.**

*Comment*: The US Environmental Protection Agency (EPA) has developed a list of hazardous substances based upon corrosiveness, reactivity, and toxicity. Hazardous substances include, but are not limited to, inorganic mineral acids or sulfur, fluorine, chlorine, nitrogen, chromium, phosphorous, selenium, and arsenic and their common salts; lead, nickel, and mercury and their inorganic salts, or metallo-organic derivatives; coal; tar acids such as phenol and cresols and their salts; and all radioactive materials.

*Legal Annotation*: "CERCLA defines '**hazardous substance**' to include a variety of chemicals and toxins including those designated by EPA as air pollutants, water pollutants, and solid wastes. § 9601(14)." *Burlington North & Santa Fe RY v. US* (U.S., 2009).

## HAZARDOUS SUBSTANCE DISPOSAL

**A method for the safe disposal of hazardous substances.**

*Legal Annotation*: "CERCLA makes four classes of people liable for response costs or contribution: the current owner or operator of a facility, 42 U.S.C. § 9607(a)(1); any person who owned or operated the facility 'at the time of **disposal**' of a **hazardous substance** . . . any person who arranged for disposal or treatment, or arranged for transport for disposal or treatment of hazardous substances at the facility . . . and any person who accepts or accepted hazardous substances for transport to sites selected by such person." *US v. CDMG Realty Co.* (3rd Cir., 1996).

## HAZARD TYPES

***Natural Hazard*: Any hazard produced primarily by forces of nature that result in an impact to humans or property of sufficient severity to be deemed an emergency (see *Emergency*). Natural hazards include hurricanes, tornados, storms, floods, wind-driven water, tidal waves, earthquakes, drought, fire, infectious disease epidemics, and others.**

***Technological Hazard*: A hazard created primarily by man-made technology or unplanned and non-malicious actions, which result in human or property impact of sufficient severity to be deemed an emergency. Technological hazards include industrial, nuclear, or transportation accidents; unintentional natural gas and other explosions; conflagration; building collapse from primary structural failure (insufficient supports during construction or renovation, corrosion or other predictable materials deterioration, overload of structural elements, etc.); power failure; financial and resource shortage; oil and other hazardous materials spills and other injury-threatening environmental contamination. Note the interface between technological, natural, and intentional origins: a structural collapse secondary to an earthquake is a natural hazard emergency; one secondary to a deliberate methane explosion is an intentional hazard emergency; one secondary to construction error is a technological hazard emergency.**

***Intentional Hazard*: A hazard produced primarily by threatened or executed intentional actions, threatening or resulting in human or property impact of sufficient severity to be deemed an emergency. Intentional hazards cover a very wide range of forces (chemical, biological, radiations, incendiary and explosive, cyber, disruption of services or products, and others). The intent may be sabotage, criminal actions, conflict and civil disobedience or disturbance, or acts of terrorism. http://www.gwu.edu/~icdrm/publications/PDF/GLOSSARY%2002-19-2007.pdf**

## HAZARD VULNERABILITY ANALYSIS

**A systematic approach to identifying all hazards that may affect an organization and/or its community, assessing the risk (probability of hazard occurrence and the consequence for the organization) associated with each hazard and analyzing the findings to create a prioritized comparison of hazard vulnerabilities.**

***Comment***: The consequence, or "vulnerability," is related to both the impact on organizational function and the likely service demands created by the hazard impact. http://www.gwu.edu/~icdrm/publications/PDF/GLOSSARY%2002-19-2007.pdf

***Legal Annotation***: "According to JCAHO standards, health care providers should first perform a **hazard vulnerability analysis** in order to decide the best methods in which to respond to disasters." *Serou v. Touro Infirmary* (La. Ct. App., 2013).

## HAZARDOUS USE

**A building or structure, or any portion thereof, that is used for the storage, manufacture, or processing of highly combustible or explosive products or materials that are likely to burn with extreme rapidity or that may produce poisonous fumes or explosions; for the storage or manufacturing that involves highly corrosive, toxic, or noxious alkalies, acids, or other liquids or chemicals producing flame, fume, or poisonous, irritant, or corrosive gases; and for the storage or processing of any materials producing explosive mixtures of dust or that result in the division of matter into fine particles subject to spontaneous ignition.**

***Legal Annotation***: "This court has never decided whether a municipality may validly enact a zoning ordinance creating a distinction based solely on public versus private ownership of an arguably noxious or **hazardous use** of land. . . . Testimony was given in the trial court concerning various safety hazards and disturbances associated with a gas well, such as gas emerging from a hole, fire, explosion, and noise." *Mahony v. Township of Hampton* (Pa., 1994).

"Industrial districts under the 1954 plan are defined as: . . . 2. Any process or assembly, manufacture or treatment constituting a **hazardous use**, including but not limited to such things as the manufacture or bulk storage of fireworks and explosives; and the manufacture of illuminating gas and other explosive or poisonous gases, except as may be incidental to a permitted industrial process." *Trans Rail Am., Inc. v. Hubbard Twp.* (Ohio Ct. App., 2007).

## HAZARDOUS WASTE

**Those wastes that can cause or help to cause illness or death, or that, in the absence of proper management, represent a significant threat to either human health or environment.**

***Legal Annotation***: "'**Hazardous waste**' is defined as 'a solid waste, or combination of solid wastes, which . . . may . . . pose a substantial present or potential hazard to human health or the environment when improperly treated, stored, transported, or disposed of, or otherwise managed.'" *Burlington North & Santa Fe RY v. US* (U.S., 2009).

## HAZMAT

**The common acronym for "hazardous materials." See *Hazardous Substances*. http://www.gwu.edu/~icdrm/publications/PDF/GLOSSARY%2002-19-2007.pdf**

***Legal Annotation***: "Other firefighters are given additional incentive when they actually serve on the **HazMat** Team and are placed in a more dangerous situation. The City obviously has an interest in cleaning up hazardous materials and having a team of firefighters to clean up the materials is an interest that is furthered by the incentive pay." *Morgan v. City of Shreveport* (La. Ct. App., 2011).

## HEALTH-CARE FACILITY

**A facility or institution, whether public or private, principally engaged in providing services for health maintenance and the treatment of mental or physical conditions. See *Health-Care Services*.**

***Comment***: Health-care facilities include general or special hospitals, public health centers, diagnostic centers, treatment centers, rehabilitation centers, extended care facilities, long-term care facilities, nursing homes, outpatient clinics, and dispensaries. Accessory uses include laundries, restaurants, gift shops, laboratories, pharmacies, and medical offices.

***Legal Annotation***: "Further, our conclusion is consonant with the public's perception of the modern hospital as a multifaceted, **health-care facility** responsible for the quality of medical care and treatment rendered. The community hospital has evolved into a corporate institution, assuming 'the role of a comprehensive health center ultimately responsible for arranging and coordinating total health care.'" *Elam v. College Park Hospital* (Calif. Ct. App., 1982).

## HEALTH-CARE SERVICES

**Establishments providing support to medical professionals and their patients, such as medical and dental laboratories, blood banks, oxygen, and miscellaneous types of medical supplies and services.**

*Legal Annotation:* "'[B]asic **health care services**' are defined in HRS § 432D-1 as 'preventive care, emergency care, inpatient and outpatient hospital and physician care, diagnostic laboratory services, and diagnostic and therapeutic radiological services.'" *Alohacare v. Ito* (Haw. 2012).

## HEALTH CLUB

**An establishment that houses exercise equipment and space for the purposes of physical exercise. See *Gym*.**

***Comment***: Also referred to as a fitness club or fitness center, and also a gym, although the latter typically refers to facilities provided in schools. Health clubs have evolved substantially in the past few years, and most of the larger ones now provide a vast array of equipment and services, including a main workout area (with exercise machines and free weights); a cardio area (including cardiovascular-related training equipment such as rowing machines, stationary bikes, elliptical trainers, and treadmills); group exercise classes (such as aerobics, cycling, martial arts, Pilates, and yoga); sports facilities (such as swimming pools, squash courts, and basketball courts); and other services such as snack bars, cafes, child-care facilities, and lounges. Some even offer spa facilities, including various massage treatments, and beauty salons, saunas, and steam showers. Most of the larger health or fitness clubs that are established today are part of regional or national chains and offer a variety of memberships and pricing.

The size and parking requirements of health clubs vary substantially, from small, neighborhood-oriented clubs of a few thousand square feet and one or two employees, to those of over one hundred thousand square feet employing over one hundred full- and part-time staff and open virtually 24/7. As a result, communities should be judicious in how and where health clubs of different types should be permitted, as well as parking required to accommodate peak periods of use.

***Legal Annotation***: "For the purposes of the Act, '**health club**' is defined as 'any enterprise organized for profit . . . which offers on a regular, full-time basis services or facilities for the development or preservation of physical fitness through exercise, weight control, or athletics.'" *State v. Southern Fitness and Health, Inc.* (Tenn., 1987).

## HEALTH PLANNING

**The study of the provision, distribution, and financing of health facilities and services for present and future populations.**

***Legal Annotation***: "Under Georgia's Health Planning and Development Act of 1983, all health care facilities are required to obtain a certificate of need (CON) from the State **Health Planning** Agency (SHPA) prior to the implementation or expansion of any health service. [2] Each CON application is reviewed individually according to a process which requires consideration of a number of **health planning** issues, including the existing services in an area and the need for additional services." *St. Joseph's Hospital v. Hospital Corp. of America* (11$^{th}$ Cir., 1986).

## HEAT-ISLAND EFFECT

**An air-circulation problem peculiar to urban areas whereby heat from buildings, structures, pavements, and concentrations of pollutants creates a haze dome that prevents rising hot air from being cooled at its normal rate.**

***Legal Annotation***: "According to the EPA, '[t]he term "**heat island**" describes built up areas that are hotter than nearby rural areas. . . . **Heat islands** can affect communities by increasing summertime peak energy demand, air conditioning costs, air pollution and greenhouse gas emissions, heat-related illness and mortality, and water quality.'" http://www.epa.gov/hiri/

"The Project shall incorporate a light colored 'cool roof' membrane to reduce surface temperature, **heat island effect**, and heat transfer to the interior of the structure." *Coalition for Clean Air v. VWR International, LLC* (E.D. Calif., 2013).

## HEAVY INDUSTRY

**See *Industry, Heavy*.**

## HEDGE

**A row of bushes or small trees planted close together, especially when demarcating a boundary or forming a barrier.**

*Legal Annotation:* "A *hedge* is '[a] row of closely planted shrubs or low-growing trees forming a fence or boundary.'" American Heritage Dictionary, supra, at 602.Bubis v. Kassin (N.J., 2005).

## HEDGEROW

**Shrubs, plants, and trees, closely planted, grown, and cultivated to form a boundary between fields to delineate grazing areas for livestock, or to separate fields from roads.**

***Comment***: Typically found in agrarian landscapes. More common in the UK and Western Europe than in the USA.

*Legal Annotation:* "This Court notes that the row of trees was not specifically planted by either party in order to serve as a boundary marker nor is there any allegation that they consist of either arborvitae or a **hedgerow** that may be commonly understood to denote a boundary." *Banville v. Brennan* (R.I., 2014).

## HEIGHT

**See *Building Height; Grade, Finished.* See *Figure 17*.**

## HELIPAD

**A landing area or platform for helicopters.**

***Comment***: May be located at airports, helistops, or heliports, and typically including lighting and windsocks.

***Legal Annotation***: "Because hospitals are expressly permitted in a Multi-Family District, they are also permitted in a Local Retail Business District. **Helipads** are not expressly permitted in a Multi-Family District, so a **helipad** is permissible only if it is an accessory use permitted in a Multi-Family District." *Cleveland Clinic Found. v. Bd. of Zoning Appeals* (Ohio Ct. App., 2012).

## HELIPORT

**An area including a helipad that, either at ground level or elevated on a structure, is licensed by the Federal Aviation Administration for the landing and takeoff of helicopters and that includes auxiliary facilities, such as parking, waiting rooms, and maintenance equipment.**

***Comment***: Heliports and helistops (see definition below) are utilized for a variety of purposes, including emergency purposes, trauma centers at major hospitals, for business purposes, to serve the needs of executives or clients, or as a quick transportation option (for example, shuttling passengers between downtowns and major airports within metropolitan areas). Their establishment often encounters neighborhood resistance, primarily related to noise and safety concerns.

***Legal Annotation***: "A consultant hired by the City found the **heliport** would be compatible with adjacent land uses, and concluded that Condor's proposed site was 'an ideal location for a **heliport**.'" *Condor Corp. v. City of St. Paul* (8th Cir., 1990).

## HELISTOP

**A heliport but without auxiliary facilities, such as parking, waiting room, fueling, and maintenance equipment.**

***Comment***: Helistops are often constructed by major office and industrial uses and can be considered an accessory to the principal use. Many municipalities ban them because of concerns relating to nuisance and safety. From a planning point of view, controls relating to hours of operation and the number of daily flights may be reasonable. A single helistop in an office park or industrial park may be a more viable alternative than one for each building.

***Legal Annotation***: "After its initial review, DCLU determined neither SEPA nor the City's conditional use criteria were met based on its conclusion the **helistop** would result in noise and land use impacts that could not be mitigated, and the **helistop** was not a business necessity." *Development Serv. of America v. Seattle* (Wash., 1999).

## HERTZ (Hz)

**A unit that measures frequency in all physical systems that have a wave pattern.**

***Legal Annotation***: "Heinrich Hertz, a German scientist, was the discoverer of electromagnetic radiation (radio waves), and his name has been used for many years in foreign countries as the unit of frequency. One cycle per second is called one '**hertz**.'" *Rio Grande Family Radio Fellowship, Inc. v. FCC* fn. 1 (D.C. Cir., 1968).

## HIGH-OCCUPANCY VEHICLE (HOV)

**A vehicle carrying more than a specified number of people.**

***Comment***: In many states, certain highways restrict traffic in one of its lanes to high-occupancy vehicles, at rush hours or at all times, to encourage commuters to share vehicles rather than to ride alone. Success of these HOV-restricted lanes has been somewhat mixed. In many cases HOV-restricted access lanes have either been abandoned or the HOV restrictions have been loosened, for example by dropping its restrictions for the minimum number of passengers from three to two.

***Legal Annotation***: "In November 1980 defendant was issued a summons for driving in a **High Occupancy Vehicle (H.O.V.)** lane on the Garden State Parkway without the minimum of three passengers in his car then required by [statute]." *State v. Barcheski* (N.J. App. Div., 1981).

## HIGH-RISE

**See *Dwelling, High-Rise*.**

## HIGH-SPEED RURAL ROADWAY

**The access classification for roadways in rural environments where the posted speed limit is fifty miles per hour or greater. See *High-Speed Urban Roadway*.**

*Legal Annotation:* "Rural Zone. The rural zone is defined as a high-speed, rural roadway outside of a developed community. It has a high design speed (≥ 45 mph), little roadside development, few access points, and is designed to facilitate high-speed, longer distance travel. There are relatively few features or potential conflicts that require driver attention in this zone. The design within this zone should be consistent with the high design and posted speeds." *Appendix B to NCHRP Report 737 Design Guidance Document.*

## HIGH-SPEED URBAN ROADWAY

**The access classification for roadways in urban environments where the posted speed limit is forty-five miles per hour or greater.**

***Comment***: Both the "high-speed rural" and "high-speed urban" classifications are part of highway access codes that establish standards for driveway access to roads. See *High-Speed Rural Roadway.*

## HIGH-VOLUME (HI-VOL) SAMPLER

**A device used in the measurement and analysis of suspended particulate pollution.**

***Legal Annotation***: "Air sampling is a method of evaluating the concentration of airborne beryllium in a particular area. There are several different methods for air sampling, which produce divergent measures of beryllium exposure. In one method, a '**high volume sampler**' is used to draw air through a filter placed in the breathing zone of a worker. The filter is then analyzed for beryllium contaminants. Another method is referred to as 'personal sampling,' and aims to determine the amount of beryllium to which each individual worker is exposed." *Genereux v. American Beryllia Corp.* (1st Cir., 2009).

## HIGHER EDUCATIONAL INSTITUTION

**A university, college, community college, junior college, two-year college, or other institution offering post-high school training and education.**

***Comment***: The definition above provides for a wider array of educational institutions beyond colleges and universities, in that vocational or business schools are included. In some zoning ordinances, the term is defined in such a manner as to only include colleges and universities so as to recognize the significant difference in impacts between the two types of facilities. The development ordinance must consider the fact that colleges and universities, unlike a secretarial school or vocational training center, are actually mini-cities with concerns relating to circulation, services, utilities, on-campus housing, and significant potential impacts during special events, such as a football game or graduation. Colleges and universities may require and support a major number of off-campus retail stores and service establishments. They may also significantly impact surrounding areas and generate increased competition for housing.

***Legal Annotation***: "**HIGHER EDUCATIONAL INSTITUTION**. Any university, college, junior college or similar public or nonprofit private educational organization or institution for post-high-school training and education, including secretarial, business, trade, technical and professional education." *Town of Barrington, RI Zoning Sec. 185.55.*

## HIGHEST AND BEST USE

**The reasonably probable and legal use of vacant land or an improved property that is physically possible, appropriately supported, and financially feasible and that results in the highest value.**

***Comment***: An appraisal concept that determines the use of a particular property likely to produce the greatest net return in the foreseeable future (Johnsich 1991: 76). The term "highest and best use" has little validity in planning or zoning studies but is germane in condemnation or eminent domain, where a governmental entity takes a property or a portion of a property and is thereby obligated to provide just compensation based upon the property's "highest and best use." Another application is where it is used for comparing several alternative potential uses of a specific piece of property to determine which is more profitable. See *Taking*.

***Legal Annotation***: "The existing use of the land, in this case, cotton farming, is its presumed **highest and best use**, but the landowner can rebut this presumption by showing a reasonable probability that when the taking occurred, the property was adaptable and needed or would likely be needed in the near future for another use." *Exxon Pipeline Co. v. Zwahr* (Texas, 2002).

## HIGHWAY

**See *Street, Freeway*.**

## HIGHWAY CAPACITY

**See *Capacity, Roadway*.**

## HIGHWAY-ORIENTED BUSINESS

**A commercial use dependent on both a large flow of traffic and convenient access.**

***Comment***: Typical highway-oriented businesses include hotels and motels, restaurants, automobile service uses, auto sales (new and used), and retail centers. These uses often require large land parcels for vehicle storage and circulation that may be disruptive or unavailable in many urban settings. Zoning controls for such areas might preclude the individual small user, unless part of a larger complex of related uses. Site design standards for highway access spacing, landscaping, signage, and site design objectives are essential to avoid the clutter and unattractive commercial highway strip development found at the entrances to many cities.

***Legal Annotation***: "The intent of an H[ighway] S[ervice] district is 'to establish areas for **highway-oriented business** and to provide development standards that will not impair or obstruct the traffic carrying capabilities of abutting roads and highways.' Permitted uses include such things as hotels, restaurants, retail businesses, and commercial recreation and amusement structures." *Schrank v. Pennington County Board* (S. Dak., 1998).

## HISTORIC AREA

**A district, zone, or area designated by a local, state, or federal authority within which the buildings, structures, appurtenances, and places are of basic and vital importance because of their association with history; or because of their unique architectural style and scale, including color, proportion, form, and architectural detail; or because of their being a part of or related to a square, park, or area, the design or general arrangement of which should be preserved and/or developed according to a fixed plan based on cultural, historical, or architectural motives or purposes. See *National Register of Historic Places and Historic District*.**

***Comment***: Local historic districts or zones are usually implemented as overlay zones; that is, the historic district often covers several use districts, and the overlay zone usually regulates only the exterior appearance of the property and its existing and proposed structures, not its use. These zones usually require local agency design review and approval for any exterior building changes or new construction. Local historic district regulations must conform to state enabling legislation, and the district may include nonhistoric properties if such properties are essential to the preservation and protection of the district. The delineation of historic districts, and their design standards, should be supported by appropriate studies and incorporated in the local master plan. See *Historic Building Styles; National Register of Historic Places; Overlay Zone.*

***Legal Annotation***: "Under § 8.05 of the [Enabling] Act '[b]efore the construction, alteration, reconstruction, moving, or demolition of any structure is made' within the **historic area** 'if any changes are involved which would affect the exterior appearance of a structure visible or intended to be visible from an adjacent public way' in the historic district it is necessary to apply to the Commission 'for permission to build, alter, reconstruct, move, demolish, or make the addition.'" *Faulkner v. Town of Chestertown* (Md. Ct. App., 1981).

## HISTORIC BUILDING

**Any building or structure that is historically or architecturally significant. See *Historic Property*.**

***Legal Annotation***: "A project will normally have a significant effect on the environment if it will . . . [d]isrupt or adversely affect . . . a property of historic or cultural significance to a community or ethnic or social group. Thus, the significant impacts of a discretionary project upon a **historic building** must be considered in an EIR." *League For Protection of Oakland's Architectural & Historic Resources v. City of Oakland* (Calif. Ct. app., 1997.

## HISTORIC BUILDING STYLES

**Recognized architectural styles from the past (in most cases, in the USA from fifty years or more), such as Colonial, Early and Late Georgian, Federal, Greek Revival, Victorian, Victorian Gothic, Carpenter Gothic, Italianate, Tudor, Mission, Prairie, and Art Moderne. *See Figures 56–60.***

**Figure 56**

COLONIAL (1700-1720)

*Spartan design; large central chimney; narrow clapboards (bricks in the South); simple frames around doors and windows; small window panes (often twelve-over-twelve)*

EARLY GEORGIAN (1720-1760)

*Symmetrical design; set on high foundation, with emphasis on entrance bay; columns frame entry, with pediment above; often classical features in cornice; executed in brick or wood*

---

**Figure 57**

LATE GEORGIAN (1760-1780)

*Lavish use of classical details; doorways surrounded with pilasters or columns; Palladian window on second floor in center, cornice on simple window caps; corners marked with quoins or pilasters*

FEDERAL (1780-1820)

*Doorways with pilasters and columns, often topped with flat entablature; elliptical fanlight over entry; frames; hipped roofs, often with window balustrade*

---

**Comment:** The definition is actually a partial listing of major American historic building styles. For purposes of historic district zoning for a particular area, this listing might be revised as appropriate and detailed architectural definitions of each style added.

***Legal Annotation***: "In contrast to discriminatory zoning, which is the antithesis of land-use control as part of some comprehensive plan, the New York City law embodies a comprehensive plan to preserve structures of **historic** or aesthetic interest wherever they might be found in the city, [28] and as noted, over 400 landmarks and 31 **historic** districts have been designated

**Figure 58**

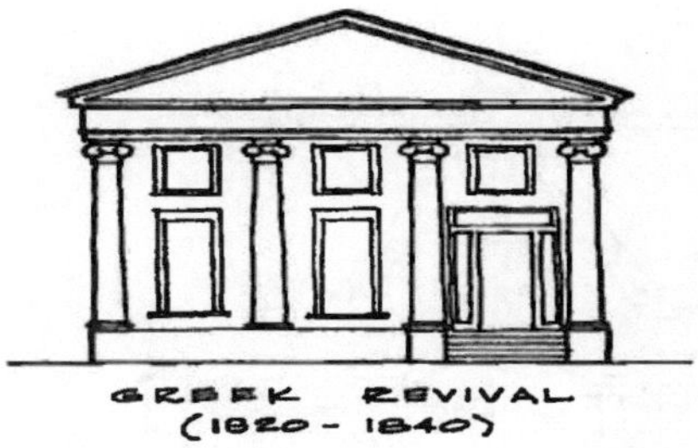


*Emphasis on columns, capitals, and low triangular gabled pediment to create Greek temple appearance; strong vertical windows, with six-over-six panes; simple lines*

*Emphasis on vertical effect, with many sharply pointed gables; steeply pitched roofs; slender, tall windows; decorated woodwork*

**Figure 59**

*Medieval building characteristics; heavy use of decoration; tall windows with leaded panes*

*Sawn-wood ornament at peaks of gables, in verge under gables, and on porches; sawn brackets on porch posts and on cornice*

pursuant to this plan. . . . Opened in 1913, it is regarded not only as providing an ingenious engineering solution to the problems presented by urban railroad stations, but also as a magnificent example of the French beaux-arts **style**. . . . 'Historic district.' Any area which: (1) contains improvements which: (a) have a special character or special **historical** or aesthetic interest or value; and (b) represent one or more periods or styles of architecture typical of one or more eras in the history of the city; and (c) cause such area, by reason of such factors, to constitute a distinct section of the city; and (2) has been designated as a '**historic** district pursuant to the provisions of this chapter.' § 207-1.0 (h). The Act also provides for the designation of a 'scenic landmark,' see § 207-1.0 (w), and an 'interior landmark.' See § 207-1.0 (M). . . . The Commission's report stated:

**Figure 60**

VICTORIAN GOTHIC (1850-1880)

*Two or three stories; low-pitched hip roof with widely overhanging eaves supported by large brackets; a center cupola or tower; balanced facades; decorative lintels over narrow-hung windows; double doors*

CARPENTER GOTHIC (1880-1910)

*Steeply pitched end-gabled roofs; gabled entryway; multi-paned narrow windows in bands of three; tall chimneys; masonry stuccoed construction; half-timbering*

---

'Grand Central Station, one of the great buildings of America, evokes a spirit that is unique in this City. It combines distinguished architecture with a brilliant engineering solution, wedded to one of the most fabulous railroad terminals of our time. Monumental in scale, this great building functions as well today as it did when built. In style, it represents the best of the French Beaux Arts.' Record 2240." *Penn Central Transp. Co. v. New York City* (U.S., 1978).

## HISTORIC DISTRICT

**See *Historic Area and Historic Property*.**

***Legal Annotation***: "The Commission first performs the function, critical to any landmark preservation effort, of identifying properties and areas that have 'a special character or special historical or aesthetic interest or value as part of the development, heritage or cultural characteristics of the city, state or nation.' If the Commission determines . . . that a building or area satisfies the ordinance's criteria, it will designate a building to be a 'landmark,' . . . or will designate an area to be a '**historic district**.'" *Penn Central Transp. Co. v. New York City* (U.S., 1978).

## HISTORIC OBJECT

**A material object of functional, aesthetic, cultural, historical, or scientific value that may be, by nature or design, movable yet related to a specific setting or environment. See *Historic Property*.**

***Comment***: Examples of historic objects are: Delta Queen Steamboat, Cincinnati, Ohio; Adams Memorial, Rock Creek Cemetery, Washington, DC; Sumpter Valley Gold Dredge, Sumpter, Oregon. See *Historic Area; Historic Properties*.

***Legal Annotation***: "The City of Pasco asserts that the old bridge is merely an **historic 'object'** but not an historic site within the meaning of 4(f) which the cities contend is implicated only in D.O.T. projects involving use of 'land' from the historic site." *Benton Franklin Riverfront Trwy. v. Lewis* (E.D. Wash., 1981).

## HISTORIC PRESERVATION

**An endeavor which seeks to preserve and protect features in the built environment such as buildings, districts, neighborhoods or**

**Figure 61**

(Mission, top) Stucco walls; round arches supported by piers; continuous wall surface forming parapets; hip roof of red tiles; overhanging eaves with exposed rafters

**communities which are of particular historic significance.**

***Comment***: Historic preservation efforts at the national level are effectuated by listing a property on the National Register of Historic Places. Buildings and districts are generally required to be fifty years old or more, unless a property's historical significance is of "exceptional importance." A listing on the National Register makes properties eligible for a federal tax credit of 20 percent of the cost of rehabilitation if undertaken in accordance with the secretary of the interior's Standards for Rehabilitation of Historic Buildings. Historic preservation includes managing, stabilizing, and sensitive reuse of historic buildings. It also includes conserving scenic views and natural landscapes (New Jersey Office of State Planning 1996).

***Legal Annotation***: "Furthermore, judgments of historical significance made by the Advisory Council on **Historic Preservation**, the expert regulatory body concerned with preserving, restoring, and maintaining the historic and cultural environment of the Nation . . . deserve great weight. However, compliance with the NHPA, even when it exists, does not assure compliance with NEPA. Each mandates separate and distinct procedures, both of which must be complied with when historic buildings are affected." *Preservation Coalition, Inc. v. Pierce* (9th Cir., 1982).

## HISTORIC PROPERTY

**Any prehistoric or historic district, site, building, structure, or object included in or eligible for inclusion on a register of historic places. See *Historic Bulding Styles; Historic Area*.**

***Comment***: As defined by the National Historic Preservation Act (NHPA) of 1966, *historic properties* (or resources) means any "prehistoric or historic district, site, building, structure, or object included in, or eligible for inclusion on the National Register of Historic Places."

The resources noted above—building, district, object, site, and structure—are defined and illustrated as follows:

(a) Building

A building is a structure created to shelter any form of human activity, such as a house, barn, church, hotel, or similar structure. "Building" may refer to a historically related complex such as a courthouse and jail or a house and barn. Examples: Molly Brown House, Denver, Colorado; Meek Mansion and Carnage House,

**Figure 61**

(Art Moderne, bottom) Streamlined appearance; smooth wall surfaces with rounded corners; little ornamentation; flat roof; windows that wrap around corners; often a curved canopy over the front door

---

Hayward, California; Huron County Courthouse and Jail, Norwalk, Ohio; Fairntosh Plantation, Durham vicinity, North Carolina.

(b) District

A district is a geographically definable area, urban or rural, possessing a significant concentration, linkage, or continuity of sites, buildings, structures, or objects united by past events or aesthetically by plan or physical development. A district may also comprise individual elements separated geographically but linked by association or history. Examples: Georgetown Historic District, Washington, DC; Martin Luther King Historic District, Atlanta, Georgia; Durango-Silverton Narrow-Gauge Railroad, right-of-way between Durango and Silverton, Colorado.

(c) Object

An object is a material thing of functional, aesthetic, cultural, historical, or scientific value that may be, by nature or design, movable yet related to a specific setting or environment. Examples: Delta Queen Steamboat, Cincinnati, Ohio; Adams Memorial, Rock Creek Cemetery, Washington DC; Sumpter Valley Gold Dredge, Sumpter, Oregon.

(d) Site

A site is the location of a significant event, a prehistoric or historic occupation or activity, or a building or structure, whether standing, ruined, or vanished, where the location itself maintains historical or archaeological value regardless of the value of any existing structure. Examples: Cabin Creek Battlefield, Pensacola vicinity, Oklahoma; Mound Cemetery Mound, Chester vicinity, Ohio; Mud Springs Pony Express Station Site, Dalton vicinity, Nebraska.

(e) Structure

A structure is a work made up of interdependent and interrelated parts in a definitive pattern or organization. Constructed by humans, it is often an engineering project and large in scale. Examples: Swanton Covered Railroad Bridge, Swanton vicinity, Vermont; Old Point Loma Lighthouse, San Diego, California; North Point Water Tower, Milwaukee, Wisconsin; Reber Radio Telescope, Green Bay vicinity, Wisconsin.

***Legal Annotation***: "The regulations offer three options to mitigate an otherwise adverse effect so that it is 'considered as being not adverse,' two of which are implicated here. 36 C.F.R. § 800.9(c). First, an agency may conduct appropriate research '[w]hen the **historic property** is of value only for its potential contribution to archeological, historical, or architectural research, and when such value can be substantially preserved through the conduct of appropriate research.' 36 C.F.R. § 800.9(c)(1) (emphasis added). Second, an adverse effect becomes 'not adverse' when the undertaking is limited to the 'transfer, lease, or sale of a **historic property**, and adequate restrictions or conditions are included to ensure preservation of the property's significant historic features.' 36 C.F.R. § 800.9(c)(3) (emphasis added). The Tribe insists that the Forest Service elected the wrong remedy. We agree." *Muckleshoot Indian Tribe v. US Forest Service* (9th Cir., 1999).

## HISTORIC SITE

See *Historic Property*.

*Legal Annotation*: "'Historic property' is defined [in the Indiana Code] as 'any **historic site** or structure,' I.C. 14-3-3.4-1, and '**historic site**' or 'historic structure' is any site or structure important to the 'general, archeological, agricultural, economic, social, political, architectural, industrial, or cultural history of Indiana.'" *Whitacre v. State* (Ind. Ct. App., 1993).

## HISTORIC STRUCTURE

See *Historic Property*.

## HOLDING CAPACITY

**The maximum amount of development that a lot can accommodate based on applicable zoning requirements. See *Carrying Capacity*.**

*Legal Annotation*: "The Objection to Lifting Invalidity asserted that Ordinance No. 03-0323-09 failed to comply with the GMA because . . . (6) the County had conducted a faulty population **holding capacity** analysis. . . . On May 26, before the Western Growth Board issued the 2009 Compliance Order, ICAN filed a new petition for review, also challenging ordinance No. 03-0323-09. This petition raised 10 alleged violations . . . (8) the **holding capacity** analysis did not comply with the GMA." *Irondale Community Action Neighbors v. Western Washington Growth Management Hearings Board* (Wash. Ct. App., 2011).

## HOLDING ZONE

**A temporary low-density zoning that governs until a decision is reached by a community as to how the area should be rezoned (uslegal.com). See *Interim Zoning*.**

*Comment*: In some states, holding zones are considered illegal, whether established on a de facto basis or surreptitiously to thwart undesirable development until proper zoning can be put in place.

*Legal Annotation*: "The farmland in the eastern part of the city was placed in a **holding zone**, to be rezoned for residential use on an as-needed basis." *1000 Friends of Oregon v. City of Dundee* (Ore. Ct. App., 2005).

## HOMELAND SECURITY

**A concerted national effort to prevent terrorist attacks *within* the United States, reduce America's vulnerability to terrorism, and minimize the damage and recover from attacks that do occur (Office of Homeland Security, 42). http://www.gwu.edu/~icdrm/publications/PDF/GLOSSARY%2002-19-2007.pdf**

*Legal Annotation:* "Part of the 'primary mission' of the Department of **Homeland Security** is to 'prevent terrorist attacks within the United States' and 'reduce the vulnerability of the United States to terrorism.' 6 U.S.C. § 111(b)(1)." *Tabbaa v. Chertoff* (2nd Cir., 2007).

## HOME OCCUPATION

**Any activity carried out for gain by a resident and conducted in the resident's dwelling unit ("When Home Is Where the Business Is," *Zoning News,* December 1991; *Planning*, June 1993, 16; Julie Bennett, "Home Bodies," *Planning*, May 1999; Wunder 2000).**

*Comment*: The above definition is the broadest possible one covering all home occupations. It simply states that any activity that is carried out for gain by a resident in his or her dwelling unit is a home occupation. It does not mean that a municipality must permit home occupations or that controls and limits cannot be placed on home occupations. Home occupations are best controlled through performance standards rather than listings of permitted home occupations or professions. In those zones where home occupations are permitted, the development ordinance may impose reasonable restrictions, including the number of nonresident employees (usually a maximum of two), sign control (one sign, with the name of the resident and the home occupation and not to exceed the size of any residential identification sign permitted in the zone), and a maximum on the amount of square footage that may be used for the home occupation (25 percent or four hundred feet, whichever is less).

Other controls are also appropriate. These include:

- The home occupation must be carried out indoors, without any outdoor storage.
- The residential appearance of the structure may not be altered
- Any commercial vehicles for the use must be garaged.
- Noise, glare, fumes, odors, and electrical interference are prohibited.
- Not more than one client, customer, or patron is permitted on the premises at any time.
- Deliveries and pickups by tractor-trailers are prohibited.

An applicant for a home occupation should be required to submit a site plan to the appropriate municipal official (engineer, planner, or zoning official) to ensure that all zoning requirements are met. If additional parking is required, a site plan should be submitted to the approving authority to determine what landscaping and setback requirements are needed.

The home occupation should also be customary, incidental, and accessory to the principal residential use. "Customary" is subject to change, however, as modern technology reduces the need for face-to-face communication.

***Legal Annotation***: "Section 302 of the [Abington Township Zoning] Ordinance defines a '**home occupation**' as follows: '**HOME OCCUPATION**: Any use customarily conducted entirely within a dwelling . . . and carried on by the inhabitants residing therein, providing that the use is clearly incidental and secondary to the use of the dwelling for dwelling purposes.'" *Reynolds v. Zoning Hearing Board* (Pa: Commonwealth Court 1990).

## HOME OFFICE

See *Home Occupation*.

## HOME PROFESSIONAL OFFICE

**A home occupation consisting of the office of a practitioner of a recognized profession. See *Home Occupation*.**

***Comment***: The major question is defining a recognized profession. The granting of a state license in and by itself is not an indication of a recognized profession. Customary home professional offices usually include attorneys, medical practitioners, engineers, and architects. As noted in the definition of "home occupation," performance standards are preferable to distinctions between occupations and professions and/or listings of acceptable occupations.

Home professional offices may be of greater intensity than home occupations, and as such require different treatment. Because a greater proportion of the structure may be devoted to the business, more employees and visitors are present, and the exterior appearance is likely to reflect the inclusion of offices, their presence is often restricted to locations (along arterial roads of residential areas) and sites that are large enough to accommodate the additional parking that is required to accommodate these uses.

Additional controls on these offices should include a maximum on the amount of floor area in the residence that can be used for the home office (typically 25 percent), maximum number of non-resident employees (usually two or three), hours of operation (not later than 8:00 pm), adequate on-site parking appropriately screened, and a requirement for site plan review so that the residential character of the neighborhood is not impaired.

***Legal Annotation***: "Airmont Code provides: 'Permissible "**home professional office**" uses include, but are not limited to, the following: clergymen, lawyers, physicians, dentists, architects, engineers or accountants, if said use meets the other requirements of this Local Law. . . . It is the intent of this Local Law that the **home professional office** shall only be an accessory use and that the residential character of the neighborhood involved shall be maintained at all times.'" *LeBlanc-Sternberg v. Fletcher* (2nd Cir., 1995).

## HOMELESS SHELTER

**A facility providing temporary housing to indigent, needy, or homeless persons.**

***Legal Annotation***: "Community House contained both a **homeless shelter** and a low income housing unit. The **homeless shelter** could hold, in separate dormitories, sixty-six men, thirteen women, and ten families." *Community House, Inc. v. City of Boise* (9th Cir., 2007).

## HOMEOWNERS' ASSOCIATION

**A community association, other than a condominium association, that is organized in a development in which individual owners share common interests and responsibilities for costs and upkeep of common open space or facilities.**

***Comment***: Homeowners' associations (HOAs) are typically governed by a volunteer board of directors. Property management may be carried out by a mix of private management firms, HOA-employed contractors, and resident volunteers. The homeowners' association usually holds title to certain common property, whereas condominium associations do not (Goodno 2005).

***Legal Annotation***: "Common interest developments are required to be managed by a **homeowners association** (§ 1363, subd. [a]), defined as 'a nonprofit corporation or unincorporated association created for the purpose of managing a common interest development' (§ 1351, subd. [a]), which homeowners are generally mandated to join." *Villa De Las Palmas Homeowners v. Terifaj* (Calif., 2004).

## HOMES FOR THE AGED

**See *Adult Retirement Community; Assisted Living Facility; Congregate Residences; Continuing Care Retirement Community; Housing For The Elderly; Residential Health-Care Facilities; Retirement Community*.**

***Comment***: An obsolete term, no longer used.

***Legal Annotation***: "In determining whether the proposed project would qualify as a permitted use under such a classification we note that the term **home for the aged** is defined by statute in Illinois as: 'any home operated not for profit under the auspices of a religious, fraternal, charitable or other non-profit organization, or by a county * * * or operated not for profit under an endowment, which * * * as its principal objective, provides maintenance, personal care, nursing, or sheltered care to * * * three or more persons over 60 years of age.' *Pioneer Trust & Sav. Bk. V. County of Cook* (Ill. App. Ct., 1977).

## HORSE FARM

**A farm that is primarily used for the breeding and boarding of horses. See *Boarding Stable; Agriculture*.**

***Comment***: Under the principal definitions of "farms" and "agriculture," horse farms would typically be listed as permitted uses. The problem with listing horse farms as a permitted use in an agriculture district is that some horse farms include such activities as races, horse shows, auctions, and riding classes as accessory uses. Races, shows, and auctions can generate significant amounts of traffic and crowds where food and drinks are sold. Consequently, many ordinances identify horse farms as conditional uses and limit the number of horse shows, races, and other events. They may even require site plans to show how access, parking, circulation, and sanitary facilities are proposed to be accommodated. Some towns require special permits regulating the maximum number of shows and length of time for each show.

***Legal Annotation***: "In addition, the evidence shows that Rouse, after acquiring the farm in a run-down condition, had expended sums of money improving the quality of the 150 acres of sod by fertilizing and otherwise caring for it and that he incurred other expenses in grading, filling and preparing all of the land for the use to which it was being put—as a cattle and **horse farm**." *United States v. Carroll* (4th Cir., 1962).

## HORTICULTURE

**The cultivation of a garden or orchard. See *Agriculture*.**

*Legal Annotation*: "The same authority defines '**horticulture**' as follows: 'The cultivation of a garden or orchard; the science and art of growing fruits, vegetables, and flowers or ornamental plants. **Horticulture** is one of the main divisions of agriculture.'" *Jordan v. Stark Bros. Nurseries & Orchards Co.* (W.D. Ark., 1942).

## HOSPICE

**A facility specializing in the care of terminally ill persons.**

*Legal Annotation*: "**Hospice** programs, as currently structured, are designed to provide comprehensive 'palliative and supportive services . . . [to] dying persons and their families.'" *Cianciotto v. Hospice Care* (N.Y. Dist. Ct. 2011).

## HOSPICE CARE

**The care of terminally or seriously ill patients that focuses on relieving their pain and suffering but attending to their emotional and spiritual needs as well.**

*Comment*: Hospice care may be carried out in a patient's home, within a hospital or nursing home, or in a hospice home or facility whose sole focus is hospice care.

*Legal Annotation*: "The application listed the proposed uses as '**Hospice**/social work and services.' On August 17, Valetutto approved this application, with the following explanation: 'Approval for use as **hospice care**, including counseling, social work and services, with stays of approximately twenty-five days or less, as defined by the appropriate State agency.' . . . Valetutto rescinded both permits for Eldercare, noting his approvals were based on the stated use of '**hospice care**,' which is a permitted use in the MMC Redevelopment Area, but there was 'conflicting and confusing information' and 'continued confusion as to the exact proposed use' by Eldercare." *Rocky Top, LLC v. City of South Amboy, NJ* (N.J. App.Div., 2012).

## HOSPITAL

**An institution providing primary health services and medical or surgical care to persons suffering from illness, disease, injury, deformity, and other abnormal physical or mental conditions and including inpatient and outpatient services institution-related facilities, such as diagnostic and treatment facilities, laboratories, training facilities, medical offices, and staff residences.**

*Comment*: State agencies usually regulate the size, scale, type, and location of hospitals. Before one can be built, a "certificate of need" or similar instrument is required. In most urban and suburban areas, new hospital construction is rare, as state agencies attempt to reduce costs by limiting new facilities. However, reconstruction, rehabilitation, and new construction for older hospitals to meet new demands are increasing.

From a zoning perspective, hospitals are extremely intensive uses. They operate twenty-four hours per day, generate significant traffic volumes, and have many employees on different shifts. Some estimates indicate that the average hospital has three employees per bed, plus volunteers, visitors, and doctors. Because hospitals are often located in residential areas, particular attention should focus on entrances and exits; location of power plants, laundries, and other support uses; parking; and overall neighborhood impact.

Hospital care is changing rapidly, and this will have an impact on the future design of hospital campuses. For instance, outpatient surgery, which accounted for less than 3 percent of all surgery twenty years ago, now constitutes more than 75 percent of all surgical procedures. The result is a general downsizing of bed and long-term functions and more outpatient facilities.

Another change is the construction of medical office buildings on hospital campuses. They bring doctors closer to hospitalized patients, reduce traffic and congestion, and generate some taxes from otherwise tax-exempt facilities.

*Legal Annotation*: "The ordinary meaning of '**hospital**' is a place where sick or injured persons, not animals, are treated. . . . *Black's Law Dictionary* (5th ed. 1979) defines **hospital** as '[a]n institution for the treatment and care of sick, wounded, infirm or aged persons.'" *State v. Hartsough* (Colo., 1990).

## HOSTEL

**See *Youth Hostel*.**

## HOTEL

**A facility offering transient lodging accommodations to the general public and that may include additional facilities and services, such as restaurants, meeting rooms, entertainment, personal services, and recreational facilities. See *Bed And Breakfast; Boardinghouse; Conference Center; Inn; Motel; Resort; Tourist Home*.**

***Comment***: Hotels can generally be classified as either limited-service or full-service. Limited-service hotels provide only lodgings and do not provide any restaurant or food service, recreation facilities, and the like. Full-service hotels always have restaurants and possibly a bar or lounge with entertainment, personal services, health club, and retail stores.

Another variant of hotel that has become more commonplace over the past decade is the extended-stay hotel. As a general rule, extended-stay facilities are limited-service hotels but with larger rooms (approximately 425 square feet) and with refrigerators, cooktops, microwave ovens, dishes, and utensils, and with washers and dryers on premises. The extended-stay facility is for transients staying five or more days, with an average of seven to ten days. The average stay for traditional transient facilities (non-extended stay) is 1.5 days. Extended-stay hotels will have a variety of room types, including studios and one- and two-bedroom suites.

Another type of hotel, which can be a full- or limited-service hotel, is an all-suites hotel. These can be extended-stay or traditional but, as the name implies, consist mostly of suites.

The principal zoning concern is whether the extended-stay hotels can, with very long-term occupancies, become semipermanent residential dwellings or apartment houses. According to representatives of the industry, this is highly unlikely because the average room rental, on a monthly basis, is too expensive for long-term occupancy. In addition, the BOCA National Building Code classifies hotels with occupancies of thirty days or more as apartment houses and requires significantly greater and more expensive materials and construction techniques. However, fueling this fear is the use of some extended-stay hotels by some governmental agencies for temporarily housing the homeless or disaster victims.

Other concerns relate to the number and size of ancillary facilities, such as restaurants, bars, lounges, and health clubs. For example, a full-service hotel might be too intensive a use for a residential neighborhood. But an extended-stay facility, without any restaurant, bar, or lounge, might easily be accommodated.

***Legal Annotation***: "The ordinance defines '**hotel**' as follows: 'A building or group of buildings having ten (10) or more guest rooms in which lodging, or meals and lodging, are offered for compensation.' . . . Thus, the Ellsworth ordinance defines '**hotel**' as an establishment with residence units that are temporary and shorter term." *Jordan v. City of Ellsworth* (Maine, 2003).

## HOTEL, CASINO

**Establishments primarily engaged in providing short-term lodging in hotel facilities with a gambling casino on premises.**

***Comment***: The casino on premises typically includes table wagering games and other gambling activities, such as slot machines and sports betting. These establishments generally offer a range of services and amenities, such as food and beverage services, entertainment, valet parking, swimming pools, spas, and personal services in addition to lodging and the casino itself.

***Legal Annotation***: "The Venetian Casino Resort is a large **hotel and casino** complex located on the former site of the Sands Casino on Las Vegas Boulevard South—'the Las Vegas Strip'—in Clark County, Nevada." *Venetian Casino v. Local Joint Executive Board* (9th Cir., 2001).

## HOTEL, MICRO-UNIT

**See *Dwelling, Micro-Unit*.**

## HOUSE OF WORSHIP

See *Place of Worship*.

## HOUSE TRAILER

See *Manufactured Home*.

## HOUSEHOLD

**All the people who occupy a housing unit.**

***Comment***: A household includes the related family members and all the unrelated people, if any, such as lodgers, foster children, wards, or employees who share the housing unit. There are two major categories of households: "family" and "nonfamily." A person living alone in a housing unit, or a group of unrelated people sharing a housing unit such as partners or roomers, are also counted as a household. Group quarters such as fraternity or sorority houses or dormitories are not included as households (Source: 2010 US Census).

***Legal Annotation***: "The tradition of uncles, aunts, cousins, and especially grandparents sharing a **household** along with parents and children has roots equally venerable and equally deserving of constitutional recognition." *Moore v. East Cleveland* (U.S., 1977).

## HOUSEHOLD PET

**Smaller domesticated animals, residing within a dwelling unit and not raised for commercial gain. See *Animal, Domestic*.**

***Comment***: The real problem is not in defining household pets but in limiting the number and size to prevent them from becoming nuisances. For example, the definition might limit household pet to one hundred pounds to prevent large animals, such as fully grown pigs or goats, from becoming household pets. A reasonable number of household pets, excluding fish and birds, might be not more than three per dwelling unit.

For lots in excess of an acre outside of urban areas but used primarily as residences, as opposed to farms, a different standard, limiting the number of "animal units," can be used. For example, on lots of one acre or more, one animal unit per acre could be permitted. An animal unit would be defined as the equivalent of one cow, four hogs, ten sheep, ten goats, one hundred poultry, one horse, one pony, one mule, or one hundred rabbits, or combinations thereof.

***Legal Annotation***: "The term '**household pet**' is defined in § 20A of the town regulations as 'any domesticated animal kept for pleasure rather than utility or profit which is normally kept within a residence and includes among others dogs, cats, gerbils, guinea pigs, hamsters, reptiles, birds, turtles, and tropical fish.'" *Graff v. Zoning Board of Appeals* (Conn., 2006).

## HOUSING, ECHO

**A small housing unit on a concrete foundation or slab in the rear or side yard of a dwelling.**

***Comment***: Echo housing is also known as "granny" flats or elder cottage housing. It permits an older person to live independently but close to relatives. The cottage typically consists of one bedroom, a bathroom, a living room, and a kitchen and is connected to the utility system of the main unit (Andrews 2005: 7).

***Legal Annotation***: "Section 15.2. Definitions

A. **ECHO** Lot: Land occupied or to be occupied by **ECHO** units and accessory buildings permitted herein, together with such open spaces as are required under this Ordinance and having its principal frontage upon a street.

B. **ECHO** Unit: A single family residential dwelling unit with full facilities for residential self-sufficiency in each individual dwelling unit which has a resident who is an elderly person.

C. **ECHO** Village: An ECHO Village is a housing development which meets the unique needs of the elderly through the provision of significant facilities and services specifically designed to meet the physical or social needs of such residents." *Zoning Ordinance Hamburg Township, Livingston County, Michigan Article 15.00 2 E.C.H.O.* Printed on: 3/2008. http://www.hamburg.mi.us/lawroom/PDFS/ZONING%20ORDINANCE/ART15-Elderly%20Cottage.pdf

## HOUSING ELEMENT

**That portion of the master plan consisting of reports, statements, proposals, maps, diagrams, and text designed to meet the municipality's fair share of its region's present and prospective housing needs, particularly with regard to low- and moderate-income housing.**

*Comment*: Housing elements usually include a good deal of other information as required by state law. In New Jersey, for example, the following information is required in a housing element:

- An inventory of the municipality's housing stock by age, condition, purchase or rental value, occupancy characteristics, and type, including the number of units affordable to low- and moderate-income households and substandard housing capable of being rehabilitated;
- A projection of the municipality's housing stock, including the probable future construction of low- and moderate-income housing, for the next six years, taking into account, but not necessarily limited to, construction permits issued, approvals of applications for development, and probable residential development of lands;
- An analysis of the municipality's demographic characteristics, including, but not limited to, household size, income level, and age;
- An analysis of the existing and probable future employment characteristics of the municipality;
- A determination of the municipality's present and prospective fair share for low- and moderate-income housing and its capacity to accommodate its present and prospective housing needs, including its fair share for low- and moderate-income housing; and
- A consideration of the lands that are most appropriate for construction of low- and moderate-income housing and of the existing structures most appropriate for conversion to, or rehabilitation for, low- and moderate-income housing, including a consideration of lands of developers who have expressed a commitment to provide low-and moderate-income housing.

*Legal Annotation*: "The **housing element** 'shall contain an analysis demonstrating that it will provide . . . a realistic opportunity [for its fair share of low- and moderate-income housing], and the municipality shall establish that its land use and other relevant ordinances have been revised to incorporate provisions for low and moderate income housing.'" *The Hills Development Co. v. Bernards Township* (N.J., 1986).

## HOUSING, MULTIGENERATIONAL

**Housing designed to accommodate separate households consisting of two or more generations of related family members, such as elderly parents or parent, recently married offspring, recent graduates, etc., in separate attached, connected, or internal dwelling units.**

*Comment*: According to the Pew Research Center, over 16 percent of the US population now lives in households with two or more adult generations, and all indications are that it will continue to increase. Multigenerational housing is designed to accommodate these families. It affords both independence and privacy, as well supervision and assistance where needed.

About 75 percent of a multigenerational house is occupied by the primary resident, and the remainder by other relatives, with their own kitchen, bathroom, and bedrooms. Some housing now being built to accommodate multigenerational living (Lenmar Builders, KB Homes, for example) calls for two or more households in one structure with separate entrances yet with inner connections as needed.

Zoning issues for this housing type might best be addressed by providing appropriate development and design standards (density, height, coverage, parking, aesthetics, etc.) as part of a conditional use category in specific zones. In addition, the standards might require that the homeowner live in the main or a secondary dwelling. The multigenerational units offer communities a method to meet the need for smaller and less expensive housing.

One additional point that should be noted: A multigenerational unit not occupied by a family member, and with its own bedroom, bathroom, kitchen, and a separate ingress and egress, might cause the house to be classified as a two-family home. This could pose problems if it is located in a single-family zoning district (Abrams 2013; Graham and Niederhaus 2013).

***Legal Annotation***: "[T]hey allege that all parties involved knew that the square footage was important because the Plaintiffs intended to demolish the house and construct a much larger one to accommodate their **multi-generational** family." *Kermali v. Belli* (N.Y. Sup. Ct., 2010).

## HOUSING, RETIREMENT

**See *Housing for the Elderly*.**

## HOUSING, SHARED

**Two or more unrelated persons living in a single dwelling unit.**

***Comment***: Shared housing is primarily used to reduce costs to increase the supply of housing for individuals who cannot afford to live alone, such as students, the elderly, recent graduates, etc. Some municipalities have set up formal mechanisms where persons with extra room in their dwelling units are matched up with individuals seeking housing.

A distinction can be made between shared housing and boardinghouses. Boardinghouses generally lease a specific room to the tenant, and kitchen privileges are not usually available. Shared housing allows for much greater use of all rooms (except bedrooms). It is clearly not a fraternity house. **See *Fraternity House*.**

***Legal Annotation***: "24 C.F.R. § 982.615 (2009) provides: '(a) Sharing a unit. An assisted family may reside in **shared housing**. In **shared housing**, an assisted family shares a unit with the other resident or residents of the unit.'" *Welke v. Dakota County Community Development Agency* (Minn: Court of Appeals 2010).

"IH has been attempting to develop two sites in Fairfax for more than a decade. Eventually, after various proposals, IH sought administrative approval of a '**shared housing**' development on the sites, to consist of nineteen bedrooms in six buildings, with each of five buildings containing one shared kitchen and other common facilities. The project required a series of permits and variances." *Park Area Neighbors v. Town of Fairfax* (Calif. Ct. App., 1994).

## HOUSING FOR THE ELDERLY

**Multifamily housing designed for older people. See *Adult Retirement Community; Assisted Living Facility; Congregate Residences; Continuing Care Retirement Community; Retirement Community*.**

***Legal Annotation***: "Moreover, that ruling is unquestionably correct; the zoning ordinance specifically provides that **housing for the elderly** is a permitted special use in multiple-family zones." *Smith & Lee Associates v. City of Taylor* (6th Cir., 1996).

## HOUSING REGION

**That geographic area surrounding or adjacent to a municipality from which the bulk of the employment within the municipality is drawn; or the area surrounding or adjacent to the municipality where most of the residents of the municipality are employed.**

***Comment***: The issue of housing region has assumed even greater importance in recent years because of its application in exclusionary housing cases. In the *Mt. Laurel I* case (*Southern Burlington County NAACP v. Township of Mt. Laurel*, 67 N.J. 151, 1975), the court determined the Mt. Laurel housing region as a twenty-mile radius from Camden but stopping at the state boundary. Norman Williams, Jr., in *After Mt. Laurel: The New Suburban Zoning* (Rose and Rothman 1977), defined the housing region as "the area of continuous settlement which coincides roughly with the area within which substantial numbers of people commute to work in the old center." In *Oakwood at Madison v. Township of Madison* (72 N.J. 481), the court noted the region as "the area from which, in view of available employment and transportation, the population of the township would be drawn absent invalidly exclusionary zoning." In many other exclusionary zoning cases, the work/resident/trip destination forms the basis of the housing region from which fair share allocations can then be made.

*Legal Annotation*: "On the other hand, § 4(b) of the act defines '**housing region**' as 'a geographic area of no less than two nor more than four contiguous, whole counties which exhibit significant social, economic and income similarities.' . . . There is an element of arbitrariness in any method of delineating **housing regions** for the purpose of determining a municipality's regional fair share obligation." *Morris County Fair Housing Council v. Boonton Township* (N.J., 1985).

## HOUSING UNIT

**A room or group of rooms used by one or more individuals living separately from others in the structure, with direct access to the outside or to a public hall and containing separate bedroom, bathroom and kitchen facilities. See *Dwelling Unit*.**

*Comment*: The Census 2010 definition of "housing unit" drops the requirement for cooking facilities and allows above-the-garage quarters and group homes to be defined as housing units. The census defines a housing unit as a house, an apartment, a mobile home, a group of rooms, or a single room that is occupied (or if vacant, intended to be occupied) as separate living quarters.

*Legal Annotation*: "The majority concludes that the Plainfield zoning ordinance prohibiting more than four unrelated individuals from sharing a single **housing unit** violates . . . the New Jersey Constitution." *State v. Baker* (N.J., 1979).

## HUMAN-CENTERED DESIGN

**See *Universal Design*.**

## HUMAN SCALE

**The proportional relationship of a particular building, structure, open space enclosure, or streetscape element to the human form and function.**

*Comment*: Designing to the human scale has assumed greater importance in the urban environment because of the predominance of the automobile. In US cities, the predominance of highways, streets, parking lots, and driveways and the impact they have had in separating buildings and other elements in the urban form have created built forms that dwarf human beings. Designing spaces that are oriented to the human scale—buildings spaced closely apart, and narrow, automobile-free pathways—allows humans to feel more closely related and more comfortable in such environments. Medieval cities in Europe are examples of environments built to human scale.

*Legal Annotation*: "This section is intended to promote the design of an urban environment that is built to **human scale** and to encourage street fronts that create a pedestrian-conducive environment, while also accommodating vehicular movement." *Wal-Mart Stores v. City of Oregon City* (Ore. Ct. App., 2006).

## HUMUS

**Decomposed organic material.**

*Legal Annotation*: "The biologically active portion of the forest floor consists of the following: the litter (or topmost layer, comprised of leaves and large pieces of plant matter); the duff layer (organic matter in a more advanced state of decomposition than the litter layer); and the **humus** layer (most commonly known as soil, which is divided for descriptive purposes into the A-horizon (topmost) and the B-horizon)." *Sierra Club v. Glickman* (E.D. Texas 1997).

## HYBRID ZONING

**See *Zoning, Hybrid*.**

## HYDRAULIC FRACTURING

**A mining technique that employs pressurized fluid to create fractures in a rock layer or tight shale formation, to permit the release of petroleum, natural gas, or other substances for extraction.**

*Comment*: Also known as "fracking," this horizontal mining technique is particularly useful in shale formations that do not have sufficient permeability to economically extract oil or gas with a vertical well. Hydraulic fracturing has raised environmental concerns, including contamination from the fluids used, risks to air quality from methane gas leakage, the migration of gases and hydraulic fracturing chemicals to the surface, the mishandling of process wastes, and ground and subsurface water contamination (Bust 2012).

From a zoning and planning perspective, hydraulic fracturing requires substantial environmental and development studies to determine the necessary safeguards needed to mitigate expected impacts.

*Legal Annotation:* "Applying for a permit is a process; drilling is a process; casing is a process; **hydraulic fracturing** is a process; pumping is a process; storing fluids is a process; separating oil and water is a process; transporting oil and gas is a process; and conditioning gas to a marketable standard is a process. It does not make any sense to find all of the above 'processes' to be production, except for the conditioning of the gas." *In re Bradford v. Tp. Zoning Hearing Board* (Pa. Common. Ct., 2012).

## HYDROLOGY

**The science dealing with the properties, distribution, and circulation of water and snow. *See Figure 6.***

***Legal Annotation***: "Scientists and legislators have recognized the unique ecological and economic value that wetlands provide in protecting water quality, regulating local **hydrology**, preventing flooding, and preventing erosion." *R&Y, Inc. v. Municipality of Anchorage* (Alaska, 2001).

## HYDROPHYTIC VEGETATION

**Wetlands vegetation consisting of plant life adapted to growth and reproduction under periodically saturated root-zone conditions during at least a portion of the growing season.**

*Legal Annotation*: "**Hydrophytic vegetation** is present if greater than fifty percent of the dominant plant species are obligate wetland plants, facultative wetland plants, or facultative plants (excluding facultative negative)." *US v. Bailey* (8th Cir., 2009).

# I

## IESNA

**Illuminating Engineering Society of North America.**

*Comment*: Also referred to as IES, their most important contribution to land use regulation is the publication of lighting standards that many zoning ordinances reference as standards that must be met by development. Their most important publication is *The Lighting Handbook*, now in its 10th edition.

*Legal Annotation*: "Section 281-48.C(2)(b) of the Land Development Ordinance requires lighting fixtures to meet '**IES**NA [**Illuminating Engineering Society** of North America] full-cutoff criteria.' Section 281-48.C(3)(f) provides that '[t]he amount of illumination projected onto any nonresidential property line from another property shall not exceed 1.0 vertical foot candle measured line-of-sight from any point on the property.'" *In Re Appeal of Main Street at Exton, LP* (Pa. Comm. Ct., 2010).

## ILLUMINATED SIGN

**See *Sign, Illuminated*.**

## IMAGE

**The mental picture or impression of a community or place held in common by members of the community or place. See *Branding*.**

## IMPACT ANALYSIS

**A study to determine the potential direct or indirect effects of a proposed development on activities, utilities, stormwater runoff, circulation, surrounding land uses, community facilities, environment, and other factors. See *Fiscal Impact Analysis; Environmental Impact Statement*.**

*Comment*: The impact analysis also can include fiscal, aesthetic, social, and legal impacts. The impact analysis serves a variety of functions. It should point out what impact the proposed development will have on the factors considered and what steps are needed to mitigate the impact. This is particularly true for environmental considerations, stormwater management, and utility needs. For projects that require variances, the impact analysis can be used to determine whether substantial detriment would result—an important criterion in the granting of a variance. Finally, impact analysis allows the municipality to plan. If, for example, a development of houses is expected to generate a given number of school-age children, an impact analysis can alert the local board of education of the need to accommodate the additional load.

*Legal Annotation*: "Most important, it performs no cumulative **impact analysis** of 'reasonably foreseeable future actions' outside the Sandy-Remote Area that, in combination with the Sandy-Remote timber sales, could constitute 'collectively significant actions . . . over a period of time.'" *Kern v. US Bureau of Land Management* (9th Cir., 2002).

## IMPACT FEE

**A fee imposed on a development to help finance the cost of public improvements.**

*Comment*: Developers have long been required to pay for the cost of improvements necessitated by a development. These improvements include on- and off-site roads, utilities, and stormwater management facilities. Developers have also been required to pay for their fair share of off-tract facilities that are needed as a result of their development. Through this method, off-tract intersections may be improved, water and sewer mains enlarged, and additional off-tract drainage basins constructed.

Impact fees are an extension of the philosophy that developments should pay their own way. Thus, where permitted by state legislation and local ordinance, an impact fee may be imposed on development for roads, schools, parks, fire stations, libraries, and other such public facilities. Where impact fees are permitted, they must be specific, based on a reasonable formula, and uniformly applied.

*Legal Annotation*: "With respect to the calculation of development **impact fees**, the statute states that the governmental entity considering adopting development **impact fees** 'shall conduct a needs assessment' for the types of public facilities for which fees are to be levied, and it states that the amount of the development **impact fees** 'shall be based upon actual cost of public facility expansion or improvements, or reasonable estimates of the cost, to be incurred.' . . . The statute further provides that the amount of the development **impact fees** 'must be reasonably related to or reasonably attributable to the development's share of the cost of infrastructure improvements made necessary by the development,' and it sets forth factors to be considered in order to ensure that the fees do not 'exceed a proportionate share' of the costs incurred by the governmental entity in accommodating the development." *North End Realty, LLC v. Mattos* (R.I., 2011).

## IMPERMEABLE

**Not permitting the passage of water.**

*Legal Annotation*: "The critical question, according to NGWC, is whether the bed and banks are sufficiently **impermeable** that they 'prevent the transmission of all but relatively minor quantities through the channel boundary.'" *North Gualala Water v. State North Resources Control Board* (Calif. Ct. App., 2006).

## IMPERVIOUS COVERAGE

**See *Lot Coverage.***

*Legal Annotation*: "The upsurge of development in the area has caused 'increased nutrient loading of the lake largely because of the increase in **impervious coverage** of land in the Basin resulting from that development.' . . . '**Impervious coverage**—such as asphalt, concrete, buildings, and even packed dirt—prevents precipitation from being absorbed by the soil. Instead, the water is gathered and concentrated by such coverage. Larger amounts of water flowing off a driveway or a roof have more erosive force than scattered raindrops falling over a dispersed area—especially one covered with indigenous vegetation, which softens the impact of the raindrops themselves.'" *Tahoe-Sierra Preservation Council, Inc. v. Tahoe Regional Planning Agency* (U.S., 2002).

## IMPERVIOUS SURFACE

**A surface that has been compacted or covered with a layer of material so that it is highly resistant to infiltration by water. *See Figure 62.***

***Comment***: One method by which impervious surfaces can be defined is in terms of a percolation rate in minutes per inch. For example, the New Jersey State Standards for Construction of Individual Subsurface Sewage Disposal Systems define impervious formations as having a percolation rate slower than 120 minutes per inch. Retention and detention basins and dry wells allowing water to percolate directly into the ground usually are not considered impervious surfaces. Graveled areas

**Figure 62**

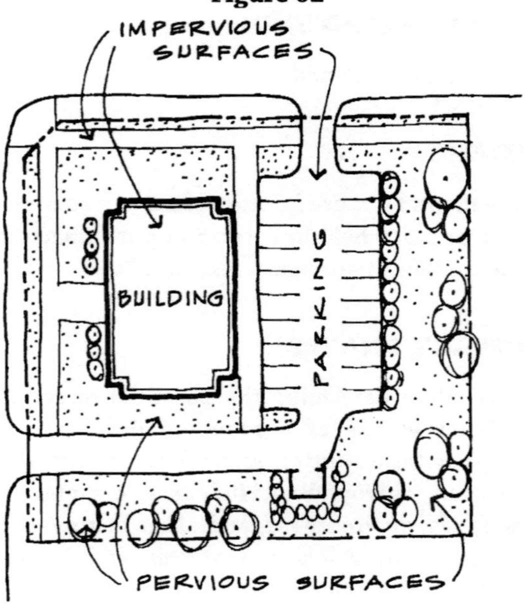

initially allow a significant amount of percolation, but with heavy traffic and use, they become less pervious. Local ordinances often allow not more than 50 percent of graveled areas to be counted as pervious. Concerns relating to the amount of a site that is covered by impervious surfaces include increasing the rate and pollutant load from stormwater runoff, contributions to the "heat-island effect," and deprivation of tree roots of aeration.

See *Detention Basin; Retention Basin.*

*Legal Annotation*: **"Impervious surface** is surface which has been improved so it no longer absorbs and delays rainfall runoff." *Zelinger v. City and County of Denver* (Colo., 1986).

"It is axiomatic that increasing the amount of **impervious surface** will increase the quantity and rate of storm water flow from petitioner's property." *Dolan v. City of Tigard* (U.S., 1994).

## IMPLEMENTATION

**The carrying out or fulfillment of plans and/or proposals.**

*Legal Annotation*: "The heart of the Amendments is the requirement that each State formulate, subject to EPA approval, an **implementation** plan designed to achieve national primary ambient air quality standards—those necessary to protect the public health—'as expeditiously as practicable.'" *Union Elec. Co. v. EPA* (U.S., 1976).

## IMPOUNDMENT

**A body of water, such as a pond, confined by a dam, dike, floodgate, or other barrier.**

*Legal Annotation*: "The Central and South Florida Flood Control Project (Project) consists of a vast array of levees, canals, pumps, and water **impoundment** areas in the land between south Florida's coastal hills and the Everglades." *South Florida Management Dist. v. Miccosukee Tribe* (U.S., 2004).

## IMPROVED PARKING AREA

**An area for the parking of motor vehicles that has been modified from its natural condition by excavation, fill, paving, or deck or structure.**

*Legal Annotation*: "[T]he 'History' section of the report provides, 'The subject property now consists of the parking lot on Parcel 1, the Maple Island Hardware store building (including the Wrap and Ship store) on Parcel 2, and a 51,360 square foot **improved parking area** donated by the city.'" *Federal Deposit Insurance Corporation v. Prill (D. Minn., 2014).*

## IMPROVED PUBLIC STREET

**See *Street, Improved Public.***

## IMPROVEMENT

**Any permanent structure that becomes part of, is placed upon, or is affixed to real estate.**

*Legal Annotation*: "Relevant criteria for determining what constitutes an '**improvement** to real property' include: whether the addition was meant to be permanent or temporary, whether it became an integral component of the overall system, whether the value of the property was increased, and whether the use of the property was enhanced." *St. Louis v. Rockwell Graphic Systems, Inc.* (Ill., 1992).

## INCENTIVE ZONING

**See *Zoning, Incentive.***

## INCIDENTAL

**Subordinate and minor in significance and bearing a reasonable relationship to the primary use.**

*Legal Annotation*: "Zoning ordinances which permit 'customarily **incidental**' accessory uses to the main activity permit, by implication, any use that logic and reason dictate are necessary or expected in conjunction with the principal use of the property." *Charlie Brown of Chatham, Inc. v. Board of Adjustment for Township of Chatham* (N.J. App. Div., 1985).

## INCINERATION

**A process in which all of the combustion factors related to burning waste substances—**

**temperature, retention time, turbulence, and combustion air—can be controlled.**

*Legal Annotation*: "The plain meaning of this language is that so long as a facility recovers energy by **incineration** of the appropriate wastes, it (the facility) is not subject to Subtitle C regulation as a facility that treats, stores, disposes of, or manages hazardous waste." *Chicago v. Environmental Defense Fund* (U.S., 1994).

## INCINERATOR

**A furnace or similar apparatus for burning waste, trash, or garbage.**

*Legal Annotation*: "Since 1971, petitioner city of Chicago has owned and operated a municipal **incinerator**, the Northwest Waste-to-Energy Facility, that burns solid waste and recovers energy, leaving a residue of municipal waste combustion (MWC) ash." *Chicago v. Environmental Defense Fund* (U.S., 1994).

## INCLUSIONARY DEVELOPMENT

**A residential housing development in which a percentage of the dwelling units are affordable to low- and moderate-income households.**

*Comment*: Depending on state law, inclusionary developments may include specific percentages of lower-income dwelling units (20 percent, for example) and specify a reasonable affordable income range (low income, up to 50 percent of median family income; moderate, up to 80 percent of median family income).

*Legal Annotation*: "N.J.A.C. 5:93-8.10(c) 'authorizes the imposition of development fees on owners of sites zoned for **inclusionary development** and provides that: "[m]unicipalities may allow developers of sites zoned for **inclusionary development** to pay a fee in lieu of building low and moderate income units . . . The fee may equal the cost of subsidizing the low and moderate income units that are replaced by the development fee."' *Bi-County Inc. v. Borough of High Bridge* (N.J.2002).

## INCLUSIONARY ZONING

**See *Zoning, Inclusionary*.**

## INDIGENOUS NEED

**Existing deficient housing units within a municipality that are occupied by low- and moderate-income households. See *Surrogate*.**

*Comment*: Indigenous need refers to those dwelling units in a municipality that are deemed deficient (formerly known as dilapidated) and occupied by lower-income households. In fair-share programs, indigenous housing is part of the present need, as opposed to a prospective need.

*Legal Annotation*: "Present need consists of the **indigenous need** of a municipality and the fair share of the reallocated excess need of the municipality's present need region. **Indigenous need** is defined as substandard housing currently existing in any municipality." *AMG Realty Co. v. Warren Township* (N.J. Super Ct., 1984).

## INDIRECT SOURCE

**A pollution source that by its nature attracts large numbers of polluting sources while not actually releasing the pollutant itself.**

*Comment*: Indirect sources of pollution may include parking lots, roofs, and retention and detention basins.

*Legal Annotation*: "An **indirect source** is defined in the [Clean Air Act] as 'a facility, building, structure, installation, real property, road, or highway which attracts, or may attract, mobile sources of pollution. Such term includes parking lots, parking garages, and other facilities subject to any measure for management of parking supply.'" *Sierra Club v. Larson* (1st Cir., 1993).

## INDIVIDUAL SEWAGE DISPOSAL SYSTEM

**A system for the treatment and disposal of sanitary sewage in the ground of the lot upon which the primary use is located. *See Figure 32*.**

*Comment*: Also referred to as "on-site septic systems." Septic systems are designed and constructed to treat sewage in a manner that will retain most of the settleable solids in a septic tank and discharge the liquid portion to a disposal field.

***Legal Annotation***: "That in areas not currently served by public sewer systems it is the responsibility of the subdivider to provide adequate information to prove that the area of each lot is adequate to permit the installation and operation of an **individual sewage disposal system**." *Smith v. Town of Wolfeboro* (N.H., 1992).

## INDOOR RECREATION CENTER

**A permanent structure housing facilities for recreational activities such as tennis, platform games, swimming, exercise rooms, handball, and similar activities.**

***Comment***: The definition does not differentiate between recreational centers operated by public or semipublic agencies such as a local board of education, YMCA, or commercial recreation center. Indoor recreation centers may also include facilities for lectures, arts and crafts, and special events. They may include child-care centers, snack bars, retail shops, and instruction in various games. Zoning and site design considerations include parking, circulation, aesthetics, hours of operation, and impact on surrounding areas (Schultz and Kasen 1984).

***Legal Annotation***: "She admitted that the city has provided a swimming pool, baseball and softball fields, a gym, tennis courts, and a recreation center in an area of town that is predominantly black. . . . [T]he city's director of planning . . . testified that the city converted a garbage dump into the area now served by tennis courts, baseball fields, and the **indoor recreation center**." *Houston v. Haley* (N.D. Miss., 1987).

## INDOOR TENNIS FACILITY

**A building or structure containing one or more roofed and enclosed tennis courts.**

***Legal Annotation***: "[T]he board of appeals of the town of Longmeadow (board) granted a special permit . . . for the use of land in a residence zone for the construction of a building to house an eight court **indoor tennis facility** to be operated by the Meadows Racquet Club, a club not conducted for profit." *Kiss v. Board of Appeals of Longmeadow* (Mass., 1976).

## INDUCED TRAVEL DEMAND

**In traffic engineering, the creation of traffic demand by adding road or highway capacity.**

***Comment***: Proponents of mass transit point out that widening roads actually increases congestion by inducing travel demand. In addition, development often follows road improvements, further adding to traffic volumes.

***Legal Annotation***: "Sierra Club next argues the FEIS did not adequately address **induced travel [demand]**. According to various studies, increased highway capacity attracts increased levels of vehicle traffic. **Induced travel** occurs when the supply of available highway space lowers the cost of travel, particularly in terms of time, thereby inducing travelers to take trips they otherwise would not take because of the concomitant costs." *Sierra Club v. US Dept. of Transportation* (D. Nev., 2004).

## INDUSTRIAL PARK

**A tract of land that is planned, developed, and operated as a coordinated and integrated facility for a number of separate industrial uses, with consideration for circulation, parking, signage, utility needs, aesthetics, and compatibility.**

***Comment***: Modern industrial parks include support facilities for the principal uses, such as hotels, restaurants, recreation, banking and business services, child-care centers, and telecommunications facilities. Individual uses are often subdivided for financing purposes, but cross easements are required to ensure that circulation, utilities, signage, parking, and other facilities are maintained and available to all uses in the industrial park. A good reference for industrial park development standards is the *Business Park and Industrial Development Handbook*, published by the Urban Land Institute (Frej et al. 2001). See *Warehouse*.

***Legal Annotation***: "The precise nature of the **industrial park** is now uncertain, for the park's eventual shape depends on what businesses choose to locate there." *Sierra Club v. Marsh* (1st Cir., 1985).

## INDUSTRIAL PROPERTY

**Any parcel of land containing an industrial use or any building containing such uses.**

*Legal Annotation*: "The property is devoted to a fruit orchard and is improved by a five room residence, windmill, tankhouse and barn, but has been zoned as '**industrial property**.'" *Rose v. State of California* (Calif., 1942).

"Reget contends, however, that his property was the only heavy **industrial property** targeted for rezoning. He complained, and the City eventually agreed to abandon its attempt to rezone Reget's property in exchange for his agreement to abide by the junk-dealer ordinance. More specifically, in a covenant signed in 1997, Reget promised to install a fence on several sides of his business to hide his outdoor auto storage from the view of nearby residences. He also agreed to abide by the City's noise restrictions by limiting his nighttime operations." *Reget v. City of La Crosse* (7th Cir., 2010).

## INDUSTRIAL SEPARATOR

**An air pollution control device that uses the principle of inertia to remove particulate matter from a stream of air or gas.**

*Comment*: Also referred to as "cyclonic separators."

*Legal Annotation*: "The proposal for revision included three **cyclonic separators** as means of air pollution control." *Weyerhaeuser Co. v. Southwest Air Pollution Control* (Wash., 1979).

## INDUSTRIAL WASTE

**Liquid, gaseous, chemical, and solid residue or by-products of an industrial process.**

*Legal Annotation*: "The zoning ordinance in effect when Blue Circle commenced its fuel conversion project in the early 1980s required industrial operators to obtain a conditional use permit to establish an '**industrial waste** disposal' site." *Blue Circle Cement v. Board of County Commissioners* (10th Cir., 1994).

## INDUSTRY

**Those fields of economic activity including forestry, fishing, hunting, and trapping; mining; construction; manufacturing; transportation, communication, electric, gas, and sanitary services; and wholesale trade.**

*Legal Annotation*: "The EPA noted that it considered input from environmental, **industry**, engineering, and governmental entities, held symposia to discuss research and costs of proposed technologies, and considered the materials from the Phase I and II rule makings." *ConocoPhillips Co. v. USEPA* (5th Cir., 2010).

## INDUSTRY, HEAVY

**Industrial uses engaged in heavy manufacturing, sewage treatment and disposal facilities, electric generating plants and facilities, incinerators and landfills, water purification facilities, automobile and truck body shops, junkyards and salvage yards, human and animal crematories, motor freight terminals, used motor vehicle storage and impoundment yards, and firing ranges. See *Industry, Light; Manufacturing, Heavy*.**

*Comment*: As indicated in the commentary under INDUSTRY, LIGHT, there are two approaches to defining industrial uses. The first approach is to specifically list those uses that are so classified (in the case above), in addition to heavy manufacturing, such as solid waste disposal and treatment facilities, electric generation plants and facilities, and incinerators and landfills. The second approach is a "performance-standard based approach," where performance, bulk, and other standards are included in the ordinance, and where the ordinance would indicate that uses that meet such standards would be classified as "heavy industrial uses." It should be noted that industrial zoning is still for the most part "cumulative," in that light industrial zoning typically allows light manufacturing and other related uses that have minimal impacts, whereas heavy industrial zones permit both light industrial uses and heavy manufacturing. It is typically the inclusion of the "heavy manufacturing" and other, more noxious, uses that distinguishes heavy from light industrial zones.

*Legal Annotation*: "Thus the statute defines **heavy industry** use not only in terms of its physical characteristics but also in terms of its potential to pollute in the event of equipment failure or human error." *Kreshtool v. Delmarva Power & Light Co.* (Del. Super. Ct., 1973).

## INDUSTRY, LIGHT

**Industrial uses engaged in light manufacturing, packaging, storage, and distribution of products, including warehousing, wholesaling, and shipping and receiving, and scientific research development and training, kennel and animal hospitals, new vehicle storage, and vehicle transportation service establishments. See *Industry, Heavy; Manufacturing, Light.***

*Comment*: Light industry can be defined in two ways. One way, as in the definition above, provides a list of specific uses that fall into this category, including "light manufacturing," which is specifically defined in this book and for which a number of examples are provided in the comment under the definition. This definition is useful for those who wish to simply plug a definition into a zoning ordinance. An alternate approach, as discussed in the introduction to the book under "The Purpose of Definitions," is to define *light industry* as the "industrial uses that meet specific performance standards, bulk controls, and other requirements," which standards are then included in other sections of the ordinance. This would include "performance standards" (another term that is defined in this book) as well as other standards, such as "employing fewer than five hundred persons, with an emphasis on activities other than manufacturing," as suggested in the Institute of Transportation Engineers (ITE) *Trip Generation Handbook*, now in its tenth edition.

For those who are intent on using the definition above and utilizing an approach wherein specific activities are listed, as opposed to using a "performance-standard based approach," the key is to only include those industrial uses that do not produce any corrosion; toxic, noxious fumes; glare; electromagnetic disturbances; radiation; smoke, cinders, odors, dust, or waste; undue noise or vibration; or other objectionable features so as to be detrimental to the public health, safety, or general welfare.

*Legal Annotation*: "'**Light Industry**' is defined in Section 202 of the [Hazlet Township] Zoning Ordinance as: 'A use engaged in the manufacture, predominantly from previously prepared materials, of finished products or parts, including processing, fabrication, assembly, treatment, packaging, incidental storage, sales and distribution of such products, but excluding basic industrial processing.'" *Hawbaker, Inc. v. Zoning Hearing Board of Hazlet Township* (Pa: Comm. Ct., 2011).

## INFILL

**The act of encouraging, planning for, or approving development of new housing or other uses on scattered vacant sites in a built-up area.**

*Comment*: Infill is an important component of smart growth (Shigley 2006; Listokin et al. 2007).

## INFILL DEVELOPMENT

**Development that takes place on vacant or underutilized parcels within an area that is already characterized by urban development and has access to urban services. http://www.pgplanning.org/Resources/Tools_On-line/Glossary.htm**

*Legal Annotation*: "The new code permitted development of any number of substandard lots, regardless of common ownership of adjacent lots. The purpose of liberalizing the code was to encourage **infill development** of housing on vacant lots in single-family zones." *Tekoa Construction v. City of Seattle* (Wash. Ct. App., 1989).

## INFILTRATION

**(1) The flow of water into soil; (2) unplanned and unwanted stormwater flow into a sanitary sewer system. *See Figure 6.***

*Legal Annotation*: "**Infiltration** is water which leaks from the ground into the sewer through such sources as broken pipes, defective joints, and leaky manhole barrels. . . . As a result of excessive infiltration, raw or untreated sewage has been discharged into the Shenango River and its tributaries during periods of heavy rainfall." *Pymatuning Water Shed Citizens v. Eaton* (W. D. Penn., 1980).

## INFRASTRUCTURE

**Facilities and services needed to sustain all land-use activities.**

***Comment***: Infrastructure includes water and sewer lines and other utilities, streets and roads, communications, and public facilities, such as firehouses, parks, and schools.

***Legal Annotation***: "Thus, we cannot conclude that the statutory language unambiguously excludes cities' and states' physical **infrastructure** as distinct from the panoply of less tangible benefits cities and states offer to their residents, even though it is often through and by these **infrastructures** that the services are delivered." *Frame v. City of Arlington* (5th Cir., 2010).

## INGRESS

**A place or means of gaining access or entry into a property. See Egress.**

***Legal Annotation***: "As a rule, where the intention in granting an easement is to afford only a right of **ingress** and egress, it is the right of passage, and not any right in a physical passageway itself, that is granted to the easement holder." *Lewis v. Young* (N.Y., 1998).

## INHERENTLY BENEFICIAL USES

**(1) Uses that clearly promote the public good; (2) uses of land or buildings having well-recognized value or benefit to a community and that therefore deserve special consideration in the administration of local zoning.**

***Comment***: Inherently beneficial uses are those uses that are essential to society. These uses include schools, child-care centers, medical facilities and nursing homes, public housing, lower-income housing, public utility installations, sewage treatment plants, and places of worship.

Since ordinances do not often zone for many types of inherently beneficial uses, they may require use variances in order to locate in the municipality. In New Jersey, the designation as an inherently beneficial use relieves the applicant of the obligation of proving special reasons for the use. The use still must meet the negative criteria that it will not be substantially detrimental to the public good and will not substantially impair the intent and purpose of the zone plan and zoning ordinance (N.J.S.A. 40:55D-70d).

Because of the potential diversity, size, and complexity of such uses, a recommended approach to their regulation is to classify them as conditional uses in the local development ordinance and include appropriate development standards for each use.

***Legal Annotation***: "New Jersey statute 'defines '**inherently beneficial use**' as 'a use which is universally considered of value to the community because it fundamentally serves the public good and promotes the general welfare.'" *Dalessio v. Township of Upper Deerfield* (N.J. App. Div., 2011).

## INN

**An establishment where travelers are provided lodging, food, and drink.**

***Comment***: An inn is commonly distinguished from a hotel or motel by its size and its purportedly more personal atmosphere. Inns often are contained in whole or in part in buildings that were previously private residences. See *Bed And Breakfast; Hotel; Motel.*

***Legal Annotation***: "Appellant fails to demonstrate, and we are unable to determine a significant difference between a small motel and a bed and breakfast **inn**. The *Webster's New World Dictionary*, Third College Edition (1988), defines '**inn**' as 'an establishment or building providing lodging, and usually food or drink for travelers; hotel or motel especially one in the country or along a highway.'" *Robins v. Walter* (Fla. Ct. App., 1995).

## INOPERABLE VEHICLE

**Any vehicle at present inoperable but capable of being repaired to place it in operating condition without exceeding its present estimated value and repair cost.**

*Legal Annotation*: "Municipal Code of the City of Des Moines defines '**inoperable vehicle**' as: 'Any motor vehicle, recreational vehicle, boat, trailer, or semitrailer which lacks a current registration or component part which renders the vehicle unfit for legal use.'" *City of Des Moines v. Gruen* (Iowa, 1990).

## INSTITUTIONAL USE

**A nonprofit, religious, or public use, such as a religious building, library, public or private school, hospital, or government-owned or operated building, structure, or land used for public purpose.**

*Legal Annotation*: "And, the evidence showed that the property was worth $230,000 as zoned for single-family residential use; whereas the property was worth $760,000 if rezoned for neighborhood shopping, and office and **institutional use**, which was its highest and best use." *Jebco Ventures v. City of Smyrna* (Ga., 1989).

## INTANGIBLE PERSONAL PROPERTY

**"Personal property that cannot be felt or touched, including securities, bonds, certificate of deposit, and other intangible assets". http://biztaxlaw.about.com/od/glossaryp/g/personalprop.html**

*Legal Annotation*: "According to the Appraisal Institute, the value of a going concern is comprised of . . . 3) **intangible personal property**, which includes residual intangibles. See Appraisal Institute, supra, p. 642. Simply put, the calculation 'necessarily involve[s] an allocation among the component parts of real property and tangible and **intangible [personal property]**.' . . . Included in the residual intangible category is capitalized economic profit, or business enterprise value, which is defined as 'the present worth of an entrepreneur's economic (pure) profit expectation.'" *Redding Life Care, LLC v. Town of Redding* (Conn., 2013).

## INTEGRATED LOGISTICS CENTER

**An intermodal (e.g., sea, rail, and highway) transportation, storage, and distribution complex designed to handle goods brought in by ship, train, and truck for transfer to on-site warehouses or storage facilities for later shipment to retail chains, distribution centers, manufacturers, and industrial suppliers.**

*Comment*: Also known as "freight villages," these facilities are usually located with direct and close access to seaports and often airports, as well as the interstate highway system and rail lines. They occupy large land areas (as much as five thousand acres) and generate significant vehicular traffic. They are also major employment centers.

*Legal Annotation*: "The LM Agreement states that Market is in the business of 'providing **integrated logistics management** services, including arranging for and furnishing transportation. . .'" *First National Bank of Danville v. System Transport* (N.D. Ill., 2005).

## INTELLIGENT TRANSPORTATION SYSTEM (ITS)

**A method to maximize the efficiency of the existing roadway system by using computer-based interactive management elements that provide information to motorists and/or are responsive to changing demands. (Adapted from the *New Jersey State Development and Redevelopment Plan* 2002.)**

*Legal Annotation*: "Additionally, DOT has developed an **Intelligent Transportation System (ITS)**, which monitors traffic flow, weather and road conditions . . . [and] the collection of such data aids DOT and public safety entities in being able to 'respond to emergency situations, manage and divert traffic, and provide real-time traffic information to motorists,' thereby improving the safety of the traveling public and reducing travel times." *Crown v. Department of Transportation* (N.Y., 2005).

## INTENSITY OF USE

**The number of dwelling units per acre for residential development and floor area ratio (FAR)**

**for nonresidential development, such as commercial, office, and industrial.**

*Comment*: In small- to medium-sized-lot residential development (lots under one acre), FAR is a very useful tool in maintaining an appropriate relationship between building bulk and lot size.

*Legal Annotation*: "Of course, where the plan adopts general parameters of long term growth with a provision that the **intensity of use** or the density of living units shall not exceed a certain amount, a more restrictive zoning ordinance may be in accord with that plan." *Baker v. City of Milwaukie* (Ore., 1975).

## INTERCEPTOR DRAIN

**Underground drainage system designed to catch and divert stormwater runoff away from a slope or other area sensitive to water erosion or impact.**

*Legal Annotation*: "After assuring Congress that the Department of the Interior had made provision to construct an **interceptor drain** of sufficient capacity to serve the drainage requirements of the San Luis Unit, the Secretary did not have unlimited discretion to determine whether the construction of a drain was necessary at all." *Firebaugh Canal Co. v. US* (9th Cir., 2000).

## INTERCEPTOR SEWER

**Sewers used to collect the flows from main and trunk sewers and carry them to a central point for treatment and/or discharge.**

*Legal Annotation*: "An **interceptor sewer** is '[a] sewer that receives the flow from collector sewers and conveys the wastewater to treatment facilities.'" *Spokane v. Washington Department of Revenue* (Wash., 2002).

## INTERCHANGE

**A grade-separated, bridged system of access to and from highways where vehicles may move from one roadway to another without crossing streams of traffic. See *Grade Separation. See Figure 92.***

*Legal Annotation*: "Reconstruction was undertaken because the design of the exit and entry ramps of the **interchange** is confusing, requiring drivers in some instances to leave one parkway to obtain access to the other, and the road capacity, particularly east of the **interchange**, is inadequate and produces excessive traffic congestion." *Westbury v. Dept. of Transportation* (N.Y., 1989).

## INTERESTED PARTY

**(1) In a criminal or quasi-criminal proceeding, any citizen of the state; (2) in a civil proceeding, in any court, or in an administrative proceeding before a municipal agency, an individual, whether residing within or without the municipality, whose right to use, acquire, or enjoy property is or may be affected by any action taken under any law of the municipality or state or the United States.**

*Legal Annotation*: "*Black's Law Dictionary* thus defines '**interested party**' as '[a] party who has a recognizable stake (and therefore standing) in a matter.'" *Clark Sand Co., Inc. v. Kelly* (Miss., 2011).

## INTERIOR LOT

**See *Lot, Interior.***

## INTERIM ZONING

**See *Zoning, Interim.***

## INTERMEDIATE CARE FACILITY (ICF)

**A facility that provides health-related and personal care services to chronically ill, disabled, or elderly people, including assistance with dressing and eating.**

*Comment*: Intermediate care facilities are provided to those people who require a fairly high degree of assistance but who do not require the degree of care and treatment that a hospital or skilled nursing facility provides. Most states regulate ICFs, which are often grouped under the general term "nursing home" or "long-term care facility." Unlike nursing homes or hospitals, ICFs provide only limited medical supervision, such as the administration of medication or medical treatment by qualified personnel. See *Long-Term Care Facility*.

***Legal Annotation***: "The Health and Safety Code states, '[a]n **intermediate care facility**' means a health facility that provides inpatient care to ambulatory or nonambulatory patients who have recurring need for skilled nursing supervision, but who do not need such care continuously.'" *Kotler v. Alma Lodge* (Calif. Ct. App., 1998).

## INTERMITTENT SOUND

**Sound that is not continuous but of a cyclical or repetitive nature.**

***Legal Annotation***: "They pulled out of the parking place, turned on the turret lights and activated the horn and the siren for **intermittent sound**." *People v. Genn* (N.Y., Sup. Ct., 1989).

## INTERMITTENT STREAM

**A stream that normally flows for at least thirty days after the last major rain of the season and is dry a large part of the year (*California General Plan Glossary* 1997).**

***Legal Annotation***: "Put most starkly, the question is whether a seasonally **intermittent stream** which ultimately empties into a river that is a water of the United States can, itself, be a water of the United States. . . . [W]e answered that question in the affirmative, when we held [that] . . . [e]ven tributaries that flow intermittently are 'waters of the United States.'" *US v. Moses* (9th Cir., 2007).

## INTERMODAL FACILITY

**A facility or system that transfers people, goods, or information between two or more transport modes or networks between an origin and destination ( *New Jersey State Development and Redevelopment Plan 2000*).**

***Legal Annotation***: "The Board found that 'based on careful consideration of the entire record, this is a legitimate rail transportation project, which should be allowed to go forward'. It observed that 'RTR has developed specific plans for constructing an **intermodal facility** for which there is evidence of a current demand . . . [and] taken reasonable steps to prepare for the commencement of rail operations.'" *City of Riverview v. Surface Transp. Bd.* (6th Cir., 2005).

## INTERNAL STREET OR ROAD

**A private street, within a tract or development, meeting all municipal standards used for internal vehicular circulation.**

***Legal Annotation***: "The orientation of buildings and layout of the **internal street** network were heavily considered in this Application. The Applicant did front retail buildings on Seneca Meadows Parkway and Observation Drive consistent with the Sector Plan's recommendations where the topography is flat enough. . . . For the rest of the development, the Applicant ultimately established a primary **internal main street** with smaller blocks that are pedestrian oriented as envisioned by the Sector Plan." *Pringle v. Montgomery Co. Planning Bd.* (Md. Ct. Spec. App., 2013).

## INTERSECTION

**The location where two or more roadways cross at grade without a bridge. See *Junction*. *See Figure 92*.**

***Legal Annotation***: "The transportation code defines '**intersection**' as the common area at the junction of two highways, other than the junction of an alley and a highway." *Krug v. State* (Texas Ct. App., 2002).

## INTERSTATE HIGHWAY

**A countrywide, federally supported network of controlled and limited-access highways.**

***Legal Annotation***: "Indeed, the condition imposed by Congress is directly related to one of the main purposes for which highway funds are expended—safe interstate travel. This goal of the **interstate highway** system had been frustrated by varying drinking ages among the States." *South Dakota v. Dole* (U.S., 1987).

## INTERSTATE WATERS

**(1) Rivers, lakes, and other waters that flow across or form a part of state or international boundaries; (2) waters of the Great Lakes; (3) coastal waters, including ocean waters seaward to the territorial limits and waters along the coastline (including inland streams) influenced by the tide.**

***Legal Annotation***: "The Corps' current regulations interpret 'the waters of the United States' to include, in addition to traditional interstate navigable waters, all **interstate waters** including interstate wetlands; all other waters such as intrastate lakes, rivers, streams (including intermittent streams), mudflats, sandflats, wetlands, sloughs, prairie potholes, wet meadows, playa lakes, or natural ponds, . . . tributaries of [such] waters; and wetlands adjacent to [such] waters." *Rapanos v. US* (U.S., 2006).

## INTERTIDAL AREA

**The land area between high and low tide, also called a beach. See *Beach*. See *Figure 11*.**

***Legal Annotation***: "For these users of the coastal wetland, the pier would be a significant visual intrusion, traversing the entire width of the **intertidal area** (approximately 95 feet) at a height above grade of between ten feet (at the shoreline) to 17 feet (at mean low water). While persons walking the intertidal area would be able to pass beneath the dock, the dock would . . . partially obstruct and/or fragment the view along the **intertidal area**." *Uliano v. Board of Environmental Protection* (Maine, 2009).

## INTRUSIVE SOUND

**Noise that is over and above the existing ambient noise level.**

***Comment***: Noise that is intrusive is obviously "louder" than the ambient noise level. Other factors affecting the intrusive nature include amplitude, duration, frequency, and time of occurrence.

***Legal Annotation***: "E. Unreasonably **intrusive sound**. The making, creation or maintenance of any unreasonably **intrusive sound** is prohibited." *City of Peekskill, NY Chapter 3091: NOISE.*

## INVERSE CONDEMNATION

**The taking or reduction in value of private property as a result of governmental activity without any formal direct exercise of eminent domain.**

***Comment***: An example of an inverse condemnation is the expansion of an airport flight path that brings airplanes so low over residences as to make them uninhabitable.

***Legal Annotation***: "We will conclude that although a landowner so aggrieved may challenge both the constitutionality of the ordinance and the manner in which it is applied to his property by seeking to establish the invalidity of the ordinance . . . he may not recover damages on the theory of **inverse condemnation**." *Agins v. City of Tiburon* (Calif., 1979).

"The chief difference between a condemnation claim and an **inverse condemnation** claim is that the former is initiated by a government entity while the latter is initiated by the landowner." *B & B Enterprises v. City of Lebanon* (Tenn., 2010).

## INVERSION

**An atmospheric condition in which a layer of cool air is trapped by a layer of warm air so that it cannot rise.**

***Comment***: Also referred to as "temperature inversion." Certain cities, such as Los Angeles, have microclimatic conditions that lead to frequent occurrences of temperature inversion, exacerbating air pollution problems.

***Legal Annotation***: "According to Amos's testimony, an **inversion** is a reversal of normal atmospheric temperature gradient in which 'colder air [is] at the surface and it warms up [with a] rise in elevation,' holding surface air and pollutants down." *Mendoza v. Washington State Dept. of Agriculture* (Wash. Ct. App., 2006).

## ISLAND

**(1) A land area totally surrounded by water; (2) in road and parking lot design, a raised planting area, usually curbed, and placed to guide traffic, separate lanes, limit paving (impervious surface), preserve existing vegetation, and increase aesthetic quality.**

***Legal Annotation*:** "'**Island**' means a naturally-formed area of land surrounded by water, which is above the level of mean high water." *US v. California* (U.S., 1966).

"In 1990 the [Department of Natural Resources] added a second lane to the boat ramp and constructed a concrete parking area with lighting . . . [and] installed a six inch curbed **island** in the parking area." *Schaller v. State* (Iowa: Supreme Court 1995). http://tinyurl.com/me5enmc

## ISOLATED LOT

**An undeveloped, undersized lot in separate ownership from surrounding property and not meeting area or bulk requirements for the zone in which it is located. (Cox 2003).**

***Comment*:** The isolated lot invariably becomes the subject of a variance application. Many ordinances address the issue by "grandfathering" such lots or allowing such lots to be developed with any use permitted in the zone, provided that the applicant does not own any adjacent land or has not owned any adjacent land since the ordinance made the lot nonconforming. Where "grandfathering" is not permitted, a New Jersey Supreme Court decision (*Chirichello v. Zoning Board of Adjustment, Borough of Monmouth Beach*, 78 N.J. 544, 1979) offers some guidelines on how to deal with the problem, as follows:

- Did the owner purchase the property knowing, either in fact or constructively, of the deficiency? For example, if the lot became nonconforming by reason of a change in the zoning regulations after the property was purchased, the owner could not have known of the potential disablement.
- Was an offer made to purchase the property at a fair price? If so, there is no hardship. (The court indicated that the fair market value should be based on the assumption that the variance would be granted. Otherwise, the value of the unusable lot would be zero.)
- Conversely, can vacant land be purchased at a fair price that would make the lot conforming?

In addition to proving hardship, the applicant also must satisfy that what is being proposed will not have an adverse impact on surrounding properties or the neighborhood and that the proposed development is consistent with the intent and purpose of the zone plan and ordinance.

***Legal Annotation*:** "It is settled in this State, as well as in other jurisdictions, that a municipality may not destroy the economic value of an **isolated lot** by retroactively prohibiting the erection thereon of a single-family dwelling through adoption of a zoning ordinance prescribing minimum lot size requirements unless relief is available to the owner of such undersized lot." *Dallmeyer v. Lacey Township Board of Adjustment* (N.J. Super. Ct., 1987).

# J

## JET SKI

See *Personal Watercraft*.

## JETTY

See *Breakwater*.

## JOINT OWNERSHIP

**The equal estate interest of two or more persons.**

***Legal Annotation***: "A viable tenancy by the entirety, with regard to either realty or personalty, must possess always and at the same time the following characteristics of form: unity of possession (**joint ownership** and control); unity of interest (the interests must be the same); unity of title (the interests must originate in the same instrument); unity of time (the interests must commence simultaneously); and, the unity of marriage." *First National Bank of Leesburg v. Hector Supply Co.* (Fla., 1971).

## JOURNEY TO WORK

**The worker's daily trip from residence to place of employment and back, by whatever mode of transportation.** ***See Figure 63***.

**Figure 63**

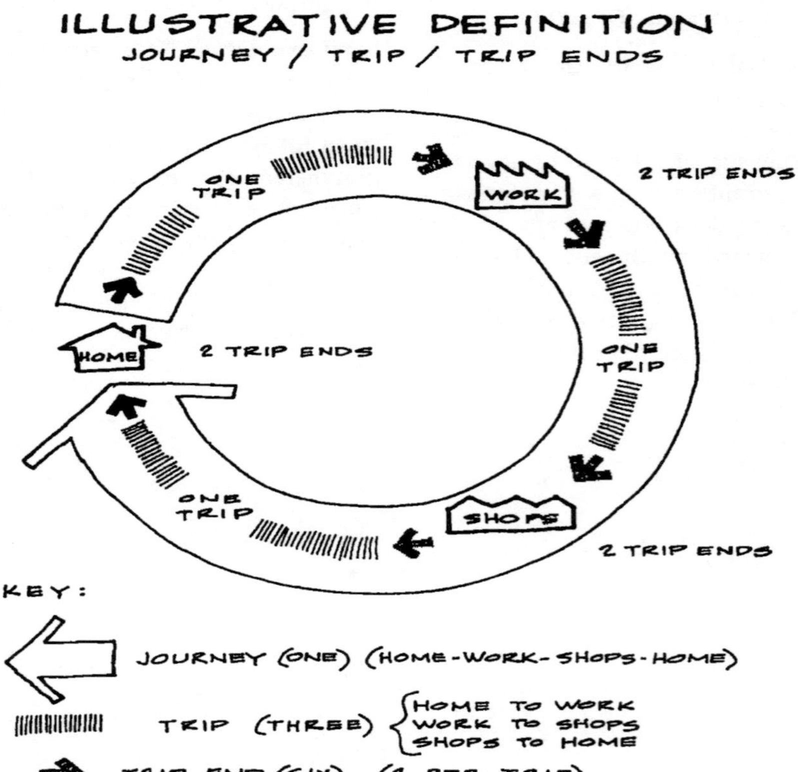

***Legal Annotation***: "The journey home is obviously as foreseeable and essential a part of the special service which an employee is called upon to perform after his regular hours as is the **journey to work** in the case of an early special duty assignment." *Safeway Stores, Inc. v. Workers' Comp. Appeals Board* (Calif. Ct. App., 1980).

## JUNCTION

**A place of joining or crossing of streets or railroads. See *Intersection*.**

***Legal Annotation***: "The bill sets forth the act . . . requiring railroad companies to perform certain duties, among others to stop passenger trains at the **junction** or intersecting points of other railroads." *Herndon v. Chicago Rock Island & Pacific Railway Co.* (U.S., 1910).

## JUNK

**Any scrap, waste, reclaimable material, or debris, whether or not stored, for sale or in the process of being dismantled, destroyed, processed, salvaged, stored, baled, disposed of, or for other use or disposition.**

***Comment***: The definition can also include examples of what constitutes junk, such as unregistered and inoperable vehicles, tires, vehicle parts, equipment, paper, rags, metal, glass, building materials, household appliances, machinery, brush, wood, and lumber. See *Garbage; Solid Waste*.

***Legal Annotation***: "[T]he term **junk** is defined in the Indiana Department of Transportation Act, [which states] '[j]unk means old or scrap copper, brass, rope, rags, batteries, paper, trash, rubber debris, waste, or junked, dismantled, or wrecked automobiles or automobile parts, iron, steel, and other old scrap ferrous or nonferrous material.'" *Saurer v. Board of Zoning Appeals* (Ind. Ct. App., 1994).

## JUNK VEHICLE

**See *Vehicle, Junk*.**

## JUNKYARD

**Any lot, land, parcel, building, or structure, or part thereof, used for the storage, collection, processing, purchase, sale, salvage, or disposal of junk.**

***Comment***: In some jurisdictions, junkyards are prohibited altogether. However, if they are permitted as-of-right or by special exception or as conditional uses, regulations relating to appropriate setbacks, screening, and buffering are required, in addition to meeting performance standards (relating to noise, glare, smoke, fumes, etc.).

***Legal Annotation***: "The **[Fairbanks North Star Borough]** defines '**junkyard**' as 'the use of more than five hundred square feet of the yard of any lot or parcel for the storage or keeping of junk.' 'Junk' is defined as 'dismantled or wrecked automobiles, aircraft, motor vehicles or machinery, mobile homes or trailers; used appliances or furniture; scrap building material.'" *Balough v. Fairbanks North Star Borough* (Alaska, 2000).

## JUST COMPENSATION

**Payment made to a private property owner by an agency with power of eminent domain when private property is taken for public use. See *Eminent Domain; Highest And Best Use; Taking*.**

***Legal Annotation***: "The Takings Clause of the Fifth Amendment, made applicable to the States through the Fourteenth, provides that private property shall not 'be taken for public use, without **just compensation**.' . . . The paradigmatic taking requiring **just compensation** is a direct government appropriation or physical invasion of private property. . . . Our precedents stake out two categories of regulatory action that generally will be deemed per se takings for Fifth Amendment purposes. First, where government requires an owner to suffer a permanent physical invasion of her property—however minor—it must provide **just compensation**. A second categorical rule applies to regulations that completely deprive an owner of 'all economically beneficial us[e]' of her property." *Lingle v. Chevron USA, Inc.* (U.S., 2005).

# K

## KENNEL

**An establishment in which dogs or domesticated animals are housed, groomed, bred, boarded, trained, or sold, all for a fee or compensation.**

***Comment***: Since kennels include animal runs, care must be taken to locate them away from residential areas and provide noise buffers or barriers. Odors and water runoff from cleaning, boarding, or play areas are of similar concern. Many communities license kennels, establishing a minimum number of animals after which a license is required

***Legal Annotation***: "Scott County Zoning Ordinance §2.1.45 defines **'kennel'** as '[a] commercial business for the sale or temporary boarding of three (3) or more dogs over the age of six (6) months, not including those owned by the resident or property owner.'" *McIntosh v. Scott County Board of Adjustment* (Ky.Ct. App., 2013).

## KENNEL, PRIVATE

**The keeping, breeding, raising, showing, or training of four or more dogs over six months of age for personal enjoyment of the owner or occupant of the property.**

***Comment:*** This provision identifies individuals who breed, raise, train, and show dogs. Because of the potential nuisance and neighborhood impact, the primary control should be the size of the property where they are permitted.

***Legal Annotation***: "The zoning ordinance . . . permitted the operation of a **private kennel** as an accessory use and prohibited the operation of a commercial kennel. While in all respects the kennel operated by respondents could have been used as a commercial kennel, the Board of Adjustment found that because the dogs were adopted and not sold, the kennel was not a commercial kennel but a **private kennel** permitted as an accessory use under the zoning ordinance." *Dobo v. Zoning Board of Adjustment of Wilmington* (N.C. Ct. App., 2002).

## KIOSK

**(1) A freestanding structure upon which temporary information and/or posters, notices, and announcements are posted (*See Figures 20 and 64*); (2) an open booth or other structure where items are sold or where a service is performed.**

**Figure 64**

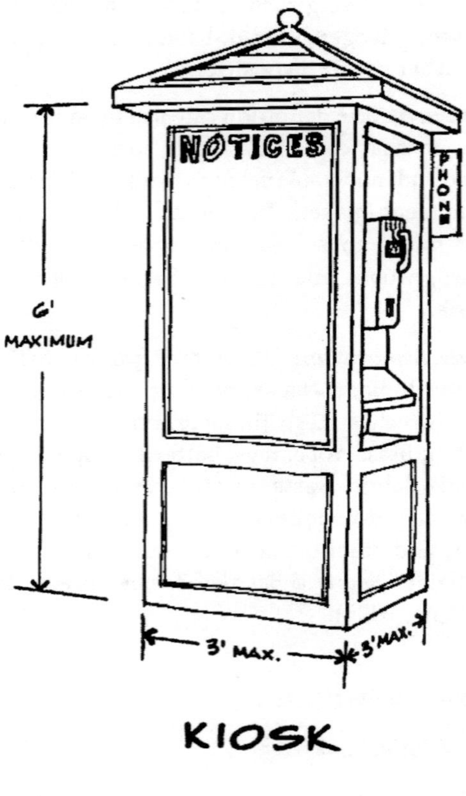

*Comment:* An information kiosk may incorporate a public pay phone and a trash receptacle. Its design should reflect community character. Kiosks that perform retail functions include newsstands, telephone booths, and hot dog stands. The term "kiosk" is sometimes also applied to ATMs or airport self-service check-in booths.

***Legal Annotation***: "The Oxford English Dictionary defines '**kiosk**' to include a 'structure . . . used for the sale of newspapers' and a 'telephone kiosk.' . . . The specification further defines those 'convenient locations' to include, e.g., an airport terminal, a bank, a shopping area, or a store. All of these locations—consistent with the ordinary meaning of 'kiosk' — indicate public accessibility.'" *Decisioning.com, Inc. v. Federated Department Stores, Inc.* (Fed. Cir., 2008).

## KNOLL

**A small, natural round hill or mound.**

***Legal Annotation***: "In February 2007, residents of the Westport subdivision complained to the Mayor of Leland that HWW left a large mound of dirt and debris, approximately ten to fifteen feet in height, in a portion of the recreation area ('the **knoll**')." *Town of Leland, NC v. HWW, LLC* (N.C. Ct. App., 2010).

# L

## LABOR FORCE

**All the population sixteen years of age or older having the potential for active work for wages.**

*Legal Annotation*: "The civilian **labor force** consists of all individuals aged 16 years or older employed or seeking employment in the United States." *Earl v.Vnu USA* (E.D. Calif., 2009).

## LAGOON

**In wastewater treatment, a shallow, artificial pond where sunlight, bacterial action, and oxygen interact to restore wastewater to a reasonable state of purity.**

*Legal Annotation*: "In 1969, the City of Martin built a **lagoon** into which raw sewage is piped from the city's sewer system. Theoretically, in a properly constructed and maintained sewage **lagoon**, sewage sinks to the bottom of a lagoon, where it is decomposed through bacterial action." *Pate v. City of Martin* (Tenn., 1981).

## LAKE

**An inland waterbody fed by springs or surrounding runoff.**

*Legal Annotation*: "The Lakeshore Program . . . defines '**lake**' as: '[A] body of standing water and the area within its lakeshore occurring naturally rather than by virtue of constructed impoundments . . . having a water surface of at least 160 acres for at least 6 months in a year of average precipitation as such averages are determined by the United States geological survey, not used exclusively for agricultural purposes, and navigable by canoes and small boats.'" *Paulson v. Flathead Conservation District* (Mont., 2004).

## LAND

**Ground, soil, or earth, including structures on, above, or below the surface.**

*Legal Annotation*: '**[L]and**' is defined as 'any ground, soil, or earth whatsoever regarded as the subject of ownership and everything annexed to it whether by nature . . . or by man (as buildings . . .) extending indefinitely vertically upwards and downwards.'" *Lake Saint Louis Community Association v. Ravenwood Properties* (Mo. Ct. App., 1988).

## LAND BANK

**An inventory of vacant and/or underutilized publicly owned properties that may be made available for private development, provided requirements of sale can be met.**

*Comment*: The purpose of a municipal land bank is to consolidate a community-wide inventory of largely distressed and often tax-delinquent properties into more attractive packages for potential buyers that are committed to making needed improvements. Land-banked properties might also be retained by the public agency to meet future public needs; e.g., school sites, recreation fields, public buildings, etc.

*Legal Annotation*: "A city may not, under the guise of the police power, require a property owner to dedicate private property for some future public purpose as a condition of obtaining a building permit without paying the property owner just compensation, when the requested dedicated property is to be placed in a **land bank** for future use by the city and such future use is not directly occasioned by the construction sought to be permitted." *Simpson v. City of North Platte* (Nebr., 1980).

## LAND DISTURBANCE

**Any activity involving the clearing, cutting, excavating, filling, or grading of land, or any other activity that alters land topography or vegetative cover.**

***Legal Annotation***: "On 17 February 1998, Greenbriar applied to the City for a **land disturbance** permit (the 'Permit'), which the City issued on 18 March 1998. The Permit seemed to authorize the clearing of a commercial site." *Greenbriar Village, LLC v. Mountain Brook* (11th Cir., 2003).

## LANDLOCKED

**A lot or parcel of land without direct access to a public road.**

***Comment***: Local development regulations should preclude approval of any subdivision or site plan that results in any property becoming landlocked.

***Legal Annotation***: "As a result of such conveyance parcel C, which was retained by plaintiffs, became **landlocked** without any means of ingress or egress to or from Witherly Lane." *Reese v. Borghi* (Calif. Ct. App., 1963).

## LAND RECLAMATION

**(1) The process of creating new land from oceans, riverbeds, or lakes through drainage, regrading, or fill, or a combination of these methods; (2) returning damaged and disturbed lands to a stable and usable state. See *Filling*.**

***Comment***: In the first definition above, where new land is added, the process is also sometimes referred to as "infilling" but should not be confused with the terms "infill" or "infill development" as defined in this book. In the second definition, where disturbed or damaged land is "reclaimed," such as when landfills or quarries are closed, land reclamation returns such land to a more useful, environmentally healthy, and aesthetically pleasing state.

***Legal Annotation***: "In light of the flexible approach taken in the case law toward application of the 'beneficial use' concept, and given the legislative expressions of concern for reclamation of mined land and abatement of dust pollution, we believe that **land reclamation** and dust control are beneficial uses." *State v. Southwestern Colorado Water Conservation District* (Colo., 1983).

## LAND SURVEYOR

**One who is licensed by the state as a land surveyor and is qualified to make accurate field measurements and to mark, describe, and define land boundaries.**

***Legal Annotation***: "'**Land Surveyor**' is defined as a 'person who, by reason of his special knowledge of mathematics and surveying principles and methods which are acquired by education and practical experience, is qualified to engage in the practice of land surveying as attested by his registration as a land surveyor.' . . . (emphasis added)." *State Board of Registration for Land Surveoyrs v. Bender* (Ind. Ct. app., 1993).

## LAND SWAPS

**An exchange of land between two or more separate owners ("Colorado County" 2011).**

***Legal Annotation***: "In December 2005, Reserves executed an Assignment of Rights to Conveyance by Deed, which satisfied the October Land Sales Contract. The December Assignment provided that Reserves could satisfy future invoices from Fresh Cut by transferring additional lots to Glenn at a rate of one lot per $250,000 of invoiced work. By April 2006, Reserves had transferred 8 lots to Glenn (the '**land swaps**')." *Reserves Dev. LLC v. Severn Sav. Bank, FSB* (Del., 2008).

## LAND TRUST

**A nonprofit organization dedicated to the acquisition of land, usually for farmland or conservation/preservation purposes, but also to provide for the protection of cultural resources, landmarks, water resources, wildlife habitat, and the like.**

***Comment***: Acquisitions by land trusts may involve outright land acquisition or just the acquisition of conservation easements, development rights, or mining rights, depending on the objectives sought to be achieved. In many but not all cases, land that is acquired by a land trust is deed-restricted and eventually turned over to a public entity for ongoing ownership and maintenance. Land trusts may also assist private and public organizations with their land acquisition and preservation efforts.

*Legal Annotation*: "Those guidelines provide that, for 20-acre or greater parcels, 'farmland mitigation shall be satisfied by direct acquisition of a farmland conservation easement as allowed by these guidelines and the Land Trust's program. . . .' Further, under the FMP guidelines the interest 'shall be held in trust by the **land trust** and/or the County in perpetuity.' A **land trust** is defined as '[a] nonprofit public benefit 501(c)(3) corporation or other appropriate legal entity operating in Stanislaus County for the purpose of conserving and protecting land in agriculture, and approved for this purpose by the Board of Supervisors. The County may be designated as a Land Trust.' This **land trust** qualifies as one of the limited entities or organizations that may acquire and hold conservation easements under section 815.3." *Building Industry Assn. of Central California v. County of Stanislaus* (Calif. Ct. App., 2010).

## LAND USE

**A description of how land is occupied or used.**

*Legal Annotation*: "'**Land use**' is defined by statute as: (1) The placement or erection of any solid material on land; (2) The grading, removing, harvesting, dredging, mining, or extraction of any material or natural resource on land; (3) The subdivision of land; or (4) The construction, reconstruction, demolition, or alteration of any structure, building, or facility on land." *Hou v. University of Hawaii* (Hawaii Ct. App., 2012).

## LAND-USE INTENSITY (LUI) STANDARDS

**A system of bulk regulations, designed primarily for large-scale developments, and based on the physical relationships between specific development factors.**

*Comment*: LUI standards attempt to correlate the land area, floor area, open space, recreation space, and car storage of a project. Details of the system were first published in the Federal Housing Administration's *Land Planning Bulletin No. 7, Land Use Intensity Rating* (1996). They have never been fully appreciated or gained wide-scale acceptance.

*Legal Annotation*: "No national standards exist to describe what constitutes low-, medium-, and high-intensity land use, and **land use intensity standards** used by land use planners vary considerably." *Lemon v. McHugh* (D. D.C., 2009).

## LAND-USE PLAN

**(1) A plan designed to guide and control the future use of lands; (2) a geographic-specific element of the community master plan or comprehensive plan containing proposals for the physical, economic, and social development of the community.**

*Comment*: Any plan, whether it is part of a master or comprehensive plan or not, that sets forth guidelines or policies for the future use of land can be termed a "land-use plan." However, when the land-use plan is one of several elements of a master plan, it is usually the most important and central element and takes into account the other master plan elements. It shows the existing and proposed location, extent, and intensity of development of land for residential, commercial, industrial, open space, agricultural, recreational, or educational uses, and other public and private purposes. In many states, the local zoning ordinance must be consistent with the adopted land-use plan element of the master plan.

*Legal Annotation*: "[T]he main tool that BLM employs to balance wilderness protection against other uses is a **land use plan**—what BLM regulations call a 'resource management plan.' **Land use plans**, adopted after notice and comment, are 'designed to guide and control future management actions.' Generally, a **land use plan** describes, for a particular area, allowable uses, goals for future condition of the land, and specific next steps." *Norton v. Southern Utah Wilderness Alliance* (U.S., 2004).

## LANDFILL

**A disposal site in which refuse and earth, or other suitable cover material, are deposited and compacted in alternating layers of specified depth in accordance with an approved plan. See *Sanitary Landfill*.**

***Comment***: Landfills are usually regulated and licensed by the state or another public agency to accept certain types of waste. Landfills differ from dumps in that refuse is compacted and covered in the landfill.

***Legal Annotation***: "The Indiana Code defines '**landfill**' . . . as 'a solid waste disposal facility at which solid waste is deposited on or beneath the surface of the ground as an intended place of final location.'" *Killbuck Concerned Citizens v. JM Corp.* fn. 9 (Ind., 2011).

## LANDMARK

**(1) Any site, building, structure, or natural feature that has visual, historic, or cultural significance; (2) a permanent marker, usually called a "monument," designating property boundaries. See *Historic Property*.**

***Legal Annotation***: "A **landmark** is defined as: '[a]ny improvement, any part of which is thirty years old or older, which has a special character or special historical or aesthetic interest or value as part of the development, heritage or cultural characteristics of the city, state or nation, and which has been designated a landmark pursuant to the provisions of this chapter.'" *9th & 10th Street LLC v. New York City Landmarks Preservation Commission* (N.Y. Sup. Ct., 2008).

## LANDSCAPE

**(1) An expanse of natural scenery; (2) elements used in the alteration and/or ornamentation of open space, including lawns, trees, plants, and other natural materials, such as rock and wood chips, and decorative features, including sculpture, patterned walks, fountains, and pools. See *Landscape Plan*.**

***Comment***: As noted in the definition, landscaping treatments can include some non-natural elements, such as a fountain. However, they do not include artificial trees or other artificial plants. Natural materials used in landscaping often are referred to as "softscape," while non-natural elements incorporated into a landscape, such as gazebos, benches, and fountains, are referred to as "hardscape."

***Legal Annotation***: "According to *The Architecture Book*, '**landscape**' means '[a] pictoral (and hence perspective) concept of one's on-land surrounds, as opposed to an abstract design idea . . . hence the idea of the pictoral or picturesque.' . . . One dictionary defines '**landscape**' as: 'a section or portion of rural scenery, usually extensive, that may be seen from a single viewpoint . . . to improve the landscape of . . . to improve the appearance of (an area of land, a highway, etc.), as by planting trees, shrubs, or grass, or altering the contours of the ground.'" *Keith v. Volpe* (C.D. Calif., 1996).

## LANDSCAPE PLAN

**A component of a development plan on which are shown:**

- **proposed landscape species (such as number, spacing, size at time of planting, and planting details)**
- **proposals for protection of existing vegetation during and after construction**
- **proposed treatment of hard and soft surfaces**
- **proposed decorative features**
- **grade changes**
- **buffers and screening devices**
- **any other information that can reasonably be required for an informed decision to be made by the approving authority**

**(Rouse and Bunsten-Ossa 2013.)**

***See Figures 65 and 66.***

***Legal Annotation***: "A conceptual **landscape plan** needs to indicate the areas of existing landscaping and areas of proposed landscaping. The plan shall also identify the major types of plant material to be used (e.g., [t]he species of trees and parking lot trees to be used, species of shrubbery to be used to screen parking lots, etc.)." *San Jose Christian College v. Morgan Hill* (9th Cir., 2004).

**Figure 65**

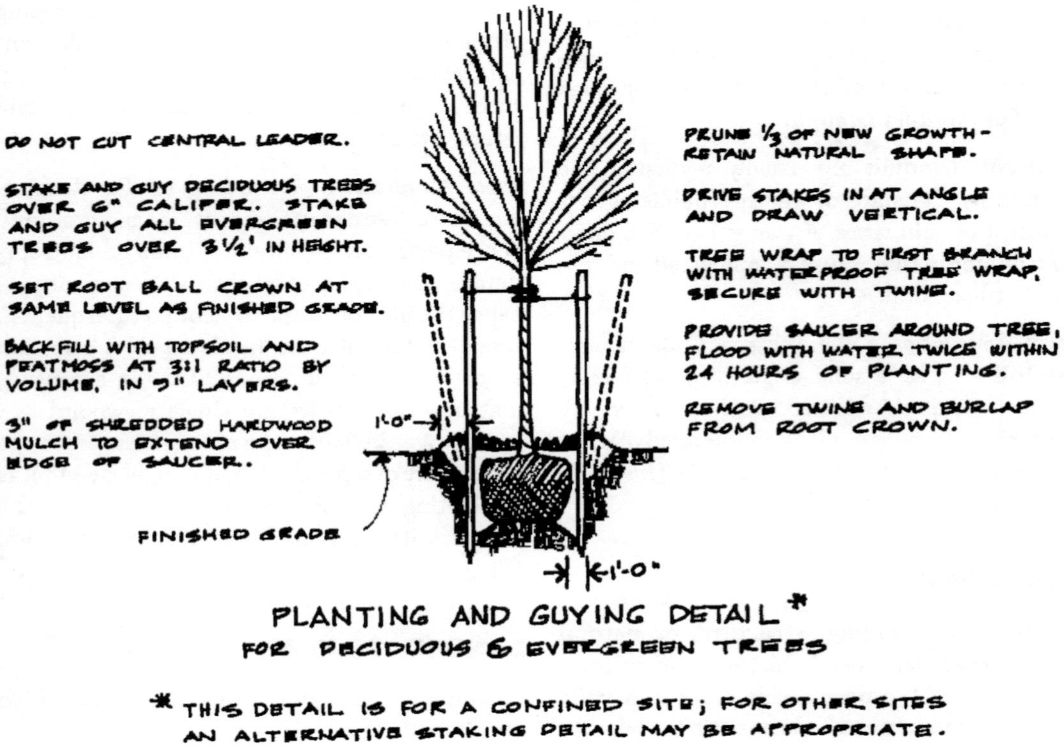


**Figure 66**

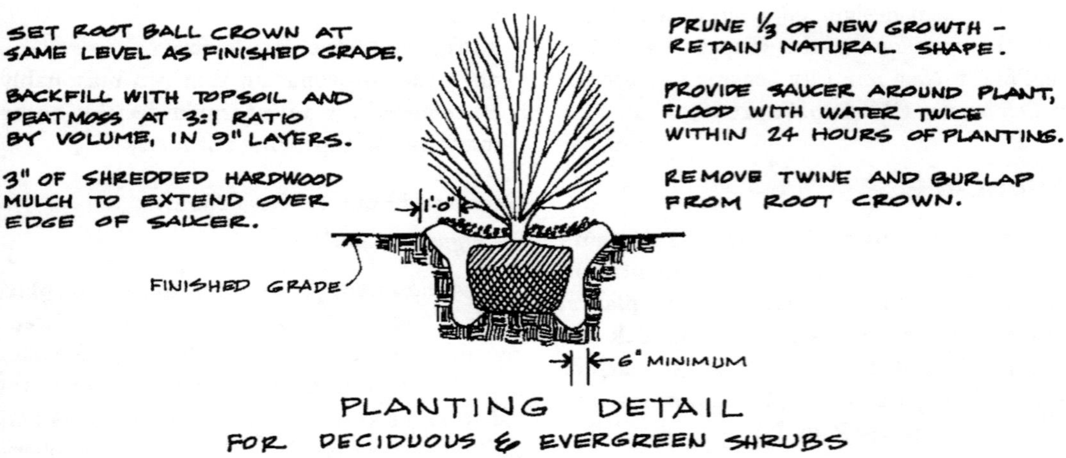

## LANE

**A street or easement providing vehicular and service access to the rear of individual lots. See *Alley*.**

*Legal Annotation*: "Although the potential public right-of-way in the **lane** is lost as a result of the passage of time and lack of acceptance, the purely private easement rights of individual property owners in the plan of lots to use the **lane** is not extinguished." *Loch v. Zoning Hearing Board* (Pa: Comm. Ct., 1990).

## LARGE-LOT ZONING

**Low-density residential development that requires a large parcel of land for each dwelling.**

*Comment*: While there is no set definition of what constitutes a "large lot," "low density" usually refers to subdivisions of land into lots of one acre or more. While many jurisdictions still practice or permit large-lot zoning, their exclusionary, energy-consumptive, and sprawl-inducing impacts have led many to reevaluate the merits of this form of land-use regulation.

*Legal Annotation*: "Ecological and environmental considerations were also advanced by the municipality in Mount Laurel to justify **large lot zoning** throughout the township. We pointed out there that while such factors and problems were always to be given consideration in zoning . . . 'the danger and impact must be substantial and very real (the construction of every building or the improvement of every plot has some environmental impact)—not simply a make-weight to support exclusionary housing measures or preclude growth.'" *Oakwood at Madison, Inc. v. Township of Madison* (N.J. 1977).

## LATENT DEMAND

**In traffic engineering, the increase in traffic demand as highway congestion decreases.**

*Legal Annotation*: "Since all the major coastal cities from southern California to northern Washington have readily available access to the 1-5 and Route 99 corridors, which have straighter alignments and faster travel times, the opening of STAA access to US Route 101 through Richardson Grove is not expected to generate a substantial amount of diverted truck traffic. In addition, a traffic study performed for the projects to lift STAA restrictions on Routes 197 and 199 in Del Norte County also found that there was very little **latent demand** expected with the removal of the STAA restriction. That study estimated that providing STAA access could add about eight truck round trips per day on Routes 199 and 197." *Lotus v. Department of Transportation* (Calif. Ct. App., 2014).

## LATERAL SEWERS

**Pipes conducting sewerage from individual buildings to larger pipes called "trunk" or "interceptor" sewers. See *Common Lateral Sewer*.**

*Legal Annotation*: "No submain or **lateral sewers** have been constructed from the main trunk sewer in the direction of any of the lands owned by plaintiffs." *Hurley v. Board of County Commissioners* (Kan., 1961).

## LAUNDROMAT℠

**An establishment providing washing, drying, or dry-cleaning machines on the premises on a pay-per-use basis to the general public.**

*Legal Annotation*: "A **laundromat** basically derives its value from the . . . service of a commercial nature. That is, it gives working men and women ready access to automatic washing procedures whenever they need them just as if they were more fortunate and could afford their own washing machines. This service should be permitted in a commercial district, ordinarily located on the fringes of residential districts, so that it is readily available to the users thereof." *Van Sciver v. Zoning Board of Adjustment* (Pa., 1959).

## LEACHATE

**Liquid that has percolated through solid waste or other mediums from which dissolved or suspended materials have been extracted.**

*Legal Annotation*: "**Leachate** is produced when liquids, such as rainwater, percolate through wastes stored in a landfill. The resulting fluid will contain suspended components drawn from the original waste. Proper **leachate** management involves the storage of wastes in lined containers so that **leachate** may be collected before it seeps into soil or groundwater. The **leachate** will periodically be pumped out of the container and subsequently treated." *Chemical Waste Management, Inc. v. USEPA* (D.C. Cir., 1989).

## LEACHING

**The process by which soluble materials in the soil, such as nutrients, pesticide chemicals, or contaminants, are washed into a lower layer of soil and are dissolved and carried into groundwater.**

*Legal Annotation*: "These wastes began **leaching** through the sandy soil beneath them and into the groundwater aquifer below." *United States v. Waste Industries, Inc.* (4th Cir., 1984).

## LEASE

**In a land development context, a lease is a contractual agreement for the use of lands, structures, buildings, or parts thereof for a fixed time and consideration.**

*Legal Annotation*: "This reflects the ancient notion that a **lease** is a conveyance of an 'estate in land,' in which the respective covenants—a tenant's to pay rent, the landlord's to repair—were deemed independent of each other. This approach was appropriate in the feudal culture in which property law evolved. But this feudal notion of landlord-tenant law—rooted in the special needs of an agrarian society—has not been a realistic approach to landlord-tenant law for many years, and has been replaced by what eminent authorities have described as 'a predominately contractual' analysis of leasehold interests" *Lindsey v. Normet* (U.S., 1972).

## LEAST-COST HOUSING

**Housing that sells for prices substantially below median housing prices in an area and built in accordance with local codes and ordinances that have been carefully screened to eliminate cost-generating provisions and any requirements not related to health, safety, and welfare. See *Manufactured Home*.**

*Comment*: Least-cost housing does not have affordability controls or income limits as in the case of low- and moderate-income housing, but it is an attempt to provide housing affordable to those whose incomes are slightly above such limits, where conventional market rate housing is beyond their means. Where a jurisdiction eliminates cost-generating requirements, developers can build cheaper, more affordable housing. Some of the cost-generating requirements found to be unrelated to health, safety, and welfare include large-lot zoning, unrealistic densities for various housing types, minimum building areas, garages, and oversized utilities or infrastructure (thirty-six-foot-wide local streets, for example).

Many of the impediments to least-cost housing are identified in the 1991 report of the President's Advisory Committee on Regulatory Barriers to Affordable Housing, *Not in My Back Yard: Removing Barriers to Affordable Housing* (Kemp Report).

*Legal Annotation*: "**Least cost housing** is that housing which is consistent with minimum health and safety requirements, yet unfettered by unnecessary cost-generating requirements. Id. at 512. The logic behind this requirement is the hope that building new housing within the reach of moderate income families will have a beneficial "filtering down" impact on housing for lower income families." *Montgomery Associates v. Township of Montgomery* (N.J. Super. Ct., 1977).

## LEED (LEADERSHIP IN ENERGY AND ENVIRONMENTAL DESIGN)

**A rating system intended to encourage the design, construction, operation, and maintenance of buildings and neighborhoods so as to minimize their consumption of energy and to lessen their impact on the environment.**

*Comment*: This acronym stands for the green building certification system developed by the US Green Building Council in 1998 as a rating system for all types of new construction. The mission of the council is to transform the way buildings and communities are designed, built, and operated, enabling an environmentally and socially responsible, healthy, and prosperous environment that improves the quality of life. Buildings can qualify for four levels of certification: "certified," "silver," "gold," and "platinum." (See Garde 2009 and Knack 2010.)

*Legal Annotation*: "The Commission found that the PUD would provide several public benefits, including the addition of 138 multifamily units and eight townhomes, ten percent of which would be set aside as affordable housing, improved pedestrian features, efficient and safe vehicular and pedestrian access, a new 56,000-square foot supermarket and 80,000 square feet of new neighborhood-serving retail and commercial space, thirty parking spaces during off-peak hours for patrons of the neighborhood restaurants and retail uses, new traffic signals, construction using a high environmental standard under the **Leadership in Energy and Environmental Design** ('**LEED**')-Neighborhood Development ('ND') system, and employment and training opportunities for the District." *Wisconsin-Newark Neighborhood Coalition v. District of Columbia Zoning Commission* (D.C. Ct. App., 2011).

## LEISURE SERVICES

**Activities for people other than employment or mandatory functions and including activities relating to recreation, social and cultural events, religion, and education.**

*Legal Annotation*: "Some consider **leisure activities** to be play and recreation. **Leisure** implies a less serious purpose without necessarily producing a product or skill. It implies joy, enthusiasm opportunity and energy. Some view leisure to be the opposite of work, i.e., 'smelling the roses.' We tend to associate **leisure** with retirement, and leisure activities may well occur within retirement. They are, however, often practiced in other areas of one's life." *Activity and Leosure*, Univ. of Missouri, Kansas City. http://cas.umkc.edu/casww/sa/activity.htm

## LESS-THAN-FEE ACQUISITION

See *Easement*.

## LETTER OF CREDIT

**A letter issued by a bank permitting the person or agency named in it to draw a certain amount of money from another specified bank. (Adapted from Johnsich 1991: 121.)**

*Comment*: Letters of credit are now accepted in the same manner as cash or bonds to ensure the installation or construction of required improvements. See *Performance Guarantee*.

*Legal Annotation*: "A typical **letter of credit** transaction . . . involves three separate and independent relationships—an underlying sale of goods contract between buyer and seller, an agreement between a bank and its customer (buyer) in which the bank undertakes to issue a letter of credit, and the bank's resulting engagement to pay the beneficiary (seller) providing that certain documents presented to the bank conform with the terms and conditions of the credit issued on its customer's behalf." *Voest-Alpine International Corp. v. Chase Manhattan Bank* (2nd Cir., 1983).

## LEVEE

**A structure designed and constructed to contain, control, or divert the flow of water so as to provide protection from temporary flooding.**

*Legal Annotation*: "The NFIP defines a '**levee**' as a 'a man-made structure, usually an earthen embankment, designed and constructed in accordance with sound engineering practices to contain, control, or divert the flow of water so as to provide protection from temporary flooding.'" *City of Alexandria v. Federal Emergency Management Agency* (W.D. La., 2011).

## LEVEL OF SERVICE

**A quality measure describing operational conditions within a traffic stream, generally in terms of such service measures as speed and travel time, freedom to maneuver, traffic interruptions, and comfort and convenience (Transportation Research Board 2000: 2-2).**

*Comment*: The level of service ranges from A (free flow of traffic with minimum intersection delay), which is the best, to F (forced flow, jammed intersections, long delays), which is the worst. It reflects factors such as speed, travel time, freedom to maneuver, traffic interruptions, and delay. See *Capacity, Roadway*.

*Legal Annotation*: "The Final Environmental Impact Statement/Report . . . defined more precisely the desired **Level of Service**, an industry traffic category, setting Level of Service C as a project goal. . . . Traffic conditions are ranked between **Level of Service** A ('free flow, with low volumes and high speeds') and **Level of Service** F ('forced flow operation at low speeds, where volumes are below capacity')." *Carmel-By-The-Sea v. US Department of Transportation* (9th Cir., 1997).

## LIBRARY

**A place containing books and other research materials for reading, study, and research.**

*Comment*: The above definition is the classical and largely outdated definition of a library. If most people can't define a library, everyone can probably describe one and how it functions. Libraries today still have books for reading, study, and research on-site or to borrow. They now also have newspapers, magazines, artwork, books on tape, videos, CDs, and computer terminals to allow the public to access the Internet. Libraries feature lectures, classes, concerts, and recitals. They may include day-care centers, homework centers, and meeting facilities for clubs, neighborhood associations, and outreach groups.

Libraries play key roles as community centers. They are strong anchors for downtowns and neighborhoods, and planners have found them important in revitalization efforts. They have returned to their original roles as social centers and promote and schedule conferences, exhibits, and shows. Many, going toe to toe with some of the large book retailers, have restaurants and snack bars.

Libraries can be located anywhere, but they obviously function best near schools (particularly high schools), retail locations, and other central places with people. As noted earlier, they can be important neighborhood centers. Libraries have traditionally been part of civic centers and still function well in those locations, bringing after-hours activity in an area that often closes down after business hours. Many libraries have found retail malls ideal locations, scheduling reading hours and preschool activities so parents can drop off children while shopping (Fulton and Jackson 1999: 4).

The previous editions of this publication included floor space area standards for public libraries, based on population to be served, using as its source the State Library of New Jersey. But arbitrary standards based on population are no longer valid as a result of the additional functions that libraries perform and cooperative agreements between libraries that permit interlibrary borrowing of books, documents, Internet information, etc.

More recently, rather than endorsing such prescriptive standards, the American Library Association, and its division the Public Library Association, now advocates an outcomes-assessment process in determining such individual library needs. For example, a library serving a community with a high percentage of young families may well have a need for different facilities and services than that of a library serving a similar-size population but with a high percentage of empty-nesters and retirees.

For more information on library standards appropriate to local conditions and needs, see the website of the American Library Association, **www.ala.org,** and specifically "ALA Library Fact Sheet, No. 11, Building Libraries and Additions." (Discussion with Valerie Hawkins, library reference specialist, American Library Association, Chicago, Illinois.)

*Legal Annotation*: "The front room of the building was used as a public library facility where patrons might obtain **library** services. It was a small room, containing two tables and one chair . . . a card catalogue, and open book shelves. . . . The **library** permitted 'registered borrowers' to 'browse' among the books in the room or to borrow books." *Brown v. Louisiana* (U.S., 1966).

## LIFE CYCLE

**The phases, changes, or stages an organism passes through during its lifetime.**

***Legal Annotation***: "Some of this silt settles in the streams and marsh and thereby physically interferes with the **life cycle** of tiny organisms upon which other animals of the marsh depend for their food supply." *Texas Eastern Transmission Corp. v. Wildlife Preserves, Inc.* (N.J., 1966).

## LIFE-CARE COMMUNITIES

See *Continuing Care Retirement Community (Ccrc).*

## LIFE-CYCLE HOUSING

**A variety of housing types that meet the need of households over a normal life span.**

***Comment***: A typical household might start out in a rental apartment, then move to a small detached home or townhouse, then to a larger detached home, then to a townhouse or apartment, and then eventually to an assisted living environment.

***Legal Annotation***: "We first examine whether the condemnation was for a public purpose. The district court affirmed that '[t]he Redevelopment of Cedar Grove will serve public purposes. It will provide new **life-cycle housing** options for existing Eagan residents, enhance public transportation infrastructure . . . increase the tax base, and increase employment.'" *Eagan Economic Development Authority v. U-Haul Company of Minnesota* (Minn. Ct. App., 2010).

## LIFT

**In a sanitary landfill, a compacted layer of solid waste and the top layer of cover material.**

***Legal Annotation***: "Specifically, SCA hooked up utilities at the site . . . grubbed a portion of the site to prepare it for the clay cap, compacted existing landfill at the site to prepare for the clay cap, and excavated, transported and stockpiled clay for construction of the clay cap. In addition to these activities, SCA placed the first **lift** of clay for the clay cap on the site on September 18, 1990." *US v. Navistar International Transportation Corp* (7th Cir., 1998).

## LIGHT INDUSTRY

See *Industry, Light.*

## LIGHT PLANE

See *Sky Exposure Plane.*

## LIGHT RAIL TRANSIT (LRT)

See *Transit, Light Rail.*

## LIGHT TRESPASS

**The shining of light produced by a luminaire (light fixture) beyond the boundaries of the property on which it is located.**

***Legal Annotation***: "The Planning Board further found that **light trespass** from car headlights and exterior lighting would be minimal and would not result in a significant adverse impact." *Calogrias v. Town of Southhampton* (N.Y. Sup. Ct., 2011).

## LIGHTING PLAN

**A plan showing the location, the height above grade, the type of illumination, the type of fixture, the source lumens, and the luminous area for each source of light proposed.**

***Comment***: The lighting plan should spell out the required standards, including maximum foot-candles permitted; the location and maximum height of light poles (usually eighteen to twenty-five feet maximum in nonresidential areas and twelve to fifteen feet in residential areas); requirements for shielding; and style of luminaire if in a historic district or part of an overall neighborhood plan. *The Lighting Handbook*, now in its tenth edition and published by the Illumination Engineering Society of North America, is the most authoritative source on lighting standards. See *Diffused Lighting; Foot-Candle; Iesna.*

*Legal Annotation*: "[T]he Ordinance requires that an applicant for a use authorized by special exception submit . . . an exterior **lighting plan**, including 'a detailed grid of illumination levels, a calculation as to the average illumination levels, the number of lighting fixtures, the height and location of the mounting fixtures . . . and required details of how lighting will be . . . to show that the outline and roofline provisions have been met.'" *Elizabethtown v. Mount Joy Township Zoning Hearing Board* (Pa. Comm. Ct., 2007).

## LIMITED-ACCESS HIGHWAY

**A highway, especially designed for through traffic, with limited or no access to adjacent property.**

*Comment*: Interstate highways, toll roads, parkways, and freeways are considered limited-access highways.

*Legal Annotation*: "In our opinion, and we so hold, a 'controlled-access facility,' as defined in the 1957 Act, is a **limited access highway** where the Highway Commission acquires the legal right to cut off entirely the abutting owner's right of direct access to and from the highway on which his property abuts." *Barnes v. North Carolina State Highway Commission* (N.C., 1962).

## LIMITS OF CLEARING

**The boundaries of that area of land to be cleared of trees and other vegetation in conjunction with a proposed development or land use.**

*Legal Annotation*: "The **limits of clearing** depicted on the site plan clearly extend well beyond the area designed for the playing field surfaces and appear to encompass the work that Plaintiff contends required additional compensation." *H.E. Contracting v. Franklin Pierce College* (D. N.H., 2005).

## LIMNOLOGY

**The study of the physical, chemical, meteorological, and biological aspects of freshwater bodies.**

*Legal Annotation*: "Posekany, an expert in **limnology** (scientific study of biological conditions in fresh-water bodies), testified that he had originally recommended that the Conservation Department oppose the dam." *State v. Public Service Commission* (Wis., 1962).

## LINES

See *Lot Line*.

## LINKAGE PROGRAMS

**Developer contributions, either by construction, actual provision of the service, or in-lieu fees, toward community amenities and needs—such as affordable housing, open space, child-care facilities, transit improvements, and related community services—in return for obtaining development approval.**

*Comment*: Linkage programs require developers to contribute money for or actually to build housing, transit improvements, recreation, or other amenities as a prerequisite for approvals. In some cases, the linkage programs allow for an increase in allowable density or intensity of development in return for providing the amenity. In order for linkage to work, there should be some relationship to what is being built and what is required—a rational nexus. For example, a new office building may generate a demand for more transit capacity, child care, and affordable housing. The impact can be determined and the linkage computed. Linkage formulas must be permitted by state law, be based on a local ordinance with clear and equitable requirements, and be applied fairly and uniformly.

*Legal Annotation*: "Under the **linkage program**, the commission was authorized to adopt zoning regulations to condition zoning relief for developers of 'new large-scale commercial real estate' 'upon action, or promised action, by the developer' to contribute an 'affordable housing exaction' and 'employment exaction' to mitigate the effects of the project 'upon the availability of affordable housing within the city' and 'upon the availability of jobs for low and moderate income residents of the city.'" *South Boston Betterment Trust Corp. v. Boston Redevelopment Authority* (Mass., 2002).

## LIQUEFACTION

**The transformation of loose, water-saturated, granular materials (such as sand or silt) from a solid into a liquid state (*California Central Plan Glossary*).**

*Comment*: Earthquake tremors can create a loss of soil structure, causing soil liquefaction. Modern building codes require that consideration be given to the effects of soil liquefaction in the design of new buildings, bridges, dams, and retaining structures.

*Legal Annotation*: "**Liquefaction** occurs when saturated soil is transformed from a solid to a liquefied state, particularly as the result of an earthquake. Ground failure caused by **liquefaction** can damage roads, pipelines, underground cables, and buildings with shallow foundations. The project site is located within a Seismic Hazard Zone for **liquefaction**, as designated by the California Geological Survey (CGS)." *Oakland Heritage Alliance v. City of Oakland* (Calif. Ct. App., 2011).

## LITTORAL

**Pertaining to the shore of seas, oceans, and lakes.**

*Comment*: Note that this is distinct from "riparian," which relates to streams and rivers.

*Legal Annotation*: "*Black's Law Dictionary* (6th Ed. 1990) defines littoral rights as: 'Rights concerning properties abutting an ocean, sea or lake rather than a river or stream (riparian). [T]here is often confusion between the terms littoral and riparian as applied to the water rights of property owners. **Littoral** is the proper term for describing the rights that shoreline owners possess to make exclusive use of the land lying seaward of the mean high water mark'" *Carminis v. Troy* (Conn., 2011).

## LITTORAL DRIFT

**The transportation of grains of sand on a shoreline, resulting from water action produced by winds and currents.**

*Legal Annotation*: "[D]efendant's jetties proximately caused the erosion of the shoreline by diverting sand from its natural path in the **littoral drift** by collecting it on the jetties. The court found that the north to south **littoral drift**, i.e., the natural flow of water and sand, would have replenished plaintiffs' shoreline absent the construction of the jetties and that the deprivation of the sand led to the property's erosion." *Peterman v. Department of Natural Resources* (Mich., 1994).

## LITTORAL LAND

**Land that abuts a large body of water, such as an ocean, sea, or lake.**

*Legal Annotation*: "Lands such as plaintiff's which border on a lake or ocean are called **littoral lands**. Riparian lands border rivers or streams." *101 Ranch v. United States* (8th Cir., 1990).

## LITTORAL RIGHTS

**The right of shoreline owners to make exclusive use of land abutting an ocean, sea, or lake, lying seaward of the mean high-water mark.**

*Legal Annotation*: "The District Court of Appeal for the First District concluded that, contrary to the Act's preservation of 'all common-law riparian rights,' the order had eliminated two of the Members' **littoral rights**: (1) the right to receive accretions to their property; and (2) the right to have the contact of their property with the water remain intact." *Stop the Beach Ren. v. Fla. Dept. of Env. Prot.* (U.S., 2010).

## LIVING QUARTERS, SEPARATE

**Those in which the occupants live separately from any other individuals in the building and which have direct access from outside the building or through a common hall (Census 2010).**

*Legal Annotation*: "The blueprint, in truth, did not reflect an 'addition,' but, instead, reflected another **separate living quarters** connected only by a common roof, in other words, a duplex." *Miller v. City of Lake City* (Ark., 1990).

## LOADING SPACE

**An off-street space or berth used for the loading or unloading of cargo, products, or materials from vehicles.**

*Legal Annotation*: "Section 33.03 of the Code of the City of Clearwater (the zoning ordinance) provides in part: '(4) Required off-street parking or loading area shall not be reduced or changed to any other use unless the permitted use which it serves is discontinued or modified, except where equivalent parking or **loading space** is provided to the satisfaction of the building official upon which evidence a parking lot occupancy permit will be issued.'" *Rebholz v. Floyd* fn. 2 (Fla. Ct. App., 1976).

## LOCAL AUTHORITY

**Any city, town, village, or other legally authorized agency charged with the administration and enforcement of land-use regulations. See *Municipality*.**

*Comment*: In many states, the county or regional planning agencies are charged with the administration and enforcement of land-use regulations.

*Legal Annotation*: "However, it is fundamental and not to be forgotten that the zoning power is a police power of the state and the **local authority** is acting only as a delegate of that power and is restricted in the same manner as is the state." *Southern Burlington County NAACP v. Township of Mount Laurel* (N.J., 1975).

## LOCAL HOUSING AUTHORITY

**Any public body authorized to engage in the development and/or administration of subsidized or public housing.**

*Legal Annotation*: A **local Housing Authority** is created . . . following a determination by the State Board of Housing . . . of the need for such local Housing Authority. The purpose for which such Authorities are created is to engage in low-rent housing and slum-clearance projects which . . . are declared to be 'public objects essential to the public interest.'" *Wilmington Housing Authority v. Williamson* (Del., 1967).

## LOCAL IMPROVEMENT

**A public improvement provided to a specific area benefiting that area and usually paid for by special assessment on the benefiting property owners.**

*Legal Annotation*: "A **local improvement**, although it may incidentally benefit all the property in the municipality and the public at large, is made primarily for the accommodation and convenience of inhabitants of a particular area in the community whose property receives a special benefit from the improvement either in the form of service or of enhancement of the value." *Duncan Development Corp. v. Crestview Sanitary Dist.* (Wis., 1964).

## LOCAL ROAD

*See Street, Local.*

## LOCAL STREET

**A roadway whose primary function is to provide access to abutting properties.**

*Legal Annotation*: "Originally, the Town intended Tolbert Lane to be substantially used as a cut-through to connect Battlefield Parkway with Sycolin Road. However, as other roads in the Town developed, Tolbert Lane evolved into a **local street**, serving as an access street for the parcels in the original High Point 38.37 acres." *Town of Leesburg v. Long Lane Associates* (Va., 2012).

## LODGE

**(1) The place where members of a local chapter of an association or a fraternal, cultural, or religious organization hold their meetings; (2) the local chapter itself. See *Private Club*.**

*Legal Annotation*: "The Constitution and Statutes of the National Order of Elks . . . provided that 'A **Lodge** may establish and maintain a home or club, for the social enjoyment of its members . . . and set forth in some detail the mode of controlling and managing such a home or club.'" *Security-First National Bank v. Cooper* (Calif. Ct. App., 1944).

## LODGER

**A person who pays rent in return for accommodation in someone else's house. See *Boarder*.**

*Legal Annotation*: "A '**lodger**' has only the right to use the premises, subject to the landlord's retention of control and right of access to them." *Stowe v. Fritzie Hotels, Inc.* (Calif., 1955).

## LODGING HOUSE

See *Boardinghouse*.

*Comment*: The term for a boardinghouse in the UK, derived from the Victorian era; a house in which cheap accommodation in one or more rooms is provided to unrelated individuals.

*Legal Annotation*: "The YWCA owns and operates a 97-room housing facility . . . [that] is classified as a '**lodging house**' under Minnesota law. See Minn.Stat. § 157.01, subd. 1 (1990) (defining a '**lodging house**' as a place 'where sleeping accommodations are furnished to the public as regular roomers, for periods of one week or more, and having five or more beds to let to the public')." *Donaldson v. YWCA* (Minn., 1995).

## LOGGIA

**A colonnaded or arcaded space within the body of a building but open to the outside of the building on one side, often at an upper story overlooking a courtyard.**

*Legal Annotation*: "In the proposal the applicants indicated that they would provide and maintain a water system, swimming pool, an auditorium and an administration building, with a fountain and a **loggia** for adornment." *MacDonald v. Board of County Commissioners* (Md. Ct. App., 1965).

## LONG-TERM CARE FACILITY

**An institution or a part of an institution that is licensed or approved to provide health care under medical supervision for twenty-four or more consecutive hours to two or more patients who are not related to the governing authority or its members by marriage, blood, or adoption.**

*Comment*: A long-term care facility may be either a skilled nursing facility, where patients receive a minimum number of hours of nursing care daily (New Jersey requires 2.75 hours), or an intermediate care facility, where patients receive less than the specified number of hours of nursing care daily. Besides nursing homes, other long-term care facilities are governmental medical institutions or nursing units in a home for the aged. Long-term care facilities can provide, in addition to maintenance care, restorative services and specialized services such as intravenous feeding, tube feeding, injected medication, and daily wound care. Hospices are also examples of long-term care facilities. See *Extended Care Facility; Intermediate Care Facility*.

*Legal Annotation*: "[T]he Act defines a covered 'facility' or '**long-term care facility**' as any 'private home, institution, building, residence, or any other place . . . which provides . . . personal care, sheltered care or nursing for 3 or more persons, not related to the applicant or owner by blood or marriage.' *Illinois Health Care Ass'n v. Illinois Dept. of Public Health* (7th Cir., 1989).

## LOOP DETECTOR

**An inductive (wire) loop embedded in the pavement that detects the presence of a vehicle at a signalized intersection to activate a signal change.**

*Comment*: Diagonal quadruple loops typically provide the best bicycle detection. http://safety.fhwa.dot.gov/ped_bike/tools_solve/fhwasa12018/#chap1.6

*Legal Annotation*: "There was a **loop detector** switch on Portland to detect vehicles and change the traffic light from red to green. This device consisted of wires buried in the pavement at the stop bar and extending back over an area 6 × 30 feet in dimension. If a vehicle stopped at a red light on Portland, the device would detect the vehicle and notify the controller to change the Portland traffic light to green. The City had no records from the **loop detector** device showing that Taylor's car had stopped at the red light on Portland before the collision occurred." *Lampe v. Taylor* (Mo. Ct. App., 2011).

## LOT

**A designated parcel, tract, or area of land established by plat, subdivision, or as otherwise permitted by law, to be separately owned, used, developed, or built upon.** ***See Figures 10 and 107.***

*Legal Annotation*: [T]he word '**Lot**' is defined as: 'The plot or parcel of land on which a principal building and its accessories are placed, together with the required open spaces.'" *Sanfilippo v. Board of Review* (R.I., 1963).

## LOT, CORNER

**A lot or parcel of land abutting on two or more streets at their intersection or on two parts of the same street, forming an interior angle of less than 135 degrees.** ***See Figures 10 and 107.***

*Comment*: The major problem with corner lots is the designation of the yards adjacent to the street frontages. Most ordinances require that the minimum front yard be maintained on both frontages for purposes of providing adequate sight distances, safety, air, and light to abutting residences, and for aesthetic considerations. There remains the question of how to treat the two remaining yards. Some ordinances call them side yards and require them to meet the minimum required side yard dimension. Unfortunately, this deprives the corner lot of any adequate backyard area and encroaches on one or both adjacent residences. A better approach is to permit the applicant to designate one of the street frontages as the front, require the house to be built facing the front, and then require the yard opposite the designated front to meet the minimum rear yard requirement. Both street frontages would still meet the minimum required front yard setback, one yard would meet side yard standards, and the lot would have a rear yard. The corner lot would have to be larger than the interior lots to provide the minimum required setbacks.

*Legal Annotation*: "A '**corner lot**' is a 'lot fronting on two or more streets at their intersection.'" *Seymour v. City of Alexandria* (Va., 2007).

## LOT, DEVELOPABLE

**See** ***Developable Land.***

## LOT, DEVELOPED

See *Lot, Improved*.

## LOT, DOUBLE FRONTAGE

See *Lot, Through*.

## LOT, FLAG

**A lot not meeting minimum frontage requirements and where access to the public road is provided by a narrower extension of the lot encompassing a driveway, or by a private right-of-way or easement.** ***See Figures 10 and 67.***

*Comment*: Flag lots are so named because typically the portion of the lot located away from the road is rectangular, the "flag" itself, while the driveway is located along a narrow extension to the roadway (the "flag pole"), thus resembling a flag. Flag lots are usually permitted in rural and developing municipalities to allow development of backland areas while still maintaining their rural character. The usual requirements for a flag lot are as follows: minimum lot area at least twice the area of standard lots in the zone where located; exclusive of the "pole" connecting the lot to the public road; minimum setbacks from property lines, as opposed to the usual front, side, and rear yard requirements; all setbacks measured from the projected right-of-way; minimum of twenty feet and maximum of fifty feet width for the right-of-way; not more than one flag lot for each private right-of-way (the pole); and minimum distance between flag lot rights-of-way at least equal to the minimum lot frontage in the particular zone.

While flag lots can assist in retaining the rural character of an area, they are subject to abuses. The most prevalent is when the flag lot owner wants to further subdivide and use the private right-of-way for access. The municipality then has a major subdivision without adequate access. Many towns do not permit flag lots of a size where the flag lot can be subdivided into an additional lot or lots.

*Legal Annotation*: "[T]he Torrington zoning regulations defines a **flag lot** as 'a lot which has

Figure 67

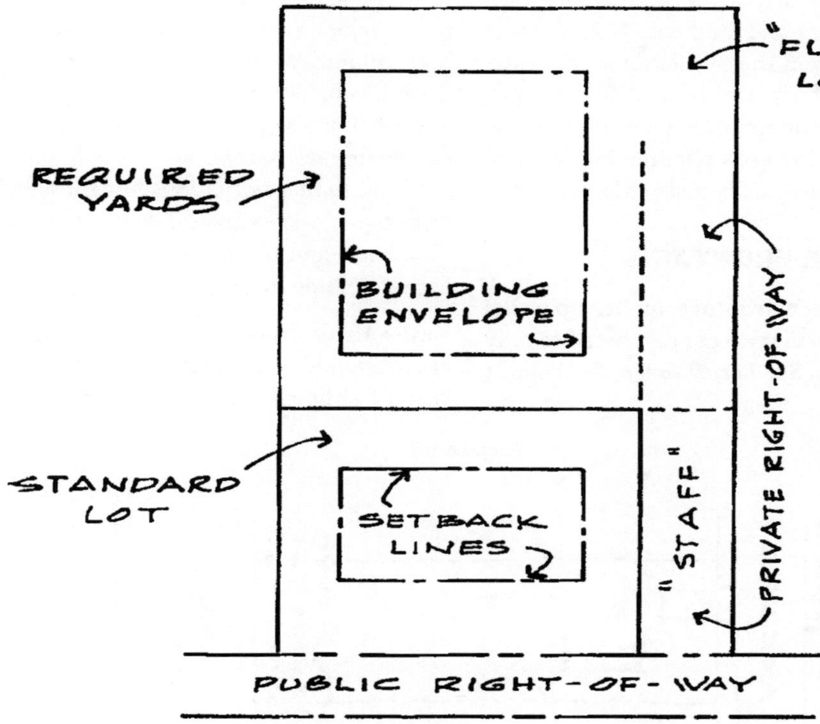


FLAG LOT

less than the minimum required lot width on a city accepted street and which is accessed by an accessway.' *CRRA v. Planning & Zoning Commission* (Conn. App. Ct., 1997).

## LOT, IMPROVED

**A lot with buildings or structures.**

*Legal Annotation*: "The property contained an **improved lot** with a building on it (the front lot) and one unimproved lot (the back lot)." *Tamco Supply v. Pollard* (Tenn. Ct. App., 2000).

## LOT, INTERIOR

**A lot that has frontage on only one street or, if so defined, a lot that does not meet the minimum frontage requirement.** ***See Figures 10 and 107.***

*Legal Annotation;* "In contrast, an '**interior lot**' is a '[a] lot with frontage on but one street." Zoning Ordinance § 2-169.'" *Seymour v. City of Alexandria* (Miss., 2007).

[T]he Litchfield zoning regulations provides in relevant part: 'An **interior lot** is defined as a lot that does not meet the requirement for minimum lot width." *Irwin v. Planning and Zoning Commission* (Conn., 1998).

## LOT, ISOLATED

**See *Isolated Lot*.**

## LOT, MINIMUM AREA OF

**The smallest lot area established by the zoning ordinance on which a use or structure may be located in a particular district.**

*Legal Annotation*: "The amendment, which applies only to residential zones, excludes wetlands, watercourses and land with a 25 percent slope or greater from the calculation of the total horizontal area of a parcel of land for the purposes of determining whether a parcel conforms to the **minimum lot area** required for development." *Harris v. Zoning Commission* (Conn., 2002).

## LOT, REVERSE FRONTAGE

**A through lot with frontage on two parallel streets, with vehicular access restricted to only one of the streets. See *Lot, Through*. *See Figures 31 and 68.***

*Comment*: As illustrated in Figure 68, reverse frontage lot layouts are often used in residential developments abutting an arterial or other high-volume roadway. With the reverse frontage design, vehicular access can be restricted to the lower-volume street frontage, eliminating undesirable driveway access along the higher-volume roadway. In these situations, the through lot may be designed with a greater depth to permit space for a berm and/or landscaped buffer next to the higher-volume roadway.

Yard-setback dimensions for the reverse frontage lot should be consistent with ordinance regulations, although the setback for the restricted

**Figure 68**

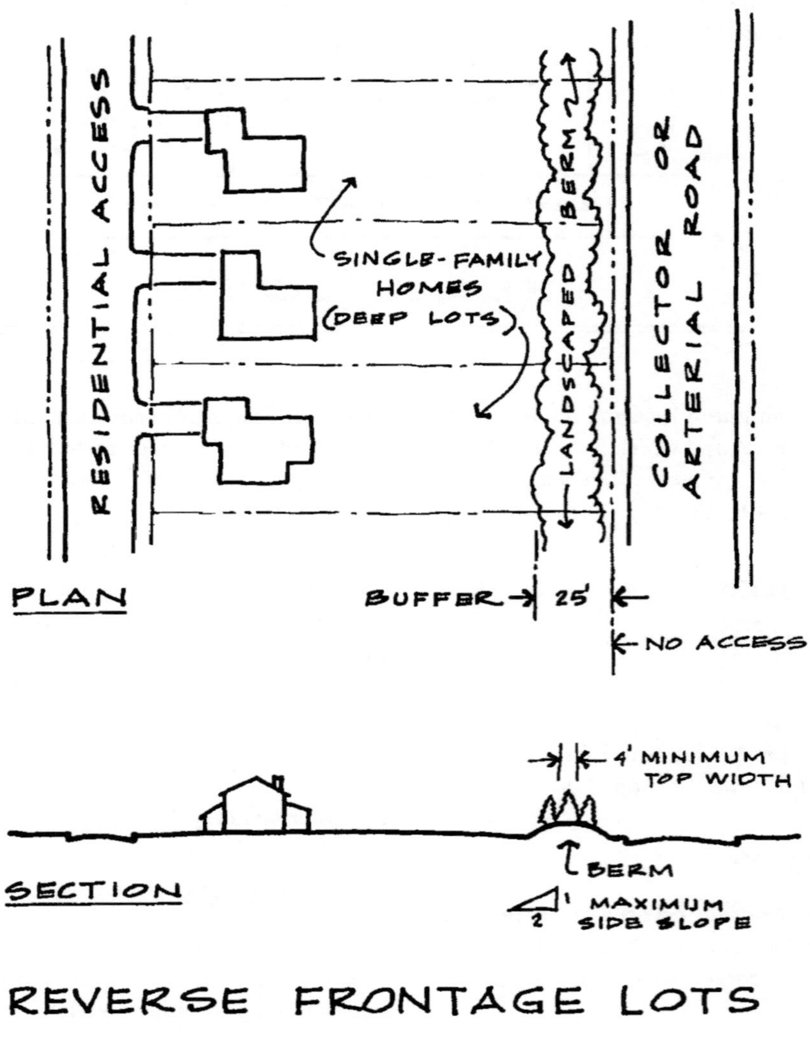

access frontage could be designated as a rear yard. The prohibited vehicular access should be a deed restriction on the lot.

***Legal Annotation***: "The County Planning Enabling Act provides: 'Where a proposed subdivision abuts a county road . . . such improvements shall be subject to recommendations of the county engineer . . . and may include additional pavement widths, marginal access streets, **reverse frontage** and other county highway and traffic design features necessitated by an increase in traffic volumes, potential safety hazards or impediments to traffic flows.'" *Builders League of South Jersey v. Burlington County Planning Board* (N.J. App. Div., 2002).

## LOT, SUBSTANDARD

**A parcel of land that has less than the minimum area or minimum dimensions required in the zone in which the lot is located.**

***Legal Annotation***: "Brunelle . . . was aware that the three-and-a-half acre parcel that he and Penn-Central had carved out of Penn-Central's larger land holdings would for zoning purposes constitute a **substandard lot** because it lacked sufficient lot street frontage on a public roadway." *Brunelle v. Town of South Kingstown* (R.I., 1997).

## LOT, THROUGH

**A lot that fronts on two parallel streets or that fronts on two streets that do not intersect at the boundaries of the lot. *See Figure 10.***

***Legal Annotation***: "[A] **through lot** is defined as an interior lot with frontage on two streets, it means a lot that runs from a street on one end to a street on the opposite end); 1 Salkin, American Law of Zoning (5th ed), § 9:61, p 9-198 (a **through lot** is an interior lot fronting on a street at either end)." *Richie v. Gladwin County* (Mich. Ct. App., 2009).

## LOT, TRANSITION

**(1) A lot in one zoning district abutting another district and designated as a transition lot; (2) a lot in a transition zone. *See Figure 69.***

**Figure 69**

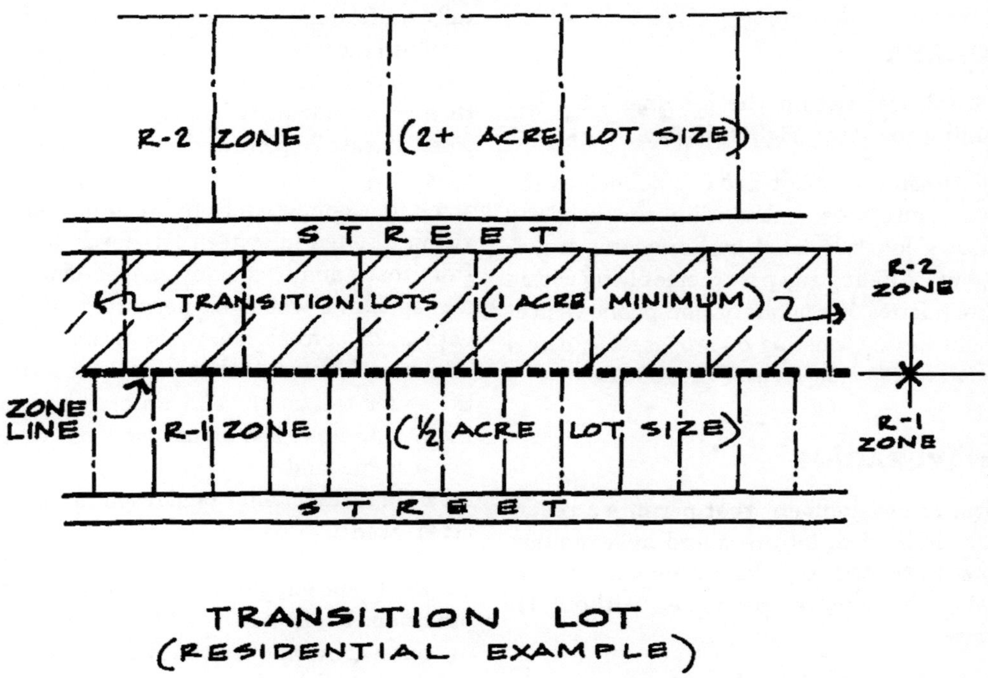

*Comment*: Transition lots (or lots in transition zones) serve as logical "change" between areas, lots, or zones whose uses are incongruous or incompatible. For example, a lot between a business and residential zone might allow parking for the business use (with adequate setbacks, buffering, and landscaping) or a higher-density residential use. The zoning ordinance may also establish an intermediate size for the transition lot. For instance, if located between a forty-thousand-square-foot residential zone and a twenty-thousand-square-foot residential zone, the transition lot might be required to have a minimum of thirty thousand square feet. The transition lot also might be part of a lot-averaging design. See *Lot Averaging; Transition Zone*.

*Legal Annotation*: "17.08.260 Zone **transition lot**. 'Zone **transition lot**' means a parcel of land abutting a district boundary where the district boundary is not a street upon which more restrictive or less restrictive standards are affixed. The width of such parcel shall be the width of the lot, if platted, but not exceed one hundred feet in any instance. (Ord. 440, Att. A (part) 1997).'" *Bingen (Washington) Municipal Code,* Chapter 17.08, "Definitions.".

## LOT AREA

**The total area within the lot lines of a lot, excluding any street rights-of-way.**

*Legal Annotation*: "'**Lot area**' is defined as the '[t]otal contiguous area within the property lines of a lot, calculated by horizontal projection, but excluding any part thereof lying within the boundaries of a public or non-public vehicular right-of-way, existing or proposed.'" *Route 4 Associates v. Planning Com'n* (Vt., 1990).

## LOT AVERAGING

**A form of development that permits a reduction in individual lot areas and bulk requirements, provided that the number of lots remains the same as permitted without lot averaging.**

*Comment*: Lot averaging has proven to be an excellent and much simpler way of preserving open space than other techniques such as transfer of development rights, which often requires the establishment of sending and receiving zones and the establishment of a transfer bank. Lot averaging is basically the same as cluster development, except that cluster development usually requires that the common open space be designated for the use and enjoyment of the residents and owners of the development and generally is owned by a homeowners' association. While lot averaging also allows the open space to be so designated, it also permits, for example, that the open space be permanently deed-restricted for agricultural purposes and sold to a farmer or retained by a single property owner for his or her own open space use.

In Cranbury Township (Middlesex County), New Jersey, the lot-averaging provision has permanently saved considerable acreage for farming. The technique works as follows in the Farm Preservation Zone (areas currently farmed without public water or sewers): The bulk regulations in this zone call for a minimum of six acres for each dwelling unit. An applicant wanting to develop a parcel of land using the lot-averaging technique must first lay out the property in a conventional, fully conforming, six-acre-per-lot subdivision to establish the maximum number of lots that could be devolved without lot averaging. The township then grants a density bonus of 25 percent, provided at least 70 percent of the land is preserved in open space or agriculture. If the parcel is 120 acres, for example, and a fully conforming subdivision resulted in sixteen lots (excluding losses from roads and irregularly shaped boundaries), the applicant would be permitted to develop with a 25 percent bonus, or twenty lots. The minimum lot size would be consistent with septic, water treatment, and water requirements. In the example, the actual lot sizes would be between one and 1.8 acres. The 70 percent preservation requirement would result in eighty-four acres saved.

The key to encouraging lot averaging is the bonus provision. It offsets the additional cost of laying out a conventional subdivision plat and any reduction in value by allowing smaller lots. But as builders have pointed out, the local market for one-acre lots is much greater than for six-acre lots, so the present value may be as much for the smaller lots as for the larger ones. In addition, the conventional layout required to determine the maximum lot yield does not call for detailed engineering plans.

While the example used is a farm zone, lot averaging works in all residential zones as long as the density in the developed parts of the tract can be accommodated.

***Legal Annotation***: "The ordinance has a **lot averaging** provision that permits residential lots as small as 1.5 acres and an 'open land' subdivision option, which allows a 50% density bonus for cluster development on 1.5 acre residential lots in exchange for the landowner's promise to preserve the remainder as agricultural land." *NJ Farm Bureau, Inc. v. Township of East Amwell* (N.J. App. Div., 2005).

## LOT COVERAGE

**That part of the lot that is covered by impervious surfaces. See *Building Coverage; Impervious Surface*.**

***Legal Annotation***: "Assuming that the hoop houses are impervious surfaces as well as structures, the **lot coverage** substantially exceeded the 10% maximum impervious surface ratio." *Township of Franklin v. Hollander* (N.J. App. Div., 2001).

"Lot width, yards and building height and **lot coverage** requirements for these uses shall be the same as those for similar size minimum lots in the respective districts. . . . Even if this argument was not waived, the method used to calculate the 5.2% deviation is the one provided in Section 2.295 of the Ordinance (defining the maximum ground coverage as '[t]he maximum ratio obtained by dividing the total impervious area . . . on a lot by the total area of the lot upon which the impervious surfaces are located') and Suburban's own engineer, Mr. Mancinelli, agreed that the deviation amount was 5.2%." *Suburban Realty, LP v. Zoning Hearing Board of Stroud Township* (Pa. Comm. Ct., 2011).

## LOT DEPTH

**The average distance measured from the front lot line to the rear lot line. *See Figure 10*.**

***Comment***: For lots where the front and rear lot lines are not parallel, the lot depth should be measured by drawing several evenly separated lines from the front to rear lot lines, at right angles to the front lot line, and averaging the length of these lines.

***Legal Annotation***: "The zoning ordinance contains the following pertinent provisions: . . . '**LOT DEPTH**—The mean distance between the front and rear lot lines, measured in the general direction of the sidelines of the lot.'" *Kaplan v. Linwood* (N.J. Super. Ct., 1991).

## LOT FRONTAGE

**The length of the front lot line measured at the street right-of-way line. *See Figure 10*.**

***Comment***: On corner lots, each side abutting the street is considered the frontage, and in many ordinances, such lots have two front yards, two side yards, and no rear yards. *See* **Comment** under LOT, CORNER.

***Legal Annotation***: "[T]he Rhode Island General Laws defines '**Lot Frontage**' as '[t]hat portion of a lot abutting a street.'" *Fisher v. Zoning Board of Review of Town of Warren* (R.I. Super. Ct., 2009).

"'Zoning **lot frontage**' is defined as 'the length of all the property of such zoning lot fronting on a street, measured between side lot lines.'" *Berger v. Town of New Denmark* (Wis. Ct. App., 2012).

## LOT LINE

**A line of record bounding a lot that divides one lot from another lot or from a public or private street or any other public space. *See Figures 10 and 16*.**

***Legal Annotation***: "These provisions prohibit the location of buildings within twenty-five feet of the **lot line**. The action of the board permitted the applicant to extend a building being erected to be used as a bowling alley to a point only ten feet from the **lot line**." *Reynolds v. Zoning Board of Lincoln* (R.I., 1963).

## LOT LINE, FRONT

**The lot line separating a lot from a street right-of-way. *See Figure 16.***

***Legal Annotation***: "The Pittsburgh zoning ordinance provides that the '**front lot line**' is the 'line which is along a front street.'" *Patricca v. Zoning Board of Adjustment* (Pa., 1991).

## LOT LINE, REAR

**The lot line opposite and most distant from the front lot line. In the case of triangular or otherwise irregularly shaped lots, a line ten feet in length entirely within the lot, parallel to and at a maximum distance from the front lot line. *See Figure 16.***

***Comment***: The ten-foot minimum length is not sacrosanct. On wider lots, it could be a percentage of the minimum lot width, say 10 percent.

***Legal Annotation***: "The City of Annapolis Zoning Code defines **rear lot line** as 'that boundary of a lot which is most distant from or is most nearly parallel to the front lot line.'" *Bennett v. Zelinsky* fn. 11 (Md. Spec. Ct. App., 2005).

## LOT LINE, SIDE

**Any lot line other than a front or rear lot line. *See Figure 16.***

***Legal Annotation***: "The City of Annapolis Zoning Code defines **side lot line** as 'any boundary of a lot that is not a front or rear lot line.'" *Bennett v. Zelinsky* (Md. Spc. Ct. App., 2005).

## LOT OF RECORD

**A lot that exists as shown or described on a plat or deed in the records of the local registry of deeds.**

***Legal Annotation***: "**Lot of record**: A lot which is part of a subdivision, the plat of which has been recorded in the office of the county clerk, or a parcel of land, the deed for which has been recorded in the office of the County Clerk of Harrison County." *SDM. v. Zoning Bd. of City of Marshall* (Texas Ct. App., 2012).

## LOT WIDTH

**The horizontal distance between the side lines of a lot measured at right angles to its depth along a straight line parallel to the front lot line at the minimum required building setback line. *See Figure 10.***

***Legal Annotation***:"The Smithfield Land Development Zoning Ordinance defines '**lot width**' as '[t]he horizontal distance between the side lines of a lot measured at right angles to its depth along a straight line parallel to the front line at the minimum front setback line.'" *RE Partnership Services, Inc. v. Town of Smithfield Zoning Board* fn. 9 (R.I., 2007).

## LOWEST ADJACENT GRADE

**The lowest point of the ground level next to a building.**

***Legal Annotation***: "Accu-Line Surveying, Inc. prepared an updated elevation certificate on or about September 18, 2007, which is dated March 12, 2006, which indicated that the Base Flood Elevation was 9.0 feet and Advisory Base Flood Elevation was 10.0 feet for the Nunez home. (See Plaintiff's Exhibit. No. 1). The elevation certificate also included the **lowest adjacent grade** at 4.61 feet and the highest adjacent grade at 5.48 feet." *Nunez v. Pinnacle Homes, LLC* (La. Ct. App., 2014).

## LOW-INCOME HOUSING

**Housing that is economically feasible for families whose income level is categorized as low within the standards promulgated by the US Department of Housing and Urban Development (HUD) or the appropriate state housing agency.**

***Comment***: Generally speaking, low income is defined as 50 percent or less of the median family income in a particular market area. "Economically feasible" can be defined as housing costs of

28 percent of gross family income for sale housing and 30 percent of gross family income for rental housing. HUD also uses the term "very low" to identify families earning up to 50 percent of median family income for the area, "low" as between 50 and 80 percent, and "moderate" as between 80 and 120 percent.

*Legal Annotation*: "The [Fair Housing] Act defines **low income housing** as housing affordable, under recognized guidelines, to householders earning fifty percent or less of the median income in the region." *Non-Profit Affordable Housing v. COAH* (N.J. App. Div., 1993).

## LOW-SPEED RURAL HIGHWAY

**The access classification for roadways in rural environments where the posted speed limit is forty-five miles per hour or less.**

*Legal Annotation*: "[T]he design criteria used provides for a **low speed rural highway** which meets current BC MoT standards." Peace River (British Columbia) Site C Hydro Project (July 2009). http://tinyurl.com/nchw23d

## LOW-SPEED URBAN HIGHWAY

**The access classification for roadways in urban environments where the posted speed limit is forty miles per hour or less.**

*Legal Annotation*: "1.2 Curb or Curb and Gutter. The design of curbs is based on whether the improved roadway will be defined as **'low speed urban**,' 'transitional,' or, 'high speed urban.' The designer must therefore first determine the type of roadway, then use the guidelines for that roadway type to determine the curb design that may be needed. A roadway is defined as 'low speed,' 'transitional,' or, 'high speed' based on two characteristics:

- Cross-section
- Posted speed (regulatory speed)

(Source: *Facilities Development Manual Wisconsin Department of Transportation,* Chapter 11, "Design," Section 20, "Cross Section Elements for Urban Highways.") http://roadwaystandards.dot.wi.gov/standards/fdm/11-00toc.pdf

## LUMBERYARD

**A retail establishment whose primary products include finished or rough-cut lumber and lumber products that are stored on-site.**

*Legal Annotation*: "'**Lumberyard**' is defined as a 'place where lumber is ordered, delivered or sold.'" *Seigles, Inc. v. City of St. Charles* (Ill. App. Ct., 2006).

## LUMEN

**A unit of measure of the quantity of light that falls on an area of one square foot, every point of which is one foot from the source of one candela.**

*Comment:* A light source of one candela emits a total of 12.57 lumens.

*Legal Annotation*: "A **lumen** is a metric unit of measure used to measure the rate at which light energy falls on a surface." *Stewart v. Beard* (M.D. Pa., 2010).

## LUMINAIRE

**A complete lighting unit consisting of a light source, pole, and all mounting brackets, if appropriate, and all necessary mechanical, electrical, and decorative parts. (Adapted from Kendig 1980.)**

*Legal Annotation*: "When Holton put tension on the line connected to the sling attached to the light pole, the sling slid up the tapered pole and pulled the **luminaire**, or lighting unit, off the top of the pole." *Beatty Construction, Inc. v. Board of Safety Review* (Ind. Ct. App., 2009).

# M

## MADE LAND

**Land previously unsuitable for development because of a high water table, open waters, flooding, unstable subsurface conditions, or similar impairments and made suitable by corrective action. See *Filling; Land Reclamation*.**

***Comment***: Reclaiming land unsuitable for development usually involves filling and draining, activities that require state and often federal permits.

***Legal Annotation***: "Because the jetty construction caused fairly rapid accretion, and, but for the construction of the jetties, the subject land would have remained submerged, California submits the accretion-formed land is **'made' land**, whose title rests in California by virtue of the Submerged Lands Act." *California ex rel. State Lands Commission v. US* (U.S., 1982).

## MAGNET STORE

**See *Retail, Magnet Store*.**

***Legal Annotation***: "The provisions and circumstances that have been taken into account include whether the leased store is a **magnet store** for the shopping center, and whether the parties based the lease agreement on past performance of a specific type of store." *Rothe v. Revco DS, Inc.* (S.D. Ind., 1997).

## MAIN

**The principal artery in any system of continuous piping to which branches may be connected (N.J.A.C. 5:21-1.4).**

***Legal Annotation***: "The court found no practical distinction between a leak in a reservoir and a break in a 20" **main** leading therefrom, saying: 'The duty to keep the destructive agency confined is as great in the one case as in the other.'" *Lubin v. Iowa City* (Iowa, 1964).

## MAINTENANCE GUARANTEE

**Any security that may be required and accepted by a governmental agency to ensure that necessary improvements will function as required for a specific period of time. See *Performance Guarantee*.**

***Comment***: The maintenance guarantee takes effect after the municipality has accepted the improvements. The maintenance guarantee usually runs for a period of one to two years. If something malfunctions, the obligor is required to correct the deficiency.

***Legal Annotation***: "The purpose of a **maintenance guarantee** is to insure the completed improvements. A **maintenance guarantee** may be in the form of a surety bond or cash, or an irrevocable letter of credit issued by a banking or savings institution authorized to do and doing business in this State." *RJP Builders, Inc. v. Township of Woolwich* (N.J. App. Div., 2003).

## MAJOR LIFE ACTIVITIES

**Functions such as caring for oneself, performing manual tasks, walking, seeing, hearing, breathing, learning, and working. See *Americans With Disabilities Act*.**

***Legal Annotation***: "A regulation implementing the Rehabilitation Act interprets the term '**major life activities**' to include 'functions such as caring for one's self, performing manual tasks, walking, seeing, hearing, speaking, breathing, learning, and working.' . . . We have identified other '**major life activities**,' including, but not limited to, 'sitting, standing, lifting, or reaching.' *Colwell v. Suffolk County Police Dept.* (2nd Cir., 1998).

## MAJOR TRAFFIC GENERATOR

**The use or uses that generate a total of five hundred or more vehicle trips per day to and from the use or uses.**

*Comment*: The five-hundred-vehicle trip is the generally accepted standard. The developer of a proposed use classified as a major traffic generator would usually be required to undertake impact studies on intersections and roadways surrounding the proposed use.

*Legal Annotation*: "Given the volume of traffic on Lindbergh Boulevard, respondent's proposal would not be a **major traffic generator**." *Despotis v. City of Sunset Hills* (Mo. Ct. App., 1981).

## MALL

**(1) A shaded walk or public promenade; (2) a shopping center where stores front on both sides of a pedestrian way, which may be enclosed or open.**

*Legal Annotation*: "Moreover, our case law indicates that we regard public pedestrian **malls** and commercial zones as the type of property traditionally used as a public forum." *American Civil Liberties Union, NV v. City of Las Vegas* (9th Cir., 2003).

"The **Mall** is a regional shopping center. . . . In addition to the five anchor stores, about 130 other retail and service establishments are tenants of the **Mall**, including a film theatre." *Bock v. Westminster Mall Co.* (Colo., 1991).

## MANHOLE

**An inspection chamber whose dimensions allow entrance, exit, and working room, located at changes in horizontal and vertical directions for underground utility conduits (N.J.A.C. 5:21-1.4).**

*Legal Annotation*: "The ordinance further requires: 'In order to provide for accurate sampling and measurement of industrial wastes, each industrial plant shall provide, on each of its industrial waste outlet sewers, a large **manhole** or sampling chamber.'" *Chicago Allis Mfg. Corp. v. Metropolitan Sanitary Dist. of Greater Chicago* (Ill., 1972).

## MANNING EQUATION

**A method for calculating the hydraulic capacity of a conduit to convey water.**

*Legal Annotation*: "Turner applied the **Manning Equation**, a civil engineering mathematical formula, to compare the conveyance capacity of ditches containing un-engineered rip-rap to that of ditches with fine sand bottoms. In concluding that water flow is more impeded in rough than in smooth channels, he asserted that MRGCD's use of un-engineered rip-rap in ditches resulted in the 'significant reduction in ditch conveyance capacity [which] means that farmers are unable to obtain adequate water supplies.'" *New Mexico Bd. of Licensure v. Turner* (N.M. Ct. App., 2013).

## MANSE

**See *Clergy Residence*.**

## MANUFACTURED HOME

**A factory-built, single-family structure that meets the Federal Manufactured Home Construction and Safety Standards Act (42 U.S.C. Sec. 5401), commonly known as the *HUD* (US Department of Housing and Urban Development) *Code* (Sanders 1998). See *Factory-Built Housing*.**

*Comment*: Such houses are often referred to as modular homes, and formerly, mobile homes. The latter term was originally coined to describe trailers that were equipped to function as truly mobile homes. The mobile home of years past has long since become a fixed, in-place house that is mobile only at the time it is moved from the factory to the site. Besides losing its mobility, the "mobile home" has also become larger, and the safety and quality have been significantly improved as a result of the passage of the Federal Manufactured Home Construction and Safety Standards Act in 1976. Units built to this code are properly referred to as "manufactured homes" as a result of the 1976 act.

Along with the name change, the appearance of manufactured housing has also changed. Many new manufactured units are designed to look like site-built housing and have pitched roofs and conventional roofing and siding materials. In addition, many manufactured houses are "customized" with site-built amenities, such as patios, garages, and decks.

As manufactured housing has become less mobile, there has been a gradual shift in development approaches from the mobile home park system, where land was rented on a long-term lease, to subdivisions, where lots are purchased. Although some manufactured housing subdivisions have comparatively large lot sizes, attractive developments can be created at densities typical of multifamily housing development if creative design techniques are used. The combined cost savings of manufactured housing and small lot sizes can produce affordable single-family housing. In 1993, the US Census Bureau found that the retail cost of factory-built homes was half that of traditional site-built housing.

Manufactured housing developments usually require special zoning provisions. In many states, however, state planning and zoning enabling legislation has been amended to make double-wide manufactured units on permanent foundations a permitted use in all areas zoned for residential development. See *Factory-Built Housing, Manufactured Housing Community; Modular Home; Mobile Home.*

***Legal Annotation***: "Under Texas law, a 'HUD-code **manufactured home**' has characteristics identical to those of a mobile home except that a HUD-code **manufactured home** is built after June 15, 1976, and is constructed according to HUD standards." *Texas Manufactured Housing Association v. Nederland* (5th Cir., 1996).

## MANUFACTURED HOUSING COMMUNITY

**A private community of single-family homes that are built in accordance with the Federal Manufactured Home Construction and Safety Standards Act and transported, sited, and installed in compliance with the act and the State Uniform Construction Code. See *Manufactured Home*.**

***Legal Annotation***: "Aberdeen at Ormond Beach, L.P., owns Aberdeen at Ormond Beach **Manufactured Housing Community** (Aberdeen), a mobile home park in Ormond Beach that provides housing for persons at least 55 years of age or older." *Volusia County v. Aberdeen at Ormond Beach* (Fla., 2000).

## MANUFACTURING

**Establishments engaged in the mechanical or chemical transformation of materials or substances into new products, including the assembling of component parts, the creation of products, and the blending of materials, such as oils, plastics, resins, or liquors.**

***Comment***: The term "manufacturing" covers all mechanical or chemical transformations, whether the new products are finished or semifinished as raw material in some other process. Manufacturing production usually is carried on for the wholesale market rather than for retail sale, although retail sale to the ultimate consumer is becoming more prevalent. Processing on farms is not usually classified as manufacturing if the raw material is grown on the farm. The manufacturing is accessory to the primary use of farming.

***Legal Annotation***: "The rule defines **manufacturing** to include every operation from the beginning of production until the product is completed and packaged for sale." *Texas Citrus Exchange v. Sharp* (Texas Ct. App., 1997).

## MANUFACTURING, HEAVY

**An establishment engaged in basic processing and manufacturing of materials or products predominately from extracted or raw materials into new products, including assembling, converting, altering, finishing of component parts, or the manufacture of such products, and the storage and/or blending of large volumes of materials of a heavy nature, including but not limited to metal, concrete, plastic, petrochemicals and heavy machinery. See *Manufacturing, Light*.**

*Comment*: Heavy manufacturing involves the manufacture or compounding process of raw materials. These activities or processes may necessitate the storage of large volumes of highly flammable, toxic matter or explosive materials needed for the manufacturing process. In this situation, the handling of such materials must be in a controlled environment and have certification from state and federal agencies that have jurisdiction over such activities. Typical heavy manufacturing uses include but are not limited to: concrete batch plants; concrete, tile, or brick manufacturing; automobile, truck, and tire assembly; ammonia or chlorine manufacturing; metal casting or foundries; gas manufacturing; dye stuffs; grain milling or processing; metal or metal ore production; refining, smelting, or alloying; petroleum or petroleum product refining; boat, pool, and spa manufacturing; slaughtering of animals; glass manufacturing; paper manufacturing; and wood or lumber processing. What distinguishes heavy manufacturing from light manufacturing is that the assembly, fabrication, or processing of goods and materials uses processes that ordinarily have greater than average impacts on the environment, or that ordinarily have significant impacts on the use and enjoyment of adjacent property in terms of noise, smoke, fumes, odors, glare, or health and safety.

In practice, the exact delineation of type of manufacturing and industry (e.g., "heavy" versus "light") is contextually influenced, so what is considered "light" in a central city may very well be classified as more intense in a rural hamlet. Further, there may be many industrial and manufacturing zones, as illustrated in the following Fairfax County ordinance: http://www.fairfaxcounty.gov/dpx/zoningordinance/articles/art05.pdf

*Legal Annotation*: "The primary purpose of the M3, **Heavy Industrial** district is to accommodate high-impact manufacturing and industrial uses, including extractive and waste-related uses." Chicago (Ill.) Zoning Ordinance Chap. 17-5 http://tinyurl.com/683gpe

## MANUFACTURING, LIGHT

**An establishment engaged in the transformation of finished products or parts into new products, including assembling, converting, altering, and finishing of component parts; or the manufacture of products and the blending of materials of a light nature, including paper, wood, or food products and light machinery. See *Manufacturing, Heavy*.**

*Comment*: Light manufacturing means manufacturing predominantly from previously prepared materials or finished products or parts, including processing, fabrication, assembly, and treatment of such products, but excluding basic industrial processing. Typical light manufacturing uses include but are not limited to: electronic goods; food and bakery products; nonalcoholic beverages; paper imprinting and publishing; household appliances assembly; and clothing apparel. What distinguishes light from heavy manufacturing is that the assembly, fabrication, or processing of goods and materials uses processes that ordinarily do not create noise, fumes, smoke, odors, glare, or health and safety hazards outside of the building or lot where such processes occur (assuming that such processes are housed entirely within a building).

*Legal Annotation*: "A **light industrial** use where all processing, fabricating, assembly, or disassembly of items takes places wholly within an enclosed building. Typical items for processing, fabricating, assembly, or disassembly under this use include but are not limited to apparel, food, drapes, clothing accessories, bedspreads, decorations, artificial plants, jewelry, instruments, computers, and electronic devices." *Dallas (Texas) Zoning Use Regulations* http://tinyurl.com/pz6vrl6

## MAP, CONTOUR

**A map that displays land elevations in graphic form with lines connecting areas of equal elevation. See *Topographic Map*. See *Figure 24*.**

*Legal Annotation*: "The Coalition cites evidence in the form of a **contour map** showing geologic units on the west side of the map at a higher elevation than those on the east side to assert that the landfill site is situated within 200 feet of a fault that has had displacement in Holocene time." *Coalition for Long Point v. Texas Commission on Environmental Quality* (Texas Ct. App., 2003).

## MAP, OFFICIAL

See *Official Map*.

## MAPPED STREET

**A street appearing on the official map of the municipality or county.**

***Comment***: Mapped streets are planned streets. By placing them on the official map, the integrity of the right-of-way is preserved, since most enabling acts prevent the issuance of a building permit for a structure in the bed of a mapped street.

***Legal Annotation***: "General City Law § 36 (1) requires only that a proposed new building have reasonable access to a **mapped street** or highway, in order to provide adequate means of coping with fires and other emergencies." *Matter of Brancato v. Zoning Board of Appeals of City of Yonkers* (N.Y. App. Div., 2006).

## MARGINAL ACCESS STREET

See *Street, Marginal Access*.

## MARINA

**A facility for the storing, servicing, fueling, berthing, and securing of boats and which may include eating, sleeping, and retail facilities for owners, crews, and guests.**

***Legal Annotation***: "The [Gerrish Township zoning] ordinance defines '**marina**' as '[a] facility which is owned or operated by a person, extends into or over an inland lake or stream and offers services to the public or members of the marina for docking, loading or other servicing of recreational watercraft.'" *Soupal v. Shady View, Inc.* (Mich., 2003).

## MARKET GARDEN

**Term used to describe smaller growing operations similar in scale and intensity to a community garden, but that also sell food commercially.**

***Legal Annotation***: "Section 2 (A) of the zoning by-law of the town of Sharon provides: 'In the single residence districts, no new building or structure or part thereof shall be designed, constructed or used and, except as provided in Section 6, no building or structure or part thereof shall be altered, enlarged, extended, reconstructed, or used and no premises shall be used for any organized business, trade, manufacturing or commercial enterprise, or except for one or more of the following purposes: . . . 6. Farm, **market garden**, nursery or greenhouse; including the sale of products raised on the premises only.' The trial judge ruled '[t]hat the proposed sale of dairy products aforesaid does not come within the contravention and intent' of the above zoning by-law or of G.L.c. 40A, § 5; '[t]hat the granting of the building permit would not be contrary to the provisions and intent of the Zoning By-Laws of the Town of Sharon'; and that 'the Building Inspector and the respondent Board of Appeals acted arbitrarily and capriciously in denying said permit.'" *Parrish v. Board of Appeal of Sharon* (Mass., 1967).

## MARKETABILITY STUDY

**A study that measures the need for a particular land use or activity within a defined geographic area.**

***Comment***: A marketability study is also referred to as a "market study" and usually involves a proposal to locate a specific use on a specified site. The study determines how many people can be expected to patronize the facility and how many similar facilities are located in the market area.

***Legal Annotation***: "Sterling had conducted a **marketability study** that indicated that the growth in residential development that had typified the early 1980s had ended by 1986." *Township of West Windsor v. Nierenberg* (N.J., 1997).

## MARQUEE

**Any hood, canopy, awning, or permanent construction that projects from a wall of a building, usually above an entrance.**

***Comment***: Marquees are usually exempt from setback requirements and are allowed to project over the sidewalk, particularly in central business districts. Consideration should be given, however, to potential problems with firefighting and the need to get ladders and equipment above the first floor. Also, there is the matter of aesthetics, and any permanent marquee extending along the sidewalk in the central business district should be designed and installed in accordance with an overall plan to ensure design continuity.

***Legal Annotation***: "Section 364(f) of Ordinance No 697 of the city of Highland Park, provides as follows: . . . 'No **marquee** or fixed awning shall hereafter be erected or maintained so as to project over any public sidewalk, street or alley except with the official approval of the city council.'" *Ver Hoven Woodward Chevrolet, Inc. v. Dunkirk* (Mich., 1958).

## MARSHLANDS

**Low-lying tracts of land characterized by high water tables and soils and extensive vegetation peculiar to and characteristic of wet places. See *Wetland, Freshwater*.**

***Legal Annotation***: "Additionally, '"[c]oastal **marshlands**" or "**marshlands**" means any marshland intertidal area, mud flat, tidal water bottom, or salt marsh in the State of Georgia within the estuarine area of the state, whether or not the tidewaters reach the littoral areas through natural or artificial watercourses. OCGA § 12-5-282(3).'" *Center for a Sustainable Coast v. Coastal Marshlands Protection Committee* fn. 2 (Ga., 2008).

## MASKING

**Covering over of one sound or element by another.**

***Comment***: Masking is the amount the audibility threshold of one sound is raised by the presence of a second, masking sound. Also used with regard to odors.

***Legal Annotation***: "A '**masking** threshold' reflects what sounds are inaudible when other sounds are present." *Lucent Technologies, Inc. v. Gateway, Inc.* (Fed. Cir., 2008).

## MASS

**See *Building Mass*.**

## MASSAGE

**Pressing, squeezing, stretching, or stimulating the face, scalp, neck, limbs, or other parts of the human body with or without cosmetic preparation, either by hand or with mechanical or electrical appliances.**

***Comment***: Massage is normally part of the services offered by physical therapists, beauty parlors, spas, gyms, or similar establishments. As such, it normally falls into the category of retail services. Many states require separate licenses, requiring exams and experience for personnel giving massages. Others include massage as part of the license granted to physical therapists, barbers, or beauticians.

***Legal Annotation***: "We hold that the occupation of a massagist and the business of **massage** parlors and similar establishments are proper subjects for regulation under the police power of the City of Charlotte." *Cheek v. City of Charlotte* (N.C., 1968).

## MASS GATHERING

**Any event, held outdoors or in a temporary structure or tent, over a fixed period of time, and attended by three thousand or more persons over the period the mass gathering is scheduled to run. See *Temporary Outdoor Activity*.**

***Comment***: Mass gatherings may include music festivals, concerts, theatrical exhibitions, public shows, entertainment, amusement, speeches, circuses, carnivals, rallies, swap-and-shop markets, and flea markets. They are distinctly different from events held in permanent outdoor amphitheaters or stadiums with permanent parking, clearly delineated circulation, and adequate restroom facilities. Many states require a license to be secured from the local government for any mass gathering and often define them in terms of the number of persons expected to attend over a specified period of time (three thousand persons over eighteen hours in New Jersey; five thousand persons over eighteen hours in Indiana).

Mass gatherings that are regularly scheduled at a fixed location can be controlled by zoning. Other mass gatherings are probably best regulated by a local licensing ordinance rather than by zoning. But the requirements are similar, whether controlled by zoning or by the issuance of a license. A site plan showing access, parking, and circulation, particularly for emergency vehicles, should be reviewed. Health and sanitary facilities, litter control, police protection, and noise impacts should be considered. Some local ordinances require one parking space for every four persons expected to be in attendance at any one time or provision for shuttle buses to and from nearby parking lots. Health requirements in one ordinance required one toilet for each 250 persons in attendance. Finally, many ordinances require the promoters to post indemnity or performance bonds to protect the local government against personal injuries and property damage (American Planning Association, "Fireworks, Farmstands, and Concerts—Summer's Here," *Zoning News*, July 1990).

***Legal Annotation***: "The [Oregon Mass Gathering] Act regulates any 'outdoor **mass gathering**,' defined as a gathering of more than 3,000 persons in an open space for more than 24 hours but fewer than 120 hours." *Southern Oregon Barter Fair v. Jackson County Oregon* (9th Cir., 2004).

## MASS TRANSIT

**A public common carrier transportation system having established routes and fixed schedules.**

***Legal Annotation***: "The San Antonio Transit System 'operated until 1978, when the city transferred its facilities and equipment to appellee San Antonio Metropolitan Transit Authority (SAMTA), a public **mass-transit** authority organized on a countywide basis.'" *Garcia v. San Antonio Metropolitan Transit Authority* (U.S., 1985).

## MASTER DEED

**A legal instrument under which title to real estate is conveyed and by which a condominium is created and established.**

***Comment***: The master deed is the key document in establishing a condominium. It is required to be filed in the office of the county recording officer. The contents of the master deed are usually prescribed by the appropriate state legislation covering condominium ownership.

Master deeds usually contain the following information:

- A statement placing the land described in the master deed under the provisions of the condominium act
- The official title of the condominium
- A legal description of the land
- A survey of the land showing the improvements to be erected, common elements, and units to be sold, in sufficient detail and shown in their respective locations with dimensions
- Identification of each unit
- A description of the common elements and limited common elements, if there are any
- The proportion of the undivided interests in the common elements, including rights of owners
- Bylaws
- Methods of amending and supplementing the master deed
- The name and nature of the association
- The manner of sharing common expenses
- Whatever other provisions may be desired, such as restrictions or limitations of use, occupancy, transfer leasing, or other disposition of a unit or the limitations on the use of common elements

***Legal Annotation***: "The condominium's **master deed** purported to authorize each unit owner, with the written approval of a majority of the trustees of the owners' association, 'to construct additions to his Unit.'" *Strauss v. Oyster River Condominium Trust* (Mass., 1994).

## MASTER PLAN

**A comprehensive, long-range plan intended to guide the growth and development, usually of a community or region, for a set period**

**of time and that typically includes inventory and analytic sections leading to recommendations for the community's land use, future economic development, housing, recreation and open space, transportation, community facilities, and community design, all related to the community's goals and objectives for these elements.**

***Comment***: The term "master plan" (also referred to in some jurisdictions as the *general* or *comprehensive plan*) has almost become a work of art. The principle underlying its analysis and preparation is the comprehensive nature of the document, integrating all of the various parts into a single, unified, coherent plan that includes implementation proposals.

State enabling legislation specifies the legal requirements of a master plan, including its preparation, contents, modifications, adoption, and implementation. Although certain plan elements may be required, there are no limits to the number or type of plan elements, areas, or subplans that may constitute a master plan. In many states, zoning ordinances must be based on the master plan, and where discrepancies occur, the master plan takes precedence. A comprehensive master plan can foster sustainability (Godschalk and Anderson 2012).

***Legal Annotation***: "By using proven sound planning concepts the Division of State and Regional Planning, statutorily charged with the obligation, developed a **master plan** (the SDGP and the Concept Map) for the purpose of guiding the future growth and development of this state." *Southern Burlington County N.A.A.C.P. v. Mount Laurel Township* (N.J., 1983).

## MAXIMUM YIELD

See *Carrying Capacity*.

## McMANSION

**A single-family home whose appearance significantly differs from homes in the immediate area by virtue of its considerably larger floor area and mass (Myers 2008). See *Bulk Regulations; Floor Area Ratio; Compatible Design; Development Context*.**

***Comment***: McMansions, sometimes referred to as "bulky houses" or "mega mansions," are usually substantially higher and wider than existing homes in the immediate vicinity and thus visually overpower the neighboring homes. They are often criticized as "out of place." In neighborhoods of similar-sized lots and homes, the use of floor area ratio controls, which make house size a function of lot size, can help to limit their intrusion in the neighborhood. Another technique is to require a part of the added floor area to be located to the rear of the dwelling, or to be located to the side and set back from the main part of the structure, thus reducing their visual impact on the streetscape. Aside from visual impacts, McMansions often engender animosity based upon socioeconomic differences—"old" versus "new" and "middle class" versus "affluent"—where McMansions can be seen as "upper middle-class gentrification."

***Legal Annotation***: "One resident testified that she did 'not want any McMansions' *[as Seymour notes in his brief, "(t)he word 'McMansion' is usually used in a pejorative sense to refer to houses that some people consider to be too large"]* and that 'the community should have the opportunity for input as to the design of any houses to be built at 227 North Latham so that we avoid McMansions, including written specifics as to height, mass, bulk, lot coverage, and value.' Another resident testified that the resubdivision would detract from the value of adjacent properties and that 'building two very large houses' on the resubdivided lots would be 'totally incompatible with the neighborhood character.' A third resident testified that he did not want construction of big houses in his neighborhood. Finally, a fourth resident testified that building two large houses on the Seymour lot would adversely affect his property value." *Seymour v. City of Alexandria* (Va., 2007).

## MEAN

**The average of a series of figures computed by adding up all the figures and dividing by the number in the series.**

***Legal Annotation***: "According to defendant's expert, the **mean** sales price of the wetland land sales was $6,714 per acre as adjusted, and the median was $6,681 per acre." *Odra Land Co., Inc. v. Monroe Twp.* (N.J. Tax Ct., 2012).

## MEAN HIGH WATERLINE

**The line formed by the intersection of the tidal plane of mean high tide with the shore.**

*Legal Annotation*: "The **mean high water line** is the line representing the average height reached by high tide over the preceding 18.6 years." *US v. Boccanfuso* (2nd Cir., 1989).

## MEANS OF INGRESS AND EGRESS

**The portal that serves as the entrance and exit point from a site or building.**

*Comment*: Specifically, the means of ingress and egress consists of the paths of travel to and from an entrance and exit.

*Legal Annotation*: "It seems fairly well settled that, while access may not be entirely cut off, an owner is not entitled, as against the public, to access to his land at all points between it and the highway. If he has free and convenient access to his property and the improvements on it and his **means of ingress and egress** are not substantially interfered with by the public he has no cause for complaint. . . . The only way in which this driveway could be utilized as a **means of ingress and egress** for the residential site to the west is by constructing an outer roadway or private service road parallel to the south side of Hubbell Avenue between the residential site and the driveway the commission has provided." *Iowa State Highway Commission v. Smith* (Iowa, 1957).

## MECHANICAL TURBULENCE

**The erratic movement of air caused by local obstructions, such as buildings.**

*Legal Annotation*: "The court further finds what the evidence in this case clearly shows, namely, that an area of severe random clear air turbulence existed to the lee of Elephant Mountain between the hours of 2 and 3 p. m. on January 24, 1963 just as could have been expected for that time of year and as the Westover Metro had predicted, the historical weather data tended to show and the airmen discovered; and that B-406 flew into this area of severe turbulence wherein the vertical tail separated from the aircraft. Compare, for example, the testimony of Colonel Bulli with Exhibit H31. . . . The court also finds that B-406 was flying low enough to have been affected by whatever **mechanical turbulence** there might have been within this area. . . . Mr. Lappe, for one, was 'quite satisfied' that **mechanical turbulence** existed within the vicinity of Elephant Mountain." *O'Keefe v. Boeing Company* (S.D. N.Y., 1971).

## MEDIAN

**(1) The middle number in a series of items in which 50 percent of all figures are above the median and 50 percent are below; (2) an island in the center of a highway that separates opposing traffic flows.** *See Figure 2.*

*Legal Annotation*: "According to defendant's expert, the mean sales price of the wetland land sales was $6,714 per acre as adjusted, and the **median** was $6,681 per acre." *Odra Land Co., Inc. v. Monroe Twp.* (N.J. Tax Ct., 2012).

"Under this test, the first step instructs the bankruptcy court to compare the debtor's annualized current monthly income to the **median** family income of a similarly sized family in the debtor's state of residence." *Schultz v. United States* (6th Cir., 2008).

"U.S. Highway . . . is being widened from a two lane highway with no **median** to a four lane highway with a traffic **median** separating the northbound from the southbound lanes." *South Carolina State Highway Dept. v. Wilson* (SC: Supreme Court 1970).

## MEDIAN BARRIERS

See *Traffic Calming.*

## MEDIAN ISLAND

**A barrier placed between lanes of traffic flowing in opposite directions. See *Barrier. See Figure 97.***

***Legal Annotation***: "The Turnpike roadway proper is 48 feet wide at this point with four traffic lanes, two northbound and two southbound, separated by a ten foot **median island**." *Vespe v. DiMarco* (N.J. 1964).

## MEDIATION

**A structured process in which parties involved in a conflict meet with a trained person (mediator) to resolve differences.**

***Comment***: The use of mediation is relatively new to the planning field but has proved to be effective. A study by the University of Montana in 2007 found that between 50 and 80 percent of cases brought to mediation resulted in a formal settlement. Parties in dispute (proponents and opponents to a new project, for example) meet with a mediator to discuss differences and attempt to resolve issues. The mediator might restrict the number of participants and establish ground rules at the beginning of the process. Experts (usually attorneys, planners, and engineers) are often excluded. Mediation determinations are not legally binding on the parties (unlike arbitration) but can result, at the least, in narrowing issues. Some agencies encourage mediation before the matter is formally presented to a planning board or board of adjustment. Others reserve the option of mediation only for after the matter is formally presented to an agency. (See Abrams 2011.)

## MEDICAL BUILDING

**A building that contains establishments providing medical and health-care services. See *Health Care Services*.**

***Legal Annotation***: "In 2007, Buonauro and Sottile planned to open a new methadone clinic in the City and reached an initial agreement to lease space in an existing **medical building** there. The lease contained an agreement requiring the clinic to obtain a business license from the City to operate such a facility. The clinic applied for the license, but the City denied it on January 24, 2008, noting that it required zoning approval and directing the clinic to seek a variance from the Berwyn Zoning Board of Appeals." *Buonauro v. City of Berwyn* (N.D. Ill., 2011).

## MEDICAL DISTRICT

**A zoning district or redevelopment district that has as its anchor a major hospital, medical school, and/or medical complex and that includes or permits a variety of other high-density mixed uses, including medical offices, parking facilities, retail and commercial uses, dormitories, hotels, and residential uses, all intended to support the medical anchor.**

***Comment***: Medical districts are "mini-cities" usually in operation around the clock and logically located in close proximity to mass transit. They impose impacts on surrounding areas that have to be considered in the planning and development of the medical district (Krohe 2006).

***Legal Annotation***: "Specifically, the City Council reasoned that, although the Comprehensive Plan suggests that higher intensity office uses should be located around downtown Spokane and the **Medical District**, the zoning code permits office use in general in an Office zone, and the Office zone does not restrict or define 'higher intensity' offices. . . . Again, the Comprehensive Plan employs precatory language. None of the provisions that Chinn cites prohibit Office zone building heights above 35 feet. Instead, the quoted language merely 'encourage[s]' buildings up to three stories, and it suggests that higher intensity office areas 'should be located around downtown Spokane in the North Bank and **Medical District**.'" *Chinn v. City of Spokane* (Wash. Ct. App., 2013).

## MEDICAL MARIJUANA DISPENSARY

**A licensed establishment or facility that sells marijuana and related supplies and may also (if permitted by local or state law) plant, grow, cultivate, and process marijuana, and manufacture products that contain marijuana.**

***Comment***: A significant number of states have now legalized the sale of medical marijuana. While state laws vary, most states have established overall controls; for example, who can purchase marijuana, the amount that can be purchased, the number of dispensaries that are permitted based on population (similar to liquor licenses), and distance between dispensaries and schools, child-care centers, and other dispensaries (usually one thousand feet). Some cities have established these controls through their licensing powers, others by zoning, and some by both. Most municipalities restrict the location of dispensaries to retail or commercial areas. None permit on-site consumption of marijuana.

The above definition is all-encompassing, including growing, cultivating, and processing of marijuana and manufacture of products containing marijuana. Some municipalities permit only the sale of marijuana and related products in retail zones and restrict the other activities to industrial zones that allow food manufacturing. (**See *Kiser 2011. Interview With Janice Talley, PP, AICP, Planning Director, Montclair, NJ***, 2013).

***Legal Annotation***: "As noted above, the Riverside ordinances at issue declare as a 'prohibited use' within any city zoning classification (1) a '**[m]edical marijuana dispensary**'—defined as '[a] facility where marijuana is made available . . . in accordance with' the CUA—and (2) any use prohibited by state or federal law. . . . The RMC further provides that any condition caused or permitted to exist in violation of the ordinance is a public nuisance which may be abated by the city. . . . In January 2009, the planning division of Riverside's Community Development Department notified Swerdlow by letter that the definition of '**medical marijuana dispensary**' in Riverside's zoning ordinances 'is an all-encompassing definition, referring to all three types of medical marijuana facilities, a dispensary, a collective and a cooperative,' and that, as a consequence, 'all three facilities are banned in the City of Riverside.'" *City of Riverside v. Inland Empire Patients Health and Wellness Center, Inc.* (Calif., 2013).

## MEDICAL WASTE

**See *Waste, Medical*.**

## MEGACHURCH

**A house of worship with a seating or holding capacity of ten thousand or more persons.**

***Comment***: Megachurches (or any large house of worship, regardless of the denomination or religion) are a relatively new phenomenon. They draw from a regional area, have a variety of activities that take place over the entire week, and generate significant amounts of traffic.

The size and scope of these megachurches raise serious questions as to their appropriateness in low-density residential areas. In fact, many of them have become established in once-vacant industrial buildings in industrial areas (Schwab 1996).

The federal Religious Land Use and Institutionalized Persons Act of 2000 (Public Law 106-274, 114 Stat. 803, 42 U.S.C. §2000cc et seq.) places severe restrictions on land-use regulations that affect religious institutions. However, given the potential impact of these intense uses on the surrounding areas, reasonable controls on location, access, parking, lighting, signs, hours of operation, noise and buffers—traditional site plan concerns—may be appropriate (Schwab 1996). **See *Place Of Worship; Religious Use*.**

***Legal Annotation***: "Another witness, Regina Hyatt, testified that she approached a County commissioner about the possibility of building a synagogue but was told that the County would only allow 100 seats because 'there will never be another **mega church** . . . in Boulder County.'" *Rocky Mountain Christian Church v. Board of County Commissioners* (10th Cir., 2010).

## MEGAPLEX

**A motion picture theater, with ten or more screens, that may include retail stores and restaurants. See *Cineplex; Motion Picture Theater*.**

***Comment***: Large movie theaters, with ten (a somewhat arbitrary number) or more screens, are becoming the norm in movie entertainment, often crowding out smaller theaters. They generate a significant amount of traffic, both pedestrian and vehicular, but properly located, they can become strong anchors in downtown locations and assist in rejuvenating failing commercial centers.

Lincoln, Nebraska, for example, adopted a zoning amendment that essentially restricted movie theaters to commercial districts and the downtown area (sidebar in Langdon 2000). Many megaplexes are designed to include retail stores and service establishments, particularly restaurants. A West Palm Beach, Florida, megaplex includes an on-site child-care center to attract parents who might otherwise stay home (Langdon 2000). Attracting megaplexes downtown, however, may require relaxing parking requirements and reducing the "financial, regulatory, political, and physical barriers to downtown infill development" (A. Ricker, quoted in Langdon 2000).

As noted in the Langdon article, one of the major hurdles is "how to accommodate large, windowless theatre buildings and hundreds of parking spaces, which make surroundings unappealing for pedestrians." In Miami Beach, the Lincoln Cinema megaplex has a five-story-high lobby facade of colored glass "which dazzles passersby with views of people, activity, and décor. . . . It gives something back to the street" (B. Zyscovich, quoted in Langdon 2000). Parking is designed to bring people to the theater by walking on sidewalks and by passing shops rather than directly from parking spaces to the theater.

***Legal Annotation***: "The lease agreement, including a September 1996 amendment thereto, required defendant to provide to plaintiff by November 15, 1996 a pad site with utilities on which plaintiff would construct a '**megaplex**' movie theater—the Southroads 20." *American Multi-Cinema, Inc. v. Southroads, LLC* (Dist. Court, D. Kan., 2000).

## MEGALOPOLIS

**An extended metropolitan area created from the merging of once separate and distinct metropolitan areas.**

***Legal Annotation***: "New Jersey is the most densely populated state in the nation and lies at the midpoint of the emerging **megalopolis** that extends from Boston to Richmond." *Gardner v. New Jersey Pinelands Commission* (N.J. 1991).

## MEMBERSHIP ORGANIZATION

**A group of persons who have come together on a formal basis, usually with bylaws and membership requirements, with the object of promoting the interests of the group's members.**

***Comment***: Membership organizations differ from professional organizations in that anyone who ascribes to the goals and objectives of the organization can become a member. Payment of a membership fee and/or annual dues is usually required. If a requirement of membership is a college degree, passing an exam, or achieving a formal and recognized level of proficiency (master plumber or electrician, for example), the organization is considered a professional organization. Many organizations have two levels of membership: one open to all who support the goals of the organization and a second level achieved through a formal examination process. For example, the American Planning Association (APA) is open to all who pay the membership fee and annual dues. Membership in the American Institute of Certified Planners (AICP), the APA's professional subsidiary, can be achieved only by passing an examination and thus qualifies as a professional organization.

Some organizations do not fit easily into a particular category. For example, military veterans' organizations may require a military affiliation or overseas duty or the winning of certain awards in order to join. These may be more logically classified as clubs or fraternal organizations.

Most membership organizations operate out of office buildings and are treated as such. Others, however, have large buildings designed for their specific use, which often produces a large turnout on meeting nights. In addition, the buildings are often rented out to other organizations for events, parties, weddings, flea markets, and the like. It is doubtful that they belong in residential zones, unless they are located on major streets and careful consideration is given to site-plan issues such as landscaping, parking, lighting, and circulation. **See** ***Club; Fraternal Organization***.

***Legal Annotation***: "The Jaycees was a nonprofit **membership organization** 'designed to inculcate in the individual membership . . . a spirit of genuine Americanism and civic interest,' [and] ... was divided into local chapters, described as 'young men's organization[s],' in which regular membership was restricted to males between the ages of 18 and 35." *Boy Scouts of America v. Dale* (U.S., 2000).

## MERGED LOTS

**Two or more contiguous lots, in single ownership, that individually do not conform to zoning ordinance bulk standards.**

***Comment***: In many states, the doctrine of merger treats separate lots under the same ownership as a single lot if either of the lots fails to meet the zoning requirement for area or frontage. The fact that the lots may have been purchased separately and may have been legally conforming lots at some time does not vest development rights in perpetuity.

***Legal Annotation***: "Sometime in the 1980s, pursuant to a provision in the Town's zoning ordinance that automatically merged contiguous non-conforming lots, the Town **merged lots** 9 and 10 to create a single lot, known as lot 7." *Sutton v. Town of Guilford* (N.H., 2010).

## MESOTROPHIC LAKES

**Lakes that are intermediate in characteristics between *oligotrophic* (clear waters and relatively free of nutrients) and *eutrophic* (high levels of growth and nutrients) lakes. See *Eutrophic Lakes; Oligotrophic Lakes*.**

***Legal Annotation***: "The Administrator decided that colored lakes and clear, high-alkalinity **lakes** should maintain a **mesotrophic** state, as these lakes receive natural nitrogen and phosphorus input but still support a healthy diversity of aquatic life. For these two classes, then, the rule sets the allowable chlorophyll-a concentration at 0.020 mg/L. In contrast, clear, low-alkalinity lakes do not receive natural nitrogen and phosphorus input from underlying geological formations, support less algal growth, and have lower chlorophyll-a levels than the other two lake classes. The rule sets the chlorophyll-a criterion for these lakes at 0.006 mg/L." *Florida Wildlife Federation, Inc. v. Jackson* (N.D. Fla., 2102).

## METER

**A metric scale measure equal to 3.28 feet.**

***Legal Annotation***: "Lastly, the Ninth Circuit stated that a 2,200-yard shutdown zone was feasible because the Navy had previously adopted a 2,000-**meter** zone for low-frequency active (LFA) sonar." *Winter v. Natural Resources Defense Council, Inc.* (U.S., 2008).

## METES AND BOUNDS

**A method of describing the boundaries of land by directions (bounds) and distances (metes) from a known point of reference.**

***Legal Annotation***: "An interest in real property is defined by the **metes and bounds** that describe its geographic dimensions and the term of years that describes the temporal aspect of the owner's interest." *Tahoe-Sierra Preservation Council, Inc. v. Tahoe Regional Planning* Agency (U.S., 2002).

## METROPOLIS

**The major city in a designated area; generally, any large city.**

***Legal Annotation***: "Stripped of its remaining historically unique structures, New York City would be indistinguishable from any other large **metropolis**." *Penn Central Transportation Company v. City of New York* (N.Y. Sup. Ct. App. Div., 1975).

## METROPOLITAN AREA

**An area whose economic and social life is influenced and boundaries are roughly defined by the commuting limits to the center city.**

***Comment***: While commuting patterns usually define a metropolitan area, other factors can be used, such as newspaper circulation or retail trade areas.

***Legal Annotation***: "However, the evidence of record in City of Parma—absent in the present case—demonstrated a pervasive pattern and practice of racial discrimination in housing decisions by Parma officials, including: Parma's 'small fraction of one per cent' Black population compared to the 16% Black population in the Cleveland **metropolitan area**, Parma's reputation for hostility toward Blacks, 'statements of elected officials of Parma which were either overtly racist or were found to have racist meanings[,]' and a history of challenged housing decisions, all of which were 'based on a desire to keep minorities out of the community and . . . had an acute and foreseeable segregative effect on this virtually all-white city.'" *White Oak Property Dev. v. Washington Tp., Ohio* (6th Cir., 2010).

## METROPOLITAN STATISTICAL AREA (MSA)

**A geographic area consisting of a large population nucleus together with adjacent areas having a high degree of economic and social integration.**

***Comment***: The major purpose of the MSA designation is to provide federal agencies with a common base in tabulating and publishing data for metropolitan areas. Data are available for individual metropolitan areas on population, housing, industry, trade, employment, payrolls, and labor markets. To that end, MSAs are defined in terms of counties and the smallest geographical unit for which a wide range of statistical data can be obtained.

***Legal Annotation***: "In principal markets such as Chicago, the **Standard Metropolitan Statistical Area** is coterminous with the housing market area." *Hills v. Gautreaux* (U.S., 1976).

## MEZZANINE

**An intermediate level between the floor and ceiling of any story and covering not more than 33 percent of the floor area of the room in which it is located. *See Figure 8.***

***Comment***: In this definition, mezzanines are counted as part of the floor area ratio calculation. The BOCA Code (BOCA 1996) does not include mezzanines in FAR calculations.

***Legal Annotation***: "In the fall of 1981, Carolan began constructing a **mezzanine** overhanging the kitchen section of the restaurant although a **mezzanine** had not been included in the plan submitted for the building permit." *Carolan v. City of Kansas City* (8th Cir. 1987).

## MGD

**Millions of gallons per day.**

***Legal Annotation***: "When the state first required consumptive use permits for water in 1977, this wellfield had a production rate of 6.9 million gallons per day (**mgd**)." *Harloff v. City of Sarasota* (Fla. Ct. App., 1991).

## MICROBREWERY

See *Brew Pub*.

## MICRO-HOTEL

**A hotel consisting of small rooms as a lower-priced alternative to luxury hotels.**

***Comment***: Micro-hotels are loosely based upon the concept of the Japanese "capsule hotel": short-stay, pay-by-the-hour cabins or boxes, most often found in airport terminals (London, Moscow, Philadelphia, Dubai) where travelers can rest or sleep without leaving the terminal or paying the full expense of a hotel room. Newer types of micro-hotels are being developed in larger cities such as New York and Boston, based upon the same concept but containing rooms of between one hundred sixty and two hundred square feet, about half the size of rooms at conventional hotels.

***Legal Annotation***: "Ansley presented Hazard with an unsolicited letter revealing in more detail the 'trade secret' or what he described as the '**Micro-tel**' concept, that is, a small-size, upscale hotel room that purported to result, when built, in reduced maintenance cost, less land utilization, and reduced construction cost." *Hudson Hotels Corp. v. Choice Hotels Intern.* (2nd Cir., 1993).

## MICRO-UNITS

See *Dwelling, Micro-Unit*.

## MICROWAVE

**That part of the electromagnetic spectrum from the infrared to the radio wavelength.**

***Legal Annotation***: "RF emissions are a form of electromagnetic radiation that have separate electric and magnetic components which are linked together, and travel as a wave at a frequency which is expressed in hertz (Hz). Higher frequencies are described in terms of kilohertz (KHz or 1,000 Hz), megahertz (MHz or one million Hz) or gigahertz (Ghz or one billion Hz). . . . Most wireless technology operates at the 800 to 900 MHz or 1,850 to 1,990 MHz frequencies. These frequencies are in the **microwave** spectrum or radio-frequency range." *Stanley v. Amalithone Realty* (N.Y., 2011).

## MID-RISE

**A building of three to seven stories. See *Dwelling, Mid-Rise. See Figure 37*.**

***Legal Annotation***: "The lower court held that the Appellee had shown that **mid-rise** apartments constitute a separate residential usage and that the township's failure to provide for **mid-rise** apartments constitutes exclusionary zoning." *Board of Supervisors of Northampton Township v. Gentsch* (Pa. Comm. Ct., 1980).

## MIGRATION

**The movement of people from one domicile to another.**

***Comment***: The key word is *domicile*. It implies a permanent as opposed to a temporary movement, such as daily commuting to a job.

***Legal Annotation***: "However, in light of the unquestioned historic acceptance of the principle of free interstate **migration**, and of the important role that principle has played in transforming many States into a single Nation, we have not felt impelled to locate this right definitively in any particular constitutional provision." *Attorney General of NY v. Soto-Lopez* (U.S., 1986).

## MILE

**A linear measure equal to 5,280 feet, 1,760 yards, or 1.6 kilometers.**

***Legal Annotation***: "We therefore conclude that low-tide elevations situated in the territorial sea as measured from bay-closing lines are part of the coastline from which the three-**mile** grant of the Submerged Lands Act extends." *US v. Louisiana* (U.S., 1969).

## MINE

**(1) A cavity in the earth from which minerals and ores are extracted; (2) the act of removing minerals and ores.**

***Legal Annotation***: "The coal was not extracted and prepared until it was taken from the **mine** to the place where it was processed and graded so as to be in condition for delivery to distributors and consumers." *Roberts v. Weinberger* (4th Cir., 1975).

## MINERAL RIGHTS

**One of a number of distinct and separate rights associated with real property that give the owner of rights certain specified privileges, such as to extract, sell, and receive royalties with respect to the minerals.**

***Comment***: The holder of mineral rights, in some cases, may be able to exercise those rights to the detriment of all other rights. For example, if the mineral rights owner has the right to explore or mine the minerals, it could severely affect the remainder of the land. See *Extractive Industries*.

***Legal Annotation***: "In this state when property is conveyed and the **mineral rights** are reserved, the party reserving the minerals is vested with a real right, the right to go upon the land and produce the minerals." *Leiter Minerals, Inc. v. California Co.* (La., 1961).

## MINI-MALL

**A shopping center of between eighty thousand and one hundred fifty thousand square feet on a site of eight to fifteen acres, where tenants are located on both sides of a covered walkway with direct pedestrian access to all establishments from the walkway. See *Shopping Center; Shopping Mall; Specialty Shopping Center*.**

***Legal Annotation***: "This **mini-mall** consisted of seven or eight retail establishments, including appellee Grand Union Supermarket." *Dopico-Fernandez v. Grand Union Supermarket* (1st Cir., 1988).

## MINI-MART

See *Retail Store, Convenience*.

## MINI-WAREHOUSE

See *Self-Storage Facility*.

## MINIMUM ACCESSIBILITY

See *Accessible Design*.

## MINIMUM PARKING STANDARDS

**A set of requirements included in land-use regulations that require a certain minimum ratio or parking standard that particular development is required to meet on-site in order to obtain development approval.**

***Comment***: Minimum parking standards are commonly found in land development regulations as a means of ensuring that a development includes some means, typically on-site, of providing for the parking needs generated by a specific use at full occupancy, at times of peak usage. Sources for minimum parking regulations in most zoning ordinances are derived from comparable communities, but the Institute of Transportation Engineering's "Parking Generation," now in its fourth edition, which bases its standards on case studies from around the United States, is a more authoritative source. Like other standards, the use of and reliance on minimum parking requirements has become controversial, with criticisms ranging from a suburban bias, to the production of large areas of pavement that are only rarely fully occupied, inefficient use of scarce land resources, sprawl, and abetting the continued dependency on the automobile. Proponents indicate that such requirements should only be used as "guidelines" and that they should be tailored and varied to meet particular circumstances and purposes, and as such, are still a necessary and useful regulatory tool.

***Legal Annotation***: "The proposed use (a place of worship) incorporates a build-out of the existing lower level parking deck to create a new sanctuary, additional office space and classrooms. An analysis was prepared by staff comparing the proposed uses within the building and **minimum parking standards** from Article 18.2.1 of the Zoning Ordinance associated with each use. According to this analysis (see Table 1), the site at full build-out would not provide the minimum number of parking spaces required per code. Because of this, staff recommends the total building area be limited to 32,053 square feet unless the applicant receives a variance from the minimum parking requirements or can demonstrate a reduction is warranted due to the operation of use such that parking spaces could be shared." *Church of Scientology v. City of Sandy Springs* (N.D. Ga., 2012).

## MINIMUM REQUIRED DISTANCE

**The shortest distance measured from one point, line, building, structure, or object to another point, line, building, structure, or object, measured in feet or meters.**

***Comment***: Minimum required distance is probably the most common standard in zoning, generally used to define how close a building can be built to a property line (front, side, and rear yards) or to an adjacent building. It is also used to establish minimum distances between incompatible uses, or to require specific design standards for construction located close to historic buildings or districts. Traditionally, the minimum required distance is measured "as the crow flies," or in a straight line between the two measuring points. However, a recent court case in New Jersey, still being litigated, finds the owner of a sexually oriented business claiming it had met the municipality's requirement that such uses be at least one thousand feet from the closest residence by measuring the one thousand feet along established walking and driving pathways or roads abutting the club and not in the traditional straight line. If the owner prevails, it might suggest that setback requirements clearly set forth how the distance is to be measured.

*Legal Annotation*: "Sandalwood deed restrictions means the setback lines depicted on the recorded property plats that reflect the minimum building lines from particular streets established by the City of Houston. Section 9 thus simply ensures that a fence or wall will not be built nearer to a street than the **minimum distance required** by the applicable City of Houston's building setback ordinance, by prohibiting it from being nearer the street than the 'minimum building setback line' reflected on the recorded plat. The evidence at trial established that the minimum building setback line for the Uptegraphs' property along Sandalwood Drive was 25 feet. Accordingly, the trial court did not err in so finding. (Section 9 also provides that the ACC may approve a fence or wall closer to the street than the minimum building setback distance. That portion of section 9, if exercised, would appear to place the homeowner in violation of the applicable City minimum building line ordinance, notwithstanding any approval on the part of the ACC, when the fence or wall is one which requires a building permit.)" *Uptegraph v. Sandalwood Civic Club SW 3d* (Texas Ct. App., 2010).

## MINING

**The extraction of minerals, including solids, such as coal and ores; liquids, such as crude petroleum; and gases, such as natural gases. See *Extractive Industries*.**

*Legal Annotation*: "A **mining** claim on public lands is a possessory interest in land that is 'mineral in character' and as respects which discovery 'within the limits of the claim' has been made." *Best v. Humboldt Placer Mining Co.* (U.S., 1963).

## MINOR SITE PLAN

**See *Site Plan, Minor*.**

## MINOR SUBDIVISION

**See *Subdivision, Minor*.**

## MINOR TRAFFIC GENERATOR

**The use or uses that generate less than a total of five hundred vehicle trips per day. See *Major Traffic Generator*.**

*Legal Annotation*: "**Minor traffic generator** means a traffic generator, which attracts at least 25,000 persons per year (only on conventional routes)." *903.8 freeway and expressway guide signs, Missouri Department of Transportation.*

## MIST

**Liquid particles suspended in air and formed by condensation of vaporized liquids.**

*Legal Annotation*: "The air and water are mixed in the snow guns and shot into the atmosphere as mist. The **mist** falls to the surface forming snow if the proper meteorological conditions are present." *Vail Associates, Inc. v. Commissioner* (Tax Ct., 1987).

## MITIGATION

**Methods used to alleviate or lessen the impact of development.**

***Comment***: One of the purposes of requiring an environmental impact statement is to determine the potential impacts from any development proposal and to propose mitigation methods to alleviate and minimize the impacts. These might include soil erosion measures and buffers, the creation of new wetlands to compensate for those that are filled or lost, or contributions for expanded public facilities.

*Legal Annotation*: "In its discussion of air-quality **mitigation** measures, the EIS identified actions that could be taken by the county government to mitigate the adverse effects of development, as well as those that the Forest Service itself could implement at the construction stage of the project." *Robertson v. Methow Valley Citizens Council* (U.S., 1989).

## MITIGATION, WETLAND

**An activity or activities carried out to compensate for impacts to freshwater wetlands, state open waters, or coastal wetlands caused by development, construction, or other activities.**

***Comment***: Wetland mitigation is currently required under the Federal Freshwater Wetland Protection Act and Coastal Zone Management rules. Mitigation for wetlands may take the following forms: creation of new wetlands, restoration or enhancement of existing wetlands, mitigation bank credit purchase, monetary contribution, or a land donation. (Source: NJ Department of Environmental Protection; Interview with Cathleen Marcelli, PE.) See *Mitigation Bank*.

***Legal Annotation***: "Leimco and the EPA entered into a Consent Agreement and Final Order ('CAFO') on April 25, 2005. . . . The CAFO required Leimco to submit a **Wetland Mitigation** Replacement Plan. . . . Plaintiff alleges that

[t]he CAFO provided that Leimco was to submit a **Wetland Mitigation** Replacement Plan which provided for, among other things the following items:

(a) Identification of the **wetlands mitigation** project involving Leimco and other unrelated third parties that will occur at the 340 acre Site located in Lake County, Leroy Township, Ohio (hereinafter 'Mitigation Site');

(b) A plan to create, restore, enhance and preserve no less than 38.72 acres of the 67 acres of wetlands and aquatic habitat, located within areas 1, 2, 3 and 4 consistent with a Preliminary Wetlands Assessment and Mitigation Site Evaluation submitted by Leimco in June of 2004 as amended;

(c) A plan to be conducted, in concert with unrelated third parties, to restore, enhance and preserve the biological wetland functions existing on no less than 71 acres of additional wetland acres, excluding buffer, of the Mitigation Site;

(d) Compliance with the Mitigation and Monitoring Guidelines, prepared by the Corps;

(e) A plan providing for the restoration of biological and habitat functions for the 23-acre abandon/prior-converted agricultural field within the Mitigation Site; and

(f) The transfer by deed of ownership interest in the Mitigation Site, including all upland buffer areas to Defendant Metroparks, when [the] project [is] completed and accepted by Defendant Corps."

*Leimco Development Co., Ltd. v. Jackson* (N.D. Ohio, 2011).

## MITIGATION BANK

**A wetland area that has been restored, established, enhanced, or preserved, which is then set aside to compensate for future conversions of wetlands for development activities (EPA, *Wetlands Compensatory Mitigation Fact Sheet*).**

***Comment***: Applicants seeking to destroy or denigrate a wetland area, upon approval of regulatory agencies, can purchase credits from a mitigation bank to meet their requirements for compensatory mitigation. The value of the credits is determined by quantifying the wetland functions or acres created or restored. The mitigation bank sponsor is ultimately responsible for the success of the project. The mitigation bank is almost always off the site of the project but in the same watershed (EPA, *Wetlands Compensatory Mitigation Fact Sheet*).

Mitigation banks are big business. In 2005, over 450 banks had been created, with another 198 proposed. Many of the banks are created by public agencies. For example, a state transportation department proposing improvements through a wetlands area will purchase land and establish a mitigation bank to compensate for the on-site damage to the wetlands (Pittman 2007; http://water.epa.gov/lawsregs/guidance/wetlands/mitbankm.cfm; http://www.mitigation banking.org/mitigationbanks/index:html).

***Legal Annotation***: "A **mitigation bank** is an offset of preserved and restored wetlands used to compensate for the environmental impact of more destructive land use." *Hearts Bluff Game Ranch v. U.S.* (Fed. Cir., 2012).

## MIXED-USE DEVELOPMENT (MXD)

**Mixed-use developments that have the specific designation as an "MXD" have the following three characteristics: (1) three or more significant revenue-producing uses (such as retail, office, residential, hotel/motel, entertainment/cultural/recreation) that in well-planned projects are mutually supporting; (2)**

**significant physical and functional integration of project components (and thus a relatively intensive use of land), including uninterrupted pedestrian connections; and (3) development in conformance with a coherent plan (which frequently stipulates the type and scale of uses, permitted densities, and related items) (ULI, *Mixed-Use Development Handbook*, 1987).**

***Comment***: Mixed-use developments with the designation of MXD are a distinct development phenomenon, different from developments that simply contain a mix of more than two uses, as defined below. Rockefeller Center in New York City is considered to be the original MXD, and it set the precedent for all MXDs that followed. Other MXDs include Penn Center in Philadelphia, Midtown Plaza in Rochester, and Charles Center in Baltimore.

## MIXED-USE DEVELOPMENTS

**The development of a neighborhood, tract of land, building, or structure with a variety of complementary and integrated uses, such as, but not limited to, residential, office, manufacturing, retail, public, and recreation, in a compact urban form.**

***Comment***: Central business districts are examples of mixed-use development, but they generally develop over long periods of time and often without a plan. Mixed-use developments, which generally include several land uses, are mixed vertically and horizontally in compact, integrated form and are encouraged as a form of "smart growth" because they reduce traffic congestion by locating homes and jobs within easy commuting distance and integrate shopping and related facilities into residential neighborhoods. Ideally, every neighborhood should be a mixed-use development providing a variety of housing types and sizes, and places to work, shop, and recreate. (Source: Jackson (2006) and Schultz (2004).)

***Legal Annotation***: "The County of Sacramento (County) approved a community plan for a large, **mixed use development** project proposed by real parties in interest in this mandate action (real parties), as well as a specific plan for the first portion of that development." *Vineyard Area Citizens v. City of Rancho Cordova* (Calif., 2007).

## MIXED-USE ZONING

**Regulations that permit a combination of different uses within a single development or zone.**

***Comment***: An example of mixed-use zoning is allowing residential apartments above ground floor retail uses.

***Legal Annotation***: "Section 410-2 (F)(3) of the Zoning Ordinance for the City of Pawtucket provides: The purpose of the RD3 Riverfront **Mixed-Use Zoning** District is to promote a mix of residential, commercial and light industrial uses that are compatible with uses along the river, including housing and commercial buildings; preserve and adaptively reuse existing mill-type structures; promote variations in the siting of structures and amenities; and to enhance view corridors to the river." *City of Pawtucket v. Pawtucket Zoning Board of Review* (R.I. Super. Ct., 2010).

## MOBILE HOME

**A residential dwelling that was fabricated in an off-site manufacturing facility, designed to be a permanent residence, and built prior to enactment of the Federal Manufactured Home Construction and Safety Standards. See *Factory-Built Housing; Manufactured Home; Modular Home.***

***Legal Annotation***: "Earlier that year, the General Assembly had authorized the council to adopt an ordinance which would license the operation of mobile home parks and regulate the use of a **mobile home** whether it was placed along with other **mobile homes** in a park or parked by itself elsewhere in the town." *Town of Gloucester v. Olivo's Mobile Home Court, Inc.* (R.I., 1973).

## MOBILE HOME PARK

**A property containing sites with required improvements and utilities that are leased for the long-term placement of mobile homes or manufactured houses, which may or may not**

**include services and facilities for the residents. See *Manufactured Home Community*.**

*Comment*: Mobile home parks, frequently referred to as manufactured housing parks or communities, often are licensed by the municipality or county, and compliance with local regulations is a prerequisite to annual license renewal. The regulations may specify a minimum area for the house pad, such as three thousand to four thousand square feet, and other required amenities. The spaces may be rented, owned individually, or sold as condominiums. Mobile home parks usually ban recreational vehicles, campers, or trailers.

*Legal Annotation*: "A county planning commission sued to enjoin the operation of a **mobile home park** that did not comply with the county's Private Act. At trial, the successor-in-interest stipulated to the mobile home park's noncompliance but claimed the park was grandfathered as a prior legal commercial use pursuant to Tennessee Code Annotated section 13-7-208(b)(1), arguing that a previous owner had established the park before the Private Act took effect. The trial court granted injunctive relief to the planning commission, finding both that the park was not in operation prior to the Private Act, and that the park was later abandoned. The Court of Appeals determined that the mobile home park was a residential use to which section 13-7-208(b)(1) did not apply but nonetheless affirmed the trial court's findings concerning abandonment. We hold that this **mobile home park** is a commercial use within the scope of section 13-7-208(b)(1). We further hold that the evidence does not preponderate against the trial court's finding that the **mobile home park** was not grandfathered because it was not yet in operation when the Private Act took effect. This finding was sufficient to warrant the injunction, and we need not reach the issue of abandonment. Accordingly, we affirm the judgment of the trial court." *Smith Cty. Planning Com'n v. Hiwassee LLC* (Tenn., 2010).

## MOBILE HOME SPACE

**A plat of land or site for the placement of a single mobile home within a mobile home park. See *Pad*.**

*Legal Annotation*: "The ordinance also includes a 'vacancy control' provision that prohibits park owners from raising the rent on any **mobile home space** by more than fifteen percent after a tenant vacates that space." *Besaro Mobile Home Park, LLC v. City of Fremont* (N.D. Calif., 2013).

## MOBILE SOURCE

**A moving source of pollution, such as an automobile.**

*Legal Annotation*: "Because the regulation of **mobile source** emissions is a federal responsibility, Congress has expressly preempted states from setting emissions standards for mobile sources." *Jensen Farms v. Monterey Bay Air Pollution Ctrl* (9th Cir., 2011).

## MODAL SPLIT

**The breakdown of how people travel by type of conveyance.**

*Comment*: An example of a modal split for commuting traffic might indicate 85 percent private auto, 10 percent bus, and 5 percent pedestrian or bike.

*Legal Annotation*: "This study undertook a '**modal split**' projection between transit and other types of trips." *Movement Against Destruction v. Volpe* (D. Md., 1973).

## MODE

**In statistics, the value or number that occurs most frequently in a given series.**

*Legal Annotation*: "Approximately 95 moving companies responded to the survey, representing about 2,241 employees. According to the petition, all statistical indicators in the data collected by the Comptroller showed that the wages that actually prevailed in the region were between $10 and $20 per hour. The average wage received by movers surveyed was $19.19; the median wage was $15; and the **mode** (i.e., the most commonly paid wage) was $12.00. . . . And, as noted earlier, no matter what statistical method is chosen—average, median or **mode**— the survey results reveal figures substantially lower than the wages chosen by the Comptroller." *Matter of Metropolitan Movers Association, Inc. v. Liu* (N.Y. Sup. Ct. App. Div., 2012).

## MODERATE-INCOME HOUSING

**Housing that is economically feasible for families whose income level is categorized as moderate within the standards promulgated by the US Department of Housing and Urban Development (HUD) or the appropriate state housing agency.**

***Comment***: Generally speaking, moderate income is defined as between 50 and 80 percent of the median family income in a particular market area. Economically feasible can be defined as housing costs of 28 percent of gross family income for sales housing and 30 percent of gross family income for rental housing. HUD also uses the term "very low" to identify families earning 50 percent or less of median family income, "low" as between 50 to 80 percent of median family income, and "moderate" as 80 to 120 percent of median family income.

***Legal Annotation***: "We set forth in that case, for the first time, the doctrine requiring that municipalities' land use regulations provide a realistic opportunity for low and **moderate income housing**." *South Burlington Cty. NAACP v. Mount Laurel Tp.* (N.J., 1983).

## MODERNISM

**In urban design, the antithesis of "urbanism," characterized by soaring skyscrapers situated on super blocks of open space, and linked by a system of mostly underground transportation modes.**

***Comment***: Modernism as applied to city planning is best characterized by the work and theories of Le Corbusier, the French architect. His disciples were Lucio Costa and Oscar Niemeyer, principal planners and architects of the Brazilian capital Brasilia. His work, and the "modernism" concept, was roundly criticized by Jane Jacobs in *The Death and Life of Great American Cities*.

***Legal Annotation***: "Professor Allison's focus on the MTC Building's aesthetic, architectural, and historic value as one of the finest products of **modernism** in the International Style from the mid-twentieth century unquestionably embodies the interest the LPL is intended to protect and perpetuate, quite apart from property, contractual, business, or financial interests. Any uprooting of the building's value by failing to preserve it directly causes an irreplaceable loss to his civic pride in and professional use and study of the building as a beautiful, magnificent, and renowned accomplishment in the city's cultural and architectural history. Nothing in the current record suggests that his use, study, and enjoyment of the MTC Building has been of less frequency, intensity, or duration than the petitioners' visits to the Pine Bush or is otherwise distinguishable so as to negate his standing." *Allison v. NYC Landmarks* (N.Y. Sup. Ct., 2011).

## MODULAR BUILDING

**A building that is usually transported to its site on a steel frame or special trailer because it does not have a permanent chassis like a manufactured (mobile) home (*FEMA Glossary*).**

## MODULAR HOME

**A structure intended for residential use and manufactured off-site in accordance with the local or state code. See *Factory-Built Housing; Manufactured Home*.**

***Comment***: This definition differs from the one for *manufactured home* in that it refers to the code that governs the construction of modular homes if other than the Federal Manufactured Home Construction and Safety Standards Code. Where the Code is used, the definition is the same as for *manufactured home*.

***Legal Annotation***: "An 'industrialized' or **'modular' home** is built off-site in modular components that are then transported to a residential site and erected on a permanent foundation." *Texas Manufactured Housing Ass'n v. Nederland* (5th Cir., 1996).

## MODULAR-ASSEMBLY-UNIT NEWSRACK

**Two or more newsracks assembled in a single housing unit that is supported by one or more pedestals and permanently attached to a sidewalk or concrete pad. See *Newsrack*. See *Figure 70*.**

*Comment*: Modular units are now available in a variety of designs, shapes, and sizes. These units can be selected to reflect community values and eliminate the problem of unsightly clutter and installation control. The illustration shows a double-deck design that requires less sidewalk area; a less expensive design would be a simple metal rack, elevated about eight inches, and capable of holding several newsracks in place.

## MORATORIUM

**The legally authorized delay of new construction or development.**

*Comment*: Local moratoriums to halt development activity while local master plans and/or development regulations are prepared or amended are not permitted in many states. However, a United States Supreme Court decision on a development moratorium in *Tahoe-Sierra Preservation, Inc. v. Tahoe Regional Planning Agency* (2002) permits such a moratorium. See *Comment Under Taking*.

***Legal Annotation***: "The question presented is whether a **moratorium** on development imposed during the process of devising a comprehensive land-use plan constitutes a per se taking

**Figure 70**

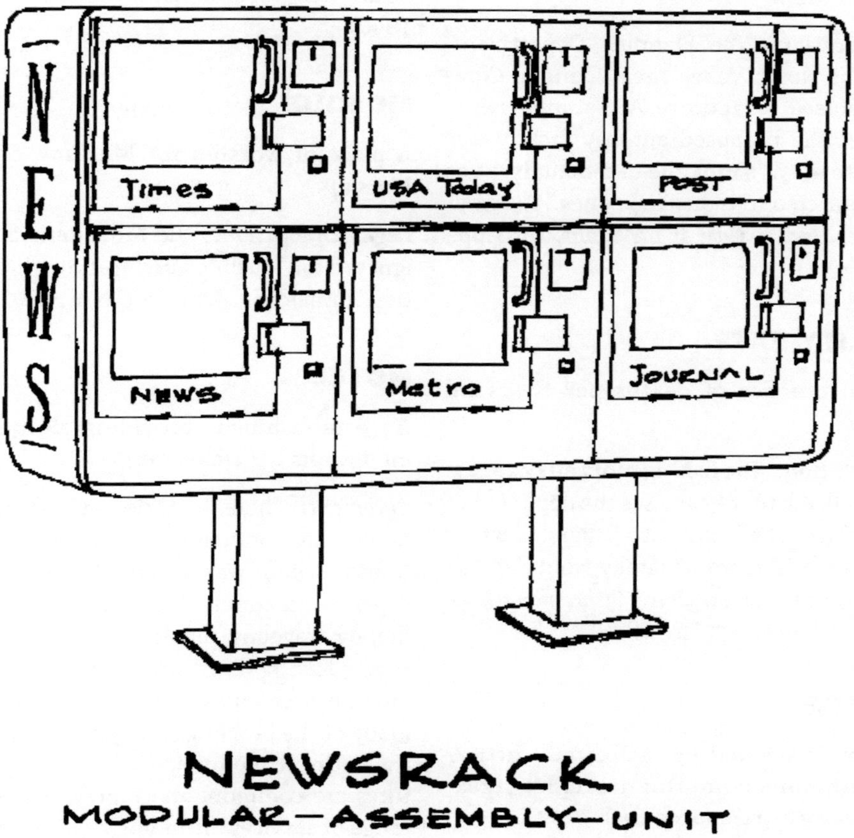

of property requiring compensation under the Takings Clause of the United States Constitution." *Tahoe-Sierra Preservation Council, Inc. v. Tahoe Regional Planning Agency* (U.S., 2002).

## MORBIDITY RATE

**The incidence of a specific disease per specified unit of population.**

*Legal Annotation*: "Such mortality information, the complaint alleged—especially the statistical **morbidity rate** of pancreatic cancer—was material to Mr. Arato's decision whether to undergo postoperative treatment." *Arato v. Avedon* (Calif., 1993).

## MORGUE

**A place for the storage of human bodies prior to autopsy, burial, or release to survivors, family, or next of kin.**

*Legal Annotation*: "The Planning Department, and later the North Valley Area Planning Commission, refused to approve APS's application, finding that the proposed autopsy facility was equivalent to use as a **morgue** or mortuary, a use which is restricted to industrial zones." *Autopsy/Post Services, Inc. v. City of LA* (Calif. Ct. App., 2005).

## MORTALITY RATE

**The annual number of deaths per thousand population.**

*Legal Annotation*: "The fishing **mortality rate** is a statistic called F that expresses the depletion of the stock of fish attributable to fishers, whether by capture or by discard of fatally wounded fish or otherwise, in a given year." *Fishermen's Dock Co-Op., Inc. v. Brown* (4th Cir., 1996).

## MORTGAGE

**A loan that is secured by real estate. http://www.realtor.com/homefinance/mortgages/terms-glossary.aspx?source=web**

*Legal Annotation*: "'**Mortgage**' is defined as 'an interest in land created by a written instrument providing security for the performance of a duty or the payment of a debt.' . . . Notably, '[t]he **mortgage** operates as a conveyance of the legal title to the mortgagee, but such title is subject to defeasance on payment of the debt or performance of the duty by the mortgagor.'. . . In other words, the mortgagee's title is defeated when the debt is paid." *Residential Funding v. Saurman* (Mich. Ct. App., 2011).

## MORTUARY

**A place for the storage of human bodies prior to their burial or cremation.**

*Legal Annotation*: "Manifestly the operation of a **mortuary** where bodies are prepared for interment or cremation is a much closer and more intimate incident of burial. . . . We therefore, conclude that cemetery lands may be used for such purposes as are incident to the burial of the dead." *Wing v. Forest Lawn Cemetery Assn.* (Calif., 1940).

## MOSQUE

**A place of worship for Muslims. See *Place of Worship*.**

*Legal Annotation*: "The **Mosque** is an area designated for Muslim worship and religious activities." *Crawford v. Artuz* (S.D.N.Y., 2001).

## MOTEL

**An establishment providing sleeping accommodations for transients.**

***Comment***: There is little distinction between hotels and motels. Traditionally, the motel (motor-hotel) was a one- or two-story, less expensive accommodation catering to the automobile traveling public, with a majority of all rooms having direct access to the outside without the necessity of passing through the main lobby of the building. Today, motels range across the entire economic spectrum. Multistory structures are common, and motels may offer a full range of services, including restaurants, meeting rooms, entertainment, and recreational facilities. See *Hotel*.

*Legal Annotation*: "More specifically, the pertinent portion of the former City of Key West Code of Ordinances section 35.07(14)(b), which applied to Planned Redevelopment Districts, such as the Truman Annex, provided as follows: Transient Housing is commercially operated housing principally available to short term visitors for less than twenty-eight (28) days; transient housing includes hotels, **motels**, guest houses, and time shares. A transient housing unit may consist of up to two (2) hotel 'locked-out' rooms (i.e., two (2) 'keys' per unit)." *Allen v. City of Key West* (Fla. Ct. App., 2011).

## MOTION PICTURE THEATER

**A place where motion pictures are shown to the public for a fee. See *Megaplex*.**

*Legal Annotation*: "This case involves a constitutional challenge to a zoning ordinance, enacted by appellant city of Renton, Washington that prohibits adult **motion picture theaters** from locating within 1,000 feet of any residential zone, single- or multiple-family dwelling, church, park, or school." *Renton v. Playtime Theaters, Inc.* (U.S., 1986).

## MOTOR FREIGHT TERMINAL

**See *Freight-Handling Facilities*.**

## MOTOR VEHICLE, ABANDONED

**A motor vehicle that (1) is physically inoperable, or missing essential parts to be operable, and that has been stored on private property for more than forty-eight hours; (2) lacks a current license plate and is not stored within a completely enclosed structure or is not currently for sale and stored at a facility licensed for such sales. See *Vehicle, Junk*.**

*Legal Annotation*: "[V].A.T.C. Transp. Code, § 683.002, defines '**Abandoned motor vehicle**' to include a motor vehicle that has remained on private property without the consent of the owner or person in control of the property for more than 48 hours." *McDuff v. State* (Texas Ct. Crim. App., Appeals 1997).

## MOUNTABLE CURB

**See *Curb, Mountable*.**

## MOVING LANE

**Any traffic lane where traffic movement is the primary, if not sole, function (N.J.A.C. 5:21-1.4).**

*Legal Annotation*: "The street, running generally north and south, was wide enough (between twenty-seven and twenty-nine feet) to accommodate the parking of automobiles on both sides and leave room for a **moving lane** of traffic between them." *Wheeler Transportation, Co., Inc. v. Katzoff* (Md. Ct. App., 1966).

## MULCH

**A layer of wood chips, dry leaves, straw, hay, plastic, or other material placed on the surface of the soil around plants to retain moisture, to prevent weeds from growing, to hold soil in place, and to aid plant growth.**

*Legal Annotation*: "The BZA upheld the inspector's decision on the grounds that the **mulch** was not grown on Lawson's land, in that Lawson bought tree bark from a commercial sawmill and simply processed it on his property into a finer form of **mulch**." *Lawson v. Foster* (Ohio Ct. App., 1992).

## MULCHING

**The application of mulch.**

*Legal Annotation*: "In 2000 the petitioners acquired the property and established a landscaping and **mulching** business, which involved processing trees and stumps through industrial wood chippers, and stirring large piles of mulch with bulldozers." *Matter of Urban Forest Products, Inc. v. Zoning Board of Appeals for Town of Haverstraw* (N.Y. App. Div., 2002).

## MULTIFAMILY DWELLING

**See *Dwelling, Multifamily*.**

## MULTIGENERATIONAL HOUSING

**See *Housing, Multigenerational*.**

## MULTIPHASE DEVELOPMENT

**A development project that is constructed in stages, each stage being capable of existing independently of the others.**

***Legal Annotation***: "On or about April 1, 2004, Buckskin submitted a land use application to Valley County, seeking to develop The Meadows, a **multiphase development** project consisting of six phases." *Buckskin Properties, Inc. v. Valley County* (Idaho, 2013).

## MULTI-SERVICE CENTER

**A building containing a variety of social services convenient and readily available to the residents of the neighborhood where located.**

***Comment***: Such services may include education, counseling, legal aid, recreation, and health care. It is often associated with and may be located in a church, school, or similar facility (Schultz and Kasen 1984).

***Legal Annotation***: "**Multi-service centers** are City-owned buildings run by sponsor community-based organizations." *Mandry v. City of New York* (N.Y. Sup. Ct., 2010).

## MULTIUSE BUILDING

**A building containing two or more distinct uses.**

***Comment***: A multiuse building might include retail stores on the first floor and offices and/or apartments on the upper floors.

***Legal Annotation***: "WRP is the owner and developer of a **multi-use building**, which includes parking, commercial space, and 20 residential units." *WRP Lake Union v. Exterior Services* (Wash. Ct. App., 1997).

## MULTIUSE PATH

**See *Shared Use Path*. http://safety.fhwa.dot.gov/ped_bike/tools_solve/fhwasa12018/#chap1.6**

## MUNICIPALITY

**The political subdivision that can adopt and enforce the development ordinances if so empowered by state legislation.**

***Comment***: The development regulations would, under this definition, note the specific legal name of the municipality. In some states, the county or state itself may adopt and enforce development regulations. See *Local Authority*.

***Legal Annotation***: "A **municipality** is merely a department of the State, and the State may withhold, grant or withdraw powers and privileges as it sees fit." *Trenton v. New Jersey* (U.S., 1923).

# N

## NARROW LANE

A travel lane less than fourteen feet in width, which therefore does not allow bicyclists and motorists to travel side by side within the same traffic lane and maintain a safe separation distance. http://safety.fhwa.dot.gov/ped_bike/tools_solve/fhwasa12018/#chap1.6

## NATIONAL AMBIENT AIR QUALITY STANDARDS (NAAQS)

**Standards promulgated by the US Environmental Protection Agency for specified air pollutants, including suspended particulates, sulfur dioxide, carbon monoxide, nitrogen dioxide, ozone, hydrocarbons, and lead (Schultz and Kasen 1984).**

*Legal Annotation*: "The first step toward establishing **national ambient air quality standards** for a particular pollutant is its addition to a list, compiled by EPA's Administrator, of pollutants that cause or contribute to air pollution 'which may reasonably be anticipated to endanger public health or welfare.'" ***Lead Industries Ass'n, Inc. v. Environmental Protection Agency*** (D.C. Cir, 1980).

## NATIONAL ENVIRONMENTAL POLICY ACT (NEPA)

**A 1969 federal act that established the Council on Environmental Policy and whose purposes include the promotion of efforts to prevent or eliminate damage to the environment and biosphere and to enrich the understanding of the ecological systems and natural resources important to the nation.**

*Legal Annotation*: "After unsuccessfully urging TVA to consider alternatives to damming the Little Tennessee, local citizens and national conservation groups brought suit in the District Court, claiming that the project did not conform to the requirements of the **National Environmental Policy Act** of 1969 (NEPA)." ***TVA v. Hill*** (U.S., 1978).

## NATIONAL FLOOD INSURANCE PROGRAM

**A federal program that provides flood insurance. See *Flood*.**

*Legal Annotation*: "The National Flood Insurance Act of 1968 established a **national flood insurance program** that enables property owners to purchase insurance against flood risks at reasonable rates." ***Hanover Bldg. Materials, Inc. v. Guiffrida*** (5th Cir., 1984).

## NATIONAL HISTORIC PRESERVATION ACT

**A 1966 federal law that established a National Register of Historic Places and the Advisory Council on Historic Preservation and authorized grants-in-aid for historic properties preservation.**

*Legal Annotation*: "[C]ongress has determined that 'the historical and cultural foundations of the Nation should be preserved as a living part of our community life and development in order to give a sense of orientation to the American people,' **National Historic Preservation Act** of 1966, 80 Stat. 915, 16 U. S. C. § 470 (b) (1976 ed.), and has enacted a series of measures designed to encourage **preservation** of sites and structures of **historic**, architectural, or cultural significance." ***Penn Central Transp. Co. v. New York City*** (U.S., 1978).

## NATIONAL HISTORICAL LANDMARK

**A site with national historic significance included on the National Register of Historic Places. See *National Register of Historic Places*.**

*Legal Annotation*: "(f) Prior to the approval of any Federal undertaking which may directly and adversely affect any **National Historic Landmark**, the head of the responsible Federal agency shall, to the maximum extent possible, undertake such planning and actions as may be necessary to minimize harm to such **landmark**, and shall afford the Advisory Council on **Historic** Preservation a reasonable opportunity to comment on the undertaking." ***National Trust for Historic Preservation v. Blanck*** (D.D.C., 1996).

## NATIONAL HISTORIC SITE

**Sites that are a part of the National Park System that commemorate historic events, activities, or persons associated with the history of the United States.**

***Comment***: National historic sites include battlefields, monuments, and memorials.

***Legal Annotation***: "John Dillinger, Public Enemy No. 1, died on July 22, 1934, at the Biograph Theater in Chicago. He emerged from the air conditioned movie palace into a sweltering evening accompanied by two women, one wearing a bright red dress. The 'lady in red', Anna Sage, had agreed to betray his presence for $10,000. Agents of the FBI were waiting. Alerted by Polly Hamilton, the other woman, Dillinger wheeled to fire, but it was too late. A hail of bullets cut him down, his .45 automatic unused. William C. Sullivan, ***The Bureau*** 30-33 (1979). Now a **national historic site**, the Biograph bears a plaque commemorating the event. It still shows movies, and the air conditioning is no better now than in 1934." ***Nash v. CBS, Inc.*** (7th Cir., 1990).

## NATIONAL REGISTER OF HISTORIC PLACES

**The official list, established by the National Historic Preservation Act, of sites, districts, buildings, structures, and objects significant in the nation's history or with unique artistic or architectural value.**

***Comment***: Listing on the National Register does not restrict any activities or actions of the private property owner using private funds. It does, however, place limits on any action of the federal government that might damage the historic nature of the property. Some states have a similar register, and listing on these registers does not apply to private property owners using private money. Only local historic district ordinances can place limits on the actions of a private property owner with respect to a property in that district. **See *Historic Area; Historic Building; Historic Building Styles; Historic Preservation; Historic Site; National Historic Preservation Act*.**

***Legal Annotation***: "The Pueblo asserts that the New Mexico canyon contains numerous sites of religious and cultural significance to the tribe, qualifying the canyon as a 'traditional cultural property' eligible for inclusion in the **National Register of Historic Places**." ***Pueblo of Sandia v. US*** (10th Cir., 1995).

## NATIVE VEGETATION

**See *Vegetation, Native*.**

***Legal Annotation***: "For example, the State has instituted a mamane replanting program that is meeting with some success. Since 1979, the State has planted over 6000 mamane trees on 70 acres of the critical habitat, and they have maintained nine fenced enclosures of 4.5 acres each. They have begun a fog drip project to capture moisture to encourage **native vegetation**." ***Palila v. Hawaii Dept of Land & Natural Resources*** (D. Hawaii, 1986).

## NATURAL CONDITION

**A condition that arises from or is found in nature and not altered by human intervention.**

***Legal Annotation***: "The ordinance had a public purpose to preserve the **natural condition** of the area." ***Just v. Marinette County*** (Wis., 1972).

## NATURAL DRAINAGE FLOW

**The pattern of surface and stormwater drainage from a particular site before the construction or installation of improvements or prior to any regrading.**

***Legal Annotation***: "And although the basic civil rule held that no one may change the **natural**

**drainage flow**, some courts have recognized that the upper owner may change the natural flow by collecting the water at one point thereby not increasing the amount of overall flow but causing greater volume at one point rather than another, so long as the increased flow is in a natural water course and injury is not too great to the lower land." *Butler v. Bruno* (R.I., 1975).

## NATURAL GRADE

See *Grade, Natural.*

## NATURAL GROUND SURFACE

**The ground surface in its original state before any grading, excavation, or filling. See *Grade, Natural*.**

*Legal Annotation*: "In the course of the construction of this new channel the earth removed was placed to the right of the new channel and formed a mound or levee of a height above the **natural ground surface**." *Montgomery v. Downey* (Ill., 1959).

## NATURAL MONUMENT

**(1) A natural feature or object used to define or mark a boundary; (2) any noteworthy natural feature.**

*Legal Annotation*: "It is established as a general rule of law both in our own court and in the courts of the United States that, where by the original survey and government plat a tract of land appears to have as its boundary a body of water, such body of water is a **natural monument**, and will constitute the boundary." *Calder v. Hillsboro Land Company* (Fla. C. App., 1960).

## NATURAL RECHARGE

**Adding water to an aquifer by natural means, such as precipitation, or from lakes and rivers.**

*Legal Annotation*: "Without human intervention, the surface/ground water interconnected system 'exists in a state of approximate equilibrium' which implies 'a long-term balance between **natural recharge** and discharge processes in a groundwater basin.'" *Board of County Commissioners v. Park County* (Colo., 2002).

## NATURAL RESERVE AREA

**A designated area with physical features and natural constraints that make conditions unsuitable for development or that contain sensitive ecological systems.**

*Comment*: Such physical features may include streams and their buffers, including the hundred-year floodplain and nontidal wetlands, severe and steep slopes associated with highly erodible soils, and other ecologically sensitive features. Natural reserve areas are usually shown on state or regional master plans. http://www.pgplanning.org/Resources/Tools_On-line/Glossary.htm

*Legal Annotation*: "On October 15, 1985, the Puerto Rico Secretary of the Natural Resources Department filed a petition at the Puerto Rico Superior Court requesting an expedited judicial order permitting various government agencies, including PREPA, to enter plaintiffs' property in Finca La Picúa for the purpose of conducting civil, criminal or administrative investigations. The Natural Resources Department has under its custody the area of Finca La Picúa. (Finca La Picúa is part of Espíritu Santo River, a **natural reserve area**.)" *Paris v. Puerto Rico Elec. Power Authority* (D.P.R., 1988).

## NATURAL RESOURCES INVENTORY (NRI)

**A survey of existing natural elements, including land, water, air, plant, and animal life, and the interrelationship of these elements.**

*Comment*:The NRI (also known as the environmental resources inventory) usually includes data on soils, geology, topography (including watershed and flood areas), and vegetation. The NRI can be an important part of master plan preparation, particularly for municipalities in rural areas where development is anticipated on heretofore undeveloped land. It also can be useful in the review of subdivision and other development plans. Such studies primarily indicate which areas are environmentally suitable for development and which are not. Depending on study detail, they also can provide: (1) assessment of development capacity; (2) background information useful in the preparation of environmental impact statements; (3) disclosure of current imbalances between development and the environment; and (4) information to residents on the environmental impacts of development.

The NRI is an areawide inventory, and as such, its data may not be sufficiently precise for use in the preparation or detailed review of specific development projects. One of the initial steps in the design review procedure, though, is a check of the proposed plans against the findings of the NRI. This check may provide some design direction or at least alert the reviewing authority to potential environmental problems. This review may also suggest that an environmental impact statement might be necessary.

*Legal Annotation*: "After holding a hearing on the final plat for the second application, the Board determined that Eagle's Nest was not included on the map when the **natural resources inventory** maps were prepared and for that reason the development was not scored." ***Cowan v. Board of Commissioners of Fremont County*** (Idaho, 2006).

## NATURE PRESERVE

**An area in which human activities are very limited and where the natural environment is protected from human changes.**

***Comment***: Nature preserves may be large holdings protected by governmental ownership or small parcels restricted by conservation easements. Their purpose is to protect endangered species, critical environmental features, and viewsheds or other natural elements. In some nature preserves, activities are limited to hiking and walking trails. **See *Conservation Easement*.**

***Legal Annotation***: "This case proves the maxim that, in appellate briefing, bluster is inversely proportional to merit. . . . In the spring of 2000, The Nature Conservancy (the 'Conservancy') purchased 6,660 acres of farmland from Wilder Corporation of Delaware ('Wilder') for $16,350,000. Wilder had conducted agricultural operations on the land, and the Conservancy intended to use the property as a **nature preserve**. . . . The sales contract . . . required Wilder to remove from the property all rubbish, hazardous or toxic substances, petroleum contamination, and cattle sewage, among other things." ***Nature Conservancy v. Wilder Corp. of Delaware*** ($7^{th}$ Cir., 2011).

"Plaintiff maintains that because utilization of L-C district land as a **nature preserve** is a permitted 'use' under the Town of Clifton Park Zoning Code, his activities consistent with such a purpose may not be restricted. We do not agree. While there is no question that the establishment of a **nature preserve**, game preserve or similar use is allowed pursuant to Town of Clifton Park Zoning Code . . . the plain language of a different provision . . . states specifically that the uses delineated in section 208-69.2 require a threshold area of 100,000 square feet of property in a L-C district. . . . Since it is undisputed that only 72,000 square feet of plaintiff's property is in the L-C district, his property cannot meet this requirement." ***Sarris v. Town of Clifton Park*** (N.Y. App. Div., 2007).

## NATURE RESERVE

**See *Nature Preserve*.**

## NATURAL SELECTION

**The natural process by which organisms best adapted to their environment survive and those less well adapted are eliminated.**

***Legal Annotation***: "Moreover, Congress was also told that the primary cause of this trend was something other than the normal process of **natural selection**: '[M]an and his technology has [sic] continued at an ever-increasing rate to disrupt the natural ecosystem.'" ***TVA v. Hill*** (U.S., 1978).

## NAVIGABLE WATERS

**Waterways that are or may be used for recreational, travel, or commercial purposes, such as the transporting of goods.**

*Legal Annotation*: "Section 3(8) of the FPA defines **navigable waters** as those parts of streams . . . which either in their natural or improved condition notwithstanding interruptions between the navigable parts of such streams or waters by falls, shallows, or rapids compelling land carriage, are used or suitable for use for the transportation of persons or property in interstate or foreign commerce." ***FPL Energy Maine Hydro LLC v. FERC*** (D.C. Cir., 2002).

## NECKDOWNS

See *Traffic Calming*.

## NEGATIVE EASEMENT

See *Easement, Negative*.

## NEIGHBORHOOD

**An area of a community with characteristics that distinguish it from other areas and that may include distinct ethnic or economic characteristics, housing types, schools, or boundaries defined by physical barriers, such as major highways and railroads, or natural features, such as water bodies or topography.**

*Comment*: Historically, the neighborhood was defined as the area served by an elementary school, with shopping and recreation facilities to serve neighborhood residents. While the description is probably dated, the neighborhood designation is useful in analyzing the adequacy of facilities and services and in identifying factors affecting the quality of the built environment. In addition, as distinct and identifiable areas, often with their own names, neighborhoods are recognized as fostering community spirit and providing a sense of place—factors recognized as important in community planning. **See** ***Traditional Neighborhood Development***.

*Legal Annotation*: "Pursuant to State Tax Department Administrative Notice 2006-16 (Jan. 31, 2006), a '**neighborhood**' is defined as a 'geographical area exhibiting a high degree of homogeneity in residential amenities, land use, economic and social trends, and housing characteristics.'" ***Mountain America LLC v. Huffman*** (W.Va, 2009).

## NEIGHBORHOOD BUSINESS AREA

**A commercial area, usually located on an arterial or collector street, providing convenience goods and services for residents of the surrounding area. See** ***Strip Commercial Development; Shopping Center.***

*Comment*: The neighborhood business area usually serves residents within a half-mile radius. The stores include food, drugs, hardware, and sundries; services include banks, offices, barber and beauty parlors, cleaners, and laundry facilities. The major characteristic of the neighborhood business area is its scale. It usually does not contain any large stores or uses designed to serve several neighborhoods. Zoning can protect the scale of such areas by placing restrictions on use sizes.

*Legal Annotation*: "Both sides were in accord that for many years before the takings the general area at the intersections of the various local and State roads heretofore noted had been a general **neighborhood business area**, consisting in the main of service establishments such as gasoline stations, automobile repair shops, art studios, antique shops, grocery stores and similar small businesses." ***Yochmowitz v. State of New York*** (N.Y. Ct. Cl., 1965).

## NEIGHBORHOOD PARK/ PLAYGROUND

**A park area designed to serve the active recreational needs of the neighborhood, including, but not limited to, field games, crafts, playground apparatus, and picnicking.**

*Comment*: The National Recreation and Park Association (NRPA) publishes guidelines and general development standards for a variety of park and recreation facilities. For this use level, NRPA recommends one to two acres per one thousand population, located within safe and easy walking and bike access to the neighborhood population, and which may be developed as part of a local school facility. **See** ***Recreation Facility***.

*Legal Annotation*: "That portion of section 277 of the Town Law, as amended by chapter 846 of the Laws of 1959, here attacked, reads as follows: 'If the planning board determines that a suitable park or parks of adequate size cannot be properly located in any such plat or is otherwise not practical, the board may require as a condition to approval of any such plat a payment to the town of an amount to be determined by the town board, which amount shall be available for use by the town for **neighborhood park, playground** or recreation purposes including the acquisition of property.'" *Gulest Assoc. v. Town of Newburgh* (N.Y. Sup. Ct., 1960).

## NEIGHBORHOOD PLAN

**The master or specific design plan for a particular neighborhood or district that provides recommended standards and guidelines for future land use and development, open space and recreation areas, streets and circulation, and community facilities. See *Traditional Neighborhood Development*.**

*Legal Annotation*: "The regular design of subdivision, with ingress and egress to and from Sepulveda Boulevard, would have been out of harmony with the **neighborhood plan** and traffic needs." *Ayres v. City Council of Los Angeles* (Calif., 1949).

## NEIGHBORHOOD SHOPPING CENTER

See *Neighborhood Business Area; Shopping Center*.

## NEIGHBORING LOT

**The first lot on each side of the subject lot on the same side of the street and any lot that fronts directly across from the subject lot and the lots adjacent thereto.**

*Comment*: The phrase is used in zoning to establish a prevailing setback line or to enforce anti-look-alike clauses. In some ordinances, two lots on either side of the subject lot are used to establish the prevailing setback. When a neighboring lot is vacant, the required setback is assumed and an average distance determines the setback.

*Legal Annotation*: "And it is no more realistic to ignore that characteristic of the property (the fact that state foreclosure law permits the mortgagee to sell it at forced sale) than it is to ignore other price-affecting characteristics (such as the fact that state zoning law permits the owner of the **neighboring lot** to open a gas station)." *BFP v. Resolution Trust Corporation* (U.S., 1994).

## NEOTRADITIONAL DESIGN

**See *Traditional Neighborhood Development*. See *Also White And* Jourdan 1997.**

## NET AREA OF LOT (NET ACREAGE)

**(1) The area of the lot excluding those features or areas that the development ordinance excludes from the calculations; (2) the area of the lot remaining after areas devoted to infrastructure, including streets and utilities, are deducted from the total lot area.**

*Comment*:In regard to the former definition above, a development ordinance might exclude, for density or area calculation purposes, undevelopable or critical areas such as floodways, wetlands, areas with steep slopes, or other constrained areas or easements. However, in recent years, court cases have sharply restricted the ability to exclude these lands, particularly where a state land-use law defines this term differently. For example, an ordinance might establish the maximum permitted residential density as fifteen dwelling units per acre. If the proposed development is located in a state where wetlands cannot be excluded from the area measurement and half of the parcel is wetlands, the density would have to be reduced to 7.5 dwelling units per acre in order to maintain the level of development intensity anticipated by the ordinance.

*Legal Annotation*: "Under the 2001 general plan, **net acreage** was defined as 'the remainder of land left after land devoted to streets, roads, and utilities are deducted from the parcel.'" *Inyo Citizens for Better Planning v. Inyo County Board of Supervisors* (Calif. Ct. App., 2009).

## NET FLOOR AREA

See *Floor Area, Net*.

*Legal Annotation*: "The plans for the four-story building proposed by the intervenors call for a gross floor area of 38,480 square feet and a **net floor area** of 30,784 square feet. Under the village zoning ordinance, net commercial space is defined as '[t]he space in a given commercial building used for the principal use to which the building is put (e.g. offices in an office building, selling space in a department store), excluding areas used for storage, utilities, and other accessory functions' . . . Although it is unclear from the record how the intervenors arrived at the figure of 30,784 square feet for 'net commercial space', we have accepted their figure, which is 20% less than their gross commercial area, for the purposes of this appeal." ***Mtr. of Devore v. Cazalet*** (N.Y. App. Div., 1979).

## NET RESIDENTIAL DENSITY

**The number of dwelling units relative to the net land area used for residential purposes.**

*Comment*: Net land area used for residential purposes should include local access streets, tot lots or local recreation areas, and a limited amount of open space around the residences. **See *Net Area Of Lot*.**

*Legal Annotation*: "As Mr. Lachowicz explained in his report, **net residential density** is calculated by dividing the number of dwelling units by the 'site area.' 'Site area' is the total parcel acreage of the site, less the acreage on which building is prohibited or otherwise inappropriate." ***East Bay Community Development Corp v. Zoning Board of Barrington*** (R.I., 2006).

## NET-ZERO BUILDING

**A building with zero net energy consumption and zero carbon emission.**

*Comment*: Traditional buildings in the United States and Europe consume 40 percent of the total fossil fuel energy and are significant contributors of greenhouse gases. Most zero-energy buildings use alternative energy sources, such as wind and solar, to reduce overall consumption through highly efficient HVAC and lighting technologies. Although net-zero buildings are uncommon, buildings that are designed to be close to zero energy are becoming more commonplace. Also referred to as zero-energy building, zero-net energy (ZNE) building, and net-zero energy building (NZEB).

*Legal Annotation*: "Chevron argues that this is a case in which CEQA allows the EIR to specify 'performance standards' rather than choose the specific mitigation methods in advance. Chevron states that 'the EIR concludes the Project's GHG emissions will have a potentially significant environmental effect on climate change. The EIR adopts a strict numeric performance standard ("**net-zero**," which is a 100% reduction). . . . To enforce this performance standard, the EIR provides a list of potential mitigation strategies.'" ***Communities for a Better Environment v. City of Richmond*** (Calif. Ct. App., 2010).

## NEW CAR AGENCY

**See *Automobile Sales*.**

## NEW TOWN

**A planned community, usually developed on largely vacant land and containing housing, employment, shopping, industry, recreation and open space, and public facilities.**

*Comment*:The term "new town" implies a predetermined population level and phased development over a period of time. Reston, Virginia, and Columbia, Maryland, are excellent examples of completed new towns.

*Legal Annotation*: "Obviously, it is the assemblage of sufficient land that permits the type of overall planning for the entire site that the General Assembly sought to encourage. Although SDAT maintained before the Tax Court that the exemption was limited to '**new town**' development, it abandoned that position at oral argument. The use of the word 'particularly' in § 8-220(b)(5) would suggest that the PDA is not limited to '**new town**' developments and, apparently, it has not been so limited by SDAT in its application of the statute. On the other hand, the acreage minimum supports SDAT's position that the exemption was for large developments under a common plan." ***Pleasants Investment v. Dept. of Assessment*** (Md. App., 2001).

## NEW URBANISM

**See *Traditional Neighborhood Development; Urbanism, New*.**

## NEWSRACK

**One or more self-service or coin-operated boxes, containers, storage units, or other dispensers installed, used, or maintained for the display and sale or distribution of newspapers, periodicals, or other written material. See *Modular-Assembly-Unit Newsrack*. See *Figure 70*.**

***Comment***:Great care must be used in adopting standards to control the location of newsracks located on sidewalks and along public streets. Unreasonable controls, not related to safety, run afoul of First Amendment (freedom of speech) criteria. Where location controls are imposed on newsracks, the basis for the controls has to be carefully documented. For example, accidents attributed to poorly placed newsracks that block drivers' vision would be the kind of documentation needed to support these controls.

Design standards for newsracks are probably defensible, provided they are not overly burdensome and relate to some overall design criteria established for the zone or area where the newsracks are proposed to be located (Floyd and Reed 1997).

***Legal Annotation***: "Indeed, Cincinnati's City Manager has determined that publications that qualify as newspapers and therefore ***can*** be distributed by **newsrack** are those that are published daily and/or weekly and '***primarily*** presen[t] coverage of, and commentary on, current events.'" ***Cincinnati v. Discovery Network*** (U.S., 1993).

## NEWSSTAND

**A portable structure, usually not exceeding one hundred square feet, from which newspapers, magazines, and other printed material are sold.**

***Comment***: Newsstands usually do not have water or sanitary facilities but may have electricity. They are frequently located on sidewalks at busy intersections, typically in the right-of-way and exempt from the usual building setback requirements. They are almost always licensed by the municipality.

***Legal Annotation***: "This case concerns a City of Chicago municipal ordinance designed to force **newsstand** operators, such as [the plaintiff], to either acquire a permit or face eviction." ***Graff v. City of Chicago*** (7th Cir., 1993).

## NEW URBANISM

**See *Traditional Neighborhood Development Plan; Urbanism, New*.**

***Legal Annotation***: "As it happened, the City referred Snowden's proposed amendment to the Commission; Snowden signed agreed orders dismissing the pending litigation; and upon receiving a negative recommendation from the Commission, the City rejected Snowden's proposed amendment, thereby thwarting his plan to develop a '**New Urbanism**' residential community. ('**New Urbanism**' is a design concept featuring compact, multiuse communities in which all the needs of daily life [housing, work, retail, entertainment, schools, parks and civic facilities] are within a ten-minute walk of one another.])" ***Snowden v. City of Wilmore*** (Ky. Ct. App., 2013).

## NIGHTCLUB

**An establishment that is open only late at night, in which music is provided, along with space in which dancing may be conducted.**

***Comment***: Nightclubs are now more commonly referred to simply as "clubs." Because of the need to differentiate a nightclub from other totally unrelated land uses referred to as "clubs," such establishments should still be referred to as "nightclubs" in zoning ordinances. Generally nightclubs are distinguished from bars or taverns by the inclusion of a dance floor and a DJ or VJ playing recorded music or music videos. The use of live bands is less commonplace today. Because nightclubs are open very late, serve liquor, play loud music, and often have restricted entry, which results in long lines outdoors, there is good reason to restrict them to localities where they are less likely to create nuisance impacts.

***Legal Annotation***: "A '**nightclub**' is defined as an establishment that: is open after 11:00 p.m.; has floor space available and used for dancing; and has a band, orchestra or other form of music or musical or other entertainment. If the establishment meets the foregoing requirement during any business day, it is a 'nightclub' for purpose of this section on all business days." ***Bankshot Billiards, Inc. v. City of Ocala*** (11th Cir., 2011).

## NOISE

**(1) Any undesired audible sound; (2) any sound that annoys or disturbs humans or that causes or tends to cause an adverse psychological or physiological effect on humans (City Code, Dallas, Texas).**

***Comment***:Noise standards are usually not found in zoning or land development ordinances but rather in health ordinances. In addition, many states have adopted noise codes as part of general environmental standards. The state standards often preempt local ordinances or establish maximum noise level standards that municipalities cannot exceed. Where a local ordinance controlling noise is allowed, the traditional definitions used are contained in the American National Standards Institute Standard ANSI S1.1-1971, "Acoustical Terminology," as amended.

A local noise ordinance would establish a maximum noise level, usually expressed as an A-weighted sound level in decibels (dBA). While the level varies by jurisdiction, 55 dBA is often cited as the maximum allowed during daylight hours and 45 dBA for evening hours. As noted earlier, many states have established maximum standards that municipalities may not exceed. In addition to maximums, a local ordinance might establish different standards for residential and nonresidential zones and indicate where sound measurements are to be made: for example, at the lot line for industries and the zone line for other uses. Finally, an ordinance should distinguish between intermittent and continuous noise, exempt certain activities (sporting events, occasional outdoor gatherings, and the like), and designate the enforcement officer or office. **See *Ambient Noise Level; A-Weighted Sound Level; Decibel; Intermittent Sound; Intrusive Sound; Noise Attenuation; Noise Disturbance; Sound-Amplifying Equipment*.**

***Legal Annotation***: "Municipal regulations govern use of amplification devices both on Madison streets in general and at the Mall in particular. Madison General Ordinance (M.G.O.) 24.04(3)(a) prohibits the use of 'any device, apparatus or instrument for the amplification of the human voice or any sound or **noise**, or other sound-making or sound reproducing device' except during the hours of 12:00–1:30 PM and 5:00–7:00 PM" ***Stokes v. City of Madison*** (7th Cir., 1991).

## NOISE ATTENUATION

**A reduction in the level of a noise source using a substance, material, or surface, such as an earth berm and/or a dense wall (California General Plan Glossary 1997).**

***Comment***: Jeffrey Grob (in an article entitled "Concrete Examples" in the April 2001 issue of ***Planning***) discusses the efficacy of, alternatives to, and aesthetic issues in noise wall installations along major highways. He notes, "The most effective barriers and those that require the least amount of space are solid walls about a foot thick. Such barriers have a dual effect. They block or deflect sound waves while also eliminating the view of the road. Studies have shown that removing the sound source visually reduces the perceived noise level. Seeing the source of the noise can be almost as distracting as hearing it" (Grob 2001 in Sorvig 2001).

***Legal Annotation***: "In 1984 Poway applied for a federal grant to provide funding for improvements to Pomerado Road, a multi-lane street running through Poway (the Pomerado Road Project or Project). Before applying for the grant, Poway's city manager had reported that '[t]he residential units [adjacent to Pomerado Road] are without an adequate system of **noise attenuation** . . . [and are] regularly impacted by adverse noise levels . . . significantly above the City's noise standard for single family residential areas.' *Craig v. City of Poway* (Calif. Ct. App., 1994).

## NOISE BARRIERS

See *Noise Attenuation*.

## NOISE DISTURBANCE

**Any noise exceeding the noise level limits established for the specific zoning district.**

*Legal Annotation*: "A '**noise disturbance**' is defined as '[t]hat level of sound which . . . [a] nnoys or disturbs a reasonable person of normal auditory sensitivities' (Islip Town Code § 35-2 [A])." *People v. Baumann & Sons* (N.Y., 2006).

## NOISE POLLUTION

**Continuous or episodic excessive noise in the human environment.**

*Comment*: Noise pollution usually is defined in terms of a maximum decibel level by frequency range.

*Legal Annotation*: "In its environmental assessments, the Parks Service acknowledged that this plan would expose the park's wildlife to increased multiple vessel encounters, **noise pollution**, air pollution, and an increased risk of vessel collisions and oil spills." *National Parks & Conservation Ass'n v. Babbitt* ($9^{th}$ Cir., 2001).

## NOISE WALL

See *Noise Attenuation*.

## NONATTAINMENT AREA

**"An area considered to have air quality worse than the National Ambient Air Quality Standards as defined in the Clean Air Act Amendments of 1970" (P.L. 91-604, Sec. 109).**

*Comment*: "Nonattainment areas must have and implement a plan to meet the standard, or risk losing some forms of federal financial assistance. An area may be a nonattainment area for one pollutant and an attainment area for others" http://en.wikipedia.org/wiki/nonattainment_area).

*Legal Annotation*: "An area in attainment for a NAAQS pollutant is 'any area . . . that meets the . . . ambient air quality standard for the pollutant.' . . . By contrast, an **area** in **nonattainment** for a NAAQS pollutant is 'any area that does not meet (or that contributes to ambient air quality in a nearby area that does not meet) the national . . . ambient air quality standard for the pollutant.' . . . Finally, an unclassifiable area is any area that 'cannot be classified on the basis of available information as meeting or not meeting the . . . ambient air quality standard for the pollutant.'" *Coalition for Responsible Regulation v. EPA* (D.C. Cir., 2012).

## NONCONFORMING LOT

**A lot, the area, dimensions, or location of which was lawful prior to the adoption, revision, or amendment of the zoning ordinance but that fails by reason of such adoption, revision, or amendment to conform to the present requirements of the zoning district.**

*Legal Annotation*: "A Land Court judge concluded that, under the clause, 'doubling the size of the structure on an undersized (**nonconforming) lot** [would] increase the nonconforming nature of the structure,' thereby requiring the plaintiffs to seek a special permit." *Bransford v. Zoning Board of Appeals of Edgartown* (Mass., 2005).

## NONCONFORMING SIGN

See *Sign, Nonconforming*.

## NONCONFORMING STRUCTURE OR BUILDING

**A structure or building, the size, dimensions, or location of which was lawful prior to the adoption, revision, or amendment of the zoning ordinance but that fails by reason of such adoption, revision, or amendment to conform to the present requirements of the zoning ordinance.**

***Legal Annotation***: "Leaving aside eminent domain and nuisance, we have often stated in our decisions that the owner of land devoted to a prior nonconforming use, or on which a prior **nonconforming structure** exists (or has been substantially commenced), has the right to continue such use, but we have never held that this right may continue virtually in perpetuity." ***Matter of Harbison v. City of Buffalo*** (N.Y., 1958).

## NONCONFORMING USE

**A use or activity that was lawful prior to the adoption, revision, or amendment of the zoning ordinance but that fails by reason of such adoption, revision, or amendment to conform to the present requirements of the zoning district.**

***Comment***:Ordinances should provide for "certificates of nonconformance" to be issued to property owners and occupants upon application to the zoning officer for a reasonable period (ninety to 180 days, for example) after the adoption of a new ordinance or major amendment. The certificate of nonconformance would officially establish the type, extent, and intensity of use taking place on a specific property. It can benefit both the property owner and the zoning authority.

The general policy with respect to nonconforming uses is to provide for their eventual elimination. To accomplish this, most local ordinances impose restrictions on the extent to which a nonconforming use may expand or change. In addition, the ability of the local zoning authority to grant variances for the expansion or change of a nonconforming use is often sharply limited.

A lawful nonconforming use exists when it meets two requirements:

1. It must have existed before the prohibitory regulation was enacted; and
2. The use must have been lawful when the change was enacted.

Thus, a use that was in violation of the zoning ordinance when the ordinance was amended does not gain status as a preexisting and lawful nonconforming use upon adoption of the amendment. It must have been a fully conforming use at the time of the amendment.

There has been considerable case law relating to permissible and impermissible changes in nonconforming uses as well as lawful and unlawful expansions. Mark S. Dennison's "Changing or Expanding Nonconforming Uses" (Dennison 1997) is an excellent article on this subject. It contains case citations and lists permissible and impermissible nonconforming use changes as well as lawful and unlawful nonconforming use expansions based on the cases.

***Legal Annotation***: "However, because it had been in existence prior to the effective date of the zoning ordinance, defendant's establishment qualified as a preexisting **nonconforming use** and, under the terms of the ordinance, was allowed to remain in operation." ***Town of Belleville v. Parrillo's Inc.*** (N.J., 1980).

## NONCONTIGUOUS PARCEL CLUSTERING

**A planning technique that allows one parcel to be preserved in its entirety for farming or open space, while its development rights are transferred to a noncontiguous parcel that is developed at a higher density than otherwise permitted, provided both parcels are considered together as a single cluster development. See *Cluster; Cluster Subdivision; Lot Averaging*.**

***Comment***: The receiving parcel must be suitable for the higher density. In addition, the total number of dwelling units and/or total floor area should not exceed the total allowed on both parcels.

***Legal Annotation***: "ARTICLE II-A Regulations for the RP Single-Family Rural Preservation District § 228-6.01 Applicability of provisions of Article

C. Planned Development Utilizing **Noncontiguous Parcel Clustering**- one (1) dwelling unit per three and one-half (3.5) acres provided that:

1. The application for development shall involve tracts with a minimum of seven (7) total acres
2. All parcels shall be in the RP Rural Preservation Zone;

3. Minimum lot area shall be thirty thousand (30,000) square feet:
4. The development is in compliance with Municipal Land Use Law 40: 55D-45 'Findings for Planned Developments';
5. Preliminary Approval shall be conditioned upon the applicant obtaining Health Department approval and Department of Environmental Protection approval (to the extent required by state law) for any proposed community septic system;
6. Seventy-five percent (75%) of the combined area of the non-contiguous parcels shall be designated as 'open lands' and deed restricted against any further development;
7. The design of a development utilizing this option and the open lands resulting from it shall promote the following Township objectives: Retention of large contiguous farmland areas, stream corridor and wetlands preservation, steep slope protection. reduction of impervious coverage, protection of the site's natural features, connections to and between approved open lands on neighboring Parcels, and compliance with the design Air lots set forth in subsection 6.10;
8. All lots created shall be deed restricted against further subdivision." Township Code Book, Chapter 228 Zoning -- East Brunswick, NJ http://tinyurl.com/p3uaq26.

## NONGOVERNMENTAL ORGANIZATION (NGO)

**An entity with an association that is based on interests of its members, individuals, or institutions and that is not created by a government but may work cooperatively with government.**

*Comment*: Such organizations serve a public purpose, not a private benefit. Examples of NGOs include faith-based charity organizations and the American Red Cross (NIMS). http://www.gwu.edu/~icdrm/publications/PDF/GLOSSARY%2002-19-2007.pdf

## NONPOINT RUNOFF

**Surface water entering a channel from no definable discharge source.**

*Legal Annotation*: "Because **nonpoint** sources of pollution, such as oil and gas runoffs caused by rainfall on the highways, are virtually impossible to isolate to one polluter, no permit or regulatory system was established as to them." ***US v. Earth Sciences*** (10th Cir., 1979).

## NONPOINT-SOURCE POLLUTION

See *Pollution, Nonpoint-Source.*

*Legal Annotation*: "('[P]oint and **nonpoint sources** are not distinguished by the kind of pollution they create or by the activity causing the pollution, but rather by whether the pollution reaches the water through a confined, discrete conveyance.'). When evaluating what constitutes a point source in the mining context specifically, we have noted that Congress intended 'runoff caused primarily by rainfall around activities that employ or create pollutants' to be a **nonpoint source**." Id. ***Greater Yellowstone Coalition v. Lewis*** (9th Cir., 2010).

## NONSLIP

**A surface that is tested or approved to be slip-resistant by a nationally recognized testing laboratory. See *Americans With Disabilities Act*.**

*Legal Annotation*: "It will be noted that the ordinance requires either roughening of the **surface**, or the use of **nonslip** material, indicating that the material to be used shall have the same effect as the roughening of the **surface**." ***Peterson v. Safeway Stores*** (Calif. Ct. App., 1960).

## NONSTRUCTURAL MANAGEMENT PRACTICES

**Controls of stormwater runoff and nonpoint-source pollution such as landscaping techniques, source controls, zoning, setbacks, buffers, or clustering (N.J.A.C. 5:21-1.4).**

*Legal Annotation*: "To meet the BAT/BCT requirement of the General Permit, SRSS must evaluate all pollutant sources at the facility and implement the best structural and **non-structural management practices** economically achievable to reduce or prevent the discharge of pollutants from the Facility." ***California Sportfishing Protection Alliance v. Santa Rosa Stainless Steel Fabricators, Inc.*** (N.D. Calif., 2013).

## NORTH AMERICAN INDUSTRY CLASSIFICATION SYSTEM (NAICS)

**A standard code system to describe and classify business establishments based on the activities in which they are primarily engaged.**

***Comment***: The NAICS became the new standard code system in 1997, when it replaced the old Standard Industrial Classification (SIC) system. It classifies business establishments into twenty two-digit broad categories as compared with the ten divisions in the old SIC. The twenty broad categories are then further subdivided into three-, four-, five-, and six-digit categories. A total of 1,170 different industries and business activities are identified.

The NAICS can be used by planners to develop various land-use categories and identify changes of use. A zoning ordinance could identify specific NAICS business sectors or subsectors as permitted uses in appropriate zones. The local ordinance would still control the intensity of development through the bulk regulations (NAICS 1997).

***Legal Annotation***: "'The **North American Industry Classification System (NAICS)** is the standard used by Federal statistical agencies in classifying business establishments for the purpose of collecting, analyzing, and publishing statistical data related to the U.S. business economy.' *See United States Census Bureau, Introduction To Naics, At http://Www.Census.Gov/Eos/Www/Naics/." Management And Training Corporation V. Us* ***(Fed.*** *C*l., 2014).

## NUISANCE

**A condition or situation that results in an interference with the use and enjoyment of property.**

***Legal Annotation***: "Whereas private **nuisance** requires an invasion of another's interest in the private use and enjoyment of land, a public **nuisance** is 'an unreasonable **interference** with a right common to the general public.'" ***Philadelphia Elec. Co. v. Hercules, Inc.*** (3rd Cir., 1985).

## NUISANCE ABATEMENT

**Programs designed to acquire, in an expedited manner, properties that are declared nuisances for all or some of the following reasons: blight, habitually used for illegal purposes, fire damage, gross neglect, disrepair, and debris.**

***Comment***: Once declared a nuisance abatement property, municipalities have the right to acquire the property and clear it and/or sell it at auction to buyers who agree to upgrade the property for eventual resale or rental. The expedited acquisition removes what many believe is a major cause of neighborhood deterioration. (*See* Dick 2007).

***Legal Annotation***: "The Ordinance declares that any cultivation of marijuana not in accordance with its provisions is a nuisance that may be abated. . . . Petitioners contend the MMP [Medical Marijuana Program] preempts the County from using **nuisance abatement** law to prohibit the use of property for medical marijuana purposes." ***Browne v. County of Tehama*** (Calif. Ct. App., 2013).

## NUISANCE ELEMENT

**Any environmental pollutant, such as smoke, odors, liquid wastes, solid wastes, radiation, noise, vibration, glare, or heat.**

***Legal Annotation***: "In determining whether a **nuisance** is temporary or permanent, the District Court held that if the source of the **nuisance** is abatable, by either discontinuing the offending activity or eliminating the **nuisance element**, it is not permanent." ***Goldstein v. Potomac Elec. Power Co.*** (Md. Ct. App., 1979).

## NURSERY, RETAIL

**The growing, cultivation, storage, and sale of garden plants, flowers, trees, shrubs, and fertilizers, as well as the sale of garden tools and similar accessory and ancillary products, to the general public. See *Greenhouse*.**

*Comment*:Also known as garden centers, retail nurseries can generate significant volumes of traffic, but only during limited periods, such as the spring planting season and some holidays. Site-plan review of parking and circulation should provide safe circulation and convenient parking, keeping in mind, however, the temporary nature of the impact.

Another issue is that of nursery greenhouses. These are enclosed, permanent structures and should be regulated in terms of setbacks, lot coverage, and other bulk controls.

***Legal Annotation***: "The nonconforming use is not merely the operation of a wholesale **nursery**, but is the operation of the entire **nursery** including both the wholesale and **retail** parts which pre-dated the zoning legislation. . . .

"**Retail**. To sell by small quantities, in broken lots or parcels, not in bulk, to sell directly to consumer. Retailer of Merchandise. A merchant who buys articles in gross or merchandise in large quantities, and sells the same by single articles or in small quantities. . . . [R]etailing. [T]he activities involved in the selling of goods to ultimate consumers for personal or household consumption." ***Hunziker v. Grande*** (Ohio Ct. App., 1982).

## NURSERY, WHOLESALE

**The growing, cultivation, storage, and sale of garden plants, flowers, trees, and shrubs to landscapers, developers, builders, and retail nurseries.**

*Comment*:Wholesale nurseries are large-scale operations, encompassing extensive land areas, a considerable amount of mechanical equipment, and selling and delivering large amounts of material to single customers, such as builders and landscapers. Many wholesalers also run retail operations, and most ordinances usually allow some retail sales. From a practical point of view, wholesalers who want to sell to the retail market should be permitted to do so as long as the site plan review process addresses the different impacts of retail operations versus wholesale.

***Legal Annotation***: "The nonconforming use is not merely the operation of a **wholesale nursery**, but is the operation of the entire **nursery** including both the wholesale and **retail** parts which pre-dated the zoning legislation. . . . '**Wholesale**. Selling to retailers or jobbers rather than to consumers. A sale in large quantity to one who intends to resell. . . . **Wholesale** Dealer. One whose business is the selling of goods in gross to retail dealers, and not by the small quantity or parcels to consumers thereof.' ***Black's Law Dictionary*** (Rev. 4 Ed. 1968)." ***Hunziker v. Grande*** (Ohio: Court of Appeals 1982).

## NURSERY SCHOOL

See *Child-Care Center*.

## NURSING HOME

See *Extended Care Facility; Intermediate Care Facility; Long-Term Care Facility*

# O

## OBJECT, HISTORIC

See *Historic Object*.

## OBSOLESCENCE

**A loss in value due to reduced desirability and usefulness of a structure because its designed construction becomes outmoded (Johnsich 1991).**

***Legal Annotation***: "This depreciation was divided into complete depreciation and incomplete depreciation. The complete depreciation represented that part of the original plant which through destruction or **obsolescence** had actually perished as useful property." *Knoxville v. Knoxville Water Co.* (U.S., 1909).

## OBSTRUCTION

**Any dam, wall, embankment, levee, dike, pile, abutment, soil, material, bridge, conduit, culvert, building, wire, fence, refuse, fill, structure, or other matter in, along, across, or projecting into any channel, watercourse, or floodplain that may impede, retard, or change the direction of the flow of water, either in itself or by catching debris carried by such water, or that is placed where the flow of water might carry the same downstream.**

***Legal Annotation***: "Without analyzing either the language or legislative history of the Act, the Court of Appeals here concluded that the Act was designed for the especial benefit of private parties who may suffer 'special injury' caused by an unauthorized **obstruction** to a navigable waterway." *California v. Sierra Club* (U.S., 1981).

## OCCUPANCY OR OCCUPIED

**The residing of an individual or individuals overnight in a dwelling unit or the storage or use of equipment, merchandise, or machinery in any public, commercial, or industrial building; (2) holding real property by being in possession (Johnsich 1991).**

***Legal Annotation***: "Because of the race or color of these petitioners they have been denied rights of ownership or **occupancy** enjoyed as a matter of course by other citizens of different race or color." *Shelley v. Kraemer* (U.S., 1948).

## OCCUPANCY PERMIT

**A required permit allowing the use of a building or structure after it has been determined that all the requirements of applicable ordinances have been met.**

***Comment***: The occupancy permit may be a temporary one for a given period of time to permit completion of certain improvements. For example, installation of landscaping may be delayed because of weather or season. Obviously, a temporary permit would not be granted if the unfinished or incomplete improvement is essential to the use or affects health or safety.

One of the problems in granting temporary permits is the difficulty in halting operations or evicting tenants if the temporary permit expires. Consequently, many jurisdictions grant temporary permits reluctantly or not at all. Also referred to as "Certificates of Occupancy."

***Legal Annotation***: "Claiming that the building's **occupancy permit** did not allow residential use of the ground floor, the inspector confronted appellant and demanded that he permit an inspection of the premises." *Camara v. Municipal Court of City and County of San Francisco* (U.S., 1967).

## OCCUPANCY RATE

**The ratio of occupied space or dwelling units to total space or dwelling units.**

*Legal Annotation*: "However, Troy took the position that the increased assessment was permitted by language in the constitutional amendment allowing adjustments for 'additions' and a subsequently enacted statutory provision, M.C.L. § 211.34d(1)(b)(vii), which defines 'additions' to include, in some circumstances, increases in the value of property attributable to an increased **occupancy rate**." *WPW Acquisition Co. v. City of Troy* (Mich., 2002).

## OCCUPANT

**The individual, family, group, or organization that lives in, occupies, or has quarters or space within a premises.**

*Legal Annotation*: "A permanent physical occupation authorized by state law is a taking without regard to whether the State, or instead a party authorized by the State, is the **occupant**." *Loretto v. Teleprompter Manhattan CATV Corp,* (U.S., 1982).

## OCCUPATION

**Gainful employment in which an individual engages to earn compensation.**

*Legal Annotation*: "However **occupation** is defined, whether in terms of primary source of income, expenditure of time and effort, or how the petitioner himself viewed his occupation, we reach the conclusion that real estate was not his occupation and that he was in fact a large-scale bootlegger." *Costello v. US* (U.S., 1961).

## ODD-LOT DEVELOPMENT

**See *Infill*.**

## ODOROUS MATTER

**Any material that produces an olfactory response in a human being.**

*Comment*: Unlike excessive light and noise, which are relatively easy to identify and measure and for which effective limits have been established, odor is difficult to measure and maximum levels of performance hard to establish. Rafson (1999) notes that when we refer to odors, we generally mean unpleasant odors, but some pleasant odors, "if omnipresent," can be an annoyance as well.

Rafson also notes that various odors can be quantified using direct measurements in a laboratory or by indirect odor measurements on-site. In most cases, the measurement uses trained panelists "who identify the level at which they can no longer tell the diluted odor from clean air." This method is called the "Dilutions to Threshold" (D/T) method, using an ASTM International procedure (E-679-91) for measuring odors. Other methods compare the odorous material to an established standard; for example, the amount of odorous material that can be detected by at least 50 percent of a group of observers. Indirect methods use mass spectroscopy and gas chromatography to identify compounds and compare them with standard concentrations.

*Legal Annotation*: "Included in the performance standards set forth in the zoning ordinance are the following: 'g. Odors—No emission shall be permitted of **odorous** gases or other **odorous matter** in such quantities as to be readily detectable at the property line of the zone lot from which they are emitted without instruments.'" *TCI, Inc. v. Town of Ghent* (N.Y. App. Div., 1991).

## OFFER

**A proposal to enter into an agreement with another party.**

*Legal Annotation*: "An **offer** is defined as 'the manifestation of willingness to enter into a bargain, so made as to justify another person in understanding that his assent to that bargain is invited and will conclude it.'" *Kloian v. Domino's Pizza* (Mich. Ct. App., 2006).

## OFFICE

**A room or group of rooms used for conducting the affairs of a business, profession, service, industry, or government and generally furnished with desks, tables, files, and communication equipment.**

*Comment*: The term "office" is almost generic, not requiring the spelling out of all the functions that may be carried out in an office. Indeed, as modern technology expands, office functions include tasks that in the past would have been considered production, industrial, or commercial. For example, desktop publishing, high-speed data transmission, and large varieties of research are now carried out in offices. While goods or merchandise are sold from offices, the transactions usually take place by phone or data transmission.

***Legal Annotation***: "In short, the space utilized by the law **office** on the one hand and the business operation on the other was for all intents and purposes commingled." *National City Trading Corp. v. U.S.* (2nd Cir., 1980).

## OFFICE HEADQUARTERS

**A very large building (five hundred thousand square feet or larger) on a large tract of land (fifty acres or more), built for a specific corporate use and/or user.**

***Comment***: Headquarters office buildings are usually single buildings that house the offices of a large corporation and often one or more major facilities of the corporation, such as corporate offices, laboratories, sales and marketing, engineering, etc. They are often located in rural or suburban areas with access to major highways. While the definition suggests a minimum of five hundred thousand square feet of building space and fifty acres of land or more, corporate headquarters are usually larger, both in building square footage and land area. They have been referred to as "Pastoral Capitalism" (Mozingo 2012). For example, in New Jersey, Bell Laboratories in Holmdel contained over two million square feet of floor area on 472 acres, Alcatel-Lucent had 1.4 million square feet of office space on 194 acres, and BASF had 2.04 million sq. ft. on 155 acres. All of the above examples have been vacant and up for sale and/or lease (Portlock 2011).

Municipalities like corporate headquarters for obvious reasons: jobs, ratables, purchasing power, and prestige. In addition, many are architectural landmarks, designed by world-famous architects. Nevertheless, a great many of these installations are now vacant for a variety of reasons. In some states, office growth has stalled, and office vacancies are up to 20 percent or even higher. At the same time, more workers are telecommuting, further reducing the need for office space. Corporations have also merged and no longer need separate corporate headquarters. Furthermore, traditional office headquarters usually were not served by transit or were located far from urban or rural centers and as such did not realize contemporary smart growth objectives.

Planning for the reuse of these very large, uniquely designed single-function buildings on large tracts of land is difficult, despite the fact that almost all have significant water, sewer, and road improvements (Sullivan 2013). They have to be "repurposed" (Hersh 2013). Some of the uses suggested for repurposing are institutional functions such as educational (colleges, high schools), cultural, or medical use; government offices and service facilities; hotels and conference centers; and continuing-care retirement communities. The sizes of the properties involved suggest the appropriateness of mixed or multiple uses, including a variety of housing (higher-density developments that include affordable housing, gated communities, etc.) as well as retail, service, and offices. In fact, the Holmdel site of Bell Laboratories has been mentioned as a possible "town center" for the township, including housing, commercial, recreation, and public uses.

Finally, one of the more innovative recommendations (McKenzie, 2013) is the possibility of declaring these sites as "Areas in Need of Redevelopment" to permit government assistance in the redevelopment process, assuming that there is a defensible basis for a finding of blight.

(See Hughes And Seneca 2012. Interviews With Mitchell Hersh, President, Mack-Cali Realty, 2013; Michael Sullivan, AICP, Clarke, Caton, Hintz Associates, 2013; And Elizabeth C. Mckenzie, PP, PA, 2013).

***Legal Annotation***: "Rice was asked by condemnor to conduct a study of the reasonable probability of rezoning the Split Rock property as of title vesting date. While the property had been zoned residential, and there had previously been some residential use of the property in the past, Rice testified that the property was currently not suited to residential use, and opined that a change of zoning to commercial, to permit commercial development, was more appropriate and would be approved. In particular, it was his opinion that a zone change to allow development of a corporate **headquarters office** or conference center was likely." *In the Matter of Application of Rockland County Sewer Dist. No. 1 v. Split Rock Partnership* (N.Y. Sup. Ct., 2012).

## OFFICE, HOME

**A home occupation in which a part of a dwelling unit is used as the resident's office. See *Home Occupation*.**

***Legal Annotation***: "There are other factors, which may from time to time weigh in the balance, such as the importance of the business functions performed by the taxpayer in the **home office**; the business necessity of maintaining a **home office**; and the expenditures of the taxpayer to establish a **home office**." *Meiers v. CIR* (7th Cir., 1986).

## OFFICE, PROFESSIONAL

**See *Professional Office*.**

## OFFICE BUILDING

**A building used primarily for conducting the affairs of a business, profession, service, industry, or government, or like activity; it may include ancillary services for office workers, such as a restaurant, coffee shop, newspaper or candy stand, and child-care facilities.**

***Comment***: Office buildings are often classified as Class A, B, or C, which generally refers to the age of the structure and amenities, although a renovated older building could be classified as a Class A building. Typical controls for offices include floor area ratio (FAR), height, setbacks, impervious surface coverage, parking, lighting, signs, and landscaping requirements. A typical suburban office building FAR may range from .15 to .30. Town and small city FARs range from 1 to 5, with FARs in major cities often in excess of 15.

***Legal Annotation***: "Before the city of New York declared Grand Central Terminal to be a landmark, Penn Central could have used its 'air rights' over the Terminal to build a multistory **office building**, at an apparent value of several million dollars per year." *Penn Central Transp. Co. v. New York City* (U.S., 1978).

## OFFICE PARK

**A development on a tract of land that contains a number of separate office buildings, with accessory and supporting uses, and open space designed, planned, constructed, and managed on an integrated and coordinated basis. See *Office Headquarters*.**

***Comment***: For mortgage or other reasons, individual buildings and parcels can be subdivided from the entire office park. However, cross easements and agreements on drainage, circulation, maintenance, parking, signage, landscaping, and access must be in place before the subdivision is permitted and made part of the resolution of subdivision approval (Portlock 2011).

***Legal Annotation***: "In this case, the environmental impact report usually measured the project's impacts by comparing it to a massive hypothetical **office park**, instead of comparing it to the vacant land that actually exists at the project site." *Woodward Park Homeowners v. City of Fresno* (Calif. Ct. App., 2007).

## OFFICIAL MAP

**An ordinance in map form adopted by the governing body that conclusively shows the location and width of existing and proposed streets, public facilities, public areas, and drainage rights-of-way.**

***Comment***: State regulations vary as to what may be shown on an official map. The purpose is to prevent private development from encroaching on sites for proposed public improvements. However, most states require that governmental entities move to acquire the land within a relatively short period of time (often one year) after approval of a development application for the land. In addition, an option fee may be required for the year. There is often a waiver of taxes on the property during the option period.

*Legal Annotation*: "Under a common sense application of this definition to the present case, a master plan is consistent with an **official map** if they share common elements, meaning that any elements addressed by both the master plan and **official map** are in agreement." *Lake City Corp. v. City of Mequon* (Wis., 1997).

## OFFICIAL SOIL MAP

**Maps that are part of a Soil Conservation Service soil survey that delineates various soil types.**

*Comment*: Soil surveys contain information on soil characteristics, including depth to bedrock, height of water table, slopes, permeability, size of rocks, erodibility, and other characteristics. The soil surveys may also contain aerial photographs on which the locations of the various types of soil within a particular geographic area are shown. More detailed on-site surveys and investigations may be needed to verify the types and locations of soils before a development plan is prepared.

*Legal Annotation*: "There is evidence in the record from which the master could conclude that the Meredith Planning Board's disapproval of Patenaude's plan was reasonable. The testimony was uncontroverted that the twenty acres devoted to recreational use in sections II and III were unsuitably steep and relatively inaccessible to those owning lots in the subdivision. There is also evidence that the board's **soil map** showed that lots No. 1 through 4 were of a soil type unsuitable for development. Significant portions of lots No. 1 through 4 were wetland." *Patenaude v. Town of Meredith* (N.H., 1978).

## OFFICIAL SOILS INTERPRETATION

**The written description of soil types and their characteristics and accompanying maps that are part of a recognized soil survey.**

*Legal Annotation*: "This conclusion was substantiated by the appraiser's report and his testimony which established no yields could be expected from soybeans or corn on Gara soils with 9 to 20 percent, the kind of land which comprises much of Debtors' Missouri property. The appraiser's opinion was substantiated by the **Soil Interpretation** Record published by the Soil Conservation Service which indicated that no expected yield from soybeans or corn on Gara soils with a slope of more than 14 percent or even on this soil with a slope of 9–14 percent if the land was severely eroded." *In re Greiman* (Bankr. Ct., N.D. Iowa, 1984).

## OFF-ROAD VEHICLE

**See *Vehicle, Off-Road*.**

## OFFSHORE FACILITIES

**Any facility floating or supported on a pier or piers, seaward of the outer harbor line, used to transfer or assemble materials for construction purposes, or for the exploration or mining of natural resources, such as natural gas or oil.**

*Legal Annotation*: "Pursuant to their agreement, the co-owners constructed on these rights-of-way an oil pipeline, a natural gas pipeline, an offshore platform and related processing facilities (collectively, the '**offshore facilities**')." *EP Operating Ltd. Partnership v. Placid Oil Co.* (5th Cir., 1994).

## OFF-SITE

**Located outside the lot lines of the lot in question but within the property (of which the lot is a part) that is the subject of a development application or within a contiguous portion of a street or other right-of-way. *See Figure 71*.**

*Legal Annotation*: "The Land Subdivision Ordinance of Princeton Township does not establish any procedures or standards by which the cost of **off-site** improvements might be apportioned to the subdivider on the basis of the benefits to the subdivision." *Longridge Builders v. Planning Board of Princeton Township* (N.J. 1968).

## OFF-SITE IMPROVEMENT

**An improvement required to be made off-site as a result of an application for development, including, but not limited to, upgrading, extending, enlarging, or improving streets, intersections, and water, sewer and**

**Figure 71**

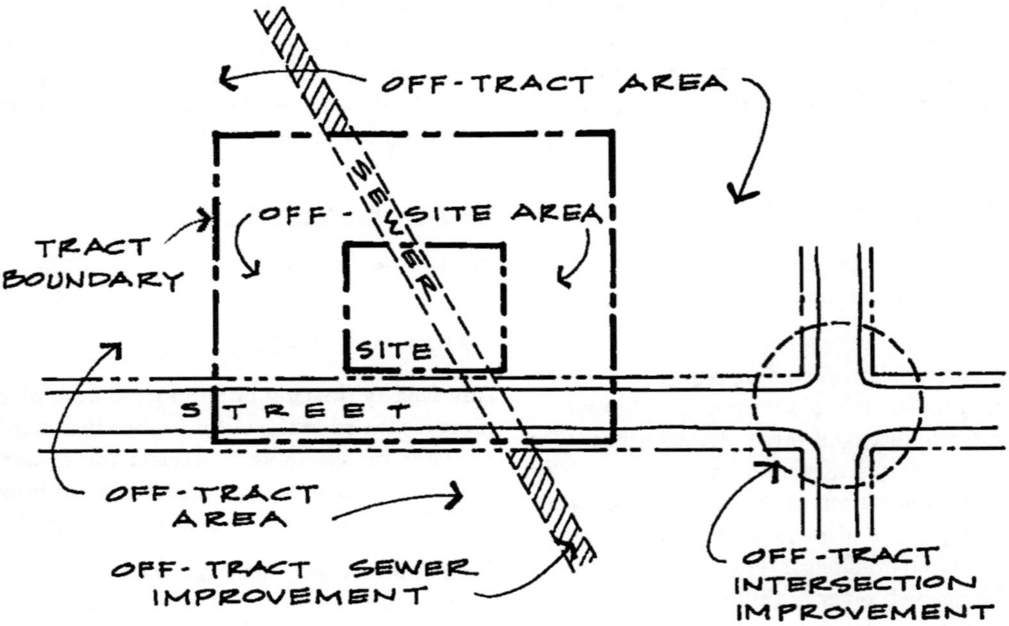


**stormwater mains or facilities.** See *Off-Tract Improvement and Figure 71.*

***Comment***: Off-site improvements are imposed as a condition of development approval. The type and extent of the improvements should be spelled out in the development ordinance. Typically, a proposed development adjacent to a narrow road would be required to widen and improve the road on the development side and install curbs and drains. When the property across from the development is not expected to be improved in the immediate future, though, municipalities often opt for requiring the developer to improve the entire width of the road to a somewhat lesser extent than normally required, rather than have one-half the width totally improved and one-half in relatively poor condition.

***Legal Annotation***: "Finally, the fact that an owner of land may 'cause' to be constructed an **off-site improvement** as a condition to its approvals should not of itself be a basis to impose such a duty upon the owner." *MacGrath v. Levin Properties* (N.J. App. Div., 1992).

## OFF-SITE PARKING

**Parking provided for a specific use but located on a site other than the one on which the specific use is located.**

***Comment***: Many ordinances permit off-site parking, provided it is located reasonably close to the use it is designed to serve. A distance of three hundred to four hundred feet is considered the maximum. Off-site parking offers an advantage in that it encourages a grouping of parking (shared parking) for more than one use. In some cases, shared parking can result in the need for fewer spaces than the sum of individual uses. See ***Parking, Shared***.

***Legal Annotation***: "Over the years, as traffic and the number of patrons have dramatically increased, the Authority has purchased or leased additional property in Falmouth and has provided shuttle bus service for its passengers between its **off-site parking** lots and the Woods Hole terminal." *Town of Bourne v. Plante* (Mass., 1999).

## OFF-STREET LOADING

**Designated areas located adjacent to buildings where trucks may load and unload cargo.**

***Comment***: A minimum dimension of fourteen by fifty-five feet is needed to accommodate modern tractor-trailers plus maneuvering space. Site design should provide wide aisles, large turning radii, and space for backing up. Since many trucks load and unload throughout the night or early in the morning, and many are refrigerator trucks requiring noisy machinery to be kept going at all times, the nature and location of adjacent uses should be taken into consideration in locating the off-street loading areas. Landscaping, berms, and solid fencing may be needed for buffering.

***Legal Annotation***: "In addition, Code section 538.200 provides that religious institutions containing 10,000 square feet of gross floor area or more must provide one **off-street loading** berth." *City of Minneapolis v. Church Universal & Triumphant* (Minn., 1983).

## OFF-STREET PARKING SPACE

**A parking space that is not located on a dedicated street right-of-way and that is directly accessible to an access aisle. *See Figure 74.***

***Legal Annotation***: "In 1959, the zoning ordinance was amended to require one **off-street parking space** for every 150 square feet of floor area in buildings, constructed in business districts." *Matter of Overhill Building Co. v. Delany* (N.Y., 1971).

## OFF-TRACT

**Not located on the property that is the subject of a development application or on a contiguous portion of a street or other right-of-way. *See Figure 71.***

***Legal Annotation***: "On June 13, 1988, defendant Township of Warren Planning Board granted preliminary major subdivision approval for the Windermere development. The approving resolution 'specifically reserved' several issues, including the 'necessity for **off tract** traffic improvements' as well as the computation of plaintiffs' 'fair share contribution for future traffic improvements on Mountain Boulevard.'" *F&W Associates v. County of Somerset* (N.J. App. Div., 1994).

## OFF-TRACT IMPROVEMENT

**An improvement required to be made off-tract as a result of an application for development. *See Figure 71.***

***Comment***: The assessment for off-tract improvements can be complicated. Most state land-use laws permit only a proportionate share assessment and require the facility to be improved to have a "rational nexus" to the project. Consequently, a developer cannot, for example, be required to pay for the entire improvement of an intersection that is seriously congested even without the new project. The developers could be made to provide for their fair share of any improvement needed to accommodate the traffic impact of the new development.

"Rational nexus" means that the project has a discernible impact on the facility proposed to be improved. The impact of a major traffic generator on adjacent intersections is obvious. The impact on one ten miles away probably does not meet the rational nexus test. **See *Rational Nexus*.**

***Legal Annotation***: "*N.J.S.A.* 40:55D-5 defines a minor subdivision as '[a] subdivision of land for the creation of a number of lots specifically permitted by ordinance as a minor subdivision; provided that such subdivision does not involve (1) a planned development, (2) any new street or (3) the extension of any **off-tract improvement** the cost of which is to be prorated pursuant to section 30 of this act.'" *Amato v. Randolph Township Planning Board* (N.J. App. Div., 1982).

## OIL CHANGE FACILITY

**An establishment that provides the lubrication and/or checking, changing, or addition of those fluids and filters necessary to the maintenance of a motor vehicle.**

***Comment***: The line between "quick lube" establishments and other types of specialized auto maintenance establishments, such as tire and muffler shops, is quickly becoming blurred.

"Service maintenance stations without fuel" may be a more appropriate term.

*Legal Annotation*: "In 1988, during construction of the **oil-change facility**, LPOM discovered the property was contaminated with petroleum and its by-products." *In Re Apex Oil Co.* (Bankr. Ct. E.D. Mo., 1992).

## OLIGOTROPHIC LAKES

**Deep lakes that have a low supply of nutrients, contain little organic matter, and are characterized by high water transparency and high dissolved oxygen.**

*Legal Annotation*: "Jenness Pond has excellent potential for recreation, being classified by the State as '**oligotrophic**' (a young lake with clear water, having average weed growth) and being approximately 232 acres in area." *In re National Environmental Systems Corp.* (Bankr. Ct. D. N.H., 1989).

## ONE-WAY CAR SHARING

**A car-sharing system where the vehicle does not have to be returned to the location from which it was rented. http://www.strc.ch/conferences/2013/Boyaci_Geroliminis_STRC13.pdf**

*Legal Annotation*: "Mr. Aderhold, a Seattleite, applied to become a car2go member in December 2012. Car2go is a **one-way** local **car-sharing** service that Defendant car2go N.A., LLC provides. In Seattle, for example, car2go provides hundreds of cars parked on city streets. Any member can use a car to drive to any location within preset boundaries, paying car2go by the minute for the use of the car. Once the member arrives at her destination, she simply leaves the car there, where another car2go member will ultimately use it to go to another destination. Car2go operates not just in Seattle, but in at least five other cities across the United States." *Aderhold v. Car2go NA, LLC* (W.D. Wash., 2014).

## ON-SITE

**Located on the lot that is the subject of an application for development. *See Figure 71.***

*Legal Annotation*: "When a programmatic EIS has already been prepared, we have held that **site**-specific impacts need not be fully evaluated until a 'critical decision' has been made to act **on-site** development." *State of Cal. V. Block* (9th Cir., 1982).

## ON-SITE WASTEWATER DISPOSAL SYSTEM

**A set of components or systems that treat, convey, and dispose of domestic wastewater on-site. See *Septic System*.**

*Comment*: The system includes septic systems, aerobic treatment systems, activated sludge systems, recirculating sand filters, gravel, pipes, and leach chambers (Bowers 2001).

*Legal Annotation*: "Plaintiffs recognize Cleary's authority to build, maintain, and regulate a 'sewer system' within the Cleary District but argue that Cleary is without authority to enact its 'Decentralized Wastewater Use Ordinance' because the Legislature granted the Mississippi State Board of Health sole authority to regulate septic tanks under the Mississippi Individual **On-Site Wastewater Disposal System** Law." *Green v. Cleary Water, Sewer & Fire Dist.* (Miss., 2005).

## ON-STREET PARKING SPACE

**A parking space that is located on a dedicated street right-of-way. *See Figure 74.***

*Legal Annotation*: "To reduce air pollution and other environmental effects of automobile commuting, a community reasonably may restrict **on-street parking** available to commuters, thus encouraging reliance on car pools and mass transit." *County Board of Arlington Cty. v. Richards* (U.S., 1977).

## ON-TRACT

**Located on the property that is the subject of a development application or on a contiguous portion of a street or other right-of-way. *See Figure 71.***

*Legal Annotation*: "The Court also determined that the defendant ought to compensate the plaintiff for any expenses incurred to maintain an adequate supply. Although still protecting **on-tract** uses over off-tract uses, the Court actually struck a balance between the two uses that attempted to ensure that both parties would have reasonable access to the common water supply." *Mich. Citizens for Water Conservation v. Nestle Waters N. Am., Inc.* (Mich. Ct. App., 2006).

## ONE HUNDRED PERCENT LOCATION

**A real estate term identifying the prime business location usually able to command the highest commercial and office rentals for a particular area or municipality.**

*Legal Annotation*: "Factors such as locational advantage, Newton's prestige reputation, and the introduction of the Massachusetts Turnpike extension combine to make Newton a desired community. These external factors can be of economic advantage. . . . They can encourage employment, broaden the tax base and restore land to high future productivity. To accomplish this will require a re-study of the zoning ordinance and adoption of substantial zoning map and ordinance changes to permit these areas to be developed to their indicated highest uses. . . . Newton Lower Falls Study area. Land within this study area is located ideally in relation to industrial and research uses along Route 128 and is considered by some developers to be close to a **100% location**." *Roach v. Newton Redevelopment Authority* (Mass. App. Ct., 1979).

## ONE-HUNDRED YEAR STORM

**The storm that is estimated to have a 1 percent chance, or one chance in one hundred, of being equaled or exceeded in any one year. See *Flood, Regulation Base*.**

*Legal Annotation*: "A **100-year storm** is a storm of such intensity that it has a one percent chance of occurring in any given year." *City of Watauga v. Taylor* (Tex. Ct. App., 1988).

## ONEROUS

**Burdensome or oppressive.**

*Comment*: (1) As a condition of development approval, an onerous requirement is one that has no clear, direct, or substantial relationship to the development; (2) in connection with deeds, titles, gifts, or contracts, the consideration given is of greater value than the one received (Johnsich 1991).

*Legal Annotation*: "The burden of establishing a prima facie case in a retaliation action is not **onerous**, but one easily met." *Nguyen v. City of Cleveland* (6th Cir., 2000).

## OPACITY

**(1) The property of a substance that renders it partially or wholly obstructive to the transmission of visible light; (2) degree of obscuration of light.**

*Comment*: The range of opacity is from 0 to 100 percent. For example, clear glass has 0 percent opacity, and a wall has 100 percent opacity.

*Legal Annotation*: **"Opacity** is one of the most basic emission limitations imposed on sources of particulate air pollution such as the Colbert plant's two smokestacks. The term '**opacity**' refers to the extent to which a plume of smoke 'reduce[s] the transmission of light and obscure[s] the view of the background.'" *Sierra Club v. Tennessee Valley Authority* (11th Cir., 2005).

## OPEN BURNING

**Uncontrolled burning of wastes in an open area.**

*Legal Annotation*: "One of Safe Air's objectives is to stop the practice of **open burning**. Safe Air asserts that smoke resulting from **open burning** endangers the public because it contains high concentrations of pollutants that create severe respiratory problems for residents in areas immediately surrounding bluegrass farms." *Safe Air for Everyone v. Meyer* (9th Cir., 2004).

## OPEN MEETING OR HEARING

**A meeting or hearing open to the public.**

*Comment*: Open meetings may be required by statute under a "sunshine law." However, the fact that a meeting is required to be open to the public does not necessarily mean that the public can participate. Public participation usually is permitted only at a public hearing, with notice duly posted and advertised.

*Legal Annotation*: "These demand 'a fair and **open hearing**,'—essential alike to the legal validity of the administrative regulation and to the maintenance of public confidence in the value and soundness of this important governmental process. Such a hearing has been described as an 'inexorable safeguard.'" *Morgan v. United States* (U.S., 1938).

## OPEN SPACE

**Any parcel or area of land or water, essentially unimproved and set aside, dedicated, designated, or reserved for public or private use or enjoyment or for the use and enjoyment of owners, occupants, and their guests.**

*Comment*: Open space may include active recreational facilities, such as swimming pools, play equipment for youngsters, ball fields, court games, and picnic tables. The improved recreation facilities, though, would be only a small part of the overall open space. The open space might include incidental parking and access roads.

*Legal Annotation*: "The State of California has determined that the development of local **open-space** plans will discourage the 'premature and unnecessary conversion of open-space land to urban uses.'" *Agins v. City of Tiburon* (U.S., 1980).

## OPEN SPACE, COMMON

**Land within or related to a development, not individually owned or dedicated for public use, that is designed and intended for the common use or enjoyment of the residents of the development and their guests and that may include such complementary structures and improvements as are necessary and appropriate. *See Figure 23.***

*Legal Annotation*: "Under the usual cluster-zoning provisions, both the size and the width of individual residential lots in a large (or medium-sized) development may be reduced, provided (usually) that the overall density of the entire tract remains constant—provided, that is, that an area equivalent to the total of the areas thus 'saved' from each individual lot is pooled and retained as **common open space**." *South Burlington County NAACP v. Township of Mount* Laurel (N.J., 1975).

## OPEN SPACE, NATURAL

**An open space area that is in an unimproved and undisturbed state, with no changes to existing grade or removal of existing vegetation. See *Green Area; Greenbelt*.**

*Legal Annotation*: "Land within the Conservation Area, which is above the 'no-development' line, is set aside solely for the conservation of permanent **natural open space**, while land within the Development Area can be developed subject to certain limitations." *Corrigan v. City of Scottsdale* (Ariz. Ct. App., 1985).

## OPEN SPACE, PRIVATE

**Open space, the use of which is limited to the occupants of a single dwelling, building, or property.**

*Legal Annotation*: "Indeed, in *Nollan* itself Justice Scalia as much as conceded that the loss of **private open space** resulting from residential beach development could lead to an adverse public impact—a diminution of coastal views—justifying a requirement that the Nollans 'provide a viewing spot on their property for passersby with whose sighting of the ocean their new house would interfere.'" *Ehrlich v. City of Culver City* (Calif., 1996).

## OPEN SPACE, PUBLIC

**Open space owned by a public entity and maintained by it for the use and enjoyment of the general public.**

*Legal Annotation*: "About eight percent of the land in Santa Monica is dedicated to **public open space**, of which 245 acres are dedicated to public parks." *Santa Monica Food Not Bombs v. Santa Monica* (9th Cir., 2006).

## OPEN SPACE ELEMENT

**That section of the master plan of the municipality or other jurisdiction that provides an inventory of public and private open space lands and proposed goals, policies, and implementation programs for the preservation, acquisition, improvement, and management of open space lands.**

*Legal Annotation*: "In 1972 City imposed a moratorium on building and development in the area, and on or about July 7, 1973, it adopted an '**Open Space Element**' to its general plan indicating that that portion of the Natomas area lying to the north of Interstate 880 was to be reserved for agricultural and open-space uses." *Furey v. City of Sacramento* (Calif., 1979).

## OPEN SPACE RATIO

**Total area of open space divided by the total site area in which the open space is located.** *See Figure* 72.

*Legal Annotation*: "According to the FEIS, the temporary loss of active open space during construction will decrease the total **open space ratio** from 26 to 23 acres per thousand residents." *US v. City of New York* (E.D.N.Y., 2000).

## OPTION

**An exclusive right to purchase, rent, or sell a property at a stipulated price and within a specified time.**

*Legal Annotation*: "The Nollans originally leased their property with an **option** to buy. . . . The Nollans' **option** to purchase was conditioned on their promise to demolish the bungalow and replace it." *Nollan v. California Coastal Commission* (U.S., 1987).

## ORDINANCE

**A law or regulation adopted by a governing body.**

*Legal Annotation*: "Stating that its purpose was 'to eliminate hazards to pedestrians and motorists brought about by distracting sign displays' and 'to preserve and improve the appearance of the City,' San Diego enacted an **ordinance** to prohibit 'outdoor advertising display signs.'" *Metromedia, Inc. v. San Diego* (U.S., 1981).

## ORGANIC

**Referring to or derived solely from living organisms.**

**Figure 72**

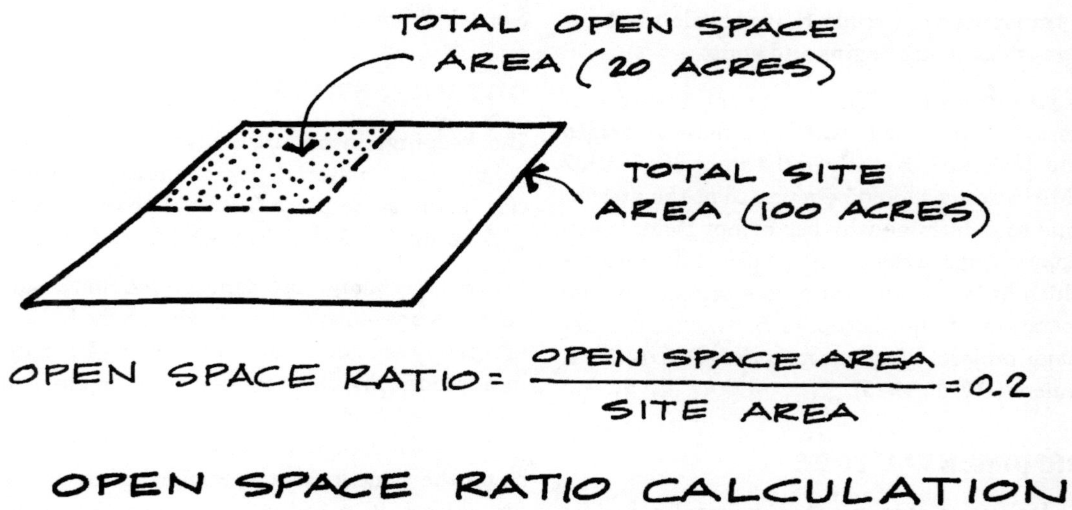

*Legal Annotation*: "The Langans are **organic** farmers: that is, they use no nonorganic fertilizers, insecticides or herbicides to aid them in their farming but rely on natural fertilizers and natural pest control agents. They had planned to can and sell their produce to **organic** food buyers." *Langan v. Valicopters, Inc.* (Wash., 1977).

## ORGANISM

**Any living human, plant, or animal.**

*Legal Annotation*: "DNA is an abbreviation for deoxyribonucleic acid, its chemical structure. It is a molecule that carries the body's genetic information. It is contained in every cell with a nucleus in every living **organism**." *Caldwell v. State* (Ga., 1990).

## ORIENTATION

**The placement of a structure on its lot with regard to other structures, natural elements such as sun and wind, and impacts from noise, glare, and similar adverse elements.**

*Legal Annotation*: "Another feature of the site plan involved the **orientation** of the structure on the far rear portion of the lot, as opposed to the front of the lot, near the street." *Barrister's, Inc. v. Westerville City Council* (Ohio Ct. App., 2004).

## ORIGIN AND DESTINATION STUDY

**A transportation study that records the location where a trip begins and ends.**

*Legal Annotation*: "There is doubt among professionals in the field whether a massive **origin and destination study** of the scope of the 1962 BMATS study should be repeated at the present time to determine whether or not there is any major change in the trip generation relationships which have been caused by the completion and operation of the Baltimore Beltway and other major projects." *Movement Against Destruction v. Trainor* (D.Md., 1975).

## ORNAMENTAL TREE

**A deciduous tree planted primarily for its beauty, color, flower, or leaf, rather than for screening purposes.**

*Comment*: Ornamental trees tend to be smaller at maturity than shade trees (American Planning Association, *Preparing a Landscaping Ordinance*, Planning Advisory Service Report No. 431, 1990).

*Legal Annotation*: "We are aware that generally, the method of estimating the value of a shade or **ornamental tree** wrongfully removed is to compare the value of the surrounding property before and after the removal." *Daniel v. Department of Transportation & Development* (La. Ct. App., 1981).

## OUTBUILDING

**A separate accessory building or structure not physically connected to the principal building.**

*Comment*: Outbuildings are smaller than the principal structure and may be used for storage or ancillary purposes. On estates, outbuildings are often the living quarters for employees.

*Legal Annotation*: "An '**outbuilding**' is defined as 'something used in connection with a main building[;] [a] small building appurtenant to a main building, and generally separated from it; *e.g.* outhouse; storage shed.' *Black's Law Dictionary* 1101 (6th ed.1990)." *Nicol v. Gonzales* (Texas Ct. App., 2004).

## OUTDOOR RETAIL SALES

See *Retail Sales, Outdoor*.

## OUTDOOR STORAGE

**The keeping, in an unenclosed area, of any goods, junk, material, merchandise, or vehicles in the same place for more than twenty-four hours. See *Retail Sales, Outdoor*.**

*Comment*: Many ordinances prohibit outdoor storage entirely or allow it only in certain restricted zones and in the rear yard only. In addition, the outdoor storage is required to be screened from public view by a fence, wall, or heavy landscaping. Where allowed, it must be on the same lot as the establishment or use for which it is providing the storage. For especially obnoxious outdoor storage uses such as junkyards, large setbacks from the street, solid fences, and a maximum height of stored material should be required.

There are uses, however, that typically and traditionally include outdoor storage and displays. These include new and used car dealers, agriculture, plant and landscaping establishments, and parking lots. Hardware stores and gas stations often display merchandise outdoors. The local ordinance should establish controls over these uses to ensure they do not become nuisances, pose safety problems, and become aesthetic disasters. These controls should include traditional site plan review, minimum setbacks from street rights-of-way and property lines, sign controls, and landscaping requirements.

*Legal Annotation*: "The City informed Big Blue that the **outdoor storage** and sale of goods was not permitted under applicable zoning ordinances and ordered Big Blue to discontinue the displays." *City of Columbus Board of Zoning Appeals v. Big Blue* (Ind. Ct. App., 1992).

## OUTFALL

**The mouth of a sewer, drain, or conduit where an effluent is discharged into the receiving waters.**

*Legal Annotation*: "The permit authorizes CRC to discharge wastewater from **outfall** number 001, the only **outfall** from which CRC discharges wastewater directly into Sand Creek." *Sierra Club v. Colorado Refining Co.* (D. Colo., 1994).

## OUTLET STORE

**See *Retail Outlet Store*.**

## OUTPATIENT FACILITY

**See *Clinic*.**

## OVERFLOW RIGHTS

**An easement that allows an owner to run excess water onto another property owner's land.**

*Legal Annotation*: "The deed reflects the transfer of riparian and **overflow rights** between the Spokane city limits and the mouth of the Little Spokane River downstream from the Nine Mile Dam, which includes the area of Mr. Ravenscroft's accident." *Ravenscroft v. Washington Water Power* (Wash. Ct. App., 1997).

## OVERFLOWED LAND

**A floodplain or land subject to frequent flooding. See *Floodplain*.**

*Legal Annotation*: "It is shown that West Greynolds Park has been extensively developed for park purposes and that eighty per cent of East Greynolds Park is mangrove swamp or what is commonly known as **overflowed land**, but it is conclusively shown that the county accepted the property." *Dade County v. City of North Miami Beach* (Fla., 1953).

## OVERHANG

**The part of a roof or wall that extends beyond a lower wall (*see Figure 20*). See *Eave*.**

*Legal Annotation*: "After finishing the garage on one house, plaintiff began to shingle a small porch **overhang**. The **overhang** extended two feet from the house and measured forty-two inches up to the peak on each side." *Hughes v. PMG Building, Inc.* (Mich. Ct. App., 1997).

## OVERLAY ZONE

**A zoning district that encompasses one or more underlying zones and that imposes additional requirements beyond those required for the underlying zone.**

*Comment*: Overlay zones deal with special situations that are not appropriate to a specific zoning district or that apply to several districts. For example, in all business zones, an overlay provision might require impact fees to provide for traffic improvements. A historic district overlay may cover parts of several zones. An overlay provision covering an entire municipality or specific zoning districts might require that all properties over a certain acreage proposed for higher-density development also provide a percentage of lower-income housing (American Planning Association, *The Administration of Flexible Zoning*

*Techniques*, Planning Advisory Service Report No. 318, 1976).

***Legal Annotation***: "Petitioners' proposed intensified use (phase I) is permitted outright in the CBD zone; however, the AA **overlay zone**, which implements the policies of the Tigard Community Development Code, allows city to attach conditions to the development in order to provide for projected transportation and public facility needs." *Dolan v. City of Tigard* (Ore., 1993).

## OWNER

**An individual, firm, association, syndicate, partnership, or corporation having sufficient proprietary interest to seek development of land.**

***Legal Annotation***: "We have repeatedly held that, as to property reserved by its **owner** for private use, 'the right to exclude [others is] "one of the most essential sticks in the bundle of rights that are commonly characterized as property."'" *Nollan v. California Coastal Commission* (U.S., 1987).

## OXIDATION POND

**An artificial lake or pond in which organic wastes are reduced by bacterial action.**

***Legal Annotation***: "The project included the creation of a 160-acre **oxidation pond**, in which sewage would be treated with chemicals and by exposure to the air." *Lindsey v. Forrest City* (Ark., 1976).

## OZONE

**A pungent, colorless, toxic gas.**

***Comment***: Ozone is a form of oxygen ($O_3$) that is formed in the ozone layer by electrical discharge or exposure to ultraviolet radiation, and is also produced in the lower atmosphere by the photochemical reaction of certain pollutants. It is both beneficial and threatening to Earth's organisms depending on how high in the atmosphere it is found. Ozone is one of the so-called greenhouse gases that are produced by the burning of fossil fuels and the cause of the greenhouse effect. Ozone is used industrially to deodorize air, purify water, and treat industrial wastes.

***Legal Annotation***: "It is therefore not conclusive for delegation purposes that, as respondents argue, **ozone** and particulate matter are 'nonthreshold' pollutants that inflict a continuum of adverse health effects at any airborne concentration greater than zero, and hence require the EPA to make judgments of degree." *Whitman v. American Trucking Assns., Inc.* (U.S., 2001).

# P

## PACKAGE TREATMENT PLANT

See *On-Site Wastewater Disposal System*.

***Legal Annotation***: "The proposed project would be located on 40 acres of land, and it would include: (1) 160 mobile home spaces, with estimated lot sizes of 0.17 an acre each; (2) a clubhouse; (3) a swimming pool; (4) a soccer field; (5) a softball field; and (6) a playground. Additionally, two linear miles of road that provided access to the mobile home community would need to be paved, and the mobile home community would need its own on-site **package treatment plant** to treat sewage." *His Light Investments, Ltd v. County of San Bernardino* (Calif. Ct. App., 2010).

## PAD

**(1) A paved space, with utility connections, in a mobile home park for the parking of a mobile home; (2) the proposed site of a freestanding use within a shopping center. See *Mobile Home Space; Pad Site*.**

***Legal Annotation***: "Mobile homes are not mobile. The term is a vestige of earlier times when mobile homes were more like today's recreational vehicles. Today mobile homes are designed to be placed permanently on a **pad** and maintained there for life." *Laurel Park Community, LLC v. City of Tumwater* (9th Cir., 2012).

## PAD SITE

**A freestanding parcel of commercial real estate usually located in the front part of a strip mall or a larger shopping center, and usually adjacent to a main artery or center access roadway.**

***Comment***: Buildings on pad sites are referred to as freestanding buildings because they are separate and apart from the larger shopping center or retail building on which the pad site is located. Pad sites are commercially desirable because of their visibility to consumers, their accessibility from within the larger center, and the ease of facilitating drive-in service. They are typically sought after by banks, casual dining establishments, and fast-food restaurants for standalone buildings. Pad sites usually range between ten thousand and sixty thousand square feet. Some pad site uses may rely upon the parking spaces of the larger center for overflow parking. See *Freestanding Building*.

***Legal Annotation***: "'**Pad site**' is understood to refer to any freestanding parcel of commercial real property located in front of or near a shopping center such that it benefits from traffic to the shopping center." *Clear Sky Car Wash LLC v. City of Chesapeake, Va.* (4th Cir., 2014).

## PAPER STREET

See *Street, Paper*.

***Legal Annotation***: "The installation of the storm drain . . . and the seasonal public use of the road does not prove an acceptance of the road where the other factors to be considered, i.e., the fact that the road remained a '**paper road**,' unpaved and not maintained by the town, and the tax collector's taking of the road as a result of non-payment of taxes by the then owner supports the conclusion that there was no acceptance. . . . *Black's Law Dictionary* (8th Ed. 2004) defines **paper street** or road as '[a] thoroughfare that appears on plats, subdivision maps, and other publicly filed documents, but that has not been completed or opened for public use.' But see . . . (describing **paper street** as one never paved, not developed as public road, not used by abutting owners for access, no formal dedication for use as highway and no formal or informal acceptance by town)." *Kores v. Calo* (Conn: App. Ct., 2011).

## PARAPET

**A barrier, wall, or railing along the edge of a balcony, bridge, terrace, or roof where there is a drop and sudden danger of falling; or a wall or hip-roof extension along the edge of the roof to visually and acoustically screen rooftop mechanical and HVAC equipment. *See Figure 20.***

***Comment*:** In addition to providing protection and visual screening, parapets can be part of the aesthetic design of a building and provide some acoustical shielding. Zoning ordinances often permit parapet walls to extend beyond the maximum building height permitted by the zoning regulations.

***Legal Annotation***: "At that time, plaintiff was approximately three feet from the roof **parapet**, which was approximately two-feet high. . . . This shove was significant enough to cause plaintiff to stumble backwards over the **parapet** and fall to the ground in the alleyway below." *Lewis v. City of New York* (E.D.N.Y., 2010).

## PARATRANSIT

**A form of public transportation service characterized by the flexible routing and scheduling of small vehicles such as taxis, vans, and small buses, to provide shared-occupancy, door-step, or curbside personalized transportation service.**

***Legal Annotation***: "Handi-Van and Village Carry are companies that formerly contracted with Broward County, Florida, to provide **paratransit** services for disabled residents of the County who are unable to use other public transit services." *Handi-Van Inc. v. Broward County* (Fla. Ct. App., 2011).

## PARCEL

**(1) A piece or area of land formally described and recorded with block and lot numbers, by metes and bounds, by ownership, or in such a manner as to specifically identify the dimensions and/or boundaries; (2) informally, as land in general.**

***Comment***: The term is often used generically to describe a piece of land often without specific boundaries, such as "that hilly parcel" or "all agricultural parcels."

***Legal Annotation***: "'Lot' means the **parcel** of land on which a principal use or building and its accessory buildings are placed, together with the required open spaces. For the purposes of determining the location of required yards, a lot shall be considered to be as shown on the official recorded plat of the property." *City of Osburn v. Randel* (Idaho, 2012).

## PARISH HOUSE

**(1) A building used by a church primarily for administrative or social purposes; (2) in the Roman Catholic Church, it refers to the residence of the cleric.**

***Legal Annotation***: "The Building Inspector's letter further stated that the **parish house** was a legal residence and the church building was a legal accessory structure and, thus, the property was in compliance with the applicable 1965 Zoning Ordinance. In addition, shortly after the owner's purchase, the Building Inspector responded to the petitioner's inquiry and concluded that the property owner's use of the church building as an 'artist's office/studio' complied with the applicable zoning ordinance. It is uncontroverted that the present zoning ordinance, adopted in 1987, does not permit the owner's use of the property." *Matter of Kennedy v. Zoning Bd. of Appeals of Town of North Salem* (N.Y. Sup. Ct., 1994).

## PARK ACCESSIBILITY

**The distance community residents live from the nearest park (Harnik and Simms 2006). See *Also Playground, Accessibile*.**

## PARK, DOG

**A parcel or tract of public or privately owned land set aside or designated for use by dog owners as "off-leash" areas for exercising their canine pets.**

*Comment*: Dog parks, also known as dog runs or off-leash areas, should be enclosed by dog-proof barriers and offer shade and water for the animals and benches for their owners, dog waste bags and containers for waste disposal, and a double-gated entry area. A one-acre minimum size is suggested, and larger parks might have separate areas for large and small dogs. The involvement of a committed owner group is desirable for a successful dog park (Krohe 2005). See *Also Park, Private; Park, Public*.

*Legal Annotation*: "After arguing that the dog park is a 'residential' use, the dissent further concludes that, even if the **dog park** is not 'residential,' it does not constitute a 'more serious' violation of the deed restriction. The dissent principally relies on Cherry to conclude that a 'more serious' violation did not occur because a 'dog park is of the same nature as a park.'" *Bloomfield Estates Improvement Ass'n, Inc. v. City of Birmingham* (Mich., 2007).

## PARK, PRIVATE

**A tract of land owned or controlled and used by specific and designated entities or persons for active and/or passive recreational purposes.**

*Legal Annotation*: "This conclusion is buttressed by the nature of the service rendered the community by a park. The service rendered even by a **private park** of this character is municipal in nature. It is open to every white person, there being no selective element other than race." *Evans v. Newton* (U.S., 1966).

## PARK, PUBLIC

**A tract of land owned by a branch of government and available to the general public for recreational purposes.**

*Comment*: Public parks may also be owned by private entities and made available to the public. For example, a service club or nonprofit institution may dedicate land for park or open space purposes. As long as the land is available to the general public in the same manner as parks owned by a branch of government, it can be considered a public park (Crompton 2001; Gavin 2000; Lewis 2008).

*Legal Annotation*: "In Reinhart, the court found that the actions of a private organization in restricting political campaigning at its art festival could not be attributed to the city, even though the festival took place in a **public park**. Id. Reinhart, however, lacked the presence of state officials who enforced the speech restriction." *Bays v. City of Fairborn* (6th Cir., 2012).

## PARK-AND-RIDE FACILITY

**A parking lot designed for drivers to leave their cars and use mass transit facilities beginning, terminating, or stopping at the park-and-ride facility.**

*Comment*: Park-and-ride facilities are often called "intercept facilities."

*Legal Annotation*: "She knew, from her more than twenty years of experience at the MBTA, that people usually park in the lot in order to '**park and ride**,' leaving their cars and then riding either a bus or the subway. People use a specific area, on the side of the parking lot nearest the station, to stop briefly to pick up or discharge passengers." *US v. Ramos* (1st Cir., 2010).

## PARKING, BANKED

**Required parking, the construction of which is permitted to be deferred until needed.**

*Comment*: Many municipalities permit or even encourage a part of the required parking for a development to be landscaped and not constructed until the demand for the parking materializes. The applicant receives all necessary planning and engineering approvals for the banked parking at the time the development receives its original approval. Only when the additional parking is needed, as determined by the applicant or required by the approving authority, is a construction permit secured and the parking installed. The advantages to the municipality are less runoff, more landscaping, and better aesthetics, even if temporary. The applicant saves money by not having to construct the improvement.

*Legal Annotation*: "When asked if he anticipated anyone attempting to park on 75th Street, Day responded that ILC's goal was to ensure adequate parking on site, and that the twelve additional **banked parking** spaces were included in the plan in case the number of spaces required by the code became insufficient." *Irshad Learning Center v. County of DuPage* (N.D. Ill., 2013).

## PARKING, SHARED

**Joint utilization of a parking area for more than one use.**

***Comment***: Shared parking involves parking spaces that are used at different times by different uses. A shared parking space serves several stores so that a vehicle does not have to be moved from place to place. The classic example is the mall movie theater that, because of off-peak-hour use, may not generate any additional parking demand. Each type of joint use reduces the total number of spaces needed. Shopping center parking is an example of a shared parking facility. Instead of computing the parking requirement for each use, a single, overall parking ratio is used. See *Parking Ratio. (Source: American Planning* Association 2006, 247.)

*Legal Annotation*: "The entire 43,246 square feet could be recommended for approval by staff if the applicant can demonstrate that the on-site parking will be sufficient to meet the full use of the proposed building including the expansion through either a parking study or **shared-parking** analysis." *Church of Scientology v. City of Sandy Springs* (N.D. Ga., 2012).

"The 2002 amendments also added section 36.310.060, which allows '**shared parking**' among separate commercial parcels:

A. Applicability. Separate commercial uses on separate parcels not more than 1,500 feet from each other within any commercial zoning district may jointly use parking facilities subject to the approval of a Parking Use Permit in compliance with Section 36.410.090 when the review authority determines that either of the following conditions exist:

1. Different peak hour parking demands exist between the separate uses; and
2. Single vehicle trips are likely to be made to two or more of the businesses proposed to share the parking." *Cook v. Kilby* (Calif. Ct. App., 2009).

## PARK, WATERFRONT

**A generally linear public area or publicly accessible area created along a body of water and including such amenities as public walking and/or cycling paths as well as larger communal areas, and potentially also including commercial uses and marina services.**

***Comment***: One significant benefit of a waterfront park is to make use of potentially flood-prone space for recreation in a manner that allows for the absorption and dissipation of floodwater in a flood emergency, through the use of permeable pavers and creation of open space and by the removal of older buildings and paved areas constructed close to the water's edge. Waterfront parks can be part of marina facilities and planned residential and commercial development.

*Legal Annotation*: "The [Thea Foss] Waterway visually and physically connects surrounding districts. The Waterway's historic past and working waterfront, combined with new cultural, recreational, residential, office and retail uses, will create a lively, urban environment. A linear **waterfront park** will link together a variety of attractive, ground level public activities and uses accessible to all of Tacoma's citizens and to the region." *KS Tacoma Holdings, LLC v. Shorelines Hearings Board* (Wash. Ct. App., 2012).

## PARKING ACCESS

**The part of a parking lot or parking area that allows motor vehicles ingress and egress from the street. *See Figure 74.***

*Legal Annotation*: "There were 'no gates, fences, security devices, or any other type of obstruction blocking either driveway, or the **parking access** in the rear of the duplex.' The parking area behind the duplex was a concrete slab surface and was 'open to the rear parking area of the adjacent duplex to the west,' and this parking area was 'not blocked by fences, gates, or any other type of obstructions and share[d] primarily the west driveway as access, but [was] also accessible from the east driveway.'" *McClintock v. State* (Texas Ct. App., 2013).

## PARKING AREA

**Any public or private area, under or outside of a building or structure, designed and used for parking motor vehicles, including parking lots, garages, private driveways, and legally designated areas of public streets. See *Garage*.**

***Legal Annotation***: "The County proposed an overnight and day-use facility, with camping sites for recreational vehicles and tent campers, a day-use area, a boat ramp and trailer **parking area**, a 90-space **parking area**, comfort facilities, an environmental education area, a beach area, and walking trails." *Forsyth County v. US Army Corps of Engineers* (11th Cir., 2011).

## PARKING AREA, PRIVATE

**A parking area for the exclusive use of the owners of the lot on which the parking area is located or whomever else they permit to use the parking area.**

## PARKING AREA, PUBLIC

**A parking area available to the public, with or without payment of a fee.**

***Legal Annotation***: "General Obligations Law § 9-103, however, does not apply to supervised municipal parks. Ferres v City of New Rochelle, supra [Suburban, municipal park with a supervisor and 24 employees which included a **public parking area**, guard house, beach, pavilion, and a place to eat]; Sena v Town of Greenfield, 91 NY2d 611 (1998) [Park included sledding hill, baseball fields and pavilion and was regularly maintained, inspected, and supervised by the Town]." *McKown v. Town of Waterford* (N.Y. Sup. CT., 2011).

## PARKING BAY

**The parking module consisting of one or two rows of parking spaces and the aisle from which motor vehicles enter and leave the spaces. *See Figure 74.***

***Legal Annotation***: "The above definitions establish that the underground area is comprised of two components. Each unit's designated **parking bay** is considered a part of the unit, itself. It is neither a common element nor a limited common element." *334 Barry in Town Homes, Inc. v. Farago* (Ill. App. Ct., 1990).

## PARKING LANE

**A lane designed to provide on-street parking.**

***Comment***: Parking lanes are usually located on one or both sides of the street. On very wide streets, however, the parking lane can be in the center of the cartway. In areas where traffic volumes are high, parking lanes may be restricted during rush hours and used only for vehicular travel.

***Legal Annotation***: "And so what is going on here is [defendant] is driving, he is driving down the road, he crosses the white line, he goes back in. I don't think the state would argue that one would legally be able to park all the way out to the edge of that white line and be called a **parking lane**. That clearly would not be true. The white line is, again, just there and it allows him to drive out to the pavement and keep his identification." *State v. Wentworth* (Ore. Ct. App., 2012).

## PARKING LOOP

**A private street with perpendicular parking.**

## PARKING LOT

**An off-street, ground-level open area that provides temporary storage for motor vehicles. See *Parking Area*.**

***Comment***: Parking lots may provide access to other uses, such as dwellings, offices, stores, and so on. They are not designed for permanent storage unless permitted by the local ordinance.

***Legal Annotation***: "On June 5, 2005, the defendant Home Depot U.S.A., Inc. (hereinafter Home Depot), was displaying barbecue grills for sale in the **parking lot** of its store in Freeport. The **parking lot** was separated from the entrance to the store by two lanes of traffic, a fire lane, and a sidewalk. . . . The Supreme Court precluded the plaintiffs from introducing prior complaints made against Home Depot, alleging that its placement of merchandise in the **parking lot** violated a zoning code provision requiring it to keep parking spaces clear for its patrons." *Sydnor v. Home Depot USA, Inc.* (N.Y. App. Div., 2010).

## PARKING METER

**A device operated by the insertion of coins or other acceptable payment method, installed adjacent to a vehicle parking space on streets or parking areas for the purpose of limiting the amount of time a vehicle can park.**

***Comment***: Newer parking meters accept credit cards, and some municipalities are now using single meters for entire parking lots or on-street parking. These meters disperse slips of paper, which are displayed on the dashboard of vehicles and show when the authorized time has expired.

***Legal Annotation***: "In the meantime, Concerned Citizens was required to install **parking meters**, set up a **parking meter** zone and conduct a traffic study. These events caused a lengthy delay, exacerbated by a hiring freeze reducing available manpower at the City." *State v. Concerned Citizens of South Central Los Angeles* (Calif. Ct. App., 2013).

## PARKING RATIO

**The minimum number of off-street parking spaces required for various types of land use. See *Minimum Parking Standards*.**

***Comment***: For nonresidential uses, parking ratios are usually expressed in terms of one space per unit of floor area—for example, one space for each 250 square feet of floor area for offices. Some ordinances base the ratio on net floor area, excluding bathrooms, hallways, stairwells, cellars and similar areas from the count. Gross floor area is easier to compute and more accurately reflects parking demand. Basements and attics are usually excluded from gross floor area unless they are occupied. However, a basement used for storage frees up other space for workers and thus contributes to the total parking demand. While the general practice is to compute parking ratio on a floor area basis, other standards have been used, such as number of classrooms, seats in a theater, hospital beds, or motel rooms. But practices change. For example, a majority of medical and surgical procedures are now accomplished on an outpatient basis, sharply reducing demand for visitor spaces. The ITE handbook *Trip Generation* (Institute of Transportation Engineers, 4th Edition, 2010) suggests that local surveys are the most accurate method for determining parking needs.

For nonresidential uses, floor area remains the most widely used standard. Typical ratios for nonresidential uses are as follows:

| Use | Parking Ratio (Spaces per 1,000 feet |
|---|---|
| General Office Use | 4.0 |
| Industrial | 2.5 |
| Medical Office | 5.0 |
| Retail (Individual) | 4.5 |
| Retail mall | 5.5 |
| Wholesale | 1.0 |

For residential land uses, most ordinances require a specific number of spaces for each dwelling-unit type. For example:

| Dwelling-Unit Type | Spaces Required (per unit) |
|---|---|
| Single-family | 2.5 |
| Townhouse | 2.0 |
| Garden apartment | 1.5 |
| High-rise | 1.0 |

The ratios should be adjusted downward, or a cap placed on the number of off-street spaces, when a specific area is served by mass transit, shared parking is available, or the municipality, as a land-use policy, uses on-street parking to meet parking demand. A study by Rutgers University (Listokin et al. 2006) described a methodology for adjusting conventional parking ratios downward for infill development, as these locations typically were better served by mass transit. Additional parking, often 10 percent of the required number of spaces, is needed for visitor parking for multifamily developments. Driveway space (ten feet by twenty feet), provided it clears the sidewalk, can be counted toward the required off-street parking for single- or two-family houses. Garages also can be counted as part of the required parking, despite the fact that in many situations, the garage becomes a storage area.

Finally, many municipalities encourage applicants, particularly in the case of nonresidential development, to bank a part of the parking and construct it only when the need is apparent. See *Parking, Banked. (American Planning Association, Off-Street Parking Requirements: A National Review of Standards, Planning Advisory Service Report No. 432, 1990; American Planning Association, Parking Standards, Planning Advisory Service Report 510/511 2002.)*

***Legal Annotation***: "The Church submitted a set of alternate conditions to its Application proposing a limitation on the occupancy of the building to 283 people, based on the 81 parking spaces provided after conversion of the basement, and applying a **parking ratio** of 3.5 people per vehicle ('the First Alternate Conditions')." *Church of Scientology v. City of Sandy Springs* (N.D., Ga., 2012).

## PARKING SPACE

**A space for the parking of a motor vehicle within a public or private parking area. See *Off-Street Parking Space; On-Street Parking Space; Stall. See Figures 73 and 74.***

***Legal Annotation***: "During a zoning inspection in May 2006, the inspector found two zoning violations. First, she sent Gerry Drackett notice on May 10, 2006, that the property at issue violated the Danbury Township Zoning Resolution that requires that lot owners to have two off-street parking places per dwelling unit, which must be 9' × 18' in size. The zoning inspector testified that upon inspection she discovered that the Dracketts had actually followed the original plans, which only provided for one **parking space**." *Drackett v. Danbury Twp. Zoning Bd. of Appeals* (Ohio Ct. App., 2010).

## PARKING SPACE, HANDICAPPED

**See *Handicapped Parking Space; See Figure 5, Americans With Disabilities Act (Ada)*.**

***Legal Annotation***: "Section 27-710.1.E—requiring one handicapped parking space for every one to twenty-five parking spaces, and one additional **handicapped parking space** for every additional one to twenty-five parking spaces." *Gould v. Zoning Hearing Board of Bristol Borough* (Pa. Comm. Ct., 2011).

## PARKING STALL

**The parking space in which vehicles park. *See Figures 55, 73, and 74.***

***Comment***: The sizes of stalls vary. The typical automobile stall is nine by eighteen feet. However, where there is a large turnover and drivers have packages, such as in a shopping center, a ten-foot wide stall is sometimes required. The wider stall permits easier vehicular access for shoppers burdened with packages. In low-turnover situations, such as office parking, an 8.5- by eighteen-foot stall may suffice. Hairpin marking is recommended in such situations to center vehicles in such stalls. See Hairpin Marking. If spaces are assigned, compact car parking can be as small as seven by seventeen feet. The typical parallel parking space is eight feet by twenty-two feet. See *Parking Space*.

***Legal Annotation***: "The Board also granted several sign variances and a design exception to permit a **parking stall** of 10 ft. × 19 ft." *Stewart v. Plan. Bd. of Manalapan* (N.J. Super. Ct., 1999).

## PARKING STRUCTURE

**A building or structure consisting of more than one level and used to store motor vehicles. See *Garage; Garage, Municipal; Garage, Public*.**

***Legal Annotation***: "The Plan acknowledged the amount of area dedicated to surface commercial parking and recommended that commercial parking needs should be provided by **structured parking** in accordance with delineated design standards. . . . In the meantime, plaintiffs undertook further construction to convert a

**Figure 73**

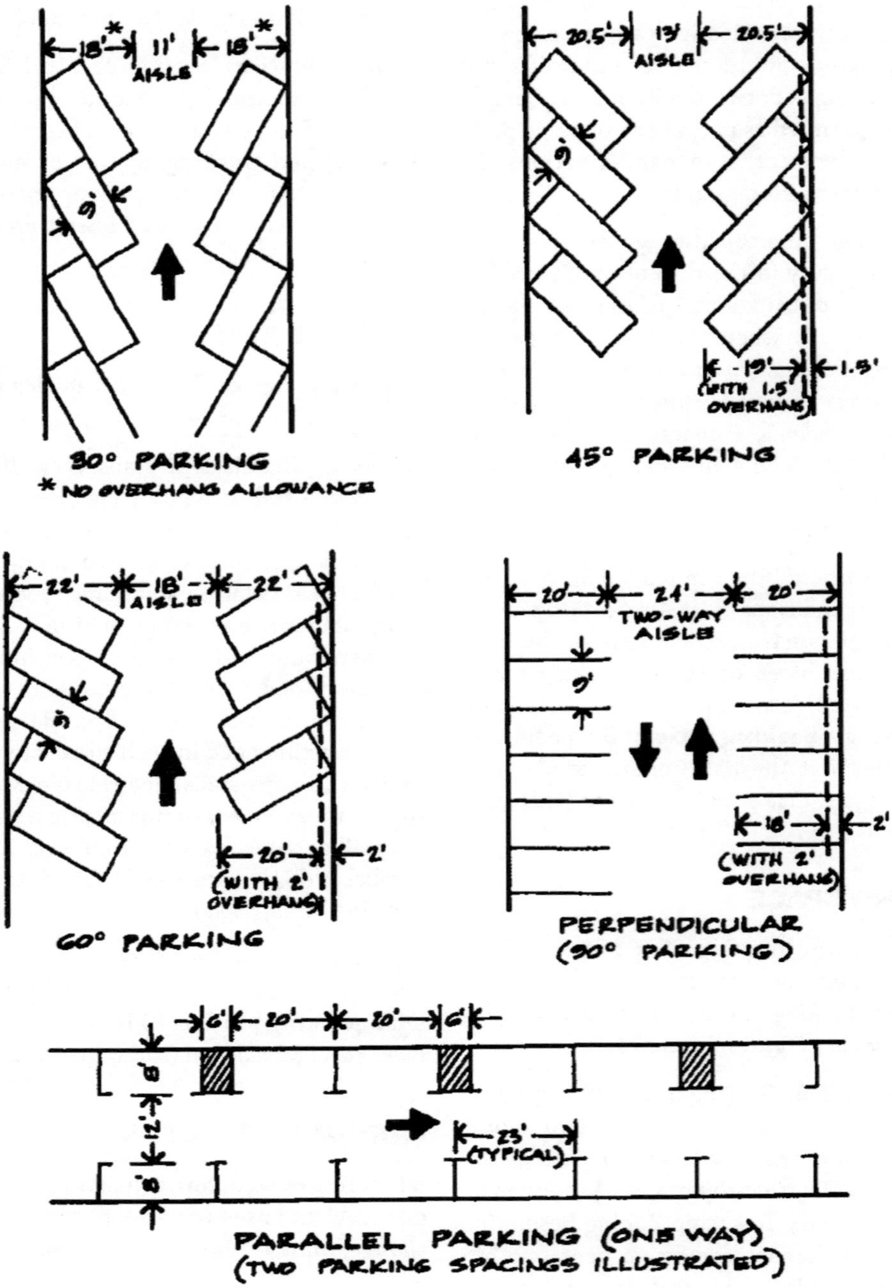


PARKING AREA DIMENSIONS
(FOR STANDARD-SIZE VEHICLES)

**Figure 74**

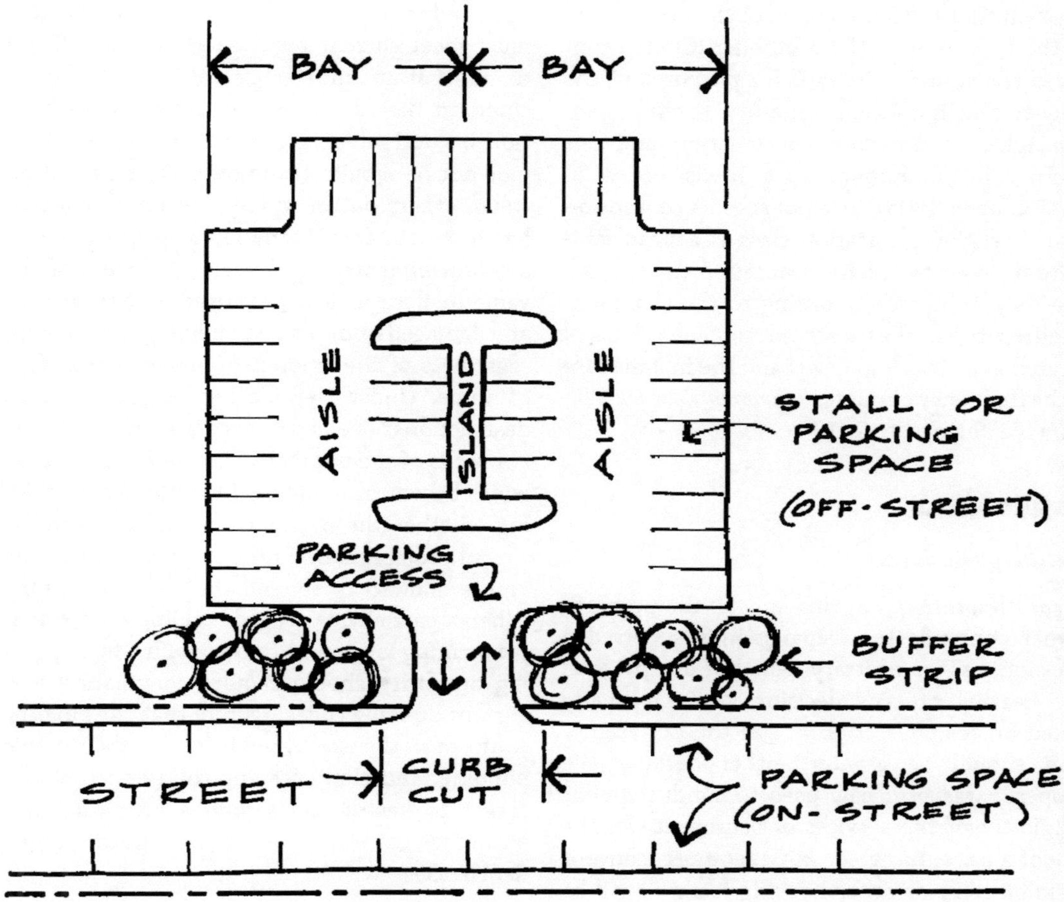


pre-existing building to an open **parking structure** to increase the number of parking spaces to 1050 and the Town issued a license for 1050 spaces in May 2008." *Comprelli v. Town of Harrison* (N.J. App. Div., 2012).

## PARKLETS

**The conversion of a small number of on-street parking spaces or other small sites in the public right-of-way into "public park" space, with such improvements as seating, tables, and landscaping.**

***Comment***: An increasingly popular program in progressive cities, such as San Francisco and New York, having started as single-day conversions, but now becoming permanent improvements. (Source: Berg 2010.)

***Legal Annotation***: "Comitta concluded that the Township's intention to use the Property for open space or a park with a memorial is a **parklet**, a passive recreational use, which is a viable and practical use for the Property. . . . Whether termed a 'park,' 'vest pocket park,' 'pocket park,' or '**parklet**,' we find the Township's taking of the Property for public park purposes within its statutory authority." *Condemnation of Lands of Laughlin* (Pa. Common. Ct., 2003).

## PAROCHIAL SCHOOL

**See *School, Parochial***

*Legal Annotation*: "It is the Commonwealth's position that the Sunday school class conducted in the basement of the Methodist Church rendered the church a 'school' for purposes of the drug-free school zone mandatory. It relies upon principles of statutory construction and our decision in Commonwealth v. Lewis, 885 A.2d 51 (Pa.Super. 2005), in support of its contention that a religious education class is a **parochial school** under the plain meaning of the statute. The only difference according to the Commonwealth between the preschool and Sunday school located in a church in Lewis and the instant case is the frequency of classes." *Commonwealth v. Wilhelm* (Pa. Super. Ct., 2013).

## PARSONAGE

See *Clergy Residence*.

*Legal Annotation*: "In this appeal, the property owner contends the Department's superseded decision was an arbitrary denial of due process, the hearing officer's decision was improperly based on religious criteria, and the tax exemption should be granted either because the property was primarily used to conduct public religious worship services or because it was the site of a **parsonage**. . . . 'A **parsonage**, convent or monastery or other housing facility shall be considered under this Section to be exclusively used for religious purposes when the persons who perform religious related activities shall, as a condition of their employment or association, reside in the facility.' 35 ILCS 200/15-40(b) (West 2006)." *Armenian Church of Lake Bluff v. Department of Revenue of State of Illinois* (Ill. App. Ct., 2011).

## PARTIAL DESTRUCTION

**A building or structure that, because of fire, flood, explosion, or other calamity, requires the rebuilding of less than half of the original floor area.**

*Comment*: The rebuilding of partially destroyed buildings becomes an issue when the building or use does not conform to current development regulations. Most ordinances stipulate that if a substantial part of a building or structure is damaged and requires rebuilding, the new structure must meet current requirements. It is difficult to arrive at an enforceable and easily applicable standard that describes the extent of destruction beyond which a nonconforming structure may not be rebuilt. Some ordinances base it on value, others on the amount of floor area that has to be replaced. Many municipalities require a conforming structure when 50 percent of the value or floor area is destroyed. Others permit any damaged or destroyed building to be rebuilt, regardless of the amount of area or percentage of value. Under New Jersey case law, partial destruction is deemed to have occurred if at least two walls of the original structure remain intact, which becomes an important factor in determining whether the owner is entitled to grandfathered protection of a nonconforming structure and is allowed to rebuild the home as before. When a partially destroyed building that is nonconforming is allowed to be rebuilt, the approving authority should require compliance with current building codes, require that the building conform to the exact dimensions of the original building, and eliminate any condition that is a threat to health and safety. Some ordinances encourage the mitigation of some of the zoning deficiencies.

*Legal Annotation*: "According to the Zoning Officer, the pre-existing nonconforming use had been extinguished pursuant to §27-705 of the Ordinance, entitled '**Partial Destruction** of a Nonconforming Use,' which states:

Any nonconforming use or structure damaged less than 50 percent of its existing floor area may be restored, reconstructed or used as before; provided, that the volume of such use or structure shall not exceed the floor area which existed up to the time of such damage; and, provided further, that such restoration shall be in accordance with the following:

A. It shall be completed within 1 year of such damage.
B. Except for the previous nonconformance, it shall be in accordance with all other requirements of this Chapter.

. . . The Zoning Officer found that the 2006 fire at the property destroyed more than 50 percent of the building's existing floor area and Landowners failed to complete the restoration of the building within one year of the damage; therefore, the pre-existing nonconforming use had been extinguished." *Kraynak v. Zoning Hearing Board of Forty Fort* (Pa. Comm. Ct., 2011).

## PARTIAL TAKING

**The taking of a part of a property under the power of eminent domain (uslegal.com). See *Taking*.**

***Comment***: Typically such taking occurs when a part of a property is required for public use, such as for the widening of a roadway. In such cases compensation must be paid to the owners of the remainder property considering damages and/or special benefits. Damages in partial taking are known as "severance damages."

***Legal Annotation***: "The central question on this appeal is whether public construction of an enormous oceanfront beach dune, for which plaintiff condemned an easement on defendants' land, conferred a special benefit on defendants' beach front property in Harvey Cedars. . . . We begin by considering the issue of special benefits. In the case of a **partial taking**, the owner 'is entitled to be compensated not only for the value of the land taken but also for any diminution in the value of [the] remaining land which may be attributable to the taking.'" *Borough of Harvey Cedars v. Karan* (N.J. App. Div., 2012).

## PARTICULATES

**Finely divided solid or liquid particles in the air or in an emission, including dust, smoke, fumes, mist, spray, and fog.**

***Legal Annotation***: "As its second issue, the Sierra Club claims that DEQ, in its decision to issue an air quality permit to Medicine Bow, failed to consider fine **particulate** matter emissions from the facility. DEQ asserts that it did consider fine **particulates**, but because emissions of fine **particulates** are difficult to measure, model, and control, the agency used measurements, models, and controls of coarse particles as a surrogate to determine that Medicine Bow also complied with requirements relating to fine particulates." *Sierra Club v. Wyo. Dept. of Envt'l Quality* (Wyo., 2011).

## PARTY DRIVEWAY

**A single way providing vehicular access to two or more properties. See *Common Passageway. See Figure 3.***

***Comment***: Also often referred to as a "common driveway" or "shared driveway."

## PARTY IMMEDIATELY CONCERNED

**For purposes of notice, "party immediately concerned" means any applicant for development, the owners of the subject property, and all owners of property and government agencies entitled to notice under a zoning ordinance, subdivision regulations, or other development regulations.**

***Legal Annotation***: "'**Party immediately concerned**' means for purposes of notice any applicant for development, the owners of the subject property and all owners of property and government agencies entitled to notice under section 7.1 of P.L.1975, c.291 (C.40:55D-12). New Jersey Permanent Statutes - Municipal Land Use Law - Section 3.3 of P.L.1975, c.291 (C.40:55D-6)."

## PARTY WALL

**A common wall shared by two attached structures, buildings, or dwelling units. *See Figure 3.***

***Legal Annotation***: "'A common definition of a **party wall** is a division wall between two adjacent properties belonging to different persons and used for the mutual benefit of both parties, but it is not necessary that the wall should stand partly upon each of the adjoining lots; it may stand wholly upon one lot.' . . . '[T]he only restriction upon its use by either is that [the] use shall not be detrimental to the other.' . . . It is well settled that 'if one of the owners carries the wall several stories higher, the other party has no right to complain . . . and the latter has an equal right to use the addition.' . . . However, neither party has a right to do anything on top of the **party wall** 'which would exclude the other party from its equal use.' . . . Further, it is permissible for an adjoining property owner to make commercial use of a **party wall** so long as it does not weaken or encroach on the other party." *145 West 10 Realty LLC v. Whelan* (N.Y. App. Div., 2013).

## PASEO

**A connecting walkway that links streets and parking areas, open plazas, courtyards, and residential and business uses within an urban center.**

***Legal Annotation***: "Breadhead operates the D'Angelo Bakery which is located on a **paseo**, or walkway, running between Parker Way and Gutierrez Street in Santa Barbara. A martial arts studio is also located on the **paseo**. On the morning of October 18, 2003, Ceder walked along the **paseo** toward the bakery." *Ceder V. Breadhead, Inc.* (Calif. Ct. App., 2008).

## PASSENGER VEHICLE

**See *Vehicle, Passenger*.**

***Legal Annotation***: "see clerk's papers at 65 (the definitions section of the national merit policy defines 'auto' as 'a private **passenger vehicle** having four wheels on the road.')." *Black v. National merit ins. Co.* (Wash. Ct. App., 2010).

## PASSIVE RECREATION

**See *Recreation, Passive*.**

***Legal Annotation***: "Section 112, of the Zoning Ordinance defines 'Parks and Playgrounds' as follows: . . . 3. Outdoor **passive recreation** facilities, including picnic pavilions, hiking, biking and fitness trails, park benches, fountains, statues and other memorials, barbeque grills, ponds, natural and cultural exhibits, amphitheaters, and other similar uses." *Keener v. Rapho Township Zoning Hearing Board* (Pa. Comm. Ct., 2013).

## PATH

**A cleared way for pedestrians and/or bicycles that may or may not be improved.**

***Legal Annotation***: "*1.1 Overview.* The Planned United Development, known as The Pines (hereinafter 'THE PINES') is proposed to consist of a series of integrated residential communities offering a variety of single family types and densities. Each residential community shall feature a coordinated landscaping theme, amenities, including open space/landscape areas, access to a pedestrian **path** and an 837*837 open space network available to all residents of THE PINES." *Village Pines v. Pines of Greenwood* (Ind. Ct. App., 2010).

## PATHOGENIC

**Causing or capable of causing disease.**

***Legal Annotation***: "The regulations in question do have a zoning quality about them, but as Respondent points out, and as exhibited in the record here, there is a font of case law and technical information illustrating the health hazards related to hog facilities. Ground water pollution, **pathogenic** organisms, and disease have all been linked to livestock animals and their waste. It is quite clear that Linn County's regulation of the structures and lagoons of Appellant's hog facility, including distance requirements of animal waste from streams, water supply and buildings occupied by people, is rationally related to the purpose of public health enhancement and disease prevention. . . . The purpose of the ordinance was to regulate for health concerns rather than for a uniform development of real estate." *Borron v. Farrenkopf* (Mo. Ct. App., 1999).

## PATIO

**A level area covered by a hard surface, directly adjacent to a principal building at or within three feet of the finished grade and not covered by a permanent roof. See *Terrace*.**

***Legal Annotation***: "Pursuant to Merriam-Webster's Online: Dictionary and Thesaurus, a '**patio**' is 'a flat area of ground that is covered with a hard material (such as bricks or concrete), is usually behind a house, and is used for sitting and relaxing.'" *Baruk v. Heritage Club Homeowners' Assn.* (Ohio. Ct. App., 2014).

## PATIO HOME

See *Dwelling, Patio Home*.

*Legal Annotation*: "'Patio home' is defined as '[a] single-family home . . . often with one outside wall of the structure sitting on the property line. Patio homes have no common structural walls with adjoining properties.' . . . The affidavits before the trial court at this stage of the litigation indicated that standard industry usage of the terms '**patio home**' and 'cluster home' do not include town homes or condominiums." *Southland Development Corp. v. Battle* (Ga. Ct. App., 2005).

## PAVED SHOULDER

**The portion of the roadway contiguous with the traveled way for accommodation of stopped vehicles, for emergency use, and for lateral support of sub-base, base, and surface courses.**

*Comment*: Use by cyclists may be allowed or prohibited based upon specific State laws. http://safety.fhwa.dot.gov/ped_bike/tools_solve/fhwasa12018/#chap1.6

*Legal Annotation*: "The plans for the northbound cross-over and diversion depicted a one foot paved berm, an 11 foot lane, a second 11 foot lane, a one foot **paved shoulder**, and two feet of aggregate shoulder. . . . Around 10:20 PM on November 30, 2006, Isaiah Killen drove his semi-trailer truck through the construction zone and while he was in the cross-over, his semi-trailer truck went off the edge of the road and traveled down an embankment. Then, at 11:10 PM, York was driving his semi-trailer truck through the cross-over and York's vehicle also went off the road, down into the embankment, and hit Killen's semi-trailer truck. York was transported to a hospital in Akron, Ohio, where he died in January 2007. . . . ODOT's decision not to incorporate the two foot **paved shoulder** is the type of discretionary decision that is entitled to the protection discretionary immunity. . . . The court concludes that ODOT is entitled to discretionary immunity for its decisions surrounding the incorporation of subsequent design guidelines." *York v. Ohio Dept. of Transp.* (Ohio Ct. Cl., 2012).

## PAVEMENT

**(1) A created surface, such as brick, stone, concrete, or asphalt, placed on the land to facilitate passage; (2) that part of a street having an improved surface. *See Figures 27 and 28*.**

*Legal Annotation*: "Section I of the regulations defines 'garage' and 'attached garage' as follows: 'Garage. A structure designed principally for shelter, enclosure or protection of vehicles. Attached Garage. A garage that is part of a dwelling by being physically connected to it by means of any permanent structural connection other than **pavement** or fences.'" *Lowney v. Zoning Board Of Appeals Of Black Point Beach Club Association* (Conn. App. Ct., 2013).

## PAVERS

**Preformed paving blocks that are installed on the ground to form patterns while at the same time facilitating pedestrian and vehicular travel.**

*Comment*: Pavers provide an attractive alternative to concrete or asphalt for walkways, driveways, and residential or light-duty parking areas.

*Legal Annotation*: "What the photos show is a portion of a concrete sidewalk made up of large **pavers**. Between the sidewalk and the crosswalk is a segment comprised of bricks; to the right of the sidewalk in the top photo, there is a brick area running up to the base of the statue of Congressman Powell. The sidewalk **pavers** are gray and the bricks red, according to trial testimony." *Locario v. State* (N.Y. Ct. Cl., 2010).

## PAYMENT IN LIEU OF TAXES (PILOT)

**A financial arrangement where a payment is made to a municipality, county, state, or other taxing entity in place of the usual obligated taxes.**

*Comment*: There are two general forms of PILOTs. One is a negotiated annual payment by a nonprofit entity, such as a private school, college, hospital, or religious institution, that is normally exempt from property taxes but may use public facilities, services, and infrastructure. The PILOT picks up some of that public cost. The other type of PILOT, where permitted by state law, is to offer a PILOT to a business or industry as an incentive to locate within the state or municipality. Here again, the PILOT is for a specific annual amount and for a mutually agreed-upon time. However, where a PILOT is offered as an inducement to locate or relocate to a state or municipality, the business or industry often has to guarantee that it will create or establish a minimum number of jobs as the quid-pro-quo.

*Legal Annotation*: "The plaintiff, SDCO St. Martin ('St. Martin'), owns a building that is located partly in the City of Marlborough (the 'City') and partly in the Town of Southborough, straddling the border between those municipalities. For a number of years, St. Martin has made payments to the City under an agreement made between the City and a prior owner of the parcel on which the building sits that were characterized then (and still are by the City) as '**payments in lieu of taxes**' ('PILOT'). St. Martin by this action seeks a declaratory judgment that the payments are an illegal tax under Massachusetts law." *SDCO St. Martin, Inc. v. City of* Marlborough (D. Mass., 2014).

## PEAK-HOUR TRAFFIC

**The largest number of motor vehicles passing over a designated section of a street or roadway during the busiest one-hour period.**

*Comment*: Separate peak hours are designated for the weekly AM hours, weekday PM hours, and weekend hours.

*Legal Annotation*: "Turtle Bay Resort continues to expand beyond the Year 2008, the **peak hour traffic** operations at the intersection of Kamehameha Highway and Alpha Road are expected to deteriorate below satisfactory levels of service [(LOS)]. . . . Alpha Road will be constructed as a private roadway and is expected to remain so in the foreseeable future. Traffic operations of the two-lane section of Alpha Road at **peak hour** volumes over 800 [vehicles per hour] would result in a [below satisfactory LOS]." *Unite Here! Local 5 v. City of Honolulu* (Hawaii, 2010).

## PEAT

**Partially decomposed organic material.**

*Legal Annotation*: "The trial court then adopted the description of coal composition and CBM gas as described by The United States Supreme Court. That description, which we also adopt herein, is as follows: a heterogeneous, noncrystalline sedimentary rock composed primarily of carbonaceous materials. It is formed over millions of years from decaying plant material that settles on the bottom of swamps and is converted by microbiological processes into **peat**. Over time, the resulting **peat** beds are buried by sedimentary deposits. As the beds sink deeper and deeper into the earth's crust, the **peat** is transformed by chemical reactions which increase the carbon content of the fossilized plant material. The process in which peat transforms into coal is referred to as coalification." *Bowles v. Hopkins County Coal, LLC* (Ky. Ct. App., 2011).

## PEDESTRIAN

**An individual who travels on foot.**

*Legal Annotation*: "Moreover, when traveling down a sidewalk a **pedestrian** is not required to exercise the care required in traversing a jungle, but he must exercise ordinary care, keeping in mind that irregularities exist in sidewalks." *Chambers v. Moreauville* (La., 2012).

## PEDESTRIAN-FRIENDLY STREETS

**Streets that are designed to promote walkability. See *Walkability*.**

*Legal Annotation*: "In November of 1999, a neighborhood group, the Citizens for a Loring Park Community, asked the HPC to study whether an area on and around Harmon Place, from Loring Park to 11th Street South, merited a designation as historic. The citizens' group liked the mini-downtown feel of the area, with its eclectic group of businesses in one- to four-story buildings and **pedestrian-friendly streets**." *Billy Graham Evangelistic v. Minneapolis* (Minn., 2003).

## PEDESTRIAN GENERATOR

**A development or project that will realize high facility use by people arriving on foot (N.J.A.C. 5:21-1.4).**

***Comment***: A pedestrian generator can trigger the need for sidewalks in areas where sidewalks are not normally required. For example, in a low-density residential area, sidewalks might not be required if the density is less than one dwelling unit per acre. Construction of a school, a typical pedestrian generator, would permit the approving agency to require sidewalks to be constructed.

***Legal Annotation***: "The transportation of children to and from the center will undeniably **generate 'pedestrian** or automobile traffic.'" *Staker v. Brown* (Ohio Ct. Comm. Pleas, 1974).

## PEDESTRIAN MALL

**An area of streetlike proportions devoted entirely to pedestrian traffic. See *Mall.***

***Comment***: Pedestrian malls may be open or enclosed. In urban areas they are often converted streets, with added amenities such as landscaping and street furniture. Some pedestrian malls do allow for some very limited vehicular travel.

***Legal Annotation***: "A '**pedestrian mall**' is another variation of a street; it is 'one or more "city streets" or portions thereof on which vehicular traffic is or is to be restricted in whole or in part and which is or is to be used exclusively or primarily for pedestrian travel.'" *Short Line Assoc. v. City & County of San Francisco* (Calif. App. Ct., 1978).

## PEDESTRIAN-ORIENTED DESIGN

**Land-use activities that are designed and arranged in a way that emphasizes travel on foot rather than by car.**

***Comment***: The factors that encourage people to walk are often subtle, but they most regularly focus upon the creation of a pleasant environment for the pedestrian. Elements include compact, mixed-use development patterns with facilities and design that enhance the environment for pedestrians in terms of safety, walking distances, comfort, and the visual appeal of the surroundings. Pedestrian-friendly environments can be created by locating buildings close to the sidewalk, by lining the street with trees, and by buffering the sidewalk with planting strips or parked cars, small shops, street-level lighting and signs, and public art or displays. See *Walkability; Pedestrian Scale; Pedestrian Walkway.* http://www.pgplanning.org/Resources/Tools_On-line/Glossary.htm

***Legal Annotation***: "It added that alternative 3 'would place the building at the back of the site, with the surface parking lot dominating the southwest corner of Tequesquite and Brockton Avenues. This . . . is not compatible with the City's goals and policies for **pedestrian-oriented design** and walkability by keeping buildings oriented toward the streets in the Downtown Health Care District.'" *Save Our Chinatown Com. v. City of Riverside* (Calif. Ct. App., 2012).

## PEDESTRIAN SCALE

**The proportional relationship between an individual and his or her environment. See *Human Scale.***

***Comment***: Pedestrian scale is an informal and subjective standard. It suggests that the relationship between the person and his or her environment, whether natural or created, is comfortable, intimate, and contributes to the individual's sense of accessibility.

***Legal Annotation***: "For example, the City's Urban Renewal Plan, which is incorporated as one of the main purposes of the Lease, stated with respect to the Faneuil Hall area: 'This area is one of the most valuable historic assets to the City of Boston, to the State of Massachusetts, and to the Nation. . . . It is intended that the historic uniqueness of this area be retained through a thoughtful blend of new construction, rehabilitation and conservation. . . . It is intended that the space formed by Faneuil Hall, the new Boston City Hall, the rehabilitated buildings along Faneuil Hall Square, and the proposed new building . . . be so designed that the intimate **pedestrian scale** that once existed in this area again be recaptured.'" *Citizens to End Animal Suffering v. Faneuil Hall* (D. Mass., 1990).

## PEDESTRIAN TRAFFIC COUNT

**The number of people who walk past a single point during a specified period of time.**

***Legal Annotation***: "Petitioner adduced as an expert a professor of transportation and planning, who made a **pedestrian traffic count** at eight different time periods on one working day. He found that a peak traffic there were 11.3 pedestrians per foot width of sidewalk per minute. He testified further that recognized criteria as to the adequacy of pedestrian facilities varied from 25 pedestrians per foot width per minute for the New York City Transit Authority to 28 pedestrians per foot width per minute for the Chicago Transit System and 27 pedestrians per foot width per minute for London." *Matter of Schneider v. Myerson* (N.Y. Sup. Ct., 1973).

## PEDESTRIAN WALKWAY

**A right-of-way for pedestrians, separate from vehicular traffic and including access ramps, stairs, mechanical lifts, and routes through buildings and other areas that are available for public use.**

***Legal Annotation***: "In response to MDR's argument that such access was unreasonable, the circuit court expressly found 'that a **pedestrian walkway** is necessary for the reasonable use and enjoyment of [MDR's] riparian rights in the Chesapeake Bay." *Stansbury v. MDR Development* (Md. Ct. Spec. App., 2005).

## PENINSULA

**A projection of land surrounded on three sides by water.**

***Legal Annotation***: "The Court stated: . . . 'At the point where plaintiff's property and other property in the subdivision join this low tidal flat, a *man made channel* has been dug running from the channel of Taylor Bayou on the west in an easterly direction and forming the south and east boundaries of the *tidal* flat, connecting with Taylor Lake. Thus the area is now completely surrounded by navigable water and in effect what was a **peninsula** is now rendered an island by the cutting of the *manmade channel, and the channel is navigable water of the United States.*'" *US v. Sexton Cove Estates, Inc.* (S.D. Fla., 1975).

## PENINSULA LOT

**A lot surrounded on three sides by roads or water. *See Figure 75.***

***Comment***: Peninsula lots for residential use should be avoided whenever possible. They lack privacy, and since they "front" on three streets, front yard setbacks are required on three sides. Accessory structures (sheds, swimming pools, and so on) are prohibited in any of the front yards unless allowed by variance. In addition, the lot is subjected to traffic from three roads and abuts two intersections.

**Figure 75**

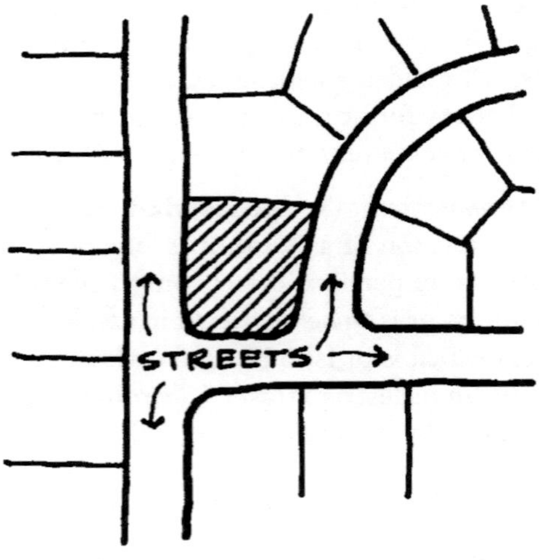


PENINSULA LOT

***Legal Annotation***: "Although the McNitts purchased two backlots when they purchased the **peninsula lot**, the backlots are not contiguous to the **peninsula lot**. Thus, the access lot provisions of the zoning ordinance do not apply." *Voedisch v. Town of Wolfeboro* (N.H., 1992).

## PENTHOUSE

**An enclosed structure located on the roof of a building. *See Figure 20*.**

***Comment***: Penthouses may be used for a variety of purposes, such as offices, apartments, or for mechanical equipment serving the building. Penthouses housing mechanical equipment are often excluded from building-height requirements. Penthouses designed for occupancy, such as offices or apartments, are usually counted as another story, although some ordinances allow penthouses to occupy up to 20 percent of the roof area without being counted. They would, however, be included within maximum floor area ratio calculation. In modern, multistory buildings, penthouses have been designed and used for swimming pools and/or recreation purposes. (Source: Haughney 2010.)

***Legal Annotation***: "Petitioner also argues that provisions in the New York City Building Code which relate to building height support its position. Thus, it notes that a **penthouse** is defined under the Building Code as 'an enclosed structure on or above the roof of any part of a building which is designed or used for human occupancy.'" *In the Matter Of 515 East 5th Street, LLC v. New York City Board of Standards and Appeals* (N.Y. Sup. Ct., 2008).

## PEOPLE MOVER

**A conveyor system designed for carrying pedestrians.**

***Legal Annotation***: "Under the present proposal, the mid-field terminal complex consists of a main terminal building which is connected to four rectangular concourses by an underground tunnel. The concourses, which contain the loading gates of the various carriers, are parallel to each other and connected only by the tunnel. This underground connecting tunnel is carefully designed to allow passengers to move efficiently from place to place within the terminal complex and contains a vehicle known as the **'people mover'** as well as a pedestrian walkway." *Southern Airways, Inc. v. City of Atlanta* (N.D. Ga., 1977).

## PERSONS WITH DISABILITIES

**Persons with impairments of a physical, cognitive, mental, sensory, emotional, or developmental nature, or some combination of such impairments. See *Accessible Design; Universal Design*.**

***Comment***: This term has replaced the term "handicapped," which is now considered offensive. "Disabilities" is an umbrella term, covering a range of impairments that limit an individual's ability to execute a task or function or make it difficult for the individual to do so.

***Legal Annotation***: "[T]he term "**persons with disabilities**" is defined as persons . . . includes 'persons who have a physical or mental impairment that limits one or more of the major life activities, have a record of such an impairment, or are regarded as having such an impairment.'" *Russell v. Crawford* (Calif. Ct. App., 2013).

## PERCOLATION

**Downward flow or infiltration of water through the pores or spaces of rock or soil.**

***Comment***: Also sometimes used in connection with the absorption of sewage in a disposal field.

***Legal Annotation***: "**Percolation** is a process whereby sewage is disseminated into the surrounding soil." *Lonning v. Jim Walter Homes, Inc.* (Tenn. Ct. App., 1986).

## PERCOLATION TEST

**A test designed to determine the ability of ground to absorb water and used to determine the suitability of soil for drainage or for septic system use.**

***Legal Annotation***: "The Cape Isle of Wight subdivision was established in the early 1950's and is comprised of land created by excavating canals in a tidal marsh and sidecasting the excavated material on both sides to cover the marsh and create uplands. Cape Isle of Wight contains 625 lots and, as of 1972, approximately 128 homes existed in the subdivision. Each of these homes used a septic system that was approved based on

**percolation tests** that could be completed at any time throughout the year. . . . A **percolation test** is used to determine if the soil will absorb and drain water adequately enough to install and use a domestic sewage-disposal system. The testing procedure, generally speaking, involves digging several holes, filling them with water, and measuring the rate at which the water-level decreases." *Neifert v. Dept. of Environment* (Md. Ct. App., 2006).

## PERFORMANCE GUARANTEE

**Any security that may be accepted by a governmental entity to ensure that improvements required as part of an application for development will be satisfactorily completed.**

***Comment***: Performance guarantees may be cash, surety bond, or letter of credit (Feiden and Burby 2002). In fact, the performance guarantee may be any security permitted by state or local ordinance. See *Maintenance Guarantee*.

***Legal Annotation***: "As the terms imply, the **performance guarantee** is a contract between the developer-obligor and its surety to guarantee completion of the stipulated improvements. Implicit in that agreement is an obligation on the part of the municipality to approve and accept them if they are properly installed, and a right to reject them if they are not and to compel correction of any defects." *Tp. of Wyckoff v. Sarna* (N.J. App. Div., 1975).

## PERFORMANCE STANDARDS

**A set of criteria or limits relating to certain characteristics that a particular use or process may not exceed.**

***Comment***: The standards regulate the characteristics of an activity rather than the activity itself. The standards usually cover noise, vibration, glare, heat, air or water contaminants, and traffic. The performance-standard approach is based on the technical ability to identify activities by impact and to measure them to determine if they meet ordinance requirements. Performance standards are often located in a separate section of a local jurisdiction's code, and not in its land-use or zoning regulations. See *Performance Zoning*.

***Legal Annotation***: "The New Source **Performance Standards** are designed to enhance air quality by forcing all newly constructed or modified buildings, structures, facilities, or installations to employ pollution control systems that will limit emissions to the level 'achievable through application of the best technological system of continuous emission reduction which . . . the Administrator determines has been adequately demonstrated.'" *Asarco Inc. v. Environmental Protection Agcy.* (D.C. Cir., 1978).

## PERFORMANCE ZONING

**Zoning regulations that permit uses based on a particular set of standards rather than on a particular type of use (American Planning Association, *Performance Standards for Growth Management*, Planning Advisory Service Report No. 461, 1996). See *Performance Standards*.**

***Legal Annotation***: "In 1987, the Town of McCandless (Town) amended its Ordinance, rezoning a portion of Town along McKnight Road into a newly created D-Development District (D-District). The Ordinance employs a zoning technique called '**performance zoning**' in the D-District. **Performance zoning** is designed to permit a wide range of uses which gives the developer flexibility in developing land. The zoning technique protects adjacent properties by requiring bufferyards of varying sizes depending on the uses involved. The Ordinance also established standards for the preservation of sensitive natural resources such as woodlands, streams, and steep slopes." *Jones v. Zoning Hearing Bd.* (Pa: Comm. Ct., 1990).

## PERGOLA

**A structure of parallel colonnades supporting an open roof of crossing rafters or trelliswork.**

***Legal Annotation***: "Clearly the ZBA reasonably may insist upon the preparation of acceptable plans establishing, inter alia, that the manner in which the **pergola** is supported by columns and is affixed to the house complies with appropriate construction methods." *Matter of Baker v. Brownlie* (N.Y. App. Div., 2000).

## PERIMETER

**The boundaries or borders of a lot, tract, or parcel of land.**

***Legal Annotation***: "In September of 1968, the Szaleskis investigated the possibility of financing the unpaid purchase price by a borrowing secured by a mortgage and discovered that a survey would be required. In March of 1969, Mr. Goodman had a survey made which developed the **perimeter** of a lot having a road frontage of 74 feet and a water frontage of 72 feet. By July, Szaleski had taken the position that this was not what he had bargained for, because the water frontage should have been 89 feet, and that if he could not get what he had bought, he would 'terminate the contract.'" *Szaleski v. Goodman* (Md. Ct. App., 1970).

## PERIMETER ROADWAYS

**Roadways along the perimeter of buildings, lots, parcels, and/or tracts of land.**

***Legal Annotation***: "Upon receipt of these permits, the plaintiffs began to work on the proposed development. In addition to remodeling the old farmhouse, they excavated and graded fairways for the proposed golf course, began building **perimeter roadways**, and excavated and performed transit readings for the clubhouse." *Kmiec v. Town of Spider Lake* (Wis., 1973).

## PERMAFROST

**A permanently frozen soil layer.**

***Legal Annotation***: "Another geographical and geological feature of great significance from the standpoint of the present litigation is that the Ladd Air Force Base is located within the discontinuous **permafrost** zone. **Permafrost** is ground that is permanently frozen (i.e., its temperature has been below zero degrees centigrade for 2 years or more). There are three **permafrost** zones—the continuous **permafrost** zone, the discontinuous **permafrost** zone, and the sporadic **permafrost** zone. In the continuous **permafrost** zone, **permafrost** underlies the surface of the ground everywhere; and there is certainty that anyone drilling or excavating below the surface to a substantial depth at any point will encounter **permafrost**." *Morrison-Knudsen Company v. US* (Cl. Ct., 1965).

## PERMEABILITY

**The speed with which water can drain through soil. See *Percolation; Percolation Test*.**

***Legal Annotation***: "**Permeability** is the soil's ability to prevent the flow of water. The degree or coefficient of **permeability** is influenced by the PI, but soil with a low PI may attain the same degree of permeability because of greater density of its compaction." *Mayor & City Council, Etc. v. Clark-Dietz, Etc.* (N.D. Miss., 1982).

## PERMEABLE PAVEMENT SYSTEM

**An alternate or supplemental stormwater management system using cast-in-place or precast modular units, both of which create voids for gravel or grass. *See Figure 76.***

***Comment***: Cast-in-place systems are very strong when reinforced with welded wire mesh. They are more expensive and labor-intensive than are systems using the precast modular pavers. Plastic flexible systems have less intrinsic strength than concrete pavers, but with adequate base and subgrade preparation, they are fully capable of supporting heavy loads. Flexible pavers are also more easily laid over irregular surfaces.

Grass infill (sodding for plastic, seeding for concrete) is more labor-intensive and expensive than gravel. In addition, a period of one to two months is required to allow the grass to become established, and the traffic on grass should not exceed one to two trips per day.

In research reported by Booth and Leavitt (1999), the differences in runoff from permeable and impermeable surfaces is "quite dramatic," and "where soil conditions are suitable, permeable pavements are quite successful at managing runoff from small and moderate storms." The authors note that both types of permeable pavements accomplish the hydrologic goal of infiltration well but point out that they differ in how well they can handle high traffic volumes and in their appearance.

*Legal Annotation*: "Appellants also challenge the district court's inclusion in the record of four DNR documents: (1) an office memorandum on impervious surfaces in shoreland areas; (2) an office memorandum on pervious pavers; (3) a guidance document on the use of **permeable pavement systems** in shoreland areas; and (4) an e-mail from a DNR staff member to the land management staff in Douglas County. . . . The county's inclusion of pervious pavers in the definition of impervious surfaces reflects an internally consistent interpretation of the impervious-surface requirement with the corresponding policy section on shoreland management, which favors water runoff and percolation standards in shoreland areas deemed sensitive to erosion and environmental degradation. Courts in other jurisdictions have cited ordinances with language reflecting this policy. See, e.g., Bolt v. City of Lansing, 587 N.W.2d 264, 267 (Mich. 1998) (citing an ordinance stating that '[i]mpervious land area includes, but is not limited to, surface areas covered by buildings, porches, patios, parking lots, driveways, walkways, and other structure' and that generally, 'all non-vegetative land areas shall be considered impervious'). Further, state regulations require that a 25% impervious-surface lot-coverage limitation be incorporated in local shoreland management controls. . . . [S]ee also Minn. R. 6120.2600 (2003) (stating purpose of shoreland management standards to preserve and enhance the quality of surface waters and conserve the natural environment). Therefore, we conclude that the board did not err in interpreting the impervious-surface requirement in the zoning ordinance to include pervious pavers as impervious surfaces." *O'Brien v. Douglas County Board of Commissioners* (Minn. Ct. App., 2005).

## PERMIT

**Written governmental permission issued by an authorized official, empowering the holder thereof to do some act not forbidden by law but not allowed without such authorization.**

**Figure 76**

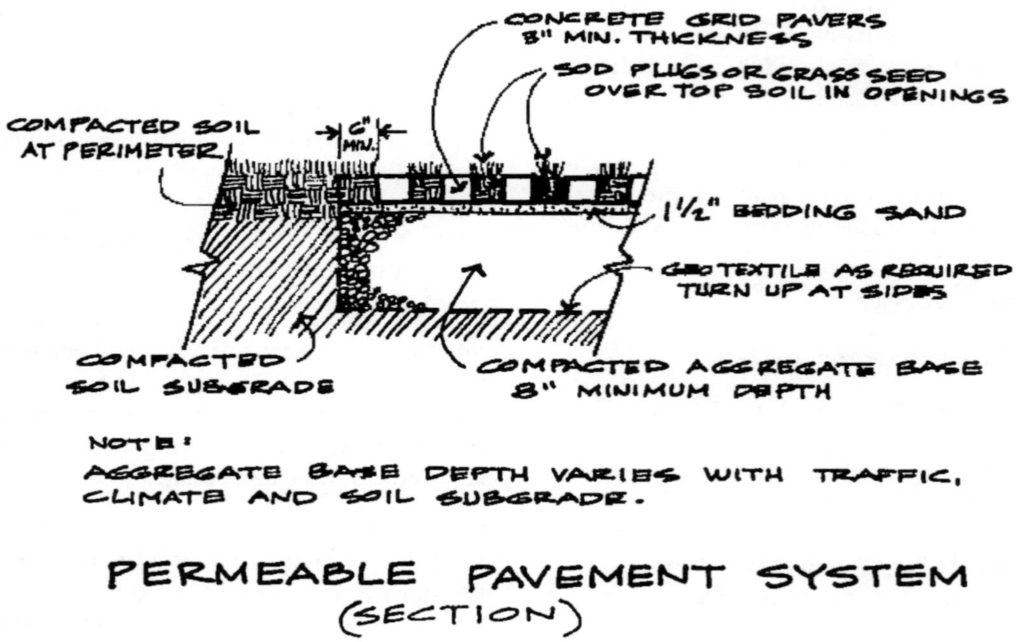

*Legal Annotation*: "A zoning **permit** is specifically required when someone '[c]onstructs, places or relocates a structure' or '[s]ubstantially changes or expands the use of lands. . . . Thus, there are two key questions to address: (1) whether the track was a structure and, if not, (2) whether it constituted a substantial change in the use of the property." *In re Laberge Moto-Cross Track* (Vt., 2011).

## PERMITTED USE

**Any use allowed in a zoning district as a matter of right. See *Conditional Use*.**

*Comment*: Although the use itself is permitted as-of-right, it is still required to meet bulk and other controls pertaining to the district in which such a use is permitted.

*Legal Annotation*: "A **permitted use** of property differs from a conditional use in that a permitted use is a matter of right, whereas a conditional use is one that a municipality will allow, but only in a controlled manner." *Hussein v. Germantown Bd. of Zoning Appeals* (Wis. Ct. App., 2011).

## PERMITTEE

**Any person to whom a permit is issued.**

*Legal Annotation*: "The basic facts are undisputed. Applicant is the **permittee** of a 236-acre Resort PUD. Issues have arisen since the Resort PUD was initially granted, and this Court has entertained several appeals in the matter. . . . As explained in the past, limitations 'that are not stated on the permit may not be imposed on the **permittee**.'" *In Re Stowe Highlands Merger/Subdivision* (Vt, 2013).

## PERPETUITY

**Lasting forever; continuous and eternal; unlimited in respect to time (*Black's* 1999).**

*Legal Annotation*: "During the summer of 2003, Hynolds acquired a piece of real property in Carlisle Township and began operating an adult-entertainment establishment, later known as The Brass Pole. After Hynolds sought to update a portion of the building and expand The Brass Pole's entertainment area, Carlisle Township passed several zoning resolutions to regulate the zoning of adult-entertainment businesses and to prohibit the operation of such businesses within general business districts. . . . The trial court . . . recognized this when it wrote that 'that *portion* of The Brass Pole in which nude dancers were already performing is a valid non[-]conforming use[.]' (Emphasis added.) The court in that case only enjoined Hynolds from using another '*portion* of the property for nude dancing[.]' (Emphasis added.) Were it otherwise, The Brass Pole would be for forever locked into zoning **perpetuity**, never capable of alteration, no matter what that alteration might be, because any alteration or expansion would violate the non-conforming use doctrine." *Rowe v. Carlisle Twp. Bd. of Zoning Appeals* (Ohio Ct. App., 2011).

## PERSON

**A corporation, company, association, society, firm, partnership, or joint stock company, as well as an individual, a state, and all political subdivisions of a state or any agency or instrumentality thereof.**

*Legal Annotation*: "First, we examine the meaning of the word '**persons**.' The plain and ordinary meaning of the word '**persons**' is very broad. See black's law dictionary 1257 ($9^{th}$ ed. 2009) (Defining '**person**' as '[a] human being' or '[a]n entity . . . That is recognized by law as having most of the rights and duties of a human being'); see also american heritage dictionary 1310 ($4^{th}$ ed. 2006) (Recognizing the legal definition of '**person**' as '[a] human or organization with legal rights and duties'). We discern no legislative intent to limit the word '**persons**' to the parties to the lawsuit. Had the legislature intended to do so, it could have done so expressly. Further, a broad interpretation is consistent with the common law principle that several liability is examined at the time the tort is committed. Therefore, we interpret the word '**persons**' to mean not only 'parties to the lawsuit,' as urged by appellant and the dissent, but also to extend to the 'parties to the transaction,' as urged by respondent." *Staab v. Diocese of St. Cloud* (Minn., 2012).

## PERSONAL PROPERTY

**Property that is movable and is not affixed to or associated with the land.**

***Comment***: "Basically, personal property is all property except real property. Personal property for a business would include equipment, office furniture and equipment, cars/trucks purchased and used by the business, and, basically, everything that isn't 'nailed down'. In other words, personal property is movable, while real property typically is not" (http://biztax.about.com/od/glossaryp/g/personalprop.htm). See *Tangible Personal Property*.

***Legal Annotation***: "'[T]angible **personal property**' is defined, in part, under Section 7201(m) of the Code as '[c]orporeal personal property including, but not limited to, goods, wares, merchandise . . . electricity for non-residential use, prepaid telecommunications, premium cable or premium video programming service . . . [and] interstate telecommunications service originating or terminating in the Commonwealth.'" *Dechert LLP v. Com.* (Pa., 2010).

## PERSONAL RAPID TRANSIT TECHNOLOGY (PRT)

**Taxi-like mobility with no-wait express service.**

***Comment***: PRTs include the following:

(1) Pod cars—robotic vehicles traveling at low speeds in protected environments
(2) Bike expressways—wide pavement and passing lanes, well lit and cleared of snow to facilitate year-round use
(3) Busway loop systems
(4) Moving sidewalks.

***Legal Annotation***: "The EIS considered the following nine alternatives to the Tunnel: an alternative alignment of the proposed location; a **personal rapid transit** consisting of a modified loop bus, moving sidewalks, and/or an underground or overground system; utilization of existing freight lines for passenger service in the northeast section of Philadelphia County; expansion of the subway system; expansion of the trolley or bus system; construction of a monorail system; administrative controls to discourage use of automobiles in the center city; expansion of the highway system; and a no-action alternative." *Philadelphia Council of Neighborhood Organizations v. Coleman* (E.D. Pa., 1977).

## PERSONAL SERVICES

**Establishments primarily engaged in providing services involving the care of a person or his or her personal goods or apparel.**

***Comment***: Personal services usually include the following: laundry, including cleaning and pressing service; linen supply; diaper service; beauty shops; barbershops; shoe repair; funeral services; steam baths; reducing salons and health clubs; clothing rental; locker rental; porter service; and domestic services.

***Legal Annotation***: "A facility for the sale of **personal services**. Typical **personal service** uses include a barber/beauty shop, shoe repair, a tailor, an instructional arts studio, a photography studio, a laundry or cleaning pickup and receiving station, a handcrafted art work studio, safe deposit boxes, a travel bureau, and a custom printing or duplicating shop." Dallas (Texas) Zoning Districts. http://www.dallascityhall.com/zoning/html/retail_personal_services_use.html

## PERSONAL WATERCRAFT

**A small vessel that uses an outboard or inboard motor to power a water jet pump as its primary source of motive power and that is designed to be operated by a person sitting, standing, or kneeling on the vessel.**

***Legal Annotation***: "Apparently, **personal watercraft** have become increasingly popular on Maryland's waters. In the Department's view, the greater numbers of these vessels, as well as their unique characteristics, have led to dangerous boating conditions. In recommending the promulgation of the regulation, the Department's Director of Boating Administration stated that **personal watercraft** are 'small, agile, extremely responsive to forward throttle, virtually unsinkable, and have extremely shallow drafts. . . . [They] are intended for fast, quick maneuvering where the operator often has spray in his/her face and the operator and passenger have the probability of falling off.'" *Christ v. Department* (Md. Ct. App., 1994).

## PERVIOUS SURFACE

**Any material that permits full or partial absorption of stormwater into previously unimproved land. See *Impervious Surface; Permeable Pavement System. See Figure 62.***

***Legal Annotation*:** "Third, the proposed driveway would be made of gravel, a **pervious surface** which would allow rainwater to enter the ground below." *Perrotti v. Zoning Board of Jamestown* (R.I., 2008).

## PESTICIDE

**An agent used to control pests.**

***Comment*:** Pesticides include insecticides for use against harmful insects; herbicides for weed control; fungicides for control of plant disease; rodenticides for killing rats, mice, and such; and germicides used in disinfectant products, algaecides, and slimicides. Some pesticides, particularly if they are misused, can contaminate water, air, or soil and accumulate in humans, animals, and the environment.

***Legal Annotation*:** "In vacating the EPA's Final Rule, the Sixth Circuit held that the application of **pesticides** '"above" or "near" waterways' that leave 'excess' or 'residual' pesticide in navigable waters meets the CWA's definition of 'chemical waste.'" *Peconic Baykeeper, Inc. v. Suffolk County* (2nd Cir., 2010).

## PESTICIDE TOLERANCE

**A scientifically and legally established limit for the amount of chemical residue that can be permitted to remain in or on a harvested food or feed crop as a result of the application of a chemical for pest-control purposes.**

***Legal Annotation*:** "First, FQPA established a new safety standard for **pesticide tolerances**. Under FQPA, a **pesticide tolerance** is 'safe' when 'there is a reasonable certainty that no harm will result from aggregate exposure to the pesticide chemical residue, including all anticipated dietary exposures and all other exposures for which there is reliable information.'" *Natural Resources Defense Council v. USEPA* (2nd Cir., 2011).

## pH

**A measure of the acidity or alkalinity of a material, liquid, or solid.**

***Comment*:** A pH of 7 is considered neutral. Below 7 is acidic; above 7 is alkaline.

***Legal Annotation*:** "The symbol '**pH**' is 'used for convenience in expressing both acidity and alkalinity usu[ally] on a scale of 0 to 14.' Webster's II New College Dictionary 1692 (1999)." *Wm. Dickson Co. v. State Department of* Ecology (Wash. Ct. App., 2010).

## PHARMACY

**A place where drugs and medicines are prepared and dispensed. See *Drugstore*.**

***Legal Annotation*:** "The Board enacted the original ordinance on August 5, 2008. It provided that 'no person shall sell tobacco products in a **pharmacy**.' The word '**pharmacy**' was defined as 'a retail establishment in which the profession of **pharmacy** by a pharmacist licensed by the State of California in accordance with the Business and Professions Code is practiced and where prescriptions are offered for sale. A **pharmacy** may also offer other retail goods in addition to prescription pharmaceuticals.'" *Safeway Inc. v. City and County of San Francisco* (N.D. Calif., 2011).

## PHASING

**Development undertaken in a logical time and geographical sequence.**

***Comment*:** The approving authority must ensure that each phase can exist as a separate entity if the project does not continue to buildout. Improvements for any phase that are geographically located in other phases must be installed and maintained prior to or coincident with construction of the phase to be served. Both objectives can be ensured by establishing deadlines, requiring performance guarantees, and withholding occupancy permits until all required improvements are installed and operating. See *Concurrency*.

***Legal Annotation***: "Furthermore, while the MZO allows for phased development, the emphasized language in Section 4.071 indicates that discretion to permit **phasing** lies with the Planning Commission, which 'may permit' phased development in light of 'existing surroundings and available facilities and services.'" *Christmas v. Town of Smyrna* (Tenn. Ct. App., 2010).

## PHOTOCHEMICAL SMOG

**Air pollution associated with oxidants rather than with sulfur oxides, particulates, or similar materials.**

***Legal Annotation***: "The staff report—made available to the parties well before the hearing—referred to published Japanese reports (apparently in Japanese) and contained a lengthy discussion of Japanese studies of incidents in which **photochemical smog** had produced significant adverse respiratory effects." *Western Oil & Gas Assn. v. Air Resources Board* (Calif., 1984).

## PHYSICAL DISABILITY

**A physical impairment that confines a person to a wheelchair; causes a person to walk with difficulty or insecurity; affects the sight or hearing to the extent that a person functioning in a public area is insecure or exposed to danger; causes faulty coordination; or reduces mobility, flexibility, coordination, and perceptiveness to the extent that facilities are needed to provide for the safety of that person. See *Americans With Disabilities Act*.**

***Legal Annotation***: "Plaintiff does not respond to defendants' counterargument that a **physical disability** is far different from a characteristic such as race, which does not bear upon one's ability to perform. Defendants contend, and this Court agrees, that a physical handicap is a trait far more analogous to age, which only evokes the rational basis test, than to race, which has long been considered a suspect classification. This Court agrees with the reasoning employed in . . . where the court expressed the view that the visually handicapped should not be considered a suspect class." *Upshur v. Love* (N.D. Calif., 1979).

## PICNIC AREA

**A place equipped with tables, benches, grills, and trash receptacles for people to assemble, cook, eat, and relax.**

***Comment***: Picnic areas are passive recreation areas and could include rest rooms, play facilities, and open shelters.

***Legal Annotation***: "One Hinerwadel, the owner of a tract of land of about 32 acres in the town of Clay, had conducted a clambake **picnic area** for over 40 years and a clam chowder processing operation for over 5 years, on such property. In 1955, a zoning ordinance was enacted by the town, which placed this property in a 'residential' zone. The owner applied for a building permit to erect certain additions to existing buildings." *Mtr. of Gerling v. Bd. of Zoning Appeals* (N.Y. Div., 1958).

## PIER

**(1) A column, used to support a structure; (2) any fixed or floating structure for securing vessels, loading or unloading persons or property, or providing access to the water, including wharves, docks, floats, or other landing facilities, and dry docks (American Planning Association, *Glossary of Zoning, Development and Planning Terms*, Planning Advisory Service Report 491/492, 1999).**

***Legal Annotation***: "We hold that a **pier** is not a principal structure within the meaning of the Zoning Ordinance of Mecklenburg County, North Carolina." *Harry v. Mecklenburg County* (N.C. Ct. of App., 1999).

## PIERHEAD LINE

**A line beyond which no structure may extend out into navigable waters.**

***Legal Annotation***: "Pursuant to the Rivers and Harbors Act of 1899 . . . the Army Corp of Engineers established harbor lines in front of the Alexandria waterfront. These 1939 harbor lines consist of a bulkhead line and a **pierhead line**. A bulkhead line is a line beyond which no solid fill may be constructed. A **pierhead line** is a line beyond which no open pile structures may be constructed." *US v. Robertson Terminal Warehouse, Inc.* (D.D.C., 2008).

## PILASTER

**A column partially embedded in a wall and usually nonstructural.**

***Legal Annotation***: "The concrete block construction is also faulty. Usually in such construction a **pilaster** is put every 20 feet with a construction joint in it, but here they were installed only every 40 feet and did not have built-in expansion joints. This has caused the walls to crack and they will continue to do so." *Frenzel v. Commissioner* (Tax Ct., 1963).

## PILING

**A vertical support member of wood, steel, or precast concrete that is driven or jetted into the ground and supported primarily by the friction between the pilings and surrounding earth.**

***Comment***: Pilings often cannot act as independent support units and therefore are often braced with connections to other pilings.

***Legal Annotation***: "The duties of a leads man pertain to the installation of **pilings** for bridges and overpasses. When a **piling** is to be driven, it is placed by a crane into a steel guide called a 'leads,' which holds the piling in a vertical position while the piling is driven into the ground." *Clark v. Floyd* (Ala., 1987).

## PILOT PLANT

**A facility used to test out concepts and ideas, to determine physical layouts, material flows, type of equipment required, and costs, and to secure other information prior to full-scale production.**

***Comment***: The pilot plant is usually an intermediate step between research and full-scale production. It requires monitoring and supervision by other than the usual production personnel and may involve frequent changes in physical layout, natural flow, or even processes. Pilot plants may produce production-grade goods, especially during the latter stages of the pilot process. However, if the pilot plant is switched to full production and operation and used for other than testing, it should be treated as a principal permitted use. Most development ordinances allow some percentage of research facilities, usually not more than 25 percent of the floor area, to be used for pilot plant operations.

***Legal Annotation***: "The first use of the process by R & H was in 1973 in an experimental or **pilot plant** operation in Philadelphia in which a relatively small amount (about 200 pounds) of the catalyst was required." *Standard Oil v. Nippon Shokubai Kagaku Kogyo Co.* (Fed. Cir., 1985).

## PLACE OF WORSHIP

**(1) A church, synagogue, temple, mosque, or other facility that is used for prayer by persons of similar beliefs; (2) a special-purpose building that is architecturally designed and particularly adapted for the primary use of conducting formal religious services on a regular basis.**

***Comment***: The major concern associated with places of worship is that very often the accessory uses may create greater impact than the primary use. Places of worship may include schools, meeting halls, recreational facilities, day care, counseling, homeless shelters, and kitchens capable of feeding hundreds of persons. They are often rented out for weddings and other social events. In previous years, churches drew primarily from the neighborhoods in which they were located. Today, the area they serve may be considerably larger. Care should be taken in drafting any ordinance regulating places of worship, to ensure that the accessory uses do not become nuisances.

While such uses may be desirable in residential areas, conditional use controls on lot size, parking, access, setbacks, and buffering may be appropriate to avoid adverse neighborhood impacts. Depending on a facility's size and outreach, its specific location should be controlled—for example, frontage on a major road or location as a transitional use between a residential and nonresidential zone. See *Comment Under Conditional Use*.

Some places of worship enjoy greater popularity during certain holidays. While it is not necessary to plan for peak use, there should be some consideration given to the several holidays or holy days within the year when occupancy will be two to three times that of normal worship services (Traggorth 2006: 35).

Importantly, the Religious Land Use and Institutionalized Persons Act (RLUIPA) of 2000 (Public Law 106-274, 114 Stat. 803, 42 U.S.C. §2000cc et seq.) states, as a general rule, that:

> No government shall impose or implement a land use regulation in a manner that imposes a substantial burden on the religious exercise of a person, including a religious assembly or institution, unless the government demonstrates that imposition of the burden on that person, assembly, or institution, is in furtherance of a compelling government interest; and is the least restrictive means of furthering that compelling governmental interest.

RLUIPA clearly places the burden on the municipality to prove that any regulation that imposes restrictions on houses of worship is needed and necessary. Some attorneys suggest that RLUIPA almost precludes the prohibition of houses of worship, whether in the form of bulk controls or location. However, provided houses of worship are: (1) treated no differently than other similar institutions (such as schools); (2) that they are not prohibited altogether; (3) that the land-use regulation does not discriminate between one type or place of worship and another; and (4) that do not interfere with religious worship or practices, such regulations are likely to be upheld. For a detailed discussion on religious land-use issues, see the September 2001 issue of the American Planning Association's *Land Use and Zoning Digest*, Vol. 53, No. 9. See *Megachurch; Religious Use; Religious Land Use; Institutionalized Persons Act*.

***Legal Annotation***: "In this case, the principal factual question resolved by the defendant was whether the proposed facility constituted a church or other **place of worship**. It is clear that, if the facility were composed solely of the convent and chapel, the question would be whether the proposed convent and chapel constituted a church or other **place of worship**. It is also clear that, conversely, if the facility were composed solely of the book and audiovisual center, the plaintiff would have no valid claim that it constituted a church or other **place of worship**. Where the two uses are combined, therefore, the factual question resolved by the defendant breaks down into two separate but related issues: (1) whether the convent and chapel constitute a church or other **place of worship**; and (2) if so, whether the presence of the book and audiovisual center renders the dominant use of the building to be something other than as a church or other **place of worship**. We therefore consider whether the record reasonably supports either a negative answer to the first question or a positive answer to the second question. If so, the defendant's determination must be upheld. We conclude that under the facts of this case the defendant could not reasonably conclude (1) that the convent and chapel do not constitute a church or place of worship, and (2) that the dominant use of the facility was other than for a church or other **place of worship**." *Daughters of St. Paul, Inc. v. Zoning Board of Appeals* (Conn. App., 1988).

## PLANNED DEVELOPMENT (PD)

**An area of a minimum contiguous or noncontiguous size, planned, developed, operated, and maintained as a single entity and containing one or more structures to accommodate retail, service, commercial, industrial, office, and residential uses or a combination of such uses, and appurtenant common areas and accessory uses, customary and incidental to the predominant uses. See *Planned Development, Commercial; Planned Development, Industrial; Planned Unit Residential Development*.**

***Comment***: The local land development ordinance should specify the minimum area required for a planned development. Many ordinances require a minimum of five acres for planned-unit residential development (PURD), where the predominant use is residential, and ten acres for other types of planned developments.

All planned developments have a number of features in common, and the definition emphasizes those features. They are planned, developed, operated, and maintained as a single entity. The resolution of approval of a planned development establishes the parameters by which the PD operates, including parking and circulation, landscaping, signage, lighting, security, and waste disposal. Where a lot or parcel in the PD is to be subdivided out for mortgaging or financing purposes (a fairly common occurrence), cross-easements are required to allow all the conditions of approval to be enforced. Where the local ordinance permits noncontiguous lands to be considered as part of the PD, the location and use of the noncontiguous parcels should be rationally related; that is, close enough to permit all the conditions of approval to be uniformly and reasonably applied.

While many ordinances list specific conditions for various types of PDs, the current trend is to consider them all as planned unit developments (PUDs) without any preconditions on the mix of uses. Many PUDs have a mix of housing, office, commercial, and industrial uses, along with retail and service facilities. The local ordinance would still establish maximum floor area ratios (FARs) for nonresidential uses and maximum densities for residential uses, as well as bulk controls, so that the overall intensity of development is controlled. This type of planning requires that the proposed PD be planned and developed within the context of an overall master plan for the municipality.

Since PDs are developed over many years, with a significant upfront expenditure in infrastructure, the local ordinance usually permits approvals extending well beyond the usual three to five years for preliminary and final approvals for conventional development, with twenty years not uncommon. In addition, the local ordinance permits changes in the mix of uses, based on market demands. If the overall number of dwelling units and the square footage of nonresidential uses remains the same, or is reduced, the changes can be achieved without the necessity of additional expensive and often time-consuming public hearings and the many exhibits required for new applications (Mandelker 2007).

***Legal Annotation***: "A **planned development** is defined under Section III of the ordinance as a 'lot, parcel or tract of land which is developed as an integrated unit and contains two or more principal buildings'. The ordinance also states that planned developments must be necessary, desirable, and appropriate with respect to the primary purpose of the development, and not be of such a nature or so located as to exercise a detrimental influence on the surrounding neighborhood." *Kraegel v. Village of Wood* Dale (Ill. App. Ct., 1973).

## PLANNED COMMERCIAL DEVELOPMENT (PCD)

**An area of at least ten contiguous or noncontiguous acres in size to be planned, developed, operated, and maintained as a single entity and containing one or more structures with appurtenant common areas to accommodate office, retail, and commercial uses, and other uses incidental to the predominant commercial use.**

***Comment***: The ordinance spells out the details, including limitations on land use and bulk controls. See *Comment Under Planned Development*.

***Legal Annotation***: "Developer filed a preliminary subdivision application on or about August 8, 2007, seeking to subdivide the Property into five commercial lots. ... Objectors asserted in their appeal to the trial court that a **planned commercial development** is not an appropriate use on the part of the tract. . . . *Joseph v. North Whitehall Township Board of Supervisors* (Pa. Common. Ct., 2010).

## PLANNED INDUSTRIAL DEVELOPMENT (PID)

**An area of at least ten contiguous or noncontiguous acres in size to be planned, developed,**

**operated, and maintained as a single entity and containing one or more structures with appurtenant common areas to accommodate industrial, manufacturing, warehousing, office, retail, and commercial uses, and other uses incidental to the predominant industrial use.**

***Comment***: The ordinance could specify the percentage of land to be used for various uses. For example, it may limit retail use to reduce traffic and may also limit the percentage of warehousing use to encourage office development.

***Legal Annotation***: "Acorn owns property in the town in a so-called **industrial planned development** (IPD) zone. On its own motion, the defendant 'submitted to itself its own petitions to amend the Zoning Regulations and Zoning Map.' One of the proposed amendments was to create a planned village district (PVD) that would apply to the Acorn site and would apparently contain industrial, commercial and residential uses." *Acorn Tech. Campus v. Planning & Zon. Com'n.* (Conn. Super. Ct., 2007).

## PLANNED-UNIT DEVELOPMENT (PUD)

See *Planned Development*.

## PLANNED-UNIT RESIDENTIAL DEVELOPMENT (PURD)

**An area of at least five contiguous or noncontiguous acres in size to be planned, developed, operated, and maintained as a single entity and containing one or more residential clusters, which may include appropriate commercial, public, or quasi-public uses primarily for the benefit of the residential development.**

***Comment***: The land development ordinance could include limitations on the various housing types to be located in the PURD and the maximum densities permitted by housing type.

***Legal Annotation***: "**Planned unit residential development** is not defined, but § 1007 accords to uses enumerated 'the common meaning of the term.' A planned unit development is usually thought of as involving development of a large tract of land, frequently large enough to constitute a new community. 2 R. Anderson, American Law of Zoning §§ 11.12, 11.13 (2d ed. 1976). It is commonly restricted to developments exceeding a specified number of units or acres." *Stevens v. Essex Junction Zoning Bd.* (Vt., 1981).

"'Planned development' means planned unit development [PUD], **planned unit residential development** [PURD], residential cluster, planned commercial development or planned industrial development. N.J.S.A. 40:55D-6." *Schride Assoc. v. Wall Tp.* (N.J. App. Div., 1983).

## PLANNING BOARD

**The duly designated planning agency of the municipality, county, or region.**

***Comment***: The planning board (also known as planning agency or planning commission) is created by ordinance with the responsibility for reviewing and approving applications for development, preparation of master plans, and other duties as specifically provided for in the state enabling act.

***Legal Annotation***: "It will be observed that the function of a **planning board** is to make a preliminary investigation, to determine if the area studied is blighted, and to report to the governing body." *Wilson v. City of Long Branch* (N.J., 1958).

"A **planning board** is charged with the responsibility of preparing, adopting and amending a master plan 'to guide the use of lands within the municipality in a manner which protects public health and safety and promotes the general welfare.'" *Manalapan Realty v. Township Committee of the Township of Manalapan* (N.J., 1995).

## PLANNING OMBUDSMAN

**An official appointed by the mayor to help resolve disputes between builders and applicants and the public.**

***Comment***: The ombudsman serves as a facilitator, often gathering facts, presenting positions, suggesting alternatives, and making recommendations to the approving authority. While the definition calls for the position to be filled by the mayor, it can be a planning board appointment or one appointed by the governing body or as specified in the enabling legislation.

*Legal Annotation*: "For guidance in resolving the issue, the Commission contacted the State **Ombudsman's** Office, which recommended sending new written ballots to each voting member." *The City of Postville v. Upper Explorerland Regional Planning Commission* (Iowa, 2013).

## PLATOON FLOW

**A group of vehicles, moving along a roadway facility together, with significant gaps between one such group and the next.**

## PLAT

**(1) A map representing a tract of land, showing the boundaries and locations of individual properties and streets; (2) a map of a subdivision.**

*Legal Annotation*: "A '**plat**' is defined as: A map or delineated representation of the subdivision of lands, being a complete exact representation of the subdivision and other information in compliance with the requirement of all applicable sections of this chapter and of any local ordinances." *Graves v. Pompano Beach ex rel. City Com'n* (Fla. Ct. App., 2011).

## PLAT, FINAL

**A map of all or a portion of a subdivision that is presented to the approving authority for final approval. See *Final Approval*.**

*Comment*: Approval of the final plat usually is granted only on the completion or installation of all improvements or the posting of performance guarantees ensuring the completion or installation of such improvements. The final approval is generally required before property can be transferred or building permits issued.

*Legal Annotation*: "There are a host of requirements that the developer must meet between sketch plan and **final plat**; while the **final plat** is to be *consistent* with the sketch plan, it need not be *identical* to it, or the entire process could end after the sketch plan was approved. Changes are anticipated. For instance, the Development Standards and Regulations provide that, at the sketch plan phase, the planning coordinator is 'to alert the applicant to . . . any issues which need to be addressed prior to final plat submittal.'" *Northfork v. Board* (Wyo., 2010).

## PLAT, PRELIMINARY

**See *Plat; Preliminary Approval*.**

*Legal Annotation*: "Thus, we conclude that the County Commission's decision to deny Alexander's **preliminary plat** was arbitrary, unlawful, and not based upon substantial and competent evidence. In so ruling, we want to emphasize the fact that a **preliminary plat** is just that—*preliminary*. . . . The approval of a **preliminary plat** merely gives the subdivider authorization to proceed with the planning and development phase of the project. . . . The Subdivision Regulations still require that the subdivider's final plat comply with all Subdivision Regulations and be approved by the Director of Zoning and Planning, the Planning and Zoning Commission, and the County Commission if the Planning and Zoning Commission disapproves of the final plat." *State ex rel. Alexander & Lindsey, LLC v. Planning and Zoning Commission of Platte County* (Mo. Ct. App., 2011).

## PLAT, SKETCH

**A layout of a proposed subdivision of sufficient accuracy and detail to be used for the purpose of discussion and classification.**

*Comment*: Many planning boards and development review agencies encourage applicants to submit sketch plats for informal, conceptual, and nonbinding reviews prior to the preparation of detailed plans.

*Legal Annotation*: "The term, 'plat,' as used in this opinion, is defined as '[a] graphic and written description of a lot or lots with survey reference ties to permanent survey monuments.' . . .

In order to obtain subdivision approval, a developer must submit three such plats: a **sketch plat**, followed by a preliminary plat, and then a final plat. . . . The sketch plat is first submitted to the City, which makes recommendations that are later reflected in the preliminary plat. When the preliminary plat is approved, the City has made a 'commitment . . . that a final plat conforming to the approved preliminary plat and any conditions will be approved.' The final plat is the recorded, 'legal instrument which will allow transfer of land within the subdivision to take place.'" *Andalucia Dev't v. City of Albuquerque* (N.M. Ct. App., 2010).

## PLAYGROUND

**An active recreational area with a variety of facilities, including equipment for younger children as well as court and field games. See *Neighborhood Park/ Playground; Recreation Facility.***

***Comment***: The playground is usually located next to an elementary school and serves the neighborhood (a half-mile radius). Playgrounds vary in size, depending on the type of equipment and games.

***Legal Annotation***: "A '**playground**' is 'an area used by children for outdoor recreation, usually containing play equipment such as slides and swings.' Random House Webster's College Dictionary (2001 ed). Although swimming pools are used for outdoor recreation, a **playground** is an area that may contain structures for play purposes, whereas a swimming pool is a structure itself. The common lay understanding of what constitutes a '**playground**' simply does not include swimming pools. While ambiguity must be construed strictly against enforcement of a restriction, the courts do not strain to find or create an ambiguity, and we find none here." *Millpointe of Hartland Condominium Association v. Cipolla* (Mich. Ct. App., 2010).

## PLAYGROUND, ACCESSIBLE

**A playground, play area, or recreational facility that complies with the accessibility guidelines of the Americans with Disabilities Act (ADA) so as to be readily accessible to, and usable by, individuals with disabilities**

***Comment***: All new or altered public recreational facilities must comply with the accessibility standards of the ADA. Facilities may include ramped play equipment, ground-level play features, accessible swings, wheelchair-accessible tables and drinking fountains, and adjustable basketball backboards. Specific standards and information are available from the US Access Board, 1131 F Street NW, Suite 1000, Washington, DC, 20004-1111.

***Legal Annotation***: "Mr. Cortez's granddaughter suffers from significant disabilities; including, a chromosomal disorder, lack of motor skills, visual and hearing impairments, and epilepsy. She uses a wheelchair for mobility. . . . Mr. Cortez carried his granddaughter from the parking facility to the football field and to the **playground** which caused him physical difficulty and frustration. . . . Specifically, Mr. Cortez alleges that there are no **accessible** pedestrian pathways from the parking facilities to the playing fields and playground." *Cortez v. City of Porterville* (E.D. Calif., 2014).

## PLAZA

**An open space that may be improved and landscaped; usually surrounded by streets and buildings. See *Court; Square. See Figure 20.***

***Legal Annotation***: "The second alternative preferred by Song would involve a shopping center without a gas station/car wash or a big-box retailer, but would include two 30-foot landscaped setbacks with a **plaza** along two perimeters, so that the development would be approximately 50 percent of that proposed for the project." *Save Our Neighborhood Group v. City of Lancaster* (Calif. Ct. App., 2011).

## PLOT

**(1) A single-unit parcel of land; (2) a parcel of land that can be identified and referenced to a recorded plat or map.**

***Legal Annotation***: "It was suggested that the word 'parcel' could also refer to a single lot, if a property historically consisted of only one lot. However, as the deed specifically refers to two plots and cites an historical plan recorded in the land evidence records that identifies the property as consisting of two plots, this Court finds that the term Parcel, as used within this deed, was intended to refer to a property consisting of more than one lot or **plot**." *Kieltyka v. Town of New Shoreham Zoning Board of Review* (R.I. Super. Ct., 2011).

## PLUME

**The visible emission from a flue or chimney.**

***Comment***: Although most often used in connection with air emissions, plumes can also be used to describe emissions into groundwater, particularly those containing contaminants.

***Legal Annotation***: "However, the EPA report cited by plaintiffs shows that it found unacceptable levels of EDB in wells in the area of Evans' home. . . . The EPA estimates a **plume** of groundwater EDB contamination, the southern edge of which appears to pass under Evans' property, or at least very close to it." *Evans v. Shoshone-Bannock Land Use Policy Commission* (D. Idaho, 2012).

## POCKET NEIGHBORHOOD

**A small (six to twelve) group of houses and/or apartments tightly clustered around common open space such as a small park, community garden, courtyard, and/or pedestrian street, walk, or alley.**

***Comment***: "A neighborhood within a neighborhood" is how Ross Chapin, FAIA, architect, advocate, and designer of over fifty pocket neighborhood projects describes them. An important part of the design is to increase interaction between neighbors and develop a sense of community while preserving privacy. According to Chapin, pocket neighborhoods lend themselves to a mix of housing types and income levels (Chapin 2011). The pocket neighborhood is also advocated as an antidote to sprawl, social isolation, and the expense associated with automobile-centric developments typical of suburbia. Pocket neighborhoods typically include smaller homes built at higher densities and in close proximity to one another, and segregated from parking lots and roadways. (Source: Abrams 2012; http://www.pocket.neighborhoods.net/whatisaPN.html; *AARP Bulletin* 2012.)

***Legal Annotation***: "The general purposes of the pocket neighborhood housing development design concept are:

A **pocket neighborhood** housing development is an alternative type of detached housing providing small residences for households. This is provided as part of the Town's overall housing strategy which intends to encourage affordability, infill development, innovation and variety in housing design and site development while ensuring compatibility with existing neighborhoods, and to promote a variety of housing choices to meet the needs of a population diverse in age, income, household composition and individual needs. *Pittsboro, NC Zoning Ordinance.*"

## PODs

**See *Portable On-Demand Storage*.**

## POINT OF TANGENCY

**The point at which a curved line meets a straight line. *See Figure 30*.**

***Legal Annotation***: "Thence along a side curve a distance of 134.11 feet to a **point of tangency**." *Hill-Shafer Partnership v. Chilson Family Trust* (Ariz., 1990).

## POINT SOURCE

**A stationary source of an individual emission, generally of an industrial nature. See *Area Source; Stationary Source*.**

***Legal Annotation***: "A **point source** is 'any discernible, confined and discrete conveyance . . . from which pollutants are or may be discharged.'" *EPA v. California ex rel. State Water Resources Control Bd.* (U.S., 1976).

## POLLUTANT

**Any introduced gas, liquid, or solid that makes a resource unfit for a specific purpose.**

*Legal Annotation*: "The term '**pollutant**' is defined in the insurance contract to mean 'any solid, liquid, gaseous or thermal irritant or contaminant, including smoke, vapor, soot, fumes, acids, alkalis, chemicals, and waste.'" Id *Westchester Fire Ins. Co. v. City of Pittsburg, Kan.* (D. Kan., 1991).

## POLLUTION

**The presence of matter or energy whose nature, location, or quantity produces undesired environmental effects.**

*Legal Annotation*: "Perhaps the most noticeable damage caused by oil **pollution** is the fouling of recreational beaches and shorefront property. One-half million tons of oil are washed ashore each year, rendering beaches unfit for swimming and filling the air with unpleasant odors. Besides the annoyance that this causes a vacationing public seeking relief from urban life, economic loss may be considerable. It is estimated, for example, that a serious oil spill off Long Island during the summer months would cost resort and beach operators thirty million dollars. Oil spills also create navigational and fire hazards in harbors, ports and marinas." *Askew v. American Waterways Operators, Inc.* (U.S., 1973).

## POLLUTION, NONPOINT SOURCE

**Pollution from any source other than from any discernible, confined, or discrete conveyances. This includes, but is not limited to, pollutants from agricultural, silvicultural, mining, construction, subsurface disposal, and urban runoff sources.**

*Legal Annotation*: "**Nonpoint source pollution** is not specifically defined in the Act, but is pollution that does not result from the 'discharge' or 'addition' of pollutants from a point source. Examples of nonpoint source pollution include runoff from irrigated agriculture and silvicultural activities." *Oregon Natural Res. Council v. US Forest Service* (9th Cir., 1987).

## POPTOPS

**Second-story or higher additions, at least one story higher than surrounding structures. See *Compatible Design*.**

*Legal Annotation*: "Additional space can be created in a number of ways.

It can be as simple as adding dormers to an attic; or, it can be as complex as adding a '**pop-top**,' or new floor." San Jose, California Zoning Ordinance Chap. 4 Additions. https://www.sanjoseca.gov/DocumentCenter/View/6117

## POP-UP STORES

**Retail space that is temporary, utilized for short-term sales, ranging from one day to several weeks.**

***Comment***: Sometimes such spaces are leased on a short-term basis in a down economy until the market picks up, or they are seasonally related, such as Halloween stores that sell costumes and decorations for a month or two. However, pop-up stores also provide venues for single events, such as a one-day sample sale and a private cocktail party the next evening. Others provide limited-edition products from niche retailers and close once the product is sold out, only to reopen later when more product is received, or reopen at another location to generate consumer interest (Louie 2012).

*Legal Annotation*: "A&S bought overstock, returns and remainder books and related merchandise from sellers such as Nationwide. It then sold the merchandise in its 'temporary' bookstores at a deep discount. A&S also operated **pop-up stores** which sold Halloween and related merchandise." *Nationwide Book Industries, LLC v. Weiss* (D. Mass., 2013).

## PORK CHOP LOT

**A lot with inadequate frontage and/or width at the front of the lot but of sufficient size to meet the minimum lot area requirements. See *Flag Lot*.**

***Comment***: So named because the shape of such lots resembles that of a pork chop.

***Legal Annotation***: "The locus is a 'double **pork chop' lot** having a shape 'so unusual that it also differs from most, if not all, of the lots in the zoning district.' Moreover, the locus is about ten times larger than the surrounding lots fronting on Fairview Street." *Gordon v. Zoning Board of Appeals of Lee* (Mass. App. Ct., 1986).

"The lot for which the variance was granted is a **'pork chop' lot**. Somewhat larger than most of the surrounding developed lots to the east of the locus but only ninety feet wide, it has a fifteen-foot wide strip, four hundred feet in length, running from the street to the main portion of the lot. The bulk of the lot is well back from any street nearby. The frontage required by the town by-law on a public way is thirty feet, fifteen feet more than the lot provides. The width requirement is one hundred fifty feet. See *The Accompanying Sketch. The Lot Was Created In Its Present Form In The 1920'S, As Far As Appears Prior To The Adoption By The Town Of Any Zoning By-Law." Paulding V. Bruins (Mass. App.* Ct., 1984).

## PORTABLE ON DEMAND STORAGE (POD)

**Portable, lightweight storage containers that provide temporary storage for homeowners in yards or driveways**

***Comment***: PODs are usually stored on the yard or driveway, filled by the homeowners, and then stored on the property or transported to a self-storage warehouse. Resistance to this use is based upon unsightliness and the length of time the container remains on the property.

***Legal Annotation***: "In 2003, appellants engaged realtor Michael Linder ('Linder') to search for commercial real estate in Columbus, for the purpose of operating a **Portable On Demand Storage** franchise on the site." *Corey v. Big Run Industrial Park, LLC* (Ohio Ct. App., 2009).

## PORCH

**A roofed, open area, which may be screened, attached to or part of a building, and with direct access to or from it. See *Portico. See Figure 9.***

***Legal Annotation***: "The record shows that the **porch** could not be built on the north side of the home because it would violate the zoning ordinance as it does now." *Snyder v. Waukesha County Zoning Board* (Wis., 1976).

## POROSITY

**A measure of the amount of space between grains or cracks that can fill with water.**

***Legal Annotation***: "Additionally, the soil **porosity** in the area was such that a septic tank could not be supported. Plaintiffs had to construct a water well and water system for the restaurant and install a sewage holding tank on the premises which was used until sewage facilities were made available by the S.I.D." *Dodds v. Gibson Products Co. of W. Mont.* (Mont., 1979).

## POROUS PAVEMENT

**A permeable pavement that allows stormwater runoff to infiltrate directly into the soil below. See *Permeable Pavement System*.**

***Comment***: Porous paving is being encouraged and even mandated in some jurisdictions, both to reduce the extent of stormwater runoff (increasing groundwater recharge and reducing downstream flooding) and avoid contaminating streams with nonpoint pollutants. While porous paving appears at the surface to be the same as traditional asphalt or concrete, it is manufactured with fine materials, leaving voids that allow water to infiltrate into the soil below. A stone "reservoir" or sub-base is provided to temporarily store surface runoff. More systematic management or maintenance (Best Management Practices) is required than with conventional paving, to ensure that the voids are not clogged, which prevents or inhibits infiltration. While significant strides have been made in recent years, some concerns about their use persist. While they are appropriate in cold weather climates, they should be avoided where activities generate highly contaminated runoff, in areas of low soil permeability or with high seasonal water tables, or in areas close to drinking-water supply wells. Also, porous paving is significantly more expensive than conventional impervious paving.

*Legal Annotation*: "The Plan called for construction of five recharge basins, two detention basins, three rain gardens, seven water quality structures, six vegetated swales, **porous pavement**, parking stalls and dry wells." *Sentinel Ridge Development, LLC v. DEP* (Pa: Common. Ct., 2010).

## PORTICO

**(1) An open-sided structure attached to a building and sheltering an entrance or serving as a semienclosed space (Nelessen 1994); (2) a roofed area supported by columns, forming a front porch (Johnsich 1991). See *Porch*.**

*Legal Annotation*: "Upon the completion of the hearing the board took the application under advisement and on March 14, 1961 rendered their decision granting a variance subject to the following conditions: '. . . 8. A semicircle **portico** with an ornamental rail on the roof is to be erected at the front door.'" *Gemma v. Zoning Bd. of Cranston* (R.I., 1962).

## POST

**A long, vertical support member of wood or steel set in holes that are backfilled with compacted materials.**

*Comment*: Posts often cannot act as independent support units and therefore are often braced with connections to other posts.

*Legal Annotation*: "The house and its porches were constructed of white or soft pine wood about thirty years ago. It was built on wooden **post** supports on the side of a hill, and had porches on the east and west sides." *Caudill v. Gibson Fuel Co.* (Va., 1946).

## POTABLE WATER SUPPLY

**Water suitable for drinking or cooking purposes.**

*Legal Annotation*: "The Zoning Board concluded that Developer's application must be rejected because of:

1. The question of the continuance of a safe and **potable water supply** and the impact of the park's water use on the surrounding land owners." *East Manchester Tp. v. Dallmeyer* (Pa. Comm. Ct., 1992).

## POWER CENTER

**An unenclosed shopping center with three or more big-box retail stores and with shared parking. See *Retail Store, Big-Box*.**

## PPM

**Parts per million.**

*Comment*: A measurement commonly used to represent the amount of pollutant concentration in a liquid or gas.

*Legal Annotation*: "Carbon monoxide data is attacked as unreliable. EPA determined that its national primary standard requiring the average amount of carbon monoxide in the air over an eight hour period not to exceed 9 PM is not being met in the Boston core and will not be met by mid-1975." *South Terminal Corp. v. Environmental Protection Agcy.* (Ist Cir., 1974).

## PRECIPITATE

**A solid that separates from a solution because of some chemical or physical change.**

*Legal Annotation*: "The most frequently observed by-product of acid mine water run-off is 'yellow boy', a slightly soluble iron hydroxide which **precipitates** out into the streambeds. Broughton, Koza, & Selway, Acid Mine Drainage and the Pennsylvania Courts, 11 Duq.L.Rev. 495, 496-97 (1973) [hereinafter cited as Acid Mine Drainage]." *Commonwealth v. Barnes & Tucker Co.* (Pa., 1977).

## PRECIPITATION

**(1) In meteorology, any product of the condensation of atmospheric water vapor (e.g., rain, snow, hail, sleet, etc.); (2) in pollution control work, any of a number of air-pollution control devices, usually using mechanical or electrical means, to collect particulates from an emission. *See Figure 6*.**

*Legal Annotation*: "Appellants' geologist testified that in his opinion normal **precipitation** should replenish the water table adequately but that a drought would reduce the amount of water available to all users." *Diehl et Ux. v. Milford Twp. Zoning Bd.* (Pa., 1981).

## PREEMPTIVE RIGHT

**The right of a riparian owner to a preference in the acquisition of lands under tidewaters adjoining the owner's upland. See *Riparian Land*.**

*Legal Annotation*: "This right in a riparian owner to a preference in the acquisition of the lands under tidewater adjoining his upland, in the event the State decided to convey them at all, later extended to other actions as we shall note, has come to be called by our courts a '**preemptive right**' or 'right of preemption.'" *Bailey v. Driscoll* (N.J. App. Div., 1955).

## PREEXISTING USE

**The use of a lot or structure prior to the time of the enactment of a zoning ordinance or amendment thereto.**

*Comment*: At the time a new zoning or development ordinance is adopted, some municipalities will attempt to survey existing uses in order to provide an accurate record of preexisting uses. The preexisting nonconforming use, legal at the time of the passage of the ordinance but made nonconforming as a result of the ordinance, has a legal right to continue. Future problems arise because of confusion as to the extent and nature of the uses at the time of passage. Hence, an inventory is often necessary to ensure that nonconforming uses do not expand illegally.

*Legal Annotation*: "The basis on which their license was refused was that although after the enactment of a zoning ordinance their business had been licensed as a nonconforming **preexisting use**, nevertheless in 1953 the zoning ordinance was amended to outlaw nonconforming uses of this nature at the expiration of three years from the effective date of the amendment." *Matter of Harbison v. City of Buffalo* (N.Y., 1958).

## PRELIMINARY APPROVAL

**"Preliminary approval" of an application means the conferral of certain rights prior to final approval, after specific elements of a development plan have been approved by the approving authority and agreed to by the applicant.**

*Comment*: Preliminary approval freezes the terms and conditions, including design and layout of an application, for a specified period of time, often three to five years. It protects against any changes in zoning or other conditions of approval during that period. Preliminary approval involves public hearings and serious planning-board input to the design. All specific conditions of approval are spelled out during the preliminary approval phase. See *Preliminary Plan*.

*Legal Annotation*: "The basic issues raised are: . . . (4) whether an environmental impact statement pursuant to RCW 43.21 is a necessary prerequisite for **preliminary approval** of the plat. We therefore conclude the plat cannot be granted **preliminary approval** since on its face it violates the controlling zoning ordinances." *Loveless v. Yantis* (Wash., 1973).

## PRELIMINARY FLOOR PLANS AND ELEVATIONS

**Architectural drawings, prepared during the early and introductory stages of a project, illustrating the scope, scale, and relation of the project to its site and immediate environs.**

*Legal Annotation*: "B.Y. submitted color drawings of the project and **preliminary floor plans**, a site plan, and **elevations** to the City to review on June 7. The City suggested changes, which B.Y. incorporated into the plans, and on June 18, B.Y. submitted updated plans." *In re BY Development, Inc.* (S.D., 2000).

## PRELIMINARY PLAN

**A map or plan, with supporting documentation, showing the proposed layout of the subdivision or site plan that is submitted for preliminary approval. See *Preliminary Approval*.**

*Comment*: While the term is "preliminary," the submission requirements for preliminary plan approval are detailed and extensive. The preliminary plan requires detailed engineering drawings of the proposed development, road profiles, utility layouts, drainage calculations, stormwater control plans, soil erosion and sediment control plans, environmental and community impact statements, and landscaping plans. For site plans, requirements include lighting plans, signage, circulation, parking plans, and building plans and elevations.

***Legal Annotation***: "In Moreland, for instance, the zoning appears much more akin to approval of a final development plan than to approval of a **preliminary plan**, leading the court to conclude the county lacked the discretion to deny final approval." *Jordan-Arapahoe, LLP v. Board of County Com'rs* (10th Cir., 2011).

## PRELIMINARY PLAT

**See *Plat; Preliminary Approval*.**

***Legal Annotation***: "A **preliminary plat** application is meant to give local governments and the public an approximate picture of how the final subdivision will look. It is to be expected that modifications will be made during the give and take of the approval process." *Knight v. City of Yelm* (Wash., 2011).

## PREMATURE SUBDIVISION

**Land legally subdivided into building lots for which: (1) a limited or no market exists; (2) the developer has gone bankrupt and/or abandoned the project; and (3) few or no homes have been constructed.**

***Comment***: Also known as "zombie subdivisions," premature subdivisions are often forced into bankruptcy, and lenders will acquire the property and attempt to repackage the project for resale. Municipalities may be able to acquire the property, through condemnation or through their redevelopment powers, at relatively low prices. Other options include rezoning for commercial or nonresidential uses and economic incentives such as increasing densities and providing for a mix of housing and retail uses (Elliot 2010).

***Legal Annotation***: "RSA 36:21 (Supp. 1975) provides that town planning boards may promulgate regulations which 'provide against such scattered or **premature subdivision** of land as would involve danger or injury to health, safety, or prosperity by reason of the lack of . . . transportation . . . or other public services, or necessitate an excessive expenditure of public funds for the supply of such services.'" *Garipay v. Town of Hanover* (N.H., 1976).

## PREMISES

**A lot, parcel, tract, or plot of land together with the buildings and structures thereon.**

***Legal Annotation***: "The building inspector, who is responsible for enforcing the zoning ordinance, testified that three establishments located in commercial zones of the Borough offered live music. However, he stated that they were permitted to do so only because this use of the **premises** preceded the enactment of the zoning ordinance and thus qualified as a 'nonconforming' use under the ordinance." *Schad v. Mount Ephraim* (U.S., 1981).

## PREPAREDNESS

**Activities, programs, and systems developed and implemented prior to a disaster/emergency that are used to support and enhance mitigation of, response to, and recovery from disasters/emergencies *(NFPA 1600,* 2004).**

***Comment***: Preparedness involves efforts at all levels of government and between government and private-sector and nongovernmental organizations to identify threats, determine vulnerabilities, and identify required resources. Within the NIMS, preparedness is operationally focused on establishing guidelines, protocols, and standards for planning, training and exercises, personnel qualification and certification, equipment certification, and publication management (NIMS). http://www.gwu.edu/~icdrm/publications/PDF/GLOSSARY%2002-19-2007.pdf

*Legal Annotation*: "The provisions of zoning ordinances shall be designed: '(1) To promote, protect and facilitate any or all of the following: the public health, safety, morals, and the general welfare; coordinated and practical community development and proper density of population; emergency management **preparedness** and operations, airports, and national defense facilities.'" *In re Appeal of Burger* (Pa. Ct. Comm. Pleas, 1992).

## PRESCRIPTION

**The securing of a title to property by adverse possession of land by right of continuous use without protest from the owner (Johnsich 1991).**

*Comment*: The time period for a prescription is usually twenty years. See *Adverse Possession*.

*Legal Annotation*: "An easement by **prescription** is created by adverse, open, continuous, notorious, and uninterrupted use of land for the prescriptive period—in Pennsylvania, twenty-one years." *Haddad v. Adlof* (Pa. Super. Ct., 2013).

## PRESERVATION

**The Secretary of the Interior Standards for the Treatment of Historic Properties define preservation, rehabilitation, restoration, and reconstruction as follows.**

1. *PRESERVATION*

The act or process of applying measures necessary to sustain the existing form, integrity, and materials of an historic property. Work, including preliminary measures to protect and stabilize the property, generally focuses upon the ongoing maintenance and repair of historic materials and features rather than extensive replacement and new construction. New exterior additions are not within the scope of this treatment; however, the limited and sensitive upgrading of mechanical, electrical, and plumbing systems and other code-required work to make properties functionally is appropriate within a preservation project.

2. *REHABILITATION*

Rehabilitation, the second treatment, emphasizes the retention and repair of historic materials, but more latitude is provided for replacement because it is assumed the property is more deteriorated prior to work. Both Preservation and Rehabilitation standards focus attention on the preservation of those materials, features, finishes, spaces and spatial relationships that, together, give a property its historic character.

3. *RESTORATION*

Restoration, the third treatment, focuses on the retention of materials from the most significant time in a property's history, while permitting the removal of materials from other periods.

4. *RECONSTRUCTION*

Act or process of depicting, by means of new construction, the form, features, and detailing of a non-surviving site, landscape, building, structure, or object for the purpose of replicating its appearance at a specific period of time and in its historic location.

*Legal Annotation*: "The project as proposed violates **Preservation** Standard 4; the abandonment of the easement will lead to the alteration of the character of the registered property." *In Re Princeton Railroad Station Track Removal Project* (N.J. App. Div., 2014).

## PRESERVATION, HISTORIC

**See *Historic Preservation*.**

## PRESERVE, NATURE

**See *Nature Preserve*.**

## PRETREATMENT

**In wastewater treatment, any process used to reduce the pollution load before the wastewater is introduced into a main sewer system or delivered to a treatment plant.**

*Legal Annotation*: "'**Pretreatment**' is defined to include 'the reduction of the amount of pollutants . . . in wastewater prior to or in lieu of discharging such wastewater into the publicly owned treatment works (POTW).'" *Pharmacia Hepar, Inc. v. City of Franklin* (Ohio Ct. App., 1996).

## PRIMARY TREATMENT

**The first stage in wastewater treatment, in which substantially all floating or settleable solids are removed by screening and sedimentation.**

***Legal Annotation***: "**Primary treatment** is 'the first stage in wastewater treatment where substantially all floating or settleable solids are removed by flotation and/or sedimentation. . . . Sludge is solid material that is removed from sewage during treatment." *Natural Resources v. US Environ. Protection* (D.C. Cir., 1981).

## PRINCIPAL BUILDING

**See *Building, Principal. See Figure 3.***

***Legal Annotation***: "A '**principal building**' is defined as 'a building designed to be used as the main dwelling house or building on the lot'." *Inc. Vil. of Upper Brookville v. Torr* (N.Y. Sup. Ct., 1956).

## PRINCIPAL ENTRANCE

**The place of ingress and egress used most frequently by the public.**

***Legal Annotation***: "Section 155-36(C) of the Ordinance states: Front yard. There shall be a setback from the street toward which the **principal entrance** is oriented which shall not be less than 35 feet in depth and within no other buildings, gasoline pumps or *outdoor displays shall exist.*" *Caln Nether v. Bd. of Sup'rs, Thornbury* (Pa. Common. Ct., 2004).

## PRINCIPAL USE

**The primary or predominant use of any lot or parcel. See *Accessory Use*.**

***Legal Annotation***: "Although the Killingworth zoning regulations do not define '**principal use**,' the prevalent meaning ascribed to that term in other jurisdictions, consistent with the definition set forth under the Killingworth zoning regulations for an 'accessory use,' is the dominant, main or primary use of the land." *Graff v. Zoning Board of Appeals* (Conn., 2006).

## PRIVACY HEDGE

**Dense shrubs, foliage, plants, and low-growing trees formed into a fence-like structure to provide privacy, block views, establish boundaries, and mitigate noise.**

***Comment***: The type of shrub or foliage depends on local growing conditions. Some of the more common hedge material includes pine trees, Norway spruce, firs, arborvitae, lilac, etc. They should be fast-growing and dense, grow low to the ground, and be easily trimmed.

***Legal Annotation***: "Rogers' seven and one-half acre residence/farm is surrounded by a wooden fence and a **privacy hedge** which blocks the visibility of his property from the private road." *Rogers v. Pendleton* (4th Cir., 2001).

## PRIVATE CLUB

**A building and related facilities owned or operated by a corporation, association, or group of individuals established for the fraternal, social, educational, recreational, or cultural enrichment of its members and not primarily for profit and whose members pay dues and meet certain prescribed qualifications for membership. See *Lodge*.**

***Comment***: Private clubs may include sleeping and dining facilities for members and guests. In some cases, the dining facilities may be open to the public.

***Legal Annotation***: "[A] **private club** is 'a building and facilities or premises, owned and operated by a corporation, association, person or persons for social, educational or recreational purposes, but not primarily for profit and not primarily to render a service which is customarily carried on as a business.'" *Midrash Sephardi, Inc. v. Town of Surfside* (11th Cir., 2004).

## PRIVATE SCHOOL

See *School, Private*.

## PRO-RATA SHARE

**A proportional share of costs associated with the construction of improvements.**

***Comment***: "Pro-rata share" refers to sharing the cost of improvements, required to be constructed by developers, that benefit more than one development. For example, when a road or sewer main is extended through several developments, each developer must pay their pro-rata share of the improvement cost.

***Legal Annotation***: "The City Council held a meeting on May 22, 2006, which Alex Garth attended. Doc. 9, Ex. 11. Whereas Mr. Garth wanted the City to approve the zone change to a PUD before discussing the financing of the Elks Drive improvements, representatives of the City first wanted to discuss the Elks Drive issue. They expressed concerns about how Plaintiffs would pay for their **pro-rata share** of $208,840 given their status in bankruptcy proceedings." *Zia Shadows, LLC v. City of Las Cruces* (D.N.M., 2011).

## PROBABILITY

**A statistical method that calculates the chance that a specific event will occur.**

***Legal Annotation***: "The objectors cannot meet their burden by merely speculating as to possible harm, but instead must show a high degree of **probability** that it will substantially affect the health and safety of the community." *544 Church Lane, LLC v. Zoning Hearing Board of Borough of Yeardon* (Pa. Common. Ct., 2010).

## PROCESS WEIGHT

**The total weight of all materials, including fuels, introduced into a manufacturing process.**

***Comment***: Process-weight regulations are used to prescribe the allowable rate of emission of pollutant matter from the process.

***Legal Annotation***: "The EPA then adopted a substitute '**process weight**' regulation, prescribing limitations on the amount of particulate emissions from process sources such as those of the Hayden facility." *Asarco, Inc. v. USEPA* (9th Cir., 1980).

## PROCESSING

**A series of operations, usually in a continuous and regular action or succession of actions, taking place or carried out in a definite manner.**

***Comment***: The term "processing" is usually associated with the chemical transformation of materials or substances into new products and may include the blending and combining of gases and liquids. However, the term also may be applied to a specific industrial or manufacturing operation.

***Legal Annotation***: "The Township contended that the compressor station was ***processing*** gas, and 'oil and gas refining, processing, storage and transmission' can only be done in the Township's General Manufacturing District. . . . Jack Carnes, the Zoning Officer, also testified. He reiterated that oil and gas production is permitted in the Forest District, but oil and gas **processing** are not permitted. . . . We agree that '**processing**' is a flexible term, but so are 'production' and 'gas pumping operations.'" *In Re Bradford, Tp. Zoning Hearing Board* (Pa: Comm. Ct., 2012).

## PROCESSING AND WAREHOUSING

**The storage of materials in a warehouse or terminal, and where such materials may be combined, broken down, or aggregated for trans-shipment or storage and where the original material is not chemically or physically changed.**

***Comment***: "Processing and warehousing" is a single term and must be defined as such. Otherwise, the word "processing," which is akin to manufacturing, describes a manufacturing facility, which could also contain warehousing space, not uncommon in a manufacturing operation. The term "processing and warehousing" as defined refers essentially to a storage and shipment place as opposed to a manufacturing establishment.

*Legal Annotation*: "The terminal facilities with which we are concerned came into existence as a result of a program initiated by Southern in 1954, designed to promote a produce terminal facility, shortly thereafter expanded into promotion of a fully integrated food wholesale, **processing, and warehousing facility**." *Southern Railway Company v. US* (N.D. Ala., 1960).

## PROFESSIONAL OFFICE

**The office of a member of a recognized profession, maintained for the conduct of that profession. See *Home Occupation; Home Professional Office*.**

*Legal Annotation*: "A **professional office** is one that provides services of a professional as distinguished from a business nature. . . . This distinction is applied only in describing the type of office that can be maintained in a residential zone. . . . In describing business zones the regulations make no distinction between a professional office and a business office." *DiBlasi v. Zoning Board of Appeals* (Conn., 1993).

## PROHIBITED USE

**A use that is not permitted in a zone district.**

*Comment*: Older zoning ordinances usually listed those uses specifically prohibited in each zone. Over time, changes in technology have created new types of land uses that were clearly inappropriate for certain zones, but because they were unknown at the time the zoning was adopted, they were not listed as prohibited. As such, they became permitted uses. This has prompted a change in the way zoning is written. Most ordinances now specify that if a use is not specifically permitted, it is prohibited.

*Legal Annotation*: "This is not to say that prohibitory statutes are not presumed valid. We recognize the presumption that the statute was intended to prohibit an illegitimate business. However, in the case before us the **prohibited use** is that of a gasoline service station. Such a business is capable of being regulated so that its operations are not inherently nor consequentially injurious to the general welfare." *Beaver Gas Co. v. Zon. Bd. of Osborne Boro.* (Pa. Comm. Ct., 1971).

## PROJECTION

**(1) A prediction of a future state based on an analysis of what has happened in the past; (2) part of a building or structure that projects from a wall or roof.**

*Comment*: Projections are often exempt from complying with setback or height requirements, if such projections are not excessive. This typically includes bay windows, steps, and chimneys that often project into required yards, and parapet walls and mechanical equipment on roofs that may exceed the height limitation.

*Legal Annotation*: "LCDC began its analysis by comparing the projected land need (in buildable acres) based on employment **projections** and an employee-per-acre calculation—viz., 311 acres—with the projected land need based on the target-industries approach used by the city—viz., 362 acres." *1000 Friends of Oregon v. Land Conservation and Development Commission* (Ore. Ct. App., 2014).

"This section of the Ordinance provides that '[a] cornice, eaves, belt course, sill, canopy or other similar architectural feature (not including bay window or other vertical **projection**) may extend or project into . . . a required front, side, or rear yard not more than 30 inches.'" *Dwight v. York* (R.I., 2014).

## PROPERTY

**Anything that is owned by a person or entity.**

*Comment*: Property includes both "real property" and "personal property," both "tangible" and "intangible" personal property (*The Free Dictionary* by Farlex).

*Legal Annotation*: "The **Property** includes a two-story structure comprised of 46,016 square feet that had been used by Majestic Sportswear (Majestic) as a clothing manufacturing facility, a nonconforming use, until 2007." *4154 Roosevelt Street, LLC v. Zoning Hearing Board of Township of Whitehall* (Pa. Common. Ct., 2014).

## PROPERTY LINE

See *Lot Line*.

*Legal Annotation*: "In contrast, the proposed Sonic restaurant's drive-in canopy area is located at least 105.6 feet from the **property line**, is oriented perpendicular to the existing residences (thereby minimizing exposure to adjacent residences), and will be separated from the nearest residences by an approximately 60 foot naturally vegetated buffer to be supplemented by two rows of evergreen trees." *Matter of Serota Smithtown LLC v. Town of Smithtown Bd. of Zoning Appeals* (N.Y. Sup. Ct., 2014).

## PROPERTY TAXES

**Taxes conditioned on ownership of property and measured by its value.**

*Legal Annotation*: "The words 'real property,' 'real estate' and 'land' as used in ch. 70 entitled 'General **Property Taxes**,' include 'not only the land itself but all buildings and improvements thereon, and all fixtures and rights and privileges appertaining thereto.'" *Waste Management v. Kenosha County Rev. Bd.* (Wis., 1994).

## PROPERTY TAX RATE

**The percentage or share of the value of property that is obligated for property tax payment.**

*Comment*: The property tax rate of a given jurisdiction is derived by dividing the dollars raised from the property tax (i.e., the property tax levy) by the jurisdiction's total property valuation. The property tax levy, divided by the jurisdiction's property valuation as assessed for tax purposes or assessed value (the assessed valuation may or may not be equal to true market value), generates the nominal (or assessed or posted) property tax rate. (The nominal rate is the actual or posted millage rate used in calculating the tax bill.) For example, if a local government has a property tax levy of $2 million and the community has a local assessed tax base of $100 million, then the nominal (or assessed or posted) property tax rate would be $2.00 per $100 of assessed valuation (or 2 percent of assessed value). A property assessed for $100,000 would therefore pay $2,000 in annual property taxes. The property tax rate can be expressed in many forms (e.g., percentage, mills, and/or dollars owed per $100 or $1,000 of property value).

*Legal Annotation*: "The State's concession in the district court read as follows: 'If Plaintiffs are successful in challenging the restrictions on assessment ratios in Amendment 373 to the Alabama Constitution, and an injunction is issued, property in every classification would automatically be assessed at 100%, as opposed to the 10%, 20%, and 30% current ratios for residential, commercial, and utility property, respectively. . . . By way of example, Alabama taxpayers with a $100,000 home in a county with a **property tax rate** of 50 mills would see their annual property tax bill increase from $300 to $3,000, after taking into account the homestead exemption and the change in assessment ratio.'" *IL v. Alabama* (11th Cir., 2014).

## PROSPECTIVE NEED

**A projection of low- and moderate-income housing needs based on the development and growth that are reasonably likely to occur in a region or municipality.**

*Legal Annotation*: "Silver asserts that the Upper Southampton Township Zoning Ordinance results in a de facto exclusion of multi-family dwelling units because the area zoned for multi-family use is so small a percentage of the total area of the township that it constitutes a mere token response to the directive of the Pennsylvania Supreme Court in exclusionary zoning cases such as Girsh Appeal, 437 Pa. 237, 263 A.2d 395 (1970), that municipalities provide a 'fair share' of the region's present and **prospective need** for low and moderate income housing." *Silver Appeal* (Pa. Common. Ct., 1978).

## PROTECTED LANDSCAPE

**Defined geographic regions, usually lying within multiple jurisdictions, that possess common characteristics or resources in need of protection and that are subject to a uniform**

**set of land management policies and efforts administered by a regional, state, or federal entity.**

***Comment***: The National Wild and Scenic Rivers program (a federal initiative) is an example of the type of land included in a protected landscape program. (Source: Watson 2010: 14.)

***Legal Annotation***: "Plaintiffs challenge Defendants' no-use determination as to Irwin Park, claiming that Defendants never analyzed noise impacts on Irwin Park and that Defendants did not analyze the project's impact on **protected landscape** features of the park." *Honolulu Traffic Com v. Federal Transit Administration* (D. Hawaii, 2012).

## PROTECTED VIEW

**A legal requirement in land-use planning that seeks to preserve the view of a specific place or historic building from another location. See *Viewshed; Easement, Scenic; See Figure 106.***

***Comment***: Protected views are accomplished by limiting the height of new buildings within or adjacent to the sightline between two places so as to preserve the ability to view a landmark or scenic vista. For example, in Portland, Oregon, the height of buildings in certain downtown blocks is limited to preserve views of Mount Hood from the West Hills. Also referred to as "protected vista."

***Legal Annotation***: "The View Corridor was identified correctly as the Public View Corridor, compatible with the map under the revised legislation. The revised ordinance applied to the parties and all other similarly situated Oakland residents so that they would have a **protected view**. The parties then proceeded on the claim of a right to a view based on the changed ordinance." *Bishop v. Hanes* (Calif., Ct. App., 2011).

## PROTECTIVE COVENANT

See *Restrictive Covenant*.

***Legal Annotation***: "The restrictive or **protective covenant** is generally created by a grant in a deed or by reference in a deed to a general plan of development. Restrictive covenants have been interpreted to be covenants running with the land and enforceable not only between the original parties, but also upon subsequent owners of the realty." *Perry v. Bridgetown Cmty. Ass'n, Inc.(1230, 1232 (Miss., 1986).*

## PUB

See *Bar; Tavern*.

## PUBLIC ADMINISTRATION

**Legislative, judicial, administrative, and regulatory activities of federal, state, local, and international governmental agencies.**

***Comment***: Government-owned and -operated business establishments are excluded from this category and are classified in accordance with the major activity.

***Legal Annotation***: "The rationale of official immunity rests on the postulate that an effective **public administration** is best achieved when public officials, who are given discretionary functions to perform, are free from the intimidation of litigation and damages for the exercise of that function." *Newson v. City of Kansas City* (Mo. Ct. App., 1980).

## PUBLIC AREAS

**Parks, playgrounds, trails, paths, and other recreational areas and open spaces; scenic and historic sites; schools and other buildings and structures; and other places where the public is directly or indirectly invited to visit or permitted to congregate.**

***Comment***: Historically, all public areas were owned by a governmental agency. This is not necessarily the case any longer. For example, malls and shopping areas and private plazas with benches are public areas in the sense that they invite the public in to browse, sit, walk, and congregate. Shopping malls, for instance, have become popular meeting places for people. While legally private property, they are functionally public areas.

*Legal Annotation*: "**Public areas** are those to which the general public may readily gain admittance. In this case the regulations legitimately exclude certain specified locations." *Intern. Soc. for Krishna Consc. v. Rochford* (7th Cir., 1978).

## PUBLIC ASSEMBLY AREA

**Any area where large numbers of individuals collect to participate or to observe programs of participation.**

*Comment*: The most common public assembly areas are squares, auditoriums, stadiums, gymnasiums, or comparable facilities under different names—for example, field house, banquet room, and theater.

*Legal Annotation*: "The area in which petitioning, leafletting, demonstrating and soliciting [is] prohibited during permitted events and the designated public assembly area during permitted events [is] described below. . . . Union Square—The prohibited area is the western half (Powell Street side) of the Square. The **public assembly area** is the eastern half (Stockton Street side) of the Square." *Cuviello v. City and County of San Francisco* (N.D. Calif., 2013).

## PUBLIC BUILDING

**(1) Any building used exclusively for public purposes by any department or branch of government; (2) buildings of an institutional nature and serving a public need, such as houses of worship; hospitals; schools; libraries; museums; post offices; and police, rescue, and fire stations.**

*Legal Annotation*: "In determining whether a **public building** is open for use by the public, we must consider the nature of the building, the building's use, and any limiting criteria on the public's right to access." *Tellin v. Forsyth Township* (Mich. Ct. App., 2011).

## PUBLIC DEVELOPMENT PROPOSAL

**A master plan, redevelopment plan, capital improvement program, or other land development proposal or plan adopted by the appropriate public agency and including possible implementation options.**

*Comment*: A public development proposal identifies a concept plan, sketch, idea, or suggestion that has moved beyond the preliminary phase toward implementation.

## PUBLIC DOMAIN

**(1) Lands that are owned directly by the government; (2) the realm embracing property rights that belong to the community at large (www.merriam-webster.com/dictionary/public%20domain).**

*Legal Annotation*: "The fact that the path of glide taken by the planes was that approved by the Civil Aeronautics Authority does not change the result. The navigable airspace which Congress has placed in the **public domain** is 'airspace above the minimum safe altitudes of flight prescribed by the Civil Aeronautics Authority.'" *United States v. Causby* (U.S., 1946).

## PUBLIC DRAINAGE WAY

**Land owned or controlled by a governmental agency that is reserved or dedicated for the installation of stormwater sewers or drainage ditches, or is required along a natural stream or watercourse for preserving the channel and providing for the flow of water so as to safeguard the public against flood damage, sedimentation, and erosion.**

*Legal Annotation*: "For purpose of preserving the integrity of the official map of a municipality no permit shall be issued for any building or structure in the bed on any street or **public drainage way**, flood control basin or public area reserved pursuant to section 23 hereof as shown on the official map, or shown on a plat filed pursuant to this act before the adoption of the official map, except as herein provided." *Barsel v. Woodbridge Tp. Bd. Adj.* (N.J. App. Div., 1983).

## PUBLIC FACILITY

**A facility such as a road, school, or sewage treatment plant financed by public revenues**

**and available for use by the public. http://www.pgplanning.org/Resources/Tools_Online/Glossary.htm**

***Legal Annotation***: "The legislature, however, has recently defined the term '**public facility**' in a statutory provision entitled 'Water Conservation Board and Compacts.' . . . This provision states: '**Public facility**' means any facility operated by an instrument of government *for the benefit of the public* including, but not limited to, a governmental building, park or other recreational facility, school, college, university, or other educational institution, highway, hospital, or stadium. . . . Hence, the determinative factor in defining a **public facility** is whether the facility is operated 'for the benefit of the public.'" *City and County of Denver v. Gallegos* (Colo., 1996).

## PUBLIC GARAGE

**See *Garage, Public*.**

## PUBLIC HEARING

**A meeting announced and advertised in advance and open to the public, with the public given an opportunity to ask questions, comment, and participate.**

***Comment***: Public hearings are often required before adoption or implementation of a master plan, project, ordinance, or similar activity that will have an effect on the public.

***Legal Annotation***: "A '**public hearing**' is defined as 'a formal meeting held pursuant to public notice by the governing body or planning agency, intended to inform and obtain public comment, prior to taking action.'" *Gladstone Partners, LP v. East Union Tp*. (Pa: Common. Ct., 2011).

## PUBLIC HOUSING

**Housing that is constructed, bought, owned, or rented and operated by a local housing authority for households meeting designated income limits. See *Local Housing Authority; Low-Income Housing*.**

***Legal Annotation***: "After concluding that the housing authority was engaged in a governmental function, the Moore Court considered the exceptions to immunity. . . . The Court wrote, 'We conclude that a unit of **public housing** is a building "used in connection with the performance of a governmental function" within the meaning of [statute]. [The housing authority] is therefore liable for negligence if the deaths in this case were due to physical defects occurring on its property within the meaning of [statute].'" *DeMartino v. Poland Local School District* (Ohio Ct. App., 2011).

## PUBLIC IMPROVEMENT

**Any improvement, facility, or service, together with its associated site or right-of-way, necessary to provide transportation, drainage, utilities, or similar essential services and facilities and that is usually owned and operated by a governmental agency.**

***Comment***: The requirement that public improvements be owned and operated by a governmental agency is changing. Public improvements may be owned by a governmental agency and leased to a private entity to provide the service or operate a facility. Conversely, the government may lease a private facility to carry out a governmental function. In both situations, the improvement, facility, or service is still considered a public improvement.

***Legal Annotation***: "The phrase '**public improvement**' is defined in R.C. 4115.03(C) to include 'all buildings, roads, streets, alleys, sewers, ditches, sewage disposal plants, water works, and all other structures or works constructed by a public authority of the state or any political subdivision thereof or by any person who, pursuant to a contract with a public authority, constructs any structure for a public authority of the state or a political subdivision thereof.'" *Ohio Valley Associated v. DeBra-Kuempel* (Ohio Ct. App., 2011).

## PUBLIC NOTICE

**The advertisement of a public hearing in a paper of general circulation, and through other**

**media sources, indicating the time, place, and nature of the public hearing and where the application and pertinent documents may be inspected.**

***Legal Annotation***: "Defendants argue that zoning ordinance BT-1 is void because the City of Killeen failed to provide proper **public notice** of the zoning ordinance prior to its adoption as required by Article 1011d, Tex.Rev.Civ. . . . : 'The legislative body of such municipality shall provide for the manner in which such regulations and restrictions and the boundaries of such districts shall be determined, established, and enforced, and from time to time amended, supplemented, or changed. However, no such regulation, restriction, or boundary shall become effective until after a public hearing in relation thereto, at which parties in interest and citizens shall have an opportunity to be heard. At least 15 days' notice of the time and place of such hearing shall be published in an official paper, or a paper of general circulation, in such municipality.'" *Hitchcock v. City of Killeen* (Texas Ct. App., 1977).

## PUBLIC RESTROOMS

**A room or small building containing one or more toilets, and possibly also urinals, which are available for use by the general public, or by customers of other services. (Source: Akoi 2009, 36.)**

***Legal Annotation***: "In this case, the hypothetical posed by the ALJ did not realistically set forth all of the limitations that this particular plaintiff possesses. Initially, the ALJ did not address the problems associated with periodic catheterization other than conclusory statements regarding the fact that **public restrooms** are as clean as private restrooms." *Taylor v. Bowen* (D. Idaho, 1988).

## PUBLIC OPEN SPACE

**See *Open Space, Public*.**

***Legal Annotation***: "The landowners spent most of the next year revising their proposal and taking other steps to fulfill the city's conditions. Their final plan, submitted in 1985, devoted 17.9 of the 37.6 acres to **public open space** (including a public beach and areas for the restoration and preservation of the buckwheat habitat), 7.9 acres to open, landscaped areas, and 6.7 acres to public and private streets (including public parking and access to the beach). Only 5.1 acres were allocated to buildings and patios." *Monterey v. Del Monte Dunes at Monterey, Ltd.* (U.S., 1999).

## PUBLIC/PRIVATE PARTNERSHIP (PPP)

**The provision of a public service or project where there is cooperation between the public and private sectors.**

***Comment***: Such partnerships are undertaken via a contract between a governmental entity and a private party. In many cases the cost is borne by those using the service or those who benefit from the project, and not by the taxpayer. In other cases, the cost of providing the service may be borne partially or wholly by the government. An example of a PPP would be a parking garage financed and constructed by a private developer and then leased to a parking authority. The private developer acts as landlord, providing maintenance, while the parking authority operates the garage itself.

***Legal Annotation***: "As we understand the term, a '**public-private partnership**' is 'a project in which there is cooperation between the public and private sectors in one or more areas of the design, development, construction, operation, ownership or financing of infrastructure assets, or in the provision of services. Compared to traditional procurement methods, the private sector assumes a greater role in the planning, financing, design, construction, operation and maintenance of public facilities or service delivery.'" *Coastside Fishing Club v. Cal. Resources Agency* (Calif. Ct. App., 2008).

## PUBLIC SERVICE

**A service relating to the health, safety, and welfare of the population.**

***Comment***: The term is often used in defining inherently beneficial uses or public utilities.

*Legal Annotation*: "In expanding upon the first factor of this test, we suggested that a '**public service**' is one that exhibits some or all of the following characteristics: (1) it concerns a business of a type generally thought suitable for public regulation;

(2) the party seeking exculpation is engaged in performing a service of great importance to the public and which is often a matter of practical necessity for some members of the public;

(3) such party holds itself out as willing to perform this service for any member of the public who seeks it, or at least for any member coming within certain established standards;

(4) because of the essential nature of the service, and the economic setting of the transaction, the party invoking exculpation possesses a decisive advantage of bargaining strength against any member of the public who seeks such service;

(5) in exercising a superior bargaining power, the party confronts the public with a standardized adhesion contract of exculpation, and makes no provision whereby a purchaser may pay additional reasonable fees to obtain protection against negligence;

(6) the person or property of members of the public seeking such services must be placed under the control of the furnisher of the services, subject to the risk of carelessness on the part of such furnisher or its servants." *Brown ex rel. Brown v. Genesis Healthcare* (W.Va., 2011).

## PUBLIC SEWER SYSTEM

**Any sewer system that is operated by a municipality, governmental agency, or public utility for the collection, treatment, and disposal of wastes.**

*Legal Annotation*: "A **public sewer system** is a public utility the same as a water system." *Ripperger v. City of Grand Rapids* (Mich., 1954).

## PUBLIC TRANSIT SYSTEM

**Any vehicle or transportation system owned, operated, or regulated by a governmental agency and used for the mass transport of people.**

*Legal Annotation*: "[B]ecause the MBTA is a **public transit system** operating in a public place and uses cameras, the two alleged victims here were not in a place and circumstance where they reasonably would or could have had an expectation of privacy." *Commonwealth v. Robertson* (Mass., 2014).

## PUBLIC UTILITY

**A closely regulated enterprise with a franchise for providing to the public a utility service deemed necessary for the public health, safety, and welfare.**

*Comment*: All states regulate public utilities, but the kinds of uses that are classified as a public utility differ from state to state. For example, cellular telephone service is classified as a public utility in New York but not in New Jersey. The threshold question as to whether a use is a public utility is whether it is so defined in the applicable state legislation. When it is, it obviously must be considered a public utility; even if it is not defined as such, it may still be a public utility for zoning purposes if it has the following characteristics:

- Provides a service that is essential to the public health, safety, and general welfare. This critical criterion rules out radio stations, which, while important, are not essential to public health, safety, and general welfare.
- Is regulated by a governmental agency. The regulatory agency may be a federal or state agency. (In the example of cellular phones, the Federal Communications Commission is the regulatory agency, regardless of whether the state also regulates them.)
- Is granted an exclusive or near-exclusive franchise for a specific geographic area. (At one time, public utilities were given exclusive rights to provide the service in the franchised area. In recent years, more than one utility may be permitted to operate in a geographic area.)
- Is required to provide service to all who apply within its franchised area.
- May have the right of condemnation.

- Is usually exempt from local development requirements or can appeal such requirements to an administrative agency.

***Legal Annotation***: "It is an essential requirement that a business or enterprise must in some way be impressed with a public interest before it may become a public utility. Accordingly, whether the operator of a given business or enterprise is a **public utility** depends on whether or not the service rendered by it is of a public character and of public consequence and concern, which is a question necessarily dependent on the facts of the particular case." *US Steel Corp. v. Northern Ind. Pub. Serv.* (Ind. Ct. App., 1985).

## PUBLIC UTILITY EASEMENT

**A right granted by an owner of property to a public utility or governmental agency to erect and maintain poles, wires, pipes, or conduits on, across, or under the land, for telephone, electric power, gas, water, sewers, or other utility services. See *Easement, Utility*.**

***Legal Annotation***: "Ardmore subdivision, located north of McNichols road and east of Evergreen road in the city of Detroit, consists of 212 residential lots on 4 streets running north from McNichols. Three of these streets are 60 feet wide, one is 80 feet wide, and the lots generally have a 40-foot frontage. There are no alleys in the rear, but a **public-utility easement** is provided." *Ardmore Association v. Bankle* (Mich., 1951).

## PUBLIC UTILITY FACILITIES

**Buildings, structures, and facilities, including generating and switching stations, poles, lines, pipes, pumping stations, repeaters, antennas, transmitters and receivers, valves, and all buildings and structures relating to the furnishing of utility services, such as electric, gas, telephone, water, sewer, and public transit, to the public.**

***Legal Annotation***: "The public interest also favors moving very cautiously in condemning private property for uses that are only questionably public. Eminent domain is commonly used to acquire land to build highways and railways. **Public utility facilities** such as power plants, water treatment facilities also have the traditional public use character, as does the construction of government buildings." *Cottonwood Christian Center v. Cypress Redev. Ag.* (C.D. Calif., 2002).

## PUBLIC WATER SYSTEM

**Any system, other than an individual well, that is operated by a governmental entity, agency, or utility for the furnishing of potable water.**

***Legal Annotation***: "Pursuant to statutes enacted to govern the public health system, a '**public water system**' is defined as 'any water supply or system that regularly supplies or offers to supply water for human consumption through pipes or other constructed conveyances, if serving at least an average of twenty-five individuals per day for at least sixty days per year, or which has at least fifteen service connections, and shall include: (1) Any collection, treatment, storage and distribution facilities under the control of the owner or operator of such system and used primarily in connection with such system; and (2) any collection or pretreatment storage facilities not under such control which are used primarily in connection with such system.'" *Jefferson Utilities v. Jefferson County* (W.Va., 2005).

## PUBLIC WIRELESS ACCESS (WI-FI)

**The provision of wireless Internet access so that it is available to anyone throughout a specific defined area.**

***Comment***: This is a highly controversial effort to provide free Internet access to residents, visitors, and businesses, as a means of spurring economic development. It is opposed by private companies that provide the same service for a fee. (Source: Gale 2009, 24.)

***Legal Annotation***: "Literally billions of contacts from the address books of tens of millions of unsuspecting wireless mobile device owners have now been accessed and stolen. The surreptitious data uploads—occurring over both cellular networks and open, **public wireless access** nodes in homes, coffee shops, restaurants, bars, stores and businesses all across the nation—have, quite literally, turned the address book owners' wireless mobile devices into mobile radio beacons broadcasting and publicly exposing the unsuspecting device owner's address book data to the world." *Opperman v. Path, Inc.* (W.D. Texas, 2012).

## PUBLIC WORKS

**Things constructed by the government at public expense for general public use, such as highways and public buildings (Johnsich 1991).**

***Legal Annotation***: "'**Public works**' are defined in pertinent part in section 1720, subdivision (a) as:

'(1) Construction, alteration, demolition, installation, or repair work done under contract and *paid for in whole or in part out of public funds. . . .* For purposes of this paragraph, "construction" includes work performed during the design and preconstruction phases of construction including, but not limited to, inspection and land surveying work.

(2) Work done for irrigation, utility, reclamation, and improvement districts, and other districts of this type. . . .

(3) *Street, sewer, or other improvement work* done under the direction and supervision or by the authority of any officer or public body of the state, or of any political subdivision or district thereof.'" *Azusa Land Partners v. Department of Industrial Relations* (Calif. Ct. App., 2010).

## PULVERIZATION

**The crushing or grinding of material into small pieces.**

***Legal Annotation***: "In light of the general rule provided by section 613(c)(5) that **pulverization** is a nonmining process, and Congress' refusal to extend the **pulverization** exception in section 613(c)(4)(E) to tripoli, we must carefully examine petitioner's contentions that fine pulverization of 'Seneca Standard' tripoli is, nevertheless, a mining process, or necessary or incidental thereto under either section 613(c)(4)(C) or section 613(c)(4)(D)." *Carborundum Co. v. Commissioner* (Tax Ct., 1978).

## PUMPING STATION

**A building or structure containing the necessary equipment to pump a fluid to a higher level.**

***Legal Annotation***: "The only mention of other permitted uses came during the following exchange between a Board member and counsel for the Archdiocese: 'Mr. Gonzales: Just looking at the other permitted uses, if the Archdiocese so chose to use this within the R-10A, what is allowed in the R-10A district, you could have professional offices. You could have art galleries. You could turn this into a place of worship, a library, telephone exchange building. You could have a surgical hospital here. You could have a medical hospital. You could have a water and sewage **pumping station**, most of which I think would provide more congestion to the neighborhood in terms of parking and traffic.'" *Marshall v. City of Philadelphia* (Pa. Common. Ct., 2012).

## PUTRESCIBLE

**Capable of being decomposed by microorganisms with sufficient rapidity to cause nuisances from odors or gases.**

***Legal Annotation***: "'**Putrescible** waste' is defined in paragraph (7.1) of the ordinance as 'those wastes which are capable of being quickly decomposed by microorganisms.' These wastes include 'kitchen wastes, animal manure, offal, hatchery and poultry processing plant wastes and garbage' as well as 'those wastes which have the capacity to create noxious odors or to attract flies and other flying insects.'" *Mullis Tree Service, Inc. v. Bibb County, Ga.* (M.D. Ga., 1993).

# Q

## QUADRUPLEX

See *Dwelling, Quadruplex.*

## QUARRY

**An open pit mine from which building materials (sand, gravel, construction aggregate) and dimension stone are excavated from the ground. See *Extractive Industries*.**

***Legal Annotation***: "Sukut contends that **Quarry** is a 'mine' and the hard rock products extracted from it are 'minerals' within the meaning of the Public Resources Code; therefore, Sukut was entitled to record and enforce a mining lien under Civil Code section 3060. . . . The California Supreme Court stated that a **quarry** 'is distinguished from a mine in the fact that it is usually open at the top and front . . . and, in the ordinary acceptation of the term, in the character of the material extracted. . . . It is a place, generally open at top and front, from which rock or stone is extracted solely because of its value for use elsewhere, just as gold or other precious metals are removed from a mine.'" *Sukut Construction, Inc. v. Rimrock CA LLC* (Calif. Ct. App., 2011).

## QUALITY OF LIFE

**The attributes or amenities that combine to make an area a desirable place to live.**

***Comment***: Examples of attributes or amenities include the availability of political, educational, and social support systems; good relations among constituent groups; a safe and healthy physical environment; and economic opportunities for both individuals and businesses.

***Legal Annotation***: "In his dissent, however, Justice Lambert disputed the constitutionality of a statute 'which has as its only standard the subjective requirement of `best interest of the child,' adding that 'mere improvement in **quality of life** is not a compelling state interest and is insufficient to justify invasion of constitutional rights.'" *Hawk v. Hawk* (Tenn., 1993).

## QUARTER-SECTION

**A tract of land one-half mile square, 2,640 feet by 2,640 feet, or 160 acres.**

***Legal Annotation***: "The disputed northern boundary of the Lanhams' property, however, lies along a line which is 86 poles 9 links north and running parallel to the southern boundary of the same quarter section. Since a **quarter section** is, by definition, 160 poles square, there is an overlapping of the boundaries by 6 poles 9 links (approximately 35 yards)." *Lanham v. Marley* (Ind. Ct. App., 1985).

## QUASI-JUDICIAL

**Public officials whose acts are functionally comparable to those of a judge, and hence are personally immune from lawsuits.**

***Comment***: Their three features are: (1) performing a traditional adjudicating function, deciding facts, applying law, and resolving disputes on the merits; (2) deciding cases that can be so controversial that without immunity would be subject to suits for damages; (3) operated under a system of safeguards designed to protect the parties' constitutional rights.

***Legal Annotation***: "A zoning board engaged in **quasi-judicial** determinations, as this one was, is subject to constraints that do not apply to a legislature. When we review the constitutionality of its actions, we must do so on the basis of its actual conduct and the facts in the record before it. The constitutionality of the **quasi-judicial** action of an administrative agency is not reviewed with the deference given legislative enactments, and the actions of such a board are not sanitized by post-hoc conjecture concerning the factual determinations it might conceivably have made. When a challenge creates a genuine dispute of material fact relating to the rationality of the actions of a zoning board, the plaintiff's right to a trial on the merits must not be buried in a shroud of affidavits." *Shelton v. City of College Station* (5th Cir., 1986).

## QUASI-PUBLIC USE

**A use owned or operated by a nonprofit, religious, or eleemosynary institution and providing educational, cultural, recreational, religious, or similar types of programs.**

*Legal Annotation*: "Plaintiff, Mount Elliott Cemetery Association, appeals from the entry of summary judgment in favor of defendant, the City of Troy (City), in this action to challenge the City Council's refusal to rezone certain property for use as a Catholic cemetery. . . . At a regular meeting held May 22, 1995, the City Council followed the recommendation of the Planning Commission and denied the rezoning request by a vote of 6-1, offering the following six reasons in support of denial: . . . (6) abuts developed land and is not considered a **quasi-public** use." *Mount Elliott Cemetery Ass'n v. City of Troy* (6th Cir., 1999).

## QUIET ENJOYMENT

**The right of an owner or occupant to the use of property without interference of possession (Johnsich 1991).**

*Legal Annotation*: "Under the village's zoning requirements, Blackhawk could not build on the parcel. Blackhawk's **quiet enjoyment** of the parcel would not be impermissibly disturbed by increased traffic whether on the new access drives or on several lanes of through traffic." *Blackhawk Dev. Corp. v. Village of Dexter* (Mich., 2005).

## QUIET ZONE

**A section of a rail line where trains are prohibited from sounding their horns as they approach grade crossings as a result of the installation of approved alternate safety features.**

*Comment*: By federal law, all trains approaching street-level grade crossings are required to sound their horns four times for fifteen to twenty seconds at a sound level of between ninety to one hundred twenty decibels. The law also provided that the Federal Railroad Administration (FRA) develop procedures whereby a quiet zone could be established without compromising safety. In 2005, the so-called "Final Rule" was published (Title 49 Code of Federal Regulation, parts 222 and 229), which established national standards and uniform procedures for communities seeking quiet-zone designations.

Establishing a quiet-zone designation is costly and must be borne by the public entity seeking the designation. It may require for, example, the installation of supplementary safety measures such as four quadrant gates, median barriers, automatic gates, and flashing lights. The requirements are set forth in the Federal Highway Administration's *Manual on Uniform Traffic Control Devices* (FHWA-under Title 23 CFR, Part 655, Subpart F).

*Legal Annotation*: "On February 19, 2009, the City of Flagstaff ('City') filed an application for approval to upgrade two crossings by installing additional audible warning devices, wayside horns. The City sought to create a Quiet Zone in accordance with title 49, section 222 of the Code of Federal Regulations ('C.F.R'). The two crossings, the Steves Boulevard crossing and the Fanning Drive crossing, would be included in this **Quiet Zone**. The application also indicated that three other crossings would be included in the **Quiet Zone**; however, they would not require modifications subject to the Commission's approval." *BNSF Railway Company v. Arizona Corporation Commission* (Ariz. Ct. App., 2012).

## QUORUM

**A majority of the full authorized membership of a board or agency.**

***Comment***: In general, no public agency meeting may be held in the absence of a quorum, except to adjourn the meeting to a specified date and time. Once a quorum is present, all actions may be taken by a majority vote of those present and eligible to vote. Failure to receive the number of votes required for approval constitutes a denial. In those applications for development in which a simple majority of the vote would suffice, a tie vote amounts to a denial.

A member of a public body who abstains from voting is, under the common law rule, counted toward a quorum and is regarded as having assented to the vote of the majority. However, when a statute requires the *affirmative* vote of a majority to approve a measure, it has been held that one who abstains from voting cannot be considered as having voted affirmatively (Cox 2003).

***Legal Annotation***: "The Township's Open Records Officer must first determine, by conducting a good faith review, if the requested emails were exchanged for the purpose of deliberation of the Township's business by a **quorum** of the Supervisors within the meaning of the Sunshine Act. . . . Section 704 of the Sunshine Act provides that '[o]fficial action and deliberations by a **quorum** of the members of an agency shall take place at a meeting open to the public unless closed under section 707 (relating to exceptions to open meetings), 708 (relating to executive sessions) or 712 (relating to General Assembly meetings covered) . . . A **quorum** is two members of a three-member board of supervisors.'" *Mollick v. Township of Worcester* (Pa. Common. Ct. 2011).

# R

## RACQUET SPORTS

**Court games played with a racquet and ball, either indoors or outdoors, on various surfaces.**

*Legal Annotation*: "Because no abuse is manifest in the board's conclusion that the location was in fact devoted to Shannopin's non-conforming use, Shannopin is therefore entitled to erect a structure in furtherance of that use. Clearly, the construction of tennis courts is a natural expansion of Shannopin's country club activity; the increasing demand for **racquet sports** facilities as alternative recreational activities is plain in our society today." *Muse et al. v. ZHB, Ben Avon Hts. Boro. et al.* (Pa. Common. Ct., 1980).

## RADIAL STREET SYSTEM

**A pattern of streets converging on a central point or area. *See Figure* 77.**

*Legal Annotation*: "Both sides called expert witnesses—the Government's experts premised their opinions on the height and bulk of the

**Figure 77**

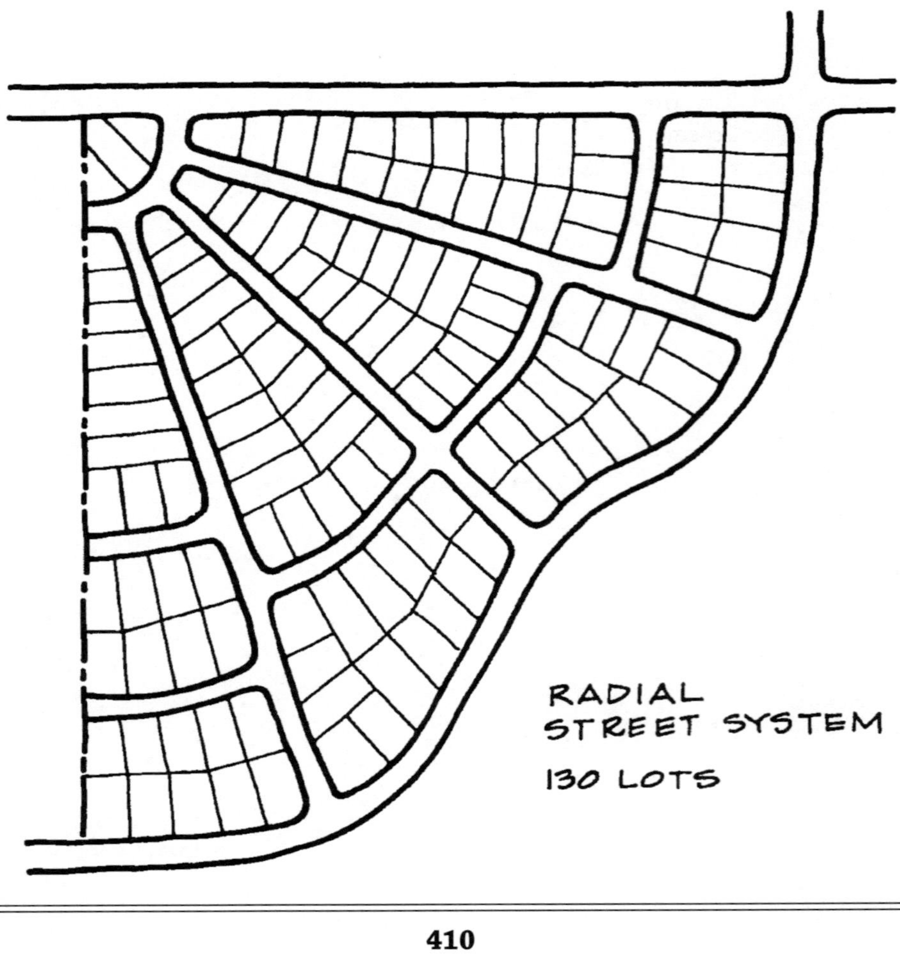

buildings protruding over the tree line on the Virginia Ridge—one said the [high buildings] tend to interfere with the perception of the general visitor to Washington and its immediate area in terms of its historical role as a horizontal city dominated by the dome of the Capitol, and as a pilgrimage site for the great national memorials of this Nation. Another said they would detract from the enjoyment of the basic principal of the plan developed over the last 100 years, which was, essentially, the radial vistas, the **radial street** plan, and the horizontal nature of the Capital as a whole within the region. Another said they would dominate the background—all said they would be visual intrusions on the monumental core." *US v. County Bd. of Arlington County* (E.D. Va., 1979).

## RADIATION

**Energy that propagates through space.**

***Comment***: While laypeople use the term with particular reference to ionizing radiation (as produced by a nuclear reactor, for example), the energy can be in any form: acoustic (as in ultrasonic radiation), light (as from a flashlight), high-energy particles (as cosmic radiation), high-energy photons (as X-rays), and radio-frequency electromagnetic fields.

***Legal Annotation***: "According to the FCC, however, 'the evidence for production of harmful biological effects [from low-level RF **radiation**] is ambiguous and unproven.' OET Bulletin 8. Results from studies have been 'inconclusive,' and 'while the possibility of "non-thermal" biological effects may exist, whether or not such effects might indicate a human health hazard is not presently known.' Id. In light of the present state of the science, the FCC has stated that any cell phone legally sold in the United States is a 'safe' phone." *Farina v. Nokia, Inc.* (3rd Cir., 2010).

## RADIATION STANDARDS

**Regulations that include exposure standards, permissible concentrations, and regulations for transportation of radioactive material.**

***Legal Annotation***: "'To date the Commission has declined to preempt on health and safety matters. However, the Commission has noted that should non-Federal RF **radiation standards** be adopted that adversely affect a licensee's ability to engage in Commission-authorized activities, the Commission would consider reconsidering whether Federal action is necessary.' . . . The FCC has always reserved the question of the preemptive authority of its RF regulations pending the existence of an actual conflict, and its current position is consistent with that approach. Accordingly, we think the FCC's position on preemption merits deference." *Farina v. Nokia, Inc.* (3rd Cir., 2010).

## RADIO AND TELEVISION BROADCASTING STATION

**An establishment engaged in transmitting oral and visual programs to the public and which consists of a studio, transmitter, tower, and antenna(s). See *Studio*.**

***Comment***: The studio for a radio or television broadcasting station may be located some distance from the transmitter and antenna. The transmitter and antennas must be located close to each other. See *Wireless Telecommunications Towers And Facilities*.

***Legal Annotation***: "It is alleged in the complaint that on February 18, 1952, plaintiff leased from the defendant certain premises of the Towne Hotel in Milwaukee for the purpose of conducting a **radio and television broadcasting station** and studios." *Midwest Broadcasting Co. v. Dolero Hotel Co.* (Wis., 1956).

## RADIO FREQUENCY

**That part of the electromagnetic spectrum employed by many communications and broadcast applications.**

***Comment***: The exact frequency range to which this refers is defined variously by different authors. The Federal Communications Commission refers to radio-frequency energy as that part of the electromagnetic spectrum between 300 kilohertz (KHz) and 100 gigahertz (GHz).

***Legal Annotation***: "We further hold that the City's order to remove the tower antenna is supported by substantial evidence and is in compliance with state and federal laws in that it does not constitute an undue interference with amateur radio communications permitted by state and federal law. But to the extent the ordinance purports to regulate **radio frequency** interference, such regulation is preempted by federal law." *Zubarau v. City of Palmdale* (Calif. Ct. App., 2011).

## RADIOACTIVE WASTES

**The by-products of nuclear reactors and military, industrial, and medical activities using radioactive material.**

***Comment***: Disposal and storage of radioactive wastes is a major concern. Storage sites should be safe from natural disasters (such as hurricanes and earthquakes), away from population centers, and accessible without traversing heavily populated areas (Schultz and Kasen 1984).

***Legal Annotation***: "'**Radioactive waste**' means all material which is discarded, unwanted or has no present lawful economic use, and contains mined or refined naturally occurring isotopes, accelerator produced isotopes and by-product material, source material or special nuclear material . . ." *Forelaws v. Bd. of Energy Fac. Siitng Coun.* (Ore., 1988).

## RAILBANKING

**"One mechanism for converting rail corridors that are not currently being used as active railroads to other purposes without actually 'abandoning' the line". http://www.ibike.org/engineering/glossary.htm. See *Rails-To-Trails*.**

***Comment***: "Railbanking is a procedure and series of agreements where the railroad puts the corridor into 'savings' with a local government which 'lends' it out and allows the public intermediate use of the corridor. Under the agreement it is understood that should the railroad want to use the corridor again for a railroad they can 'withdraw' the corridor from the 'bank'. The law providing for railbanking was upheld unanimously by the United States Supreme Court in 1990". http://www.ibike.org/engineering/glossary.htm.

***Legal Annotation***: "RLTD owns a railroad corridor, approximately one hundred feet wide and fifteen miles long, that traverses plaintiff. The National Trails System Act (NTA) provides that jurisdiction over such rail corridors is vested with the Interstate Commerce Commission, which has subsequently become known as the Federal Surface Transportation Board (STB). . . . Pursuant to the NTA, RLTD sought permission from the STB to abandon the rail line so that it could be used by defendant LTA as a rail-trail (a process known as '**railbanking**')." *Township of Bingham v. RLTD Railroad Corporation* (Mich. Ct. App., 1998).

## RAILROAD YARD

**An area for the storage and repair of trains.**

***Comment***: Railroad yards may include open storage yards, rail-switching equipment, roundhouses, and workshops.

***Legal Annotation***: "A **railroad yard** is not a nuisance per se. Ga. R. & Bkg. Co. v. Maddox, 116 Ga. 64 (42 SE 315). In the last cited case several residents in a residential section of the City of Atlanta sought to restrain the defendant railroad from operating a terminal yard located on its right of way near the residences of the plaintiffs. It was there held that where a railroad terminal yard is located and its construction authorized under statutory powers, if it be constructed and operated in the proper manner it cannot be adjudged a nuisance." *City of Doraville v. Southern Railway Company* (Ga., 1971).

## RAILS-TO-TRAILS

**"The conversion of abandoned railroad rights-of-way to non-motorized trails". http://www.ibike.org/engineering/glossary.htm. See *Railbanking*.**

***Comment***: "Such trails may be public or private; free or requiring a user fee. In the USA, much of this effort is being spearhead by the Rail-To-Trails Conservancy". http://www.ibike.org/engineering/glossary.htm.

***Legal Annotation***: "Although we conclude King County, upon these allegations, has violated

Const. art. 1, § 16, we do not find both RCW 64.04.180 and RCW 64.04.190 offensive. RCW 64.04.180 merely states the public interest in maintaining railroad rights of way as public thoroughfares. To the extent it may be argued this statute is also meant to suggest that '**rails to trails**' is a permissible change in use, we have already rejected that suggestion. We hold RCW 64.04.190 unconstitutional as applied insofar as it purports to authorize King County to acquire without payment of just compensation existing reversionary interests which follow easements for railroad purposes only. It is unnecessary for us to decide whether the statute can be constitutionally applied to some more remote and speculative type of interest." *Lawson v. State* (Wash., 1986).

## RAINFALL, EXCESS

**The portion of rainfall that becomes direct surface runoff.**

***Legal Annotation***: "On June 12, 2003, water and sewage began flowing into Hubbell's home in Xenia through drains in a shower, a toilet, and a bathroom sink. The sewage included human waste, tampons, and cigarette butts. Believing that the problem was likely caused by a malfunction in the public sewer system maintained by Xenia, to which her house was connected, Hubbell placed a telephone call to an Emergency Services number provided by the City of Xenia Public Services Department. . . . His [an on-call sewer and waste maintenance worker] belief that the problem resulted from **excess rainfall** is an individual determination." *Hubbell v. Xenia* (Ohio Ct. App., 2008).

## RAISED CROSSWALKS

**See *Traffic Calming*.**

***Legal Annotation***: "The record was finally closed on October 14, 2009, and the Board issued a lengthy decision approving the revised final stadium plan subject to several conditions, including requirements that the parking lot exit drive be reconfigured to prohibit right turns onto Anderson Road and two **raised crosswalks** be installed to comply with the Ordinance." *Jeff v. Buckingham Township* (Pa. Common. Ct., 2012).

## RAISED INTERSECTIONS

**See *Traffic Calming*.**

***Legal Annotation***: "A cold patch was applied to **raised intersections** and man-hole covers resulting in a tapered surface for vehicles to pass over. On the date of the accident, construction was going on and various pieces of construction equipment and supplies were scattered along the transit way." *Farnese v. Southeast. Penn. Transp. Auth.* (Pa., 1985).

## RAMP

**(1) A sloping walkway, roadway, or passage used to join and provide a smooth transition between two levels of different elevations; (2) a driveway leading to a parking aisle. *See Figure 30.***

***Comment***: For ramps accessible to persons with disabilities, the Americans with Disabilities Act specifies a maximum slope of one to twelve (8.33 percent).

***Legal Annotation***: "By letter on or about July 20, 2007, the Long Island Housing Services ('LIHS') sent Fairfield a reasonable accommodation specification. . . . The following accommodations were requested by the LIHS: (1) accessible building entrance on an accessible route; (2) curb **ramps** or access aisles at the dwelling entrances. . . . [T]he Court has already determined that the ordinary and plain meaning of the terms rule, policy, practice, or service do not encompass the installation of **ramps** or the widening of doorways, [and] the Court finds that the text and structure of § 3604(f)(3) as a whole also supports the same conclusion." *Reyes v. Fairfield Properties* (E.D.N.Y., 2009).

## RANCH

**A place where livestock are bred and/or raised but that does not include a concentrated animal feeding operation. See *Concentrated Animal Feeding Operation*.**

***Legal Annotation***: "The second governing statutory provision is section . . . which defines a '**Ranch**' as a 'parcel of land which is used for grazing livestock for the primary purpose of obtaining a monetary profit.'" *Douglas Co. Bd. of Equalization v. Clarke* (Colo., 1996).

## RANCHETTE

**(1) A single dwelling unit occupied by a non-farming household on a parcel that has been subdivided from agricultural land; (2) a small ranch, typically only a few acres, used more for leisure or retirement purposes than for commercial farming.**

***Comment*:** This term, in the first definition, is used by developers to give some cachet to relatively large lots located in rural or exurban areas. To qualify as a farm for tax assessment purposes, state regulations establish minimum acreage and annual farming income that have to be met.

***Legal Annotation*:** "The rural residential designation, of which five acre lots are a component, functions as an intermediary or buffer between the large-lot agricultural (range and timberland) areas and the more urban (estate and single-family) residential areas. It affords residents the opportunity to live near agricultural areas in a '**ranchette**' type of environment, thus serving as an integral component in the spectrum of housing types and densities provided by the MDGP." *Twain Harte Homeowners Assn. v. Cty. of Tuolumne* (Calif. Ct. App., 1982).

## RASP

**A device used to grate solid waste into a more manageable material, ridding it of much of its odor.**

## RATABLE

**An improvement producing revenues to the taxing authority.**

***Legal Annotation*:** "Further, Hillburn was looking for a tax **ratable**, as well as a way to provide new jobs to the community. Hillburn, in fact, had shown considerable interest in placement of a corporate headquarters, or some other type of prestigious, Class A office building, on the site, given the visibility of the parcel, and thus any structure thereon, from the neighboring highways." *In the Matter of Application of Rockland County Sewer Dist. No. 1 v. Split Rock Partnership* (N.Y. Sup. Ct., 2012).

## RATABLE PROPERTY

**Real property subject to tax by a municipality or other taxing district.**

***Legal Annotation*:** "Plaintiffs rely on the Black's Law Dictionary definition of 'assessment' to argue that the 'date of assessment' is solely the date when the value of the **ratable property** is determined and not the actual date that the tax is imposed." *Andrade v. Town of Lincoln* (R.I. Super. Ct., 2014).

## RATIONAL METHOD

**A method of surface water runoff calculation.**

***Legal Annotation*:** "Speedway argues the circuit court erred by affirming the Board's decision that the ALJ erred by concluding the **rational method** was appropriately used to calculate stormwater runoff rates. It claims the applicable regulation provides OCRM with the flexibility to permit use of the rational method even when the project site is greater than 20 acres. Speedway further claims there is substantial evidence in the record which supports use of the rational method for its project and, therefore, OCRM properly applied its discretion to grant the permit application which used this method. We agree." *Brown v. SC DHEC* (S.C., 2002).

## RATIONAL NEXUS

**A clear, direct, and substantial relationship between a particular development and the off-tract public improvement needs generated by the development.**

***Comment*:** Rational nexus is an important method for apportioning the cost of off-tract improvements. See *Linkage Programs; Off-Tract Improvement.*

***Legal Annotation*:** "In Count Four, entitled 'Inverse Condemnation', the Plaintiff complains that the City demanded exactions that were unlawful because there 'was no **rational nexus** or rough proportionality between the actual impacts of the projects and the financial responsibility demanded by the City from Weiss.'" *Weiss v. City of Gainesville* (N.D. Fla., 2010).

## RAVINE

**(1) A long, deep hollow in the earth's surface; (2) a valley with sharply sloping walls created by the action of stream waters.**

***Legal Annotation***: "The court also determined that the lots would ordinarily 'merge' into a single parcel once they were subsequently brought into common ownership, but that merger of Lots 19 and 20 was not appropriate because the 'steepness, size, and placement' of a **ravine** located on the dividing line between the two lots 'prevents them from being used functionally as one property.'" *Appeal of Weeks* (Vt., 1998).

## RAW LAND

**Land in its natural state before development. See *Unimproved Land*.**

***Legal Annotation***: "In the Integra report, the experts opine that residential use of the property is the highest and best use. They value the property at $3,340,000 on the assumption that a 174-unit condominium project would be built on the property. Using that scenario, the report concludes that the conservation easement that would preclude the assumed development is to be valued at $3,270,000. As an alternative scenario, the report considers the value of the parcel as '**raw land**', concluding that to be $68,000. But the report does not determine the highest and best use of the property after the easement is granted, as the Integra experts acknowledge in the April 2010 letter to petitioner's counsel submitted as part of their report for trial." *Boltar, LLC v. Commissioner* (Tax CT., 2011).

## RAW SEWAGE

**Untreated wastewater.**

***Legal Annotation***: "[T]he Court here finds that there can be no serious question that 'other hazardous materials,' 'dangerous toxins,' 'chemicals' and 'other contamin[ants]' are unambiguously pollutants. Thus, the remaining issue is whether '**raw sewage**' is unambiguously a pollutant. . . . [T]he Court finds that **raw sewage** is unambiguously a pollutant as used in the Absolute Pollution Exclusion." *Figuli v. State Farm Mut. Fire & Cas.* (Colo. Ct. App., 2012).

## REAL ESTATE

**Land, tenements, and other hereditaments or rights therein, and whatever is made part of or is attached to it by nature or by humans; the land and all improvements thereon (Johnsich 1991).**

***Legal Annotation***: "'Real property' is synonymous with '**real estate**.' See Black's Law Dictionary 1378 (9th ed. 2009). Under the Colorado Common Interest Ownership Act (CCIOA), which applies to condominium complexes such as the one at issue here, '**real estate**' is defined as: any leasehold or other estate or interest in, over, or under land, including structures, fixtures, and other improvements and interests that, by custom, usage, or law, pass with a conveyance of land though not described in the contract of sale or instrument of conveyance. '**Real estate**' includes parcels with or without horizontal boundaries and spaces that may be filled with air or water." *Village at Treehouse, Inc. v. Property Tax Administrator* (Colo. Ct. App., 2014).

## REALIGNED INTERSECTION

**See *Traffic Calming*.**

## REALLOCATED PRESENT NEED

**That part of a municipality's present affordable-housing need that is redistributed to other municipalities in the region.**

***Comment***: Affordable-housing need consists of a municipality's indigenous or existing need, reallocated present need, and prospective need. The reallocated present need is that part of a region's present need that has been proportionally reallocated from municipalities with obligations in excess of the regional average.

*Legal Annotation*: "**Reallocated present need** is 'that portion of a housing region's present need that is redistributed throughout the housing region.'" *Fair Share Housing Center v. Township of Cherry Hill* (N.J., 2002).

## REAL PROPERTY

**Land and typically immovable constructed improvements, such as buildings and structures.**

*Comment*: Real property is sometimes referred to as real estate.

*Legal Annotation*: "'**Real property**' is synonymous with 'real estate.' See Black's Law Dictionary 1378 (9th ed. 2009). Under the Colorado Common Interest Ownership Act (CCIOA), which applies to condominium complexes such as the one at issue here, 'real estate' is defined as: any leasehold or other estate or interest in, over, or under land, including structures, fixtures, and other improvements and interests that, by custom, usage, or law, pass with a conveyance of land though not described in the contract of sale or instrument of conveyance. 'Real estate' includes parcels with or without horizontal boundaries and spaces that may be filled with air or water." *Village at Treehouse, Inc. v. Property Tax Administrator* (Colo. Ct. App., 2014).

"Under T.P. § 1-101(dd)(1), **real property** is defined as 'any land or improvements to land.' See also Black's Law Dictionary 1218 (6th ed. 1990) (defining '**real property**' as '[l]and, and generally whatever is erected or growing upon or affixed to land.'). Improvements are 'such things as are placed thereon by the way of betterments which are of a permanent nature and which add to the value of the property as **real property** . . . includ[ing] buildings and structures of every kind.'" *Baltimore Cnty. v. Greater Baltimore Med.* (Md. Ct. Spec. App., 2011).

## REAR LANE

See *Alley*.

*Legal Annotation*: "The subject site is a corner interior lot with limited and lot with a four-[l]ane access perhaps no public street on one frontage and . . . access at the **rear lane** street access on the other frontage." *B & C Investments of Arkansas, Inc. v. City of Fort Smith* (W.D. Ark., 2007).

## REAR LOT LINE

See *Lot Line, Rear*.

*Legal Annotation*: "The reason for defining a **rear lot line** is to assist in describing a rear yard. A rear yard is: An open space between the side lot lines of a lot, extending from the **rear lot line** to a line on the lot parallel to the **rear lot line**, to a depth measured horizontally, as specified in this title." *Talbot v. Gray* (Wash, Ct. App., 1974).

## REAR YARD

See *Yard, Rear*.

*Legal Annotation*: "**Rear Yard** is defined: 'A space on the same lot with a building, between the extreme rear line of said building and the rear line of the lot and open and unoccupied except by an unenclosed porch not exceeding sixty square feet in area." *Brookline v. Co-Ray Realty Co. Inc.* (Mass., 1950).

## REASONABLE ACCOMMODATION

See *People with Disabilities*.

*Legal Annotation*: "Next, the AOAO argues that the FHA does not require accommodations that provide an increased benefit or greater opportunity beyond those provided to a person without a handicap. It argues that a **reasonable accommodation** is only necessary if, without the accommodation, the disabled person will likely be denied an equal opportunity to enjoy the housing of their choice." *Apartment Owners of Liliuokalani Gardens v. Taylor* (D. Hawaii, 2012).

## REASONABLE-USE DOCTRINE

**A common law principle that prohibits the use of one's property in such a way as to deprive others of the lawful enjoyment of their property.**

*Legal Annotation*: "According to the doctrine, [d] rainage of surface waters from one's own land onto another's is a 'reasonable use' if there is a reasonable necessity for such drainage, if regard is taken to avoid unnecessary injury to others, if the utility or benefit to the land drained outweighs the harm to the land receiving the water, and if, where practicable, the drainage is done by improving the natural system or providing a feasible artificial one. . . . The **reasonable-use doctrine** is 'a flexible doctrine, presenting a question of fact to be resolved according to the circumstances of each case.' *Sundae v. Kulhanek* (Minn. Ct. App., 2012).

## RECEIVING WATERS

**Rivers, lakes, oceans, or other waterbodies, including underground aquifers, that receive treated or untreated wastewaters.**

*Legal Annotation*: "'**Receiving waters**' are defined as all surface water bodies in the Los Angeles Region that are identified in the Basin Plan. Permittees are to assure that storm water discharges from the MS4 shall neither cause nor contribute to the exceedance of water quality standards and objectives nor create conditions of nuisance in the **receiving waters**, and that the discharge of non-storm water to the MS4 has been effectively prohibited. The Permit incorporates and adopts the Basin Plan, which sets limits on bacteria and contaminants for the **receiving waters** of Southern California. The water-quality standards limit, among other pollutants, the levels of ammonia, fecal coliform bacteria, arsenic, mercury, and cyanide in Southern California's inland rivers." *Natural Resources Defense v. County of Los Angeles* (9th Cir., 2010).

## RECHARGE

**The addition to, or replenishing of, water in an aquifer.**

*Legal Annotation*: "'**Recharge**' is defined as '[a]ddition of water, especially to a groundwater aquifer, to replace that which is withdrawn.' 5 Robert E. Beck & Amy K. Kelley, Waters and Water Rights, at G-45 (3d ed.2009)." *Pyramid Lake Paiute Tribe v. Ricci* (Nev., 2010).

## RECLAIMED LAND

**See *Land Reclamation; Made Land*.**

*Legal Annotation*: "The defendants have acquired ownership of and title to the land reclaimed by filling in below high water mark and landward of the bulkhead line. This results from a proper exercise of riparian rights by defendants and their predecessors in title. The title to such **reclaimed land** is one which may be encumbered or conveyed by the defendants and is subject to taxation by the taxing authorities. The defendants may not be deprived of their property therein except for public purposes and then only upon due process of law and with just compensation." *US v. Groen* (D.D.C., 1947).

## RECREATION, ACTIVE

**Leisure-time activities, usually of a formal nature and often performed with others, requiring equipment and taking place at prescribed places, sites, or fields.**

*Comment*: The term "active recreation" is more a word of art than one with a precise definition. It obviously includes swimming, tennis and other court games, baseball, and track, and other field sports and playground activities. There is a legitimate difference of opinion as to whether park use per se may be considered active recreation, although obviously some parks contain activity areas that would qualify.

*Legal Annotation*: "Explaining that 'the tentative plan did not devote at least 25% of open space to acceptable **active recreation** and associated facilities, an open space performance standard' set forth by ordinance." *Robal Assocs., Inc. v. Bd. of Supervisors of Charlestown Twp.* (Pa. Cmmw. Ct. 2010).

"Further, the tentative plan did not devote at least 25% of open space to acceptable **active recreation** and associated facilities, an open space performance standard set forth in Section 1504.E of the Ordinance. . . . The open space performance standard was not met because the proposed Frisbee Golf Course and the sledding hill near the residential buildings did not demonstrate safe and acceptable active open space." *Robal Assoc. v. Bd. of Sup'rs Charlestown* (Pa: Common. Ct., 2010).

## RECREATION, PASSIVE

**Activities that involve relatively inactive or less energetic activities, such as walking, sitting, picnicking, and board and table games.**

***Comment***: The reason for the differentiation between active and passive recreation is their potential impacts on surrounding land uses. Passive recreation can also mean open space for nature walks and observation.

***Legal Annotation***: "Zebulon argues that we should not construe the words 'recreation' and 'amusement' according to their natural import, but that we should limit their meaning to active, rather than passive, activities. In support of this argument, Zebulon notes that several kinds of businesses that provide **passive recreation** and amusement were explicitly listed as permitted uses in a B4 district, e.g., 'Taverns' and 'Theaters (not outdoor).' . . . Because the specific permitted uses included both active and **passive recreations** and amusements, however, we do not consider the inconsistencies to be a valid basis for limiting the meaning of the general classification to passive activities." *Zebulon Enterprises, Inc. v. County of Du Page* (Ill. App. Ct., 1986).

## RECREATION FACILITY

**A place designed and equipped for the conducting of sports and leisure-time activities. See *Health Club*.**

***Comment***: The National Recreation and Park Association publishes general standards for a variety of recreational facilities (see column 1 in Table R-1). These standards can be used in all types of jurisdictions. A selective survey of municipalities in New Jersey and the standards they use is shown

**Table R-1: General Standards For Recreational Facilities**

| Type of Facility | National Recreation and Park Standards[a] | Outdoor Recreation Facility Standards[b] |
|---|---|---|
| Baseball fields | 1/5,000 population | 1/5,000 population |
| Basketball courts | 1/5,000 population | 1/2,000 population |
| Community centers | 1/25,000 population[c] | 1/20,000 population |
| Field hockey fields | 1/20,000 population | 1/20,000 population |
| Football fields | 1/20,000 population | 1/10,000 population |
| Little League fields | 1/5,000 population | 1/3,000 population |
| Paddle tennis courts | No standard | 1/5,000 population |
| Playgrounds/tot lots | No population-based standard | 1/1,000 population |
| Running track (quarter-mile) | 1/20,000 population | 1/20,000 population |
| Soccer fields | 1/10,000 population | 1/4,000 population |
| Softball fields | 1/5,000 population | 1/1,500 population |
| Swimming pools | 1/20,000 population | 1/20,000 population |
| Tennis courts | 1/2,000 population | 1/1,500 population |
| Trails | 1 system per region | 1 mile/3,000 population |
| Volleyball courts | 1/5,000 population | 1/3,000 population |

Sources:

a. National Recreation and Park Association, *Recreation, Park and Open Space Standards and Guidelines*. (Alexandria, VA: National Recreation and Park Association, 1983).

b. Standards derived from a variety of municipalities.

c. Joseph DeChiara and Lee E. Koppelman, *Urban Planning and Design Criteria* (New York: Van Nostrand Reinhold, 1982): 405.

in column 2. These two sets of standards provide benchmarks, but the specific recreation preferences of residents based on current and future needs should be considered. Accessibility and convenience are important criteria in determining the adequacy of existing facilities. In addition, smaller municipalities with fewer than five thousand persons may have many of the listed facilities.

*Legal Annotation*: "Use of the pole barn as a basketball facility *changed the use of the Property from a farm to one which hosts a community indoor **recreation facility***. An indoor **recreation facility** is more akin to commercial activity." *Northampton Township v. Parsons* (Pa. Common. Ct., 2011).

## RECREATION FACILITY, COMMERCIAL

**A recreation facility operated as a business and open to the public for a fee.**

*Legal Annotation*: "A '**commercial recreation facility**' is '[a]n activity operated as a business, open to the public, for the purpose of recreation and entertainment.' . . . Facilities open to the general public include parks and community recreation facilities operated as non-commercial ventures (Ordinance, §112). These facilities are open to everyone. On the other hand, facilities open to the public include drive-in movie theaters, bowling alleys and health clubs are operated as commercial ventures. (Id.). These facilities are open to anyone who pays the owner for their use. Viewing the sections of the ordinance at issue in this context, the Board's interpretation of the term 'general public' to apply to any individuals and 'public' to apply only to individuals who pay to use a particular facility are not unreasonable and fall within the scope of deference to be afforded by a reviewing court." *Keener v. Rapho Township Zoning Hearing Board* (Pa. Common. Ct., Court 2013).

## RECREATION FACILITY, PERSONAL

**A recreation facility provided as an accessory use on the same lot as the principal permitted use and designed to be used primarily by the occupants of the principal use and their guests.**

*Legal Annotation*: "Nila and Charles Damitz bought two adjoining lots; on one, they built a $400,000 home and on the other a Little League baseball practice **facility**. The developer-builder and neighbors brought an action against the Damitzes, seeking to enjoin their use of the practice field. The trial court entered judgment in favor of the Damitzes. We affirm . . . 'An accessory use must be subordinate in area, extent, and purpose to the primary use of the lot.' . . . In the present case, the Damitzes purchased a double lot parcel upon which they built a home costing well over $400,000; their expenditure to develop the practice **facility** was about ten percent of that amount. The Damitzes built their home as a residence ('single family dwelling,' in the language of the zoning ordinance), in which they live with their three children on a full time basis. Clearly, the primary Damitz use of the double lot is residential. The use of the practice **facility** for approximately 8.75 hours a week (three and one-half hours on an average of two and a half times a week) for about ten weeks of the year is subordinate to their primary residential use." *Bagko Development Co. v. Damitz* (Ind. Ct. App., 1994).

## RECREATION FACILITY, PRIVATE

**A recreation facility operated by a private organization and open only to bona fide members and guests.**

*Legal Annotation*: "In this action, the plaintiffs Larry R. and Katherine Kaiser, Margaret Schraeder, and Anthony and Helen Stepanek sought to permanently enjoin the defendants, Western R/C Flyers, Inc., and Jay and Elaine Startzer, from operating a model airplane airfield near the village of Springfield, Sarpy County, Nebraska. . . . The defendants have not applied for a special use permit to operate a model airplane airfield on the Startzer property. The plaintiffs contend the defendants are required to obtain a special use permit because the lease of 1 acre by Startzers to the club constituted a commercial recreation area as defined in the ordinance. The defendants contend that their use of the land is that of a **private recreation facility**, which is a principal permitted use, and that they are not required to have a special use permit." *Kaiser v. Western R/C Flyers, Inc.* (Neb., 1991).

## RECREATION FACILITY, PUBLIC

**A recreation facility open to the general public.**

*Comment*: Public recreation facilities are usually owned and operated by a governmental agency, but not necessarily so. For example, ball fields owned by industry might be available for public use at certain times.

*Legal Annotation*: "The Forest Service has designated the Snowbowl as a **public recreation facility** under the Coconino Forest Service Plan. In doing so, the Forest Service found that the Snowbowl represented an opportunity for the general public to access and enjoy public lands in a manner that the Forest Service could not otherwise offer in the form of a major facility anywhere in Arizona." *Navajo Nation v. US Forest Service* (D. Ariz., 2006).

## RECREATIONAL DEVELOPMENT

**A residential development planned, maintained, operated, and integrated with a major recreation facility, such as a golf course, ski resort, or marina.**

*Legal Annotation*: "Cross-Up, Inc. (Cross-Up) appeals the April 7, 2010 order of the Court of Common Pleas of Clinton County (trial court) affirming the decision of the Zoning Hearing Board of Porter Township (Board) denying Cross-Up's application to use a portion of its property as a private motorcross riding track. . . . Section 8.08 of the Ordinance provides that types of recreational uses permitted in **recreational development** areas are: boating and fishing; golf courses; hiking and horseback riding; parks and arboretums; play fields; playgrounds; picnic areas; skating rinks; swimming pool; tennis courts; woodlands; and lakes. . . . [T]the Board did not abuse its discretion or err as a matter of law in denying the application." *Cross-Up, Inc. v. The Zoning Hearing Board of Porter Township* (Pa. Common. Ct., 2011).

## RECREATIONAL VEHICLE

**A vehicular-type portable structure without permanent foundation that can be towed, hauled, or driven and is primarily designed as a temporary living accommodation for recreational and camping purposes. See *Camping Vehicle*.**

*Comment*: Recreational vehicles include, but are not limited to, travel trailers, truck campers, camping trailers, and self-propelled motor homes.

*Legal Annotation*: "On September 21, 2010, however, the Township amended Article II of its zoning ordinance to define a '**recreational vehicle**' as follows (italics within paragraph indicate additions made to the previous ordinance):

A transportable or vehicular type of unit initially designed as temporary living quarters for recreational camping or travel use that does not require a special highway moving permit when transported which either has its own motive of power or is mounted on or drawn by another vehicle. The types of recreation vehicles or units are:

a. Travel Trailers—A vehicular unit, mounted on wheels, of such size or weight as not to require special highway moving permits when drawn by motorized vehicles (8.5 feet wide maximum) designated and constructed to provide temporary living quarters for recreational, camping, or travel use, *and not larger than four hundred (400) square feet when used for camping (in set up mode)*. [The previous Ordinance only allowed for 300 square feet.]

b. Truck Camper—A portable unit, designed to be loaded onto, or affixed to, the bed or chassis of a truck and constructed to provide temporary living quarters for recreational, camping or travel use *and not larger than 400 square feet*. [The previous Ordinance did not provide for any limit on square footage.]

c. Motor Homes—A vehicular unit built on a self-propelled motor vehicle chassis, designed to provide temporary living quarters for recreation, camping or travel use *and not larger than 400 square feet. All such vehicles in use for camping shall have a current state license, inspection sticker and registration and be titled in the name of the current owner*. [The previous Ordinance did not provide for any limit on square footage.]

d. Camper Trailer—A vehicular unit mounted on wheels and constructed with collapsible partial side walls which fold for towing by another vehicle and unfold on the campsite and designed to provide temporary living quarters for recreational, camping or travel use *and not larger than 400 square feet*. [The previous Ordinance did not provide for any limit on square footage.]

e. Tent—A movable shelter made of canvas or other similar material and supported by a pole or poles and designed and manufactured to provide temporary living quarters for recreational and camping use.

f. Self-Contained Unit—A unit that can operate independent of connections to external sewer, water and electrical systems; has a toilet and holding tank for liquid waste; contains water storage facilities; and may contain a lavatory, kitchen sink and/or both bath facilities connected to the holding tank *and of a size not greater than 400 square feet*. [The previous Ordinance did not provide for any limit on square footage.]" *Lake Adventure Community Association, Inc. v. Dingman Township* (Pa. Common. Ct., 2012).

## RECREATIONAL VEHICLE PARK

**Any lot or parcel of land upon which two or more sites are located, established, or maintained for occupancy by recreational vehicles for a fee as temporary living quarters for recreation or vacation purposes. See *Campground*.**

***Comment***: Many ordinances define "temporary" in terms of length of continuous occupancy permitted, in order to prevent these facilities from becoming permanent homesites. Some developments also contain recreational vehicle parking areas for the use of their residents.

***Legal Annotation***: "As the trial judge recognized, a travel trailer or **recreational vehicle park** is a different category of use under the ordinance, in that it specifically limits the use of such parks to temporary occupancy by recreational vehicles, as distinct from the relatively permanent occupancy characteristic of mobilehome park use. *The applicant has not challenged the validity of the provisions which limit the travel trailer park designation on the basis of temporary occupancy*. Hence, a mobilehome park clearly is not a permitted use under the current Resort/ Business District classification." *BAC, INC. v. ZHB, Millcreek Twp. et al.* (Pa. Common. Ct., 1985).

## RECTILINEAR STREET SYSTEM

**A pattern of streets that is characterized by right-angle roadways, grid pattern blocks, and four-way intersections. See *Gridiron Pattern*. See *Figure 78*.**

***Legal Annotation***: "Oral argument revealed the critical nature of these elements, especially where the lots are odd-shaped and not **rectilinear**; the streets are curved; cul-de-sacs exist, and the structures are customized and not uniform in configuration, or canted or angled to the street, or indeed all of the these conditions exist." *Damurjian v. Board of Adjustment* (N.J. App. Div., 1997).

## RECTORY

**See *Clergy Residence*.**

***Legal Annotation***: "It is clear that the **rectory** here is, first and foremost, the residence of the parish priests. The mere fact that parts of the **rectory** are used for nonresidential purposes in connection with certain Church-related work does not automatically deprive the Church of the benefit of the exemption." *Muniz v. Church of Our Lady of Mt. Carmel* (N.Y. App. Div., 1997).

## RECYCLABLE

**A waste product capable of being reused or transformed into a new product.**

***Legal Annotation***: "The ordinance provides: 'No Affected Retail Establishment, Restaurant, Vendor or Non-Profit Vendor shall provide Plastic Carry-Out Bags to customers at the point of sale. Reusable Bags and Recyclable Paper Bags are allowed alternatives.' (City of Manhattan Beach Ord. No. 2115, § 2(b)A.) '**Recyclable**' is defined as: 'material that can be sorted, cleansed, and reconstituted using Manhattan Beach's available recycling collection programs.'" *Save the Plastic Bag Coalition v. City of Manhattan Beach* (Calif., 2011).

## RECYCLING

**The process by which waste products are reduced to raw materials and transformed into new and often different products.**

**Figure 78**

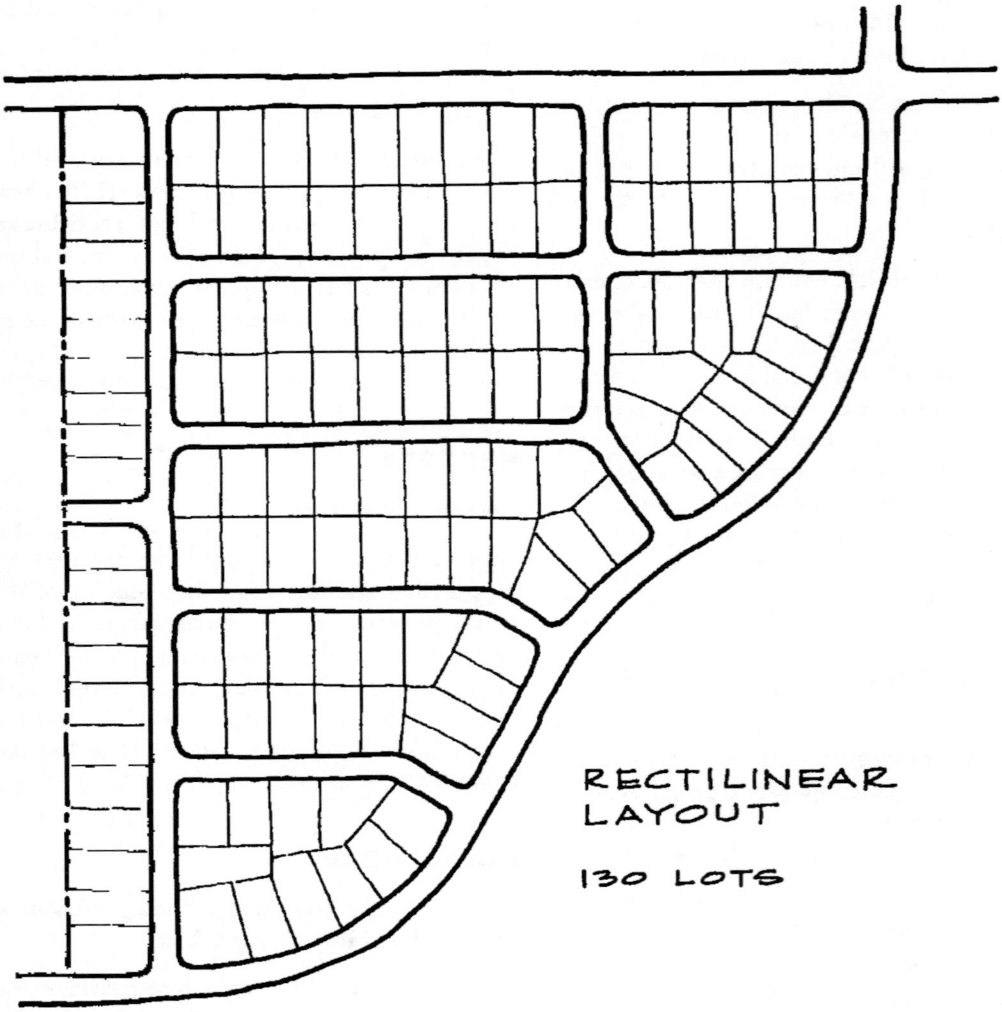


***Comment***: "Recycling" also has a broader meaning, referring to all activities related to recycling, including the collection, separation, and storage of materials. (Source: Friedman 2003: 5.)

***Legal Annotation***: "In March 1996, JTE proposed to begin a **recycling** operation at the site. This recycling operation would entail receiving CCDD at the site, separating and processing it, and returning the material to the economic mainstream. In response to JTE's proposal, Edwin Bakowski, the manager of the permit section for the Bureau of Land at the Agency, sent a letter to JTE to the attention of Janice in which he explained the circumstances under which a **recycling** facility could operate without a permit. He was concerned because JTE's proposal indicated it would accept nonrecyclable materials and he informed JTE that it could operate the facility without a permit only if it revised its proposal to accept solely CCDD. At the time, CCDD was defined as uncontaminated concrete, brick, stone, and reclaimed asphalt." *People ex rel. Madigan v. JT Einoder, Inc.* (Ill. App. Ct., 2013).

## RECYCLING AND RECOVERY FACILITY

**Land and buildings used for the sorting and reshipment of solid waste. See *Recycling Center; Recycling Collection Point; Recycling Plant*.**

***Comment***: A state court decision ruled that recovery of construction material was not an industrial or manufacturing use as provided in the local ordinance, which listed permitted uses as those that "involve a process of manufacturing, fabrication, or production of useful goods" (*Atlantic Container, Inc. vs. Township of Eagleswood Planning Board*, Superior Court of N.J., Appellate Division, decided May 18, 1999, 728 A. 2d 849 and reported in *Zoning Digest*, Vol. 52, No. 1, Case #5).

***Legal Annotation***: "The case *sub judice* involves THA's project to upgrade and modernize the Harrisburg Materials, Energy, **Recycling and Recovery Facility**, a trash-to-steam waste treatment facility ('the incinerator')." *Harrisburg Authority v. CIT Capital USA, Inc.* (M.D. Pa., 2010).

## RECYCLING CENTER

**A lot or parcel of land, with or without buildings, upon which recyclable materials are separated and processed for shipment for eventual reuse in new products.**

***Comment***: Most recycling centers are publicly owned. If they are privately owned, it may become difficult to distinguish recycling centers from junkyards, with all their attendant problems. All recycling centers should be planned with adequate buffers, unloading areas, and safe and convenient access. Larger ones belong in industrial zones.

***Legal Annotation***: "The matter pending before the Board was whether Spainhoward's **recycling center** is a retail business and, thus, a permitted use in a general business district. The Board voted that it was not." *Spainhoward v. Henderson, Henderson Cty. Bd.* (Ky. Ct. App., 1999).

## RECYCLING COLLECTION POINT

**A neighborhood drop-off point for the temporary storage of recyclables.**

***Comment***: No processing of recyclables takes place at the collection point. Approving authorities should determine and approve recycling collection points as part of their review of major development applications.

***Legal Annotation***: "However, 'transfer station' is specifically defined in 329 IAC 2-2-1(58) as follows: '(58) "Transfer station" means a facility at which solid waste is transferred into larger capacity vehicles or containers for further transportation but shall not include **neighborhood recycling collection** centers or transfer activities at generating facilities.'" *Nat. Salvage v. Com'r of Ind. D. of Em.* (Ind. Ct. App., 1991).

## RECYCLING PLANT

**A facility in which recyclables, such as newspapers, magazines, books, and other paper products; glass; metal cans; and other products are recycled, reprocessed, and treated, so as to return such products to a condition in which they may be used again in new products.**

***Comment***: Recycling plants are intensive uses that generate truck traffic, noise, and waste. They should be located in heavy (or intensive) industrial districts.

***Legal Annotation***: "McGuire was employed by Ready Help, Inc., a temporary employment agency. Tenneco operated a paper **recycling plant** in Kansas City and frequently obtained temporary workers from Ready Help. On August 7, 1986, Tenneco requested four laborers from Ready Help for the following day in anticipation of a large volume of paper products and a need for additional 'sorters.' The sorter's duties included sorting paper into various grade classifications, removing paper products from conveyor belts, and sweeping the warehouse floor." *McGuire v. Tenneco, Inc.* (Mo., 1988).

"Waste water treatment to a grease **recycling plant** is a critical element of environmental concern and regulation that has to be met and which requires special expertise." *Malone v. Div. of Admin., State, Dept. of Transp.* (Fla. Ct. App., 1983).

## REDEVELOPMENT

**The removal and replacement, rehabilitation, or adaptive reuse of an existing structure or structures, or of land from which previous improvements have been removed.**

***Comment***: Replacement may include construction of residential, commercial, industrial, public, or other uses as well as provisions for streets, parks, and other public facilities.

*Legal Annotation*: "To establish physical blight under this provision, the **redevelopment** proponent must 'show how these [incompatible] uses are preventing economic development.' . . . 'A primary purpose of **redevelopment** is to eliminate blight which private enterprise cannot.'" *County of Los Angeles v. Glendora Redevelopment Project* (Calif. Ct. App., 2010).

## REFORESTATION

**The planting or replanting of forest plant materials, resulting in the creation of a biological community dominated by trees or other woody plants. See *Afforestation*.**

*Legal Annotation*: "The cut timber, the fallen timber, and the underbrush are to be destroyed by the use of a crusher, and the land is to be burned off in a controlled burn to get rid of all of the wood and underbrush. Then something over 1,300,000 pine seedlings are to be planted for reforestation. . . . It is hard to conclude that the stay would serve the public interest when the purpose of the **reforestation** is to improve the forest rather than replace it with buildings, industry, highways, or the like. We must conclude that the State has not made a showing of likelihood of success on the merits or a substantial case in which the balance of the equities weighs heavily in favor of a stay." *State of Tex. v. US Forest Service* (5th Cir., 1986).

## REFUSE

**See *Solid Waste*.**

*Legal Annotation:* "In addressing this problem, the Committee recognizes that Solid Waste, the traditional term for trash or refuse is inappropriate. The words solid waste are laden with false connotations. They are more narrow in meaning than the Committee's concern. The words discarded materials more accurately reflect the Committee's interest." *Safe Air for Everyone v. Meyer* (9th Cir., 2004).

## REFUSE RECLAMATION

**The process of converting solid waste to salable products.**

*Comment*: An example of refuse reclamation is the composting of organic solid waste to yield a salable soil conditioner.

*Legal Annotation*: "The legislature has determined that **refuse reclamation** facilities are a desirable part of its environmental scheme. . . . WLSSD facility specifically benefits the community by providing a consistent source of fuel for the sewage sludge incineration plant which, in turn, reduces pollution of the St. Louis River area, as well as providing a preferred method of waste disposal." *Zenith/Kremer v. Western Lake Sanitary* (Minn., 1997).

## REGION

**A geographic area defined by some common feature, such as a river basin, housing market, commuter shed, economic activity, or political jurisdiction. See *Housing Region*.**

*Legal Annotation*: "NobelBiz argues that 'geographical **region**' needs no definition because it can be readily understood by a person of ordinary skill in the art. . . . NobelBiz further contends that Defendants' proposed construction contradicts the plain and ordinary meaning of the term in an attempt to render the term meaningless. In rebuttal, Defendants argue that the term 'geographic **region**' is inherently indefinite (Doc. No. 89 at 17). Citing online dictionary definitions of '**region**,' Defendants argue that a person of ordinary skill in the art would only know that 'geographic **region**' refers to an indefinite and unbounded area. . . . Defendants also cite to an online dictionary definition of 'geographic **region**' as 'a demarcated area of the earth.'" *Nobelbiz, Inc. v. Global Connect, LLC* (E.D. Texas, 2013).

## REGIONAL CENTER

**Concentrations of regionally marketed commercial and retail centers, office and employment areas, some higher-education facilities, and possibly sports and recreational complexes. http://www.pgplanning.org/Resources/Tools_On-line/Glossary.htm**

*Comment*: Regional centers are, or can be, effectively served by mass transit.

***Legal Annotation***: "Goal LU-1 sets a goal for the City to: Maintain a land use pattern that (1) protects and enhances the quality of life in the city's residential neighborhoods; (2) fosters redevelopment and revitalization of blighted or declining areas; (3) promotes and facilitates economic development and the growth of job opportunities in the city; (4) fosters the growth and development of downtown as a **regional center** of domestic and international commerce, culture and entertainment; (5) promotes the efficient use of land and minimizes land use conflicts; and (6) protects and conserves the city's natural and coastal resources." *Payne v. City of Miami* (Fla. Ct. App., 2010).

## REGIONAL SHOPPING CENTER

**See *Shopping Center*.**

***Legal Annotation***: "**A regional shopping center** is defined in the industry as one that 'provides shopping goods, general merchandise, apparel, furniture and home furnishings in full depth and variety. It is built around the full-line department store, with a minimum GLA [gross leasable area] of 100,000 square feet, as the major drawing power. For even greater comparative shopping, two, three or more department stores may be included. In theory a regional center has a GLA of 400,000 square feet, and can range from 300,000 to more than 1,000,000 square feet.' [National Research Bureau, Shopping Center Directory 1994, Eastern Volume (1993).]" *New Jersey Coalition v. JMB* (N.J., 1994).

## REGIONAL TAX BASE SHARING

**The sharing of the tax base over a regional area encompassing a number of local government entities (municipalities, school districts, etc.), rather than each one of these entities constituting a separate public finance system unto itself with a local-focused tax base.**

***Comment***: Regional tax base sharing is relatively rare in the United States. The two major examples that are cited with this system in place over many years are the Twin Cities (Minnesota) and the Meadowlands area (New Jersey).

***Legal Annotation***: "APPENDIX B—STEPS IN **TAX BASE SHARING**: 1. Determine net growth in commercial-industrial assessed valuation in each community in the metropolitan area over 1971. Take 40 percent of the result. This is the amount of assessed valuation which each community will share with the entire metropolitan area." *Village of Burnsville v. Onischuk* (Minn., 1974).

## REGULATORY BASE FLOOD

**See *Flood, Regulatory Base*.**

***Legal Annotation***: "*Flood Fringe Area*—That portion of the flood hazard area outside of the floodway based on the total area inundated during the **regulatory base flood** plus twenty-five percent of the **regulatory base flood** discharge." *Terner v. Spyco, Inc.* (N.J. App. Div, 1988).

## REGULATORY BASE FLOOD DISCHARGE

**See *Flood, Regulatory Base Discharge*.**

***Legal Annotation***: "*Flood Fringe Area*—That portion of the flood hazard area outside of the floodway based on the total area inundated during the regulatory base flood plus twenty-five percent of the **regulatory base flood discharge**." *Terner v. Spyco, Inc.* (N.J. App. Div, 1988).

## REGULATORY FLOODWAY

**See *Floodway; Floodway, Regulatory*.**

***Legal Annotation***: "In a flood insurance study commissioned by the city in 1990, the creek was designated as a '**regulatory floodway**.' A floodway 'is the channel of a stream plus any adjacent flood plain areas that must be kept free of encroachment so that [a] 100-year flood can be carried without substantial increases in flood heights.'" *Schneider v. State* (Iowa, 2010).

## REHABILITATION

**The restoration of a property, previously in a dilapidated or substandard condition, for human habitation or use, without drastically changing the plan, form, or style of architecture.**

***Legal Annotation***: "After the Planning Commission certified the 'Federal Anderson' area as blighted, no further action of any kind was taken by the Planning Commission or the Urban Redevelopment Authority with respect to the project. Subsequent to that certification of blight in 1964, conditions in the 'Federal Anderson' area changed in that buildings in the 'blighted' area were demolished (R.Rec. 357a & 358a), there was new construction in the 'blighted' area (R.Rec. 358a), and there was **rehabilitation** of existing buildings in the 'blighted' area." *Matter of Urban Redevelopment Auth* (Pa., 1991).

## REHABILITATION CENTER

See *Convalescent Center*.

*Legal Annotation*: "Central Nebraska Council on Alcoholism, Inc., proposes to use the premises for what is referred to as a **rehabilitation center** or recovery house for alcoholics where room and board would be furnished." *Beckman v. City of Grand Island* (Neb., 1968).

## RELICTION

**An increase in land area by the permanent withdrawal of a waterbody (Johnsich 1991).**

*Comment*: Reliction is different from land reclamation, in which water is drained or land is purposely filled in to create new land. See *Land Reclamation*.

*Legal Annotation*: "Generally, the common-law doctrine of **reliction** would parcel the dry lake bed to the adjoining land owners as riparian owners. **Reliction** is the process of gradual exposure of land by the permanent recession of a body of water. 6 Powell on Real Property, ¶ 983 (1970); 5A Thompson on Real Property, § 2560 (1957 Replacement). When the land under the water becomes exposed permanently, simply stated, it belongs to the adjoining land owners." *State Engineer v. Cowles Brothers, Inc.* (Nev., 1970).

## RELIGIOUS LAND USE AND INSTITUTIONALIZED PERSONS ACT (RLUIPA)

**A federal law that makes it illegal to unreasonably discriminate against religious institutions.**

*Comment*: RLUIPA makes certain zoning practices illegal under the following provisions:

- Substantial Burden Provision: When making an individualized assessment, a governmental entity cannot "substantially burden" a religious institution unless it (a) is in furtherance of a compelling governmental interest; and (b) it is the least restrictive means of furthering that compelling governmental interest.
- Equal Terms Provision: Imposing or implementing a land use regulation in a manner that treats a religious assembly or institution on less than equal terms with a nonreligious assembly or institution.
- Exclusion Provision: Prohibiting a religious institution or unreasonably limiting such institutions from a jurisdiction or discriminating against a particular belief system.

(Sources: Starkey; Giamo and Merriam 2003.)

*Legal Annotation*: "The **Religious Land Use and Institutionalized Persons Act** of 2000 (**RLUIPA**) provides: 'No government shall impose a substantial burden on the religious exercise of a person residing in or confined to an institution . . . even if the burden results from a rule of general applicability, unless the government demonstrates that imposition of the burden on that person—(1) is in furtherance of a compelling government interest; (2) is the least restrictive means of furthering that compelling government interest.'" *Hodges v. Sharon* (E.D. Calif., 2014).

## RELIGIOUS USE

**A structure or place in which worship, ceremonies, rituals, and education pertaining to a particular system of beliefs are held. See *Place of Worship; Megachurch*.**

*Legal Annotation*: "We recognize, as have other courts, that the right to establish and maintain a **religious use** includes the right to establish and maintain accessory uses. See Annot., 11 A.L.R.4th 1084 (1982)." City of Las Cruces V. Huerta (N.M. Ct. App., 1984).

## RELOCATE

**To move an individual, household, use, building, or structure from its original place to another location.**

*Legal Annotation*: "After the amendment, the Ordinance § 155.163(A) stated, in relevant part: 'No sign shall hereafter be erected, attached to, suspended from, or supported on a building or structure; nor shall any existing sign be enlarged, **relocated**, or otherwise altered; nor shall any building permit be issued for such purposes until a sign permit for same has been issued by the Zoning Administrator." *Morris Communications Corporation v. City of Bessemer City Zoning Board of Adjustment* (N.C. Ct. App., 2010).

## REMEDIATION

**The action or measures taken, or to be taken, to lessen, clean up, remove, or mitigate the existence of hazardous materials present on a property to such standards or requirements as may be established by federal, state, or local statute or regulation.**

*Legal Annotation*: "'As if remediated' is slightly different than 'as if clean' insofar as it incorporates a so-called **remediation** stigma discount. . . . One commentator has described the notion of stigma by way of example: a house with an intact roof would be slightly more valuable to a buyer than a house with a roof that has been properly repaired because of the fear of further leaks and possible hidden damage in the house. Robert N. Sechen, Relevance and Admissibility of Evidence of Environmental Contamination in an Eminent Domain Valuation Trial, 25 Stetson L.Rev. 823, 831-32 (1996)." *Housing Auth. v. Suydam Investors* (N.J., 2003).

## REMODEL

**To construct an addition or alter the design or layout of a building or make alterations or structural changes.**

*Legal Annotation*: "Section 921.03.A.1 of the Zoning Code provides that a nonconforming structure may be maintained, **remodeled**, and repaired 'without a variance and without special exception approval, provided that such maintenance, **remodeling** or repair does not increase the degree of nonconformity.'" *Lench v. Zoning Bd. of Adjustment of City of Pittsburgh* (Pa: Common. Ct., 2011).

## RENT

**A periodic payment, made by a tenant, to a landlord for the use of land, buildings, structures, or other property, or portions thereof.**

*Legal Annotation*: "The **rent** includes 'all housing services, maintenance, utilities and appliances to be provided and paid by the owner in accordance with the lease' and the 'owner may not charge the tenant extra amounts for items customarily included in **rent** to owner in the locality.' HUD-52641, Part C, ¶ 5(e) and (6)(c); see also 24 C.F.R. § 982.510(c)." *Khan v. Bland* (7th Cir., 2010).

## RENTAL HOUSING

**Housing that is occupied by a tenant paying rent to an owner, with no part of the rent being used to acquire equity in the property.**

*Legal Annotation*: "The City of Hazleton, Pennsylvania . . . is appealing a permanent injunction that the district court entered prohibiting Hazleton's enforcement of two local ordinances that attempt to regulate employment of, and provision of **rental housing** to, certain aliens. . . . In sum, we find the housing provisions of Hazleton's ordinances pre-empted regulations of immigration, and both field and conflict pre-empted by the INA." *Lozano v. City of Hazleton* (3rd Cir., 2010).

## REPAIR, MAJOR

**Any improvement that requires a building permit or that requires the replacement of a roof, wall, or other major building element. See *Alteration*.**

*Comment*: The reason for the distinction between major and minor repairs is to facilitate and expedite minor repairs with a minimum of red tape. Major repairs, on the other hand, should be more carefully reviewed to determine whether existing variances or site plan deficiencies can be ameliorated or reduced as part of the project.

*Legal Annotation*: "The AGV wires are installed in small recesses cut in the concrete floor. These recesses are approximately two inches deep and wide. After installation of the wires, the recesses are refilled with concrete. Defendant has failed to demonstrate that the removal of the AGV wires will cause any material injury to the wires. Removal requires breaking up the concrete and refilling the small recess or slot. This does not constitute a **major repair**." *General Motors Corp. v. City of Linden* (N.J. Tax Ct., 2002).

## REPAIR, MINOR

**Improvements to correct deficiencies resulting from normal wear and tear, or improvements not requiring a building permit. See *Repair, Major*.**

*Legal Annotation*: "It also looked at sidewalks, curbs and gutters, and streets, and identified lots without structures. It classified buildings as satisfactory, requiring minor repair, requiring major repair, and beyond repair. The survey identified twenty-eight percent of the buildings within the survey area as beyond repair, forty-three percent as requiring rehabilitation, and the remainder as either requiring **minor repair** or as satisfactory." *W. & G. CO. v. Redevelopment Agency* (Utah. Ct. App., 1990).

## REPLACEMENT COST

**The cost of constructing a substitute structure having utility equivalent to the structure being appraised but composed of modern materials according to current standards, design, and layout (Johnsich 1991).**

*Comment*: Replacement cost is often used as a standard in determining whether a nonconforming structure or use may be rebuilt after a fire. One frequently applied standard is that when the replacement cost is 50 percent or more of the value of the structure after repairs, the structure can be rebuilt only as a conforming one. From a practical point of view, it is often difficult to prevent a structure or use from being rebuilt unless the destruction is total. The approving authority should attempt to reduce the degree of nonconformity in any permitted rebuilding. See *Partial Destruction*.

The "equivalent" is not necessarily an exact replica of the original. The cost of providing a replica with the same or very similar materials is called "reproduction cost."

*Legal Annotation*: "Section 195-80(c) states: 'In conformity with its general power to grant variances as provided in this article, and pursuant to the guiding principles stated in this article, the Zoning Board of Appeals is hereby specifically empowered . . . (3) To grant a building permit for the reconstruction, structural alteration, restoration or repair of a structure used for a nonconforming use, to an extent exceeding in aggregate 50% of the **replacement cost** of such structure.'" *Valley Housing LP v. City of Derby* (D. Conn., 2011).

## REPURPOSE

**To use or convert from one use to another. See *Office, Headquarters; Adaptive Reuse*.**

*Legal Annotation*: "Because Moyer was without a dealer's license to sell vehicles on the property, and his tenants had a certificate permitting the property's **repurpose** to detailing and tinting, we believe the board could properly infer discontinued use as a display lot for at least six months or a year between 2006 and 2009. . . . We find substantial circumstantial evidence allowing the board to find Moyer abandoned the property's nonconforming use." *Moyer v. Zoning Board of Adjustment* (Iowa Ct. App., 2013).

## RES JUDICATA

**A common law doctrine meant to prevent relitigation of cases (or of applications for variances) between the same parties regarding the same issues, and to preserve the binding nature of the court (or quasi-judicial body's) decision.**

*Comment*: Taken from Latin, meaning "a thing decided." Judges or zoning boards of appeal who are presented with a lawsuit or a variance application that is identical to or substantially the same as the earlier one will apply the doctrine of *res judicata* to uphold the effect of the first decision. To apply *res judicata*, criteria as set forth below should be applied:

- The second application is substantially similar to the first.
- The same parties or their privies are involved.
- There must be no substantial change in the application itself or conditions surrounding the property.
- There must have been a decision on the merits of the first application.
- Both applications must involve the same cause of action.

***Legal Annotation***: "The Latin phrase '**res judicata**' means '**a thing adjudicated**.' The common-law doctrine of **res judicata** precludes relitigation of a claim formerly made. . . . **Res judicata**, or its modern term, claim preclusion, prohibits 'splitting' a claim or cause of action. . . . Claims that could have been raised by a prevailing party in the first action are merged into, and are thus barred by, the first judgment. To determine whether a claim is barred by a former judgment, the question is whether the claim arises out of the same 'act, contract or transaction.'" *Chesterfield Village v. City of Chesterfield* (Mo., 2002).

## RESEARCH LABORATORY

**A facility for investigation into the natural, physical, or social sciences, which may include engineering and product development.**

***Comment***: Research laboratories imply physical activities usually associated with "wet" labs or places with running water, gases, special ventilation devices, chemicals, special heating and electrical or electronic equipment, or use of animals or human subjects under controlled conditions.

Research facilities often include pilot plant operations, and development ordinances usually permit a certain percentage of the floor area (25 percent, for example) for pilot plant use. See *Pilot Plant*.

***Legal Annotation***: "The plaintiffs have appealed from a judgment of the Court of Common Pleas dismissing their appeal from the action of the defendant commission in amending the zoning regulations of Ridgefield to permit the use of land by **research** and development **laboratories** under a special permit to be issued by the commission. . . . A **research** and development **laboratory** is defined as a 'private commercial enterprise engaged exclusively in the pursuit of scientific research and development, including research concerning, and development of, manufactured, processed or compounded products.' . . . Whether a **research laboratory** as defined by § 9A constitutes an industrial use may be open to debate." *Summ v. Zoning Commission* (Conn., 1962).

## RESEARCH PARK

**A research facility or group of buildings dedicated to scientific research or business purposes, often linked to a major research facility. See *Office, Headquarters; Office Park*.**

***Comment***: Buildings within the park often share resources such as telecommunications hubs, uninterruptible power supply, data storage, security management, restaurants, child-care facilities, banks, entertainment, recreation and sports facilities, parking, and internal transportation. They are often encouraged by local governments, to expand the tax base and employment associated with the presence of a major university or college. Also referred to as "science parks" or "science and technology parks."

***Legal Annotation***: "The document further states that 'a preliminary program has been developed for the approximately 1,920-acre property Palm Beach County Biotechnology **Research Park** [.]' . . . The Scripps Research Institute (TSRI) is described as the 'centerpiece' of the project. . . . The County describes its intent as the master developer as follows: '[T]o develop a project that is sustainable and economically viable by creating a master plan that clusters the uses to promote intellectual exchange between the researchers and scientists at TSRI and other related companies, provides for a range of workforce housing to help minimize traffic impacts on surrounding roadways and provide obtainable housing for administrative and support staff, provides convenient retail, restaurant and other shopping opportunities for the workforce and residents, and promotes an integrated development that incorporates transportation alternatives to the automobile by incorporating a connected pathway, bikeway and multi-use rail system throughout the project.'" *Florida Wildlife Federation v. US Army Corps of Engineers* (S.D. Fla., 2005).

## RESERVATION

**(1) A provision in a deed or other real estate conveyance that retains a right for the existing owner even if other property rights are transferred; (2) a method of holding land for future public use by designating public areas on a plat, map, or site plan as a condition of approval.**

***Legal Annotation***: "On November 2, 2009, Appellants filed for a declaratory judgment, claiming the **reservation** of rights in the deed's exception included Marcellus shale gas and disputing Appellees' claim of adverse possession." *Butler v. Charles Powers Estate* (Pa. Super. Ct., 2011).

"The county's refusal to approve plats with no park land reserved is consistent with the zoning regulations which required a **reservation** of park land but permitted and did not require a dedication of such land to the county." *Smith v. Gwinnett County* (Ga., 1982).

## RESERVOIR

**A pond, lake, tank, or basin, natural or man-made, used for the storage, regulation, and control of water.**

***Legal Annotation***: "It is said that the valley fill is not a **reservoir** or lake, and therefore is not within Sec. 1 of the Act; that 'no one ever heard of a lake or **reservoir** with a sloping water table.' One definition of a **reservoir** is 'A place where water is collected and kept for use when wanted.' (Webster). Whether the water table 'slopes' we need not determine. We will assume that the law of gravitation will take care of that. We know that the valley fill is a **reservoir** from which billions of gallons of water are pumped to irrigate annually 45,000 acres of land, so it must be collected there; and the legislature aptly called such containers of water, **reservoirs** or lakes." *State v. Dority* (N.M., 1950).

## RESIDENCE

**A home, abode, or place where an individual is actually living at a specific point in time.**

***Comment***: One may have a number or residences, but the permanent home is called the "domicile." See *Domicile*.

***Legal Annotation***: "The FHA does not define the term '**residence**,' and therefore, the Court must construe the term according to its ordinary meaning. . . . As defined in Merriam-Webster's Online Dictionary, a **residence** is 'the place where one actually lives as distinguished from one's domicile or a place of temporary sojourn.' Courts have held the FHA applicable to homeless shelters, shelters for battered women, group homes for recovering drug addicts and alcoholics, seasonal bungalows, hospice facilities but not to lodging for transient guests such as hotels. Villegas v. Sandy Farms, Inc., 929 F. Supp. 1324, 1327 (D. Or. 1996) (citing cases)." *Drazen v. Town of Stratford* (D. Conn., 2013).

## RESIDENCE DISTRICT

**An area where the buildings used exclusively for residential purposes occupy more than 50 percent of the total street frontage.**

***Comment***: The term "residence district" is derived from motor vehicle statutes in defining areas where the maximum speed limit is 25 miles per hour. It also provides a specific standard that can be applied in a variety of situations to describe predominantly residential areas. Note that this term is different than a designated zoning district in which the predominant use, or predominantly permitted uses are residential, hence often referred to as a "residential district."

***Legal Annotation***: "Accordingly, the underlying standard set forth in the New York City Zoning Resolution for a **residence district** is not whether individuals reside in buildings within the district boundaries but, rather, what types of land uses are permitted within such district. It is evident from the zoning scheme that all uses of land in a **residence district** are not limited to residential dwelling units, and that some uses, such as community facilities and cemeteries, which do not consist of residential inhabitants, are permitted in **residence districts**." *City of NY v. Scandals* (N.Y. Sup. Ct., 1998).

## RESIDENT MANAGER

**An agent of the owner of a building, living on the premises, who exercises general supervision of the building.**

***Legal Annotation***: "(c) Fraternity houses, sorority houses and student cooperative houses as a special exception use pursuant to Section 5:104 if 350 square feet of lot area is provided per occupant, a **resident manager** is employed or appointed if the owner does not reside in the house, and if the floor area of the structure exceeds 5,000 square feet." *North Burns Park Assoc. v. City of Ann Arbor* (Mich. Ct. App., 1986).

## RESIDENTIAL ACCESS STREET

**See *Street, Local.***

***Legal Annotation***: "Residential streets are classified pursuant to Table 4.2, as provided in N.J.A.C. 5:21-4.1. N.J.A.C. 5:21-4.1(c). The '**Residential Access**' street, as stated in Table 4.2, '[p]rovides frontage for access to lots and carries traffic with destination or origin on the street itself[,]' and '[a]ll, or the maximum number of housing units, shall front on this class of street.'" *Northgate Condominium Association, Inc. v. Borough of Hillsdale Planning Board* (N.J. Super. Ct., 2011).

## RESIDENTIAL AREA

**A generic term describing an area that gives the impression that it is predominantly a place where people live. See *Residence District*.**

***Comment***: The definition does not provide any standard by which an area is described as residential. It is, at best, a visual impression, and the area may include a significant amount of commercial or industrial uses.

***Legal Annotation***: "The Executive Director of the Erie Zoological Society, James Rhea, testified that tigers are 'predators' capable of getting 'out of hand at any given time,' regardless of whether the tiger is declawed. He further stated that it is not possible to domesticate a tiger, and explained that professional care is the key to possessing a tiger safely. Rhea also agreed that a **residential area** is not an appropriate place for a tiger to reside because it poses a threat to the safety and welfare of area residents." *Fairview Tp. v. Schaefer* (Pa. Common. Ct., 1989).

## RESIDENTIAL CLUSTER

**A form of planned-unit residential development to be built as a single entity and containing residential housing units that have private or public open-space area as an appurtenance. See *Cluster*.**

***Comment***: Residential clustering is utilized as an alternative to large-lot zoning as an antidote to the harmful effects of suburban sprawl. In most "residential cluster developments," the lots provided for each home are reduced in size and are clustered together in one portion of the tract (often the least environmentally constrained and closest to public utilities), thereby allowing a portion of the tract to be set aside as open space or continued farming. In most cluster developments, the overall density (homes per acre) is maintained, or in some cases is slightly increased, as an incentive to preserve more of the tract as open space or for farming. Residential clustering is appropriate for exurban areas or as a means of preserving farmland at the fringe of suburbanizing areas.

The open space may be used for agricultural activities, parks, or recreation. A question that should be addressed during the approval process is whether the open space is restricted to residents of the residential cluster or open to the general public. Another question is whether residents and/or the general public can be charged for the use of facilities such as swimming pools, tennis courts, or golf.

***Legal Annotation***: "Section 225-25 B defines a 'cluster development' as a 'planned residential tract, subdivision or area where individual lots and/or buildings are arranged in clusters or groups, where access is gained entirely by internal streets, with open areas between such lots or building groups, which areas are either publicly or privately owned and maintained in a park-like appearance.'... Section 225-52 outlines 'A-1 cluster development[s].' A. Where applicable. Cluster development may be permitted in the A-1 Agriculture-Rural District, for **residential cluster** purposes, subject to the standards contained in Subsection F hereof, entitled 'Development standards.'" *Pomeranc-Burke, LLC V. Wicomico Environmental Trust, Ltd.* (Md. Ct. Spec. App. 2011).

## RESIDENTIAL DENSITY

**The number of dwelling units per acre of residential land.**

***Comment***: The density must be further defined in terms of net or gross. In some zoning ordinances, residential density is expressed as the number of bedrooms per acre of land. Floor-area ratio controls are also considered to be an alternative or supplementary methodology of controlling residential density. See *Density; Net Residential Density; Floor Area Ratio.*

***Legal Annotation***: "The residential aspects of the project were addressed in specific proffers that limited the **residential density** of the Country Club Proffer Section to 400 total bedrooms and permitted no more than 48 bedrooms per acre should that section of the property be subdivided." *Hale v. Board of Zoning Appeals, Town of Blacksburg* (Va., 2009).

## RESIDENTIAL HEALTH-CARE FACILITY (RHCF)

**Residences, usually occupied by the frail elderly, that provide rooms, meals, personal care, and health monitoring services under the supervision of a professional nurse and may provide other services, such as recreational, social, and cultural activities, financial services, and transportation.**

***Comment***: RHCFs may be independent facilities but are most often developed in conjunction with long-term care facilities. In many states, a certificate of need, which is required for an RHCF, is issued only when the RHCF is part of a long-term care facility, although not necessarily on the same lot as the RHCF. RHCFs are almost always licensed by the state, and most have communal dining rooms and other communal space. The professional nurse may be a registered or a licensed practical nurse. In general, all residents must be ambulatory and free of communicable diseases. Rooms and baths may be either private or shared.

***Legal Annotation***: "Other provisions in our statutes demonstrate that the legislature is aware that there are various types of different **residential healthcare facilities** and that it knows how to make specific reference to a 'nursing home' when it intends to do so. For instance, the legislature has identified several types of **residential healthcare facilities** and included nursing homes in the definition of '[i]nstitutions' that are licensed by the state. See General Statutes § 19A-490(A) ('"[I]Nstitution" Means A Hospital, Residential Care Home, Health Care Facility For The Handicapped, Nursing Home, Rest Home . . . Substance Abuse Treatment Facility'). The Text Of § 19A-490(A) Thus Indicates That The Legislature Knows How To Use The Specific Term 'Nursing Home' In Our Statutes When It Intends To And Thus Suggests To Us That Its Failure To Use That Term in § 12-62N Was Purposeful." Hartford/Windsor Hlth. V. City of Hartford (Conn., 2010).

## RESIDENTIAL UNIT

**See *Household; Residence*.**

***Legal Annotation***: "The City responded to a complaint in early 2008 that the garage had been illegally converted. The property is zoned Single Family Residential, Bungalow Heaven Landmark District, and so a second or third **residential unit** is not currently permitted by the Zoning Code. Ramirez complied with the City's order to return the garage to what was allowed in 1945 by removing the first and second floor kitchens and returning the first floor to a garage. The City was satisfied." *Thoreen v. City of Pasadena* (Calif. Ct. App., 2012).

## RESORT

**A facility for transient guests where the primary attractions are recreational features or activities.**

***Legal Annotation***: "Whether the properties are designated as **resorts** is irrelevant because, as was noted by the district court, '[w]hile the use of the properties may meet the definition of a **resort** in the current ordinance, a **resort** is not specifically identified as either a permitted or conditional use anywhere in the ordinance.' As described above, a PUD involves multiple units on a single parcel, and although a '**resort**' is listed as an example of a PUD, the examples merely identify ways in which such multiple-unit developments may be organized, rather than dictating that any structure that falls within the definition of a **resort** is of itself a PUD. The zoning ordinance does not restrict the rental of single-family dwellings on a short-term basis, and the use of the Owens' properties here does not compel the conclusion that the properties are PUDs." *County of Douglas v. Owen* (Minn. Ct. App., 2009).

## RESOURCE RECOVERY

**The process of obtaining materials or energy, particularly from solid waste.**

***Comment***: Typically resource recovery is conducted in facilities that are specifically designed and operated for such purposes, known as "resource recovery facilities." Due to the nature of the activities conducted and the emissions related thereto, they are considered heavy industrial uses.

***Legal Annotation***: "The FEIS challenged by petitioners in the instant proceeding concerns the construction of a proposed **resource recovery** facility (hereinafter facility) in the Town of Poughkeepsie in Dutchess County. Resource recovery is broadly defined in the FEIS as the 'recovery of waste materials for use in a productive manner'. The proposed facility approved by the Dutchess County Legislature will utilize the technology known as 'mass burning', whereby refuse is incinerated at high temperatures in the condition it is delivered without prior processing, other than screening to eliminate materials defined as '[u]nacceptable [w]astes'." *Aldrich v. Pattison* (N.Y. App. Div., 1985).

## RESPONDER, FIRST

**Refers to individuals who in the early stages of an incident are responsible for the protection and preservation of life, property, evidence, and the environment, including emergency response providers as defined in Section 2 of the Homeland Security Act of 2002 (6 U.S.C. 101).**

***Comment***: First responders include emergency management, public health, clinical care, public works, and other skilled support personnel (e.g., equipment operators) who provide immediate support services during prevention, response, and recovery operations. http://www.gwu.edu/~icdrm/publications/PDF/GLOSSARY%2002-19-2007.pdf

***Legal Annotation***: "A '**first responder**' is the first person to arrive on the scene who provides emergency care and treatment to ill and injured people." *Firefighter's Institute v. City of St. Louis* (8th Cir., 2000).

## RESPONDER, SECOND

**Personnel intended to arrive later during incident response, to augment or relieve first responders, or to provide additional, specialized expertise that is less common in first response.**

***Comment***: Second responders also include small contractors and day laborers. (Source: *New York Times*, 11/6/13, editorial.) http://www.gwu.edu/~icdrm/publications/PDF/GLOSSARY%2002-19-2007.pdf

***Legal Annotation***: "Adam Garland, Sr., the assistant chief with the Embreeville Volunteer Fire Department ('Embreeville Fire Dept.'), testified for Plaintiffs. The Embreeville Fire Dept. services the properties involved in this lawsuit as a primary responder with the Jonesborough Fire Department serving this area as a **second responder**." *Shew v. Bawgus* (Tenn. Ct. App., 2007).

## REST HOME

See *Nursing Home*.

*Legal Annotation*: "A **rest home** is defined by the ordinance as '[a] home operated as a boarding house, and in which nursing, dietary and other personal services are furnished to convalescents, invalids and aged persons, *but in which no persons suffering from a mental sickness, disease, disorder or ailment* or from a contagious or communicable disease are kept, and in which no surgical or other primary treatments such as are customarily provided in sanitariums or hospitals are performed.'" *City of Jewell Junction v. Cunningham* (Iowa, 1989).

## RESTAURANT

**An establishment where food and drink are prepared, served, and consumed, mostly within the principal building. See *Carry-Out Restaurant; Drive-In Restaurant; Fast-Food Restaurant; Retail Food Establishment*.**

***Comment***: The term *restaurant* is all-encompassing and includes many variations, some of which are defined in this book. A restaurant may have limited forms of musical entertainment to accompany the dining experience; however, restaurants that provide stage shows are called cabarets. See *Cabaret*.

*Legal Annotation*: "A **restaurant** is defined in Webster's International Dictionary as 'An establishment where refreshments or meals may be procured by the public; a public eating house,' and while this no doubt assumes that the refreshments are to be eaten on the premises, that qualification is here complied with since the food will be consumed there even though it be in automobiles stationed thereon. The applicant was clearly entitled to a permit for the erection and the use of a building as and for a 'restaurant, cafe or catering.'" *Food Corp. v. Zoning Bd. of Adjustment* (Pa., 1956).

## RESTAURANT, DRIVE-IN

**An establishment where food or drink is served to and consumed by a customer in an automobile while parked on the premises. See *Drive-Through Restaurant*.**

*Comment*: Drive-in restaurants had their heyday in the 1950s. Apart from a few chains that still provide drive-in services—such as Sonic and some A&W restaurants—they have mostly disappeared from the American rural and urban environment. Drive-in restaurants are distinguished from drive-through (or drive-thru) restaurants by the fact that cars are actually parked on the premises—as opposed to using a designated lane for ordering and for paying at a drive-thru window—where food is both served and consumed within the automobile. Because so few chains provide drive-in services, most communities omit them from their zoning regulations altogether.

*Legal Annotation*: "This is also the meaning of 'drive-in' that is used in the next clause of the ordinance, which states that one of the permitted uses in a C-2 commercial district is '**[d]rive-in restaurants** or *similar uses that provide goods and services to patrons in automobiles*.' Kandiyohi County, Minn., Zoning Ordinance § 1-328, subd. 2.6 (emphasis added). Describing uses that provide goods and services to patrons in automobiles as being similar to a **drive-in restaurant** implies that a **drive-in restaurant** is a restaurant that provides goods and services to patrons in automobiles." *State v. Rose* (Minn. Ct. App., 2005).

## RESTAURANT, DRIVE-THROUGH

**An establishment in which food or drink is served to customers within automobiles outside of the confines of the building and where the consumption of such food or drink is intended to occur off the premises. See *Drive-in Restaurant*.**

***Comment***: Drive-through restaurants have replaced drive-in restaurants and are now found in the vast majority of stand-alone fast-food restaurants. Their popularity and use has increased substantially over the past decade. In many fast-food restaurants, half or more than half of their transactions occur via the drive-through. Because of their circulatory needs (the need to circulate in a counterclockwise direction so that the drive-through window is on the driver's side of the car) and the need to allow cars awaiting their time to order (which can add up to ten or more cars in the queue at peak times), design standards for drive-through restaurants must be provided to properly accommodate such needs. Design standards are also needed to address signage (to direct vehicles to the drive-through lanes and separate them from cars whose customers are parking and eating within the restaurant), as well as loading, lighting, landscaping, etc. Most fast-food franchises have made advances in the technology, operation, and design to address a myriad of concerns associated with drive-through operations. For example, to address noise concerns, two-way speakers at low volumes at drive-through windows, and separate menu boards, are provided. To speed up service and minimize stacking in the drive-through lanes, two windows, one for paying and the second for pickup, and the use of wireless headsets have been instituted. Some chains even have two drive-through lanes—one on each side of the building. Such innovations have helped drive-through restaurants to operate more efficiently and quietly.

***Legal Annotation***: "The Plaintiff argues that a **drive-through restaurant** is akin to a hotel or motel because 'the nature of defendants' business was to offer a service of a type normally found in one's own home.' Plaintiff argues '[t]he nature of defendants' invitation was to come to a specific business (a restaurant) for the purpose of eating. The relationship between the defendants and plaintiff was, therefore, more direct and more intimate than the *Cornpropst* invitation to come to a public parking lot for the purpose of browsing in or making purchases at one or more of the various retail establishments available. Plaintiff's argument is without merit. We find nothing homey or intimate about selling hamburgers to motorists at a drive-through window.'" *Gray v. McDonald's Corp.* (Tenn. Ct. App., 1993).

## RESTAURANT, DRIVE-THRU

**See *Restaurant, Drive-through*.**

***Legal Annotation***: "SECTION 1: That this Council does hereby regulate the use of **drive-thru restaurant** facilities by adopting the following provisions:

'(a) No person being the owner, operator, tenant, employee or agent of any restaurant shall sell or offer for sale any of its products through a drive-thru facility before 6:00 AM and after 11:00 PM Sunday through Thursday, and not before 6:00 AM and after 12:00 midnight on Friday and Saturday, if said restaurant is located within 250 (two hundred fifty) linear feet of any residential structure.

'(b) Any person violating the provisions of this regulation shall be guilty of a minor misdemeanor, the fine of which shall not exceed $100.00 (one hundred dollars).'" *Franchise Operations, Inc. v. City of North Olmsted* (Ohio Ct. App., 1987).

## RESTAURANT, FAST-CASUAL

**Restaurants with a limited menu, limited service, or self-service format, whose food is made to order and is fresher and higher quality and has more complex flavors than fast-food restaurants, and whose décor is more upscale, unique, or highly developed (Wikipedia). See *Fast-Food Restaurant*.**

***Comment***: Fast-casual restaurants are one of the fastest-growing segments of the restaurant industry. Most fast-casual chains came into being in the 1990s but only became mainstream in the past few years. They are distinguished from fast-food restaurants, with which they share many of the same characteristics, by the use of fresher, higher-quality ingredients (such as free-range chicken or fresh-made salsa), and in terms of their food preparation. Dishes are handmade, often with views into the kitchen, rather than precooked and preheated in bulk, as is the case with fast-food restaurants. The décor and atmosphere are also more upscale and varied. Fast-casual restaurants, unlike fast-food restaurants, do not have drive-throughs. Examples of fast-casual restaurants include Panera Bread, Chipotle, Five Guys Burger and Fries, Baja Fresh Mexican Grill, and Moe's Southwestern Grill.

***Legal Annotation***: "He has previously worked as a machine operator, a material handler, and most recently as a bus boy at Red Robin, a **'fast-casual' restaurant.**" *Mendoza-Gil v. Astrue* (N.D. Ill., 2011).

## RESTAURANT, FAST-FOOD

**Restaurants whose emphasis is on convenience and speed of service, that are generally part of a restaurant chain or franchise, and that provide a limited menu and minimal table or fast counter service, and whose meals are typically inexpensive and made from standardized ingredients that are partially or fully cooked in bulk in advance and kept hot and then finished and packaged to order.**

***Comment***: Non-planning-related criticisms have been leveled against the fast-food industry, including adverse impacts on everything from agricultural practices to climate change, the environment, labor markets, and nutrition and health; yet the industry continues to thrive and grow. Land-use and planning concerns have been somewhat blunted by changes made by many of the fast-food chains in regard to architecture and site planning. However, such concerns remain at the forefront of community concerns about permitting fast-food restaurants as-of-right. This includes high-traffic generation, litter, noise, and uniformity and blandness of design. Zoning regulations and design standards can be implemented to ameliorate most of the latter issues, and most chains and franchises have become more flexible in amending their plans to conform to vernacular architectural styles and other regulations in order to be approved. Because of the extent to which fast-food chains in suburban areas rely on drive-through windows to accommodate their customers' needs, many fast-food franchises will no longer be established if drive-through service is not permitted. As much as half or more of the daily transactions occur via the drive-through. Examples of fast-food restaurants are McDonald's, Subway, Taco Bell, Pizza Hut, and KFC.

***Legal Annotation***: "The municipality, which is primarily residential, has a commercial district that contains a variety of uses, including at least three **fast food restaurants**—a Burger King, McDonald's and Kentucky Fried Chicken. Sometime after these restaurants were established, the governing body amended the zoning ordinance to prohibit **fast food restaurants** in any part of the municipality. . . . Initially, we note that Grillco's proposed **fast food restaurant** is not simply 'a use omitted from' the permitted uses listed in the zoning ordinance. . . . Instead, it is a use that the Saddle Brook governing body has expressly prohibited in every zoning district. . . . [T]he Board's grant of a use variance for a fast food restaurant in the face of the governing body's express prohibition of this use constituted a usurpation of 'the legislative power reserved to the governing body of the municipality.'" *Saddle Brook Realty, LLC. v. Township of Saddle Brook Zoning Board of Adjustment* (N.J. Super. Ct., 2006).

"A Formula **Fast-Food Restaurant** is defined under section 170-13 (C) (1) (b) of the Village Code as follows: FORMULA **FAST-FOOD RESTAURANT**—Any establishment, required by contract, franchise or other arrangements, to offer two or more of the following:

[1] Standardized menus, ingredients, food preparation and/or uniforms.
[2] Prepared food in ready-to-consume state.
[3] Food sold over the counter in disposable containers and wrappers.
[4] Food selected from a limited menu.
[5] Food sold for immediate consumption on or off premises.
[6] Where customer pays before eating." *Mead Sq. Commons v. Victor, NY* (N.Y. Sup. Ct., 2011).

## RESTAURANT, OUTDOOR

**Any part of a food establishment located outdoors, not used for any other purposes, and open to the sky, with the exception that it may have a retractable awning or umbrellas, and may contain furniture, including tables, chairs, railings, and planters that are readily moveable (American Planning Association, "Regulating Outdoor Sales," *Zoning News*, April 1995).**

***Comment***: The above definition does not distinguish between outdoor service on private land and that on public land. Most jurisdictions require special licenses or permits to use public land, such as sidewalks, for outdoor sales, including food. Site-plan review requirements for both public and private land include access, circulation, signage, noise (including controls on loudspeakers), appearance, and health considerations.

Outdoor food service on public land would also include, in addition to license requirements or special permits for using public land, particular attention to public access and circulation, public liability, obstruction to traffic, and blocking access to adjacent buildings.

***Legal Annotation***: "Pupco owns R. P. McMurphy's Irish Pub in the Oakley neighborhood of Cincinnati. In 2005, Pupco sought to expand the business by constructing a deck with an awning, columns, and a service driveway. The application for the permit listed the proposed use for the addition as a 'tavern.' . . . So, except for the awning, the addition would be almost completely open to the elements. It would therefore provide none of the barriers between the drinking area and the surrounding neighborhood that would protect residents from the potential noise and other disturbances that could arise from the operation of a tavern. Under any reasonable definition of the term '**outdoor**,' the proposed addition would be an outdoor drinking area that would violate the municipal code." *Pupco Property Mgt. v. City of Cincinnati* (Ohio Ct. App., 2007).

## RESTAURANT, TAKE-OUT

**An establishment where food and/or beverages are sold in a form ready for consumption, where all or a significant part of the consumption takes place off the premises. See *Restaurant, Drive-In; Restaurant, Drive-Through*.**

***Comment***: "Take-out restaurants" do not encompass drive-in or drive-through restaurants. One of the zoning problems with these types of restaurants occurs when tables are added for on-premises consumption of food. The additional parking area required is often not available or is otherwise inadequate. Most restaurants now provide for takeout service; if this portion of their business is not the predominant means whereby food is served and consumed, they would not be classified as "take-out restaurants."

***Legal Annotation***: "The regulation, on the other hand, applies to '**take-out**' **restaurant** service. As demonstrated by the dictionary definition of the word '**take-out**,' **restaurant** service of the take-out type is rendered in connection with 'food not to be consumed on the premises.' Webster's Ninth New Collegiate Dictionary." *Spero v. Zoning Board of Appeals* (Conn., 1991).

## RESTORATION

**The replication or reconstruction of a building's original architectural features.**

***Comment***: "Restoration" is usually used to describe the technique of preserving historic buildings. Rehabilitation, which also accomplishes building upgrading, does not necessarily retain the building's original architectural features. See *Rehabilitation; Preservation*.

***Legal Annotation***: "The house at that time was vacant and uninhabitable, with no heat, electricity, or plumbing, was in severe disrepair, and had recently been damaged by fire. The sale was for $20,100, Trussell agreeing to abide by historic preservation restrictions and to do a complete historic **restoration**. The exterior portion was to be completed in one year, failing which the society could, at its option, engage workers to complete the exterior restoration at Trussell's expense. No time limit was specified for interior **restoration**. There was no requirement that the house be opened to public viewing or that the house be occupied." *Worcester Heritage Society, Inc. v. Trussell* (Mass. App. Ct., 1991).

## RESTRICTION

**A limitation on property, which may be created in a property deed, lease, mortgage, through certain zoning or subdivision regulations, or as a condition of approval of an application for development.**

***Legal Annotation***: "The property lacks the frontage required under the by-law to permit construction of a residence. However, in 1998, before Gray Wolf acquired the property, a predecessor in interest obtained a variance permitting construction of a single-family residence on the property. The variance was conditioned on the imposition of a deed **restriction**, limiting the use of the property to a single-family dwelling." *Rosenfeld v. Zoning Board of Appeals of Mendon* (Mass. App. Ct., 2011).

## RESTRICTIVE COVENANT

**A restriction on the use of land, usually set forth in the deed.**

***Comment*:** Restrictive covenants usually run with the land and are binding on subsequent owners of the property. However, some restrictive covenants run for specific periods of time.

***Legal Annotation*:** "The Supreme Court erred in dismissing the first cause of action, seeking a judgment declaring that the defendants violated a **restrictive covenant**, the terms of which were incorporated into the amended complaint, barring them from erecting on their property any 'hedge' exceeding five feet in height, and related injunctive relief. Because 'the law favors the free and unobstructed use of real property,' a **restrictive covenant** 'must be strictly construed against those seeking to enforce it, and may not be given an interpretation extending beyond the clear meaning of its terms.'" *Ford v. Fink* (N.Y. App. Div., 2011).

## RESUBDIVIDE

**(1) The further division of lots or the relocation of lot lines of any lot or lots within a subdivision previously approved and recorded according to law; (2) the alteration of any streets or the establishment of any new streets within any subdivision made and approved or recorded according to law, but not including conveyances made so as to combine existing lots by deed or other instrument.**

***Legal Annotation*:** "Prior to the plaintiffs' action for injunctive relief, the defendants sought and received approval from the Norwalk planning commission to **resubdivide** their property and to build a second dwelling on their subdivided property. The defendants do not claim that the permission from the planning commission can override the restrictive covenant in their deed. A landowner who seeks a perpetual restriction on the use of subdivided property may limit development by the use of restrictive covenants. A municipal commission, however, does not have the power to deny an application for subdivision approval based on such a covenant if the application otherwise meets the requirements of the local subdivision regulations or the enabling statutes." *Cappo v. Suda* (Conn. App. Ct., 2011).

## RETAIL, LIFESTYLE CENTER

**An unenclosed retail center of between 100,000 and 250,000 square feet without any regional anchor and generally featuring national specialty stores and restaurants, with limited recreational facilities and services, convenient and easily accessible parking, a pedestrian-friendly ambiance, and each store fronting on and having its own entrance on the major circulation street.**

***Comment*:** Lifestyle centers are upscale versions of the traditional strip retail center, with greater emphasis on design, building material, landscaping, and street furniture. They attempt to establish a decidedly pedestrian feel, much like the traditional downtown, in a vehicle-oriented suburban setting. Because of their relatively smaller scale and pedestrian-friendly design, they are more likely to gain acceptance in suburban settings than the regional mall. The lifestyle center is popular even in less climate-friendly locales; for example, Deer Park Town Center in northern Illinois. It appeals particularly to women, who do 70 percent of the family shopping. As noted by one frequent shopper, "It is much easier to pick up or return merchandise in a lifestyle center than in an enclosed mall. You can easily spot the store you want and park close by" (Baeb 2002).

***Legal Annotation*:** "The claims were based on representations by the developers and their agents that the Legacy Shopping Center would be a '**lifestyle center**' and include upscale residential development which arguably would result in a higher traffic volume. . . . [R]epresentations were made regarding the Legacy Shopping Center being constructed as a '**lifestyle center**,' to include office space, retail development, restaurants, entertainment (a Santikos movie theater), and multi-family residences. The '**lifestyle center**' as represented would allegedly ensure a higher volume of traffic than other shopping centers like power centers which rely on big box retailers to draw traffic." *Dragon Fish, LLC v. Santikos Legacy, Ltd.* (Texas Ct. App., 2012).

## RETAIL FOOD ESTABLISHMENT

**Any fixed facility in which food or drink is sold primarily for off-premises preparation and consumption.**

*Comment*: Retail food establishments include all stores in which food is sold, including grocery stores, supermarkets, and specialty food stores. Some supermarkets now prepare and serve meals at lunch counters or tables as an accessory use.

*Legal Annotation*: "Under regulations promulgated by DER to regulate eating and drinking places, '**retail food establishment**' is defined as '[a]ny place, whether temporary or permanent, stationary or mobile, where food or drink is packaged, stored, served, sold or offered for sale directly to the consumer.' Tid Bit Alley does not contend that its Erie County store is not a retail food establishment." *Tid Bit Alley, Inc. v. Erie Co. Dept. of H.* (Pa. Common. Ct., 1987).

## RETAIL FOOD ESTABLISHMENT, MOBILE

**A vehicle, usually a van, truck, towed trailer, or pushcart, from which food and beverages are sold.**

*Comment*: Also referred to as "food trucks" or "food carts." Many municipalities choose to regulate these uses by licensing them and requiring compliance with regulations dealing with sanitation, traffic safety, and location. Typical locations are job sites; places of assembly, such as colleges, industries, or sports activities; and special events.

*Legal Annotation*: "Browne was one of eight applicants vying for six available permits to operate a **mobile food cart** in downtown Iowa City. The city created an objective matrix to score the applications. One criterion in the matrix was past satisfactory experience working with Iowa City. . . . 'Any right plaintiff has to earn a living through a **food cart**, like other intangible employment rights, arises from state law and does not spring from the fundamental guarantees of the Constitution. Municipalities in the United States have a history of stringently regulating or even prohibiting **food cart** vendors; thus, the right to freely operate a **food cart** is not "deeply rooted" in our Nation's history and traditions. Nor is the right to freely operate a **food cart** implicit in our concept of ordered liberty. Therefore, the court finds that plaintiff fails to allege a property right that is protected by the Constitution and does not state a substantive due process cause of action as a matter of law.' *Diaz v. City of Scranton,* 2012 WL 3597192, at *4 (M.D. Pa. Aug. 20, 2012)." *Browne v. City of Iowa City* (Iowa Ct. App., 2014).

## RETAIL, MAGNET STORE

**The largest retail establishment in a shopping center, which draws customers and thereby generates business for the remaining stores in the center. See *Anchor Tenant*.**

*Comment*: In a regional center, the department store is the magnet. In neighborhood centers, it is the supermarket.

*Legal Annotation*: "The mall had only one **magnet store**, of doubtful drawing power, and the layout and design were 'wanting.'" *Matter of Union Deposit Ctr. Equities Ltd. Partnership* (3rd Cir., 1981).

## RETAIL OUTLET STORE

**A retail establishment selling a single manufacturer's product.**

*Comment*: A traditional or conventional retail establishment normally handles a number of different product lines, often of the same product. An outlet store differs in that it handles the products of a single manufacturer and is usually owned by that manufacturer.

Outlet malls, essentially regional shopping centers comprising only retail outlet stores, have become very popular in the past two decades. Typically found in resort cities or in rural areas somewhat distant from urban centers, their popularity stems from the fact that many such outlet stores provide inventory that is slightly outdated or slightly flawed at discounted prices compared to merchandise sold in department stores or flagship stores in urban areas. From a planning and zoning perspective, the major difference is that outlet malls draw from a much larger service area than a typical shopping center. The service area may vary between five and fifty miles. Consequently, much of the traffic generation takes place on weekends, as opposed to the more typical daily or evening traffic flow generated by conventional shopping centers.

***Legal Annotation***: "From 1989 to 1998, White owned and operated two Lincoln businesses named 'Nebraska Spirit' and 'Team Spirit Industries.' Both businesses were engaged in screen printing, embroidering, and selling clothing and novelty items related to a theme of the University of Nebraska-Lincoln athletics. White was aware of the Department's plan to open a **retail outlet store** to sell authentic goods in February 1997. He opposed the opening of the store, fearing competition with his businesses." *White v. Board of Regents* (Neb., 2000).

## RETAIL SALES

**Establishments engaged in the selling or rental of goods or merchandise (usually to the general public for personal use or household consumption, although they may also serve business and institutional clients) and in rendering services incidental to the sale of such goods.**

***Comment***: Some of the important characteristics of retail sales establishments follow:

- The establishment is usually a place of business and is engaged in activity to attract the general public to buy.
- The establishment buys and receives as well as sells merchandise.
- It may process or manufacture some of the products, such as a jeweler or bakery, for example, but such processing or manufacturing is usually incidental or subordinate to the selling activities.
- Retail establishments sell to customers for their own personal or household use.

An important characteristic of a retail trade establishment is that it buys goods for resale. A farmer, for example, selling goods grown on his own property, would not be classified as a retailer. A farm stand that brings in goods from other farmers could be classified as a retail outlet but more typically is classified as a customary accessory use to a farm. Eating and drinking places also may be classified as retail establishments, although more often they are classified under retail services.

Lumberyards and paint, glass, and wallpaper stores usually are included as retail trade even though a substantial portion of their business may be to contractors. Establishments selling office supplies and equipment are usually classified as retail, although they sell to offices and other business establishments.

Finally, there are categories of retail trade that manufacture products and sell them on premises, such as bakeries. If the bulk of the products made in the bakery are sold on premises, it would be classified as retail trade. If the baking includes a large wholesale operation, selling to other stores, or supplying its own outlets, the operation would probably more accurately be classified as manufacturing.

***Legal Annotation***: "**Retail Sales**: Shall mean an establishment whose principal use is the sale of products for consumption or use by the customer off the premises. This shall include but not be limited to hardware, paint, office equipment, sporting goods, trading stamp and redemption outlets, televisions, satellite dishes, automotive supply and major household appliance stores." *In re Champlain Oil Company Conditional Use Application* (Vt., 2014).

## RETAIL SALES, OUTDOOR

**The display and sale of products and services, primarily outside of a building or structure, including vehicles; garden supplies, flowers, shrubs, and other plant materials; gas, tires, and motor oil; food and beverages; boats and aircraft; farm equipment; motor homes; burial monuments; building and landscape materials; and lumberyards. See *Restaurant, Outdoor; Sidewalk Sales*.**

***Comment***: The major characteristic of outdoor retail sales establishments is that the material sold is usually stored outdoors and customers examine and inspect the materials outside of a building or structure. Outdoor retail establishments usually have buildings in which sales may be consummated or products displayed; however, most of the items sold outdoors are too large, there are too many of them to be stored indoors, or they require light, air, and water.

From a planning and zoning perspective, site-plan considerations include the visual impact of the stored materials, outdoor lighting, signage, noise generation (including amplifiers), banners and attention-gathering devices, vehicular and pedestrian circulation, parking, and litter control.

The outdoor area where the material is stored should be improved or dust-free, except for plant materials. The stored material should be kept a reasonable distance from all lot lines, and less "tidy" items, such as building materials and lumber stacks, could be restricted to rear or side yards with adequate screening or fencing. The maximum height of the stored material should be specified.

***Legal Annotation***: "On May 8, 2009, Costco wrote to the Zoning Officer for Montgomery Township proposing to install 16 gasoline fueling pumps in the parking lot next to its existing store, which it believed to be permitted as an accessory use. The Zoning Officer responded that the Expressway Corridor Preservation Overlay District (Overlay District), where Costco's store is located, permits indoor retail sales, but not **outdoor retail sales**, such as gasoline filling stations. . . . The trial court construed the provision of the Zoning Ordinance that permits 'shops, stores or other indoor facilities' for retail sales not to include a gasoline service station, which is an outdoor facility. Because stand-alone gasoline filling stations are not permitted as of right, the trial court held they could not be permitted as an accessory use. Discerning no error in the trial court's holding, we affirm." *In re Costco Wholesale Corp.* (Pa. Common. Ct. 2012).

## RETAIL SERVICES

**Establishments providing services or entertainment, as opposed to products, to the general public for personal or household use, including eating and drinking places; hotels and motels; finance, real estate, and insurance offices; personal services; theaters; amusement and recreation services; health, educational, and social services; museums; and galleries.**

***Comment***: Services may involve some products, like restaurants, for example. The difference, though, is that the products are part of the overall service and are usually consumed on the premises. Retail services may also include personal services, such as cleaners, shoemakers, and beauty parlors. Services to businesses or industry are not usually included under retail services.

In addition, not all retail services are appropriate in all zones. For example, hotels and large multiplex movie theaters may not be appropriate for neighborhood business zones because of heavy traffic generation and hours of operation. See *Personal Services; Services.*

***Legal Annotation***: "Patricia and Michael Fowler asked the Muscatine County Zoning Commission to have their property rezoned from A-1 agricultural to C-1 commercial to permit the operation of a seasonal deer processing facility and retail counter. . . . The Fowlers, the zoning administrator, and the zoning commission chairperson executed an agreement restricting use of the Fowlers' real estate to '[o]nly wild game processing,' '[r]etail products in the wild game category . . . and supporting wild game products,' as well as a single family residence. . . . The board contends the Fowlers were not authorized to provide year-round **retail services** on their property." *Fowler v. Muscatine County Board of Supervisors* (Iowa Ct. App., 2013).

## RETAIL STORE, BIG-BOX

**See *Big-Box Store*.**

***Legal Annotation***: "The City of Turlock (City) adopted a zoning ordinance that prohibited the development of **'big box' retail stores** containing a full service grocery department." *Wal-Mart Stores, Inc. v. City of Turlock* (Calif. Ct. App., 2006).

## RETAIL STORE, CATEGORY KILLER

**A big-box store that specializes in one type of merchandise; for example, electronics, office**

**supplies, furniture, or recreation and sports equipment.**

***Legal Annotation***: "Starting in 2000 however, the company began to face intense pressure from large discount retailers such as Wal-Mart and Target, or '**category killer**' specialty stores, such as Best Buys and Toys 'R' Us." *Eldridge v. Gordon Brothers Group, LLC* (D. Mass., 2011).

## RETAIL STORE, CONVENIENCE

**A retail establishment of up to five thousand square feet selling primarily food products, beverages, newspapers and magazines, candy, cigarettes, household items, and a limited amount of freshly prepared foods such as sandwiches and salads for off-premises consumption.**

***Comment***: Convenience food stores are a fast-growing segment of the retail food industry. They are the modern equivalent of the corner grocery store—often open twenty-four hours a day, seven days a week, and containing a variety of items, providing quick and convenient service, and often touted as being compatible with and logically located in residential neighborhoods.

Convenience stores pose the usual problems of all retail establishments. These include provision of sufficient parking, lighting, litter control, access, and concern for impacts on adjacent residences. The problems are often intensified because these stores usually are open long hours. Site-plan review should pay particular attention to hours of operation, lighting impact on surrounding uses, and plans to control litter.

Convenience stores often pose unique challenges, a major one being that of design. Unfortunately, the convenience store is often a concrete-block, flat-roofed, stand-alone, one-story building with windows covered with signs, and lacking any meaningful landscaping. Parking is invariably located directly in the front of the building, disrupting the existing streetscape. Regulations should establish architectural standards, requirements for building materials, respect for existing development context and streetscape, parking layout and location, vigorous enforcement of sign standards, landscaping requirements, and litter control.

If on-site food consumption is allowed, it should be specified in the regulations, with additional requirements for parking (American Planning Association, *A Survey of Zoning Definitions*, Planning Advisory Service Report No. 421, 1989).

***Legal Annotation***: "Through the insertion of the parenthetical phrase '(including convenience)' between 'grocery' and 'stores,' section 407(22) of the Ordinance leaves no doubt that a **'convenience' store** is not a separate and distinct entity but, rather, is a species of grocery store. As such, it is apparent that the use does not encompass gasoline sales, which, in fact, are totally omitted from the 'B' Business district." *Alessi v. Millcreek Tp. Zoning Hearing Bd.* (Pa. Common. Ct., 2003).

## RETAIL STORE, EXPRESS

**Smaller version of the large-scale retail store (big-box retailer), serving rural areas or smaller urban areas.**

***Comment***: The express store, patterned after its big brother, has about 10 percent of the big-box floor area (ten thousand to twenty thousand square feet) and is usually limited to groceries and pharmaceutical products. It carries the name of and is designed to cash in on the prominence of the large-scale retail store.

## RETAIL STORE, LARGE-SCALE

**See *Retail Store, Big-Box*.**

***Legal Annotation***: "Indeed, the purpose of the amendments, as explained in the city's findings, was to 'protect Portland's industrial sanctuaries, areas that generate a high percentage of family-wage jobs, from **large-scale retail** and office uses and their negative impacts on traffic and land value.'" *Home Depot USA, Inc. v. City of Portland* (Ore. Ct. App., 2000).

## RETAIL WAREHOUSE OUTLET

**A retail use operating from a warehouse as an accessory use to the principal warehouse use.**

*Comment*: The individual terms are easily understood: a retail store in a warehouse. The major problem is how to regulate these uses, since they can cause relatively low-intensity warehouse uses and districts to become high-traffic, very intensive retail centers. Reasonable controls include the following:

- The retail establishment is accessory to and incidental to the principal warehouse use.
- The maximum area within the warehouse that can be used for retail sales is a small percentage of the warehouse and a small area (10 percent and five thousand square feet, whichever is less, for example).
- Controls on the size and location of signs should be included in the ordinance.
- Adequate parking, in accordance with retail standards, is required for the retail space (often five spaces per thousand square feet of retail space).

## RETAINING WALL

**A structure that is constructed between lands of different elevations to stabilize the surfaces, prevent erosion, and/or protect structures. See *Figure 19*.**

*Legal Annotation*: "Mr. Delekto built a drainage ditch that also serves as a **retaining wall** immediately next to the boundary between his land and the Charltons' land. The ditch/**retaining wall** is a structure pursuant to the definition contained within the Ordinance: '[A]nything built for the support, shelter or enclosure of persons, animals, goods or property of any kind, together with anything constructed or erected with a fixed location on or in the ground, exclusive of fences[,] streets and sidewalks. The term includes structures temporarily or permanently located, such as decks and satellite dishes.'" *Charlton v. Town of Oxford* (Maine, 2001).

## RETENTION BASIN

**A pond, pool, or basin used for the permanent storage of water runoff. See *Detention Basin*.**

*Comment*: Retention basins differ from detention basins in that the latter are temporary storage areas from which the water is eventually released and the basin becomes dry. In retention basins, some water remains in the basin at all times. Because of this, retention basins have the potential for water recreation and water-oriented landscaping. Both types of basins provide for the controlled release of the stored water, but typically only detention basins permit groundwater recharge. Retention basins are usually not considered impervious surfaces.

*Legal Annotation*: "The proposal also called for the small pond on the subject property to be transformed into a 1.62-acre storm water management facility in the form of a **retention basin** to capture runoff from the impervious areas of the development. The **retention basin** is not designed to provide water for use in the farming of an edible harvest. The record contains no credible evidence that the **retention basin** was used at any point after construction for farming purposes." *BMW of North America, LLC v. Borough of Woodcliff* Lake (N.J. Tax Ct., 2013).

## RETIREMENT COMMUNITY

**Any age-restricted development, which may be in any housing form, including detached and attached dwelling units, apartments, and residences, offering private and semiprivate rooms.**

*Comment*: The 1988 amendments to the Federal Fair Housing Act provide guidance on age restrictions. These amendments stipulate that a community will be considered to be "housing for the elderly," and therefore exempt from lawsuits for discriminating against children, if the minimum age for all residents is sixty-two years, or fifty-five years for one resident of each of 80 percent of the units, provided that "significant facilities and services for the elderly are provided." The term "significant facilities and services" is not specifically defined in the regulations that implement the amendments and, therefore, has been determined on a case-by-case basis as litigation has arisen.

Housing in retirement communities usually provides one-level living, or elevators in multistory buildings, and usually includes other features designed to increase safety and amenities for the elderly, such as grab bars in the bathrooms, nonskid flooring, and higher levels of lighting. The housing may also be adaptable to use by the physically impaired and, accordingly, may be built with features such as wider doorways and elevators that can accommodate wheelchairs.

Retirement communities vary from those that provide only one type of housing and one level of service to communities that provide a range, from apartments for independent living to residences for assisted living (which includes meals, personal care, housekeeping, and some health services) to long-term bed care. See *Adult Retirement Community; Assisted Living Facility; Congregate Residences; Continuing Care Retirement Community; Housing For The Elderly; Residential Health-Care Facilities.*

***Legal Annotation***: "The Housing Element states that every effort should be made to maintain the dignity, self-respect, and quality of life of mature residents in the County. This applies to mature citizens who prefer to stay in their own dwellings and those who relocate to a **retirement community**. . . . The proposed project is for a 100 percent senior living community, and it will be deed restricted for those 55 years of age and older. There are two types of living arrangements proposed—independent living and assisted living. Some independent living units would be located in the main building. Additionally, the bungalows would serve as independent living units, and are a good transition for people moving from larger homes to a senior living campus. The independent residential units do not require licensing from the State of California. The proposed project would not be a nursing facility and would not offer nursing service. This project provides two different housing types, thus enabling residents to age in one place and not have to move as circumstances change." *Foothill Communities Coalition v. County of Orange* (Calif. Ct. App., 2014).

## REUSE

See *Adaptive Reuse.*

***Legal Annotation***: "Enumerating these and other considerations, the EA concluded that adaptive **reuse** 'is expected to require substantial and impractical building modifications to allow the building to function for its intended use and bring the building into compliance with current environmental, structural, fire, safety, and energy codes.'" *Safeguarding the Historic Hanscom Areas v. FAA* (1st Cir., 2011).

## REVERBERATION

**The persistence of sound in an enclosed or confined space after the sound source has stopped.**

***Legal Annotation***: "Unlike the idealized situation represented in [Harris's Handbook], the Walmart wall is not in the middle of an open field. Rather, the Walmart store itself is only 40 [feet] away and is itself roughly 25 [feet] high. The acoustically hard space formed by the building, the pavement, and the wall will be a **reverberant** space in which sound energy will build up, effectively amplifying the level and raising the height of the noise source." *Visalia Smart Growth Coalition v. City of Visalia* (Calif. Ct. App., 2013).

## REVERSE FRONTAGE

See *Lot, Reverse Frontage.*

***Legal Annotation***: "Double frontage and **reverse frontage** lots should be avoided except where it is essential to provide separation of residential development from expressways and major arterial streets or overcome specific disadvantages or topography and orientation." *Marshall v. Bd. of Cty. Com'rs for Johnson Cty.* (D. Wyo., 1996).

## REVERSE OSMOSIS

**An advanced method of wastewater treatment relying on a semipermeable membrane to separate waters from pollutants.**

***Legal Annotation***: "In 1999–2000, La Gorce began exploring options to irrigate its golf course using a **reverse osmosis** water treatment system as an alternative to the municipal water supply." *Witt v. La Gorce Country Club, Inc.* (Fla. Ct. App., 2010).

## REVERSION

**The return of real estate to its original owner or owner's heirs.**

***Comment***: Many donations of land to a governmental agency specify that if the property is not used for the purpose for which it was donated, it reverts back to the owner. Another type of reversion is a street that may have been platted but never constructed and that is subsequently vacated by the municipality. The unused right-of-way reverts back to owners of abutting land.

***Legal Annotation***: "The deed provides for **reversion** in the event the property is not used as a County Courthouse Annex facility. Specifically, the deed provides: 'This conveyance of all of the above parcels of land by both Shalimar Village, Inc. and Barnett Bank of Pensacola is subject to and is made, executed and delivered upon the express conditions hereinbelow set forth. If these said conditions, or any one of them be violated, or if the grantee shall fail to comply with any and all of these conditions, then and in that event title to each of the parcels of real property described above shall revert to and automatically vest in the respective grantor of said parcels herein, or in its successors and assigns.'" *Meigs Properties, Ltd. v. The Board of County Commissioners of Okloosa County* (Fla. Dist. Ct., 2013).

## REZONE

**To change the zoning classification of particular lots or parcels of land.**

***Legal Annotation***: "McGlades, LLC owns a 4.2 acre tract of property located at the intersection of Day-Mt. Spokane Road and Yale Road in Spokane County, Washington. McGlades applied for a conditional use permit to expand its on-site market and deli operation. Spokane County (County) denied McGlades' application. McGlades then submitted concurrent requests to the County: (1) to amend the comprehensive plan designation from urban reserve to limited development area-commercial; and (2) to amend the County zoning map designation from an urban reserve zone to a limited development area-commercial zone. . . . The Hearings Board ruled that the County's comprehensive plan amendment violated the GMA but it did not, nor could it, zone or **rezone** McGlades' property." *Spokane County v. Growth Mngmt. Hearings* (Wash. Ct. App., 2011).

## REZONING APPLICATION

**A request for a change in zone to permit new uses, to prohibit one or more current uses, or to amend the current requirements.**

***Comment***: Some state enabling legislation will often specify how a request for a zone change is accomplished. But even in states without formal procedures, the courts have often upheld reasonable procedures designed to allow requests to be considered (*see TWC Realty v. Zoning Bd. Of Adj.*, 315 N.J. Super. 205, 215 [Law Div. 1998)] aff'd o.b. 321 N.J. Super. 216 [App. Div. 1999]). A reasonable procedure would have the applicant apply to the planning board as a first step and the planning board then examine the request in terms of (1) consistency with the master plan; (2) changed circumstances either in the area or the nature of the new use; and (3) appropriateness of the zone for the proposed change. The planning board would then consider the request at a public meeting and forward a recommendation to the governing body.

***Legal Annotation***: "Consequently, Costal submitted a **rezoning application** for the subject property to the Nash County Board of County Commissioners requesting that the property be rezoned to a 'General Industrial' district, which would permit a variety of industrial uses, not only the use proposed by Sanderson Farms." *Morgan v. Nash County* (N.C. Ct. App., 2012).

## RIDE SHARING

**The cooperative effort between two or more people to travel together, usually to and from work. http://www.vtpi.org/tdm34.htm**

***Comment***: Car pools, vanpools, and bus pools are all examples of ride sharing.

***Legal Annotation***: "AU's TDM program employed a number of approaches to reduce vehicular traffic to and from campus, including a free shuttle service, carpooling and **ride-sharing** plans, and inducements to use public transportation and bicycles. AU's transportation impact study credited the TDM program with having achieved a decade-long decline in vehicular traffic at the Main Campus of nearly 4% a year. As part of its 2011 Campus Plan, AU planned to institute enhancements to promote the TDM program and monitor its effectiveness." *Spring Valley-Wesley Heights Citizens Association v. District of Columbia Zoning Commission* (D.C. Ct. App., 2013).

## RIDGE LINE

**(1) The intersection of two roof surfaces forming the highest horizontal line of the roof; (2) the highest elevation of a mountain chain or line of hills. See *Figures 9 and 79.***

*Legal Annotation*: "The existence of the alleged '**ridge line**' is important because the plaintiffs now assert that it formed a clear line of demarcation between the land farmed by them over the years and that farmed by the defendants." *Campbell v. Buckler* (Neb., 1974).

## RIDING ACADEMY

**An establishment where horses are boarded and cared for; and where instruction in riding, jumping, and showing is offered; and where horses may be hired for riding. See *Agriculture; Boarding Stable; Farm Or Farmland; Horse Farm.***

*Legal Annotation*: "**RIDING ACADEMY**: An establishment where horses are kept for riding or driving, or are stabled for compensation, or incidental to the operation of any club, association, ranch, or similar establishment." *Lando et ux. v. Zoning Board of Adj.* (Pa. Common. Ct., 1972).

## RIGHT OF ACCESS

**The legal authority to enter a property.**

*Comment*: In privately owned property, right of access usually means access to a public road. In rented property, right of access also could mean the landlord's right to enter the property to make repairs.

*Legal Annotation*: "The National Government is guardian of a public **right of access** to navigable waters of the United States. The navigational servitude is the legal formula by which we recognize the paramount nature of this governmental responsibility." *Kaiser Aetna v. US* (U.S., 1979).

## RIGHT-OF-WAY (ROW)

**(1) A strip of land acquired by reservation, dedication, prescription, or condemnation and intended to be occupied by a street, a crosswalk, a railroad, electric transmission lines, an oil or gas pipeline, a water line, a sanitary storm sewer, or other similar uses; (2) generally, the right of one to pass over the property of another. See *Figure 1.***

*Legal Annotation*: "'**Right-of-way**' is generally defined as 'a legal right of passage over another person's ground—compare EASEMENT, SERVITUDE.' (Emphasis added.) Webster's Third New International Dictionary; accord Black's Law Dictionary (5th Ed. 1979)." *Double I Limited Partnership v. Plan & Zoning Commission* (Conn., 1991).

## RIGHT-OF-WAY LINES

**The lines that form the boundaries of a right-of-way. See *Figure 1.***

*Legal Annotation*: "Upon going out into the field, one of our first points of items I do is locate the street **right-of-way lines**, I'm talking about Pike Street and Main Street. And the practice that we have adopted over the years is to locate the curb improvement on those two streets because those curb improvements were generally put in by a survey crew or an engineer when they constructed the streets." *Perry v. Davis* (Ohio Ct. App., 2013).

## RIGHT TO FARM

**Public policy or law designed to protect farmers against municipal (or other local governmental) regulations, private nuisance suits, and unnecessary constraints on essential agricultural management practices, if these practices are consistent with federal and state law and are not a threat to the public health and safety.**

***Comment***: The right to farm may be adopted by municipal ordinances listing permitted farming activities. A right-to-farm ordinance might include provisions allowing farming to take place on "holidays, Sundays, and weekdays, at night and in the day," and providing that "the noise, odors, dust, and fumes that are caused by them are also specifically permitted as part of the exercise of this right" (*Township of Cranbury, N.J. Code*, Chapter 81, Farming).

The Cranbury ordinance defines the right to farm to "include the use of large irrigation pumps and equipment, aerial and ground seeding and spraying, large tractors, numerous farm laborers and the application of chemical fertilizers and products for the control and elimination of insects, pests, weeds, fungus and other substances injurious to the farming process or for the purpose of producing from the land agricultural products such as vegetables, grains. . . . This right to farm shall also include the right to use land for grazing by animals, subject to the restrictions contained elsewhere in this Code for raising livestock" (ibid., § 81–2).

Finally, as if to reemphasize the point, the right-to-farm ordinance states, "It is expressly found that whatever temporary inconveniences may be caused to others by such uses and activities so conducted, they are more than offset by the benefits from farming to . . . community . . . and to society in general" (ibid., § 81–4).

States have also enacted right-to-farm laws. An example is New Jersey, the state with the highest density of population in the United States that has attempted to preserve farms and other open space. "Enacted in 1983, the New Jersey Right to Farm Act was companion legislation to The Agriculture Retention and Development Act, N.J.S.A 4:1C-1 et seq., which established New Jersey's Farmland Preservation Program. The Acts were designed to work together to preserve New Jersey's agricultural industry—by keeping land in agriculture and by protecting the ability to farm." (Green 2006, 60).

"In 1998, the Right to Farm Act was amended to strengthen the protections for farmers (P.L. 1998, c. 48.) One of the most significant changes was to provide for preemption of municipal ordinances that seek to regulate specific agricultural activities as long as the agricultural operation meets the eligibility standards in the Act. The New Jersey Supreme Court upheld the Act's municipal preemption provision, finding that farmers may conduct certain agricultural activities despite municipal regulations to the contrary ( *Township of Franklin v. den Hollander,* 172 N.J. 147" [2002]; Green 2006).

***Legal Annotation***: "Because the **Right to Farm** Act does not prohibit enforcement of ordinances in existence at the time of the adoption of the Act, we affirm in part the declaratory judgment." *Wilson v. Palm Beach County* (Fla. Ct. App., 2011).

## RING ROAD

**(1) A roadway, usually paralleling the external boundaries of a property, that interconnects access drives with parking areas; (2) a highway, or a series of major roadways, that encircles a city or major urban area.**

***Comment***: Often referred to as a beltway or loop road.

***Legal Annotation***: "As the purpose of a **ring road** is to divert public traffic around the Five Points intersection, it can easily be argued that 100% of the cost of construction of the ring road is totally a public benefit." *Charter Township of Lyon v. Huffman* (Mich. Ct. App., 2010).

## RINGELMANN SMOKE CHART

**A scale for grading the density of smoke as published by the United States Bureau of Mines or any chart, recorder, indicator, or device that is approved by the Bureau or appropriate state department as the equivalent for the measurement of smoke density.**

***Comment***: There is some indication that the Ringelmann chart is being phased out and replaced by more modern devices. Many agencies still use the Ringelmann chart, and the definition covers all situations.

***Legal Annotation***: "Similarly, while it is true that the **Ringelmann Smoke Chart** measures coloration and not opacity, it does not necessarily follow that the chart may not be reasonably used as a basis for determining opacity. The **Ringelmann Smoke Chart** has been widely accepted throughout the United States as a measurement of air pollution by both legislatures and courts, and we find ourselves in agreement with the wisdom of this acceptance." *Sittner v. City of Seattle* (Wash., 1963).

## RIPARIAN BUFFER

**A vegetated area or a buffer strip adjacent to a stream, that helps to shade and protect the stream from the impact of activities conducted on adjacent land uses.**

***Comment***: Riparian buffers help to capture sediment, nutrients, and pesticides and other pollutants in surface runoff prior to their entry into surface waterbodies. They also provide habitat and wildlife corridors in developed areas and reduce erosion by providing stream bank stabilization.

***Legal Annotation***: "Because the activity associated with both the construction of the pool and the **riparian buffer** is defined in the Darien inland wetlands and watercourses regulations as a 'regulated activity' for which a permit is required, the plaintiffs filed an application with the commission seeking such a permit. After publishing notice of and holding a public hearing on the matter of the permit, the commission granted that part of the plaintiffs' application that sought to create a **riparian buffer** along the shore of Stony Brook and denied that part of the plaintiffs' application that sought to build an in-ground swimming pool and related features in the upland review area." *Cornacchia v. Env. Protection Com'n* (Conn. App. Ct., 2008).

## RIPARIAN GRANT

**The grant by the state of lands below the mean high waterline, usually beginning at the shore and extending outward to the center of the stream or some predetermined line.**

***Legal Annotation***: "The primary issue in this appeal is whether a conveyance of real property that makes no mention of an abutting **riparian grant** can be construed under N.J.S.A. 46:3-16 to include that grant as an appurtenance. Unlike a riparian right, which is a license or privilege, a **riparian grant** is a conveyance in fee simple of real property. As such, without specific mention in the deed or other evidence that the parties intended its inclusion, a **riparian grant** will not pass as appurtenant to another distinct parcel." *Panetta v. Equity One, Inc.* (N.J., 2007).

## RIPARIAN LAND

**Areas next to the banks of a stream, lake, or wetland, and including both the area dominated by contiguous high moisture content and the adjacent upland vegetation that exerts an influence on it.**

***Legal Annotation***: "'**Riparian land**' is defined as 'a parcel of land which includes therein a part of or is bounded by a natural water course' . . . and the owners of such land enjoy certain exclusive rights . . . rights include the right to erect and maintain docks, as well as to permanently anchor boats off the shore." *2000 Baum Family Trust v. Babel* (Mich., 2010).

## RIPARIAN RIGHTS

**Rights of a landowner to the water on or bordering his or her property, including the right to make use of such waters and to prevent diversion or misuse of upstream water.**

***Legal Annotation***: "**Riparian rights**, one of which is the right to construct a pier to access navigable waters, are generally reserved for riparian landowners. . . . However, up until April 9, 1994, Wisconsin recognized the ability of a riparian landowner to convey riparian rights by easement." *Konneker v. Romano* (Wis., 2010).

## RIPRAP

**Pieces of rock added to the surface of a fill slope or added on the side of a stream, levee, or swale.**

***Comment***: The purpose of placing riprap in swales or drainage channels is to reduce the erosion-inducing effects of the rapid flow of stormwater and to act as a trap for debris and sediment.

***Legal Annotation***: "**Riprap** is a larger rock that is placed on the edge of a waterway to help control erosion." *Bucksaw Resort, LLC v. Mehrtens* (Mo. Ct. App., 2013).

## RISK

**The expectation of loss from hazards and their impact.**

***Comment***: Risk is a function of probability (likelihood) of a hazard occurrence and the impact (consequences) of a hazard on the target of the risk assessment. It connotes a relationship between the hazard and the target's vulnerability to the hazard. Risk can be addressed by managing probability (through mitigation) and/or managing impact (through mitigation, preparedness, response and recovery). http://www.gwu.edu/~icdrm/publications/PDF/GLOSSARY%2002-19-2007.pdf

***Legal Annotation***: "[O]ur Supreme Court has instructed that 'the court must determine whether the record establishes that there is more than a mere theoretical possibility, but not necessarily a likelihood, of a specific harm to the public interest if the application is granted. If the court finds that such sufficient evidence exists, then it must conduct a plenary review of the record and determine independently whether the commission's decision was necessary to protect substantial interests in health, safety or other matters that the commission legally may consider, whether the **risk** of such harm to such public interests clearly outweighs the need for affordable housing, and whether the public interest can be protected by reasonable changes to the affordable housing development.'" *Eureka V, LLC v. Planning and Zoning Commission of Town of Ridgefield* (Conn. App. Ct., 2012).

## RISK ANALYSIS

**A detailed examination performed to understand the nature of unwanted, negative consequences to human life, health, property, or the environment; an analytical process to provide information regarding undesirable events; the process of quantification of the probabilities and expected consequences for identified risks (Gratt 1987: 244). See *Hazard Vulnerability Analysis*. http://www.gwu.edu/~icdrm/publications/pdf/glossary%2002-19-2007.pdf**

***Legal Annotation***: "The Corps argues that 'floodplain' designation rests solely with FEMA, and as the project area is not in a FEMA-designated floodplain, no additional consideration of flood risks (i.e. an EIS) was required. The Corps has the better of this argument, as practically, it must rely on other agency determinations in its own **risk analysis**." *American Bottom Conservancy v. United States Army Corps of Engineers* (S.D. Ill., 2013).

## RIVER

**A natural stream of water, of greater volume than a creek, flowing in a more or less permanent bed or channel, between defined banks or walls, with a current that may be either continuous in one direction or affected by the ebb and flow of the tide.**

***Legal Annotation***: "In fact, the court limited the scope of its decision by stating that '[w]here it is admitted, or certainly not denied, as in the present case, that the water is not a lake . . . the only criterion by which to determine whether it is a **river**, is the existence of a current.' . . . We also note that the issue to be resolved in the Gilmanton case involved a waterbody flowing out of a lake, not a stream flowing into a lake, as in the case currently before us." *Lake Sunapee Protective Assoc. v. NH Wetlands Bd.* (N.H., 1990).

## RIVER BASIN

**The total area drained by a river and its tributaries. See *Basin*.**

***Legal Annotation***: "This case concerns an approximately 20,000 acre tract of land (the 'Lake Long Tract') in Avoyelles Parish, Louisiana. The tract lies within the Bayou Natchitoches **basin**, an area of approximately 140,000 acres, which, along with the Ouachita, Black and Tensas river basins, makes up the Red River backwater area. The Bayou Natchitoches **basin** is subject to flooding during the spring months, and it experiences an average rainfall of sixty inches per year. Much of the **basin** had been cleared of forest before the private defendants began their landclearing activities, but 80,000 acres were still forested. The Lake Long Tract made up a quarter of this forested area. The topography of the tract itself is uneven, resulting in some areas with permanent water impoundments and other drier areas that support a variety of plant species." *Avoyelles Sportsmen's League, Inc. v. Marsh* (5th Cir., 1983).

## ROAD

**See *Street*.**

***Legal Annotation*:** "A county **road** or highway is not the absolute property of the county. Rather, an owner of land bound by a highway is presumed to own the property to the center of the road. . . . A **road** is generally only an easement for public use while landowners have a fee interest burdened by the easement." *In re Question Submitted by Murphey* (Okla. A.G. 10-2012).

## ROADWAY

**The portion of a highway, including the shoulder, that is improved, designed, or ordinarily used for vehicular travel. See *Figure 1*. See *Roadway, Shared*. http://safety.fhwa.dot.gov/ped_bike/tools_solve/fhwasa12018/#chap1.6**

***Legal Annotation*:** "A '**roadway**' is 'that portion of a highway improved, designed, or ordinarily used for vehicular travel, exclusive of the sidewalk or shoulder.' . . . The 'shoulder' is the 'part of a highway which is contiguous to the regularly traveled portion of the highway and is on the same level as the highway . . . [and] may be pavement, gravel, or earth.'" *Wilkes v. Commissioner of Public Safety* (Minn. Ct. App., 2010).

## ROADWAY, SHARED

**A roadway that is open to both bicycle and motor vehicle travel (*1999 AASHTO Guide*). See *Bike Lane*.**

***Comment*:** As opposed to many roadways that are designed primarily for motor vehicle traffic but allow bicycles to use them, shared roadways are those that are specifically designed to carry both bicycles and motor vehicles. This ranges from providing specifically designated bike lanes to widening the curb lanes to allow motor vehicles to more easily pass bicyclists.

***Legal Annotation*:** "LPF 3 consists of a 20-foot by approximately 1,120-foot **shared roadway**. . . . LPF 3 provides public access for pedestrians and bicyclists to other LPFs including Lake Village/Echo Drive (LPF 1) and the roadway serving Kahle Park and Kingsbury Grade (LPFs 4 and 5). LPF 3 also serves as the residential access road for Sierra Colina and provides access to the dedicated 10.7 acres of open space, both for the public and for operation and maintenance by Douglas County." *League to Save Lake Tahoe v. Tahoe Regional Planning Agency* (D. Nev., 2011).

## ROD

**A lineal measure equal to 16.5 feet or 5.5 yards.**

***Comment*:** This surveyor's measure is no longer used. Four rods equal one chain. Ten chains by ten chains equals ten acres. See *Chain*.

***Legal Annotation*:** "A '**rod**' is 'a linear measure equal to 5.5 yards, 16.5 feet, or 5.03 meters.' Webster's New College Dictionary 982 (3rd ed. 2008). In turn, a 'perch' is '[o]ne square **rod** of land.' Id. at 836." *Dutch Corner Historical Society v. Stahl* (Pa. Common. Ct., 2013).

## ROOF

**The outside top covering of a building. *See Figure 79*.**

***Legal Annotation*:** **"By the time the revised building permit was issued, construction of the three-story rear addition was nearly complete, and by January 15, 2005, the new construction was under roof. 'Under roof' is defined in the zoning regulations as the 'stage of completion of a structure or part thereof when the main roof of the structure or part thereof, and the roofs of any structures on**

**Figure 79**

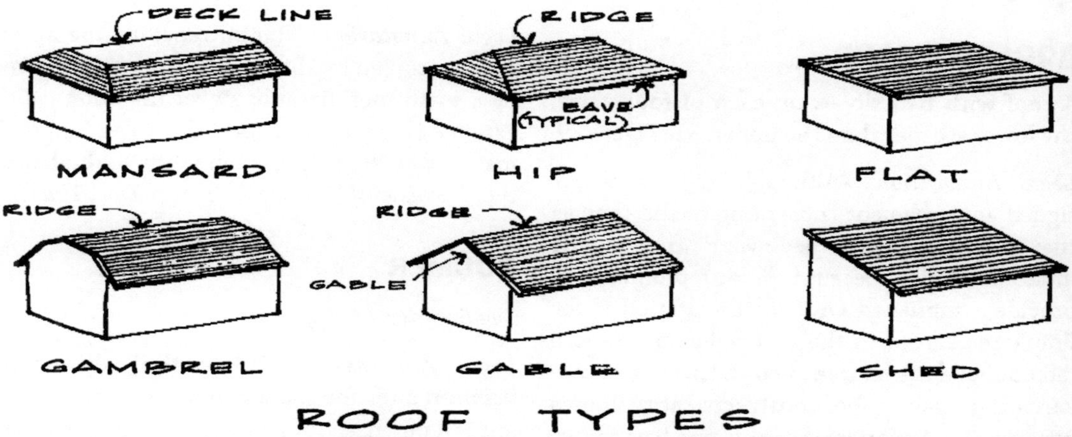


**the main roof or part thereof, are in place.' 11 DCMR § 3112.2(b)(1)."** ***Basken v. BZA*** **(D.C. Ct. App., 2008).**

## ROOF, FLAT

**A roof that is not pitched and the surface of which is generally parallel to the ground.** ***See Figure 79.***

*Legal Annotation*: "The appellees, on the contrary, do not contend that the zoning ordinance is invalid. They maintain simply that the addition in question, open on three sides and connected with the dwelling only by a **flat roof**, is not a principal building within the letter or spirit of the ordinance, but is a mere accessory building; and that, in addition, the City was estopped by the action of Brock in approving the sketch after protest had been made." *City of Cleveland v. Young* (Miss., 1959).

## ROOF, GABLE

**A ridged roof forming a gable at both ends of the building.** ***See Figure 79.***

*Legal Annotation*: "Schott in his court testimony also made reference to the change from a hip roof to a **gable roof**. However, neither he nor any other witness explained satisfactorily why a **gable roof** was objectionable or why a hip roof would be preferable. Flood had advised plaintiffs that to require this change in style of roof would be prohibitively expensive. It is especially to be noted that the trial court did not require conversion to a hip roof as one of its conditions to building of the house. The evidence does not show the insistence upon a hip roof to be reasonable." *Ashelford v. Baltrusaitis* (Mo. Ct. App., 1980).

## ROOF, GAMBREL

**A gabled roof with two slopes on each side, the lower steeper than the upper. See** ***Figure 79.***

*Legal Annotation:* "The only real issue presently in this case is how the height of a garage with a gambrel roof (apparently a sort of gabled roof) should be measured." *Albery v. Reddig* (7th Cir., 1983).

## ROOF, HIP

**A roof with sloping ends and sides. See** ***Figure 79.***

*Legal Annotation*: "A **hip roof** is a pyramid shaped roof. A reverse gable is a triangular-shaped pitched roof cut into the hip roof and usually contains a window. When the shape of the **hip roof** and reverse gables are carried through to the interior of the house, the effect is a cathedral ceiling with cut-outs, called true valleys, notched into the area where the vaulted ceiling and the walls of the room meet." *Zitz v. Pereira* (E.D. N.Y., 1999).

## ROOF, MANSARD

**A roof with two slopes on each of four sides, the lower steeper than the upper. See *Figure 79*.**

*Legal Annotation*: "Although the Frankards signed an agreement consenting to the change, they later claimed they were fraudulently induced to sign because Amoco promised to provide a **mansard roof** for the station if the Frankards agreed to the rent reduction. Amoco did not build the **mansard roof**. Later, the Frankards had a gabled roof constructed at their own expense. . . . A **mansard roof** is one having two slopes on all sides with the lower slope steeper than the upper one. It looks much like those seen on the vest majority of America's barns. See *Webster's New Collegiate Dictionary (1977)*." Frankard V. Amoco Oil Co. (Wis. Ct. App., 1983).

## ROOF PITCH

**The steepness (pitch or slope) of a roof as measured by the vertical rise (in inches) by the horizontal distance (run).**

*Comment*: In construction practice, the pitch is usually expressed in how many inches of vertical rise over twelve inches or one foot of run. For example, a 5:12 pitch would be a roof that rises five inches for each foot of horizontal distance.

*Legal Annotation*: "The standards listed in Wright County ordinances § 740 material to this appeal are: . . .

The minimum widths of the structure shall be 24 feet measured from face of exterior wall. [and] There shall be a minimum 3:12 **roof pitch** with a minimum 12 inch soffit. . . . Kennedy argues that Wright County has not proved that a 24-foot width requirement for a residential structure or a 3:12 **roof pitch** is related to achievement of the statutory purpose. . . . Wright County Ordinances . . . and 740 (1985) are invalid because they are contradictory to Minnesota statutes." *Wright County v. Kennedy*, 415 NW 2d 728 (Minn: Court of Appeals, 1987).

## ROOF, SHED

**A roof with one slope. See *Figure 79*.**

*Legal Annotation*: "The entrance to the apartment occupied by the defendants was sheltered by a small roof or canopy over the door, which extended out from under the eaves approximately four feet. This canopy was a **shed roof** type." *Skupienski v. Maly* (N.J. App. Div., 1957).

## ROOMER

**See *Boarder*.**

*Legal Annotation*: "The critical distinction between a tenant and a **roomer** is that '[a] tenant is a purchaser of an estate, entitled to exclusive legal possession, but a **roomer** has merely a right to use the premises.'" *Young v. District of Columbia* (D.C. Ct. App., 2000).

## ROOMING HOUSE

**A house in which lodgers rent one or more rooms for one or more nights, and sometimes for extended periods of time, and in which common areas or services, such as laundry, cleaning, and dining may be provided. See *Boardinghouse*.**

*Comment*: Newer forms of "rooming houses" are now being built to cater to young singles who want or need to live away from home in smaller, affordable units. Such modern rooming houses are composed of multiple apartments, as small as one hundred to two hundred square feet, including a small kitchen and compact bath.

*Legal Annotation*: "A **rooming house** is defined as 'any building or portion thereof which contains not less than three, or more than nine guest rooms which are used, or let, for occupancy by individuals for compensation paid directly or indirectly.'" *Civitans Care, Inc. v. Board of Adjustment* (Ala. Ct. App., 1983).

## ROOMING UNIT

**Any habitable room or group of rooms forming a single habitable unit, used or intended to be used for living and sleeping but not for cooking or eating.**

*Legal Annotation*: "The Code defines a 'rental unit' as 'A rented dwelling unit or **rooming unit**.' . . . A 'rental dwelling unit' is defined as 'A dwelling unit in a residential premises covered by a tenancy agreement.' . . . A '**rooming unit**' is defined as 'Any room or group of rooms forming a single habitable unit used or intended to be used for living and sleeping, but not for cooking or eating purposes.'" *City of Vincennes v. Emmons* (Ind., 2006).

## ROOMS, COMBINED

**Two or more adjacent habitable spaces that by their relationship, planning, and openness permit their common use.**

## ROOMS, HABITABLE

**A space used for living, sleeping, or eating, or combinations thereof, but not including kitchens, bathrooms, toilet compartments, closets, halls, storage rooms, laundry and utility rooms, basement recreation rooms, and similar spaces.**

*Legal Annotation*: "'A **Habitable Room**' is a room or enclosed floor space used or intended to be used for living, sleeping or eating purposes, excluding bathrooms, toilet rooms, laundries, pantries, dressing rooms, storage spaces, foyers, hallways, utility rooms, heater rooms, boiler rooms, basement recreation rooms, and areas used for kitchen purposes." *Nolden v. East Cleveland City Commission* (Ohio Ct. Common Pleas, 1966).

## ROUNDABOUTS

See *Traffic Calming*.

*Legal Annotation*: "A **roundabout** is a circular intersection in which the traffic flows in one direction around a central island. Vehicles already in the circle have the right-of-way." *People v. Troyer* (Calif. Ct. App., 2012).

## ROW HOUSE

**An attached dwelling separated from others in a row by a vertical, unpierced wall extending from basement to roof. See *Dwelling, Townhouse*.**

*Comment*: Row houses are urban housing types, usually on their own lots with little or no front yard and a small, enclosed rear yard.

*Legal Annotation*: "Section 201.2(43) of the Ordinance defines the term '**row house**' as a 'dwelling constructed or designed for, and occupied exclusively by, one dwelling unit and which is one of three or more abutting buildings or dwellings all in a row or which is one of three or more buildings or dwellings having party walls in common.' . . . To the extent that the ZHB held that Section 502.3 of the Ordinance prohibits multiple row houses on a lot, the ZHB's holding is contrary to the '**row house**' definition. By definition, a '**row house**' is one dwelling unit associated with others by abutting or party walls." *Samuel's Dell, LLC v. Borough of Lewistown Zoning Hearing Board* (Pa. Common. Ct., 2010).

## RUBBISH

**A generic term for solid waste, excluding food waste and ashes, taken from residences, commercial establishments, and institutions.**

*Legal Annotation*: "Similarly, '**rubbish**' is defined as 'miscellaneous useless valueless waste or rejected matter.'" *Crippen v. City of Cedar Rapids* (Iowa, 2000).

## RUMMAGE SALE

**The sale by a school, religious institution, trust association, fund, or foundation, organized and operated for religious, charitable, scientific, community, or educational purposes, of tangible personal property to obtain money for some charitable purpose.**

*Legal Annotation*: "There are also exemptions for real estate signs that meet the ordinance's criteria, window signs, on-premises insignia of recognized historic agencies or religious orders, and temporary on-premises signs for civic, philanthropic, educational, and religious organizations as long as the signs do not exceed the size specified in the statute and are posted within the time period specified by the ordinance. Incidental vehicular signs, neighborhood identification signs meeting the ordinance's specifications and temporary **rummage sale** signs meeting the ordinance's specifications are also exempt." *Lavey v. City of Two Rivers* (7th Cir., 1999).

## RUN WITH THE LAND

**A covenant or restriction to the use of land contained in a deed and binding on the present and all future owners of the property.**

***Comment***: For example, a restriction never to divide the land into more lots is incorporated in a deed and the prohibition against subdivision is said to "run with the land," since future owners also are bound by the restriction.

***Legal Annotation***: "A covenant is either real or personal. Covenants that **run with the land** are real as distinguished from personal covenants that do not **run with the land**." *Raintree Corp. v. Rowe* (N.C. Ct. App., 1978).

## RUNOFF

**That portion of rainfall, melted snow, irrigation water, or any other liquid that flows across ground surface and eventually is returned to streams. *See Figure 6.***

***Legal Annotation***: "To support its interpretation of section 1342(p)(3)(B)(iii), Building Industry additionally relies on the statutory provisions addressing nonpoint source **runoff** (a diffuse **runoff** not channeled through a particular source), which were also part of the 1987 amendments to the Clean Water Act." *Bldg. Indus. Ass'n v. Water Resources Bd.* (Calif. Ct. App., 2004).

## RURAL AREA

**A sparsely developed area, with a population density of fewer than one hundred persons per square mile, where the land is undeveloped or primarily used for agricultural purposes.**

***Legal Annotation***: "A '**rural area**' is defined as 'a community or area of the state in which the noncommercial, customary, and traditional use of fish or game for personal or family consumption is a principal characteristic of the economy of the community or area.' AS 16.05.940(25)." *McDowell v. State* (Alaska, 1989).

## RURAL ROAD

**See *Street, Rural*.**

***Legal Annotation***: "This act is providing only for the construction of **rural roads**, and a **rural road** is defined as 'Any continuous stretch of public way, road, thoroughfare, street or right of way, not now or as of the particular time of inquiry in the future designated as part of the State highway system in the manner provided by law and not located wholly within the boundaries of any incorporated municipality.'" *State of Ga. v. Ga. Rural Roads Authority* (Ga., 1955).

# S

## SALE

**The exchange of goods, services, or property for money or some other consideration.**

***Legal Annotation***: "This is the case of a single private house. No doubt there is a public interest even in this, as there is in every purchase and sale and in all that happens within the commonwealth. . . . And why should a **sale** of underground rights bar the State's power?" *Pennsylvania Coal Co. v. Mahon* (U.S., 1922).

## SALINE LAND

**Land with a high salt content that makes it unsuitable for agricultural cultivation.**

***Legal Annotation***: "Whether, for instance, a certain tract is swamp land or not, **saline land** or not, mineral land or not, presents a question of fact not resting on record, dependent on oral testimony; and it cannot be doubted that the decision of the Land Department, one way or the other, in reference to these questions is conclusive and not open to relitigation in the courts, except in those cases of fraud, etc., which permit any determination to be reëxamined." *Burfenning v. Chicago, St. P., M. & OR Co.* (U.S., 1896).

## SALINITY

**The degree of salt in water.**

***Legal Annotation***: "The new plan, inter alia, changed the unit of measurement for the **salinity** reading at Vernalis from a ppm standard for total dissolved solids to an electrical conductivity measure." *Central Delta Water Agency v. US* (9th Cir., 2002).

## SALTWATER INTRUSION

**The invasion of salt water into a body of fresh water, occurring in either surface or ground waterbodies. *See Figure 6.***

***Comment***: Saltwater intrusion or infiltration is generally caused by overpumping or overdrawing fresh water from an aquifer.

***Legal Annotation***: "In recent years, a combination of factors resulting from population increases and land use policies has caused both a decrease in recharge of rain and waste water back into the aquifers and an increase in the amount of water pumped out of the aquifers. This, in turn, had led to **saltwater intrusion** into the portions of the glacial, Jameco and Magothy aquifers lying under the southernmost part of Nassau County." *Town of Hempstead v. Flacke* (N.Y. App., 1981).

## SALVAGE

**The utilization of waste materials. See *Refuse Reclamation*.**

***Legal Annotation***: "At the end of their useful life, FP & L sold the transformers to Pepper's Steel and Alloys, Inc. ('Pepper's') as scrap. Pepper's **salvaged** the transformers for recovery of various metals and oil at its disposal site in Medley, Dade County, Florida. At the time of purchase, Pepper's did not know that the transformers contained PCB-contaminated mineral oil." *Florida Power & Light Co. v. Allis Chalmers Corp.* (11th Cir., 1990).

## SALVAGE YARD

**A facility or area for storing, selling, dismantling, shredding, compressing, or salvaging scrap, discarded material, or equipment. See *Junk; Junkyard*.**

***Legal Annotation***: "[T]he 1967 Ordinance provides that an automobile **salvage yard** is a public nuisance if located in a residential district established by the Ordinance and shall be abated, removed or changed to a conforming use within a period of two years." *Rives v. City of Clarksville* (Tenn. Ct. App., 1981).

## SAME OWNERSHIP

**Properties owned or controlled by the same individual, corporation, partnership, or other entity.**

***Comment***: Multi-building or multi-tract developments may be subdivided in several corporate names or owned by subsidiaries of the parent company. This definition clarifies the intent of considering all such parcels as a single parcel for zoning purposes.

***Legal Annotation***: "This Court has recognized that contiguous lots under the **same ownership** are to be considered as a whole for purposes of judging the reasonableness of zoning ordinances, despite the owner's division of the property into separate, identifiable lots." *Bevan v. Brandon Twp.*, (Mich., 1991).

## SAMPLING

**A statistical technique that involves selecting a small, random, stratified percentage of a group; analyzing it; and then drawing certain conclusions about the group.**

***Legal Annotation***: "The [Census] Bureau's announcement of its plan to use statistical **sampling** in the 2000 census led to a flurry of legislative activity. Congress amended the Census Act to provide that, '[n]otwithstanding any other provision of law, no sampling or any other statistical procedure, including any statistical adjustment, may be used in any determination of population for purposes of the apportionment of Representatives in Congress among the several States.'" *Department of Commerce v. United States House of Representatives* (U.S., 1999).

## SANDPIT

See *Extractive Industries*.

***Legal Annotation***: "The plaintiffs own and operate a **sandpit** covering approximately 7.9 acres in Alexandria. Wesley Platts, an owner of land abutting the **sandpit**, is a 'disapproving abutter' for purposes of . . . the statute that governs local regulation of excavations." *Bedard v. Town of Alexandria* (N.H., 2010).

## SANITARY LANDFILL

**A site for solid waste disposal. See *Dump; Landfill*.**

***Legal Annotation***: "A **sanitary landfill** is created by first compacting the refuse and then dumping it into trenches. The garbage is then covered with earthen material and clay sealer. A daily cover is added, and final covering layers are placed atop the garbage to complete each trench." *Cosmopolitan Nat'l Bank v. County of Cook* (Ill., 1984).

## SANITARY LANDFILLING

**A planned method of solid waste disposal in which the solid waste is spread in thin layers, compacted to reduce its volume, and covered with earthen material and clay sealer.**

***Legal Annotation***: "'Landfills are disposal facilities where solid waste is buried directly in the ground. **Sanitary landfilling** is a controlled burial operation which is intended to protect the public health, minimize environmental impacts, and prevent nuisance conditions.' Solid Waste Management Study for Faribault County at V-12." *Waste Systems Corp. v. County of Martin, Minn.* (8th Cir., 1993).

## SANITARY SEWAGE

**Any liquid waste containing animal or vegetable matter in suspension or solution or the water-carried waste resulting from the discharge of toilets, laundry tubs, washing machines, sinks, dishwashers, or any other source of water-carried waste of human origin or containing putrescible material.**

***Legal Annotation***: "'**Sanitary sewage**' is defined in turn as 'the normal water-carried household and toilet wastes from residences, business buildings, institutions, industrial and commercial establishments, exclusive of storm water runoff, surface water and [ground water].'" *Peterson v. Commonwealth* (Pa. Common. Ct., 2012).

## SANITARY SEWER

**An underground system that carries wastewater and sewerage to a treatment plant.**

**See *Combined Sewers; Sewer System And Treatment; Storm Sewer.***

***Comment***: In a sanitary sewer system, surface water (stormwater runoff) is not intentionally admitted.

***Legal Annotation***: "How or why the blockage occurred is irrelevant. The purpose of the **sanitary sewer** is to carry waste water *away* from the residence. The City's sanitary sewer failed to carry waste water away from the McKennas' residence *because* of a blockage in the City's main, and therefore, failed to function as intended." *CSAA v. City of Palo Alto* (Calif. Ct. App., 2006).

"The Wrights do correctly note that '**sanitary sewer**' is not defined. However, we have little difficulty concluding that a lateral sewer line, whose sole function is to convey sewage to the main sewer line, easily falls within the intended meaning of a '**sanitary sewer**.' To hold otherwise would be to ignore the plain and simple meaning of the term." *Wright v. Clay Tp. Regional Waste Dist.* (Ind. Ct. App., 1998).

## SANITATION

**The control of all the factors in the physical environment that exercise or can exercise a deleterious effect on human physical development, health, and survival.**

***Legal Annotation***: "The final justification suggested for warrantless administrative searches is that the public interest demands such a rule: it is vigorously argued that the health and safety of entire urban populations is dependent upon enforcement of minimum fire, housing, and **sanitation** standards, and that the only effective means of enforcing such codes is by routine systematized inspection of all physical structures." *Camara v. Municipal Court of City and County of San Francisco* (U.S., 1967).

## SANITARIUM

**A hospital used for the recuperation or the treatment of chronic and usually long-term illnesses.**

***Legal Annotation***: "[T]he Ordinance states that a hospital is: [a] place for the diagnosis, treatment or other care of humans and having facilities for inpatient care, including such establishments as a sanitarium or preventorium. . . . The Merriam Webster Collegiate Dictionary (10th ed. 2000) defines a **sanatorium** in its long accepted meaning as '1: an establishment that provides therapy combined with a regimen (as of diet and exercise) for treatment or rehabilitation; 2a: an institution for rest and recuperation (as of convalescents) b: an establishment for the treatment of the chronically ill.'" *Diversified Health Associates, Inc. v. Zoning Hearing Bd.* (Pa. Common. Ct., 2001).

## SATELLITE DISH ANTENNA

**A parabolic or dish-shaped antenna designed to send and/or receive radio waves.**

***Comment***: Many local ordinances have attempted to control the location and size of satellite dish antennas for aesthetic reasons. Court cases have ruled that Federal Communications Commission regulations have preempted local control over these devices or at least require them to be treated as any other antenna (*Alsan Technology v. Zoning Board of Adjustment,* 235 N.J. Super. 471; *Nationwide v. Zoning Board of Adjustment,* 243 N.J. Super. 18). Local control of satellite antennas may be upheld if the local ordinance is crafted to meet the following three-point test:

- The ordinance should not differentiate between satellite dish antennas and other types of antennas.
- There should be a reasonable, clearly defined health, safety, and/or aesthetic objective as the basis for the ordinance.
- The ordinance should not impose unreasonable limitations on reception or impose costs on the user disproportionate to total investment in antenna equipment and installation.

***Legal Annotation***: "This regulation does not preempt all local zoning regulation of **satellite dish antennas**. Rather, preemption may only occur where the local regulation 'differentiates' between **satellite dish antennas** and 'other types of antenna facilities.'" *Lima Partners v. Borough of Northvale* (N.J. App. Div., 1987).

## SATELLITE OFFICE

**(1) An office used by employees who are telecommuting; (2) a branch office or facility of a company or governmental agency.**

*Comment*: With respect to zoning, there is no reason to distinguish between satellite offices and any other types of business office use. **See** *Telecommuting*.

*Legal Annotation*: "The plain meaning of the statute, then, is that neither an office of the 'circuit court clerk' nor an office of the 'board of elections and registration' is a **satellite office**. Indeed, it is clear that the statute is written in the alternative and that a '**satellite office**' is any office other than an office of the circuit court clerk or the office of the Board of Elections." *Curley v. Lake Cty Bd. of Elections Regis.* (Ind. Ct. App., 2008).

## SAUNA

**A steam bath or heated bathing room used for the purpose of bathing and relaxation, with steam or hot air used as a cleansing and relaxing agent.**

*Legal Annotation*: "As background, the case arises out of a fire that occurred at the Waltham Racquet Club on March 18, 1997, as a result of the careless placement of a towel or other fabric on the rocks contained within the **sauna** heater. Defendant manufactured the **sauna** heater in 1974. A jury found that the heater had been negligently designed because of a failure to supply it with a guard or grille. Earlier, between 1978 and 1988, the Waltham Racquet Club had experienced a fire in the same **sauna** room, caused by a similar careless act." *Cigna Ins. Co. v. Oy Saunatec, Ltd.* (D. Mass., 1999).

## SCALE

**(1) The relationship between distances on a map and actual ground distances; (2) the proportioned relationship of the size of parts to one another.** ***See Figure* 7.**

*Comment*: Map scale is usually represented by a graphic scale (a visual bar) or by a ratio (or representative fraction), indicating that, for example, one inch (on the map) equals one mile (on the ground). Because maps are often enlarged or reduced, the bar scale should be used, since it is not affected by map enlargement or reduction. **See** *Area Scale*.

*Legal Annotation*: "The locations of flood limits shown on the map are only approximate because the map **scale** is small (1 inch = 2,000 feet) and the contour interval is relatively large (10 feet, supplemented by 5-foot-interval contours in some areas)." *Lombard Park Dist. v. Chicago Title & Trust Co.* (Ill. App. Ct., 1969).

"The building would have been totally out of **scale** with other structures in the neighborhood. Nonvisual impacts would also have resulted from the construction of the project. The building would have blocked sunlight and cast a shadow over surrounding properties." *Polygon Corporation v. Seattle* (Wash., 1978).

## SCALE OF DEVELOPMENT

**The relationship of a particular project or development, in terms of its size, height, bulk, intensity, and aesthetics, to its surroundings.**

*Legal Annotation*: "In order to assure that the **scale of development** in the future will result in a quality of life that would be appropriate for areas such as Friendship Heights, the approved and adopted Sector Plan allows for an additional 555,000 square feet of office use, 375,000 square feet of retail use, 1,648 residential dwelling units, and a projected total population in the Sector Plan Area of 6,000 persons." *Mont. Cty. v. Woodward & Lothrop* (Md. Ct. App., 1978).

## SCATTERED-SITE HOUSING

**Subsidized housing located on sites that are geographically dispersed throughout substantially built-up areas.**

*Comment*: The theory behind scattered-site housing is that it is preferable both for the residents of the subsidized housing as well as the community to disperse such subsidized units throughout established neighborhoods, as opposed to concentrating them in one area. See *Infill*.

*Legal Annotation*: "**Scattered site housing** differs from traditional public housing in that there is no construction of large multiunit 'project' style buildings. Instead, '**scattered-site housing** is affordable housing dispersed throughout a geographic area. This type of single-family housing typically blends in with the surroundings; it looks like any other house on a given block.' J. Cummins, 'Recasting Fair Share: Toward Effective Housing Law and Principled Social Policy,' 14 Law & Ineq. 339, 385 n.241 (1996)." *Edgewood Village, Inc. v. Housing Authority* (Conn., 2003).

## SCENIC AREA

**An open area, the natural features of which are visually significant or geologically or ecologically unique.**

*Comment*: Conservation easements are often used to preserve scenic areas. See *Easement, Conservation.*

*Legal Annotation*: "The phrase '**scenic area**' is a little more difficult to dismiss. No doubt the legislature intended that the department could, under this language, acquire property to be looked at by the travelling public as distinguished from stood upon, rested in or parked upon. But we hesitate to construe the phrase '**scenic area**' as an open-end grant of authority to the State highway department to acquire all the land which can be seen by the travelling public, even with the naked eye." *Central Advertising Co. v. State Highway Comm'n* (Mich., 1969).

## SCENIC CORRIDOR

**An area visible from a highway, waterway, railway, or major hiking, biking, or equestrian trail or publicly accessible right-of-way that provides vistas over water and across expanses of land, such as farmlands, woodlands, coastal wetlands, or mountaintops or ridges. See *Viewshed*.**

*Comment*: Scenic vistas also provide views of the built environment, such as an urban skyline.

*Legal Annotation*: "The legitimacy and reasonableness of enforcement of the ordinance are not contested; therefore, we need only address whether the ordinance is invalid because it constitutes a taking. See ***id. We conclude the scenic corridor ordinance has not deprived petitioners of 'all economically beneficial or productive use' of their property. Thus, no unconstitutional taking has occurred." JWL investments v. Bd. of adjustment (N.C. Ct.*** App., 1999).

## SCENIC EASEMENT

See *Easement, Scenic*.

## SCENIC OVERLOOK

**A designated area, usually a pullout area on the side of a road, where a scenic area or viewshed can be observed. See *Viewshed*.**

*Legal Annotation*: "The **scenic overlook** is to occupy a 36 acre tract abutting State Highway 9-W, and would also include picnic sites. The Commission found that the overlook would enable visitors to enjoy 'the scenic vistas of the Hudson River' and 'will not seriously or substantially impinge on the scenic historic or environmental qualities of the area.'" *Scenic Hudson Preserv. Conf. v. Federal Power Com'n* (2nd Cir., 1971).

## SCENIC ROADWAY

**An official designation for roadways that cross areas of natural beauty, including open-space areas, farmlands, forests, and scenic vistas. *See Figure 106*.**

*Comment*: Scenic roadway designation can provide the rationale for special design guidelines relating to land use, building design, sign standards, landscaping, and view protection.

*Legal Annotation*: "Secondly, **Scenic Road**: The size of the project with only one outlet, that on M-131, threatens the destruction of a section of **scenic roadway** running from Harbor Springs to Cross Village. The increased usage will require improvement which generally includes widening with removal of many unique trees presently along or on the right of way. Whether removed or not, the increased exhaust fumes would be detrimental to said trees." *Ray v. Mason County Drain Comm'r* (Mich., 1975).

## SCHEMATIC DRAWING

**See *Plat, Sketch*.**

***Legal Annotation***: "An illustrative **schematic drawing** is attached as Appendix 1 as an aid to understanding the location and relationships of the various parcels of property and claimed easements." *Pipkin v. Der Torosian* (Calif. Ct. App., 1973).

## SCHOOL

**Any building or part thereof that is designed, constructed, or used for education or instruction in any branch of knowledge.**

***Comment***: The above definition includes all types of schools, such as business and trade schools, schools of art, dance, theater, culture, and the martial arts, as well as academic institutions. Local ordinances can further define the kinds of schools that might be allowed in specific areas; for example, only elementary and secondary schools in residential areas. In many states, regulations affecting schools must be applied uniformly to private and public schools. See *Roman Catholic Diocese of Newark V. Borough Of Ho-Ho-Kus, 202 A.*2d 161 (1964).

***Legal Annotation***: "A '**school**' can be commonly defined as an '*institution* for the instruction of children.' Webster's II, New Riverside University Dictionary 1045 (1994) (emphasis added); and an 'institution' can be commonly defined as an 'established organization or foundation, esp[ecially] one dedicated to public service.'" *Hooks v. Clark County School Dist.* (9th Cir., 2000).

## SCHOOL, ELEMENTARY

**Any school that is licensed by the state and meets the state requirements for elementary education.**

***Legal Annotation***: "Under the IDEA and the ESEA, an '**elementary school**' is defined as 'a *nonprofit* institutional day or residential school, including a public elementary charter school, that provides elementary education, as determined under State law.' 20 U.S.C. §§ 1401(6) (IDEA), 7801(18) (ESEA) (emphasis added)." *Arizona State Bd. v. US Dept. of Educ.* (9th Cir., 2006).

## SCHOOL, PAROCHIAL

**A school supported, controlled, and operated by a religious organization. See *School, Private*.**

***Legal Annotation***: "As I said in the *Lemon* and *DiCenso* cases, a **parochial school** is a unitary institution with subtle blending of sectarian and secular instruction. . . . 'It should be clear to all that a Roman Catholic **parochial school** is an integral part of that church, as definitely so as is the service of worship. A **parochial school** is usually developed in connection with a church. In many cases the church and school monies are not even separated. Such a school is in no sense a public school, even though some children from other groups may be admitted to it. The buildings are not owned and controlled by a community of American people, not even by a community of American Roman Catholic people. The title of ownership in a public school is vested in the local community, in the elected officers of the school board or the city council. But the title of ownership in a **parochial school** is vested in the bishop as an individual, who is appointed by, who is under the direct control of, and who reports to the pope in Rome.' L. Boettner, Roman Catholicism 375 (1962)." *Tilton v. Richardson* (U.S., 1971).

## SCHOOL, PRIVATE

**Any building or group of buildings, the use of which meets state requirements for elementary, secondary, or higher education and that does not secure the major part of its funding from any governmental agency.**

***Legal Annotation***: "A **private school** is defined as '[a]ny nonpublic nursery school, kindergarten, elementary (1–8), secondary school (9–12).'" *Skelly v. Montessori Centre of Barrington, Inc.* (R.I. Super. Ct., 2011).

## SCHOOL, SECONDARY

**Any school that is licensed by the state and authorized to award diplomas for secondary education.**

***Legal Annotation***: "Similarly, the statutes define a '**secondary school**' as 'a *nonprofit* institutional day or residential school, including a public secondary charter school, that provides secondary education, as determined under State law.' . . . (emphasis added)." *Arizona State Bd. v. US Dept. of Educ.* (9th Cir., 2006).

## SCHOOL, VOCATIONAL

**See *Vocational School*.**

## SCHOOL DISTRICT

**The specific jurisdiction administrated by the elected or appointed body of a state, county, or other local governmental unit to provide educational services to its resident population.**

***Legal Annotation***: "A '**school district**' is defined as 'an area of land established as a political subdivision of the state for the administration of public schools and segregated geographically for taxation and bonding purposes.'" *Ellenberg v. New Mexico Military Institute* (10th Cir., 2007).

## SCOUR

**Removal of soil or fill material by the flow of floodwaters.**

***Comment***: The term is frequently used to describe storm-induced, localized conical erosion around pilings and other foundation supports where the obstruction of flow increases turbulence (*FEMA Glossary*).

***Legal Annotation***: "If the river flows into an excavated pit, it would deposit its sediment in the pit and any water leaving the pit (once the pit is full) would carry less sediment and flow more quickly, which could **scour** the riverbed immediately downstream of the pit." *Valley v. County of Santa Barbara* (Calif. Ct. App., 2013).

## SCRAP

**Discarded or rejected materials that result from manufacturing or fabricating operations.**

***Legal Annotation***: "'New **scrap**' is defined as the refuse produced during the manufacture of articles for ultimate consumption, including all finished and semifinished articles that are to be reworked. Typical examples of new scrap are defective castings, clippings, punchings, turnings, borings, skimmings, drosses, and slags. Finished and semifinished articles frequently are received as scrap because of excess inventory, faulty manufacture, or change in design or other causes of obsolescence, and the metal content of all such articles is included as new scrap.

"'Old scrap' is defined as scrap derived from metal articles that have been discarded after serving a useful purpose. Typical examples of old scrap are discarded trolley wire, battery plates, railroad-car boxes, automobile crankcases, cocks and faucets, and lithographers plates."

*M.W. Mack Metal Company v. Commissioner* (U.S. Tax Ct., 1954).

## SCREEN

**A structure, berm, or planting consisting of fencing and/or evergreen trees or shrubs providing a continuous view obstruction within a site or property or a portion thereof.**

***Legal Annotation***: "Alternative 2A was based on the 'use [of] landscaping and . . . an earth berm to **screen** the view of the Soundwall.' The total anticipated cost of Alternative 2A was $1,630,000." *City of Yorba Linda v. City of Anaheim* (Calif. Ct. App., 2011).

## SCREENING

**(1) A method of visually shielding or buffering one abutting or nearby structure or use from another by fencing, walls, berms, or densely planted vegetation; (2) the removal of relatively coarse floating and/or suspended solids by straining through racks or screens.**

*Legal Annotation*: "The premises shall be landscaped so that vegetative **screening** at least five feet in height shall he maintained around the perimeter of the outdoor dining area, along the outside of the curved walls and the back of the slate patio where the outdoor dining is permitted. Further, a double six-foot-high fence with sound baffling material sandwiched between the two fences shall be installed and maintained along the portions of the L-shaped northeast boundary line that stretch between the two one-story cottages. The foregoing shall be subject to Design Review Board approval." *Matter of Hamptons, LLC v. Zoning Bd. of Appeals of the Incorporated Village of East Hampton* (N.Y. Sup. Ct., 2011).

## SCRUBBER

**An air pollution control device that uses a liquid spray to remove pollutants from a gas stream by absorption or chemical reaction.**

*Legal Annotation*: "One of the ways SO can be reduced, for example, is by installing a flue gas desulfurization system, or '**scrubber**.' **Scrubbers** are large chemical plants—often larger than the power plants themselves—that remove $SO_2$—from plant exhaust and cost hundreds of millions of dollars." *North Carolina ex rel. Cooper v. Tennessee Valley Authority* (4th Cir., 2010).

## SEA LEVEL

**The level of the ocean between high and low tides, which is used as a reference for all land elevations. See *Contour Line; Intertidal Area*.**

*Legal Annotation*: "Neither party provided a definition for the technical term '**Sea Level** Datum' as part of its statement of undisputed facts. This has contributed to the Court's difficulty in discerning a 'plain meaning' for the disputed phrase. One definition of '**Sea Level** Datum' located by the Court explains that '**Sea Level** Datum' refers to the National Geodetic Vertical Datum of 1929 and 'should not be confused with mean **sea level**.' See National Oceanic and Atmospheric Administration, Tides & Currents website. . . . One court, relying upon expert testimony, defined 'mean **sea level**' as the elevation of an object relative to the 'average sea level datum.' Kelley v. United States, 2009 WL 1439896, at * 2 (E.D.Va.2009) ('"MSL" or "mean sea level" is the elevation or altitude of an object relative to the average **sea level** datum.')." ***Valley View Dev. V. US Army Corps of Engineers (N.D.*** Okla., 2010).

## SEASHORE

**The area where the land meets the sea or ocean.**

*Legal Annotation*: "'**Seashore**' is defined as 'the space of land over which the waters of the sea spread in the highest tide during the winter season.'" *Dardar v. Lafourche Realty Co., Inc.* (5th Cir., 1993).

## SEASONAL DWELLING UNIT

**A dwelling unit that lacks one or more of the basic amenities or utilities required for all-year or all-weather occupancy.**

***Comment***: In resort or seashore areas, municipalities may grant dwelling-unit certificates of occupancy that place limits on their occupancy during certain periods of time. For example, houses that lack heating might not be certified for use during winter months.

Many municipalities also recognize that houses originally built for seasonal use eventually become all-year-round dwellings and require all dwellings to be fully certified.

*Legal Annotation*: "A **'seasonal' dwelling** is defined as one used for continuous habitation only during the months of May through October." *Lebanon v. Woods* (Conn., 1965).

## SEASONAL STRUCTURE

**A temporary structure that is erected or moved into place and only utilized for the duration of a summer or winter season.**

***Comment***: An example of a temporary structure is covering erected over a recreational amenity, such as a swimming pool or tennis court, for the purpose of extending its use to cold-weather months or inclement conditions. The problem with seasonal structures is that they often become permanent. An open tennis court, for instance, may be acceptable; however, one with a plastic structure to extend the season may be visually objectionable.

*Legal Annotation*: "A **seasonal structure** placed on bottomland to facilitate private noncommercial recreational use of the water if it does not unreasonably interfere with the use of the water by others entitled to use the water or interfere with water flow. A dock which is removed at the end of the boating season is included in the definition of '**seasonal structure**'." *Thom v. Rasmussen* (Mich. Ct. App., 1984).

## SEASONAL USE

**A use carried on for only a part of the year.**

*Comment*: Typical seasonal uses are recreational activities such as outdoor swimming or skiing, but they also include farm stands and Christmas tree sales. Zoning regulations should consider the fact that the use is in place or being used for only a relatively small part of the year. Bulk controls can be waived or relaxed for many of these uses, although some site-plan review may be needed to ensure adequate parking and safe circulation.

*Legal Annotation*: "The question presented by this appeal is whether the court below erred in determining that the year-round use of trailers in a trailer park, as opposed to their **seasonal use** during the late spring, summer and early fall months, was not an extension of a nonconforming business use in violation of § 14 (2) of the zoning regulations of the town of Coventry." *Beerwort v. Zoning Board of Appeals* (Conn., 1958).

## SEAWALL

**A wall or embankment that acts as a breakwater and is used to prevent beach erosion.**

*Legal Annotation*: "'**Seawall**' is defined as '[a] structure built along the shoreline to resist the erosion of the land caused by the lake and which can also be used to moor boats and as a structure to receive and discharge boat's passengers and cargo.. . .'" *Hyatt v. Town of Lake Lure* (W.D. N.C., 2002).

## SECOND-HOME COMMUNITY

**A development consisting of vacation homes or resort residences not used as the principal domicile.**

*Legal Annotation*: "Defendant Quechee Lakes Corporation (QLC) is the developer of Quechee Lakes Development, a planned **second-home community** in Quechee." *Gannon v. Quechee Lakes Corp*. (Vt., 1994).

## SECOND MORTGAGE

**A mortgage on real estate that has already been pledged as collateral against another mortgage.**

*Legal Annotation*: "The first is that although a **second mortgage** is a conveyance of sorts, it is more significantly a security transaction that was made the subject of a complete regulatory statute that addressed itself directly and thoroughly to its particular problems." *Westervelt v. Gateway Financial Service* (N.J. Super. Ct., 1983).

## SECONDARY TREATMENT

**Wastewater treatment beyond the primary state in which bacteria consume the organic parts of the wastes.**

*Comment*: This biochemical action is accomplished by use of trickling filters or the activated sludge process. Effective secondary treatment removes virtually all floating and settleable solids and approximately 90 percent of both BOD (biological oxygen demand) and suspended solids. Customarily, disinfection by chlorination is the final state of the secondary treatment process. See *Tertiary Treatment*.

*Legal Annotation*: "First, the Agency reiterates that **secondary treatment** is concerned with the removal of carbonaceous organic material. This argument begs the question. If Maier's petition questions the EPA's earlier conclusion as to nonattainability, the Agency should explain its continued reliance on its previous explanation. The EPA has not done so, instead insisting that any new information on attainability submitted by Maier 'does not establish (or even suggest) why control of nitrogen or phosphorus should be considered **secondary treatment**.'" *Maier v. USEPA* (10th Cir., 1997).

## SECTION OF LAND

**Measured as 640 acres, one square mile, or 1/36th of a township. See *Quarter Section*.**

*Legal Annotation*: "A **section of land** is a square mile and consists of 640 acres. BLACK'S LAW DICTIONARY 1521 (4th ed. 1968)." *Sharp v. 251st Street Landfill, Inc.* (Okla., 1991).

## SECURITIZATION

**The pooling of mortgage loans into a mortgage-backed security. The principal and interest payments from the individual mortgages are paid out to the holders of the MBS security. http://www.realtor.com/home-finance/mortgages/terms-glossary.aspx?source=web**

*Legal Annotation*: "A '**securitization**' is a bundling of secured real property loans for sale as a group to institutional investors. Although the securitization technique had previously been used with first trust deeds, securitization was not commonly used with second trust deeds as of 1989. A **securitization** transaction consists of several components, involves an investment banker, rating agency and trustee, and can take a year or more to complete. A party (such as First Alliance) which originates loans which are securitized can earn higher profits than from selling loans individually. Neither Rosenfeld nor Chisick had previously been involved in a **securitization**." *Hedging Concepts, Inc. v. First Alliance Mortgage* (Calif. Ct. App., 1996).

## SEDIMENT

**Deposited silt that is being or has been removed by water or ice, wind, gravity, or other means of erosion. See *Silt*.**

*Legal Annotation*: "Additionally, it concluded that this low water velocity and extended residence time allowed suspended **sediments** to settle out of the water. It estimated that approximately 10,540 cubic yards of **sediment** is stored in the relevant portion of the Saint Brides Ditch rather than downstream in the Northwest River. It explained that this filtered **sediment** likely includes some quantity of dissolved pollutants that are thus removed from the Northwest River, improving the drinking water and fishing quality of the river." *Precon Development v. US Army Corps of Engineers* (4th Cir., 2011).

## SEDIMENT BASIN

**A pond, a dam, or a barrier built across a waterway at a suitable location to allow sediments to settle out of water.**

*Legal Annotation*: "A **sediment basin** is a temporary pond built at a construction site to protect the quality of a nearby body of water—here, Brown's Pond—by capturing eroded or disturbed soil that is washed off during rainfall; the sediment-laden soil settles in the basin before the runoff is discharged." *City of Newburgh v. Sarna* (S.D. N.Y., 2010).

## SEDIMENTATION

**(1) The depositing of earth or soil that has been transported from its site of origin by water, ice, wind, gravity, or other natural means as a product of erosion; (2) in wastewater treatment, the settling out of solids by gravity.**

*Legal Annotation*: "The Forest Service recognizes that **sedimentation** can come from many sources other than grazing, and so attempts to isolate, identify and remedy those conditions caused by grazing that lead to **sedimentation**. First and foremost is riparian grazing, that tramples streambanks and destroys stream-side vegetation. As will be discussed below, the Forest Service is monitoring riparian areas to avoid this source of grazing-caused sedimentation.

"**Sedimentation** is also caused by upland grazing and trailing on steep slopes and erodible soils, causing sediments to wash down into streams."

*Western Watershed Project v. US Forest Service* (D. Idaho, 2011).

## SEDIMENTATION TANKS

**In wastewater treatment, containers where the solids are allowed to settle or to float as scum.**

***Comment***: The scum is skimmed off, and settled solids are pumped to incinerators, digesters, filters, or other means of disposal.

***Legal Annotation***: "SSL is evaporated and burned in 'SSL recovery,' eliminating the water pollution potential and producing usable heat and sometimes reusable chemicals. The non-SSL waste solutions are pumped into **sedimentation tanks** where some of the suspended solids settle out of solution. The solutions are then pumped into other tanks and lagoons for secondary or 'biological' treatment, in which bacteria are grown in the solutions to feed on and break down the waste. Eventually, the water is drained from the bacteria-laden solutions by a variety of methods. After draining, the caked solid or 'sludge' that is left is incinerated or used for landfill." *Weyerhaeuser Co. v. Costle* (D.C. Cir., 1978).

## SEEPAGE

**Water that flows through the soil.**

***Legal Annotation***: "'**Seepage**' is 'the process of seeping,' that is, 'flow[ing] or pass[ing] slowly through fine pores or small openings.' 'Migration' is 'move[ment] from one country, place, or locality to another' or 'chang[ing] position in an organism or substance.'" *Madison Const. v. Harleysville Mut. Ins.* 735 A. 2d 100 (Pa., 1999).

## SEEPAGE PIT

**A covered pit with open, jointed lining through which septic tank effluent or stormwater runoff may seep or leach into the surrounding soil.**

***Comment***: Seepage pits are utilized both for onsite septic sewer disposal systems and for handling stormwater runoff from building roofs or other paved surfaces.

***Legal Annotation***: "The Debtor informed McCracken that there may be a '**seepage pit**,' i.e., a pit containing stones that enables a piece of land to contain more water than it otherwise would be able to, on the property where the new parking lot is to be built which may obviate the need for this variance. Regardless of whether this **seepage pit** exists, Robert expressed confidence that the land can be made to conform to the water run off requirements." *In re Temple Zion* (Bankr. Ct., E.D. Pa., 1991).

## SELF-STORAGE FACILITY

**A building or group of buildings containing separate, individual, and private storage spaces of varying sizes available for lease or rent for varying periods of time.**

***Comment***: In the 1970s, when self-storage facilities first became popular, they were often classified as mini-warehouses and limited to industrial and warehouse zoning districts. The modern self-storage facility is a multistory retail service use, located in a commercial corridor and serving individuals and small businesses, usually within a five-mile radius.

Self-storage facilities are very low traffic generators, requiring little permanent parking, often as little as one parking space per fifty to one hundred rental units for one-story buildings. Two-story buildings may require elevator access, and more parking spaces around the elevators may be needed. Many have resident managers living in on-site apartments; the newer facilities rely on enhanced automated operational and security systems.

Access is provided to the rental units from driveways, so the width between buildings should be at least twenty feet. First-generation self-storage facilities were not particularly attractive because they were often flat-roofed, one-story structures arranged in long, monotonous rows. Newer facilities have two or more stories and direct access to the units from enclosed corridors. The outer walls have significant areas of glass and other architectural treatment. Heavy perimeter landscaping may be the best way to break up building appearance, along with substantial setbacks from lot lines.

Local ordinances should address security, landscaping, fencing, lighting, and height, as well as wall treatment. The use of the storage spaces should also be regulated. Most ordinances specify that the use is for dead storage only, and flammable or hazardous chemicals and explosives are prohibited. Arlington, Texas, prohibits the following uses in self-storage facilities:

- Auctions; commercial, wholesale, or retail sales; or miscellaneous or garage sales.
- The servicing, repair, or fabrication of motor vehicles, boats, trailers, lawn mowers, appliances, or other similar equipment.
- The operation of power tools, spray-painting equipment, table saws, lathes, compressors, welding equipment, kilns, or other similar equipment.
- The establishment of a transfer and storage business.
- Any use that is noxious or offensive because of odors, dust, noise, fumes, or vibrations.

Some self-storage facilities have open areas where boats, vacant trailers, and recreation vehicles may be stored. The local ordinance should specify whether this type of storage is permitted (American Planning Association, *Standards for Self-Service Storage Facilities*, Planning Advisory Service Report No. 396, 1986). **See *Also* P**ristin 2005.

***Legal Annotation***: "A **self-storage facility** is real property 'designed and used only for renting or leasing individual storage space in [a] facility' where the occupants have access to the facility only to store and remove their personal property." *Johanns v. Minnesota Mobile Storage, Inc.* (Minn. Ct. App., 2006).

## SEMI-AMBULATORY DISABILITY

**An impairment that causes individuals to walk with difficulty or insecurity.**

***Comment***: Individuals using braces or canes; arthritics; and those with pulmonary and cardiac ills may be semi-ambulatory.

***Legal Annotation***: "The Cottages Residents must be at least **semi-ambulatory**, requiring no more than a one-person assist with transfers, not in need of 24-hour nursing care or routine professional or ancillary medical assistance, and not at risk to themselves or others." *Geary v. Life Investors Ins. Co. of America* (N.D. Texas, 2007).

"They represent a class of mobility handicapped persons who have been denied access to the publicly operated buses in Rhode Island. This class, certified on April 8, 1981, has been broken down into two subclasses: mobility handicapped persons confined to wheelchairs and mobility handicapped persons not confined to wheelchairs. This latter group is often described as **semi-ambulatory**." *RI Handicapped, Etc. v. RI Public Transit* (D. R.I., 1982).

## SEMIDETACHED

**See *Dwelling, Single-Family Semidetached*.**

***Legal Annotation***: "In the zoning regulations in defining a 'Dwelling, Semi-detached,' for example, it is stated that a dwelling, **semi-detached** is a '*building* that has two one-family housekeeping units erected side by side on adjoining lots, separated from each other by an approved masonry party wall . . . and separated from any *building* by space on all sides.' (Emphasis added)." *Feinberg v. Southland Corp. (*Md. Ct. App., 1973).

## SEMIFINISHED PRODUCT

**The end result of a manufacturing process that will become a raw material for an establishment engaged in further manufacturing.**

***Comment***: The above definition, derived from NAICS (1997), includes the following illustration of a semifinished product:

The product of the alumina refinery is the input used in the primary production of aluminum; primary aluminum is the input to an aluminum wire drawing plant; and aluminum wire is the input of a fabricated wire product manufacturing establishment (NAICS 1997).

***Legal Annotation***: "Further, the Commission examines five factors to determine whether a **semifinished product** is a like product, distinct from the finished product. These factors include: (1) the necessity and costs of further processing for the **semifinished product**; (2) the degree of interchangeability between the **semifinished** and finished **products**; (3) the extent to which the use of the **semifinished product** is dedicated to the finished product; (4) whether the two products have independent markets and uses; and (5) whether the **semifinished product** imparts an essential characteristic or function to the finished product." *Timken Co. v. US* (Ct. Intl. Trade, 1996).

## SENIOR CITIZEN HOUSING

**Housing designed for, and occupied by, at least one person fifty-five years of age or older per dwelling unit, and which has significant facilities and services specifically designed to meet the physical or social needs of older persons.**

***Comment***: The above definition is derived from § 100.306, "Significant Facilities and Services Specifically Designed for Older Persons," 24 C.F.R. part 100 (Department of Housing and Urban Development—Housing for Older Persons) or any amendments thereto. **See *Housing for the Elderly*.**

***Legal Annotation***: "It is apparent that the city council by approving the application intended that the term 'non-profit **Senior Citizen Housing** project' in the permit have the same meaning as that term is given in the application, a project 'under the requirements specified' in section 231. That section establishes the definition of nonprofit senior citizen housing. Section 231 . . . established a program for insurance of mortgages on housing for the elderly by the federal government. The purpose of the section 'is to assist in relieving the shortage of housing for elderly persons and to increase the supply of rental housing for elderly persons.' The term 'elderly person' is defined as any person who is 62 years of age or over. The word 'housing' is defined as eight or more new or rehabilitated living units, not less than 50 percent of which are specially designed for the use and occupancy of elderly persons." *Sports Arenas Properties, Inc. v. City of San Diego* (Calif., 1985).

## SENSE OF PLACE

**The characteristics of an area that make it readily recognizable as being unique and different from its surroundings and having a special character and familiarity (Schultz and Kasen 1984). See *Character; Community of Place*.**

***Legal Annotation***: "If a property owner does not consent to a historic designation, certain criteria must be satisfied before the Town Council enacts an involuntary historic designation ordinance. A. If the owner of the property does not consent to the review, approval shall require a supermajority vote, one (1) vote more than a simple majority vote, of the Town Council. In such cases, the Town Council shall use the following criteria in addition to the designation criteria listed in Section 2.18.170[sic]: The property has overwhelming historic importance to the entire community. The term overwhelming significance shall, for purposes of this Chapter, encompass: 1. Possessing such *unusual* or *uncommon* significance that the structure's potential demolition or major alteration would diminish the *character and **sense of place*** in the community of Castle Rock (emphasis added). . . . 'Character and **sense of place**' 'takes clear meaning from the observable character of the district to which it applies.' South of Second Associates v. Georgetown, 196 Colo. 89, 93, 580 P.2d 807, 810 (1978) (quoting Robert M. Anderson, Architectural Controls, 12 Syracuse L.Rev. 26, 45 [1960]) ('While determination of what is compatible with the "atmosphere" of the town may on first impression be thought to be a matter of arbitrary and subjective judgment, under consideration it proves not to be.' [quoting Town of Deering v. Tibbetts, 105 N.H. 481, 202 A.2d 232 (1964)])." *Kruse v. Town of Castle Rock* (Colo. Ct. App., 2008).

## SEPARATED BICYCLE FACILITY

See *Bicycle, Separated Facility*.

## SEPARATE OWNERSHIP

**Properties owned or controlled by different individuals, corporations, partnerships, or other entities. See *Same Ownership*.**

*Legal Annotation*: "The first issue presented to this Court is whether the ordinance requirement that a lot be in 'single and **separate ownership**' is met when the owner intends to hold his lot separately from an adjoining lot, even though there is no outward manifestation of this intention. The ordinance in question defines 'single and **separate ownership**' as: The ownership of a lot by one (1) or more persons, partnerships or corporations, which ownership is separate and distinct from that of any abutting or adjoining lot." *W. Goshen T. v. Crater et Ux.* (Pa. Common. Ct., 1988).

## SEPARATE LIVING QUARTERS

See *Living Quarters, Separate*.

*Legal Annotation*: "**Separate living quarters** are those in which the occupants live and eat separately from any other persons in the building and which have direct access from the outside of the building or through a common hall. The occupants may be a single family, one person living alone, two or more families living together, or any other group of related or unrelated persons who share living arrangements. (People not living in households are classified as living in group quarters.)" *In re Fleishman* (Bankr. Ct. D. Ore., 2007).

## SEPTIC SYSTEM

**An underground system with a septic tank used for the decomposition of domestic wastes. See *On-Site Wastewater Disposal System*. See *Figure 32*.**

***Comment***: Bacteria in the wastes decompose the organic matter, and the resultant sludge then settles to the bottom of the septic tank. The effluent flows through perforated pipe and into the ground. Sludge must be pumped out at regular intervals.

*Legal Annotation*: "Testimony at the trial established the following facts regarding the operation of a **septic system**: The purpose of a **septic system** is to convert waste material into liquid suitable for entry into ground water. Sewage is first collected in a septic tank where much of the solid waste settles. What remains after settling is liquid effluent which contains particles of solid waste. In the subject system, the effluent was collected in galleries before entry into the surrounding soil. A gallery, which is often part of a septic system, is a large trench lined with blocks or concrete and usually covered with a lid, which controls the level of effluent entering into the surrounding soil and makes way for the entry of fresh effluent into the gallery. The trench is customarily four feet wide and either two or four feet deep, depending on anticipated use. The system constructed by the defendant was two feet deep. Effluent leaches out through perforations in the sides of the gallery into surrounding soil, or leaching area, unless the soil is saturated, as was the case here." *Coburn v. Lenox Homes, Inc.* (Conn., 1982).

## SEPTIC TANK

**A receptacle that receives the discharge of sewage from a building, sewer, or part thereof and is designed and constructed so as to permit settling of solids from this liquid, digestion of the organic matter, and discharge of the liquid portion into a disposal area. *See Figure 32*.**

*Legal Annotation*: "A **septic tank** is basically a rectangular tank with a sloping bottom. As raw sewage enters the tank, those suspended solids with a specific gravity greater than water are pulled by gravity to the bottom of the tank. The suspended solids are both separated from raw sewage and permitted to decompose in the same tank. Decomposition of these removed solids (sludge) is known as anaerobic digestion; that is, the oxidation of organic material, with gases as the by-product. As gasification takes place, the specific gravity of the sludge changes and some of the sludge will rise to the surface and form a 'scum blanket' on the top of the tank. The scum blanket will be made up of hair particles and fibrous materials, as well as some of the organic materials. Thus, there are two layers of sludge build-up, residue at the bottom and the scum blanket on the top, that must be removed." *United States v. City of Asbury Park* (D. N.J., 1972).

## SERVICE ROAD

**A local street that runs parallel to a higher-order street, such as an arterial street or highway, and that provides access to abutting properties. *See Figure 97*.**

***Comment***: Service roads are usually one-way, two-lane streets with parking on one side.

***Legal Annotation***: "A frontage road or **service road** is a highway facility adjacent to and part of an access-free road designed to provide access to the abutting land which, because of the control of access on the express road, is without means of ingress or egress from that road." *State ex rel. Department of Highways v. Linnecke* (Nev., 1970).

## SERVICE STATION

**See *Automobile Service Station*.**

***Legal Annotation***: "A **service station** is 'a retail station for servicing automobiles and other motor vehicles, especially with gas and oil.' Surely, V.S.H.'s proposed gasoline business is more similar to a service station than to a retail store. There is ample evidence in the record to support the Board's finding that a portion of the business would constitute a motor vehicle service station." *VSH Realty, Inc. v. ZHB of Sharon Hill* (Pa., Common. Ct., 1976).

## SERVICES

**Establishments primarily engaged in providing assistance, as opposed to products, to individuals, business, industry, government, and other enterprises.**

***Comment***: The general category of services includes hotels and other lodging places; personal, business, repair, and amusement services; health, legal, engineering, and other professional services; educational services; membership organizations; and other miscellaneous services.

The above definition includes all types of services and would be appropriate for intensive commercial and retail districts, such as the central business district of an urban area. Development ordinances should specify different types and scale of services appropriate for neighborhood or local business areas. **See *Business Services; Personal Services; Retail Services; Social Services*.**

## SET-ASIDE

**The percentage of housing units devoted to low- and moderate-income households within an inclusionary development.**

***Comment***: The minimum required set-aside varies by state. In Florida, for example, the percentage is lower than 20 percent, and there is no requirement for a 50 percent low and 50 percent moderate split. In New Jersey, the minimum set-aside is 20 percent, with 10 percent for moderate-income and 10 percent for low-income households. See *Inclusionary Development*.

***Legal Annotation***: "Middletown's ordinance provides that all new major residential subdivision and site plan applications must **set aside** 7% of the development's total dwelling units for lower income housing. . . . For the reasons expressed above, that portion of Middletown's ordinance which imposes a mandatory development fee upon all nonresidential development is without statutory authority and therefore invalid. Since residential developments are required to **set aside** 7% of the units for affordable housing or pay an 'in lieu' development fee without receiving a reasonable density bonus or other zoning incentive in return, we conclude that that condition is also an impermissible exaction." *Holmdel Builders v. Holmdel Tp*. (N.J. App. Div., 1989).

## SETBACK

**The distance between the building and any lot line. *See Figure 16*.**

***Comment***: The minimum setbacks in a zoning ordinance define the building envelope and establish the required yards—front, rear, and side. The ordinance should also indicate what may be permitted in which yards, such as parking, fences, accessory buildings, patios, swimming pools, and other recreational uses. Certain projections, such as uncovered walks, chimneys, bay windows, and stoops, are usually exempt from setback requirements, although limits may be set.

Minimum setback standards of other site features to lot lines are sometimes also specified in zoning ordinances, such as parking areas, driveways, and accessory structures such as tennis courts or swimming pools.

*Legal Annotation*: "A **setback** is a minimum distance between developments in order to prevent the construction of buildings too close together." *Wyman v. Town of Phippsburg* (Maine, 2009).

## SETBACK LINE

**A line drawn along the required minimum setback from any lot line.**

***Comment***: By drawing all of the setback lines within a lot, the area within which the principal structure may be erected or placed can be established, often referred to as a "building envelope." **See *Setback; Building Line*. See** *Figure 16*.

***Legal Annotation***: "Under the Town's zoning ordinance an owner may build to what is called the construction **setback line** on lots abutting the Gulf. . . . For multi-family or commercial properties, the construction **setback line** is a line running generally parallel to the shoreline at points 5 feet inland of the primary dune crest line. . . . On other commercial lots, not abutting the Gulf, structures must be set back 20 feet from the property line and inland of the construction setback line." *Gulf House Ass'n, Inc. v. Town of Gulf Shores* (Ala., 1985).

## SETTLEABLE SOLIDS

**Bits of debris and fine matter heavy enough to settle out of wastewater.**

***Legal Annotation***: "Petitioners also claim that **settleable solids** are a component of total suspended solids and that the EPA should have classified **settleable solids** as a conventional rather than a nonconventional pollutant. Petitioners contend that BAT-based effluent limitations are therefore inappropriate for **settleable solids**. We disagree. In the Clean Water Act, Congress classified **suspended solids** as a conventional pollutant. . . . Congress did not classify **settleable solids**. We must determine, therefore, whether the EPA's classification of **settleable solids** as a nonconventional pollutant 'is based on a permissible construction of the [Clean Water Act].'" *Rybachek v. USEPA* (9th Cir., 1990).

## SETTLING CHAMBER

**In air-pollution control, a device used to reduce the velocity of flue gases, usually by means of baffles, promoting the settling of fly ash.**

***Legal Annotation***: "But flocculation in the process of sedimentation is not peculiar to sugar juice, as the plaintiffs' expert witness Dennis conceded. Peck No. 1,392,214 (1921), covering an apparatus for treating sewage, states that 'the treated sewage is subjected to sedimentation and decantation to settle out the flocculated particles, called the activated sludge, and to permit the escape of a relatively clear and stable effluent by overflow'. . . . Continuous sedimentation in a **settling chamber** and continuous decantation therefrom of clarified sugar juice are shown in Pickering," *Dorr Co. v. Yabucoa Sugar Co.* (1st Cir., 1941).

## SETTLING TANK

**In wastewater treatment, a tank or basin in which settleable solids are removed by gravity.**

***Legal Annotation***: "The sewage to be treated, passing from the elementary settlement through a mixing channel, is there augmented by the introduction of activated sludge and then proceeds eventually to the aeration chamber, being retained in the mixing channel for perhaps two minutes. The mixture is retained and treated in the aeration chamber for about six hours. Each of these chambers in cross-section is substantially the same as that of chamber No. 4 at Desplaines, after the modification there in 1924, containing, however, two rows of diffuser plates instead of one. At the end of the tank, the mixture, after treatment as aforesaid, passes over weirs into a **settling tank**, which is provided with a partially hoppered bottom to cause the sludge as it settles to drift toward the center of the bottom of the tank." *Sanitary Dist. of Chicago v. Activated Sludge* (7th Cir., 1937).

## SEWAGE

**The total of organic waste and wastewater generated by residential, industrial, and commercial establishments. (Source: Margil 2010 and Filsram 2010.)**

***Legal Annotation***: "Sec. 3. (1) A person [defined in § 2 (i) to mean 'an individual, partnership, firm, corporation, association or other entity'] shall not place, throw, deposit, discharge or cause to be discharged into or onto the waters of this state, any . . . **sewage** [defined in § 2 (d) to mean 'all human body wastes, treated or untreated'] . . . or other liquid or solid materials which render the water unsightly, noxious or otherwise unwholesome so as to be detrimental to the public health or welfare or to the enjoyment of the water for recreational purposes." *Lake Carriers' Assn. v. MacMullan* (U.S., 1972).

## SEWER, SANITARY

See *Sanitary Sewer*.

## SEWER, STORM

**A pipe or conduit used to collect and carry away stormwater runoff to receiving waterbodies.**

***Comment***: A sewer that conveys household, commercial, and industrial sewage is called a sanitary sewer; if it transports runoff from rain or snow, it is a storm sewer. A combined sewer is one in which stormwater runoff and sewerage are transported in the same pipe.

***Legal Annotation***: "The purpose of a **storm sewer** is to carry off flood waters. Each lot in the district is benefitted by being relieved from the dangers and damages which may be occasioned from storm waters, more or less common to the district in which it is situated. Each tract ordinarily augments the aggregate volume of storm waters in a district, in the proportion that its area bears to the entire area of lots in the district." *City of Detroit v. State of Mich.* (6th Cir., 1986).

## SEWER SYSTEM AND TREATMENT

**Devices for the collection, treatment, and disposal of sewage. See *Combined Sewers; Interceptor Sewer; Lateral Sewers; Outfall; Package Treatment Plant; Primary Treatment; Sanitary Sewage; Sanitary Sewers; Secondary Treatment; Septic System; Sewer; Tertiary Treatment*.**

***Legal Annotation***: "Notwithstanding any other provision of law, on or after January 1, 1972, waste from within the Lake Tahoe watershed shall be placed only into a **sewer system and treatment** facilities sufficient to handle and treat any such waste and transportation facilities sufficient to transport any resultant effluent outside the Lake Tahoe watershed, except that such waste may be placed in a holding tank which is pumped and transported to such treatment and transportation facilities." *Fallen Leaf Protection Assn. v. State of California* (Calif. App. Ctr., 1975).

## SEWERAGE

**(1) All effluent carried by sewers, whether it is sanitary sewage, industrial wastes, or stormwater runoff; (2) the entire system of sewage collection, treatment, and disposal.**

***Legal Annotation***: "A system of **sewerage** is defined to mean and include a system of sewers, outfalls, works, plants and facilities for sewage treatment and disposal, or any or all of such facilities." *Morse v. Wise* (Wash. Dept. Two, 1951).

## SEX SHOP

**See *Adult Use*.**

***Legal Annotation***: "Moreover, where the January 2004 Amendments defined a '**sex shop**,' inter alia, in terms of a store in which '[m]ore than 5 percent of its stock in trade consists of' or '[m]ore than 5 percent of its gross public floor area is devoted to' sexually oriented toys or novelties . . . this December 2004 Amendment does not include any triggering percentage. Instead, it defines a 'sexual device shop' as a store that 'regularly features' even one 'sexual device,' and also adds specific exceptions for 'any pharmacy, drug store, medical clinic, or any establishment primarily dedicated to providing medical or healthcare products or services,' and still more critically here, any 'commercial establishments which do not restrict access to any portion of their premises by reason of age.'" *Doctor John's, Inc. v. City of Sioux City, IA* (N.D. Iowa, 2006).

## SEXUALLY ORIENTED BUSINESS

See *Adult Use*.

*Legal Annotation*: "A **sexually-oriented business** is an 'adult arcade, adult bookstore or video store, adult cabaret, adult motion picture theater, adult theater, escort agency or nude model studio.'" *Center, Fair Public Policy v. Maricopa County, AZ* (9th Cir., 2003).

## SHADE TREE

**A tree, usually deciduous, planted primarily for its overhead canopy.**

*Comment*: Most zoning ordinances or site-plan regulations require the planting of shade trees at minimum specified distances along public streets or as a minimum ratio per number of parking spaces within parking lots over a certain size, to provide shade and greenery and to reduce heat-island effects.

*Legal Annotation*: "Plaintiffs filed their petition seeking damages for destruction of a **shade tree** wherein they, in substance, alleged that there was located on the lot line between the adjoining properties of plaintiffs and defendant a large towering oak tree which allegedly was a valuable **shade tree** for plaintiffs' lot and, in fact, for both lots." *Higdon v. Henderson* (Okla., 1956).

## SHADOW PATTERN

**(1) The impact of shade cast by a structure or building on surrounding areas during the day and over various seasons; (2) the pattern of light or shade cast by an object.**

*Legal Annotation*: "Main Street was clear and dry except for a portion thereof south of the intersection where the **shadow** of a building prevented a thin layer of ice, unobserved by plaintiff, from melting." *Wright v. Salt Lake Transportation Company* (Utah, 1957).

## SHARED DRIVEWAY

See *Party Driveway*.

*Comment*: A shared driveway may cross a side lot line, enabling a lot without direct highway access to have access to the highway. Shared driveways require access easements.

*Legal Annotation*: "In the instant case, the restrictive covenants provide no specialized definition for these words. The Merriam-Webster Online Dictionary 2009 defines 'dual' in relevant part as 'consisting of two parts or elements or having two like parts'; 'separate' as 'not shared with another'; 'entryway' as 'a passage for entrance'; and 'driveway' as 'a private road giving access from a public way to a building on abutting grounds.' An 'entryway' is different from a public road, such as Weaverville Road or Blueberry Hill Rd. The covenant's reference to 'dual and separate entryway' into the parties' respective properties plainly expresses a requirement that the parties each have their own driveway, with no **shared driveway**." *Wein II, LLC v. Porter* (N.C. Ct. App., 2009).

## SHARED HOUSING

See *Housing, Shared*.

## SHARED LANE MARKING (SLM OR "SHARROW")

See *Bicycle Facilities*.

## SHARED PARKING

See *Parking, Shared*.

## SHARED ROADWAY

See *Roadway, Shared*.

## SHARED-USE PATH

See *Bicycle, Facilities*.

*Legal Annotation*: "They show that while various agencies classified the pathway as a transportation route for purposes of project approvals and funding, all of the agencies also recognized that the pathway is a **shared-use path** with recreational use being an important use." *Camicia v. Howard S. Wright Construction Co.* (Wash., 2014).

## SHED

**An accessory structure or building used primarily for storage purposes.**

*Comment*: In general, sheds should be restricted to rear or side yards, and the local ordinance should establish limits on their size and minimum setbacks from all lot lines.

***Legal Annotation***: "[T]he word '**shed**', is defined as 'a slight structure built for shelter or storage . . . a lean-to, or separate building open in front, an outbuilding, a hut, as a wagon shed.' . . . 'A small building slightly constructed and of simple form, usually one story high, and often with front or front and sides open; also a lean-to, as a wagon shed.' . . . 'A slight or temporary building; a large open structure for *temporary* storage of goods, as a **shed** on a wharf, a railway **shed**, a sheep **shed**, cattle **shed**.' (Emphasis supplied). The dictionary's definition is consistent with the general usage of the word '**sheds**' and both are denotive of an unsubstantial structure created for a temporary purpose." *Easton v. Wash. Co. Ins. Co.* (Pa., 1957).

## SHEET FLOW

**The flow of surface water runoff over a broad expanse of land.**

***Legal Annotation***: "With regard to Thonet's criticism of Zepponi's flow data, Zepponi responded that '**sheet flow** is defined as the flow in a relatively thin sheet of generally uniformed thickness.' In a flat parking lot, for example, 150 feet may be appropriate." *Northgate Condominium Association, Inc. v. Borough of Hillsdale Planning Board* (N.J. Super. Ct.,. 2011).

## SHELTERED CARE FACILITY

**See *Boarding Home for Sheltered Care*.**

***Legal Annotation***: "The original complaint for injunction filed by the plaintiff against Ridgeview House, Inc., prayed for writs of injunction restraining the defendant, an operator of a **sheltered care home**, from housing any persons suffering from mental retardation or mental disorders and ordering the defendant to remove from the Ridgeview House any person suffering from mental retardation or a mental disorder. . . . The property in question had been a hotel located in an area of the city of Evanston that was zoned for business. **Sheltered care homes** and nursing homes were not permitted in the area. In 1970, the defendant Ridgeview House, Inc., filed an application for a special use permit to convert the hotel into a **sheltered care facility**." *City of Evanston v. Ridgeview House, Inc.* (Ill., 1976).

## SHIELD

**A wall that protects persons from harmful radiation released by radioactive materials.**

***Legal Annotation***: "An arrangement in a gamma unit, comprising a large number of radiation sources ... mounted within a radiation **shield**." *Elekta Instrument v. Our Scientific Intern.* (S.D.N.Y., 1999).

## SHOPPING CENTER

**A group of commercial establishments planned, constructed, and managed as a total entity, with customer and employee parking provided on-site, provision for goods delivery separated from customer access, aesthetic considerations and protection from the elements, and landscaping and signage in accordance with an approved plan. See *Minimall; Retail Outlet Store; Retail Store, Large-Scale; Specialty Shopping Center*.**

*Comment*: Shopping centers are further defined by size and the area their shoppers come from:

- A superregional center includes retail, office, and service uses, occupies more than one hundred acres, has four or more anchor stores, and contains more than one million square feet of gross leasable space.
- A regional shopping center contains a wide range of retail and service establishments, occupies fifty to one hundred acres of land, has

at least one or more anchor stores, and contains more than four hundred thousand square feet of gross leasable space. It draws its clientele from as much as a forty-five-minute drive away.
- A community shopping center features a discount store or supermarket, contains approximately one hundred fifty thousand square feet of gross leasable area, and has a site area of ten to twenty-five acres. Its clientele draw is approximately a ten-minute drive from the center.
- A neighborhood shopping center generally offers goods necessary to meet daily needs, occupies up to ten acres, has up to one hundred thousand square feet of gross leasable area, and draws its clientele from a five-minute driving radius from the center.

*Legal Annotation*: "This contemplated **shopping center** would include a large chain store, grocery store, drug store, five and ten cent store, hardware store, beauty shop and shoe store. The erection of such a shopping center is permissible in a 'B.L.' zone." *Hardesty v. Zoning Board* (Md. Ct. App., 1956).

## SHOPPING MALL

**A shopping center with stores on both sides of an enclosed or open pedestrian walkway.**

*Legal Annotation*: "Amalgamated Food Employees Union, Local 590 v. Logan Valley Plaza, Inc. described the 'suburban shopping center' as 'typically a cluster of individual retail units on a single large privately owned tract.' . . . A 'mall' is defined as a '**shopping mall**.' Webster's Third Int'l Dictionary 91a (1993). '**Shopping Mall**' is defined as 'a large usu[ally] suburban building or group of buildings containing various shops with associated passageways.'" *State v. Viglielmo* (Hawaii, 2004).

## SHOULDER

**That part of the roadway contiguous with the traveled way for accommodation of stopped vehicles, emergency use, and lateral support of base and surface courses.**

*Legal Annotation*: "The term '**shoulder**' is defined in the Motor Vehicle Code: 'Shoulder' means that portion of the highway contiguous to the roadway generally extending the contour of the roadway, *not designed for vehicular travel* but maintained for the *temporary accommodation of disabled or stopped vehicles* otherwise permitted on the roadway. Emphasis added." *Gregg v. State Hwy. Dep't.* (Mich., 1990).

## SHRUB

**A woody plant, smaller than a tree, consisting of several small stems from the ground or small branches near the ground.**

***Comment***: Shrubs may be deciduous or evergreen and reach a mature height of two to nine feet (American Planning Association, *Preparing a Landscaping Ordinance*, Planning Advisory Service Report No. 431, 1990).

*Legal Annotation*: "'The distinction between trees and **shrubs** is often debated.' Ernie Wasson et al., The Complete Encyclopedia of Trees and **Shrubs** 16 (2003). Trees and **shrubs** are both woody perennials that renew their growth via above-ground buds. . . . The main differences between trees and **shrubs** are the height of the plant and number of stems. . . . ('Trees are generally defined as tall plants . . . with a distinct trunk. . . . A **shrub** is by default any woody plant that meets the above test but is not big enough to be a tree. . . . **[S]hrubs** [can have] very numerous stems.'). However, those distinctions are not hard and fast. A small tree can be ten feet tall, while a large **shrub** can be well over fifteen feet tall. Ibid. Moreover, 'there are many instances of plants that remain **shrubs** in most situations . . . but when growing undisturbed in a favorable environment become small or even medium-sized trees.'" *New Jersey Shore Builders Ass'n v. Township of Jackson* (N.J., 2009).

## SIDE YARD

See *Yard, Side*.

## SIDEWALK

**The portion of a road right-of-way paralleling and usually separated from the**

**cartway, paved and designed for preferential or exclusive use by pedestrians. http://safety.fhwa.dot.gov/ped_bike/tools_solve/fhwasa12018/#chap1.6**

***Comment***: The New Jersey Residential Site Improvement Standards (RSIS) (NJDCA 2000; NJ Administrative Code, Title 5, Chapter 21) recommend that sidewalks in residential developments have a minimum width of four feet, and six feet where sidewalks abut the curb and perpendicularly parked cars overhang the sidewalk. The Standards call for a wider width near pedestrian generators and employment centers. A minimum of five feet is generally recommended to allow two adults to walk side by side. The New Jersey Department of Transportation (NJDOT 1996) guidelines recommend eight to ten feet for centers (growth areas) designated in the New Jersey State Development and Redevelopment Plan (2002) and thirteen feet for urban areas.

The RSIS does not specify any minimum distance between the curb and sidewalk. In urban areas and areas of higher density, the sidewalk should be right up to the curb. In other areas, the NJDOT guidelines recommend a setback from the curb of at least four feet and preferably eight feet to permit a physical separation from the roadway. The setback allows for car-door opening and plantings.

The RSIS requires sidewalks in developments in excess of one dwelling unit per acre, and where the development or project is within 2,500 feet of a train station, public school, school bus route, existing recreational, business, or retail use of a site where such is permitted by existing zoning. The RSIS also requires sidewalks where the proposed street connects to or extends existing streets that have sidewalks on both sides of the street.

The RSIS also mandates sidewalks where the net density of the development exceeds 0.5 dwelling units per acre and the development is located within two miles of a school. Sidewalks are not required on rural streets or rural lanes and are not required in alleys. In blocks greater than six hundred feet long, ten-foot pedestrian-way easements may be required by the approving authority through the center of the block.

Finally, sidewalks should be required on arterial and collector roads. These roads carry considerable traffic and often connect employment areas with business and retail uses. The lack of sidewalks forces workers to use vehicles to drive relatively short distances to get to restaurants and shopping. Wide sidewalks, a minimum of eight feet, should be set back ten feet from the roadway to encourage safe pedestrian travel.

***Legal Annotation***: "An ordinance enacted by the city of Carbondale (plaintiff) requires, under threat of fine, that persons in control of property fronting or abutting on paved **sidewalks** remove snow and ice from such **sidewalks** or, if the snow and ice are too hard for removal, to cover them with abrasive materials within 24 hours after a snowfall or freezing precipitation. . . . The Gridley decision was based largely upon the court's observation that a lot owner has no greater interest in the street or **sidewalk** abutting his property than any other member of the municipality. This court has since reiterated that the **sidewalk** is considered a part of the street which has been set aside for pedestrian use." *City of Carbondale v. Brewster* (Ill., 1979).

## SIDEWALK CAFÉ

**Restaurant with tables and chairs on the sidewalk in front or on the side of the premises. See *Restaurant, Outdoor; Café*.**

***Comment***: Municipalities that permit outdoor cafés usually do so by special permit or licensing, since the space occupied by tables is often part of the right-of-way. In considering outdoor cafés, the width of the sidewalk becomes a crucial criterion to ensure adequate pedestrian circulation.

***Legal Annotation***: "Petitioners commenced this CPLR article 78 proceeding against the council and DCA, seeking to annul the resolution. They argue that the determination was arbitrary and capricious because the applicable zoning resolution permits unenclosed cafes on

University Place and the determination is based on concerns that such a café would adversely affect the neighborhood. Respondents do not dispute that unenclosed cafes are permitted in the subject district pursuant to the zoning resolution. Instead, respondents argue that the determination 'is in harmony with' the general goals of such resolution. Respondents note that the zoning resolution's purpose is in part 'to promote **sidewalk cafes** as visual amenities' and 'to preserve and enhance the character of neighborhoods throughout the City.' Respondents contend that the council had authority to consider these purposes in denying consent for the proposed café." *In the Matter of Weprin v. Council of the City of New York* (N.Y. Sup. Ct., 2007).

## SIDEWALK DISPLAY

**The outdoor display of merchandise for sale by a business use on the sidewalk contiguous to the business.**

*Legal Annotation*: "While shopping at Defendant's store in Woodward, Oklahoma, Plaintiff and her husband observed a **sidewalk display** of pegboards leaning vertically against the Defendant's building. After paying for six pieces of the pegboard at the store's service desk, Plaintiff, with her husband's assistance, selected five pieces of pegboard from the display and loaded them into her husband's truck." *Brown v. Wal-Mart Stores, Inc.* (10th Cir., 1993).

## SIDEWALK SALES

**Retail sales of a short-term and temporary nature conducted on the sidewalk or adjacent to the indoor establishment of the tenant or owner without permanent improvement made to the site.**

*Comment*: The local ordinance should specify those zones in which sidewalk sales are permitted, such as commercial or business zones, and how long and how many times a year they are allowed. For example, a typical restriction might limit sidewalk sales to not more than four times a year for periods not exceeding seven days. In addition, other restrictions might include how much area can be devoted to the sales. Daytona, Florida, for example, requires that the display area not be greater than 10 percent of the lot or parcel area or five hundred square feet, whichever is smaller. Maintaining pedestrian circulation is a critical consideration in allowing sidewalk sales. Site-plan review considerations also include liability issues, aesthetics, cleanup provisions, lighting, and signs. Many municipalities require sidewalk sales to be licensed or classify them as conditional uses and require the applicant to secure a special permit.

*Legal Annotation*: "While there is evidence which indicates that at certain times of the year the city allows all of the merchants to conduct what are commonly referred to as '**sidewalk sales**,' such is not indicative of any abrogation of authority on the part of the city to prohibit the use of sidewalks for the conducting of businesses at all other times. The evidence is also clear that during such time of '**sidewalk sales**' Kleiber was permitted to operate his stand on the public sidewalks, as were other merchants." *Kliebler v. City of Idaho Falls* (Idaho, 1986).

## SIGNED SHARED ROADWAY (SIGNED BIKE ROAD)

See *Bicycle Facilities, Classification of*.

## SIGHT TRIANGLE

**A triangular-shaped portion of land established at street intersections in which nothing is erected, placed, planted, or allowed to grow in such a manner as to limit or obstruct the sight distance of motorists entering or leaving the intersection. *See Figures 1 and 80*.**

*Comment*: Also known as sight easement.

*Legal Annotation*: "A 'Clear **Sight Triangle**' is defined in section 2.2 of the Ordinance as '[a] n area of unobstructed vision at street intersections or street and driveway intersections

**Figure 80**

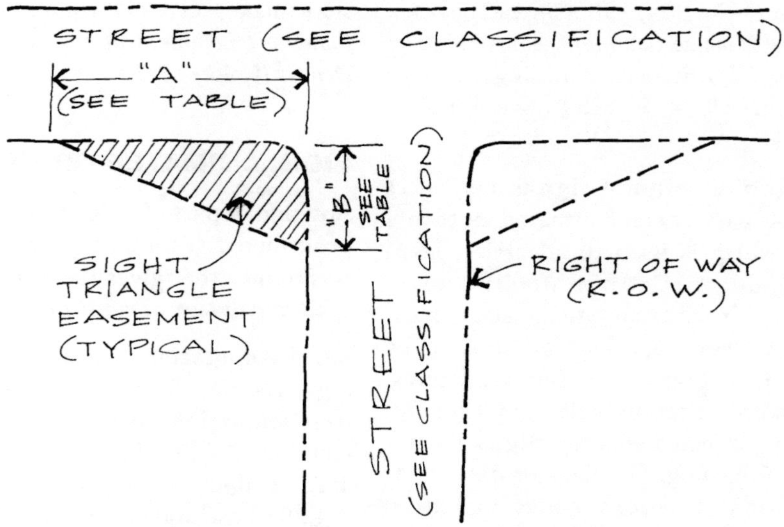


REQUIREMENT BY STREET CLASSIFICATION (MEASURED ALONG R.O.W.)

| "A" (DISTANCE IN FEET) | | "B" (DISTANCE IN FEET) LOCAL STREET | COLLECTOR STREET | ARTERIAL STREET |
|---|---|---|---|---|
| 30 | LOCAL STREET | 30 | 100 | 130-150 |
| 100 | COLLECTOR STREET | 30 | 100 | 130-150 |
| 130-150 | ARTERIAL STREET | 30 | 100 | 130-150 |

SIGHT TRIANGLE
(SIGHT EASEMENT)

defined by lines of sight between points at a given distance from the intersection of street and/or driveway lines.' (Ordinance, § 2.2.)" *Aungst v. Zoning Hearing Board* (Pa. Common. Ct., 2014).

## SIGN

**Any object, device, display, or structure, or part thereof, situated outdoors or indoors, that is used to advertise, identify, display, or direct or attract attention to an object, person, institution, organization, business, product, service, event, or location by means of words, letters, figures, design, symbols, fixtures, colors, illumination, or projected images.** ***See Figure 81.***

***Comment***: Ordinances usually exclude from the definition of signs national or state flags, window displays (but not window signs), graffiti, athletic scoreboards, or the official announcements or signs of government (American Planning Association, *The*

*Mechanics of Sign Control*, Planning Advisory Service Report No. 354, 1980; *Sign Regulation for Small and Midsize Communities: A Planners Guide and Model Ordinance*, Planning Advisory Service Report No. 419, 1989). See *Advertising Display.*

***Legal Annotation***: "**Sign**: A **sign** is any object or device or part thereof situated outdoors or indoors which is used to advertise, identify, display, direct or attract attention to an object, person, institution, organization, business, product, service, event or location by any means including words, letters, figures, designs, symbols, fixtures, colors, motion illumination or projected images. **Signs** do not include the following: (1) Flags of nations or an organization of nations, states and cities, fraternal, religious and civic organizations; (2) merchandise, pictures or models of products or services incorporated in a window display; (3) time and temperature devices not related to a product; (4) national, state, religious, fraternal, professional and civic symbols or crests; (5) works of art which in no way identify a product. If for any reason it cannot be readily determined whether or not an object is a **sign**, the Department of Zoning Administration shall make such determination. § 619.-396" *Combined Communications Corp. v. City & Cty., Denver* (Colo., 1975).

## SIGN, ANIMATED OR MOVING

**Any sign or part of a sign that changes physical position or light intensity by any movement or rotation or that gives the visual impression of such movement or rotation.**

***Legal Annotation***: "Section 9.4.203 of the Sign Law prohibits: 1. '**Moving signs**' which have animation, including 'moving, rotating' (section 9.4.203[b][2]) and '[s]igns which are portable' (section 9.4.203[c]) . . . Section 9.4.203's **animated and moving sign** prohibitions rationally relate to public safety and promotion and enhancement of the City's character. The FAC lacks facts to demonstrate the Sign Law's impossibility to relate to legitimate governmental objectives and to negate conceivable bases to support the Sign Law. The equal protection claim is subject to dismissal." *Govan v. City of Clovis* (E.D. Calif., 2013).

**Figure 81**

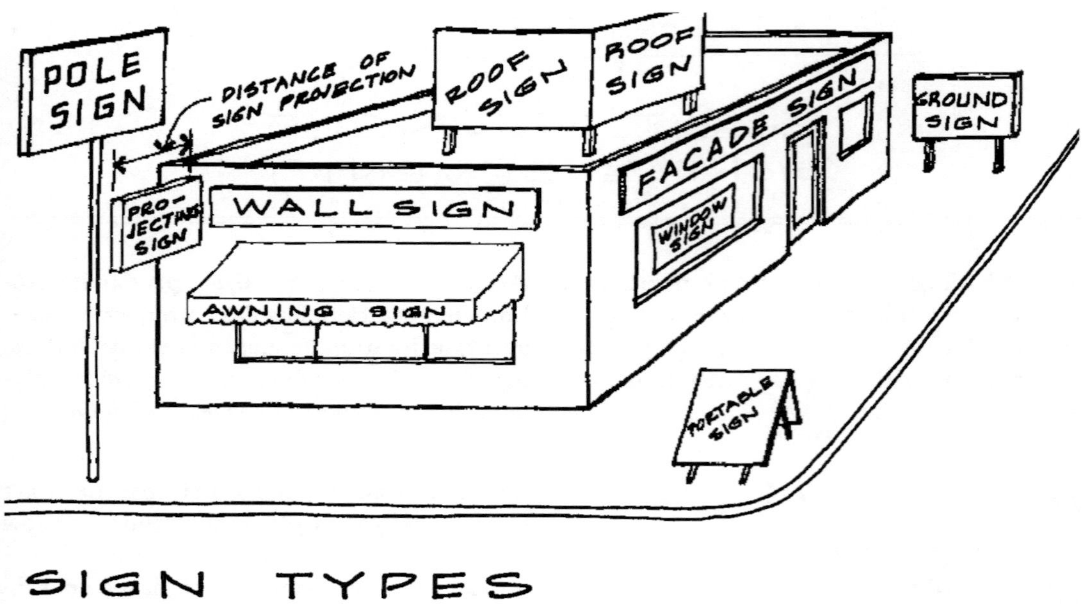

"The signs allegedly converted were a standing sign, an attraction panel, three facia of varying sizes, one menu board and one **animated sign**." *JeToCo Corp. v. Hailey Sales Co.* (Ark., 1980).

## SIGN, AWNING

**A sign that is mounted, painted, or attached to an awning or other window or door canopy that is otherwise permitted by ordinance.** ***See Figure 81.***

*Comment*: A recent merchandising trend in downtown and commercial centers is the installation of translucent awnings across an entire store frontage. These often brightly colored, transparent awnings, with lighting from below and integral signage, are used to draw shopper attention. In these circumstances the sign area could be interpreted to include the entire awning area. **See *Awning, Illuminated*.**

*Legal Annotation*: "'[E]ach tenant store front shall be limited to one wall sign, one projecting sign and one **awning sign**.' The Kroger store was identified by a permanent wall sign on the exterior of the building, over the entry vestibule." *JP Morgan Chase Bank, Inc. v. City of Dublin* (Ohio Ct. App., 2011).

## SIGN, BANNER

**A temporary sign of cloth or similar material that celebrates an event, season, community, neighborhood, or district and is sponsored by a recognized community agency or organization.** ***See Figure 82.***

*Comment*: Banner signs are often attached to lampposts in local business districts and provide an attractive streetscape feature celebrating the seasons, holidays, or special community-wide events.

*Legal Annotation*: "For example, § 16-248(a) of the Sign Code said that '[t]he following signs are prohibited anywhere in the city: . . . Animated or flashing signs . . . **Banner signs** . . . Buntings and flags . . . temporary and permanent signs, other than public interest signs, place[d] on any public property . . . [and] [a]ny sign not prescribed as a permitted sign by this article. . . . But § 16-248(a) also excepted certain signs from its prohibitions, including animated or flashing signs that display the time or temperature; temporary grand opening or special event **banner signs**; the United States flag; bus shelter or bench signs, and temporary project signs; and temporary and permanent public interest signs." *Coral Springs Street Systems, Inc. v. City of Sunrise* (11th Cir., 2004).

**Figure 82**

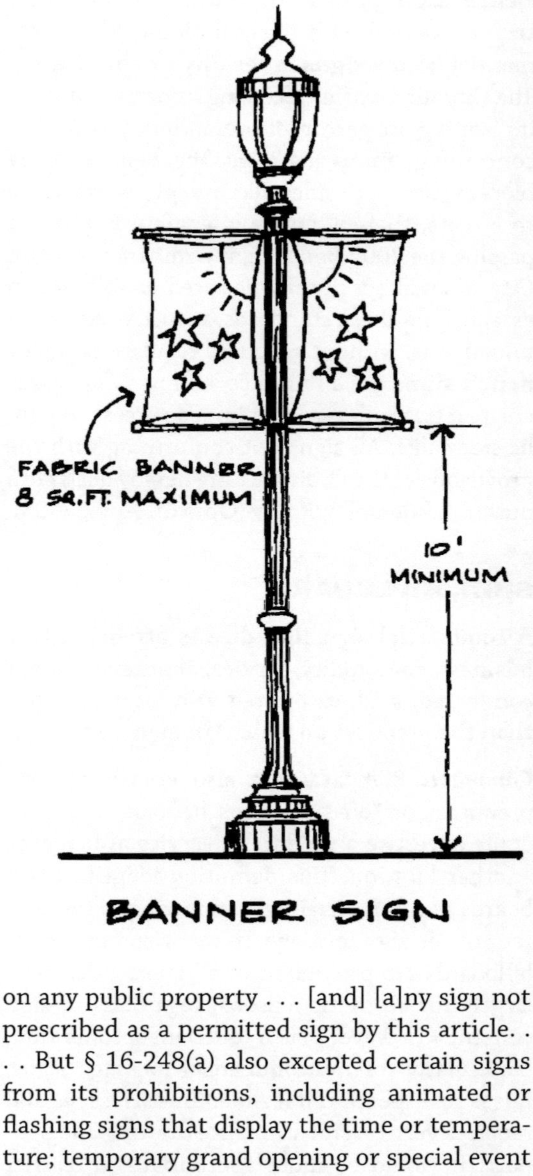


## SIGN, BENCH

**A sign painted on, located on, or attached to any part of the surface of a bench, seat, or chair placed on or adjacent to a public place or roadway.**

*Legal Annotation*: "The City enacted the 2002 **Bench Sign** Ordinance, which, after an amortization period, effectively prohibits the placement of **bench signs** in the City's right-of-ways. The City did so after receiving information from its zoning inspector of numerous complaints concerning, inter alia, that the benches were blocking access to sidewalks and placed too close to streets, thereby creating a safety hazard. In passing the 2002 Bench Sign Ordinance, Canton City Council specifically declared as follows: In establishing these standards, the City has determined that, without adequate regulation, public **bench signs** are a nuisance, and in some places create a traffic hazard and impede access to public sidewalks. All signs not conforming with the provisions of the Ordinance are hereby declared a nuisance." *Canton v. Koury* (Ohio Ct. App., 2005).

## SIGN, BILLBOARD

**A commercial sign that directs attention to a business, commodity, service, or entertainment conducted, sold, or offered at a location other than the premises on which the sign is located.**

*Comment*: Billboards are also known as "off-premises" or "off-site" signs because they generally advertise a product or service available at another location. This definition identifies billboards as commercial signs, referring to the content of the sign message. In many communities, billboards are prohibited in all zoning districts, largely for aesthetic reasons, regardless of sign content. However, such outright prohibition, particularly for noncommercial message signs, raises free speech (First Amendment) issues and requires very careful ordinance drafting and support. It would be more appropriate to restrict such signs to specific zones and regulate their size, lighting, and placement accordingly. For an excellent discussion of the legal issues of billboard regulation, *see* American Planning Association, *Aesthetics, Community Character, and the Law*, Planning Advisory Service Report No. 489/490, 1999.

*Legal Annotation*: "Morrow's sign ordinance prohibits **billboards**. Section 8-5-1(4) of the ordinance defines a **billboard** as an: [a]dvertising sign or a sign which advertises a commodity, product, service, activity or any other person, place or thing, which is not located, found, or sold on the premises upon which such sign is located; usually found along or near major roadways and of such size as to catch the attention of the motoring public and may sometimes be illuminated or animated." *Southlake Prop. Associates v. City of Morrow, Ga.* (11th Cir., 1997).

"An '**outdoor advertising sign**' is one that advertises: (a) Goods, products or services which are not sold, manufactured or distributed on or from the premises on which the sign is located; (b) Facilities not located on the premises on which the sign is located; or (c) Activities not conducted on the premises on which the sign is located." *Drayton v. Department of Transportation* (Ore. Ct. App., 2003).

## SIGN, BLADE

**A vertically oriented wall sign. See *Sign, Projecting*. See *Figure 83*.**

**Figure 83**

*Legal Annotation*: "On June 30, 1995, the LPC issued a Certificate of Appropriateness (COP) with respect to all of the exterior work to be performed by Warehouse, including the installation and appearance of the subject, projecting vertical **'blade' sign** with the name 'Burlington Coat factory' [sic] on it, which extended from the second to the third floors on the exterior of the Building (**Blade Sign**)." *Burlington Coat Factory of NY, LLC v. Majestic Rayon Corp.* (N.Y. Sup. Ct., 2013).

## SIGN, BULLETIN BOARD

**A sign that identifies an institution or organization on whose premises it is located and that contains the name of the institution or organization, the names of individuals connected with it, and general announcements of events or activities occurring at the institution, or similar messages.**

*Legal Annotation*: "1. **BULLETIN BOARD SIGN**: A sign that indicates the name of an institution or organization on whose premises it is located and which contains the name of the institution or organization, the name or names of persons connected with it and announcement of persons, events or activities occurring at the institution. Such signs may also present a greeting or similar message." *Outdoor Systems, Inc. v. City of Merriam, Kan.* (D. Kan., 1999).

## SIGN, BUSINESS

**A sign that directs attention to a business or profession conducted, or to a commodity or service sold, offered, or manufactured, or to an entertainment offered on the premises where the sign is located.**

*Legal Annotation*: "This controversy centers upon the city's distinction between a **'business sign**,' which relates to goods or services available on the premises where the sign is situated, and an 'outdoor-advertising sign,' which relates to goods or services available elsewhere. **Business signs** are not to exceed 75 square feet in size, though there may be one on each face of a building. Outdoor-advertising signs cannot be more than 25 feet long or 12 feet high, so that a maximum area of 300 square feet is possible." *Board of Adjustment, Fayetteville v. Osage Oil & Transp., Inc.* (Ark., 1974).

## SIGN, CANOPY

**A sign attached to the underside of a canopy.** ***See Figure 84.***

**Figure 84**

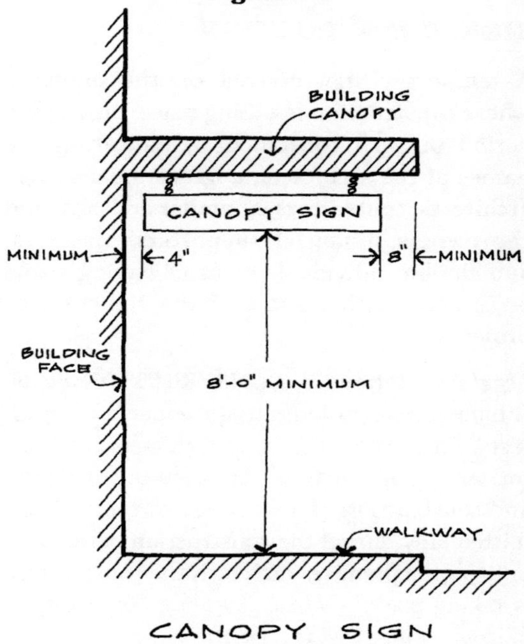


*Legal Annotation*: "The **sign** in question is prohibited by the Raleigh City Code if it is attached to a roof, but the sign is permitted if it is attached to a **canopy.** . . . The sign in question is not attached to a canopy. The words of a statute must be construed in accordance with their ordinary and common meaning unless they have acquired a technical meaning or unless a definite meaning is apparent or indicated by the context of the words. . . . The ordinary meanings of the word 'canopy' are set forth in Webster's Third New International Dictionary, which in part defines a canopy as 'a covering usu[ally] for shelter or protection . . .' Webster's Third New International Dictionary 328 (1968). Webster's includes with this definition an exhaustive list of sub-definitions. . . . This list of sub-definitions includes 'a . . . cover providing shelter and decoration (as over a door or window)' and 'an awning or marquee often stretching from doorway to curb.' . . . The structure in question is not located over a traditional type of window or door, and it doesn't extend from the doorway to the curb, so it cannot be classified as a **canopy** according to what we believe to be the ordinary and common understanding of the word '**canopy**.'" *Raleigh Place Assoc. v. Bd. of Adj.* (N.C. Ct. App., 1989).

## SIGN, CONSTRUCTION

**A temporary sign erected on the premises where construction is taking place, during the period of such construction, indicating the names of the architects, engineers, landscape architects, contractors or similar artisans, and the owners, financial supporters, sponsors, and similar individuals or firms having a role or interest with respect to the structure or project.**

***Legal Annotation***: "3. **CONSTRUCTION SIGN**: A temporary sign indicating the name of architects, engineers, landscape architects, contractors and similar artisans involved in the design and construction of a structure or project, permitted only during the construction period and only on the premises on which the construction is taking place." *Outdoor Systems, Inc. v. City of Merriam, Kan.* (D. Kan., 1999).

## SIGN, DIGITAL

**Changeable electronic variable message signs (CEVMS) that have changeable messages or displays and meet requirements related to duration of messages, transition time, lighting, and brightness.**

***Comment***: CEVMS signs are generally computer-controlled and include digital LED displays. These signs include provisions to freeze a display in one fixed position in case of malfunction. Local provisions are required to meet state and federal standards in order not to violate prohibitions against "intermittent," "flashing," or "moving" signs. The standards recommended by the US Dept. of Transportation, Federal Highway Administration in *Memorandum HEPR-20*, dated September 25, 2007, include:

- Duration of Message—between four and ten seconds; eight seconds recommended
- Transition Time—between one and four seconds; one to two seconds recommended
- Brightness—not unnecessarily bright, for the safety of motoring public. No specific level given.
- Spacing and Locations—as permitted by Federal/State Agreements (FSA)

Outdoor Advertising Associates of America, Inc. (OAAA), in a publication entitled *Digital Technology Billboards Today*, suggested "lighting levels no more than 0.3 foot candles above the level of surrounding ambient light conditions." The publication also refers to studies funded by the Foundation for Outdoor Advertising Research and Education on traffic safety and digital billboards. It also includes letters from various agencies on traffic safety and digital billboards.

The spacing and location for these types of signs, usually billboards, are usually included in local zoning ordinances. See *Sign, Control; Sign, Billboard.*

***Legal Annotation***: "On September 6, 2007, City passed ordinance number 070887 ('**Digital Sign** Ordinance'), which stated, in part, that 'No outdoor advertising sign may have any revolving, moving, flashing, blinking, or animated characteristics.'" *The Lamar Company, LLC v. City of Kansas City* (Mo. Ct. App., 2010).

## SIGN, DIRECTIONAL

**Signs limited to directional messages such as "one way," "entrance," and "exit," or symbols, such as arrows.**

***Comment***: In some jurisdictions, where a number of buildings are located within the development, the name of a business or tenant is also permitted to be included on the directional sign.

***Legal Annotation***: "The parties focus on a specific part of that statute, § 84.30(3)(a), which reads: (3) SIGNS PROHIBITED. *No sign* visible from the main-traveled way of any interstate or federal-aid highway *may be erected* or maintained, *except the following*: (a) ***Directional*** and other official ***signs***, including, but not limited to, signs pertaining to natural wonders, scenic and historical attractions, *which are required or authorized by law, and which comply with rules* which shall be *promulgated by the [Wisconsin DOT]* relative to their lighting, size, number, spacing and such other requirements as are appropriate to implement this section, *but such rules shall not be inconsistent with, nor more restrictive than, such national standards as may be promulgated* from time to time *by the secretary of transportation of the United States* under 23 USC 131(c). (Emphasis added.)." *Donaldson v. Town of Spring Valley* (Wis. Ct. App., 2008).

## SIGN, DIRECTORY

**A sign listing the tenants or occupants of a building or group of buildings and that may also indicate their respective professions or business activities. *See Figure 85*.**

## SIGN, FAÇADE

**See *Sign, Wall*.**

***Legal Annotation***: "On March 26, 1976, shortly after construction of the pylon began, plaintiff's representatives sent a letter to defendant requesting it cease that construction and submit drawings for plaintiff's review. On March 29, 1976 plaintiff sent a mailgram to defendant informing it the 'mall sign structure will totally block our store **facade sign** and further hide our store.' After receiving more detailed plans, it was obvious defendant did not intend to replace the canopy previously removed and plaintiff again requested the work to cease by letter of April 1, 1976 which protested the proposed pylon because it would block approximately two-thirds of plaintiff's **facade sign** and protested the removal of a three foot metal canopy which provided weather protection for its exterior

**Figure 85**

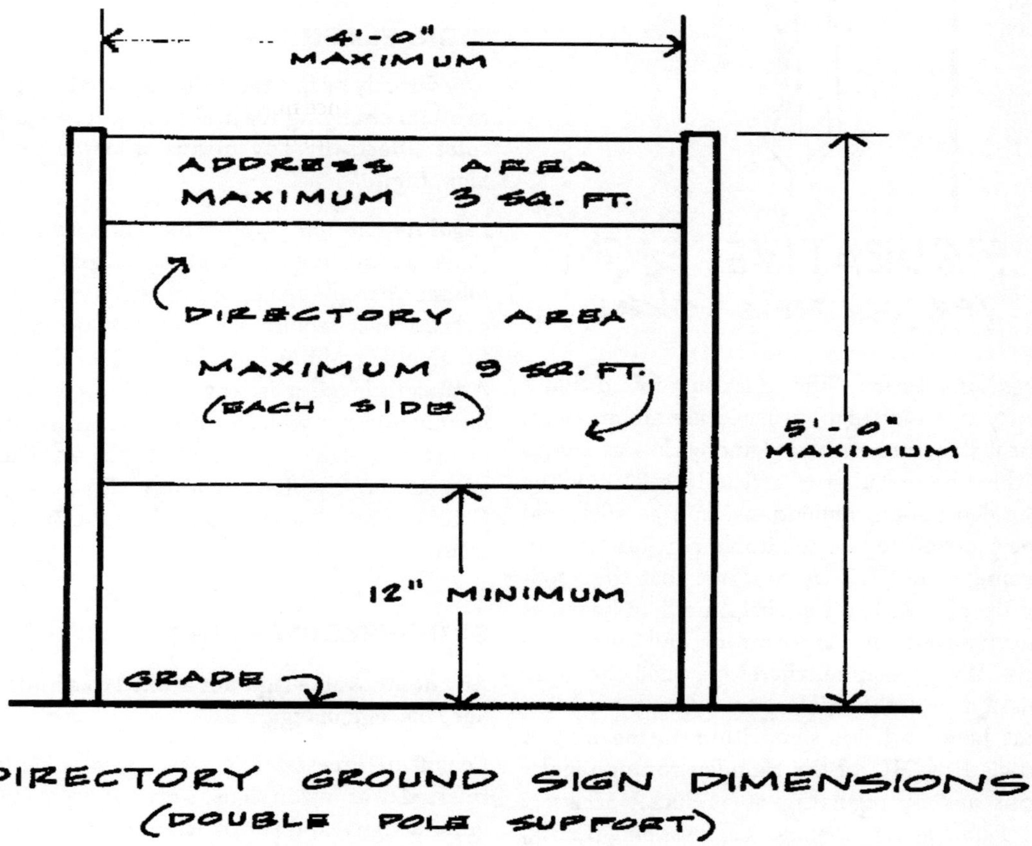

entrance." *Eckerd Drugs of LA. v. Greenland Vistas* (La. Ct. App., 1978).

## SIGN, FIGURATIVE

**Figure-shaped signs that identify a specific type of business through the use of objects as graphic symbols. *See Figure 86.***

**Figure 86**

***Legal Annotation***: "The trial court found that a thirty-two foot high, brushed aluminum cylindrical structure entitled 'Landmark' was a **sign** within the meaning of article II, § 210, of the Hamden zoning regulations, and as such, did not conform to the applicable regulations concerning signs. . . . We conclude that the application of § 210 to the sculpture 'Landmark' is unsupported and is arbitrary and unreasonable. We determine, therefore, that the commission and the trial court erred by holding that 'Landmark' is a sign within the meaning of article II, § 210, of the Hamden zoning regulations and by regulating it as such." *Schwartz v. Planning & Zoning Commission* (Conn., 1988).

"A closer question is presented by RIYA's attack on the Board's conclusion that the blade is not a **sign**, but merely functions as 'an architectural element of the proposed building.' If deemed a sign, the blade would require several variances from § 150-37, which variances were not sought by AVN Holdings. . . . Cranbury's definition of a '**sign**' is quite broad. Section 150-7 provides as follows: **SIGN**: 'Any object, device, display or structure or part thereof, situated outdoors or indoors, which is used to advertise, identify, display, direct or attract attention to an object, person, institution, organization, business, product, service, event or location by any means, including words, letters, figures, design, symbols, fixtures, colors, illumination or projected images.' This far-reaching definition characterizes almost anything that draws attention to a structure as a **sign**." *Riya Cranbury Hotel, LLC v. Zoning Board of Adjustment of Township of Cranbury* (N.J. App. Div., 2013).

## SIGN, FLASHING

**Any directly or indirectly illuminated sign that exhibits changing natural or artificial light or color effects by any means whatsoever. See *Sign, Digital*.**

***Legal Annotation***: "Under the Chanhassen City Code, all 'moving' or **'flashing' signs** are prohibited except temperature signs or barber poles, which require a conditional use permit. Chanhassen, Minn., City Code § 20-1259 (2005). A **'flashing' sign** is 'any directly or indirectly illuminated sign which exhibits changing natural or artificial light or color effects by any means whatsoever.' Chanhassen, Minn., City Code § 1-2 (2005)." *Halla Nursery, Inc. v. City of Chanhassen* (Minn., 2010).

## SIGN, FREESTANDING

**Any nonmovable sign not affixed to a building. See *Pole Sign in Figure 81*.**

***Comment***: Freestanding signs, also sometimes referred to as "pylon signs," are usually pole signs, ground signs, and construction signs. Aesthetically, pole signs tend to be the most offensive in terms of height, size, and design. The preferable alternative to the pole sign is the ground sign.

*Legal Annotation*: "A **freestanding sign** is 'a sign the principal support of which is independent of any building.' Section 8.21(10)." *Adams Outdoor Advertising v. East Lansing* (Mich., 1992).

## SIGN, GOVERNMENTAL

**A sign erected and maintained pursuant to and in discharge of any governmental functions or required by law, ordinance, or other governmental regulation.**

*Legal Annotation*: "Section 213-387 of the Babylon Ordinance defines the term '**governmental sign**' as 'any sign erected and maintained by or at the direction of any governmental body, organization, agency or corporation.' The Babylon Ordinance's definition of regulated 'signs' specifically exempts from its reach '**governmental signs**.'" *Nichols Media Group, LLC. v. Town of Babylon* (E.D. N.Y., 2005).

## SIGN, GROUND

**A freestanding sign, other than a pole sign, in which the entire bottom is in contact with or is close to the ground. See *Figure 81*. See *Also Sign, Monument; Sign, Pylon*.**

*Comment*: Also known as a pedestal or monument sign.

*Legal Annotation*: "'**Ground Sign**' shall mean a detached sign erected upon or supported by the ground'; 'Roof Sign' shall mean a sign erected upon or above a roof or parapet of a building or structure." *City of Los Angeles v. Barrett* (Calif. Ct. App., 1957).

"While Mounds View does not allow billboards in any zoning district, it does allow smaller signs in various districts. For example, residential districts may contain small signs related to the sale or lease of property, business districts may have signs no greater than 100 square feet total, and light industrial districts may have a **pedestal sign** not larger than 340 square feet." *In Re Eller Media Company's Applications* (Minn., 2003).

## SIGN, HANGING

**A freestanding sign supported by the extended arm of a single post. *See Figure 87*.**

**Figure 87**

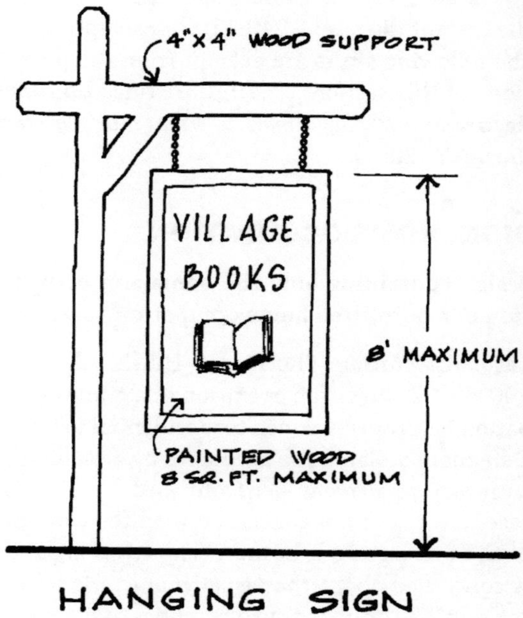


*Comment*: It is recommended that for hanging signs, the top edge of the sign face not exceed eight feet above grade level.

*Legal Annotation*: "The township maintains that the sign ordinance here under review may be justified as a reasonable exercise of the police power because, it is said, regular inspections are necessary to insure the continued safe conditions of the signs. Specifically, it is urged that inspection of a **hanging sign** may reveal a situation in which the sign may be about to fall down; similarly, an inspection of the window signs will insure that they do not completely cover the glass area so as to hamper efforts to discover and control a possible fire." *State v. Boston Juvenile Shoes* (N.J. App. Div., 1971).

## SIGN, HOLIDAY DECORATION

**Temporary signs, in the nature of decorations, and customarily and commonly associated with any national, local, or religious holiday.**

***Comment***: Due to their temporary nature, such signs are typically exempted from the sign regulations in the local zoning ordinance.

***Legal Annotation***: "The following provisions of the Town Law, Art. I, Zoning are the subject of the instant dispute: § 249-11(D). Exempt signs. The following **signs** are exempt from the provisions of this section. . . . (9) Christmas **holiday decorations."** *Sugarman v. Village of Chester* (S.D. N.Y., 2002).

## SIGN, HOME OCCUPATION

**A sign containing only the name and occupation of a permitted home occupation.**

***Legal Annotation***: "Rochester Hills Ordinance 200, § 4.02 allows the operation of a home occupation on property zoned for residential use. . . . Defendant violated the ordinance by attaching a large sign to a tree in her front yard. . . . In this case, the city is not concerned with the content of the message on a **home occupation sign**; it is concerned about the visual characteristics of the sign. The ordinance in question is designed to preserve the character of residential areas within the city. It attempts to advance this interest by prohibiting commercial signs that are at odds with this residential character." *City of Rochester Hills v. Schultz* (Mich., 1999).

## SIGN, IDENTIFICATION

**A sign giving the nature, logo, trademark, or other identifying symbol; address; or any combination of the name, symbol, and address of a building, business, development, or establishment on the premises where it is located.**

***Legal Annotation***: "No sign or signs shall be erected or maintained upon any real property in the City of Whittier zoned R-1, R-2, R-3, R-R, or P, as defined and set forth in article IX entitled 'Zoning and Planning,' chapter I, part I of the Whittier Municipal Code, except that an unlighted non-electric sign shall be permitted on any lot within said zoning classification as follows:

1. A name or **identification sign** not exceeding four (4) square feet in area shall be permitted on any building, lot or parcel of land so zoned as above set forth." *Burk v. Municipal Court* (Calif. Ct. App., 1964).

"4. **IDENTIFICATION SIGN**: A sign giving the name and address of a building, business, development or establishment. Such signs may be wholly or partly devoted to a readily recognized symbol." *Outdoor Systems, Inc. v. City of Merriam, Kan.* (D. Kan., 1999).

## SIGN, ILLUMINATED

**A sign lighted by, or exposed to, artificial lighting either by lights on or in the sign or directed toward the sign.**

***Comment***: The regulation of sign illumination is a very important element in sign control. The key to such regulation is the zone district itself and the carefully enunciated community design objectives for that district. In a New Jersey case (*State v. Calabria, Gillette Liquors*, 301 N.J. Super. 96 [Law Div. 1997]), the court applied the test enunciated in *Virginia State Bd. Of Pharmacy v. Virginia Citizens Consumer Council*, 425 U.S. 748 (1976) as follows:

(i) whether the restriction is justified without reference to the content;
(ii) whether the restrictions serve a significant governmental interest; and
(iii) whether the restrictions leave open ample alternative channels for communication of the information at issue.

The New Jersey case was an outright ban on neon signs, and the court concluded that "[t]he municipality's interest in aesthetics, while proper, was not advanced by an outright ban on the use of neon illumination rather than by some form of other restriction on the use of such lighting" (Cox 2003: 789). The court found that "[t]he municipality's expert's conclusory allegation, lacking facts or explanation, was insufficient to support the conclusion that neon in and of itself could not otherwise be regulated to meet the municipality's aesthetic standards. Ibid. at 105–108" (Cox 2003: 789).

However, a prohibition on the use of neon signs in a designated historic district is likely to be upheld, and reasonable limitations on the size and use of neon signs in other areas may be appropriate.

*Legal Annotation*: "An **illuminated sign** is defined as meaning 'a sign lighted or self-luminous by any means whatever, or giving the outward appearance of same.'" *Strauss v. Univ. of State of NY* (N.Y. App. Div., 1956).

## SIGN, INFLATABLE

**Any display capable of being expanded by air or other gas and used on a permanent or temporary basis to advertise a product or event.**

*Legal Annotation*: "The balloon is approximately ten feet tall and has no writing on it. In response to a complaint by Gold's Gym, the police were summoned. Lawrence Township Police Officer Mark Harmon went to the scene and spoke with three IBEW leaders about the balloon. The leaders removed the balloon. According to Harmon, 'approximately . . . 45 minutes later, [he] received a call from the dispatcher on the police radio. They had received a [second] call that the inflatable rat had been put back up.' He returned to the scene and issued a summons to DeAngelo, charging that the inflatable rat is a 'balloon sign or other **inflated sign**,' prohibited by Ordinance § 535(L)(2). DeAngelo moved to dismiss the summons challenging the constitutionality of the Ordinance. The State opposed the motion, stipulating to the facts and requesting that the municipal judge decide the legal issue: whether an inflatable rat is a type of sign that the Ordinance prohibits." *State v. DeAngelo* (N.J. App. Div., 2007).

## SIGN, LANDMARK

**Any sign of artistic or historic merit, uniqueness, or extraordinary significance to the community as may be identified by the local historical commission or other official agency.**

## SIGN, MARQUEE

**Any sign made a part of a marquee and designed to have changeable copy, either manually or electronically. See *Marquee*.**

*Legal Annotation*: "The ordinance defines a **marquee sign** as '[a] wall sign that is mounted on or attached to a marquee.' A marquee is defined as '[a] structure other than a roof that is attached to, supported by and projecting from a building, and that provides shelter for pedestrians.'" *Harborside Assoc. v. Parade Residence Hotel* (N.H., 2011).

## SIGN, MEMORIAL

**A sign, tablet, or plaque memorializing a person, event, structure, or site.**

*Legal Annotation*: "Coral Springs argues that the Sign Code violated this prohibition in a number of ways, including: . . . (2) permitting temporary political and roadside **memorial signs** but not other temporary noncommercial signs." *Coral Springs Street Systems, Inc. v. City of Sunrise* (11th Cir., 2004).

## SIGN, MENU BOARD

**A sign containing the menu, or a portion thereof, of the food products for sale from the restaurant with which it is associated.**

*Comment*: Menu boards can be A-frame sandwich boards temporarily placed on the sidewalk, affixed to the wall or window of a restaurant, or in the case of drive-through restaurants, a freestanding sign adjacent to the drive-through lane. **See *Sign, Sidewalk; Sign, Freestanding*.**

*Legal Annotation*: "An 'off-site directional sign' is defined as '[a] sign located off site and along an arterial street and listing the names of one or more business establishments with distance information designed to direct vehicular traffic.' An 'on-site directional sign' is defined as '[a] ny sign on the property which includes information aiding in the flow of vehicular and/or pedestrian traffic.' A '**drive-through menu board**' is defined as '[a] freestanding sign located adjacent to a drive-through lane which details the sale of products or services available on the property and which is not intended to be seen from roadways or parking lots.'" *Nittany Outdoor Advertising, LLC v. College Township* (M.D. Pa., 2014).

## SIGN, MONUMENT

See *Sign, Ground.*

*Legal Annotation*: "The zoning code defined a **monument sign** as '[a] sign where the bottom of the information panel is either in contact with the ground or mounted within two feet of the ground.'" *LT Propco, LLC v. Westland Garden State Plaza Limited Partnership* (N.J. App. Div., 2012).

## SIGN, NAKED LIGHT DISPLAY

**A string of lights or any unshielded light used to attract attention.**

*Legal Annotation*: "The 2005 Sign Ordinance continues to prohibit 'Attention-getting devices, including but not limited to balloons . . . all inflatable air signs and lights . . . [and] neon tubing or **bare bulb lights** encircling a window or outlining the structure." *Tanner Advertising Group v. Fayette County* (11th Cir., 2006).

## SIGN, NAMEPLATE

**A sign, located on the premises, giving the name and/or address of the owner or occupant of a building or premises.**

*Legal Annotation*: "5. **NAME PLATE SIGN**: A sign giving the name and/or address of the owner or occupant of a building or premises on which it is located and where applicable, a professional status." *Outdoor Systems, Inc. v. City of Merriam, Kan.* (D. Kan., 1999).

## SIGN, NEON

**A sign consisting of glass tubing, bent to form letters, symbols, or other shapes and illuminated by neon or a similar gas through which an electric voltage is discharged.**

*Comment*: See *Sign, Illuminated*.

*Legal Annotation*: "The Parkview Baptist Church constructed a new church at 17th and Elizabeth Streets in a Residence 'A' District and installed a **neon sign** on its grounds without a permit from the City. . . . It is clear that the church has a right to display a sign upon its property, and it is equally clear that the legislative arm of the city had placed no restriction upon the right of the church to erect a sign of its own choosing." *Parkview Baptist Church v. City of Pueblo* (Colo., 1959).

## SIGN, OFF-PREMISES

See *Sign, Billboard.*

*Legal Annotation*: "An '**off-premises sign**' is 'A sign which directs attention to a business, commodity, service or entertainment not conducted, sold or offered on the premises where the sign is located, or which business, commodity, service or entertainment forms only minor or incidental activity upon the premises where the sign is displayed.'" *Hoosier Outdoor Advertising Corp. v. RBL Management* (Ind. Ct. App., 2006).

## SIGN, OFFICIAL

**Any sign installed by a governmental agency and intended to direct or control traffic; identify streets, parks, and historical events; or to provide other information deemed necessary by that official agency.**

*Legal Annotation*: "If 'an **official sign** is not in proper position and sufficiently legible to be seen by an ordinarily observant person[,]' then it shall not be enforced against an alleged violator. . . . Thus, '[t]here is no criminal liability for violation of a traffic control device that is unofficial,' i.e., not 'in conformity with' the [OMUTCD]." *S. RusselL v. Blair* (Ohio Ct. App., 2006).

## SIGN, ON-SITE INFORMATIONAL

**A sign commonly associated with, and not limited to, information and directions necessary or convenient for visitors coming on the property, including signs marking entrances and exits, parking areas, circulation direction, restrooms, and pickup and delivery areas.**

*Legal Annotation*: "Sec. 13-338. Exempted signs. The following signs shall be exempted from the provisions of this article but not the building regulations as contained in this Code, when determined not to be detrimental to the health, safety, and welfare of the public: . . . (d) Menu boards which are either freestanding or affixed wall signs designed as an outdoor means to communicate orders for food and beverages contained within the business structure itself, which are not legible from any public right-of-way and which provide **on-site information** for drive-in service and not additional advertisement; provided that they do not exceed sixteen (16) square feet when located in a front yard or a side yard and twenty-four (24) square feet when located in a rear yard; provided further that there be no more than one (1) menu board per lot." *Adams Outdoor Advertising v. Newport News* (Va., 1988).

## SIGN, OPEN HOUSE

**Temporary, off-premises signs used to direct prospective purchasers to a house for sale.**

*Comment*: This type of sign is often improperly placed in the public right-of-way; the ordinance should place restrictions on their number, size, placement, use, frequency, and duration.

*Legal Annotation*: "**OPEN HOUSE SIGNS: Open House Signs**, in order to be exempt, shall comply with the requirements for real estate signs above set forth except:

a. **Open House Signs** shall advertise only property for sale and not property for rent.
b. The Open House advertised by an **Open House Sign** shall be for a maximum period of forty-eight (48) hours per event.
c. An **Open House Sign** utilized as a directional sign may be placed in the public right-of-way, provided that it does not obstruct the free passage of pedestrians or lawfully operated vehicles and further are not placed in such a manner as to cause corner sight obstructions.
d. No **Open House Sign** shall be permitted on any median.
e. No **Open House Sign** shall have attached thereto balloons, flags, or any other attention attracting attachments of any sort, kind nor description.
f. **Open House Signs** may only be displayed from 8:00 AM to 5:00 PM on the two days of a permitted Open House event." *Majer v. Township of Long Beach* (D. N.J., 2009).

## SIGN, OUTDOOR ADVERTISING

See *Sign, Billboard.*

## SIGN, PEDESTAL

See *Sign, Ground.*

## SIGN, POLE

**A sign that is mounted on a freestanding pole or other support. See *Sign, Freestanding. See Figure 81.***

*Comment*: Also referred to as a pylon sign or freestanding sign.

*Legal Annotation*: "A '**pole sign**' is 'a sign which is supported or suspended from a freestanding column or columns and designed so as to permit pedestrian or vehicular movement thereunder.'" *North Olmsted Chamber of Com. v. North Olmsted* (N.D. Ohio, 2000).

## SIGN, POLITICAL

**A temporary sign announcing or supporting political candidates or issues in connection with any national, state, or local election.**

*Comment*: Political signs can be regulated but not prohibited, regardless of the type of area or particular zoning district. The most appropriate regulations are those that limit such signs to private property and prohibit placement in public rights-of-way and attachment to utility poles and traffic signs and devices. The ordinance should require removal within a specified period of time following completion of the political event or election.

*Legal Annotation*: "The term '**political sign**' is defined as 'any sign which is designed to influence the action of the voters for the passage or defeat of a measure appearing on the ballot at any national, State, or local election.'" *City of*

*Antioch v. Candidates' Outdoor Graphic Serv*. (N.D. Calif., 1982).

## SIGN, PORTABLE

**Any sign not permanently attached to the ground or other permanent structure, or a sign designed to be transported, including, but not limited to, signs to be transported on wheels; sandwich board signs; and signs on balloons and umbrellas. *See Figure 81*.**

***Comment***: The prohibition of portable signs for aesthetic purposes has been upheld by the courts. *See* American Planning Association, *Sign Regulation for small And Midsize Communities: A Planners Guide and A Model Ordinance,* Planning Advisory Service Report No. 419 (1989) and *Aesthetics, Community Character, and the Law,* Planning Advisory Service Report No. 489/ 490 (1999).

***Legal Annotation***: "A **portable sign** is defined in the City Code as: any sign designed or constructed to be easily moved from one location to another, including signs mounted upon or designed to be mounted on a trailer, wheeled carriage, or other nonmotorized mobile structure. A **portable sign** which has its wheels removed shall still be considered a **portable sign**." *Lindsay v. City of San Antonio* (5th Cir., 1987).

## SIGN, PREEXISTING NONCONFORMING

**A sign lawfully erected and maintained prior to the adoption of an ordinance, that, because of amendments to that ordinance, no longer conforms with the requirements of that ordinance.**

***Comment***: If permitted by state law, preexisting nonconforming signs can be phased out over a period of time. This requires the establishment of an amortization schedule, commensurate with the sign's initial cost and current value. For more information *see* American Planning Association, *Sign Regulation for Small and Midsize Communities: A Planners Guide and a Model Ordinance*, Planning Advisory Service Report No. 419 (1989) and *Aesthetics, Community Character, and the Law*, Planning Advisory Service Report No. 489/490 (1999).

***Legal Annotation***: "In *Boyce* precisely the same argument was made. Removal without compensation of a **nonconforming but preexisting sign** was ordered when the Commission found that the repairs made to the preexisting sign exceeded those permitted under Commission regulations. Boyce raised the same issue, that Section 226.580 made no provision for removal of a **preexisting nonconforming sign**, which became an illegal sign because of excessive repair." *Osage Outdoor Adver. v. Mo. Highway & Transp.* (Mo. Ct. App., 1984).

## SIGN, PRIVATE SALE OR EVENT

**A temporary sign advertising private sales of personal property, such as "house sales," "garage sales," "rummage sales," and the like, or private not-for-profit events, such as picnics, carnivals, bazaars, game nights, art fairs, craft shows, and Christmas tree sales.**

***Legal Annotation***: "A '**garage sale**' sign cannot exceed 5 square feet and a homeowner is permitted to display only one such sign on his or her property; the sign may be displayed for the period of the sale only." *Quinly v. City of Prairie Village Kan.* (D. Kan., 2006).

## SIGN, PROJECTING

**A sign that is wholly or partly dependent upon a building for support and that projects more than twelve inches from such building. *See Figure 88*.**

***Comment***: Also known as a shingle sign.

***Legal Annotation***: "***Projection sign***. Any letter, work, model, sign, device or representation used in the nature of an advertisement or announcement projecting from the building and not in the same plans as the wall." *Nat. Advertising Co. v. City of Bridgeton* (E.D. Mo., 1985).

## SIGN, PYLON

**See *Sign, Pole*.**

Figure 88

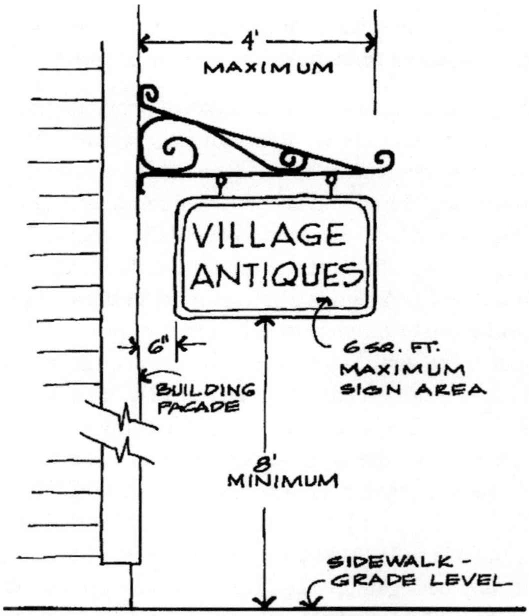


SHINGLE SIGN
(PROJECTING SIGN)

## SIGN, REAL ESTATE

**A sign pertaining to the sale or lease of the premises, or a portion of the premises, on which the sign is located.**

*Legal Annotation*: "6. **REAL ESTATE SIGN**: A sign pertaining to the sale or lease of the lot or tract of land on which the sign is located or to the sale or lease of one or more structures or a portion thereof located thereon." *Outdoor Systems, Inc. v. City of Merriam, Kan.* (D. Kan., 1999).

## SIGN, RESIDENCE DESIGNATION

**A sign or nameplate indicating the name and/or address of the occupants of a residential property.**

*Legal Annotation*: "He left the grant deeds silent on the issue of maintenance of the easement and did not intend to prohibit Lightner from placing an **address sign** at the entrance to the easement. Dudley admitted Lightner never told him that he (Lightner) would not use the easement for the construction of more than one residence, would not maintain the easement, would not surface the easement road, would not trim trees and brush within the easement, or would not install utilities, an automatic gate opener, or an **address sign** within the easement." *Wilson v. Lightner* (Calif. Ct. App., 2011).

## SIGN, ROOF

**A sign that is mounted on the roof of a building or that is wholly dependent upon a building for support and that projects above the top edge or roofline of a building with a flat roof; the eave line of a building with a gambrel, gable, or hip roof; or the deck line of a building with a mansard roof. *See Figure 81.***

*Legal Annotation*: "A **roof sign** is defined as a sign erected upon or above a roof or parapet wall of a building and which is supported by said building. Randolph Vine argues that even if it had not acquired vested rights in the amended building permit, it is entitled to continue its use because the sign as constructed squarely fits within the Philadelphia Zoning and Planning Code definition of a **roof sign** and that the Board committed an error of law in finding otherwise." *Randolph Vine Assoc. v. Zoning Bd.* (Pa. Common. Ct., 1990).

## SIGN, SEARCHLIGHT DISPLAY

**Any use of lighting intended to attract the general public by the waving or moving of light beams.**

*Legal Annotation*: "Attention Attracting Device: 'Attention attracting device' means any flashing, blinking, rotating or moving action, banner, representation of animal or human forms, **searchlight** or balloons designed or intended to attract the attention of the public to an establishment or to a sign.'" *Robert L. Rieke Bldg. Co. v. City of Overland Park* (Kan., 1983).

## SIGN, SIDEWALK

**Any temporary freestanding display located on the sidewalk or sidewalk area adjacent to a public roadway or storefront.**

*Legal Annotation*: "These Town officials noted several Town Code violations and issued plaintiff and the Zodiac Lounge several summonses for, inter alia, (1) posting a wall sign and displaying a portable **sidewalk sign** without a permit." *Rubino v. Town of Babylon* (E.D. N.Y., 2012).

## SIGN, SUSPENDED

**A sign hanging from the underside of an arcade, canopy, marquee, awning, or porch.**

*Legal Annotation*: "From the rope he also suspended a six-foot cardboard sign variously described as supporting LaRouche or urging voter registration. . . . A comparable unwillingness to distinguish between significantly different instrumentalities of communication infects the defendant's argument that his **suspended sign** was the virtual equivalent of the placard he might concededly have carried by hand, or of the display of a message on one's clothing, which was held to be protected in *Cohen v. California*, 403 U.S. 15 (1971). But the attempt to analogize these activities ignores the fact that the public owner of the lamppost and the tree has reserved them for nonexpressive purposes, whereas the placard would presumably belong to the person who carried it on the sidewalk forum, just like the jacket on which Cohen had written his opinion of the draft." *State v. Hodgkiss* (N.H., 1989).

## SIGN, TEMPORARY

**A sign or advertising display constructed of cloth, canvas, fabric, plywood, or other light material and designed or intended to be displayed for a short period of time.**

*Legal Annotation*: "**Temporary sign** is defined as '[a]ny sign, banner, pennant, valance or advertising display constructed of cloth, canvas, light fabric, cardboard, wallboard or other like materials, with or without frames, and any other type sign not permanently attached to the ground, or a structure, intended to be displayed for a short period of time only.'" *GK Ltd. Travel v. City of Lake Oswego* (9th Cir., 2006).

## SIGN, VEHICLE

**A sign on a vehicle not customarily and regularly used to transport persons or property.**

*Legal Annotation*: "The Ordinance provides that, in most districts of Rio Rancho, '[c]ommercial **vehicle signs** must be on an operable vehicle, currently registered and licensed to operate on public streets and actively used in the daily function of the business to which some signs relate.' Appendix B at 11. A sign is a 'commercial **vehicle sign**' under the Ordinance if '[t]he primary purpose for which the vehicle [on which the sign is displayed] is used is not for the stationary display of the sign.' Appendix C—Definitions at 14, filed July 25, 2013 (Doc. 15-3). The Ordinance further provides that, in most districts of Rio Rancho, '[m]obile billboards may not be parked, except for lunch from 12:00 PM to 1:00 PM on any property except where it may be legally parked for storage.' Appendix B at 11. The Ordinance defines 'mobile sign' as '[a] ny sign placed upon, applied to the surface of, or attached to a motorized vehicle or towed trailer that is driven on public streets primarily for the purpose of displaying the signage on them; signs commonly referred to as "mobile billboards."' Appendix C—Definitions at 15." *Southwest Media Mobile, LLC v. City of Rio Rancho* (D. N.M., 2014).

## SIGN, VENDING MACHINE

**Any sign, display, or other graphic attached to or part of a coin-operated machine dispensing food, beverages, or other products. See *Vending Machine*.**

*Legal Annotation*: "A specimen policy, identical with that issued, was attached to the **vending machine** for inspection by any person desiring to obtain one of the policies. And, in addition, a large placard on the face of the machine—following the caption '"Domestic" Airline Trip Insurance'—also gave notice that the insurance 'COVERS . . . FLIGHT . . . ON ANY SCHEDULED AIRLINE.'" *Lachs v. Fid. & Cas. Co. of NY* (N.Y., 1954).

## SIGN, WALL

**A sign fastened to, or painted on, the wall of a building or structure in such a manner that**

**the wall becomes the supporting structure for, or forms the background surface of, the sign and that does not project more than twelve inches from such building or structure.** ***See Figure 81.***

***Comment***: Also referred to as a "façade sign."

***Legal Annotation***: "The business district subsection contains a provision which distinguishes between 'pole or ground signs' and '**wall signs**.' . . . A **wall sign** is '[a] sign that is attached parallel to a wall on a building.' Id. The total square feet of sign area for pole or ground signs is three-quarters the building frontage in lineal feet, not to exceed fifty square feet on any pole or ground sign. Ord. § 13-1-3(A)(2)(a). **Wall signs** are limited to 'one (1) square feet for each lineal foot of building store frontage of primary use or uses, but the maximum for any one business shall be fifty (50) square feet.' Ord. § 13-1-3(A)(2)(b). In addition, [a]ll **wall signs** shall attach to the business structure and not project above the roof line. The allowed **wall signage** may be divided into not more than two (2) wall signs per business. Signage for parcels which lie on a corner lot shall be computed by using the building frontage which gives them the most signage. Id. Display case signs are included in the total signage allowed on a parcel. Ord. § 13-1-3(A)(7)." *King Enterprises, Inc. v. Thomas Township* (E.D. Much., 2002).

## SIGN, WINDOW

**A permanent sign that is painted or mounted onto a windowpane, or that is hung directly inside a window solely for the purpose or effect of identifying any premises from the sidewalk or street; or a temporary sign advertising special sales, events, or products.** ***See Figure 81.***

***Comment***: Unlimited window signs, both permanent and temporary, can result in a cluttered, unattractive appearance for the premises. Most sign regulations limit signs to 15 or 20 percent of window area.

***Legal Annotation***: "A **window sign** is defined as follows in the Phoenix Zoning Ordinance: **Sign, window**: Any sign affixed to the interior or exterior of a window, or any sign located inside a building within six feet of the interior side of a window and displayed so as to attract the attention of persons outside the building. Merchandise which is included in a window display shall not be considered as part of a **window sign**." *Austin Shea (Arizona) v. City of Phoenix* (Ariz. Ct. App., 2006).

## SIGN AREA

**The entire face of a sign, including the advertising surface and any framing, trim, or molding but not the supporting structure.** ***See Figure 89. See Sign Face.***

***Comment***: Figure 89 illustrates the measurement of a wall sign area where there is no defined sign background. For those signs with a defined background (such as sign frame, trim, molding, or color panel), the calculated sign area should include the defined background. The area for a sign with more than one face is usually computed by adding together the area of all sign faces visible from any one point. For double-sided identical signs, only one side constitutes total sign area.

**Figure 89**

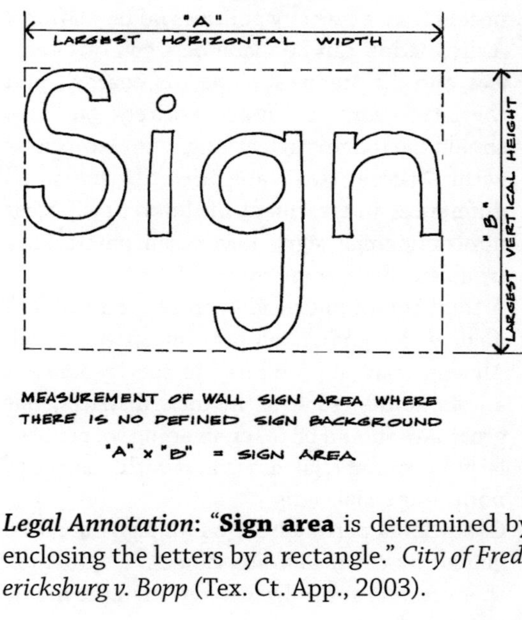


***Legal Annotation***: "**Sign area** is determined by enclosing the letters by a rectangle." *City of Fredericksburg v. Bopp* (Tex. Ct. App., 2003).

## SIGN CONTROL

**Regulations on the number, size, location, height, color, materials, lighting, and content of signs.**

***Comment***: Sign controls are difficult to prepare, enact, and enforce. American Planning Association Planning Advisory Service Report 489/490 (1999) offers important guidelines, as follows:

- First Amendment restrictions must be observed. Restrictions on speech are valid only if the regulation seeks to implement a substantial government interest, directly advances that interest, and reaches no farther than necessary to accomplish the given objective.
- Time, place, and manner restrictions generally are valid. Examples of potentially appropriate subjects for regulation include size, shape, color, height, flashing, placement, orientation, and number.
- A sign ordinance should clearly state the purposes for which it is being adopted. The promotion of aesthetic objectives alone is sufficient justification for regulating signs.
- An ordinance that is part of a comprehensive city beautification effort (including, for example, preservation, scenic roadway protection, or street tree planting) is more likely to withstand judicial scrutiny than an ordinance disconnected from other city policies and regulations.
- A distinction can be made between on-premises and off-premises signs (billboards), and the latter may be banned entirely, but care should be taken in carving out exceptions within those two categories. Unexplained differences in treatment of different kinds of noncommercial signs have been particularly troublesome to some courts.
- A total community-wide ban on political and ideological signs is likely to be unconstitutional.
- All signs can be prohibited in special areas in a community, such as historic districts, but great care should be taken in doing so, particularly in commercial zones and with respect to noncommercial signs.
- Conditional permit systems for signs must be guided by clear, definite, objective standards that prevent unbridled discretion in the hands of local officials.
- Post-campaign and post-event removal requirements are permissible, as are inspection and removal fees, if reasonably related to actual administrative costs.
- "Problem" signs, such as portable signs, can be regulated strictly, but the grounds for the special treatment should be rooted in the public welfare and should be made explicit.
- When drafting amortization provisions, be sure the amortization period selected is long enough to allow the sign owner to recoup his investment and make a profit; five- to eight-year periods have been upheld by the courts.

(American Planning Association, *Aesthetics, Community Character, and the Law*, Planning Advisory Service Report No. 489/490 [1999]: 99–100.)

Some of the more specific controls are as follows:

- *Number*: Most ordinances permit only one freestanding sign per lot, if they allow any, regardless of the number of establishments on the lot. If a lot has more than one frontage, a freestanding sign for each frontage might be appropriate.
- *Location*: Freestanding signs should be set back at least five to ten feet from the right-of-way and out of the sight easement if the property is on a corner lot or there is a driveway. A ground sign for large industrial or office properties is the recommended freestanding-type sign. An entrance sign on an island in the main driveway eliminates the need for a sign on each side of the driveway.
- *Area*: Wall signs, if allowed, should be based on a percentage of the building façade, with a maximum size. The percentage is often set at 5 to 10 percent of the principal ground-level façade, with a maximum of sixty square feet. Window signs, whether temporary or permanent, should be included in the maximum permitted sign area. The area of freestanding signs, particularly those on major arterials or highways, depends on the actual average speed limit of traffic and the nature of the land uses along the road. A maximum letter size of twelve inches for highways with speeds of fifty miles per hour or more would probably result in a sign size of between seventy-five and one hundred square feet.

- *Height*: The maximum height of the top of signs should not exceed the height of the principal structure on the site or twenty feet, whichever is lower. No signs should be permitted above the roofline.
- *Multiple-building campuses*: In industrial and office parks and shopping centers, the overall sign program should be carefully coordinated as an approved sign plan. The plan would include a sign design theme that covers location, color, size, lettering, material, content, and lighting. In a multi-tenanted industrial park, for example, there would normally be a single entrance sign and, before the first intersection within the park, a directional sign indicating the location of all the buildings and their tenants. Smaller direction signs (six square feet or less) around each building would indicate parking, loading, and unloading areas. In a single-tenant building, one freestanding sign, preferably a ground sign, should be permitted. In a multi-tenanted building, a directory sign should be located at the entrance to each building. Wall signs should be avoided, but a letter or number (spelled out) at or near the top of the building, and referred to in the main directional sign near the entrance, would be allowed.
- *Flags, banners, and pennants*: Banners and pennants are designed for instant attention. They can create a carnival-like atmosphere and should be banned except for carnivals, special temporary events, or the opening of new establishments and should require a special permit establishing sign size, location, and duration. Well-designed banner signs that identify and celebrate a community, local business district, or other special district can be attractive streetscape elements and should be encouraged. *See Figure 76*.

National flags are another matter. Many businesses, particularly car dealers, are now featuring enormous garrison-size flags on very high flagpoles. While national flags are exempt from sign controls, the height of the poles should be restricted to the maximum height of buildings in the district.

***Legal Annotation***: "Because Riverside County is a large, diverse and rapidly expanding jurisdiction, the Board of Supervisors finds that proper **sign control** is necessary for aesthetic and safety reasons. More specifically, proper **sign control** is necessary to provide for the preservation and protection of open space and scenic areas, the many natural and man-made resources, and the established rural communities within Riverside County. Proper **sign control** also safeguards the life, health, property and public welfare of Riverside County residents by providing the means to adequately identify businesses and other sign users, by prohibiting, regulating and controlling the design, location and maintenance of signs, and by providing for the removal and limitation of sign use. It is the intent of this ordinance to provide for such control." *Valley Outdoor, Inc. v. County of Riverside* (9th Cir., 2003).

## SIGN ENHANCEMENT FEATURE

**Any portion of a sign structure intended to improve the physical appearance of a sign, including roofs, moldings, railroad ties, lattice, or other decorative features. *See Figure 90*.**

***Comment***: It is not unusual for a pole or freestanding sign to be "enhanced" with decorative elements or features to increase its attention-drawing capacity while not exceeding the ordinance sign-size limitation. A comprehensive sign ordinance can include regulations on the extent of allowable sign enhancement features.

***Legal Annotation***: "The dual oversized stop signs were installed on January 23, 1980. The Commissioner's subsequent order that directed that a three-color traffic light be installed at the intersection was not predicated upon a superseding engineering study or upon a determination that the recommended **sign enhancement** was inadequate or was without reasonable support." *Stack v. State* (N.Y. App. Div., 1989).

## SIGN FACE

**The area or display surface on a sign used for the message. See *Sign Area*.**

***Legal Annotation***: "A '**sign face**' is defined as follows: The entire area on which graphic or written material or information is placed for viewing in a

Figure 90

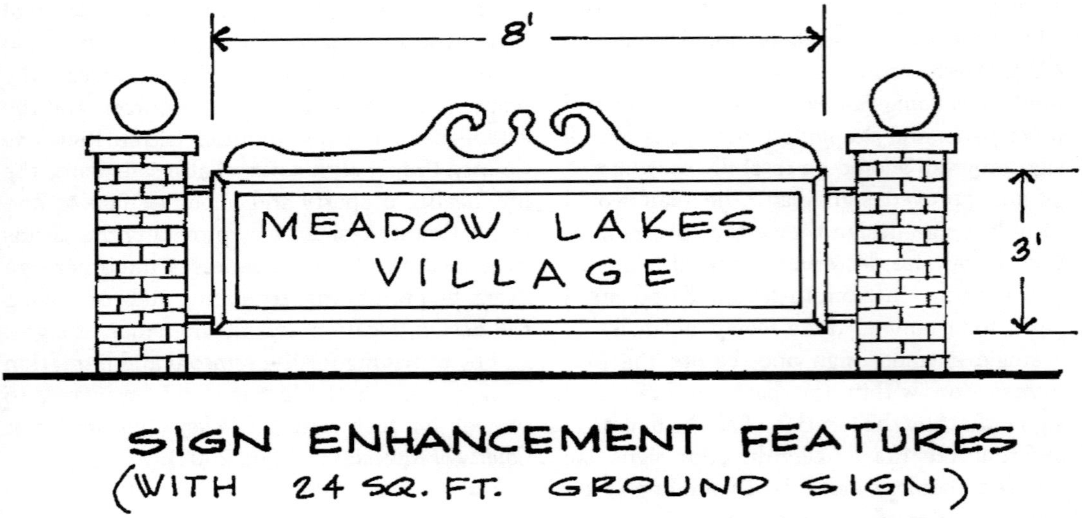


single direction." *Lamar Advertising Co. v. ZHB of Monroeville* (Pa. Common. Ct., 2007).

## SIGN PROJECTION

**On a sign attached to a wall, the distance from the exterior wall surface to the sign element farthest from such surface. *See Figure 88.***

***Legal Annotation***: "For approximately 30 years prior to 1985, Greylock Liquors was a tenant at 564 Union Avenue, Belleville, New Jersey. A projecting illuminated sign was hung to advertise the business. Although the sign was modified in the early 1970's, the sign remained when the liquor store terminated its business apparently in 1984 or early 1985. The sign contained the words 'Pepsi' on the top and 'Greylock Liquors' on the bottom. The **sign** was a nonconforming legal structure in the neighborhood retail district in that it **projected** more than six inches from the building facade or one of its side walls." *Camara v. Board of Adjustment* (N.J. App. Div., 1990).

## SIGNAL SPACING

**The distance between traffic signals along a roadway.**

*Legal Annotation*: "2.1 **Traffic Signal Spacing**

Traffic signals are allowed at one-quarter mile spacing. Any proposed **signal** at less than one-quarter mile **spacing** must be applied for, with the applicant solely responsible for the signal's cost. The applicant must provide a traffic study that shows that the additional signal can be accommodated without significantly disrupting the progressive flow of traffic in the circulation system by preserving the minimum 'through-band' width of the affected street. The traffic study shall include a simulation analysis for any new signal that is proposed to be spaced less than one-quarter mile." *City of Ontario, California Engineering Department Traffic and Transportation Division Traffic and Transportation Guidelines August 2013.*

## SIGNIFICANT INCREASE IN TRAFFIC

**Vehicular use exceeding the previously anticipated two-way traffic generated by the greater of:**

- One hundred trips during the peak hour of the highway or the development, or
- Ten percent of the previously anticipated daily movements.

*Comment*: The two standards (one hundred trips and 10 percent) are those used by the New Jersey State Department of Transportation for its highway access calculations. The term "anticipated" means that the actual and projected trips are modeled using methods in the *Trip Generation Manual,* Institute of Transportation Engineers (now in its ninth edition, 2012). A significant increase in traffic triggers more study and possibly the need for improvements to the highway system.

*Legal Annotation*: "Moreover, even evidence of a **significant increase in traffic** is not enough to defeat a special exception unless it is shown that this substantial increase would, by a high degree of probability, pose a substantial threat to the health and safety of the community. Id. We further noted as a relevant factor, when evaluating the impact of traffic, evidence that other permitted uses may generate as much or more traffic as the proposed special exception use. . . . Moreover, an increase in traffic at or near an already dangerous intersection is not a sufficient basis for denying a special exception when the proposed use would contribute less traffic than a 'normal use' of the same type. . . . Indeed, to defeat a special exception on the grounds of traffic conditions, there must be a high probability that the proposed use will generate traffic patterns not normally generated by that type of use and that such 'abnormal' traffic will pose a substantial threat to the health and safety of the community." *In re Brickstone Realty Corp.* (Pa. Common. Ct., 2001).

## SILT

**Finely divided particles of soil or rock, often carried in cloudy suspension in water and eventually deposited as sediment.**

*Legal Annotation*: "A major problem, well known to both Hendrie and the Committee was the fact that much of the soil at Rangely is very hazardous to build on, the evidence being that the soil at the pool site consists of up to forty feet of sandy and clayey **silt** with occasional thin lenses of **silty** sand and gravel. The **silt** is dry, porous and firm in its natural state but when wetted it becomes soft and compressible due to a water soluble sulphate. This unstable element apparently goes into solution when water is applied to it, destroying its solidity." *Hendrie v. Board of County Commissioners* (Colo., 1963).

## SILVICULTURE

**The development and/or maintenance of a forest or wooded preserve.**

*Legal Annotation*: "The Forest Service advises us that **silviculture** is the 'care and cultivation of forest trees.'" *League of Wilderness Defenders v. Forsgren* (9th Cir., 2002).

## SIMILAR USE

**A use that has similar characteristics to the use specifically cited in terms of the nature or type of activities conducted on the premises, as well as similar trip generation; type of traffic, parking, and circulation; utility demands; environmental impacts; physical space need; and market area. See *Change of Use*.**

*Comment*: The term "similar" refers not just to the type or nature of the use, but also to the range of impacts of the use cited, as opposed to one specific standard for each characteristic.

*Legal Annotation*: "Sandy Schultz (Schultz), the city's community development director, reviewed Kruse's permit application together with Prasse and the city manager and concluded that Kruse's proposed use as a marijuana dispensary was not allowed under the Claremont Land Use and Development Code. In reaching this conclusion, the City's planning staff relied on table 212.A of the former Land Use and Development Code, which enumerated the uses permitted within the City's commercial districts, and section 212(A) of the former Land Use and Development Code, which stated: 'In the event a use is not listed or there is difficulty in categorizing a use as one of the uses listed in table 212.A, the use shall be prohibited unless a Finding of **Similar Use** is approved by the Director of Community Development pursuant to Chapter 2, Part 7.' Neither table 212.A nor section 212(A) of the former Land Use and Development Code contained any reference to marijuana dispensaries." *City of Claremont v. Kruse* (Calif. App. Div., 2009).

## SINGLE OWNERSHIP

**See *Same Ownership*.**

***Legal Annotation***: "In effect, this township is requiring each mobile home to be sited only as if it were a single-family dwelling. In itself, that provision is not blameworthy. The physical result would be development similar to a three-per-acre subdivision of conventional single-family dwellings. Of course, such development would be quite unusual because the **single-ownership** requirement bars actual subdivision of lots by title; holding all the lots under **single-ownership** means that the development would have to involve individual lot occupancy based upon rental or possibly cooperative ownership arrangements." *Stahl v. Upper Southampton Tp.* (Pa. Common. Ct., 1992).

## SINGLE-FAMILY DWELLING

**See *Dwelling, Single-Family Detached; Dwelling, Single-Family Semidetached*.**

## SINGLE-ROOM OCCUPANCY (SRO)

**A housing type wherein one or two people are housed in single rooms, wherein tenants typically share bathrooms and kitchens.**

***Comment***: Many SROs were originally designed and used as hotels or boardinghouses that fell into disrepair, and thereafter converted to SROs—which has led to the term SRO having negative connotations. However, newer SRO buildings are composed entirely of studio apartments, with kitchenettes and bathrooms or half-baths. SROs are mostly used for lower-cost housing and housing for the homeless, without the use of direct subsidies. A relaxation of zoning, parking, and building requirements can help to bring costs down.

***Legal Annotation***: "Sister Mary believes that many residents of the transitional homes would benefit from more privacy and independence than these homes afford. Her proposed solution is a '**Single Room Occupancy**' ('SRO') which would provide small individual rooms and community kitchen facilities. The goal of such a facility is to give the resident a sense of control over his or her environment." *US v. City of Philadelphia, Pa.* (E.D. Pa., 1993).

## SITE

**Any plot or parcel of land or combination of contiguous lots or parcels of land. See *Figure 70*. See *Historic Properties*.**

***Legal Annotation***: "'**Site**' is defined as 'a parcel of land, subdivided or unsubdivided, occupied or to be occupied by a use or structure.' Ordinance § 8." *Rotter v. Coconino County* (Ariz., 1991).

## SITE IMPROVEMENTS

**Construction of, or improvement to, streets, access roadways, parking facilities, sidewalks, drainage structures, and utilities in connection with any development.**

***Legal Annotation***: "**Site improvements** include a paved parking area, an illuminated sign, spotlights, fencing and landscaping. The property is served by public water and sewer systems, and is located near three major highways and a railroad." *Alemany v. Commissioner of Transportation* (Conn., 1990).

## SITE PLAN

**The development plan for one or more lots on which is shown the existing and proposed conditions of the lot, including topography, vegetation, drainage, floodplains, wetlands, and waterways; landscaping and open spaces; walkways; means of ingress and egress; circulation; utility services; structures and buildings; signs and lighting; berms, buffers, and screening devices; surrounding development; and any other information that reasonably may be required in order for an informed decision to be made by the approving authority.**

***Comment***: Site plans are not usually required for one or two family homes on separate lots. See Site Plan, Minor.

*Legal Annotation*: "A **site plan** is a plan required to be submitted by the builder, showing the proposed location of the buildings, parking areas, and other installations on the plot, and their relation to existing conditions, such as roads, neighboring land uses, natural features, public facilities, ingress and egress roads, interior roads, and similar features' (2 Rathkopf, Zoning and Planning [4th ed])." *Riegert Apts v. Planning Bd.* (N.Y., 1982).

## SITE PLAN, MINOR

**A development plan involving a small addition or alteration to an existing development in which the increase in floor area and impervious surface coverage is insubstantial and that requires no variances, does not require a new street or the extension of an existing street, does not require off-tract improvements, and contains all the information that reasonably may be required to act on the plan.**

*Comment*: Most municipal planning or land development ordinances allow agency subcommittees, with the assistance of their experts (planner, engineer, attorney), to classify site plans as minor plans if they meet certain requirements, such as an increase of less than 5 percent of the floor area of the existing building and/or an increase of not more than 10 percent of the existing impervious surface coverage. This in turn reduces the requirements for public notice submission requirements and allows approval by the subcommittee. It is an attempt to reduce the paperwork and approval time for small and noncontroversial site plans.

*Legal Annotation*: "The Clinton Township Code defines a **minor site plan** as a conventional site plan that does not involve 'any new building, any addition to an existing building or any physical on-site improvements.'" *Brower Dev. v. Planning Bd.* (N.J. App. Div., 1992).

## SITE-PLAN REVIEW

**The review of a site plan for any public or private project by the designated review agency for the local jurisdiction.**

*Comment*: Site-plan review generally refers to a method authorized in the local development ordinance whereby a committee of the local planning board, or the board itself, reviews applications for development using established standards and criteria. One example of why site-plan review of development applications is necessary is in regard to on-site parking. Although the proposed development may include the number and size of parking spaces required in the development ordinance, it does not ensure that such spaces will function properly.

Although the local planning board is responsible for the approval of site plans, the actual task of review may be undertaken by a committee of the board or by a special committee with particular expertise in plan review. Committee members should include the municipal planner or consultant, municipal engineer, and representatives of municipal agencies such as the environmental commission. Often the planning board attorney is on the committee. See *Technical Coordinating Committee*.

The review procedure itself should be a systematic process that starts with the overall design concept and ends with design details, such as the size and type of curbs and sidewalks, and should include the following steps.

- Site inspection
- Overall design concept
  - Land use (contextual) relationships (to off-site areas)
  - Local Master Plan conformance
  - Utility considerations (need and available capacity)
  - Overall circulation (site access)
  - Support facilities (schools, shops, police, fire, and the like)
- Internal site-use relationships
- Evaluation of environmental impact
- Analysis of on-site circulation
  - Site design details
  - Parking layout
  - Landscape design
  - Lighting
  - Signage
  - Street furniture

The authority for site-plan review is found in state planning laws authorizing development ordinances. Site-plan review standards must be in conformance with state law and any guidelines established by the courts in land-use decisions. Site design standards must have a reasonable relationship to the public health, safety, or general welfare, or other proper police-power objectives.

*Legal Annotation*: "**Site plan review** is designed to ensure that uses permitted by a zoning ordinance are 'constructed on a site in such a way that they fit into the area in which they are being constructed without causing drainage, traffic, or lighting problems.' . . . **Site plan review** is also 'designed to assure that sites will be developed in a safe and attractive manner and in a way that will not involve danger or injury to the health, safety, or prosperity of abutting property owners or the general public.' . . . These purposes are 'accomplished by subjecting the plan to the very expertise expected of a planning board in cases where it would not be feasible to set forth in the ordinance a set of specific requirements upon which a building inspector could readily grant or refuse a permit.'" *Summa Humma Enters. v. Town of Tilton* (N.H., 1994).

## SKATEBOARD

**A foot board mounted on four or more wheels and usually propelled by the user, who sometimes stands, sits, kneels, or lies upon the device while it is in motion.**

**Comment**: While most skateboards are designed to be propelled by the rider, there are skateboards designed to be propelled by an electric motor or other mechanical means.

*Legal Annotation*: "The **skateboard** is described in the record. Basically, it is a board mounted on two wheels in the front and two in the back. It has no brakes, no motor and no steering device. The operator places one foot on the board and pushes the **skateboard** until it gains speed. He is then able to place both feet upon the board and to proceed at a goodly pace. The machine is propelled entirely by the rider. It has no vertical handle at the front end. The operator can change its direction only by shifting his weight. Able counsel for plaintiff makes the point 'skateboards have attained wide popularity and the trial court in its opinion recognized and took notice of their wide use.'" *Olson v. Village of Oak Lawn* (Ill. App. Ct., 1982).

## SKATEBOARD PARK

**A building, structure, or open area containing or developed with slopes, hills, passageways, and other challenges for skateboard users.**

**Comment**: Rental or sale of skateboards and related equipment may be included, and a user fee may be charged.

***Legal Annotation***: "The premises at 4267 West Loomis Road consists of a commercial, one-story building constructed in 1977 with floor space of 10,400 square feet. The building premises meets all state and local building, plumbing, and electrical code requirements. The building originally was designed to serve as a **skateboard park** with facilities to accommodate at least 400 people who would both participate in skateboarding activities and attend as spectators. The building is located more than 200 feet from Loomis Road and is serviced by a standard, paved driveway entrance from Loomis Road. The premises is not located within 500 feet of any residentially zoned district, school, or church. . . . It is no secret that the issue for members of the Greenfield Common Council was one of nudity, not public safety. This fact finds support in the Plan Commission and Common Council discussions of the proposed use. Additionally, when the premises originally was opened as a **skateboard park**, this intended use, admittedly different from an evening nude dancing establishment, generated not nearly the same fear of traffic and safety problems voiced after the subject of nudity surfaced." *Little v. City of Greenfield* (E.D. Wisc., 1983).

## SKATEPARK

**A facility that is designed for and used by persons riding skateboards, in-line skates, or roller skates.**

**Comment**: Skateparks range in size from ten thousand square feet to three acres. They consist primarily of ramps and pipes, which are designed so that skateboarders can move side to side, from vertical to horizontal and back to vertical positions through ramps, inclined surfaces, pipes in the shape of a half circle or oval, passageways, and other challenges. Ancillary facilities and uses might include rental of skateboards and skates, food, and parking. If evening use is contemplated, lighting and potential impacts on surrounding areas have to be considered.

*Legal Annotation*: "An extreme wheel sports (BMX biking, skateboarding, and in-line skating) **skate park** is also proposed, which will have a 2,000-2,500 seating capacity along with live television broadcasts." *In re Proposed Xanadu Redevelopment Project* (N.J. App. Div., 2008).

## SKETCH PLAN

**A rough sketch map of a proposed subdivision or site plan of sufficient accuracy to be used for the purpose of discussion and classification. See *Plat, Sketch*.**

*Legal Annotation*: "(b) **Sketch plan** is a nontechnical depiction of the existing features of the land and the development proposed thereon together with ownership data. A **sketch plan** serves the following two (2) purposes: 1. The developer can obtain an early determination of his prospects before he invests heavily in technical plans; and 2. The county can fully evaluate the pros and cons of the project on a before-the-fact basis, thus allowing necessary changes to be made more easily." *Chase Manhattan Mortg. & Rlty. Trust v. Wacha* (Fla. Ct. App., 1981).

## SKETCH PLAT

**See *Plat, Sketch*.**

## SKI AREA

**An area developed for snow skiing, with trails and lifts, and including ski rental and sales, instruction, and eating facilities.**

*Legal Annotation*: "A major concern of the original planners and the Bridger Canyon residents was that the existing Bridger Canyon Road would not handle the traffic that would be generated by 7,000 to 8,000 day skiers. The construction of an adequate road to handle those numbers was determined to be contradictory to the intent of the General Plan. To resolve this problem, the plan provided for full expansion of the **ski area** by designating a 400 plus acre area with a P.U.D. density of one unit per half acre. This high density area was included in order to allow enough overnight facilities to maintain a low daily traffic volume on the Bridger Canyon Road. The plan proposes 1,500 car parking lot spaces for 4,500 day visitors and a possible P.U.D. density for 800 units to serve an estimated 3,000 overnight visitors." *BCPOA v. Planning & Zoning Com'n* (Mont., 1995).

## SKI RESORT

**A ski area that also includes sales, rental, and service of related equipment and accessories; eating places; residences; and hotels and motels. See *Ski Area*.**

*Legal Annotation*: "A 1970 study conducted by the Forest Service pursuant to this congressional directive identified Sandy Butte as having the highest potential of any site in the State of Washington for development as a major downhill **ski resort**. . . . In 1978, Methow Recreation, Inc. (MRI), applied for a special use permit to develop and operate its proposed 'Early Winters **Ski Resort**' on Sandy Butte and an 1,165-acre parcel of land it had acquired adjacent to the National Forest. The proposed development would make use of approximately 3,900 acres of Sandy Butte; would entice visitors to travel long distances to stay at the resort for several days at a time; and would stimulate extensive commercial and residential growth in the vicinity to accommodate both vacationers and staff." *Robertson v. Methow Valley Citizens Council* (U.S., 1989).

## SKILLED NURSING FACILITY

**See *Long-Term Care Facility*.**

*Legal Annotation*: "The Township argues that the **skilled nursing facility** is not a 'hospital or sanatorium' based on the limited type of medical care provided, but clearly falls within the definition of group home. . . . Before the Zoning Hearing Board, Manor contended that the proposed facility is a **skilled nursing facility** as opposed to a regular nursing home. . . . Chapter 201.3 of the regulations promulgated by the Pennsylvania Department of Health for long term care facilities defines skilled care: 'Skilled care—Professionally supervised nursing care and related medical and other health services provided for a period exceeding 24 hours to an individual not in need of hospitalization, but those needs are such that they can only be met in a long term care facility on an inpatient basis, and who needs the care because of age, illness, disease, injury, convalescence or physical or mental infirmity. The term includes the provision of daily inpatient services that are needed on a daily basis by the patient, ordered by a physician, which require the skills of and are furnished directly by or under the supervision of technical or professional personnel, such as, but not limited to, registered nurses, licensed practical nurses, physical therapists, occupational therapists, speech pathologists or audiologists. The care would include nursing, skilled rehabilitation or a personal care service that because of a special medical complication of the patient require that the personal care services be performed by or under the direct supervision of skilled nursing or rehabilitative personnel.'" *Manor Healthcare v. Zoning Hearing Bd.* (Pa. Common. Ct., 1991).

## SKIMMING

**The mechanical removal of oil or scum from the surface of water.**

***Legal Annotation***: "West Suburban No. 1 treats municipal waste, primarily from sewer connections located in Bolingbrook. The basic operation of the plant begins with the influx of the sewage into two primary tanks. Solids settle to the bottom of the tanks, while floating materials rise to the top. Wooden planks called flights are chain-driven along the bottom and top of the primary tanks. Settled solids, or sludge, are pushed along the bottom into hoppers for further treatment. The flights then rotate up to **skim** the surface and push scum to the end for removal. Sewage then flows into an aeration tank, where it is bubbled with air and metabolized by the biomass." *Citizens Utilities Co. v. Poll. Cont. Bd.* (Ill. App. Ct., 1984).

## SKY EXPOSURE PLANE

**A theoretical plane beginning at a lot line or directly above a street line at a height set forth in the ordinance and rising over a slope determined by an acute angle measured down from the vertical as set forth in the ordinance. *See Figure 91.***

***Comment***: Sky exposure plane controls regulate the bulk and height of tall structures such that a predetermined level of natural light will be available to the adjacent street or other public space. Such regulations are most appropriate in highly built-up urban areas that allow tall buildings. Their original intent was to allow light to penetrate to the street level, but they have also provided the added benefit of enhancing the aesthetics of skyscrapers. The Chrysler and Empire State Buildings in New York City are prime examples of how sky exposure plane regulations created attractive "stepbacks" in the buildings' façades, particularly at the upper levels.

**Figure 91**

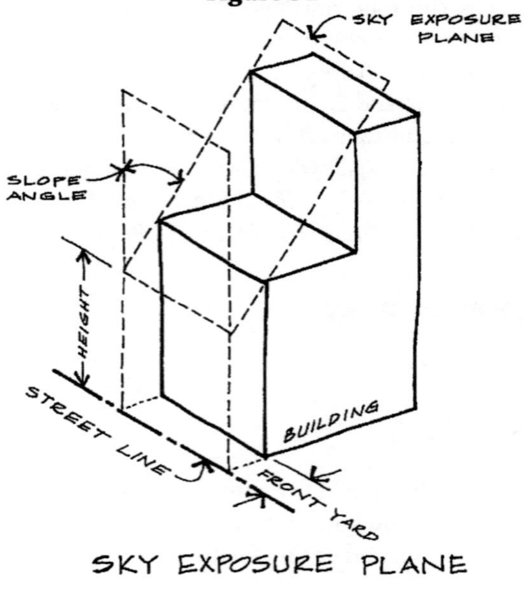


***Legal Annotation***: "The City's Department of City Planning's 'Zoning Glossary' defines '**sky exposure plane**' as 'a virtual sloping plane that begins at a specified height above the street line and rises inward over the zoning lot at a ratio of vertical distance to horizontal distance set forth in district regulations. A building may not penetrate the sky exposure plane which is designed to provide light and air at street level, primarily in medium- and higher-density districts." *Westwater v. New York City Bd. of Standards & Appeals*, 2013 NY Slip Op 32515 (N.Y. Sup. Ct., 2013).

"The CPC also found other amenities in the neighborhood, such as playgrounds, parks, and commercial venues, to be adequate. Next, the CPC turned to whether buildings allowed under the new designation, such as JBJ's six-story proposed development, would fit within the context of the surrounding area; the CPC concluded that they would: 'the proposed MX8: M1-2/R6A zoning district would impose bulk rules that would permit residential uses to a FAR of 2.7, bonusable to 3.6 and community facility uses to a FAR of 3.0. Commercial and industrial uses would be permitted to an FAR of 2.0, which is the same FAR permitted by the existing M3-1 district. The proposed district would also limit building heights to 60 feet at the street, and 70 feet after a 15-foot setback. The existing district regulates height with a **sky exposure plane** that starts 60 feet above the streetline.'" *Williamsburg Community Preserv. Coalition v. Council of the City of New York* (N.Y. Sup. Ct., 2012).

## SKY GLOW

**The illumination of the night sky from non-natural sources that causes a reduction in the overall darkness of an area. http://www.pgplanning.org/Resources/Tools_On-line/Glossary.htm. See *Lighting Plan; Foot Candles***

***Comment***: Human-produced light pollution mars our view of the stars, threatens astronomy, disrupts ecosystems, affects human circadian rhythms, and wastes energy to the tune of $2.2 billion per year in the United States alone. The International Dark-Sky Association (IDA), founded in 1988, has called attention to the hazards of light pollution and is encouraging planners, legislators, manufacturers and citizens to provide energy-efficient outdoor lighting that is directed to the objects or areas to be illuminated, and not needlessly into the sky. (*See* darksky.org.)

***Legal Annotation***: "Because Sunset Valley does not point to any authority providing that 'the right to regulate lighting and minimize **sky glow**' is considered a constitutional or vested property right, we sustain TxDOT's third issue." *Texas DOT v. City of Sunset Valley* (Texas Ct. App., 2002).

## SLOPE

**The deviation of a surface from the horizontal, usually expressed in percent or degrees. See *Grade. See Figure 52.***

***Comment***: Slope percentage is computed by dividing the vertical distance by the horizontal distance times one hundred. For example, a parcel of land one hundred fifty feet in length that rises twelve feet in height has a slope of 8 percent: $12 \div 150 \times 100 = 8$ percent. See *Topography; Contour Line*.

***Legal Annotation***: "A steep **slope** is a '[l]and area where the inclination of the land's surface from the horizontal is twelve (12) percent or greater. Article 1311.04(a)(110) of the Ordinance. The following building restrictions apply to areas of steep **slopes**: (1) Twelve (12) to less than fifteen (15) percent **slope**: no more than forty (40) percent of such areas shall be developed and/or regraded or stripped of vegetation. (2) Fifteen (15) to twenty-five (25) percent **slope**: no more than thirty percent (30) of such areas shall be developed and/or regraded or stripped of vegetation, with the exception that no more than twenty (20) percent of such areas may be disturbed in the case of landslide prone area. (3) More than twenty-five (25) percent **slope**: no more than fifteen (15) percent of such areas shall be developed and/or regraded or stripped of vegetation, with the exception that no more than five (5) percent of such areas may be disturbed in the case of landslide prone area.'" *Jones v. Zoning Hearing Bd.* (Pa. Common. Ct., 1990).

## SLOUGH

**Low-lying muddy ground, wetlands, or marshy area. See *Wetlands*.**

*Legal Annotation*: "A **slough** is an 'area of soft muddy ground' or 'swamplike region.' Random House Dictionary of The English Language 1800 (unabridged 2d ed. 1987)." *Kinder Morgan North Texas Pipeline, LP v. Justiss* (Tex. Ct. App., 2006).

"The deed description of the body of water as a 'slew' or '**slough**' is also consistent with Adamson's contention and the jury's finding that it is a stream. 'A **slough** is a side channel, inlet, or arm from a river. Webster's International Dictionary, 2d ed., p. 2369; 39 Words and Phrases, p. 523.'" *Parker v. Adamson* (Ga. Ct. App., 1964).

## SLUDGE

**Any solid, semisolid, or liquid waste generated from a wastewater treatment plant, water supply treatment plan, or air pollution control facility exclusive of any treated effluent.**

*Legal Annotation*: "'Sewage **sludge**' is defined by federal regulations as the 'solid, semi-solid, or liquid residue generated during the treatment of domestic sewage in a treatment works.' (40 C.F.R. § 503.9[w] [2005].) More generally, sewage **sludge** refers to the mud-like deposit originating from sewage and created by the treatment processes used to decontaminate wastewater before it is released into local waterways. Sewage **sludge** typically consists of water and 2 to 28 percent solids." *CSD No. 2 Of Los Angeles v. County of Kern* (Calif. Ct. app., 2005).

## SLUM

**See *Blighted Area*.**

*Comment*: "Slum" is a term that is no longer used, because of its pejorative connotations.

*Legal Annotation*: "We come, then, to the problem presented in the case at bar. It lies in three parts. 1. First, there is the **slum**. A slum is made up of houses (or substitutes for houses), the appurtenances thereto, and people. The houses and appurtenances are such that the people live in filth and breed disease and crime. A **slum** can be eliminated by tearing down the houses, destroying the appurtenances, and either building new housing on the spot for the people or moving the people away." *Schneider v. District of Columbia* (D.C. D.C., 1953). (Ed. note: The characterization is indicative of the prejudice that existed at the time.)

## SLURRY

**A "soupy" mix of fluid, often water, and a solid such as clay, cement, stone, wood pulp, etc. to stabilize unimproved areas such as dirt roads or building foundation wall trenches, until more permanent materials can be put in place.**

*Comment*: The use of slurry walls in the construction of the foundation of the World Trade Center is credited with preventing the surrounding waters from inundating the site after the buildings collapsed on September 11, 2001. The use of the slurry wall is detailed in an article by Dunlap (2013).

*Legal Annotation*: "An 'aqueous **slurry**' is a soupy mixture in which solid matter is suspended." *Intermountain Research & Eng. Co. v. Hercules Incorporated* (9th Cir., 1969).

## SMART CODE

**See *Form-Based Code*.**

*Legal Annotation*: "2.1 **Smart Code** Zoning District Descriptions. This table provides description of the general character of each Smart Code zoning district, based on the Transect concept. The Transect is a system of ordering human habitats in a range from the most natural to the most urban. The Smart Code is based upon 6 Transect Zones which describe the physical character of place at any scale, according to the density and intensity of land use and urbanism." *Germantown Smart Code Chapter 23 Article VII Draft July 19, 2013.*

## SMART GROWTH

**Policies, legislation, regulations, procedures, and strategies that attempt to achieve more**

**compact, efficient mixed-used development, tied to existing infrastructure and facilities by using such techniques as transfer of development rights, growth boundaries, targeted public and private investments, impact fees, open space and farmland preservation, and flexible zoning and subdivision regulations within established parameters (Downs 2001; Duany et al. 2000; Katz 2010; Flint 2011; Meck 2002; Weitz and Waldner 2002).**

*Comment*: Smart growth is the antithesis of sprawl, promoting development patterns that are economically sound, environmentally responsible, and socially just. Smart growth shares many of the principles found in traditional neighborhood design, including:

- A mix of land uses: stores, jobs, and homes
- A range of housing types, sizes, and costs
- A variety of transportation choices, including accessible public transit
- Compact, safe, and walkable neighborhoods
- Distinctive communities with a strong sense of place
- The preservation of open space, farmland, and critical environmental areas
- A focus of public investment on existing community assets
- Citizen participation in development decisions

According to the US Environmental Protection Agency (EPA), "smart-growth development practices support national environmental goals by preserving open spaces and parkland and protecting critical habitat; improving transportation choices, including walking, bicycling, and transit, which reduces emissions from automobiles; promoting brown field redevelopment; and reducing impervious cover, which improves water quality and reduces storm water runoff" (Poitner 2011).

*Legal Annotation*: "The statute defines '**[s] mart growth**' as follows: '**Smart growth** is a principle of land development that emphasizes mixing land uses, increases the availability of affordable housing by creating a range of housing opportunities in neighborhoods, takes advantage of compact design, fosters distinctive and attractive communities, preserves open space, farmland, natural beauty and critical environmental areas, strengthens existing communities, provides a variety of transportation choices, makes development decisions predictable, fair and cost effective and encourages community and stakeholder collaboration in development decisions.'" *DiRico v. Town of Kingston* (Mass., 2010).

## SMART PARKING

See *Smart Parking Management*.

## SMART PARKING MANAGEMENT

**The systematic application of management strategies to all parking facilities in the area, which increases their efficiency, reduces demand, and/or encourages the use of alternative transportation modes.**

*Comment*: Strategies include: increasing shared parking, so each space can serve multiple users and destinations; more efficient pricing, such as charging higher rates and varying time limits during peak periods; encouraging car sharing, bicycle usage (e.g., providing bike paths and shower facilities); improving information and marketing to help drivers find and pay for parking while reducing the hunt for empty spaces; using new technologies such as payment by credit or debit card, or pay-by-phone; and the use of smartphone apps and wireless sensors that tell drivers where spaces are open. The benefits of such strategies are to significantly reduce the number of spaces required; improve service; provide more accessible land-use patterns; reduce traffic volumes, congestion, accidents, and air pollution; improve mobility for non-driver; and provide more sustainable and attractive communities.

*Legal Annotation*: "The following bylaw provisions for implementing **smart parking** strategies are designed to address three distinct issues relative to off-street parking: 1) Reducing the standards for required parking; 2) Providing innovative solutions for shared and off-site parking; and 3) Parking area design." *Massachusetts Smart Parking Model Bylaw.* http://www.mass.gov/envir/smart_growth_toolkit/bylaws/SP-Bylaw.pdf

## SMOG

**Generally used to mean an equivalent of air pollution, particularly associated with oxidants.**

*Legal Annotation*: "**Smog** is a fog made heavier and darker by the smoke of a city. (Webster's New International Dictionary, 2d ed.). In Roget's Thesaurus 'smog' is classified with 'fog.' '**Smog**' and 'fog' are also similar in sound, and they rhyme. The word '**smog**,' itself is an American neologism from two words, 'smoke' and 'fog.' On the other hand, the registered trademark is not 'Fog' but 'London Fog' made by The Londontown Manufacturing Company. There is no doubt that if the defendant had chosen as its mark 'London Smog' that would have been intolerably confusing." *Londontown Manufacturing Co. v. Cable Raincoat Co.* (S.D. N.Y., 1974).

## SMOKE

**(1) Solid particles generated as a result of the incomplete combustion of materials containing carbon; (2) gas-borne and airborne particles arising from a process of combustion in sufficient numbers to be observable, exclusive of visible condensed water vapor.**

*Legal Annotation*: "In the case before us we think that both common knowledge and ordinary language support our recognition that **smoke** is visible, and that, as a matter beyond scientific dispute, **smoke** is visible precisely because it contains incompletely oxidized materials. Thus Webster's International Dictionary (2d ed.) defines 'smoke' as: 'The gaseous products of burning organic materials . . . when rendered visible by the presence of small particles of carbon. . . . **Smoke** is thus always the result of imperfect combustion.' And the Encyclopaedia Britannica comments, 'If complete combustion were always attainable no fuel would emit smoke, the final products in such an ideal case being limited to carbon dioxide, water vapour, and free nitrogen, all quite innocuous, and invisible unless the water vapour condenses to a cloud of steam.' (20 Encyclopaedia Britannica [1954] p. 839.) The remote possibility that in an unusual case something other than incompletely oxidized materials renders the gases from a fire visible does not detract from our reasoning." *McAllister v. Workmen's Comp. App. Bd.* (Calif., 1968).

## SNOUT HOUSE

**A house with a front entrance garage that occupies more than 50 percent of the house frontage and/or protrudes more than ten feet from the rest of the house.**

*Comment*: Snout houses dominate their lots and create unattractive "garage door" streetscapes. One approach is to require all front entrance garages to occupy less than 50 percent of the house frontage and not protrude more than ten feet closer to the street than the rest of the frontage. Other restrictions call for locating the front door not more than eight feet from the front of the garage (Knack 2001).

*Legal Annotation*: "A '**snout house**' is a residence constructed with the front door wall more than eight feet behind the front of the garage door, except as permitted in these regulations." *Municipal Code, 20.94.050 Definitions. Pacific, Washington.* http://www.codepublishing.com/wa/pacific/html/Pacific20/Pacific2094.html

## SNOW DUMP SITES

**Areas designated for the temporary storage of snow removed from public streets and facilities.**

*Comment*: Snow dump sites are particularly important in dense urban areas to facilitate the rapid clearing of public streets and facilities following a major snowstorm. Designated sites can provide sediment ponds to capture snowmelt and avoid runoff to streams and other sensitive watercourses or areas.

*Legal Annotation*: "As many Saskatchewan municipalities continue to grow and develop, their snow dump management practices will require improvements. In fact, some municipalities within the province are planning to develop existing **snow dump sites** into commercial or residential development and may require environmental remediation prior to development. The siting, design and management considerations presented in this report leverages existing knowledge and experience gained from other jurisdictions and should be considered by municipalities who want to improve or reclaim existing **snow dump sites** or develop new snow dump sites. Adopting improved snow dump siting, design and management practices can mitigate potentially adverse environmental, social and economic impacts." *Saskatchewan Snow Dump Management Guidelines.* (http://suma.org/cmsupload/fckeditor/communities_of_tomorrow/Snow%20Dump.pdf)

## SNOWMOBILE

**A self-propelled vehicle designed for travel on snow or ice or a natural terrain and steered by wheels, skis, or runners. See *Vehicle, Off-Road.***

***Legal Annotation*:** "(e) For the purposes of this Act, a **snowmobile** is defined as any motorized vehicle which is designed to operate on snow or ice. The use of **snowmobiles** in the wilderness designated by this Act is not permitted except that the Secretary may permit **snowmobiles**, not exceeding forty inches in width, on (1) the overland portages from Crane Lake to Little Vermilion Lake in Canada, and from Sea Gull River along the eastern portion of Saganaga Lake to Canada, and (2) on the following routes until January 1, 1984." *National Ass'n of Property Owners v. US* (D. Minn., 1980).

## SOCIAL SERVICES

**Establishments providing assistance and aid to those persons requiring counseling for job training, employment, psychological problems, or learning and physical disabilities.**

***Comment*:** This major group also includes organizations soliciting funds for these and related services. Additionally, it includes child day-care services, nurseries as well as residential care, and special categories for persons with limited ability for self-care but for whom medical care is not a major requirement.

***Legal Annotation*:** "The DISD's plans for the shopping center complex include a K-12 school, facilities to provide a number of education services, and facilities to provide **social services**. . . . These **social services** are to include a senior citizens program, a health services agency, family services, a parent education program, and employment agencies." *Tasby v. Estes* (5$^{th}$ Cir., 1978).

## SOIL

**All unconsolidated mineral and organic material, of whatever origin, that overlies bedrock and can be readily excavated.**

***Legal Annotation*:** "[D]isposal fields shall not be constructed in areas where the maximum ground water elevation is less than four feet below the bottom of the disposal field. Provided, that in instances where the undisturbed **soil** consists of porous sand or gravel with a percolation rate of two minutes or less per inch, the maximum ground water elevation may be not less than two feet below the bottom of the disposal field." *Glen Avenue Realty v. Dir. of Pub. Hlt. of Wilmington* (Mass., 1970).

## SOIL CEMENT

**Pulverized natural soil mixed with a small amount of portland cement and water, usually processed in a tumbler, and compacted to high density.**

***Comment*:** Soil cement is frequently used as a construction material for pipe bedding, slope protection, and road construction as a sub-base layer reinforcing and protecting the subgrade. It has good compressive and shear strength, but it is brittle and has low tensile strength, so it is prone to forming cracks.

***Legal Annotation*:** "**Soil cement** is a method of preparing the base of a road prior to surfacing it. It involves mixing the existing soil with portland cement and water. This provides a solid base and moisture barrier suitable for surfacing with asphalt. In order to utilize **soil cement** in this case, the limestone surface of the road would have had to be removed." *Hallar Enterprises, Inc. v. Hartman* (La. Ct. App., 1991).

## SOIL CONDITIONER

**A biologically stable organic material, such as humus or compost, that makes soil more**

**amenable to the passage of water and to the distribution of fertilizing material, providing a better medium for necessary soil bacteria growth.**

*Legal Annotation*: "The industrial organic wastes consisted of fruit pomace and spent diatomaceous earth (DE). Fruit pomace is a by-product of fruit juice production, and consists of the skin, seeds, and other portions of the fruit left over after juice is extracted. It can be used as mulch, animal feed, or a **soil conditioner**." *Hickle v. Whitney Farms, Inc.* (Wash., 2003).

## SOIL CONSERVATION DISTRICT

**A geographic area, usually a county, in which professionals provide advice to communities, agencies, and individuals within the jurisdiction and review development proposals for soil erosion and sedimentation control measures.**

*Comment*: The soil conservation district concept began in 1936 and is used by the US Department of Agriculture to administer its programs relating to water and soil.

*Legal Annotation*: "The creation of **soil conservation districts** is provided for in Code, 1931, 19-21A-5, as amended. Therein, the legislature has said: '(a) Any twenty-five owners of land lying within the limits of the territory proposed to be organized into a district may file a petition with the State soil conservation committee asking that a **soil conservation district** be organized to function in the territory described in the petition.' The localized nature of a **soil conservation district** is most apparent. The above quoted language requires that the establishment of a district be initiated by land owners within the territory proposed to be a district; also, it specifically provides that the district shall function only in the territory described in the petition. Nothing in this section or in any section of the code pertaining to **soil conservation districts** indicates that such districts function on a state-wide scale." *Hesse v. State Soil Conserv. Committee* (W. Va., 1969).

## SOIL ENGINEER

**A professional engineer who is qualified by education and experience to practice applied soil mechanics and foundation engineering.**

*Legal Annotation*: "Testifying for Budd was Dr. Louis J. Capozzoli, a highly qualified **soil engineer** who, as reported decisions show, has testified in many previous cases involving soil analysis. He personally visited the parking lot and reviewed the tests run by Louisiana Testing and by Gorsha. He noted that the Louisiana Testing report described the base material to a depth of three inches as 'stiff reddish brown silty clay,' rather than 'sand, clay, gravel.' Capozzoli stated that Hixson could not tell from this report that there was six inches of sand, clay, gravel, or that the percentages of these materials met the Department of Transportation and Development standards. Of course, in deference to Hixson, the Court notes he relied on the conclusion by Louisiana Testing that the base material was adequate, and in addition, as an extra precaution, he recommended further laboratory tests of the base material during construction. Of course, the owner did not require and no one performed these tests during the work." *Hanna-Abington Alexandria, Inc. v. Budd Const. Co., Inc.* (La. Ct. App., 1986).

## SOIL EROSION

**See *Erosion*.**

*Legal Annotation*: "Congress 'recognized that the wastage of soil and moisture . . . resulting from **soil erosion**, is a menace to the national welfare' and declared its policy to be 'to provide permanently for the control and prevention of **soil erosion** and thereby to preserve natural resources, control floods, prevent impairment of reservoirs, and maintain the navigability of rivers and harbors, protect public health, public lands and relieve unemployment.' It therefore authorized the Secretary of Agriculture to conduct surveys, investigations, and research relating to the character of **soil erosion** and the preventive measures needed, to carry out preventive measures." *Baboquivari Cattle Co. v. Commissioner of Internal Revenue* (Bd. Tax App., 1942).

## SOIL EROSION AND SEDIMENT CONTROL PLAN

**Strategies and procedures that describe necessary land-treatment measures for minimizing soil erosion and sedimentation. See *Erosion; Sedimentation*.**

*Legal Annotation*: "4.9 MINIMUM ACCEPTABLE STANDARDS. **Plans for soil erosion and sediment control** shall be developed in accordance with these regulations using the principles as outlined in Chapters 3 and 4 of the Connecticut Guidelines for **Soil Erosion and Sediment Control**, as amended. **Soil erosion and sediment control plans** shall result in a development that: minimizes erosion and sedimentation during construction; is stabilized and protected from erosion when completed; and does not cause off-site erosion and/or sedimentation. The minimum standards for individual measures are those in the Connecticut Guidelines for **Soil Erosion and Sediment Control**, as amended. The commission may grant exceptions when requested by the applicant if technically sound reasons are presented. The appropriate method from Chapter 9 of the Connecticut Guidelines for **Soil Erosion and Sediment Control**, as amended, shall be used in determining peak flow rates and volumes of runoff unless an alternative method is approved by the commission." *Norwich v. Norwalk Wilbert Vault Co.* (Conn., 1988).

## SOIL MAP

**A map indicating the names and spatial distribution of soil types on a site and including information relating to soil characteristics such as slope, depth to seasonal high water, depth to bedrock, permeability, natural drainage class, stoniness, and flood and stream overflow hazard.**

*Comment*: The data source for maps showing the soil types and locations of a given area is usually the official soil maps prepared by the Soil Conservation Service of the US Department of Agriculture. The information provided in the official soil maps is field-compiled by the Soil Conservation Service by testing at selected locations. However, soil maps developed from this base for use in development applications must be field-checked for accuracy and adjusted if warranted, especially in cases involving the delineation of areas where development is precluded or limited.

*Legal Annotation*: "Defendants also introduced in evidence exhibit 12, which is a soil survey of Loup County prepared by the United States Department of Agriculture in 1934, which contains a Loup County **soil map**. This map shows types of soils, drainage, secondary roads, and trails. It is significant that this map fails to show any road or trail across the Dunne property as contended herein by plaintiff." *Satterfield v. Dunne* (Neb., 1966).

"Under the land-capability classification system, the predominant soils on the Caton property, **soil map** units 26 and 27, are classified as class III and class IV. Class III soils have 'severe limitations that reduce the choice of plants or that require special conservation practices, or both.' Soil Survey, p. 146, Attach., Br. of Resp't Caton. Class IV soils have 'very severe limitations that reduce the choice of plants or that require very careful management, or both.' Soil Survey, p. 146, Attach., Br. of Resp't Caton. Other soils on the Caton property, the gorskel very stony loam, gorskel-harwood complex, and the torriorthents, steep, are class VII; the logy cobbly silt loam is class VI and the renslow silt loam is class IIIe. Subclass 'e' means that the main risk is erosion unless close-growing plant cover is maintained. Class VI soils have 'severe limitations that make them generally unsuitable for cultivation.' Soil Survey, p. 146, Attach., Br. of Resp't Caton. Class VII soils have 'very severe limitations that make them unsuitable for cultivation.' Soil Survey, p. 146, Attach., Br. of Resp't Caton." *Yakima County v. Eastern Washington Growth Management Hearings Board* (Wash. Ct. App., 2008).

## SOIL REMOVAL

**Any digging, excavation, placement, replacement, filling, grading, leveling of soil, or any activity that alters or changes the grade, location, or contour of lands and the transportation or supplying of soil.**

*Comment*: Many local jurisdictions require permits for "soil removal"—a term not only involving the exportation of soil, but also soil importation as well as the movement of large quantities of soil within a site. Permits for such activities are required because of concerns related to disturbing soil that may be contaminated; ensuring that soil imported to a site is clean; and because the disruptive impacts of truck and heavy equipment, both on- and off-site, sometimes require restrictions relating to hours of operation and routes used by such trucks.

## SOLAR ACCESS

**A property owner's right to have the sunlight shine on the owner's land. See *Sky Exposure Plane*.**

*Comment*: The enforcement of this right is through the zoning ordinance that establishes height and setback requirements. Applicants may be asked to present sun-shadow diagrams to permit an agency to determine if solar access will be impaired (Morley 2014).

*Legal Annotation*: "This appeal from a judgment of the circuit court for Waukesha County, Max Raskin, circuit judge, was certified to this court by the court of appeals, sec. (Rule) 809.61, Stats. 1979–80, as presenting an issue of first impression, namely, whether an owner of a **solar**-heated residence states a claim upon which relief can be granted when he asserts that his neighbor's proposed construction of a residence (which conforms to existing deed restrictions and local ordinances) interferes with his **access** to an unobstructed path for sunlight across the neighbor's property. This case thus involves a conflict between one landowner (Glenn Prah, the plaintiff) interested in unobstructed access to sunlight across adjoining property as a natural source of energy and an adjoining landowner (Richard D. Maretti, the defendant) interested in the development of his land. . . . Chapter 354, Laws of 1981, sec. 66.032, provides specific conditions for **solar access** permits. In part that section provides for impermissible interference with solar collectors within specific limitations: 66.032 Solar access permits. (1) . . . (f) 'Impermissible interference' means the blockage of solar energy from a collector surface or proposed collector surface for which a permit has been granted under this section during a collector use period if such blockage is by any structure or vegetation on property, an owner of which was notified under sub. (3) (b). 'Impermissible interference' does not include: 1. Blockage by a narrow protrusion, including but not limited to a pole or wire, which does not substantially interfere with absorption of solar energy by a solar collector. 2. Blockage by any structure constructed, under construction or for which a building permit has been applied for before the date the last notice is mailed or delivered under sub. (3) (b). 3. Blockage by any vegetation planted before the date the last notice is mailed or delivered under sub. (3) (b) unless a municipality by ordinance under sub. (2) defines impermissible interference to include such vegetation." *Prah v. Maretti* (Wis., 1982).

## SOLAR COLLECTOR

**A device or combination of devices, structure, or part of a device or structure that transforms direct solar energy into thermal, chemical, or electrical energy.**

*Legal Annotation*: "As amended in 2008, section 25981 provides: '(a) As used in this chapter, "**solar collector**" means a fixed device, structure, or part of a device or structure, on the roof of a building, that is used primarily to transform solar energy into thermal, chemical, or electrical energy. The **solar collector** shall be used as part of a system that makes use of solar energy for any or all of the following purposes: (1) Water heating. (2) Space heating or cooling. (3) Power generation. (b) Notwithstanding subdivision (a), for the purpose of this chapter, "**solar collector**" includes a fixed device, structure, or part of a device or structure that is used primarily to transform solar energy into thermal, chemical, or electrical energy and that is installed on the ground because a **solar collector** cannot be installed on the roof of the building receiving the energy due to inappropriate roofing material, slope of the roof, structural shading, or orientation of the building. (c) For the purposes of this chapter, "**solar collector**" does not include a **solar collector** that is designed and intended to offset more than the building's electricity demand. (d) For purposes of this chapter, the location of a **solar collector** is required to comply with the local building and setback regulations, and to be set back not less than five feet from the property line, and not less than 10 feet above the ground. A **solar collector** may be less than 10 feet in height only if, in addition to the five-foot setback, the solar collector is set back three times the amount lowered.' Thus, at least with respect to one solar access protection law, **solar collectors** are devices or structures which are fixed on the roof of a building. Alternatively, **solar collectors** are devices or structures affixed to the ground because they cannot be placed on the roof." *Toorvald v. City of West Hollywood* (Calif. Ct. App., 2010).

## SOLAR ENERGY SYSTEM

**A complete design or assembly consisting of a solar energy collector, an energy storage facility (where used), and components for the distribution of transformed energy (Best 2009).**

*Legal Annotation*: "The term '**solar energy system**' is not defined in the Municipal Code. However, some guidance may be found as to the meaning of '**solar energy system**' from state laws regulating solar access. . . . Civil Code section 801.5, subdivision (a)(1) defines a **solar energy system** as follows, 'Any solar collector or other solar energy device whose primary purpose is to provide for the collection, storage, and distribution of solar energy for space heating, space cooling, electric generation, or water heating.' There is no further explanation of what a solar collector or **solar energy** device is in the Civil Code." *Toorvald v. City of West Hollywood* (Calif. Ct. App., 2010).

## SOLAR SKY SPACE

**The space between a solar energy collector and the sun that must be free of obstructions that shade the collector to an extent that precludes its cost-effective operation. See *Solar Sky Easement*.**

**Comment**: Increasingly, planners will be asked to develop zoning requirements that protect the solar sky space. It can be done through minimum setback requirements and sky exposure planes. Site-plan review might also require a shadow analysis to ascertain whether or not any proposed tree plantings, landscaping, or structures will block off solar collectors. For single-family and two-family homes, which are usually excluded from site-plan review, the construction code official or building inspector should be given guidelines as to what may be permitted and minimum setbacks needed in order to ensure a functioning solar collector.

***Legal Annotation***: "The proposed addition to the Fontainebleau is being constructed twenty feet from its north property line, 130 feet from the mean high water mark of the Atlantic Ocean, and 76 feet 8 inches from the ocean bulkhead line. The 14-story tower will extend 160 feet above grade in height and is 416 feet long from east to west. During the winter months, from around two o'clock in the afternoon for the remainder of the day, the shadow of the addition will extend over the cabana, swimming pool, and sunbathing areas of the Eden Roc, which are located in the southern portion of its property. . . . In this action, plaintiff-appellee sought to enjoin the defendants-appellants from proceeding with the construction of the addition to the Fontainebleau (it appears to have been roughly eight stories high at the time suit was filed), alleging that the construction would interfere with the light and air on the beach in front of the Eden Roc and cast a shadow of such size as to render the beach wholly unfitted for the use and enjoyment of its guests, to the irreparable injury of the plaintiff. . . . No American decision has been cited, and independent research has revealed none, in which it has been held that—in the absence of some contractual or statutory obligation—a landowner has a legal right to the free flow of light and air across the adjoining land of his neighbor. Even at common law, the landowner had no legal right, in the absence of an easement or uninterrupted use and enjoyment for a period of 20 years, to unobstructed light and air from the adjoining land. . . . And the English doctrine of 'ancient lights' has been unanimously repudiated in this country." *Fontainebleau Hotel Corp. v. Forty-Five Twenty-Five, Inc.* (Fla. Dist. Ct., 1959). (Editors' note: Old decision, dated, illustrative of how undeveloped the law was fifty years ago, requiring statutory solutions and private contracts to protect solar access.)

## SOLAR SKY EASEMENT

**A right, expressed as an easement, covenant, condition, or other property interest, in any deed or other instrument executed by or on behalf of any landowner, that protects the solar sky space of an actual, proposed, or designated solar energy collector at a described location by forbidding or limiting activities or land uses that interfere with access to solar energy.**

***Comment***: The solar sky space must be described either as the three-dimensional space in which obstruction is prohibited or limited, or as the times of day in which direct sunlight to the solar collector may not be obstructed, or as a combination of the two methods.

***Legal Annotation***: "This section provides: (f) '**Solar skyspace easement**' means (1) a right, whether or not stated in the form of a restriction, easement, covenant, or condition, in any deed, will, or other instrument executed by or on behalf of any owner of land or **solar skyspace** or in any order of taking, appropriate to protect the **solar skyspace** of a solar collector at a particularly described location to forbid or limit any or all of the following where detrimental to access to solar energy. (a) structures on or above ground; (b) vegetation on or above the ground; or (c) other activity; (2) and which shall specifically describe a **solar skyspace** in three dimensional terms in which the activity, structures, or vegetation are forbidden or limited or in which such an easement shall set performance criteria for adequate collection of solar energy at a particular location." *O'Neill v. Brown* (Ill. App. Ct., 1993).

## SOLID WASTE

**Unwanted or discarded material, including waste material with insufficient liquid content to be free-flowing. See *Waste*.**

***Comment***: Solid waste may be categorized as follows:

- *Agricultural*—solid waste that results from the raising and slaughtering of animals and the processing of animal products and from orchard and field crops
- *Commercial*—waste generated by stores, offices, and other activities that do not actually turn out a product
- *Industrial*—waste that results from industrial processes and manufacturing
- *Institutional*—waste originating from educational, health-care, and research facilities
- *Municipal*—residential and commercial solid waste generated within a community
- *Pesticide*—the residue from the manufacturing, handling, or use of chemicals intended for killing plant and animal pests
- *Residential*—waste that normally originates in a residential environment, sometimes called "domestic solid waste"

***Legal Annotation***: "Despite the previously-noted ambiguity in the circuitous definitions, it is clear that **solid waste** is defined very broadly. Indeed, solid waste is 'any discarded material.' As broad as this definition may be, clearly it would not include materials that still are useful products." *Zands v. Nelson* (S.D. Calif., 1991).

## SOLID WASTE DISPOSAL

**The ultimate disposition of solid waste that cannot be salvaged or recycled.**

***Legal Annotation***: "The principal issues in these appeals are whether (1) the trial court improperly substituted its judgment for that of the defendant Wallingford zoning board of appeals (board) in determining that **solid waste disposal** is a valid nonconforming use of certain property that is located in the town of Wallingford, owned by the plaintiff city of Meriden and leased, in part, to the plaintiff Connecticut Resources Recovery Authority (CRRA); (2) a Wallingford zoning regulation prohibiting **solid waste disposal** over an aquifer is a valid exercise of the town's police power; (3) this regulation is preempted by state solid waste and water quality statutes; and (4) the trial court improperly determined that the decision of the defendant Wallingford planning and zoning commission (commission) to retain the regulation was not supported by the record. We reverse the judgment of the trial court in each case and remand with direction to dismiss the plaintiffs' appeals." *Connecticut Resources Recovery Auth. v. Planning & Zoning Commission* (Conn. 1993).

## SOLID WASTE STORAGE CONTAINER

**A receptacle used for temporary storage of solid waste while awaiting collection. See DUMPSTER™.**

***Legal Annotation***: "The record supports this determination. Because a **dumpster** is not a structure, and the use of a **dumpster** is not allowed as a principal use in the zoning district, an unscreened dumpster cannot be a legally nonconforming use." *In The Matter Of The Administrative Citation RFS XXXXXXXXX* (Minn. Ct. App., 2010).

## SOLID WASTE MANAGEMENT

**A planned program providing for the collection, storage, and disposal of solid waste, including, where appropriate, recycling and recovery.**

***Legal Annotation***: "As we have seen, the Legislature recognized that **solid waste management** is a matter of statewide concern, which could be effectively treated only through a comprehensive statewide policy (§ 66702). The Legislature placed responsibility in local government and the state as to **solid waste management** (§ 66730). Local **solid waste management** and planning must conform with a county plan developed in coordination with the county cities. The state scheme for **solid waste management** and disposal and the implementation of that scheme through adoption of county plans does not contemplate nor require dedication of a landfill operation for a public park or open spaces upon cessation of operations. While dedication of property for street purposes as a condition to issuance of a building permit to accommodate the increase in traffic occasioned by the proposed improvement is proper . . . the initiative dedication requirement, i.e., the taking of landfill property upon cessation of use, is the price a landowner or operator must pay in the implementation of state and local solid waste disposal plans. That price is clearly prohibited by the state statute (§ 65909)." *Wiltshire v. Superior Court* (Calif. Ct. App., 1985).

## SOLID WASTE TRANSFER FACILITY

**A place where solid waste materials are taken from a collection vehicle, temporarily stored or stockpiled, and ultimately moved to another facility.**

***Legal Annotation***: "The original language prohibited the operation of 'any treatment or disposal facility' without a certificate. . . . In 1987, the language was modified to require certification of a '**solid waste management facility**.' . . . The term '**solid waste management facility**' is undefined in statute, but the regulation definition of 'solid waste management' includes 'activities that result . . . in the disposal of solid waste.' . . . We conclude that the change in terminology did not change Towns' substantive violation in any material respect." *Agency of Natural Resources v. Towns* (Vt., 2001).

## SOOT

**Agglomerations of tar-impregnated carbon particles that form when carbonaceous material does not undergo complete combustion.**

***Legal Annotation***: "The expert evidence is that where there is incomplete combustion in burners of this character carbon monoxide is given off; that very seldom are conditions ideal for complete combustion; and that whenever carbon—**soot**—is produced it indicates that combustion is not complete." *Rumsey v. Schollman Bros. Co.* (Neb., 1952).

## SORORITY HOUSE

**See *Fraternity House*.**

***Legal Annotation***: "(47). FRATERNITY/ **SORORITY HOUSE**: A building or part thereof which has only one (1) dining facility and one (1) kitchen and which is designed, intended and/

or used primarily for the lodging or activities of any club or association, a majority of whose local members are students at the Lock Haven State College." *Mullen v. Zoning Hearing Board* (Pa. Common. Pleas Ct., 1984).

## SOUND

**See *Noise*.**

***Legal Annotation***: "The City enacted ordinance number 97-4019, which created, among other things, section 8-322.1(a) of the Sarasota Zoning Code. The portion of the ordinance challenged in this proceeding prohibits all amplified **sound** in nonenclosed structures in the area zoned Commercial Business-Newtown (CBN), during certain hours of each day, regardless of the decibel level of the **sound** being produced and regardless of whether the **sound** is audible outside the structure. The challenged portion of the ordinance provides: Amplified sound prohibited: Amplified **sound** not in a completely enclosed structure is prohibited between the hours of 10:00 PM and 7:00 AM the following morning on Sunday through Thursday, inclusive, except the day prior to a holiday, or between the hours of 11:59 PM and 10:00 AM the following morning, on Friday, Saturday, and the day prior to a holiday. This section shall not apply to structures or portions thereof used primarily for residential purposes. 'Amplified **sound**' is defined as the 'using or operating for any purpose, or permitting the operation or use for any purpose, any amplification system or any amplified radio, phonograph, tape player, television set, musical instrument, drum or similar device which is amplified.' 'Amplified' is defined as 'to increase the strength, amount of or loudness of a device.' The ordinance defines 'completely enclosed building' instead of 'completely enclosed structure' and requires all doors and windows of a business to remain closed, except for normal ingress and egress." *Daley v. City of Sarasota* (Fla. Ct. App., 2000).

## SOUND LEVEL

**The weighted sound pressure obtained by use of a meter with an A-weighting as specified in the ANSI specifications for sound level meters.**

***Legal Annotation***: "The Zoning Ordinance requires 'objectionable' noises to be muffled but to an unknown extent and by unknown means. ZONING ORDINANCE § 205-105(B). It states that noise in residential areas may not exceed the acceptable maximum **sound pressure level** for residential areas measured with a sound level meter from the closest residence and conforming to standards prescribed by [ANSI]." *HHI Trucking & Supply v. Oakmont Bor. Coun.* (Pa. Common. Ct., 2010).

## SOURCE PROPERTY

**The property from which the subject sound is originating, including public or private streets, sidewalks, or other public or open-space areas.**

***Legal Annotation***: "It was only some three years earlier that the town, in 1977, had adopted the ordinance with which we here are concerned. At its heart is its section 3.01, which, after a blanket provision that '[n]o person shall make . . . any unnecessary noise', defines the last phrase, among other things, as 'any excessive or unusually loud sound or any sound which either annoys, disturbs, injures or endangers the comfort, repose, health, peace or safety of a person'. Section 2 of the ordinance lists 10 'standards to be considered in determining whether unnecessary noise exists in a given situation', while expressly stipulating that these are not to be exclusive. The 10 are as follows: . . . (i) whether the **sound source** is temporary." *People v. NY Trap Rock Corp.*, (N.Y. 1982).

## SPECIAL ASSESSMENT

**A fee levied by a local authority for the financing of a local improvement that is primarily of benefit to the landowners who must pay the assessment.**

***Legal Annotation***: "'A **special assessment** is a levy upon property within a specified district. Although it resembles a tax, a **special assessment** is not a tax. In contrast to a tax, a special assessment is imposed to defray the costs of specific local improvements, rather than to raise revenue for general governmental purposes.' . . . In Blake v. Metro. Chain Stores . . . our Supreme Court set out the test for distinguishing the two: 'The differences between a **special assessment** and a tax are that (1) a **special assessment** can be levied only on land; (2) a **special assessment** cannot (at least in most States) be made a personal liability of the person assessed; (3) a **special assessment** is based wholly on benefits; and (4) a **special assessment** is exceptional both as to time and locality.'" *Michigan's Adventure, Inc. v. Dalton Tp.* (Mich. Ct. App., 2010).

## SPECIAL EXCEPTION USE

**See *Conditional Use*.** http://www.census.govs/local/definition.html

***Legal Annotation***: "[A] **special exception use** is an additional use which the controlling zoning ordinance states will be allowed in a given zone unless there is a showing that the use would have unique adverse effects on the neighboring properties." *MBC Realty, LLC v. Baltimore* (Md. Ct. Spec. App., 2010).

## SPECIAL FLOOD HAZARD AREA (SFHA)

**The land area covered by the floodwaters of the base flood (FEMA regulations). See *Flood Hazard Area*.**

***Comment***: The SFHA is the area where the National Flood Insurance Program's (NFIP's) floodplain management regulations must be enforced and the area where the mandatory purchase of flood insurance applies.

***Legal Annotation***: "A '**Special Flood Hazard Area**' is defined in the SFIP as '[a]n area having special flood or mudflow, and/or flood-related erosion hazards, and shown on a Flood Hazard Boundary Map or Flood Insurance Rate Map as Zone A, AO, A1-A30, AE, A99, AH, AR, AR/A, AR/AE, AR/AH, AR/AO, AR/A1-A30, V1-V30, VE, or V.' 44 C.F.R. pt. 61 app. A(1), art. II(B)(26)." *Davis v. Nationwide Mutual Fire Insurance Company* (E.D. Va., 2011).

## SPECIAL IMPROVEMENT DISTRICT (SID)

**A district, with the power to levy taxes, created by legislative act, petition, or vote of the residents or owners for a specific purpose.**

***Comment***: Special improvement districts have been very effective in assisting in the revitalization of local business areas. Their work primarily focuses on cleanliness and safety but also includes recommendations on building façades and signage, coordinating special events and programs, streetscape improvement, development of off-street parking, liaison with officials and elected representatives, and providing district maintenance. Some SIDs deploy "community service representatives," uniformed individuals who "serve as the eyes and ears for police and other code enforcement agencies." An important reason for the effectiveness of SIDs is their ability to tax themselves and channel the additional revenues into programs directly benefiting the district (Levy 2001; Houston 2004). **See *Business Improvement District*.**

***Legal Annotation***: "'Section 6. That the character of the improvements to be made in said **Special Improvement District** is hereby declared to be as follows: The construction of pipes, hydrants and hose connections for irrigating appliances and fire protection; all of which improvements are to be made in accordance with the plans and specifications to be prepared by the engineer of the town of Ryegate and to be adopted by the council of said town, and which plans and specifications will then be on file in the office of the town clerk, and to which reference is hereby made and by such reference are made a part hereof to all intents and purposes the same as though said plans and specifications were fully set forth and incorporated at length in this resolution.' The resolution also provided that the district to be created was 'for the purpose of making special improvements upon and along that portion of Railway Avenue, Second Avenue and the alley between Third and Fourth Avenues, and the alley between Fourth Avenue and the avenue next north of Fourth Avenue, from Harkins Street on the west and the street next east of Second Street on the east, including all avenues, streets and alley intersections.'" *Lumbermen's Trust Co. v. Town of Ryegate* (9th Cir., 1932).

## SPECIAL USE PERMIT

**A permit issued by the proper governmental authority, that must be acquired before a special exception use can be implemented. See *Conditional Use Permit*.**

***Legal Annotation***: "As the statute implies, the terms 'special use' and 'conditional use' are used interchangeably . . . and a conditional use or a **special use permit** 'is one issued for a use which the ordinance expressly permits in a designated zone upon proof that certain facts and conditions detailed in the ordinance exist.'" *Coastal Ready-Mix, Etc. v. Bd. of Com'rs, Etc.* (N.C., 1980).

## SPECIALTY FOOD STORE

**A retail store specializing in a specific type or class of foods, such as a bakery, butcher, delicatessen, fish market, or gourmet shop.**

***Legal Annotation***: "In 1959, the city adopted an ordinance which zoned plaintiff's property residential. Although the property is located in a residential area, plaintiff has used the property for commercial purposes since 1941. [This includes a catering service known as the Bowman Farm Cupboard, and a delicatessen and **specialty food store**.] Other uses include a picnic ground, a site for a wedding ceremonial service, and a guest house or apartment. Because of commercial use prior to enactment of the zoning ordinance, plaintiff acquired a nonconforming use which, of course, permits plaintiff to continue using the property as before, but places certain limits upon what may be done by way of altering or rebuilding structures on the nonconforming premises. When plaintiff was refused a building permit to make certain alterations, this suit was filed." *Bowman v. City of Southfield* (Mich., 1966).

## SPECIALTY SHOPPING CENTER

**(1) A shopping center whose shops cater to a specific market and are linked together by an architectural, historical, or geographic theme or by a commonality of goods and services; also known as a theme or fashion center; (2) a retail center of between one hundred thousand and two hundred thousand square feet consisting mostly of small shops with distinctive, one-of-a-kind merchandise with emphasis on arts and crafts supplied locally. See *Minimall; Shopping Center*.**

***Legal Annotation***: "Mr. Kinser proposes to develop the existing house into a specialty shopping center, consisting of small shops, the development of necessary parking facilities to be used in common with the dinner theater, possible additional retail facilities and, depending on financial feasibility, the eventual construction of apartments on presently undeveloped portions of the property." *Dixon v. Kinser* (N.C. Ct. App., 1981).

## SPECIFICATIONS

**Detailed instructions that designate the quality and quantity of materials and workmanship expected in the construction of a structure.**

***Legal Annotation***: "The agreement which the plaintiff Brodsky and the defendant corporation signed contained all of these elements, except the fourth which is not relevant to this case. The defendant contends that building **specifications** are an essential ingredient to a binding contract. The agreement, however, did not on its face leave anything to speculation but specified the amount of factory and air-conditioned office floor space. This agreement would imply a physical plant reasonably suited to defendant's manufacturing and office needs. No more certain **specifications** are needed for purposes of enforcing this lease agreement." *Brodsky v. Allen Hayosh Ind., Inc.* (Mich: Court of Appeals 1965).

## SPECIMEN TREE

**A particularly impressive or unusual example of a species because of its size, shade, age, or any other trait that epitomizes the character of the species (American Planning Association, *Preparing a Landscaping Ordinance*, Planning Advisory Service Report No. 431, 1990).**

*Legal Annotation*: "Valley Crest's business activities include buying and selling **specimen trees**, which are large trees not commonly grown in a nursery. In early 2004, Erick Serrano, a tree procurer for Valley Crest's specimen tree division, left a note on the gate to the property indicating Valley Crest was interested in purchasing some of the coast live oak trees on the property." *Lukic v. Valley Crest Tree Company* (Calif. Ct. App., 2011).

## SPEED HUMPS

**See *Traffic Calming*.**

*Legal Annotation*: "The report states that the residents of Newcomb Boulevard reported two major concerns: speeding and cut-through traffic. The report concludes that speeding exists and recommends the use of **speed humps** as a traffic calming measure. The report, however, recommends that '[f]urther study should be considered before implementation of such devices.'" *Huston v. City of New Orleans* (La. Ct. App., 2013).

## SPEED TABLES

**See *Traffic Calming*.**

*Legal Annotation*: "The enhancements included reducing the number of lanes on the avenue from four to two to promote a safer bicycle and pedestrian environment; community identity markers; traffic calming features, such as **speed tables** at crosswalks; bulb-outs at intersections to reduce crosswalk lengths; decorative pavement bands; outdoor seating areas; enhanced bicycle parking; information kiosks; newspaper racks; landscape improvements; enhanced and additional on-street parking; and redevelopment of the Caltrain plaza." *Ogawa v. City of Palo Alto* (Calif. Ct. App., 2013).

## SPEED-CHANGE LANE

**An auxiliary lane, deceleration lane, or acceleration lane, including tapered areas, primarily for the deceleration or acceleration of vehicles entering or leaving the through-traffic lanes.**

*Legal Annotation*: "Under 'Entering the Freeway,' the handbook advises: '1. You must yield the right-of-way to vehicles already on the freeway. 2. Enter the **speed change lane**, stay to the right, signal left, and when the way is clear increase your speed so you can merge with the flow of traffic.'" *Mahaffey v. State* (Tex. Ct. App., 2010).

## SPILLWAY

**A passageway through which excess water escapes from a waterbody.**

*Legal Annotation*: "In order to ensure that an inlet small enough to cause a temporary lake in the basin in light rains will nonetheless empty the basin within 2 days of heavy rains, a **spillway** is provided to carry around the barrier that water which is in excess of the volume which the inlet can handle in this period." *Karch v. US* (Ct. Cl., 1977).

## SPILLWAY, EMERGENCY

**The spillway capable of passing the spillway design storm with the principal and/or auxiliary spillway blocked.**

*Legal Annotation*: "In light of Hicks's statement that a 'standpipe and an **emergency spillway**' were constructed to guard against spoil basin overflow, we note that a 'pipe' from which pollutants are discharged may be a point source of pollution." *Sierra Club v. Abston Const. Co, Inc.* (Court of Appeals, 5th Cir. 1980). http://tinyurl.com/nec7bwt

"The **emergency spillway** is a 243.4-foot long low grassy embankment on the southwest corner of the reservoir. It was installed in 1971 and enlarged in 2002 to its current size. It is designed so that if the water in the reservoir gets too high, it will overtop the **emergency spillway** so that the reservoir does not fail. The emergency spillway has never been overtopped." *Seiler v. Norwalk* (Ohio Ct. App., 2011).

## SPLIT-LOT ZONING

**A lot or single parcel of land located in two or more zones.**

*Comment*: As a general rule, a lot should be located in a single zone. Occasionally, because of topography or platting that took place before modern subdivision techniques, single lots may be in two or more zones. One way to overcome the problem is to permit a zone line to be shifted to the lot line if the lot line and zone line are within twenty-five feet of each other.

A common example is a through lot, with half of the lot fronting on a commercial street and zoned for commercial use and the rear fronting on a residential street and zoned residential. In this example, the shifting of the lot line may not be a practical way to reconcile the problem. The lot, for example, might be too deep and the lot line and zoning boundary not within twenty-five feet of each other. In addition, if the lines were shifted arbitrarily, it might result in an inappropriate mix of land uses.

If the zone line is maintained and the lot remains split, all use and bulk requirements for the specific zone apply only to that part of the lot in that zone. The land area in the residential zone cannot be used to determine the floor area for the commercially zoned parcel, and the land in the commercial part of the lot cannot be used to establish the number of dwelling units to be built on the residential part of the lot. In addition, the setback lines are measured from the zone boundary line. If the ordinance calls for a rear yard setback of fifty feet for the commercial property, that setback is measured from the zone boundary line dividing the lot.

There are exceptions, however. For example, in *AMG Associates v. Tp. Of Springfield*, 65 N.J. 101 (1974), the New Jersey Supreme Court (the state's highest court) ruled that a property owner could use the rear part of his property, which was zoned residential, to provide parking for the commercial use on the front of the property. But in this situation, the residentially zoned parcel could be accessed only through the commercial part of the lot, and the residentially zoned part was less than the minimum required for residential development. In this case, a variance would have been justified on the basis of hardship, since the strict application of the law would have rendered the rear portion unusable.

*Legal Annotation*: "As noted, the property is '**split-zoned**', approximately 7500 square feet of lot 304 lies in the R-8 residential zone and the remaining 60,000 square feet of the property lies in the M-2 limited industrial district zone. The portion of lot 304 in the R-8 zone begins at the property's southernmost point abutting Little Falls Road and proceeds north along Little Falls Road for fifty feet, and east into the property approximately 150 feet. . . . Recchia places great emphasis on a statement in the 1997 reexamination report stating that '[a]ll **split-lot zoning** should be reviewed and modified as appropriate.' This statement is not specific enough to support a finding of substantial inconsistency simply because the property in question is **split-zoned**." *Victor Recchia Res. Const. v. Zoning Board of Adjustment of Tp. of Cedar Grove* (N.J., 2001).

## SPOIL

**Dirt, rock, or waste material that has been removed from its original location, or materials that have been dredged from the bottoms of waterways.**

*Legal Annotation*: "In performing hydraulic dredging Rambo would first use a cutter head to penetrate the bottom of the bay and suck up water and sediment, called dredge **spoil**. The **spoil** is then suspended and pumped to a spoil disposal site in a diked area. The spoil was carried by a pipe, called the dredge pipe, approximately 1,500 feet in length to the diked area." *Matter of Jackson's Marina, Inc. v. Jorling* (N.Y. App. Div., 1993).

## SPORTS COURT

**Paved surfaces, designed and built to accommodate a variety of athletic purposes or recreational pastimes, such as tennis, basketball, and roller hockey, typically located in the rear yard of a single-family residence.**

*Comment*: An increasingly popular alternative to single-purpose courts for tennis or basketball, sports courts are designed for "backyard" use for more than one sport and are not regulation-sized.

***Legal Annotation***: "Plaintiff built a **sports court** in his backyard without obtaining a building permit or the required township approvals. . . . The parties do not dispute that the **sports court** is an accessory use and a 'principal use permitted' in the residential district where it is located." *Perlman v. Charter Township of Bloomfield* (Mich. Ct. App., 2008).

## SPOT ZONING

**Rezoning of a lot or parcel of land to benefit an owner for a use that is not permitted in the surrounding area, where there is no compelling reason or public benefit, and where it does not further the comprehensive plan.**

***Comment***: The rezoning of a small parcel for a use that is not permitted in the surrounding area may not be considered as illegal spot zoning, even if this is done at the request of a single owner and accords that owner with a benefit. The key is whether there is also a compelling reason and public need or benefit, and whether it was undertaken in furtherance of a comprehensive plan or master plan.

***Legal Annotation***: "'The term "**spot zoning**" is ordinarily used where a zoning ordinance is amended reclassifying one or more tracts or lots for a use prohibited by the original zoning ordinance and out of harmony therewith.' . . . The specific facts of each case dictate whether an amendment to the ordinance is considered void. . . . The case law consistently has invalidated zoning ordinances on the basis of **spot-zoning**, where the zoning ordinances 'were designed "to favor" someone.' . . . See 1 Yokley, Zoning Law and Practice §§ 8-1 to 8-3 (3d ed. 1965). Recently, this Court stated 'an example of an arbitrary or discriminatory zoning decision is "**spot zoning**."' . . . This Court has defined **spot-zoning** as 'a small island of relatively intense use surrounded by a sea of less intense use.' . . . However, [t]he mere fact that an area is small and is zoned at the request of a single owner and is of greater benefit to him than to others does not make out a case of spot zoning if there is a public need for it or a compelling reason for it.' . . . Likewise, this Court has stated that '[w]e are of the opinion that although a zoning ordinance or amendment creates in the center of a large zone a small area or a district devoted to a different use, it is not spot zoning if it is enacted in accordance with a comprehensive zoning plan.'" *Board of Sup'rs of Panola County* (Miss., 2010).

## SPRAWL

**Poorly planned, auto-dependent growth, usually of a low-density, single-use nature, in previously rural areas and some distance from existing development and infrastructure.**

***Comment***: Sprawl is typically an automobile-dependent, single-use, resource-consuming, discontinuous, low-density development pattern (*New Jersey State Development and Redevelopment Plan* 2002). Urban sprawl is now recognized as a direct result of national policies that encourage the dispersal of urban growth and is being challenged by proponents of "smart growth." **See *Smart Growth.* See *Also*** Duany et al. 2000.

***Legal Annotation***: "Importantly, plaintiff alleges no actual injury or threat of injury to its interests arising from the construction of the water pipeline itself. Rather, it is the generalized threat of future urban development in and around Veneta and the presumed traffic increase on Highway 126 that fuels this lawsuit. However, alleged harm from urbanization or '**sprawl**' is nothing more than a 'generalized grievance' of wide public concern that courts have repeatedly found insufficient to confer standing." *Landwatch Lane County v. United States Fish and Wildlife Service* (D. Ore., 2012).

## SQUARE

**A public open space in a developed area. See *Court; Plaza.***

***Legal Annotation***: "The court said in Headley that a public **square** is commonly intended to be 'an open tract of land for use for purposes of free passage or of ornamentation and improvement as grounds of pleasure, amusement, recreation, or health' to which all members of the public have free access. . . . The court found that using the public **square** as a high school athletic field and playground would be inconsistent with the purpose for which the **square** was dedicated because it would necessitate the exclusion of the general public from the **square**. . . . Accordingly, the court enjoined the city from carrying out its plan. In the instant case, construction of a senior citizen's residence on the public **square** property would make it impossible to use the property in the manner in which a public **square** is customarily used and would entail the exclusion of the general public from the property. The trial court was therefore correct in enjoining plaintiff from selling the property or terminating or otherwise interfering with its use as a public **square**." *City of Zumbrota v. Strafford Western Em. Co.* (Minn., 1980).

## SQUATTER

**A person who settles on land without the permission of the owner.**

***Legal Annotation***: "A **squatter** is 'one who settles on another's land without legal title or authority.' See *Black's Law Dictionary 1258 (5th Ed. 1979)." Us V. Murray (D. V.I.*, 2010).

## STABILIZATION

**As pertaining to streets, the ability of a surface to resist deformation from imposed loads.**

***Comment***: Stabilization can be accomplished by adequate thickness of asphalt base and surface course, dense graded aggregates, cement-treated soil aggregates, or concrete or precast masonry units set on a base course (N.J.A.C. 5:21-1.4). Stabilization is a term also used in connection with ensuring that steeply sloped areas that have been regraded are "stabilized" so as to prevent soil erosion, or collapse in the case of mining and tunneling.

***Legal Annotation***: "[T]he combination of perched water which resulted from poor drainage, the lack of subgrade **stabilization**, and repeated dynamic loads by vehicular traffic [were] the major contributing factors to the pavement distress. . . . The repeated dynamic vehicular traffic loads usually liquefy the existing loose and wet silty sands. Once the silty sands liquefy, they lose their strength and become unable to transfer the loads to the surrounding subgrade." *LBM Investments, Inc. v. Caribe Properties, Inc.* (Tex. Ct. App., 2013).

## STABILIZED BASE COURSE (BITUMINOUS)

**Soil aggregate and bituminous material uniformly mixed and placed on a previously prepared surface.**

***Legal Annotation***: "Meco submitted a bid in the amount of $876,921. Its bid contained the following unit prices for asphalt concrete: 15,680 square yards of **Bituminous Stabilized Base** Course Mix I-2 (Item 3.1) at $13.50, totaling $211,680." *Meco, Inc. v. Township Of Freehold* (N.J. App. Div., 2011).

## STABILIZED TURF OR EARTH

**Turf or earth (soil) strengthened usually by the mixing of cement, lime, or other building material with the original soil. See *Stabilized Base Course; Soil Cement*.**

***Comment***: The mixing achieves increased strength, thereby reducing shrinkage and movement (N.J.A.C. 5:21-1.4).

***Legal Annotation***: "Among other things, the contract called for the construction of a concrete pilot channel to reroute drainage from the roadside into the river at a point away from the concrete headwalls of the bridge. The plans called for the channel to be five feet wide, with five feet of **stabilized earth** fill on each side of the channel." *Foreman v. Allen Keller Co.* (Tex. Ct. App., 2009).

## STABLE

**A structure that is used for the shelter or care of horses and cattle.**

***Legal Annotation***: "A '**stable**' may be either 'private' or 'public,' and a 'public **stable**' is defined as a 'building in which any horses are kept for remuneration, hire or sale.' Zoning Ordinance,

§ 201." *Tennyson v. ZHB of West Bradford Tp.* (Pa. Common. Ct., 2008).

## STACK

**A smokestack, vertical pipe, chimney, flue, conduit, or opening designed to exhaust gases and suspended particulate matter into the outdoor air.**

***Legal Annotation***: "The Agency issued Cargill a permit to make the modifications, but imposed several special conditions. Accord was reached on all conditions except special condition nine, which provided: 'The height of the incinerator discharge **stack** shall be raised to 100 feet above grade. The incinerator shakedown and emission testing may be performed with the existing short **stack**; however, incinerator operation will not be allowed until the stack has been raised to the specified 100 feet.' . . . Cargill attempted to obtain a variance from the Village for a 100-foot stack. The Village, however, refused to grant one. . . . Cargill next claims, in a cursory manner, that the amendment to section 39(c) is unconstitutional because it will result in a denial of due process and equal protection, and constitutes both a taking of property and special legislation." *Village of Carpentersville v. PCB* (Ill., 1990).

## STACKED FLAT

**A single-level apartment placed on top of another single-level apartment, as in a multistory apartment building.**

***Comment***: The term "flat" is synonymous with apartment.

## STACKED TOWNHOUSE

**See *Dwelling, Stacked Townhouse*.**

## STADIUM

**A large open or enclosed place used for games and major events and partly or completely surrounded by tiers of seats for spectators.**

***Comment***: Stadiums may include locker and training rooms as well as eating and drinking establishments and sports-related retail stores as accessory to the principal use.

***Legal Annotation***: "In *Martin v. City of Philadelphia* (1966) 420 Pa. 14 [215 A.2d 894], the Pennsylvania Supreme Court sustained an ordinance which authorized a loan to construct a sports stadium, declaring: 'A **sports stadium** is for the recreation of the public and is hence for a public purpose; for public projects are not confined to providing only the bare bones of municipal life, such as police protection, streets, sewers, light, and water; they may provide gardens, parks, monuments, fountains, libraries, [and] museums.'. . . Indeed, as long ago as 1930 an Ohio appellate court discovered numerous examples of such publicly owned facilities across the country: 'In fact, within the forty-eight states of the Union ninety-three municipal stadiums have been erected, or are in the process of erection.'" *City of Oakland v. Oakland Raiders* (Calif., 1982).

## STAGGERED WORK HOURS

**Work schedules that permit employees to arrive and leave at different hours, either individually or by department.**

***Legal Annotation***: "Employees value a job for many reasons besides the rate of pay, including, for example, the presence of other workers of the employee's own sex, the availability of recreational facilities at the worksite, **staggered work hours**, better health benefits, longer vacations, and so forth. What makes one job better than another varies from one employee to another." *Ford Motor Co. v. EEOC* (U.S., 1982).

## STALL

**(1) A booth, cubicle, or stand used by a vendor, such as in a market or shopping mall, in which merchandise is displayed and sometimes sold. *See* Kiosk. (2) A compartment in a barn or shed used for the accommodation of a domestic animal, such as a horse. (3) A pew in a church.**

## STALL, PARKING

**See *Parking Stall*.**

## STANDARD OF LIVING

**A measure of the adequacy of necessities and comforts in an individual's daily life in comparison to the general populace.**

*Legal Annotation*: "'**Standard of living**' is defined as 'a minimum of necessities, comforts, or luxuries that is essential to maintaining a person in customary or proper status or circumstances.' Webster's Third New International Dictionary 2223 (1986)." *Howell v. Howell* (Utah Ct. App., 1991).

## STANDPIPE

**See *Water Tower*.**

*Legal Annotation*: "A **standpipe** is an elevated tank. The capacities of the tanks range from 2 million gallons to 250 thousand gallons." *Bristol Cty. Water Co. v. Harsch* (R.I., 1978).

## STATIONARY SOURCE

**A nonmobile emitter of pollution. See *Area Source; Point Source*.**

*Legal Annotation*: "A '**stationary source**' is 'any building, structure, facility or installation which emits or may emit any air pollutant.' . . . An 'area source [is] any **stationary source** . . . that is not a major source.'" *National Min. Ass'n v. USEPA* (D.C. Cir., 1995).

## STEEP SLOPE

**Land areas where the slope exceeds 20 percent.**

***Comment***: Use of the 20 percent figure is somewhat arbitrary. The major point is that construction on slopes in excess of 20 percent requires additional safeguards against erosion and other potential problems. Some ordinances reduce the allowable intensity of development on steep slopes.

*Legal Annotation*: "A **steep slope** is a '[l]and area where the inclination of the land's surface from the horizontal is twelve (12) percent or greater. Article 1311.04(a)(110) of the Ordinance. The following building restrictions apply to areas of **steep slopes**: (1) Twelve (12) to less than fifteen (15) percent slope: no more than forty (40) percent of such areas shall be developed and/or regraded or stripped of vegetation. (2) Fifteen (15) to twenty-five (25) percent slope: no more than thirty percent (30) of such areas shall be developed and/or regraded or stripped of vegetation, with the exception that no more than twenty (20) percent of such areas may be disturbed in the case of landslide prone area. (3) More than twenty-five (25) percent slope: no more than fifteen (15) percent of such areas shall be developed and/or regraded or stripped of vegetation, with the exception that no more than five (5) percent of such areas may be disturbed in the case of landslide prone area.'" *Jones v. Zoning Hearing Bd.* (Pa. Common. Ct., 1990).

## STORAGE

**The storing of an item in a fixed location for a specific or unspecified period of time.**

*Legal Annotation*: "The common element among the definitions of '**storage**' discussed previously in this opinion is that an item must be in a fixed location for an extended period of time. As stated previously, the general comprehensive dictionaries define '**storage**' as the act of putting an item away for future use. Within the context of § 3.3.A.7, defining '**storage**' as leaving in place for more than a transient period of time on a regular or continuing basis, as occurred in this case, a commercial vehicle of over 1000 pound capacity for future use, leads to a workable result because it does not provide a definition completely divorced from the context in which the regulation was created. This definition is broader than the definition set forth in The Latest Illustrated Book of Development Definitions for which the plaintiffs advocate, but it is not limited to the storage of goods as is the definition in The Latest Illustrated Book of Development Definitions. Interpreting '**storage**' in accordance with the general dictionaries' definitions provides a reasonable interpretation of the term that harmonizes the definition with the context of [the ordinance]." *Grissler v. Zoning Board of Appeals of the Town of New Canaan* (Conn. App. Ct., 2013).

## STORAGE, OUTDOOR

See *Outdoor Storage*.

## STORM SEWER

See *Sewer, Storm*.

## STORM SURGE

**Rise in the level of the ocean that results from the increase in atmospheric pressure associated with hurricanes and other storms. (Source: FEMA, *Hazard Mitigation and the National Flood Insurance Program [NFIP]*.)**

*Legal Annotation*: "**Storm surge** is a wind driven process: the wind puts energy into the sea surface through the waves and currents. The greater the wind, the greater the storm surge will be." *In Re Katrina Canal Breaches Consolidated Litigation* (E.D. La., 2013).

## STORMWATER DETENTION

**Any storm drainage technique that retards or detains runoff, such as a detention basin, parking lot or rooftop detention, porous pavement, dry wells, or any combination thereof. See *Detention Basin; Retention Basin*.**

*Legal Annotation*: "She alleged that the City's negligent maintenance or design of a **stormwater detention** pond, located north of the intersection where Nathan drowned, had caused debris to clog a grate covering the pond's designed drainage outlet, resulting in storm waters backing up and ultimately overflowing the pond, flooding the adjacent residential area and causing Nathan's death. . . . The location and basic features of the detention pond are undisputed. The Tanglewood Forest regional detention pond (designated 'Pond 342' by the City) lies in the Slaughter Creek watershed in southwest Austin. It is bordered to the north by Slaughter Lane and by residential areas on its other sides. Designed to temporarily detain storm water, Pond 342 consists mostly of a large grassy field, roughly the size of six football fields, bordered by a grassy embankment. The large field is also used for recreational purposes like soccer. On the northern side of Pond 342 are inlet pipes designed to channel drainage from areas north of Slaughter Lane. Flow channels cross the pond leading to an outlet structure located at its southwestern corner—a 66-inch outlet pipe, leading to a grass-lined spillway channel and other drainage structures designed to divert storm water ultimately into a tributary of Slaughter Creek. Covering the outlet pipe at all relevant times has been some sort of metal grate." *City of Austin v. Leggett* (Texas Ct. App., 2008).

## STORMWATER MAINTENANCE FACILITIES

**The various improvements—such as swales, curbs, catch basins, trunk sewers, collector sewers, and detention and retention basins—composing the system that accommodates and controls stormwater runoff. See *Stormwater Detention*.**

*Comment*: While there is agreement as to what elements the stormwater maintenance system consists of, responsibility for their maintenance often generates controversy. Generally speaking, improvements on private property are the responsibility of the private party. From time to time, however, improvements on private property are taken over by a public entity because of public safety and health concerns. For example, a detention basin serving a large drainage area might become the maintenance responsibility of the public entity because of flooding concerns beyond the private property that the basin serves.

In cases where the public assumes the responsibility for the maintenance of these facilities on private property, access easements from the public road to the facilities should be provided and the facility itself included in a dedication, either by subdivision or easement, to the public entity.

*Legal Annotation*: "The trial court concluded that: [p]laintiff is entitled to complete the construction of the Cheddar Close subdivision with the **stormwater maintenance facilities**, including the VorTechnics unit, detention basin and drywells . . . that have been approved by the [NJDEP] in accordance with the permit issued to the plaintiff by the NJDEP." *Friendship, Inc. v. Township of New Hanover* (N.J. App. Div., 2012).

## STORMWATER MANAGEMENT

**The control and management of stormwater to minimize the detrimental effects of surface water runoff.**

*Comment*: For new development, stormwater management regulations usually apply only to any net increase in stormwater runoff generated by such development activity (Berkooz 2011).

*Legal Annotation*: "The Hollises and Robinsons' expert testified that **stormwater management** is a field of engineering that prevents the type of severe flooding, erosion, and sediment accumulation that eventually occurred on the Hollis and Robinson property. The plans Power Engineering prepared for Stonington included protective measures such as silt fences and detention ponds to catch eroding soil and sediment runoff. Stonington failed to follow the plans, despite its admitted responsibility to do so." *Hollis v. Stonington Development, LLC* (S.C. Ct. App., 2011).

## STORMWATER RETENTION

**A storm drainage technique that allows for detention but that retains some of the stormwater in ponds or basins at all times. See *Stormwater Detention; Retention Basin*.**

*Legal Annotation*: "Admiral complains that its property is inundated during heavy rainstorms and floods to a greater extent than occurred prior to the construction of the shopping center. Admiral also alleges that the **storm water retention** system installed for the shopping center does not adequately contain floodwaters from the river nor retard the increased flow of rainwater from the development site to the river." *Admiral Builders Corp. v. Robert Hall Village* (Ill. App. Ct., 1981).

## STORY

**That portion of a building included between the surface of any floor and the surface of the floor next above it, or if there is no floor above it, then the space between the floor and the ceiling next above it, and including basements if the basement ceiling is greater than five feet above the average adjoining grade. See *Basement*. See *Figure 8*.**

*Comment*: While "story" is often used to limit height and size of buildings, a much more effective tool is "building height" in feet, as well as FAR (floor area ratio) for nonresidential buildings and "maximum density" (dwelling units per acre) for multifamily residences. In those cases where an applicant decides to expand a basement or cellar to create additional usable space, that expansion should not be counted as a story, providing there are no changes to the exterior of the building, the original use remains the same, and FAR or maximum density limits are not violated.

*Legal Annotation*: "Under the Zoning Code, a '**story**' is defined as: that portion of a building included between the surface of any floor and the surface of the next floor above it . . . not including cellar or basement." *Lench v. Zoning Bd. of Adjustment of City* (Pa. Common. Ct., 2011).

## STORY, HALF

**A space under a sloping roof that has the line of intersection of the roof and wall face not more than three feet above the floor level and in which space the possible floor area with headroom of five feet or less occupies at least 40 percent of the total floor area of the story directly beneath. *See Figure 92*.**

**Figure 92**

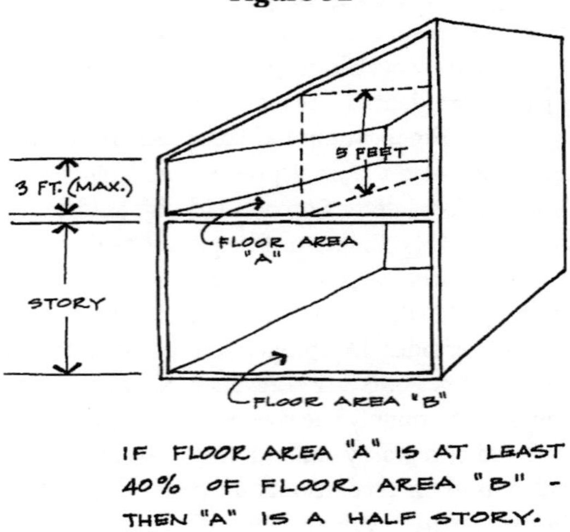

*Legal Annotation*: "A **half story** is defined in c. 26, § 1 (p), as 'a story which is situated in a sloping roof, the floor area of which does not exceed two-thirds of the floor area of the story immediately below it and which does not contain an independent apartment.'" *O'Connell v. Brockton Board of Appeals* (Mass., 1962).

## STREAM

**A watercourse having a source and terminus, banks, and a channel through which water flows continuously or periodically.**

*Comment*: Streams usually empty into other streams, rivers, lakes, or oceans but remain streams even if they are dry at certain times of the year. A watercourse that is dry at certain times of the year is known as an "intermittent stream."

*Legal Annotation*: "A **stream** is defined as 'a body of running waters of this state moving over the surface of the land in a channel or bed including stream types classified as perennial or intermittent and channelized or relocated streams.'" *Noble v. Department of Fish and Wildlife* (Ore. Ct. App., 2012).

## STREAM CORRIDOR

**Any river, stream, pond, lake, or wetland, together with adjacent upland areas, that supports protective bands of vegetation that line the water's edge.**

*Legal Annotation*: "The Metropolitan River Protection Act ('River Act') permits a planning commission for a metropolitan area with a population of one million or more persons to develop a comprehensive plan for land and water use along stream corridors when a stream supplies forty percent or more of the water for the metropolitan area. River Act, § 4. A '**stream corridor**' is all land within 2,000 feet of the water course. Sec. 2 (e). The planning commission is also authorized to develop plans for the fifty-year flood plain of the stream, land which probably will be flooded once every fifty years." *Pope v. City of Atlanta* (Ga., 1978).

## STREET

**Any vehicular way that is (1) an existing state, county, or municipal roadway; (2) shown upon a plat approved pursuant to law; (3) approved by other official action; (4) shown on a plat duly filed and recorded in the office of the county recording officer prior to the appointment of a planning board and the grant to such board of the power to review plats; (5) shown on the official map or adopted master plan. It includes the land between the street lines, whether improved or unimproved.**

*Comment*: See *Hellinovich (2008) On "Great" streets and neighborhood.*

*Legal Annotation*: "Section 19.04.515 defines a **street** as: a thoroughfare which has been dedicated or abandoned to the public and accepted by proper public authority, or a thoroughfare, not less than twenty-five feet wide, which has been made public by right of use and which affords the principal means of access to abutting property. Salt Lake County Code of Ordinances § 19.04.515 (1997). Thus, a **street** is a thoroughfare [We have defined a thoroughfare as 'a place or way through which there is passing or travel.'] that is (1) dedicated or abandoned to the public, or (2) made public by private right of use, and (3) the principal means of access to abutting property." *Culbertson v. Board of County Commissioners of Salt Lake County* (Utah, 2002).

## STREET, COLLECTOR

**A street that collects traffic from local streets and connects with minor and major arterials. See *Boulevard*. See *Figure 97*.**

*Comment*: Collector streets generally carry traffic within, but usually not between, neighborhoods. They also provide access to abutting land uses. Traffic volumes may vary between fifteen hundred and five thousand vehicles per day (ADT) but may drop as low as one thousand and go as high as seventy-five hundred, depending on the density and type of development. In some cases, where volumes are high, it may be useful to break down the category into "minor" and "major" collectors. Major collectors should not be used to provide access to abutting properties, and on-street parking is usually prohibited.

*Legal Annotation*: "A '**collector street**' is defined as: [a] street which carries traffic from minor streets to arterial or major streets, including the principal entrance streets of a residential development and the streets for circulation within such a development." *Sippel v. Franklin Park Borough* (Pa. Common. Ct., 2010).

## STREET, COMPLETE

**Roads that are planned, designed, operated, and maintained to enable safe, convenient, and comfortable travel and access for users of all ages and abilities, regardless of their mode of transportation.**

*Comment*: See *Smart Growth America, National Complete Streets Coalition, Complete Streets A To Z, For Details And Standards For "Complete Streets"; Mccann 2005: 18; Mccann And R*ynne 2010.

*Legal Annotation*: "5.18 GREEN **COMPLETE STREETS**

(A) PURPOSE

The purpose of the City's Green **Complete Street** regulation is to establish standards to safeguard life and property and promote and preserve public welfare and community aesthetics and to allow citizens to enjoy the use of streets and corridors within the city of La Crosse by the establishment of comprehensive standards, regulations and procedures governing the planning, design and construction or major construction of corridors within the City. The regulations found in this section attempt to balance the needs of all users of city streets and corridors including motorists, transit users, pedestrians and cyclists. The purpose of this ordinance is to ensure that the streets of the City of La Crosse provide safe, convenient, and comfortable routes for walking, bicycling, and public transportation, encourage increased use of these modes of transportation, enable convenient travel as part of daily activities, improve the public welfare by addressing a wide array of health and environmental problems, and meet the needs of all users of the streets, including children, older adults, and people with disabilities. This ordinance is further intended to provide a mechanism to combine the principles of **complete streets** and traffic calming with improving the stormwater quality and quantity problems that the City faces by incorporating stormwater considerations into each and every **complete street** or traffic calming activity where feasible." *La Crosse, Wisconsin Municipal Code, Chapter 5.*

## STREET, CUL-DE-SAC

**A street with a single common ingress and egress and with a turnaround at the end.** ***See Figures 93, 94, 95, and 96.***

*Comment*: Cul-de-sacs, by eliminating through traffic, provide a safe place for young children to play and can foster neighborhood social interaction. However, most designs do not encourage walking and biking, particularly when compared to the traditional neighborhood grid design. This deficiency can be remedied by including pedestrian and bikeway connections from the end of the cul-de-sac to the neighborhood grid system, to open spaces, and to other cul-de-sacs.

**Figure 93**

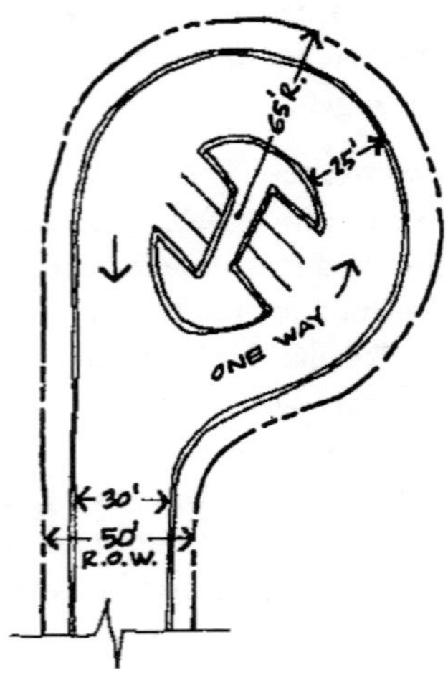


LARGE DIAMETER CUL-DE-SAC
(WITH CENTER ISLAND PARKING)

**Figure 94**

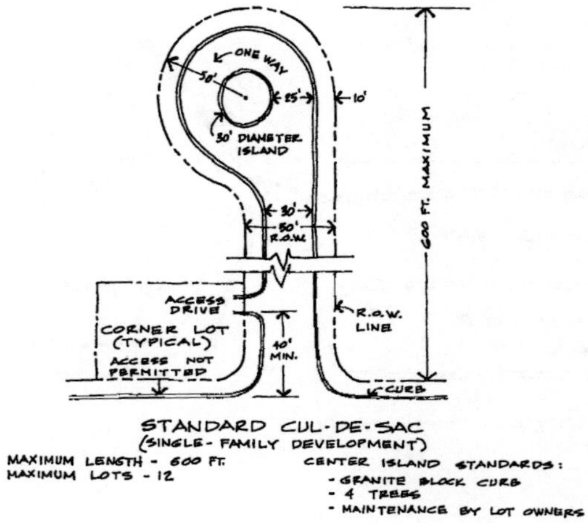


**Figure 95**

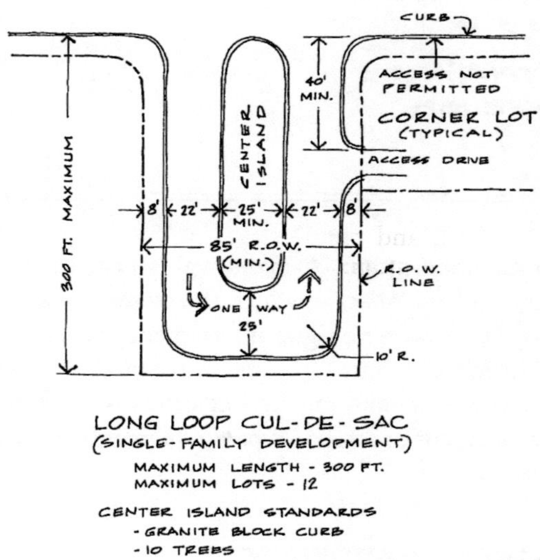


***Legal Annotation***: "Art. II, § B. A **cul-de-sac street** is defined as '[a] street connected to another street at one end only and provided with a turn-around space at its terminus.'" *Jasso v. Camas County* (Idaho, 2011).

## STREET, DEAD-END

**A street with a single common ingress and egress. See *Street, Cul-De-Sac*.**

***Legal Annotation***: "Accordingly, we agree with the dissenting justice in the Appellate Court that '[t]he language "turn-around roadway" strongly suggests that a **dead-end street** is one in which drivers would have to turn around in order to get out; hence, the minimum radius requirement for the turnaround. The language "closed end" also strongly suggests the same thing, namely, that a **dead-end street** is one that has an end that is closed to getting out; hence, the requirement that there be a right-of-way with a minimum width at the closed end.'" *Kraiza v. Planning and Zoning Com'n* (Conn., 2012).

## STREET, DUAL

**A street with opposing lanes separated by a median strip, center island, or other form of barrier, which cannot be crossed except at designated locations.**

***Legal Annotation***: "The dead-end street is designed as a **dual street** with a landscaped median over its entire length, which divides the dead-end street into two (2) distinct and separate lanes. The construction of the lanes, right-of-way, and median shall be constructed in accordance with VDOT standards. Median breaks shall be provided at every intersection and at other points at intervals of no more than three hundred (300) feet or as otherwise specified by the reviewing parties. Median breaks shall be designed to VDOT standards;" Development Standards, Article 5 Dead-End Streets, Public and Private. Sec. 17-701.05.E Streets. *Rockingham County, Virginia.* http://tinyurl.com/qjhxdo3

## STREET, EXPRESSWAY

**A divided, multilane highway for high-speed vehicular traffic with limited points of access or exit, having few if any intersections. *See Figure 97*.**

***Legal Annotation***: "An **expressway** is defined by subsection (c) of section 18 of Article 89B (1951 Code) as follows: 'The term "**expressway**" shall mean a major thoroughfare of two or more traffic lanes in each direction, designed to eliminate principal traffic hazards, and shall embrace all bridges, tunnels, overpasses, underpasses, interchanges, entrance plazas, approaches, and other

**Figure 96**

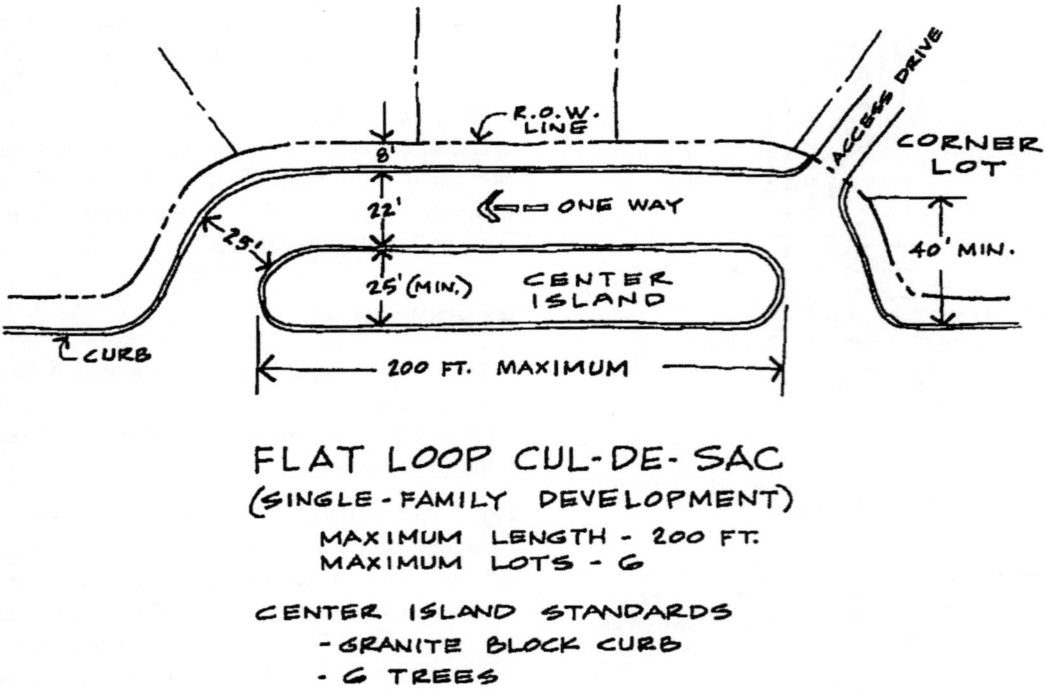


structures which the Commission may deem necessary to the operation of the **expressway**, together with all property, rights, easements, franchises and interests acquired by the Commission for the construction and operation thereof, and having the following characteristics: (a) a median divider separating opposing traffic lanes to eliminate head-on collisions and side-swiping; (b) grade separation structures to eliminate the conflict of cross streams of traffic at all intersections; (c) points of access and egress limited to predetermined locations; (d) vertical curves of lengths sufficient to provide long sight distances; and (e) shoulders of widths adequate to permit vehicles to stop or park off traffic lanes.'" *State Roads Comm. v. Franklin* (Md. Ct. App., 1953).

## STREET, FREEWAY

**A limited-access, multilane highway designed for high-speed vehicular traffic with no traffic signals, intersections, or at-grade crossings.** ***See Figure 97.***

*Legal Annotation*: "A '**freeway**' is defined as a highway in respect of which the owners of abutting lands have no right or easement of access to or from their abutting lands or in respect to which such owners have only limited or restricted right or easement of access." *People v. Thomas* (Calif. Ct. App., 1952).

## STREET HARDWARE

**Mechanical and utility systems, usually located within a street right-of-way, such as hydrants, manhole covers, tree grids, traffic signals, lighting standards, and directional signs.**

*Legal Annotation*: "Rather, because Administrative Code § 7-210 does not explicitly address this issue, the court examined the relevant sections of the Administrative Code that might address the kind of defect found here, and determined that a defective sign post was not the kind of 'hardware' referred to in Administrative Code § 19-147(d), which refers to 'hole (manhole) covers, castings, and other **street hardware**' required to be flush with the surrounding street." *Calise v. Millennium Partners* (N.Y. Sup. Ct., 2010).

## STREET HIERARCHY

**The conceptual arrangement of streets based on function. *See Figure 97.***

***Comment***: A hierarchal approach to street design classifies streets according to function, from major arterial roads that carry regional traffic between communities down to local streets where the principal function is to provide access to abutting land.

***Legal Annotation***: "Oldham Farms maintained that the residential **street hierarchy** in the subdivision regulations was only applicable to roads within the proposed subdivision plan; to find otherwise would preclude the development of any new subdivisions. . . . We likewise agree with the trial court that the Commission's interpretation was reasonable in light of the language of Articles V and VII; as a result there was no requirement that existing streets be classified using the residential **street hierarchy** found in Article I of the subdivision regulations." *Brooks v. Oldham County Planning Commission* (Ky. Ct. App., 2012).

## STREET, IMPROVED PUBLIC

**Any street that complies with the dimensional standards and construction specifications of the municipality, or a street meeting lesser standards that the municipality agrees to accept.**

***Legal Annotation***: "'Lot' is defined as: 'An area of land of sufficient size to meet zoning requirements for a permitted or special use. Such lot shall have frontage on an **improved public street**, or on an approved private street.'" *Constantine v. Village of Glen Ellyn* (Ill. App. Ct., 1991).

## STREET, LOCAL

**A street that provides frontage for access to abutting lots and carries slow-speed traffic primarily having a destination or origin on the street itself. *See Figure 97.***

***Comment***: Local streets are also known as residential access or neighborhood streets and are the lowest order of residential street, other than a rural street. They usually have rights-of-way of up to fifty feet and cartways of between twenty-four and twenty-eight feet with sidewalks and curbs. Parking is usually permitted on one side of the street if it is twenty-six feet wide, and on both sides of the street if it is twenty-eight feet or more in width. **See *Street, Cul-De-Sac; Street, Loop*.**

***Legal Annotation***: "A Class VI **local street** is defined as '[a] two-lane roadway which provides access directly to adjoining low/medium density land uses and conducts traffic to local limited and Class V streets which serve the area. The Class VI road is designed to accommodate low volumes of traffic at low speeds.'" *Myers Park Homeowners Association, Inc. v. City of Charlotte* (N.C. Ct. App., 2013).

## STREET, LOOP

**A local street that has its only ingress and egress at two points on the same collector or sub-collector street. *See Figure 97.***

***Legal Annotation***: "This is precisely why Connor, the defendant's planning consultant, advised the defendant that Eastwood Drive is not a dead-end street. See footnote 2 of this opinion. It is also the most likely explanation of why the defendant, in 1988, when it approved the eastwood subdivision, thereby approved Eastwood Drive: because it was not then, and is not now, a dead-end street within the meaning of those regulations. It is something else, namely, what can most aptly be described as a **loop street** or, perhaps, a lollipop street." *Kraiza v. Planning and Zoning Com'n* (Conn. App. Ct., 2010).

## STREET, MAJOR ARTERIAL

**A street that connects and distributes traffic to and from minor arterials, with access control, channelized intersections, and restricted parking. *See Figure 97.***

***Comment***: Major arterials carry regional traffic between communities at higher speeds and with

**Figure 97**

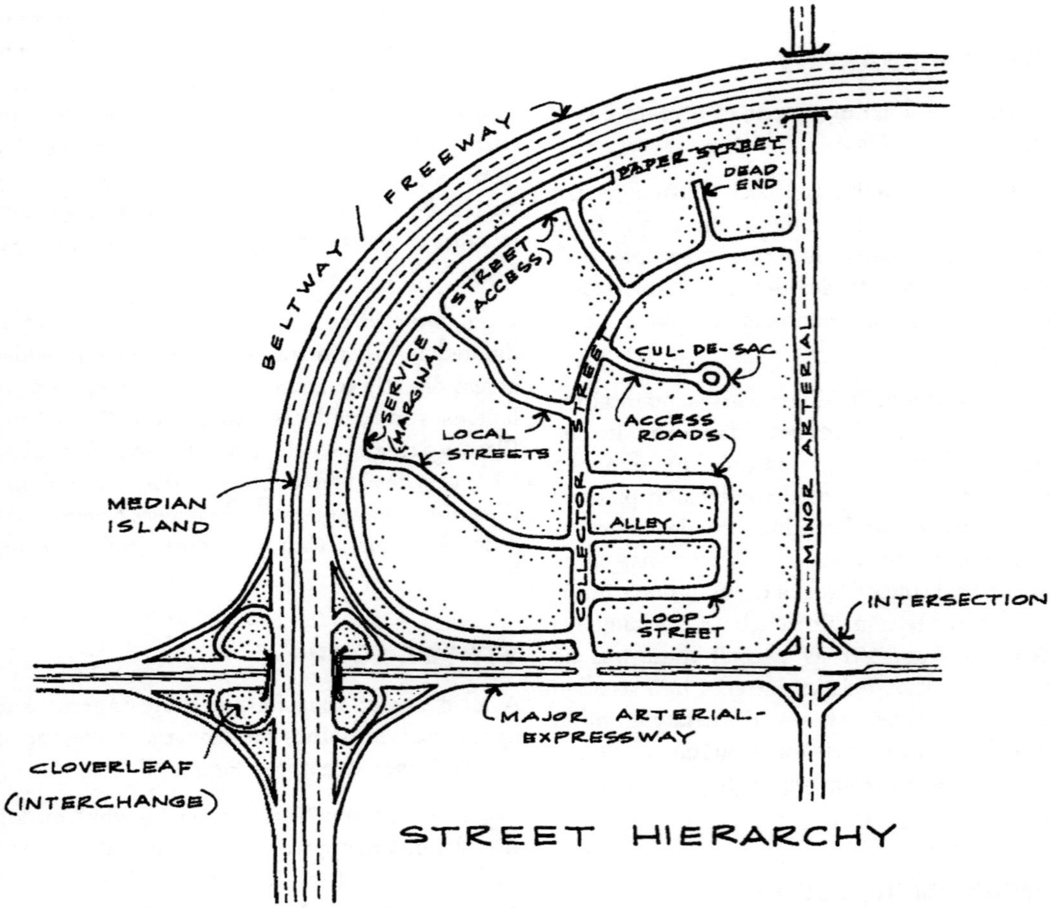


traffic volumes in excess of ten thousand vehicles per day (ADT).

*Legal Annotation*: "Although the defendants maintain that Busse Highway is a suitable road on which to build single-family homes because of its low traffic volume, the Des Plaines comprehensive plan classifies it as a **major arterial street** and anticipates higher traffic volume in the future." *Tomasek v. City of Des Plaines* (Ill. App. Ct., 1975).

## STREET, MARGINAL ACCESS

**A service street that runs parallel to a higher-order street, such as an arterial street or freeway, and that provides access to abutting properties and separation from through traffic.** *See Figure 97*.

*Comment*: Marginal access streets may be designed as residential access or collector streets, depending on traffic volumes.

*Legal Annotation*: "The subdivision regulations under Section II—Definitions, also define a marginal access street as: '**MARGINAL ACCESS STREET**. A street running parallel to and adjacent to or in the immediate vicinity of another street and which has as its principal purpose the relief of such other street from the local service of abutting properties.' We note that a **marginal access street** is synonymous with a service road. The subdivision regulations also provide that where the subdivision has frontage on a major street the subdivider shall dedicate a right-of-way forty feet wide adjacent to such major street for a service road." *City of Mobile v. Waldon* (Ala., 1983).

## STREET, MINOR ARTERIAL

**A street that interconnects and links major arterials and distributes traffic to and from collector streets. *See Figure 97*.**

*Comment*: Minor arterials overlap major collectors to some extent. Traffic volumes range between five thousand and ten thousand vehicles per day (ADT), with speeds of thirty to thirty-five miles per hour.

*Legal Annotation*: "The proposal and adjacent preliminary plat provide adequate arterial access and local access road connectivity. Cumulative traffic impacts from such developments will not result in the capacity of such roads being exceeded." *Ponderosa Neighborhood Association v. Spokane County* (Wash. Ct. App., 2007).

## STREET, MULTIFAMILY ACCESS

**A type of private residential street serving multifamily development that is either a loop street or a connecting street between streets and that permits nonparallel on-street parking that is accessed from the traveled way.**

*Comment*: The distinguishing element that defines multifamily access streets is that nonparallel on-street parking, accessed from the traveled way, is permitted. The requirement for a loop or connecting street is to differentiate the multifamily access street from the typical parking lot in a multifamily development. The usual pavement width for the access street traveled way, exclusive of the perpendicular parking spaces, is twenty-four feet, with curbs and sidewalks required.

## STREET, PAPER

**A street that has never been built but is shown on an approved plan, subdivision plat, tax map, or official map.**

*Legal Annotation*: "A **paper street** is a street which appears on a recorded plat but which in actuality has never been open, prepared for use, or used as a street." *Robidoux v. Pelletier* (R.I., 1978).

## STREET, PRIVATE

**A street that has not been accepted by the municipality or other governmental entity.**

*Comment*: Private streets may be used by the public, often as access to a development, industrial plant, or shopping area. Some states permit the municipality to remove snow on private streets without affecting their status.

*Legal Annotation*: "We affirm the judgment upholding the zoning board because we conclude that the ordinance is unambiguous and that a **private street** is a *roadway*. . . . We conclude that the eighty-by-twenty foot strip of land on the western edge of the Beidlers' lot is a roadway. The fact that it is a private roadway makes no difference. The point is that neither the Beidlers nor two of their neighbors would have access to their properties without this roadway. It is not simply a private driveway on the Beidlers' property." *St. Ex Rel. Beidler v. Williams Bay Zoning Bd.* (Wis. Ct. App., 1991).

## STREET, RURAL

**A road primarily serving as access to abutting building lots in areas with densities of less than one dwelling unit per acre.**

*Comment*: Rural streets usually have rights-of-way of forty feet and cartways of eighteen to twenty feet without curbs and sidewalks. Parking may be permitted on one side of the street only.

*Legal Annotation*: "This act is providing only for the construction of **rural roads**, and a **rural road** is defined as 'Any continuous stretch of public way, road, thoroughfare, street or right of way, not now or as of the particular time of inquiry in the future designated as part of the State highway system in the manner provided by law and not located wholly within the boundaries of any incorporated municipality.' Under the terms of the act each project leased by the Authority to the State and to the State Highway Department, will, upon the completion of its construction, 'be a part of the system of public roads of the State and of the county or counties wherein the project is located.' Such a project will not be a part of the State highway system unless it is designated as such in the way and manner provided by law. The purpose of the act is to construct **rural roads**, and not to enlarge or add to the State highway system." *State of Ga. v. Ga. Rural Roads Authority* (Ga., 1955).

## STREET, SERVICE

See *Street, Marginal Access*.

*Legal Annotation*: "Both before and after the improvement, the intervening strip was a physical and legal barrier between the **'service' street** and the through street. Indirect access to the throughway portion is available at the end of each block, i.e., at the intersection of the service street and one of the side streets which intersects with Livingston Avenue." *Schiff v. Columbus* (Ohio Ct. App., 1965).

## STREET BEAUTIFICATION

**Improving the appearance of a street in accordance with a plan, including, but not limited to, the installation of landscaping, benches, street lighting, sidewalks, wastebaskets, and signage.**

*Legal Annotation*: "Additional delays were caused by the city's June 1967 passage of the bonds for the Market **Street beautification** project." *Orpheum Bldg. v. San Francisco Bay Area Rapid* (Calif. Ct. App., 1978).

## STREET CAPACITY

See *Capacity, Roadway*.

*Legal Annotation*: "Under that provision, the Planning Commission must determine whether **street capacity** is 'adequate [to] serve the subject property with the permitted uses' that a requested zone change would allow before it approves the zone change." *Siporen v. City of Medford* (Ore., 2010).

## STREET FURNITURE

**Constructed, aboveground objects, such as outdoor seating, kiosks, bus shelters, sculpture, trash receptacles, planters, bollards, fountains, and telephone booths, that have the potential for enlivening and giving variety to streets, sidewalks, plazas, and other outdoor spaces open to and used by the public.**

*Comment*: Street furniture can include, but is generally distinct from, street hardware. **See** *Street Hardware*.

*Legal Annotation*: "**Street furniture** is defined as any structure erected or placed in the public or private ways on a temporary or permanent basis." *Globe Newspaper Company v. Beacon Hill Architectural Commission* (1st Cir., 1996).

## STREET LINE

See *Right-of-Way Lines*.

*Legal Annotation*: "'**Street-Line**' is defined as the established boundary lines of a street, alley or public thoroughfare." *Boudreau v. Albanese* (N.Y. Sup. Ct., 1951).

## STREET SPAM

**Unauthorized signs located within a public right-of-way and attached to utility poles or other right-of-way structures.**

*Legal Annotation*: "These signs are also known as **street spam**, bandit and snipe signs, vertical litter, illegal signs and utility telephone pole advertising." Citizens Against Ugly Street Spam. http://www.causs.org/index.html

## STREETCAR

**A self-powered rail vehicle that travels on tracks along urban streets or segregated from streets on a separate right-of-way.**

*Comment*: Also referred to as "tram" or "trolley." Developed in many American cities in the nineteenth century, most streetcar lines were removed in the mid-twentieth century. A few cities such as Boston, New Orleans, Pittsburgh, and San Francisco retained them. Starting in the 1980s, some American cities brought back streetcars, including Portland (OR), Memphis, Tampa, and Little Rock, and many planned to do so, including Washington, DC, Tucson, and Detroit. The advantages of streetcars are savings in fuel and less air pollution, lower noise generation, fewer drivers, and narrower rights-of-way compared to buses; swift acceleration and stopping; and a more comfortable ride. Disadvantages are the space taken up by fixed infrastructure (such as island platforms), higher initial capital costs, reduction in speed for cars and buses using the same roads, the hazard to citizens from tram tracks, and disruption by breakdowns and repair to the infrastructure.

***Legal Annotation***: "A **streetcar** is defined in Webster's New International Dictionary, second edition, as 'a car, usually a passenger car, running through the public streets.' The same authority defines a street railway as 'a street car line.'" *Dolton v. Green* (Calif. Ct. App., 1945).

## STREETSCAPE

**All the elements that constitute the physical makeup of a street and that, as a group, define its character, including building frontage; street paving; street furniture; landscaping, including trees and other plantings; awnings and marquees; signs; and lighting (Schultz and Kasen 1984).**

***Comment***: Streetscapes are an important component of the developed environment: not only are they public spaces that facilitate vehicular and pedestrian mobility, but people interact there too. Streetscapes help to define a community's aesthetic quality and identity, its economic health and level of activity, and the extent of social cohesion. If streetscapes are safe and inviting to pedestrians, people are more likely to walk, reducing automobile traffic, improving public health, stimulating local economic activity, and attracting residents and visitors to a community (Schellinger and Priest 2006).

***Legal Annotation***: "Additionally, the board had before it a letter from Jose Giner, a member of the American Institute of Certified Planners, whom the board had hired as an independent planner to look at this issue. Giner confirmed in his letter that he had inspected the neighborhood and 'noted that there is a marked contrast in the character of the **streetscape** when one turns onto High Street from South Broad Street. The predominant character of the area immediately west of the current [MCDD] line is residential in nature.' He noted that the 'residential uses appear stable and thriving [and that the] residential properties appear fully occupied and well kept.' He further opined that 'in reviewing the record, there were concerns regarding the retention of the historic character of the neighborhood in which the subject property is located. The current [z]oning regulation for the [MCDD] would not offer much if any protection for the retention of the structures [and] changing [the current zone] to [MCDD] will not promote the retention of the historic character of the neighborhood.'" *Dutko v. Planning and Zoning Board of City of Milford* (Conn. App. Ct., 2008).

## STRIP COMMERCIAL DEVELOPMENT

**Commercial or retail uses, usually one story high and one store deep, that front on a major street.**

***Comment***: Strip commercial development is typically characterized by street-frontage parking lots serving individual stores or strips of stores. Some older commercial strips, however, are dependent on on-street parking and, in some cases, parking lots interspersed among or positioned behind the buildings. Strip commercial developments differ from central business districts and shopping centers in at least two of the following characteristics: (1) there are no provisions for pedestrian access between individual uses; (2) the uses are only one store deep; (3) the buildings are arranged linearly rather than clustered; and (4) there is no design integration among individual uses.

While strip commercial developments are universally criticized as ugly, the problem with them may be inadequate local regulations. For example, landscaped parking lots, including trees and landscaped island separations between bays, can significantly improve overall appearance and soften building impact. Other requirements that significantly improve the aesthetics of these uses include peaked rather than flat roofs, wide sidewalks abutting the storefronts, with canopy or roof overhangs over pedestrian areas, and controlled and integrated signage. Features such as kiosks, benches, and sculpture can help humanize these developments and make them more attractive.

In addition, adjacent residential areas can be shielded from strip commercial uses by requiring walls and berms with heavy landscape treatment. Functional and attractive pedestrian access from adjacent residential areas should be provided.

***Legal Annotation***: "The subject property is located on the east side of Wisconsin Avenue and bordered to the north by the Page Building complex and a Dart Drug store, to the south by the Jelleff's Boy's Club recreational complex, and to the east by Dumbarton Oaks Park. Immediately across Wisconsin Avenue to the west of the subject property are located Gordon Junior High School and some **strip commercial development** which includes miscellaneous small shops and business facilities." *Citizens Ass'n v. District of Columbia Zoning* (D.C. Ct. App., 1979).

## STRIP MINING

**A process of recovering ore or fuel deposits by mechanically scraping the overhanging rock and strata.**

***Comment***: Strip mining is also known as surface mining.

***Legal Annotation***: "**Strip mining** is effected through steam shovels and bull dozers which turn up the top layer of the earth as easily as a can opener lays bare the contents of a box of sardines." *Rochez Bros., Inc. v. Duricka* (Pa., 1953).

## STRIP ZONING

**See *Strip Commercial Development*.**

***Legal Annotation***: "The Court of Appeals has noted that zoning experts now reject the idea that '**strip zoning**' is 'good zoning.' The shoddy vestiges of an earlier, contrary expert view, offend the eye in almost every village, town and city in the State. The County Commissioners clearly were entitled to consider the fact that the vacant B-1 land on the west side of the highway was still undeveloped twelve years after original zoning." *Quinn v. County Comm'rs* (Md. Ct. App., 1974).

## STRUCTURAL ALTERATION

**Any change in either the supporting members of a building, such as bearing walls, columns, beams, and girders, or in the dimensions or configurations of the roof or exterior walls.**

***Legal Annotation***: "A '**structural alteration**' is a change in an existing building which constitutes such a change or changes in an old building as converts the existing building into a new or substantially different structure." *Hanna v. Board of Adjustment* (Pa., 1962).

## STRUCTURE

**A combination of materials that form a construction for use, occupancy, or ornamentation, whether installed on, above, or below the surface of land or water.**

***Comment***: By this definition, all buildings are structures; however, not all structures are buildings. **See *Building*.**

***Legal Annotation***: "A **structure** is defined as 'anything constructed or erected on the ground or attached to something on the ground.' The appellant-landowner was enjoined from maintaining in his front yard a satellite television antenna used for personal and business purposes. He sells these antennas out of his home under a valid business license from the City." *Gouge v. City of Snellville* (Ga., 1982).

## STUB STREET

**A street that runs up to the property line and is designed to be extended when the adjacent property is developed.**

***Comment***: Dead-end or cul-de-sac streets are purposely designed not to be extended into the adjacent property, whereas stub streets, whether they have temporary turnarounds or not, are designed to be extended into the adjacent property.

*Legal Annotation*: "Under the Greensboro Ordinance § 30-2-2.12, a '**stub street**' is '[a] street having one (1) end open to traffic, but which is neither a cul-de-sac street nor a permanent dead-end street.'" *Elikins v. City of Greensboro Board of Adjustment* (N.C. Ct. App., 2005).

## STUD FARM

**A farm where a stallion stands at stud and mares are bred to him, and where breeding, pasturing, and foaling may take place. See *Horse Farm*.**

*Legal Annotation*: "John Keblusek and William D. McCarthy, neighboring landowners, testified for the plaintiffs. Keblusek said the subject property was being used as a **stud farm** for raising and breeding horses at the time he bought his house. Later it became a horse stable." *Dietz v. Village of Midlothian* (Ill. App. Ct., 1980).

## STUDIO

**(1) The workshop of an artist, sculptor, photographer, or craftsperson; (2) a place for radio or television production; (3) a place where movies are produced. See *Artist Studio*.**

*Comment*: The studio for radio or television broadcasting is that part of the station from which the signal originates. It could be an office or a home and is often separate and some distance from the transmitter and antennas.

From a zoning perspective, the local ordinance should clearly identify the type of studio permitted. Workshops of craftspersons, for instance, would be appropriate for residential areas, as would small studios for radio productions. Large-scale television or movie production studios clearly belong in nonresidential areas.

*Legal Annotation*: "The City filed a petition seeking an injunction on October 17, 1990 to stop Mrs. Miller from using a 5 h.p. industrial air compressor in conjunction with her 'home occupation.' The petition claims that the use of the air compressor constituted an illegal extension of an art **studio** or home occupation in violation of the City's Comprehensive Zoning Ordinance, Ordinance 4264 (the 'CZO'), as amended. The City maintains that while an art **studio** is a permitted land use within a 'RD-2' Zoning District as a home occupation, the use of mechanical equipment that is not 'normally used for family, domestic or household purposes' in conjunction with a home occupation is prohibited." *City of New Orleans v. Miller* (La. Ct. App., 1993).

## STUDIO APARTMENT

**See *Dwelling Unit, Efficiency*.**

*Legal Annotation*: "[Defense Counsel]: For a bath. So this is what you would call a **studio apartment**; is that correct?

[Officer]: Yeah, I guess you could use it as a studio.

[Defense Counsel]: There's no particular area set aside for a bedroom.

[Officer]: Not that I could see, no. It's a combination of everything." *Commonwealth v. Muscheck* (Pa., 1975).

## SUBDIVIDER

**Any person having an interest in land that is the subject of an application for subdivision. See *Applicant*.**

*Legal Annotation*: "A '**subdivider**' is defined in Government Code section 66423 as one 'who proposes to divide, divides or causes to be divided real property into a subdivision for himself or for others.'" *Pescosolido v. Smith* (Calif. Ct. App., 1983).

## SUBDIVISION

**The division of a lot, tract, or parcel of land into two or more lots, tracts, parcels, or other divisions of land for sale, development, or lease.**

*Comment*: Many state enabling laws exclude certain subdivisions from this definition. For example, in New Jersey, the following are not considered subdivisions, providing no new streets are created: (1) divisions of land for agricultural purposes where all resulting parcels are five acres or larger in size; (2) divisions of property by testamentary or intestate provisions; (3) divisions of property upon court order, including, but not limited to, judgments of foreclosure; and (4) conveyances so as to combine existing lots by deed or other instruments.

*Legal Annotation*: "The Subdivision Map Act defines a subdivider as a 'person, firm, corporation, partnership or association who causes land to be divided into a **subdivision** for himself or for others' . . . and a **subdivision** is defined as 'any real property . . . shown on the latest adopted county tax roll as a unit or as contiguous units, which is divided for the purpose of sale or lease, whether immediate or future, by any subdivider into five or more parcels'" *Pratt v. Adams* (Calif. Ct. App., 1964).

## SUBDIVISION, ANTIQUATED

**See *Premature Subdivision*.**

## SUBDIVISION, CLUSTER

**See *Cluster Subdivision*.**

## SUBDIVISION, CONSOLIDATION

**The combining of individual recorded lots to form a single tract in single ownership. See *Assemblage; Consolidation*.**

*Legal Annotation*: "The judge found that there was no provision in the MLUL, or the Development Regulations that required that the **consolidated subdivision** be split into two lots along the zone lines." *Mt. Hill, LLC v. Zoning Bd. of Adjustment of Township of Middletown* (N.J. Super. Ct., 2008).

## SUBDIVISION, MAJOR

**Any subdivision not classified as a minor subdivision.**

*Legal Annotation*: "Bentwood Acres contained four lots and would be classified as a minor subdivision under the definition contained in the County subdivision regulations because it contained no more than five lots. Bentwood Estates was classified as a **major subdivision** because it contained more than five lots." *Basinger v. Boone County* (Mo. Ct. App., 1990).

## SUBDIVISION, MINOR

**A subdivision of land that does not involve any of the following: (1) the creation of more than the maximum number of lots specifically permitted by ordinance as a minor subdivision; (2) a planned development; (3) any new street; or (4) the extension of any off-tract improvements.**

*Comment*: Many ordinances further restrict minor subdivisions to land incapable of further subdivision. Any parcel that could be further subdivided would be classified as a major subdivision. The purpose is to ensure that required improvements are installed and are not avoided by a series of minor subdivisions. The number of lots permitted to be subdivided and classified as a minor subdivision varies but is typically not more than five lots.

*Legal Annotation*: "Bentwood Acres contained four lots and would be classified as a **minor subdivision** under the definition contained in the County subdivision regulations because it contained no more than five lots. Bentwood Estates was classified as a major subdivision because it contained more than five lots." *Basinger v. Boone County* (Mo. Ct. App., 1990).

## SUBDIVISION, PREMATURE

**See *Premature Subdivision*.**

## SUBGRADE

**The prepared surface upon which pavement and shoulders are constructed.**

*Legal Annotation*: "A roadbed is constructed by excavating and embankment, or 'cut and fill' operations. Prior to placing the pavement structure on the subgrade, it is necessary to 'finish' or 'prepare' the **subgrade**. The **subgrade** is defined as the 'top surface of the roadbed upon which the pavement structure and shoulders including curbs are constructed.' **Subgrade** tolerance, as used in this dispute, is the amount of variation in the **subgrade** plane." *T. Brown Constructors, Inc. v. Pena* (Fed. Cir., 1998).

## SUBMERGED LAND

**Those lands situated below the mean low waterline or all of the lands covered by the mean high waterline.**

***Legal Annotation***: "The tide is not the only factor changing the boundary. It also can be changed by nature's forces—primarily water—that add to or subtract from a body of land. Additions to land generally are created by accretion or reliction. . . . With accretion, land increases gradually and imperceptibly when water deposits solid material so that land once covered by water becomes dry. . . . Reliction occurs when previously **submerged land** is uncovered by permanently receding water. . . . Decreases in tidal lands generally are caused by erosion, which gradually and imperceptibly wears away the land. . . . All of these processes may cause a riparian or littoral owner to gain or lose title to the land." *TH Investments, Inc. v. Kirby Inland Marine* (Tex. Ct. App., 2007).

## SUBSIDENCE

**The sinking or downward shift of land as a result of natural or artificial causes.**

***Comment***: The potential for ground subsidence is of concern to geologists, geotechnical engineers and surveyors. Subsidence can be caused by mining, dissolution of subsurface limestone, natural gas extraction, or the drainage of coastal or delta plains.

***Legal Annotation***: "Coal mine **subsidence** is the lowering of strata overlying a coal mine, including the land surface, caused by the extraction of underground coal. This lowering of the strata can have devastating effects. It often causes substantial damage to foundations, walls, other structural members, and the integrity of houses and buildings. **Subsidence** frequently causes sinkholes or troughs in land which make the land difficult or impossible to develop. Its effect on farming has been well documented—many subsided areas cannot be plowed or properly prepared. **Subsidence** can also cause the loss of groundwater and surface ponds. In short, it presents the type of environmental concern that has been the focus of so much federal, state, and local regulation in recent decades." *Keystone Bituminous Coal Assn. v. DeBenedictis* (U.S., 1987).

## SUBSIDIZED HOUSING

**Housing priced below market cost as a result of the use of subsidies and limited to occupancy by households in specified income ranges. See *Low-Income Housing; Moderate-Income Housing; Public Housing*.**

***Comment***: Subsidized housing is usually restricted to households earning 80 percent or less of the median income of the area in which the housing is located. Rental and sales prices are usually based on the income of the occupant. The US Department of Housing and Urban Development regulations for rental housing stipulate that rents, including utilities, cannot exceed 30 percent of the occupant's gross annual income. In New Jersey, where subsidized housing is often made available on a sales basis, mortgage principal and interest, condo fees (if applicable), taxes, and insurance cannot exceed 28 percent of the occupant's income.

***Legal Annotation***: "Other statutory and regulatory provisions support this definition of subsidized housing. In the low and moderate income housing sections of G. L. c. 40B, subsidized housing means 'housing subsidized by the federal or state government under any program to assist the construction of low or moderate income housing.'" *Gross v. Prudential Insurance Company of America, Inc.* (Mass. App. Ct., 1999).

## SUBSOIL

**The layer of soil just below the surface of the ground.**

***Legal Annotation***: "Natural organic matter in the **subsoil** decays at a slower rate, but it is not replenished with much plant litter. Thus, burying

**topsoil** particles will likely result in decline of their initially relatively high natural organic matter levels, down to the relatively low levels characteristic of subsurface particles. If the natural organic matter concentration is decreased, the particles may have less of a 'hold' on pesticide residues bound to them. Thus, according to this scenario, burial could possibly result in release of pesticide residues. In practice, such release might be so slow as to have no net impact on water quality. On the other hand, there is the possibility that the quality of the natural organic matter in the **subsoil** is different than that in the topsoil, such that the natural organic matter in the subsoil has a higher affinity for the pesticide." *River Bend Associates, Inc. v. Conservation and Inland Wetlands Commission* (Conn., 2004).

## SUBURBAN CORPORATE CENTER

**See *Office Headquarters; Office Park*.**

## SUBSTANDARD STRUCTURE/ DWELLING

**A term used in the 1960s and preceding the US *Census of Housing* to indicate a lack of some or all plumbing facilities and/or the presence of physical inadequacies. See *Deficient Unit*.**

*Legal Annotation*: "Grafton City Ordinance 5-346 defines a **substandard structure**, identifying nine types of defects that constitute a basis for declaring a structure substandard. The authority to order demolition of a **substandard structure** is found under Grafton City Ordinance 5-347, providing:

All **substandard buildings and structures** within the terms of Section 5-346 of this article are hereby declared to be public nuisances and shall be repaired, vacated, or demolished as herein before and herein after provided. The standards used to determine whether a structure should be repaired, vacated, or demolished are found under Grafton City Ordinance 5-350, providing: (1) If the **substandard building or structure** can reasonably be repaired so that it will no longer exist in violation of the terms of this article it shall be ordered repaired. . . . (3) In any case where a **substandard building or structure** is fifty (50) percent or more damaged or decayed or deteriorated from its original value or structure it shall be demolished." *Pic v. City of Grafton* (N.D., 1998).

## SUPER-REGIONAL SHOPPING CENTER

**A facility including retail, office, and service uses occupying over one hundred acres, having four or more anchor stores, and containing over one million square feet of gross leasable space. See *Retail Store, Big-Box*.**

*Legal Annotation*: "Experts for Raley's testified that five types of retail facilities currently exist: (1) the **super-regional shopping center**, such as the Arden Fair Mall in Sacramento, designed to serve around 300,000 people within a 12 mile radius and occupying between 500,000 and 1,500,000 square feet; (2) the regional facility, such as the Downtown Plaza and the County Fair Mall, designed to serve around 150,000 persons within an 8- to 10-mile radius and occupying between 300,000 and 1,000,000 square feet; (3) the community shopping center, designed to serve between 100,000 and 150,000 people within a 5- to 10-mile radius and taking up between 100,000 and 150,000 square feet; (4) the neighborhood shopping facility designed to serve 40,000 people within a 1.5 mile radius and taking up 30,000 to 100,000 square feet; and (5) the freestanding store, which has a similar trade area to the neighborhood shopping center." *Young v. Raley's, Inc.* (Calif. Ct. App., 2001).

## SUBSTANTIAL IMPROVEMENT

**Any extension, repair, reconstruction, or other improvements of a property, the cost of which equals or exceeds 50 percent of the fair market value of a property either before the improvement is started or, if the property has been damaged and is being restored, before the damage occurred.**

*Comment*: "Substantial improvement" is often used to define the point beyond which a nonconforming use or structure cannot be repaired. The

Federal Insurance Administration also requires flood-proofing measures to be installed when a structure in a floodway undergoes "substantial improvement."

*Legal Annotation*: "The term '**substantial improvement**' is defined in section E(17) of the appellant City's Flood Damage Prevention Regulations as follows: **Substantial improvement** means any repair, reconstruction, or improvement of a structure, the cost of which equals or exceeds fifty percent (50%) of the market value of the structure either before the improvement or repair has started or if the structure has been damaged and is being restored, before the damage occurred." *City of Webster v. Signad, Inc.* (Texas Ct. App., 1984).

## SUBSTANTIALLY DIFFERENT

See *Change of Use*.

## SUBSURFACE DISPOSAL SYSTEM

**A collection of treatment tanks, disposal areas, holding tanks and ponds, surface spray systems, cesspools, wells, surface ditches, alternative toilets, or other devices and associated piping designed to function as a unit for the purpose of disposing of wastes or wastewater on or beneath the surface of the ground. See *Septic System; Wastewater System*.**

*Legal Annotation*: "Three specific disposal problems were dealt with: (1) a **subsurface disposal system** for the overflow from the Bonderizer tanks, consisting of a septic tank and leach beds lying to the northeast of defendant's building. This, it was complained by the department and by at least one neighbor, resulted in pollution of groundwater, specifically wells used for drinking water in the vicinity of the plant." *Commonwealth v. Dresser Mfg. Co.* (Pa. Common. Pleas, 1973).

## SUBURBAN AREA

**A predominantly low-density residential area located immediately outside of an urban area or a city and associated with it physically and socioeconomically.**

*Comment*: Suburban areas have population densities ranging from five hundred to one thousand persons per square mile.

*Legal Annotation*: "Plaintiff, relying on Wymer's exclusion for 'urban, **suburban**, and subdivided lands' . . . asserts that whether defendant's land was **suburban** is a question of fact. We disagree. Plaintiff's evidence on this issue consists of some census figures, a map, and a property survey. The mere presence of homes near a large, undeveloped tract of land does not make the land '**suburban**.' A suburb is 'an outlying part of a city or town; a smaller place adjacent to or sometimes within commuting distance of a city; the residential area on the outskirts of any city or large town.' Webster's Third New International Dictionary, Unabridged Edition (1965)." *Ellsworth v. Highland Lakes Development Associates* (Mich. Ct. App., 1993).

## SUITABLE SITE

**A site that is adjacent to compatible land uses, has access to appropriate streets, and is consistent with state environmental policies.**

*Comment*: "Suitable site" may have different meanings in different jurisdictions, as the legal annotation below indicates. The definition above is derived from the New Jersey Council on Affordable Housing pertaining to sites deemed "suitable" for lower-income housing but may have wider applicability. The broad criteria have been further refined in a series of court cases by judges and planners. In *Orgo Farms and Greenhouses v. Colts Neck Township*, 192 N.J. Super. 559 (1984), and *Orgo Farms and Greenhouses v. Colts Neck Township*, 204 N.J. Super. 585 (1985), the court cited the importance of state and regional planning designations for growth and limited-growth areas as criteria in determining suitable sites. The court-appointed planning master in the same case proposed five criteria as tests for suitable sites:

(1) regional accessibility; (2) proximity to goods and services; (3) availability of water and sewers; (4) environmental suitability; and (5) land-use compatibility.

Another special master added further criteria, as follows: (1) has access to appropriate streets; (2) avoids historic sites; (3) avoids restricted agricultural lands; (4) avoids wetlands and required buffers; (5) avoids flood hazard areas; (6) avoids steep slopes (in excess of 15 percent); (7) avoids reserved recreation, conservation, and open space; (8) has clear title, free of encumbrances that would preclude the development of low- and moderate-income housing; (9) lacks intangible factors likely to delay or hinder development of low- and moderate-income housing; and (10) is owned by or under contract or sale to a developer who is ready, willing, and able to build a substantial amount of low-and moderate-income housing.

*Legal Annotation*: "The plaintiffs claim that the action of the commission in rejecting the Stamford site was arbitrary because public convenience and necessity 'can require the use of a particular site in violation of zoning only if no other reasonably **suitable site** is available.' Chief Justice Andrews, in In re Application of Shelton Street Ry. Co. . . . in discussing the meaning of 'public convenience and necessity,' stated . . . 'Public necessity . . . is that urgent, immediate public need arising from existing conditions which, in the judgment of the legislature, justifies a disturbance of private rights that otherwise might be legally exempt from such interference. The term is therefore a relative one. It determines, in each case that may arise, the relation of the duty implied in the broad grant of legislative power to promote by appropriate action the interests of the commonwealth, to the limitations of that power established for the protection of private rights. . . . Sometimes . . . the necessity is one which does not affect the whole body politic the same way, but may or may not exist in different localities, for reasons peculiar to each. . . . When [a question of public necessity is] involved it is commonly called a question of "public convenience and necessity," or "common convenience and necessity."' The term 'means a condition existing at the time of the application . . . that, in the judgment of the trier, will justify the interference with private rights involved.' . . . Manifestly, it is not necessary that justification for the action of the commission rest upon a finding that there is no alternative. It is enough if, in the deliberate, carefully considered judgment of the commission, the site approved serves the public convenience and necessity better than any alternative offered." *Wilson Point Property Owners Assn. v. Connecticut Light & Power Co.* (Conn., 1958).

## SULFUR DIOXIDE ($SO_2$)

**A heavy, pungent, colorless gas, formed primarily by the combustion of fossil fuels, that damages the respiratory tract as well as vegetation and certain materials and is considered a major air pollutant.**

*Legal Annotation*: "**Sulfur dioxide** is a primary pollutant produced by the burning of oil and coal and, uncontrolled, is emitted in large quantities through the smokestacks of large consumers of oil and gas, e.g., public utilities. It is an acidic substance whose acidity can be neutralized by interaction with lime, an alkaline substance." *National Lime Ass'n v. EPA* (D.C. Cir., 1980).

## SUMMER CAMP

**A location away from home, often in a rural or country setting, where campers spend all or part of the summer living in tents, barracks, or dormitories, participating in organized activities, sports, and arts and crafts, and usually eating together in a central dining facility.**

*Comment*: The term "summer camp" may be a misnomer, since these facilities operate throughout the year in all seasons and many are located in urban areas. Some are geared to the elderly or to persons with disabilities. Housing includes "camp-type" dormitories and cabins.

*Legal Annotation*: "Edward Lashins appeals the environmental court order authorizing Timothy Gore to reopen a children's **summer camp** as a pre-existing and conditional use under the Town of Wilmington's zoning ordinance. Appellant maintains that Gore's proposed **summer camp** is actually a nonconforming use subject to a discontinuance provision included in the ordinance that prohibits resurrecting nonconforming uses once those uses have changed to permitted uses." *In re Appeal of Lashins* (Vt., 2002).

## SUMP

**A depression or tank that serves as a drain or receptacle of liquids for salvage or disposal.**

*Legal Annotation*: "A '**sump**' is a pit or well constructed to collect liquids such as oil or water. A '**sump** pump' is a pump set to drain a **sump**. Webster's New Universal Unabridged Dictionary at 1825 (2d ed. 1983)." *Blumenstock v. Gibson* (Pa. Super. Ct., 2002).

## SUPERCENTER

**A type of department store that is physically extremely large and combines the sale of department store merchandise with a full-scale grocery.**

*Legal Annotation*: "Appellant Bakersfield Citizens for Local Control (BCLC) has challenged development of two retail shopping centers in the southwestern portion of the City of Bakersfield (City), alleging violations of the California Environmental Quality Act (CEQA). The shopping centers are located 3.6 miles apart. . . . When complete, they will have a combined total of 1.1 million square feet of retail space. Each shopping center will contain a Wal-Mart Supercenter (Supercenter) plus a mix of large anchor stores, smaller retailers, and a gas station. An environmental impact report (EIR) was prepared and certified for each project. . . . In *Bakersfield Citizens* we stated '**Supercenters** are . . . unique.' . . . *American Canyon* quoted this language from *Bakersfield Citizens* . . . and stated 'A **supercenter** is a unique type of retail operation.' . . . Arguably, however, any type of retail operation is unique, just as '[a] rendering plant has different environmental impacts than a chandler.' . . . For purposes of CEQA, the significant inquiry is whether an agency proposes or intends to carry out or approve a 'project' which 'may have a significant effect on the environment.' Under those circumstances, the agency 'shall prepare, or cause to be prepared . . . an environmental impact report' for that project." *BCLC v. City of Bakersfield* (Calif. Ct. App., 2004).

## SUPERMARKET

**A large, self-service retail establishment selling a wide variety of food as well as other convenience and household goods.**

*Comment*: Supermarkets usually vary in size, from approximately thirty-five thousand square feet to over seventy-five thousand square feet, and provide parking at a ratio of about five to six off-street spaces per thousand square feet of gross leasable space. Supermarkets are now selling an ever-increasing array of goods, including prepared foods for on- and off-site consumption; beer, wine, and liquor; flowers; gifts; pharmaceutical goods; cosmetics; pet supplies; pool supplies and equipment; sporting supplies; clothing; furniture; home and garden supplies and even auto parts, tires and batteries; and cameras, televisions, computers, and video games. The larger supermarkets include branch banking facilities, pharmacies, and eating areas (Fischler 2006).

*Legal Annotation*: "Finally, we address the defendants' claim that the trial court improperly concluded that a Super Stop & Shop does not fall within the ambit of the 'Food Shops, Retail' classification contained within the city zoning regulations. The defendants argue that because the proposed **supermarket** will contain a bakery, a pharmacy and a bank, 'it should not be classified as "Food Shop[s], Retail" but rather as a "Department Store," "Shopping Center" or "Retail Store, Discount," which are not permitted uses' on the Cytec property, which is zoned as 'light industrial.' We disagree." *Alvord Inv. v. Zon. Bd. of App. of Stamford* (Conn., 2007).

## SURFACE COURSE

**The placement of asphalt or concrete on the previously prepared base course.**

*Legal Annotation*: "Apparently, I-4 **surface course** is composed of an asphalt mixture. Although its cost is substantially less than that of pure asphalt, a significant change in the market costs of asphalt will produce a corresponding significant change in the costs of I-4 **surface course**." *American Asphalt Company, Inc. v. Delaware River Port Authority* (N.J. Super. Ct., 2011).

## SURFACE WATER

**Water on the earth's surface exposed to the atmosphere as oceans, lakes, rivers, streams, and ponds. See *Groundwater*.**

*Legal Annotation*: "The issues in this appeal are governed by the common enemy doctrine, which has directed the law of **surface water** in Washington since 1896. . . . **Surface water** is 'vagrant or diffused [water] produced by rain, melting snow, or springs.' . . . The Currenses contend that Sleek is liable for the damage brought about when the grading and construction on Sleek's property caused **surface water** to flow off of the property and to collect in a low point on the Currenses' land." *Currens v. Sleek* (Wash., 1999).

## SURGICAL CENTER

**An outpatient facility for medical procedures and simple surgery.**

***Comment***: Surgical centers are more elaborate than a doctor's office but less equipped and more limited in the services they perform than a hospital. The maximum stay at an outpatient surgical center is twenty-three hours.

***Legal Annotation***: "An ambulatory **surgical center** is a healthcare facility 'that operates primarily to provide surgical services to patients who do not require overnight hospital care.' Tex. Health & Safety Code Ann. § 243.002 (West 2001)." *Texas Workers' Comp. Comm'n v. East Side Surgical Center* (Texas Ct. App., 2004).

## SURROGATE

**A census indicator of deficient housing used in the calculation of present need.**

***Comment***: Surrogates for deficient housing include age of structure, no elevators in a midrise building, no central heat, overcrowding, nonexclusive use of complete plumbing facilities, inadequate kitchen facilities, and access. Usually any deficiency, together with age, constitutes evidence of deficient housing.

***Legal Annotation***: "It is not clear whether Hintz and Kasler view overcrowding as simply a surrogate for dilapidation or an independent standard of housing inadequacy. In any event, this question would be of only academic interest under their methodologies, since the presence of a single **surrogate** is sufficient to designate a unit as deficient." *Countryside Properties, Inc. v. Mayor and Council of Bor. of Ringwood* (N.J. Super. Ct., 1984).

## SURVEILLANCE SYSTEM

**(1) A monitoring system to determine environmental quality; (2) a monitoring system to maintain security.**

***Comment***: Environmental surveillance systems are established to monitor all pollution and other aspects of progress toward attainment of environmental standards. Surveillance systems identify potential episodes of high pollutant concentrations in time to take preventive action.

***Legal Annotation***: "A visible emissions standard for coal-fired plants limits the amount of opacity of emissions exiting a particular smoke stack, which is measured by a **continuous system** monitoring that complies with the EPA's standards." *Sierra Club v. Wisconsin DNR* (Wis. Ct. App., 2010).

"She discussed with Beattie ways in which Risky Business was not in compliance with the Ordinance, namely the doors, windows, and other openings were not covered with an opaque material and the video **surveillance system** was not functional. . . . She informed Beattie that he had ten working days to bring the store into compliance or his license application would be denied." *Risky Business Novelties and Videos, Inc. v. County of Crow Wing* (D. Minn., 2013).

## SURVEY

**(1) The process of precisely ascertaining the area, dimensions, and location of a piece of land; (2) determining the characteristics of persons, land, objects, buildings, or structures by sampling, census, interviews, observations, or other methods.**

***Legal Annotation***: "Miller commissioned John Kimpel & Associates ('Surveyor') to perform a land **survey** of the portion of the land that Anderson was purchasing. The Surveyor marked the boundaries of Anderson's property on the **survey**, but no visible exterior markers, flags, or pins were placed on the property to designate the common property line." *Anderson Property Management LLC v. H. Anthony Miller* (Ind. Ct. App., 2011).

"The only evidence against Imperial's bona fide intent to alienate the lots in its park is the **survey** of residents. There are 225 spaces or resident households in Imperial's park. Of the 225 households in Imperial's park, only 83 returned ballots. Of those, 18 supported conversion, 46 opposed conversion, 3 did not mark their ballots, 15 declined to state their votes, and 1 ballot was returned after the deadline. As in Chino, a majority of residents did not care enough about conversion to respond to the survey. This low response was insufficient to show the conversion was a sham." *218 Properties, LLC v. City of Carson* (Calif. Ct. App., 2014).

## SUSPENDED SOLIDS

**Small particles of solid pollutants in sewage that contribute to turbidity and that resist separation by conventional means.**

***Comment***: The examination of suspended solids and the BOD (biological oxygen demand) test constitute the two main determinations for water quality performed at wastewater treatment facilities.

***Legal Annotation***: "Defendant's waste discharge permit authorizes discharges from defendant's slaughterhouse to the Mount Vernon sanitary sewer and POTW under certain conditions. In particular, defendant's effluent is limited to a maximum consecutive three-day average of 1430 pounds of biochemical oxygen demand ('BOD') per day, a maximum consecutive three-day average of 825 pounds of total **suspended solids** ('TSS') per day, and a pH between 6.0 and 11.0 standard units. It is undisputed that defendant exceeded one or more of these limitations at various times throughout the limitations period." *Waste Action Project v. Draper Valley Holdings LLC* (W.D. Wash., 2014).

## SUSTAINABILITY

**Sustainability is "meeting the needs of the present without compromising the ability of future generations to meet their own needs" (United Nations Bruntland Commission).**

***Comment***: "The concept of sustainability is an important goal that can be applied at all scales of planning from global through municipal and down to corridors and individual sites.

"At each scale, the issues affecting sustainability will vary. For instance, on a global scale issues of climate change and destruction of the rain forests may dominate. Sustainability at the regional scale may focus on protection of water resources and control of urban sprawl. At the local level, one community may focus on reducing energy consumption. Another may adjust maintenance and operational plans to increase recycling, reduce embodied energy, and use more environmentally friendly products and services. At all scales, both the issues and resources will change, but the principles remain: reduce energy consumption and greenhouse gas emissions (especially as related to building operations and transportation); reduce the amount of solid waste through reuse and recycling of material resources; ensure that communities provide for all members; eliminate pollution; increase "green" areas and open space; and protect biodiversity" (Pointner 2011). (See also *Beatley 2009; Feiden And Hamin* 2011.)

***Legal Annotation***: "The trial court was apparently referring to the EIR's statement that: 'Based on the current scientific literature, it would be speculative to determine whether the contribution *of any particular project or plans* to greenhouse gas emissions and climate changes is significant. Based on an investigation of [the project's] compliance with local air quality thresholds, future long-term operational impacts, and Wal-Mart's commitment to increasing the company's environmental **sustainability** goals and policies . . . *the project would still have the potential to result in impacts associated with greenhouse gas emissions and global climate change.* However, there is significant uncertainty involved in making predictions of the extent [to] which the project operations have on greenhouse gas emissions and global climate change.' (Italics added)." *Rialto Citizens for Responsible Growth v. City of Rialto* (Calif. Ct. App., 2012).

## SUSTAINABLE DEVELOPMENT

**Development that maintains or enhances economic opportunity and community well-being while protecting and restoring the natural environment upon which people and economies depend (Schwab and Brower 1997).**

*Comment*: Sustainable development is development that meets the needs of the present without compromising the ability of future generations to meet their own needs. http://www.epa.gov/greenkit/sustain.htm; Berke and Conroy 2000

*Legal Annotation*: "The University's master plan has the following specific project objectives: (1) enhance the campus learning environment within a walkable campus core and accommodate growth in campus enrollment up to the long-standing master plan ceiling of 18,000 full-time equivalent students; (2) create supportive student neighborhoods and foster a sense of community, increase on-campus housing to accommodate 5,000 students and identify locations on campus for faculty housing; (3) implement design improvements, including improved campus entryway and pedestrian promenades; (4) implement comprehensive environmentally **sustainable development** and operation strategies; and (5) maintain the original master plan design criteria to preserve views while protecting users from the elements. To achieve these objectives, the master plan proposes to accommodate growth through in-fill development of new facilities and replacement of seismically deficient or functionally obsolete facilities. In total, this involves 1,039,000 square feet of new/replaced academic, administrative and support space; 3,770 new student beds; and up to 220 faculty/staff housing units. These new and expanded facilities will be accommodated within the campus's existing land use configuration, consisting of an academic core surrounded by student residences and open space." *City of Hayward v. Trustees of California State University* (Calif. App. Ct., 2012).

## SUSTAINABLE TRANSPORTATION PLANNING

**An approach to transportation planning that places an emphasis on environmental impact as well as system effectiveness and efficiency, and promotes the use of renewable energy and other renewable measures.**

*Comment*: Traditional transportation planning focuses primarily on improving mobility, especially for automobiles, while often failing to consider wider impacts, such as energy consumption, carbon dioxide emissions, accidents, and physical inactivity. Sustainable transportation planning, which promotes fuel efficiency, emissions controls, and the use of renewable energy and resources, aims to meet the mobility requirements of the population while at the same time reducing environmental and social impacts, as well as reducing traffic congestion.

*Legal Annotation*: "Petitioners further argue that the EA is inadequate for failing to consider a reasonable range of alternatives. In her comments, petitioner Barnes recommended that the monies earmarked for aviation be redirected 'towards high-speed rail and environmentally **sustainable transportation** alternatives that provide protection for urban and rural communities from the negative impacts of aviation.'" *Barnes v. US Dept. of Transp.* (9th Cir., 2011).

## SWALE

**Low-lying or depressed land area, commonly wet or moist, that can function as an intermittent drainage-way.**

*Legal Annotation*: "A **swale** is a grassy depression in the ground designed to collect stormwater runoff." *Cleveland v. McCarthy* (Ohio Ct. App., 2011).

## SWAP MEET

**See *Flea Market, Temporary Outdoor Activity*.**

## SWIMMING POOL

**A water-filled enclosure, permanently constructed or portable, having a depth of more than eighteen inches below the level of the surrounding land; or an above-surface pool, having a depth of more than thirty inches;**

**designed, used, and maintained for swimming and bathing.**

*Comment*: The eighteen-inch exclusion would be effective in permitting landscaping and other shallow, not-for-swimming, pools. The thirty-inch height for surface pools marks the usual break between portable and non-portable pools beyond which some codes require fencing and gates.

*Legal Annotation*: "In addition, the Board did not address the conflicting provisions in the Zoning Ordinance. The Ordinance requires a fence to surround a **swimming pool**. If a **swimming pool** is allowed in a rear, side or front yard, then it follows that a fence must also be erected in that same yard." *McClay v. Zoning Hearing Board of Upper Chichester* (Pa. Common. Ct., 2010).

## SYNAGOGUE

**A place of worship for Jewish religious services. See *Place of Worship*.**

*Legal Annotation*: "The statement of principles recited that the **synagogue** is a house of prayer where the worship of God is carried on in accord with the Jewish tradition; that the **synagogue** is a house of study wherein religious teachings for adults, as well as children, are carried on; that the **synagogue** is a place of fellowship and friendship among its adherents wherein there is present a men's group, a sisterhood (women's group), and a junior high school age youth group, and that the **synagogue** is also a place where services for the community are performed, such as Red Cross work, Boy Scout work and work of other such organizations." *Matter of Cmty. Synagogue v. Bates* (N.Y., 1956).

## SYNDICATE

**A group formed to combine capital or other assets for future investment.**

*Legal Annotation*: "8.2(C) To evidence the availability to Borrower of a facility for purposes of financing its development and construction of the Spire Building, Borrower shall obtain from a lender or **syndicate** of lenders, (i) on or prior to March 1, 2008 a letter of intent evidencing same." *Bank of America, NA v. Shelbourne Development Group, Inc.* (N.D. Ill., 2011).

## SYNERGISM

**The cooperative action of separate substances so that the total effect is greater than the sum of the effects of the substances acting independently.**

*Legal Annotation*: "The Junction City-Ogden-Manhattan area has been ripe for residential and commercial development as our country's participation in the Iraq and Afghanistan wars has intensified over the past nine years and additional forces are trained at and deployed from Fort Riley. Some additional **synergy** is provided by the proximity of this area to Kansas State University, Interstate 70, and the anticipated National Bio Agro-Defense Facility (NBAF)." *In Re Rim Development, LLC* (Bankr. Ct. D. Kan., 2010).

# T

## TAILINGS

**Second-grade or waste material derived when raw material is screened or processed.**

***Legal Annotation***: "The House Report described the need for such legislation in the following terms: Uranium mills are a part of the nuclear fuel cycle. They extract uranium from ore for eventual use in nuclear weapons and power plants, leaving radioactive sand-like waste—commonly called uranium mill **tailings**—in generally unattended piles." *Kerr-McGee Chemical Corp. v. US Nuclear Regulatory Commission* (D.C. Cir., 1990).

## TAKING

**To take, expropriate, acquire, or seize property without compensation. See *Eminent Domain; Just Compensation*.**

***Comment***: The question of taking has become increasingly important as a result of recent US Supreme Court decisions, including the so-called 1987 Trilogy of *First English Evangelical Lutheran Church v. County of Los Angeles*, *Nollan v. California Coastal Comm'n*, and *Keystone Bituminous Coal Ass'n v. DeBenedictis*; the categorical taking case of *Lucas v. South Carolina Coastal Council* (1992); and most recently the 2014 trilogy of *Arkansas Game and Fish v. U.S.*, *Horne v. Dept. of Agric.*, and *Koontz v. St. Johns River Management District*.

The best and most readable exposition of the takings issue is set out in the last opinion written by Justice O'Connor in *Lingle v. Chevron USA, Inc.* (2005):

> The Takings Clause of the Fifth Amendment provides that private property shall not "be taken for public use, without just compensation." As its text makes plain, the Takings Clause "does not prohibit the taking of private property, but instead places a condition on the exercise of that power." In other words, it "is designed not to limit the governmental interference with property rights per se, but rather to secure compensation in the event of otherwise proper interference amounting to a taking." While scholars have offered various justifications for this regime, we have emphasized its role in "bar[ring] Government from forcing some people alone to bear public burdens which, in all fairness and justice, should be borne by the public as a whole."
>
> The paradigmatic taking requiring just compensation is a direct government appropriation or physical invasion of private property. Indeed, until the Court's watershed decision in Pennsylvania Coal Co. v. Mahon (1922), "it was generally thought that the Takings Clause reached only a 'direct appropriation' of property, or the functional equivalent of a 'practical ouster of [the owner's] possession.'" ("[E]arly constitutional theorists did not believe the Takings Clause embraced regulations of property at all".)
>
> Beginning with Mahon, however, the Court recognized that government regulation of private property may, in some instances, be so onerous that its effect is tantamount to a direct appropriation or ouster—and that such "regulatory takings" may be compensable under the Fifth Amendment. In Justice Holmes' storied but cryptic formulation, "while property may be regulated to a certain extent, if regulation goes too far it will be recognized as a taking." The rub, of course, has been—and remains—how to discern how far is "too far." In answering that question, we must remain cognizant that "government regulation—by definition—involves the adjustment of rights for the public good," and that "Government hardly could go on if to some extent values incident to property could not be diminished

without paying for every such change in the general law."

Our precedents stake out two categories of regulatory action that generally will be deemed per se takings for Fifth Amendments purposes. First, where government requires an owner to suffer a permanent physical invasion of her property—however minor—it must provide just compensation. A second categorical rule applies to regulations that completely deprive an owner of "all economically beneficial us[e]" of her property. We held in Lucas that the government must pay just compensation for such "total regulatory takings," except to the extent that "background principles of nuisance and property law" independently restrict the owner's intended use of the property.

Outside these two relatively narrow categories (and the special context of land-use exactions), regulatory takings challenges are governed by the standards set forth in Penn Central Transp. Co. v. New York City (1978). The Court in Penn Central acknowledged that it had hitherto been "unable to develop any 'set formula'" for evaluating regulatory takings claims, but identified "several factors that have particular significance." Primary among those factors are "[t]he economic impact of the regulation on the claimant and, particularly, the extent to which the regulation has interfered with distinct investment-backed expectations." In addition, the "character of the governmental action"—for instance whether it amounts to a physical invasion or instead merely affects property interests through "some public program adjusting the benefits and burdens of economic life to promote the common good"—may be relevant in discerning whether a taking has occurred. The Penn Central factors—though each has given rise to vexing subsidiary questions—have served as the principal guidelines for resolving regulatory takings claims that do not fall within the physical takings or Lucas rules.

***Legal Annotations***: "The **Takings** Clause of the Fifth Amendment of the United States Constitution, made applicable to the States through the Fourteenth Amendment . . . provides: '[N]or shall private property be **taken** for public use, without just compensation.'" *Dolan v. City of Tigard* (U.S., 1994).

"Lastly, the character of the governmental action also weighs against finding an unconstitutional **taking**. A **taking** is more readily found when the government action is 'characterized as a physical invasion,' and less likely when the 'interference arises from some public program adjusting the benefits and burdens of economic life to promote the common good.' . . . In Penn Central, the Supreme Court upheld comprehensive governmental regulation of private property designed to preserve historic buildings in the City of New York. . . . Likewise, our Supreme Court has recognized that states and cities may enact land-use restrictions or controls to enhance the quality of life by preserving the character and desirable aesthetic features of a city. . . . Here, the purpose of the City's ordinance is 'to promote the educational, cultural and general welfare of the citizens of New Albany and . . . to ensure the viability of the [d]owntown and other historic commercial activities and to enhance tourism.' . . . As such, the ordinance serves a substantial public purpose. We conclude that no taking has occurred and affirm the trial court's denial of Bradford's request for summary judgment on his claim of inverse condemnation." *Historic Preservation v. Bradford Realty* (Ind. Ct. app., 2012).

## TANGIBLE PERSONAL PROPERTY

**Personal property that can be felt or touched.**

***Comment***: "Tangible personal property includes furniture, business equipment, vehicles, household goods, clothing, collectibles, and jewelry." http://biztax.about.com/od/glossaryp/g/personalprop.htm

***Legal Annotation***: "An examination of the statute in question and the objectives intended to be accomplished thereby clearly indicates that the General Assembly when using the word **tangible** in referring to **personal property** had in mind the ordinary and popularly understood meaning of such term as indicated in Webster's first definition thereof, which is 'Capable of being touched; also, perceptible to the touch; tactile; palpable.'" *Farrand Coal Co. v. Halpin* (Ill., 1957).

## TANK FARM

**An open-air facility containing large, aboveground containers for the bulk storage of material in liquid, gaseous, powder, or pellet form.**

***Legal Annotation***: "The **tank farm** consisted of storage tanks and pumps and was used by Esso as a distribution station for 'white' petroleum products, i. e., diesel fuel, kerosene, and regular and premium gasoline." *U.S. v. Esso Standard Oil Co. of Puerto Rico* (3rd Cir., 1967).

## TATTOO PARLOR

**An establishment in which people receive permanent decorative tattoos from a tattoo artist.**

***Comment***: Aside from providing tattoos, many tattoo parlors today also provide body piercing. Until the 1990s tattooing was considered a form of deviance. It has now entered the mainstream as an acceptable form of expression, common among both sexes, and all economic classes, from later teen years to middle age. Despite the cultural transformation, tattoo parlors often carry the stigma associated with other "undesirable" land uses such as massage parlors, pawn shops, check cashing stores, methodone clinics, and medical marijuana dispensaries. The institution of training and certification requirements as well as adherence to health-related and operational requirements has begun to make such uses more acceptable. Also referred to as "tattoo studios" or "tattoo shops."

***Legal Annotation***: "Finally, the court concluded that because the sale of the tattoo is intertwined with the process of creating it, the business of a **tattoo parlor** is also pure speech subject only to reasonable time, place, or manner restrictions." *Coleman v. City of Mesa* (Ariz. Ct. App., 2011).

"[T]he City's zoning ordinance did not specifically permit the operation of a **tattoo parlor** as a matter of right in any particular zoning district. Rather, the right to operate such an establishment in a particular zoning district, specifically the RT-2 Resort Tourist District, depended on its classification under the City's zoning ordinance. As already noted, that determination was a discretionary act." *Ancient Art Tattoo Studio v. Virginia Beach* (Va., 2002).

## TAVERN

**An establishment in which alcoholic beverages are served, primarily by the drink, and where food or packaged liquors may also be served or sold. See *Pub*.**

***Comment***: Liquor laws vary by state, and the above definition may not be applicable in all states or areas. Zoning regulations should make a distinction between taverns that have live entertainment or permit dancing and those that do not. Those with live entertainment and dancing may require considerably more parking and need additional setbacks because of noise.

***Legal Annotation***: "In so far as applicable, these provide in substance as follows: No premises shall be used 'for the sale of alcoholic liquor under any **tavern**, restaurant or all-alcoholic liquor package store permit' within 1500 feet of any other premises 'used for the sale of alcoholic liquor under any **tavern**, restaurant, druggist or all-alcoholic liquor package store permit.'" *Cohen v. Board of Appeals on Zoning* (Conn., 1953).

"In April, 1936, the city of Danbury legally adopted an amendment to § 1 of its zoning ordinance which added the following definitions: '(v) A "**Tavern**" is a place where beer or alcoholic liquor is sold under a tavern permit issued by the State Liquor Control Commission. (w) A "Grill" is a place where beer or alcoholic liquor is sold under a restaurant permit issued by the State Liquor Control Commission. (x) A "Hotel" is a place where beer or alcoholic liquor is sold under a hotel permit issued by the State Liquor Control Commission. (y) A "Package Store" is a place where beer or alcoholic liquor is sold under a package store permit issued by the State Liquor Control Commission.'" *Danbury v. Corbett* (Conn., 1953).

## TAX ABATEMENT

**Full or partial exemption from real estate taxes for a defined period of time.**

***Comment***: Tax abatements can be used for a variety of purposes, including encouraging development, historic preservation, natural resource conservation, urban redevelopment, enterprise zones, or some other public objective. In many states, tax abatements are limited to those uses or geographic areas listed in applicable state legislation.

***Legal Annotation***: "Because property **tax abatement is** an equitable remedy utilized to correct errors in property tax levies . . . it is subject to the equitable defense of laches." *Paras v. Portsmouth* (N.H., 1975).

## TAXES

**Compulsory contributions exacted by a government for public purposes, except employee and employee assessments for retirement and social insurance purposes, which are classified as insurance trust revenue.**

***Comment***: All tax revenue is classified as general revenue and comprises amounts received (including interest and penalties but excluding protested amounts and refunds) from all taxes imposed by a government. Note that local government tax revenue excludes any amounts from shares of state-imposed and collected taxes, which are classified as intergovernmental revenue. http://www.census.gov/govs/local/definitions.html

***Legal Annotation***: "A **tax** is defined to be 'a contribution imposed by government on individuals for the service of the State.'" *Morgan's SS Co. v. Louisiana Bd. Of Health* (U.S., 1886).

## TAX-EXEMPT PROPERTY

**Property that, because of its ownership or use, is not subject to property taxation.**

***Legal Annotation***: "These cases hold that normally **tax exempt property** is taxable if used for a non-public purpose. The use is not taxable; rather the property is made taxable because of its use." *Wanamaker v. Phila. Sch. Dist.* (Pa, 1971).

"In 2001 the Legislature enacted an amendment to Section 7-36-7, which states that **property exempt from property taxation**: includes property of a museum that: 1) has been granted exemption from the federal income tax by the United States commissioner of internal revenue as an organization described in Section 501(c)(3) of the Internal Revenue Code of 1986, as amended or renumbered; 2) is used to provide educational services; and 3) grants free admission to each student who attends a public school in the county in which the museum is located." *Georgia O'Keefe Museum v. County* (N.M. Ct. App., 2002).

## TAX INCREMENT FINANCING (TIF)

**A form of public financing that is used for subsidizing redevelopment, infrastructure, or other public improvement projects.**

***Comment***: TIF utilizes increases in future anticipated tax revenues to finance the debt that is issued to pay for the project. TIF programs are most often designed to channel funding toward improvements in distressed, underdeveloped, or undeveloped parts of a jurisdiction without which development is unlikely to occur. With the reduction of federal funding for redevelopment, reductions of municipal budgets, and/or caps on municipal property tax collections, TIFs are increasingly being used by local governments as a way to strengthen their tax bases, attract private investment, and increase overall economic activity.

***Legal Annotation***: "**Tax increment financing** is a tool used by cities and other development authorities to finance the development or redevelopment of a particular geographic or project area. . . . It operates by enabling the city or authority to capture the additional real estate tax revenue or tax increments generated by a new development instead of allowing these tax increments to go to other taxing jurisdictions such as the county or the local school district. . . . The city or authority then uses these tax increments to finance the cost of the development." *Brookfield Trade Ctr. v. Cty. Of Ramsey* (Minn., 1998).

## TECHNICAL COORDINATING COMMITTEE (TCC)

**A committee consisting of one or more persons to review all applications for development. See *Design Review; Design Standards; Site-Plan Review*.**

***Comment***: TCCs may also be known by a variety of other names, such as "development review committee," "application review committee," "technical review committee," or "professional staff review." The TCC, if permitted by enabling legislation and established by the municipality, can save both applicants and approving authority time, money, and energy. The exact makeup of the TCC and members' duties should be carefully spelled out in the land development ordinance.

In general, TCCs may consist of the municipal engineer, planner, planning board or zoning board attorney, building inspector, zoning official, and one or two members of the approving authority (planning board or zoning board). The members are usually appointed by the chairman of the approving authority, although the engineer and planner are often specified by ordinance as ex-officio members.

Their job may consist of any one or more of the following:

- Determine whether the application is a minor or major development application.
- Determine compliance with municipal development standards and regulations.
- Make recommendations on the design and technical elements of any application.
- Determine whether the application is complete and ready for public hearing.
- Conduct formal hearings on minor development applications.

The TCC meetings are less formal than the planning board meeting and, as a result, allow for informal exchanges of ideas and recommendations on design and layout to make the application more acceptable to the municipality. TCCs usually do not get involved in policy matters, such as when variances are requested. They generally confine themselves to the technical aspects of the application.

In some states, TCCs can approve minor applications for development. In such situations, more formal procedures, including hearings, notices, and the publication of decisions, are often required.

***Legal Annotation***: "The county further notified appellant that following the **Technical Coordinating Committee's** review, the county planning commission would meet in joint session with the **Technical Coordinating Committee** in order to receive technical input relative to the preliminary plat. This meeting was scheduled for June 7, 1989." *Emerald Acres Inv. C. Bd. Of Cty. Com'rs* (Fla. Ct. App., 1992).

## TELECOMMUNICATIONS CELL SITE

**See *Wireless Telecommunications Towers And Facilities*.**

***Legal Annotation***: "Defendant New York SMSA Limited Partnership, Inc. cross moves for: (1) for a declaratory judgment to the effect that the Plaintiff is not entitled to remove its telecommunications equipment from the May Place Tower; and (2) an injunction restraining the Plaintiff from interfering with its ability to operate the subject **wireless telecommunications cell site** and/or compelling the Plaintiff to cooperate in good faith by, inter alia, authorizing a temporary **cell cite** while tower repairs progress. . . . According to the providers, during negotiations which ensued concerning the dispute, the District rejected several allegedly viable alternatives, including: (1) a 'phased' or staged rehabilitation procedure obviating prolonged equipment removal and/or service disruption; (2) the on-site placement of separate, 'cells-on-wheels' ('COWS'); and/or (3) the installation of a temporary, ballast-mounted 'monopole' tower for all providers, which would be situated on the southwest corner of the enclosed May Place site." *Massapequa Water District v. New York SMSA Limited Partnership* (N.Y. Sup. Ct., 2008).

## TELECOMMUTING

**An arrangement for performing work at a location other than the primary work location, such as at home or in a satellite office, and sending and receiving material by phone, e-mail, or other electronic means.**

*Legal Annotation*: "Wieliczko, who does not own or run a business of any sort, is an employee like many other individuals who work, own homes and do much of their office work at home. This has become so popular that it has spawned a new form of employment—**telecommuting**. It is now common for employers to economize on workspace and have part of their staff work at the company headquarters and part at home, with the schedule varying from day to day." *Wasserman v. WR Grace & Co.* (N.J. App. Div., 1995).

## TEMPERATURE INVERSION

**See *Inversion*.**

## TEMPLE

**A building used for religious practice.**

*Comment*: "Temple" is the name sometimes given to houses of worship of Reform and some Conservative Jewish congregations, for Mormon sacred ordinances, and for local lodges of various fraternal orders.

*Legal Annotation*: "Such a house of God, called a **temple**, is defined as: 'a house of prayer, a house of fasting, a house of faith, a house of learning, a house of glory, a house of order, a house of God.'" *Theodore M. Burton, Conference Report*, pp. 42–44 (April 1967), http://tinyurl.com/kmjuvuz.

## TEMPORARY OUTDOOR ACTIVITY

**Happenings that are carried out primarily out-of-doors for a fixed period of time; these include flea markets, fireworks, displays, speeches, farm stands, seasonal sales, swap meets, racing meets, circuses, carnivals, concerts, and parades. See *Mass Gathering*.**

*Comment*: Some forms of temporary outdoor activities are clearly addressed by zoning. These include weekend flea markets, farm stands, racing meets, and so forth. Others are more transitory, such as parades, carnivals, and fireworks, and are probably best controlled by permit or license from the municipality.

*Legal Annotation*: "Wilson & Son Ranch LLC appeals a judgment determining that Phillip and Shannon Hintz hold both an express easement that partly coincides with a gravel road running across Wilson's estate as well as an easement by prescription to use the portions of that road not covered by the express easement. Wilson also challenges the trial court's ruling that the Hintzes' use of their property for hosting **temporary outdoor events** such as weddings does not exceed the scope of the express easement. Because we find that the Hintzes' business does not exceed the scope of the easement and that Wilson's other arguments have not been properly preserved for review, we affirm." *Wilson & Son Ranch, LLC v. Hintz* (Wash. Ct. App., 2011).

## TEMPORARY PERMIT

**Authorization for a land-use activity for a limited period of time.**

*Comment*: The local zoning ordinance should spell out what activities can be authorized by a temporary permit, what municipal official or office can issue the temporary permit, and what is required to be submitted for the temporary permit.

Activities usually covered by temporary permits include yard sales, construction trailers, temporary signs, carnivals and circuses sponsored by nonprofit organizations, and seasonal or outdoor sales.

The usual officials authorized to issue the temporary permit are the zoning officer, planner, or municipal engineer. Material to be submitted usually includes a site plan showing access, parking, location, use of structures, and, where appropriate, lighting, sanitary facilities, and security arrangements. Some ordinances require the posting of bonds to ensure compliance with the provisions of the grant of the temporary permit (Jaffee 1999).

*Legal Annotation*: "The **temporary permit** provisions were also constitutional as they were not substantially broader than necessary to achieve the government's aesthetic interest in prompt removal of the signs." *Messer v. City of Douglasville* (11th Cir., 1992).

## TEMPORARY PROTECTION

**Stabilization of erosive or sediment-producing areas by temporary measures until permanent measures are in place.**

*Legal Annotation*: "Unlike the situation in *Laguna Beach Taxpayers' Assn. v. City Council* . . . in which the 'initiative architectural policy ordinance . . . propose[d] a policy that all future buildings in the city should conform to a type of architecture to be adopted' . . . the ordinance here does not provide for future permanent zoning but establishes a **temporary protection** against interim changes in zoning." *Fletcher v. Porter* (Calif. Ct. App., 1962).

## TEMPORARY RETAIL FOOD ESTABLISHMENT

**A retail food establishment that operates at a fixed location for a limited period of time in connection with a fair, carnival, circus, picnic, concert, public exhibition, or similar transitory gathering.**

***Comment***: Temporary retail food establishments are accessory to the principal permitted use—for instance, a fair or carnival—and are not the same as a food cart or food truck. **See *Food Cart, Food Truck*.**

*Legal Annotation*: "N.J.S.A. 26:3E-1 defines a restaurant as 'any facility or part thereof in which food is prepared and provided or served for consumption on the premises but shall not include mobile food establishments or any **temporary food establishment** which operates at a fixed location for a limited period of time in connection with a fair, carnival, public exhibition or similar transitory gathering or charitable fundraising event.'" *LDM, Inc. v. Princeton Reg. Health Comm.* (N.J. Super. Ct., 2000).

## TEMPORARY STRUCTURE

**A structure that is erected without any foundation or footings and is removed when the designated time period, activity, or use for which the temporary structure was erected has ceased.**

*Legal Annotation*: "The import of the term 'temporary', used in describing the construction, is synonymous with the term 'removable' in that the plastic dome which covers the pool is capable of being taken down during the summer months and put up again in the fall, similar to an outdoor awning or storm windows and screens. It does not imply a '**temporary structure**' in the sense that the construction will be demolished at the conclusion of a fixed period of time." *Suburban Club of Larkfield v. Town of Huntington* (NY, 1968).

## TEMPORARY USE

**A use established for a limited duration with the intent to discontinue such use upon the expiration of the time period.**

***Comment***: Temporary uses usually do not involve the construction or alteration of any permanent building or structure, although the authorization of the temporary use does not necessarily preclude such construction.

*Legal Annotation*: "He relied on the definition of '**temporary use**' in the 2006 International Zoning Code, which the Township adopted in 2008. According to that definition, a '**temporary use**' is an activity conducted for a fixed period of time such as 'the sale of agricultural products, contractors' offices and equipment sheds, fireworks, carnivals, flea markets, and garage sales.'" *Bucks Cove Rod & Gun Club, Inc. v. Texas Township Zoning Hearing Board* (Pa. Common. Ct., 2011).

## TENANT

**An occupant of land or premises who occupies, uses, and enjoys real property for a fixed time, usually through a lease or rental arrangement with the property owner.**

*Legal Annotation*: "New York City's Rent Control Law broadly defines '**tenant**' as 'tenant, subtenant, lessee, sublessee, or other person entitled to the possession or to the use or occupancy of any housing accommodation'" *Sullivan v. Brevard Assoc.* (NY Ct. of App., 1985).

"For the purposes of the LTRA, a **tenant** is defined as 'any person who occupies a rental unit for residential purposes with the landlord's consent for an agreed upon consideration.'" *De Bruyn Produce Co. v. Romero* (Mich. Ct. App., 1993).

## TENEMENT HOUSE

**A multifamily building most commonly located in the center of a large city, often overcrowded and occupied with low-income families and generally characterized as aging and substandard.**

*Legal Annotation*: "A **tenement house** is defined by the Licensing Regulations of the District of Columbia as 'any building or part thereof containing three or more tenements [a tenement means one or more habitable rooms other than an apartment . . . under the exclusive control of the occupant or occupants thereof] occupied or offered for occupancy for a consideration, or any building or part thereof containing any combination of three or more tenements and apartments, of which not more than two are apartments, occupied or offered for occupancy for a consideration.'" *Bernstein v. Lime* (D.C. Munic. Ct. App., 1952).

## TENNIS COURT

**A firm, rectangular surface with a low net stretched across the center, where the sport of tennis is played.**

*Comment*: In residential areas, impacts from noise and lighting can be of concern. Standards related to lighting, buffers, and setbacks are appropriate.

*Legal Annotation*: "In support of their appeal the petitioners contend that it should be ruled that a **tennis court** is a structure for which a building permit is required, that mandamus lies to compel the inspector of buildings to require an application for a permit, so that, by an appeal from his decision granting or denying such application, the board of appeals of the town, as the appropriate tribunal for initial action, may determine whether a **tennis court** is a customarily incidental accessory use under the zoning by-law." *Williams v. Inspector of Buildings of Belmont* (Mass., 1960).

## TENT

**A portable structure usually made of cloth, canvas, plastic, or similar material stretched over poles and secured to a wooden platform or surrounding ground with ropes or cable.**

*Legal Annotation*: "This controversy concerns the Society's proposed erection of a **tent** on The Breakers property. The controversy began in 2001. During the spring, summer, and fall months of 2001 the Society had a large **tent** erected on the lawn. The ostensible purpose of the **tent** was to sell tickets to The Breakers and to the Society's other mansions, to advertise these other mansions to visitors, and to provide shelter to potential ticket purchasers. Previously, tickets were sold from a small, two person booth which was not accessible by the public. The new forum would have six ticket-selling stations, as well as two plasma television screens running advertisements.

"In creating this new forum, the Society constructed a 2000 square foot platform anchored to the ground with cement pilings, and which included access ramps and decorative pergolas. Admittedly, this construction was done without any permission. Subsequently, however, the Zoning Officer for the City of Newport, Guy Weston . . . received complaints from neighbors of The Breakers and from the Historic District Commission regarding the tent. . . . Upon inspection, Weston informed the Society that the platform, ramps, and pergolas were unauthorized and that both Historic District Commission and zoning approval were needed for these structures." NI, *LTD. v. Duncan* (R.I., Super. Ct., 2004).

## TENT CITY

**A temporary housing area or site that uses tents and other temporary structures. See *Tent*.**

*Comment*: After Hurricane Katrina, FEMA set up temporary housing sites for Gulf Coast residents left homeless by the storm. These sites, in the form of wooden structures covered by tents, were referred to as "tent cities." Most have access to light, air, and heat and are designed for occupancies of up to six months. **See *Disaster Housing*.**

Informal tent cities are often set up by homeless people or protesters without authorization. While many have been forced to shut down, some inhabitants of tent cities have organized and legally fought for the right to exist at least temporarily, by instituting measures to limit crime or drug use.

*Legal Annotation*: "**Tent City** 4 is an encampment of homeless people that moves to a new location on the east side every 90 days. In 2004, Share/Wheel and the Church agreed to host **Tent City** 4. They negotiated with the City of Woodinville to secure City property (the Lumpkin property) for **Tent City**, subject to certain terms and conditions. The parties executed the Temporary Property Use Agreement in August 2004 to memorialize their agreement. The Church then hosted **Tent City** in accordance with that agreement. . . . Hosting a 90-day encampment not within the primary or accessory buildings of the church is not within the allowed 'accessory use' of church property. It is not incidental to a residence, and it is not an accessory use inside a church building. Therefore, the Church's failure to obtain a permit for **Tent City** 4 was a code violation for which the City was entitled to obtain injunctive relief." *City of Woodinville v. Northshore United Church of Christ* (Wash. Ct. App., 2007).

## TERMINAL, TRUCK

**(1) A place where transfers between modes of transportation take place; (2) a terminating point where goods are transferred from a truck to a storage area or to other trucks or another form of transportation. See *Distribution Center; Truck Terminal; Warehouse*.**

*Legal Annotation*: "The term '**truck terminal**' is not defined in the Dane County Zoning Ordinances as they existed at the time pertinent to this litigation. Secs. 10.01 and 10.01 (15) of the Dane County Zoning Ordinances specify that any words not defined in the ordinance should be construed as defined in the Wisconsin Building Code and, if not defined therein, by reference to dictionary usage or to a common understanding of the term. It is agreed that the Wisconsin Building Code does not define '**truck terminal**,' nor have we been persuaded that there is any common understanding of the meaning of the term. Webster's New Third International Dictionary defines '**terminal**' as: '6a. either end of a carrier line (as a railroad, trucking or shipping line, or airline) with classifying yards, dock and literage facilities, management offices, storage sheds, and freight and passenger stations b: a freight or passenger station that is central to a considerable area or serves as a junction at any point with other lines.' Under that dictionary definition, which includes **terminals** related to trucking, it is clear that the term, '**truck terminal**,' includes the concept of facilities for storage or loading." *Cohen v. Dane County Board of Adjustment* (Wis., 1976).

## TERMINAL VISTA

See *Visual Termination*.

## TERRACE

**An external, raised, open, flat area either around a building or in a park or open space.**

*Comment*: Used primarily for leisure activities, terraces may be supported by an embankment or solid foundation, or supported by columns, but with the space below filled in, and always open to the sky. Such terraces may or may not be paved. **See *Patio*.**

Terraces are also created to permit the cultivation of crops or rice on steeply sloped lands. However, terrace farming is less common in the United States than in Asia and Europe.

*Legal Annotation*: "A '**Terrace**' is defined in the 'Definitions' section of the Offering Plan as any **terrace**, balcony or garden which is appurtenant to a residential unit. The Offering Plan stated that all **terraces** and roof set backs adjacent to apartments would be paved with concrete pavers, even for those roof setbacks that are not accessible . . . Schedule A to the Offering Plan is a table that provides a general description of each unit, including area, offering price and percentage of common interest. In provides a column titled 'Approx. Exterior Sq. Ft **Terrace**', which is blank for all but eight units, suggesting very few units had appurtenant outdoor space." *Pappas v. New 19 W., LLC* (N.Y. Sup. Ct., 2008).

## TERTIARY TREATMENT

**Wastewater treatment, beyond the secondary or biological stage, that includes removal of nutrients, such as phosphorus and nitrogen, and a high percentage of suspended solids.**

***Comment***: The standards utilized for classifying treatment as "tertiary" are typically found in local state or federal regulations.

***Legal Annotation***: "**Tertiary treatment** is treatment that will, for the purpose of this permit, produce an effluent that will contain an organic load, as measured by the 5-day bio-chemical oxygen demand test, of not more than 10 mg/1 as an average of five consecutive samples or 20 mg/1 at any time; will limit the total suspended solids to 25 mg/1 or less; will limit the volatile suspended solids to 10 mg/1 or less; will provide effective disinfection to control disease producing organisms; will provide satisfactory disposal of sludge; and will reduce the quantities of oil, grease, acids, alkalis, toxic, taste and odor producing substances inimical to the public interest to levels that will not pollute the receiving stream." *Appeal of Deguffroy* (Pa. Ct. Comm. Pleas, 1974)

## TEXTURE

**The quality of a surface, ranging from mirror-finish, smooth to coarse and unfinished.**

***Legal Annotation***: "Moreover, the very Ordinance upon which the plaintiff claims the Planning Commission unlawfully and illegally relied in denying his permit . . . specifically includes window replacement and grants the Commission the authority to deny permits for the same. Specifically, that provision provides: 'In reviewing all plans required to be submitted by this Section . . . the Commission shall give consideration to: (1) the historic or architectural value and significance of the structure and its relationship to the historic value of the surrounding area; (2) the relationship of the exterior architectural features [which includes "the type, design and character of all windows"] of the structure to the remainder of the structure and to the surrounding area; (3) the general compatibility of exterior design, **texture** and materials proposed to be used; (4) any other factors including aesthetic factors which the Commission deems to be pertinent.'" *Struna v. Shepherdstown Planning Commission* (N.D. W. Va., 2011).

## TEXTURED PAVEMENT

**See *Traffic Calming*.**

***Legal Annotation***: "Toll Middle School is located on Glenwood Road between Concord Street and Virginia Avenue. There are marked crosswalks at both ends of Glenwood Road and a mid-block crosswalk, which consisted of two parallel, 12-inch-wide yellow stripes painted with yellow thermoplastic paint and reflective glass beads located 18 feet apart, running perpendicular to the north and south curbs of Glenwood road. The pavement surface within crosswalk was **textured 'stamped' red asphalt**." *Nalbandyan v. City of Glendale* (Calif. Ct. App., 2012).

## THEATER

**A building or part of a building used to show motion pictures or for drama, dance, musical, or other stage performances.**

***Legal Annotation***: "The term '**theater**' is not defined in the Township zoning ordinance. As a result the Court must look to the term's ordinary meaning since no other source is available from which to discern legislative intent. Upon review of the common definition of **theater**, the Court finds that there are few if any circumstances in which the booths proposed by Executive could fall within the ordinary meaning of that term. Certainly, in terms of parking and traffic problems, there is nothing from which to infer that the associated problems would be even remotely similar. A **theater** has been defined as 'a building for showing motion pictures; something resembling a theater in form or use; a room, often with rising tiers of seats for lectures, surgicals demonstrations or other assemblies or exhibitions.' Webster's Third New International Dictionary, Unabridged (4th ed. 1976). The Random House College Dictionary defines the term **theater** as '[a] building, part of a building, or outdoor area for housing dramatic presentations, stage entertainments, or motion-picture shows. . . . [a] room or hall, fitted with tiers of seats rising like steps, used for lectures, anatomical demonstrations, etc.' (Rev. ed. 1980)." *Executive Art Studio v. Charter Tp. of Kalamazoo* (W.D. Mich., 1987).

## THEATER, DRIVE-IN

**An open lot devoted primarily to the showing of motion pictures or theatrical productions on a paid-admission basis to patrons seated in automobiles.**

***Comment***: Drive-in theaters are diminishing in number and popularity in the United States. Where they still exist, they are being used until demand for other, more remunerative uses materialize. Drive-in theaters include refreshment stands and amusement rides. Since drive-in theaters operate only at night, many sites are used for other purposes during the day, such as flea markets.

***Legal Annotation***: "The definitions section of the Zoning Code, § 11-1-3, defines '**Theater, Outdoor Drive-In**' but does not define the term 'motion picture' nor the term 'amusement enterprise.' The meaning of these latter two terms is thus unclear from the plain language of the ordinance." *Tovar v. Billmeyer* (Idaho, 1978).

## THEME PARK

See *Amusement Park*.

***Legal Annotation***: "It was Mr. Bensen's testimony that the claimant intended to recreate these various old buildings and to establish an additional **Theme Park** attraction which would be known as Frontiers of Industry. Exhibits '9' and '26' were artistic renderings illustrative of what could have been done in the Palmer Pond Section. We should point out that, in consideration of subject property, we must keep in mind we are in the field of entertainment. Certainly, if we were treating the problem of a real estate subdivision, the production of an artist's rendering would not be of substantial assistance. However, as stated by Mr. McGoodwin, one of claimant's **Theme Park** experts: 'The **theme park** is a conception of architecture, and the biggest practitioners of the construction of theme parks came from the movie lots and sets, mostly of southern California. They are truly sets. These people are used to drawing a picture of an 1880 log cabin, or an 1890 fire station. They do research and they come up with a rendering as authentic, but as attractive, not necessarily—absolute historical veracity is not what they are after, necessarily." *Frontier Props. v. State of NY* (N.Y. Ct. Cl., 1968).

## THEORETICAL DRIVEWAY LOCATION

**The center of the highway frontage of any lot; used to calculate whether a lot is conforming for highway access purposes.**

***Comment***: Used in highway access ordinances or part of state highway access regulations.

***Legal Annotation***: "'Theoretical driveway location (TDL)' means the center of the State highway frontage of any lot. It is used to calculate whether a lot is conforming." Title 16. New Jersey Department of Transportation Chapter 47. State Highway Access Management Code. http://www.state.nj.us/transportation/about/rules/pdf/chapter47.pdf

## THERMAL POLLUTION

**Degradation of water quality by the introduction of a heated effluent.**

***Comment***: Thermal pollution is primarily the result of the discharge of cooling waters from industrial processes, particularly from electrical power generation.

***Legal Annotation***: "'**Thermal pollution**' is used to designate the effects on a river—its water, flora and fauna—of the injection of heated water." *State of New Hampshire v. Atomic Energy Commission* (1st Cir., 1969).

## THREATENED SPECIES

**Wildlife species that may become endangered if conditions surrounding them deteriorate and that are so designated by a governmental agency.**

*Legal Annotation*: "A '**threatened species**' is 'any species which is likely to become an endangered species within the foreseeable future.' 16 U.S.C. § 1532(20)." *Sierra Club v. Clark* (8th Cir., 1985).

## THROUGH LOT

**See *Lot, Through.***

*Legal Annotation*: "The subject property is a **through-lot** located at 600 West Stratford Place, Chicago. A **through-lot** is one which goes from one street to another without an alley in between." *Bayer v. Zoning Bd. of Appeals* (Ill. App. Ct., 1970).

## TIDE

**A periodic rise and fall of the surface of ocean waters caused by gravitational pull. *See Figure 11.***

*Legal Annotation*: "The 'head of **tide**' is defined by the National Oceanic and Atmospheric Administration as '[t]he inland or upstream limit of water affected by the **tide**.' NOAA Shoreline Website: A Guide to National Shoreline Data and Terms, http://shoreline.noaa.gov/glossary.html (last visited Jan. 25, 2011)." *Critical Area Commission v. Moreland, LLC* (Md. Ct. App., 2011).

## TIDELAND

**Land between low and high tide. See *Intertidal Area*. See *Figure 11*.**

*Legal Annotation*: "The land in controversy consists principally of reclaimed **tide land** which was filled as a result of certain dredging operations carried on by the city between 1918 and 1923. In 1917 the United States War Department established a bulkhead line in the bay which was located parallel to and about 260 feet northerly of the center line of the alley. The material from the dredging operations was deposited in the area between such bulkhead line and the northerly boundary of block 109. After the land was filled, the City of Newport Beach constructed a street designated as Bay Avenue, which is 50 feet in width, parallel to and 100 feet northerly of the center line of the alley shown on the subdivision map. Ninth and Tenth Streets, which constitute the easterly and westerly boundaries of block 109, were likewise extended through such filled area to the bulkhead line." *City of Newport Beach v. Fager* (Calif. Ct. App., 1940).

## TILLABLE LAND

**Land capable of being tilled or plowed for cultivating crops.**

*Legal Annotation*: "Plaintiffs complain that the trial court admitted evidence as to the meaning of the term 'tillable acres,' implying that the introduction of testimony on that point led to confusion. The record shows, however, that plaintiffs' counsel stated during the course of the questioning: 'There is only one question, what does a farmer in the town of Adrian call **tillable land**?' Answering that question, Edmund Neas, plaintiffs' son, testified that **tillable land** is land that can be worked with a tractor. The same definition was given by the witness, Dwyer, and by the Siemens' son, Bernhard Alfred." *Neas v. Siemens* (Wis., 1960).

## TIMBERLAND

**Land covered by harvestable trees and wooded areas.**

*Legal Annotation*: "'**Timberland**' is defined as 'land, other than land owned by the federal government . . . which is available for, and capable of, growing a crop of trees of any commercial species used to produce lumber and other forest products, including Christmas trees.' (§ 4526.) The parties do not dispute that the land involved in this controversy is properly categorized as

**timberland**." *Hewlett v. Squaw Valley Ski Corp.* (Calif. Ct. app., 1997).

## TIME-SHARE

**A property in which multiple parties hold rights to use the property for an allotted period of time. (Also known as "Universal Lease Programs.")**

***Comment***: These properties are typically condominium units, usually located in resort areas. These units may be on a partial ownership, lease or "right to use" basis, in which the sharer holds no claim to ownership of the property. Often time-share owners may exchange their scheduled use time, usually one week, through an exchange agency; or, less often, through a direct exchange by locating an owner with the location and weeks both mutually desire.

***Legal Annotation***: "Defendants do not identify the specific ruling in the 58 page decision that they seek to reconsider. Instead, they request reconsideration: to the effect that [a] **Time Share** is anything other than a form of title to real estate, substantially similar if not equal to ownership of a condominium and are both controlled pursuant to the same Chapter M.G.L. 183. The form of ownership does not affect the form or process of operation of a resort. The primary determination in the Memorandum and Order vis-à-vis a **time share** consists of the finding that **time share** ownership 'is distinct and materially different from owning a property that does not include **time share** estates.' . . . The plain language of Massachusetts General Laws chapter 183A applies to condominiums whereas chapter 183B applies to **time share** estates. Thus, as correctly explained in the Memorandum and Order, 'Listing a percentage of "ownership" of these two properties' in Narbonne's personal financial statement 'while omitting their operation as time shares is materially misleading with respect to the loan.' . . . Defendants' argument that both **time share** and resort ownership are covered under Massachusetts General Laws chapter 183 ignores the statutory distinctions and the materiality of the financial implications of operating a **time share** resort as opposed to a condominium/hotel. Defendants do not provide any newly discovered evidence or identify a manifest injustice resulting from this court's ruling. Reconsideration is therefore improper." *Wells Fargo Bank, NA v. Narbonnd* (D. Mass., 2013).

## T-INTERSECTION

**An at-grade intersection where two roads meet at the end of one of the roads and form the shape of the letter *T*.**

***Legal Annotation***: "A **'T' intersection** is formed where two roads meet at the end of one of the roads forming a 'T'; and the driver must make either a right or a left turn." *Jones v. Mississippi Dept. of Transp.* (Miss., 1999).

## TOPOGRAPHIC MAP

**A map of a part of the earth's surface showing elevations from sea level or some other fixed reference point.**

***Comment***: Topographic maps often include natural and artificial features, such as structures, rivers, and wooded areas. **See *Map, Contour And*** *Figure 24.*

***Legal Annotation***: "[A] distance of approximately 534 feet to the intersection of said private road right-of-way with the contour line identifying an elevation of 2,350 feet as depicted on a **topographic Map** No. 36-32 of Buncombe County, compiled by Fairchild Aerial Survey, Inc., and updated by Piedmont Aerial Survey, Inc." *Garland v. City of Asheville* (N.C. Ct. App., 1983).

## TOPOGRAPHY

**The physical land surface relief describing terrain elevation and slope. See *Contour Line*.**

***Legal Annotation***: "'**Topography**' is defined in the dictionary as 'the configuration of a surface including its relief and the position of its natural *and man-made* features.' (Webster's New Internat. Dict. (3d ed. 1986) p. 2411, italics added)." *Denny's, Inc. v. City of Agoura Hills* (Calif. Ct. App. 1997).

## TOPSOIL

**(1) The natural, undisturbed surface layer of soil having more organic material than subsequent layers, having a pH of 5.0 to 7.5, and being suitable for satisfactory growth and maintenance of permanent, locally adapted vegetation; (2) where the original surface layer has been removed, the reapplication of soil material used to cover an area so as to improve soil conditions for establishment and maintenance of adapted vegetation (NJDCA 2000, N.J.A.C. 5:21-1).**

*Comment*: The above source also provides standards for when the surface layer has been removed and new soil material brought in, as follows: "[T]he new soil must be friable, loamy soil, reasonably free of debris, objectionable weeds and stones, have a natural pH of 5.0 to 7.5, have an organic matter content greater than 2.0 percent and contain no toxic substances which may be harmful to plant growth." Topsoil usually has a depth of six to ten inches, although it may be less in certain regions and more in others. Since topsoil is needed to support plant growth and is relatively poor in terms of providing a stable base for buildings or structures, builders will often scrape off the topsoil on a construction site and stockpile it on the site until the final permanent landscaping phase of development, when it is re-spread. Many local ordinances prohibit the export of topsoil from building sites.

*Legal Annotation*: "In contrast, '**topsoil**' is defined as 'soil on the surface prior to mining that will support plant life[.]' Wyo. Stat. § 35-11-103(e)(xiv). This definition is pivotal in the regulatory scheme governing reclamation efforts in the mining process because topsoil must be separately preserved and managed. Thus, in accord with industry usage, the DEQ did not include '**topsoil**' when calculating the 'overburden' restrictions in the annual operations of a small mine." *Platte Development Co. v. State, EQC* (Wyo., 1998).

## TOT LOT

**An improved and equipped play area for small children, usually up to elementary school age.**

*Comment*: Tot lots generally do not exceed twenty-five hundred square feet and are usually equipped with swings, sandboxes, and other playground equipment suitable for small children. They include benches and tables and are usually fenced.

*Legal Annotation*: "Speer Recreation Center has a fully-equipped, fenced '**tot lot**' with many varieties of play structures for children and shaded sitting areas with picnic tables for adults. The black community has absolutely no facilities for younger children, at Smith-Brown or elsewhere. This is perhaps the most needed recreational improvement in black Arcadia." *Johnson v. City of Arcadia, Fla.* (M.D. Fla., 1978).

## TOURISM

**The attracting and serving of people visiting an area for recreation and vacations (Krone 2010).**

*Legal Annotation*: "'**Tourism**' is defined as 'tourist travel, especially when regarded as a source of income for a country, business, etc.' 'Tourist' includes 'one who makes a tour; one who makes a journey for pleasure.' 'Travel' is defined as 'the act or process of traveling[,]' with 'traveling' relating to 'a passing from place to place; the act of performing a journey.'" *Fountain Place Cinema 8, LLC v. Morris* (W.Va., 2011).

## TOURIST HOME

**An establishment in a private dwelling that supplies temporary accommodations to overnight guests for a fee. See *Bed And Breakfast*.**

*Legal Annotation*: "At the time, Woodford County's zoning ordinance recognized '**tourist home**' as a permitted conditional use, but the ordinance did not define that term. Patricia Wilson, the Planning Director, supplied the definition from one of the standard reference works in the Board's library. [Harvey S. Moskowitz & Carl G. Lindbloom, The New Illustrated Book of Development Definitions (New Brunswick, N.J.: Center for Urban Policy Research, 1993).] The definition stated that a **tourist home** is '[a]n establishment in a private dwelling that supplies temporary accommodations to overnight guests for a fee. See *bed and breakfast.' Based on this definition, the board granted the previous conditional use permit." Keogh v. Woodford Cty. Bd. of Adj. (Ky. Ct. App., 2007).*

## TOWER, AMATEUR RADIO

**A tower with one or more antennas connected to radio equipment operated by a licensed amateur radio operator in accordance with applicable FCC laws and regulations.**

***Comment***: An application to install an amateur radio tower often provokes opposition because of real or perceived interference problems, potential dangers to health, and aesthetic considerations. Because amateur radio towers are usually much lower than cellular towers, opposition is usually local in nature, often limited to the street or immediate neighborhood surrounding the tower.

The Federal Communications Commission (FCC) regulates amateur radio licensing and operations, including operating frequencies, maximum radio frequency emissions, and interference. In 1985, the FCC issued a limited federal preemption of amateur radio antennas (FCC PRB-1, 101 FCC. 2d 952 [September 16, 1985]). PRB-1 states that local governments must reasonably accommodate amateur operations, but they may still zone for height, safety, and aesthetic concerns. Any regulations affecting aesthetics, location, height, and screening must "reasonably accommodate such communications and must represent the minimum practicable regulation to accomplish the stated purpose" (American Planning Association, *Aesthetics, Community Character, and the Law*, Planning Advisory Service Report No. 489/490, 1999, 121).

Amateur radio operators provide important, recognized communication support services to government and private relief agencies in times of major local and national disasters. They also provide assistance to citizens in forwarding "health and welfare" messages during periods when normal communication facilities are unavailable. To protect this valuable resource, many states have enacted specific laws providing limits on the types of controls that local government can enact affecting the placement, screening, or height of amateur radio antenna support structures.

Local ordinances should consider addressing the issue directly. For example, antennas, as permitted accessory uses, could be restricted to rear and side yards with reasonable setbacks from property lines. Landscaping can be required around the base of the tower, including the planting of trees that would provide some screening. In addition, a building permit from the local building department would be appropriate to ensure that the structure is erected in a safe manner. Finally, the maximum height could be established at seventy-five feet, which experts suggest is needed to ensure communication reliability for certain frequencies. Anything higher would require a variance. Towers on top of buildings would have to meet the maximum established for buildings in the particular zone.

These controls address issues of safety and aesthetics while still providing a reasonable accommodation for amateur radio.

***Legal Annotation***: "The defendant, the Town of Hudson (town), appeals from a Superior Court (Brennan, J.) order rescinding a building permit granted to the intervenor, Jeremy L. Muller. The town argues that the court misapplied the law on accessory uses and ordered relief that conflicted with federal objectives to allow and promote amateur ham radio facilities. We affirm in part, reverse in part, vacate and remand.

"Muller resides in a section of Hudson zoned Residential-Two (R-2), and is an amateur or 'ham' radio operator. In December 1998, when Muller applied for a building permit, the town had no regulations restricting the number or height of amateur radio towers. The town zoning administrator granted Muller a building permit to erect three ninety-foot **amateur radio towers** with antennae to be added at a later date that would bring the total height of each tower to one hundred feet.

[. . .]

"We note, however, that while New Hampshire and federal law require municipalities to accommodate amateur communications, they do not require the town to allow an amateur operator to erect any antenna he or she desires. . . . Instead, they require only that the town 'consider the application, make factual findings, and attempt to negotiate a satisfactory compromise with the applicant.'" *Marchand v. Town of Hudson* (N.H., 2001).

## TOWER, ANTENNA

**A structure that is intended to support antennas and related equipment used to transmit and/or receive wireless communication signals.**

***Comment***: The difference between telecommunications and mobile or cellular communications is that telecommunications is related to wire communications while mobile or cellular is related to wireless communications. Antennas for both are often supported by or mounted on towers.

***Legal Annotation***: "On October 5, 2010, Verizon applied to BCPC for approval of the placement of a 305 foot, self-supporting, lattice-style cellular **antenna tower** on a 10,000 square foot section of Eloise Warnke's farm (the Warnke farm)." *Hampson v. Boone Co. Planning Commission* (Ky. Ct. App., 2014).

"The ordinance also defines 1) **antenna tower** as a 'vertical structure which supports an antenna or antennae in an elevated position.'" *Ross v. Harris* (Ind. Ct. App., 2006).

## TOWER, COMMERCIAL COMMUNICATIONS

**A transmission tower that (1) serves an individual user and is not available to the general public; (2) is privately owned and operated for the purpose of leasing tower space to others; and/or (3) is a single-purpose facility and not part of a cell site network.**

***Legal Annotation***: "The Zoning Ordinance defines a '**commercial communications tower**' as '[a] structure situated on a nonresidential site that is intended for transmitting or receiving radio, television, or telephone communications (excluding those towers used exclusively for dispatch communications as an accessory to an established principal use).' Zoning Ordinance § 24-1." *Illinois RSA No. 3, Inc. v. County of Peoria* (C.D. Ill., 1997).

## TOWER STRUCTURE, ALTERNATIVE

**Antenna-mounting structures designed to look like clock towers, bell towers or steeples, silos, flagpoles, or trees, and similar antenna-mounting structures whose primary purpose is to camouflage the presence of antennas.**

***Comment***: Until new technology can eliminate the need for cellular towers, alternate tower structures will continue to be employed. The most effective means of camouflaging antennas are clock and bell towers and silos. The least effective are fake trees and flagpoles.

***Legal Annotation***: "For example, the ordinance defines **alternative tower structure** as including 'man-made trees, building walls, clock towers, bell steeples, light poles and similar alternative design mounting structures that camouflage or conceal the presence of commercial communication towers and antennas.' Zoning Ordinance Section 160.021(A)(1)." *Ross v. Harris* (Ind. Ct. App., 2006).

## TOWN

**(1) A developed community, smaller than a city and larger than a village; (2) in some states, a description of the form of local government.**

***Comment***: The New Jersey State Development and Redevelopment Plan (2002) defines a town as having an urban density of more than one thousand persons per square mile and interrelated mixed uses.

***Legal Annotation***: "If a **town** is a political subdivision then petitioners are entitled to an order validating their petitions because they have more than 500 valid signatures. . . . Elsewhere in the statutes a town is defined as a political subdivision (see, e.g., General Municipal Law, §§ 60 [subd. 2, par. b], 209-o [subd. 1, par. a]; §§ 1, 100 [subd. 1]; Executive Law, § 10 [subd. 1, par. e]; cf. § 331 [subd. 3])." *Matter of Steinberg v. McNab* (N.Y., 1969).

## TOWN AND GOWN

**In a community with an academic institution (e.g., college or university) or associated populations (e.g., college students, faculty), "town" refers to the community's non-academic entity or population, while "gown" refers to the academic entity or associated populations.**

*Comment*: "Historically colleges and universities in the United States literally walled themselves off from their host communities. This was particularly the case in urban settings in the 1960s and 1970s as cities suffered from urban decline. Community and government agencies, in turn, have often viewed colleges as having some adverse impacts, complaining about their tax-exempt status, physical encroachment, and parking and traffic problems. The term town-gown itself typically conjures up acrimony and tension which has frequently played out when academic and community stakeholders have interacted." More recently, "institutions of higher learning and their host communities have come to recognize their relationship as symbiotic" and there have been efforts to improve town-gown relations. An example in the United States is the "Campus Compact, a national coalition of over 950 college and university presidents that promotes community service, civic engagement, and service-learning" (http://www.compacat.org/resources/future-of-camus-engagement/tow). While there may be "town-gown" frictions, university spending can be important for economic development (Ortiz 2007).

*Legal Annotation*: "The relationship between universities and their neighbors—between **Town and Gown**—has been the subject of considerable controversy and litigation, and the law has evolved significantly over the years. New York (as well as other jurisdictions) long considered religious, educational and other institutions to be 'favored uses' in residential areas, allowed where other nonresidential uses are not. This approach is entirely consistent with a sort of romantic view of a traditional neighborhood, with a neighborhood park, neighborhood elementary school and two or three houses of worship all carefully integrated into an otherwise entirely residential setting." *President and Directors v. Bd. of Zon. Adj.* (D.C. Ct. App., 2003).

## TOWN CENTER

See *Central Business District*.

*Comment*: While "town center" most often refers to a community's central business district or downtown area, many suburban communities that lack them often try to create or recreate "town centers" by adopting planned development zoning, or through redevelopment. The focus is typically on recreating walkable blocks of mostly ground-floor retail development with office, entertainment, and residential development, both above the ground-floor retail uses and in separate blocks. **See *Central Business District*.**

*Legal Annotation*: "This proposal would allow for the overall development of the subject properties as a mixed-use development consisting of approximately 1.8 million square feet of new retail, commercial, office and residential space. The proposal would divide the subject properties into four sectors: a '**town center**' mixed-use community (comprised of a diverse mix of retail, office, residential, hotel and entertainment uses and public spaces in a pedestrian-oriented environment with preservation of 14 acres of open space); office building development; residential development; and, existing buildings." *BPG Real Estate v. Bd. of Sup'rs of Newtown* (Pa. Common. Ct., 2010).

## TOWN SQUARE

**The traditional center of a village or town, usually surrounded by governmental, religious, and cultural buildings.**

*Legal Annotation*: "We conclude that the sidewalks and parking lots of [the two stores] are not the modern-day equivalent of **town squares**. The scope of noncommercial invitation to these premises is limited. The stores themselves sell only home improvement items. Neither shopping center in which the stores are located provides a broad array of commercial enterprises, nor does either attempt to be a 'one stop' shopping area.

There is no evidence that the store's parking lots or sidewalks are places where the public is consistently invited to congregate for noncommercial purposes, nor is there evidence that plaintiff has extended an invitation to the public to use its sidewalks and parking lots for noncommercial activity by providing areas for the public to congregate or community bulletin boards." *Stranahan v. Fred Meyer, Inc.* (Ore. Ct. App., 1998).

## TOWNHOUSE

**See *Dwelling, Townhouse*.**

***Legal Annotation***: "The only difference between a single-family detached residence and a **townhouse** is that **townhouses** are constructed in clusters and are not detached. In each instance, however, they are single-family residences. The trial judge found from the testimony of the expert witnesses on both sides that **townhouses** on the Louk Tract would not violate 'the need for open spaces, air and room but in fact because of the peculiar nature of this tract and with its trees were better able to supply those factors than single family detached dwellings placed on pipestem lots or cul-de-sac lots'. The court stated: 'The town's expert witness could give the court no good reason for why the tract should be zoned single family detached as opposed to **townhouses**.'" *Town of Vienna Council v. Kohler* (Va., 1978).

## TOWNSHIP

**(1) A unit of territory six miles square and containing thirty-six-mile-square sections; (2) in some states, a description of the form of local government.**

***Legal Annotation***: "The Land Ordinance of 1785 also initiated a land-surveying practice that was first applied to the Northwest Territory but that was applied to all territories acquired by the United States thereafter: 'At the point where the Ohio River crosses the Pennsylvania border, a north-south line—a principal meridian—was to be run and a base line west-ward—the geographer's line—was to be surveyed; parallel lines of longitude and latitude were to be surveyed, each to be 6 miles apart, making for **townships** of 36 square miles or 23,040 acres. . . . Each **township** was to be divided into lots of one mile square containing 640 acres.' . . . Each of these 1-square-mile lots was called a 'section,' so the section numbered 16, reserved for the public schools, was the 'Sixteenth Section.'" *Papasan v. Allain* (U.S., 1986).

"A *township* is a different thing from a town in the organic law of Missouri; the latter being an incorporated municipality, the former only a geographical subdivision of a county." *Harshman v. Bates County* (U.S., 1876).

## TOXIC SUBSTANCES

**Any combination of pollutants, including disease-carrying agents, that, after discharge and upon exposure, ingestion, inhalation, or assimilation into any organism, can cause death or disease, mutations, deformities, or malfunctions in such organisms or their offspring, and that adversely affect the environment.**

***Legal Annotation***: "**Toxic substances** are defined as 'any substance whether gaseous, liquid or solid which when discharged to the sewer system in sufficient quantities will interfere with any sewage treatment process, or will constitute a hazard to human beings or animals, or will inhibit aquatic life or create a hazard to recreation in the receiving waters of the effluent from the sewage treatment works of the Sanitary District.'" *Rauland Div., Zenith Radio v. Metro. San. Dist.* (Ill. App. Ct., 1971).

## TOXICITY

**The quality or degree of being poisonous or harmful to plant or animal life.**

***Legal Annotation***: "EP **toxicity** is defined in 25 Pa.Code § 261.24(a) as follows: (a) A solid waste exhibits the characteristic of EP toxicity if . . . the extract from a representative sample of the waste contains the contaminants listed in Table I at a concentration equal to or greater than the respective value given in the table." *Baumgardner Oil Co. v. Com.* (Pa. Common. Ct., 1992).

## TRACE METALS

**Metals, usually insoluble, found in small quantities in air, water, or other materials.**

*Legal Annotation*: "Currently, suspended solids (comprised of filamentous blue-green algae and **trace metals**, including arsenic, chromium, copper, zinc and lead) are being discharged into the Alucroix Channel." *Commissioner of the Department of Planning and Natural Resources, Robert S. Mathes v. Century Alumina Company, LLC, et al.* (D. V.I., 2010).

## TRACT

**An area, parcel, site, piece of land, or property that is the subject of a development application. *See Figure 70.***

*Legal Annotation*: "Planning regulations were adopted by New Fairfield in 1948. Amendments to these regulations are not in any respect material to the question before us. Section 1 of the regulations, since 1948, has had this definition: 'Subdivision means the division of a **tract** or parcel of land into three or more lots in such a manner as to require provision for a street or streets whether immediate or future for the purpose of sale or building development, and shall include, re-subdivision of parcels already laid out and approved." *Peninsula Corporation v. Planning & Zoning Commission* (Conn., 1964).

## TRADITIONAL NEIGHBORHOOD DEVELOPMENT (TND)

**An approach to land-use planning and urban design that promotes the building of pedestrian-friendly neighborhoods with a mix of uses, housing types and costs, lot sizes and density, architectural variety, a central meeting place such as a town square, a network of narrow streets and alleys, and defined development edges. See *Neighborhood*.**

*Comment*: Traditional neighborhood development de-emphasizes dependence on the automobile by employing mixed land-use patterns that afford residents the opportunity to live, work, play, and shop within their own neighborhood. It is based on the form and design of older towns and cities (Arendt 2004; Congress for New Urbanism 2004). Porches, detached garages, alleys, and residences over retail uses are encouraged. Traditional neighborhood design promotes mass transit alternatives by allowing higher densities.

TND zoning controls will not necessarily produce their stated objectives. But Hinshaw (2000) suggests that such ordinances can be tilted toward good development by adhering to the following five principles:

- Respect for existing scale and proportions.
- A close relationship to the street, which ensures the continuity of the townscape.
- The mixing of different uses, both vertically and horizontally.
- Minimum intrusiveness from parking.
- A variety of attractive and accessible public spaces.

*Legal Annotation*: "In 2003, the then Board adopted a **Traditional Neighborhood Development (TND)** as an overlay to the Multiple Use District. The overlay allowed for a village-type development as a conditional use. In 2004, PVA applied for conditional use approval as authorized by the TND ordinance, for a mixed use, high density residential development to be called 'Pennsbury Village.' PVA sought to build 154 units and 80,000 square feet of commercial space. In addition to its own lands, PVA proposed to use a portion of land owned by the Township. The Board conducted hearings, at which Fenton and Charles Scottoline (Scottoline) appeared and made statements in person or through counsel, objecting to the plan. Fenton's primary objection was that Township property was being used for private purposes. Fenton and his wife also solicited funds to oppose PVA's plans. After concluding the hearings, the Board approved a modified version of the original plan subject to numerous conditions, which prompted appeals by both PVA (#04-08055) and Citizens (#04-08070)." *Crandell v. Pennsbury Bd. of Supervisors* (Pa. Common. Ct., 2009).

## TRAFFIC CALMING

**The use of traffic management measures such as changes in existing street alignment,**

**installation of barriers and diversions, and other physical measures to reduce traffic speeds and/or volumes in the interest of street safety and neighborhood amenity (Knack 1998; Ewing and Brown 2009).**

***Comment***: Traffic calming has the objective of reducing the negative effects of motor vehicle use on the quality of life in a residential neighborhood by altering driver behavior and thereby improving living conditions for area residents. Traffic calming includes both volume-control devices and speed-control devices. Volume-control devices largely divert traffic in order to reduce or eliminate through traffic. Speed-control devices have the objective of slowing traffic in a given neighborhood. Both types of devices are physical in nature, ranging from speed humps or bumps in streets to street closures or diversions. Examples of traffic-calming devices are defined here and illustrated in *Figures 97* and *98*.

*FULL CLOSURES* (cul-de-sacs/dead ends): Barriers or turnarounds placed across a street to completely close it to through traffic except for connecting pedestrian or bicycle pathways.

*HALF-CLOSURES* (partial closures/one-ways): Barriers that block travel in one direction for a short distance on otherwise two-way streets.

*DIAGONAL DIVERTERS* (full diverters/diagonal road closures): Barriers placed diagonally across an intersection, blocking through movement.

*MEDIAN BARRIERS* (median diverters/island diverters): Raised islands located along the centerline of a street and continuing through an intersection so as to block through movement at a cross street.

*FORCED-TURN ISLANDS* (forced-turn channelizations/right-turn islands): Raised islands on approaches to an intersection that block certain vehicular movements.

*SPEED HUMPS* (road humps/indulations): Rounded, raised areas placed across the road to slow traffic.

*SPEED TABLES* (trapezoidal humps/speed platforms): Flat-topped speed humps, often with a brick or other textured surface on the flat section.

*RAISED CROSSWALKS* (raised crossings): Speed tables with crosswalk markings and signage providing pedestrians with a level street crossing.

*RAISED INTERSECTIONS* (raised junctions): Flat, raised areas covering entire intersections, with ramps at all approaches and often with a textured surface on the flat section.

*TEXTURED PAVEMENTS:* A textured or rough road surface of brick or stone that slows traffic while adding an aesthetic dimension to the street environment.

*TRAFFIC CIRCLES* (rotaries/intersection islands): Raised islands, placed in intersections, around which traffic is forced to circulate.

*ROUNDABOUTS* (rotaries): Traffic circles for higher-volume streets.

*CHICANES* (deviations/serpentines/twists): Curb extensions or islands that alternate from one side to the other, forming S-shaped roadways.

*REALIGNED INTERSECTIONS* (modified intersections): Changes in alignment that convert T-intersections with straight approaches into curving streets meeting at right angles.

*NECKDOWNS* (nubs/bulbouts/intersection narrowing): Curb extensions at intersections that reduce roadway width.

*CENTER ISLAND NARROWING* (mid-block medians/median chokers): Raised islands located along the centerline of a street that narrow the street at that location.

*CHOKERS* (pinch points/constrictions/mid-block narrowing): Curb extensions on one or both sides of the street that narrow the street at that location.

***Legal Annotation***: "Lastly, Administrative Code § 19-179 requires the Department of Transportation to conduct a study on the feasibility of installing **traffic calming** measures, which include 'protected pedestrian phases.' This same section defines 'protected pedestrian phases' as 'traffic control indications that are adjusted to provide that all conflicting vehicular movements are stopped in order to accommodate pedestrian

**Figure 98**

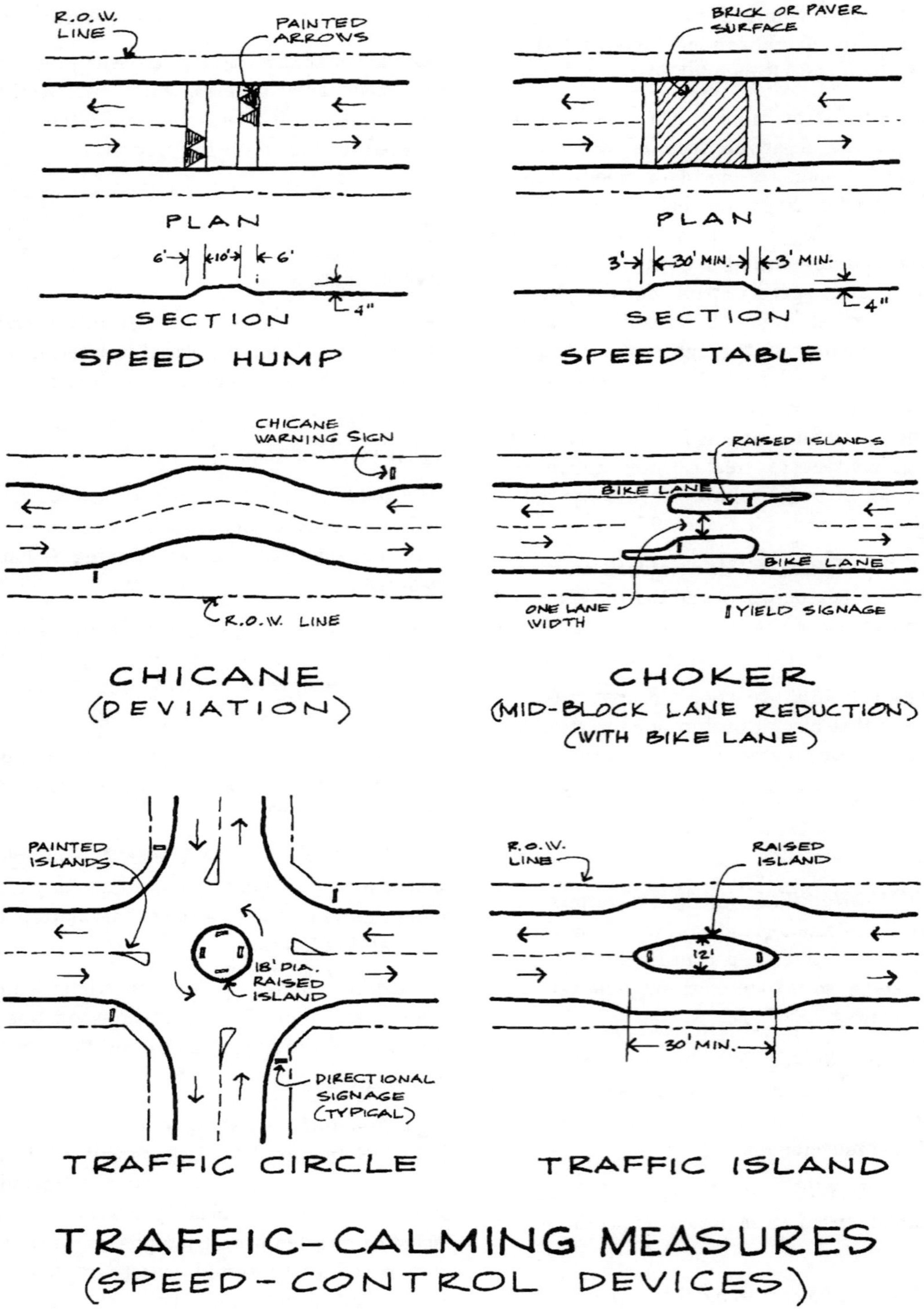
R.O.W. LINE
PAINTED ARROWS
PLAN
6' 10' 6'
4"
SECTION
SPEED HUMP
BRICK OR PAVER SURFACE
PLAN
3' 30' MIN. 3' MIN.
4"
SECTION
SPEED TABLE
CHICANE WARNING SIGN
R.O.W. LINE
CHICANE
(DEVIATION)
RAISED ISLANDS
BIKE LANE
BIKE LANE
ONE LANE WIDTH
YIELD SIGNAGE
CHOKER
(MID-BLOCK LANE REDUCTION)
(WITH BIKE LANE)
PAINTED ISLANDS
18' DIA. RAISED ISLAND
DIRECTIONAL SIGNAGE (TYPICAL)
TRAFFIC CIRCLE
R.O.W. LINE
RAISED ISLAND
12'
30' MIN.
TRAFFIC ISLAND
TRAFFIC-CALMING MEASURES
(SPEED-CONTROL DEVICES)

Figure 99

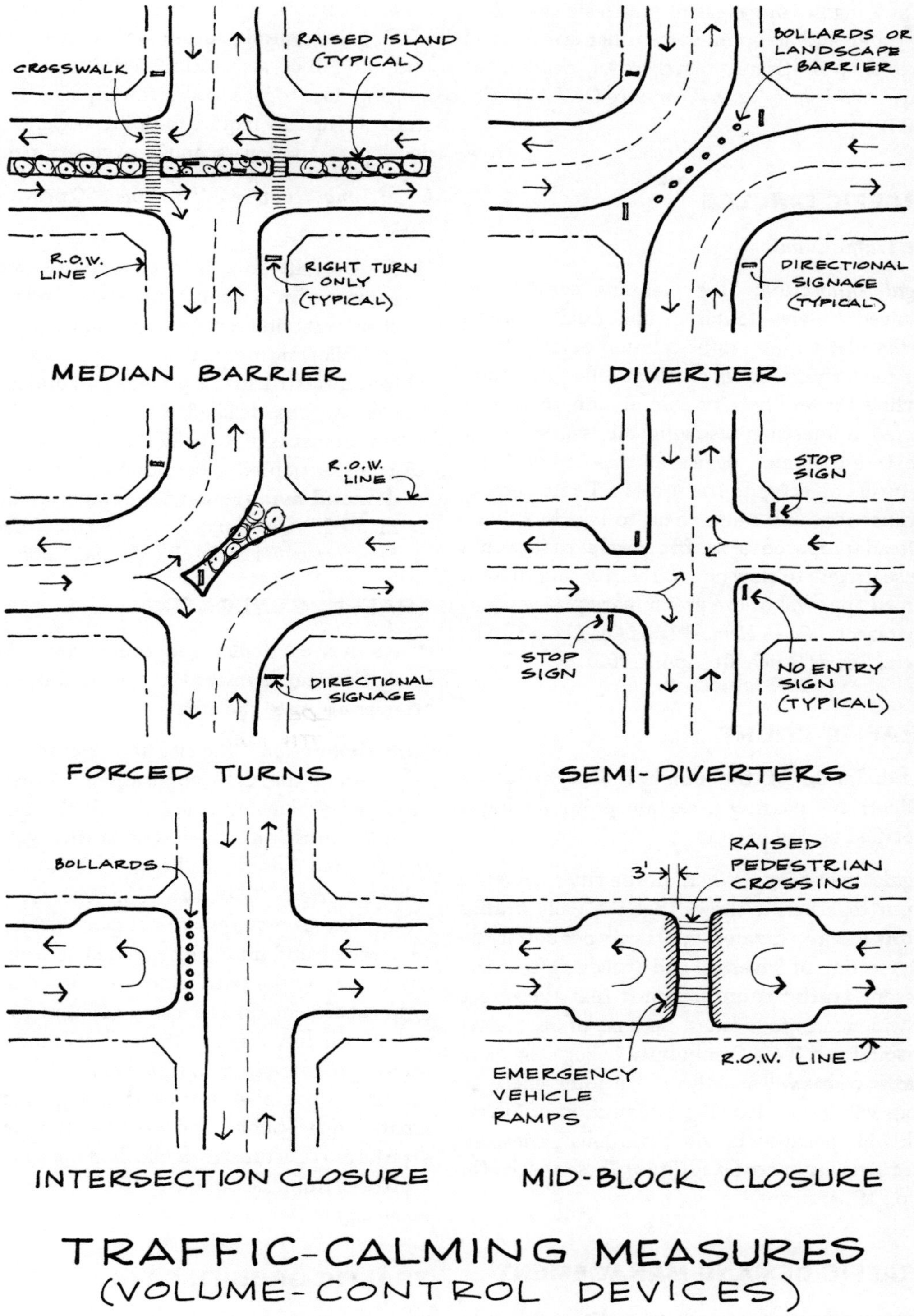
CROSSWALK
RAISED ISLAND (TYPICAL)
R.O.W. LINE
RIGHT TURN ONLY (TYPICAL)
MEDIAN BARRIER
BOLLARDS OR LANDSCAPE BARRIER
DIRECTIONAL SIGNAGE (TYPICAL)
DIVERTER
R.O.W. LINE
DIRECTIONAL SIGNAGE
FORCED TURNS
STOP SIGN
STOP SIGN
NO ENTRY SIGN (TYPICAL)
SEMI-DIVERTERS
BOLLARDS
INTERSECTION CLOSURE
3'
RAISED PEDESTRIAN CROSSING
R.O.W. LINE
EMERGENCY VEHICLE RAMPS
MID-BLOCK CLOSURE
TRAFFIC-CALMING MEASURES
(VOLUME-CONTROL DEVICES)

movement.' . . . Also, '**traffic calming**' is defined as 'any engineering measure which slows vehicular traffic and accommodates other street users such as pedestrians, bicyclists or children at play.'" *475 Ninth Ave. v. Bloomberg* (N.Y. Sup. Ct., 2003).

## TRAFFIC CIRCLES

**See *Traffic Calming*.**

***Legal Annotation***: "The planning commission resolved to give tentative and final approval of the plat with a traffic-calming device at the northern intersection of Monticello Drive and Skyline Drive. The city commission then conducted a meeting resolving all issues except the traffic-calming device at this intersection. Plaintiffs objected to the use of a T-intersection because it would cause them to lose lots. They instead proposed a **traffic circle** that would cause drivers to slow down. The city commission denied approval of the preliminary plat without any reason." *Cole's Home & Land Co., LLC v. City of Grand Rapids* (Mich. Ct. App., 2006).

## TRAFFIC COUNT

**A tabulation of the number of vehicles or pedestrians passing a certain point during a specified period of time.**

***Legal Annotation***: "When all the city's evidence is put together, it shows that the daily **traffic count** is approximately 9,691 cars per day at the intersection of Silverbell and Speedway, that the present **traffic count** requires that the street be widened to four lanes. Because of St. Mary's Hospital and Pima Community College the daily **traffic count** will shortly reach a point where six lanes will be needed. The intersection of Silverbell and Speedway is now hazardous." *Transamerica Title Insurance Co. v. City of Tucson* (Ariz. Ct. App., 1974).

## TRAFFIC DEMAND MANAGEMENT

**Strategies aimed at reducing the number of vehicle trips, shortening trip lengths, and reducing trips during peak hours.**

***Comment***: These strategies encourage the use of mass transit, car pools, vanpools, bicycling, and walking and typically focus on the home-to-work commute. They also include efforts to provide housing close to jobs to shorten trip lengths. The strategies usually require the joint cooperation of developers, employers, and local governments.

***Legal Annotation***: "RCW 36.70A.350 provides in part:

(1) A new fully contained community may be approved in a county planning under this chapter if criteria including but not limited to the following are met:

(a) New infrastructure is provided for and impact fees are established consistent with the requirements of RCW 82.02.050;

(b) Transit-oriented site planning and **traffic demand management** programs are implemented." *Quadrant Corp. v. State, Growth Management Hearings Bd.* (Wash., 2005).

## TRAFFIC GENERATOR

**A use in a particular geographic area that is likely to attract substantial vehicular or pedestrian traffic into the area.**

***Legal Annotation***: "The city argues that it properly denied the CUP application because the proposed expansion, coupled with the existing campus, constitutes a 'larger **traffic generator**' that is not located adjacent to an arterial or collector street. The city's comprehensive plan states: 'Access requirements of quasi-public uses vary widely and must be evaluated according to the nature of the particular use. Larger **traffic generators** should be located adjacent to arterial or collector streets. The city contends that the proposed expansion would conflict with the comprehensive plan because the campus is designated quasi-public and because the nearest arterial or collector street, Old Shakopee Road, is six blocks from the campus." *RDNT, LLC v. City of Bloomington* (Minn. Ct. App., 2014).

## TRAFFIC GROWTH RATE

**The rate at which traffic volumes are projected to increase over a period of time, expressed as a percentage that is compounded annually.**

*Legal Annotation*: "In addressing the problem of service along the inside route, the Board began by noting that 'if all carriers exercised their certificate rights at all the points in question, the result, at current and foreseeable traffic levels, would be wasteful and uneconomic service.' Op. 15. The Board found the Examiner's projections of traffic generally too optimistic, and disapproved his inflation of a **traffic growth rate** based upon economic stimuli which he thought would be provided by exploitation of North Slope oil resources. Op. 6. Using more conservative demand projections, the Board rejected the Examiner's conclusion that Seattle-Juneau service would support operations by two carriers, and projected losses for second-carrier service by either Western or Pan American. Op. 16 n. 20." *Western Air Lines, Inc. v. Civil Aeronautics Board* (D.C. Cir., 1974).

## TRAFFIC IMPACT STUDY

**A report analyzing anticipated roadway conditions before and after proposed development (American Planning Association, *Traffic Impact Analysis*, Planning Advisory Service Report No. 387, 1984).**

*Comment*: The report may include an analysis of mitigation measures and a calculation of fair-share financial contributions. Mitigation measures may include road widenings, intersection improvements, and traffic-control devices.

*Legal Annotation*: "As required by the Building Zone Ordinance, public hearings were held in February and March 1999. RPT introduced a report entitled '**Traffic Impact Study**' prepared by VMI/Maris, a traffic and parking consultant, predicting that the proposed expansion would increase vehicular traffic in the area of the mall by about one percent during peak evening hours and by about two percent on peak Saturday hours. According to the report and testimony by the consultant, the additional traffic would have minimal impact on traffic conditions in the area of the mall." *Retail Prop. v. Appeals Bd.* (N.Y., 2002).

## TRAFFIC ISLAND

**A raised, and often curbed and planted area, located to guide traffic, separate traffic lanes, preserve existing vegetation, and increase aesthetic quality. See *Traffic Calming*.**

*Legal Annotation*: "The **traffic island** is a long, narrow, raised concrete island located between Broad Street, a state highway, and Old York Road, a public street under the City's jurisdiction, separating traffic lanes on these streets." *Morton v. Com. of Pa. Dept. of Transp.* (Pa. Common. Ct., 2004).

## TRAIL

**An off-roadway, usually unimproved path.**

*Comment*: The word "trail" should generally be avoided as it may refer to a range of facilities, including a coarse, unpaved hiking/biking route or a paved urbanized facility. http://safety.fhwa.dot.gov/ped_bike/tools_solve/fhwasa12018/#chap1.6

*Legal Annotation*: "First, the 'paved pathway' described by Gomez constitutes a **trail** under accepted definitions because it is a 'path,' and as Carroll v. County of Los Angeles (1997) 60 Cal. App.4th 606, 609 (Carroll), observed, a path is synonymous with a '**trail**.' (Ibid. [dictionary definition of a **trail** is a 'marked or established path or route' (Webster's Collegiate Dict. [10th ed. 1995, p. 1251]; see also Treweek v. City of Napa (2000) 85 Cal.App.4th 221, 230 [a **trail** 'consist(s) primarily of a path or track'].)" *Gomez v. Padre Dam Municipal Water District* (Calif. Ct. App., 2012).

## TRAILER

**A structure standing on wheels, towed or hauled by another vehicle, and used either for short-term human occupancy; carrying of materials, goods, or objects; or as a temporary office.**

*Comment*: Development ordinances may allow for trailers on work sites to be used as temporary offices.

*Legal Annotation*: "A **trailer** is a moving container sent out onto the highway system, necessarily susceptible to a variety of regulations, weighings, and inspections, and constantly risking discovery by loading, unloading, search, or accident. A hotel room is a residence, however temporary, and our search and seizure law traditionally has protected a person's residence more vigorously than other, more public, places." *US v. Jenkins* (6th Cir., 1996).

## TRANSFER OF DEVELOPMENT RIGHTS (TDR)

**The removal of the right to develop or build, expressed in dwelling units per acre or floor area, from land in one zone district, and the transfer of that right to land in another zone where such transfer is permitted. See *Density Transfer*. See *Figure 100*.**

***Comment***: TDR, or transfer of development credits, is a development tool used to preserve open space, farmland, water resources, or vistas in one area and to direct development to other, more suitable areas. In urban areas, TDR has been used for historic preservation. TDR permits an owner of real property to sell the development rights associated with that property (the preservation or sending zone) to the owner of another property (the transfer or receiving zone) in return for compensation. Regulations governing the transfer zone would allow an increase in development intensity to accommodate the added development, all in accordance with the local master plan. **See *Lot Averaging*.**

*Legal Annotation*: "The **transfer of development rights** is an incentive to keep owners of designated properties from further developing their land. Under a **TDR** ordinance or statute, real property chosen for preservation is designated as a sending site. This allows the owner of the sending site to sever development rights from the parcel and sell them to the owner of a designated receiving site. A receiving site is a parcel of real property that is made eligible for further development through the purchase of development rights from a sending site. Under the Ordinance, purchasing development rights

**Figure 100**

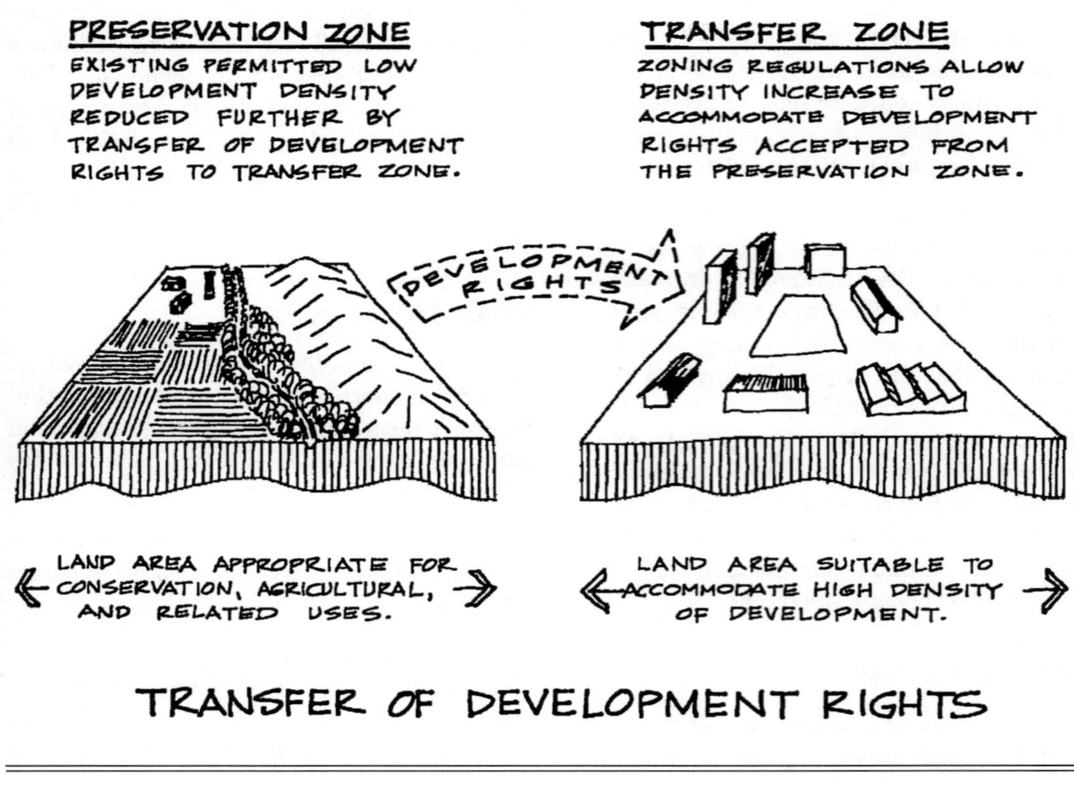

allows the owner of the receiving site to build a structure with an increased floor area ratio, meaning that the structure is allowed to exceed existing zoning standards governing the maximum height of buildings." *KGF Development, LLC v. City of Ketchum* (Idaho, 2010).

## TRANSFER STATION

**A site at which solid wastes are prepared for transport to a processing facility or land disposal site.**

***Comment***: Transfer stations may include separation of different types of waste and aggregation of smaller shipments into larger ones. They may also include compaction to reduce the bulk of the waste. These facilities are intensive uses and are properly located in heavy industrial zones. They are usually necessary because garbage trucks that pick up from houses are unsuitable for long, over-the-road hauls to distant landfills or other facilities for solid waste disposal.

***Legal Annotation***: "The Plan mandated construction of a **transfer station** and originally provided that county trash could be deposited there for compacting and subsequent transport by the **transfer station's** operator to the Warren County site for ultimate disposal. The 'key ingredient' of the Plan was an Interdistrict Waste Agreement with Warren County, approved by the DEP, under which Warren would, until at least 2005, accept all of Hunterdon's trash for processing at its planned trash-to-steam plant. . . . One of the principal functions of the **transfer station** is the compacting of trash to allow its efficient long-distance transport to landfills. In performing this function, the station is not in competition with out-of-state landfills. On the contrary, the station is their customer." *J. Filiberto Sanitation, Inc. v. State of New Jersey Dept. of Envir. Prot.* (3rd Cir., 1988).

## TRANSIT-DEPENDENT POPULATION

**Persons who are (1) without private transportation; (2) elderly (over age sixty-five) or disabled; (3) youths (under age eighteen); and (4) persons below poverty or median income levels defined by the US Census Bureau (Federal Department of Transportation).**

***Comment***: The use of census data to calculate the transit-dependent population yields a more accurate result and permits more consistent comparisons between geographic areas.

***Legal Annotation***: "Plaintiffs are resident taxpayers of Butte County who aver they are elderly, disabled, of limited means and, hence, **transit-dependent**." *Folsom v. Butte County Assn. of Governments* (Calif., 1982).

## TRANSIT-ORIENTED DEVELOPMENT (TOD)

**The concentration of development nodes, consisting of mixed-use development (high- and medium-density residential, retail and service commercial, entertainment, and downtown type uses), located along public transit corridors, (commuter and light rail, bus routes, and regional bicycle paths) and with convenient and easy access to mass transit stations. *See Figure 101*.**

***Comment***: TODs are designed to maximize transit ridership by locating employment and housing within walking distance (up to two thousand feet) of a transit stop. Urban TODs are located on main transit routes (bus and rail) and have high-density housing and employment. Neighborhood TODs should be located on a feeder bus line and contain lower-density housing and local retail/services only.

The 2012 APA National Planning Awards cited Contra Costa (California) Centre Transit Village as "A Model of Transit Oriented Development." This is an excellent resource since it goes into detail on the mechanics of putting a TOD together.

***Legal Annotation***: "Under either plan, PDR was required to dedicate all of the right-of-way for the trolley and construct all the river improvements had development occurred before construction of the trolley. Indeed, the Riverwalk Plan was specifically designed as a **transit-oriented development**, incorporating the trolley into its

**Figure 101**

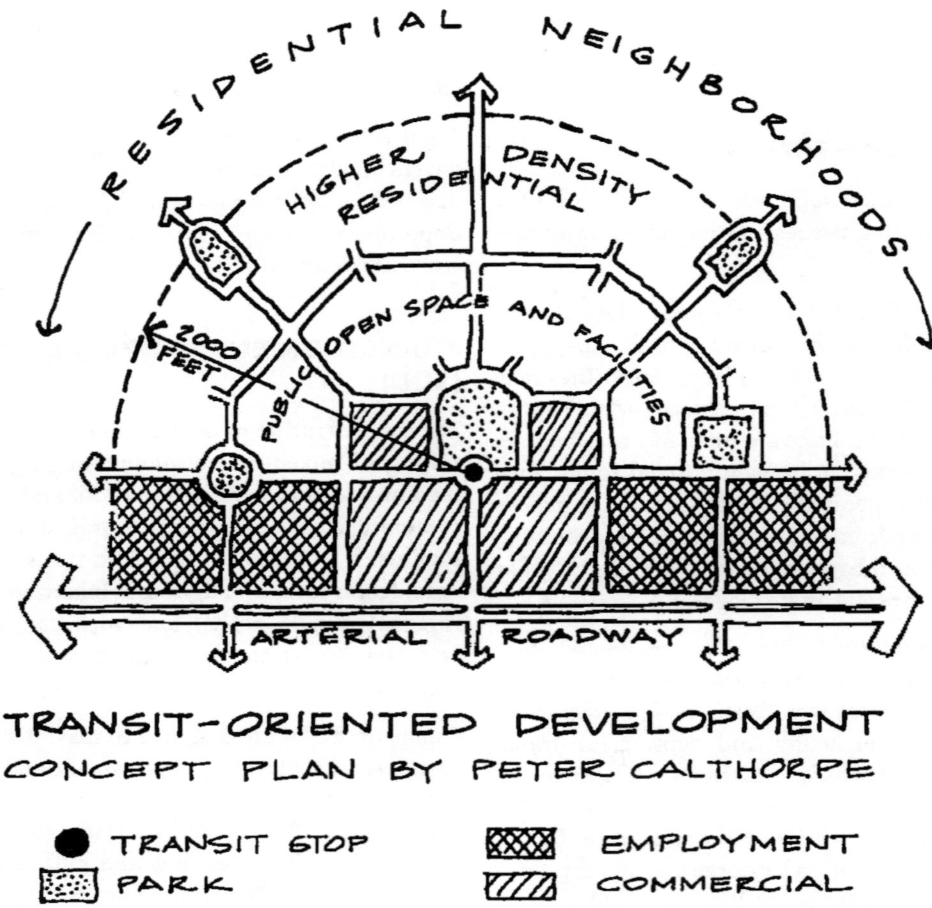


development plan." *MTBD v. Handlery Hotel, Inc.* (Calif. Ct. App., 1999).

## TRANSIT, LIGHT RAIL (LRT)

**An urban form of transportation in which electrically self-propelled passenger vehicles, operating as a single train or as multiple units coupled together, travel along exclusive rights-of-way or within reserved lanes of a street.**

*Legal Annotation*: "'**Light rail transit**' is a rail system utilizing modern versions of street cars which operate on their own rights-of-way or within reserved lanes of streets." *Macht v. Skinner* (D.D.C., 1989).

## TRANSIT SHUTTLE

**Transit service that travels over a short route or one that connects two transit systems or centers.**

*Legal Annotation*: "The case concerns federal **transit** funding under the American Recovery and Reinvestment Act of 2009 (ARRA) (49 U.S.C.

§ 53) for BART's Oakland Airport Connector Project (the project) extending BART train service directly to Oakland International Airport in place of existing AirBART bus **shuttle** service." *McKee v. San Francisco Bay Area Rapid Transit District Board of Directors* (Calif. Ct. App., 2012).

## TRANSITION ZONE

**A zoning district whose primary purpose is to buffer and protect the inhabitants or uses in one zone from that of another nearby zone, whose uses in the latter are incompatible with or would have negative impacts on that of the former zone.**

***Comment***: An example is to place a zone consisting of more benign uses, such as an office and research zone, between a low-density residential and industrial zone, or to place a townhouse zone between a high-density multifamily zone and a low-density, single-family residential zone. Originally, the term "zone of transition" was used by Ernest Burgiss in his Concentric Zone Model in the 1930s to delineate the area between the factory zone and working-class residential zone peripheral to the central business district of the City of Chicago. **See *Lot, Transition; Transitional Area*.**

***Legal Annotation***: "He stated this piece of property was a '**transition zone**' between the two areas of different land use, and the Home represented the best 'buffer' between the two uses. This Court in *Cleaver v. Zoning Board of Adjustment*, supra, recognized the validity of such '**transition zones**'. A court must be mindful of the fact that in rapidly growing cities certain pieces of property will lie between two different uses, and it is in conformity with the comprehensive plan to put this land to the best use possible. This '**transition zone**' theory, as recognized in Cleaver, in no way erodes the rejection of the argument in Schubach I, that because this land was on the border line between the two uses it should be rezoned. We in no way retreat from the view that simply because a piece of property rests on the border of a commercial zone it automatically can be rezoned commercial. Instantly, we merely recognized that to promote the orderly development of a community the zoning authorities must be allowed to put a piece of property to the use which is most beneficial to the comprehensive plan, i.e., establish a land use which best blends in with surrounding different uses." *Schubach v. Silver* (Pa., 1975).

## TRANSITIONAL AREA

**(1) An area in the process of changing from one use to another or changing from a predominant occupancy by one ethnic, racial, religious, or national-origin group to another; (2) an area that acts as a buffer between two land uses of different intensity and compatibility. See *Transition Zone; Transitional Use; And Figure 102.***

***Comment***: An example of a transitional area—more specifically, a transitional use area—is the land area between a business area along a street frontage and the adjacent residential area. Many development ordinances establish transitional districts that permit either residential or some less intensive commercial use to be located between two such disparate land uses. The less intensive commercial use might be a small office building or institutional use.

***Legal Annotation***: "The evidence in this case establishes that the normal planning and zoning practice is to move from the more intensive land uses, through transitional or less intensive land use into the residential areas, perhaps even going through multi-family residential areas before reaching the single family residential areas. An example of the **transitional area** is shown by the uses of the property in the Summit development which is across U.S. 280 to the south and east of the Property." *American Petroleum Equip. and Construction, Inc. v. Fancher* (Ala., 1997).

## TRANSITIONAL CARE CLINIC

**A facility operated as an accessory use in connection with, and on the premises of, a transitional care home to provide physical, social, and psychological therapy or counseling by qualified personnel, whose patients are limited to those who have recently resided in the**

**transitional care home or to families of those who are residing in or have recently resided in a transitional care home.**

*Legal Annotation*: "**Transitional Care Clinic**: A licensed clinic operated as a subordinate use in connection with and on the premises of a transitional care home, solely for providing physical, social and psychological therapy or counseling by qualified personnel whose patients are limited to those who have recently resided in the transitional care home or families of those who are residing or have recently resided in a transitional care home." *Codified Ordinances of the City of Mount Vernon, Ohio.* http://conwaygreene.com/MtVernon/lpext.dll/MtVernon/32ef/3608/3a1a/3a67?fn=document-frame.htm&f=templates&2.0

## TRANSITIONAL CARE HOME

**A facility in which individuals live for a short period while receiving physical, social, or psychological therapy and counseling to assist them in overcoming physical or emotional problems.**

*Comment*: The transitional care home is a form of halfway house. Residents do not require segregation from society and require only short-term shelter away from their usual residences. Professional therapy and counseling are provided on a more intensive basis than is permitted in an outpatient facility. In zoning, these facilities usually function as boarding homes. **See *Boarding Home For Sheltered Care*.**

*Legal Annotation*: "Richard Inocencio, the victim in this matter, was 57 years old at the time of trial. He had suffered a stroke two years previously and had some ongoing memory and hearing issues. He had owned a roofing company in San Leandro for about 20 years. He also owned a **transitional care home** for recovering addicts and homeless people in Hayward. According to the director of the **transitional care home**, in May 2007, approximately $2,500 in cash and some prescription medication was stolen from an unlocked file cabinet in the office of the home." *Sanders v. Adams* (N.D. Calif., 2012).

## TRANSITIONAL USE

**A permitted use or structure of an intermediate intensity of activity or scale and located between a more intensive and a less intensive use. See *Transitional Area*. See *Figure 102*.**

*Comment*: Some random examples of transitional uses include professional offices located between retail and residential uses; two-family and townhouse units located between single-family detached and apartment blocks; and private clubs or low-intensity recreational uses between industrial and residential uses.

*Legal Annotation*: "Additionally, the witnesses testified that the site was well suited for apartments, which would serve as an appropriate **transitional use** between the single-family residences to the north and west of the lot and the more industrial uses to its south and east. They also observed that the complex would be less intrusive to the residences than a fully complying office building would be." *Coventry Square v. Westwood Zoning Bd. of Adjustment* (N.J., 1994).

## TRANSPORTATION CORRIDOR

**A combination of principal transportation routes involving a linear network of one or more highways of four or more lanes, rail lines, or other primary and secondary access facilities that support a development corridor.**

*Legal Annotation*: "The 'Winona Elevator Property' is clearly adjacent to the City and is in fact surrounded by the City on three sides. While the roads leading to the 'Winona Elevator Property' are Highways 51 and 82, a traveler drives through the City to get there. In addition, the motto of the City is the 'Crossroads of North Mississippi' and numerous witnesses testified that this area is a major **transportation corridor**. In addition, even though the City's population showed a slight decrease by 300 people from 1990 to 2000, Slaughter stated that this does not indicate that the City has no path of growth. Slaughter maintains that it is more important to look at the commercial activities rather than population growth in the limited proposed annexation area. A portion of Highway 51 was expanded in 1996–1997

**Figure 102**

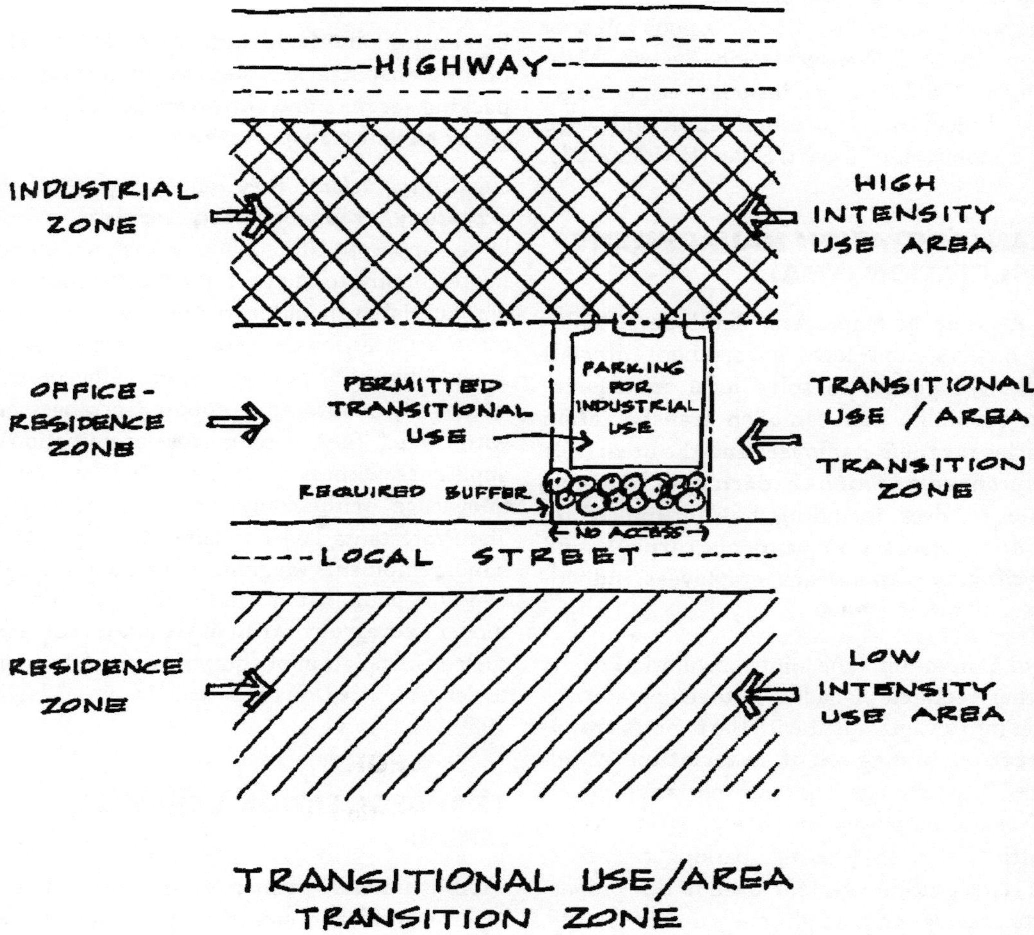


from a two-lane road to a five-lane road which is indicative of the traffic and growth. Slaughter stated that the **transportation corridor** is a major factor in attracting development." *In re Extension of Boundaries of City of Winona* (Miss., 2004).

## TRANSPORTATION DEMAND MANAGEMENT SYSTEM (TDM)

**Actions taken to reduce the number of vehicles on streets and highways during peak travel hours, as well as to reduce the total number of trips by encouraging commuters to share driving, to use alternative modes of transportation, or to change traveling hours.**

***Comment***: The transportation demand management plan's objective is to decrease the number of vehicles on the road by one or more of the following methods: increase in parking fees, requiring businesses to encourage ride sharing, allowing flexible work times and schedules, and other related programs designed to reduce the number of people who commute alone or during peak travel times.

***Legal Annotation***: "Specifically, the Plaintiffs raise three objections to the FHWA's analysis of alternatives. Plaintiffs first, largely in reliance on the opinion of their expert witness, charge that FHWA failed to adequately incorporate **Transportation Demand Management**

**('TDM')**—which includes such traffic management strategies as the promotion of alternative work schedules, and car-pool/van-pool programs—and Transportation System Management ('TSM')—which includes such management devices as signal coordination and video traffic monitoring." *Davis v. Slater* (D. Utah 2001).

## TRANSPORTATION MANAGEMENT ASSOCIATION (TMA)

**(1) A group of employers, developers, building owners, and local government officials working together to solve local transportation problems and establish transportation policies for their employees and the area; (2) a nonprofit corporation that arranges transportation services, including, but not limited to, public transportation, vanpools, carpools, and bicycling, to corporations, employees, individuals, and other groups.**

*Legal Annotation*: "The joint consultation report further required Xanadu's 'owner/operator' to enter into an agreement with the region's **transportation management association** 'Meadowlink' to manage the transportation needs of Xanadu employees, with strategies such as shuttle buses, ridesharing, parking cash-outs, and transit incentives. Moreover, noting proposals to provide train or light rail access to the site, the report stated: 'Until rail access is realized, the developer shall subsidize and/or provide shuttle bus services between the Meadowlands Xanadu/Meadowlands Sports Complex from the Secaucus Junction Train Station and from the Port Authority Bus Terminal in New York City.'" *In re Proposed Xanadu Redevelopment Project* (N.J., App. Div., 2008).

## TRANSPORTATION DEMAND MARKET (TDM)

**A general term for strategies that increase overall system efficiency by encouraging a shift from single-occupant vehicle (SOV) trips to non-SOV modes, or shifting automobile trips out of peak periods. http://tinyurl.com/kr47se6**

## TRANSPORTATION SERVICES, ACCESSORY

**Establishments furnishing services incidental to transportation, such as forwarding and packing services and the arranging of passenger or freight transportation.**

*Legal Annotation*: "They rendered none of the **accessory transportation services** offered by the applicant United. The protestants offered no testimony to support their insistence that Jordan Marsh should be required to use protestants' services for the delivery of parcels under seventy-five (75) pounds before being permitted to enter into the proposed arrangement with United. They relied on cross-examination of applicant's witnesses supplemented by 'judicial knowledge' of the content of their certificates. The Protestants laid no claim to being able to handle shipments weighing in excess of seventy-five (75) pounds, nor are they in a position to render **accessory transportation services** such as installation of equipment as an incident to delivery." *Ace Delivery Service, Inc. v. Boyd* (Fla., 1959).

## TRANSPORTATION SERVICES, LOCAL

**Establishments primarily engaged in furnishing local and suburban passenger transportation, including taxicabs, passenger transportation charter services, school buses, and terminal and service facilities for motor vehicle passenger transportation.**

*Legal Annotation*: "Taxicabs generally perform **local transportation services**, while other modes of transportation (e.g., bus, train, aircraft) provide transportation for more distant travel. Furthermore, a distance of more than seventy miles reasonably can be viewed as not local in nature." *ICC v. Mr. B's Services, Ltd.* (7$^{th}$ Cir., 1991).

## TRANSPORTATION SYSTEMS MANAGEMENT (TSM)

**An approach to congestion mitigation that seeks to identify operational and management**

**improvements to enhance the capacity of the existing transportation system.**

*Comment*: What makes TSM different is that it is low-cost but effective in nature, and includes but is not limited to: intersection and signal improvements (turning lanes, signal timing), freeway bottleneck renewal programs (acceleration/deceleration lanes, weaving sections), data collection to monitor system performance, and special events management strategies.

*Legal Annotation*: "Specifically, the Plaintiffs raise three objections to the FHWA's analysis of alternatives. Plaintiffs first, largely in reliance on the opinion of their expert witness, charge that FHWA failed to adequately incorporate Transportation Demand Management ('TDM')—which includes such traffic management strategies as the promotion of alternative work schedules, and car-pool/van-pool programs—and **Transportation System Management ('TSM')**—which includes such management devices as signal coordination and video traffic monitoring." *Davis v. Slater* (D. Utah 2001).

## TRANS-SHIPMENT

**(1) The act of transferring freight between two modes of transport, such as from a truck to a railroad car; (2) the act of transferring freight from long-haul trucks to local delivery vehicles.**

*Comment*: Trans-shipment may include aggregating or breaking down shipments into larger or smaller ones.

*Legal Annotation*: "'**[T]ranshipment**' means, after goods have been unloaded or in any way removed from the means of transportation by which they came into Canada, their loading, placing on board or within or upon the same or any other means of transportation (*transbordement*)." *Transhipment Regulations C.R.C.*, c. 606 (2014).

## TRAP

**A fitting or device so designed and constructed as to provide, when properly vented, a liquid seal that will prevent the back passage of air without materially affecting the flow of sewage or wastewater.**

*Legal Annotation*: "A 'P-trap' is defined as 'a P-shaped **trap** used especially for sinks and lavatories' (Webster's 3d New Internat. Dict. (1986), p. 1835). Here, it was located just below the shower drain." *Robertson v. Fleetwood Travel Trailers* (Calif. Ct. App., 2006).

## TRASH ENCLOSURE

**An accessory use or structure where trash and/or recycling material containers or any other type of waste or refuse containers are stored.** ***See Figure 34.***

*Comment*: The local ordinance should include specific design requirements for trash enclosures, including location, materials, gates, and screening. For large-scale developments, the enclosure should be roofed, and enclosure design should reflect principal building architecture and materials.

*Legal Annotation*: "Appellee does not seem to dispute the fact that the twenty-foot setback would pass through the proposed restaurant's **trash enclosure**. Appellee does contend that the evidence does not conclusively establish that the **trash enclosure** is subject to the required setback. This argument is precluded, however, by § 208.2 of the zoning regulations, which clearly indicates that all structures are subject to the minimum setback requirement." *In re Poole* (Vt., 1978).

## TRAVEL CENTER

**A multifaceted and integrated retail establishment located on a single lot located at the exit of a highway, that includes a long-term parking (rest) area, a gasoline station, a restaurant, a convenience store, and other services. Also known as a "truck stop."**

*Comment*: Originally composed of parking areas, a gasoline station, and a restaurant, travel centers now incorporate additional retail services for the traveling public, such as franchised food establishments, showers, and laundries.

If a particular zone permits a variety of uses, there is no reason why the various uses cannot be combined on a single parcel and developed as an integrated entity. Indeed, by combining the various uses, the result is efficiency in travel and better site design with fewer driveway openings, less impervious coverage, and closer attention to landscaping and signs. But the site must be "designed in a manner that enables each business to function without internal congestion" (Thompson 1997b: 2; http://tinyurl.com/mdks4wp).

***Legal Annotation***: "In June 2010, Ellison proposed two amendments to the County's comprehensive plan map and zoning map 'for the purpose of developing the Thorp **Travel Center** consisting of a truck stop, restaurant and hotel and RV park.' The proposed development would cover over 29 acres, comprising a 4,000 square foot fuel station, a 10,000 square foot retail store, a 5,000 square foot retail store, a 6,000 square foot restaurant, a 24,000 square foot hotel with 50 units, a 5,000 square foot recreational vehicle park with 45 spaces, and parking lots with spaces for hundreds of cars and trucks. These uses would operate 24 hours a day, employ up to 140 people, and generate $10.9 million annually. The proposed development would require new roads and a six-acre septic or sewer reserve area. Surrounding uses are mainly agricultural." *Kittitas County v. Kittitas County Cons.* (Wash. Ct. App., 2013).

## TRAVELED WAY

**The portion of the roadway, excluding shoulders, used for the movement of vehicles. http://safety.fhwa.dot.gov/ped_bike/tools_solve/fhwasa12018/#chap1.6**

***Legal Annotation***: "We note that '**traveled way**' is defined in the statute at Section 103(8) as 'the portion of the roadway for the movement of vehicles, exclusive of shoulders.'" *Penn Advertising, Inc. v. Department of Transp.* (Pa. Common. Ct., 1999).

## TRAVEL PLAZA

See *Truck Stop*.

***Legal Annotation***: "The designated evidence shows that the purpose of the **travel plaza** is to offer a place where the traveling public—whether they be in a car, truck, or RV—can obtain fuel, dine, shop, bank, and use the travelers' rest facilities. The designated evidence also reveals that there would be a separate fueling area for RVs and that the RV services would be provided at these RV fueling islands. Based on the ordinance's definition of an accessory use, we conclude that the RV services of waste tank disposal and propane refueling, which is offered to only one portion of the potential customers of the travel plaza and would be located on already existing fueling islands, is subordinate to the principal uses of travel plaza and would not change the character of the travel plaza premises." *Flying J. v. City of New Haven, Bd. Zoning* (Ind. Ct App., 2006).

## TRAVEL TRAILER

**A recreational vehicle that is towed by a car or a truck. See *Recreational Vehicle*.**

***Legal Annotation***: "By contrast, the Pittsburgh Code definition of 'trailer' refers to a vehicle (or a portable structure) which is 'equipped for and used as sleeping or living quarters.' Study of the Pittsburgh Code definition of 'trailer' shows that it is broad enough to embrace at least two different types of vehicles which are equipped for and used as sleeping or living quarters. First, the Pittsburgh Code definition of 'trailer' clearly embraces a '**travel trailer**,' which is commonly understood to be a towed vehicle equipped for sleeping and living on a non-permanent basis, e.g., at stops on a journey. And a **travel trailer** is designed and used for travel; i.e., as the definition states, it is 'used as a conveyance on highways,' conveying the travelers' living and sleeping facilities; the law prohibits the conveyance of passengers in a travel trailer. . . . In order to be thus useable on public highways without special permit, **travel trailers** have a width of eight feet or less. Even more clearly, the Pittsburgh Code definition of 'trailer' also embraces a motorhome, which the dictionary defines as an automotive vehicle built on a truck or bus chassis and equipped as a self-contained traveling home—compare MOBILE HOME. Webster's New Collegiate Dictionary 752 (1977). The Pittsburgh definition of 'trailer' includes this concept because its wording is not limited to towed vehicles but embraces a 'vehicle . . . used as sleeping or living quarters . . . and drawn by its own . . . motive power.' And a motorhome is even more definitively 'used as a conveyance on highways' because motorhomes lawfully carry passengers (and driver) as well as living facilities." *Hitchcock v. Zoning Bd. of Adjustment* (Pa. Common. Ct., 1991).

## TREE HOUSE

**A structure built above ground level, using a tree for part of its support, and not designed for continuous habitation.**

***Legal Annotation***: "The clouds of this 'perfect storm' began to gather in late 1996, when the Welches moved to 218 Kitchings Drive in Clinton. Scot (an electrical engineer) and Mary wanted a **tree house** in their front yard, so Mary sought approval from the City's building inspector and zoning official, Julion Lowther. According to Mrs. Welch's uncontradicted testimony, Lowther approved the project and indicated that no permit was required. Shortly thereafter, construction of the **tree house** began and was completed over the next several years at a cost to the Welches of over $5,000.00. . . . On September 22, 1999, the first of two building inspections by the City's building inspector took place at the Welches' home. The second took place on September 26, 2000. Neither inspector complained about, or objected to, the **tree house**. Indeed, the Welches claim, and the City does not dispute, that prior to the spring of 2002, there was no indication from the City or anyone else of a problem with, or objection to, the **tree house**." *Mayor & Bd. of Aldermen v. Welch* (Miss., 2004).

## TREE, PROHIBITED

**Any tree species that, by the nature of its fruit, root system, brittleness of wood, or susceptibility to disease, is not permitted for use in proposed development projects or as a replacement tree.**

***Legal Annotation***: "Sec. 5.01. Subject to the exceptions enumerated in Article VI no person shall remove, cause to be removed, transplant or destroy, on any land in the township to which this ordinance applies, any permitted tree having six inches d.b.h. ['diameter at breast height," defined as 4½ feet above grade] or greater, any **prohibited tree** having nine inches d.b.h. or greater, or conifer greater than 20 feet in height, without first obtaining a tree removal permit." *Huron Charter Township v. Fox* (Mich. Ct. App., 2010).

## TREE PROTECTION

**Measures taken, such as temporary fencing and the use of tree wells, to protect existing trees from damage or loss during construction. *See Figures 103 and 104*.**

*Comment:* The local land development ordinance should require, as part of the landscaping plan for major developments or during constsruction, that a tree protection plan must be submitted showing which trees are proposed to be protected and the method to be used to provide the protection. Some jurisdictions adopt tree removal and protection regulations to guard against clear-cutting or the removal or damaging of trees, not only as part of new construction or landscaping work but at all times. In such instances, the number of trees to be removed beyond a certain diameter and/or height is restricted, as are actions that might damage or destroy such trees. Such regulations often require tree replacement when trees are removed.

***Legal Annotation***: "About July 1973, the Landowner orally granted to Duke the right to remove all trees, bushes and other vegetation from the premises, at no cost to the Landowner. The City stopped Duke, claiming that Duke was violating its **tree protection** ordinance, which is a part of the City's zoning law. . . . In the absence of language clearly indicating that the legislature intended that the City could forbid landowners to cut trees and require landowners to plant trees in replacement we hold that the tree protection ordinance, as written, has not been authorized by the General Assembly." *Dunbar v. City of Spartanburg* (S.C., 1976).

**Figure 103**

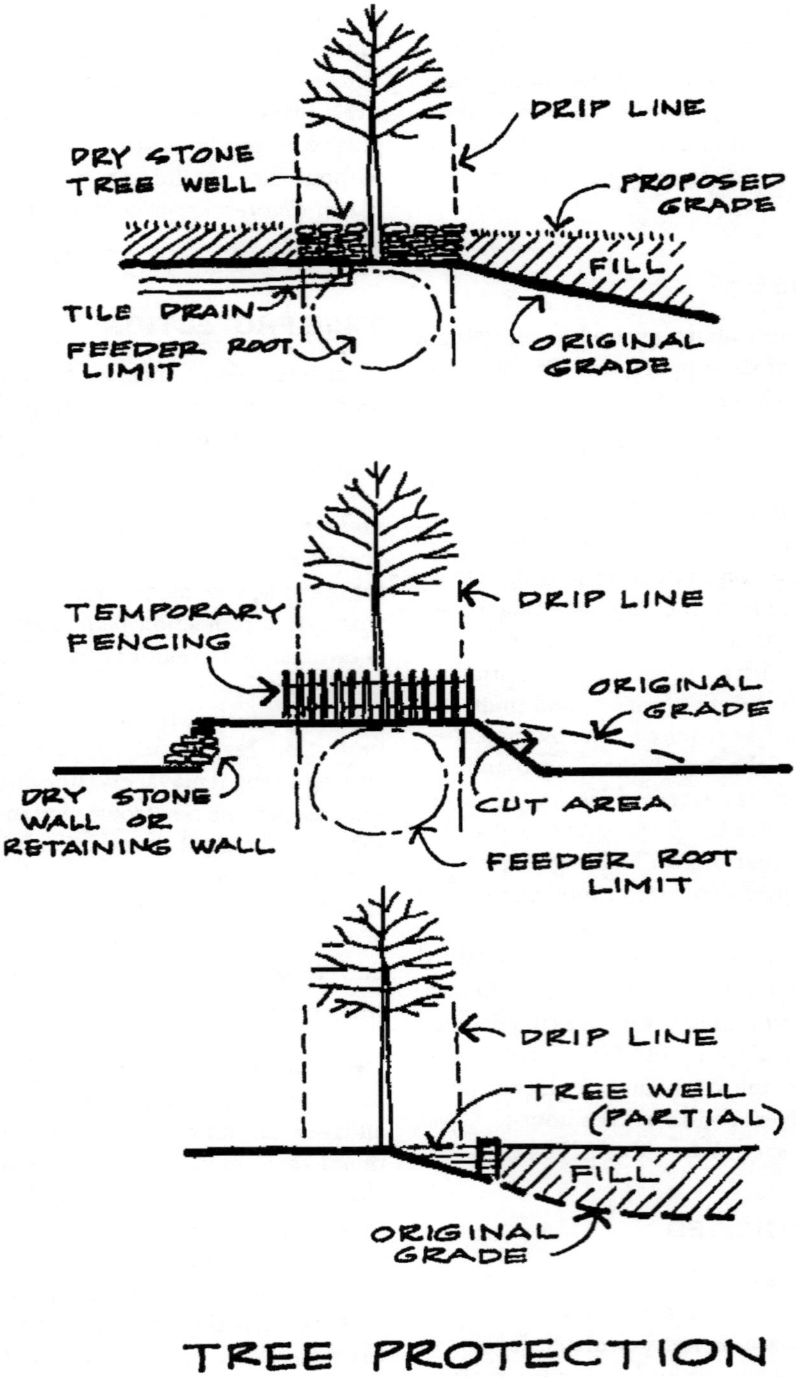
DRIP LINE
DRY STONE TREE WELL
PROPOSED GRADE
FILL
TILE DRAIN
FEEDER ROOT LIMIT
ORIGINAL GRADE
DRIP LINE
TEMPORARY FENCING
ORIGINAL GRADE
DRY STONE WALL OR RETAINING WALL
CUT AREA
FEEDER ROOT LIMIT
DRIP LINE
TREE WELL (PARTIAL)
FILL
ORIGINAL GRADE
TREE PROTECTION

**Figure 104**

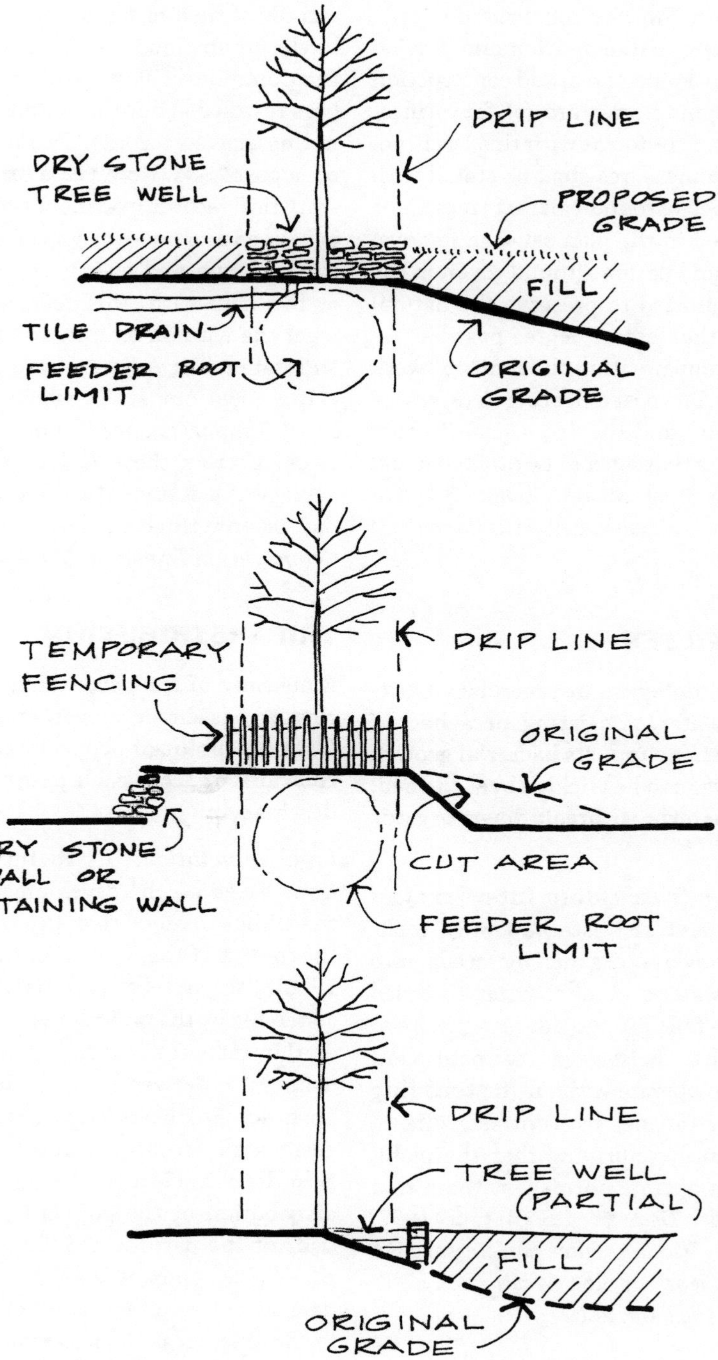


TREE PROTECTION

"A detailed plan showing landscaping improvements, open areas, limit of construction activity, edge of clearing, sedimentation and erosion controls, a soil stockpiling area, and construction staging, refueling and storage area(s), for verification that such plan conforms with this Decision. **Tree protection** measures shall be stated with details for tree wells around existing trees to be protected included in the plan set. The removal of trees, shrubs, and natural ground cover on the site shall be minimized to preserve the natural environment to the highest degree possible. All trees over 8" in caliper within the limits of work shall be flagged prior to tree clearing. A representative of the Board and the Town [sic] Planner shall identify trees that need to be protected and preserved during construction." *Zoning Board of Appeals of Amesbury v. Housing Appeals Committee* (Mass., 2010).

## TRICKLING FILTER

**A device for the biological or secondary treatment of wastewater, consisting of a bed of rocks or stones that supports bacterial growth and permits sewage to be trickled over the bed, enabling the bacteria to break down organic wastes.**

*Legal Annotation*: "A **trickling filter** provides secondary treatment of waste in sewage treatment, i.e., it converts organic materials into carbon dioxide, water and inert materials called 'sludge.'. . . Burke failed to provide any other evidence showing that the sewage treatment plant could continue to operate without the **trickling filter**. The government, by contrast, offered conclusive evidence confirming that the plant, indeed, could not operate normally without that filter. See *Strickler Decl. ¶¶ 4-5 (Aug. 5, 1997) (Stating That The Trickling Filter Is Necessary For Secondary Treatment Of The Wastewater)." Pr Burke Corp. V. Us (Fed. Cir. 2002).*

## TRIP

**A single or one-way motor vehicle movement either to or from a subject property or study area.** ***See Figure 63.***

*Legal Annotation*: "The neighbors presented records of their observations of traffic generated by the group home that were not contradicted by the Community. For example, one of the neighbors testified about the volume of traffic at trial, noting that she recorded 718 **trips** for the month of August 1993. However, a careful review of the statistical records in evidence reveals that a '**trip**' is defined as a one-way journey. Thus, every visit to the home and every errand run is counted as two trips each. This definition is contrary to what the witness indicated at the hearing when she stated, 'For August I have a total of . . . 718 **trips** down our street which would be *up and back*.' (Emphasis added). Putting these numbers in perspective, these 718 '**trips**' work out to an average of just under twelve visits or errands per day, or only three per resident each day." *Hill v. Community of Damien of Molokai* (N.M., 1996).

## TRIP DISTRIBUTION

**A measure of the percentage of the total vehicles or passenger movements that are going from one point of origin to each point of destination, or from each point of origin to one destination.**

*Legal Annotation*: "As to future traffic conditions based on the development of the project, the DEIR explained that '[i]n order to determine the impact of the project on traffic levels once it is built, the number and **distribution of trips** generated by the project was calculated. Trip generation rates for the project were forecasted by using rates derived from the Institute of Transportation Engineers Trip Generation, 7$^{th}$ Edition designated for quality restaurant use. Project **trip distribution** was based on the geographic distribution of the population from which the trips of the patrons and employees of the proposed development would originate or terminate, as well as knowledge of development trends in the area, local and sub-regional traffic routes, and regional traffic flows. . . . Distribution findings were entered into the TRAFFIX program, which calculated specific numbers and distribution of traffic (trips) for the proposed project." *Dembrowski v. City of West Hollywood* (Calif. Ct. App., 2010)

## TRIP ENDS

**The total of single or one-direction vehicle movements entering and leaving a specified land use or site over a designated period of time.** ***See Figure 62. (Adapted From Institute of Transportation Engineers, Trip Generation Manual, 9th Edition, 2012.) See Figure 63.***

***Legal Annotation***: "All subdivision and land development projects shall be evaluated to determine the impact of traffic which they generate on the Township's overall highway system. This requirement shall apply to all new subdivisions or land developments proposed and to any expansion of an existing land development which is proposed after the effective date of this ordinance. The level of traffic impact shall be determined based on the estimated '**Trip Ends**' generated by the proposed uses in the subdivision or land development. '**Trip Ends**' shall be defined as the estimated total number of motor vehicle trips entering and leaving a specific land use or uses located in subdivision or land development per day. These '**Trip Ends**" will be determined based on the estimated 'Trip Generation Rates' for various types of land uses set forth in the latest edition of the publication entitled 'Trip Generation, An Informational Report.' Information in the above publication such as local similar development counts may be used to estimate the ADT if the Township Engineer . . . considers such information as providing a more applicable estimate of the '**Trip Ends** Per Day' for the specific uses proposed." *Joseph v. North Whitehall Township Board of Supervisors* (Pa. Common. Ct., 2010).

## TRIP GENERATION

**The total number of vehicle trip ends produced by a specific land use or activity.**

***Comment***: The Institute of Transportation Engineers (2012) reports the results of more than 5,500 trip generation studies undertaken in its *Trip Generation Manual* publication. The book provides estimates on the number of vehicle trips likely to be generated by a particular land use in terms of a number of variables, such as the square footage of the structure, size of parcel, and number of employees.

Research by Fehr and Peers, reported in *Planning* magazine, noted that "trip generation is directly influenced by development scale, site density, land-use mix, urban design, transit availability, and the location of accessible travel destinations." The article further points out that not considering these factors results in significant overestimation of trip generation levels (Carter and Walters 2013; Millard-Ball and Siegman; Walters, Bochner and Ewing 2013).

***Legal Annotation***: "THE **TRIPS GENERATION** ASSESSMENT FORMULA "To determine the amount of special benefits, and therefore the assessment for each parcel, Bellevue relied exclusively on the number of vehicle trips (1) generated by existing land uses and (2) which will be generated by future land uses. The formula allocated one-third of the costs to trips generated by existing uses and two-thirds to trips estimated to be generated by future uses of the property.

[. . .]

"The number of **trips generated** by a particular use was taken from a publication of the Institute of Transportation Engineers. That document warns that extreme care must be taken in use of the data therein. The publication states that local data should be collected when using the national data, but no local data was taken or presented to the City Council." *Bellevue Plaza, Inc. v. City of Bellevue* (Wash., 1993).

## TRIPLE-WIDE UNITS

**Three manufactured housing components, attached side to side, to make one complete housing unit.**

***Legal Annotation***: "The Bersts alleged in their amended complaint that the moratorium prevented them 'from making reasonable use of their property by prohibiting any sort of development on it for a six-year period.' They also stated in their complaint that the County denied their application for a permit to replace their single-wide mobile home with a **triple-wide mobile home**. Thus the trial court erred in granting dismissal for failure to state a claim upon which relief can be granted." *Berst v. Snohomish County* (Wash. Ct. App., 2002).

## TRIPLEX

**See *Dwelling, Triplex*.**

***Legal Annotation***: "On June 24, 2008, Hamm bought a **triplex** apartment building located at 1310 West $10^{th}$ Street, Wilmington, Delaware, from the Estate of Anne Dorsey Hall. The previous owner of the **triplex**, Anne Dorsey Hall, purchased the property in 1946 and resided in the second floor apartment from 1950 until her death on September 27, 2007. During those years, Hall rented out the other two apartments. However, while the **triplex** had been originally zoned for multi-unit dwellings, in approximately 1980 the area was rezoned for single-family dwellings. Nevertheless, Hall continued to rent out the apartments as a permissible nonconforming use. . . . After his purchase of the **triplex** in June 2008, Hamm swiftly proceeded to make significant repairs on the property while obtaining the necessary permits and inspections. The repairs totaled approximately $47,000 and complied with historical parameters. In August 2008, Hamm leased two of the three apartments located in the triplex. And, in September 2008, Hamm leased the third apartment. In quickly going forward with the repairs, Hamm's intent was to make sure that he had tenants in the triplex before one year had passed from August 2007, the date the previous tenant departed. Hamm was fully aware of the Wilmington ordinance that does not permit a nonconforming use to continue if one year has passed since the discontinuance of the use." *Hamm v. City of Wilmington Zoning Board of Adjustment* (Del. Super. Ct., 2010).

## TRUCK CAMPER

**A structure designed to fit into the bed of a pickup truck and used for temporary shelter and sleeping.**

***Legal Annotation***: "'**Truck camper**' means a nonself-propelled recreational vehicle that does not have wheels for road use and is designed to be placed upon and attached to a motor vehicle. '**Truck camper**' does not include truck covers that consist of walls and a roof, but do not have floors and facilities enabling them to be used as a dwelling." *Ryncarz v. Powhatan Point* (Ohio Ct. App., 2005).

## TRUCK ROUTE

**Streets designated for use by all vehicles exceeding a certain weight.**

***Comment***: Truck routes generally follow major arterials through industrial areas, bypassing retail, commercial, and residential areas and avoiding areas with large concentrations of people, such as schools and cultural centers.

***Legal Annotation***: "Each of the above described roads is a primary road for the movement of traffic and each is unrestricted for truck use under the city **truck route** ordinance. Each of the roads is further designated as State trunk line highways with the Expressway also being designated as a Federal highway." *Lamb v. City of Monroe* (Mich., 1959).

## TRUCK SALES

**The sale of vehicles primarily designed to carry cargo and materials.**

***Comment***: Truck sales often involve the assembly of chassis and cabs and may be more appropriate in an industrial zone.

***Legal Annotation***: "The original regulations . . . had permitted automobile and **truck sales** and service in Commercial A and B Districts (which it seems would include a used car sales lot), but were silent as to the dismantling or wrecking of vehicles on the premises." *Phillips v. Zoning Commissioner* (Md. Ct. App., 1961).

## TRUCK STOP

See *Travel Center*.

***Legal Annotation***: "Appellant applied for a Zoning Certificate Building Permit to construct a **truck stop**. Because a '**truck stop**' was not explicitly referred to in the Frederick County

Zoning Regulations, appellant sought and obtained an opinion by the Zoning Administrator providing that a **truck stop** was a permitted use in the G.C. classification. The Town of New Market appealed this interpretation to the Board of Appeals, which affirmed the Zoning Administrator. The Town then appealed to the Circuit Court. . . . A '**truck stop**' is not a zoning classification, but a use within a classification, and one that was never explicitly placed in the zoning ordinance until the 1981 textual change." *Cardon Inv. v. Town of New Market* (Md. Ct. Spec. App., 1983).

## TRUCK TERMINAL

**An area and building where trucks load and unload cargo and freight and where the cargo and freight may be broken down or aggregated into smaller or larger loads for transfer to other vehicles or modes of transportation.**

***Comment***: Truck terminals are basically transshipment facilities and often include the storage or parking of trucks awaiting cargo as well as facilities for servicing of trucks. Storage facilities such as warehouses, incidental to the principal use, may also be part of a truck terminal.

Truck terminals are similar to distribution centers and warehouses, except they usually serve many manufacturing firms and are owned and operated by trucking companies. There are two types of terminals. An "end-of-line" terminal serves a small geographic area, often a city or metropolitan area. "Branch bulk" terminals serve large regional areas. Freight may be stored on the site until a full truckload for a specific area has been aggregated. Truck terminals generate more truck traffic than warehouses or distribution centers, but usually at off-peak hours. **See *Distribution Center; Warehouse*.**

*Legal Annotation*: "The question then is whether, assuming that **truck terminals** are prohibited in an A-1 zone, the use made of the property by the Cohens constitutes a '**truck terminal**,' as that term is strictly construed. The term, '**truck terminal**,' is not defined in the Dane County Zoning Ordinances as they existed at the time pertinent to this litigation. Secs. 10.01 and 10.01 (15) of the Dane County Zoning Ordinances specify that any words not defined in the ordinance should be construed as defined in the Wisconsin Building Code and, if not defined therein, by reference to dictionary usage or to a common understanding of the term. It is agreed that the Wisconsin Building Code does not define '**truck terminal**,' nor have we been persuaded that there is any common understanding of the meaning of the term. Webster's New Third International Dictionary defines 'terminal' as: '6a. either end of a carrier line (as a railroad, trucking or shipping line, or airline) with classifying yards, dock and literage facilities, management offices, storage sheds, and freight and passenger stations b: a freight or passenger station that is central to a considerable area or serves as a junction at any point with other lines.' Under that dictionary definition, which includes terminals related to trucking, it is clear that the term, '**truck terminal**,' includes the concept of facilities for storage or loading. The zoning board, on the other hand, contends that a terminal is merely a place where a journey begins or ends. Both of these interpretations are reasonable. It thus appears that the term is ambiguous. As we have stated above, an ambiguous term in a zoning ordinance must be construed in favor of the free use of private property, and unless this court can be satisfied that the use that the property has been put to by the Cohens is unambiguously a '**truck terminal**,' it is not a prohibited use. Thus, we cannot conclude as a matter of law that a place where empty trucks are parked constitutes a '**truck terminal**' as that term appears in C-2 of the zoning ordinances." *Cohen v. Dane County Board of Adjustment* (Wis., 1976).

## TURBIDITY

**A thick, hazy condition of air or water produced by the presence of suspended particulates or other pollutants.**

*Legal Annotation*: "'**Turbidity** is an expression of the optical property of water which causes light to be scattered and absorbed rather than transmitted through in straight lines. **Turbidity** is caused by the presence of suspended matter.' . . . This optical property of water is most commonly measured using the Jackson Turbidity Unit (JTU). 'A general rule of thumb guideline is that 5 JTU is the limit for drinking water, 10 JTU impairs flyfishing, 20 JTU impairs other fishing methods, and long-term 50 JTU water alters fish behavior.'" *Marsh v. Oregon Natural Resources Council* (U.S., 1989).

## TUTORING

**The provision of instruction to students.**

***Comment***: Tutoring is usually considered a home occupation. The local ordinance should specify the type of tutoring permitted, such as academic subjects, art, music, or dance, and the number of students permitted at any one time.

***Legal Annotation***: "b. The following are permitted home occupations provided they do not violate any of the provisions of the previous paragraph: . . . (5) **Tutoring**, limited to four students at a time." *City of Pekin v. Kaminski* (Ill. App. Ct., 1987).

## TWO-FAMILY DWELLING

**See *Dwelling, Two-Family*.**

# U

## UNDERGROUND UTILITIES

**The placement of electric, telephone, cable, and other utilities, customarily carried on poles, in underground vaults or trenches.**

***Legal Annotation***: "The Kansas Underground Utility Damage Prevention Act, K.S.A. 66-1801 *et seq.*, governs the procedures for excavating in areas containing underground natural gas pipelines. This Act creates a statutory duty to the public to ensure the safety and integrity of **underground utilities**." *Double M Const., Inc. v. State Corp Com'n* (Kan., 2009).

## UNDERSIZED ISOLATED LOT

**See *Isolated Lot*.**

## UNDERUTILIZED LAND

**Land parcels with any of the following characteristics:**

- **More than 80 percent of the parcel in a nonbuilding use, such as surface parking or storage yard.**
- **Land parcels containing structures that are at least 50 percent vacant.**
- **Land parcels with buildings with a floor area ratio of less than .10.**
- **Land parcels with buildings that are abandoned, dilapidated, or otherwise seriously impaired by physical deficiencies.**

***Comment***: The definition is useful in determining the redevelopment potential of a tract of land. The percentages should be adjusted to meet local needs and conditions.

***Legal Annotation***: "Therefore, the only significant opportunity for revitalization of the City is through the redevelopment of **underutilized land** mass. The challenge of the City of Perth Amboy is to provide incentive to property owners to bring these sites to market." *ERETC v. City of Perth Amboy* (N.J. App. Ct., 2005).

## UNDEVELOPED LAND

**Land in its natural state before development.**

***Legal Annotation***: "**Undeveloped land** in a community is a limited resource which is difficult to conserve in a period of increased population pressure." *Associated Home Builders Etc. v. City of Walnut Creek* (Calif., 1971).

## UNDIVIDED HIGHWAY

**A highway without any center island, median, or barrier.**

***Legal Annotation***: "In late 1969 or early 1970 the Pennsylvania Department of Transportation (PennDOT) commenced widening the route from a two-lane **undivided highway** to a four-lane divided highway." *Brill v. Dept. of Transportation* (Pa. Comm. Ct., 1975).

## UNIFORMITY

**The requirement that the regulations within a particular zone regulate each class of use or building in a uniform manner.**

***Comment***: An example is to have a building height limitation in the zone of thirty-five feet, regardless of what the building is used for.

***Legal Annotation***: "Chapter 4 of title 7 of the Government Code (65800-65907) establishes standards for the adoption and administration of zoning regulations by counties and nonchartered cities. Among such standards is that of **uniformity** within land use zones. 'All such regulations shall be uniform for each class or kind of building or use of land throughout each zone.'" *Scrutton v. County of Sacramento* (Calif. App. Ct., 1969).

## UNIMPROVED LAND

**Land without any improvement. See *Improvement; Raw Land*.**

***Legal Annotation*:** "The area in question now consists partly of vacant or **unimproved land** and land with some structures not in themselves substandard or insanitary but which have been found by the agency to be essential to the completion of an adequate unit of development." *Gohld Realty Co. v. Hartford* (Conn., 1954).

## UNIQUE NATURAL FEATURE

**That part of the natural environment that is rare or not duplicated in the community or region.**

***Legal Annotation*:** "Lake Tahoe, a **unique** high Sierra mountain lake and the dominant **natural feature** of the Tahoe basin, is losing its most valued quality, its pristine clarity. In recognition of this deterioration, the states of Nevada and California and the United States Congress ratified the Tahoe Regional Planning Compact (hereinafter Compact)." *Tahoe-Sierra Preservation v. Tahoe Reg. Planning Agency* (D. Nev., 1985).

## UNIVERSAL DESIGN

**"A design approach that seeks to create environments, objects, and systems that can be used by as many people as possible." See *People With Disabilities*.**

***Comment*:** "The term 'Universal Design' has evolved from 'Barrier Free Design' and 'Accessible Design,' design processes that focus specifically on addressing the needs of people with disabilities. Universal Design goes further by recognizing that we all exist somewhere on a wide continuum of human ability. Everyone, even the most able-bodied person passes through childhood, periods of temporary illness and injury, and old age. By designing for all of the abilities on the continuum, universal design can create environments products and services that will be easier for all people to use, regardless of their abilities, age or current state of health." http://www.universaldesign.com/about-universal-design.html

Examples of Universal Design include: in-floor lighting, tactile and guiding floor blocks, bright-colored handrails, low-set elevator control panels, children's and barrier-free toilet facilities, and diaper changing facilities (in both women's and men's restrooms) (http://en.wikipedia.org/wiki/Universal_design). *See Also* Myerson 2007: 44.

***Legal Annotation*:** "Salmen is a licensed architect, and a member of the American Institute of Architects, and the American National Standards Institute's A117 Committee. . . . He is president of Universal Designers & Consultants, Inc., an architectural design and consulting firm, specializing in **universal design**, accessibility, regulatory compliance, and facility evaluations. . . . Salmen was also the American Institute of Architects representative on the ADA Accessibility Guidelines Review Federal Advisory Committee." *Douris v. Bucks County Office of District Attorney* (E.D. Pa., 2004).

## UNIVERSITY

**An institution of higher education and research that provides both undergraduate and postgraduate education. See *College*.**

***Legal Annotation*:** "The handbook excludes from the definition of '**university** grounds' all '[c]ampus streets and adjoining sidewalks maintained by the City of Knoxville.'" *McGlone v. Cheek* (E.D Tenn., 2012).

## UNSIGHTLY AREAS

**Outdoor areas whose appearance may be considered ugly and objectionable.**

***Comment*:** The definition above is somewhat subjective but unavoidable, because what constitutes "unsightly" is in the eye of the beholder. Examples of unsightly areas include: areas outside of a building where machinery or equipment is repaired, stored, and/or serviced; outside trash storage areas; loading docks; outdoor vehicle storage areas; and utility facilities. Unsightly areas can be the subject of specific regulations to restrict their locations and/or provide for screening. For example, loading and unloading docks can be restricted to those sides of buildings that keep them from being visible from the street. Outside trash storage areas can be required to be screened with fencing or landscaping.

*Legal Annotation*: "The preamble to the ordinance sets forth the purposes thereof as follows: 'Whereas, the removal of all topsoil or loam from land involves noise and dust in the removal thereof and results in blighted, **unsightly areas** unfit for use thereby retarding development as useful districts and creating drainage problems, swamp conditions and similar dangers to public health and safety.'" *Miesz v. Mayfield Heights* (Ohio App. Ct., 1952).

## UPLAND

**(1) Land elevated above surrounding lands; (2) any non-wetland area.**

*Legal Annotation*: "These agencies all expressed concern regarding the potential environmental impacts of the Casino World development, including the potential impacts on water quality and habitat, the secondary impacts of the **upland** development, and the cumulative impacts of the numerous casino projects along the coast." *Friends of the Earth, Inc. v. US Army Corps of Engineers* (D.C.D.C., 2000).

## UPZONE

**To raise the intensity of use by increasing the permitted density or floor area ratio or otherwise increasing the extent of development previously permitted. See *Downzone*.**

*Comment*: This term and its counterpart, "downzone," are often misused. "Upzone" means to increase or raise the density (number of dwelling units per acre) or floor area ratio. "Downzone" means to decrease or lower the density or floor area ratio.

*Legal Annotation*: "We do not discuss here that it was a failure to **upzone** or rezone rather than downzoning. For the purpose of this issue, failure to **upzone** is not different from downzoning, insofar as we determine whether an action of this type is taken to reduce or lower the value of property." *Toso v. City of Sanat Barbara* (Calf. Ct. App., 1980).

## URBAN

**Relating to or constituting a city or town. See *Urban Area*.**

*Comment*: A more useful term in a development context is "urban area," which has distinct and measurable characateristics.

*Legal Annotation*: "**Urban** is defined as 'of, relating to, characteristic of, or taking place in a city . . . constituting or including and centered on a city... of, relating to, or concerned with an urban and specif. a densely populated area . . . belonging or having relation to buildings that are characteristic of cities. . . .' (Webster's Third New Internat. Dict. (unabridged 1968) p. 2520, col. 3; see also Black's Law Dictionary (5th ed. 1979) p. 1381, col. 1, defining **urban** as '[o]f or belonging to a city or town. Within city limits . . .'" *Honey Springs Homeowners v. Bd. of Supervisors* (Calif. Ct. App., 1984).

## URBAN AGRICULTURE

**See *Agriculture, Urban*.**

## URBAN AREA

**Densely developed residential and commercial and other nonresidential areas (US Census 2010).**

*Comment*: The 2010 US Census identifies two types of urban areas: urbanized areas of fifty thousand or more people; and urbanized clusters of at least twenty-five hundred and less than fifty thousand people.

*Legal Annotation*: "The billboards involved are located beyond 660 feet from the right-of-way of the Interstate Highway outside of an '**urban area**' as defined . . . as follows: (10) '**Urban areas**' means those areas which the secretary of transportation, in the exercise of his sound discretion and upon consideration being given to the population within boundaries of an area and to the traveling public, determines by official order to be urban.'" *Diemer v. Com. Transp. Cabinet* (KY, 1990).

## URBAN CENTER

**(1) An area of statewide importance; (2) a large settlement that has a high intensity of population and mixed land uses, including industrial, commercial, residential, and cultural uses; (3) the historical focus in the major urban areas of the state (*New Jersey State Development and Redevelopment Plan* 2002).**

***Legal Annotation*:** "Mansfield is approximately 25 miles east of Timken's Bucyrus facility. Mansfield is the county seat of Richland County; it is a highly industrialized **urban center** with a population of approximately 55,000 persons." *Timken Co. v. Vaughan* (N.D. Ohio, 1976).

## URBAN CONTEXT

**The combination of buildings, structures, and streetscape elements that form a distinct neighborhood or section of a city or urban place. See *Development Context*.**

***Legal Annotation*:** "Thus, the EIR correctly concluded that '[p]arking shortfalls relative to demand are not considered significant environmental impacts in the **urban context** of San Francisco.'" *San Franciscans Downtown Plan v. City of San Francisco* (Calif. App. Ct., 2002).

## URBAN DESIGN

**(1) The process of organizing the contextual elements of the built environment such that the end result will be a place with its own character or identity; (2) planning the development of the built environment in a comprehensive manner to achieve a unified, functional, efficient, and aesthetically appealing physical setting (Schultz and Kasen 1984). See *Building Mass; Building Scale; Community Design Plan; Design Standards; Development Context; Harmonious Relationship; Human Scale; Urban Context*.**

***Comment*:** Although often associated with the practice of architecture, the discipline of urban design is unique. While architects are concerned primarily with the design of individual buildings, urban designers are concerned with developing contextual design guidelines for all buildings. Design principles for new construction and existing buildings are spelled out by Segedy and Daniels (2007). They also suggest that a "design review ordinance" based on the existing predominant design and details can provide useful guidelines for new construction and renovation.

***Legal Annotation*:** "The Commission also relied upon an '**Urban Design** Plan,' containing general environmental policies for the City developed over several years to be included in the City's Master Plan." *William C. Haas & Co. v. City of San Francisco* (9th Cir., 1979).

## URBAN FRINGE

**The closely settled territory adjacent to the central place(s) of an urbanized area.**

***Comment*:** The census blocks that constitute the urban fringe generally have an overall population density of at least one thousand people per square mile of land area (US Census Bureau).

***Legal Annotation*:** "The Legislature perceived as one cause of these problems the self-fulfilling prophecy of the property tax system: taxing land on the basis of its market value compels the owner to put the land to the use for which it is valued by the market. As the **urban fringe** approaches, the farmer's land becomes valuable for residential development." *Sierra Club v. City of Hayward* (Calif., 1981).

## URBAN GROWTH BOUNDARIES

**(1) A perimeter drawn around an urban growth area (American Planning Association, *Growing Smart* project); (2) a boundary, often parcel-specific, marking the outer limit beyond which urban development will not be permitted (California Planning Roundtable).**

***Comment*:** See Avin And Bayer 2003 for suggestions as to criteria and applications to determine how to establish boundary lines.

***Legal Annotation*:** "Goal 14 specifies the requirements for conversion of rural land to urban land.

The goal provides: 'To provide for an orderly and efficient transition from rural to urban land use. **Urban growth boundaries** shall be established to identify and separate urbanizable land from rural land.'" *1000 Friends of Oregon v. Wasco County Court* (Ore., 1985).

## URBAN HOMESTEADING

**A program for selling vacant, usually substandard urban housing to people who will rehabilitate and occupy such housing.**

*Legal Annotation*: "Other laws, too numerous to describe in detail, reveal how urban rehabilitation is imbedded in public policy and the public interest. *See, e.g.*, . . . **Urban Homesteading** Act, *N.J.S.A.* 40A:12-31 to -38 (authorizing municipalities to create '**urban homesteading** programs' designed to allow for the transfer of municipally owned vacant dwellings to willing applicants for a nominal fee 'in order to facilitate their reuse and, equally, to encourage and promote the economic revitalization of this State's urban centers.')" *Davidson Bros. v. D. Katz & Sons* (N.J. App. Ct., 1994).

## URBANISM, NEW

**A term used to describe an idealized model of traditional city life that includes traditional neighborhood design; high-density, mixed-use development; heavy dependence on mass transit, pedestrian, and bicycle use (and reduced dependence on the automobile); human-scale orientation in architectural forms (particularly as to building access, storefronts, and public amenities); and diversity of land use, culture, and social interaction.**

*Comment*: The term "new urbanism" has been expanded in recent years to encompass virtually any movement or ideology that seeks to reform the top-down, centralized model city of modern times in favor of a more diverse, complex, integrative, bottom-up model. See Barnett 2011 for a discussion of more than sixty "newest urbanisms," describing models for community participation, environmental protection and sustainability, design of systems and places, political processes, and the like.

*Legal Annotation*: "'**New Urbanism**' is a design concept featuring compact, multiuse communities in which all the needs of daily life (housing, work, retail, entertainment, schools, parks and civic facilities) are within a ten-minute walk of one another." *Snowden v. City of Wilmore* (Ky. App. Ct., 2013).

## URBAN RENEWAL

**A program for the physical improvement of primarily urban areas through comprehensive planning and governmental assistance to effect rehabilitation and redevelopment.**

*Comment*: This term has been largely discredited because of the failure of federal urban renewal programs to achieve their desired outcomes.

*Legal Annotation*: "The original **urban renewal** plan, adopted in 1959, called for a combination of rehabilitation of structures by property owners in part of the area, and of site acquisition in another part." *Shannon v. United States Dept. of Housing & Urban Development* (3rd Cir., 1970).

## URBAN RUNOFF

**Stormwater from city streets, gutters, and paved surfaces.**

*Comment*: Urban runoff usually contains a significant amount of litter and organic and bacterial wastes. **See *Runoff***.

*Legal Annotation*: "**Urban runoff** has been named as the foremost cause of impairment of surveyed ocean waters. Among the sources of stormwater contamination are urban development, industrial facilities, construction sites, and illicit discharges and connections to storm sewer systems." *Environmental Defense Center, Inc. v. USEPA* (9th Cir., 2003).

## URBAN SERVICE BOUNDARY

**A defined region, not always coincidental with a municipality's corporate boundary, that delineates the geographical limit of government-supplied public facilities and services (Nelson and Dawkins 2004).**

*Legal Annotation*: "In these consolidated cases, LUBA remanded comprehensive plan amendments by the City of Beaverton and Washington County, respectively. The amendments purported to establish an **urban service boundary** (USB) that included certain unincorporated territory in the county within the area that would ultimately be annexed by and receive services from Beaverton, rather than the City of Portland." *City of Portland v. City of Beaverton* (Ore. App. Ct., 1994).

## URBAN SERVICES

**Utilities, such as water, gas, electricity, and sewer, and public services, such as police, fire, schools, parks, and recreation, provided to an urbanized or urbanizing area.**

*Legal Annotation*: "The GBO allows the extension of **urban services** to greenbelt land if such extension is consistent with the GBO and is approved by both the City Department of Water and the Department of Public Works." *Kinzli v. City of Santa Cruz* (9th Cir., 1987).

## URBAN SPRAWL

See *Sprawl*.

## URBANIZED AREA

**An area consisting of a central place or places and adjacent urban fringe that together have a minimum residential population of at least fifty thousand people and generally an overall population density of at least one thousand people per square mile. See *Urban Area*.**

*Comment*: The definition above is a more generalized definition, better suited for land development purposes. We do note, however, that the US Census has a different definition of urbanized area, as follows: "a densely settled core of census tracts and/or census blocks that have a population of at least 50,000 along with adjacent territory containing non-residential urban land uses as well as territory with a low population density included to link outlying densely settled territories with the densely settled core" (US Census 1990).

*Legal Annotation*: "The City of Scottsdale bases its standing on the provisions of Section 9-101.01, A.R.S. This statute defines **urbanized area** as that land within six miles of an incorporated city or town having a population of five thousand or more. The statute then provides that no territory within an **urbanized area** will be incorporated as a city or town (two exceptions mentioned are inapplicable herein). A segment of the District is located within the urbanized area adjacent to Scottsdale. The intent of the statute is to give existing cities and towns area in which to expand without conflicts from newly created municipalities." City of Scottsdale v. Mcdowell Mt. Irr. & D. Dist., (Ariz., 1971).

## USE

**The purpose or activity for which land or buildings are designed, arranged, or intended, or for which land or buildings are occupied or maintained.**

*Legal Annotation*: "As we have said on numerous occasions, the Fifth Amendment is violated when land-use regulation 'does not substantially advance legitimate state interests *or denies an owner economically viable **use** of his land*.'" *Lucas v. South Carolina Coastal Council* (U.S., 1992).

## USE, ACCESSORY

See *Accessory Use*.

## USE, CONDITIONAL

See *Conditional Use*.

## USE, EXISTING

See *Existing Use*.

## USE, INHERENTLY BENEFICIAL

See *Inherently Beneficial Uses*.

## USE, INSTITUTIONAL

See *Institutional Use*.

## USE, PERMITTED

See *Permitted Use*.

## USE, PRINCIPAL

See *Principal Use*.

## USE, RELIGIOUS

See *Religious Use*.

## USE, TEMPORARY

See *Temporary Use*.

## USE, TRANSITIONAL

See *Transitional Use*.

## USE VARIANCE

See *Variance, Use*.

## USER CHARGES

**A requirement of government under which those who benefit directly from a particular service pay all or part of the cost.**

***Comment***: User charges are not new, but the types and extent are increasing. Impact fees are similar, except that they are usually paid by the developer and are included in the sale or rental cost of the project.

***Legal Annotation***: "In contrast to a special assessment, a usage fee typically is charged only to those who use the goods or services. The amount of the **[user] charge** is related to the actual goods or services provided to the payer." *San Marcos Water Dist. v. San Marcos Unified School* (Calif., 1986).

## UTILITY, PRIVATE OR PUBLIC

**(1) Any agency that, under public franchise or ownership, or under certificate of convenience and necessity, or by grant of authority by a governmental agency, provides the public with electricity, gas, heat, steam, communication, transportation, water, sewage collection, or other similar service; (2) a closely regulated enterprise with a franchise for providing a needed service. See *Public Utility*.**

***Legal Annotation***: "The state-created monopoly status of a utility arises from the unique characteristics of the services that a utility provides. As recognized in *Cantor* v. *Detroit Edison Co.*, 428 U.S. 579, 595-596 (1976), '**public utility** regulation typically assumes that the private firm is a natural monopoly and that public controls are necessary to protect the consumer from exploitation.'" *Central Hudson Gas & Elec. Corp. v. Public Serv. Comm'n of NY* (U.S., 1980).

## UTILITY BOX

**Electric transformers, switch boxes, telephone pedestals and telephone boxes, cable television boxes, traffic control boxes, and similar devices.**

***Legal Annotation***: "Prior to closing, Mrs. Chilson inspected the property and discovered a **utility box** in open view on the premises. She was informed by her attorney that the utilities were being paid by the Conservation Club and that she should seriously consider the effect of that present possession on the title." *West Concord Conservation Club v. Chilson* (Minn., 1981).

## UTILITY CORRIDORS

**Rights-of-way or easements for utility lines on either publicly or privately owned property.**

***Legal Annotation***: "In June, 2001, LMJV applied to the Forest Service for rights-of-way across NFS lands for access and **utility corridors** from U.S. Highway 160 to private land it owns within the Rio Grande National Forest." *Colorado Wild, Inc. v. US Forest Service* (D. Colo., 2007).

## UTILITY EASEMENT

See *Easement, Public Utility*.

## UTILITY SERVICES

**The generation, transmission, and/or distribution of electricity, gas, steam, communications, and water; the collection and treatment**

**of sewage and solid waste; and the provision of mass transportation.**

***Legal Annotation***: "Moreover, the Miller Act requires municipalities to obtain commission approval before forcing the abandonment of nonmunicipal utility facilities or the withdrawal of nonmunicipal utility services located inside the municipality. . . . Thus, under the Miller Act, a municipality generally must seek commission approval before forcing a utility to stop serving customers or to abandon its electric lines inside the municipal limits." *Village of Grafton v. Ohio Edison Co.* (Ohio, 1996).

# V

## VACANCY

**Any unoccupied land, structure, building, or part thereof that is available and suitable for occupancy.**

***Legal Annotation***: "The pertinent provision is Denver Revised Municipal Code § 617.1-4(3)(d) which states: 'Any one of the following Specific Acts shall terminate immediately the right to operate a nonconforming use: . . . **Vacancy** for a period of 12 or more consecutive months of the structure or that part of the structure occupied by the nonconforming use.'" *Wyatt v. Board of Adjustment-Zoning* (Colo. Ct. App., 1980).

"A **vacancy** due to the inability to secure tenants does not constitute a discontinuance, interruption, or abandonment of such nonconforming commercial use." *Ward Kinard v. Glenwood Carrier* (La. Ct. App., 1965).

## VACANCY RATE

**The number of uninhabited dwelling units, or percent of unoccupied, nonresidential floor area that is available and suitable for occupancy, expressed as a percentage of the total number of dwelling units for residential use and total floor area for nonresidential use respectively. See *Occupancy Rate*.**

***Legal Annotation***: "Moreover, while the decision refers to the economic effect the proposed store would be expected to have upon other local businesses, it does so in the context of assessing the probability and extent of the change it would work upon the over-all character of the community, as a result of an increased **vacancy rate** among commercial properties in the downtown area—an entirely proper avenue of inquiry, even within SEQRA." *Wal-Mart v. Planning Board* (N.Y. App. Ct., 1998).

"[T]he municipality's expert testified that a **vacancy rate** of less than 3% indicated a serious housing shortage . . . several of plaintiffs' experts stated that a 5% vacancy rate was typical of a housing market in equilibrium; one fixed a 3% vacancy rate as indicative of a housing shortage." *Helmsley et al. v. Borough of Fort Lee* (N.J., 1978).

## VACANT LAND

**(1) Land that is undeveloped and unused; (2) any nonresidential areas with significant amounts of land not covered by nonstructural, impervious surfaces; (3) land suitable for redevelopment. See *Underutilized Land; Undeveloped Land; Unimproved Land*.**

***Legal Annotation***: "The township is now definitely a part of the outer ring of the South Jersey metropolitan area, which area we define as those portions of Camden, Burlington and Gloucester Counties within a semicircle having a radius of 20 miles or so from the heart of Camden city. And 65% of the township is still **vacant land** or in agricultural use." *South Burlington County NAACP v. Township of Mt. Laurel* (N.J., 1975).

"The bill alleges that the tract of land in question is **vacant** and has been held for years for the purpose of selling and developing it for industrial uses." *Village of Euclid et al. v. Ambler Realty Company* (U.S., 1926).

## VACATION HOME

**A second home, owned or rented, usually used seasonally, and located in an area with nearby recreational opportunities or amenities.**

***Legal Annotation***: "Defendants use their beach house as a **vacation home** and, when they are not using it themselves, they rent it for short periods of time to others, who likewise use it as a **vacation home**." *Yogman v. Parrott* (Ore. 1997).

## VALLEY

**(1) A stretch of lowland lying between mountains or hills; (2) the land area drained or watered by a major river system.**

*Legal Annotation*: "The board found, *inter alia*, that the proposed subdivision would be located in a part of the town which was a **valley** lowland having a high water table and which was productive cropland." *Matter of Neiderfofer v. Gustafson* (N.Y. App. Ct., 1974).

## VALUE MALL

**See *Retail Store, Large-Scale*.**

## VAN

**(1) A closed vehicle with a capacity of approximately eight to twelve passengers; (2) a self-propelled recreation vehicle containing sleeping facilities but not bathroom or cooking facilities; (3) a large truck for carrying cargo or freight.**

*Legal Annotation*: "Among other things, the Board reasoned that the petitioner's passenger **van** calculations and the related, on-street parking estimates, lacked credibility since the petitioner was, inter alia, speculatively assuming that each congregant utilizing the **van** would also be a separate driver. The Board also made a finding that since the parking lot curb cut lot was only 14 feet (ten feet short of the required width), this non conformity—taken together with the limited, back-up space (21 feet, where 24 is mandated)—would greatly increase 'the probability of accidents' and thereby negatively impact upon, and be substantially dangerous to, the surrounding area as well as to the 'public's health, safety and welfare.'" *Matter of Gospel Faith Mission Intl., Inc. v. Weiss* (N.Y. Sup. Ct., 2012).

## VANPOOLING

**A share-the-expense method of commuting for people who work in the same place and have the same work hours. See *Carpooling*.**

***Comment***: Vanpools differ from carpools in that the employer or sponsoring organization usually provides the passenger vans that are used in the program. Source: http://www.vtpi.org/tdm34.htm

*Legal Annotation*: "Caltech supports **vanpooling** by providing flexible work schedules, by assisting individuals to locate others who are interested in **vanpooling** and by a program that guarantees a ride home if the employee has to leave work either too early or too late to make the vanpool ride." *Wurm v. California Institute of Technology* (Calf. App. Ct., 2009).

"Indeed, the intention of the Ridesharing Act was to encourage employers to provide ridesharing and **vanpooling**, but only insofar as those terms are commonly understood. Under the facts presented *sub judice*, employer's marshaling of its employees at its place of business and subsequent dispersal to various work locations at its convenience and interest does not fall within the commonly-accepted notion of vanpooling." *Rite Care Resources v. WCAB* (Pa. Comm. Ct., 1993).

## VAPOR

**The gaseous phase of substances that are normally either liquids or solids at atmospheric temperature and pressure; for example, steam and phenolic compounds.**

*Legal Annotation*: "[P]atents relate to an apparatus and a method, respectively, for removing water **vapor** from a sample to be analyzed in a gas chromatograph." *OI Corp. v. Tekmar Co. Inc.* (US Fed. Cir., 1997).

## VAPOR PLUME

**Stack effluent consisting of condensed flue gas or flue gas made visible by condensed water droplets or mist.**

*Legal Annotation*: "However, when Con Edison applied for a building permit, the application was denied by the village's building inspector on the grounds that the size of the proposed tower exceeds the 40-foot height limitation in the zoning district, that a visible **vapor plume**

emanating from the tower would extend beyond the boundary of the immediate site in contravention of section 54-22 of the Buchanan Zoning Ordinance, and that a saline draft would be deposited, also in violation of that section." *Con Ed Co. of NY v. Hoffman* (N.Y., 1978).

## VAPORIZATION

**The change of a substance from the liquid to the gaseous state.**

***Legal Annotation***: "At some locations, TRC used a foam spray to suppress the odors caused by **vaporization** of the volatile organics exposed during the excavation." *New York v. Solvent Chemical Co., Inc.* (W.D. N.Y., 2010).

## VARIANCE

**Permission to depart from the literal requirements of a zoning ordinance.**

***Legal Annotation***: "As we discussed in Stadsvold, '[t]here are two types of **variances**: use **variances** and area **variances**. "A use **variance** permits a use or development of land other than that prescribed by zoning regulations." . . . An area **variance** controls "lot restrictions such as area, height, setback, density and parking requirements."'" *Krummenacher v. City of Minnetonka* (Minn., 2010).

## VARIANCE, AREA

**See *Variance, Bulk*.**

## VARIANCE, BULK

**Permission to depart from the dimensional requirements of a zoning ordinance. See *Variance, Hardship*.**

***Comment***: In some states a bulk variance is referred to as an "area variance." Examples include noncompliance with setbacks; building height; lot area, depth, or width; and lot and bulding coverage.

***Legal Annotation***: "This precludes 'use' variances, but apparently does not prohibit so-called **'bulk' variances**, those which prescribe setbacks, building heights, and the like." *Topanga Assn. for a Scenic Comm. v. City of Los Angeles* (Calif., 1974).

## VARIANCE, HARDSHIP

**Permission to depart from the requirements of a zoning ordinance by reason of an extraordinary and exceptional situation uniquely affecting a specific piece of property or the structures lawfully existing thereon, the strict application of which would result in peculiar and exceptional practical difficulty to or exceptional and undue hardship on the developer of such property (New Jersey Statutes Annotated, 40:55 D-70 c[1][c]).**

***Comment***: The hardship variance is granted because strict enforcement of the zoning ordinance as it applies to a specific lot would present practical difficulties in the use of the property. "Hardship" most often relates to the physical characteristics of the property, and without the variance, the property becomes unusable.

Hardship may also be used to justify a use variance. For example, in cases involving obsolete uses or outdated structures, a hardship variance may be justified so that the building can be adapted or used for a different purpose. Another example of hardship as a basis for a use variance is split lot zoning, where the zone line runs through the center of the property and a part of the property is rendered useless. Hardship variances do not typically include economic hardships. Moreover, personal hardship—that relating to the owner—is not a basis for the granting of such variances.

***Legal Annotation***: "There are essentially four factors that appellants must prove to be entitled to a variance under the applicable statute and ordinance. The factors are: (1) that an unnecessary **hardship** exists which is not created by the party seeking the variance and which is caused by unique physical circumstances of the property for which the variance is sought; (2) that a variance is needed to enable the party's reasonable use of the property; (3) that the variance will not alter the essential character of the district or neighborhood, or substantially or permanently impair the use or development of the adjacent property such that it is detrimental to the public's welfare; and (4) that the variance will afford the least intrusive solution." *Larsen v. Zoning Board of Adjustment* (Pa., 1996).

## VARIANCE, PLANNING

**A variance arising directly out of a municipality's authority to plan.**

***Comment***: Planning variances are granted to allow buildings or structures to be constructed in the bed of a proposed street, in a drainage right-of-way, or on proposed parks or playgrounds, or to build on a lot not abutting a street. Because such departures are not from the zoning ordinance but instead from the adopted official map, such variances are termed "planning variances."

***Legal Annotation***: "In deleting the conditions, the Board concluded that the improvements to the road were not necessary because, although it was difficult, emergency vehicles could service the area, and there were other homes in the area with variances. The trial judge found that the Board heard substantial testimony and thoroughly considered the granting of this **planning variance**." *Cerra v. Township of Frankford Land Use Board* (N.J. App. Ct., 2012).

## VARIANCE, USE

**A variance granted for a use or structure that is not permitted in the zone.**

***Comment***: Since the application for a use variance involves a use that is not permitted in the zone, it is often harder to obtain and is likely to encounter greater resistance from the neighboring property owners. Though the procedures and criteria for obtaining a use variance differ amongst states, use variances are typically granted where the applicant can demonstrate hardship (*see* Variance, Hardship). Typically the approving authority must weigh this hardship for the property owner against potential negative impacts that might occur in the neighborhood. In some jurisdictions, such as New Jersey, the basis upon which use (and area or bulk) variances can be granted is expanded beyond hardship. Where particular public benefits ensue and the goals and objectives of the state enabling legislation or the local comprehensive plan would be advanced, and where the negative impacts would not be substantial, use variances may then also be granted.

***Legal Annotation***: "[W]e deem it appropriate to require an enhanced quality of proof, as well as clear and specific findings by the board of adjustment, that the grant of a **use variance** is not inconsistent with the intent and purpose of the master plan and zoning ordinance. Such proofs and findings must satisfactorily reconcile the grant of a use variance with the ordinance's continued omission of the proposed use." *Medici v. BPR Co.* (N.J., 1987).

## VEGETATION

**(1) Trees, shrubs, ground cover, vines, grasses (both lawn and ornamental types), herbaceous perennials, biennials, annuals, bulbs, ferns, mosses, and lichens; (2) a living organism belonging to the vegetable kingdom, as distinguished from the animal kingdom, having rigid cell walls and characterized by growth chiefly from the synthesis of simple, usually inorganic food materials from soil, water, and air (*Funk & Wagnalls* 1968).**

***Legal Annotation***: "Indeed, the regulation could hardly state more clearly that saturation by either surface or ground water is sufficient to bring an area within the category of wetlands, provided that the saturation is sufficient to and does support wetland **vegetation**." *US v. Riverside Bayview Homes, Inc.* (U.S., 1985).

## VEGETATION, EXOTIC

**Vegetation that occurs naturally in another part of the world and does not occur locally.**

***Comment***: Introduction of exotic vegetation has been both accidental and intentional. Although many exotic plants have been used successfully, some exotic species have become nuisances because of their rapid reproduction and the lack of natural pests or diseases in the area to which they have been introduced. Other exotic species are highly susceptible to such pests and diseases. **See *Vegetation, Native*.**

***Legal Annotation***: "[T]hreats to the Listed Species [in the Florida Keys include] . . . increased traffic, illegal dumping, mortality from pets (especially cat predation), loss of fresh water (fertilizers degrading water quality), exotic fire ants, **exotic vegetation**, pesticide use." *Florida Key Deer v. Brown,* (S.D. Fla., 2005).

## VEGETATION, INDIGENOUS

**Vegetation existing in a specific geographic area at the present time.**

***Legal Annotation***: "Larger amounts of water flowing off a driveway or a roof have more erosive force than scattered raindrops falling over a dispersed area—especially one covered with **indigenous vegetation**, which softens the impact of the raindrops themselves." *Tahoe-Sierra Preservation Council, Inc. v. Tahoe Regional Planning Agency* (U.S., 2002).

## VEGETATION, NATIVE

**Vegetation that exists naturally, without intervention by humans, in a specific geographic area.**

***Comment***: All plants, except those that have been genetically modified by human actions, are native in some location; therefore, it is important that the geographic area be specified. Also, many plants that have been introduced into an area, either intentionally or accidentally, have become naturalized. Such plants are not normally considered native. The use of native vegetation has increased in recent years for reasons of habitat protection, enhancement, and restoration; preservation of regional character; superior adaptability to climate and soil conditions; and resistance to harmful insects and diseases in the area. **See *Vegetation, Exotic*.**

***Legal Annotation***: "Thus I would affirm the trial court's determination that Florida Rock's proposed mining operation is 'new development,' on which a 25% reservation of land to protect **native vegetation** is required pursuant to the Putnam County Comprehensive Planning and Land Development Act." *Florida Rock Properties v. Keyser* (Fla. App. Ct., 1998).

## VEGETATION, NATIVE AND INDIGENOUS

**Vegetation that occurs naturally in a specific geographic area or that was introduced into the area by humans.**

***Comment***: Native and indigenous vegetation is often specified as replacement vegetation in conservation areas and easements or as part of a landscape plan for development. The specific geographic area may be as small as the municipality but usually encompasses much larger areas, such as the Northwest, the Southeast, and so on. The agricultural extension service of the state department of agriculture or local nurseries can be helpful in providing lists of native and indigenous vegetation for the specific geographic area. **See *Vegetation, Exotic; Vegetation, Indigenous; Vegetation, Native*.**

***Legal Annotation***: "Where **native vegetation** is not available to create a sight-obscuring buffer between the planned development and existing county or state roads, fast-growing **native vegetation** that will grow to obscure the planned development should be planted within the buffer area." *Suquamish Tribe v. Central Puget Sound* (Wash. Ct. App., 2010).

## VEGETATION MAP

**A pictorial depiction of the location and type of plant materials that appear in a given land area (Schultz and Kasen 1984).**

***Legal Annotation***: "However, time estimates could be provided for certain interim measures listed under that task which are not even included on the chart, such as '[i]nvestigate preferred habitat[, d]etermine areas preferred for pronghorn activities . . . [,] investigate preferred forage species . . . [, c]omplete a **vegetation map** that includes all pronghorn habitat.'" *Defenders of Wildlife v. Babbitt* (D.D.C., 2001)

## VEGETATIVE PROTECTION

**Stabilization of areas vulnerable to erosion or sediment-producing areas by covering the soil with permanent or short-term seeding, mulching, or sodding.**

***Legal Annotation***: "The goal of the applicant's CMP [Compensatory Mitigation Plan] is to re-establish, restore, and/or enhance the values of each habitat parameter (i.e., embeddedness and sediment deposition, velocity/depth regime, riparian cover, bank stability and **vegetative protection**), in order to promote a general improvement in the area's existing benthic conditions." *Ohio Valley Environmental Coalition v. Aracoma Coal Co.* (4th Cir., 2009).

## VEHICLE, INOPERABLE

**Any vehicle that, while presently inoperable, is in a condition whereby repairs to the same could be made to place it in operating condition without exceeding its present estimated value and cost to repair.**

***Legal Annotation***: "'**Inoperable vehicle**' means: 'Any motor vehicle, recreational vehicle, boat, trailer, or semitrailer which lacks a current registration or component part which renders the vehicle unfit for legal use.'" *City of Des Moines v. Gruen* (Iowa, 1990).

## VEHICLE, JUNK

**Any rusted, wrecked, damaged, dismantled or partially dismantled, inoperative, or abandoned motor vehicle in such a condition that it is economically infeasible to restore the vehicle to an operating condition.**

***Comment***: "Economically infeasible" means that the cost of restoring the vehicle to an operating condition exceeds the market value of the vehicle.

***Legal Annotation***: "In part, it provides that '**Junk vehicle**' means 'any vehicle legally placed in storage with the County Treasurer or unlicensed and which has any of the following characteristics[.]' Then follows a list of conditions that will cause a vehicle to be considered junk. If the vehicle has broken glass; a broken, loose, or missing part; houses nuisance animals; contains any flammable fuel; or if it is 'inoperable' or in a 'defective or obsolete condition,' it fits the definition." *Kistler v. City of Perry* (Iowa, 2006).

## VEHICLE, MOTOR

**A self-propelled device licensed as a motor vehicle and used for transportation of people or goods over roads.**

***Legal Annotation***: "A quiet place where yards are wide, people few, and **motor vehicles** restricted are legitimate guidelines in a land-use project addressed to family needs." *Village of Belle Terre v. Boraas* (U.S., 1974).

## VEHICLE, OFF-ROAD (ORV)

**Vehicles, including dune buggies and all-terrain vehicles, snowmobiles, trail bikes, mopeds, and motorbikes, designed for use on unimproved surfaces.**

***Comment***: ORVs are also known as all-terrain vehicles (ATVs). As recreational vehicles, ORVs can be detrimental to the landscape and trails. Many of them are noisy and pose dangers to wildlife.

***Legal Annotation***: "These regulations not only prescribed the procedure and criteria to be employed in designating areas and trails; they went one step further, declaring that all public land not restricted or closed to **ORV** use 'remain open to **off-road vehicle** use and are hereby designated as open use areas and trails except that restrictions and closures regarding the use of public lands that result from authority other than part 6290 shall not be affected by the open use designation of this paragraph.'" *National Wildlife Federation v. Morton* (D.D.C., 1975).

## VEHICLE OVERHANG

**The portion of a vehicle extending beyond the wheel stops or curbs *(see Figures 73 and 105)*.**

***Comment***: In parking lot design, an overhanging car may interfere with pedestrian travel. In such cases, the adjacent sidewalks or planting island should be made wider by at least two feet, and any shrubs or trees should not be planted within the overhang area.

*Legal Annotation*: "SEC. 10-2.625 **VEHICLE OVERHANG**. Where a parking lot is designed so that cars may overhang low landscaping, the stall depth for a standard-sized car may be reduced by 2½ feet. The stall depth for a compact space may be reduced by 2 feet. The area overhung shall not be included in required landscape setback. In areas where **vehicles overhang** a sidewalk or walkway, the width of the sidewalk or walkway shall be increased by the overhang width to provide a minimum unobstructed width of the sidewalk or walkway of 4 feet. Parking stalls adjacent to walls shall be increased in width from the standard by at least one foot to accommodate door swing." *Hayward, Calif., Article 2 Off-Street Parking Regulations.*

## VEHICLE, PASSENGER

**A motor vehicle with no more than two axles and/or four wheels, not more than forty-five hundred pounds in gross weight, and designed primarily for the transport of persons.**

*Legal Annotation*: "Under the term 'motor vehicle' the following definition appears: 'A motor vehicle is *any* ***passenger vehicle***, truck, truck-trailer, trailer or semi-trailer propelled or drawn by mechanical power.'" *Heerey v. Zoning Board of Appeals* (Ill. App. Ct., 1980).

## VEHICLE, RECREATIONAL

See *Recreational Vehicle*.

## VEHICLE SALES AREA

**An open area, other than a right-of-way or public parking area, used for display, sale, or**

**Figure 105**

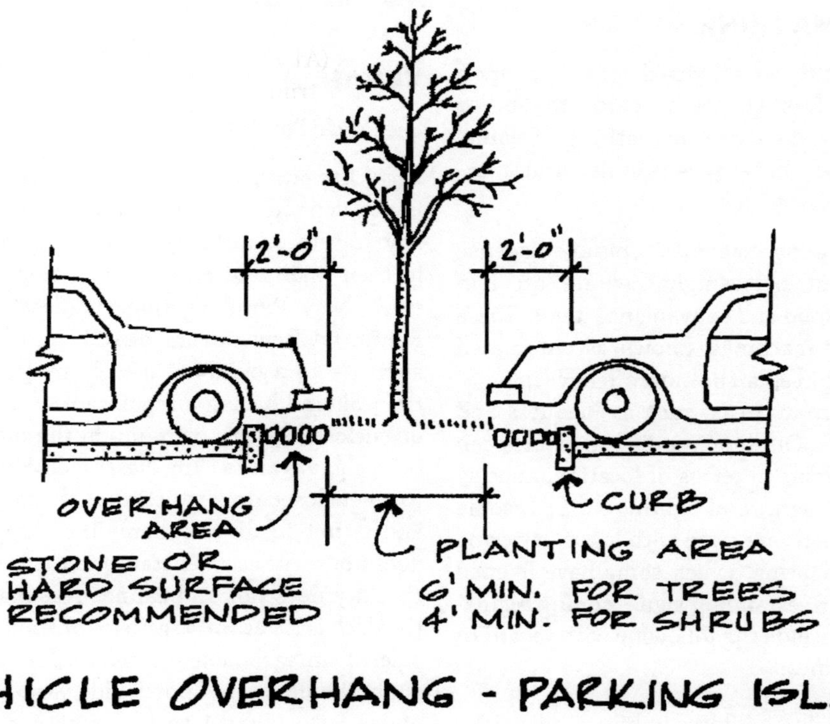


VEHICLE OVERHANG - PARKING ISLAND

**rental of new or used vehicles in operable condition and where no repair work is done.**

*Legal Annotation*: "There, the trial court permitted a realtor to testify regarding the value of a commercial complex that included a restaurant, manufacturing facilities for a specific type of car, an auto body and painting shop, and a used **car sales area**." *Mann v. Brandelli* (Calif. Ct. App., 2013).

## VEHICLE TRIP

**An event in which a motor vehicle moves from a point of origin to a point of destination. See *Trip*.**

*Legal Annotation*: "Nevertheless, there is authority elsewhere that a municipality is empowered to pass an ordinance requiring taxicab operators to be licensed by it for accepting or discharging passengers therein, regardless of whether or not the **vehicle's trip** occurs entirely within the city." *Village of Schaumburg v. Franberg* (Ill. App. Ct., 1981).

## VENDING MACHINE

**Any unattended self-service device that, upon insertion of money, credit card, token, or similar means, dispenses something of value, including food, beverages, goods, and merchandise. See *Newsrack*.**

*Comment*: Vending machines typically dispense soft drinks, but increasingly they are larger in size and offer food and convenience items. These super vending machines, known as automated convenience stores, can be most effective in high-density pedestrian areas, such as business and office locations. Outdoor vending machines can generate problems in terms of location, appearance, number, signs, and lighting. In fact, some vending machiens are large with logos, lettering and internal lighting, which some have likened to a de facto "freestanding sign." Zoning regulations should include the following with regard to vending machines:

- They should be prohibited in historic districts.
- They should be allowed in areas with high pedestrian activity, such as office and business zones.
- They should be allowed as accessory uses to specific permitted uses, such as gas stations or newsstands.
- Locations should be specified in such a way as to ensure they do not impede pedestrian or vehicular traffic flows or interfere with sight triangles.
- In developed areas with established setbacks, vending machines (other than newsracks) should not be permitted to encroach into the setback.
- Signage or logos on vending machines should be limited and lighting designed to control spillage.
- There should be special controls and design standards for newspaper vending machines, as discussed under the definition of NEWSRACK.

*Legal Annotation*: "The presence of a milk **vending machine**, such as the ones used here, in the basement of an apartment building which is not accessible to the general public, can have little, if any, adverse application to the character of the residential neighborhood." *Dellwood Co. v. City of New Rochelle* (N.Y. App. Ct., 1960).

## VERANDA

See *Porch; Portico*.

*Legal Annotation*: "The term 'uncovered **porch**' is not defined in the ordinance. Words used in any statute or ordinance are to be understood in their plain and ordinary meaning. . . . Webster's New World Dictionary (Second College Edition) defines **porch**: '**porch** . . . 1. A covered entrance to a building, usually projecting from the wall and having a separate roof. 2. An open or enclosed gallery or room on the outside of a building; **veranda**.' The Nesses' deck is adjacent to an enclosed deck which the City has approved and is not in dispute here. The disputed deck does not serve as an entrance to the house. Also, the City does not and cannot reasonably argue the deck is a **veranda**, gallery, or room. We consider it unreasonable, therefore, for the City to apply the uncovered porch side yard limitations under Subsection 4 to the Nesses' deck when that structure clearly is covered under Subsection 3 which permits its location in the side yard without restriction." *City of Fargo v. Ness* (N.D., 1996).

## VERNAL POOL

**A temporary pool or pond that is devoid of fish but that supports distinctive plants and animals adapted to ephemeral aquatic conditions, and that dries up at certain times of the year.**

***Comment***: Vernal pools are typically inundated by surface runoff and have no permanent flowing outlet. These conditions are ideal for amphibians such as frogs and salamanders, particularly because there is no competition from fish. Vernal pools are often considered critical environmental features and as such are afforded protection from development in many states.

***Legal Annotation***: "The site contains a fragile wetland area and **vernal pool**, which is a small hardpan-floored depression that fills with water during the winter and engenders plant growth as it dries." *Mira Monte Homeowners Assn. v. County of Ventura* (Calif. App. Ct., 1985).

## VEST-POCKET PARK

**A small land area, usually in a built-up neighborhood, developed for active or passive recreation.**

***Legal Annotation***: "The Property's immediate use as a 'park' or 'parklet' for passive and aesthetic recreation may then evolve into a more physical or interactive recreational park. Whether termed a 'park,' '**vest pocket park**,' 'pocket park,' or 'parklet,' we find the Township's taking of the Property for public park purposes within its statutory authority." *In re Condemnation of Lands of Laughlin* (Pa., 2003).

## VESTED RIGHT

**A right that cannot be changed or altered by changes in regulations.**

***Comment***: A development application that has been granted approval typically has a vested right for a certain period of time. During that period of time, changes in zoning do not apply to that development. Changes to the approved plan by the developer are typically not protected against such zoning changes. In such cases, the applicant is obligated to build in accordance with the new regulations or seek variances. However, a landowner cannot argue it was proceeding in good faith once a formal action to change the zoning has taken place. Thus, if a developer learns of a legislator's intention to introduce a zoning change and proceeds anyway, it does not necessarily mean the developer no longer proceeded in good faith.

***Legal Annotation***: "Applying the foregoing principles, plaintiff's application for registration of its tanks should be judged by the law as amended at the time of the appeal, unless doing so would interfere with a **vested right**. Whether a particular expectation rises to the level of a **vested right** is not capable of precise definition. In recognizing the conclusory nature of the inquiry, this court has defined a **vested right** as an expectation that is so far perfected that it cannot be taken away by legislation. . . . Although not capable of precise definition, a **vested right** is a complete and unconditional demand or exemption that may be equated with a property interest." *First of America Trust Co. v. Armstead* (Ill., 1996).

## VETERINARY HOSPITAL

**A place where animals are given medical care and the boarding of animals is limited to short-term care incidental to the hospital use.**

***Comment***: Some veterinary hospitals include animal boarding, breeding, and/or laboratories. A zoning ordinance should distinguish between veterinary hospitals, which can be located in any nonresidential area, and animal care facilities, which may or may not include a medical treatment component. Facilities that breed and/or board animals, particularly dog kennels, need special noise-deadening construction and/or deep open-space buffering to avoid sound transmission beyond property boundaries.

***Legal Annotation***: "Under this zoning classification a **veterinary hospital** operated in conjunction with boarding kennels was a permitted use provided a use permit was granted by the Board after a public hearing." *McClung v. County of Henrico* (Va., 1959).

## VICARAGE

**See *Clergy Residence*.**

## VIDEO VIEWING BOOTHS

**See *Adult Use*.**

***Legal Annotation*:** "Mannheim Video ('Mannheim') operates a video arcade and gift shop within Cook County, Illinois. A portion, less than half, of Mannheim's business is comprised of sexually explicit materials, including books, magazines and novelties. The Mannheim video arcade houses individual, coin-operated **booths**, which feature sexually explicit selections. . . . Mannheim's three-count complaint sought declaratory and injunctive relief and alleged that: (1) the term 'substantial or significant portion of its stock' is unconstitutionally vague; (2) its **video viewing booths** are not theatres within the definition of the zoning ordinance; and (3) the zoning ordinance otherwise impermissibly infringes upon Mannheim's First Amendment rights." *Mannheim Video, Inc. v. County of Cook* (7th Cir., 1989).

## VIEW-PROTECTION REGULATION

**Requirements to ensure that development does not interfere with scenic views. See *Viewshed and Figure 106*. (See American Planning Association, *Aesthetics and Land-Use Controls: Beyond Ecology and Economics,* Planning Advisory Service Report No. 399, 1986; *Aesthetics, Community Character, And the Law,* Planning Advisory Service Report no. 489/490, 1999.)**

***Comment*:** As noted in PAS 489/490, to deflect potential taking claims, view-protection ordinances often allow for, or encourage, mechanisms to transfer development out of protected areas, including cluster development and transfer of development rights.

***Legal Annotation*:** "Additionally, as the trial court correctly reasoned, SJCC 18.50.140 assists in defining what views are at issue here. This provision generally addresses public views with one exception. SJCC 18.50.140(D) describes **view protection** for 'surrounding properties to the shoreline and adjoining water.' But that protection applies when there is 'development on or over the water.' In the instant case, there is no 'development on or over the water.' Thus, harmonizing the provisions at issue, the visual impacts language on which Durland relies does not apply to adjacent property owners." *Durland v. San Juan County* (Wash. Ct. App., 2013).

## VIEWSHED

**An elevated or unobstructed location, position, or area that permits an unhindered panoramic vista of particular interest or pleasure or unique view to or from a particular point. See *Vista*. See *Figure 106*.**

***Comment*:** Viewsheds may be identified as part of a comprehensive community design study, master plan, or development application. Viewsheds may be protected from loss or damage by appropriate development regulations such as special viewshed protection easements, viewshed protection regulations, building setbacks, floor area ratio limits, height restrictions, or similar bulk controls. The community design study, which should be part of the local master plan, provides the basis for the regulations that implement viewshed preservation. Viewshed protection regulations should limit obstructions to the viewpoint area and also include development controls within the viewshed vista area itself.

***Legal Annotation*:** "A prominent and controversial feature of the FEIS and the Findings involved the visual impact of the project upon observation points along a **viewshed** between nearby Buttermilk Falls State Park and the project site." *East Coast Dev. Co. v. Kay* (N.Y., 1996).

## VILLAGE

**A small, compact center of predominantly residential character with a core of mixed-use commercial, residential, and community services. See *Neighborhood*.**

**Figure 106**

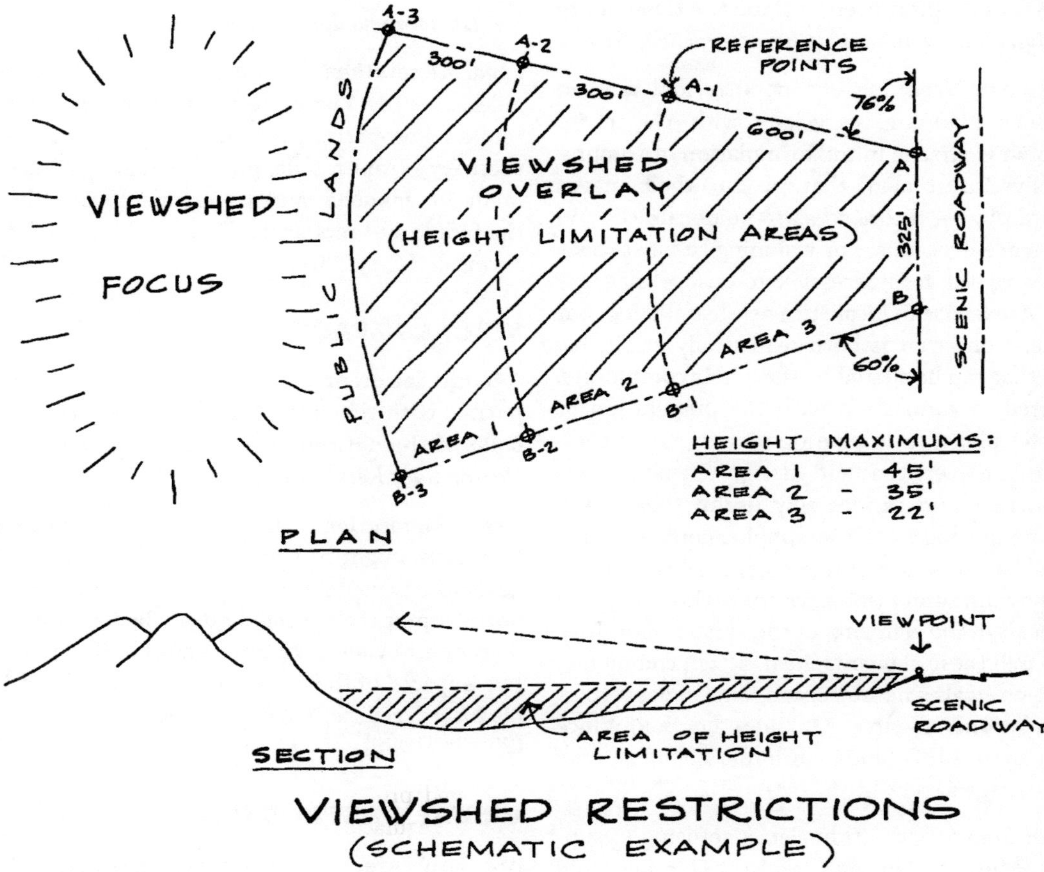


*Comment*: Mary Winder, PP, AICP for the Heritage Group of Sarasota County, Florida, describes the role of neighborhoods in achieving the traditional village form, as follows:

> The principles call for each neighborhood to have a central area of mixed uses, an interconnected street network, and walkable distance. The walkability standard limits the area of a neighborhood to a quarter-mile radius based on a standard of a five-minute walk. This standard results in an area of 125 acres. In some cases, the size might go up to 200 acres due to special environmental characteristics such as wetlands. The principles call for the neighborhood center to contain a mix of uses, including apartments and townhouses. The overall housing density should be at least three dwelling units per acre and preferably four to six. (These density standards would produce 375 to 750 dwelling units in a 125-acre neighborhood.) There should be an integrated network of streets to facilitate driving, walking, and biking. There should also be locations for civic buildings and spaces such as schools and parks. (Winder 2001.)

***Legal Annotation***: "The other section is AS 35.30.040. It provides: In this chapter . . . (2) '**village**' means an unincorporated community of the unorganized borough where at least 25 people reside as a social unit." *Native Village of Eklutna v. Alaska RR* (Alaska, 2004).

## VISIONING

**The process by which a community articulates its desired future image and expresses it in**

**the form of words and graphics, often as part of a master plan preparation. See *Community Design Plan; Community Character; Focus Group*.**

***Comment***: Visioning is a popular tool used in modern planning, especially with respect to involving citizens in the formulation of comprehensive future plans that tap into their images of a desirable future so as to guide choices and influence decisions. For visioning to be successful or useful, it is necessary to ensure that it is not an exercise in idealistic wish-list making, but instead one that is both realistically attainable and that can be shared by the whole community. If used in connection with the preparation of master plans, the visioning process can encompass both written and design elements. An important and increasingly useful tool in the visioning process is the appointment of a citizens' advisory committee composed of citizens in the community who have special knowledge or interest in the elements of the master plan. They research these elements, hear citizen comments, develop goals and objectives, and make recommendations. (Source: Outside the Box, Vince Papsidero, AICP, Linda LaClorda, *Planning*, May 2008, page 42.)

***Legal Annotation***: "In his letter refusing to support Mutual Housing's project, Garofalo told CHFA that Derby was planning to commence a '**visioning** and planning process' for the Caroline Street neighborhood . . . and testified that the public process should include the whole neighborhood; however, no plan was ever actually put in place." *Valley Housing LP v. City of Derby* (D. Conn., 2011).

## VISTA

**A unique view to or from a particular point.**

***Comment***: The view may be one of great natural beauty, farmlands, settlements (such as villages), or spectacular urban scenes. Many ordinances attempt to develop vista protection provisions to ensure that unique vistas are preserved and not encroached upon by development. **See *Viewshed*.**

***Legal Annotation***: "'**Vista**' means view." *Techworld Development v. DC Preservation League* (D.D.C., 1986).

## VISUAL COMPATIBILITY

**See *Harmonious Relationship*.**

***Legal Annotation***: "As noted, Chapter 64 provides: . . . (d) **Visual compatibility** with surrounding properties, including proportion of the property's front facade, proportion and arrangement of windows and other openings within the facade and roof shape." *Lusk v. Village of Cold Spring* (2nd Cir., 2007).

## VISUAL IMPACT

**A modification or change that could be incompatible with the scale, form, texture, mass, or color of the natural or built environment. See *Harmonious Relationship*.**

***Legal Annotation***: "The resolution indicated that there might be some potentially significant adverse environmental impact associated with Sprint's proposals, roughly described as impact on property values, **visual impact** and 'cumulative impacts' of the proposed facilities and possible future facilities." *Sprint Spectrum LP v. Willoth* (2nd Cir., 1999).

## VISUAL OBSTRUCTION

**Any structure, such as a building, fence, wall, or natural feature that limits visibility.**

***Comment***: Visual obstructions can be a hazard at street intersections where they interfere with traffic visibility. Many ordinances include requirements for sight easements to restrict visual obstructions.

***Legal Annotation***: "Nevertheless, where a specific regulatory provision, such as Village of Scarsdale Code § 294-1 (A), imposes upon property owners a duty to prevent vegetation from **visually obstructing** the roadway, proof of noncompliance with the regulatory provision may give rise to tort liability for any damages proximately caused thereby." *Lubitz v. Village of Scarsdale* (N.Y. App. Ct., 2006).

## VISUAL TERMINATION

**(1) A building, structure or other surface or streetscape element terminating a view; (2)**

**the placement of a building or structure for the purpose of spatial enclosure, providing a visual focal point, or giving enhanced recognition to the building or structure by such placement.**

*Legal Annotation*: "Focal points, or points of **visual termination**, shall generally be occupied by more prominent buildings and structures or landscape elements." *Village of Florida, N.Y., Article VI. Supplementary Regulations Sec. 119-50 Regulations applying to all residence districts.*

## VOCATIONAL SCHOOL

**A secondary or higher education facility, primarily teaching usable skills, that prepares students for jobs in a trade and meets the state requirements as a vocational facility.**

*Legal Annotation*: "The plain meaning of **vocational school** is a 'school, esp. one on a secondary level, that offers instruction and practical introductory experience in skilled trades such as mechanics, carpentry, and plumbing.' American Heritage Dictionary 1511 (3d ed 1997)." *Graceland College v. Dept. of Revenue* (S.D., 2002).

"The school is located in an area designated as an apartment-house district. Under the terms of the ordinance, uses permissible in such districts include grade or high school, apartment house, boarding or lodging house, hotel, hospital, home for dependents or nursing home, boarding school, **vocational school**, college or university, club, fraternity or sorority house, and a number of other specified uses." *City of Chicago v. Sachs* (Ill., 1953).

## VOIR DIRE

**A preliminary examination to test the competence of a witness or evidence (*Black's* 1999).**

***Comment***: A traditional method used in courts or before agencies to disqualify experts or to limit their areas of testimony.

***Legal Annotation***: "On the first day of trial in Jefferson Circuit Court, the judge conducted ***voir dire*** examination of the venire, excused certain jurors for cause, and permitted the parties to exercise peremptory challenges." *Batson v. Kentucky* (U.S. 1986).

## VOLATILE

**Evaporating readily at a relatively low temperature.**

***Legal Annotation***: "The method of application, suggested by the specifications, was simply to place the solution in a glass or metal, hermetically sealed vessel, on which the heat of the hand could operate so as to cause the **volatile** liquid to begin to evaporate, in turn causing internal pressure and, consequently, ejection of the liquid in a jet or spray." *Bridgeport Brass Co. v. Bostwick Laboratories* (2nd Cir., 1950).

## VOLUME-BASED WASTE DISPOSAL

**See *Waste Disposal, Volume-Based.***

# W

## WADING POOL

**An aboveground or in-ground structure containing less than eighteen inches of water.**

*Legal Annotation*: "In addition there would be a **wading pool** for small children, playground equipment, a snack shop and a shelter for use during inclement weather." *Tower Cabana Club v. City of Chicago* (Ill., 1955).

## WAIVER

**Permission to depart from the requirements of an ordinance with respect to the submission of required documents. See *Exception*.**

*Comment*: The terms "waiver" and "exception" are often used interchangeably. There are differences, however. "Waiver" refers to the submission of required documents; an "exception" is for relief of design standards or other non-zoning requirements in the ordinance. (Waiver of zoning requirements usually requires a variance.)

For example, an applicant may request a waiver of the requirement to submit an environmental impact statement for a small, isolated lot and request an exception to the sidewalk requirement if there are no sidewalks in the area. Cox (2003) notes that a request for a waiver or exception requires the approving agency to make findings and conclusions in order to "permit proper judicial review."

*Legal Annotation*: "The court analyzed and rejected respondents' argument that the definition and **waiver** provisions in the ordinances were impermissibly vague; it held that the disparate treatment of adult theaters and other theaters was justified by a compelling state interest and therefore did not violate the Equal Protection Clause; and finally it concluded that the regulation of the places where adult films could be shown did not violate the First Amendment." *Young v. American Mini Theaters, Inc.* (U.S., 1976).

## WALKABILITY

**The extent to which a neighborhood or area contains those features and elements that encourage and are conducive to walking.**

*Comment*: Also known as "neighborhood walkability," "walkable communities," and "pedestrian friendly street." See *Pedestrian-Oriented Design*. Recent Studies (Columbia University, Built Environment And Health Research Group, http://beh.columbia.edu-neighborhood walkbility) show a direct and positive relationship between walking activity and lower body mass index (BMI) and the benefits of greater physical activity. in addition to the obvious need for more sidewalks and walkways, the study focused on five "D's" as contributing to walkability: higher density, diversity (mix of land uses), design (the layout of the street grid), destination accessibility (to stores, community activities, socializing), and distance (proximity) to transit hubs. The study also indicates that aesthetics, lighting, and safety contribute to walkability.

*Legal Annotation*: "As an example, the report explained that 'community design' recognizes that . . . 'To support the characteristic of **walkability**, the area should have high enough densities and a diverse enough mix of uses within a quarter mile radius of centers to support **walkability**.'" *Bakers Five, LLC v. Land Construction and Development Comission* (Ore. Ct. App., 2014).

## WALK-UP

**An apartment building of more than two stories that is not equipped with an elevator.**

*Legal Annotation*: "The north side of the property was adjacent to a four-story **walk-up** apartment building with a restaurant and a food market, as well as a three-story factory." *In the Matter of City of New York* (N.Y., 2010).

## WALK-UP ESTABLISHMENT

**An establishment that by design of its physical facilities, service, or packaging encourages or permits pedestrians to receive a service or obtain a product without entering the establishment.**

***Legal Annotation***: "On its application, Avenue Bank described the facility as a '**walk-up**/drive-up' **facility**, with the only business to be the receipt of deposits, the cashing of checks, drafts and money orders, the changing of money and the receipt of loan payments." *First Bank of Oak Park v. Avenue Bank, Etc.* (7th Cir., 1979).

## WALL

**(1) The vertical exterior surface of a building; (2) one of the vertical interior surfaces that divide a building's space into rooms.**

***Legal Annotation***: "To the rear of their lot the ground slopes upward at a rather steep grade and between the rear **wall** of the building and the beginning of the slope is a rectangular open area." *Mack Zoning Appeal* (Pa., 1956).

## WAREHOUSE

**A building used primarily for the storage of goods and materials. See *Distribution Center; Truck Terminal*.**

***Comment***: In addition to the storage of goods and materials, modern warehouses function as distribution centers. Products are received, broken down into smaller quantities, often reassembled, and then reshipped. In the modern warehouse, the holding time is generally short.

Truck terminals differ from both warehouses and distribution centers, although they have certain common characteristics. The function of the truck terminal is to move packages on a contingent basis. Packages are picked up from a given geographic area at different addresses, often by smaller trucks, and then reassembled for shipment by larger trucks for delivery to other geographical areas. Common carriers may pick up tractor-trailer loads from specific manufacturers and then break down the load for subsequent delivery. They may also pick up from different locations, aggregate the loads at their terminals, send them out (often by air), and then break down loads for delivery.

Warehouses and distribution centers employ very few workers; a ratio of one worker per five thousand square feet of building area is not uncommon. Buildings often contain from 3 to 5 percent office space. Large companies may use small areas within the warehouse for other functions, such as employee training. These can be considered customary accessory uses. In addition, some retail activities may take place but under very strict controls. See *Retail Warehouse Outlet*.

The major planning issue with respect to warehouses (and distribution centers) is that the industry trend is for larger and larger buildings. One-million-square-foot buildings are no longer uncommon. For obvious reasons, interchange areas on major highways are highly desirable locations for these activities. Another trend is the provision of loading docks along the entire length of the two longest exterior walls of the building, plus an equivalent number of trailer storage spaces opposite the loading spaces. The availability of this number of loading doors and trailer spaces facilitates the twenty-four hour nature of some of the more intensely utilized warehouses—those used for big-box retailers and Internet-oriented retailers.

Municipalities can mitigate and reduce the visual impact of large-scale warehouses by requiring site improvements and building wall treatment. These include the following:

- Extensive use of landscaping and berms to shield and break up building mass and shield the loading and trailer storage areas
- Variations and articulation to overall building façades by changes in the façade plane
- Use of subdued wall coloration, patterning, texture, and reveals

- Creating or enhancing topographical changes on the site to create visual interest and provide shielding
- Adding elements that draw focus, introduce scale, and provide three-dimensional effects

One New Jersey municipality (Cranbury Township, Middlesex County), experiencing a large influx of very large warehouse buildings, amended its land development ordinance to address the visual impact of these buildings. The ordinance requires staggered building walls. The staggered walls must include a setback or bump-out of at least four feet, a minimum of fifty feet in length, at least every 150 to 180 feet, depending on bay width.

Other requirements include use of painted panels, reveals, awnings or canopies, wall openings, wall texture changes, changes in building height, and variations in rooflines. Building entries and building corners must be readily identifiable through the use of canopies, marquees, architectural treatments, and the use of different materials, such as glass.

The ordinance also requires that the front and two side elevations of all buildings and structures be constructed of brick, architectural block, architectural precast concrete, or tilt-up construction using similar material of equally high quality and aesthetic value. Utility-standard concrete panels or masonry units may be used on rear elevations and/or loading dock areas only if the rear elevations and loading docks are not visible from any public right-of-way after berming, fencing, or landscape treatment.

Color and texture are addressed. Texture patterns must be provided to create shadow patterns to reduce the visual impact and mass of the building. Variations in color are to be kept to a minimum, and accent colors should be consistent in color, size, and location on all buildings in the industrial park.

Location and siting requirements mandate that all buildings front on internal roadways. To the extent practical, warehouses located along arterial roads must be situated so that they are perpendicular to, or at an angle to, the arterial road, with the short side of the building parallel or at an angle to the road. Loading and unloading bays in multiple-building industrial parks are required to be located between the buildings so that a single means of ingress and egress serves both buildings.

Extensive landscaping is required for these large warehouses. Applicants are required to present computer-generated plans showing how the landscaping looks at various time intervals.

***Legal Annotation***: "Built in 1926, the entire premises were situated in a retail zoning district and, in compliance with the certificate of occupancy and applicable zoning regulation, served as a storage and **warehouse** facility." *Toys "R" Us v. Silva* (N.Y., 1996).

## WAREHOUSE OUTLET

See *Retail Warehouse Outlet*.

## WAREHOUSING, PRIVATE

**A building used primarily for the storage of goods and materials by the owner of the goods or operated for a specific commercial establishment or group of establishments in a particular industrial or economic field.**

***Legal Annotation***: "(b) The property is located in public or **private warehousing** facilities in this state which are not subject to the control of or under the supervision of the owner of the property or manned by its employees and from which the property is to be shipped to any person, including a customer, outside this state." *Fichtel & Sachs Industries, Inc. v. Wilkins* (Ohio, 2006).

## WAREHOUSING, PUBLIC

**A building used primarily for the storage of goods and materials and available to the general public for a fee.**

***Comment***: Public warehouses may be bulk warehouses, such as those with tank storage; commodity warehouses, such as grain elevators; refrigerated warehouses; or general-merchandise warehouses. See *Self-Storage Facility*.

***Legal Annotation***: "In 1978, C.F. Sales, a company engaged in the business of **public warehousing** and the unloading of bulk materials at Clinton, Iowa, entered into an agreement with IMC for the lease of storage space in its warehouse on the Clinton municipal dock." *CF Sales, Inc. v. Amfert, Inc.* (Iowa, 1983).

## WASTE

**Any unusable or unwanted substance or material.**

***Comment***: "Waste" is a generic term and can be disaggregated into different types of waste, as follows:

- *Bulk waste*—Items whose size precludes or complicates their handling by normal collection, processing, or disposal methods.
- *Construction and demolition waste*—Building materials and rubble resulting from construction, remodeling, repair, and demolition operations.
- *Hazardous waste*—Wastes that require special handling to avoid illness or injury to persons or damage to property.
- *Medical waste*—Includes isolation wastes; infectious agents; human blood and blood products; pathological waste; needles and sharp instruments; body parts; contaminated bedding; and surgical wastes.
- *Special waste*—Wastes that require extraordinary management.
- *Wood pulp waste*—Wood or paper fiber residue resulting from a manufacturing process.
- *Yard waste*—Plant clippings, prunings, and other discarded material from yards and gardens.

***Legal Annotation***: "Petitioner, the Solid Waste Agency of Northern Cook County (SWANCC), is a consortium of 23 suburban Chicago cities and villages that united in an effort to locate and develop a disposal site for baled nonhazardous solid **waste**." *Solid Waste Agency of Northern Cook Cty. v. Army Corps of Engineers* (U.S., 1981).

## WASTE DISPOSAL, VOLUME-BASED

**Garbage collection program where residents pay for each bag of trash, but where recycling is free.**

***Comment***: Also known as "pay-as-you-throw." A variant known as "modified volume-based," or "basic service," charges residents a set fee for weekly trash pickup but an additional amount for each bag dumped over a set limit. The intent of the program is to encourage recycling, and also for residents to compact their garbage before throwing it out. Some programs also separately collect yard waste and food scraps for composting purposes.

***Legal Annotation***: "We hold that there is no discriminatory purpose underlying the waste management tax scheme. The tax scheme was adopted to ensure the financial survival of the waste facility while maintaining a **volume based** system to encourage waste reduction." *Zenith/Kremer v. Western Lake Sanitary* (Minn., 1997).

## WASTELAND

**Land that is barren and uncultivated.**

***Legal Annotation***: "It was significant to the discussion in the case that the defendant's property was a swampy **wasteland** that had been abandoned by the logging industry, and it was bordered on one side by the city's odiferous refuse dump and on another side by a primary water well for the city." *Kyser v. Kasson Tp.* (Mich. Ct. App., 2008).

## WASTEWATER

**(1) Water carrying wastes from homes, businesses, and industries that is a mixture of water and dissolved or suspended solids; (2) excess irrigation water that is runoff to adjacent land. See *Gray Water*.**

***Legal Annotation***: "In August, 1995, the pollution control commission and G & B jointly filed an application with the zoning commission for a special permit and site plan approval for the construction of a **wastewater** treatment facility." *Keiser v. Zoning Commission* (Conn. Ct. App., 2001).

## WASTEWATER MANAGEMENT PLAN

**A description of existing and future wastewater-related jurisdictions, wastewater service**

**areas, and selected environmental features and domestic treatment works subject to approval by the appropriate state agency.**

*Legal Annotation*: "Generally, those regulations provide that a **wastewater management plan** should provide wastewater services for land uses allowed in the zoning ordinance or reasonably contemplated by the master plan." *Sod Farm Associates v. Springfield Tp. Planning Bd.* (N.J. Super. Ct., 1995).

## WASTEWATER SYSTEM

**Any device or system in public or private ownership used in the storage, treatment, recycling, or reclamation of sewage generated by two or more individual units of development (*New Jersey State Development and Redevelopment Plan* 2002).**

*Legal Annotation*: "In 1983, the commission granted Upjohn's application for permits to improve its **wastewater** treatment **system**, subject to numerous conditions, one of which was that Upjohn submit a plan and timetable for the removal of all existing sludge." *Upjohn Co. v. Planning & Zoning Commission* (Conn., 1992).

## WATERBODIES

**Any natural or artificial collections of water, whether permanent or temporary.**

*Legal Annotation*: "In regulatory provisions that remain in effect, the Corps had concluded that wetlands perform important functions such as filtering and purifying water draining into adjacent **water bodies** . . . slowing the flow of runoff into lakes, rivers, and streams so as to prevent flooding and erosion . . . and providing critical habitat for aquatic animal species." *Rapanos v. US* (U.S., 2006).

## WATER-CARRYING CAPACITY

**The ability of a pipe, channel, or floodway to transport flow as determined by its shape, cross-sectional area, bed slope, and coefficient of hydraulic friction.**

*Legal Annotation*: "The construction of the levees on each side of the creek banks merely increased the size and **water carrying capacity** of the Wakenda watercourse." *Smithpeter v. Wabash R. Co.* (Mo., 1950).

## WATERCOURSE

**Any natural or artificial stream, river, creek, ditch, channel, canal, conduit, culvert, drain, waterway, gully, ravine, or wash in which water flows in a definite direction or course, either continuously or intermittently; has a definite channel, bed, and banks; and includes any area adjacent thereto subject to inundation by reason of overflow or floodwater.**

*Legal Annotation*: "It is thus distinguishable from water flowing in a fixed channel, so as to constitute a **watercourse**, or water collected in an identifiable body, such as a river or lake." *Keys v. Romley* (Calif., 1966).

## WATERFRONT PARK

**See *Park, Waterfront*.**

## WATER POLLUTION

**The addition of pollutants to water in concentrations or in sufficient quantities to result in measurable degradation of water quality.**

*Legal Annotation*: "In EPA's view, the Act divides the causes and control of **water pollution** into two categories, point sources of pollutants (regulated through the § 402 permit program) and nonpoint sources of pollution (regulated by the states through 'areawide waste treatment management plans' under § 208, 33 U.S.C. § 1288)." *National Wildlife Federation v. Gorsuch* (D.C. Cir., 1982).

## WATER QUALITY CRITERIA

**The levels of pollutants that affect the suitability of water for a given use.**

*Comment*: Generally, water-use classification includes public water supply, recreation, propagation of fish and other aquatic life, agricultural use, and industrial use.

*Legal Annotation*: "A state water quality standard 'shall consist of the designated uses of the navigable waters involved and the **water quality criteria** for such waters based upon such uses.' 33 U. S. C. § 1313(c)(2)(A)." *PUD No. 1 of Jefferson Cty. v. Washington Dept. of Ecology* (U.S., 1994).

## WATER QUALITY MANAGEMENT PLAN (WQMP)

**The identification of strategies, policies, and procedures for managing water quality and wastewater treatment and disposal in a geographical area.**

*Comment*: A plan for water quality management contains four major elements:

- The use to be made of water (recreation, drinking water, fish and wildlife propagation, industrial, or agricultural).
- Criteria to protect the water to keep it suitable for use.
- Implementation plans (for needed industrial-municipal waste treatment improvements) and enforcement plans.
- An antidegradation statement to protect existing high-quality waters.

*Legal Annotation*: "Once established and approved, a state must incorporate the TMDLs into its 'continuing planning process,' (CPP) which is the state's overall **water quality management plan** that brings together and coordinates all aspects of the state's water pollution control program." *Missouri Soybean v. Missouri Clean Water* (Mo., 2003).

## WATER RIGHTS

**A property owner's right to use surface or underground water from adjacent lands.**

*Comment*: The western and eastern United States have different water laws. Riparian rights are applicable mainly to eastern areas. Western law generally provides that the first to claim the water has the use of it. See *Riparian Rights*.

*Legal Annotation*: "Within a year of that treaty, the California gold rush began, and the settlers in this new land quickly realized that the riparian doctrine of **water rights** that had served well in the humid regions of the East would not work in the arid lands of the West." *California v. United States* (U.S., 1978).

## WATERSHED

**An area of land that drains into a body of water such as a river, lake, stream, or bay and is separated from other watersheds by topographic features such as hills or slopes (NJ Department of Environmental Protection).**

*Comment*: The watershed of a lake would not include only the streams entering the lake, but also the land area that drains into these streams. Large watersheds, referred to as drainage basins, include the watersheds of many smaller rivers and streams (NJ Department of Environmental Protection; http://www.pgplanning.org/Resources/Tools_On-line/Glossary.htm). See *Basin; Drainage Area.*

*Legal Annotation*: "Reliez Creek is a natural watercourse which drains a **watershed** of approximately 2,291 acres. It is several miles long, and runs from the hills to a confluence with Las Trampas Creek. . . . Over the last 50 years development in the **watershed** has transformed an essentially rural environment into one in which 1,294 acres are developed." *Locklin v. City of Lafayette* (Calif., 1994).

## WATER SUPPLY SYSTEM

**The system for the collection, treatment, storage, and distribution of potable water from the source of supply to the consumer.**

*Legal Annotation*: "That the supply of water to a city is a public purpose cannot be doubted, and hence the condemnation of a **water supply system** must be recognized as within the unquestioned limits of the power of eminent domain. It matters not to whom the **water supply system** belongs, individual or corporation, or what franchises are connected with it—all may be taken for public uses upon payment of just compensation." *Long Island Water Supply Co. v. Brooklyn* (U.S., 1897).

## WATER TABLE

**The upper surface of groundwater or the level below which the soil is seasonally saturated with water.**

***Legal Annotation***: "The **water table** was raised both by the percolation of the water which rose and fell with the river and by the resulting blockade of the drainage of the land's surface and subsurface water." *United States v. Kansas City Life Ins. Co.* (U.S., 1950).

## WATER TOWER

**A water storage facility, usually above ground and often spherical or cylindrical in shape.**

***Legal Annotation***: "In Taber v. City of Benton Harbor, 280 Mich. 522, 274 N.W. 324, the city proposed to erect a steel **water tower** and tank 140 feet high with a storage capacity of 6,000,000 gallons as an improvement to an existing municipally-owned water system, the proposed site for such **water tower** being in a residence district of the city." *Baltis v. Village of Westchester* (Ill., 1954).

## WATER TRANSPORTATION

**Establishments engaged in freight and passenger transportation on the open seas or inland waters and in the furnishing of incidental services, such as lightering, towing, and canal operation.**

***Comment***: This major group includes excursion boats, sightseeing boats, and water taxis, as well as cargo and hauling operations.

***Legal Annotation***: "By § 500 of Transportation Act, 1920 (Feb. 28, 1920, c. 91, 41 Stat. 499; 49 U.S.C. § 142) 'it is declared to be the policy of Congress to promote, encourage and develop **water transportation**, service, and facilities in connection with the commerce of the United States, and to foster and preserve in full vigor both rail and **water transportation**.'" *Miss. Valley Barge Co. v. US* (U.S., 1934).

## WATERFRONT PROPERTY

**A property that has frontage on a waterbody.**

***Legal Annotation***: "This matter is of great public importance, particularly in view of population pressures, demands for recreational property, and the increasing development of seashore and **waterfront property**." *Marks v. Whitney* (CA, 1971).

## WATERS OF THE UNITED STATES

**Waters including territorial seas, navigable waters including tidal waters, and their tributaries, including lakes, rivers, and streams, and wetlands adjacent to these waters.**

***Comment***: Placement of dredged or fill material in "waters of the United States" is regulated by the US Army Corps of Engineers under Section 404 of the Clean Water Act.

***Legal Annotation***: "And, most relevant here, the CWA defines 'navigable waters' as 'the **waters of the United States**, including the territorial seas.'" *Rapanos v. US* (U.S., 2006).

## WATERSHED MANAGEMENT

**The implementation of a plan or plans for managing the quality and flow of water within a watershed, the naturally defined area with which water flows into a particular lake or river or its tributary.**

***Comment***: The aims of watershed management are holistic and concern the maintenance of water quality, the minimization of stormwater runoff, and the preservation of natural drainage patterns. Watershed management is, in many ways, an enlargement of most of the concerns that underlie floodplain management (*FEMA Glossary*).

***Legal Annotation***: "The State concedes, quite correctly on the Court's own theory, that even in this case 'the United States is not barred from asserting that rights to minimum instream flows might be necessary for erosion control or fire protection on the basis of the recognized purposes of **watershed management** and the maintenance of timber.'" *US v. New Mexico* (U.S., 1978).

## WAYFINDING SYSTEM

**A comprehensive and coordinated signage system that provides coherent regulatory and directional signs.**

***Comment***: The wayfinding system should be based on an overall design theme that is consistent in colors, sizes, and types of signage and is aesthetically pleasing, easily recognizable, and pedestrian-oriented. It should be part of the comprehensive design plan for residential neighborhoods as well as business districts. The system should serve to integrate and facilitate various modes of transportation and be expandable to new venues (Finucan 1999).

***Legal Annotation***: "The combined judgment of the Board and DOT about **wayfinding** needs, by contrast, has everything to do with their specific areas of technical expertise: evaluating technologies and accommodations for those with disabilities and transportation issues, respectively." *George v. Bay Area Rapid Transit* (9th Cir., 2009).

## WEAVING

**In traffic engineering, the crossing of two or more traffic streams traveling in the same general direction along a significant length of highway without the aid of traffic-control devices.**

***Legal Annotation***: "(f) The construction or installation of minor road and street improvements such as pavement marking . . . widening of a highway by less than a single lane width where capacity is not significantly increased and no new right of way is required, adding auxiliary lanes for localized purposes, (**weaving**, climbing, speed change, etc), where capacity is not significantly increased and no new right of way is required, channelization and elimination of sight restrictions at intersections, street lighting, guardrail and barricade installation, installation of catch basins and culverts, and reconstruction of existing road bed (existing curb to curb in urban locations), including adding or widening of shoulders, addition of bicycle lanes, paths and facilities, and pedestrian walks and paths, but not including additional automobile lanes." *Downtown Traffic Planning v. Royer* (Wash. Ct. App., 1980).

## WEIR

**A barrier (dam, fence, enclosure, rocks) set in a waterway to alter the flow, raise water levels, protect banks, or enhance fishing.**

***Legal Annotation***: "In March 1968, Ventron engaged the firm of Metcalf & Eddy to study the effects of mercury on the land, and three months later, Ventron constructed a **weir** to aid in monitoring the effluent." *NJ Dept. of Environ. Protect. v. Ventron Corp.* (N.J., 1983).

## WELL

**A hole or shaft sunk into the earth to tap an underground supply of water.**

***Legal Annotation***: "A **well** physically located on the Nebraska tract pumps ground water for irrigation of both the Nebraska tract and the Colorado tract." *Sporhase v. Nebraska ex rel. Douglas* (U.S., 1982).

## WETLAND BUFFER

**Abutting areas that surround and protect a wetland from adverse impacts to its function and value. See *Wetland Transition Area*.**

***Legal Annotation***: "It is also well established that, in furtherance of those interests, the town may include requirements in its **wetlands** bylaw that are more stringent than those in the act, as Blackstone has done by requiring a notice of intent for any work in the 100-foot buffer **zone**, and by barring building within the **buffer zone**." *FIC Homes of Blackstone, Inc. v. Conservation Commission of Blackstone* (Mass. App. Ct., 1996).

## WETLAND, COASTAL

**A wetland that is regularly inundated by the tides, with inundation frequency ranging from twice daily to twice monthly.**

***Comment***: The US Army Corps of Engineers regulates activities in coastal wetlands under Section

404 of the Clean Water Act and Section 10 of the Rivers and Harbors Act.

*Legal Annotation*: "For the purpose of this chapter, a '**coastal wetland**' means any salt marsh bordering on the tidal waters of this state, whether or not the tidal waters reach the littoral areas through natural or artificial watercourses, and those uplands directly associated and contiguous thereto which are necessary to preserve the integrity of that marsh." *R.I. Gen. Laws § 46-23-6(2)(iii)(e).*

## WETLAND, DEGRADED

**(1) A wetland in which there is impaired surface water flow or groundwater hydrology, or excessive drainage; (2) a wetland that has been partially filled or excavated and/or contaminated with hazardous substances; (3) a wetland that has an ecological value substantially less than that of undisturbed wetlands in the region.**

*Comment*: Improvement of the ecological value and restoration of wetland hydrology to degraded wetlands is termed "enhancement" and is a form of wetland mitigation.

*Legal Annotation*: "Mitigation measures were required to ensure that Phase 1 did not substantially conflict with LCP policies against significant habitat disruption, including . . . '[p]hasing of site remediation and wetland restoration [to] minimize the amount of time that both the existing **degraded wetlands** and the wetlands in the southwest corner of the site (slated for restoration) are non-functional.'" *Citizens for a Better Eureka v. California Coastal Commission* (Calif. App. Ct., 2011).

## WETLAND, FRESHWATER

**An area that is inundated or saturated by surface water or groundwater at a frequency and duration sufficient to support—and that under normal circumstances does support—a prevalence of vegetation adapted for life in saturated soil conditions.**

*Comment*: Wetlands are identified by one of three parameters: certain soil types, aquatic plants, and hydrology. Federal and state legislation makes the filling or dredging of wetlands extremely difficult (McElfish 2006). Many states also require buffer or transition areas to provide additional protection to wetlands.

*Legal Annotation*: "**Freshwater wetlands** are areas inundated or saturated by surface water or ground water at a frequency and duration sufficient to support a prevalence of vegetation typically adapted for life in saturated soil conditions (hydrophytic vegetation)." *Matter of Freshwater Wetlands Rules* (N.J. App. Div., 1989).

## WETLAND MITIGATION

**Activities carried out in order to compensate for freshwater wetlands or state openwaters loss or disturbance caused by regulated activities.**

*Comment*: Wetland mitigation may include creation, restoration, enhancement, and preservation of high-quality wetlands and uplands.

*Legal Annotation*: "The Corps determined that some impact on the wetlands was unavoidable, and so, the permit was conditioned on the implementation of a **wetland mitigation** plan, intended to minimize any negative effects." *Sierra Club v. Slater* (6th Cir., 1997).

## WETLAND SWALE

**A freshwater wetland that is a linear topographic depression that conveys surface water runoff, generally not more than fifty feet wide and draining an area of less than fifty acres.**

*Comment*: Under the New Jersey Freshwater Wetland Protection Act, no transition area is required adjacent to most swales, and they may be filled under a general permit in some circumstances.

*Legal Annotation*: "Among the lands of Chompist Farm are approximately three acres of **wetlands** lying in a natural **swale**. The wetlands are surrounded on the south and east by pastures that slope into the swale, and on the north by a barn and house." *Buxton v. USEPA* (D.C.D.C., 1997).

## WETLAND TRANSITION AREA

**A buffer of upland adjacent to a wetland that serves to minimize adverse impacts on the wetland or serves as an integral component of the wetland ecosystem.**

***Comment***: Transition areas can filter out pollutants from upland areas before they would enter a wetland. Transition areas can also serve as wildlife corridors and sanctuary for wildlife during times of wetland inundation. Activities in transition areas are regulated under state and local wetland protection programs. Transition-area widths may vary depending on the quality of the wetland. In New Jersey, wetland transition areas may range from fifty to one hundred fifty feet under the New Jersey Freshwater Wetlands Protection Act, and they may be as much as three hundred feet in the New Jersey Pinelands.

***Legal Annotation***: "N.J.S.A. 13:9B-3 defines **transition area** as 'an area of land adjacent to a freshwater **wetland** which minimizes adverse impacts on the wetland or serves as an integral component of the wetlands ecosystem.'" *New Jersey Dept. of Environmental Protection v. Bello* (N.J. App. Ct., 2013).

## WETLANDS

See *Wetland Buffer; Wetland, Coastal; Wetland, Degraded; Wetland, Freshwater; Wetland Mitigation; Wetland Swale; Wetland Transition Area*.

## WHARF

See *Pier*.

## WHEEL STOPS

See *Bumper Blocks*.

## WHOLESALE TRADE

**Establishments or places of business primarily engaged in selling merchandise to other businesses, including retailers; industrial, commercial, institutional, or professional business users; and other wholesalers; or acting as agents or brokers and buying merchandise for, or selling merchandise to, such individuals or companies.**

***Comment***: Lumber, plywood, and millwork yards, such as building-materials establishments, are generally classified as wholesale unless the primary operation is directly to the general public rather than to building contractors. In such cases, they are classified as retail operations.

***Legal Annotation***: "The Bureau of the Budget, in its *Standard Industrial Classification Manual,* likewise classifies '**wholesale trade**' to include 'all establishments or places of business engaged primarily in selling merchandise to retailers, to industrial or commercial users, or to other wholesalers.'" *Roland Electrical Co. v. Walling* (U.S., 1946).

## WIDE CURB LANE

See *Bicycle Facilities*.

## WI-FI

See *Public Wireless Access (Wi-Fi)*.

## WILDLIFE HABITAT

**A place with specific environmental characteristics in which a particular species, or wildlife in general, is able to thrive.**

***Legal Annotation***: "In summary, all management activities undertaken by the Forest Service must comply with the forest plan, which in turn must comply with the Forest Act, which requires that **wildlife habitat** must be managed to maintain viable populations of native and desired non-native wildlife species." *Idaho Sporting Congress, Inc. v. Rittenhouse* (9th Cir., 2002).

## WILDLIFE MANAGEMENT

**The management or control of wildlife for the well-being of wildlife but balanced with the needs of people using the best available science.**

***Comment***: Wildlife management has become a multidisciplinary, integrated science aimed primarily at conserving wildlife by taking into consideration ecological principles such as carrying capacity, disturbance, and succession; and environmental conditions such as physical geography, pedology, and hydrology; so as to preserve and improve wildlife habitats.

*Legal Annotation*: "Moreover, in addition to the six GTRs, the plan establishes a program for intense **wildlife management** throughout the entire project area. The **wildlife management** plan includes: selective clearing of 466 acres of wooded swamp; creation of small pools of standing water; planting of oak trees; development of an emergency access road; construction of firebreaks and prescribed burning to manage sand ridge areas; selective thinning and burning of planted and natural pine areas; and staged disking, seeding and mowing of old fields, pastures and rights-of-way." *National Wildlife Federation v. Marsh* (11th Cir., 1983).

## WILDLIFE CROSSINGS

**Underpasses or overpasses on highways of a variety of sizes and designs, with both roadside fencing and strategic plantings to allow wildlife to cross highways safely, reducing collisions and roadkill. Also known as a "critter crossing."**

*Legal Annotation*: "The Applicant shall be responsible for funding the construction of all **wildlife crossings** in the general location and design identified on Map H-2. The minimum design of the **Wildlife Crossings** to be provided at each location shall comply with the following:

All other **Wildlife Crossing** identified on Map H-2 will be constructed as identified on Map H-2 by Type as set forth below.

Type A **Wildlife Crossing** at a minimum shall include a 6' by 16' crossing under C.R. 210. The crossing shall be located landward of the jurisdictional wetland line or will include a contiguous dry portion of at least 50 percent of the total width of the crossing which is above the 10 year mean base flow of the drainage system.

Type B **Wildlife Crossing** at a minimum shall include a 6 ft x 6 ft crossing under the roadway. The crossing shall be located landward of the jurisdictional wetland line or will include a contiguous dry portion of at least 50 percent ofthe total width of the crossing which is above the 10 year mean base flow of the drainage system.

Type C **Wildlife Crossing** is an at grade crossing with a traffic calming design, posted speed limit signs of not to exceed 35 miles per hour and the placement of signs identifying the area as a wildlife crossing and other traffic calming measures which may be approved by the County.

Type D **Wildlife Crossing** at minimum will include a 3 ft x 3 ft crossing under C.R. 210." Northeast Florida Regional Council Planning & Growth Management Policy Committee (Nov. 7, 2013).

## WINDBREAK

**Berms, vegetation, landscaping, fences, or a combination of all four to provide a barrier against wind, snow, dust, or other natural elements.**

*Legal Annotation*: "An integral part of the agricultural property is a **windbreak** of cypress and eucalyptus trees situated on the condemned strip of property." *Ventura County Flood Control Dist. v. Security First National Bank* (Calif. App. Ct., 1971).

## WIND FARM

**A grouping of several wind-powered turbines in the same general location and used for the production of electric power.**

*Comment*: A large wind farm may consist of several hundred wind turbines and cover an area of several hundred acres. The land area between the turbines may be used for agricultural or other low-intensity use purposes. A wind farm may also be located offshore to take advantage of strong and usually constant winds blowing over a large body of water.

Impacts to consider in the location of wind farms include aesthetic factors, bird mortality, noise created from rotating turbine blades, and changes to the microclimate in the immediate area. However, given the public good that would result from the construction of a wind farm, it is probably unlikely that an application for a wind farm could be denied because of the impacts. Alternate compensation may be in order for those directly affected by the negative impacts of the facility (Filsram 2010; Homsy 2007; Rynne et al. 2011).

*Legal Annotation*: "As described in the record, the **wind farm** would consist of 130 wind turbine generators and an electrical service platform." *Alliance to Protect Nantucket Sound, Inc. v. Energy Facilities Siting Board* (Mass., 2006).

## WINDROW

**(1) Vegetative debris piled into long continuous rows; (2) a long row of cut hay or grain left to dry in a field before being bundled.**

*Legal Annotation*: A snow windrow is a long low ridge of snow that has been scraped off the road and deposited along the curb during snowplowing operations. See Webster's Third New International Dictionary 2620 (1976)." *Damaschke V. City Of Racine* (Wis. Ct. App., 1989).

## WINDROWING

**Composting in which large rows of vegetative waste are turned from time to time to encourage aeration.**

*Legal Annotation*: "After the shearing was completed in a section, bulldozers outfitted with rake blades pushed the felled trees into windrows. . . . However, in the process of **windrowing** the trees and debris, soil and leaf litter was also scraped into the windrows." *Avoyelles Sportsmen's League, Inc. v. Marsh* (5th Cir., 1983).

## WIRELESS TELECOMMUNICATIONS TOWERS AND FACILITIES

**(1) A parcel of land containing a tower, sending and receiving antennas attached to the tower, and a prefabricated or modular structure or cabinets containing electronic equipment; (2) a Federal Communications Commission (FCC)-licensed facility, designed and used for the purpose of transmitting, receiving, and relaying voice and data signals from various wireless communication devices and equipment.**

***Comment***: The definition applies to all personal wireless services covered in the Federal Telecommunications Act of 1996 (§332(c)(7))—"the Act." The Act defines personal wireless services as including commercial mobile services, which in turn is defined to cover cellular telephone services, personal communications services, all types of mobile radio, and paging services. It does not include any amateur radio facility that is owned and operated by a federally licensed amateur radio station operator or is used for "receive only" or noncellular telephone service facilities. For purposes of zoning definitions, the more familiar "cellular antenna tower site" is often used, although the site may also contain equipment designed to provide other commercial mobile services.

For a new tower location, the parcel of land is usually small, often ten thousand to twenty thousand square feet in area. The tower may be eighty to two hundred feet high, or even higher, depending on the area to be served, local topography, and the equipment to be placed on the tower. The shorter towers are usually monopoles; the higher towers usually employ a lattice design.

Telecommunication sites can also be located in or on new or existing buildings. The antennas can be located on the roof or flush with the façade and the electronic equipment placed inside the building. In some cases, the antennas themselves can be located in "alternative tower structures," such as artificial trees, clock towers, silos, steeples, flagpoles, and similar structures that camouflage or conceal the presence of antennas or towers.

Antennas are usually panel types, about eight to twelve inches in width and three to six feet in height, but may also include whip antennas (six to fifteen feet in height) and satellite dish antennas.

The modular unit may vary between four hundred and twelve hundred square feet in area and contains the electronic equipment to enable the system to operate effectively. The equipment can also be located in secure existing buildings. Since the units are unstaffed, there is no traffic activity except for periodic maintenance.

The major conflict between service providers and municipalities is one of aesthetics and the appropriateness of the proposed site for the facility. The Act specifically excludes any denials based on health considerations if the emission from the facility complies with FCC emission regulations.

Since the Act states that state and local government regulations cannot unreasonably prohibit personal wireless services or discriminate between providers (Section 704(c)(7)), municipalities should plan for this use and, if possible, the specific location where these facilities can be located. With the exception of certain existing towers, buildings, and structures, the exact location would probably not be known until more-specific site location studies related to coverage and capacity are undertaken, usually by the provider.

Certainly, existing wireless telecommunications towers represent the most logical location for any proposed new facilities. All approvals of a tower site should provide that the owner/operator must make space available at a "reasonable" fee for any subsequent applicants. Other existing structures that are logical locations for cellular antennas include water towers and industrial and commercial building roofs. Many towns encourage their location on municipally owned land where appropriate, because of lease fees as well as an opportunity to relocate municipal radio facilities to the new, often higher tower.

These uses can also be accommodated in industrial and commercial zones and remote areas or sites, away from existing residences, although mid-rise and high-rise residential buildings are also logical locations. Other possible locations include the interior of church steeples, water tanks, barn silos, fire and clock towers, utility poles and towers, billboards, and lighting standards.

When these facilities are located on existing buildings, placing the equipment toward the center of the roof and erecting parapet walls can reduce the visual impact.

While there has been some controversy regarding parks and forests as possible sites for these uses, the fact remains that the visual and aesthetic impact in these areas is less than in built-up areas, and the trees effectively block at least part of the view of the tower.

Applicants can provide, through the use of either photography or computer graphics, what the view of a proposed tower will be from various locations in the community.

Safety and environmental factors also are legitimate concerns with respect to these facilities. Although the possibility of the tower collapsing is slight (all are built to code standards), setbacks should be established to provide some protection from ice or falling debris. Studies have shown that debris usually falls within 50 percent of the tower's height (Abrams 1998: 4). The Act provides for environmental impact assessments when the tower is proposed for areas with endangered species or critical habitats, when it could affect historic sites, impact wetlands, or cause water diversion or deforestation.

Coloration and landscaping are legitimate concerns and are part of the site-plan review process. Landscaping around the site can screen street-level visual impacts. While some attempts have been made to incorporate the antennas in fake trees, the result has been less than satisfactory and often draws attention to the obvious.

Wireless telecommunications facilities generate no traffic, noise, lighting, odor, or other adverse impacts. Abrams suggests that they be considered in three broad zoning categories as follows:

1. As permitted uses
    - On existing structures such as towers and buildings.
    - When located in industrial or commercial areas.
    - When located within moderate- to large-sized public parkland areas or other appropriate public facilities areas, such as maintenance depots or storage areas.

2. As special exception and conditional uses when located in
   - Residentially zoned or developed areas.
   - Agricultural and farmland preservation areas.
   - Areas with transitional zoning and development.
   - Historic districts and sites.
3. As prohibited in environmentally sensitive areas such as floodplains, wetlands, and areas with steep slopes and erodible soils

Still, approval of these facilities is not a given. The Act provides that state and local governments must act on requests for siting permits within a reasonable time, put denials in writing, and support the decision by substantial evidence contained in a written record (paragraph 7). The denial must be based on specific, not general concerns. Among the reasons for denial: The service can be provided by (1) less-intrusive means; (2) a lower tower; or (3) use of an existing structure or an "alternative structure." The local government can deny an application for more towers than the minimum required to provide wireless services (*Sprint Spectrum, L.P. v. Willoth*, US Court of Appeals for the Second Circuit; reported in Lawlor 1999).

For additional materials on cellular towers and facilities, *see*: Abrams 1998, p. 3; and American Planning Association, *Aesthetics, Community Character, and the Law*, Planning Advisory Service Report No. 489/490 (1999), Chapter 6, Telecommunications Facilities.

***Legal Annotation***: "In other words, local governments may reasonably take the location of the telecommunications tower into consideration when deciding whether: (1) to require a more probing inquiry, and (2) to approve an application for construction of **wireless telecommunications facilities**, even though this may result in discrimination between providers of functionally equivalent services." *Sprint Spectrum LP v. Willoth* (2nd Cir., 1999).

## WORKING DRAWINGS

**Detailed, precise drawings by an engineer or architect from which construction may be undertaken.**

***Comment***: Working drawings for buildings are required for issuance of a building permit. For roads and other structures, working drawings are usually required as part of the final approval process.

***Legal Annotation***: "He [the contractor] is then called upon to contribute his practical expertise during the development of the **working drawings**, and subsequently apply this expertise during construction, in order to achieve maximum economies. He is expected to provide cost estimates from time to time during development of **working drawings** to determine that the project is within budget so that some of the early phases of construction can proceed prior to completion of all of the drawings." *City of Inglewood-LA Cty. Civic Ctr v. Superior Court* (Calif., 1972).

# X

## XERISCAPE

**Landscape design encouraging the use of drought-resistant plants and ground cover, as well as water conservation and retention techniques.**

***Comment***: Xeriscape landscaping is used in semi-arid and arid environments. Advantages are less water consumption and more rainwater retention. Disadvantages are that xeriscape landscaping may not be suitable for traditional lawn uses, such as athletic fields, and may create adverse aesthetic responses. *See* Koerth-Baker (2012) and Weinstein (1999).

***Legal Annotation***: "The MND stated that the project would not have a significant effect upon the environment provided the potential impacts were mitigated to a level of insignificance through implementation of certain conditions imposed on the granting of the land use determination, and by application of existing City ordinances, such as the Sewer Ordinance, Grading Ordinance, Flood Plain Management Specific Plan, and **Xeriscape** Ordinance, which are specifically intended to mitigate such potential impacts of all projects." *Baldwin v. City of Los Angeles* (Cal Ct. App., 1999).

# Y

## YARD

**An open space that lies between the principal building or buildings and the nearest lot line. See *Buildable Area; Lot Line; Yard, Required; Yard Depth; Yard Line. See Figures 16 and 107.***

***Comment***: Uses and structures that are typically permitted in required residential yards include accessory structures and swimming pools (rear or side yards only), patios and open porches, bay windows, open steps, driveways, fences, and permitted signs and lighting. In nonresidential zones, parking lots are typically permitted in side and rear yards, usually with requirements for setbacks and buffers from adjoining properties.

***Legal Annotation***: "As can be seen from these definitions, a **yard** is generally considered to be an open, unoccupied and unobstructed space subject to a few well-defined exceptions." *Elsaesser v. Hamilton Bd. of Zoning Appeals* (Ohio Ct. App., 1990).

## YARD, FRONT

**A space extending the full width of the lot between any building and the front lot line and measured perpendicular to the building at the closest point to the front lot line. *See Figures 16 and 107.***

***Comment***: Note that this term defines a space and not a required setback. The definition specifies that the line of measurement is perpendicular to the building and extends to the lot line. If the line of measurement were perpendicular to the lot line, there would be problems with pie-shaped and irregular lots.

Typically, many ordinances require that the minimum required yard remain open and unoccupied, regardless of whether the principal structure is set farther back than required. Other ordinances allow parking in the front yard, provided that the parking is set back beyond the minimum front-yard setback.

***Legal Annotation***: "The regulations contain the following definitions: A **front yard** is 'an open space extending across the full width of the lot between the front wall of the principal building and the front lot line.'" *McCrann v. Town Plan & Zoning Commission* (Conn., 1971).

## YARD, REAR

**A space extending across the full width of the lot between the principal building and the rear lot line and measured perpendicular to the building to the closest point of the rear lot line. See *Comment Under Yard, Front And Figures 16 and 107.***

***Legal Annotation***: "The regulations contain the following definitions: a **rear yard** is 'an open space extending across the full width of the lot, between the rear wall of the principal building and the rear lot line.'" *McCrann v. Town Plan & Zoning Commission* (Conn., 1971).

## YARD, REQUIRED

**The minimum open space between a lot line and the yard line, within which no structure is permitted to be located except as provided in the zoning ordinance. *See Figures 16 and 107.***

***Legal Annotation***: "The provision regarding yard encroachments in section 2.6.4.1 reinforces this concept by requiring '[e]very part of every **required yard** [to] be open and unobstructed from 30 inches above the general ground level of the graded lot upward to the sky.'" *Vanderbilt Shores Condo. v. Collier County* (Fla. Ct. App., 2004).

**Figure 107**

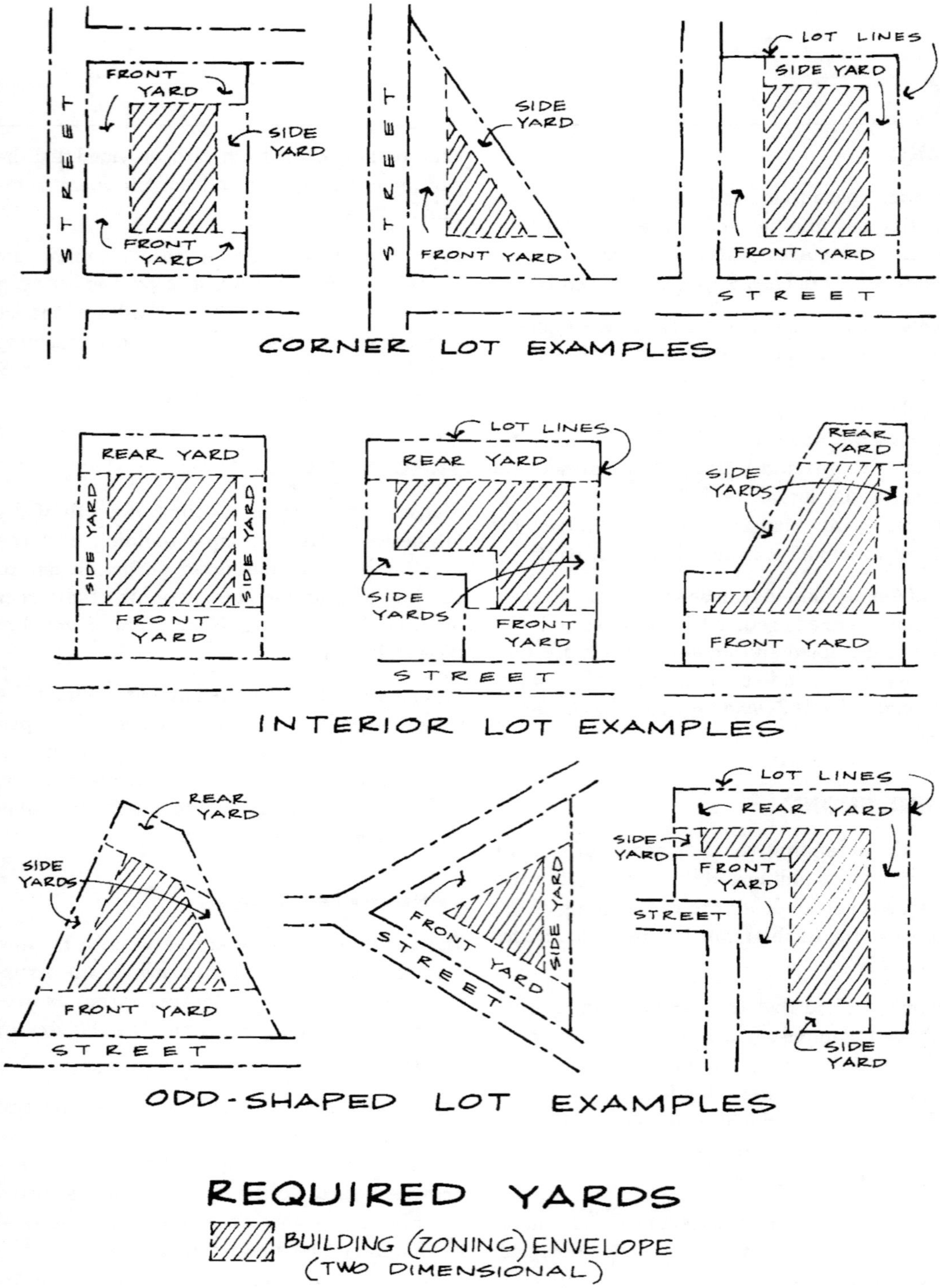
FRONT YARD
SIDE YARD
STREET
LOT LINES
CORNER LOT EXAMPLES
REAR YARD
SIDE YARDS
INTERIOR LOT EXAMPLES
ODD-SHAPED LOT EXAMPLES
REQUIRED YARDS
BUILDING (ZONING) ENVELOPE (TWO DIMENSIONAL)

## YARD, SIDE

**A space extending from the front yard to the rear yard between the principal building and the side lot line and measured perpendicular from the side lot line to the closest point of the principal building.** ***See Figures 16 and 107.***

*Legal Annotation*: "A **side yard** is defined in Municipal Code section 12.03: 'A yard more than six (6) inches in width between a main building and the side lot line, extending from the front yard or front lot line where no front yard is required, to the rear yard. The width of the required side yard shall be measured horizontally from the nearest point of the side lot line toward the nearest part of the main building.'" *Mock v. Shulman* (Calif. Ct. App., 1964).

"The regulations contain the following definitions: A **side yard** is 'an open space extending from the front to the rear yard, between the principal building and the side line of the lot.'" *McCrann v. Town Plan & Zoning Commission* (Conn., 1971).

## YARD DEPTH

**The shortest distance between a lot line and a yard line.**

*Legal Annotation*: "The change to an R-30 zone increased the requirements to 30,000 square feet per lot, with a minimum frontage of 150 feet, a minimum front-**yard depth** of 50 feet, side yards of a minimum of 25 feet, and a 25-foot minimum rear yard." *Petersen v. Town Plan & Zoning Commission* (Conn., 1967).

## YARD LINE

**A line drawn parallel to a lot line at a distance therefrom equal to the depth of the required yard.** ***See Figure 16.***

*Legal Annotation*: "'Front **yard line**' is defined as 'a line drawn parallel to a front lot line at a distance therefrom equal to the depth of a required front yard.'" *Matter of Golia v. Srinivasan* (N.Y. App. Div. 2012).

## YARD SALE

See *Garage Sale*.

## YOUTH CAMP

**Any parcel or parcels of land having the general characteristics of a camp as the term is generally understood, used wholly or in part for recreational or educational purposes and accommodating five or more children under eighteen years of age for a period of, or portions of, two days or more; the term includes a site that is operated as a day camp or as a resident camp.**

*Legal Annotation*: "According to the Boy Scouts, the Township's new zoning classification only allows the Boy Scouts to use their 4,748 acres located in Blue Lake Township for the single purpose of operating a **youth camp**." *Chicago Area Council, Inc. v. Blue Lake Township* (Mich. Ct. App., 2010).

## YOUTH HOSTEL

**An establishment providing transient, overnight accommodations, typically characterized by low cost, shared use of a self-service kitchen, common areas, sleeping rooms, and bathroom facilities.**

*Comment*: While primarily youth- and student-oriented, these facilities cater to all age groups. In addition to the dormitory-style accommodations, private rooms and baths are often available. Establishments meeting the standards of the International Youth Hostel Federation (IYHF) in terms of facility standards, operating policies, and programs display the blue triangle logo with a hut-and-tree trademark and receive the seal of approval of the IYHF (Canon 2003).

*Legal Annotation*: "As evidenced by the New York City Zoning Map 6a, the premises is located within an R7-2 zoning district. This is a general residential district in which the only uses permitted are residential and community facility uses. Commercial uses, such as **youth hostels**, are prohibited in an R7-2 zoning district." *Jazz on 129th LLC v. Christ Temple of the Apostolic Faith, Inc.* (N.Y., 2012).

# Z

## ZERO LOT LINE

See *Dwelling, Zero Lot Line.*

*Legal Annotation*: "The homes in the Woodridge Escondido development (development) are a type known as '**zero lot line**.' One exterior side wall of each home is built on one of the side yard property lines of the lot on which the home is located (the lot on which the home is located is sometimes referred to as the dominant tenement). Each lot has a five-foot easement over the side yard of the adjacent lot that belongs in fee to the owner of that neighboring lot (which is sometimes referred to as the servient tenement)." *Woodrbridge Escondidio Property v. Nielsen* (Calif. Ct. App., 2005).

## ZIPCAR

See *Car Sharing.*

*Legal Annotation*: "**Zipcar** provides a car-sharing service to members who, upon approval of their application, sign a membership agreement and pay an annual membership fee. For predetermined hourly rates, members may reserve cars, which are parked throughout various metropolitan areas, in half-hour increments for periods of one hour or more." *Blay v. Zipcar* (D. Mass. 2010).

## ZIPPER LOT

**A division of property using zero lot-line design with offset rear-lot lines to permit each lot a more usable rear yard.** *See Figure 108.*

*Legal Annotation*: "b. **Interlocking lot**. In this case, the location of the dwelling unit is such that the side and rear walls of the garage both rest directly on the lot line. No other exterior walls of the dwelling unit shall have a zero setback. This concept can be used with a **zipper lot** (z-lot) design or on a standard lot in which the garages of the abutting lots are connected at the side and the rear while the living areas of the dwelling units are set back from the property lines." *Wood County, West Virginia, Comprehensive Planning Program Land Use Regulations, Part I: Subdivision Regulations.* http://tinyurl.com/lygnfbf

## ZOMBIE SUBDIVISION

See *Premature Subdivision.*

## ZONE

**A specifically delineated area or district in a municipality within which uniform regulations and requirements govern the use, placement, spacing, and size of land and buildings.** See *Floating Zone.*

*Legal Annotation*: "The Supreme Court of Illinois, in *City of Aurora v. Burns*, in sustaining a comprehensive building zone ordinance dividing the city into eight districts . . . said: 'The segregation of industries, commercial pursuits and dwellings to particular districts in a city, when exercised reasonably, may bear a rational relation to the health, morals, safety and general welfare of the community. The establishment of such districts or **zones** may, among other things, prevent congestion of population, secure quiet residence districts, expedite local transportation, and facilitate the suppression of disorder, the extinguishment of fires and the enforcement of traffic and sanitary regulations.'" *Village of Euclid v. Ambler Realty Co* (U.S., 1926).

## ZONE, TRANSITION

See *Transition Zone.*

*Legal Annotation*: "He stated this piece of property was a '**transition zone**' between the two areas of different land use, and the Home

**Figure 108**

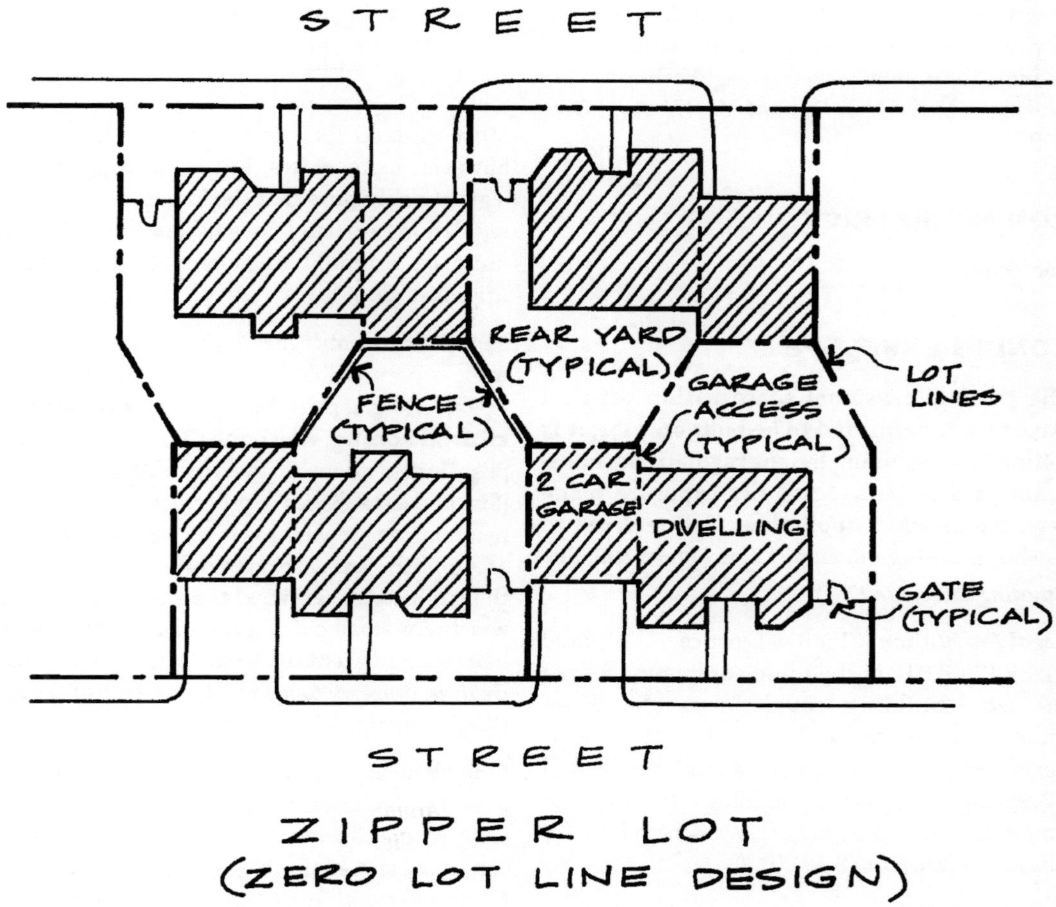


represented the best 'buffer' between the two uses. . . . A court must be mindful of the fact that in rapidly growing cities certain pieces of property will lie between two different uses, and it is in conformity with the comprehensive plan to put this land to the best use possible." *Schubach v. Silver* (Pa., 1975).

## ZONING

**The delineation of districts and the establishment of regulations governing the use, placement, spacing, and size of land and buildings.**

***Legal Annotation***: "**Zoning** is defined as 'governmental regulation of the uses of land and buildings according to districts or zones.' 8 McQuillin Municipal Corporations § 25.01, at 12 (3d ed. 1965)." *Miller v. City of Albuquerque* (N.M., 1976).

## ZONING BOARD

**See *Board Of Adjustment*.**

## ZONING, CONTEXTUAL

**The requirement that new construction and rehabilitation of existing properties in largely built-up areas reflect the characteristic bulk, height, and style of existing buildings. See *Compatibility, Development Context*.**

***Legal Annotation***: "This area was being rezoned, as were other portions of the city, to implement

**contextual zoning**, which encourages the maintenance of a street wall of buildings, instead of plazas, and which requires that new buildings be built 'in context' with the neighborhood." *One Beekman Place, Inc. v. City of NY* (N.Y. App. Div., 1991).

## ZONING DISTRICT

See *Zone*.

## ZONING ENVELOPE

**The three-dimensional space within which a structure is permitted to be built on a lot; it is defined by maximum height regulations, minimum yard setbacks, and sky exposure plane regulations when applicable. Also referred to as the "building envelope." See *Figure 109*. See *Building Envelope*.**

***Legal Annotation***: "The trial justice . . . [n]oted that § 17.08.010 of the zoning ordinance defines the term '**building envelope**' as 'the three-dimensional space within which a structure is permitted to be built on a lot and which is defined by regulations governing building setbacks, maximum height, and bulk.'" *Lloyd v. Zoning Board of Review for Newport* (R.I., 2013).

## ZONING, EXTRATERRITORIAL

**The extension of zoning authority by an incorporated municipal entity (city, town, etc.) to adjacent unincorporated land beyond the boundary of the incorporated entity.**

***Comment***: The states that permit an incorporated municipality to extend its zoning authority to surrounding unincorporated land usually impose restrictions, as follows:

- The zoning extension has to be based on master-plan recommendations and/or specific zoning studies.
- It has to be periodically reviewed.
- The maximum distance of the extraterritorial zoning may be limited by state statute.
- If the unincorporated land becomes part of an incorporated entity, the extraterritorial zoning becomes null and void and subject to the zoning authority of the newly incorporated entity.

Most states do not permit extraterritorial zoning; however, many states, in their zoning enabling legislation, require that the impact of any zoning regulations on land in adjacent municipalities must be carefully considered ("Condominium Approval" 2009).

***Legal Annotation***: "The City's ordinance purports to be a permissible land division restriction on extraterritorial plats, but in effect it is **extraterritorial zoning**, which the City may not accomplish independent of the Town of Delavan. . . . [Statute] establishes a procedure for a city and neighboring towns to work cooperatively to accomplish **extraterritorial zoning** within the city's **extraterritorial zoning** jurisdiction, which, for small cities, extends for one and one-half miles adjacent to the city's boundaries." *Lake Delavan Property Company, LLC v. City of Delavan* (Wis., Ct. App., 2014).

"The obvious purpose of this statutory mandate is that boundaries be defined, to the extent feasible, so that owners of property outside the city can easily and accurately ascertain whether their property is within the area over which the city exercises its **extraterritorial zoning** authority." *Sellers v. City of Asheville* (NC Ct. of App. 1977).

## ZONING, HYBRID

**Zoning codes that incorporate components of both conventional "Euclidian" zoning and form-based codes. See *Form-Based Code*.**

***Comment***: Most hybrid zoning codes combine conventional use-based standards with form-based standards.

***Legal Annotation***: "A PUD is **hybrid zoning** which is site particular and subsequent changes in the general zoning codes of the Village do not impact it (e.g., the 1988 setback requirements in the Village code do not impact the setback requirements..." *Kirk Corp. v. Village of Buffalo Grove* Ill. App. Ct., 1993).

**Figure 109**

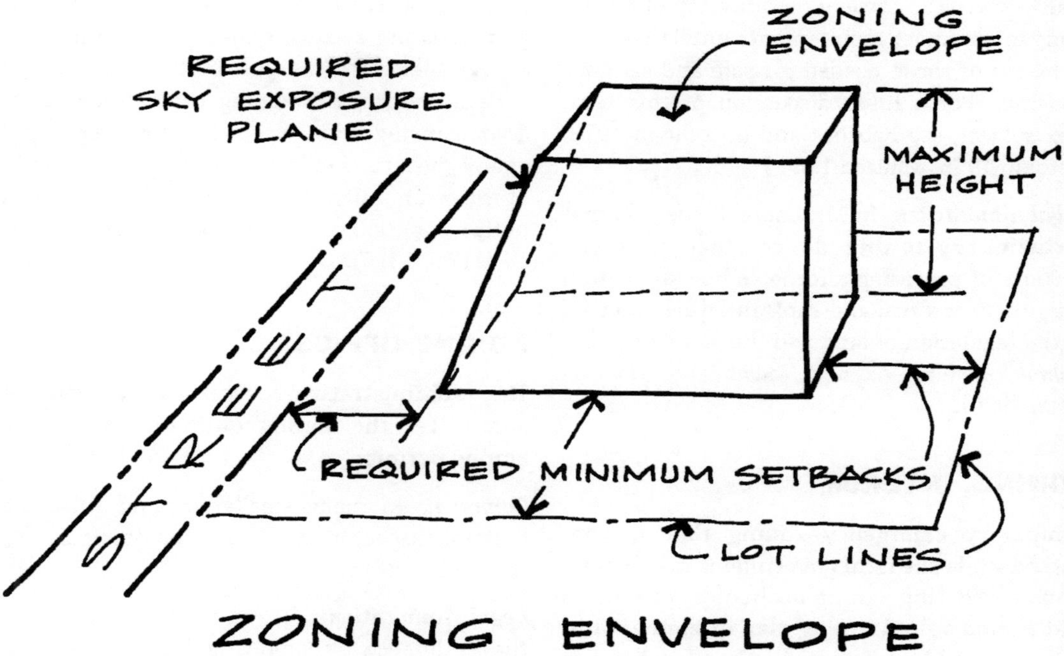


## ZONING, INCENTIVE

**The granting by the approving authority of additional development capacity in exchange for the developer's provision of a public benefit or amenity.**

*Comment*: In urban areas, developers are granted additional height and floor area in exchange for the development of public plazas and similar urban open spaces. In some developing suburbs and urban areas, developers are offered additional dwelling-unit density if lower-income housing units are created.

Incentive zoning should not be confused with off-tract improvements or impact fees. These represent attempts to correct deficiencies in infrastructure or to ensure that infrastructure needs created by a project are adequate. Incentive zoning is a quid pro quo—more development for some benefit, the need for which may not necessarily be created by the development itself. The local ordinance would have to clearly spell out the bonuses and the benefits (Morris 2000).

*Legal Annotation*: **"Incentive zoning** is based on the premise that certain uneconomic uses and amenities will not be provided by private development without economic incentive. The economic incentive frequently used, and the one used in the Manhattan Bridge District amendment, is the allowance of greater density within a proposed building, more floor area than permitted under general zoning rules, if developers provided certain amenities for the community." *Asian Americans v. Koch* (N.Y., 1988).

## ZONING, INCLUSIONARY

**Regulations that increase housing choice by establishing requirements and providing incentives to construct housing to meet the needs of low- and moderate-income households.**

*Comment*: Inclusionary techniques include specific requirements for a minimum percentage of low- and moderate-income housing as part of any development and density bonuses for building low- and moderate-income units. Another technique designed to provide more affordable housing is the removal or modification of regulations to eliminate requirements unrelated to or in excess of those needed for safe and sanitary housing. (For a fuller discussion of this complex subject, see Babcock and Bosselman 1973; Listokin 1976; Mallach 1984.)

*Legal Annotation*: "In Mt. Laurel II, we held that **inclusionary-zoning** devices that serve the purpose of providing affordable housing within a region bear a real and substantial relationship to the regulation of land and the zoning power." *Holmdel Builders Ass'n v. Township of Holmdel* (N.J., 1990).

## ZONING, INTERIM

**Temporary emergency zoning that is conducted while the local government makes revisions to existing zoning ordinances or creates and adopts a final zoning plan or zoning ordinance, or addresses some other local policy issue (uslegal.com). See *Holding Zone*.**

*Comment*: Interim zoning has three main purposes: it permits planning and ordinance preparation to proceed relatively free of development pressures; it prevents uses that will not conform to the adopted ordinances; and it engenders public debate on the issues. When interim zoning controls have been found to be a subterfuge for a more or less permanent effort to halt growth, the courts have thrown them out (American Planning Association, *The Language of Zoning,* Planning Advisory Service Report No. 322, 1976).

*Legal Annotation*: "The orderly process of **interim zoning** allows the issues to have the benefit of full public debate, at the same time protecting the affected area from unwise exploitation prior to agreement and formulation of new zoning restrictions which may be more restrictive." *Collura v. Arlington* (Mass., 1975).

## ZONING MAP

**The map or maps that are a part of the zoning ordinance and delineate the boundaries of zone districts.**

*Legal Annotation*: "While it is undoubtedly true that a property owner has no vested interest in an existing **zoning map** and, accordingly, is always subject to the possibility of a rezoning without notice, the zoning ordinance and its accompanying zoning maps should nevertheless at any given time reflect the current planned use of the community's land so as to afford as much notice as possible." *Eves v. Zoning Bd. Of Adjustment* (Pa., 1960).

## ZONING OFFICER

**The administrative officer designated to administer the zoning ordinance and issue zoning permits.**

*Comment*: In many smaller communities, the building inspector or construction official is also the zoning officer.

*Legal Annotation*: "If an applicant violates the Ordinance by supplying false or misleading information or by failing to secure inspection or approval of structural modifications, the **zoning officer** is permitted to 'take any enforcement action, whether by legal process or otherwise,' to address the violation and 'to prevent the occupancy of [the] building.'" *Taylor Inv., Ltd. v. Upper Darby Tp.* (3rd Cir., 1993).

## ZONING PERMIT

**A document signed by a zoning officer, as required in the zoning ordinance, as a condition precedent to the commencement of a use or the erection, construction, reconstruction, restoration, alteration, conversion, or installation of a structure or building, that acknowledges that such use, structure, or building complies with the provisions of the municipal zoning ordinance or authorized variance therefrom.**

*Comment*: Where a building permit is required, the building permit often includes a zoning permit.

*Legal Annotation*: "A property owner who intends to develop a residential lot of less than three acres normally must obtain subdivision approval from the PZC before Ridgefield will issue a **zoning permit** for the lot." *Natale v. Town of Ridgefield* (2nd Cir., 1999).

## ZOO

**A place where animals are kept, often in a combination of indoor and outdoor spaces, and are viewed by the public.**

***Legal Annotation***: "The scope of the Master Plan, and what had taken place at the time this suit was filed is as follows: The **zoo**, as of 1971 consisted of 12.7 acres on the western side of the middle park, known as Merz Memorial Zoo, and an additional two acres which housed the sea lions and reptiles, located across and beyond Natatorium Drive, east of the main part of the **zoo**." *State ex rel. Guste v. Audubon Park Commission* (La. Ct. App., 1978).

# REFERENCES


Abrahms, Sally. 2012. "Sharing Common Ground." *AARP Bulletin* (May).

Abrahms, Sally. 2013. "Three Generations Under One Roof." *AARP Bulletin* Vol. 54 No. 3 (April).

Abrams, Joshua. 2011. "The Zoning Dispute Whisperer." *Planning* 20 (November).

Abrams, Stanley D. 1998. "Update on the 1996 Telecommunications Act: Personal Wireless Services." *Land Use Law & Zoning Digest* (April).

Akoi, Chris. 2009. "Dealing With a Dirty Little Secret." *Planning* (April).

Alexander, Christopher, Sara Ishikawa, and Murray Silverstein. 1977. *A Pattern Language*. New York, NY: Oxford University Press.

American Planning Association. 1992. "APA Recommends Proactive Regulation of Electromagnetic Fields." *Zoning News* (August): 13.

American Planning Association. 2004. "Agritourism." *Zoning Practice* (March).

American Planning Association. 2006. *Planning and Urban Design Standards*. New York, NY: John Wiley.

Amiton, Rian. 2011. "Biking Catches Up." *Planning* (January).

Amur, Tayfun. 2007. "Fighting CEQA with CEQA." *Planning* (March).

Andrews, James. 2005. "Not Your Grandmother's Granny Flat." *Planning* (March).

Arvidson, Adam. 2008. "Pedal Pushers." *Planning* (March).

Arvidson, Adam. 2012. "Power to the Pedalers." *Planning* (May/June).

Avin, Uri and Michael Baer. 2003. "Right Sizing Urban Growth Boundaries." *Planning* (February).

Babcock, Richard F. and Fred P. Bosselman. 1973. *Exclusionary Zoning: Land Use Regulation and Housing in the 1970s*. New York, NY: Praeger.

Baeb, Edie. 2002. "Upstart Mall Holds Its Own." *Crain's Chicago Business* (July 8): 3.

Bailkey, M. and J. Nasr. 2000. "From Brownfields to Greenfields: Producing Food in North American Cities." *Community Food Security News* 6 (Fall/ Winter).

Barnett. 2011. "A Short Guide to 60 of the Newest Urbanisms." *Planning* (April).

Barrette, Michael. 1996. "Hog-Tied by Feedlots." *Zoning News* (October).

Beatley, Timothy. 2009. "Sustainability 3.0: Building Tomorrow's Earth-Friendly Communities." *Planning* 16 (May).

Beckman, John, Richard Bartholomew, and Paul Rookwood. 2006. "On the Ground in New Orleans." *Planning* (April).

Berg, Nate. "From Parking to Parklets." *Planning* (July).

Berke, Philip and Maria Conroy. 2000. "Are We Planning For Sustainable Development?" *Journal of the American Planning Association* 66:1 (Winter).

Berkooz, Corry. 2011. "Green Infrastructure Storms Ahead." *Planning* (March).

Best, Allen. 2009. "A Run to the Sun." *Planning* (April).

Bieszcat, Alice and Joe Schwieterman. 2012. "My Car, Your Car." *Planning* (May/June).

*Black's Law Dictionary* (Bryan A. Garner, ed.). 7th ed. 1999. St. Paul, MN: West Group.

Blakeley, Edward J., and Mary Gail Snyder. 1997. *Fortress America: Gated Communities in the United States*. Washington, DC: The Brookings Institution, 1997.

Blanchard, B. Wayne. 2007. "Guide to Emergency Management and Related Terms, Definitions, Concepts, Acronyms, Organizations, Programs, Guidance, Executive Orders & Legislation. A Tutorial on Emergency Management, Broadly Defined, Past and Present." http://training.fema.gov/hiedu/docs/terms%20and%20definitions/terms%20and%20definitions.pdf.

Blanton, Whit. 2004. "Air Front." *Planning* (May).

Booth, Derek B. and Jennifer Leavitt. 1999. "Field Evaluation of Permeable Pavement Systems for Improved Stormwater Management." *Journal of the American Planning Association* 65: 3 (Summer).

Bowers, Fred H. 2001. *A Protocol for Testing, Assessing and Approving Innovative or Alternative Onsite Wastewater Disposal Systems*. Trenton, NJ: New Jersey Department of Environmental Protection, Division of Wastewater Quality.

Brennan, Dean and Al Zelinka. 1997. "Safe and Sound." *Planning* (August).

Brodeur, Mark. 2003. "Ten Tips for Designing a Consumer Friendly Downtown." *Planning* (April).

Bruch, Megan and Mathew Ernst. 2010. *Choosing Direct Marketing Channels for Agricultural Products.* University of Tennessee Institute of Agriculture (December).

Building Officials and Code Administrators (BOCA). 1996. *The Boca National Energy Conservation Code 1996: Model Building Regulations for the Protection of Public Health, Safety and Welfare*, 8th ed.

Burchell, Robert W. and David Listokin. 1980. *The Practitioner's Guide to Fiscal Impact Analysis.* New Brunswick, NJ: Center for Urban Policy Research.

Bust, David. 2012. "Planning Practice." *Planning* (April).

*California General Plan Glossary*. 1997. Palo Alto, CA: California Planning Roundtable.

Canon, John. 2003. Interview by the authors with John Canon, Hosteling International USA, Silver Spring, Maryland.

Carney, Kristin. 2009. "Creating Jobs Over Coffee." *Planning* (December).

Carter, Peter and Jerry Walters. 2013. "Livability 2.0." *Planning* (May/June).

Census 2000 (US). Washington, DC: US Department of Commerce, Bureau of the Census.

Center for Universal Design. 2006. "Definitions, Accessible, Adaptable, and Universal Design." North Carolina State University, HDFS.4.91.

*Coffee Creek Center Design Code Book*. 2003. Chesterton, IN: Lake Erie Land Company.

Chapin, Ross. 2011. *Pocket Neighborhoods: Creating Small Scale Communities in a Large Scale World.* Newton, CT: Taunton Press.

"Colorado County Sets Rules for Land Swaps." 2011. *Planning* (April).

"Compatibility Defined" 2009. *Planning* (January).

"Condominium Approval in Municipality's Extraterritorial Zone is De Facto Rezoning." 2009. *Planning.* Legal News (December).

Connor, Susan M. 1998. "How the Federal Fair Housing Act Protects Persons with Handicaps in Group Homes." *Land Use Law* (January).

Corum, Vance, Marcie Rosenzweig, and Eric Gibson. 2001. *The New Farmers Market*. Auburn, CA: New World Publishing.

Cox, William M. with Donald M. Ross. 2003. *New Jersey Zoning and Land Use Administration*. Newark, NJ: Gann Law Books.

DeChiara, Joseph and Lee E. Koppelman. 1982. *Urban Planning and Design Criteria.* New York. NY: Van Nostrand Reinhold.

Dennison, Mark S. 1996. "Zoning and the Comprehensive Plan." *Zoning News* (August).

Dennison, Mark S. 1997. "Changing or Expanding Nonconforming Uses." *Zoning News* (March).

Dick, Andrews. 2007. "Blight Fight." *Planning* (June).

Downey, David. 2006. "All in a Day's Work." *Planning* (April).

Downs, Anthony. 2001. "What Does 'Smart Growth' Really Mean?" *Planning* (April).

Duany, Andres, Elizabeth Plater-Zyberk, and Jeff Speck. 2000. *Suburban Nation: The Rise of Sprawl and the Decline of the American Dream*. New York, NY: North Point Press (Farrar, Straus and Giroux).

Duerksen, Christopher. 1996. "Site Planning for Large-Scale Retail Stores." *PAS Memo.* Chicago, IL: American Planning Association (April).

Dulap, David. 2013. "On September 11, A Wall Limited the Devastation." *The New York Times* (September 12, A29).

Elliot, Donald. 2010. "Premature Subdivisions and What to Do About Them." Cambridge, MA: Lincoln Institute of Land Policy (Working Paper).

Ernst, Matt and Tim Woods. 2013. "Community Supported Agriculture." University of Kentucky Cooperative Extension Service (April).

Ewing, Reed and Steven Brown. "Traffic Calming Progress Report." 2009. *Planning* (November).

Federal Emergency Management Agency. *Glossary*. training.femagov/EMIWEBeb/emischool/EL361ToolKit/glossary.htm

Federal Emergency Management Agency (FEMA). 2008. Homeland Security Exercise and Evaluation Program (HSEEP).

Filsram, Greg. 2010. "Favorable Disposal." *Planning* (August/ September).

Filsram, Greg. 2010. "Wind Farm Proposal Stir Up Great Lakes." *Planning* (November).

Finkel, Ed. 2005. "Affordable Forever." *Planning* (November).

Finn, Robin. 2013. "The Great Air Race." *The New York Times* (Real Estate Section, February 22.)

Finucan, Karen. 1999. "Way to Go." *Planning* (November).

Fischler, Marcelles. 2006. "Super-Duper Markets." *The New York Times* (Section 14, July 30).

Flint, Anthony. 2011. "Smart Growth." *Planning* (January).

Floyd, Charles F. and O. Lee Reed. 1997. "Controlling Newsbox Clutter." *Land Use Law* (September).

Frej, Anne et al. 2001. *Business and Industrial Development Handbook*. Washington, DC: Urban Land Institute.

Friedman, Andrew. 2003. "Recycling Redux." *Planning* (November).

Frizell, David J. and Harry S. Pozycki, Jr. 1989. *New Jersey Practice*. Volume 36, *Land Use Law*. St. Paul, MN: West Publishing.

Fulton, William and Chris Jackson. 1999. "Let's Meet at the Library." *Planning* (May).

*Funk & Wagnalls Standard College Dictionary*. 1968. New York, NY: Funk & Wagnalls.

Gale, Daryl. 2005. "In Philly, Wi-Fi Means Willing to Fight." *Planning* (July).

Gallagher, Mary Lou. 1993. "A Small Room at the Inn." *Planning* (June).

Garde, Asay. 2009. "Sustainable by Design: Insights from the U.S. LEED-ND Pilot Projects." *Journal of the American Planning Association*. Vol 74, No. 4 (Autumn).

Garreau, Joel. 1991. *Edge City: Life on the New Frontier*. New York, NY: Anchor Books.

Giamo, Michael and Dwight Merriam. 2003. "Church v. State." *Planning* (April).

Goodno, Jim. 2005. "Homeowners Associations are Growing in Numbers and Power." *Planning* (April).

Graham, John and Sharon Graham Niederhaus. 2013. *A Practical Guide to Successful Multigenerational Living*. Linham, MD: Taylor Trade Publishing.

Greco, Joanne. 2012. "Body and Soul Centers." *Planning* (March).

Green, Joann. 2007. "We're So Cool." *Planning* (2007).

Green, Marci. 2006. "What is the Municipality's Role in Farm Regulation?" *New Jersey Municipalities* 60 (January).

Grob, Jeffrey. 2001. "Concrete Examples." In Kim Sorvig (2001), "A Sound Solution?" *Planning* (April).

Groe, Isabelle. 2005. "Weaving a Useful Web." *Planning* (July).

Groe, Isabelle. 2008. "Growers Gamble." *Planning* (March).

Hagman, D. G. 1975. *Urban Planning and Land Development Control Law*. St. Paul, MN: West Publishing.

Harnik, Peter and Jeff Simms. 2004. "How Far Is Too Far?" *Planning* (December).

Harville, Brian. 2005. "New Tech, New Trouble." *Planning* (July).

Haughey, Richard. 2008. *Getting Density Right*. Washington, DC: Urban Land Institute.

Haughney, Christine. 2010. "The Penthouse Apartment Is Taken Down a Notch." *The New York Times* (New York/ Dec 27).

Hayes, Anna. 2001. "Using Visioning in a Comprehensive Planning Process." University of Wisconsin–Extension.

Hecimovich, Jim. "Greenbelts or Green Wedges." 2008. *Planning* (March).

Hedman, Richard. 1984. *Fundamentals of Urban Design*. Chicago, IL: Planners Press.
Henderson, Harold. 2005. "Cohousing Again." *Planning* (August/September).
Hendrickson, Mary and Mark Porth. 2012. *Urban Agriculture: Best Practices and Possibilities*. University of Missouri, Extension, Division of Applied Sciences (June).
Hinshaw, Mark. 2000. "Rezone or Dezone." *Planning* (June).
Hinshaw, Mark. 2006. "Reforming Regulations." *Planning* (December).
Homsy, George. 2007. "Earth, Wind, and Fire." *Planning* (August/ September).
Houston, Lawrence. 2004. "Capitalist Tool." *Planning* (January).
Hughes, James and Joseph Seneca. 2012. "Reinventing the New Jersey Economy." New Brunswick, NJ: Bloustein School of Planning and Public Policy.
Hunterdon County (New Jersey) Planning Board. 2000. *Preserving Community Character in Hunterdon County: A Community Design Handbook*. Flemington, NJ: Hunterdon County Planning Board (February).
Institute of Real Estate Management of the National Association of Realtors. 1985. *Income/Expert Analysis, Office Buildings, Downtown and Suburban*. Chicago, IL: IREM.
Institute of Transportation Engineers (ITE). 1997. *Trip Generation*. 6th ed. Washington, DC: Institute of Transportation Engineers. (*Editor's note:* ITE has published the ninth edition of *Trip Generation* in 2012.)
Jackson, Randy. 2006. "A Redevelopment Revolution." *Planning* (January).
Jacobs, Allan, Elizabeth MacDonald, and Yodam Rofe. 2002. *The Boulevard Book: History, Evolution, Designs of Multiway Boulevards*. Cambridge, MA: MIT Press.
Jacobs, Jane. 1961. *The Death and Life of Great American Cities* New York, NY: Random House.
Jaffee, Martin. 1999. "The Case for Temporary Permits." *Land Use Law* (February).
James Duncan and Associates. 1996. *Planning for Agricultural Land Preservation in Minnesota: A Handbook for Planning under Minn. Statutes, Chapter 40A*. Report prepared with Iowa State University for the Minnesota Department of Agriculture.
Johnsich, John Robert. 1991. *The Real Estate Dictionary of Terms and Definitions*. 3d ed. Sacramento, CA: Real Estate Publishing Co.
Karney, Kristen. 2009. "Creating Jobs Over Coffee." *Planning* (December).
Kaser, Libby. 2010. "Denver Launches Bike Sharing." (July).
Katz, Peter. 2004. "Form First." *Planning* (November).
Katz, Peter. 2010. "Saratoga's Smart Growth Dividend." *Planning* (December).
Kelly, Eric Damian. 1999. "Beyond Regulation: Implementing Comprehensive Plans in the New Millennium." *Law and Zoning Digest* 51: 5 (May).
Kendig, Lane with Susan Connor, Cranston Byrd, and Judy Heyman. 1980. *Performance Zoning*. Washington, D.C.: Planners Press.
Kiser, Libby. 2011. "Cannabusiness Comes to Town." *Planning* (March).
Knack, Ruth Eckdish. 1998. "Drive Nicely." *Planning* (December).
Knack, Ruth Eckdish. 2001. "Love Me, Love My Garage." *Planning* (June).
Knack, Ruth Eckdish. 2002. "Dense, Denser, Denser Still." *Planning* (August).
Knack, Ruth. 2005. "Power to the Women." *Planning* 8 (March).
Knack, Ruth. 2010. "LEEDS-ND: What the Skeptics Say." *Journal of the American Planning Association* (December).
Koerth-Baker, Maggie. 2012. "Bloom Town." *New York Times Magazine* December 2, 18–19.
Kohut, John. 2004. "Thinking at the Edge." *Planning* (January).
Konsoulis, Mary. "Over 70 and Still Kicking." 2008 *Planning* (November).
Krohe, James. 2005. "Who Let the Dogs Out?" *Planning* (February).
Krohe, James. 2006. "Medical Districts to the Rescue." *Planning* (April).
Krohe, James. 2010. "Back to the Good Life." *Planning* (July).

LaClorda, Linda and Vince Papsidero. 2008. "Outside the Box." *Planning* (May).
Lang, Robert. 2003. *Edgeless Cities: Exploring the Elusive Metropolis*. Washington DC: Brookings Institution.
Langdon, Philip. 2000. "Flix, Nix, Stix: Megaplex Theaters Go Downtown." *Planning* (August).
Langdon, Phillip. 2006. "The Not So Secret Code." *Planning* (January).
Lardner/Klein Landscape Architects, PC. 1998. *Summary Report: Simsbury Center Design Charrette*. Alexandria, VA.
Lawlor, James. 2004. "Court Voids Zoning Changes Because Public Notice is Inadequate." *Planning* (February).
Lawlor, James. 2006 "Ordinance Leaves No Place for Adult Business." *Planning* (October).
Lawlor, Jim. 1999. "Act Two for Telecommunications." *Planning* (September).
Lennertz, Bill. 2006. "A Charratte Is the Best Way to Share." *Planning* (August/September).
Lennertz, Bill. 2011. "High-Touch/ High-Tech Charrattes." *Planning* (October).
Levy, Paul R. 2001. "Making Downtown Competitive." *Planning* (April).
Linowes, Lisa. 1985. "Farmers Markets." *Planning Advisory Service Memo*. American Planning Service (July).
Listokin, David and Carole Walker. 1989. *The Subdivision and Site Plan Handbook*. New Brunswick, NJ: Center for Urban Policy Research.
Listokin, David, Carole Walker, Schoor DePalma, and National Center for Smart Growth Research and Education. 2006. *Infill Development Standards and Policy Guide*. Study prepared by the Rutgers University Center for Urban Policy Research (New Brunswick: NJ) for the New Jersey Department of Community Affairs.
Listokin, David. 1976. *Fair Share Housing Allocation*. New Brunswick, NJ: Center for Urban Policy Research.
Litman, Tod. 2006. "London Congestion Pricing: Implications for Other Cities." Victoria Transport Policy Institute (January).
Little, Charles E. 1990. *Greenways for America*. Baltimore, MD: Johns Hopkins University Press.
Louie, Elaine. 2013. "How a Pop-Up Store Pops Up." *The New York Times* September 13.
Lucero, Lora. 2011. "Property Owners Prevail in Texas Beach Restoration Case." *Planning* (January).
Lynch, Kevin and Gary Hack. 1984. *Site Planning*. Cambridge, MA: MIT Press.
Magers, Vince. 2006. "Savings Accounts." *Planning* (September).
Mallach, Alan. 1984. *Inclusionary Housing Programs: Policies and Practices*. New Brunswick, NJ: Center for Urban Policy Research.
Mandelker, Daniel R. 1994. "Zoning Discrimination Against Group Homes under the Fair Housing Act." *Land Use Law* (November).
Mandelker, Daniel R. and William R. Ewald. 1988. *Street Graphics and the Law*. Chicago, IL: Planners Press.
Margil, Marl. 2010. "Slinging Sludge." *Planning* August/ September).
McCann, Barbara. 2005. "Complete the Streets." *Planning* (May).
McCarty, Kathryn Shane, ed. 1991. *Local Officials Guide: Complying with the Americans with Disabilities Act of 1990*. Washington, DC: National League of Cities.
McElfish, James. 2006. "It's Legal." *Planning* (August September).
McGowan, Leslie and Betty Richter-Reba. 1998. "'Buy-Downs': A New Direction in Affordable Housing." *New Jersey Planners' Journal* 4, 2 (Summer).
McHarg, Ian. 1969. *Design With Nature*. Garden City, NY: Doubleday Natural History Press. (1992 Second Edition. New York, NY: Wiley.)
McKeon, Aaron. 2010. "Save It All." *Planning* (December).
Meck, Stuart, ed. 2002. *Growing Smart Legislative Guidebook: Model Statutes for Planning and the Management of Change*. Chicago, IL: American Planning Association.

Meltz, Robert; Dwight H. Merriam; and Richard Frank. 1999. *The Taking Issue: Constitutional Limits on Land Use Control and Environmental Regulation.* Washington, DC: Island Press.

Menton, Eric. 2003. "Staying in the Swim." *Planning* (March).

Merriam, Dwight H., and Herbert J. Sitkowski. 1999. "The Seven-Nun Conundrum: Seeking Divine Guidance in the Definition of 'Family.'" *Land Use Law* (June).

Merriam, Dwight. 2011. "Zoning Isn't a Cure-All." *Planning* (July).

Millard-Ball, Alan and Patrick Siegman. 2006. "Playing the Numbers Game." *Planning* (May).

Minton, Eric. 2006. "Hey Big Spender." *Planning* (April).

Morgan, M. Granger. 1989. *Electric and Magnetic Fields from 60 Hertz Electric Power: What Do We Know About Possible Health Risks?* Pittsburgh, PA: Department of Engineering and Public Policy, Carnegie-Mellon University.

Mozingo, Louisa. 2012. *Pastoral Capitalism: A History of Suburban Corporate Landscapes.* Cambridge, MA: MIT Press.

Mukherji, Nina and Alfonso Morales. 2010. "Zoning for Urban Agriculture." *Zoning Practice Issue Number 3, American Planning Association (March).*

Myers, Phylis. 2008. "Megamansions Threaten Cape Cod National Seashore." *Planning* (November).

Myerson, Deborah. 2007. "The Ultimate in Accessibility." *Planning* (December).

National Complete Streets Coalition. "Complete Streets: A to Z." *Smart Growth America*. Smart Growth America, n.d. Web. 16 Jan 2014. <http://www.smartgrowthamerica.org/complete-streets/a-to-z>.

Nelessen, Anton C. 1994. *Visions for a New American Dream: Process, Principles, and an Ordinance to Plan & Design Small Communities*. Chicago, IL: American Planning Association.

New Jersey Council on Affordable Housing. 1993. *Substantive Rules of the New Jersey Council on Affordable Housing* (NJAC 5:93-1.3). Trenton, NJ: New Jersey Department of Community Affairs, Council on Affordable Housing.

New Jersey Department of Community Affairs (NJDCA), Division of Codes and Standards. 2000. *Residential Site Improvement Standards (RSIS).* Trenton, NJ: NJDCA.

New Jersey Department of Transportation (NJDOT). 1996. *Pedestrian Compatible Planning and Design Guidelines*. Trenton, NJ: NJDOT (April).

New Jersey Office of State Planning. 1995. Memo, "Big Box Retail." Vol. 1, No. 2. Trenton, NJ: Office of State Planning (December).

New Jersey Office of State Planning. 1996. Memo, "Historic Preservation." Vol. 2, No. 3. Trenton, NJ: Office of State Planning (April).

*New Jersey State Development and Redevelopment Plan*. 2002. Trenton, NJ: New Jersey State Planning Commission.

Newcomb, Tim. 2011. "Vancouver Embraces Bikes, Adds Lanes." *Planning* (February).

Newman, Oscar. 1996. *Creating Defensible Space*. Washington, DC: US Department of Housing and Urban Development.

*North American Industry Classification System (NAICS)*. 1997. Washington, DC: Executive Office of the President, Office of Management and Budget.

O'Connor, Robert. 2004. "Congestion Charges Reduces Central London Traffic in First Year." *Planning* (February).

Ortiz, David. 2007. "College and Town." *Planning* (February).

Oser, Alan. 2003. "How Zoning Works." *The New York Times* December 16, p. 7.

Papsidero Vince and Linda LaClorda, 2008. "Outside the Box." *Planning* (May).

Paquette, Carole. 2004. "New Designs Allow for Courtyards." *The New York Times* In the Region, September 5: 11.

Parolek, Daniel, Karen Parolek, and Paul Crawford. 2008. *Form Based Codes: A Guide for Planners, Urban Designers, Municipalities, and Developers.* Hoboken, NJ: Wiley.

Pittman, Craig. 2007. "Banking on a Loss." *Planning* (December).

Pointner, Peter. 2011. "What's In a Name? Sustainability, Smart Growth, New Urbanism." *The Commissioner.* American Planning Association (Summer).
Portlock, Sarah. 2011. "Wide Open Spaces." *Sunday Star-Ledger* February 20: 1.
President's Advisory Commission on Regulatory Barriers to Affordable Housing. 1991. *"Not in My Back Yard": Removing Barriers to Affordable Housing.* Report to President Bush and Secretary Kemp by the Advisory Commission. HUD-5806. Rockville, MD.
Pristin, Terry. 2005. "Moving Into the Neighborhood." *The New York Times* C8, July 27.
Pruetz, Rick. 2013. "Prosperity Comes in Cycles: Bicycle Trails Can Bump Up Local Economies." *Planning* (Fall).
Purdy, Jeffrey. 2007. "Form-Based Codes: New Approach to Zoning." *Smart Growth Tactics*. Michigan Association of Planning (January).
Rafson, Harold J. 1999. "About Odor." *Zoning News* (December).
Replogle, Michael. 2008. "Is Congestion Pricing Ready for Prime Time." *Planning* (May).
Robbins, Elaine. 2006. "Teed Off over the Aquifer." *Planning* (February).
Rose, Jerome G. and Robert E. Rothman, eds. 1977. *After Mount Laurel: The New Suburban Zoning*. New Brunswick, NJ: Center for Urban Policy Research.
San Diego (California) Planning Commission. 2013. "Report on PC-13-0145."
Sawicki, David S. 1989. "The Festival Marketplace as Public Policy: Guidelines for Future Policy Decisions." *Journal of the American Planning Association* 55: 3 (Summer).
Schellinger, David and Sharon Priest. 2006. "Getting Streetscape Design Right." *Planning* (June).
Schultz, Jim and Kelly Kline. 2004. "Getting to the Bottom of Mixed Use." *Planning.*
Schultz, Marilyn Spigel and Vivian Loeb Kasen. 1984. *Encyclopedia of Community Planning and Environmental Managemen*t. New York, NY: Facts on File.
Schwab, Anna K. and David J. Brower. 1997. "Sustainable Development: Implementation at the Local Level." *Land Use Law* (April).
Schwab, James. 1996. "Zoning and Big Box Religion." *Zoning News* (November).
Schwab, James. 1998. *Planning and Zoning for Concentrated Feed Lot Operations.* Planning Advisory Service Report 482 (Chicago, IL: Planners Book Service).
Schwanke, Dean. 1987. *Mixed-Use Development Handbook*. Washington, DC: Urban Land Institute.
Scotthanson, Chris and Kelly Scotthanson. 2005. *The Cohousing Handbook: Building a Place for Community.* Gabriola Island, BC: Canada New Society Publishers.
Segedy, Jim and Tom Daniels. 2007. "Small Town Design: Getting It Right." *Planning* (July).
Seliger, Susan. 2012. "Keeping an Ailing Relative at Home, Almost." *The New York Times* D5 (May).
Shigley, Paul. 2001. "Round 3 for Eminent Domain." *Planning* (2007).
Shigley, Paul. 2006. "California Goes Vertical." *Planning* (April).
Shirley, Lori. 1999. "Chesapeake Challenge." *Planning* (August).
Skinner, Jon. 2008. "Taking Accessible Design to the Next Level." *Planning* (July).
SmartCode©. 2003. Unified development ordinance developed by Duany Plater-Zyberk & Company, Miami, Florida. Viewable at http://www.smartcode.org/.
Snodgrass, Edmund, Nigel Dunnett, Dusty Gedge, and John Little. *Small Green Roofs: Low Tech Options for Greener Living.* 2011. Kindle Book.
Sorvig, Kim. 2001. "A Sound Solution?" *Planning* (April).
Starkey, Kevin. 2006. "Land Use and Religious Institutions." New Jersey Institute of Local Government Attorneys *Municipal Law Review.* 29(4)1.
Stein, Clarence. 1989. *Toward New Towns for America* Cambrige, MA: MIT Press.
Stephensen, Gary. 2008. *Farmers Markets: Success, Failures and Management*. Amherst, NY: Cambria Press.
Swope, Christopher. 2006. "L.A. Banks on Buses." *Planning* (May).
"Taking Off the Stabilisers." 2013. *The Economist* (October 12).

*The New Lexicon Webster Dictionary of the English Language*. Bernard S. Cayne, ed. 1989. New York, NY: Lexicon Publications.
Thibert, Joel. 2012. "Making Local Planning Work for Urban Agriculture in the North American Context: A View From the Ground." *Journal of Planning Education and Research* 32 (3): 349 (Fall).
Thompson, Laura. 1997a. "The Conflict at the Edge." *Zoning News* (February).
Thompson, Laura. 1997b. "Zoning for Dual Fueling." *Zoning News* (August).
Toenjes, L. P. 1989. *Building Trades Dictionary.* Homewood, IL: American Technical Publishers.
Traggorth, Dave. 2006. "Church and State." *Planning* (April).
Transportation Research Board, National Research Council. 2000. *Highway Capacity Manual*.Washington, DC: Transportation Research Board.
Untermann, Richard. 1989. "Grade Easy." American Society of Landscape Architects.
Walters, Jerry, Brian Bochner, and Reid Ewing. 2013. "Getting Trip Generation Right." *PAS Memo* (May/June).
*Watershed Watch*. 2001. Pennington, New Jersey: Stony Brook-Millstone Watershed Association (June).
Watson, Elizabeth. 2010. "Lasting Landscapes." *Planning* (February).
Webster's *Third New International Dictionary* (1976), Springfield, MA: G & G Merriam Co.
Weinstein, Alan. 2006. "Kelo and Counting." *Planning* (June).
Weinstein, Gayle. 1999. *Xeriscare Handbook*. Golden CO: Fulcrum Publishing.
Wells, Ken. 2003. "It's In the Air." *Planning* (November).
White, S. Mark and Dawn Jourdan. 1997. "Neo-Traditional Development: A Legal Analysis." *Land Use Law* (August ).
Williams, Norman Jr. 1977. "On 'From *Mount Laurel*: Guidelines on the Regional General Welfare,'" in J. G. Rose and R. E. Rothman (1977), *After Mount Laurel: The New Suburban Zoning.* New Brunswick, NJ: Center for Urban Policy Research.
Winder, Mary. 2001. Speech before the Heritage Group, Sarasota, Florida (June 4).
Wolcott, Barbara. 2004. "Interest in Alternative Energy." *Planning* (December).
Zelinka, Al and Jenny Johnson. 2005. "Accidental Spaces." *Planning* (December).
Zelinka, Al and Wendy Beattie. 2003. "How to Turn Alleys into Allies." *Planning* (November).
Ziegler, Edward H. Jr. 1991. *Rathkopf's The Law of Zoning and Planning.* New York, NY: Clark Boardman.

## AMERICAN PLANNING ASSOCIATION, *PLANNING ADVISORY SERVICE (PAS) REPORTS*

(Listed by author's name; PAS Report number follows bibliographic data.)

American Society of Planning Officials. 1955. *Zoning Ordinance Definitions*. 72.
Arendt, Randall. 2004. *Crossroads, Hamlet, Village, Town: Design Characteristics of Traditional Neighborhoods*, Old and New (revised edition). 142pp.
Bergman, David. 1991. *Off-Street Parking Requirements: A National Review of Standards*. 432.
Browne, Carolyn. 1980. *The Mechanics of Sign Control*. 354.
Burrows, Tracy. 1989. *A Survey of Zoning Definitions*. 421.
Congress for New Urbanism. 2004. *Codifying New Urbanism*. 526.
Crompton, John L. November 2001. *Parks and Economic Development*. 502
Davidson, Michael and Fay Dolnick (eds). 2004. *A Planners Dictionary*. 521/522.
Davidson, Michael and Fay Dolnick. November 2002. *Parking Standards*. 512.
Davidson, Michael and Fay Dolnick, eds. 1999. *A Glossary of Zoning, Development and Planning Terms*. 491/492.
DeGrogh, Teresa and Rachel German. 1986. *Standards for Self-Service Storage Facilities*. 396.Duerksen, Christopher J. 1986. *Aesthetics and Land-Use Controls: Beyond Ecology and Economics*. 399.
Duerksen, Christopher J. and R. Matthew Goebel. 1999. *Aesthetics, Community Character, and the Law*. 489/490.

Elliot, Donald L., Matthew Goebel, and Chad B. Meadows, 2012. *The Rules That Shape Urban Form*. 570.
Feiden, Wayne and Raymond Burby. July 2002. *Performance Guarantees for Government Permit Granting Authorities*. 508.
Feiden, Wayne M. with Elisabeth Hamin. 2011. *Assessing Sustainability: A Guide for Local Governments*. 565.
Fleming, Robert Lee. 1994. *Saving Face: How Corporate Franchise Design Can Respect Community Identity*. 452.
Fleming, Ronald Lee. February 2002. *Saving Face: How Corporate Franchise Design Can Respect Community Identity*. 503/504.
Gavin, Alexander. December 2000. *Parks, Recreation and Open Space: A Twenty-First Century Agenda*. 497/498.
Glassford, Peggy. 1983. *Appearance Codes for Small Communities*. 379.
Godschalk, David R. and William R. Anderson. 2012. *Sustaining Places: The Role of the Comprehensive Plan*. 567.
Greenberg, Froda with Jim Hecimovich. 1984. *Traffic Impact Analysis*. 387.
Handy, Susan, Robert G. Paterson, and Kent Butler. 2003. *Planning for Street Connectivity: Getting from Here to There*. 515.
Hecimovich, James (ed.). 2008. *Great Places in America: Great Streets and Neighborhoods, 2007 Designees*. 552.
Hinshaw, Mark L. 1995. *Design Review*. 454.
Hodgson, Kimberley, Marcia Caton Campbell, and Martin Bailkey. 2011. *Urban Agriculture: Growing Health, Sustainable Places*. 563.
Johnson, Laurie, Dwelley Laura Samant, and Suzanne Frew. 2005. *Planning for the Unexpected: Land-Use Development and Risk*. 531.
Kendig, Lane. 2004. *Too Big, Boring or Ugly: Planning and Design Tools to Combat Monotony, the Too-big House, and Teardowns*. 528.
Knapp, Gerrit, Stuart Meck, Terry Moore, and Robert Parker. 2007. *Zoning as a Barrier to Multifamily Housing Development*. 548.
Lewis, Megan (ed.). 2008. *From Recreation to Re-creation: New Directions in Parks and Open Space: System Planning*. 551.
Mandelker, Daniel. 2007. *Planned Unit Developments*. 545.
McCann, Barbara and Suzanna Rynne. 2010. *Complete Streets*. 559.
Meck, Stuart, Rebecca Retzlaff, and James Schwab. 2003. *Regional Approaches to Affordable Housing*. 513/514.
Moore, Terry, Stuart Meck, and James Ebenhoh. 2006. *An Economic Development Toolbox*. 541.
Morley, David. 2014. *Planning for Solar Energy*. 575.
Morris, Marya (ed.). 2006. *Planning Active Communities*. 543/544.
Morris, Marya (ed.). 2009. *Smart Codes: Model Land-Development Regulations*. 556.
Morris, Marya. 2006. *Integrating Planning and Public Health*. 539/540.
Morris, Marya. September 2000. *Incentive Zoning: Meeting Urban Design and Affordable Housing Objectives*. 494.
Nelson, Chris and Casey Dawkins. 2004. *Urban Containment in the United States: History, Models, and Techniques for Regional Metropolitan Growth Management*. 520.
Orton, Cabot, Keith Spiegel, and Eddie Gale. June 2001. *Lights, Camera, Community Video: Engaging Citizens in Creating a Community Documentary and Vision*. 500/501.
Rouse, David C. and Ignacio F. Bunster-Ossa. 2013. *Green Infrastructure: A Landscape Approach*. 571.
Rynne, Suzanne, Larry Flowers, Eric Lantz, and Erica Heller. 2011. *Planning for Wind Energy*. 566.
Schalk, Susan M. and Stephanie A. D. Ward. 2010. *Planners and Planes: Airports and Land-Use Compatibility*. 562.
Schoup, Donald C. 2005. *Parking Cash Out*. 532.

Schwab, James C (ed.). 2010. *Hazard Mitigation: Integrating Best Practices into Planning*. 560.
Shuford, Scott, Suzanne Rynne, and Jan Mueller. 2010. *Planning for a New Energy and Climate Future*. 559.
Weitz, Jerry and Leora Susan Waldner. November 2002. *Smart Growth Audits*. 512.
Wunder, Charles. December 2000. *Regulating Home-Based Businesses in the Twenty-First Century*. 499.

# LAND MEASURES

| | **Equals** |
|---|---|
| **1 mile** | 5,280 feet |
| | 1,760 yards |
| | 320 rods |
| | 80 chains |
| **1 chain** | 66 feet |
| | 100 links |
| | 4 rods |
| **1 rod** | 25 links |
| | 16.5 feet |
| | 1 perch |
| | 1 pole |
| **1 link** | 7.92 inches |
| **1 township** | 36 sections |
| **1 full section** | 640 acres |
| **1 square mile** | 640 acres |
| | 1 full section |
| **1 acre** | 43,560 square feet |
| | 4,840 square yards |
| | 160 square rods |
| | 10 square chains |
| **1 square chain** | 10,000 square links |
| **1 square rod** | 30.25 square yards |
| **1 square yard** | 9 square feet |
| **1 square foot** | 144 square inches |